Who's Who
in the
Classical World

EDITED BY

Simon Hornblower and Tony Spawforth

OXFORD
UNIVERSITY PRESS

OXFORD
UNIVERSITY PRESS

Great Clarendon Street, Oxford OX2 6DP

Oxford University Press is a department of the University of Oxford.
It furthers the University's objective of excellence in research, scholarship,
and education by publishing worldwide in

Oxford New York

Athens Auckland Bangkok Bogotá Bombay Buenos Aires Calcutta
Cape Town Chennai Dar es Salaam Delhi Florence Hong Kong Istanbul
Karachi Kuala Lumpur Madrid Melbourne Mexico City Mumbai
Nairobi Paris São Paulo Singapore Taipei Tokyo Toronto Warsaw
and associated companies in Berlin Ibadan

Oxford is a registered trade mark of Oxford University Press
in the UK and certain other countries

Published in the United States
by Oxford University Press Inc., New York

© Oxford University Press 2000

Database right Oxford University Press (maker)

First published 2000

British Library Cataloguing in Publication Data
Data available

Library of Congress Cataloging in Publication Data
Data available

ISBN 0-19-280107-4

1 3 5 7 9 10 8 6 4 2

Typeset by Selwood Systems, Frome
Printed in Great Britain by
Cox & Wyman Ltd
Reading, Bucks

SIMON HORNBLOWER is Professor of Classics and
Ancient History at University College London. He is
editor with Tony Spawforth of the acclaimed third
edition of the *Oxford Classical Dictionary* (1996) and
The Oxford Companion to Classical Civilization (1998),
and is an editor of and contributor to volume 6 of
the *Cambridge Ancient History* (1994). His other
books include a major commentary on Thucydides.

TONY SPAWFORTH is Professor of Ancient History
at the University of Newcastle upon Tyne. He is also a
well-known presenter of television programmes on
archaeological and classical subjects in the BBC series
'Ancient Voices'. In addition to the *Oxford Classical
Dictionary* and *The Oxford Companion to Classical
Civilization*, his publications include *Hellenistic and
Roman Sparta, A Tale of Two Cities*.

Oxford Paperback Reference

Contents

List of maps

Introduction

This book aims to fill a felt student need for a generous selection of the biographical entries from the third (1996) edition of the *Oxford Classical Dictionary* (*OCD³*). In the 1998 *Oxford Companion to Classical Civilization* (*OCCC*) we published a representative selection from all the areas covered by *OCD³*; inevitably, there were many biographical casualties, including such major figures as Theophrastus and Jugurtha. The present book restores to life a large number of such *OCD³* individuals 'killed off' for the purposes of *OCCC*. But biographical entries accounted for no less than one quarter of the two-million words of *OCD³*, so that we have, regretfully, had to make many exclusions, usually of very short entries, for the purposes of the present 300,000 word book. But we hope that the coverage will amply satisfy the needs of students and of the general reader.

The aim of this book is, unpretentiously, the desire to provide a handy reference guide to the bewildering number of ancient individuals whose names have come down to us; this is not the place to engage in an argument about biographical versus other and no doubt more sophisticated approaches to the study of the ancient world. On the issue of balance between biographical and non-biographical, our view is implied by the shift in emphasis brought in our 1996 edition of *OCD*: the one-quarter proportion mentioned above, large though it may seem, was in fact a considerable reduction of the fraction of *OCD* given over to human individuals in earlier (1949 and 1970) editions, because in 1996 we greatly increased the number of thematic and other non-biographical entries—many were completely new in 1996—while retaining the biographical element at roughly its previous level. We would however make the following point: 'biographical' is really a misnomer for many of the entries in the present book, as in *OCD³* and *OCCC*. The entries on 'Plato' and 'Aristotle', for instance, do provide at the outset the necessary biographical information as a factual framework, but for most of their extent they are in effect authoritative essays on the philosophy of those two thinkers; and arguably that is the correct approach to the study of ancient philosophy (talk of philosophical 'schools' or 'movements' can be seriously misleading). Again, one engine driving ancient historiography was undoubtedly the polemical aim of doing better than, and showing up the alleged limitations of, an identifiable predecessor. With the possible exception of religion (and even here such shadowy figures as King Numa were invoked by the ancients themselves to explain their religious institutions), it is a simple truth that you can get a long way towards understanding the ancient world by considering the careers, including the thought and writings, of individuals. But naturally, for a rounded view, we refer readers to OCD^3 or $OCCC$.

Finally, a word about the scope of this book. We have included only historical individuals, not gods, heroes or mythical figures. The line is usually easy to draw, though one could argue about e.g. Lycurgus the Spartan lawgiver; and even a definitely historical figure like Croesus, who dedicated column-bases at Ephesus which can now be seen in the British Museum, was in some ways turned into a mythical figure. Our principle of exclusion would hardly be worth stating but for the different policy followed in Betty Radice's Penguin *Who's Who in the Ancient World*, which for instance includes the god Dionysus but not the Athenian reformer Cleisthenes.

We acknowledge with gratitude Rowley Hudson's assistance with proof-reading.

SIMON HORNBLOWER
TONY SPAWFORTH
2000

Index to initials of contributors

R.L.Hu.   Richard L. Hunter
S.H.   Simon Hornblower
S.E.H.   Stephen E. Hinds
S.J.Ha.   Stephen J. Harrison
S.J.Ho.   Stephen J. Hodkinson
T.Hon.   Tony Honoré

B.I.   Brad Inwood

A.H.M.J.   Arnold Hugh Martin Jones
H.D.J.   H. D. Jocelyn

C.F.K.   Christoph F. Konrad
C.H.K.   Charles H. Kahn
D.K.   David Konstan
I.G.K.   Ian Gray Kidd
R.A.K.   Robert A. Kaster

A.B.L.   Alan Brian Lloyd
A.W.L.   Andrew William Lintott
B.M.L.   Barbara M. Levick
D.G.L.   D. G. Lateiner
H.S.L.   Herbert Strainge Long
J.F.L.   John Francis Lockwood
J.F.La.   John F. Lazenby
R.O.A.M.L. R. O. A. M. Lyne
W.L.   W. Liebeschuetz

A.M.   Arnaldo Momigliano
B.C.McG.   Brian C. McGing
D.M.M.   Douglas Maurice MacDowell
H.Ma.   Herwig Maehler
J.F.Ma.   John F. Matthews
J.L.Mo.   John L. Moles
K.M.   Klaus Meister
M.J.M.   Martin J. Millett
P.K.M.   Peter Kenneth Marshall
R.H.M.   Ronald Haithwaite Martin
S.M.   Stephen Mitchell

A.N.   Alexander Nehamas
M.C.N.   Martha C. Nussbaum
V.N.   Vivian Nutton

D.O.   Dirk Obbink
G.E.L.O.   Gwilym Ellis Lane Owen

C.B.R.P.   C. B. R. Pelling
D.S.P.   David S. Potter
J.G.F.P.   Jonathan G. F. Powell
N.P.   Nicholas Purcell
P.J.P.   P. J. Parsons
S.R.F.P.   Simon R. F. Price

C.C.R.   Christopher C. Rowland

D.A.R.   Donald Andrew Frank Moore
            Russell
G.W.R.   Geoffrey Walter Richardson
H.J.R.   Herbert Jennings Rose
J.C.R.   John Carew Rolfe
J.M.Ri.   John M. Riddle
J.S.R.   Jeffrey Stuart Rusten
J.W.R.   John William Rich
L.D.R.   Leighton Durham Reynolds
P.R.   Philip Rousseau
P.J.R.   P. J. Rhodes
R.B.R.   R. B. Rutherford
R.H.R.   R. H. Robins
T.R.   Tessa Rajak
W.D.R.   William Davis Ross

A.Schi.   Alessandro Schiesaro
A.Sm.   Andrew Smith
A.F.S.   Andrew F. Stewart
A.H.S.   Alan Herbert Sommerstein
A.J.S.S.   Antony J. S. Spawforth
C.E.S.   Courtenay Edward Stevens
D.R.S.   Danuta R. Shanzer
E.M.S.   Edith Mary Smallwood
E.T.S.   Edward Togo Salmon
G.S.   Gisela Striker
H.H.S.   Howard Hayes Scullard
H.P.S.   Hans Peter Syndikus
J.B.S.   John B. Salmon
J.H.S.   John Hedley Simon
J.H.D.S   J. H. D. Scourfield.
K.S.S.   Kenneth S. Sacks
M.Sch.   M. Schofield
M.S.S.   Martin Stirling Smith
M.S.Sp.   M. Stephen Spurr
R.B.E.S.   Rowland B. E. Smith
R.J.S.   Robin J. Seager
R.R.K.S.   Richard R. K. Sorabji
R.W.S.   Robert William Sharples
S.S.-W.   Susan Mary Sherwin-White

C.C.W.T.   Christopher C. W. Taylor
C.J.T.   Christopher J. Tuplin
D.J.T.   Dorothy J. Thompson
G.B.T.   Gavin B. Townend
G.J.T.   G. J. Toomer
M.B.T.   Michael Burney Trapp
P.T.   Piero Treves
R.T.   Rosalind Thomas
R.A.T.   Richard Allan Tomlinson
S.C.T.   Stephen C. Todd

P.N.U.   Percy Neville Ure

H.v.S.   Heinrich von Staden

J.T.V.	J. T. Vallance	J.Wi.	Josef Wieshöfer
		L.C.W.	Lindsay Cameron Watson
A.J.W.	A. J. Woodman	L.M.W.	L. Michael Whitby
A.M.W.	Anna M. Wilson	M.W.	Michael Winterbottom
B.H.W.	Brian Herbert Warmington	M.Wil.	Margaret Williamson
D.E.W.W.	Donald Ernest Wilson Wormell	M.L.W.	Martin Litchfield West
F.W.	Frederick John Williams	M.M.W.	M. M. Willcock
G.C.W.	George Clement Whittick	N.G.W.	Nigel Guy Wilson
H.D.W.	Henry Dickinson Westlake	S.R.W.	Stephanie Roberta West
H.T.W.-G.	Henry Theodore Wade-Gery		

Abbreviations

A. GENERAL

app.	appendix	lb.	pound/s
app. crit.	apparatus criticus	l., ll.	line, lines
b.	born	lit.	literally
bk.	book	m.	metre/s
c.	*circa*	mi.	mile/s
cent.	century	mod.	modern
cm.	centimetre/s	MS	manuscript
comm.	commentary	Mt.	Mount
d.	died	n., nn.	note, notes
end	at/nr. end	n.d.	no date
ed.	editor, edited by	no.	number
ed. major/	major/minor	NS	new series
minor	edition of critical text	NT	New Testament
edn.	edition	Ol.	Olympiad
esp.	especially	OT	Old Testament
f., ff.	and following	oz.	ounce/s
fl.	floruit	pref.	preface
fr.	fragment	prol.	prologue
ft.	foot/feet	ps.-	pseudo-
g.	gram/s	repr.	reprint, reprinted
Gk.	Greek	Suppl.	Supplement
i.a.	*inter alia*	T	*testimonium* (i.e. piece of
ibid.	ibidem, in the same work		ancient evidence about
introd.	introduction		an author)
kg.	kilogram/s	trans.	translation, translated by
km.	kilometre/s	yd.	yard

B. AUTHORS AND BOOKS

Note: [--] names of authors or works in square brackets indicate false or doubtful attributions
A small number above the line indicates the number of an edition

AA	see Syme, *AA*	*Sept.*	*Septem contra Thebas*
AE	*L'Année Épigraphique*, published	*Supp.*	*Supplices*
	in *Revue Archéologique* and	Aeschin.	Aeschines
	separately (1888–)	*In Ctes.*	*Against Ctesiphon*
Ael.	Aelianus	*In Tim.*	*Against Timarchus*
VH	*Varia Historia*	*AJPhil.*	*American Journal of Philology*
Aesch.	Aeschylus	Alc.	Alcaeus
Ag.	*Agamemnon*	Alcm.	Alcman
Cho.	*Choephoroe*	Anecd. Bekk.	*Anecdota Graeca*, ed. I. Bekker, 3
Eum.	*Eumenides*		vols. (1814–21)
Pers.	*Persae*	Anon.	Anonymus *De Comoedia*
PV	*Prometheus Vinctus*	*De com.*	

ANRW	Aufstieg und Niedergang der römischen Welt (1972–)	Asc.	Asconius
Anth. Pal.	Anthologia Palatina	Mil.	Commentary on Cicero, Pro Milone
Ant. Lib.	Antoninus Liberalis	Astin, Scipio	A. E. Astin, Scipio Aemilianus (1967)
Met.	Metamorphoses		
AO	see Develin, AO	Ath.	Athenaeus
APF	see Davies, APF	Ath. pol.	Athenaion politeia (Aristotelian); see also Xen. for 'Old Oligarch' i.e. Ps.-Xen. Ath. Pol.
Apollod.	Apollodorus mythographus		
App.	Appian		
B Civ.	Bella civilia	August.	Augustine
Syr.	Συριακή	Conf.	Confessions
Apul.	Apuleius	Ep.	Epistulae
Apol.	Apologia	Auson.	Ausonius (see Green)
Flor.	Florida	Grat. act.	Gratiarum actio
Ap. Rhod.	Apollonius Rhodius	Austin	M. M. Austin, The Hellenistic World from Alexander to the Roman Conquest (1981)
Argon.	Argonautica		
Ar.	Aristophanes		
Ach.	Acharnenses	Austin, CGFP	C. Austin, Comicorum Graecorum fragmenta in papyris reperta (1973)
Av.	Aves		
Eccl.	Ecclesiazusae		
Eq.	Equites		
Lys.	Lysistrata	Bacchyl.	Bacchylides (ed. B. Snell and H. Maehler, 1970)
Nub.	Nubes		
Plut.	Plutus	BGU	Berliner Griechische Urkunden (Ägyptische Urkunden aus den Kgl. Museen zu Berlin)
Ran.	Ranae		
Thesm.	Thesmophoriazusae		
Vesp.	Vespae	BHisp.	Bellum Hispaniense
Archil.	Archilochus	BICS	Bulletin of the Institute of Classical Studies, London
Archim.	Archimedes, Method of Mechanical Theorems		
Method		Blass, Att. Ber.	F. Blass, Die Attische Beredsamkeit, 2nd edn. (1887–98)
Ar. Did.	Arius Didymus		
Arist.	Aristotle		
An. post.	Analytica posteriora	BM Coins, Rom. Emp.	British Museum Catalogue of Coins of the Roman Empire (1923–)
Eth. Eud.	Ethica Eudemia		
Eth. Nic.	Ethica Nicomachea		
Gen. an.	De generatione animalium	Broughton, MRR	T. R. S. Broughton, The Magistrates of the Roman Republic (1951–2); Suppl. (1986: supersedes Suppl. 1960)
Gen. corr.	De generatione et corruptione		
Metaph.	Metaphysica		
Ph.	Physica		
Poet.	Poetica		
Pol.	Politica	Caes.	Caesar
Rh.	Rhetorica	B Civ.	Bellum Civile
Top.	Topica	B Gall.	Bellum Gallicum
Aristid. Or.	Aristides, Orationes	Callim.	Callimachus
Aristox.	Aristoxenus	Aet.	Aetia
Fr. hist.	Fragmenta historica	Epigr.	Epigrammata
Harm.	Harmonica	Hymn 1	Hymn to Zeus
Arn.	Arnobius	" 2	" " Apollo
Adv. nat.	Adversus nationes	" 3	" " Artemis
Arr.	Arrian	" 4	" " Delos
Anab.	Anabasis	" 5	" " Athena
Cyn.	Cynegeticus	" 6	" " Demeter
Epict. diss.	Epicteti dissertationes		
ARV	J. D. Beazley, Attic Red-Figure Vase-Painters, 2nd edn. (1963)	Ia	Iambics
		Calp. Ecl.	Calpurnius Siculus, Eclogues

Carm. epigr.	Carmina epigraphica ('pars posterior' of Anthologia Latina)
Carm. pop.	Carmina popularia in Diehl's Anth. Lyr. Graec. 2, pp. 192–208
Cass. Dio	Cassius Dio
Catull.	Catullus
Chron. Pasch.	Chronicon Paschale
Cic.	Cicero (Marcus Tullius)
Acad.	Academicae quaestiones
Acad. post.	Academica posteriora (=Plasberg, Bk. 4)
Att.	Epistulae ad Atticum
Balb.	Pro Balbo
Brut.	Brutus or De Claris Oratoribus
Cat.	In Catilinam
Corn.	Pro Cornelio de maiestate (fragmentary)
De or.	De oratore
Div.	De divinatione
Dom.	De domo sua
Fam.	Epistulae ad familiares
Fin.	De finibus
Font.	Pro Fonteio
Har. resp.	De haruspicum responso
Leg.	De legibus
Mil.	Pro Milone
Off.	De officiis
Orat.	Orator ad M. Brutum
Phil.	Orationes Philippicae
Pis.	In Pisonem
Q Fr.	Epistulae ad Quintum fratrem
Rep.	De republica
Scaur.	Pro Scauro
Sest.	Pro Sestio
Tim.	Timaeus
Tog. cand.	Oratio in senatu in toga candida (fragmentary)
Tusc.	Tusculanae disputationes
Verr.	In Verrem
CIL	Corpus Inscriptionum Latinarum (1863–)
CJ	Classical Journal
Clem. Al.	Clemens Alexandrinus
Strom.	Stromateis
Cod.	Codex
Cod. Theod.	Codex Theodosianus
Columella, Rust.	Columella, De re rustica
C Phil.	Classical Philology
Courtney, FLP	E. Courtney, The Fragmentary Latin Poets (1993)
CQ	Classical Quarterly

Cron. Erc.	Bolletino del Centro internazionale per lo studio dei papyri ercolanesi
Davies, APF	J. K. Davies, Athenian Propertied Families 600–300 BC (1971)
Dem.	Demosthenes
De fals. leg.	De falsa legatione
Dessau, ILS	H. Dessau, Inscriptiones Latinae Selectae (1892–1916)
Develin, AO	R. Develin, Athenian Officials 684–321 BC (1989)
Diels, Dox. Graec.	H. Diels, Doxographi Graeci (1879)
Dig.	Digesta
Din.	Dinarchus
Dio Chrys. Or.	Dio Chrysostomus Orationes
Diod. Sic.	Diodorus Siculus
Diog. Laert.	Diogenes Laertius
Dion. Hal.	Dionysius Halicarnassensis
Ant. Rom.	Antiquitates Romanae
Comp.	De compositione verborum
De imit.	De imitatione
Lys.	De Lysia
Pomp.	Epistula ad Pompeium
Thuc.	De Thucydide
DK	H. Diels and W. Kranz, Fragmente der Vorsokratiker, 6th edn. (1952)
Donat.	Aelius Donatus
Vit. Verg.	Vita Vergilii
EJ	V. Ehrenberg and A. H. M. Jones, Documents Illustrating the Reigns of Augustus and Tiberius, 2nd edn. (1976)
Enc. Virg.	Enciclopedia Virgiliana, 5 vols. (1984–90)
Enn. Ann.	Ennius, Annales
Ep.	Epistula
Epictetus, Diss. Schenkl	Epicteti Dissertationes, ed. H. Schenkl (1894)
Epicurus	Epicurus
Ep.	Epistulae
Ep. Hdt.	Epistula ad Herodotum
Ep. Men.	Epistula ad Menoeceum
Ep. Pyth.	Epistula ad Pythoclem
Sent. Vat.	Vatican Sayings, = Gnomologium Vaticanum
RS	Ratae sententiae
Epigr. Gr.	G. Kaibel, Epigrammata Graeca ex lapidibus conlecta (1878)
Epit.	Epitome

Eratosth.	Eratosthenes	Gow–Page,	A. S. F. Gow and D. L. Page, *The*
Etym. Magn.	*Etymologicum Magnum*	*HE*	*Greek Anthology: Hellenistic*
Euc.	Euclid		*Epigrams*, 2 vols. (1965)
Eur.	Euripides		
Alc.	*Alcestis*	*Harv. Stud.*	*Harvard Studies in Classical*
Andr.	*Andromache*		*Philology*
Bacch.	*Bacchae*	*HCT*	A. W. Gomme, A. Andrewes, and
Beller.	*Bellerophon*		K. J. Dover, *A Historical*
Cyc.	*Cyclops*		*Commentary on Thucydides*,
El.	*Electra*		5 vols. (1945–81)
Hec.	*Hecuba*	Hdn.	Herodianus
Hel.	*Helena*	Hdt.	Herodotus
Heracl.	*Heraclidae*	Heraclid.	Heraclides Ponticus
HF	*Hercules furens*	Pont.	
Hipp.	*Hippolytus*	Hermog.	Hermogenes
Hyps.	*Hypsipyle*	*Id.*	Περὶ ἰδεῶν
IA	*Iphigenia Aulidensis*	Hes.	Hesiod
IT	*Iphigenia Taurica*	*Cat.*	*Catalogus mulierum*
Med.	*Medea*	*Op.*	*Opera et Dies*
Or.	*Orestes*	*[Sc.]*	*Scutum*
Phoen.	*Phoenissae*	*Theog.*	*Theogonia*
Rhes.	*Rhesus*	Hieron.	Hieronymus, see Jerome
Sthen.	*Stheneboea*	Hippol.	Hippolytus
Supp.	*Supplices*	*Haer.*	*Refutatio omnium haeresium*
Tro.	*Troades*	*Hist.*	*Historia*
Euseb.	Eusebius	*Hist. Aug.*	*Historia Augusta* (see SHA)
Chron.	*Chronica*	Hom.	Homer
Hist. eccl.	*Historia ecclesiastica*	*Il.*	*Iliad*
Praep.	*Praeparatio evangelica*	*Od.*	*Odyssey*
evang.		Hor.	Horace
Eust.	Eustathius	*Ars P.*	*Ars poetica*
Prooem.	*Eustathii prooemium*	*Carm.*	*Carmina* or *Odes*
ad Pind.	*commentariorum*	*Carm. saec.*	*Carmen saeculare*
	Pindaricorum, ed. F. W.	*Epist.*	*Epistulae*
	Schneidewin (1837)	*Epod.*	*Epodi*
		Sat.	*Satirae* or *Sermones*
FGrH	F. Jacoby, *Fragmente der*	hyp.	hypothesis
	griechischen Historiker		
	(1923–)	Iambl.	Iamblichus
Fornara	C. W. Fornara (ed.), *Archaic*	*VP*	*Vita Pythagorae*
	Times to the End of the	*IG*	*Inscriptiones Graecae* (1873–)
	Peloponnesian War, 2nd edn.:	*ILabraunda*	J. Crampa (ed.), *Labraunda*
	Translated Documents of		*Swedish Excavations and*
	Greece and Rome 1 (1983)		*Researches* 3 (1 and 2): *The*
Fulg.	Fulgentius		*Greek Inscriptions* (1969 and
Myth.	*Mitologiae tres libri*		1972)
Serm. Ant.	*Expositio sermonum*	*ILLRP*	*Inscriptiones Latinae Liberae Rei*
	antiquorum		*Republicae*, ed. A. Degrassi,
			vol. 1^2 (1965), 2 (1963)
G&R	*Greece and Rome*, NS (1954/5–)	*ILS*	see Dessau
Gai. *Inst.*	Gaius, *Institutiones*	*IMylasa*	W. Blümel, *Die Inschriften von*
Gal.	Galen		*Mylasa* (2 vols., 1987–8)
Libr. Propr.	Περὶ τῶν ἰδίων βιβλίων	*Inscr. Ital.*	*Inscriptiones Italiae* (1931/2–)
Gell.	Aulus Gellius		
NA	*Noctes Atticae*	*JACT*	Joint Association of Classical
GL	see Keil, *Gramm. Lat.*		Teachers

Jer.   Jerome

Ab. Abr.   *Ab Abraham,* the chronological reckoning from the first year of Abraham followed in Jerome's translation and enlargement of Eusebius' Chronicle

Chron.   *Chronica = Ab Abr.*

Ep.   *Epistulae*

JHS   *Journal of Hellenic Studies*

Joseph   Josephus

AJ   *Antiquitates Judaicae*

BJ   *Bellum Judaicum*

Vit.   *Vita*

JRS   *Journal of Roman Studies*

Just. *Epit.*   Justinus, *Epitome* (of Trogus)

Justin, *Apol.*   Justin Martyr, *Apologia*

KA   see Kassel–Austin

Kassel–Austin, PCG   R. Kassel and C. Austin, *Poetae Comici Graeci,* vol. 1 (1983), 2 (1991)

Keil, *Gramm. Lat.*   H. Keil, *Grammatici Latini,* 8 vols. (1855–1923; repr. 1961)

Kl. Schr.   *Kleine Schriften* (of various authors)

Körte, *Men. Rel.*   A. Körte, *Menandri Reliquiae*

Kühn   K. G. Kühn, *Medicorum Graecorum Opera*

Lactant.   Lactantius

Div. inst.   *Divinae institutiones*

Lib.   Libanius

[Longinus], *Subl.*   [Longinus], Περὶ ὕψους

LP   E. Lobel and D. L. Page, *Poetarum Lesbiorum Fragmenta* (1955)

Lucian

Alex.   *Alexander*

Anach.   *Anacharsis*

Macr.   *Macrobii*

Lucil.   Lucilius

Lucr.   Lucretius

Malcovati, *ORF*   H. Malcovati, *Oratorum Romanorum Fragmenta* (2nd edn. 1955; 4th edn. 1967)

Marm. Par.   *Marmor Parium* (*IG* 12 (5), 444)

M. Aur. *Med*   Marcus Aurelius, *Meditations*

Mette   H. J. Mette, *Urkunden dramatischer Aufführungen in Griechenland,* Texte und Kommentare no. 8 (1977)

Michel   C. Michel, *Recueil d'inscriptions grecques* (1900–27)

Migne, *PG*   Migne, *Patrologiae Cursus, series Graeca*

PL   *Patrologiae Cursus, series Latina*

ML   R. Meiggs and D. Lewis, *A Selection of Greek Historical Inscriptions to the End of the Fifth Century BC,* rev. edn. (1988)

Nash, *Pict. Dict. Rome*   E. Nash, *Pictorial Dictionary of Ancient Rome* (1961–2; 2nd edn. 1989)

Nauck   see *TGF*

Nauck/Snell   see *TGF*

Nemes.   Nemesianus

Cyn.   *Cynegetica*

Ecl.   *Eclogae*

Nep.   Nepos

Att.   *Atticus*

Nov. Theod.   *Novellae Theodosianae*

OCT   Oxford Classical Texts

Od.   *Odyssey*

OGI   *Orientis Graeci Inscriptiones Selectae*

'Old Oligarch'   see Xen. for *Ath. Pol.* attributed to Xenophon (see entry OLD OLIGARCH)

Or.   *Oratio*

ORF and *ORF*⁴   see Malcovati, *ORF*

Ov.   Ovid

Am.   *Amores*

Ars am.   *Ars amatoria*

Fast.   *Fasti*

Hal.   *Halieuticon liber*

Her.   *Heroides*

Ib.   *Ibis*

Medic.   *Medicamina faciei*

Met.   *Metamorphoses*

Pont.   *Epistulae ex Ponto*

Tr.   *Tristia*

Page, *FGE*   D. L. Page *Further Greek Epigrams* (1981)

PMG   *Poetae Melici Graeci* (1962)

Parth.   Parthenius

Amat. narr.   *Narrationum amatoriarum libellus* (Ἐρωτικὰ παθήματα)

Paus.   Pausanias

PBrux.   *Papyri bruxellenses graeci* 1:
                Papyrus du nome Prosopite,
                Nos. 1–21, by G. Nachtergael
                (1984); 2: *No. 22,* by M. Huys
                (1991). For *PBrux.* 7616 see C.
                Préaux and M. Hombert,
                Recherches sur le recensement
                dans l'Égypte romaine,
                Papryologica Lugduno-Batava 5
                (1952)
PCG   see Kassel–Austin
PCPS   *Proceedings of the Cambridge*
                Philological Society
Peter, *HRRel.* H. Peter, *Historicorum*
                Romanorum Reliquiae, vol. 1²
                (1914), 2 (1906)
Pf.   R. Pfeiffer
Philo   Philo Judaeus
  Leg.   *Legatio ad Gaium*
Philol.   *Philologus*
Philostr.   Philostratus
  V S   *Vitae sophistarum*
Phot.   Photius
  Bibl.   *Bibliotheca*
Pind.   Pindar (ed. B. Snell and H.
                Maehler, 1987–8)
  Isthm.   *Isthmian Odes*
  Nem.   *Nemean   "*
  Pyth.   *Pythian   "*
  Pae.   *Paeanes   "*
PIR   *Prosopographia Imperii Romani*
                Saeculi I, II, III, 1st edn. by E.
                Klebs and H. Dessau (1897–8);
                2nd edn. by E. Groag, A. Stein,
                and others (1933–   )
PL   see Migne
Pl.   Plato
  Ap.   *Apologia*
  Chrm.   *Charmides*
  [Hipparch.] *Hipparchus*
  Phd.   *Phaedo*
  Prm.   *Parmenides*
  Prt.   *Protagoras*
  Resp.   *Respublica*
  Symp.   *Symposium*
Platon.   Platonius
  Diff. com. *De differentia comoediarum*
Plaut.   Plautus
  Amph.   *Amphitruo*
  Mil.   *Miles gloriosus*
  Mostell.   *Mostellaria*
PLille   *Papyrus grecs* (Institut
                papyrologique de l'Université
                de Lille, 1907–12)
Plin.   Pliny (the Elder)
  HN   *Naturalis historia*

Plin.   Pliny (the Younger)
  Ep.   *Epistulae*
  Pan.   *Panegyricus*
Plotinus,   Plotinus, *Enneades*
  Enn.
PLRE   *Prosopography of the Later*
                Roman Empire 1, ed. A. H. M.
                Jones and others (1970); 2 and
                3, ed. J. R. Martindale
                (1980–92)
Plut.   Plutarch
  Mor.   *Moralia*
  De exil.   *De exilio*
  De fac.   *De facie in orbe lunae*
  De glor.   *De gloria Atheniensium*
    Ath.
  [De mus]   *De musica*
  Quaest.   *Quaestiones convivales*
    conv.
  Vit.   *Vitae Parallelae*
    Alc.   *Alcibiades*
    Ant.   *Antonius*
    Arat.   *Aratus*
    Brut.   *Brutus*
    Cam.   *Camillus*
    C. Gracch. *Gaius Gracchus*
    Cic.   *Cicero*
    Cim.   *Cimon*
    Luc.   *Lucullus*
    Lyc.   *Lycurgus*
    Lys.   *Lysander*
    Mar.   *Marius*
    Marc.   *Marcellus*
    Nic.   *Nicias*
    Num.   *Numa*
    Pel.   *Pelopidas*
    Per.   *Pericles*
    Sol.   *Solon*
    Sull.   *Sulla*
    Them.   *Themistocles*
    Ti. Gracch. *Tiberius Gracchus*
    X orat.   *Vitae decem oratorum*
Polyb.   Polybius
Porph   Porphyry
  Plot.   *Vita Plotini*
Pow.   see Powell, *Coll. Alex.*
Powell, *Coll.* J. U. Powell, *Collectanea*
  Alex.   *Alexandrina* (1925)
P Oxy.   *Oxyrhynchus Papyri* (1898–   )
  praef.   *praefatio*
Prisc. *Inst.* Priscian, *Institutio de arte*
                grammatica

Procl.   Proclus
 Hypotyp.   Hypotyposis
 Comm. in   Commentary on the first book
   Eucl.   of Euclid's Elements
Prop.   Propertius
PSI   Papiri Greci e Latini,
                Pubblicazioni della Società
                italiana per la ricerca dei papiri
                greci e latini in Egitto (1912–)
PSorbonn.   Papyrus de la Sorbonne 1,
                nos. 1–68, ed. H. Cadell (1966)
P Teb.   Tebtunis Papyri (1902–76)
Ptol.   Ptolemaeus mathematicus
 Harm.   Harmonica
P Vat. II   Il Papiro Vaticano Greco II, ed.
                M. Norsa and G. Vitelli (1931)
PVS   Proceedings of the Vergil Society

Quint.   Quintilian
 Inst.   Institutio oratoria

RE   A. Pauly, G. Wissowa, and
                W. Kroll, Real-Encyclopädie d.
                klassischen Altertumswissenschaft
                (1893–)
Rev. Arch.   Revue archéologique
Rhet. Her.   Rhetorica ad Herennium
Rh. Mus.   Rheinisches Museum für
                Philologie (1827–), NS
                (1842–)
RRC   M. H. Crawford, Roman
                Republican Coinage (1974)

Sall.   Sallust
 [Ad Caes.   Epistulae ad Caesarem senem
   sen.]
 Cat.   Bellum Catilinae or De
                Catilinae coniuratione
 Hist.   Historiae
 Iug.   Bellum Iugurthinum
Satyr.   Satyrus Historicus
 Vit. Eur.   Vita Euripidis
Sherk,   The Roman Empire: Augustus to
 Hadrian   Hadrian, Translated
                Documents of Greece and
                Rome 6 (1988)
Sid. Apoll.   Sidonius Apollinaris
 Carm.   Carmina
 Epist.   Epistulae
SIG   see Syll.³
Sil.   Silius Italicus
 Pun.   Punica
Simpl.   Simplicius
 in Cael.   in Aristotelis de Caelo
                Commentarii

in Phys.   in Aristotelis de Physica
                Commentarii
Smallwood,   E. M. Smallwood, Documents
 Docs.   illustrating the Principates of
 … Nerva   Nerva, Trajan and Hadrian
                (1966)
 Docs.   Documents illustrating the
  … Gaius   Principates of Gaius, Claudius
                and Nero (1967)
Snell–   see Bacchyl. and Pind.
 Maehler
Socrates,   Socrates, Historia ecclesiastica
 Hist. eccl.
Stat.   Statius
 Achil.   Achilleis
 Silv.   Silvae
 Theb.   Thebais
Steph. Byz.   Stephanus Byzantius or
                Byzantinus
Suda   Greek Lexicon formerly known
                as Suidas
Suet.   Suetonius
 Dom.   Domitianus
 Gram.   De grammaticis
 Iul.   Divus Iulius
 Ner.   Nero
 Rel. Reiff. Reliquiae, ed. Reifferscheid
 Tib.   Tiberius
 Tit.   Divus Titus
 Vesp.   Divus Vespasianus
 Vit.   Vitellius
 Vita Hor.   Vita Horatii
Suppl. Hell. H. Lloyd-Jones and P. Parsons
                (eds.), Supplementum
                Hellenisticum, Texte und
                Kommentare no. 11 (1983)
Schmitt, SdA H. H. Schmitt (ed.), Die
                Staatsverträge des Altertums 3:
                Die Verträge der griechisch-
                römischen Welt von 338 bis 200
                v. Chr. (1969)
schol.   scholiast or scholia
Schol. Bob.   Scholia Bobiensia
Schol. Flor. Scholia Florentina in
 Callim.   Callimachum
SEG   Supplementum epigraphicum
                Graecum (1923–)
Sen.   Seneca (the Elder)
 Controv.   Controversiae
 Suas.   Suasoriae
Sen.   Seneca (the Younger)
 Apocol.   Apocolocyntosis
 Ep.   Epistulae
 Q Nat.   Quaestiones naturales
Serv.   Servius
 Praef.   Praefatio

Sext. Emp.	Sextus Empiricus	Tod	M. N. Tod. *Greek Historical*
Math.	*Adversus mathematicos*		*Inscriptions* vol. 1² (1946),
Pyr.	Πυρρώνειοι ὑποτυπώσεις		2 (1948)
SHA	Scriptores Historiae Augustae		
Ant. Pius	*Antoninus Pius*	Val. Max.	Valerius Maximus
Hadr.	*Hadrian*	Varro, *Ling*	Varro, *De lingua Latina*
Prob.	*Probus*	*Rust.*	*De re rustica*
CLA	D. R. Shackleton Bailey (ed.),	*Sat. Men.*	*Saturae Menippeae*
	Cicero's Letters to Atticus, 7	Vell. Pat.	Velleius Paterculus
	vols. (1965–70)	Verg.	Virgil
SVF	H. von Arnim, *Stoicorum*	*Aen.*	*Aeneid*
	Veterum Fragmenta (1903–)	*Ecl.*	*Eclogues*
*Syll.*³	W. Dittenberger, *Sylloge*	*G.*	*Georgics*
	Inscriptionum Graecarum, 3rd	*Vit. Aesch.*	*Vita Aeschyli* (OCT of Aeschylus)
	edn. (1915–24)	*Vit. Ar.*	*Vita Aristophanis*
Syme	R. Syme	*Vit. Eurip.*	*Vita Euripidis* (OCT of
AA	*The Augustan*		Euripides)
	Aristocracy (1986)		
		W	see West, *GLP* and *IE*²
Tac.	Tacitus	Wallbank,	F. W. Wallbank, *A Historical*
Agr.	*Agricola*	*HCP*	*Commentary on Polybius*, 3
Ann.	*Annales*		vols. (1947–79)
Dial.	*Dialogus de oratoribus*	Wehrli	F. Wehrli (ed.), *Die Schule des*
Germ.	*Germania*		*Aritoteles 7*, 2nd edn. (1969)
Hist.	*Historiae*	West, *GLP*	M. L. West, *Greek Lyric Poetry*
TAPA	*Transactions of the American*		(1993)
	Philological Association	*GM*	*Greek Metre* (1982)
Ter.	Terence	*IE*²	*Iambi et Elegi*, 2nd edn. (1989)
Ad.	*Adelphoe*		
An.	*Andria*	Xen.	Xenophon
Eun.	*Eunuchus*	*An.*	*Anabasis*
Haut.	*H(e)autontimorumenos*	*Ap.*	*Apologia Socratis*
Hec.	*Hecyra*	*Hell.*	*Hellenica*
Phorm.	*Phormio*	*Mem.*	*Memorabilia*
TGF	A. Nauck, *Tragicorum*	*Symp.*	*Symposium*
	Graecorum Fragmenta, 2nd	*Vect.*	*De vectigalibus*
	edn. (1889); Suppl. by B. Snell		
	(1964)	*YClS*	*Yale Classical Studies*
Them. *Or.*	Themistius, *Orationes*		
Theoc.	Theocritus	Zonar.	Zonaras
Epigr.	*Epigrammata*	*ZPE*	*Zeitschrift für Papyrologie und*
Id.	*Idylls*		*Epigraphik*
Theophr.	Theophrastus		
Sens.	*De sensibus*		

How to use this book

This book is designed for easy use but the following notes may be helpful to the reader.

Chronological span The period covered is from the middle of the second millennium BC to the 6th century AD, with the main concentration of coverage focused on 800 BC to AD 300. For a brief outline, see the Chronology on pp. 435–40.

Alphabetical arrangement Entries are arranged in letter-by-letter alphabetical order of their headwords, which are shown in bold type.

Names In all cases the forms of names used are those that are the most familiar. Thus, Roman individuals of the Republican and imperial periods (up to about AD 275) are listed under their surname (*cognomen*) rather than the family name (*nomen*). For example, Cicero is listed under C rather than under his family name of Tullius, and the great general Publius Cornelius Scipio Aemilianus Africanus is listed under the familiar form 'Scipio Africanus', rather than under his family name of Cornelius. Similarly, Roman emperors, who often had long names, are listed under their usual short form, such as Nero, and the full name follows in parentheses.

In antiquity, the Latin alphabet did not contain the letter J and only in medieval times were many Roman names, such as Iulius, written with a J. In this book, we have retained the 'I' spellings except for those names which occur as headwords, which the reader would naturally look for under J.

Note that the Roman forename (*praenomen*) Gaius is conventionally abbreviated C. (not G.) and similarly Gnaeus is abbreviated Cn. not Gn.

Greek names are normally spelt in their more familiar Latinized or Anglicized forms (that is, 'Pericles' not 'Perikles').

Transliteration of Greek Except where its use was thought essential to the subject matter or context of the entry, Greek has been transliterated, with long vowels indicated by macrons ($\bar{o}$, $\bar{e}$).

Cross-references An asterisk (*) in front of a word in the text signals a cross-reference to a related entry which may be interesting to look up. Similarly, 'see' or 'see also' followed by a headword in small capitals is used to cross-refer when the precise form of headword to which the reader is being pointed does not occur naturally in the text.

References to classical texts and commentaries are given in abbreviated form in the entries, for the benefit of classics students and others who may wish to follow them up. Details of these sources are given in full at the front of the book (pp. xii–xix).

Contributors' initials are given at the end of each entry, and a key to these initials is provided on pp. ix–xi.

Aa

Accius, Lucius (170–*c*.86 BC), stage poet and literary scholar of municipal freedman birth. His family's lands were at Pisaurum in Umbria. He attached himself in Rome to Decimus Junius Brutus Callaicus (consul 138). Although of conservative political views, he believed that literary talent demanded in its context more respect than nobility of birth (cf. the anecdote about Gaius Julius Caesar Strabo Vopiscus at Val. Max. 3. 7. 11). He had a touchy sense of his own importance, always avenging insults (*Rhet. Her.* 1. 24). Contemporaries were amused by the outsize statues of himself he had placed in the temple of the Muses (Plin. *HN* 34. 19).

Over 40 tragic titles and not one unmistakably comic title are transmitted. (*Achilles, Aegisthus, Agamemnonidae, Alcestis, Alcmeo, Alphesiboea, Amphitruo, Andromeda, Antenoridae, Antigona, Armorum iudicium, Astyanax, Athamas, Atreus, Bacchae, Chrysippus, Clytemestra, Deiphobus, Diomedes, Epigoni, Epinausimache, Erigona, Eriphyla, Eurysaces, Hecuba, Hellenes, Medea, Melanippus, Meleager, Minotaurus, Myrmidones, Neoptolemus, Nyctegresia, Oenomaus, Pelopidae, Persidae, Philocteta, Phinidae, Phoenissae, Prometheus, Stasiastae vel Tropaeum Liberi, Telephus, Tereus, Thebais, Troaides*). A relatively large number concerned the Trojan cycle of legends. The earliest, probably the *Atreus*, was performed in 140 (Cic. *Brut.* 229). The year 104 saw the première of the *Tereus*. The *Brutus* dramatized the tyrannical deeds of the second Tarquin (L. *Tarquinius Superbus). It could have glanced at the ambitions of the *Gracchi. The *Aeneadae vel Decius* centred on the defeat of the Gallo-Etrusco-Samnite alliance at Sentinum in 295. It must have given prominence to the non-Italian origin of the Romans; possibly in conscious criticism of the demands being formulated by the Italian allies (*socii*) in the last part of the 2nd cent.

A lengthy hexameter poem, the *Annales*, found Greek origins for Roman religious festivals. The trochaic septenarii of the *Pragmatica* had something to do with the theatre. In the case of the *Parerga* and the *Praxidica* neither the style nor the range of content is clear. The *Didascalica* ran to at least nine books and comprehended among other things the history of both the Athenian and the Roman theatre. Accius cast his discourse here in a mixture of prose and diverse poetical metres. Later researchers demonstrated his dates for the activities of *Livius Andronicus to be too low (Cic. *Brut.* 72) and disputed his judgement that the *Gemini lenones, Condalium, Anus bis compressa, Boeotia, Agroecus* and *Commorientes* then attributed to Plautus were spurious (Gell. *NA* 3. 3). Various attempts by him to make the Latin orthographical system reflect more closely the actual pronunciation of the language were not taken up. His desire to kill off the practice of giving Greek names Latin terminations (Varro, *Ling.* 10. 70) had more influence. Varro admired his learning sufficiently to dedicate to him his *De ambiguitate litterarum.* More respect for old Roman tradition was shown by his composition in Saturnian verses of an *elogium* for his patron Brutus (*schol. Bob. Cic.* p. 179). Somewhat out of character with his dignified public mien seems a work of obscure content but clearly frivolous form cited by *Gellius and Diomedes, the *Sotadica.* *Pliny the Younger put him among the Latin erotic poets (*Ep.* 5. 6).

The grandeur of Accius' tragic style caused some contemporaries to laugh (Porphyrio, *Hor. Serm.* 1. 10. 53). *Cicero, however, who was proud to have known him personally, admired his plays almost as highly as he did those of *Pacuvius and cited extensive passages in his rhetorical and philosophical dialogues. Performances are known of the *Eurysaces, Clytemestra, Tereus,* and *Brutus* on the mid-1st-cent. BC stage. The likes of *Columella and *Seneca the Younger continued to read him. In late antiquity Nonius Marcellus had access to at least 30 of his scripts, and a writer on old Latin metre could cite four at first hand (*Priscian, ed. Keil, *Gramm. Lat.* 3. 418 ff.). H.D.J.

Achilles Tatius Greek novelist from Alexandria, author of 'The Story of Leucippe and Cleitophon' (*Ta kata Leukippēn kai Kleitophōnta*) in eight books. Shown by papyri to be circulating by the late 2nd cent. AD, it can hardly antedate AD 150. Of three other works ascribed to Achilles by the *Suda* (a Byzantine lexicon), two are lost (an *Etymology* and a *Miscellaneous History of Many Great and Illustrious Men*), and the ascription of that partly preserved, *On the Sphere*, is debated. The *Suda*'s story that later he became a Christian, and even a bishop, is probably false. Achilles varies patterns common to the genre: the enamoured couple elope and survive shipwreck, attacks by pirates and brigands, and complicated adventures in Egypt; they are eventually reunited in Ephesus after Leucippe has passed a chastity-test (cf. *Heliodorus). The story is presented as Cleitophon's autobiographic narrative, told to the writer in a temple grove at Sidon (cf. *Longus). Unusually (but again cf. Longus) he succumbs (once) to the advances of a suitor, the married Ephesian Melite. Melodramatic effects include false deaths (three times Leucippe 'dies' and comes to life) and Achilles shares Heliodorus' and *Philostratus' fondness for learned digressions, some remote from his theme (e.g. on the phoenix, 3. 25, and the elephant, 4. 4), others making important if oblique contributions, like the description of the painting of Europa(1. 1) and the debate on the respective attractions of homosexual and heterosexual love (2. 35–8). His diction atticizes (i.e. was modelled on classical Athenian speech), though not consistently; his short, asyndetic sentences, sometimes of equal length and similar rhythm (*isokola*), class him with Gorgias, 'Asianic' orators, and contemporaries like Polemon, Longus, and Aelian while a sophistic background is reflected in his characters' readiness to declaim. Ancient and modern critics alike have found him hard to evaluate. Some see his strained effects as humorous parody, but his attention to emotions and character-development is commended as realistic, and he handles sex

explicitly enough to attract charges of pornography. Photius (*Bibl.* cod. 87, cf. *Anth. Pal.* 9. 203) praised Achilles' style but condemned his licentiousness; most moderns, uncertain how to evaluate him, prefer Longus and Heliodorus. E.L.B.

Aelius Seianus See SEJANUS.

Aemilius Lepidus See LEPIDUS.

Aemilius Papinianus See PAPINIAN.

Aemilius Paullus See PAULLUS.

Aemilius Scaurus See SCAURUS.

Aeschines (*c.*397–*c.*322 BC), Athenian orator whose exchanges with *Demosthenes in the courts in 343 and 330 provide a large part of the evidence for the relations of Athens and Macedon in the 340s and the 330s. His origins were sufficiently obscure to allow Demosthenes' invention full play. He probably did not receive the usual formal training in rhetoric, but after hoplite service of some distinction in the 360s and early 350s, and a period as an actor, he embarked on a public career as a supporter first briefly of Aristophon and then of *Eubulus, during whose supervision of the city's finances Aeschines' brother, Aphobetus, was a theoric commissioner (treasurer of the fund from which grants were made to enable citizens to attend the theatre). In 347/6 both Aeschines and Demosthenes were members of the *boulē* (Council of Five Hundred) and their disagreements led to sixteen years of enmity. Early in 346 (though many have dated the affair to 348/7) when alarming news reached Athens of the extension of Macedonian influence to Arcadia, Eubulus supported by Aeschines took the lead in urging Athens to protest to Arcadia and to seek to organize a Common Peace, which would provide for common action against aggressors and so make it unnecessary for any state to seek Macedonian help. Aeschines was sent on an embassy to Megalopolis where he sought to dissuade the assembly of the Arcadians from dealings with *Philip II. Whether through the indifference of the Greek states or through the new threat to Greece caused by the refusal of the Phocian tyrant, Phalaecus, to permit access to Thermopylae, the key-point for the defence of Greece, the initiative of Eubulus and Aeschines proved abortive. An embassy of ten, including Aeschines and Demosthenes, was hastily sent to negotiate peace terms with Philip. Their return to the city was closely followed by a Macedonian embassy, and on the 18th and 19th Elaphebolion, when the peace was debated and voted, Aeschines played a notable if ineffectual part. Demosthenes, realizing that peace was essential and that the only form of peace which Philip would accept was a plain alliance with Athens and her allies of the Second Athenian Confederacy, made himself responsible for getting the decree of Philocrates passed: Aeschines strove without success for a Common Peace open to all the Greeks. The ten ambassadors then set off again to secure Philip's oath to the treaty which he did not render until his forces were in position to attack Phocis. When the ambassadors returned with this alarming news, it was decided in the *boulē* to recommend an expedition to save Phocis, but by 16th Skirophorion, when the people met, it was known that Philip had occupied Thermopylae; Demosthenes' proposal was not even read out and he was himself shouted down. Aeschines then made a speech, which Demosthenes chose to regard as proof that Aeschines had been won over by Macedonian bribery. The truth was probably far different; since Phocis could not be saved, Aeschines sought to reconcile the Athenians to the fact by reporting vague suggestions of Macedonian proposals for central Greece which were very much what Athens was seeking.

From that day Demosthenes was implacably opposed to Aeschines as well as determined to destroy the Peace, while Aeschines was gradually won over to support it and seek its extension into a Common Peace. In 346/5 Demosthenes with the support of Timarchus began a prosecution of Aeschines for his part in the peace negotiations; Aeschines replied by charging Timarchus with breach of the law forbidding those whose misconduct was notorious from addressing the assembly; the *Against Timarchus* was successful and Demosthenes was forced to recognize that the time was not ripe to attack Aeschines. By mid-343 the mood of Athens had clearly begun to change; early in the year Philocrates had been successfully prosecuted by *Hyperides and in the *De falsa legatione*

Demosthenes attacked Aeschines, the advocate of merely amending a discredited peace, as if he had been the orator really responsible in 346 for Athens' accepting the Peace. Aeschines replied in a speech of the same title and, supported by Eubulus and Phocion, was narrowly acquitted. Aeschines continued to have some influence in the assembly, and in 340/39 was sent as one of Athens' representatives to the Amphictionic Council (the body which controlled the affairs of the sanctuary of Delphi), on which occasion he appears to have displayed a serious lack of judgement in relation to the affairs of central Greece: at a time when the war against Philip had recommenced and there was a clear need to avoid exacerbating the divisions of Greece, Aeschines replied to Locrian charges against Athens with such a vigorous attack on the conduct of the Amphissans that hostilities began and Philip was the more easily able to intervene.

Aeschines was a member of the embassy sent to negotiate with Philip after the battle of Chaeronea (338), but from then on he withdrew from politics only to re-emerge on two occasions when circumstances seemed favourable for an attack on Demosthenes. The first was in early 336 when Ctesiphon proposed that Demosthenes should be crowned in the theatre at the Dionysia (festival of Dionysus) for the excellence of his services to the city: earlier Demosthenes had been similarly honoured without protest but, at a time when Demosthenes' gloomy predictions after Chaeronea seemed mocked by the opening of the Macedonian invasion of Persia, Aeschines indicted the decree under the *graphē paranomōn* (law against unconstitutional proposals). However, the murder of Philip made the future too uncertain for Aeschines to be confident of success, and he decided not to proceed with the indictment for the moment. In 330 after the defeat of Persia at the battle of Gaugamela (331) and the failure of the Spartan king Agis III's revolt, which Demosthenes had chosen not to support, Athens was in almost complete isolation with no prospect of liberation from Macedon, and Aeschines thought the moment suitable for him to proceed with his prosecution of Ctesiphon. In the *Against Ctesiphon*, after adducing minor, if perhaps valid, legalistic considerations concerning the details of the original decree, he reviewed the career of Demosthenes, somewhat selectively, and sought to show that Demosthenes was unworthy of the crown. In the *De corona* Demosthenes replied with all the devastating effect that his great rhetorical gifts could command, and Aeschines failed to secure the necessary fifth of the jury's votes to save him from a fine and the limitation of the right to prosecute. He chose to retire from Athens to Rhodes, where he taught rhetoric.

The supremacy of Demosthenes as an orator has to a large extent beguiled posterity into the opinion that he alone fully appreciated the menace of Macedon and correctly diagnosed the causes of Philip's success, and Aeschines has been represented as an opportunist with little judgement and less principle. In fact, there was no obvious way of saving Athens and Greece, and it is probable that Aeschines no less than Demosthenes sought to maintain his city's power and independence.

SPEECHES The only genuine speeches of Aeschines known to the critics of the Roman period were the three that we have: a fourth, concerning Delos, was rejected by the rhetor and historian Caecilius. Aeschines was a man of dignified presence and fine voice, who deprecated the use of extravagant gestures by an orator, preferring a statuesque pose. Proud of his education, he displays it by frequent quotation of poetry. In the use of historical argument he cannot compare with Demosthenes, but in a battle of wits he more than holds his own. His vocabulary is simple but effective, though occasional obscurities may be found in his sentences. Ancient critics ranked him lower than he deserves; the fact is that he was not aiming at literary perfection; his object was to produce a powerful effect on his audiences, and he was justified by the result.   G.L.C.

Aeschylus, Athenian tragic dramatist

LIFE (?525/4–456/5 BC) Aeschylus was probably born at Eleusis near Athens in 525/4 BC (*Marm. Par.*). He fought at the battle of Marathon in 490 (*Marm. Par.*; *Vita* 4, 11) and probably at Salamis in 480 (Ion of Chios, *FGrH* 392 F 7). His first tragic production was in 499 (*Suda* αι 357 with π 2230), his first victory in 484 (*Marm. Par.*); thereafter he may have been almost invariably victorious, especially after the death of *Phrynichus c.473 (he gained thirteen victories altogether, *Vita* 13). Of his surviving plays, *Persians* was produced

in 472 (his *chorēgos* or financial backer being the young *Pericles) and *Seven against Thebes* in 467. *Suppliants*, part of a production which won first prize over *Sophocles (*POxy.* 2256. 3), must be later than *Seven* (despite the predominant role of the chorus and other features once thought to prove it very early); its exact date is uncertain. The *Oresteia* (comprising *Agamemnon*, *Choephori* ('Women Bearing Drink-offerings') and *Eumenides*, with the lost satyr-play *Proteus*) was Aeschylus' last production in Athens, in 458. He had already visited Sicily once, possibly twice, at the invitation of Hieron of Syracuse, composing *Women of Aetna* in honour of Hieron's newly founded city of Aetna (*Vita* 9) and producing *Persians* at Syracuse (ibid. 18; Eratosth. in schol. Ar. *Frogs* 1028); after the production of the *Oresteia* he went there again, dying at Gela in 456/5. *Prometheus Bound*, if by Aeschylus (see below), may have been composed in Sicily and produced posthumously. His epitaph (*Vita* 11) makes no reference to his art, only to his prowess displayed at Marathon; this estimate of what was most important in Aeschylus' life—to have been a loyal and courageous citizen of a free Athens—can hardly be that of the Geloans and will reflect his own death-bed wishes (cf. Paus. 1. 14. 5) or those of his family.

Two sons of Aeschylus themselves became dramatists, Euphorion (who also restaged many of his father's plays) and Euaeon. A nephew, Philocles, was the founder of a dynasty of tragedians that lasted over a century.

WORKS (° denotes a known satyr-play). Aeschylus' total output is variously stated at between 70 and 90 plays. Seven plays have survived via medieval manuscripts, of which *Prometheus Bound* is of disputed authenticity (it was possibly composed by Euphorion and produced by him as Aeschylus' work). In addition there survive substantial papyrus fragments of °*Netfishers* (*Diktyoulkoi*) and °*Spectators at the Isthmian Games* (*Theōroi* or *Isthmiastai*).

Many of Aeschylus' productions were connected 'tetralogies', comprising three tragedies presenting successive episodes of a single story (a 'trilogy') followed by a satyr-play based on part of the same or a related myth. This seems to have been common practice in his day, though the production of .472

(*Phineus, Persians, Glaucus of Potniae* and °*Prometheus the Fire-kindler*) is an exception. Four tetralogies are securely attested: (1) the *Oresteia* (see above); (2) *Laius, Oedipus, Seven against Thebes,* °*Sphinx*; (3) *Suppliants, Egyptians, Danaids,* °*Amymone*; (4) a *Lycurgeia* comprising *Edonians, Bassarids, Young Men* (*Neaniskoi*) and °*Lycurgus*. At least seven other tetralogies can be reconstructed with a fair degree of probability: (5) *Myrmidons, Nereids, Phrygians* (satyr-play unknown), based on *Iliad* 16–24; (6) *Ghost-Raisers* (*Psychagōgoi*), *Penelope, Bone-Gatherers* (*Ostologoi*), °*Circe*, based on the *Odyssey* but apparently with an innovative ending; (7) *Memnon, The Weighing of Souls* (*Psychostasia*), *Phrygian Women* (satyr-play unknown), based on the cyclic *Aethiopis*, ending with the funeral of Achilles; (8) *The Award of the Arms* (*Hoplon Krisis*), *Thracian Women, Women of Salamis* (satyr-play unknown), centring on the death of Ajax; (9) *Semele, Wool-Carders* (*Xantriai*), *Pentheus*, and perhaps °*The Nurses of Dionysus*, on the birth of Dionysus and his conflict with Pentheus (cf. *Euripides' Bacchae*); (10) *Eleusinians, Women* (?) *of Argos, Epigoni*, and perhaps °*Nemea*, on the recovery of the bodies of the Seven against Thebes and their sons' war of revenge; (11) *Lemnian Women, Argo, Hypsipyle,* °*Cabiri*, on the story of Hypsipyle and Jason. In some cases two tragedies seem to be connected but no third related one can be identified: (12) *Prometheus Bound* and *Prometheus Unbound* (if, as is likely, the title *Prometheus the Fire-bearer* (*Pyrphoros*) is no more than a variant form of °*Prometheus the Fire-kindler* (*Pyrkaeus*)); (13) *Phorcides* and *Polydectes* (with °*Netfishers*), with Perseus the slayer of Medusa as hero; (14) *Mysians* and *Telephus*.

Aeschylean plays not mentioned above include *Archer-Nymphs* (*Toxotides*), on the death of Actaeon; *Athamas; Atalanta; Callisto; Carians* or *Europa;* °*Cercyon; Chambermakers* (*Thalamopoioi*); *Children of Heracles; Cretan Women* (on the story of Polyidus); *Daughters of the Sun* (*Heliades*); *The Escort* (*Propompoi*); *Glaucus the Sea-god;* °*Heralds* (*Kerykes*); *Iphigenia; Ixion;* °*The Lion; Niobe;* °*Oreithyia; Palamedes; Perrhaebian Women* (whose central character was Ixion); *Philoctetes* (see Dio Chrys. *Or.* 52); *Priestesses* (*Hiereiai*); °*Sisyphus the Runaway* and *Sisyphus the Stone-roller* (if these two are different plays).

TECHNIQUE Aeschylus was the most innovative and imaginative of Greek dramatists. His extant plays, though covering a period of only fifteen years, show a great and evolving variety in structure and presentation.

The three earlier plays (*Persians, Seven,* and *Suppliants*) are designed for a theatre without a *skēnē* but containing a mound or elevation (tomb of Darius, Theban acropolis, Argive sanctuary, the two latter with cult-images on them). There are two actors only; the main interactions are less between character and character than between character and chorus (often expressed in 'epirrhematic' form, i.e. dialogue between singing chorus and speaking actor), and in two cases the chorus open the play in marching anapaests. There is a wide variety of structural patterns, some of them (like *Sept.* 375–676, with its seven pairs of speeches punctuated by short choral stanzas) probably unique experiments, but all built round the basic framework of a series of episodes framed by entries and exits and separated by choral songs. The pace of the action is usually rather slow.

By 458 the dramatist had available to him a *skēnē* (stage-building) and probably an *ekkyklēma* (wheeled platform) and *mēchanē* (crane) also, as well as a third actor. Aeschylus makes imaginative, and once again very varied, use of the new opportunities. After composing the first half of *Agamemnon* entirely in his old style (with no actor–actor dialogue whatever), he centres the play on a verbal trial of strength between Agamemnon and Clytemnestra, meanwhile keeping Cassandra long silent and then making her narrate Agamemnon's death prophetically before it happens. The house and its entrance are firmly controlled throughout by the 'watchdog' Clytemnestra. In the second half of *Choephori* the action increasingly accelerates as the climax approaches, and then abruptly slows as Clytemnestra for a time staves off her doom with brilliant verbal fencing. In *Eumenides* a series of short scenes, full of surprises and changes of location, and including a trial-scene with some virtuoso four-sided dialogue, leads to a conclusion mainly in the old epirrhematic mode for one actor and chorus (with a second chorus at the very end).

Aeschylus' plots tend to be characterized, not by abrupt changes of direction (*peripeteiai*), but by a build-up of tension and expectation towards a climax anticipated by the audience if not by the dramatis personae. He was quite capable of contriving *peripeteiai* when he wished, as witness *Seven against Thebes* where the whole action pivots on Eteocles' discovery that he has unwittingly brought about a combat between himself and his brother and thus fulfilled his father's curse; the trilogy form, however, encourages sharp changes of direction and mood between plays rather than within them.

In general the central interest in Aeschylean drama is in situation and event rather than in character. Even quite major figures in a play (like Pelasgus or Orestes) can be almost without distinctive character traits: if their situation gives them effectively no choice how to act, their personal qualities are irrelevant and are ignored. On the other hand, characters who make (or have previously made) decisions vitally affecting the action, when alternative choices were possible, are portrayed as far as is necessary for illuminating these decisions: Eteocles is usually calm and rational but can be carried away by strong emotions, Agamemnon is one who values prestige above all other considerations. The character most fully drawn is Clytemnestra, because the plot requires her to be a unique individual, 'a woman with a man's mind'. In the *Oresteia* several minor characters are drawn with marked vividness, less perhaps for their own sake than to focus special attention on what they have to say.

For similar reasons, Aeschylean choruses nearly always have a strong and distinctive personality. Their words are often of the utmost importance in drawing attention to the deeper principles underlying events (even when they do not themselves fully understand these principles or their implications) and, together with their music and dance, in establishing the mood and theme of a whole play. The women of *Seven*, dominated almost throughout by fear, contrast sharply with the Danaids, utterly determined in their rejection of marriage and coercing Pelasgus by a cool threat of suicide; the Argive elders of *Agamemnon*, enunciators of profound moral principles yet unable to understand how these principles doom Agamemnon to death, share a trilogy with the Erinyes, hellish blood-

suckers yet also divine embodiments of these same principles. Aeschylus' choruses often have a substantial influence on the action; the Danaids and the Erinyes are virtually the protagonists of their plays, the women's panic in *Seven* causes Eteocles' promise to fight in person, while in *Choephori* it is the chorus who ensure that Aegisthus is delivered unguarded into Orestes' hands. Sometimes a chorus will surprise the audience near the end of a play (as when the Argive elders defy Aegisthus); it is a distinctly Aeschylean touch in *Prometheus Bound* when the hitherto submissive Oceanids resolve to stay with Prometheus despite Hermes' warning of apocalyptic destruction impending.

Aeschylus' lyric style is smooth and flexible, and generally easier of immediate comprehension than that of *Pindar or Sophocles, provided the listener was attuned to a vocabulary that tended towards the archaic and the Homeric. In iambic dialogue, where he had fewer models to follow, he sometimes seems stiff compared with Sophocles or Euripides, though he can also create an impression of everyday speech through informal grammar and phraseology. He excels at devising patterns of language and imagery, elaborating them down to minute detail, and sustaining them all through a play or a trilogy.

Patterns of metre (and presumably of music) are likewise designed on a trilogic scale; in the *Oresteia* ode after ode ponders the workings of justice in syncopated iambics and lecythia, with variations and deviations to suit particular contexts (epic-like dactyls for the departure of the expedition to Troy, ionics for Helen's voyage and her welcome by the Trojans). Aeschylus' lyrics are mostly simple and perspicuous in structure, here too resembling Alcman or *Stesichorus more than Pindar or Sophocles. He makes extensive use of marching anapaests as preludes to (and occasionally substitutes for) choral odes, and also in quasi-epirrhematic alternation with lyrics. The regular speech-verse is the iambic trimeter, but the trochaic tetrameter (characteristic of early tragedy according to Arist. *Poet.* 1449ᵃ22) appears in *Persians* and *Agamemnon*.

Aeschylus is consistently bold and imaginative in exploiting the visual aspects of drama. The contrast between the sumptuous dress of Atossa at her first, carriage-borne entry and the return of Xerxes alone and in rags; the chaotic entry of the chorus in *Seven*; the African-looking, exotically dressed Danaids and their confrontation with brutal Egyptian soldiers; the purple cloth over which Agamemnon walks to his death, and the display of his corpse in the bath-tub with Cassandra beside him and Clytemnestra 'standing where I struck' (a scene virtually repeated in *Choephori* with a different killer and different victims); the Erinyes presented anthropomorphically on stage (probably for the first time), yet tracking Orestes like hounds by the scent of blood; the procession that ends the *Oresteia*, modelled on that at the Great Panathenaea (festival of Athena) these are far from exhausting the memorable visual images in only six or seven plays, quite apart from numerous careful touches of detail (e.g. at the end of *Agamemnon* where Aegisthus, that 'woman' of a man, alone of those on stage has neither weapon nor staff in his right hand).

THOUGHT Aeschylus, like all truly tragic writers, is well aware of, and vividly presents, the terrible suffering, often hard to justify in human terms, of which life is full; nevertheless he also believes strongly in the ultimate justice of the gods. In his surviving work (leaving aside *Prometheus*), all human suffering is clearly traceable, directly or indirectly, to an origin in some evil or foolish action—Xerxes' ill-advised decision to attempt the conquest of Greece; Laius' defiance of an oracular warning to remain childless; the attempt by the sons of Aegyptus to force the Danaids to be their wives; the adultery of Thyestes with Atreus' wife; the abduction of Helen by Paris. The consequences of these actions, however, while always bringing disaster to the actors, never end with them, but spread to involve their descendants and ultimately a whole community; some of these indirect victims have incurred more or less guilt on their own account, but many are completely innocent. In some of Aeschylus' dramas, like *Persians* or the Theban trilogy, the action descends steadily towards a nadir of misery at the end. In the *Oresteia*, however, presumably also in the Odyssean trilogy, and not improbably in the Danaid trilogy, it proves to be possible to draw a line under the record of suffering and reach a settlement that promises a better future; each time a key element in the final

stages is the substitution of persuasion for violence, as when in the *Oresteia* a chain of retaliatory murders is ended by the judicial trial of Orestes, and the spirits of violent revenge, the Erinyes, are persuaded to accept an honoured dwelling in Athens.

In dramas of the darker type described above, the gods are stern and implacable, and mortals often find themselves helpless prisoners of their own or others' past decisions; though they may still have considerable freedom to choose how to face their fate (compare the clear-sighted courage of Pelasgus or Cassandra with Xerxes or Agamemnon). Elsewhere, especially perhaps in Aeschylus' latest work, a different concept of divinity may appear. In the *Oresteia* ethical advance on earth, as the virtuous Electra and an Orestes with no base motive succeed the myopic Agamemnon and the monstrous Clytemnestra, is presently answered by ethical advance on Olympus as the amoral gods of *Agamemnon* and *Choephori* turn in *Eumenides* into responsible and even loving (*Eum.* 911, 999) protectors of deserving mortals. Something similar may well have happened in the Prometheus plays.

Aeschylus is intensely interested in the community life of the *polis*, and all his surviving genuine works have strong political aspects. He seems to be a strong supporter of democracy (a word whose elements first appear together in the phrase *dēmou kratousa cheir* 'the sovereign hand of the people', *Supp.* 604) and of Athens' wars of the early 450s, while recognizing the overriding importance of avoiding civil conflict by conciliating rival interests (*Eum.* 858–66, 976–87). To later generations, who from time to time continued to see his plays (cf. Ar. *Ach.* 10), Aeschylus, who may have come of age in the year of *Cleisthenes' reforms and whose death coincided with the peak of Athenian power, was (as in Aristophanes' *Frogs*) the poet of Athens' greatness, of the generation of Marathon where he had lived what to him was the supreme day of his life.   A.H.S.

Aesop, as legendary a figure as *Homer. What we now call fables (Gk. *ainoi*, *mythoi*, *logoi*), i.e. stories clearly fictitious (often about speaking animals), which illustrate a point or support an argument, are first alluded to by Hes. *Op.* 202–12 and Archil. fr. 174 West, but by the 5th and 4th cents. such fables in prose are regularly attributed to Aesop (Ar. *Vesp.* 566, *Av.* 471; Arist. fr. 573 Rose; a black-figured portrait of Aesop with talking fox, Beazley, *ARV²* 2 p. 916 no. 183, K. Schefold, *Die Bildnisse der antiken Dichter, Redner und Denker* (1943) 57.4). Hdt. 2. 134–5 places him in the 6th cent. BC as the slave of Iadmon, a Samian later murdered by Delphians (cf. Ar. *Vesp.* 1446–8); Plato Com. fr. 70 KA has his soul returning from the grave (cf. Plut. *Sol.* 6); the legend suggests a ritual scapegoat (*pharmakos*).

A biography, serving as a context for the fables he told, may have existed already in the 5th century, but the extant biography, written no earlier than the Roman empire, is a romance on these themes. Beginning with a miracle (Isis grants him speech, the Muses give him inspiration in storytelling) and concluding with a martyr's death (Delphic priests kill him because he denounces their greed), it is largely a repository of slave-savant anecdotes about Aesop and his hapless Samian master, the 'philosopher' Xanthus, followed by Aesop's career as adviser to the Lydian king Croesus and the king of Babylon (cf. the Assyrian Ahiqar).

The first known collection of Aesopic fables was made by the early hellenistic ruler of Athens, Demetrius of Phaleron (Diog. Laert. 5. 5. 80). The medieval tradition (which includes moral epilogues) is in three parts, of which the oldest (*Collectio Augustana*) dates to the 3rd cent. AD, or even earlier.   J.S.R.

Agathias, also referred to as **Agathias Scholasticus** ('lawyer'), historian and poet in Constantinople, *c.*AD 532–*c.*580. A native of Myrina in Asia Minor, where his father was a rhetor, he was educated at Alexandria and Constantinople, where he later practised law, a profession about whose conditions he complains in his *Histories*. His poetic activity began early, with a lost *Daphniaca*, amatory hexameters, and he is the author of numerous epigrams in classical style on personal and traditional subjects, including love poems; *Nonnus was a major influence in style, vocabulary, and versification. Many of these, as well as poems by his contemporaries, including Paul the Silentiary and other officials, were included by him in a collection known as the *Cycle*, compiled, or at any rate completed, in the early years of Justin II (AD 565–78), and modelled on the earlier *Garland*

of Meleager. The epigrams of the *Cycle* reflect the technical literary accomplishments of members of the office-holding élite in Constantinople in the latter part of the reign of Justinian (AD 527–65), as well as their classicizing tastes. Agathias' *Histories*, a continuation in five books of *Procopius' *History of the Wars*, covers only the years AD 553–9, and is likewise highly literary and rhetorical, an aim which Agathias defends himself (*Hist.* 3. 1), including also digressions and speculative passages about the meaning of the events narrated. The work is important also for its long excursuses on the Franks and the Sasanids, each of which draws on good information, however much imbalance they introduce to the work as a whole. Though apparently a Christian and a moralist, Agathias' work is literary and secular. Unlike Procopius, he was not a participant in the events he describes, nor did he have military experience. Nevertheless, his work made sufficient impact for it to be continued by Menander Protector, and to take its place in the line of early Byzantine secular historians.   A.M.C.

Agathocles, tyrant, later king of Syracuse, born 361/0 BC in Thermae, Sicily. His father Carcinus, an exile from Rhegium, received Syracusan citizenship under *Timoleon 343/2 and owned a large pottery manufactory. The young Agathocles took part in various military enterprises and early on nurtured political ambitions. The oligarchy of six hundred that ruled Syracuse after Timoleon's death distrusted the active young man with popular tendencies and he was banished *c.*330. During his exile he attempted to obtain a power base in southern Italy, operating as a *condottiere* in Croton or Tarentum. He successfully relieved Rhegium when it was besieged by the six hundred, thereby toppling the oligarchy. Recalled by the people in Syracuse he was exiled again after the oligarchs had been reinstated. Subsequently he threatened the oligarchs and their Carthaginian allies with a private army of mercenaries from the Sicilian inland. Hamilcar changed sides and through his mediation Agathocles was able to return to Syracuse and in 319/8 was made 'stratēgos (general) with absolute power in the cities of Sicily' (*FGrH* 239 B 12). A military coup in 316 (cf. Diod. Sic. 19. 5. 4–9, from *Timaeus) resulted in the murder and banishment of the six hundred and to Agathocles was entrusted 'the generalship with absolute power and the care of the city' (Diod. Sic. 19. 9. 4). The new rule, chiefly reliant on mercenaries, was a tyranny in all but name.

During the following years Agathocles concentrated on the cities that had given refuge to the banished oligarchs, especially Acragas, Gela, and Messana. Messana appealed to Carthage for help and in 314 concluded a peace treaty with Agathocles; Hamilcar again acted as mediator. Carthage retained the 'epicraty' (area of control) west of the Halycus (mod. Platani), Syracuse the hegemony over the otherwise autonomous Greek cities (Schmitt, *SdA* 3, no. 424). When Agathocles in contravention of the treaty invaded Carthaginian territory he suffered a crushing defeat at the southern Himera in the summer of 311. While the Carthaginians were advancing against Syracuse Agathocles entrusted the city's defence to his brother Antander and made his way through the enemy blockade to Africa (14 August 310). His objective was to defeat the Carthaginians in their own country and to make them withdraw troops from Sicily (Diod. Sic. 20. 3–5). He burned his ships, defeated the enemy in the field, and advanced against Carthage. In Sicily Antander was holding out against the Carthaginians, but Acragas had organized an alliance of Greek cities promising them their liberty. Agathocles in Africa had been in contact with Ophellas, the governor of Cyrene, since 309. Ophellas was planning a great North African empire (Diod. Sic. 20. 40). On his assassination his army enlisted with Agathocles, who in 308/7 returned to Sicily where matters had been deteriorating. Soon afterwards the army in Africa was almost completely wiped out. Agathocles returned to Africa for a short time only to abandon the rest of his soldiers and to flee back to Sicily. The peace of 306 again named the Halycus as the border between the Carthaginian epicraty and Greek Sicily (Schmitt, *SdA* 3, no. 437). Agathocles later defeated the exiles' army and ruled Greek Sicily—with the exception of Acragas. In 305 he assumed the title of king (Diod. Sic. 20. 54, 1) and not long afterwards married Theoxene, one of *Ptolemy I's stepdaughters.

From *c*.300 he concentrated his efforts on southern Italy (Diod. Sic. 21. 4 ff.). In two campaigns he briefly brought Bruttium under his control and supported Tarentum in 298/7 against the native Lucanians and the Messapians. He conquered Croton 295 and concluded alliances with other cities in southern Italy; he even captured Corcyra (Diod. Sic. 21. 2) and held it for a short time. Agathocles' aim seems to have been the union of Sicilian and south Italian Greeks under his rule. His preparations for another campaign against Carthage were cut short when he was assassinated in 289/8. His attempt to establish a dynasty failed owing to family rivalries, he therefore 'restored to the people their self-government' (Diod. Sic. 21. 16. 5). Agathocles was on no account the popular tyrant often depicted by historians, but rather a cruel careerist and an unscrupulous adventurer. Modern historians have frequently overestimated his historical importance: he achieved nothing of lasting impact—on the contrary, immediately after his death anarchy erupted both in Syracuse, where a *damnatio memoriae* (motion by the senate to erase all traces of a person's memory) was decreed (Diod. Sic. 21. 16. 6), and other places (Diod. Sic. 21. 18).   K.M.

Agathon, son of Tisamenus of Athens, was the most celebrated tragic poet after the three great masters, *Aeschylus, *Sophocles, and *Euripides. He won his first victory at the Lenaea (a festival sacred to Dionysus) in 416 BC, and the occasion of *Plato's *Symposium* is a party at his house in celebration of that victory. Plato emphasizes his youth in the *Symposium* and portrays him as a boy in the *Protagoras* (315d), of which the dramatic date is about 430, so he must have been born after 450. In the *Protagoras* he is seen in the company of the sophist (itinerant teacher) Prodicus, and he appears to have been influenced in style by Gorgias. In 411 he heard and approved *Antiphon's speech in his defence (Arist. *Eth. Eud.* 3. 5)—this suggests antidemocratic sentiments—and in the same year he was caricatured in *Aristophanes (1)'s *Thesmophoriazusae.* The play ridicules him for effeminacy and passive homosexual tastes, and Plato, portraying him as the long-term boyfriend of one Pausanias, partly confirms the charge. Before 405 he left Athens (like Euripides) for the court of King Archelaus of Macedon (Ar. *Ran.* 83–5 and other sources), and he died there, probably before 399.

The parody of his lyrics at Ar. *Thesm.* 101–29 is elaborately decorative, and his speech at Pl. *Symp.* 194e–197e is a florid rhetorical exercise in the manner of Gorgias. His fragments (less than 50 lines) are in a pointed, epigrammatic style, probably due to sophistic influence. *Aristotle says that he wrote a tragedy (probably *Antheus* rather than *Anthos*) in which all the characters were invented, not taken from legend (*Poet.* 9); that he wrote a tragedy which failed because he tried to include too much material, as if writing an epic (*Poet.* 18); and that he was the first to write choral odes that were mere interludes, unconnected with the plot (*Poet.* 18). All these developments can be seen as exaggerations of tendencies found in the later work of Euripides; and one of Agathon's fragments (fr. 4, where an illiterate character describes the letters THESEUS) is an attempt to cap a virtuoso Euripidean passage (fr. 382 Nauck). He is also said to have introduced the chromatic scale into the music of tragedy (Plut. *Quaest. conv.* 3. 1. 1).   A.L.B.

Agesilaus II (*c.*445–359 BC), Spartan king of the junior, Eurypontid line. Son of *Archidamus II by his second wife, he was not expected to succeed his older half-brother Agis II and so went through the prescribed educational curriculum (*agōgē*) like any other Spartan boy. In 400 he unexpectedly secured the succession, with the aid of his former lover *Lysander, ahead of Agis' son Leotychides, whose parentage was suspect (rumour had it that his true father was the exiled *Alcibiades).

The first king to be sent on campaign in Asia, where his proclaimed aim was to liberate the Greeks from Persian suzerainty, Agesilaus achieved some success against the Persian viceroys Pharnabazus and Tissaphernes in 396–5 before his enforced recall to face a coalition of Sparta's Greek enemies in central and southern Greece. The battle of Coronea (394) was a Pyrrhic victory, and, despite some minor successes of his around Corinth and in Acarnania (391–388), the coalition was defeated not on land by Agesilaus but at sea by the Spartan nauarch Antalcidas with a Persian-financed fleet. Agesilaus, however, threw himself wholeheartedly behind the Peace of Antalcidas, or King's Peace (386), which he interpreted to suit what he took to be Sparta's best interests. Pro-Spartan oligarchs were brought to power in Mantinea, Phlius, and Olynthus, but the most flagrant violation

of the autonomy clause of the peace was the occupation of Thebes (382). By condoning that breach and securing the acquittal of Sphodrias (father of his son's beloved), who was on trial for an illegal attempt to seize the Piraeus, the main harbour of Athens (378), Agesilaus provoked a further anti-Spartan coalition supported by Persia. Despite some success of Agesilaus in Boeotia in 378 and 377, the Thebans and their Boeotian federation eventually proved too strong for an enfeebled Spartan alliance at Leuctra in 371. The Theban ascendancy of 371 to 362, presided over by Epaminondas and *Pelopidas, and the consequent liberation of Messenia from Sparta, are directly attributable to Agesilaus' unremitting hostility to Thebes. Agesilaus nevertheless did not lose face or influence at home, and continued to direct Spartan counsels in the years of his city's humiliation. He organized the defence of the city against Epaminondas' coalition in 370 and 362, and sought to augment the state's revenues by foreign service as a mercenary (in Asia Minor with the Persian satrap Ariobarzanes in 364, and in Egypt with King Nectanebis II in 361–59). He died in Cyrenaica on the return journey from Egypt, aged about 84.

Though born lame in one leg, and displaying a streak of romanticism, Agesilaus was typically Spartan in his qualities and limitations. He was an efficient soldier, but a better tactician than strategist, who failed to understand the importance of siegecraft and sea power. At home, no Spartan king ever exploited better than he the resources of charisma and patronage available to a blue-blooded Heraclid king (i.e. one supposedly descended from Heracles). But the narrowness of his personal loyalties and political sympathies dissipated those moral assets by which alone Sparta might have maintained her Greek hegemony, in the face of a sharply dwindling citizen population and the constant hostility of the helots at home and Sparta's Greek and non-Greek enemies beyond her borders.   P.A.C.

Agricola (Gnaeus Julius Agricola) (AD 40–93), son of Lucius Julius Graecinus, a senator from Forum Iulii (mod. *Fréjus*), was brought up by his mother after his father's execution by *Gaius (1) (Caligula). After study at Massalia (Marseille), he was *tribunus laticlavius* (senatorial military tribune) in Britain during the *Boudiccan revolt (60–1). He then married Domitia Decidiana, was quaestor of Asia (63–4), tribune of the *plebs* (66), and praetor (68). Appointed by *Galba to recover temple property, after joining the Flavian side he recruited troops in Italy. Commanding Legio XX in Britain, he saw action under the governor Petillius Cerialis (71–3). He was made a patrician, served as legate of Aquitania for 'less than three years' (73–6), became consul (76?) and *pontifex* (member of one of the four major colleges of the Roman priesthood), then legate (military governor) of Britain for seven years (77–84), winning *ornamenta triumphalia* (the insignia normally carried by a general in his triumphal procession).

Apart from mentions by *Cassius Dio, a lapidary inscription at Verulamium (St Albans), and inscribed lead pipes from Chester, Agricola is known entirely from the biography by his son-in-law *Tacitus. He was certainly exceptional: the only senator known to have served three times in one province; unusually young as governor of Britain; the longest known tenure there. Favour from *Vespasian and *Titus may be surmised. In his first season (77) he conquered Anglesey; in the second he was in northern England and southern Scotland. Measures to promote Romanization in his second winter are stressed by Tacitus. In his third season (79) he advanced to the Tay, leading to (following Cass. Dio) Titus' fifteenth imperatorial acclamation; in the fourth (80) he consolidated along the Forth–Clyde. His fifth season (81) was in the west of Scotland: he drew up his forces facing Ireland, which he told Tacitus could easily have been conquered. He then tackled the Caledonians, victory narrowly eluding him in the sixth season (82) but being won at a great battle late in the seventh, mons Graupius, probably September 83. He ordered the fleet to circumnavigate Britain, finally proving that it was an island. Recalled, presumably in spring 84, he was denied further appointments because of *Domitian's jealousy, according to Tacitus.
A.R.Bi.

Agrippa, Marcus Vipsanius, the lifelong friend and supporter of *Augustus, was born in 64, 63, or even 62 BC of obscure but probably well-to-do family (he neglected his undistinguished family name). He accompanied Octavius (the future Octavian and Augustus) to Rome from Apollonia after *Julius Caesar's murder, helped him to raise a private army, prosecuted *Cassius in the court set up by Quintus Pedius in 43, and was prominent in the war against Lucius Antonius (Pietas). After holding the tribunate of the *plebs* in 43 or a little later, and so entering the senate, he was urban praetor in 40. As governor of Gaul in 38 he suppressed a rebellion in Aquitania, led a punitive expedition across the Rhine, and either now or in 20 settled the Ubii on the left bank. As consul (37) he fitted out and trained a new fleet for Octavian's war against Sextus *Pompey, converting Lake Avernus near Cumae into a harbour (portus Iulius) for the purpose, and in 36 won two decisive naval engagements at Mylae and Naulochus, where his improved grapnel was highly effective. In 35–34 he took part in the Illyrian War. Although an ex-consul he held the aedileship in 33, contributing greatly to Octavian's popularity. In 31 his vigorous naval operations were the primary cause of Mark *Antony's defeat; at Actium he commanded the left wing. He next (31–29), with *Maecenas, managed affairs in Italy in Octavian's absence. On Octavian's return he helped carry out a purge of the senate and a census (29–8) and he held second and third consulships in the crucial years 28 and 27. In 23 Augustus, ill and embroiled in political controversy, handed him his signet-ring, conferring an unofficial status (most importantly in the eyes of the armies) that would have meant his supremacy if Augustus had died. He was entrusted with a mission in the eastern half of the empire, probably with proconsular power, which he carried out from Mytilene. The claim that rivalry with Augustus' nephew Marcus Claudius Marcellus had sent him into virtual exile cannot be substantiated. More likely it was a constitutional crisis, with Agrippa put in easy reach of the armies of the Balkans and Syria if Augustus' position were undermined or his life threatened. He was recalled in 21 to represent Augustus in Rome; in 20 he proceeded to Gaul and in 19 to Spain where he quelled the Cantabri. In 18 he was given tribunician power for five years, a power held otherwise only by Augustus, and his *imperium* (overriding military and civil authority) was renewed for the same period. In 13 his tribunician power was renewed for five more years, and his *imperium* apparently made superior to that of all other holders, like that of Augustus (the extent and development of Agrippa's powers, outlined in the fragmentary papyrus (*Kölner Pap.* 1 (1976), 10 = EJ 366) that contains part of Augustus' funerary elogium on him, remains controversial). As a *quindecimvir sacris faciundis*, one of the guardians of the Sibylline oracles (from before 37), he assisted in the celebration of the Secular Games in 17. His second mission to the east (17/16–13) is notable for the establishment of Polemon of Pontus in the Bosporan kingdom, the settlement of veterans at Berytus and Heliopolis, and his friendship with *Herod and benevolent treatment of the Jews. Early in 12 he went to Pannonia where there was a danger of revolt, but fell ill on his return and died about the end of March. After a public funeral he was buried in the mausoleum of Augustus.

Agrippa's wealth was spent freely in the service of the Roman people and the empire, winning him lasting popularity. He restored the sewers of Rome and reorganized the water supply, constructing two new aqueducts (Julia, 33 BC, and Virgo, 19 BC), and a network of distribution installations. Virgo fed Rome's first public baths, close to his Pantheon, and the expanded Saepta Julia (26 BC), all in a huge recreational area. He also built a granary (horrea Agrippiana) behind the Forum and a new bridge over the Tiber. Constructions in the provinces included buildings at Nemausus and a road system radiating from Lugdunum. By his will Augustus received the greater part of his property, including the Thracian Chersonese; he also made generous bequests to the people of Rome.

He wrote an autobiography (now lost) and a geographical commentary (also lost, but used by *Strabo and *Pliny the Elder) from which a map of the empire was constructed, to be displayed after his death on the porticus Vipsaniae.

Agrippa was married three times: in 37 to Caecilia Attica, in 28 to Augustus' niece the elder Marcella, whom he divorced in 21 to marry Augustus' daughter *Julia. The first two wives produced daughters, Attica's including Vipsania Agrippina, the first wife of the later emperor *Tiberius, Marcella's the Vipsania who married *Quinctilius Varus. Julia had three sons, Gaius Julius Caesar and Lucius Julius Caesar, who were adopted by

Augustus in 17, and Agrippa Julius Caesar (Agrippa Postumus); and two daughters, Julia and *Agrippina the Elder; through her he was grandfather and great-grandfather respectively of the emperors *Gaius (1) and *Nero.

Agrippa, portrayed as upright, simple, and modest, a man who subordinated his ambitions to those of Augustus, was by 12 BC a partner nearly equal in power. Refusing three triumphs (19 BC onwards) and failing even to report his Spanish successes inhibited private men from applying and contributed to the end of such triumphs. Like his advocacy of public display of works of art (he was a noted collector), it went against the interests of the ruling class, who boycotted his funeral games. To Augustus he may sometimes have been an embarrassment.

G.W.R.; T.J.C.; B.M.L.

Agrippa I, II, kings of Judaea. See JULIUS AGRIPPA.

Agrippina the Elder (Vipsania Agrippina) (*c*.14 BC–AD 33), the daughter of Marcus Vipsanius *Agrippa and of *Julia (daughter of *Augustus). She married *Germanicus (probably in AD 5), to whom she bore nine children. She was with Germanicus on the Rhine from 14 to 16 and in the east from 18 until his death in the following year. From 19 to 29 she lived in Rome, the rallying point of a party of senators who opposed the growing power of *Sejanus. With *Tiberius, whom she suspected (without evidence) of causing her husband's death, her relations were consistently bad, and he refused her request in 26 for leave to marry again. She was arrested in 29 on the instruction of Tiberius and banished by the senate to the island Pandateria, where she starved to death in 33. She was survived by one son, the future emperor *Gaius (1), and three daughters, *Agrippina the Younger (see next entry), Julia Drusilla, and Julia.

J.P.B.; A.J.S.S.

Agrippina the Younger (Julia Agrippina) (AD 15–59), eldest daughter of *Germanicus and *Agrippina the Elder, was born on 6 November AD 15 at Ara Ubiorum. In 28 she was betrothed to Gnaeus Domitius Ahenobarbus, to whom she bore one son, the later emperor *Nero, in 37. During the principate of her brother *Gaius (1) (37–41) her name, like those of her sisters, was coupled with the emperor's in vows and oaths; but when she was discovered at Mogontiacum late in 39 to be involved in the conspiracy of Gnaeus Cornelius Lentulus Gaetulicus, she was sent into banishment. She was recalled by her uncle *Claudius, who married her in 49. Aided by the financial secretary Marcus Antonius Pallas, *Seneca (the Younger), and the guard-prefect Sextus Afranius Burrus, she quickly achieved her ambitious purpose. Receiving for herself the title Augusta, she persuaded Claudius to adopt Nero as guardian of his own son Britannicus. She was generally believed to have poisoned Claudius, to make room for Nero (54). In the first years of Nero's rule she was almost co-regent with him but, after Pallas had fallen in 55 and Burrus and Seneca turned against her, she lost her power. In March 59 she was murdered at Baiae by a freedman, Anicetus, acting on Nero's instructions. She wrote an autobiography.   J.P.B.; A.J.S.S.

Alcaeus, lyric poet, of Mytilene on Lesbos. Probably born c.625–620 BC, since he was old enough to participate in the struggle against Athens for Sigeum near Troy in the last decade of the century in which Pittacus (see below) distinguished himself (fr. 428; Hdt. 5. 95; Diog. Laert. 1. 74; Strabo 13. 1. 38). Lesbian politics at this period were violent and confused. The ruling dynasty, the Penthilidae, who traced their descent from Agamemnon's son Orestes, were weakened and finally overthrown by two successive coups (Arist. *Pol.* 1311[b]26, 29). Power passed to a tyrant named Melanchrus, who was overthrown by a faction headed by Pittacus and Alcaeus' brothers c.612–609 (*Suda*, entry under Πιττακός; Diog. Laert. 1. 74); Alcaeus (perhaps too young—fr. 75) was not involved (Diog. Laert. 1. 74). A new tyrant, Myrsilus, emerged, who was opposed unsuccessfully by a faction of exiles including Pittacus and Alcaeus (frs. 129, 114); Pittacus subsequently allied himself with Myrsilus, while his former comrades continued the struggle in exile (frs. 129, 70). After Myrsilus' death the people elected Pittacus *aisymnētēs* (dictator) to ward off Alcaeus' faction (frs. 70, 348; Arist. *Pol.* 1285[a]35 ff.). Internal divisions within the faction contributed to its failure to oust Pittacus (fr. 70). Pittacus' marriage alliance with the Penthilidae probably belongs to this

period (fr. 70), as may Alcaeus' journey to Egypt and his brother Antimenidas' service abroad (frs. 432, 350). An ancient critic (*POxy.* 2506. 98) indicates at least three periods of exile. Alcaeus' poetry is full of attacks on and abuse of Pittacus, for perjury and faithlessness, low birth (probably false), drunkenness, unbridled ambition, and physical defects (frs. 72, 129, 348; Diog. Laert. 1. 81). Popular opinion was with Pittacus, as in general is that of posterity. The tradition that Pittacus subsequently pardoned Alcaeus (Diog. Laert. 1. 76) is suspect.

Alcaeus' poetry was divided by the scholars of Hellenistic Alexandria into at least ten books. It was monodic, and was composed in a variety of lyric metres in two- or four-line stanzas, including the alcaic stanza, named after him. The dialect is predominantly Lesbian vernacular, but epicisms are admitted. His range is rivalled only by *Archilochus in the Archaic period. He dealt with politics, war, wine, love, hymns to the gods, moralizing, and myth (though possibly both moralizing and myth were always subordinated to specific contexts). There is considerable variety in the treatment of each theme. Politics may be dealt with through personal abuse or the grandeur of myth and ritual or both (frs. 72, 129, 298; Diog. Laert. 1. 81); the invitation to drink may be supported by myth (fr. 38A) or the imperatives of the weather (frs. 338, 347). He is open to a range of influences. In his use of lyric for abuse he blurs the difference between lyric and iambus. His hymns are influenced by the rhapsodic tradition. Fr. 347 recasts a passage of *Hesiod in lyric form. He has a vivid descriptive power and an impressive vigour, particularly in his arresting openings; his control of form and mood (the developed contrasts of frs. 42 and 338, the changes of mood and register in fr. 129, the extended metaphor of storm for civil strife in fr. 326, the accelerating tempo of the list in fr. 140) is often underrated. He was popular at Attic symposia and a favourite with *Horace (*Carm.* 1. 32. 5 ff., 2. 13. 26 ff.).   C.C.

Alcibiades (451/0–404/3 BC), son of Cleinias, Athenian general and politician. Brought up in the household of his guardian *Pericles, he became the pupil and intimate friend of *Socrates. A flamboyant aristocrat, he com-

peted in politics with the new-style demagogues, and his ambitious imperialism drew
Athens into a coalition with Argos and other
enemies of Sparta. This policy, half-heartedly
supported by the Athenians, was largely discredited by the Spartan victory at Mantinea
(418). Though Alcibiades temporarily allied
with *Nicias to avoid ostracism, the two were
normally adversaries and rivals, and when
Alcibiades sponsored the plan for a major
Sicilian expedition, Nicias unsuccessfully
opposed it. Both were appointed, together
with Lamachus, to command this expedition
(415). After the mutilation of the herms (see
ANDOCIDES), Alcibiades had been accused of
involvement in other religious scandals, and
soon after the fleet reached Sicily he was
recalled for trial. He escaped, however, to
Sparta, where he encouraged the Spartans to
send a general to Syracuse, and to establish a
permanent Spartan post at Decelea in Attica
(which was eventually done in 413).

In 412 he was involved in Sparta's decision
to concentrate on the Aegean rather than the
Hellespont, but he soon lost the confidence
of the Spartans and fled to the Persian satrap
Tissaphernes. He tried to secure his return to
Athens by obtaining the support of Persia
and bringing about an oligarchic revolution,
but the negotiations with Persia were unsuccessful. The Athenian fleet at Samos
appointed him general, and for several years
he skilfully directed operations in the Hellespont, winning a brilliant victory at Cyzicus
in 410. On returning to Athens in 407 he was
cleared of the religious charges hanging over
him and was appointed to an extraordinary
command; but when a subordinate was
defeated by *Lysander at Notium (406) he
withdrew to Thrace, and his approach to the
Athenians before Aegospotami was rebuffed
(405). After he had taken refuge with the
Persian Pharnabazus, he was murdered in
Phrygia through the influence of the Thirty
Tyrants (the extreme oligarchic group who
controlled Athens at that time) and of Lysander.

Alcibiades was a competent military leader
and a master of intrigue, but his personal
ambition and the excesses of his private life
aroused the distrust of the Athenians, and he
was not given the chance to show whether
his ambitious policies, carried out under his
leadership, could bring about success.

H.D.W., P.J.R.

Alcman, lyric poet, active in the mid- to late
7th cent. BC in Sparta. His birthplace was
disputed. Some believed him a Laconian (i.e.,
in effect, Spartan), while a number of ancient
authors made him a Lydian from Asia Minor
(*Anth. Pal.* 7. 18, 19, 709; Ael. *VH* 12. 50; *Suda*,
entry under *Ἀλκμάν*, *POxy.* 2389, 2506, 3542;
Vell. Pat. 1. 18. 2); the latter version (derived
from fr. 16) was further embroidered to make
him a freed slave (Heraclid Pont. *Excerp. Polit.*
9). The *Suda* credits him with six books of
lyric songs (*melē*); a group called 'Diving
women'/'Swimming women' (*kolymbōsai*),
of which no certain trace survives, may have
made up one of these or a seventh book. The
lyric songs, mostly choral, included maiden-
songs (*partheneia*), which were probably
arranged into two books by Alexandrian
scholars (Steph. Byz. entry under *Ἐρυσίχη*).
We also hear of hymns and wedding-songs
(*hymenaioi*). The *Suda* credits him with love-
poetry, and fragments with erotic content
survive (58, 59a).

The most important surviving works are
fragments of two maiden-songs found on
papyri. The first (fr. 1) shows many features
of the developed choral lyric: a myth (1–35),
gnomic moralizing (36 ff.), and (probable but
not certain, since the opening is lost) framing
reference to the present occasion. An account
of the death of the sons of Hippocoon is followed by a gnomic transition (36 ff.) on
divine punishment and mortal limitation.
The rest of the fragment is devoted to praise
of two females who play a major role in the
ritual (Hagesichora and Agido) and description (with humorous self-deprecation) of the
chorus. The song was performed at dawn
(41 f., 60 ff.). The identity of the goddess honoured (87, *Aotis*, lit. 'the goddess at the dawn')
is unclear (conjectures include Helen,
Artemis Orthia, Phoebe daughter of Leucippus, likewise the nature of the festival,
though many scholars detect a reference to a
rival choir (60 ff.); there is uncertainty about
the details of the myth and its relevance to
the occasion. The second (fr. 3), more fragmentary, poem also concentrates on the
actions of the leading figure (Astymeloisa).
Both poems share a richness of sensuous
imagery and a pronounced homoerotic
tenor. There is an evident taste for puns, and
a proliferation of proper names, many of significance only to the original audience.
Alongside this parochiality we find a taste for

the distant and exotic (1. 59, 100; cf. frs. 90, 148 ff.). Together the two songs show a gaiety and humour not usually associated with Sparta. Some other fragments come from maiden-songs (16, 26, 29, 38, 59b, 60), but many defy classification. Alcman's descriptive power is shown in an account of the sleep of nature (fr. 89, context unknown). Mythic narrative is attested by a number of fragments (e.g. fr. 69 Niobe; fr. 77 addressed to Paris; fr. 69 the stone of Tantalus; fr. 80 Odysseus and Circe). The songs are composed in the Laconian vernacular, with intermittent epic and aeolic forms. The poetry had achieved classic status by the late 5th cent. (Ar. *Lys.* 1247 ff.).

C.C.

Alexander of Abonuteichos in Paphlagonia. He was a contemporary of *Lucian whose bitterly hostile account, *Alexander or the False Prophet*, remains the most important source of information, although it must now be read against the evidence of inscriptions, coins, and works of art.

Alexander claimed to have a new manifestation of Asclepius in the form of a snake called Glycon. A number of statues and statuettes have been discovered showing Glycon as a serpent with human hair—applied by Alexander, according to Lucian. Coins reveal that the birth of Glycon, described in detail by Lucian, took place in the reign of *Antoninus Pius and that his cult gained very rapid acceptance. According to Lucian, this was the result of the oracles that Glycon provided in a variety of forms. After the cult was established, Alexander, who served as Glycon's prophet, or interpreter, created mysteries from which unbelievers, especially Christians and Epicureans, were excluded. *Marcus Aurelius recognized the cult by conferring status on Abonuteichos (thereafter known as Ionopolis) and Lucian mentions several consultants from the ranks of the imperial aristocracy, including Servianus, governor of Cappadocia in AD 161, and Rutilianus, governor of Moesia around 150 and Asia between 161 and 163. Alexander also sent Marcus Aurelius an oracle of Glycon at the beginning of the German Wars (probably in 168). The cult seems to have been particularly important around the Black Sea and in the Balkans. Alexander himself married the daughter of Rutilianus, and seems to have fathered at least one child by a woman of

Caesarea Trochetta. He died probably in the 170s. Lucian's attack on him dates to the reign of *Commodus, while inscriptions and excavation show that Glycon continued to be honoured well into the 3rd, and possibly the 4th, cent. AD.

D.S.P.

Alexander of Aphrodisias, commentator on *Aristotle. Appointed public teacher of Aristotelian philosophy, probably though not certainly in Athens, at some time between 198 and 209 AD (his treatise *On Fate* being dedicated then to *Septimius Severus and *Caracalla); referred to by later writers as '*the* commentator' on Aristotle. Commentaries on *Metaphysics A–Δ, Prior Analytics* 1, *Topics, Meteorologica,* and *De sensu* survive; others are extensively quoted by later writers. The commentaries on *Metaph. E–N* and on *Sophistical Refutations* are, in their present form, spurious. In a number of short treatises (*On the Soul, On Fate, On Mixture* surviving in Greek; *On Providence* in Arabic translation) Alexander presents as Aristotelian his own developments of Aristotelian material. There are also numerous short discussions, some preserved in Greek (*Quaestiones, Ethical Problems*) and others only in Arabic, which seem linked with his teaching activity but whose authenticity is debatable. The *Medical Puzzles and Physical Problems* (ed. J. L. Ideler, *Physici et Medici Graeci Minores* (1841)), *(Unpublished) Problems* (ed. U. C. Bussemaker, *Aristotelis Opera* (1857) 4. 291; H. Usener (1859)), and *On Fevers* (ed. Ideler, as above) are certainly spurious.

Alexander explained Aristotle in Aristotelian terms; he is better at producing ingenious explanations of particular points than at seeing the broader implications. He has been accused—perhaps unjustly—of a tendency to materialistic and mechanistic explanations, and to nominalism; but he recognizes the specific forms of things that possess matter as real, though separable from the matter only in thought. He denied individual immortality, and identified the Aristotelian Active Intellect with God, an interpretation adopted by Averroes but rejected by Aquinas. The (differing) explanations of how God can be the source of our understanding in his *On the Soul* and in the short piece *On the Intellect*, immensely influential in the Middle Ages but doubtfully authentic, are suggestive rather than convincing. Providence he interprets as the influence of the heavens on the sublunary world, ensuring the continuity of physical change and the survival of species, while denying any divine concern for individuals as such. In emphasizing the dependence of time on thought he was closer to Aristotle than were *Straton or Boethus of Sidon, who made time exist in its own right. R.W.S.

Alexander the Great, king of Macedon, 356–323 BC, son of *Philip II and *Olympias. As crown prince he was educated by *Aristotle (from 342); he was his father's deputy in Macedon (340) and fought with distinction at the battle of Chaeronea (338). Philip's last marriage created a serious rift, but a formal reconciliation had been effected by the time of his death (autumn 336), and Alexander was proclaimed king against a background of dynastic intrigue, in which his rivals (notably Amyntas, son of Perdiccas, and the faction of Attalus) were eliminated. A show of force in southern Greece saw him acknowledged Philip's successor as *hēgemōn* of the League of Corinth; and in 335, when the Thebans took advantage of his absence campaigning on the Danube and rebelled, he destroyed the city and enslaved the survivors. The exemplary punishment enabled him to leave the Greek world under the supervision of Antipater with little fear of revolt, while he turned to the war of revenge against Persia.

2. In early 334 Alexander led his grand army across the Hellespont. In all some 43,000 foot and 5,500 horse (including the expeditionary force under Parmenion, it was the most formidable array ever to leave Greek soil. The Macedonians were its indispensable nucleus. The infantry phalanx, *c.*15,000 strong and armed with the fearsome six-metre (19½-foot) pike (*sarisa*), comprised a guard corps (hypaspists) and six regionally levied battalions (*taxeis*); and the cavalry, originally 1,800 strong, was also divided into regional squadrons (*ilai*). In pitched battle the phalanx (infantry-of-the-line), in massed formation, was practically unbreakable on level ground, and Alexander was able to generate a cavalry charge from the flank which had decisive momentum. The men of the hypaspists, usually supplemented by Agrianian javelin-men and the corps of archers, were deployed in rapid-moving columns along with the cavalry, and were an irresistible combination in mountain warfare. These units were far

superior to any they encountered (except arguably the armoured cavalry of Bactria, and, supplemented by a large reserve of secondary troops (Thracians, Illyrians, and the hoplites of the Corinthian League), they gave Alexander an overwhelming military advantage.

3. Alexander's superiority was immediately asserted at the Granicus (334), where a composite satrapal army was outmanœuvred and its large mercenary phalanx exterminated. That allowed him to march directly to occupy Sardis, Ephesus, and Miletus. The most serious threat came from a superior Persian fleet, which sustained the stubborn defence of Halicarnassus, and Alexander took the gamble of demobilizing his own fleet and abandoning the coast. He moved east via Lycia, Pamphylia, and Phrygia (where he 'cut' the Gordian knot, fulfilling a presage of empire), and largely ignored a major Persian counter-offensive in the Aegean, which—fortunately for him—the Great King of Persia (Darius III) crippled by withdrawing a large segment of the fleet to swell his royal army (summer 333). Alexander made Cilicia his base for the critical campaign and lured the vast Persian army into the narrow coastal plain south of Issus, where its numbers were ineffective. He disrupted the front line with his standard cavalry charge from the right and gradually forced the entire Persian army into panic retreat. This overwhelming victory (*c.* November 333) gave him control of the near east as far as the Euphrates. There was some resistance, notably at Tyre and Gaza, which he crushed in exemplary fashion, preferring protracted and costly sieges (seven months at Tyre) to diplomacy and negotiation. All challenges were met directly, whatever the human cost.

4. After a winter (332/1) in Egypt, which was surrendered peacefully, he invaded Mesopotamia and won his crowning victory at Gaugamela (village in mod. Iraq) on 1 October 331. Darius' forces were outmanœuvred again, on chosen ground and unrestricted plain; Alexander sacrificed his left wing, leaving it to be enveloped while he extended the enemy line to the right, created a gap and drove inwards at the head of his cavalry. Again a general rout ensued, and Mesopotamia in turn lay open to him. Babylon and Susa fell without resistance, and he forced the Persian Gates against deter-

mined opposition to occupy the heartland of Persis (winter 331/0). At Persepolis he acquired the accumulated financial reserves of the Persian empire and incinerated its great palace during (it would seem) an orgiastic symposium (drinking session), subsequently representing it as the final act of the war of revenge. That in effect came during the summer of 330 when Darius fled from his last refuge at Ecbatana, to be murdered by his closest entourage (led by Bessus, satrap of Bactria). Alexander honoured his rival's body and closed the war by discharging his Hellenic troops *en masse*.

5. A new challenge arose when Bessus, who had withdrawn to his satrapy, proclaimed himself King of Kings under the regnal name Artaxerxes v. He appointed counter-satraps in central Asia and fomented revolt. Alexander left his satraps to cope with the insurgency, while he moved in a great swathe through Areia, Drangiana, and Arachosia (east Iran and west Afghanistan) and crossed the Hindu Kush to invade Bactria (spring 329). Bessus was soon gone, arrested in his turn by his nobles and surrendered to Alexander for exemplary punishment. Shortly afterwards, when Alexander reached the north-eastern limit of the empire (the Syr-Darya), a new uprising began in Sogdiana (Uzbekistan), rapidly spreading south to Bactria. One of Alexander's (non-Macedonian) columns was ambushed by the insurgents' nomad auxiliaries west of Marakanda (Samarkand), a military and moral reverse which impressed the need for slow, systematic pacification. The conquest of the area fortress by fortress witnessed deliberate massacre, enslavement, and transplantation of recalcitrant populations, and, when the revolt ended (spring 327), the north-eastern satrapies were left exhausted under a large garrison of mercenaries and a network of new city foundations, in which a Hellenic military élite was supported by a native agrarian work-force—the invariable model for the dozens of Alexandrias he founded in the eastern empire.

6. From Bactria Alexander moved into India at the invitation of the local dynasts of the Kabul valley and Punjab. He was nothing loath to reaffirm the traditional Achaemenid claims to the Indus lands. Resistance was treated as rebellion, and his progress through Bajaur and Swat was marked by massacre and

destruction, as in Sogdiana. Even the remote rock-fortress of Aornus (Pir-sar) was reduced by siege at the cost of prodigious hardship, to demonstrate that there was no escape from his dominion. The spring of 326 saw him at Taxila, east of the Indus, poised for a campaign against Porus, who held the Jhelum (Hydaspes) against him. After a series of diversionary manœuvres he crossed the river under cover of a spring thunderstorm and defeated Porus, whose war elephants could not compensate for his cavalry inferiority. The victory was commemorated in two city foundations (Bucephala and Nicaea), and a remarkable issue of silver decadrachms depicts Alexander (crowned by victory) in combat with Porus and his elephant. Alexander continued eastwards, crossing the rivers of the Punjab in the face of an increasing monsoonal deluge, until his troops' patience was exhausted. They refused to cross the Hyphasis (Beas) and invade the Ganges river system, and Alexander reluctantly acceded. A river fleet (commissioned in the summer) was ready at the Hydaspes by November 325, and the army proceeded by land and water to the southern Ocean. The journey was marked by a singularly vicious campaign against the Malli, unprovoked except for their failure to offer submission, and Alexander's impetuousness cost him a debilitating chest wound. Further south the kingdoms of Sambus and Musicanus were visited with fire and slaughter when their allegiance wavered, and, as he approached his base in the Indus delta (Patalene), the natives fled in terror (July 325).

7. Alexander now returned to the west, deputing Nearchus to take his fleet across the southern coastline while he led the main army through the Gedrosian desert (Makran), in emulation—so Nearchus claimed—of Cyrus the Great and Semiramis. The horrors of heat and famine which ensued were considerable, but perhaps exaggerated in the sources, which attest no great loss of life among the Macedonian army. Reunited with the fleet in Carmania (*c.* December 325), he returned to Persepolis and Susa (March 324), where some 80 of his staff joined him in taking wives from the Persian nobility. For the next year there was a lull in campaigning (except for a punitive expedition against the Cossaeans of the Zagros), but there were grandiose preparations in the Levant, where

he commissioned a war fleet allegedly 1,000 strong, some of which was conveyed to Babylon in summer of 323. The first stage of conquest was certainly the Persian Gulf and Arabian littoral, which Alexander intended to conquer and colonize, but the sources, in particular the memoranda (*hypomnēmata*) reported by *Diodorus Siculus, refer to projects of conquest in the western Mediterranean aimed at Carthage and southern Italy—and plans are even alleged of a circumnavigation of Africa. The reality is perhaps beyond verification, but it is likely enough that Alexander conceived no practical limit to his empire.

8. Alexander's monarchy was absolute. From the outset he regarded Asia Minor as liberated territory only in so far as he displaced the Persians, and he announced the fact of possession by imposing his own satraps upon the erstwhile Persian provinces. By 332 he regarded himself as the proper ruler of the Persian empire, and after Gaugamela he was acclaimed king of Asia. From 330 his status was displayed in his court dress, which combined the traditional Macedonian hat (*kausia*) and cloak with the Persian diadem, tunic, and girdle. He used Persian court ceremonial and promoted Persian nobles, but there is no evidence of a formal 'policy of fusion' with Persians and Macedonians assimilated into a single ruling class. Except for a brief moment at Opis the Macedonians were entrenched in a position of superiority. The Susa marriages would indeed give rise to a mixed offspring (as would the liaisons of his soldiers with native women), but in both cases the ultimate aim was probably to counter the regional and family loyalties which had been the curse of both Persian and Macedonian monarchs. At another level he had cut across the traditional regional basis of his army and introduced Iranians even to the élite Companion cavalry. There was to be a single loyalty—to the crown.

9. Alexander naturally experienced opposition in various forms. His Macedonian troops proved increasingly reluctant to be enticed into further conquest. He gave way once, at the Hyphasis, but at Opis (324) he confronted their contumacious demands for repatriation with summary executions and a devastating threat to man his army exclusively from Persians. He had deliberately made his Macedonians dispensable and dem-

onstrated the fact. The same ruthlessness marked his reaction to opposition at court. He isolated and struck down Parmenion because of his resistance to imperial expansion, and the adolescent pages, who seriously threatened his life for reasons which are obscure (but probably based on antipathy to the new absolutism), were tortured and stoned to death. Insubordination was as intolerable as conspiracy. Alexander's return to the west in 325/4 witnessed a spate of executions of satraps who had exceeded their authority or arrogated power (e.g. Astaspes in Carmania, Orxines in Persis). Misgovernment as such was a secondary consideration, as is shown by his remarkable offer of pardon to Cleomenes, the financial administrator of Egypt. Relations with the Greek world became increasingly strained. At first the machinery of the Corinthian League was effective; and the challenge by Agis III of Sparta had limited support and was quickly crushed (? spring 330). But Alexander undermined the provisions of the league by his Exiles' Decree (324), which threatened Athens' possession of Samos and gave almost every city the problem of repatriating long-term exiles. The last year of his reign was punctuated by tense and heated diplomacy, and his death was the catalyst for general war in southern Greece.

10. Given Alexander's uncompromising claims to sovereignty it can be readily understood how he came to conceive himself divine. A Heraclid by lineage, he believed himself the descendant of Heracles, Perseus, and (ultimately) Zeus, and by 331 he had begun to represent himself as the direct son of Zeus, with dual paternity comparable to that of Heracles. He was reinforced in his belief by his pilgrimage (in 331) to the oracle of Ammon in Egypt (recognized as a manifestation of Zeus at Siwa), and thereafter styled himself son of Zeus Ammon. But divine sonship was not divinity, and by 327, after conquest had followed conquest, Alexander was encouraged (particularly in the liberated atmosphere of the symposium) to believe that his achievements deserved apotheosis at least as much as Heracles'. *Proskynēsis*, the hierarchical prostration of inferior to superior, was *de rigueur* at the Persian court, but Alexander attempted to extend it to Macedonians and Greeks, for whom the gesture was an act of worship. The experi-

ment failed, thanks to the resistance of Callisthenes, but the concept remained, and there is an anecdotal (but probable) tradition that he wrote to the cities of Greece in 324, suggesting that it would be appropriate for divine honours to be voted him along with a hero-cult for his deceased favourite, *Hephaestion. Cults were certainly established, predominantly in Asia Minor, and persisted long after his death, eclipsing the largely ephemeral worship of his successors.

11. Portraits of Alexander tend to follow the model created by his favourite sculptor, *Lysippus, who perpetuated the leftward inclination of his neck and the famous *anastolē* (hair thrown back from a central parting). His profile, first illustrated on the 'Alexander sarcophagus' (311), appears repeatedly on coins, most strikingly on the commemorative tetradrachms of *Lysimachus. His personality is far more elusive, thanks to the tendency in antiquity to adduce him as a moral example of good or evil and the propensity of moderns to endue him with the qualities they would admire in themselves. His reputation for invincibility, which he studiously fostered, has been a source of fascination (notably for *Pompey, *Trajan, and Napoleon), mostly for ill. The process began when he died (10 June 323) after a ten-day illness (which contemporaries ascribed to poison), and the marshals who sought to emulate him rapidly dismembered his empire.   A.B.B.

Alexis, *c.*375–*c.*275 BC, poet of Middle and New Comedy, born at Thurii in south Italy (*Suda* α 1138), but apparently living most of his long life in Athens. He wrote 245 plays (*Suda*); the first of his two, three, or four victories at the Lenaea (a festival sacred to Dionysus) came probably in the 350s (six after Eubulus, four after Antiphanes in the victors' list, *IG* 2². 2325. 150 = 5 C 1 col. 3. 11 Mette), and he won a victory in 347 at the Dionysia (*IG* 2². 2318. 278 = 1. 14. 64 and 3 B 1 col. 2. 119 Mette). The good anonymous tractate on comedy (2. 17 p. 9 Kaibel, 3. p. 10 Koster) makes *Menander a pupil of Alexis—a relationship more plausible than that of blood alleged in the *Suda*. About 140 titles and 340 fragments survive, but it is difficult to assess from them the part played by Alexis in the transition from Middle to New Comedy. However, four interesting points

emerge: some signs of influence on Menander (e.g. the comparison of life to a carnival, Alexis fr. 222 KA = 219 K, Menander fr. 416 Körte–Thierfelder) are suspected but not proved; Alexis used both the older form of chorus which could be addressed by an actor (fr. 239 KA = 237 K) and the later form familiar from Menander (fr. 112 KA = 107 K); the *parasitos* (parasite) almost certainly received this name from Alexis (fr. 183 KA = 178 K); and Alexis' *Agonis*, dating probably to the 330s, was an early example of the type of plot especially associated with New Comedy, involving a love affair with a courtesan, and probably a confidence trick and recognition. The fragments sometimes show a lively imagination and beauty of language: e.g. 70 KA and K, carnal passion a crime against real Love; 222 KA = 219 K; 230 KA = 228 K, old age as life's evening. Pleasant wit is revealed in frs. 107 KA = 102 K and 168 KA = 163 K (cf. W. G. Arnott, *Hermes* 1965, 298 ff.). Of interest also are frs. 46 KA = 45 K, a verbally clever comparison of man and wine; 103 KA = 98 K, a long description of aids to female beautification; 113 KA = 108 K, part of a postponed prologue of New-Comedy type; 129 KA = 124 K, a cook's cure (in pseudomedical language) for burnt pork; 140 KA = 135 K (from the *Linus*, one of about a dozen mythological burlesques in Alexis), Heracles' teacher with a library of classical Greek authors; 247 KA = 245 K, a man philosophizing about the nature of Eros.

Alexis' fame continued down to Roman times. A. *Gellius (*NA* 2. 23. 1) notes that his plays were adapted by Roman comedians; Turpilius used Alexis' *Demetrius* as a model, and *Plautus' *Poenulus* may derive at least in part from his *Carchedonius*.   W.G.A.

Alfenus Varus, Publius, suffect consul 39 BC. Born at Cremona, he was the first Cisalpine to gain a consulship, and the only one under Augustus. (His son, consul AD 2, was presumably born in Rome, and of consular descent.) Porphyrio, on Hor. *Sat.* 1. 3. 130, identifies *Alfenus vafer*, a cobbler who has given up his trade, with Alfenus Varus from Cremona. The identification is doubtful, but the scholiast (ancient commentator) knew Varus' origin. In 41 Varus, with two other men, was concerned with confiscating land in northern Italy, or extorting money in lieu of land, for distribution to veterans. His title is variously given by different scholiasts, and there is no other information. He was harsh in treating Virgil's Mantua (see the anxious flattery of *Ecl.* 9. 26 ff.), but may have aided Virgil in regaining his land or getting compensation. *Ecl.* 6. 6 f. shows that Varus (it must be Alfenus) had been an officer in a war, which was to be expected, in view of his extraordinary promotion. (The scholiast's 'explanation' is useless.) He studied law under Servius Sulpicius Rufus and became an eminent jurist: he composed 40 books of *Digesta* ('Ordered Abstracts'), a title he was the first to employ. Of this work 70 excerpts survive in *Justinian's compilation of the same name, the earliest coherent passages of legal writing to be preserved. Citing consultative opinions (*responsa*) of his teacher Servius along with his own, Alfenus lacks logical rigour but is prepared to see legal remedies extended to new situations. He analyses the facts of the cases in which he is consulted in greater detail than do later lawyers.

E.B.; T.Hon.

Ambrose (Ambrosius) Born *c.* AD 340, son of a praetorian prefect of Gaul, Ambrose was well educated and achieved official success under the patronage of the great prefects Sextus Claudius Petronius Probus and Quintus Aurelius Symmachus. Until his early death, his brother Uranius Satyrus showed equal promise. His sister Marcellina became well known for her practice of consecrated virginity, dating from the time of Liberius, bishop of Rome (AD 352–66). Ambrose was appointed governor of Aemilia and Liguria in 374. Already experienced, therefore, in the affairs of Milan (Mediolanum), he was chosen to be the city's bishop in the same year, while intervening in what had become a disputed election. He died in 397 (see Paulinus of Milan, *Life of St Ambrose* 3–5 for his early career and, more generally, *PLRE* 1. 52 'Ambrosius' 3).

Ambrose is famous for his confrontations with the emperor *Theodosius I. Imperial orders to rebuild in 388 a synagogue at Callinicum destroyed by a Christian mob were rescinded after his intervention (*Epp.* 40, 41); and in 390 he excommunicated the emperor, following the calculated massacre of thousands in the circus at Thessalonica (*Ep.* 51 provides more reliable information than Paulinus). But those triumphs reflected force

of personality without precedent or institutional significance. Nor is it easy to judge what direct contribution Ambrose made to Theodosius' laws against paganism. His earlier relationships with Gratian and Valentinian II, close and affectionate, did more to form and reflect his attitudes to civil authority, as also did his embassies to Trier during the usurpation of Maximus, 383–4 and 386 (*Ep.* 24). His abiding preoccupations in the public sphere were the defeat of Arianism (which brought him into famous conflict with the empress Justina in 386: see *Ep.* 20) and the inhibition of pagan cult (symbolized by his successful encouragement of imperial resistance to Symmachus over the restoration of the altar of Victory in the senate-house in 384, recorded in *Epp.* 17 and 18).

Ambrose was a master of oral instruction. Deeply learned in Greek traditions—both those stemming from *Plotinus and those indebted to *Philo and *Origen—and familiar with his near-contemporary *Basil of Caesarea, he made his own contribution to theological development by binding both exegesis and philosophy more closely to sacramental cult. Not content with mere typology, his 'mystagogic' skills harnessed the erudition of the Church to its growth as a community through baptism and homily. *Augustine was the most famous example of his success. His preaching was reinforced by a keen appreciation of ceremonial, hymnody, and architecture, together with veneration for the martyrs. He also devoted enormous energy to the spiritual health and ecclesial discipline of other churches in north Italy, not least through his correspondence and his attendance at synods. His sympathetic morality is revealed in his writings on virginity (closely associated with his sister) and in his *De officiis.*

P.R.

Ammianus Marcellinus (*c.* AD 330–95), the last great Latin historian of the Roman empire, was born at Syrian Antioch. His early entry, *c.*350, into the élite corps of *protectores domestici* (imperial bodyguard) may indicate family connections with the imperial service at Antioch, in which case an early acquaintance with the Latin language could be inferred, as well as the Greek which formed the base of his literary education. Assigned by Constantius II to the personal staff of the general Ursicinus, Ammianus saw service in north Italy, Gaul, and Germany (the early campaigns of *Julian), Illyricum and Mesopotamia. It was here, in the siege and capture by the Persians of Amida (mod. Diarbekir) in 359, that the first phase of Ammianus' military career came to an end. He escaped from the city, but Ursicinus was dismissed from office in the aftermath of its fall. Ammianus seems to have returned to Antioch, but subsequently participated in the disastrous Persian campaign of Julian (363). In later years he travelled—to the Black Sea and Egypt, southern Greece, possibly to a Thracian battlefield from the Gothic invasions of 376–8—before he came to Rome in the mid-380s. It was here that he completed his history. The work is composed in 31 books, of which the first thirteen, covering the period from Nerva to 353, seem from the nature of a reference to them by the grammarian Priscian already to have been lost by the early 6th cent. The earlier of the lost books were apparently not very full or original, but the scale of the narrative enlarged as Ammianus approached his own day. The surviving books describe in great detail the events and personalities of Ammianus' active lifetime through a period of just 25 years, covering the reigns of Constantius II and Julian (353–63), the brief tenure of Jovian (363–4), the joint reigns of Valentinian I (364–75) and Valens (364–78), and the usurpation of Procopius (366). The culmination of the work is the Gothic invasions of 376–8 and the battle of Hadrianople (9 August 378) at which Valens was killed. The period from 378 to the time of publication is alluded to only in passing references which are, however, of value in judging the date of composition of the work; the latest datable events referred to are of 390 and 391, and the history was probably completed very soon after this.

In the earlier books, narrating his service under Ursicinus, Ammianus' own experiences form a major element, and events are largely seen through the often biased eyes of his patron; with their vivid narrative of sometimes very detailed events and the subjectivity of their judgements, these books have seemed to readers to resemble personal memoir rather than formal history. Despite his own participation—which was at a less privileged level than his experiences with Ursicinus—his narrative of the Persian campaign of Julian is less personally involved, relying sometimes on written sources, and

the books on Valentinian and Valens are less detailed, and despite moments of intense involvement, not focused on the author's own experiences. The centre-piece of the history was the government, first in Gaul as Caesar and then in the east as sole Augustus, of Julian the Apostate. Ammianus deeply admired Julian, particularly for his military and administrative abilities. He was openly critical of other aspects of Julian's regime, not least his religious policies.

Himself a pagan of a more traditional cast, Ammianus disliked Julian's intolerance, and was hostile to the emperor's devotion to excessive sacrifice, and of his submission to the influence of philosophers who, in the end with disastrous results, indulged Julian's interest in Neoplatonic techniques of divination. The extent to which Ammianus was himself a polemical writer is debated. He did not adopt the openly ideological stance against Christianity taken by his younger contemporary Eunapius (whose work he seems to have used from time to time). He is however scathing, in satirical fashion, about the ostentation of the bishops of Rome, criticizes those of Alexandria for their ambition, and ironically refers to the failure of Christianity to live up to its 'pure and simple' professions.

Ammianus' elaborate, individual, and often very intense style is notable for its strong pictorial sense and for its ability to portray character, in which it displays the influence of physiognomical writing and exploits often very vivid comparisons of human character with that of wild beasts. It contains many passages, especially of military narrative, in which individuals are shown at close quarters and in situations of personal stress and great danger. It is influenced too by the language of satire, as when Ammianus denounces the behaviour of the nobility and common people of Rome, or the behaviour of lawyers. The subject-matter is wide, and the history contains many geographical and ethnographical digressions (describing the non-Roman as well as the Roman worlds), as well as scientific and antiquarian excursuses, in which the author's Greek culture is acknowledged, sometimes with quotations of Greek words in which Ammianus refers to Greek as his 'own' first language. The sources for the lost books are not known, except that Ammianus' back-references do not indicate the large-scale use of Greek sources that would have been possible for him, and there are occasional traces of the lost Latin history known as 'Enmann's *Kaisergeschichte*' which can be seen in other Latin writers of the period such as Aurelius Victor and Eutropius. For the contemporary period, Ammianus' narrative was based on personal knowledge and the accounts of eyewitnesses—those 'versati in medio' referred to in the preface of book 15; some of these, such as the eunuch Eutherius and the senator Praetextatus can be convincingly identified. Ammianus does not mention the orator *Symmachus, and was certainly not the anonymous historian addressed by Symmachus in *Epistolae* 9. 110. In general, his affinities with Roman 'senatorial' circles have been much exaggerated by historians.

Ammianus' work, justly admired by Gibbon, is a classic of Latin historiography, though whether the influence of *Tacitus is more than formal (it would explain the starting-point at the reign of Nerva) is debated. The influence of *Sallust is indicated from time to time, but the most persuasive literary influence is clearly that of *Cicero, whose writings are constantly referred to and alluded to. Greek authors, like *Herodotus, *Thucydides (2), and *Polybius, are acknowledged at suitable moments but do not seem otherwise to have exercised any real influence upon Ammianus' manner. *Homer and *Virgil are effectively used to give epic scale and colour to the narrative. Affinities with contemporary Latin prose writers are not obvious or extensive; the most obvious, both as to style and content, is perhaps the imperial legislation collected in the Theodosian Code (see THEODOSIUS II), a comparison by which Ammianus, a lover of settled government and respect for institutions, might not have been offended.   J.F.Ma.

Anacreon, lyric poet, native of Teos in Ionia (western Asia Minor). Little is known of his life. Born perhaps *c.*575–570 (Eusebius gives his *floruit* as 536/5), he probably joined in the foundation of Abdera in Thrace by the Teans fleeing before the threat of the Persian general Harpagus in 545 (Strabo 14. 1. 310; Aristox. fr. 12 Wehrli. Hdt. 1. 168). He joined the court of *Polycrates, tyrant of Samos (Hdt. 3. 121), the most illustrious Greek of his day; Strabo claims that his 'whole poetry is full of men-tions of Polycrates' (14. 1. 16), though there is no reference in surviving fragments. Tradition made Anacreon and Polycrates rivals for the love of a Thracian boy, Smerdies, whose hair Polycrates cut off in a fit of jealousy (Stob. 4. 21. 24; Ath. 12. 540e; Ael. *VH* 9. 4); this may be false inference from Anacreon's poetry. After the murder of Polycrates by the Persian satrap Oroites he joined the Pisistratid court at Athens (see PISISTRATUS); allegedly Pisistratus' younger son Hipparchus sent a warship to fetch him ([Pl.] *Hipparch.* 228c). According to Plato (*Chrm.* 157e) he praised the family of Critias (grandfather of the oligarch Critias), whose lover he was (scholion on Aesch. *PV* 128). After Hipparchus' murder he may have gone to Thessaly (*Anth. Pal.* 6. 136, 142, if correctly attributed). The fragments suggest that he lived to old age, though the figure of 85 years ([Lucian] *Macr.* 26) cannot be verified. The tradition that he died by choking on a grape (Val. Max. 12) displays the myth-making typical of ancient biography.

He composed in a variety of rhythms; the dialect is Ionic vernacular with some epic features. The range of what survives is narrow. Wine and love (both homosexual and heterosexual) figure prominently. His control of form produces an appearance of effortlessness. Many poems have an epigrammatic quality. Words are positioned with great effect, as in fr. 357, a prayer to Dionysus, with the play on the beloved's name and closing revelation that this is a love poem; 358 with the contrast between the fluent first and staccato second half reflecting the move from enchantment to rejection; 395 with its closing wordplay; and 360 with the closing image of the beloved boy as a charioteer of the poet's soul. Striking images for love abound (396, 398, 413). Delicacy, wit, paradox, irony and self-mockery are prominent, as in 417, addressed to a coy girl, represented as a reluctant filly, 347 which laments the loss of a boy's hair in mock-epic terms, the bathos of 359, the idea of riotous decorum in 356a. He also produced biting abuse in the iambic tradition (346, 372, 388). Later sources ascribe maidensongs to him (Ath. 13. 600d); a possible fragment survives (501). His work inspired a corpus of frivolous imitations in and after the Hellenistic period, the Anacreontea, which until the 19th cent. were believed to be his work.   C.C.

Anaxagoras (probably 500–428 BC), son of Hegesibulus, and a native of Clazomenae in western Asia Minor; the first philosopher known to have settled in Athens. The evidence for his biography, although relatively plentiful, is confused and confusing. The best critical study (by J. Mansfeld) has him arrive in Athens in 456/5 in the archonship of Callias and philosophize there for 20 years or so, until his prosecution and trial on a charge of impiety (dated to 437/6). He resettled in Lampsacus, probably with the aid of his patron *Pericles. There he died and was buried with high honours. His name was associated with the fall of a large meteorite at Aegospotami in Thrace (c.467); his explanations of other physical phenomena are already reflected in *Aeschylus' *Supplices* (c.463) and *Eumenides* (458).

The Neoplatonist Simplicius (6th cent. AD) preserves extensive fragments of Anaxagoras' one book, which famously began with the words: 'All things were together' (fr. 1 DK). The longest and most eloquent surviving passage explains how our differentiated *kosmos* was created from the original *mélange* by the action of mind, an entirely discrete principle, unmixed with any other substances but capable of ordering and controlling them (fr. 12). Anaxagoras' most striking and paradoxical claim is the thesis that, despite the consequent separation of dense from rare, hot from cold, etc., 'as things were in the beginning, so now they are all together' (fr. 6): 'in everything—except mind—a portion of everything' (fr. 11). Ancient commentators (e.g. Arist. *Ph.* 187ᵃ36–ᵇ7) supplied examples: what we call black contains a predominance of portions of black (cf. fr. 12 end.), but portions of white also, for how else could water turn into snow? Similarly sperm contains flesh, hair, and indeed everything else, for hair cannot come from not-hair, flesh from not-flesh (fr. 10), etc.

If analysis or division were thoroughgoing, would it not be possible to reach particles of pure flesh or pure black? This idea is explicitly rejected by Anaxagoras: 'the small is unlimited' (there are no theoretical minima), and as complex as the large (frs. 3 and 6). The ultimate constituents of the world never exist as discrete physical entities, only as stuffs or powers of which—hence the designation 'portions'—such entities consist. When Anaxagoras talks of an infinity of 'seeds' both

in the beginning and now in our world (fr. 4), we should probably think not of particles but of the potentiality of latent portions to become manifest.

To Anaxagoras is attributed the maxim: 'The appearances are a sight of what is not apparent' (fr. 21a). Infinite variety in phenomena reflects infinite variety in seeds; things as we perceive them are very like things as they really are. This position is far removed from Parmenidean metaphysics and epistemology. (See PARMENIDES.) Yet engagement with Eleatic ideas is evidently responsible for some key features of Anaxagoras' thought, e.g. the doctrine of the fundamental homogeneity of reality, his 'all together' echoing Parmenides' own words (fr. 8. 5), and the explicit rejection of the concepts of birth and death in favour of mixture and dissolution (fr. 17). Modern scholars have been fascinated by the subtlety with which these ontological principles are applied in Anaxagoras' system. By contrast his cosmology is perceived as a mere reworking of *Anaximenes', even if the claim that the sun is a huge incandescent stone shocked contemporary opinion (Diog. Laert. 2. 12). More original is Anaxagoras' theory of mind, as both Plato (*Phd.* 97b ff.) and Aristotle (*Metaph.* 984ᵇ15 ff., 985ᵃ18 ff.) recognize, while lamenting its failure to offer teleological explanations of natural processes.   M.Sch.

Anaximander, of Miletus in western Asia Minor (died soon after 547 BC), said to be an associate or disciple of *Thales, was the first Greek to write a prose treatise 'On the Nature of Things' (*Peri physeōs*). He thus initiated the tradition of Greek natural philosophy by elaborating a system of the heavens, including an account of the origins of human life, and by leaving his speculation behind in written form. He was the first to make a map of the inhabited world; some sources also credit him with a *sphairos* or plan of the heavens.

Anaximander's view of the cosmos is remarkable for its speculative imagination and for its systematic appeal to rational principles and natural processes as a basis for explanation. The origin of things is the *apeiron*, the limitless or infinite, which apparently surrounds the generated world and 'steers' or governs the world process. Symmetry probably dictates that the world-order will perish into the source from which it has arisen, as symmetry is explicitly said to explain why the earth is stable in the centre of things, equally balanced in every direction. The world process begins when the opposites are 'separated out' to generate the hot and the cold, the dry and the wet. By a process that is both biological and mechanical, earth, sea, and sky take shape and huge wheels of enclosed fire are formed to produce the phenomena of sun, moon, and stars. The size of the wheels was specified, corresponding perhaps to the arithmetical series 9, 18, 27. The earth is a flat disc, three times as broad as it is deep. Mechanical explanations in terms of the opposites are offered for meteorological phenomena (wind, rain, lightning, and thunder) and for the origin of animal life. The first human beings were generated from a sort of embryo floating in the sea.

The *apeiron* is ageless, deathless, and eternal; unlike the anthropomorphic gods, it is also ungenerated. The cosmos, on the other hand, is a world-order of coming-to-be and perishing according to a fixed law of nature, described in the one quotation from Anaximander's book (perhaps the earliest preserved sentence of European prose): out of those things from which beings are generated, into these again does their perishing take place 'according to what is needful and right; for they pay the penalty and make atonement for one another for their wrongdoing (*adikia*), according to the ordinance of time'.

C.H.K.

Anaximenes, of Miletus in western Asia Minor (traditional *floruit* 546–525 BC) followed in the footsteps of *Anaximander in composing a treatise in Ionian prose in which he developed a world system on the basis of an infinite or unlimited principle, which he identified as *aēr*. His system differed from that of his predecessor in several respects. Instead of suspending the earth in the centre of the universe by cosmic symmetry, he supported it from below by cosmic air. And instead of leaving the infinite starting-point for world formation indeterminate in nature, he specified it as elemental air, which he probably conceived as a kind of vital world-breath that dominates the world order as our own breath-soul rules over us. Anaximenes also offered a mechanistic explanation for world

formation and change in terms of the condensation and rarefaction of the air. Air becomes fire by rarefaction; by motion it becomes wind; by condensation it becomes water and, by more condensation, earth and stones.

It was the Milesian cosmology as reformulated by Anaximenes that became standard for Ionian natural philosophy in the 5th cent. *Heraclitus reacts against this system by replacing air with fire. *Anaxagoras and *Democritus follow Anaximenes in regarding the earth as a flat disc supported by air. Diogenes of Apollonia, the most conservative 5th-cent. physicist, retains the cosmic air as divine principle of life and intelligence, controlling the world-order.

C.H.K.

Andocides (*c*.440–*c*.390 BC), a member of a distinguished aristocratic family, whose grandfather had been one of the ten Athenian envoys who negotiated the Thirty Years Peace of 446 between the Athenians and Spartans. In 415, shortly before the great expedition to Sicily was due to depart, the Athenians were greatly dismayed one morning to discover that in the night the statues of Hermes around the city ('herms') had been mutilated: Hermes being the god of travellers, this act was presumably intended to affect the progress of the expedition, but it was also taken, curiously, as a sign that the democracy itself was in danger. In the subsequent accusations the young Andocides and his associates in a club, which was probably suspected of oligarchic tendencies, were named as having shared both in the mutilations and in profane parodies of the Eleusinian mysteries, and were arrested. Andocides, to secure immunity and, as he claimed, to save his father, confessed to a share in the mutilations and gave an account of the whole affair which, though it may have been far from the truth, was readily accepted by the Athenians. This secured his release, but shortly afterwards, when the decree of Isotimides, aimed at him especially, forbade those who had confessed to an act of impiety to enter temples or the Agora (market area), Andocides preferred to leave the city and began to trade as a merchant, in which role he developed connections all over the Aegean and in Sicily and Italy. In 411, seeking to restore himself to favour at Athens, he provided oars at cost price to the fleet in Samos, and shortly afterwards returned to Athens to plead for the removal of the limitation on his rights. Unfortunately for him, the oligarchic revolution of the Four Hundred had just installed in power the very class of citizens whom his confession had affected, and he was put into prison and maltreated. Released, perhaps at the fall of the Four Hundred, he returned to his trading, in the course of which he was for a while imprisoned by *Evagoras, the king of Cyprus. At some time after the re-establishment of the democracy in 410, he returned to the city to renew his plea (the speech *De reditu* belongs to this occasion) but he was again unsuccessful. Returning finally under the amnesty of 403, he resumed full participation in public life, and in 400 (or 399) successfully defended himself in the *De mysteriis* against an attempt to have him treated as still subject to the decree of Isotimides: the sixth speech of the Lysian corpus (see LYSIAS), *Against Andocides*, was delivered by one of his accusers. In 392/391 he was one of the Athenian envoys sent to Sparta to discuss the making of peace, and on his return in the debate in the assembly he delivered the *De pace* urging acceptance of the proffered terms, which were in fact very similar to those of the King's Peace of 387/386. The Athenians, however, rejected the peace, and Andocides and the other envoys were prosecuted by the young Callistratus. Andocides anticipated condemnation by retiring into exile, and we hear no more of him.

SPEECHES In addition to the three speeches mentioned above, there is a fourth speech, *Against Alcibiades*, preserved under his name, which purports to be concerned with an ostracism in 415; most scholars regard this as a forgery. Fragments of four other speeches are preserved.

Greek and Roman critics discovered in Andocides faults which, according to their canons, were serious; and admittedly the faults are there. He sometimes carries the use of parenthesis to absurd extremes; he cannot keep to one point at a time; his style is so loose that the argument is hard to follow. On the other hand, this inconsequential method of expression is at times effective, giving the impression of an eagerness which outruns premeditated art. He possessed a natural gift of expression, a fine flow of words, and a good narrative style. He was not a profes-

sional rhetorician, and if he neglected scholastic rules, it can at least be claimed for him that he was successful on his own unconventional lines.   G.L.C.

Annaeus Lucanus, Marcus See LUCAN.

Annaeus Seneca, Lucius See SENECA THE ELDER and SENECA THE YOUNGER.

Annius Milo See MILO.

Antigonus Doson (*c*.263–221 BC), regent and king of Macedonia 229–221. His nickname means 'the man who will give'. He was son of Demetrius the Fair, who was half-brother of *Antigonus Gonatas. Antigonus Doson ruled at first as regent for Demetrius II's young son Philip (later *Philip V), but after some initial military successes against invading Dardanians and Aetolians and rebellious Thessalians he was granted the royal title. He had already married Philip's mother Chryseis and adopted the boy, so dispelling suspicions that he might wish to usurp Philip's ultimate claim to succeed. Doson's reign is characterized by careful restorative diplomacy, in Thessaly, where he allowed the Thessalian League to be reconstituted, but especially in the Peloponnese, leading to the restoration of Macedonian influence, which had largely vanished during Demetrius II's reign. He also visited Caria around 227 and constructed a position of influence in the area around Mylasa—his reasons are obscure—which Philip V could inherit. In the Peloponnese the Achaean Confederacy was so oppressed by the Spartan king *Cleomenes III that *Aratus (2) felt forced to approach Antigonus in 226. It was a fine opportunity for Antigonus to regain the Acrocorinth, which Aratus duly promised. In 224 Antigonus marched south, organized his allies into a Hellenic League under Macedonian presidency, restored Achaean influence in Arcadia and in 222 invaded Laconia. At Sellasia he crushed Cleomenes' army, occupied Sparta and supervised the reorganization of the revolutionary city. His sudden death, after bursting a blood vessel in battle with Dardanians in 221, left Macedonia to the 17-year-old Philip V; but before his death Antigonus arranged for experienced advisers to occupy the most important functions of state, thus confirming his reputation as a careful administrator who put public interests first.   R.M.E.

Antigonus Gonatas (*c.*320–239 BC), king of Macedonia (*c.*277/6–239 BC), son of *Demetrius the Besieger and Phila; the meaning of the nickname Gonatas is unknown. He served under his father in Greece in 292, commanded his possessions there from 287, and took the royal title on Demetrius' death in 282, though he failed to gain Macedonia until 277/6. Before then his military ability won widespread recognition, not only in Macedonia, through a major victory near Lysimacheia in 277 over Celts who had overrun Macedonia and Thrace. Cassandreia still resisted him for ten months but his dynastic alliance with *Antiochus I Soter, whose sister Phila he married, ended Seleucid competition. *Pyrrhus occupied western Macedonia and Thessaly in 274 but his death in 272 removed this threat. In Greece Demetrius' old naval bases—Piraeus, Chalcis in Euboia, Corinth, and Demetrias—guaranteed Antigonus' influence, and although an alliance led by Athens and Sparta and supported by *Ptolemy II Philadelphus tried to eject the Macedonians (in the 'Chremonidean War' of *c.*267–261), Athens finally had to capitulate. Subsequently Antigonus, in alliance with Antiochus II, took the offensive in Ptolemy's preserve, the SE Aegean—a naval victory near Cos (perhaps 254) caused a modest spread of Macedonian influence which was reinforced by Antigonus' son Demetrius's marrying Antiochus II's sister Stratonice. In Greece Antigonus became notorious for controlling cities by supporting tyrants, a practice which saved garrison troops but provoked serious local opposition, especially in the Peloponnese, where the Achaean Confederacy exploited dissatisfaction to extend its influence, even taking Corinth in 243. Nevertheless Demetrias, Chalcis, and the Piraeus remained Macedonian. In Macedonia Antigonus seems to have aimed at restoring the court tradition of *Philip II. In particular his own intellectual interests, fostered in his youth in southern Greece, led to frequent visits to Pella by historians, poets, and philosophers. The larger cities of the kingdom— at least Amphipolis, Pella, Cassandreia, and Thessalonica—encouraged by the stable conditions, acquired some limited rights of self-government, which were widely recognized

before Antigonus' death. Antigonus also helped establish his dynasty by regulating the succession. His son Demetrius (the future king Demetrius II) played a major part, from the 260s onwards, both in military and civil capacities; some historians even think he used the royal title in Antigonus' last years. Antigonus' long period of rule—37 years— and cautious policies provided a desperately needed consolidation for Macedonia. Characteristic for his later reputation is his reported comment, even if not authentic, that kingship is honourable servitude.

                                                R.M.E.

Antigonus the One-eyed (Monophthalmos), (*c.*382–301 BC), Macedonian noble, was prominent under *Philip II and governed Greater Phrygia for *Alexander the Great (334–323). Victorious in three battles over Persian refugees from the battle of Issus (332), he remained unchallenged in his satrapy until he fell foul of the regent *Perdiccas whom he denounced to Antipater in Macedon (322), unleashing the First Coalition War. For his services he was given command of the campaign against *Eumenes of Cardia and the remnants of the Perdiccan factions. In 319 he defeated both groups spectacularly, and Antipater's death, on the heels of his victories, encouraged him in his supremacist ambitions. He supported *Cassander against the regent *Polyperchon, and took the war against Eumenes (Polyperchon's appointee as royal general) into central Asia. The victory at Gabiene (316) gave him control of territory from the Hindu Kush to the Aegean, but his success brought immediate war with his erstwhile allies: Cassander, *Lysimachus and *Ptolemy I (315). The 'Peace of the Dynasts' (summer 311) briefly ratified the status quo, but it was a dead letter from the first. *Seleucus I invaded Babylon in 311 with Ptolemy's support, provoking full-scale war, and Ptolemy resumed hostilities in 310. Antigonus directed his attention to the Greek world, broadcasting his predilection for freedom and autonomy, and ultimately reactivated the Corinthian League of *Philip II as a weapon against Cassander (303/2). Athens welcomed him and his son, *Demetrius the Besieger, with open arms and exaggerated honours (307), and in the following year the two had themselves proclaimed kings (*basileis*). But the achievements belied the propaganda. The invasion of Egypt (306) was abortive, as was Demetrius' year-long siege of Rhodes (305/4). Finally the coalition of 315 was reforged. At the battle of Ipsus (in Phrygia) in 301 the combined Antigonid forces were defeated decisively and Antigonus died in battle. His ambitions had been too patent, his resources inadequate to contain the reaction they provoked.   A.B.B.

Antimachus, of Colophon in western Asia Minor, Greek poet and scholar (fl. 400 BC). He may have been taught by Stesimbrotus of Thasos; Plutarch, *Lys.* 18. 8 says he competed at the Lysandreia festival in Samos in *Lysander's presence (therefore before 395 BC); his younger friend and admirer *Plato sent *Heraclides Ponticus (fr. 6 Wehrli) to Colophon to collect his poems.

WORKS Small fragments survive: the *Thebais* was an epic, probably in 24 books, narrating the first expedition against Thebes, and exhibiting a wide knowledge of earlier poetry. *Lyde* was a narrative elegy in at least two books, allegedly composed after the death of his wife or mistress Lyde. It included very diverse mythological episodes, e.g. the Argonautica, Demeter's wanderings, Oedipus, and Bellerophon; unhappy love may have been one of its connecting themes. Other poems, *Deltoi, Artemis,* and *Iachine* (the title is probably corrupt), are mere names to us. Antimachus also produced an edition of *Homer and wrote on his life, claiming him as a fellow Colophonian; Homeric glosses, along with scholarly neologisms and obscure periphrases, are prominent in his poetry. In his combination of the roles of scholar and poet Antimachus is the precursor of the great Hellenistic poets of the next century, who however took very varied views of his work. *Callimachus criticized the *Lyde* as 'fat and inelegant' (fr. 398 Pf.), but the form of his own *Aetia* may be in part modelled on it; Posidippus of Pella and Asclepiades of Samos (both of whom were allegedly among a group of literary enemies whom Callimachus attacked) praised it. *Apollonius Rhodius alluded to his poems in the *Argonautica,* and explained one of his rare words in a scholarly work. But it appears that Callimachus' condemnation prevailed, and Antimachus' works were apparently not frequently read in antiquity: though *Quintilian

10. 1. 53 commends him, with reservations, as a writer of epic, the admiration felt for the *Thebais* by the emperor *Hadrian (Cass. Dio 69. 4. 6 = test. 31 Wyss) was clearly eccentric. (The tendency to use Antimachus' name as the antithesis to another poet, usually Homer, admired by the author does not necessarily imply familiarity with Antimachus' works.)   F.W.

Antiochus I Soter (Soter) (*c.*324–261 BC), eldest son of *Seleucus I and the Bactrian Apame, crown prince (*mār šarri*) in Babylonia before he became co-regent with Seleucus I (292–281/0); then held responsibility for the 'Upper Satrapies', when he married Seleucus' second wife, Stratonice, daughter of *Demetrius the Besieger, for political as well as romantic reasons, since Demetrius still posed a threat. This apparent division of royal power (coins from the eastern satrapies, e.g. Bactria, were still minted under the names of both Seleucus and Antiochus, and in inscriptions Seleucus' name took precedence) perhaps indicates both Seleucus' perception of the importance of the eastern part of the empire and of the need for royal authority there, and also of Antiochus' potential acceptability there as a half-Iranian king.

Antiochus was, with Seleucus I and *Antiochus III the Great, one of the most dynamic and successful of the Seleucid kings and played a crucial part in consolidating the empire, both territorially and institutionally. His huge colonizing and consolidating activity through the Seleucid empire, apart from many city foundations in Anatolia, include in the east, the oasis city of Antioch Margiana, not far from modern Merv (Strabo 11. 10. 2), Soteira in Aria (region of Herat), and continued input for foundations such as Ai Khanoum, in northern Afghanistan and Antioch-Persis, probably modern Bushire.

Antiochus' continuation of Seleucus I's work in Babylonia, using the Babylonian kingship as a political and religious focus for support, is mirrored in the famous building inscription from the temple of Esida in Borsippa, near Babylon (268), which also refers to the rebuilding of the temple of Esagila at Babylon, in the rituals of which Antiochus also took part. The note of concord with Babylonian traditions and with Babylonian gods can be understood as intentional Seleucid policy of using Babylonian kingship as a vehicle for rule in Babylonia, the core of the empire.

At his accession (281), Antiochus had to restore control of his father's empire, by military force, in many regions, e.g. revolts in Syria and in Anatolia, where dynasts in Bithynia and Pontus became independent, and reinforce Seleucid claims to Thrace, which the kingdom continued to reiterate until the reign of Antiochus III. In this period Sardis in Lydia became one of the Seleucid royal capitals (besides Antioch in Syria, Seleuceia on Tigris in Babylonia), as a base for political and military operations in the western parts of the empire. Antiochus was the first of the Hellenistic kings to organize an army to deal with the incursions into Anatolia of the Celts (Galatians) and their disruption of life in country and city. He is famous for his decisive victory over the Celts at the battle of Elephants, penning them back to a small area in the Halys region. Antiochus was also in conflict with *Ptolemy II over Coele-Syria and Phoenicia, but by the end of the 270s, peace had been restored with Coele-Syria and Phoenicia remaining under Ptolemy's rule and the Seleucid eastern empire apparently under control.   G.T.G.; S.S.-W.

Antiochus III the Great (c.242–187 BC), second son of *Seleucus II, succeeded to the Seleucid throne as a young man, after the assassination of his elder brother, Seleucus III. He faced many problems within the empire: in the east, a rebellion in Media led by the satrap Molon (222), with the support of the satrap of Persis, Alexander (brother of Molon); Molon invaded Babylonia, seized the royal capital, Seleuceia on Tigris, and took the title 'king'. In the west, Achaeus, viceroy of Seleucid Asia Minor, was in revolt and in control of the royal capital of Sardis. The Ptolemies still retained control of Seleuceia-Pieria in north Syria.

Within the next 25 years, Antiochus, 'restitutor orbis', overcame the revolt of Molon (Polyb. 5. 51–4), regained Seleuceia-Pieria (219), re-established control over Sardis (213), and in 212 began his *anabasis* to the 'Upper Satrapies', bringing Commagene and Armenia under direct Seleucid rule; he restored Seleucid suzerainty over Parthia and Bactria (210–206), renewed links with the India of the Mauryas (Polyb. 11. 39. 11–12) and,

on his return, mounted a naval expedition to the Persian Gulf, where the Seleucids controlled the island of Icaros (mod. Failaka, off Kuwait), and waged a campaign against Gerrha, but in the end agreed a treaty that allowed the former status of the Gerrhaeans as independent to continue (Polyb. 13. 9. 4–5). It was as a result of these campaigns that Antiochus was given the epithet *megas* (Great), the *terminus ante quem* of which is 202 BC. In campaigns (202–198) Antiochus finally established lasting Seleucid control over southern Syria, Phoenicia, and Judaea after initial invasions (221, 219, 217, when he was defeated by *Ptolemy IV at the battle of Raphia). Then (198) Antiochus launched an onslaught against Ptolemaic possessions in Lycia and Caria, which he took over (new inscriptions attest to the disruption and turmoil that this caused to the local populations). He moved thence to Thrace (197/6), where he refounded Lysimachea (Livy, 33. 38; App. *Syr.* 1). The campaign into Thrace, always (since Seleucus I) claimed as Seleucid, brought Antiochus up against the imperialistic Roman republic. In the protracted diplomatic exchange of 196–193, he and the senate were at cross purposes, and finally he invaded Greece. He was defeated by the Romans in two land battles, at Thermopylae in Greece and at Magnesia in Asia Minor (190). He also lost a naval campaign to them.

By the peace of Apamea (188), Antiochus ceded Seleucid satrapies in Anatolia, north of the Taurus (e.g. Lydia, Phrygia, Mysia, Caria), retaining in southern Anatolia Pamphylia and Rough and Smooth Cilicia. He still ruled a huge realm, from southern Turkey, through Syria and Palestine to Babylonia, Iran, and central Asia. After his defeat by Rome, Antiochus was again on campaign to the 'Upper Satrapies', where, disastrously, he pillaged the temple of Bel/Zeus in Elymais, and died from his injuries.

Antiochus stands out as one of the most dynamic and successful of the Seleucid kings. The centrality of Babylon (and so of Babylonia) and of his eastern empire is mirrored in a newly published Babylonian astronomical diary (188/7), which shows Antiochus participating in rituals in the temple of Esagila (Babylon), before he embarked on his ill-fated, second *anabasis*.

Antiochus was married (221) to *Laodice,

daughter of Mithradates of Pontus, who gave Antiochus four sons, of whom Seleucus IV and *Antiochus IV Epiphanes ruled as kings.

His reign was marked by continuous military campaigns to reconsolidate the Seleucid empire. He was also the first Seleucid to have organized, on a satrapal basis, a state ruler-cult for the king, the *progonoi* (his ancestors) and, by 193, his queen, Laodice.

G.T.G.; S.S.-W.

Antiochus IV Epiphanes (*c*.215–164 BC), third son of *Antiochus III the Great, became king in 175. He sought actively to reconsolidate the remaining huge Seleucid empire, from Cilicia and Syria eastwards, after the Peace of Apamea (188) had precluded the Seleucids from their possessions north of the Taurus mountain range. His attempt to incorporate Ptolemaic Egypt and Cyprus (170–169/8) failed because Rome's victory over *Perseus of Macedon enabled Rome to order Antiochus from Egypt. His intervention in Jerusalem, overturning Antiochus III's 'charter for Jerusalem' (following Antiochus III's capture of it from the Ptolemies), guaranteeing the worship of Yahweh and the extensive privileges of all those involved in the cult, in co-operation with an 'hellenizing party', has, from the viewpoint of Seleucid historiography, resulted in a distorted and hostile picture of the king, presented in Maccabees 1–3, whereas in reality Judaea was strategically and economically of minor importance. Antiochus was active as a benefactor of cities of Aegean Greece and of indigenous cities within the Seleucid empire. The great resources of military manpower remaining are reflected in accounts of the famous procession mounted by him at Daphne (166/5), prior to his *anabasis* to the 'Upper Satrapies', a major military campaign, in which he met his death.

G.T.G.; S.S.-W.

Antiochus of Ascalon (b. *c*.130 BC), Academic philosopher (i.e. he belonged to the school originally founded by *Plato) who studied under *Philon of Larissa, but later founded his own school. He joined L. *Lucullus on a mission to Alexandria and the eastern provinces in 87/6. L. *Cicero heard Antiochus' lectures at Athens in 79 and held him in high esteem throughout his life. Antiochus died in 69/8 BC, shortly after the battle of Tigranocerta, which he witnessed, again in the company of Lucullus.

According to Cicero, Antiochus left Philon's Academy because of its scepticism, and embraced a version of dogmatism hardly distinguishable from Stoic doctrine. Antiochus himself maintained that the Stoics, together with the Peripatetics (the followers of *Aristotle), were the legitimate heirs of Plato's philosophy, while the scepticism of the Academics from *Arcesilaus on had been an aberration. He therefore called his school the Old Academy.

Antiochus is known to have written a work on epistemology in two volumes (*Kanonika*); the *Sosus*, probably a dialogue, in which he argued against the thesis of his teacher Philon that the tradition of the Academy had been uninterrupted throughout its sceptical period; and a book about the gods. Cicero tells us that he also wrote on other subjects, notably ethics. While Antiochus' epistemology was undoubtedly Stoic (see Cicero's *Lucullus*), he adopted some Peripatetic views in his ethics (Cicero, *Fin*. 5), claiming that the difference between Stoic and Peripatetic ethics was merely terminological.

His school does not seem to have continued beyond the time of his brother and successor Aristus. It is not clear whether Antiochus had any influence on the newly developing Platonism of his time.

G.S.

Antipater (?397–319 BC), Macedonian statesman. Trusted lieutenant of *Philip II, he represented the king at Athens in 346 and 338, and governed Macedon during the Danubian campaign of *Alexander the Great (335). From 334 he acted as viceroy in Europe and in 331/0 dealt competently with a revolt in Thrace and the subsequent war in the Peloponnese which Agis III of Sparta instigated. Later his relations with Alexander were soured, and in 324 *Craterus was sent to replace him in Macedon. Alexander's death (323) resolved the tension but unleashed the Lamian War in which a formidable Hellenic coalition, headed by the Athenians and Aetolians, came close to victory. The advent of Craterus and his veterans redressed the balance, and the critical victory at Crannon (August 322) allowed Antipater to impose the settlement which brought oligarchy and a Macedonian garrison to Athens. At the news of *Perdiccas' dynastic intrigues he declared war and invaded Asia Minor with Craterus (321). After Perdiccas' death he presided over the conference at Triparadeisus where—in turbulent circumstances—he assumed the regency and returned to Europe early in 319 with the kings in his custody. His death shortly afterwards left a legacy of civil war, thanks to his preference of *Polyperchon over his own son, *Cassander.   A.B.B.

Antiphon of Rhamnus (one of the constituent demes or villages of Attica, the territory of Athens) (c.480–411 BC), the first Attic orator whose works were preserved. From a prominent family, he participated in the intellectual movement inspired by the sophists (itinerant professors of higher education), taking a particular interest in law and rhetoric; he reportedly taught *Thucydides, among others. Many (though not all) scholars are now inclined to identify him with *Antiphon 'the Sophist' (Xen. *Mem.* 1. 6), fragments of whose work *Truth* are concerned with the nature of justice and the relationship between *nomos* ('law, convention') and *phusis* ('nature'); see next entry.

Thucydides (8. 68) praises Antiphon highly for ability (*aretē*), intelligence, and power of expression, adding that he stayed in the background himself but made his reputation giving advice to others. He credits Antiphon with planning the oligarchic coup that overturned the democratic constitution of Athens for a few months in 411 BC (the so-called regime of the Four Hundred). When democracy was restored, most leaders of the coup fled, but Antiphon and Archeptolemus remained to stand trial for treason; both were convicted and executed. Antiphon's speech in his own defence, a small papyrus fragment of which survives, was the finest speech Thucydides knew. When congratulated by *Agathon on its brilliance, Antiphon replied that he would rather have satisfied one man of good taste than any number of common people (Arist. *Eth. Eud.* 1232^b 7).

Antiphon was apparently the first to compose speeches for other litigants and thus the first to write them down. His clients included well-known political figures and foreign allies of Athens. We have six complete works: three courtroom speeches and three *Tetralogies*. All concern homicide cases, though the fragmentary speeches treat many other issues. The courtroom speeches and the

datable fragments come from the last two decades of Antiphon's life (430–411). In *Against the Stepmother* (1) a young man accuses his stepmother of having employed a servant-woman to poison his father. He may have brought the case from a sense of duty, for he offers little evidence. In *The Murder of Herodes* (5) a Mytilenean is accused of murdering Herodes during a sea voyage: Herodes went ashore one stormy night and never returned. He defends his innocence by appeal both to facts and to probabilities (*eikota*), and accuses his opponent of trumping up the charge for political reasons and personal gain. In *On the Chorus Boy* (6) a *chorēgos* (producer and financial backer of a play) is accused of the accidental death of a boy who was given a drug to improve his voice. The *chorēgos* argues that he was not even present at the time and that the prosecution is politically motivated.

The *Tetralogies* are Antiphon's earliest works. Their authenticity is disputed, but their arguments concerning probability, causation, and similar issues fit the period and Antiphon's interests. Using the sophistic method of contrasting arguments (cf. *Protagoras' Antilogiae) and displaying a self-conscious virtuosity, the *Tetralogies* illustrate methods of argument that could be applied to a wide variety of cases. Each consists of four speeches for hypothetical cases, two on each side. In the *First Tetralogy* (2) a man is murdered and circumstantial evidence points to the accused, who argues that others are more likely (*eikos*) to be the killers. In the *Second Tetralogy* (3) a boy is accidentally killed by a javelin; the defence argues that the boy himself, not the thrower, is guilty of unintentional homicide because he was the cause of his own death. In the *Third Tetralogy* (4) a man dies after a fight and the accused argues that the victim is to blame because he started it.

Antiphon stands at the beginning of the tradition of literary Attic prose. He is an innovator and experimenter; he is fond of antithesis (in both word and thought), poetic vocabulary, the use of participles, and occasionally extreme asyndeton. In comparison to successors like *Lysias, Antiphon lacks grace of expression, clarity of organization, and the vivid presentation of character, but the force and variety of his arguments may account for his success.   M.Ga.

Antiphon the sophist (i.e. itinerant professor of higher education) of Athens (5th. cent. BC). Scholars are divided on whether he was identical with the orator (see preceding entry). Works attributed to him include *Concord* and *Truth*; of the latter some papyrus fragments survive (DK B 44), critical of conventional morality from a standpoint of self-interest.   C.C.W.T.

Antisthenes (mid-5th–mid-4th cent. BC), associate of *Socrates, one of those named by *Plato as having been present at his final conversation. A professional teacher, he continued the sophistic tradition by writing voluminously on many subjects, including ethics, politics, natural philosophy, epistemology, language, literature, and rhetoric, and in a variety of genres, including Socratic dialogues, declamations, and diatribes against various people, including Plato.

He followed Socrates in holding that virtue can be taught and that it is sufficient for happiness, 'requiring nothing more than Socratic strength' (Diog. Laert. 6. 11). Consequently he stressed the austerity of the Socratic lifestyle, and was vehemently hostile to pleasures except those of a hard and simple life. This emphasis on the self-sufficiency and detachment of the virtuous agent was taken up by the Stoics and (with special emphasis on physical austerity) the Cynics; later writers treat Antisthenes as the founder of the Cynic tradition.

He shared with Cratylus, Prodicus, and others an interest in the nature of language and its relation to reality. He is among those (including Protagoras and Prodicus) reported as having denied the possibility of contradiction. *Aristotle represents him (*Metaph.* 1024^b 32–4) as having derived this thesis from the view that anything can be referred to only by a unique formula specifying its nature. Aristotle also ascribes to 'followers of Antisthenes' (*Metaph.* 1043^b 23–32) the theory that only complex things can be defined, whereas simple entities are indefinable (a theory criticized in Plato's *Theaetetus*).

Following *Xenophanes and others, he was critical of conventional religion, maintaining that while in common belief (*kata nomon*) there are many gods, in reality (*kata phusin*) there is only one.   C.C.W.T.

Antistius Labeo See LABEO.

Antoninus Pius, Roman emperor AD 138–61, born at Lanuvium in Latium in 86, was the son of Titus Aurelius Fulvus (consul 89) and grandson of another Aurelius Fulvus (consul 70 and 85), from Nîmes (Nemausus). His mother Arria Fadilla was daughter of Arrius Antoninus (consul 69 and 97), whose names he bore as well as Boionius from his maternal grandmother: T. Aurelius Fulvus Boionius Arrius Antoninus. He married Annia Galeria Faustina, and became consul in 120. Apart from the traditional magistracies, his only posts were those of imperial legate in Italy (an innovation of *Hadrian), in his case in Etruria and Umbria, where he owned land, and proconsul of Asia (135–6).

His links with the Annii Veri, combined with his wealth, popularity, and character, led Hadrian to choose him as adoptive son and successor on the death of Lucius Aelius Caesar. Given *imperium* (a grant of supreme military and civil authority) and the *tribunicia potestas* (tribunician power) on 25 February 138, he became Imperator Titus Aelius Aurelius Antoninus Caesar and at Hadrian's wish adopted both the young son of L. Aelius (the future emperor Lucius Verus) and his nephew by marriage Marcus Annius Verus (*Marcus Aurelius). His accession at Hadrian's death, 10 July 138, was warmly welcomed by the senate, which overcame its reluctance to deify Hadrian at Antoninus' insistence and named him Pius in acknowledgment of his loyalty. His wife Faustina was named Augusta, and his only surviving child, also Annia Galeria Faustina, was betrothed to Marcus Aurelius Caesar, his nephew and elder adoptive son. Pius became consul for a second term and Pater Patriae ('father of the fatherland') in 139, consul for a third term in 140 with Marcus Aurelius as colleague, and held one further consulship, in 145, again with Marcus Aurelius, whose marriage to the younger Faustina took place the same year. On the birth of a child to this couple in late 147, Marcus Aurelius received *tribunicia potestas* and Faustina (whose mother had died in 140) became Augusta. The dynastic succession thus clearly established—but, despite Hadrian's intention, the younger adoptive son received neither any powers nor the name Caesar—Antoninus' longevity and steady hand made 'Antonine' a byword for peace and prosperity. This impression is largely influenced by Publius Aelius *Aristides' *To Rome*, delivered in 143 or 144, by the portrayal of the tranquil life of the imperial family, entirely confined to Italy, in *Fronto's *Letters*, by the impressive tribute to Antoninus in Marcus Aurelius' *Meditations*, and by the uniformly favourable attitude of the scanty historical sources.

Hadrian's policies were rapidly changed in some areas: the consular legates for Italy, unpopular with the senate, were abolished, and southern Scotland reconquered by the governor Lollius Urbicus, Hadrian's Wall being replaced by the 'wall of Antoninus' between Forth and Clyde. This campaign, for which Antoninus took the acclamation 'Imperator' for the second time in late 142, was the only major war, but Moorish incursions in North Africa were dealt with by sending reinforcements to Mauretania in the 140s, minor campaigns kept the peace in Dacia, a show of force at the beginning of the reign deterred a Parthian invasion, and in the late 150s a minor extension of territory in Upper Germany was marked by the construction of a new 'outer' *limes* (physical frontier). Direction of military policy (and much else) was doubtless left to the guard prefect Marcus Gavius Maximus, who held office for almost the entire reign. The statement in the SHA (*Ant. Pius* 5. 3) that he kept 'good governors in office for seven or even nine years' seems to be mistaken; the senatorial *cursus honorum* (career path)—and other parts of the imperial system—settled down in a stable pattern, contributing to the emperor's popularity with the upper order. Two conspiracies against him are mentioned in the SHA (*Ant. Pius* 7. 3–4), the second, that of Cornelius Priscianus, 'who disturbed the peace of the province of Spain' being thus referred to in the *fasti Ostienses* for 145, but no further details are known. A highlight of the reign was the celebration of Rome's 900th anniversary in 148, when Antoninus' otherwise thrifty financial policy was relaxed (by a temporary debasement of the silver coinage). He cut down on excess expenditure, although relieving cities affected by natural disasters, and left a surplus of 675 million denarii at his death. In spite of his conservatism and sceptical attitude towards Greek culture, Greeks advanced to the highest positions in his reign (Tiberius Claudius Atticus Herodes,

consul 143, being the best-known case); other provincials also rose, not least from Africa, helped by the prominence of Fronto, a native of Cirta. The long, peaceful reign allowed the empire a breathing-space after Trajan's wars and Hadrian's restless travels. Antoninus' last watchword for the guard, 'equanimity', sums up his policy well; but he was angry with 'foreign kings' in his last hours and clouds were looming. He died at Lorium near Rome on 7 March 161 and was deified 'by universal consent'.   A.R.Bi.

Antony, Mark, Roman statesman and general. The truth of his career and personality has been heavily overlaid by legend, as first hostile propaganda presented him as a villain, then romantic biography turned him into a figure of tragic self-destruction.

2. Eldest son of Marcus Antonius (Creticus), he was born in 83 (or, less likely, 86) BC. His youth was allegedly dissipated. He distinguished himself as cavalry commander under Aulus Gabinius in Palestine and Egypt (57–4), then joined *Julius Caesar in Gaul, where, apart from an interval in Rome (53–2), he remained till the end of 50; in 51 he was quaestor. As tribune of the plebs in 49 he defended Caesar's interests in the senate, fled to his camp when the *senatus consultum ultimum* was passed (the 'ultimate decree' of the senate, in effect a declaration of emergency), took part in the fighting in Italy, and was left in charge of Italy during Caesar's Spanish campaign. In 48 he served in Greece and commanded Caesar's left wing at the battle of Pharsalus. Caesar then sent him to impose order on Italy as his *magister equitum* ('master of the horse', i.e. dictator's lieutenant and deputy) till late in 47, but he was only partly successful, and he held no further post till 44 when he was Caesar's consular colleague. On 15 February 44 he played a prominent role in the incident of the Lupercalia, offering a diadem which Caesar refused.

3. After the Ides of March he at first played a delicate game, combining conciliation of the Liberators with intermittent displays of his popular and military support. He acquired and exercised a strong personal dominance, but this was soon threatened by the emergence of Octavian (the future *Augustus), and the two locked in competition for the Caesarian leadership. Octavian deftly acquired support and allies, and by

early 43 Antony faced an armed coalition consisting of Decimus Junius Brutus Albinus, whom he was blockading in Mutina (mod. Modena in north Italy), the consuls Aulus Hirtius and Gaius Vibius Pansa Caetronianus, both moderate Caesarians, and Octavian, backed by the senate's authority and Cicero's eloquence. In April he was compelled by reverses at Forum Gallorum and Mutina to retreat into Gallia Narbonensis. He was however joined there by the governors of the western provinces, *Lepidus, Gaius Asinius Pollio, and Lucius Munatius Plancus, and subsequently reconciled with Octavian.

4. By the *lex Titia* (November 43) Antony, Lepidus, and Octavian were appointed 'triumvirs for the restoration of the state' for five years. The proscription (publication of a list of citizens who were declared outlaws and whose goods were confiscated) of their enemies (especially the wealthy) was followed in 42 by the defeat of *Cassius and *Brutus at Philippi, which firmly established Antony's reputation as a general. By agreement with Octavian he now undertook the reorganization of the eastern half of the empire; he also received Gaul, strategically vital if there were to be any renewal of fighting in the west. In 41 he met *Cleopatra at Tarsus and spent the following winter with her in Egypt. Their twins Alexander Helios and Cleopatra Selene were born in 40. The defeat of his brother Lucius Antonius (Pietas) in the Perusine War (named from Perusia, mod. Perugia in Umbria) compelled him to return to Italy early in 40, despite the Parthian invasion of Syria; but a new agreement was reached at Brundisium whereby Antony surrendered Gaul, which Octavian had already occupied, and married Octavian's sister *Octavia. The division of the empire into east and west was becoming more clear-cut. At Misenum in 39 the triumvirs extended their agreement to Sextus *Pompey, after which Antony returned with Octavia to the east. By 38 his lieutenant Publius Ventidius had expelled the Parthians from Syria. In 37, new differences between Antony and Octavian were settled at Tarentum, and the Triumvirate was renewed for another five years; but this time he left Octavia behind when he left for the east, and renewed his association with Cleopatra on a firmer basis. Their third child Ptolemy Philadelphus was born in 36.

5. This liaison had political attractions.

Egypt was one of several important kingdoms which Antony strengthened and expanded; nor did he grant all that Cleopatra wished, for he refused to take territory from *Herod the Great of Judaea, another able and valued supporter. The allegiance of the east was courted by religious propaganda. By 39 he had already presented himself as Dionysus in Athens, and he and Cleopatra could now be presented as Osiris and Isis (or Aphrodite), linked in a sacred marriage for the prosperity of Asia (cf. Plut. *Ant.* 26). But in 36 Antony's Parthian expedition ended in a disastrous reverse, while the defeat of Sextus Pompey and the elimination of Lepidus correspondingly strengthened Octavian. It still seems to have been some time before Antony accepted that a decisive clash with Octavian was inevitable. At first he continued to concentrate on the east, planning a further invasion of Parthia and annexing Armenia in 34: this was marked in Alexandria by a ceremony (hostile sources regarded it as a sacrilegious version of a Roman triumph) after which Cleopatra and her children—including Caesarion, whom Antony provocatively declared to be Caesar's acknowledged son—were paraded in national and regal costumes of various countries, just as if they might inherit them dynastically. The propaganda exchanges with Octavian intensified in 33, then early in 32 Octavian intimidated many of Antony's supporters, including the consuls Gnaeus Domitius Ahenobarbus and Gaius Sosius, into leaving Rome. Antony divorced Octavia; then Octavian outrageously seized and published Antony's will, in which he allegedly left bequests to his children by Cleopatra and requested burial in Alexandria. Octavian proceeded to extract the annulment of Antony's remaining powers and a declaration of war against Cleopatra: Antony would now seem a traitor if he sided with the national enemy.

6. The spring and summer of 31 saw protracted military engagements in western Greece. Antony's initial numerical superiority was whittled away by *Agrippa's skilful naval attacks, then during the summer Antony was deserted by most of his most influential Roman supporters, including Plancus, Marcus Titius, and Domitius Ahenobarbus: they had allegedly been alienated by Cleopatra's presence. In September 31 Cleopatra and Antony managed to break the blockade at Actium and escape southwards,

but the campaign was decisively lost, and their supporters defected to Octavian in the following months. Antony committed suicide as Octavian entered Alexandria (August 30).

7. For all its romanticism, much of Plutarch's portrayal of Antony carries some conviction—the great general, with unusual powers of leadership and personal charm, destroyed by his own weaknesses. But it is easy to underestimate his political judgement. True, Octavian won the war of propaganda in Italy, but till a late stage Antony continued to have strong support from the east and from influential Romans (many old republicans preferred him to Octavian). He looked the likely winner until the Actium campaign itself, and it is arguable that military rather than political considerations sealed his downfall. His administrative arrangements in the east were clear-sighted, and most were continued by Augustus.

8. His only literary publication was a pamphlet of *c*.33, 'On his own Drunkenness', evidently a reply to Octavian's aspersions rather than a tippler's memoir. Specimens of his epistolary style can be seen in *Cicero's correspondence, the thirteenth *Philippic*, and *Suetonius' *Augustus*.

9. Antony was married ?(1) to Fadia, though this is more likely to have been a careless affair; (2) to his cousin Antonia, daughter of Gaius Antonius 'Hybrida', whom he divorced in 47; (3) in 47 or 46, to Fulvia; (4) in 40, to Octavia. By Antonia he had a daughter Antonia; by Fulvia two sons, Marcus Antonius Antyllus and Iullus Antonius; by Octavia two daughters, Antonia *maior* and Antonia *minor*, through whom he was the ancestor of the emperors *Gaius (1), *Claudius, and *Nero. His 'marriage' to Cleopatra would not have been seen as such by an Italian audience. C.B.R.P.

Apelles, painter, of Colophon, later of Ephesus, both in western Asia Minor (sometimes called Coan because of the Coan 'Aphrodite'). He is mentioned more frequently, and generally considered better, than any other painter. *Pliny the Elder dates him 332 BC (from the portrait of *Alexander the Great). He was taught first by Ephorus of Ephesus, then by Pamphilus of Sicyon. When in the Sicyonian school, he helped Melanthius to paint the victorious chariot of the

tyrant Aristratus. He painted portraits of *Philip II, Alexander (who allowed no other artist to paint him), and their circle, and a self-portrait (probably the first). Anecdotes connect him with Alexander, *Ptolemy I, and Protogenes. He died in Cos while copying his 'Aphrodite', probably early in the 3rd cent.

About 30 works are recorded. He showed Alexander mounted and with a thunderbolt; also with the Dioscuri and Victory; and in triumph with War personified as a bound captive. Thus he fully reflected the eastern aspects of Alexander's rule in a Greek medium. His 'Aphrodite Anadyomene' (rising from the sea wringing out her hair) was in Cos, later in Rome. 'Sacrifice', also in Cos, was described by *Herodas (4. 59). He is probably the Apelles who painted the 'Calumny' described by Lucian. The tone of his pictures was due to a secret varnish. He wrote a book on painting: he claimed to know when to take his hand from a picture (unlike Protogenes, his friendly rival), and that his works had charm, *charis* (unlike Melanthius'). His 'Nude Hero' was said to challenge nature herself; horses neighed only at Apelles' horses. K.W.A.

Apollodorus, of Athens (*c*.180–after 120 BC), studied in Athens with the Stoic Diogenes of Babylon, collaborated with *Aristarchus (2) in Alexandria, perhaps fled (in 146 ?), probably to Pergamum, and later lived in Athens. A scholar of great learning and varied interests, he was the last of a series of intellectual giants in Alexandria.

WORKS 1. *Chronicle* (*Chronika*) was based on the researches of *Eratosthenes, although it extended coverage beyond the death of *Alexander the Great to Apollodorus' time. Written in comic trimeters which made it easy to memorize, it covered successive periods of history, philosophical schools, and the life and work of individuals from the fall of Troy (1184) to 146/5; later it was continued to 119 or 110/9 BC. Apollodorus frequently synchronized events and used archon lists for dating. *Diodorus Siculus employed it, but Castor's *Chronika* became more popular in the Roman period. 2. *On the Gods* (*Peri theōn*), a rationalistic account of Greek religion, much used by later writers, including *Philodemus. 3. A twelve-book commentary on the Homeric *Catalogue of Ships* based on Eratosthenes and Demetrius of Scepsis which accounted for Homeric geography and subsequent changes. *Strabo used it extensively in books 8 to 10 in discussing contemporary sites. His several other possible works include commentaries and perhaps critical editions of the comic poets *Epicharmus and Sophron and an etymology, perhaps the first by an Alexandrian grammarian. Although some of his works display a rationalizing tendency, it is doubtful whether he was a Stoic.

Apollodorus' authority gave rise to forgeries: a geographical guidebook (*Gēs periodos*) in comic trimeters (1st cent. BC) and the extant *Bibliotheca*, a study of Greek heroic mythology which presents an uncritical summary of the traditional Greek mythology (1st or 2nd cent. AD).   K.S.S.

Apollonius Dyscolus, son of Mnesitheus, of Alexandria (2nd c. AD). 'Dyscolus', 'bad-tempered', is a nickname. Of his life little is known; apart from a short visit to Rome, he did not leave Alexandria, and it is not certain that he taught in a school. His works are distinguished, even among grammarians, for obscurity of style and asperity of manner; but his method is genuinely critical, and his zeal for correcting errors extends to his own (cf. *Syntax*, p. 231. 15 Bekker). For the history of grammar from *Dionysius Thrax, to his own day he is our chief source of information, especially for Stoic linguistic philosophy.

Of some 20 works, mostly on syntax, named in the *Suda*, four survive (thanks to a single MS, Paris. gr. 2548): on the *Pronoun, Conjunction, Adverb,* and *Syntax*. A conspectus of his doctrines is given in the *Syntax*, which deals mainly with article, pronoun, verb, preposition, and adverb, successively. He approaches syntax from the parts of speech, not the sentence, beginning with the establishment of the 'correct' order of these, assuming that there must be a proper order for them as there is, in his view, for the alphabet; and he has much argument disproving such current opinions as that the function of the article is to distinguish genders, and that ὦ is its vocative. As a result, although he correctly settles many details, acutely arguing from function, not form, he nevertheless achieves no comprehensive, organic, system of syntax. His work is marked by a constant quest for principle. 'We must investigate what *produces* solecisms, and not merely adduce examples.' '*Why* do some verbs take the geni-

tive, not the accusative?' In discussing forms and constructions he makes much use of alleged ἀναλογία (see CRATES OF MALLUS), e.g. insisting on ἴμι, not εἴμι, by 'analogy' from the plural and dual; also τεθείκωμαι (pf. pass. subj.). He also makes use of what he recognizes to be false analogy (συνεκδρομή), as when he explains that the usage γράφει τὰ παιδία (nominative) is permitted because it sounds the same as when παιδία is accusative, in which case the syntax is normal.

He himself writes Hellenistic κοινή (standard Greek), as befitted a technical writer; Atticism (imitation of classical Athenian authors) was confined to belles-lettres. So we find such typical turns of syntax as ἐὰν with indicative, εἰ with subjunctive, ἐπεὶ μή, etc. Apollonius takes no thought for style, and his work is marked by frequent pleonasm, anacoluthon, etc. He had a wide knowledge of literature and was familiar with Latin. Inevitably he falls short of the comparative and historical methods available today. But it is notable that he achieved an understanding of the difference between time and aspect in non-indicative moods of the verb. He had great influence on later Greek and Latin grammarians, notably *Priscian, who called him, 'maximus auctor artis grammaticae' ('the founding father of grammar').
P.B.R.F.; R.B.; N.G.W.

Apollonius of Perge, mathematician (fl. 200 BC). Born at Perge in Pamphylia, he composed the first version, in eight books, of his *Conics* in Alexandria 'somewhat too hurriedly' (*Conics* 1 pref.). He visited Ephesus and Pergamum, where he stayed with the Epicurean Eudemus, to whom he subsequently sent the first three books of the revised version of the *Conics*. After Eudemus' death the remaining books were sent to Attalus (perhaps Attalus of Rhodes).

Of the *Conics* (*Kōnika*) the first four books survive in Greek and the next three in Arabic translation; the eighth is lost. Apollonius states (*Conics* 1 pref.) that the first four books form an elementary introduction, while the remainder are particular extensions (*periousiastikōtera*). He claims no originality for the content of *Conics* 1–4, but says that he expounds the fundamental properties 'more fully and generally' than his predecessors. This is fully justified: earlier writers on conics, including *Archimedes, had defined them as sections of a right circular cone by a plane at right angles to a generator, and hence the parabola, ellipse, and hyperbola were called 'section of a right-angled cone', 'of an acute- angled cone', and 'of an obtuse-angled cone' respectively. Apollonius generates all three sections from the most general type of circular cone, the double oblique, and defines the fundamental properties by the 'application of areas' familiar from *Euclid, using the terms *parabolē*, *elleipsis*, and *hyperbolē*, according to whether the applied figure exactly fits, falls short of, or exceeds that to which it is applied.

Apollonius did for conics what Euclid had done for elementary geometry: both his terminology and his methods became canonical and eliminated the work of his predecessors. Like Euclid, too, his exposition follows the logical rather than the original sequence of working. Investigation of the latter has revealed how 'algebraic' his methods are. His silence on some features of conics (e.g. the focus of the parabola) is not due to ignorance, but to the elementary nature of the treatise; the specialized investigations of books 5–7 cover only a selection of possible topics, but book 5 in particular reveals Apollonius as an original mathematical genius.

Commentaries to the *Conics* were written by Serenus and Hypatia. That by Eutocius on books 1–4 is extant but superficial. *Pappus provides lemmata, including some to the lost book 8.

Of other works by Apollonius there survives only the *Logou apotomē* ('Cutting-off of a Ratio'), in two books, in Arabic translation. Pappus (bk. 7) describes incompletely the contents of five other lost works: (1) *Chōriou apotomē* ('Cutting-off of an Area'); (2) *Diōrismenē tomē* ('Determinate Section'); (3) *Epaphai* ('Tangencies'); (4) *Neuseis* ('Inclinations'); (5) *Topoi epipedoi* ('Plane Loci'). Apollonius also wrote works on the *Cylindrical Helix* (*Proclus on Euc. 105), the *Comparison of the Dodecahedron and Eicosahedron* (Hypsicles, *Euclid bk. 14*, 2), and on unordered irrationals (Pappus on *Euc. 10*, 218 Junge–Thomson). In his *Ōkytokion* ('Quick Delivery') he calculated limits for π closer than those of Archimedes (Eutocius on Arch. 258). His *Katholou pragmateia* ('General Treatise') dealt with the foundations of geometry (Marinus on *Data Euc.* 234). Pappus (bk. 2) gives excerpts from a work

in which Apollonius sets out a system for expressing large numbers by, in effect, using 10,000 instead of ten as a base (cf. Archimedes' *Sand-reckoner*). The ascription to Apollonius of a work *On the Burning-Mirror* is probably a mistaken attribution of the extant work of Diocles.

Apollonius did important work in theoretical astronomy. Ptolemy, *Almagest* 12. 1 gives a theorem of Apollonius for establishing the stationary points of planets from the epicyclic/eccentric hypothesis. He also worked on lunar theory, but references to his 'lunar tables' arise from scribal confusion with the later astronomer Apollinarius.

G.J.T.

Apollonius Rhodius, a major literary figure of 3rd-cent. BC Alexandria, and poet of the *Argonautica*, the only extant Greek hexameter epic written between *Homer and the Roman imperial period.

LIFE Our main sources are: *POxy.* 1241, a 2nd-cent. AD list of the librarians of the Royal Library at Alexandria; two Lives transmitted with the manuscripts of *Argon.* which probably contain material deriving from the late 1st cent. BC; an entry in the *Suda*. (1) All four state that Apollonius was from Alexandria itself, though two 2nd-cent. AD notices point rather to Naucratis. The most likely explanation for the title 'Rhodian' is thus that Apollonius spent a period of his life there, which would accord well with what we know of his works (cf. below), though it remains possible that he or his family came from Rhodes. (2) Apollonius served as librarian and royal tutor before *Eratosthenes (*POxy.* 1241), and probably in succession to Zenodotus thus *c.*270–45. It is to this period that the *Argonautica* should be dated. (3) All four sources make him a pupil of *Callimachus, which probably reflects beliefs about the indebtedness of his poetry to Callimachus (cf. below). (4) The *Lives* give confused and contradictory accounts of withdrawal to Rhodes after a poor reception for his poetry in Alexandria. Nothing of value can be retrieved from these stories, which may well be fictions based on the existence of a text of at least *Argon.* 1 which differed significantly from the vulgate (the *proekdosis*, cited six times by the scholia to *Argon.* 1). (5) Very flimsy ancient evidence has been used by some scholars to construct a 'quarrel' between Apollonius and Callimachus concerning poetic questions, particularly the value and style of epic. The many striking parallels between the works of Callimachus and the *Argonautica*, however, argue against, rather than for, any serious dispute; moreover, Apollonius does not appear in the list (*PSI* 1219) which seeks to identify Callimachus' literary opponents, and Roman poets clearly align Apollonius with, rather than against, Callimachus. Two episodes in the *Argonautica* handle the same material as two poems of *Theocritus (Hylas, cf. *Id.* 13; Amycus and Polydeuces, cf. *Id.* 22), and this offers no reason to doubt the dating derived from other sources.

LOST WORKS (1) Poems (cf. Powell, *Coll. Alex.* 4–8). *Canobus*: choliambic poem on Egyptian legends. *Foundation Poems* in hexameters on Caunus, Alexandria, Naucratis, Rhodes, and Cnidus; poems of this type reflect the deep Alexandrian interest in local history and cult. Many other lost poems may also be assumed, including probably epigrams (cf. Ant. Lib. *Met.* 23); an extant epigram attacking Callimachus (*Anth. Pal.* 11. 275) is very doubtfully ascribed to Apollonius. (2) Prose Works. Apollonius' scholarly interests were reflected in many works (cf. R. Pfeiffer, *History of Classical Scholarship* 1 (1968) 144–8), including a monograph on Homer (*Against Zenodotus*). *Archilochus and *Hesiod were also among the poets discussed by Apollonius; he defended the authenticity of the *Shield of Heracles* (*hypothesis* A to the poem) and probably rejected Hesiodic authorship of the *Ornithomanteia* which was transmitted after *Works and Days* (corrupt scholium to *Op.* 828).

ARGONAUTICA Hexameter epic on the Argonautic legend in four long books totalling 5,835 preserved verses. Fifty-two manuscripts are known, and a large body of papyri attests to the popularity of the poem in later antiquity. It was very important at Rome, where it was translated by Publius Terentius Varro Atacinus, is a major influence on *Catullus 64 and *Virgil's *Aeneid*, and, with the *Aeneid*, forms the basis of *Valerius Flaccus' *Argonautica*.

Books 1–2 deal with the outward voyage, to recover the golden fleece, from Iolcus in Thessaly to the Colchian city of Aia at the extreme eastern edge of the Black Sea (in modern Georgia), which is ruled over by Aeëtes, the cruel son of Helios, the sun-god. The major events of this voyage are a stay at Lemnos where the local women, who have murdered the entire male population, seize the chance for procreation, and Jason sleeps with Queen Hypsipyle(1. 609–910); the loss of Heracles from the expedition (1. 1153–1357); a boxing-match between Amycus, king of the Bebrycians, and Polydeuces (one of the Dioscuri, twin of Castor: 2. 1–163); meeting with the blind prophet Phineus whom the Argonauts save from the depredations of the Harpies and who, in return, tells them of the voyage ahead (2. 168–530); passage through the Clashing Rocks (the 'Symplegades') which guard the entrance to the Black Sea (2. 531–647); meeting on the island of Ares with the sons of Phrixus, who fled Greece on the golden ram (2. 1030–1230). In Book 3 Jason asks Aeëtes to grant him the fleece; this the king agrees to do on the condition that Jason ploughs an enormous field with fire-breathing bulls, sows it with dragon's teeth, and slays the armed warriors who rise up from the ground. Jason succeeds in this, because, at the instigation of Jason's protector Hera, the king's daughter, Medea, falls in love with the hero and supplies him with a magic salve to protect him and give him superhuman strength. In Book 4 Medea flees to join the Argonauts and secures the fleece for them from the grove where it is guarded by a sleepless dragon. The Argonauts flee via a great river (the Danube) which is pictured as flowing from the Black Sea to the Adriatic; at the Adriatic mouth, Jason and Medea lure her brother, Apsyrtus, who commands the pursuing Colchians, to his death, a crime for which Zeus decides that they must be purified by Medea's aunt Circe who lives on the west coast of Italy. They reach Circe via rivers (the Po (Padus) and the Rhône) imagined to link NE Italy with the western Mediterranean. From there they sail to Drepane (Corfu), Homer's Scheria, where Jason and Medea are married, and are then driven to the wastes of Libya where they are again saved by divine intervention. They finally return home by way of Crete, where Medea uses her magic powers to destroy the bronze giant Talos who guards the island.

The central poetic technique of Apollonius is the creative reworking of *Homer. While the Hellenistic poet takes pains to avoid the repetitiveness characteristic of Archaic epic, Homer is the main determinative influence on every aspect of the poem, from the details of language to large-scale narrative patterns, material culture, and technology (e.g. sailing) which is broadly 'Homeric' (but note 'Hellenistic' architectural features at 3. 215 ff.). This is most obvious in set scenes such as the Catalogue of Argonauts (1. 23–233), corresponding to Homer's Catalogue of Ships, the description of the cloak Jason wears to meet Hypsipyle (1. 721–67), corresponding to the Shield of Achilles, the meeting of Hera, Athena, and Aphrodite on Mt. Olympus at the start of book 3 which finds many forerunners in Homer, the scenes in the palace of Aeëtes, corresponding to the scenes of the *Odyssey* on Scheria, and the voyage in the western Mediterranean, corresponding to Odysseus' adventures on his way home. These scenes function by contrast: the Homeric 'model' is the base-text by which what is importantly different in the later poem is highlighted. Individual characters too owe much to Homeric predecessors, while also being markedly different from them: e.g. Jason/Odysseus, Medea/Nausicaa and Circe. After Homer, the two most important literary influences are Pindar's account of the Argonauts (*Pyth.* 4) and Euripides' *Medea*; the events of the tragedy are foreshadowed in a number of places in the epic—perhaps most strikingly in the murder of Apsyrtus who goes to his death 'like a tender child' (4. 460)—and in one sense the epic shows us that the events of the tragedy were 'inevitable', given the earlier history of Jason and Medea.

A fundamental principle of composition for Apollonius is discontinuity, a feature shared with the poetics of Callimachus. The *Argonautica* is constantly experimental. This shows itself, for example, in the organization of the narrative both within books (e.g. book 2 where scenes of action—Amycus, the Harpies—stand in sharp contrast to long passages of ethnography and geography, and book 4 where different Argonauts and Medea take turns to play leading roles) and between books (thus book 3 stands apart as a tightly-knit drama of its own). Apollonius' principles of characterization have also frequently been misunderstood; the two main sides of Medea's character—impressionable virgin and dangerous sorceress—are only confusing if viewed from the perspective of that 'consistency' which *Aristotle prescribed for dra-

matic character. Apollonius is rather interested in the similarities and differences between the power of love, the power of persuasion, and the power of drugs, and this interest is explored through the presentation of Medea, whose character is thus a function of the narrative. Jason's character, on the other hand, brings persuasion and stratagem to the fore (cf. esp. his testing (*peira*) of the crew after the passing of the Clashing Rocks (2. 607–49), and the praise of *muthos* (speech) and *mētis* (stratagem, cunning plan) at 3. 182–93. His story is of the familiar type of rite of passage (cf. Orestes, Theseus, etc.) in which a young man must accomplish a dangerous set of tasks before assuming his rightful position (in this case a kingship which had been usurped by Pelias); that Jason seems often overwhelmed (*amēchanos*) by the enormity of what he must do and only finally accomplishes it through Medea's help finds many parallels in related stories, but also marks the difference between his exotic story and that of the Homeric heroes. With the partial exception of some of Odysseus' adventures, magic and fantasy have little role in Homer, whereas they had always had a prominent position in the Argonautic myth and are very important in the *Argonautica*. Discontinuity is also seen in the divine element of the epic where different Olympian gods—Athena, Apollo, and Jason's main protector, Hera—and other minor divinities are all prominent at one time or another.

In common with other Alexandrian poetry, the aetiology of cult and ritual is very important in the *Argonautica*. Apollonius' scholarly learning, visible also in his detailed manipulation of earlier texts, here emphasizes how the Argonautic voyage is in part a voyage of acculturation establishing Greek tradition. The repeatedly positive evaluation of Greek culture (including cult and ritual) should be connected with the Ptolemaic context of the work; the Ptolemies (see PTOLEMY) promoted themselves as the true heirs and champions of Classical Greek culture, and this strain should not be overlooked in the epic. It is even possible that the characters of King Alcinous and Queen Arete owe not a little to *Ptolemy II Philadelphus and his sister/wife. Just as Ptolemaic ideas are thus inscribed into prehistory, Apollonius also mixes the temporal levels of his poem in other ways too. One is by emotional authorial 'intrusions' (e.g. 1. 616–19, 2. 542–5, 4. 445–9) which strongly differentiate the *Argonautica* from the 'impersonal' Homeric poems; these are one manifestation of the strong literary self-consciousness of an epic which is much concerned with displaying the problems of *how* one writes epic poetry. Another is by reflections of Hellenistic science within the mythical material of the poem; Aphrodite bribes her son with a ball which is also a cosmic globe of a kind familiar in Apollonius' time (3. 131–41), Medea's suffering reflects contemporary physiological theories (3. 762–3), and Mopsus' death from snakebite (4. 1502–36) is a very typical mixture of Alexandrian medicine and myth.

The language of Apollonius is based on that of Homer, constantly extended and varied by analogy and new formation, but Apollonius also draws upon the vocabulary of the whole high poetic tradition. Metrically, his hexameter shows similar developments to Callimachus' and Theocritus', and dactylic rhythm is more predominant than in Homer. Complex, enjambed sentences and syntactically sophisticated indirect speech reveal the possibilities open to the poet of written, rather than oral, epic.

The *Argonautica* is a brilliant and disturbing achievement, a poem shot through with intelligence and deep ironies. Its reception at Rome is in stark contrast to its reception by modern critics who have tended to see it as a failed attempt to write like Homer; more recently, however, it has become the subject of serious literary study, and is thus coming into its own.   R.L.Hu.

Appian, of Alexandria, Greek historian. Born in Alexandria at the end of the 1st cent. AD, he experienced the Jewish rising of AD 116/7, became a Roman citizen, moved to Rome as an advocate and eventually gained, through the influence of his friend *Fronto, the *dignitas* of a procurator under *Antoninus Pius, which enabled him to devote his time to writing a Roman History. After the preface and book 1 on early Rome in the period of the kings, this work is arranged ethnographically, dealing with the individual peoples as Rome conquered them: book 2, Italians; 3, Samnites; 4, Celts; 5, Sicilians; 6, Iberians; 7, *Hannibal; 8, Carthaginians (Libyans and Nomads); 9, Macedonians and Illyrians; 10, Greeks and Ionians; 11, Syrians

(Seleucids) and Parthians; and 12, *Mithradates VI.; 13–17 treat the Civil Wars; 18–21, the wars in Egypt; 22, the century up to *Trajan; 23, Trajan's campaigns against Dacians, Jews, and Pontic peoples; and 24, Arabians. A survey of Rome's military and financial system was apparently not yet written when Appian died in the 160s. The preface, books 6–9, and 11–17 survive complete, apart from 8b on the Nomads and 9a on the Macedonians (of which only fragments exist) as well as 11b on the Parthians (11b was perhaps unfinished at Appian's death; the textual tradition preserves a Byzantine fake instead); 1–5 are fragmentary, 10 and 18–24 lost.

In order to accommodate a millennium of Roman history in a single work, Appian greatly, but not always successfully, reduced the material he chose from a variety of Greek and Latin authors, among them *Hieronymus of Cardia, *Polybius, and Roman annalists like Asinius Pollio, *Julius Caesar, and *Augustus. Since some of his valuable sources, especially on the Civil Wars, are otherwise lost, his work gains historical importance for us, even though it does not simply reproduce these sources. Recent research has stressed Appian's own conscious contribution not only in choosing, reducing, and organizing the material, but also in the independent composition of speeches, in the introduction of episodes from the rhetorical repertoire, and in detailed interference with the sources in view of his avowed aims: a proud citizen of Alexandria, Appian makes events in Egypt the climax of his work; a convinced monarchist, he explains, not always correctly, Roman republican institutions to his Greek audience (papyri show that his work was read in Dura-Europus (a town on the river Euphrates); a stout conservative, he regards a lack of popular concord, as witnessed in the Civil Wars, as cataclysmic; unusually interested in administration and finance, he preserves more social and economic information than most historiographers; above all, an ardent admirer of Rome, Appian explains her success through reference to the Romans' good counsel, endurance, patience, moderation, and, especially, overall virtue.   K.B.

Appius Claudius Caecus See CLAUDIUS CAECUS, APPIUS.

Appuleius Saturninus See SATURNINUS.

Apuleius, writer and orator, born *c.* AD 125 of prosperous parents (*Apol.* 23) at Madaurus in Africa Proconsularis, and educated in Carthage, Athens, and Rome (*Flor.* 18, 20, 16); at Athens he gained enough philosophy to be called *philosophus Platonicus* by himself and others. He claims to have travelled extensively as a young man (*Apol.* 23), and was on his way to Alexandria when he arrived at Oea, probably in the winter of AD 156. The story from that point is told by Apuleius himself in his *Apologia*, no doubt in the most favourable version possible; at Oea he met an ex-pupil from Athens, Pontianus, who persuaded him to stay there for a year and eventually to marry his mother Pudentilla in order to protect her fortune for the family. Subsequently, Apuleius was accused by various other relations of Pudentilla of having induced her to marry him through magic means; the case was heard at Sabratha, near Oea, in late 158 or early 159. We can deduce from the publication of the *Apologia* (see below) that he was acquitted. The *Florida* (see below) make it clear that Apuleius was active as a public speaker and philosophical lecturer in Carthage in the 160s AD, and he seems to have been made priest of the imperial cult for his province (*Flor.* 16); nothing is known of him after 170, though the disputed *De mundo* and *De Platone* (see below) are both addressed to the (unnamed) writer's son Faustinus. Of Apuleius' undisputed writings, only the *Apologia* and the *Florida* can be dated with any accuracy; scholars disagree on whether the *Metamorphoses* is a late or early work, though more think it late than early.

WORKS (1) The *Apologia*, Apuleius' speech of defence against charges of magic (see above), sometimes called *De magia* in older editions and later MSS, is an extraordinary rhetorical *tour de force*. In rebutting the charges Apuleius digresses hugely in order to show a vast range of literary and other learning, and presents himself as a committed intellectual and philosopher. The title recalls *Plato's Apology, the argumentation Cicero at his most colourful.

(2) The *Metamorphoses*, sometimes called the *Golden Ass*, is the only Latin novel which survives whole. On an epic scale (eleven books) and full of narratological cleverness, erotic, humorous, and sensational by turns, it is a remarkable and fascinating work. The basic story is that of the young man Lucius, who through his curiosity to discover the secrets of witchcraft is metamorphosed into an ass and undergoes a variety of picaresque adventures before being retransformed through the agency of the goddess Isis. This plot is punctuated by a number of inserted tales, which have in fact a close thematic relation to the main narrative; the most substantial and best-known of them is that of Cupid and Psyche ('Soul' in Greek), which parallels the main story of Lucius by presenting a character (Psyche) whose disastrous curiosity causes troublesome adventures before her rescue through divine agency. The last book provides a much-discussed and controversial double twist: after his rescue by Isis, Lucius' low-life adventures are interpreted in a new religious and providential light (11. 15. 1–5), and the identity of the narrator seems to switch from Lucius to Apuleius himself (11. 27. 9), a final metamorphosis. The novel's literary influences are various, including much Greek and Latin poetry; the main ass-tale is partly paralleled by the *Onos* dubiously ascribed to *Lucian (which has no Isiac conclusion or inserted tales but is evidently an epitome), and the two may well have a common source in the lost Greek *Metamorphoses* of 'Lucius of Patrae' (Phot. *Bibl.* cod. 129). Many of the stories may derive from the tradition of bawdy Milesian Tales (see ARISTIDES), and that of Cupid and Psyche, with its element of Platonic allegory, may owe at least something to a Greek source (cf. Fulg. *Myth.* 3. 6).

(3) The *Florida* are a short collection, derived from a longer one, of choice excerpts from Apuleius' showy declamations given at Carthage in the 160s, containing passages of narrative, description, and anecdote which show considerable rhetorical and stylistic talent.

(4) The *De deo Socratis* is a declamation on the *daimonion* of *Socrates, probably based on a Greek original (note Plutarch's similar *De genio Socratis*), showing Apuleius' Platonic interests as well as his oratorical skills. For the *daimonion* see SOCRATES.

(5) Lost works: collections of speeches from which the *Florida* are a selection, other speeches and poems, *Ludicra* (minor poems), *De proverbiis, Hermagoras* (another novel), *Phaedo* (version of Plato), *Epitome historia-*

rum, De republica, De medicinalibus, De arboribus, Eroticus (cf. ps.-Lucian *Amores*), *Quaestiones conviviales*, works on astronomy, zoology, agriculture, music, and arithmetic.

(6) Disputed works: controversy continues on the authenticity of two extant works ascribed to Apuleius. (*a*) *De dogmate Platonis* or *De Platone*, two books of mediocre exposition of the philosophy of Plato. The extant *Peri hermēneias* (On Interpretation), a treatise on formal logic, has been by some ascribed to Apuleius as the third book of this work, but many regard it as spurious. (*b*) *De mundo*, a translation of the pseudo-Aristotelian *Peri kosmou.*

(7) Spurious works: *Asclepius, Herbarius, De remediis salutaribus, Physiognomonia.* Of these the *Asclepius* has some interest as a Latin version of a Hermetic treatise.

The style of Apuleius is admired by many; it owes little to his African origin (the idea of 'African Latin' is now largely discredited), but is the apex of 'Asianism' (florid style) in Latin, full of poetic and archaic words and apparent coinages, rhythmical and rhyming cola, and coloured with colloquialism and Graecisms; it is best seen in the great set pieces of the *Metamorphoses* (e.g. 11. 1–6). His literary personality is strongly projected in all his works, and in the extraordinary range they cover: proud of his abilities as a speaker and writer, possessed of certitude and a vast if indiscriminate and vicarious learning, he is best seen as a Latin sophist, matching in the Roman west the extraordinarily extrovert and self-promoting characters who were his contemporaries in the Greek Second Sophistic (the revival of Greek oratory in the 2nd cent. AD). Some of his subsequent fame is initially owed to St *Augustine, his fellow-African, who was aware of Apuleius' prestige in his home province and was careful to attack him, but the *Metamorphoses* have been deservedly popular from the early Renaissance on.   S.J.Ha.

Aratus (1), *c.*315 to before 240 BC, poet. Born at Soloi in Cilicia, he was taught by the grammarian Menecrates of Ephesus, and studied at Athens, where he probably first became acquainted with *Callimachus and the philosophers Timon of Phlius and Menedemus. He there imbibed Stoicism from *Zeno (2) and was introduced to *Antigonus Gonatas of Macedonia, who invited him to the court at Pella. There he celebrated the king's marriage to Phila, half-sister of the Seleucid *Antiochus I Soter, and composed a *Hymn to Pan* glorifying Antigonus' victory over the Celts (277). Later he migrated to Antiochus' court in Syria, where he is said to have undertaken editions of *Homer's *Odyssey* and *Iliad.* Returning to Macedonia, he died there some time before the death of Antigonus (240/39).

Aratus' best-known work, and the only one still extant, is a poem entitled *Phaenomena*, undertaken at the suggestion of Antigonus. The first and longest part of this is a versification of a prose treatise by *Eudoxus of Cnidos which gave a detailed description of the make-up and relative positions of the constellations. After a proem to Zeus (1–18), Aratus describes the poles and the northern constellations (19–318), the southern constellations (322–453), refuses to describe the five planets, enumerates the principal circles of the celestial sphere (462–558), and lists the simultaneous risings and settings of many combinations of the constellations, supposedly for telling the time at night (559–732). The second part of the poem (733–1154) deals with weather signs. Although it has a separate title (*Diosēmeiai*), and is derived from a different source (perhaps a work of *Theophrastus), it is an integral part of the poem. After enumerating the days of the lunar month, and mentioning the seasons and Meton's 19-year calendarical cycle, Aratus gives weather prognostications, not only from the celestial bodies, but also from terrestrial phenomena and animal behaviour. The poem is enlivened by frequent mythological allusions and picturesque digressions, the longest being the descriptions of the golden age (98–136) and of storms at sea (408–35). The author's Stoicism is apparent especially in the proem, where 'Zeus' is the Stoic all-informing deity.

The *Phaenomena* achieved immediate fame (cf. *Anth. Pal.* 9. 25 (Leonidas of Tarentum); Callim. *Epigr.* 27), and lasting popularity beyond the circle of learned poets: it became the most widely read poem, after the *Iliad* and *Odyssey*, in the ancient world, and was one of the very few Greek poems translated into Arabic. Latin translations were made by Publius Terentius Varro Atacinus, Cicero, Germanicus, and Avienus. It was read more for its literary charm than its astronomical content, but some of the numerous commentaries on it criticized the many grave astronomical errors which it contains, especially the commentary of *Hipparchus (which, alone of his works, has survived, because of its connection with this popular poem).

Aratus wrote many other poems, all lost except for two epigrams preserved in the Greek Anthology (Gow–Page, *HE* 760–7); for new fragments see *Suppl. Hell.* 83–120. A collection entitled *Ta kata lepton* gave its name to the *Catalepton* attributed to *Virgil.

G.J.T.

Aratus (2) (271–213 BC), statesman from Sicyon west of Corinth. He fled to Argos after the murder of his father Cleinias in 264 and was educated there. In 251 he expelled the tyrant Nicocles from Sicyon and joined the city to the Achaean Confederacy. From 245 on he occupied a dominant position amongst the Achaeans, normally holding the generalship of the confederacy in alternate years. His policy was for long based upon opposition to Macedon, especially Macedonian influence in the Peloponnese, and co-operation with Egypt, where he visited *Ptolemy II Philadelphus and whence he obtained substantial subsidies. He seized the Acrocorinth from a Macedonian garrison in 243 and united Corinth to the Achaean Confederacy. In 241 he defeated *Antigonus Gonatas' Aetolian allies at Pellene and thereafter, in alliance with Aetolia against Macedon (239–229), frequently attacked Athens and Argos; in 229 Argos was brought into the Achaean Confederacy and Athens, with Aratus' help, was freed from Macedonian control. These years also saw the addition of Megalopolis (235) and Orchomenus to the confederacy. The growth of Spartan power under *Cleomenes III changed much, especially against the backdrop of Aratus' failure to organize a strong Achaean army. After defeats by Cleomenes in 227, Aratus opened negotiations with *Antigonus Doson of Macedon. The arrival of Doson in the Peloponnese in 224 and victory over Cleomenes at Sellasia (222) preserved the Achaean Confederacy from disruption but at the price of a Macedonian garrison on the Acrocorinth and the re-establishment of Macedonian influence in the Peloponnese. On the accession of *Philip V, Aratus called in Doson's Hellenic League against Aetolian aggression (220). In the ensuing Social War he exposed the treachery of the Macedonian

court cabal under Apelles, and after the Peace of Naupactus (217) resisted Philip's anti-Roman policy and proposed seizure of Ithome in Messenia. His death (213), probably from consumption, was widely blamed upon Philip. His ability as a guerrilla leader early on and his success at diplomacy (both within and without the Peloponnese) establish his reputation as the real architect of the Achaean Confederacy. He wrote *Memoirs* (*Hypomnēmatismoi*: Polyb. 2. 40), pro-Achaean and apologetic in tone, and less reliable than Polybius claims (cf. Plut. *Arat.* 3).

P.S.D.

Arcesilaus or **Arcesilas** (both forms given in the sources), of Pitane in Aeolia, 316/5–242/1 BC, head of the Academy (the philosophical school founded by *Plato) from *c.*268. In his youth, Arcesilaus studied mathematics with Autolycus at Pitane. His older brother wanted him to study rhetoric, but Arcesilaus escaped to Athens to study philosophy. He first attended the lectures of *Theophrastus, but then formed a close friendship with Crantor, whom he followed to the Academy. There he also met Polemon and Crates. On the death of Crates, Socratides, an older member of the school, resigned in favour of Arcesilaus, and he was elected scholarch. *Diogenes Laertius' biography (4. 28–45) describes him as a kind and urbane man, respected and admired by his contemporaries.

From the 1st cent. BC on Arcesilaus was known as the founder of the Middle Academy (Diog. Laert. 1. 14; Sext. Emp. *Pyr.* 1. 220)— the philosopher who introduced scepticism into Plato's school. We do not know whether he was influenced in this by his older contemporary *Pyrrhon of Elis, though the famous satirical line of the Stoic Ariston, 'Plato in front, Pyrrhon behind, in the middle Diodorus' (Diog. Laert. 4. 33) shows that people recognized some similarities. Arcesilaus, who is said to have owned a private copy of Plato's dialogues, seems to have appealed to the examples of *Socrates and Plato. Like Socrates, Arcesilaus would examine or argue against any given thesis and make no assertions of his own. His professed attitude of withholding assent (*epochē*) was adopted to avoid error and rashness of judgement. Stories about his alleged esotericism, according to which he taught the positive doctrines of Plato to an inner circle of advanced students (Sext. Emp. *Pyr*. 1. 234; August. *contra Academicos* 3. 20. 43), are certainly later inventions. Arcesilaus published nothing, and what we learn about his arguments must have been handed down in the Academy or through the writings of his opponents.

Arcesilaus' most influential and famous argument was directed against the Stoic theory of knowledge. He argued that given the definition of the Stoic criterion of truth, the so-called cognitive impression (*katalēptikē phantasia*), one could show that nothing could be grasped or apprehended, since it was impossible to find an impression of such a kind that it could not be false. For any true and clear impression one could describe a situation in which an otherwise indistinguishable impression would be false. Since the Stoics held that the wise man would never assent to a false impression, it followed that the Stoic sage must withhold judgement on all matters. To the Stoic objection that suspension of judgement would make action, and hence life, impossible, Arcesilaus replied that it was possible to act without assenting to anything, and that in the absence of certain knowledge a wise man could be guided by 'what is reasonable' (to *eulogon*).

The thesis that 'nothing can be grasped' (*akatalēpsia*) has been described by ancient as well as modern authors as a doctrine of the sceptical Academy, but this is a mistake: Arcesilaus and his successors down to *Carneades insisted that they did not know or assert that nothing could be known, any more than they knew or asserted any other philosophical thesis (Cic. *Acad*. 1. 45; *Acad. post*. 28).   G.S.

Archidamus, 'leader of the *damos*' or people, was the name of several Eurypontid kings of Sparta, of whom the most notable were:

ARCHIDAMUS II, who married an aunt and reigned for over 40 years (?469–427 BC), in succession to Leotychidas II. He first distinguished himself by his resolute response to the great earthquake of 464, which had prompted a massive revolt of the helots aided by a couple of the communities of the *perioikoi* in Messenia. But even his seniority was insufficient to dissuade the Spartan assembly from voting for war with Athens in 432, and

he led the allied forces in invasions of Attica on three occasions (431, 430, 428); in 429 he inaugurated the siege of Plataea in Boeotia. Twice married, he was allegedly fined on the first occasion for marrying a too short wife (the mother of Agis II); his second marriage produced *Agesilaus II.

ARCHIDAMUS III, son of *Agesilaus II and lover of the son of Sphodrias, reigned from 360/59 to 338 BC. He was born about 400 but did not fight at Leuctra (371), after which disastrous defeat he was charged with escorting back to Sparta the remnant of the Spartan army. He commanded troops successfully against the Arcadians in 368 and 365, and distinguished himself in the defence of Sparta against *Epaminondas in 362. In the Third Sacred War he took the Phocians' part against Thebes, but withdrew Spartan forces in disgust at the duplicity of their commander Phalaecus (346). Now that Sparta had lost an empire and failed to find a role, he aped his father's later career as a mercenary, responding to an appeal from Sparta's Italian daughter-city Tarentum against the non-Greek Lucanians (*c*.342). But in 338, when other Greek leaders were preoccupied with the threat of *Philip II of Macedon, Archidamus died in battle at Manduria in southern Italy. If the *Archidamus* of *Isocrates (a speech placed in the mouth of the then crown prince at a dramatic date of 366) is to be credited, Archidamus like his father was an irredentist believer in Sparta's futile mission to regain Messenia.   P.A.C.

Archilochus, Greek iambic and elegiac poet, from Paros, one of the Cyclades. He mentioned the Lydian king Gyges, who died *c*.652 BC (fr. 19), and a total solar eclipse which was almost certainly that of 6 April 648 (fr. 122); a memorial to his friend Glaucus, son of Leptines (fr. 131), in late 7th-cent. lettering, has been found on Thasos, where Archilochus spent part of his life (*SEG* 14. 565). His poetry was concerned with his personal affairs and with contemporary public events—politics, shipwrecks, war, etc. Its tone varied widely, from grave to gay, from pleasantly bantering to bitter. Archilochus was famous throughout antiquity for the stinging wit with which he lashed his enemies and sometimes his friends, and for what appeared to be carefree admissions of outrageous conduct such as fleeing from battle and abandoning his shield (fr. 5), or compromising young ladies. He repeatedly attacked one Lycambes, who had (or so the ancients understood) betrothed his daughter Neobule to Archilochus but later revoked the agreement. The vengeful poet then produced a series of poems in which he recounted in the most explicit detail the sexual experiences that he and others had enjoyed with both Neobule and her sister. This (so the legend goes) induced Lycambes and his daughters to hang themselves for shame. We have several fragments from sexual narratives (e.g. frs. 30–48). However, in the 'Cologne Epode' discovered in 1974 (fr. 196a) Neobule is represented as available for Archilochus but he dismisses her as over-blown and promiscuous, while gently seducing the younger sister. The whole business has to be considered against the background of the Ionian *iambos* (a term originally associated with jesting and ribaldry) and its conventions of bawdy narrative and abuse of individuals.

The ancients arranged Archilochus' work in four sections: Elegiacs, (iambic) Trimeters, (trochaic) Tetrameters, and Epodes, with a couple of inauthentic pieces (frs. 322–4) tagged on at the end. Most celebrated were the Epodes, songs in simple strophes usually made up of a hexameter or iambic trimeter plus one or two shorter cola. Most famous of all was the first Epode, in which Archilochus remonstrated with Lycambes using the fable of the fox and the eagle (frs. 172–81). He used an animal fable in at least one other Epode (frs. 185–7). The lubricious material is concentrated in the Trimeters, though they also contained some serious pieces. The Tetrameters and Elegiacs were also of mixed character, but Archilochus clearly favoured tetrameters for elevated subjects such as accounts of battles (e.g. frs. 94, 98) and warnings of political dangers (frs. 105–6). Several of the elegiac fragments (8–13) lament men drowned at sea.   M.L.W.

Archimedes, mathematician and inventor (*c.*287 to 212 or 211 BC). Born at Syracuse, son of an astronomer Phidias, and killed at the sack of the city by the Romans under Marcellus, he was on intimate terms with its king *Hieron II. He visited Egypt, but lived most of his life at Syracuse, corresponding with the mathematician and astronomer Conon, *Eratosthenes, and others. Popular history

(see Plut. *Marc.* 14–19) knew him as the inventor of marvellous machines used against the Romans at the siege of Syracuse, and of devices such as the screw for raising water (*Kochlias*); for his boast 'give me a place to stand and I will move the earth' (Simpl. *In phys.* 1110. 5); for his determination of the proportions of gold and silver in a wreath made for Hieron ('*Eureka*! I have discovered it!' Vitr. 9 pref. 9–12); for his construction of two 'sphaerae' (a planetarium and a star globe) which were taken to Rome (Cic. *Rep.* 1. 21–2); and for his tomb, which by his wish depicted a cylinder circumscribing a sphere, with the ratio 3:2 which he discovered between them (Cic. *Tusc.* 5. 64–6).

His extant works, with the principal features of each, are, in Greek: (1) *On the Sphere and Cylinder*, two books: formulae for the surface-area and volume of a sphere and any segment of it. (2) *Measurement of the Circle*: by inscribing and circumscribing regular polygons of 96 sides, upper and lower limits of $3\frac{1}{7}$ and $3\frac{10}{71}$ are found to the value of π; Archimedes incidentally gives a rational approximation to the square root of 3 and of several large numbers. (3) *On Conoids and Spheroids*: determination of the volumes of segments of solids formed by the revolution of a conic about its axis. (4) *On Spirals*: properties of tangents to the 'Archimedean' spiral and determination of its area. (5) *Equilibriums of Planes* or *Centres of Gravity of Planes*, two books: the theory of the lever is propounded and the centres of gravity of various rectilinear plane figures (bk. 1) and of segments of conics (bk. 2) are established. (6) *Quadrature of the Parabola*: the area of a parabola is determined first by 'mechanical' (see below) and then by geometrical means. (7) *The Sandreckoner*: description of a system for expressing enormously large numbers in words (in effect a notation in which 100,000,000 is used as a base as we use 10). Archimedes employs it to express the number of grains of sand which, on certain assumptions, the universe is calculated to contain. It is the only surviving work of Archimedes touching on astronomy, and is our best source for the heliocentric system of *Aristarchus (1). (8) *Method of Mechanical Theorems*: description of the method invented by Archimedes for finding by 'mechanical' means the areas and volumes of the parabola, sphere, etc. (9) *On Floating Bodies*: deals with the positions which segments of a solid of revolution can assume when floating in a fluid; for this Archimedes invented a science of hydrostatics *ab ovo*. The Greek text of the latter two works was discovered only in 1906, although *On Floating Bodies* was already known in Latin translation.

Extant works in Arabic translation are: (1) *On the Heptagon in a Circle*: geometrical construction of the regular heptagon. (2) *Book of Lemmas* (available only in Latin translation). (3) *On Touching Circles*. (4) *Book of Assumptions*. All of these have undergone alteration in transmission, and the authenticity of the last three is doubtful.

The most notable characteristic of Archimedes' mathematical work is its freedom from the trammels of traditional Greek mathematics. It is true that in the *proofs* of those theorems for which the integral calculus is now used (e.g. those determining the surface-area and volume of a sphere or the area of a parabola) he uses the standard Greek method of bypassing infinitesimals (invented by *Eudoxus and employed in Euclid bk. 10, misnamed 'method of exhaustion' in modern works). But the *Method* (no. 8 above) reveals that for the *discovery* of these theorems he used a technique which consists of dividing two figures into infinitely thin strips, weighing these strips against each other, and then summing them to get the ratio of the two whole figures. This is analogous to the practice of the developers of the integral calculus in the 17th cent., but unlike them Archimedes recognized its lack of rigour, and used it only as a heuristic procedure. The same freedom of thought appears in arithmetic in the *Sandreckoner*, which shows an understanding of the nature of a numerical system immeasurably superior to anything else from antiquity. It is this breadth and freedom of vision, rather than the amazing ingenuity which Archimedes displays in the solution of particular problems, which justifies calling him the greatest mathematician of antiquity. His work in hydrostatics (see (9) above) was epoch-making (although the effect in antiquity was negligible). The same is true of statics, though here he probably had predecessors.

All of his work in astronomy is lost except for an ingenious method of finding the sun's apparent diameter described in the *Sandreckoner*, and a passage giving the distances of

the heavenly bodies preserved in Hippolytus (*Haer.* 41. 18 ff. Wendland). This corrupt passage suggests that he had no mathematical theory of astronomy. However, his construction of a planetarium implies the reverse. On this he wrote a work (*Kata tēn sphairopoiian*, Pappus 8. 3), now lost. Other lost works include treatises on the semi-regular polyhedra (Pappus 5. 34), on elementary mechanics (*Peri zygōn* or *Peri isorropiōn*, Pappus 8. 24) and on reflection in mirrors (*Katoptrika*, Theon, comm. on Ptolemy's *Almagest* 1. 347 f.). An epigram preserves a 'cattle-problem' attributed to Archimedes; this poses a problem in indeterminate analysis with eight unknowns. There is no evidence that Archimedes found the solution. Fragments of a work entitled *Stomachion*, dealing with a square divided into fourteen pieces for a game, are preserved in Greek and Arabic.

Commentaries by Eutocius to *Sphere and Cylinder*, *Measurement of the Circle*, and *Equilibriums of Planes* survive.   G.J.T.

Aristagoras, deputy tyrant of Miletus (western Asia Minor) *c.*505–496 BC in *Histiaeus' absence and influential rebel with too many causes. Trying to extend Miletus' Aegean power, he promoted a joint Ionian–Phoenician expedition of 100 ships against prosperous, independent Naxos in 500 (Hdt. 5. 30). Failing in the four-month siege, facing large military debts, and perhaps contemplating an independent east Aegean empire, he arrested and deposed fellow autocrats before demobilization (and thereby curried favour with ordinary Greeks along the coast), seized the Persians' Ionian fleet, abdicated Histiaeus' *de iure* tyrannical powers at Miletus, and promoted revolt against Persia from the Black Sea to Cyprus (Hdt. 5. 37–8). Control of land and sea was quickly achieved. Seeking allies and cash, Aristagoras sailed to Europe (499/8). Spartans declined, Athenians and Eretrians (from Euboia) briefly enlisted, but, faced with Phoenician sea-power and Persian access by land, the Ionian Revolt faltered. Although Aristagoras superficially united Ionian communities during the six-year revolt, his authority over Miletus and allied forces remained anomalous. As financial support diminished and allies bickered, he secured refuge and resources in strategically important Myrcinus, Histiaeus' base of operations (Hdt. 5. 124; 497/6 BC). While expanding power and revenues there, he was ambushed and killed by Thracians (5. 126).

Herodotus calls Aristagoras the originator of the Ionian Revolt. He scored impressive early successes, but he later proved an easy scapegoat for self-justifying survivors, victims of Persian retribution, and Athenian and Spartan self-glorification. Subsequent events confirmed his belief (5. 49) in the possibility of Anatolian Greek independence, but his revenues, diplomatic skills, and strategic planning proved inadequate. History vilifies losers and tyrants, especially when exemplified in one man.   D.G.L.

Aristarchus (1), of Samos, astronomer, is dated by his observation of the summer solstice in 280 BC. He was a pupil of the Peripatetic *Straton of Lampsacus. He is famous as the author of the heliocentric hypothesis, that 'the fixed stars and sun remain unmoved, and that the earth revolves about the sun on the circumference of a circle, the sun lying in the middle of the orbit' (Archimedes, *Sandreckoner* 4–5); he also assumed that the earth rotates about its own axis (Plut. *De fac.* 6). His only extant treatise, *On the Sizes and Distances of the Sun and Moon*, is, however, on the geocentric basis. Starting with six 'hypotheses', the treatise has eighteen propositions displaying the author's facility in both geometry and arithmetic. The ratios of sizes and distances which have to be calculated are equivalent to trigonometric ratios, and Aristarchus finds upper and lower limits to their values starting from assumptions equivalent to well-known theorems in geometry. The results are grossly discrepant from reality: this is due not only to Aristarchus' method, which, though mathematically correct, is ill-suited for its purpose (see HIPPARCHUS), but also to errors in the hypotheses, notoriously a figure of 2° for the moon's apparent diameter. He probably wrote the treatise more as a mathematical exercise than as practical astronomy. He is said to have invented a type of sundial known as the *skaphē* (Vitr. 9. 8), and to have estimated the year-length as $365\frac{1}{4} + \frac{1}{1623}$ days (a value which he must have derived from Babylonian astronomy).   G.J.T.

Aristarchus (2), of Samothrace (*c.*216–144 BC), belonged to the school of *Aristophanes (2) of Byzantium at Alexandria and was tutor of Ptolemy VII son of Ptolemy Philometor (see PTOLEMY). He succeeded Apollonius *ho eidographos* ('classifier of literary genres') as head of the Alexandrian Library (*c.*153 BC). On the accession of Ptolemy VIII (145 BC) he left Alexandria for Cyprus, where he died. With him scientific scholarship really began, and his work covered the wide range of grammatical, etymological, orthographical, literary, and textual criticism. He was styled *ho grammatikos*, 'extremely scholarly' (Ath. 15. 671 f.), and for his gift of critical divination was nicknamed *mantis* ('seer') by Panaetius (Ath. 14. 634c). His name has often been used to typify the complete critic (e.g. Cic. *Att.* 1. 14. 3. Hor. *Ars P.* 450). In matters of language he was an Analogist and an opponent of *Crates of Mallus. The school which he founded at Alexandria and which lasted into the Roman imperial period had many distinguished pupils, e.g. *Apollodorus and *Dionysius Thrax. He was the first scholar to write numerous commentaries, and the first to write about prose authors. His writings fall into three main groups:

1. Critical recensions (*diorthōseis*) of the text of *Homer, *Hesiod, *Archilochus, *Alcaeus, *Anacreon, *Pindar. For his recension of the *Iliad* and *Odyssey*, and elsewhere, he used symbols to indicate his suspicions of the genuineness of verses, wrongful repetition, confused orders of verses, etc. The *disiecta membra* of his commentaries surviving in medieval scholia often enable us to reconstruct his apparatus of critical signs. In his treatment of textual problems in Homer he was more cautious than his Alexandrian predecessors and sought to remove corruption, conjecture, and interpolation by scrupulous regard for the best manuscript tradition, by careful study of the Homeric language and metre, by his fine literary sense, by emphasis on the requirements of consistency and appropriateness of ethos, and by his practice of interpreting a poet by the poet's own usage (*Homēron ex Homērou saphēnizein*). He avoided allegorical interpretation, as practised by the Stoics. But his work seems to have had comparatively little influence on the traditional text of Homer.

2. Commentaries (*Hypomnēmata*) on Homer, Hesiod, Archilochus, *Alcman, Pindar, *Aeschylus, *Sophocles, *Aristophanes (1), *Herodotus, and perhaps *Euripides and *Ion.

3. Critical treatises (*Syngrammata*) on particular matters relating to the *Iliad* and *Odyssey*, e.g. the naval camp of the Greeks; and polemics against other writers and scholars, e.g. against Philitas and the 'chorizontes' (who ascribed the two poems to separate authors), especially Xenon.

J.F.L.; R.B.; N.G.W.

Aristides, Publius Aelius (AD 117–after 181), sophist (of the so-called Second Sophistic, the revival of Greek oratory in the 2nd cent. AD) and man of letters. Born at Hadrianotherae in Mysia (north-western Asia Minor), he was a pupil of Alexander of Cotiaeum and studied in Athens and Pergamum. At the age of 26, he suffered the first of a long series of illnesses, which ended his hopes of a great public career and drove him to spend much of his time as a patient at the Asclepieum (sanctuary of the healing god Asclepius) of Pergamum. The rest of his life was passed mainly in Asia Minor, where he made his home in Smyrna and in the intervals of illness occupied himself in writing and lecturing.

His many-sided literary output (built on an intimate knowledge of the Classical literary heritage) made him a giant in his own day and, through its subsequent popularity, a 'pivotal figure in the transmission of Hellenism' (Bowersock). It includes addresses delivered on public and private occasions, declamations on historical themes, polemical essays, prose hymns to various gods, and six books of *Sacred Discourses* (*Hieroi logoi*). Two rhetorical treatises transmitted under his name (ed. Schmid, 1926) are wrongly attributed. Among the public addresses, *To Rome* (26 Keil) paints an impressive picture of the Roman achievement, as seen by an admiring provincial, while the *Panathenaic Oration* (1 K) provides a potted history of Classical Athens, much used as a Byzantine school text. The historical declamations (the *Sicilians*, 5–6 K, and the *Leuctrians*, 11–15 K) show an equal facility with Classical oratorical style and with the fine details of 5th and 4th cent. BC history. Of the polemical works, the most interesting are *On Rhetoric* (2 K) and *In Defence of the Four* (3 K), which answer *Plato's attack on rhetoric and orators (politicians) in the *Gorgias*. The prose hymns (37–46 K), though Aristides did not invent the genre, revealed new possibilities in both a Platonizing and an Isocratean vein (see

ISOCRATES), and were an influential model for later writers. The *Sacred Discourses* (47–52 K), finally, are in a class apart. A record of revelations made to Aristides in dreams by the healing god Asclepius, and of his obedience to the god's instructions, they are of major importance, both as evidence for the practices associated with temple medicine, and as the fullest first-hand report of personal religious experiences that survives from any pagan writer.   E.R.D.; M.B.T.

Aristogiton Athenian tyrannicide. He and Harmodius, both of the family of Gephyraei, provoked, according to *Thucydides, by amorous rivalry, plotted along with others to kill the tyrant Hippias (elder son of *Pisistratus) at the Panathenaic festival (the great Athenian festival of Athena) of 514 BC and end the tyranny. The plot miscarried, only Hippias' younger brother Hipparchus was killed, and the 'tyrannicides' were executed.

After the expulsion of Hippias in 510 by Sparta and the famous Athenian family the Alcmaeonids, the 'tyrannicides' were elevated as heroes. Bronze statues of them by Antenor were erected, probably quite early (Pliny, *HN* 34. 16–17, gives 510/9); carried off by the Persian king Xerxes in 480, they were replaced in 477/6 by a second group by Critius and Nesiotes; the epigram inscribed on the base was composed by *Simonides (fr. 76 Diehl; *SEG* 10. 320). Their tomb was placed in the Ceramicus (the great extramural cemetery of Athens); the *polemarchos* (a senior magistrate) sacrificed annually to them, and their descendants received free meals in the *prytaneion* (town hall). Certain *scolia* (drinking songs) were sung claiming that they brought Athens *isonomia* (freedom or democracy) (Page, *PMG* nos. 893–6). It was thus a popular belief, famously rebutted by Thucydides (1. 20, 6. 53 ff.), that Hipparchus was the tyrant at the time. Other conflicting claims clustered round the role of the tyrannicides, but Jacoby's view that 5th-cent. popular tradition literally thought they, rather than Sparta and the Alcmaeonids (as in Hdt. 5. 55–65), ended the tyranny, is undermined by Thucydides (6. 53) and comedy. It is likely that all parties concerned concurred in honouring them from early on as a convenient, simple, and patriotic symbol for the defeat of tyranny. Later, they are seen as having ended the tyranny.   R.T.

Aristophanes (1), the greatest poet of the Old Attic Comedy, was the son of Philippus and the father of Araros. It has been inferred (wrongly, perhaps) from *Ach.* 652 ff. that he lived, or owned property, on Aegina. Since he considered himself too young in 427 BC (Ar. *Nub.* 530 f. with schol.) to produce a play himself, he is unlikely to have been born earlier than 460 and may have been born as late as 450. He died in or shortly before 386. Eleven of his plays survive; we have in addition 32 titles (some of them alternative titles, and some certainly attributed to other authors) and nearly a thousand fragments and citations. The surviving plays, and the datable lost plays (°) are:

427: °*Banqueters*, produced by Callistratus. It contained (frs. 198 and 222 and *Nub.* 529 with schol.) an argument between a profligate son and his father and also between the profligate and a virtuous young man.

426 (City Dionysia i.e. the main festival of Dionysus at Athens): °*Babylonians*, produced by Callistratus. Dionysus was a character in the play (fr. 70), and by its 'attacks on the magistrates' it provoked a prosecution—apparently unsuccessful—by *Cleon (schol. Ar. *Ach.* 378).

425 (Lenaea, another Athenian festival of Dionysus; first prize): *Acharnians* ('*Ach.*'), produced by Callistratus; the 'hero' makes, and enjoys to the full, a private peace-treaty.

424 (Lenaea, first prize): *Knights* ('*Eq.*'), produced by Aristophanes himself; Cleon is savagely handled and worsted in the guise of a favourite slave of Demos, and a sausage-seller replaces him as favourite.

423 (City Dionysia, bottom prize): *Clouds* ('*Nub.*'), ridiculing *Socrates as a corrupt teacher of rhetoric. We have only the revised version of the play, dating from the period 418–416; the revision was not completed and was never performed (schol. *Nub.* 552).

422 (Lenaea, second prize): *Wasps* ('*Vesp.*'), produced by Philonides, ridiculing the enthusiasm of old men for jury service.

421 (City Dionysia, second prize): *Peace* ('*Pax*'), celebrating the conclusion of peace with Sparta.

414 (Lenaea): °*Amphiaraus*, produced by Philonides (hyp. 2 Ar. *Av.*).

414 (City Dionysia, second prize): *Birds* ('*Av.*'), produced by Callistratus, a fantasy in which an ingenious Athenian persuades the birds to build a city in the clouds and compels the gods to accept humiliating terms.

411: *Lysistrata* ('*Lys.*'), produced by Callistratus, in which the citizens' wives in all the Greek states compel their menfolk, by a 'sex strike', to make peace; and *Thesmophoriazusae* ('*Thesm.*')—datable in relation to *Euripides' *Helena* and *Andromeda*, and by political references—in which the women at a festival called the Thesmophoria plan to obliterate Euripides, and an elderly kinsman of his takes part in their debate, disguised as a woman.

408: the first °*Plutus* (schol. Ar. *Plut.* 173).

405 (Lenaea, first prize): *Frogs* ('*Ran.*'), in which Dionysus goes to Hades to bring back Euripides, finds that he has to be the judge in a contest between *Aeschylus and Euripides, for the throne of poetry in Hades, and ends by bringing back Aeschylus.

392: *Ecclesiazusae* ('*Eccl.*'); the date depends on a partially corrupt scholium (on *Eccl.* 193) and on historical references, and a case can be made for 391. In this play the women take over the running of the city and introduce community of property.

388: the second *Plutus* ('*Plut.*'), in which the god of wealth is cured of his blindness, and the remarkable social consequences of his new discrimination are exemplified.

After 388: °*Aiolosikon* and °*Cocalus*, both produced by Aristophanes' son Araros (hyp. 4 Ar. *Plut.*). *Cocalus* anticipated some of the characteristics of *Menander, according to *Vit. Ar.* 1 pp. 1, 3.

In the first period, down to 421, Aristophanes followed a constant procedure in the structure of his plays, particularly in the relation of the parodos (entry of the chorus) and the parabasis (address by the chorus to the audience) to the rest of the play. From *Av.* onwards we see significant changes in this procedure, culminating, in *Eccl.* and *Plut.*, in the introduction of choral songs irrelevant to the action of the play (indicated in our texts by the word *chorou*), and in *Plut.* the chorus seems, for the first time, something of an impediment to the unfolding of the plot. At the same time *Eccl.* and *Plut.* show a great reduction (though not a disappearance) of strictly topical reference. The evidence suggests that Aristophanes was a leader, not a follower, in the changes undergone by comedy in the early 4th cent. BC. Aristophanes' language is colourful and imaginative, and he composes lyric poetry in every vein, humorous, solemn, or delicate. He has a keen eye and ear for the absurd and the pompous; his favoured weapons are parody, satire, and exaggeration to the point of fantasy, and his favourite targets are men prominent in politics, contemporary poets, musicians, scientists, and philosophers, and—as is virtually inevitable in a comedian writing for a wide public—manifestations of cultural change in general. His sympathetic characters commonly express the feelings of men who want to be left alone to enjoy traditional pleasures in traditional ways, but they are also ingenious, violent, and tenaciously self-seeking in getting what they want. Having been born into a radical democracy which had been created and strengthened by his father's and grandfather's generations, Aristophanes nowhere advocates oligarchic reaction, least of all in 411, when this reaction was an imminent reality. His venomous attack on Cleon in *Eq.* is adequately explained by Cleon's earlier attack on him (see above), and his treatment of other politicians does not differ significantly from the way in which 'we' satirize 'them' nowadays. No class, age-group, or profession is wholly exempt from Aristophanes' satire, nor is the citizen-body as a whole, and if we interpret his plays as moral or social lessons we never find the lesson free of qualifications and complications. In *Eq.* Cleon is worsted not by an upright and dignified man but by an illiterate and brazen cynic who beats him at his own game. In *Nub.* Socrates' 'victim' is foolish and dishonest, and in the contest between Right and Wrong, Right, who is characterized by bad temper, sexual obsession, and vacuous nostalgia, ends by 'deserting' to the side of Wrong. In *Thesm.* Euripides, sharply parodied in much of the play, triumphs in the end. In *Ran.* the end of the contest between Aeschylus and Euripides finds Dionysus in a state of complete irresolution. Modern sentiment admires the heroine of *Lys.*, but possibly Aristophanes and his audience found preposterous much in her which seems to us moving and sensible. Aristophanes' didactic influence (as distinct from his influence in raising the intellectual and artistic standards of comedy) does not seem to have been significant. Plato (*Ap.* 18bc, 19d) blames him for

helping to create mistrust of Socrates. On the other hand, *Ach.* and *Lys.* do not seem to have disposed the Athenians to negotiate for peace (*Pax* did not mould public opinion, but fell into line with it), and Cleon was elected to a generalship shortly after the first prize had been awarded to *Eq.* The fact that Aristophanes survived not only Cleon's attacks but also (with other comic poets) two oligarchic revolutions and two democratic restorations should not be forgotten.

Aristophanes was intensively studied throughout antiquity, and the plays which are now lost, as well as those which have survived, were the subject of commentaries (cf. schol. Ar. *Plut.* 210).   K.J.D.

Aristophanes (2) of Byzantium (probably *c.*257–180 BC) succeeded *Eratosthenes as head of the Alexandrian Library (*c.*194 BC). He was a scholar of wide learning, famous for his linguistic, literary, textual, and scientific researches, and he is credited with the innovation of writing Greek accents.

His edition of *Homer's *Iliad* and *Odyssey* made a distinct advance on the work of Zenodotus and *Rhianus. Despite some capriciousness and boldness of treatment, due to a subjective method of criticism, his work showed much critical acumen; e.g. he was the first to put the end of the *Odyssey* at 23. 296. In his textual criticism he used symbols to show his doubts of the genuineness or satisfactoriness of verses.

Besides editions of *Hesiod's *Theogony*, *Alcaeus, and *Alcman, he produced the first properly ordered edition of *Pindar, in seventeen books; in his texts of the lyric poets Aristophanes used signs to mark the ends of metrical *cola*; but *PLille* 76a and 73 of *Stesichorus prove that his predecessors had recognized the importance of *cola*. Scholia (ancient notes and commentaries) and papyri attest his work on *Sophocles and *Euripides; he also compiled the first critical edition of the comedies of *Aristophanes (1); but to a later date belong the metrical *hypotheseis* (scholarly introductions prefixed to the texts of Greek dramas), traditionally ascribed to him, on seven of these comedies. He may have proposed a somewhat unsatisfactory grouping of fifteen dialogues of *Plato in trilogies.

His select lists of the best Classical poets seem, along with those of *Aristarchus (2), to have provided the basis for the classification of writers in the Alexandrian canon. He corrected and supplemented the biographical and literary information contained in the *Pinakes* of *Callimachus. Introductions (attributed to Aristophanes) to some plays of *Aeschylus, Sophocles, and Euripides, based on the *Didascaliae* (lists of dramatic productions) of Aristotle and on Peripatetic research, are extant in an abbreviated form. In the *Peri prosōpōn* he treated the character-types in Greek Comedy. His interest in *Menander led him to compile the treatise *Parallēloi Menandrou te kai aph' hōn eklepsen eklogai* ('Parallels between Menander and the people he stole from'), possibly the first treatise on plagiarism.

Of his lexicographical works the most important was the *Lexeis* (or *Glōssai*), which perhaps consisted of a series of special studies classified according to dialect or to subject and dealt with prose as well as verse. He produced two books of proverbs in verse (schol. Soph. *Aj.* 746) and four in prose (schol. Ar. *Av.* 1292).

The work *Peri zōōn* appears to have been based on the ('on animals') studies of Aristotle, Theophrastus, and the Paradoxographers (collectors of marvels). Excerpts survive in Byzantine miscellanies. There is no good reason to attribute to him a grammatical treatise *Peri analogias* ('on analogy').

J.F.L.; N.G.W.

Aristotle (384–322 BC) was born in Stagira in Chalcidice (northern Greece). His father Nicomachus, a member of the medical guild of the Asclepiadae (who took their name from the healing god Asclepius), was court physician to king Amyntas II of Macedonia, and Aristotle may have spent part of his childhood at the court in Pella. Although his interest in biology may have developed early because of his father's career, there is no evidence that he began systematic study. Asclepiad doctors taught their sons dissection, but Aristotle probably did not receive this training, since both of his parents died when he was extremely young.

2. At the age of 17 he travelled to Athens and entered *Plato's Academy, remaining until Plato's death in 348/7 BC. Plato's philosophical influence is evident in all of Aristotle's work. Even when he is critical (a great part of the time) he expresses deep respect

for Plato's genius. Some scholars imagine that no dissent was tolerated in the Academy; they therefore conclude that all works in which Aristotle criticizes Plato must have been written after Plato's death. This is implausible. Plato's own work reveals a capacity for searching self-criticism. Frequently these criticisms resemble extant Aristotelian criticisms. An attractive possibility is that the arguments of his brilliant pupil were among the stimuli that led Plato to rethink his cherished positions.

3. At Plato's death Aristotle left Athens, probably because of political difficulties connected with his Macedonian ties. (He may also have disapproved of the choice of *Speusippus as Plato's successor.) Accepting an invitation from Hermias, ruler of Assos and Atarneus in the Troad and a former fellow student in the Academy, he went to Assos, where he stayed until Hermias' fall and death in 345, marrying his adopted daughter Pythias. While at Assos, and afterwards at Mytilene on Lesbos, he did the biological research on which his later scientific writings are based. (The treatises refer frequently to place-names and local species of that area.) His observations, especially in marine biology, were unprecedented in their detail and accuracy. (His work remained without peer until the time of Harvey (1578–1657), and was still much admired by Darwin.)

4. Invited by *Philip II of Macedon to Pella in 342 BC, he became tutor to Philip's son *Alexander the Great. His instruction focused on standard literary texts, but probably also included political theory and history. Aristotle's opinion of his pupil's philosophical ability is unknown, but in later years their relationship was distant. In the *Politics* Aristotle writes that rule by a single absolute monarch would be justified only if the person were as far superior to existing humans, in intellect and character, as humans are to beasts. He conspicuously fails to mention any case in which these conditions have been fulfilled.

5. In 335, after a brief stay in Stagira, Aristotle returned to Athens. As a resident alien (*metic*) he could not own property, so he rented buildings outside the city, probably between Mt. Lycabettus and the Ilissus. Here, in what was called the Lyceum, he established his own school. (The school later took its name from its colonnade or *peripatos*.) He

delivered some popular lectures, but most of his time was spent in writing or lecturing to a smaller group of serious students, including some, such as *Theophrastus and Eudemus, who achieved distinction. He amassed a considerable library, and encouraged his students to undertake research projects, especially in natural science and political history (where he projected a collection of historical and comparative descriptions of 158 regimes).

6. Pythias died early in this period; they had one daughter. For the rest of his life Aristotle lived with a slave-woman named Herpyllis, by whom he had a son, Nicomachus. Although in his will Aristotle praises Herpyllis' loyalty and kindness, he freed her from legal slavery only then. On the death of Alexander in 323 BC, an outbreak of anti-Macedonian feeling forced Aristotle to leave Athens once again. Alluding to the death of *Socrates, he said that he was leaving to prevent the Athenians from 'sin[ning] twice against philosophy'. He retired to Chalcis on Euboea, where he died in 322 of a digestive illness.

7. Aristotle left his papers to Theophrastus, his successor as head of the Lyceum. *Strabo reports that Theophrastus left them to Neleus of Scepsis (in Asia Minor), whose heirs hid them in a cellar, where they remained unused until a rich collector, Apellicon, purchased them and brought them to Athens early in the first century BC. This is seriously misleading. There is copious evidence that some of Aristotle's major works were used by his successors in the Lyceum, as well as by *Epicurus and numerous Alexandrian intellectuals. At this stage the works were not edited in anything like the form in which we know them. A list of Aristotle's works, probably dating from the 3rd cent. BC, appears to cover most of the major extant texts under some description, as well as a number of works now lost. Among the lost works are dialogues, some of which were still well known in *Cicero's Rome. Apparently their style was different from that of the extant works: Cicero describes it as 'a golden river'. We can reconstruct portions of several lost works through reports and citations.

8. When *Sulla captured Athens (86 BC), Apellicon's collection was brought to Rome, where it was edited around 30 BC, by Andronicus of Rhodes, whose edition is the basis for all subsequent editions. Andronicus grouped

books into works, arranged them in a logical sequence, and left copious notes about his views on authenticity. We possess most of the works he considered genuine and important, in manuscripts produced between the 9th and 16th cents. The transmission during the intervening period is represented by several papyrus fragments, plus the extensive papyri from which the (dubious) *Athenaion politeia* (Athenian Constitution) has been edited. Several of the Greek commentaries produced between the 3rd and 6th cents. AD show evidence of access to now lost elements of the manuscript tradition, and can prove useful in establishing the text.

9. The extant works may be classified as follows:

(a) Logic and Metaphysics: *Categories, De interpretatione, Prior Analytics, Posterior Analytics, Topics, Sophistici elenchi* (= *Top.* 9), *Metaphysics*.

(b) Nature, Life, and Mind: *Physics, De caelo, De generatione et corruptione, Meteorologica* (bk. 4 of dubious authenticity), *Historia animalium, De partibus animalium, De motu animalium, De incessu animalium, De generatione animalium, De anima, Parva naturalia* (including *De sensu, De memoria, De somno, De somniis, De divinatione per somnum, De longitudine et brevitate vitae, De iuventute, De respiratione*).

(c) Ethics, Politics, Art: *Eudemian Ethics, Nicomachean Ethics, Politics; Magna moralia* (probably not written up by Aristotle, but closely based on Aristotelian lectures); *Athenaion politeia* (authorship disputed); *Rhetoric; Poetics*.

Of the works surviving only in fragments, the most important and substantial is *Peri ideōn* (*On the Forms*), a critical discussion of Plato's theories; also significant are the dialogues *On Philosophy* and *On the Good*, and the *Protrepticus*.

Clearly spurious works transmitted along with the corpus include *De mundo, De spiritu, De coloribus, De audibilibus, Physiognomonica, De plantis, De mirabilibus auscultationibus, Mechanica, Problemata* (a compilation of materials from the school), *De lineis insecabilibus, Ventorum situs, De Melisso, Xenophane, Gorgia, De virtutibus et vitiis, Oeconomica, Rhetorica ad Alexandrum*.

10. Many questions have been raised about the status of the 'Aristotelian corpus'. The most plausible view is that the extant treatises

are written lectures. The exact wording of most of the material is Aristotle's. We cannot rely on the order of books within a treatise as Aristotelian, or even the grouping of distinct books into a single treatise. All titles and many introductory and concluding sentences are likely to be the work of later editors. Cross-references may be genuine if well integrated with their context. Throughout we are faced with textual problems, some of which require the transposition of substantial passages for their solution. Some sections, furthermore, may have been left poorly organized by Aristotle himself, and are best regarded as assorted notes that were never worked into a finished discussion (for example, *De anima* 3. 6–7). The most serious philosophical problems raised by the state of the corpus come from its duplications: (*a*) multiple discussions of a single problem, and (*b*) a single discussion repeated in more than one context. There are many cases of the first type; here we must ask whether differences amount to incompatibility or are best explained by a difference of perspective or starting point. Doublets of the second type may be very brief, or they may be several books long; sometimes repetition is verbatim, sometimes with changes. *Metaphysics* 1 and 13 have many chapters in common, with small but significant changes. *Metaphysics* 11 compiles material from other books of the *Metaphysics* and the *Physics*. Books 5–7 of the *Nicomachean Ethics* also appear as books 4–6 of the *Eudemian Ethics*. In each case, we must ask how likely it is that Aristotle himself would have put the repeated portion in both contexts himself. If such a hypothesis creates problems with the overall argument of the work, we should ask whether it is clear that Aristotle himself must have noticed those problems.

11. The medieval tradition led us to view Aristotle's work as a closed, consistent system without internal chronological development. This view of the corpus was overthrown early in the 20th cent. by Werner Jaeger's important work, which convincingly presented evidence of development and stressed the flexible undogmatic character of Aristotle's philosophizing (whether or not one agrees with Jaeger's particular chronological story). Thereafter, however, scholars sometimes went to an opposite extreme, hastily assuming incompatibility and making irresponsible

use of developmental explanations. In general, it is crucial to recognize the extent to which Aristotle's problems and questions in a particular work dictate his approach to an issue.

12. Aristotle was the first Greek philosopher to attempt a general account of validity in inference. The *Prior Analytics* is thus a towering achievement; though displaced in the Hellenistic period by Stoic propositional logic, it became the dominant account of formal logic from the early Middle Ages until the early 20th cent. The *Topics* and the *Sophistici elenchi* show Aristotle's keen interest in methods of dialectical argumentation and in the analysis of common fallacies and paradoxes; they give us a vivid picture of the philosophical culture of Aristotle's time.

13. In the *Posterior Analytics* Aristotle sets out the conditions under which scientific demonstration will convey genuine understanding (*epistēmē*). Conclusions must be deducible, ultimately, from first principles that are true, basic, necessary, and explanatory of the other conclusions of the science. The scientist has understanding when he is able to show how the more basic principles of his science explain the less basic. (In this sense, understanding must always be of the universal, since particulars cannot become part of a deductive explanatory structure of this sort; this does not mean, however, that Aristotle thinks our grasp of particulars shaky or prone to sceptical doubt.) *Posterior Analytics* 2. 19 argues that understanding is based on the experience of many particulars, and requires the achievement of *nous* concerning the first principles. Although *nous* has often been taken to be a special faculty of mind that grasps first principles a priori, it is probably best understood to be mental insight into the explanatory role of principles that the thinker knows and uses already on the basis of experience. Thus Aristotelian science does not require an a priori foundation.

14. In *Metaphysics* 4, Aristotle undertakes the defence of two especially basic logical principles: the Principle of Non-Contradiction and the Principle of the Excluded Middle. Non-Contradiction, which is called 'the most basic starting point of all', is established not by a proof from other principles, but by an 'elenctic demonstration', i.e. one that establishes that the opponent who challenged this law actually must rely on it if he

is to think and speak at all. For to say anything definite he must rule something out—at the least, the contradictory of what he sets forth.

15. Throughout his work Aristotle is intensely concerned with experience, including the record of experience contained in what people say. It is common for an inquiry, in science as well as in ethics, to begin by 'setting down the *phainomena*', the 'appearances', which usually include perceptual observation and the record of reputable belief, frequently as embodied in language. Aristotle clearly believes that scientific inquiry involves examining common conceptions as well as looking at the world; indeed the two frequently interpenetrate, as in the inquiries into time and place in the *Physics*. Aristotle is also very careful to survey the views of the reputable thinkers who have approached a problem. As he states at the start of his inquiry into number in *Metaphysics* 13, he can hope in this way to avoid making the same mistakes, and can perhaps hope to progress a little beyond what the tradition has already accomplished. Although we may find fault with his treatment of one or another previous thinker, he was the first Greek thinker to make engagement with the books of others a central part of his method.

16. 'Metaphysics' is not an Aristotelian term (it refers to the placement of that work 'after the *Physics*' in ancient editions), but Aristotle's study of the most general characteristics of things gives subsequent metaphysics its agenda. Aristotle holds that the central question about that which is (*to on*), for both his predecessors and himself, has been a question about *ousia*, usually translated 'substance'. Since *ousia* is a verbal noun formed from the participle *on*, this is not a perspicuous statement. But from Aristotle's procedures we can get a better idea of his problem. Two questions appear to drive the search for substance: a question about *change*, and a question about *identity*. Since a central part of our experience of nature is that of change—the cycle of the seasons, changes in living bodies—an account of nature needs to find a coherent way to speak about process. Following Plato's *Theaetetus*, Aristotle holds that this, in turn, requires the ability to single out some entities as (relatively) stable 'subjects' or 'substrates' (*hupokeimena*) of change, things to which the change happens. At the same time, discourse about the world

also requires asking and answering the question 'What is it?' about items in our experience. This means being able to say what it is about an individual that makes it the very thing it is, and to separate that aspect from more superficial attributes that might cease to be present while the individual remained the same. This question, Aristotle holds, leads us to search for (what we now call) the thing's 'essence' (here we borrow a Ciceronian rendering of Aristotle's odd yet homely term, *to ti ēn einai*, 'the what it is to be'). The two questions might seem to point in opposite directions: the first in the direction of matter as the basic substance, since that persists while animals and people are born and die; the second in the direction of the universal, since 'human being' or 'tree' seem promising accounts of the 'what is it' of particulars. But it is Aristotle's view that in reality the two must be held closely together and will ultimately converge on a single account of the basic substances. For any adequate theory of change must single out as its substrates items that are not only relatively enduring, but also definite and distinct; and any account of the essence of a particular should enable us to say what changes it can undergo while still remaining one and the same. Aristotle pursues the two prongs of his question through several treatises, with results that appear to undergo development and are always difficult to interpret.

17. In the early *Categories*, Aristotle argues that the 'primary substances' and substrates of change are physical individuals, such as 'this human being' and 'this horse' (as contrasted both with individual qualities, quantities, relations, etc., and also with universals of all types). On the other hand, we can only individuate and identify them via 'secondary substances', species universals such as 'human being' and 'horse'. Unlike Platonic forms, secondary substances have no existence apart from physical individuals, but they are fundamental to our grasp of them. In *Physics*, and *Gen. corr.*, Aristotle brings matter into the picture and asks about its relation to form or organization. Although he ultimately rejects the notion that a thing's matter is substance, and more basic than its organization, he is apparently driven to grant that some cases of change—the comings-to-be and passings-away of substances—have to be explained with reference to material substrates.

18. Aristotle's culminating inquiry into substance, in *Metaph.* 7–8, is the subject of endless interpretative controversy. On one plausible reading, Aristotle concludes that the most basic substrates are also the essences of things, and that both of these are identical with the *form* (*eidos*) of a thing as a member of a certain species, for example, the human-ness (characteristic human organization) of Socrates. This form is a particular in the sense that Socrates is a distinct human being from Coriscus; on the other hand, the account of Socrates' essence or form mentions only those features he shares with other species members. In other words, what Socrates really is, and what must remain the same about him while other attributes change, is his characteristic species organization.

19. Other major topics in Aristotle's meta-physical work include *potentiality* and *actuality* (concepts linked to substance and invoked in explaining the forms of living things); *number* (Aristotle attacks the Platonist separation of numbers from things); *unity* (organic living beings have more than artefacts); and the nature of the *study of being* itself (it may become a general study with substance as its focal point). In *Metaphysics* 12, Aristotle articulates his idea of god as an eternally active and unaffected substance, whose activity is thinking and who inspires movement in the heavenly spheres by becoming an object of their love.

20. The *Metaphysics* describes the develop-ment of philosophy as a search for explan-ations of natural events that inspire wonder. In the *Physics* Aristotle describes the types of explanation a natural philosopher should be prepared to give. He begins from the question 'Why?' (*dia ti*)—asked either about a thing or a complex state of affairs; he suggests that there are four basic ways in which we can answer such a 'why' question. First, we may cite the materials of which a thing is com-posed. This answer is inadequate on its own, since we need to be able to pick out the thing as a structure of a certain sort before we can enumerate its constituents. Second, we may mention a thing's form or characteristic organization. Third, we may mention some agent or event that made the event or thing come about—this sort of answer is called by Aristotle 'the origin of change', and by the tradition 'the efficient cause'. Finally, we may mention 'the end' or 'that for the sake of

which' a thing is. Aristotle insists frequently that we should explain processes or subsys-tems of creatures by showing how they con-tribute to the overall functioning of the creature. The characteristic organization of a species is in that sense an 'end' towards which processes should be seen as contributing. Whether Aristotle invokes teleological explanations to relate one species to another species is highly uncertain, as is the question whether such explanations apply to the non-living. The *Physics* also contains valuable dis-cussions of place, time, and the nature of change.

21. Aristotle's work on *psychē* (*De anima*) is a general study of life and the living. After criticizing materialist and Platonist accounts of *psychē*, he defends the view that *psychē* is the substance of a living thing; he argues that this substance will be not its material con-stituents but its species-form. His working definition is that *psychē* is the 'first entelechy of a natural organic body'. 'First entelechy' takes the place of 'form' in order to stress the fact that it is not actual functioning (e.g. seeing or thinking) that is the *psychē*, but the organization-to-function. 'Organic' seems to mean 'equipped with materials that are suit-able for performing these functions'. Aristotle goes on to give more concrete accounts of self-nutrition, reproduction, perceiving, imagining, and thinking; these inquiries are further developed in the *Parva naturalia* and, in some cases, the biological writings.

22. Aristotle's ethical treatises search for an adequate account of *eudaimonia*, a term usually translated 'happiness', but which might more perspicuously be understood as 'human flourishing'. There is general agree-ment that *eudaimonia* is the 'target' of human choice, and that it involves being active. Reflection, Aristotle holds, will show common candidates such as pleasure and honour to be inadequate accounts of what *eudaimonia* is; it must be understood as 'activity of soul in accordance with complete excellence'. This complex end has many con-stituent elements; Aristotle investigates a long list of excellences of character (such as courage, moderation, generosity, justice), which are, in general, stable dispositions to choose activities and to have responses that are neither excessive nor deficient in each area of choice; this 'mean' standard is given by looking to the choices of the 'person of prac-

tical wisdom', i.e. to paradigms of human excellence. Excellence of character requires and is required by practical wisdom, an excellence of the intellect.

23. Aristotle stresses the fact that practical wisdom requires a grasp of many particulars, which must be derived through experience. Like medicine and navigation, good judgement (in law as well as in ethics) requires a grasp of rules laid down in advance, but also the ability to adjust one's thinking to the complex requirements of the situation that is at hand. His account of 'equity' (*epieikeia*) in public judgement is continuous with reflections on that theme in the Greek orators; it has had enormous influence in the history of western law. Closely connected to Aristotle's accounts of practical wisdom are his reflections on voluntary action and excusing factors, and on choice (*prohairesis*), which is involved, it seems, in the specification of *eudaimonia* into its constituent parts as well as in more concrete operations.

24. Friendship (*philia*), Aristotle holds, is one of the most important elements in a good human life. Even if one were free of need and doing well in all other respects, one would still view life as not worth living without friends. Aristotle seems to hold that any genuine friendship requires mutual awareness and mutual activity seeking to benefit the other for the other's own sake. Friendships, however, come in different types, according to the characteristics of the parties that are the ground or basis for the friendship. There are friendships of pleasure, of utility, and of character, the last being both the most stable and the richest.

25. In two separate discussions Aristotle argues that pleasure is not equivalent to the good. (His accounts of pleasure differ, and may not be compatible.) In the final book of the *Eth. Nic.* he then goes on to praise the life that is devoted to contemplating the eternal. He appears to praise this activity not just as one among the other constituents of *eudaimonia*, but as something of supreme value, to which maximal attention should be given where possible. Scholars have long disagreed about whether these chapters are consistent with the more inclusive picture of *eudaimonia* that appears to emerge from the rest of the work; incompatibilist interpretations have much force. But however we resolve these questions, the chapters give evidence of

Aristotle's high evaluation of the contemplative life, and complicate the task of describing the relationship between Aristotle's ethical thought and Plato's.

26. The investigation of human flourishing is a part of the science of politics, since legislators need to know about human ends in order to design schemes that promote these ends. But political theory requires, in addition, a critical and empirical study of different regimes, and an attempt, on that basis, to consider what the best form of government would be. In the process, Aristotle makes Greek philosophy's most distinguished contribution to economic theory.

27. Aristotle's great rhetorical treatise argues, against Platonic strictures, that rhetoric can be a systematic science. Defining rhetoric as 'the capability of recognizing in each case the possible means of persuasion', he argues for its autonomy and offers a comprehensive discussion of persuasion through speech. The work includes many discussions of broader interest, including a survey of ordinary beliefs about many ethical topics, and an analysis of the major emotions.

28. Aristotle's *Poetics* should be read in close connection with his ethical writings, which insist, against Plato, that good people can sometimes fall short of *eudaimonia* through disasters not of their own making. Tragic action, Aristotle holds, inspires two emotions in its audience: *pity* (a painful emotion felt at the undeserved and serious suffering of another person), and *fear* (a painful emotion felt at the thought of serious disasters impending). We pity the tragic hero as someone undeserving of his misfortune, and fear for him, seeing him as someone similar to ourselves. (Plato's *Republic* had argued that both of these emotions are pernicious: literature that inspires them should be removed.) In this way, poetry proves more philosophical than historical narration, since it presents universals, things 'such as might happen' in a human life. Like other forms of representation (*mimēsis*), it gives rise to the pleasure of learning and recognition. The tragic hero's reversal inspires pity if it is due not to wickedness of character but rather to some *hamartia*, by which Aristotle seems to mean some error in action, sometimes blameworthy and sometimes not. Scholars will never agree on the proper interpretation of the *katharsis* through pity and fear that is

the result of watching tragic action. But it should be observed that 'purgation' is only one possibility, and a problematic one; another possibility, perhaps more in keeping with the rest of Aristotle's argument, is that the emotional experience, by removing obstacles to our recognition of the mutability of human life, 'cleans up' or 'clears up' our muddled view of human fortunes. The central concepts of this work remain disputed and in need of close scholarly argument.

29. Aristotle's achievements have been fundamental to a great deal of the subsequent history of western philosophy. His undisputed greatness has produced at times an attitude of deference that he probably would have deplored. On the other hand, few if any philosophers have so productively stimulated the inquiries of other distinguished philosophers; few philosophers of the remote past, if any, are so conspicuously alive in the range of questions they provoke and in the resourcefulness of the arguments they offer.

M.C.N.

Aristoxenus, of Tarentum in south Italy (b. *c.*370 BC), best known for musical writings but also a philosopher, biographer, and historian. He was trained in music, possibly to professional standards, by his father Spintharus and Lampon of Erythrae (perhaps while living in Mantinea). Later, probably at Athens, he studied with the Pythagorean (see PYTHAGORAS) Xenophilus, pupil of Philolaus, before joining *Aristotle's Lyceum. Here his success made him expect to inherit the headship; and when Aristotle bequeathed it to *Theophrastus instead, his remarks about Aristotle (according to the *Suda*, our main biographical source) were memorably rude. The waspishness of criticisms levelled at others in his writings makes this believable; but his intellectual orientation is unmistakably Aristotelian, and his one surviving reference to Aristotle (*Harm.* 31. 10–16) is also the one unqualified compliment paid to anyone in that work. Nothing is known of him after 322 BC. Perhaps he devoted himself to writing: much of his enormous output (453 books, on the *Suda*'s reckoning) may come from this period. We are equally in the dark about the date and place of his death.

WORKS Aristoxenus' known works can be divided into five groups.

(*a*) Writings on harmonics, of which three incomplete books survive under the title *Elementa harmonica.* Repetitions, along with shifts in style and conceptual apparatus, suggest that book 1 belonged to a different work from books 2–3 (for a contrary view see Bélis (1986), in bibliog. below): the hypothesis, based on references in *Porphyry, that the former was called *Principles* (*Archai*), the latter *Elements* (*Stoicheia*) is uncertain. Aristoxenus saw himself as pioneering a wholly new and scientific approach to harmonics. Pythagoreans had conceived pitches as quantities, and studied their mathematical relations. Earlier empiricists had sought merely to tabulate various forms of attunement and scale. Aristoxenus takes his subject, melody (*melos*) or attunement (*to hērmosmenon*), to be a 'nature' existing solely in the audible domain; and he holds that the science must therefore represent it as it appears to the ear, not through a physicist's conception of sounds as movements of the air, since sounds are not heard in that guise, and specifically harmonic or musical properties attach only to what is heard. (This explains, among other things, his treatment of notes as points in a quasi-spatial continuum of pitch accessible to the ear, not, like the Pythagoreans, as magnitudes of some physical variable; for it is not as such magnitudes that notes become elements in melody.) The main task of harmonics is to identify the components of audible *melos*, to abstract the principles governing their relations, and to demonstrate that aesthetic distinctions between melodic and unmelodic sequences and structures are determined by these principles. Harmonics is to be a science of the sort analysed in Aristotle's *Posterior Analytics*: Aristoxenus' conceptions of melodic movement, continuity, space, and much else have an equally Aristotelian pedigree. Books 1–2 discuss basic components and structures (intervals, notes, genera, etc.), and introduce the fundamental principles governing harmonic organization: both books, especially book 2, offer challenging reflections on method. Book 3 derives from the principles a set of theorems about melodic sequences. Gaps exist in all three books, and the third breaks off in mid-flow. Aristoxenus' works on harmonics were very influential: much that is missing from *Harm.* can be reconstructed from later sources, especially Cleonides, Baccheius Geron, and Aristides Quintilianus.

(*b*) Writings on rhythmics. Part of book 2 of an *Elementa Rhythmica* survives. It argues that rhythm is a temporal structure imposed on, not inherent in, what is 'rhythmized' (*to rhythmizomenon*); and it defines rhythmic forms, by reference to a 'primary duration' (*prōtos chronos*), in terms of the ratio between arsis (*anō chronos*, up-beat) and thesis (*katō chronos*, down-beat). Another fragment on rhythm is *POxy.* 2687: later authors including Baccheius, Aristides Quintilianus, and the 11th-cent. Byzantine Michael *Psellus preserve further Aristoxenian material. A work *On the Primary Duration* is quoted by Porphyry (*On Ptolemy's Harmonics* 78. 21–79. 28).

(*c*) Other works survive only in brief quotations. Musical treatises included *On Music, On Melodic Composition* (each in at least four books, Ath. 619d; Porph. *On Ptol. Harm.* 125. 24), *On Listening to Music, On Tonoi, On Auloi and Instruments, On the Boring of Auloi, On Auletes, On Tragic Poets, On Tragic Dancing*, and perhaps *Praxidamanteia*. Aristoxenian passages in the pseudo-Plutarchan *De musica* show that he worked extensively on musical history.

(*d*) Biographies, including Lives of at least four philosophers, Pythagoras, Archytas of Tarentum, *Socrates, and *Plato. Fragments on the latter two (frs. 25–30, 33) are scurrilous and vituperative; but his work on Pythagoras probably underlies much of the later tradition, and substantial reports about Archytas drawn from Didymus by Claudius Ptolemaeus and Porphyry may originate with him.

(*e*) Other writings. Recorded titles demonstrate the variety of Aristoxenus' interests: *Educational Customs* (or 'laws', *nomoi*), *Political Nomoi* in at least eight books (Ath. 648d), *Pythagorean Maxims, Historical Notes, Brief Notes, Miscellaneous Notes* in at least sixteen books (Phot. *Bibl.* 176), *Random Jottings* (*Ta Sporadēn*), *Miscellaneous Table Talk*.

Aristoxenus' assorted memoranda left only minor traces in later historical gossip. In musicology, especially harmonics, he remained authoritative throughout ancient times. Harmonic theory became polarized into two main camps, 'Aristoxenian' and 'Pythagorean', but even Pythagorean and Platonist writers drew freely on his analyses. His conservative attitude to musical history became canonical, and authors of the imperial period still echoed his nostalgia for the pure styles of the Greek 5th cent. long after their sounds had died.   A.D.B.

Arnobius, a teacher of rhetoric at Sicca Veneria in Proconsular Numidia (north Africa), said by *Jerome to have taught *Lactantius and to have suddenly become a Christian (*c.*295). A year or two later, at his bishop's instance, he wrote seven books, *Adversus nationes*, as a proof of full conversion. He attacked those who argued, like the later opponents of Augustine, that 'ever since the Christians have been on earth, the world has gone to ruin' (*Adv. nat.* 1. 1), and that Christ was a mortal magician, not superior to Apollonius of Tyana or Zoroaster (1. 52–3). His answer, although conventional in tenor, is not so in content, since he amasses much valuable antiquarian learning, designed to prove that Roman institutions were subject to change, and that therefore Christianity was not bad because it was new. Incidentally he reveals something of pagan beliefs current in Africa. He does not look for prefiguration of the Gospel even in the Old Testament. His attack on the *viri novi* (newcomers) in book 2 shows him abreast of recent developments in Platonism (i.e. Neoplatonism); but, while he cites several dialogues and applauds *Plato's notion of God, he (characteristically) rejects the hypothesis of innate ideas. His own teaching on the soul may be of Stoic origin. He cites the New Testament little, and indeed, apart from hope of his soul's salvation through Christ and his hostility to paganism, Arnobius shows little trace of Christian theology. Writing before the council of Nicaea, he speaks of Christ as a secondary deity. His easy and fluent Latin yields the first use of the word *deitas* and of *atheus* as applied to Christianity.   W.H.C.F.; M.J.E.

Arrian (Lucius Flavius Arrianus), *c.* AD 86–160. Born in Nicomedia in Bithynia, he held local office and pursued studies with *Epictetus, whose lectures he later published (allegedly verbatim) as the *Discourses* and summarized in the *Encheiridion* ('Manual'). In Greece between 108 and 112 he attracted the friendship of *Hadrian, who later gave him senatorial rank and after his consulate (?129) employed him for six years (131–7) as legate (governor) of Cappadocia. Subsequently he retired to Athens, where he held the archonship (145/6), and perhaps survived into the reign of *Marcus Aurelius.

One of the most distinguished writers of his day, Arrian represented himself as a second *Xenophon and adopted a style which fused elements of Xenophon into a composite, artificial (yet outstandingly lucid) diction based on the great masters, *Herodotus and *Thucydides. The *Cynegeticus* is an explicit revision of Xenophon's monograph in the light of the revolution in hunting brought by the Celtic greyhound; and Xenophon's influence is demonstrable in the short essays he wrote in Cappadocia: the *Periplus* (c.131), the *Essay on Tactics* (136/7), and, most remarkable, the *Order of Battle against the Alans* (135), which expounds his tactics to repel the incursion of the Alans (nomadic pastoralists from north Pontus) in the style of Xenophon's *Cyropaedia*.

Celebrated as a philosopher in his lifetime, Arrian is today principally known as a historian. Works now lost include the eight-book *Bithyniaca*, the history of his native province from mythical times to its annexation by Rome, and the seventeen-book *Parthica* with its detailed narrative of *Trajan's campaigns (probably the source for *Cassius Dio). His most famous work deals with the age of *Alexander the Great. The period after Alexander's death (323–319 BC) was covered expansively in the ten books of *Affairs after Alexander* (significant fragments of which survive on palimpsest and papyrus). The only extant history is the so-called '*Anabasis of Alexander*', a history of Alexander the Great in seven books from his accession to his death. A short companion piece, the *Indike*, provides a digest of Indian memorabilia, based explicitly upon Megasthenes, *Eratosthenes, and Nearchus, and recounts Nearchus' voyage from south India to Susa. Arrian's work is conceived as a literary tribute to Alexander's achievements, to do for him what *Homer had done for Achilles, and the tone is eulogistic, mitigating standard criticisms and culminating in a panegyric of extraordinary intensity. The sources Arrian selected were *Ptolemy I and Aristobulus, contemporaries and actors in the events and appropriately favourable to Alexander; and the narrative is in the main worked up from material they provided, supplemented by *logoi* ('stories'), mostly from late rhetorical sources and chosen for their colour. Arrian's priority was excellence of style, not factual accuracy. Consequently his account is rich in detail and eminently readable, but is marred by demonstrable errors and misunderstandings.

A.B.B.

Arsinoë II Philadelphus ('Brother-loving') (c.316–270 BC), daughter of *Ptolemy I and his mistress Berenice, was married first (300/299) to *Lysimachus whom she aided in his bid for the Macedonian throne. Following Lysimachus' death at Corupedium, she next married (281/280) her half-brother Ptolemy Ceraunus; he murdered her younger sons. Arsinoë fled to Samothrace and then to Egypt where (mid-270s) she finally married her full brother *Ptolemy II. This royal couple set a precedent for later Ptolemaic brother–sister marriages; the dynastic cult they instituted strengthened the monarchy. In her lifetime Arsinoë was granted a priestess ('basket-bearer', *kanēphoros*) in the Alexandrian dynastic cult; the couple were later incorporated as *Theoi Adelphoi* ('Sibling Gods'). In 270 Arsinoë became the first Ptolemaic ruler to enter the Egyptian temples as 'temple-sharing goddess'. Whatever its nature, Arsinoë's influence on her brother was internationally recognized (*Syll.*[3] 434–5. 15). In her honour, the *Fayūm was renamed the Arsinoite nome and Philadelphia so named. Her career was marked by ambition and political deftness, her death memorialized by *Callimachus (fr. 228 Pf.) and the festival of the Arsinoeia. A recent attempt to redate her death to 268 (Grzybek, *Calendrier macédonien* (1990) 103–20) has not met universal acceptance.

D.J.T.

Artemisia (1), early 5th-cent. BC ruler, under Persian suzerainty, over Halicarnassus, Cos, Nisyrus, and Calymnos: Hdt. 7. 99 (which implies 6. 43 is exaggerated: 'democracies' installed in Ionia and Caria (west and southwest Asia Minor) after the Ionian Revolt from Persia of 499–494 BC). In the Persian Wars, Artemisia accompanied Xerxes' expedition with five ships. According to the Halicarnassian *Herodotus she was a 'warner' figure, who unsuccessfully urged Xerxes not to fight at Salamis, but fought bravely and escaped by sinking a ship in her way. The ship was Calyndian (*not* Calymnian), from a place on the border between Caria and Lycia. Xerxes remarked 'my men have become women and my women men' (Hdt. 8. 88). Afterwards she urged him to retreat and transported part of his family to Ephesus. Her son or nephew Lygdamis was still in power at Halicarnassus *c*.465–450 (ML 32 = Fornara 70).   P.T.; S.H.

Artemisia (2), daughter of Hecatomnus, ruled Caria (south-west Asia Minor) with her full brother and incestuous husband *Mausolus in the mid-4th cent. BC: *Ilabraunda* (1972), no. 40, joint decree in Greek ('it seemed good to Mausolus and Artemisia') conferring honours on Cnossus in Crete. He certainly used the Persian title satrap and she probably did too. At his death in 353 (when she succeeded him, ruling until 351) she was grief-stricken, supposedly drank his ashes (Gell. *NA* 10. 18), and organized a rhetorical funeral competition at which Theodectes, *Theopompus (the winner), and others performed; but the participant 'Isocrates' may not be the famous man of that name. She held down Rhodes, already absorbed into the Hecatomnid sphere of influence by Mausolus, and was the target of *Demosthenes' speech 15 (351) 'On the Freedom of the Rhodians', urging an attack on Caria to free the Rhodian democrats. She should share with her satrapal brothers and sister (Mausolus, Idrieus, Pixodarus, Ada) the responsibility for spreading Hellenism in Caria, while retaining the native cultural element, in the generation before *Alexander the Great.

S.H.

Asconius Pedianus, Quintus (AD 3–88: probable meaning of Jer. *Chron.* on 76, his death coming 12 years after the onset of blindness; the earliest reference to his activities may be Servius' remark (on *Ecl.* 4. 11) that Gaius Asinius Gallus (d. AD 33) told Asconius that *Virgil's fourth Eclogue was written in his honour); from Padua (Patavium) (*Livius noster* p. 77. 4 Clark; also Quint. 1. 7. 24). It is not known whether he had a public career, although he was certainly familiar with senatorial practice (e.g. 43. 27). His intimate knowledge of the city of Rome indicates that he spent many years there and possibly also composed his written work there. The only surviving work is part of a commentary (written AD 54–7) on *Cicero's speeches, preserved in the order *Pis.*, *Scaur.*, *Mil.*, *Corn.*, *Tog. Cand.*, and apparently much abbreviated. It is not known precisely how many

speeches received such attention, but it was certainly a considerable number. This commentary was written for his two sons, in preparation for public life. The sources used include Cicero himself (some speeches now lost) and the invaluable *acta* (a gazette, whose publication dates from before 59 BC) for speeches after 59 BC. Although his reliability has occasionally been impugned, the consensus still regards him as a priceless resource, both for his chronological proximity to Cicero and for the variety of important sources accessible to him. Other works attributed to Asconius are: (1) *Vita Sallustii* (ps.-Acron on Hor. *Sat.* 1. 2. 41); (2) a work possibly entitled *De longaevorum laude* or *Symposium* (Pliny, *HN* 7. 159; *Suda*, entry under Ἀπίκιος); (3) *Contra Vergilii obtrectatores* (Donat. *Vit. Verg.* 191, ed. C. Hardie, OCT). The manuscripts of the commentary on Cicero also contain a mainly grammatical work on *Verr.*, but this has been shown by Madvig to be a 5th-cent. compilation.

P.K.M.

Astydamas, the name of two tragic poets of the 4th cent. BC, father and son. The father was the son of Morsimus, son of *Aeschylus' nephew Philocles. It appears that some of the information attached to the father in our sources properly belongs to the son. In that case all we know of the father is that he produced his first play in 398 and lived to be 60 (Diog. Laert. 4. 43. 5); and it was the son who was said to have been a pupil of *Isocrates before turning to tragedy, to have written 240 tragedies (but the number can hardly be right), and to have won fifteen victories.

The younger Astydamas was one of the most successful poets of his day. He won his first victory in 372, and others are recorded in inscriptions. After the success of his *Parthenopaeus* (340) the Athenians honoured him with a statue in the theatre (part of the base survives), but he was not allowed to inscribe on it the conceited epigram which made him a byword for vanity (D. L. Page, *Further Greek Epigrams* (1990), 33–4). *Aristotle (*Poet.* 14) tells us that his *Alcmaeon* made the hero kill his mother unwittingly (when the usual version makes him do so deliberately). An especially famous play was the *Hector*, based on parts of *Homer's *Iliad*: it is believed to be depicted on an Apulian vase and attested in three papyri, and *Plutarch speaks of it (*De glor. Ath.* 7) in the same breath as Aeschylus and *Sophocles.

A.L.B.

Athenaeus (fl. *c.* AD 200), of Naucratis in Egypt. His only extant work, *Deipnosophistai* ('The Learned Banquet'), was probably completed in the years immediately following the death of the emperor Commodus in AD 192; other chronological inferences are uncertain. It belongs to the polyhistoric variety of the symposium form, practised earlier by *Aristoxenus and *Didymus. It is now in fifteen books (originally perhaps 30); there is also an Epitome, which covers existing gaps. At the 'banquet', which extends over several days, philosophy, literature, law, medicine, and other interests are represented by a large number of guests, who in some cases bear historical names (most notably *Galen); a Cynic philosopher is introduced as a foil. The Roman host, Larensis, probably the author's patron, is attested epigraphically (*CIL* 6. 212). The sympotic framework, if not devoid of occasional humour, is subordinate in interest to the collections of excerpts which are introduced into it. These relate to all the materials and accompaniments of convivial occasions; they are drawn from a vast number of authors, especially of the Middle and New Comedy, whose works are now lost; they are valuable both as literature and as illustrating earlier Greek manners. The order of these extracts sometimes suggests the use of lexica (Didymus, Pamphilus) or of *didaskaliai* (lists of dramatic productions), as well as of lists of *Kōmōdoumenoi* (people made fun of in comedy); but Athenaeus has collected much independently from the great writers; he cites some 1,250 authors, gives the titles of more than 1,000 plays, and quotes more than 10,000 lines of verse.

W.M.E.; R.B.; N.G.W.

Attalus I (269–197 BC), ruler of Pergamum (241–197), the first Pergamene to use the royal title. Cousin and adopted son of *Eumenes I, Attalus expanded and consolidated his kingdom through active self-defence policies, successfully fighting against some of the Galatians before *c.*230 (to whom he had first refused customary payments) and against the Seleucid king Antiochus Hierax before 227, a success which temporarily brought all Seleucid Asia Minor north of the Taurus into his sphere of influence. Most of this he lost again

to Seleucus III and Achaeus from 223–212, though an agreement with *Antiochus III the Great against Achaeus (216) seems to have recognized Attalus' rights to Mysia and Aeolis, where Pergamene rule was re-established or consolidated. Friendly contacts with cities in Ionia and Hellespontine Phrygia were established, though hostility to the Bithynian kingdom was permanent. In Pergamum itself victories were celebrated by Attalus' taking the title 'Soter' ('Saviour') and with monuments of spectacular expense and artistic quality (e.g. the 'Dying Gaul'); demonstrative investment at Delphi (a prominent stoa might be connected with these victories) brought friendship with Aetolia, where he financed at least one fort before 219. At Athens he dedicated on the Acropolis a series of statues setting his Galatian victory into the Greek context of victory against Giants, Amazons, and Persians (though this dedication might be later). These Greek connections involved him with Aetolia and Rome in the First Macedonian War. He provided ships, gained Aegina (209), became honorary *stratēgos* (chief magistrate) of the Aetolian Confederacy and was included among Roman friends in the Peace of Phoenice (205). He instrumentalized his Roman connection when *Philip V developed his Aegean policy after 204, largely at the expense of Pergamum and Rhodes. Attalus' appeal (with Rhodes) helped bring Rome back to Greece for the Second Macedonian War (200–197), in which Attalus personally and his fleet actively participated. His diplomacy brought Athens (where a tribe was named Attalis after him), the Achaeans, and Sparta into alliance with Rome. He died suddenly at Thebes while courting Boeotia (spring 197). He left four sons, *Eumenes II, *Attalus II, Philetaerus, and Athenaeus.

R.M.E.

Attalus II (220–138 BC), king of Pergamum (158–138), second son of *Attalus I, called 'Philadelphus' ('Brother-loving'). Attalus served under his brother *Eumenes II as loyal general against *Antiochus III the Great, the Galatians, Prusias I of Bithynia, and Pharnaces I of Pontus, and as diplomat, especially in Rome, where after 167 some senators favoured him against Eumenes. As king—he bore the title already in Eumenes' lifetime—he married Eumenes' widow Stratonice and adopted her son Attalus. He recognized

Roman paramountcy and acted accordingly: he restored Ariarathes V to Cappadocia, supported Alexander Balas against Demetrius I in Syria (153–150), Nicomedes II of Bithynia against Prusias II (149), whom with Roman help he had recently defeated, and sent troops against Andriscus (148) and to Corinth (146). He founded Philadelphia in Lydia and Attaleia (Antalya) in Pamphylia, continued Eumenes' building programme at Pergamum and the tradition of magnificent gifts to Greek cities and shrines (e.g. the 'Stoa of Attalus' at Athens).   R.M.E.

Attalus III (c.170–133 BC), son of *Eumenes II, last king of Pergamum (138–133), who bequeathed his kingdom to Rome. Called 'Philometor' ('Mother-lover') because of his close relationship to Stratonice, he was allegedly unpopular and had a reputation for being brutal and uninterested in public affairs, though given early experience by *Attalus II, devoting himself rather to scientific study, especially botany and pharmacology. His will, modelled on that of *Ptolemy VIII, may have been a dramatic attempt by the childless king to curb opposition, which however broke out with violence under Aristonicus after Attalus' premature natural death in 133.   R.M.E.

Atticus, Titus Pomponius, b. 110 BC as the son of a cultured *eques* (Roman Knight) of a family claiming descent from the legendary Roman king Pompilius Numa, was later adopted by a rich uncle (Quintus Caecilius), whose wealth he inherited. He was a friend of *Cicero from boyhood (Cicero's brother Quintus married Atticus' sister), and Cicero's *Letters to Atticus*, probably published in the reign of *Nero (though parts were known to some before), are the best source for his character, supplemented by an encomiastic biographical sketch by his friend Nepos (see CORNELIUS NEPOS). In 85 Atticus left Italy after selling his assets there, in order to escape the civil disturbances he foresaw. He lived in Athens until the mid-60s (hence his *cognomen* or surname), among other things studying Epicurean philosophy (see EPICURUS), to which however he never wholly committed himself. Henceforth he combined a life of cultured ease (*otium*) with immense success in various business activities and an infallible instinct for survival. He privately urged

Cicero to determined action on behalf of the optimates (lit. 'the best men'), with whom he sympathized, but himself refused to take sides in politics and personally assisted many prominent politicians from *Marius to Octavian (see AUGUSTUS), without regard for their differences and conflicts. He was Cicero's literary adviser and had his works copied and distributed. He himself wrote a *Liber Annalis* (a chronological table of world, and especially Roman, history), which became a standard work, eulogistic histories of some noble families, and minor works. (All are lost.) He lived to become a friend of *Agrippa, who married his daughter. In 32 he committed suicide when incurably ill.

        E.B.

Augustine, St (Aurelius Augustinus) (AD 354–430), was born at Thagaste (mod. Souk Ahras, Algeria), son of Patricius, a modest town councillor of pagan beliefs, and a dominant Catholic mother, Monica. Educated at Thagaste, Madauros, and Carthage, he taught rhetoric at Thagaste, Carthage, and Rome and (384–6) as public orator at Milan, then the capital of the emperor Valentinian II. Patronized at Rome by *Symmachus, the pagan orator, he hoped, by an advantageous marriage (to which he sacrificed his concubine, the mother of a son, Adeodatus—d. c.390) to join the 'aristocracy of letters' typical of his age (see AUSONIUS). At 19, however, he had read the *Hortensius* of *Cicero. This early 'conversion to philosophy' was the prototype of successive conversions: to Manicheism, a Gnostic sect promising Wisdom, and, in 386, to a Christianized Neoplatonism patronized by *Ambrose, bishop of Milan. Catholicism, for Augustine, was the 'Divine Philosophy', a Wisdom guaranteed by authority but explored by reason: 'Seek and ye shall find', the only scriptural citation in his first work, characterizes his life as a thinker.

Though the only Latin philosopher to fail to master Greek, Augustine transformed Latin Christianity by his Neoplatonism: his last recorded words echo *Plotinus. Stimulated by abrupt changes—he was forcibly ordained priest of Hippo in 391, becoming bishop in 395—and by frequent controversies, Augustine developed his ideas with an independence that disquieted even his admirers. He has left his distinctive mark on most aspects of western Christianity.

Augustine's major works are landmarks in the abandonment of Classical ideals. His early optimism was soon overshadowed by a radical doctrine of grace. This change was canonized in an autobiographical masterpiece, the *Confessions* (*c.*397–400), a vivid if highly selective source for his life to 388 and, equally, a mirror of his changed outlook. *De doctrina Christiana* (begun 396/7) sketched a literary culture subordinated to the Bible. *De Trinitate* (399–419) provided a more radically philosophical statement of the doctrine of the Trinity than any Greek Father. *De civitate Dei* (413 to 426) presented a definitive juxtaposition of Christianity with literary paganism and Neoplatonism, notably with *Porphyry. After 412, he combated in Pelagianism views which, 'like the philosophers of the pagans', had promised men fulfilment by their unaided efforts. In his *Retractationes* (427) Augustine criticized his superabundant output of 93 works in the light of a Catholic orthodoxy to which he believed he had progressively conformed—less consistently, perhaps, than he realized.

Letters and verbatim sermons richly document Augustine's complex life as a bishop; the centre of a group of sophisticated ascetics (notably Paulinus of Nola, the 'slave' of a simple congregation, he was, above all, a man dedicated to the authority of the Catholic Church. This authority had enabled his restless intellect to work creatively: he would uphold it, in Africa, by every means, from writing a popular song to elaborating the only explicit justification in the early Church of a policy of religious persecution.

J.F.Ma.

Augustus (63 BC–AD 14), the first emperor at Rome, who presided over the inception of much of the institutional and ideological framework of the imperial system of the first three centuries AD. The long survival of his system, and its association with a literary milieu that came to be regarded as the golden age of Latin literature, make him a uniquely important figure in Roman history, but no narrative history of his lifetime survives except for the account of *Cassius Dio (incomplete 6 BC–AD 14), and the rest of the evidence is very deeply imbued with partisan spirit of various kinds. An estimation of his personal contribution is hard to achieve.

Born Gaius Octavius, son of a *novus homo*

or first man of his family to reach the senate (C. Octavius, praetor 61, d. 59) from Velitrae in the Alban Hills, as a young man he was typical enough of the milieu of junior senators in the third quarter of the 1st cent., perceiving that the way to success lay through the support of the great dynasts for their agents and followers. In this he had a head start: his mother Atia (of a family from Aricia, next door to Velitrae) was the daughter of *Julius Caesar's sister, which made Gaius Octavius one of the closest young male relatives of the dictator, a connection emphasized when in 51 BC he gave the funeral oration for his maternal grandmother. In 47 he was made *pontifex* (priest); with Caesar in Spain in 45, he was enrolled as a patrician, and when the dictator drew up his will (13 September 45) he adopted the 17-year-old Octavius and made him his heir. The young man spent the winter in study at Apollonia in Dalmatia, but reacted with decision and alacrity when Caesar was murdered and the will read. Over the next months he consolidated his position as the leader of the friends of Caesar, commemorating his adoptive father, and wooing his veterans; a course of action which brought him into conflict with Mark *Antony, and support of the cause against him which was victorious at Mutina (April 43), after which he seized the consulship by force. At Bononia the differences between him, Antony, and M. *Lepidus were resolved and the Triumvirate established. The next years were marked by the crushing of Antony's brother Lucius Antonius (Pietas) and *Fulvia at Perusia (Perugia), with singular violence, the settling of veterans on confiscated land, and the proscriptions (published lists of citizens who were declared outlaws and whose goods were confiscated), in which he was as ruthless as the others. He married Scribonia as a gesture to Sextus *Pompey, and she bore his only child *Julia (in 39 he divorced her to marry *Livia); to seal the political dispositions made at Brundisium in October 40 Antony married his sister Octavia. All the politicians of the time made use of *imperium* (supreme military and civil authority), one of the only surviving constitutional principles of any potency, and Caesar's heir now took the first name Imperator.

Over the 30s, events combined with astute responses enabled Imp. Caesar to represent himself as defender of an Italian order. His principal local rival for this position, Sex. Pompeius (finally defeated at Naulochus in 36), he represented as a pirate-leader. He took advantage of his control of the ancient centre of *imperium* and (especially through the singular post-consular aedilate of *Agrippa in 33) maintained the favour of the disaffected and volatile *populus* (people) who still in theory granted it. After a half-hearted attempt to attain some military reputation against a foreign enemy (the Illyrians) he turned to representing Antony in Alexandria as alien, immoral, and treacherous. In 32 a formal oath expressed the mass loyalty of Italy to his cause. The advantages of this policy were not wholly symbolic. Italy offered material resources, manpower, and the land with which to reward its loyalty. Imp. Caesar and his close supporters of these years and afterwards (especially Agrippa, Titus Statilius Taurus, and *Maecenas) were victorious against Antony, whose pro-Egyptian policy and failure in Armenia had lost him much of his eastern support. The battle of Actium (31 BC) was the turning-point; the capture of Alexandria in the next year ended the war and led to the incorporation of Egypt in the *imperium*. Victory in the east, the vindication of his political promises in Italy, and the booty of the Ptolemies gave him an unassailable position, soon expressed in terms of divinity.

From his consulship of 31 (he held it every year down to 23) there began a down-playing of the irregularity of the triumviral system, which culminated in a formal restitution of the *res publica* (constitutional organs of state), a restoration in the sense of repair or revival rather than a return to a different constitution. He returned to Rome in mid-29, triumphed, beautified the city by the dedication of important temples, and signalled an end to war by the closing of the temple of Janus. Agrippa was his colleague in the consulship for 28 and 27: at the beginning of 27 he made the formal gesture of reinstating the magistrates, senate (reduced in numbers through a purge of undesirable elements), and people in their old constitutional role. In return he received a major grant of proconsular *imperium*, and many honours, including the name Augustus, and departed to carry out the military duties of his new command.

Before 7 BC Augustus spent a great deal of time in the provinces (only in 23, 18, 17, and 12 did he spend the whole year in Rome, and he was absent for the whole of 26/5, 21/0, and 15/4). The Civil Wars had shown that power at Rome was to be won in the provinces, and with ever greater numbers of Roman citizens outside Italy, Augustus had to form an empire-wide system. The creation of a huge proconsular province on the model of the commands of Pompey and the triumvirs, which gave Augustus *imperium* over most of the troops of the *res publica*, was the core of this, and the most important part of the 'settlement' of 27. Delegation was essential in so unwieldy an entity, and, like his predecessors, Augustus appointed senatorial legates and equestrian prefects to serve his *imperium*. If these men ran units which were analogous to the *provinciae* of the proconsuls who continued to be sent to the parts of the Roman dominion that lay outside Augustus' command, that is not to say that the settlement envisaged two types of province. Such an innovation would have been far less subtle than the skill with which the legal flexibility of the assignment of proconsular commands and the convenient precedents of the previous generation were adapted to Augustus' purpose.

There were difficulties, since holders of *imperium* had been accustomed to a greater independence than Augustus could afford to allow them. Already in 30 the claim of M. Licinius Crassus to the *spolia opima* (spoils offered by a Roman general who had slain an enemy leader in single combat) had tested the limits of self-determination; this bid for an antique honour was, characteristically, thwarted by a display of greater erudition from Augustus. Egypt's temptations proved too much for even the equestrian prefect C. *Cornelius Gallus (26). M. Primus came to grief because his informal instructions were inconsistent (*c.*24). In 23, again following the precedent of *Pompey, the proconsular *imperium* was clearly labelled *maius* (superior), which also clarified the position of the other holders under Augustus of wide-ranging commands, such as Agrippa and Gaius Julius Caesar, the elder son of Agrippa and Julia.

The maintenance of the loyalty of the soldiers finally depended on Augustus' capacity to pay them. That in turn depended on the organization of revenues so that they would regularly accrue to him directly. A simple fiscal logic thus operated which transformed the empire: previously, the maintaining of cash flows to the centre, where they might be squandered by one's enemies, was of little interest to provincial governors. Now, the efficiency of the exaction system was the only guarantee of the survival of the new order. The whole world was enrolled, and noticed it (Luke 2: 1, even if the process was not so sudden as the experience of Judaea implied). Taxation was reformed and new provinces made so that their tribute might swell Augustus' takings. The enthusiastic imposition of such burdens caused rebellion and disaster, especially in Germany. A military treasury on the Capitol announced the theoretical centrality of the fiscal arrangements to the whole empire from AD 6.

The incorporations of this period doubled the size of the provincial empire: NW Spain and the provinces of the Alps and the Alpine foreland, Raetia, Noricum, and Pannonia, with Germania and Moesia beyond them, saw most of the military aggression, the provincialization of Galatia and Judaea being relatively peaceful. A reasonably high level of military activity was a sensible ingredient in Augustan political strategy, and provided the glory which fuelled the *auctoritas* (prestige) of the ruling cadre. Some of this took the form of expeditions which bore no fruit in terms of the all-important taxation, either directly (or in some cases ever): like Augustus' own trip to the Danube (35–33 BC), Aelius Gallus' Arabian campaign (25–24), and the wars in southern Egypt of Cornelius Gallus (29) and Gaius Petronius (25). The main point of such trips was the glamour of the geography and ethnography, celebrated in poetry and on Agrippa's map, which propagated the belief that Augustus' Rome ruled the whole inhabited world. This impression was reinforced by Augustus' generally successful use (continued in the east from Antony's careful practice) of the traditional diplomatic relations with local magnates, kings, or communities, in places outside the direct *imperium* of a Roman governor. Ritual courtesies on both sides could suggest that the empire included India or Britain, and had a practical role in settling outstanding issues with Parthia in 20 in a negotiation which Augustus made a great deal of. When a serious military threat appeared, in the shape of the Pannonian Revolt, 'the worst war since those against Carthage', or the German war that followed the massacre of *Quinctilius Varus and his three legions, the system all but collapsed.

For all his absences, Rome itself was at the heart of Augustus' vision. City-foundations in the provinces, and benefactions to existing *coloniae* (colonies) and *municipia* (municipalities), encouraged the imitation of the metropolis and the recognition of that constituency of Italians spread across the Mediterranean world that had played such a vital part in the Civil Wars. He could not avoid a real concern for the urban populace of Rome itself, who caused major disturbances of the traditional kind at intervals throughout his ascendancy. In 23, the choice of *tribunicia potestas* (tribunician power) as the 'indication of the highest station', and the way in which Augustus counted the years of his 'reign' thereafter, signalled also his descent from the *populares* (popular politicians) of the late republic, many of whose policies he continued (albeit sometimes with a show of reluctance): he made provision against famine, fire, and flood, and reorganized the districts of the city (spreading his own cult in the process). The popular assembly duly ratified his legislation, and was represented *en masse* in displays of loyalty at important moments.

*Varro had taught the Romans to be at home in their own city, and Augustus was an eager interpreter of the process. The ancient messages of cult and civic ritual offered many opportunities, which he was making use of already in the 30s. After Actium the serious development of the cult of Palatine Apollo as a parallel for Capitoline Jupiter, and the restoration of dozens of Rome's ancient sanctuaries; after 12 – when he finally became *Pontifex Maximus* (head of the college of priests) on the death of Lepidus – the formation of the House of the Pater Patriae, in 2 BC the inauguration of a replacement forum, to which many state ceremonies were removed; throughout the creation of a 'suburb more beautiful than the city' on the Campus Martius, for the amenity of the populace: the reduplication of Rome's glories cleverly allowed him to be a new founder without damaging the old system, and to surpass all past builders and benefactors without the solecism of departing from or belittling their precedent. He thus underlined his relationship with the previous centuries of Roman history in a Roman Whig history that culminated in his ascendancy.

His management of *lex* (statute) was equally historic: giving his name to far more *leges* than any legislator before him, and announcing his control of the legislative assembly in the process, he became the city-founding lawgiver of the new Rome. The control of religion, that mirror of the *res publica*, was the interpretative vehicle of much of this, and learning, interpretation, and doctrine, of law or ritual precedent, history or geography, were the indispensable servants of all these projects. Hence the cultural and literary acme that later generations of Romans perceived at this epoch. These processes came together in the pivotal years 19–17 BC, when he had made the last modifications to his position in the *res publica*, settled the eastern and western provinces, and acquired his first grandson (Gaius Caesar). Now came the ethical and social laws, and in 17 the great celebration of the divine diuturnity that the Fates had given to Rome by making her populace virtuous and therefore fecund, in the *ludi saeculares* or Secular Games.

His concern for the institutions of state allowed him to insert himself into the annals of Roman history as a continuator or reformer rather than as an intruder or revolutionary, while the inherent flexibility of the institutions gave him a wonderful repertoire of gambits both for shaping opportunities for political success for his supporters and for social promotion, of which the most important form of all was the identification of a successor to his office. The very happy accident of his long life allowed readjustment of many of his innovations in a process of trial and error, a refining process which explains the success and long survival of many of them: the city prefect (*praefectus urbi*), the public postal service, the fire brigade (*vigiles*), and so on.

The arrangement of a successor proved the most difficult task of all. The calculation of *auctoritas* in which he excelled, and which his very name evoked, entailed that no merely dynastic principle could be guaranteed; it would belittle his own carefully constructed practical reputation for real ability to have a successor who owed everything, as he had done, to a name. At the same time he had been unable (and had perhaps not wanted) to avoid accumulating honours for his family, and using for that very consolidation of *auctoritas* the image of a Father and the model of the state as a super-household, one conducted like his own and under his benign but omnicompetent tutelage. There was in the end a dissonance between the role of those who had to be permitted to acquire the necessary *auctoritas* to maintain the image of effective governance, especially through largely factitious military escapades, and the need to rely on his own blood-line to keep alive the charisma of his own divine associations. Agrippa was a compliant assistant in the public sphere, and Livia happy and expert at propagating the necessary pictures in the private; but *Tiberius and *Drusus, Livia's children by her first marriage, were not good at being second fiddle, and Julia, his daughter and only child, on whom the whole dynastic construction relied, nearly wrecked the whole thing by probably calculated sexual misbehaviour. This called into question the credentials of the model family, the legitimacy of her offspring, and the feasibility of using ethics as a constitutional strategy, while potentially irradiating her partners (who included Antony's son Iullus Antonius) with her share of the ancestral charisma.

The dynastic policy was not overtly monarchic either, however, and what saved Augustus was the fact that he had (since he did not have the option of destroying them wholesale) re-created the Roman aristocracy and given them a new role in his social system. As an antidote to the Civil War social mobility was to be curbed; freedmen were discouraged from promotion, the *plebs* was indulged but controlled; the two upper classes were encouraged to procreate, and each had its precise place in the religious system, at the theatre, and in government. As an ornament to the whole thing, and to camouflage the prerogatives that he ascribed to his own family, survivors of the great lines of the historic Roman past were encouraged to live up to their ancestors' images, and given an honorific but circumscribed part to play in a system whose regulation, through his censorial function, it was Augustus' job to manage. Hence—and the power derived also from his fatherly pretensions—the ethical content of much of his legislation, which did the nobility the credit of thinking them worthy of the past while giving their arbiter a useful way of coercing them if they failed to live up to it. The seeds of the disastrous use of the laws on adultery and *maiestas* (treason) over the next generations were therefore sowed by Augustus, who was not himself faced by any very coherent opposition.

Later authors dated the establishment of the imperial monarchy to 31 or 27 BC. In many ways, as Augustus probably saw, and Tacitus appreciated, the new arrangements, many times modified, and threatened by diverse instability, could not be regarded as established until someone had succeeded to them, and then shown himself willing to continue their essentials. Although the *optimus status* ('best state of affairs') was in most respects in place by the climax of the legislative phase and the announcement of the *saeculum* in 17, and the pinnacle of *auctoritas* was commemorated in 2 BC, the Augustan empire could have been dissolved in AD 14. The achievement of Augustus lay in the flexibility with which he and his advisers responded to a period of striking social change in the Mediterranean world, the legacy of the Roman/Italian diaspora of the previous century. But in controlling a dynamic process there is more continuity and less revolution than is usual in the foundation of a monarchy, and that may well help to account for the stability of the system that Augustus' successors developed out of his innovations.

N.P.

Aurelian (Lucius Domitius Aurelianus) (*c.* AD 215–75), a man of humble origin from the Danubian region, achieved high military rank under *Gallienus, but helped organize the plot that destroyed him. Appointed by Claudius II Gothicus (emperor AD 268–70) to the chief command of the cavalry, he served with distinction against the Goths. Though Aurelian was the obvious successor to Claudius, he did not immediately declare himself on the latter's death, allowing the throne to pass to Quintillus. However, it was not long before he was hailed as emperor by his troops and disposed of his rival (*c.* September 270).

Barbarian invasions first claimed his attention. He defeated the Vandals in Pannonia and then repulsed a dangerous incursion into Italy by the Alamanni and Iuthungi, pursuing the latter over the Danube. On his return to Rome, he surrounded the city with walls to protect it against further barbarian attacks (the 'wall of Aurelian'). With characteristic ruthlessness, he also disposed of early political opponents to his rule.

He next dealt with Palmyra. *Zenobia, ruling for her young son, Septimius Vaballathus, had recently exploited Roman civil war to occupy Egypt and Asia Minor up to Bithynia (autumn 270). Coins and papyri show that she was now calling Vaballathus Imperator, but not Augustus, and was projecting him as the—albeit junior—colleague of Aurelian. Aurelian tolerated the compromise for only as long as he had to; early in 272 he marched east. Following defeat at Antioch on the Orontes, Zenobia withdrew south, and proclaimed Vaballathus Augustus (spring 272). Aurelian pursued the rebels to Emesa, broke their main strength, and forced them to take refuge in Palmyra, which he then besieged. In summer 272, Zenobia was captured on her way to seek aid from Persia, and Palmyra surrendered.

Marching back westward, Aurelian defeated the Carpi on the Danube, but was recalled by a further revolt in Palmyra (spring 273). He quickly crushed the uprising, and then proceeded to Egypt to suppress violent disturbances possibly associated with the rebellion in Palmyra.

Aurelian now turned west and ended the Gallic empire at Châlons, defeating Tetricus (early 274). Tetricus and Zenobia headed the captives from all Aurelian's victories in a magnificent triumph.

Early in 275 Aurelian set out against Persia, but was murdered at Caenophrurium, near Byzantium, in a household plot. Some time passed before Tacitus was appointed to succeed him—the army offering the choice to the senate, the senate shirking the dangerous responsibility.

Aurelian's energy and military talents restored the unity of the empire after a decade of division; and he was more than just a successful general. Towards the end of his reign (274) he had the courage to abandon the old province of Dacia—by now reduced to the Transylvanian highlands—and relocate its garrison, civilian administrators, and those of the rest of the population able and willing to join the evacuation, south of the Danube. He sought to reform the silver coinage, much damaged by 40 years of continual debasement. And, with the help of the booty won from Palmyra, he attempted to establish the worship of Sol Invictus—with himself as this deity's chosen vicegerent—at the centre of Roman state religion (see ELAGABALUS). Thus in many ways he pioneered the work of Diocletian and Constantine I; yet he lacked the originality to bring the period of 'crisis' to its conclusion. His murder was followed by a further ten years of uncertainty.

J.F.Dr.

Aurelius, Marcus See MARCUS AURELIUS.

Aurelius Antoninus, Marcus See (1) CARA-CALLA, (2) ELAGABALUS.

Aurelius Severus Alexander See SEVERUS ALEXANDER.

Ausonius, Decimus Magnus, of Bordeaux (Burdigala), statesman, teacher, and writer, enjoyed one of the more meteoric careers of the 4th cent. AD. The son of a humble doctor, he taught grammar and rhetoric for 30 years before being appointed tutor of the emperor's son and heir and summoned to Trier (Augusta Treverorum) in the mid-360s. When in 375 Valentinian I died and Gratian duly succeeded, Ausonius enjoyed a remarkable political ascendancy, placing family and friends in positions of influence and gaining for himself a praetorian prefecture and the consulship of 379. Most of his retirement he spent cultivating literary friendships in Aquitaine and writing poems which shed interesting light on his outlook and environment.

His rather obscure politics have always attracted less attention than his writings, which apart from a panegyric of Gratian and a few of his letters and dedications, are all in verse. His longest and most famous poem is the *Moselle*, a lively and colourful description relatively untouched by contemporary tendencies to flatter or plagiarize. Experiences in Trier supposedly also inspired *Cupido cruciatus* ('Cupid in Torment') based on a wall-painting, and the *Bissula*, both (for him) mildly erotic. The later *Ordo urbium nobilium* ('Catalogue of Famous Cities') shows in an extreme form his tendency to enumerate, as do his *Caesares* and *Fasti* (on the Roman consuls). Works such as the *Technopaegnion* ('game of skill'—poem whose form mimics the shape of an object), the *Ludus Septem Sapientum* ('Play of the Seven Sages'), *Griphus ternarii numeri* ('Riddle of the Number Three'), and the so-called *Eclogues*, may derive from classroom practice. He compiled an ingenious and provocative Virgilian 'nuptial cento' (poem made up of recognizable extracts from existing poems), and his epigrams include translations from the Greek and a few Greek compositions of his own. More solemn are various poems about his close family, a commemoration of deceased relatives in the *Parentalia*, and the obituaries of local teachers in the *Professores*. The *Ephemeris* ('Daily Round') is a kind of self-portrait, but one more notable for its literary colour and metrical variety than any intimate personal detail; consul or not, Ausonius likes to put on the traditional guise of the easily contented man. The long and powerful Christian prayer embedded in this work is by no means the only evidence of a Christian allegiance, evidently combined with a lively interest in the traditional Graeco-Roman deities.

Ausonius often asks to be read in a jovial spirit and small doses. Together with great wit and originality, he shows a strong local patriotism and an appreciation of his classical heritage unsurpassed in late antiquity.

R.P.H.G.

Bb

Bacchylides (*c.*520–450 BC), lyric poet, of Iulis in Ceos, son of Midon (or Midylus, *Etym. Magn.* 582, 20), nephew of *Simonides (Strabo 486, *Suda*, entry under Βακχυλίδης). His floruit was given as 480 by *Chron. Pasch.* 162b (304. 6), as 467 and 451 by *Eusebius–Jerome (the entry in Eusebius, *Chron.* Ol. 87.2 = 431 BC, refers to a flute-player Bacchylides mentioned by the comic poet Plato in his *Sophistai*, fr. 149 KA, *PCG* 7. 494, see G. Fatouros, *Philol.* 1961, 147). The assumption that he was younger than *Pindar (Eust. *Prooem. ad Pind.* 25 = schol. Pind. 3, p. 297. 13 Dr.) is unfounded and unlikely in view of the early date of his poem in praise of the young prince Alexander, son of Amyntas (fr. 20b Snell–Maehler), who succeeded his father as king of Macedonia in *c.*494. Although Bacchylides was one of the canonical nine lyric poets (*Anth. Pal.* 9. 184 and 571; schol. Pind. 1, p. 11. 20 Dr.), and although he was well known in Hellenistic and Roman times (imitated by Horace *Carm.* 1. 15, quoted by Strabo, Plutarch, [Longinus], *Subl.* and by the emperor *Julian who 'enjoyed reading him', as Amm. Marc. 25. 4. 3 says), only a handful of lines had survived in quotations when a papyrus containing his book of victory odes almost complete and the first half of his book of dithyrambs was found at Meïr, near Al-Kussīah, south of Hermopolis, in 1896 and published by F. G. Kenyon in 1897. Since then, remains of fifteen more papyri have been attributed to him, and two papyri contain scholia on his epinician odes and dithyrambs. The known dates of his epinician odes are: 476 (5, for Hieron's horse-race victory at Olympia, also celebrated by Pindar, *Ol.* 1), 470 (4, for Hieron's chariot victory at Delphi, for which Pindar sent *Pyth.* 1), 468 (3, for Hieron's chariot victory at Olympia), and 452 (6, for Lachon's sprint victory as a boy at Olympia); likely dates are: *c.*485 (13) and 454 or 452 (1 and 2); the Third Dithyramb (17, 'The Youths' or 'Theseus') seems to date from the early 490s; it is really a paean sung by a Cean choir at Delos. Bacchylides spent some time in exile in the Peloponnese (Plut. *De exil.* 14). Like Simonides and Pindar, he may have stayed at Syracuse as Hieron's guest (Ael. *VH* 4. 15), but the alleged rivalry between him and Pindar seems to be a figment of some ancient biographers.

His patrons, apart from Hieron of Syracuse, included athletes from Ceos, Aegina, Phlius in the Peloponnese, Metapontum in south Italy, and Thessaly; a poem in honour of a magistrate of Larissa seems to have been added at the end of the book (14b, cf. Pindar's *Nem.* 11). Several of his dithyrambs were composed for competitions at Athens (15?, 18, 19, 23?), one for Sparta (20). The Alexandrian editors gave them titles and arranged them in alphabetical order. Stylistically, his dithyrambs are like ballads, using lively narrative, often allusive and selective, as well as direct speech. They exploit the pathetic potential of the myths, as do those epinician odes which contain a mythical narrative as their centre-piece. *Dith.* 2 (16, 'Heracles' or 'Deianira'?) appears to assume familiarity with *Sophocles' *Trachiniai*; *Dith.* 4 (18, 'Theseus') is unique in being a dialogue between the chorus as people of Athens and the chorus leader, their king, Aegeus; this may have been influenced by Attic drama (plays like Aesch. *Supp.* or *Pers.*), rather than being an archaic form of dithyramb. Bacchylides also wrote hymns (frs. 1–3), paeans, of which fr. 4 + 22 contains a fine eulogy of peace, processional songs (frs. 11–13), maiden-songs (Plut. [*De mus.*] 17), dancing-songs (hyporchemata, frs. 14–16), songs about love (erotica, frs. 17–19) and songs of praise (encomia?, frs. 20–20f). *Didymus wrote a commentary on the epinician odes and probably also on other books. The textual transmission must have broken off sometime in the Roman period; later authors like *Athenaeus and *Clement of Alexandria seem to quote from anthologies.

H.Ma.

Basil of Caesarea (in Cappadocia), *c*. AD 330–79 (the dates are debated but not disproved). He is honoured as the chief architect of monastic life in the Greek Church. His early education was completed at Athens, where he came under the influence of Himerius and Prohaeresius. He was also instructed briefly by *Libanius. Those experiences marked him out for a teaching career, upon which he may have embarked. However, the influence of Eustathius of Sebaste and of travel in the eastern provinces inclined him to the practice of asceticism, which he undertook in the company of his friend Gregory of Nazianzus. His education bore fruit, nevertheless, in his *Address to Young Men*, which discussed the adaptation of the classical curriculum to Christian use and enjoyed lasting influence. His ascetic experience was distilled chiefly in his *Long Rules* and *Short Rules*.

A growing interest in Church affairs drew him into the moderate party of Basil of Ancyra and encouraged him in lifelong loyalty to Meletius of Antioch. Within the general context of the Arian controversy, those associations made him less acceptable to both Alexandria and Rome. Nevertheless, he was remembered for his courageous resistance to the Arian emperor Valens and he did much to damage the reputation of the Arian theologian Eunomius.

He spent the whole of his priestly and episcopal career in Caesarea. In spite of his orthodoxy, he attracted the favour of Valens, who supported financially his extensive works of charity and sent him on an important mission to Armenia in 373. As a churchman, he strongly advocated and worked for unity but in conservative terms that were less convincing to ambitious peers.

His numerous letters are an important source for eastern provincial life at the time and reveal a man of delicacy, insight, and power. His homilies are much neglected and show a skilful combination of learning, style, and clarity. His crowning achievement was his *Hexaemeron*, which Ambrose paraphrased.   P.R.

Boethius, Anicius Manlius Severinus (*c*. AD 480–*c*.524). The Ostrogothic king Theoderic appointed this leading nobleman consul (510), and *magister officiorum* ('master of the offices', a very senior official with extensive responsibilities for the working of the central bureaucracy) (?522). Boethius resisted official oppression, was implicated in a senatorial conspiracy, imprisoned, and executed. His *De consolatione philosophiae* is a prison dialogue with Philosophy, a mixture of prose and verse, owing much to *Martianus Capella and *Augustine. It justifies providence on a Stoic and Neoplatonic basis, without overt Christianity; its reconciliation of free will and divine prescience is philosophically notable; it shows high literary genius, and an astounding memory for classical texts under trying conditions. Boethius' Greek scholarship was rare in Italy; he planned introductions and translations for the mathematical and logical disciplines, and complete translations of *Plato and *Aristotle. The project was never completed, and much is lost or fragmentary. Survivors: *De arithmetica* and *Institutio musica* (on which see below); a commentary on *Cicero's *Topics*, translations and commentaries for *Porphyry's *Isagoge*, and Aristotle's *Prior Analytics*, *Categories*, and *Perihermeneias*; translations of Aristotle's *Topics* and *Sophistici elenchi*. Five treatises give Boethius' own introduction to Peripatetic logic. Literal translation and repetitive explanation made the philosophic corpus inelegant but serviceable; excepting *De syllogismis hypotheticis*, it is generally unoriginal. Boethius owed much to Alexandrian and Athenian Neoplatonists (especially Ammonius), but personal contact is unprovable. Involved in Christological controversies which had divided Rome and Constantinople, he wrote five theological *Tractates*; the fifth, the most original, favours the Theopaschite formula, aimed at reconciling Monophysites. Undervalued in his own day, Boethius wielded vast influence from Carolingian times onward, especially on Abelard; *De consolatione* was translated by King Alfred, Chaucer, and Elizabeth I.

                                                                                        S.J.B.B.

MUSICAL WRITINGS Boethius' *Institutio musica*, mainly paraphrased from Greek sources, deploys Pythagorean harmonics (see PYTHAGORAS), within the quadrivium, to promote understanding of music's extraordinary powers. Books 1–3 (introduction and mathematical demonstrations) and possibly book 4 (divisions of the monochord, modes) derive from a lost work by Nicomachus. Book 5 (incomplete) renders Claudius *Ptolemy *Harm.* 1, very selectively: perhaps *Harm.* 2–3 were intended to follow. Boethius' eloquent but difficult text became the foundation of medieval music theory.   A.D.B.

Boudicca (name uncertain, but 'Boadicea' has neither authority nor meaning), wife of Prasutagus, who was established as client king of the Iceni (East Anglia) by the Romans. On his death (AD 60/1) he had left the emperor co-heir with his daughters, but imperial agents maltreated his family. Under Boudicca the Iceni, assisted by the Trinov-antes (Essex), rose in rebellion while the gov-ernor, Suetonius Paulinus, was occupied in the west. Camulodunum (Colchester), Lond-inium (London), and Verulamium (St Albans) were successively sacked. Venturing a battle, however, with Paulinus' main force, Boudicca's troops were easily routed, and she herself took poison.   C.E.S.; M.J.M.

Brutus, Marcus Junius, son of Marcus Junius Brutus and of *Servilia, born (probably) 85 BC, was adopted by his uncle (?) Quintus Servilius Caepio by 59 and was henceforth called Quintus Caepio Brutus. Brought up by *Cato the Younger, he was educated in oratory and philosophy and long retained a fierce hatred for his father's mur-derer *Pompey. In 58 he accompanied Cato to Cyprus and in 56 lent a large sum to (Cypriot) Salamis at 48 per cent interest p.a., contrary to the Gabinian law, procuring a senate decree to validate the loan. As moneyer (perhaps 55) he issued coins showing Libertas and portraits of his ancestors Lucius Junius Brutus (who overthrew *Tarquinius Superbus) and Gaius Servilius Ahala, the tyr-annicide (*RRC* 433). As quaestor 53 he went to Cilicia with Appius Claudius Pulcher, whose daughter he had married, and there lent Ariobarzanes I a large sum, probably to enable him to pay interest on his huge debt to Pompey. When *Cicero succeeded Appius, he found that an agent of Brutus had been made prefect of cavalry to extort money from Salamis and that five Salaminian senators had been killed. He cancelled the appointment, but to avoid offence to Brutus gave a similar post to Brutus' agent in Cappadocia and rec-ognized the validity of the loan to Salamis (Cic. *Att.* 5. 21–6. 1). In 52 Brutus defended *Milo and in a pamphlet attacked Pompey's wish for a dictatorship, but in 50 they both defended Appius against Publius Cornelius

*Dolabella, and in 49 he joined the Repub-lican cause and was formally reconciled with Pompey. After the battle of Pharsalus he suc-cessfully begged Caesar for pardon and, no doubt through Servilia's influence, became one of his protégés. He was made a *pontifex* (member of one of the four chief colleges of the Roman priesthood) and in 47 sent to govern Cisalpine Gaul, while Caesar went to Africa to fight Cato and the republicans. During this time he developed relations with Cicero, who dedicated various philosophical and rhetorical works to him and, at his request, wrote a eulogy of Cato after Cato's death. (Finding it unsatisfactory, Brutus wrote one himself.) Although he now divorced Claudia and married Cato's daugh-ter *Porcia, widow of Marcus Calpurnius Bibulus, he remained on good terms with Caesar, met him on his return from Munda, assured Cicero of Caesar's laudable optimate intentions, and was made urban praetor for 44 and designated consul for 41. But when Caesar became dictator for life (February 44), Brutus, reminded of his heritage, joined, and *ex officio* took the lead in, the widespread conspiracy that led to Caesar's assassination before his departure for his Parthian War. Outmanœuvred by Mark *Antony, whose life he had spared on the Ides of March, he and *Cassius had to leave Rome and, failing to win popular approval, left Italy for Greece (August 44). With Antonius now openly against them, Brutus collected close to 400 million sesterces from the treasuries of Asia and Syria and confiscated the supplies Caesar had prepared for his campaign. He and Cassius gradually seized all the eastern prov-inces, building up large armies, partly of vet-erans. When Cicero, in his *Philippics*, swung the senate behind them, they received *imper-ium maius* (authority greater than that of other Roman magistrates in the east) in the east. Brutus captured, and later executed, Antony's brother Gaius Antonius; after Dola-bella's death he acquired Asia and completed its conquest, and during 43 and 42 squeezed it dry for his armies. The money was turned into a large coinage (*RRC* 500–8) and Brutus, alone among the republicans, put his own head on one of the gold coins. He also won the title of *imperator* ('commander', a title of honour) in Thrace. In 42 he and Cassius, with about 80,000 legionaries plus auxiliaries, twice met Antony and Octavian (the future

*Augustus) at Philippi (in northern Greece). In the first battle Cassius, defeated by Antony, committed suicide, while Brutus impressively defeated Octavian. In a second battle, forced on Brutus, he was defeated, deserted by his soldiers, and also committed suicide. His body was honourably treated by Antony.

Arrogant, rapacious, calculatingly ambitious, Brutus yet professed a deep attachment to philosophy. Cicero admired but never liked him, and ignored his warnings not to trust Octavian. A renowned orator, with an austere and dignified style, he despised Cicero's as 'effeminate and spineless' (Tac. *Dial.* 18. 5). His literary works (philosophy, historical epitomes, poetry) are lost, as are his letters, except for a few surviving among Cicero's. With Cassius, he was officially condemned under the empire, but revered by many as the last defender of Roman freedom.

E.B.

Cc

Caecilius Metellus Macedonicus See METELLUS MACEDONICUS.

Caecilius Metellus Numidicus See METELLUS NUMIDICUS.

Caelius Rufus, Marcus, born (probably) 88 or 87 BC at Interamnia (mod. Teramo), son of an *eques* or knight, did his *tirocinium fori* (apprenticeship to public life) under *Cicero and *Crassus. As one of a band of upper-class youths he was attracted to *Catiline, but did not join in his conspiracy. In 59 he successfully prosecuted Gaius Antonius Hybrida for extortion. Known for a dissolute and extravagant lifestyle, he was also active in politics and in 57/6 was somehow involved in the murder of an Alexandrian embassy opposing Ptolemy XII's restoration. For this he was prosecuted in 56 for violence by the son of Lucius Calpurnius Bestia, whom he had unsuccessfully prosecuted; a Publius Clodius, perhaps the famous *Clodius, joined as co-accuser. A vigorous orator, he defended himself and was defended by Crassus and (in a surviving speech) by Cicero, who depicted the prosecution as a plot hatched by *Clodia, with whom Caelius had had an affair. Caelius was acquitted and, in revenge, supported *Milo as tribune 52, and after Milo's conviction joined Cicero in securing the acquittal of Clodius' actual murderer. During Cicero's proconsulate Caelius was aedile (50) and vainly hoped for Cilician panthers or money from Cicero, whom he informed, in a series of letters written in a delightful, informal style, of gossip and political events in Rome (Cic. *Fam.* 8). Joining *Julius Caesar as the probable victor in civil war (see 8. 14. 3) and from contempt for *Pompey, he served in Spain (49) and became *praetor peregrinus* (i.e. praetor with responsibility 'over foreigners') 48. Against the opposition of the consul Publius Servilius Isauricus and the urban praetor Gaius Trebonius, he proposed a radical programme of debt relief, was suspended from office, and, joined by Milo, raised an insurrection in which he was killed.

E.B.

Caesar See JULIUS CAESAR.

Caligula See GAIUS (1).

Callimachus, of Cyrene, Greek poet and scholar, 'Battiades' (*Epigr.* 35), i.e. son (or descendant?) of Battus; his grandfather was a general (*Epigr.* 21). He flourished under *Ptolemy II (285–246 BC) and continued into the reign of *Ptolemy III (*Suda*); he mentions the Celtic invasion of 279 (*Hymn* 4. 171 ff.; fr. 379); the marriage (*c.*275) and apotheosis (270? 268?) of *Arsinoë II Philadelphus (frs. 392, 228); and the Laodicean War of 246/5 (fr. 110). Other work for Berenice II (*Epigr.* 51?, frs. 387–8, *Suppl. Hell.* 254 ff.), and perhaps the *Victory of Sosibius* (fr. 384), belong to the same late period. Callimachus stood close to the Alexandrian court; it may be accident that we have no works datable between Arsinoë's death and the accession of Berenice (herself a princess of Cyrene).

Callimachus was credited with more than 800 books (*Suda*). Michael Choniates, *c.* AD 1200, may still have possessed copies of *Aetia* and *Hecale*. But, apart from the six hymns and some sixty epigrams, and a selection from the prose *Paradoxa* (fr. 407), only fragments now survive. The Milan *Diegeseis*, a papyrus of *c.* AD 100, contains summaries of the poems, in the order *Aetia*, *Iambi*, *Lyrica*, *Hecale*, *Hymns*.

WORKS 1. *Aetia*, in four books (some 4,000 lines in all?): a miscellany of elegiac pieces, from extended epigrams (fr. 64, on the tomb of *Simonides; fr. 114, on the Delian statue of Apollo to narratives of 100–200 lines (frs. 67–75, Acontius and Cydippe; *Suppl. Hell.* 254–69, *Victory of Berenice*). The common subject is 'origins': the origins in myth or history of Greek cults, festivals, cities, and the like. Episodes are chosen and rehearsed with antiquarian relish. In the 'prologue' (fr. 1) the poet answers the critics who complain that he does not compose a 'continuous poem' on the deeds of kings or heroes: poetry should be judged by art, not quantity; Apollo recommended the slender Muse, the untrodden paths; better be the cicada than the braying mule. Like *Hesiod, he had met the Muses, in a dream, and they related the *Aetia* to him (fr. 2). Books 1 and 2 were structured, at least in part, by a dialogue between the poet-researcher and the Muses; books 3 and 4 are framed by the substantial court-poems *Victory of Berenice* and *Lock of Berenice*. Within books, poems may be grouped thematically. The 'epilogue' (fr. 112) recalls *Hesiod's meeting with the Muses; and leads over to the 'pedestrian field of the Muses', i.e. (probably) to the *Iambi*. It is generally (but controversially) argued that the *Aetia* went through two editions: the poet in old age added 'prologue' and 'epilogue', and perhaps books 3–4 entire.

2. *Iambi*: thirteen poems, written in scazons or other iambic metres. In the first, Hipponax speaks, returned from the dead; in the last, the poet names Hipponax as the exemplar of the genre. Personal invective (1–5), and the fable (2, 4), play their part, as in the traditional *iambus*. But these poems range much wider: 6 (the statue of Zeus at Olympia) reads as an epodic epigram, 8 as an iambic epinician; 7–11 record various *aitia*; 12 celebrates a birth. The framing poems continue literary polemic: in 1 against quarrelling scholars, in 13 against those who think that an author should confine himself to a single genre.

3. Miscellaneous poems include the lyric *Apotheosis of Arsinoë* (fr. 228), and the elegiac epinician for Sosibius (fr. 384).

4. *Hecale*, a hexameter narrative of something over 1,000 lines. Theseus leaves Athens secretly to face the bull of Marathon; a storm breaks; he takes shelter in the cottage of the aged Hecale; he leaves at dawn and subdues the bull; he returns to Hecale, finds her dead, and founds the deme Hecale and the sanctuary of Zeus Hekaleios in her memory. This heroic (but not Homeric) material was deviously elaborated, with Hecale rather than Theseus at the centre. The scene of rustic hospitality became famous; talking birds

diversify the narrative; the action ends in another *aition*, perhaps drawn from the *Atthis* (the name given to the genre of local histories of Athens and Attica).

5. The *Hymns* reanimate the traditional (Homeric) form, but with no view to performance. The hymns to Zeus, Artemis, and Delos (nos. 1, 3, 4) elaborate the god's birth and virtues with quizzical learning and virtuoso invention. Those to Apollo (no. 2), Athena (no. 5), and Demeter (no. 6) are framed as dramas, in which the narrator-celebrant draws the hearer into an imagined ritual; 6 (Doric hexameters) and still more 5 (Doric elegiacs) deliberately cross generic boundaries.

6. The *Epigrams* (a selection preserved in Meleager's anthology, *Garland*, c.100 BC) cover the full range of literary, erotic, dedicatory, and sepulchral themes; scattered fragments (frs. 393–402) hint at more.

7. Callimachus wrote prose works on nymphs; on athletic contests; on the foundation of islands and cities; on winds, on rivers, on 'marvels', and on birds; on 'barbarian customs' and on local names of fish and of months. He was among the founders of lexicography and paradoxography (literary collections of marvels). The *Pinakes* ('Tables of Those who have Distinguished themselves in Every Form of Culture and of What they Wrote') presented, in 120 books, a bibliography of Greek literature and a catalogue of the Alexandrian Library, organized by subject ('rhetoric', 'laws', 'miscellaneous prose'); they included some biographical notes, and cited the first line of each work, and the number of lines. Callimachus also 'arranged' the poems of *Pindar and *Bacchylides (fr. 450, *Suppl. Hell.* 293).

Callimachus often states his preferences in poetry and among poets. He defends shorter (and discontinuous) poems (fr. 1), the small drop from the pure spring (*Hymn* 2. 107 ff.), diversity of genre (*polyeidia*) (fr. 203); 'a big book equals a big evil' (fr. 465), 'slim' poetry (fr. 1. 24) is better than 'thick' (fr. 398). This 'new' aesthetic (which might seem less novel if we had the poetry of the 4th cent.) quotes the example of past poets. Callimachus invokes Hesiod (frs. 2, 112; *Epigr.* 27), and condemns the Epic Cycle (*Epigr.* 28); Homer is all-present, but formal emulation and verbal pastiche are rigorously avoided. From Pindar he borrows the critical images of the 'fine flower' (*Hymn* 2. 112, *Isthm.* 7. 18) and the 'carriage road' (fr. 1. 25–8, *Pae.* 7b. 11). *Mimnermus and Philitas exemplify the short poem, Ion of Chios *polyeidia.* *Antimachus, *Plato, and Praxiphanes are variously dispraised (frs. 398, 589, 460). Of contemporaries, Callimachus commends *Aratus (1) (*Epigr.* 27, fr. 460); the story of his quarrel with *Apollonius Rhodius (and of the *Ibis*, frs. 381–2) is now generally discounted.

Callimachus says little about Egypt (though some have tried to find Pharaonic ideology in *Hymn* 4). From Alexandria he looks to Greece, and the Greek past; he has a scholar's systematic knowledge of the Greek literary inheritance, an exile's feeling for the old country and its links (through *aitia*) with the contemporary world. His work often reaches out to the archaic world, crossing the centuries of drama and prose—to Hesiod, Hipponax, Pindar. But this past is transmuted. Verbal borrowing is rare; genres are shifted or mixed, myth transformed by mannerism, words and motifs juxtaposed in postmodern incongruities. *Victoria Berenices* may serve as an example. This epinician is also an *aition* (the foundation of the Nemean Games). It borrows words from Pindar, and story from Bacchylides, in the wrong dialect (Ionic) and the wrong metre (elegiac). The narrative dwells not on Heracles but on the rustic hospitality of the peasant Molorcus; Molorcus' war with the mice parallels Heracles' fight with the lion. Callimachus' poems are (by epic standards) short; various in style, metre, and genre; experimental in form, recondite in diction, polished in versification, devious, elaborate, allusive, and sometimes obscure (the earliest surviving papyrus, within a generation of Callimachus' death, includes an explanatory paraphrase). To Roman poets he became the exemplar of sophistication, *princeps elegiae* ('master of elegy', Quint. *Inst.* 10. 1. 58): *Catullus translated him (66), *Propertius invokes him (3. 1. 1). The *Aetia* in particular stands behind *Ovid's *Fasti* and Propertius 4; *Georgic* 3 begins with an allusion to it. But classicizing snobbery took him to represent technique without genius (Ov. *Am.* 1. 15. 14).

Callimachus commands an extraordinary variety of tone: tongue-in-cheek epic (*Hecale* fr. 74 Hollis), versified statistics (*Iambus* 6), classic pathos (*Epigr.* 19), Catullan elegance (fr. 401). The scholarship is integral to the poetry, which even quotes its own sources (frs. 75. 54, 92. 3, *Schol. Flor. Callim.* 35?). But irony and invention dominate. P.J.P.

Calpurnia (1), daughter of Lucius Calpurnius Piso Caesoninus, married *Julius Caesar in 59 BC, cementing an alliance between her husband and father. Though Caesar was prepared to divorce her to marry *Pompey's daughter in 53, her affection for him was great, and she attempted to keep him from the senate on the Ides of March (Plut. *Caes.* 63). After the murder she handed his papers and 4,000 talents to Mark *Antony.

G.E.F.C.; R.J.S.

Calpurnia (2), third wife of *Pliny the Younger, whom she accompanied to Bithynia (*Ep.* 10. 120–1). She was granddaughter of Lucius Calpurnius Fabatus, a Roman knight of Comum (*ILS* 2721), to whom Pliny excused her miscarriage on grounds of her youth and inexperience (*Ep.* 8. 10–11). His affectionate letters to her (6. 4. 7; 7. 5) established the theme of conjugal love in Latin literature.

G.E.F.C.; M.T.G.

Calpurnius Siculus The author of seven pastorals, Calpurnius may be dated with reasonable security to the Neronian age. The crucial pieces of evidence are *Eclogue* 1. 75 ff., which seemingly allude to the comet that foretold *Claudius' death and *Nero's accession in AD 54, and *Eclogue* 7, which celebrates the construction of a wooden amphitheatre in the Campus Martius, and, almost certainly, the *Munus Neronis* (Neronian Games) which inaugurated it in 57. Nevertheless, attempts continue to ascribe Calpurnius to a later period, on internal, stylistic, metrical, and lexical grounds. Of the author's life virtually nothing is known: his cognomen *Siculus* may not refer to his homeland, but symbolize his debt to *Theocritus. He is sometimes credited with the *Laus Pisonis* ('Panegyric on Piso').

Of the *Eclogues*, 1, 4, and 7 are court-poems, dealing in ascending chronological order with the early years of Nero's reign. All three contain extensive monologues. By contrast, 2, 3, 5, and 6 are in dialogue form, and are concerned with rustic matters of a more traditional kind. In 1, two shepherds, Ornytus and Corydon—who is generally identified with Calpurnius—discover verses inscribed by Faunus on the bark of a tree, prophesying a new golden age. In contrast to Calpurnius' model, Virgil *Eclogue* 4, the prophecy incorporates detailed references to contemporary politics. In 2, a shepherd and a gardener (an innovation in pastoral) sing without rancour of the love which they share for Crocale. *Eclogue* 3, which is structured around a parallel between a wayward woman and a wayward heifer, presents a contrasting view of love. In it Lycidas, an unpleasant personage as are several of Calpurnius' characters, attempts to recover the affections of Phyllis, whom he has beaten in a jealous rage. His pleas for forgiveness combine the roles of elegiac lover and shepherd-poet; he also exhibits resemblances to the elegist's *bête-noire*, the *dives amator* or rich rival. *Eclogue* 4, the longest and most fulsome of the poems, celebrates the pacifying and fructifying effect which the divine Nero has had on rural life. Corydon's opening statement that the times are now more propitious for literary endeavour is balanced by a concluding plea for imperial patronage. *Eclogue* 5 reports old Micon's advice on how to keep sheep and goats. Both the subject-matter and the insistence on hard work are georgic rather than pastoral. In *Eclogue* 6 a singing-contest is, unusually, aborted by the extreme quarrelsomeness of the competitors, Lycidas and Astylus, who stake prizes of a most unpastoral kind. *Eclogue* 7 describes Corydon's bedazzlement at the *Munus Neronis*, and his resultant alienation from his rural existence.

L.C.W.

Camillus (Furius Camillus, Marcus), consular tribune 401, 398, 394, 386, 384, 381, supposedly censor 403, and dictator 396, 390, 389, 368, 367 BC. His alleged campaigns against the Falisci and Capenates in 401 and 398 hardly account for his appointment as dictator in 396 to complete the seizure of Veii. After the victory he built a temple to the Veientan Juno Regina on the Aventine. He also reputedly restored the temple of Matuta Mater in the forum Boarium, but whether this can be reconciled with the archaeological evidence from the S. Omobono sanctuary is contentious.

In 394 he supposedly secured the surrender of Falerii, after refusing the offer of a Faliscan schoolmaster to hand over his charges as hostages. Against this are set suggestions that

his success at Veii attracted divine envy or (particularly in Livy (5. 23. 5 f.)) that by using the white horses of Jupiter and Sol in his triumph he set himself above his fellow citizens. These attempts to explain his subsequent fall are supplemented by stories of growing political tensions between Camillus and the *plebs*, culminating in his trial and exile in 391 (though *Diodorus Siculus (14. 117. 6) records a tradition dating it after the Gallic sack of Rome in 390. However, the different accounts of Camillus' prosecutors and the charges against him (misappropriation or inequitable distribution of the Veientan booty or the triumph with white horses) support the view that this entire narrative was invented as an explanation for Camillus' apparent inability to prevent the Gallic sack and is partly modelled on the fate of Achilles and Scipio Africanus.

Similarly, the varying accounts of the departure of the Gauls in 390 and recovery (or non-recovery) of the gold paid as ransom suggest that the story of Camillus' recall, appointment as dictator, and dramatic intervention at the moment the ransom was weighed out is patriotic fiction, perhaps of late date (the Lucius who saved Rome according to *Aristotle (Plut. *Cam.* 22) can hardly be Marcus Camillus). Also fictitious will be the story of his decisive opposition to a renewed proposal of settlement at Veii, though this may go back to *Ennius (*Ann.* 154 f. Skutsch with comm.). Accounts of his actions in 390 may be influenced by parallels with *Sulla; they enable Livy to depict him in Ciceronian terms as a 'second founder' of Rome and 'father of his country' (*parens patriae*), who articulates a highly traditionalist conception of the Roman identity, particularly in its religious dimension (5. 51 ff.).

Though Camillus' campaigns against the Volsci and recovery of Sutrium under 389 and 386 may be duplicates and the rapidity of Rome's recovery after the Gallic sack exaggerated, these advances and the absorption of Tusculum in 381 may plausibly symbolize Roman resurgence, whatever Camillus' own role in them. However, his (apparently late) introduction into the trial of Marcus Manlius Capitolinus is a dramatizing invention, as may be the dictatorships of 368 and 367 (when he supposedly defeated the Gauls and restored domestic harmony): his alleged cre-

ation of a temple of Concord (367) is almost
certainly anachronistic.　　　　　　　A.D.

Caracalla, named Marcus Aurelius
Antoninus (AD 188–217), nicknamed Caracalla, emperor AD 198–217. Elder son of L.
*Septimius Severus, originally called Septim-
ius Bassianus; renamed after *Marcus Aurelius and made Caesar in 195. Augustus in 198,
he was consul for the first time with his father
in 202 and for the second time with his
brother Publius Septimius Geta in 205, when
he had his hated father-in-law Gaius Fulvius
Plautianus killed. Consul for the third time
in 208, again with Geta, whom he also hated,
he accompanied his father to Britain, sharing
command against the Caledonians. When
Severus died, he and Geta abandoned Scotland, making the wall of *Hadrian the frontier again, and returned to Rome. After
having Geta killed (26 December 211), a
drastic purge followed. To conciliate the soldiers, he raised their pay, creating financial
problems. One solution was the 'Antonine
*constitution' which made all free men and
women in the empire Roman citizens; he
simultaneously doubled the inheritance tax
paid only by citizens, which funded the *aerar-
ium militare* (military treasury). In 215 a new
coin was struck, the so-called *antoninianus*,
evidently tariffed at two denarii, but weighing
only 1.5: this was to lead to inflation.

In 213 he fought the Alamanni (the first
time they are mentioned), evidently gave the
Raetian *limes* (frontier) a stone wall, and
became Germanicus Maximus. In 214 he
attacked the Danubian Carpi and reorganized Pannonia, each province now having two
legions (Britain was split into two provinces
at this time; Hither Spain was also
subdivided). Obsessed by *Alexander the
Great, he raised a Macedonian phalanx and
went east in his footsteps, through Asia and
Syria to Alexandria, where large numbers
who had mocked him were killed. When his
offer to marry a Parthian princess was
rejected, he attacked Media. While preparing
a further campaign he was murdered near
Carrhae (8 April 217). Macrinus deified him
as Divus Antoninus Magnus.　　　　A.R.Bi.

Carneades from Cyrene (214/3–129/8 BC),
the most important representative of the
sceptical Academy (the school founded by
*Plato), often called the founder of the New

Academy as distinct from the Middle
Academy of *Arcesilaus. He studied philosophy in the Academy under Hegesinus, but
also took lessons in Stoic dialectic from Diogenes of Babylon. Carneades became
scholarch some time before 155, when he was
sent by Athens on an embassy to Rome
together with the Stoic Diogenes and the
Peripatetic Critolaus. He resigned as head of
the Academy in 137/6 and was succeeded by a
younger namesake. Carneades was famous
for his dialectical and rhetorical skills. He
attracted many students, and his lectures
drew large audiences, even from the schools
of the orators. He left no writings, but his
arguments were recorded in many volumes
by his pupil Clitomachus.

Carneades used the method of arguing for
and against any given view to criticize all dogmatic philosophies, covering not only epistemology, but also physics, theology, and
ethics. He also continued the debate between
the Academy and the Stoa, whose doctrines
had been defended against earlier sceptical
objections by Chrysippus. In the dispute
about the criterion of truth, he expanded the
argument about the impossibility of distinguishing between cognitive and non-cogni-
tive impressions. Most influential became his
reply to the standard objection that sceptical
withholding of assent (*epochē*) makes life
impossible. He confronted the Stoics with a
dilemma: if there is no cognitive impression,
then either the wise man will hold opinions—an alternative abhorred by the
Stoics—or else he will suspend judgement on
everything. In the latter case, he will still be
able to act, since it is possible to follow
impressions without full assent, and the wise
man may make reasonable decisions if he is
guided by impressions that are plausible or
convincing (*pithanon*, Lat. *probabile*) and
checked for consistency with other relevant
impressions. Carneades' account of the
pithanon was introduced to refute the Stoic
claim that life is impossible without cognitive
impressions. But it also presented an attractive alternative to Stoic epistemology and was
adopted by some of Carneades' successors as
the basis of a new theory of fallibilism, which
made it possible for the Academics to
abandon strict suspension of judgement and
develop their own doctrines.

Carneades' criticisms of the belief in gods
and divination were extensively used by

Cicero (*Nat. D.*; *Div.*) and *Sextus Empiricus (*Math.* 9). In ethics, he is credited with a classification of all possible views about the highest good (*Carneadea divisio*), invented no doubt in order to argue that none of these options can be conclusively defended. Again his main target was Stoicism, and echoes of the debate can be found e.g. in *Cicero and *Plutarch. On the occasion of the famous embassy to Rome, he gave speeches for and against justice on two consecutive days. Carneades' performance was so impressive that *Cato the Elder demanded a speedy departure of the Athenian delegation in order to protect Roman youths from the subversive influence of the philosophers.   G.S.

Cassander (d. 297 BC), son of *Antipater, represented his father at Babylon (323), where *Alexander the Great treated him with naked hostility. In the struggles of the Successors he first impinges at Triparadeisus (late 321), where he was appointed chiliarch (cavalry commander and grand vizier). Chiliarch he remained at Antipater's death (autumn 319), subordinate to the regent *Polyperchon; but he defected to *Antigonus the One-eyed and with Antigonus' support established bases in Piraeus and the Peloponnese (318/7). An inconclusive invasion of Macedon (?early 317) was followed by a wholly successful one which overthrew the tyrannical dowager, *Olympias. From 316 he was master of Macedon and promoted the memory of *Philip II (whose daughter, Thessalonice, he married) over that of Alexander. He ceremonially refounded Thebes (316), and had the young Alexander IV (son of Alexander the Great and Roxane) secretly killed at Amphipolis (*c.*310). A leading figure in the coalition war against Antigonus (315–311), he secured recognition of his position as general in Europe in the 'peace of the dynasts' (311) and later (*c.*305) had himself proclaimed 'King of the Macedonians', subsequently his official title. When war resumed, he lost ground in southern Greece as the oligarchies he had supported (most notably at Athens) were undermined by Antigonus' propaganda of autonomy, and only the outbreak of war in Asia saved him from a devastating invasion at the hands of *Demetrius the Besieger (302). His death (?May 297) left Macedon temporarily stable, to be soon convulsed by the quarrels of his heirs.   A.B.B.

Cassian Born in what is now Romania in *c.* AD 360, Cassian had the advantage of a Latin upbringing in the Greek world. Like his master Evagrius of Pontus, he travelled through Syria, Palestine, and Egypt, making extensive contact with the masters of eastern asceticism and gaining a thorough grounding in the theory of the ascetic life.

With the Egyptian condemnation of *Origen in 399, he enjoyed the protection of John Chrysostom in Constantinople, together with many other exiled admirers of the Alexandrian master. After an obscure interval, he settled in southern Gaul in *c.*415 under the patronage, in particular, of Proculus of Arles. He served and moulded the ascetic enthusiasms of several bishops and founded two monasteries of his own near Marseilles.

For the resulting communities he wrote his *Institutes* and *Conferences*, which gained widespread and permanent influence in the west. The *Institutes* were more practical, important for liturgical detail and for their systematic treatment of the vices, reflecting eastern practice and the theology of Evagrius. The *Conferences* reported conversations with ascetics of northern Egypt and gave new Christian vigour to the dialogue form. Their setting appeared solitary but Cassian's intentions were coenobitic: he encouraged virtues and practices proper to community life. While respecting Egyptian tradition, he adapted it to the new monasteries of Gaul.

Cassian's writings were charged with an Alexandrian optimism. The ascetic was made in the image of God and perfection was in some sense a natural expectation based on the development of inherent qualities. Virtues formed a unity, so that any step forward would find its reward in an integrated drama of self-possession. The result was a genuine freedom—not only from inadequacy but from fear of submission to others. In making such emphases, Cassian had a role to play on a broader stage. He wrote a treatise on the Incarnation against Nestorius; and his views on freedom had a lasting influence in Gaul among those who sympathized more with *Pelagius than with *Augustine. His ascetic teaching was highly valued by Benedict and was mentioned explicitly in the latter's *Rule*. He died *c.*435.   P.R.

Cassiodorus (Magnus Aurelius Cassiodorus Senator), politician, writer, and monk (c. AD 490–c.585). His Bruttian family had a tradition of provincial leadership and official service. He assisted his father, praetorian prefect of Italy, 503–7, under the Ostrogothic king Theoderic. Writing Theoderic's diplomatic letters in 506, he was *quaestor sacri palatii* (rhetorical draftsman and legal adviser), 507–12. Consul in 514, in 523 he replaced his disgraced kinsman *Boethius as *magister officiorum* ('master of the offices', a very senior official with extensive responsibilities for the working of the central bureaucracy, but also with draftsman's duties); he served into 527, aiding the new reign of Athalaric and Amalasuintha. Prefect of Italy from 533, he was again both administrator and royal draftsman. With Pope Agapitus (535–6), he planned an abortive school of Christian higher education at Rome. Remaining prefect under kings Theodahad and Witigis, and made patrician, he retired in 537/8 during the Gothic wars. Moving to Constantinople, he assisted Pope Vigilius in the Three Chapters controversy (550). Soon after, he withdrew permanently to his monastery of Vivarium on his ancestral estate at Scylacium. There he organized translations and manuscript copying, partly to support the Three Chapters against official condemnation, partly to promote Christian education. Vivarian texts soon circulated widely, but the monastery quickly shared in the decay of Italian civilization.

Among his works: (1) a short chronicle of the world and Rome, ordered by Theoderic's son-in-law Eutharic, when consul in 519. (2) A lost, tendentious Gothic history, extensively used in Jordanes' *Getica* (c.551). Notable for its untrustworthy pedigree of Theoderic's Amal family and use of Gothic legend, it is the first known ethnic history from the barbarian kingdoms, integrating Goths into the classical past. (3) Panegyrics (fragmentary) on Gothic royalties, last of the Latin prose genre. (4) *Variae*: twelve books of state papers, edited c.537, an invaluable source for Ostrogothic Italy, and the structures, culture, and ideology of late-Roman government. The collection was both an apology for the Ostrogoths and their Roman collaborators, and a moral, rhetorical, and practical guide for future rulers and ministers; Cassiodorus' blending of *ekphrasis* (extended literary description of a real or imaginary object) and learned digression into official discourse is remarkable. (5) The appended *De anima* grounded the *Variae* in religious reflections on human nature and society. (6) *Expositio Psalmorum*: this exegetical and literary commentary developed the Psalms as a Christian rhetorical handbook and encyclopaedia of liberal arts, superseding pagan classics. (7) *Institutiones*: an intellectual Rule for Vivarium (but also meant for a wider public), this short encyclopaedia and bibliography of Christian and secular studies renewed the project of Christian higher education, and depicted reading (including the liberal arts) and copying as central to monastic life. (8) *De orthographia*: a guide for Vivarian copyists. Among influential Vivarian translations were Josephus' *Antiquitates*, and the ecclesiastical *Historia tripartita*, combining Socrates Scholasticus, Sozomen, and Theodoret. Cassiodorus did not save classical culture, as is sometimes claimed; but, especially from Carolingian times, *Variae*, *Expositio*, and *Institutiones* were widely read, and helped to maintain and integrate the Christian and Roman inheritances in western Europe.

S.J.B.B.

Cassius (Gaius Cassius Longinus) the tyrannicide (killer of *Julius Caesar), was quaestor 54 BC and proquaestor under *Crassus in 53. He escaped from Carrhae (where the Parthians defeated Crassus in 53 BC), collected the remnants of the army, and organized the defence of Syria, staying on as proquaestor till 51: in 52 he crushed an insurrection in Judaea and in 51 repelled a Parthian invasion. As tribune 49 he supported *Pompey and was appointed by him to a naval command; in 48 he operated in Sicilian waters but on the news of Caesar's defeat of Pompey at Pharsalus abandoned the war and (perhaps at Tarsus, spring 47) obtained Caesar's pardon and the post of *legatus*. Praetor 44, he played a leading part in the conspiracy against Caesar. Soon after the deed he was forced by popular hostility to leave Rome, and was assigned by the senate in June the task of importing corn from Sicily, and later the unimportant province of Cyrene. After quarrelling with Mark *Antony he sailed instead for Asia (September or October) and from there to Syria, where, early in 43, the governors of Bithynia and

Syria, Quintus Marcius Crispus and Lucius
Staius Murcus, put their armies at his disposal. Quintus Caecilius Bassus, whom they
had been besieging, followed suit; a force
under A. Allienus on its way from Egypt to
*Dolabella was intercepted and made to join
him; and after the capture of (Syrian) Laodicea he took over Dolabella's army too. After
Mutina the senate had given him, with
*Brutus, command over all the eastern prov-
inces and probably also *imperium maius*
(overriding military authority); but in the
autumn they were outlawed for the murder
of Caesar under the law of Quintus Pedius.
After raising more troops and money and
subduing the Rhodians, who had refused
their support, Cassius crossed with Brutus
to Thrace in summer 42 and encountered
Antony and Octavian (SEE AUGUSTUS) at
Philippi. In the first battle his camp was captured and, probably under the impression
that the day was altogether lost, he killed
himself.

More keen-sighted and practical than
Brutus, Cassius seems nevertheless to have
been less respected and less influential. He
was a man of violent temper and sarcastic
tongue, a strict disciplinarian, and ruthless
in his exactions. The charge of covetousness
may have been well founded; but there is no
convincing evidence that he was influenced
by petty motives in the conspiracy against
Caesar. He married Brutus' half-sister Junia
Tertia (Tertulla), who survived till AD 22 (Tac.
Ann. 3. 76).   T.J.C.; R.J.S.

Cassius Dio (*c.* AD 164–after 229), Greek
senator and author of an 80-book history of
Rome from the foundation of the city to AD
229. His full name was perhaps Lucius
Cassius Dio, as on M. M. Roxan, *Roman Military Diplomas* 2 (1985), no. 133 ('Cl.' on *AE*
1971, 430, could attest the further name 'Claudius', but is probably a stone-cutter's error;
'Cocceianus' may have been added in Byzantine times through confusion with Dio of
Prusa). Dio came from a prominent family
of Nicaea in Bithynia (modern Iznik). His
father, Cassius Apronianus, entered the
senate, attaining a consulship and several
governorships. Dio's senatorial career was
even more distinguished. He was praetor in
194 and suffect consul probably *c.*204. From
218 to 228 he was successively *curator* (an
imperial financial official) of Pergamum and

Smyrna, proconsul of Africa, and legate
(governor) first of Dalmatia and then of
Upper Pannonia. In 229 he held the ordinary
consulship with *Severus Alexander as colleague and then retired to Bithynia. Dio lived
through turbulent times: he and his fellow
senators quailed before tyrannical emperors
and lamented the rise of men they regarded
as upstarts, and in Pannonia he grappled with
the problem of military indiscipline. These
experiences are vividly evoked in his account
of his own epoch and helped to shape his
view of earlier periods.

Dio tells us (72. 23) that, after a short work
on the dreams and portents presaging the
accession of *Septimius Severus, he went on
to write first a history of the wars following
the death of *Commodus and then the
Roman History, and that for this work he
spent ten years collecting material for events
up to the death of Severus (211) and a further
twelve years writing them up. Nothing survives of the early works or of other historical
writings attributed to Dio by the Suda (a
Byzantine lexicon). The dates of composition
of the *Roman History* are disputed, but the
most natural interpretation of Dio's words is
that he began work *c.*202. His plan was to
continue recording events after Severus'
death as long as possible, but absence from
Italy prevented him giving more than a
cursory account of the reign of Severus Alexander and he ended the history with his own
retirement (80. 1–5).

The *Roman History* is only partially extant.
The portion dealing with the period 69 BC to
AD 46 (36. 1. 1–60. 28. 3) survives in various
MSS, with substantial lacunae after 6 BC. For
the rest we depend on excerpts and the epit-
omes of *Zonaras (down to 146 and 44 BC to
AD 96) and Xiphilinus (from 69 BC to the
end).

Like its author, the work is an amalgam of
Greek and Roman elements. It is written in
Attic Greek, with much studiedly antithetical
rhetoric and frequent verbal borrowings
from the classical authors, above all *Thucydides. The debt to Thucydides is more than
merely stylistic: like him, Dio is constantly
alert to discrepancies between appearances
and reality. In its structure, however, the
history revives the Roman tradition of an
annalistic record of civil and military affairs
arranged by the consular year. Dio shows
flexibility in his handling of the annalistic

framework: there are many digressions, usually brief; external events of several years are sometimes combined in a single narrative cluster; introductory and concluding sections frame the annalistic narratives of emperors' reigns.

For his own times Dio could draw on his own experience or oral evidence, but for earlier periods he was almost entirely dependent on literary sources, chiefly earlier histories. Attempts to identify individual sources are usually futile. Dio must have read widely in the first ten years, and in the ensuing twelve years of writing up he probably worked mainly from his notes without going back to the originals. Such a method of composition may account for some of the history's distinctive character. It is often thin and slapdash; errors and distortions are quite common, and there are some surprising omissions (notably the conference of Luca in 56 BC, for which see *JULIUS CAESAR). However, Dio does show considerable independence, both in shaping his material and in interpretation: he freely makes causal links between events and attributes motivations to his characters, and many of these explanations must be his own contribution rather than drawn from a source.

One notable feature of the work is the prominence of the supernatural: Dio believed that divine direction played an important part in his own and others' lives and he devoted much space to portents. Another is the speeches, which are free inventions and sometimes on a very ample scale. Many of them are commonly dismissed as mere rhetorical set-pieces, but they generally have a dramatic function, often heavily ironic. In *Maecenas' speech of advice to *Augustus (52. 14–40) Dio combines an analysis of the problems facing Augustus and of the imperial system as it evolved under the emperors with a sketch of how he himself would have liked to see the empire governed.

The *Roman History* is dominated by the change from the republic to the monarchy of the emperors, repeatedly endorsed by Dio on the grounds that only monarchy could provide Rome with stable government. The late republic and the triumviral years (see AUGUSTUS) are accorded much more space than other periods. Dio anachronistically treats the conflicts of the late republic as struggles between rival contenders for

supreme power. His account of the settlement of 27 BC perceptively explores the ways in which it shaped the imperial system under which he still lived (53. 2. 6–21. 7). Dio's treatment of individual emperors' reigns reflects the values and interests of the senator: his overriding concern is with the respects in which emperors measured up to or fell short of senators' expectations.   J.W.R.

Catiline (Lucius Sergius Catilina), of patrician, but not recently distinguished, family, served with *Pompey and *Cicero under Gnaeus Pompeius Strabo in the Social War (91–89 BC). He next appears as a lieutenant of *Sulla both in the *bellum Sullanum* after Sulla's invasion of Italy and in the proscriptions (outlawing of political enemies and confiscation of their property) when, incited by *Lutatius Catulus (2), he killed his brother-in-law Marius Gratidianus. There is no further record of him until his praetorship (68 BC), after which he governed Africa for two years. Prosecuted *repetundarum* (i.e. for provincial extortion) on his return, he was prevented from standing for the consulship for 65 and 64, but was finally acquitted with the help of his prosecutor *Clodius Pulcher. In 66/5 he was said to be involved in a plot with Publius Autronius and Publius Cornelius Sulla; the details are obscured by gossip and propaganda, and his involvement is doubtful. Frustrated ambition now became his driving force. In the elections for 63 he made a compact with Gaius Antonius 'Hybrida' and gained the support of *Julius Caesar and Marcus Licinius *Crassus, but was defeated by Cicero. He then began to champion the cause of the poor and dispossessed: dissolute aristocrats, bankrupt Sullan veterans, and those whom they had driven from their lands. Again defeated for 62, he organized a widespread conspiracy with ramifications throughout Italy. Cicero, kept informed by his spies, could not take decisive action owing to lack of sufficient support, for Catiline—an old Sullan, a patrician, and now a demagogue—was both popular and well connected. In November Cicero succeeded in frightening Catiline into leaving Rome to join a force of destitute veterans in Etruria. Soon afterwards, some Allobrogan envoys, carelessly given letters by conspirators in Rome, provided Cicero with the written evidence he needed. The leaders of the conspiracy in

Rome were arrested and, after a long debate and a vote in the senate, executed. The consul Antonius marched out against Catiline, who was caught between two armies and was defeated and killed by Marcus Petreius near Pistoria (early January 62). Cicero was hailed as saviour of Rome, but was open to the charge of having executed citizens without trial.   E.B.

Cato the Elder (Marcus Porcius Cato), 'Cato the Censor' (234–149 BC) ('Censorius') was a dominant figure in both the political and the cultural life of Rome in the first half of the 2nd cent. BC. A *novus homo* (roughly, the first man in his family to become a senator and/or consul), he was born at Tusculum, but spent much of his childhood in the Sabine country, where his family owned land. He served in the Hannibalic War (see HANNIBAL), winning particular praise for his contribution at the battle of the Metaurus in 207. He embarked on a political career under the patronage of the patrician Lucius Valerius Flaccus, who was his colleague in both consulship and censorship. As quaestor 204 he served under *Scipio Africanus in Sicily and Africa; a constant champion of traditional Roman virtues, he looked with disfavour on Scipio's adoption of Greek customs and relaxed military discipline in Sicily, but the story that he came back to Rome to express his criticisms should be rejected. He is said to have returned from Africa via Sardinia, bringing thence the poet *Ennius to Rome. He was plebeian aedile 199 and praetor 198, when he may have carried the Porcian law which extended the right of *provocatio* (appeal to the people against the action of a magistrate) to cases of scourging. He governed Sardinia, expelling usurers and restricting the demands made on the Sardinians for the upkeep of himself and his staff. He reached the consulship in 195: after unsuccessfully opposing the repeal of the Oppian law, he went to Spain, where, in a campaign which may have extended into 194, he suppressed a major rebellion, extended the area under Roman control, and arranged for the exploitation of the gold and silver mines; he returned to Rome to celebrate a triumph. In 191, as military tribune, he played an important part in the defeat of *Antiochus III at Thermopylae, and was sent to Rome by Manius Acilius Glabrio to report the victory. Cato was constantly engaged in court

cases, both as prosecutor or prosecution witness and as defendant. He was an instigator of the attacks on the Scipios (Africanus and his brother Lucius Cornelius Scipio Asiagenes), and two of his other targets, Quintus Minucius Thermus and Glabrio, can be seen as allies of the Scipios. The attack on Glabrio was connected with the censorial elections of 189, when Cato and Flaccus stood unsuccessfully. Five years later they were elected, having stood on a joint programme of reversing the decline of traditional morality. They were severe in their review of the rolls of the senate and the *equites* (knights), removing *Flamininus from the senate and depriving Scipio Asiagenes of his public horse. High levels of taxation were imposed on what the censors regarded as luxuries, and the public contracts were let on terms most advantageous for the state and least so for the contractors. They undertook extensive public works, including major repairs and extensions to the sewage system. The controversies caused by his censorship affected Cato for the rest of his life. But he courted conflict and spoke his mind to the point of rudeness. He rigidly applied to himself the standards he demanded of others and made a parade of his own parsimony: when in Spain he had made a point of sharing the rigours of his soldiers.

Though he held no further public offices Cato continued to play an active role in politics. He was probably an augur (*MRR* 3. 170). He opposed the modification of the Baebian law of 181 which had provided for the election of only four praetors in alternate years, and of the Orchian law, a sumptuary law. Soon after 179 he attacked Marcus Fulvius Nobilior, and in 171 was one of the patrons chosen by the peoples of Spain to present their complaints against Roman governors. A critical remark about *Eumenes II of Pergamum in 172 and speeches in 167 against declaring war on Rhodes and in favour of leaving Macedonia free are probably part of a general reluctance to see Rome too directly involved in eastern affairs. It was also in 167 that he opposed the attempt by Servius Sulpicius Galba to block the triumph (victory procession of a Roman general) of Aemilius *Paullus; Cato's son later married a daughter of Paullus, and it thus seems that the old enmity between Cato and the family of the Scipios was at an end. In the last years of his life, after serving on an embassy to Carthage in 153, Cato convinced himself that the existence of Carthage constituted a serious danger to Rome; he ended each speech in the senate by saying that Carthage must be destroyed. Despite the opposition of Publius Cornelius Scipio Nasica Corculum war was eventually declared in 149. Shortly afterwards came the last speech of Cato's life, against Sulpicius Galba.

Cato has rightly been called the 'virtual founder of Latin prose literature'. Among works that were known to later generations—though not necessarily intended for publication by Cato himself—but of which we know little, are the *Ad filium* ('to his son'), perhaps no more than a brief collection of exhortations, a letter to his son, the *De re militari* ('on military matters'), a work dealing with civil law, the *Carmen de moribus*, probably a prose work on behaviour, and a collection of sayings.

Cato was the foremost orator of his age, and made many speeches. Over 150 were known to *Cicero, and we possess fragments of eighty. There can be little doubt that he intended his speeches to survive, though it is an open question whether he revised them for publication and conceived of himself as creating Latin oratory as a literary genre.

Previous Roman historians, starting with Quintus Fabius Pictor, had written in Greek; Cato's *Origines*, begun in 168 and still in progress at the time of his death, was the first historical work in Latin. It consisted of seven books. The first dealt with the foundation of Rome and the regal period; Cato had little or nothing to say about the early republic. The second and third covered the origins and customs of the towns of Italy (the title of the work is appropriate only for these three books). His approach was probably influenced by Greek *ktisis* (foundation) literature and/or *Timaeus. The remaining books described Rome's wars from the First Punic war onwards. Cato is said to have written in a summary fashion, though some episodes were given detailed treatment, and he devoted more space to the events of the period during which he was writing; the last two books cover less than twenty years. He chose to omit the names of generals and included at least two of his own speeches (those on behalf of the Rhodians and against Sulpicius Galba).

The only work of Cato which survives intact is the *De agri cultura* ('on agriculture'). It is concerned not with agriculture as a whole, but principally with giving advice to the owner of a middle-sized estate, based on slave labour, in Latium or Campania, whose primary aim was the production of wine and olive oil for sale. It also includes recipes, religious formulae, prescriptions, and sample contracts. The work is disordered and some have wondered whether Cato himself is responsible for the shape of the text as we have it. See further Appendix, below.

Cato sometimes expressed great hostility to all things Greek: in the *Ad filium* he called the Greeks a vile and unteachable race; in 155, worried by the effect their lectures were having on Roman youth, he was anxious that an embassy of Athenian philosophers should leave Rome rapidly. But he knew Greek well and had a good knowledge of Greek literature. His objections were to an excessive philhellenism and he probably thought that contemporary Greeks were very different from the great figures of the past.

Cato was married twice, to Licinia and to Salonia (daughter of one of his clients), and had a son by each wife; the first died as praetor-designate in 152; the second, born when his father was 80, was the grandfather of Cato the Younger; see next article.

                                                                    J.Br.

APPENDIX: CATO THE ELDER, *de agri cultura* 'Cato first taught agriculture to speak Latin' (Columella *Rust.* 1. 1. 12). The work (*c*.160 BC) was both innovative and part of an established Greek genre. Indications of acquaintance with Greek technical literature are clear, while the largely shapeless structure of the treatise reflects the infancy of Roman prose writing. Later authors (Varro *Rust.* 1. 2. 12–28) defined and systematized agriculture, discarding Cato's recipes and encomium of cabbage. Cato wrote for the young man who expected to make money and to enhance his public reputation by successful agriculture (3. 2). Thus the villa (rural estate) should be sited near good access routes (1. 1. 3), and wine and oil stored until prices are high (3. 2). The treatise's essential subject is the slave-staffed villa in Latium and Campania practising mixed farming with an emphasis on vines and olives. The archaeological record documents a gradual spread of villa sites in these regions from the beginning of the 2nd cent.

BC and a remarkable diffusion of Italian wine-amphorae in the western Mediterranean from the mid-2nd cent. BC.   M.S.SP.

Cato the Younger (Marcus Porcius Cato), 'of Utica' ('Uticensis') (95–46 BC), great-grandson of Cato the Elder (see preceding entry), nephew of *Livius Drusus (2), and brought up in the Livian household with the children of his mother's marriage to Gnaeus Servilius Caepio. Quaestor probably in 64, in 63 he became tribune-designate in order to check Quintus Caecilius Metellus Nepos, supported Lucius Licinius Murena's prosecution, and intervened powerfully in the senate to secure the execution of the Catilinarians (see CATILINE). As tribune he conciliated the mob by increasing the numbers eligible to receive cheap corn, but in all else remained uncompromising; *Cicero (*Att.* 1. 18. 7; 2. 1. 8) deplores his lack of realism which prevented revision of the Asian tax-contracts (61)—thus alienating the *equites* (knights)—and which frustrated every overture of *Pompey until the coalition between Pompey, *Julius Caesar, and *Crassus was formed. In 59 he opposed Caesar obstinately and was temporarily imprisoned, but next year *Clodius removed him by appointing him to undertake the annexation of Cyprus. Though King Ptolemy of Cyprus (an illegitimate son of *Ptolemy IX and brother of *Ptolemy XII Auletes) killed himself and Cato's accounts were lost on the voyage home, his reputation for fairness remained unimpaired. After Luca (see POMPEY) he persuaded his brother-in-law Lucius Domitius Ahenobarbus not to give up hope of being elected consul for 55, but Domitius' candidature collapsed because of physical intimidation by the supporters of Pompey and Crassus. Publius Vatinius defeated Cato for the praetorship by bribery, but Cato was eventually praetor in 54. In 52, abandoning his constitutional principles, he supported Pompey's election as sole consul; he himself stood for 51 but failed. In the war he tried to avoid citizen bloodshed but resolutely followed Pompey: he served in Sicily, but was expelled from there by Gaius Scribonius Curio. Then he served in Asia, and held Dyrrachium during the campaign of Pharsalus. After Pompey's defeat, Cato joined the quarrelling Pompeians in Africa and reconciled them; he had Quintus Caecilius Metellus Pius Scipio made general. During

the war he governed Utica with great moderation, and was honoured by the city's inhabitants when after Thapsus in April 46 he committed suicide rather than accept pardon from Caesar, an act which earned him the undying glory of a martyr.

Cato's constitutionalism, a mixture of Stoicism and old Roman principles, was genuine. After death he was more dangerous than ever to Caesar, who in his *Anticato*, a reply to Cicero's pamphlet *Cato*, pitched the hostile case too high, and allowed the fame of Cato's life and death to give respectability to the losing side, and to inspire later political martyrs: 'the victors had their cause approved by the gods, the vanquished by Cato' (Lucan 1. 128).   G.E.F.C.; M.T.G.

Catullus (Gaius Valerius Catullus) came from a distinguished propertied family of Verona but spent most of his life in Rome. The dates of his life are incorrectly transmitted in the *Chronicle* of Jerome but can be approximately reconstructed. He was probably born in 84 BC or a little earlier, and probably died in 54 BC: at any rate, there is no trace in his work of events subsequent to 55 BC. Since he was sent to Rome as a young man, his family were probably thinking of a political career, but he seems to have had no great ambitions in this area. His only public activity, so far as we know, was service on the staff of the propraetor Memmius who was governor of Bithynia in 57–6 BC. In general, the political events of the turbulent decade he passed in Rome are little mentioned in his work. On one occasion his politically active friend Gaius Licinius Calvus involved him in a literary campaign against the triumvirs, especially *Julius Caesar (with his minion, Mamurra, but this outburst of ill-humour did not last and when Caesar magnanimously offered him his hand in reconciliation, he did not refuse it (Suet. *Iul.* 73).

If Catullus was only marginally involved in politics, he was at the centre of the radical social change that marked the end of the republic. He lived in the circles of the *jeunesse dorée* (the *delicata iuventus* as Cicero called them) who had turned away from the ideals of early Rome and embraced Hellenistic Greek culture. This environment affected not only Catullus' outlook and views but also his language, which acquired a facility previously unknown in Roman literature. In a literary sense also Catullus was surrounded by like-minded individuals. A whole group of young poets, the so-called 'neoterics', shared the same rejection of traditional norms and the same search for new forms and content, and, as in their lifestyle, Hellenistic culture provided the most important. In these same aristocratic circles Catullus met the married woman whom he called 'Lesbia'. He depicts her as self-assured, beautiful, and cultured, and regards her becoming his lover as the peak of felicity. But when he realizes that she has been false to him with a succession of partners, his happiness turns to despair. The ups and downs of this affair provide Catullus with the central theme of his poetry. His love poetry is completely different from the light-hearted frivolity of Hellenistic literature, as presented in the epigrams of the *Greek Anthology*; he sought in love not sexual transport but a deep human union which would last a whole lifetime. Apuleius (*Apol.* 10) tells us that behind the name Lesbia was a Clodia, and this seems to offer a secure historical context, since we know of a Clodia with similar characteristics living in Rome at this time, the sister of *Clodius and wife to the consul of 60 BC, Quintus Caecilius Metellus Celer. Cicero gives a picture of her in his *Pro Caelio* which for all its bias must have had some basis in life. The identity of Lesbia and Clodia was for a long time thought secure, but has often been questioned in the 20th cent. Nevertheless, even if the identification cannot be proved, Cicero's picture of the historical *Clodia is instructive for the social background to Catullus' poetry.

Catullus died young, and left behind only a slim corpus of work amounting to 114 poems of extremely varied length and form. The book is primarily ordered on metrical grounds. Sixty short poems in lyric or iambic metres are followed by poems 61–8, which are long poems in a variety of metres: the remainder of the book consists of epigrams. Another structural principle groups the elegies and epigrams together—that is, all the poems in elegiacs (65–116). Within these major sections, the ordering is again not random. In the short poems, as far as possible, a succession of poems in the same metre is avoided: the only exceptions are the many poems in phalaecean hendecasyllables, which often of necessity must be placed together, and the two short closural poems, 59 and

60. In the long poems, the first and last are metrically related to the neighbouring shorter poems: poem 61 is in lyric metre, 65–8 in elegiacs. A series of cycles may also be noticed in the content; the most important of these is the Lesbia cycle at the beginning of the book (2, 3, 5, 7, 8, 11), telling the story of Catullus' love affair from their first courtship through the height of passion to estrangement and the final break up of the affair. It is then up to the reader to place the rest of the Lesbia poems, which are not ordered chronologically, within this framework. There is another Lesbia cycle in the epigrams (70–87), though it is more loosely constructed and not completely chronological. Further cycles of related poems include those dealing with the dubious pair of friends Furius and Aurelius (15–26) and with Gellius (74–91, and 116). Other motives, such as the trip to Bithynia, the Iuventius poems, and the invectives against Caesar, are distributed throughout the book. This apparently careless arrangement has led some to believe that Catullus did not order the book himself, but that it is the result of posthumous publication. The principles of ordering mentioned above, however, seem more likely to go back to the poet himself, and a similar variety may be discerned in various reconstructions of Hellenistic books, such as the *Garland* of Meleager.

The three major groupings of poems within the corpus differ considerably in their approach. The short poems (1–60) contain much that one might term 'social poetry' from a thematic point of view, though they also include expressions of stronger emotions. These poems are certainly not, as has sometimes been thought, artless productions of a moment's reflection: Catullus models himself in them on the elegance and facility of the shorter Hellenistic forms. The group of longer poems in more elevated style begins with two wedding poems (61–2): poem 63 describes the fate of a young man who has become a devotee of Cybele, the 'epyllion' (mini-epic) 64 contrasts happy and unhappy love in the stories of Peleus and Ariadne, and 65–8 are a series of elegiac poems on various themes. Poem 66 (with the introductory poem 65) contains a translation of the *Lock of Berenice* which concludes *Callimachus' Aetia*: 68 (possibly two connected poems) is often seen as a precursor of the love elegies of *Propertius and *Tibullus. The epigrams (69–116) differ radically from the other poems. Even when they deal with the painful circumstances of the poet's own life, they are never simply representations of a momentary emotion, but rather reflective analyses of a situation or the poet's own experience.   H.-P.S.

Catulus See LUTATIUS CATULUS.

Cersobleptes (or **Cersebleptes**, *IG* 2. 65 b), the Odrysian king (i.e. he ruled in Thrace), son of Cotys I. Cersobleptes found himself, when he came to the throne in 360 BC, engaged in a war, which he had inherited from his father, with Athens, and with two pretenders to the throne, Berisades and Amadocus. Charidemus, the Athenian general, married Cersobleptes' sister, and continued to advise him, as he had done his father. In 359 BC the Athenian commander, Cephisodotus, was forced to make a treaty with Cersobleptes, which the Athenians repudiated. In the following year, Berisades and Amadocus joined forces, and, with Athenian help, forced Cersobleptes to sign a treaty dividing the kingdom of Cotys between the three princes, the Thracian Chersonese being ceded to Athens; Cersobleptes' share seems to have been the eastern part, Cypsela, Cardia, and the Propontis. Charidemus, however, persuaded Cersobleptes to renounce the treaty, and it was not till 357 that he was forced by the Athenian commander, Chares, to surrender the Chersonese, and agree to the partition of Thrace. In the following years *Philip II of Macedon proposed an alliance with Cersobleptes for the expulsion of the Athenians from the Chersonese, but nothing came of it. Meanwhile, through the agency of Charidemus, Athens secured Cersobleptes' goodwill, while his rival Amadocus (Berisades was now dead) turned to Philip. Philip invaded Thrace, and it was only his severe illness that prevented its subjection. In the peace of 346 BC between Athens and Philip, Cersobleptes was not included. The last war between Philip and Cersobleptes took place in 342 BC, and in that year or the next the Odrysian kingdom passed into the control of Macedonia. His name is inscribed on a silver vessel from Rogozen (Bulgaria).   J.M.R.C.; S.H.

Chariton, Greek novelist, author of the eight-book *Chaereas and Callirhoë* (*Ta peri*

Chairean kai Kallirhoën). He opens by naming himself and his city, Aphrodisias in Caria, claiming to be secretary to an orator Athenagoras. All three names have been suspected as appropriate fictions, but both personal names appear on inscriptions of Aphrodisias, Athenagoras recurring in two prominent families. Papyri date Chariton not later than the mid-2nd cent. AD, but although scholars agree in making his, or Xenophon Ephesius', the earliest of the novels surviving complete, dates are canvassed between the 1st cent. BC and *Hadrian's reign. His use of a historical character (Callirhoë's father is the Syracusan Hermocrates, victor over the Athenians in 413 BC) suggests an early stage in the genre's development. The historical *mise-en-scène*, much quotation of *Homer, and allusion to many other classical authors (notably *Thucydides and the more famous *Xenophon) show some literary ambition, confirmed by careful avoidance of hiatus; yet Chariton's diction does not Atticize (imitate classical Athenian Greek); hence Papanikolaou dated him in the 1st cent. BC.

Chariton begins at Syracuse: Chaereas and Callirhoë, both outstandingly beautiful, fall in love and marry. Soon after marriage Chaereas, driven to jealousy by disappointed rivals, kicks his pregnant wife. Taken for dead she is buried, but tomb-robbers find her alive, and in Miletus sell her to the rich and educated Dionysius. Chaereas learns of Callirhoë's abduction, and, searching for her, is himself enslaved. Callirhoë marries Dionysius to protect the child she expects by Chaereas, but her beauty overwhelms the satrap Mithradates, then Artaxerxes, the Persian king, at whose court Mithradates and Dionysius dispute their claims to her, and she and Chaereas again meet. Eventually the couple, reunited, return to Syracuse, to live happily ever after.

Chariton deploys traditional elements of the genre (travel, false deaths, pirates, enslavements, shipwrecks, happy ending) in a clear, linear narrative whose components are adroitly joined; key twists he ascribes to Fortune (*Tychē*), occasionally directing readers' responses by authorial comment (e.g. 8. 1. 4).   E.L.B.

Cicero, Marcus Tullius, the famous orator.
LIFE The first of two sons of a rich and well-connected *eques* (Roman knight) of

Arpinum (mod. Arpi), he was born on 3 January 106 BC, the year following the first consulship of *Marius, with whose family (also from Arpinum) his grandmother Gratidia had marriage connections. His intelligent and ambitious father (who was to die in the year of Cicero's canvass for the consulship), advised perhaps by Lucius Licinius Crassus, gave his two sons an excellent education in philosophy and rhetoric in Rome and later in Greece, with their two first-cousins as their fellow students. Cicero did military service in 90/89 under Pompey's father, Gnaeus Pompeius Strabo, and attended legal consultations of the two great Scaevolae (see SCAEVOLA). He conducted his first case in 81 (*Pro Quinctio*) and made an immediate reputation through his successful defence of Sextus Roscius of Ameria on a charge of parricide in 80, a case which reflected discreditably on the contemporary administration of the dictator Sulla. Cicero was then from 79 to 77 a student of philosophy and oratory both in Athens and in Rhodes, where he heard *Posidonius; he visited *Rutilius Rufus at Smyrna.

He returned to Rome, his health greatly improved, to pursue a public career, and was elected quaestor for 75, when he served for a year in western Sicily, and praetor for 66, in each case at the earliest age at which he could legally become a candidate. By securing the condemnation of *Verres for extortion in Sicily in 70 he scored a resounding success against Quintus Hortensius Hortalus, eight years his senior, whom he was to replace as the leading figure at the Roman bar. In a cleverly disarming speech delivered during his praetorship (*De imperio Cn. Pompei*) he supported, against strong opposition from the so-called optimates ('best men', i.e. the office-holding upper class), the tribune Gaius Manilius' proposal to transfer the command in the war against *Mithradates to *Pompey; this was the first public expression of his admiration for Pompey who was, with occasional short interruptions, henceforward to be the focus of his political allegiance. He was elected consul for 63, the first man from his family to reach the consulship—in fact, the first *novus homo* with no political background whatever since 94—because, in a poor field (including *Catiline), who had tried for the office twice before), his reputation as an orator and his cultivation of aristo-

crats, *equites*, and prominent Italians paid off. Hampered by a weak and indeed suspect colleague, Gaius Antonius 'Hybrida', Cicero did very well to secure evidence which convinced the senate of the seriousness of Catiline's conspiracy. After the *senatus consultum ultimum* ('last decree', in effect the declaration of a state of emergency) was passed, and Catiline left Rome for his army in Etruria, five conspirators prominent in Roman society and politics, including a praetor, Publius Cornelius Lentulus Sura, were arrested and executed on 5 December (the Nones). Although, after debate, the senate, influenced by *Cato the Younger, had recommended their execution, the act itself, a violation of the citizen's right to a trial, could be justified only by the passing of the last decree and was Cicero's personal responsibility. Though approved in the first moment of panic by all classes of society in Rome, its legality was strictly questionable, and Cicero was unwise to boast as loudly of it as he did (even in a long and indiscreet letter to Pompey in the east, *Pro Sulla* 67, *Pro Planc.* 85, cf. *Fam.* 5. 7). He published his speeches of 63, including those against Catiline, in 60, wrote of his action in prose and verse, in Greek and Latin, and invited others, including Posidonius, to do the same; and to the end of his life he never wavered in his belief that he had acted rightly and had saved Rome from catastrophe.

Though it was unlikely that he would escape prosecution, Cicero refused overtures from *Julius Caesar, which might have saved him at the price of his political independence. In 58 *Clodius, whom he had antagonized in 61 when Clodius was charged with incest, moved a bill as tribune re-enacting the law that anyone who had executed a citizen without trial should be banished. Without awaiting prosecution Cicero fled the country, to Macedonia, and Clodius passed a second bill, which Cicero regarded as unconstitutional, declaring him an exile. His house on the Palatine was destroyed by Clodius' gangsters, part of its site to be made a shrine of Liberty, and his villa at Tusculum was also badly damaged. With Pompey's belated support and with the support of the tribune *Milo, who employed violence as irresponsibly as Clodius had done in the previous year, Cicero was recalled by a law of the people on 4 August 57 and was warmly welcomed on his return both in Italy and in Rome, which he reached on 4 September.

He returned to a busy winter, fighting to secure adequate public compensation for the damage to his property and, in the senate and in the courts, supporting those chiefly responsible for his recall. Hopes of dissociating Pompey from his close political connection with Caesar, attempts which Clodius was employed by Caesar to interrupt, were at an end when Caesar, Pompey, and *Crassus revived their political union at Luca in April 56, and Cicero was sharply brought to heel (*Att.* 4. 5, on his 'palinode' or recantation; cf. *Fam.* 1. 9 for his later account of his conversion). He at once spoke warmly in the senate (e.g. in *De provinciis consularibus*) and on the public platform in favour of Caesar, as of a long-standing political friend. He claimed that it was the act of a realist, a *sapiens*, to accept the indisputable predominance of the Three ('temporibus adsentiendum', *Fam.* 1. 9. 21) and only revealed in conversation and in letters to such close friends as *Atticus the deep wound which his pride—his *dignitas*—had suffered. He took no more part in the collapsing world of republican politics, devoting himself to writing, which he never regarded as anything but a poor substitute for active political life (the *De oratore* was published in 55, and the *De republica* finished in 51); and he was humiliated by briefs which, under pressure from Pompey and Caesar, he was forced to accept. He defended Publius Vatinius successfully and Gabinius unsuccessfully in 54. He was humiliated too by his failure, in a court packed with troops, to defend Milo adequately when, with the case already prejudiced, Milo was impeached for the murder of Clodius early in 52. The period brought him one consolation, when he was elected augur in 53 or 52 in the place of his earlier protégé, young Publius Licinius Crassus, who had been killed at Carrhae.

Cicero was out of Rome during the eighteen months preceding the outbreak of the Civil War, being selected under regulations following Pompey's *lex de provinciis* of 52 to govern Cilicia as proconsul from summer 51 to summer 50. He was a just, if not a strong, governor, but he regarded his appointment with horror as a second relegation from Rome. However, his dispatches recording the successful encounter of his troops with brigands on mons Amanus earned a *supplicatio* at Rome and he returned, the *fasces* of his lictors wreathed in fading laurels, hoping that he might celebrate a triumph. Instead he was swept into the vortex of the Civil War.

Appointed district commissioner at Capua by the government, he did not at first follow Pompey and the consuls overseas. Caesar saw him at Formiae on 28 March 49, and invited him to join the rump of the senate in Rome on terms which with great resolution Cicero refused to accept (*Att.* 9. 11 a, to Caesar; 9. 18). His long indecision up to this point which was anything but discreditable was now at an end, and he joined the republicans in Greece, irritating their leaders by his caustic criticism, himself dismayed by the absence of any idealistic loyalty on their part to the cause of republicanism. After Pharsalus, in which he took no part, he refused Cato's invitation to assume command of the surviving republican forces and, pardoned by Caesar, he returned to Italy. But political life was at an end, and he was utterly out of sympathy with Caesar's domination. All that he could do was to return to his writing, his only important speech being that delivered in the senate in 46 (the year in which the *Brutus* was written) in praise of Caesar's pardon of Marcus Claudius Marcellus (consul 51), who had done so much to precipitate the outbreak of the Civil War.

That Cicero was not invited to participate in the conspiracy to kill Caesar in 44 is not insignificant. He hailed the news of the murder on 15 March with intemperate delight (e.g. *Fam.* 6. 15). Political life began again, and Cicero had all the prestige (*auctoritas*) of a senior consular. Within three months he was saying openly that Mark *Antony should have been killed too (*Att.* 15. 11. 2). He accepted the overtures of the young Caesar (Octavian; see AUGUSTUS), uncritical of the lawlessness of many of his acts, misled by his youth into a mistaken underassessment of his political acumen, and he closed his eyes to the fact that Octavian could never be reconciled to *Brutus and *Cassius. He struggled in speech after speech (the *Philippics*, the first delivered on 2 September 44, the last on 21 April 43) to induce the senate to declare Antony a public enemy. After Antony's defeat in Cisalpine Gaul in April 43, Octavian fooled Cicero for a time, perhaps with the suggestion that they might both be consuls together.

But Octavian's intentions were different. After his march on Rome to secure the consulship for himself and his uncle Quintus Pedius, and the formation of the Triumvirate, he did not oppose Antony's nomination of Cicero as a victim of the proscriptions which were the inauguration of the new regime. The soldiers caught Cicero in a not very resolute attempt to escape by sea. His slaves did not desert him, and he died with courage on 7 December 43.

In politics he hated Clodius, with good reason, and he hated Crassus and, at the end of his life, Antony. For the character of Cato, eleven years his junior, he had unqualified respect, and he published a panegyric of Cato in 45, after his death; but in politics, especially in the years following Pompey's return from the east in 62, he thought Cato's uncompromising rigidity (his *constantia*) impolitic, and Cato never concealed his distaste for Cicero's policy of temporizing expediency, both at this period and when he capitulated to the Three in 56. With Pompey Cicero never established the intimacy to which, particularly after Pompey's return in 62, he aspired, suggesting that he might play a second Laelius to Pompey's Scipio (see SCIPIO AEMILIANUS). Few of his contemporaries, perhaps, held him in higher esteem than did his constant opponent Caesar who, though often with an imperiousness which Cicero could not tolerate, was always friendly in his approach. Cicero was not a discriminating judge of the political intentions of others, being far too susceptible to, and uncritical of, flattery; and he was inevitably condemned to a certain political isolation. Loyally and not very critically devoted to the existing republican constitution, and fascinated by the mirage of a political consensus ('concordia ordinum'), he was never a liberal reformer (*popularis*); yet he was never completely acceptable to the established *optimates*, the worst of whom despised his social origin, while the rest mistrusted his personality as much as he mistrusted theirs. And, not having the *clientela* of the noble or of the successful general, he lacked *auctoritas*. It was this political isolation which (cf. *Att.* 1. 17; 1. 18. 1, of 61/60 BC) enhanced the importance for him of his close association with the knight Titus Pomponius Atticus, a man of the highest culture in both languages, his banker, financial adviser, publisher, and most generous and tolerant friend.

His marriage to Terentia had issue: Tullia, to whom he was devoted, whose death in 45 was the hardest of the blows which afflicted his private life, and Marcus Tullius Cicero. His marriage survived the storms and stress of thirty years, until he grew irritated with Terentia and divorced her in winter 47/6, to marry the young Publilia, from whom in turn he was almost immediately divorced. Cicero was a good master to his slaves and, with the rest of his family, was devoted to Tiro, to whom twenty-one of his letters in *Fam.* 16 are addressed. He gave him his freedom in 53, 'to be our friend instead of our slave', as Quintus *Cicero wrote (*Fam.* 16. 16. 1).

Cicero, who was never a really rich man, had eight country residences, in Campania, at Arpinum, at Formiae, and, his suburban villa, at Tusculum; in Rome he was extremely proud of his house on the Palatine hill, which he bought in 62 for $3\frac{1}{2}$ million sesterces (*Fam.* 5. 6. 2).

Apart from the surviving histories of the late republic and, in particular, Plutarch's Lives of Cicero and of his outstanding contemporaries, the bulk of our knowledge of him derives from his own writings, in particular from his letters, only a minority of which was written with any thought of publication. His reputation has therefore suffered from the fact that we have intimate knowledge of the most private part of his personal life; in this respect he has been his own worst enemy, and his critics have given undue prominence to his extremes of exaltation and depression and to the frequent expression of his evident vanity. (See J. P. V. Balsdon, 'Cicero the Man', in T. A. Dorey (ed.), *Cicero* (1965).) J.P.B.; M.T.G.

WORKS *SPEECHES* Fifty-eight of Cicero's speeches survive in whole or part; numerous others were unpublished or lost (88 are recorded by J. Crawford, *M. Tullius Cicero: The Lost and Unpublished Orations* (1984)).

Cicero's normal practice, if he decided to publish a speech, was to 'write up' (*conficere*) a version after the event. In one case we know that he delivered a speech from a script (*Post reditum in senatu*); otherwise it seems that only a few important passages, chiefly the exordium and peroration, were written out *in extenso* beforehand. The published versions of court speeches in many instances certainly represent a shortened version of the actual proceedings, as shown by Humbert; the examination of witnesses is largely omitted, and some sections of argumentation are represented only by headings. The extent to which Cicero changed the content or emphasis of his speeches when preparing them for publication is disputed. It has been thought that the speeches were regularly altered to suit the political circumstances of the time of publication, rather than the time of delivery. On the other hand, it has been pointed out that Cicero's overt reason for publication was to provide examples of successful oratory for posterity to imitate and admire, and this would naturally place limits on the degree of alteration that could reasonably be made, as would the presence among his readership of a substantial number of those who had been present at the delivery of the speech.

In certain cases there is firm evidence that our text does not represent a speech that was actually delivered. The five speeches of the *Actio secunda in Verrem* were prepared for use in court but were never actually delivered, since *Verres withdrew into exile after the *Actio prima*. The second *Philippic* was not delivered as a speech, but circulated as a pamphlet, although it observes the conventions of a senatorial speech. But these are exceptions. The *Pro Milone* is an exception in another way, being a rare example of an unsuccessful speech that was nevertheless published; our sources claim or imply that they had access to a transcript (complete with interruptions) of the actual speech, which differed from Cicero's published version, although it is not proved that the difference in content was much greater than in the case of most of Cicero's other speeches (J. N. Settle, *TAPA* 1963, 268–80).

Cicero's reputation as an orator depended on consistent practical success, although his detractors in antiquity made as much capital out of his relatively rare failures as their modern equivalents have done. In these successes a large part must have been played by his manner of delivery, of which virtually no impression can be given by a written speech; yet it is possible to see in the published versions something of the powers of advocacy that made Cicero the leading courtroom orator of his time (this has been brought out particularly clearly by Stroh). The political speeches are perhaps more difficult for a

modern reader to appreciate: Cicero's self-glorifications and his unbridled invectives tend to repel those brought up in a modern western society, while adverse judgement of his political position can hinder appreciation of his oratory. It is easy to be cynical about what *Juvenal called the 'divine Philippic' (the Second) without coming to terms with the historical circumstances that produced this and other speeches, and the oratorical qualities that made them into objects of near-universal admiration.

The style of Cicero's speeches did not remain entirely uniform. As he himself observed, in his youth he had a tendency to exuberance (so-called Asianism), best exemplified in the *Pro Roscio Amerino* (cf. F. Solmsen, *TAPA* 1938, 542–56); this was later tempered by increasing maturity and by a change in oratorical fashion. The style also depended to some extent on the occasion; there are variations in manner between Cicero's addresses to senate and people, to a full jury, and to a single arbitrator, and Cicero himself talks of the different styles appropriate for the different sections of a speech (plain for narration, grand for the final appeal to the emotions, etc.). However, Cicero's speeches throughout his life are consistent in their rhythmical regularity, their smooth and balanced sentence-construction, and their careful choice of vocabulary and idiom (on the style of the speeches, see L. Laurand, *Étude sur le style des discours de Cicéron*, 3 vols., 2nd edn. (1925–7)). Cicero's style was criticized by some of his contemporaries for lacking vigour (Tac. *Dial.* 18) and by later rhetoricians for longwindedness and lack of quotability (ibid. 22).

Cicero made good use of the theories of rhetoric current in his time, and, still more, of the great classical models of Athenian oratory. Most of the ancient structural conventions, figures of speech, and standard modes of argument can be exemplified from his writings, and some of the speeches were consistently taken as copy-book examples by later rhetoricians such as *Quintilian; but Cicero never merely followed the rules for their own sake, and examples can be found of highly effective departures from the recommended practice of the rhetoricians.

Of the extant speeches, three belong to the period before Cicero's Sicilian quaestorship (*Pro Roscio Amerino*, from Cicero's first major public trial in 80 BC, together with *Pro Quinctio* and *Pro Roscio Comoedo*). Then follows the series of speeches from the trial of Verres in 70: *Divinatio in Caecilium*, the *Actio prima in Verrem*, and the five speeches of the *Actio secunda* generally referred to as the Verrines. The *Pro Tullio*, *Pro Fonteio*, and *Pro Caecina* date from 69. Two of the extant speeches belong to Cicero's praetorship, the *Pro lege Manilia* (alias *De imperio Cn. Pompei*) and the *Pro Cluentio*. Of the 'consular' orations which Cicero himself published (a collection of twelve according to *Att.* 2. 1. 3; but see W. C. McDermott, *Philologus* 1972, 277–84), we have the three speeches *De lege agraria contra Rullum*, the *Pro Rabirio perduellionis reo*, and the four Catilinarians; the *Pro Murena* also dates from this year. From the years succeeding the consulship the *Pro Sulla*, *Pro Archia* (both 62), and *Pro Flacco* (59) survive. Another group is formed by the speeches made on returning from exile in 57 and in the following year: *Post reditum in senatu*, *Post reditum ad Quirites*, *De domo sua*, *De haruspicum responsis*, *Pro Sestio*, *In Vatinium interrogatio*. To the year 56 also belong the senatorial speech *De provinciis consularibus* and the defences of Caelius Rufus and Lucius Cornelius Balbus; the invective *In Pisonem* was published in 55. From 54 we have the *Pro Plancio* and the *Pro Rabirio Postumo*. In 52, Cicero defended *Milo without success, publishing a version of the speech before departing to govern Cilicia. In 46–45, Cicero addressed the victorious Caesar on behalf of Marcus Claudius Marcellus, Ligarius and King Deiotarus of Galatia. Otherwise Caesar's dictatorship offered no opportunity for Cicero to exercise his forensic gifts, and he devoted himself to the writing of treatises on rhetoric and philosophy. During his brief return to public life in 44–43, Cicero delivered the series of speeches known (at his own joking suggestion: *Ad Brut.* 2. 3. 4) as the *Philippics*, which directly or indirectly expressed his opposition to Antony; cf. DEMOSTHENES. Fourteen of these survive; at least three more have been lost.

WORKS ON RHETORIC (*a*) *De inventione*, written in Cicero's youth, is a treatise on some techniques of rhetorical argument, which has a close resemblance to parts of the anonymous *Rhetorica ad Herennium* (once falsely attributed to Cicero).

(*b*) *De oratore* (55 BC), *Brutus*, and *Orator* (46) represent Cicero's major contribution to the theory of (Latin) rhetoric, and he himself grouped them with his philosophical works. They present an idealized picture of the orator as a liberally educated master of his art, a picture in which the technical aspects of Greek rhetorical theory still have their place, but are supplemented by knowledge of literature, philosophy, and general culture, and by the qualities of character required of the ideal Roman aristocrat. This was endorsed by later Roman authors such as *Quintilian, and it was one of the formative influences on Renaissance ideals of character and education. The *De oratore* was closely linked with the more ambitious *De republica* which followed it, and the ideal orator depicted in the former is little different from the ideal statesman in the latter. The *Brutus* is devoted largely to a history of Roman oratory, while the *Orator* deals with more technical points of style. These last two works were written against a background of controversy regarding the desirable style or styles in oratory, in the course of which Cicero had been criticized for persisting (as it seemed) in the 'Asian' fashions of his younger days, and a plain 'Attic' or 'Athenian' style had been held up as an ideal. Cicero reacts to this by attempting to demonstrate that different styles are effective for different purposes, that there was more variety in actual Athenian oratory than the 'Atticists' allowed, and that the ideal orator should be master of several styles, including (where appropriate) the Ciceronian grand manner itself, for which *Demosthenes, rather than the Asian rhetoricians, is claimed as a precedent. Although this controversy was in some senses an ephemeral one, these works contain much of interest concerning the way Roman orators regarded their art, and the *Brutus* is a mine of prosopographical information as well as of Roman rhetorical criticism.

(*c*) Cicero's minor works on the subject comprise: *Partitiones oratoriae*, a dialogue in which Cicero instructs his son in the elements of the art; the date is uncertain, but it must belong to a time at which Cicero's son was approaching maturity; *Topica*, written in 44 BC and dedicated Gaius Trebatius Testa, an exposition of the content of *Aristotle's work of the same title; and *De optimo genere oratorum*, of disputed authenticity, an introduc-

tion to translations (which may or may not
have existed) of *Aeschines' *In Ctesiphontem*
and Demosthenes' *De corona.*

POEMS Cicero early acquired a reputation
as a bad poet on the basis of two lines from
his autobiographical compositions, 'o fortu-
natam natam me consule Romam' ('O happy
Rome, born in my consulship') and 'cedant
arma togae, concedat laurea laudi' ('yield
arms to the toga, the bay to achievement')
(the variant *linguae* 'to the tongue' was probably satirical). The only obvious faults of
these lines are a naïve self-esteem and a somewhat old-fashioned taste for assonance; in
general, Cicero was a competent enough ver-
sifier, and despite his admiration for the older
poets, his verse technique is more modern
than that of his contemporary *Lucretius. He
appears at times to have had serious poetic
ambitions and to have regarded verse-writing
as more than an amateur's accomplishment.
It is perhaps less surprising in an ancient than
it would be in a modern context that he chose
to make verse a vehicle for personal propaganda, in the *Consulatus suus* (of which a
substantial passage is quoted by Cicero
himself in *Div.* 1. 17) and *De temporibus suis.*
Apart from these, Cicero composed an original (probably fairly short) epic poem on his
fellow-Arpinate *Marius; this must have been
in circulation in the 50s BC (he refers to it at
the beginning of the *De legibus*). The only
part of his poetry to survive in a manuscript
tradition is the so-called *Aratea,* 469 lines
from a verse translation of *Aratus (1)'s
Phaenomena; this is of interest as part of the
tradition of adapting Hellenistic didactic
poetry and as a precursor of *Virgil's *Georgics.* There are some other scattered fragments
of lost poems, and Cicero translated a
number of passages of Greek poetry *ad hoc*
for quotation in his philosophical works (in
preference to the original Greek).

LETTERS Cicero's surviving correspondence is an invaluable collection of evidence
for his biography, for the history of the time,
and for Roman social life. The sixteen books
Ad familiares were published after Cicero's
death by his freedman Marcus Tullius Tiro.
Cicero's letters to *Atticus were preserved
(without the replies) by the latter and seen by
*Cornelius Nepos (Nep. *Att.* 16. 2–4, referring
to a collection in 11 books). They were in
circulation in the reign of Nero and later, but
the silence of *Asconius suggests that they

were not available to him. Our present collection *Ad Atticum* consists of sixteen books,
probably an augmented version of the collection known to Nepos. We also have the
smaller collections *Ad Quintum fratrem*
(including the Commentariolum petitionis,
on the technique of electioneering) and *Ad
Brutum.* Further collections of Cicero's letters
apparently existed in antiquity. The *Ad familiares* collection contains, in addition to
Cicero's own, letters from a variety of correspondents to him.

The letters were not in any sense written
for publication; as far as is known, it was not
until 44 BC that Cicero thought of publishing
a selection of them (*Att.* 16. 5. 5; cf. *Fam.* 16.
17. 1), and it is not clear that this idea was
ever put into practice in that form. They vary
greatly in their level of formality. At the one
extreme they include official dispatches and
letters of a semi-public nature on matters of
political importance, whose style is similar to
that of the public speeches; at the other may
be found casual notes to members of the
family and informal exchanges with Atticus,
often highly allusive and colloquial.

                                                                  J.G.F.P.

PHILOSOPHICA Apart from the treatises
on rhetoric, an important part of the Hellenistic philosophical curriculum (though see
below), these fall into two parts: (*a*) the writings on political philosophy and statecraft
of the years immediately preceding Cicero's
governorship of Cilicia, and (*b*) the works on
epistemology, ethics, and theology (standing
in the place of physics) which were produced
in the incredibly short period between February 45 and November 44. Cicero gives a list
and account of his own philosophical writings at *Div.* 2. 1.

In the *De republica,* a dialogue between
*Scipio Aemilianus, Gaius Laelius, and
others, of which we have only parts of the
six books (including the *Somnium Scipionis,*
preserved as a whole by *Macrobius), Cicero
discusses the ideal state, always with an eye
on the history of the Roman republic, and
favours a constitution combining elements
of all three main forms, monarchy, oligarchy,
and democracy. His discussion reflects the
political conditions of the time and looks to
a wise counsellor (for which part Cicero may
at one time have cast *Pompey) as a remedy
for Rome's political sickness. But its chief
attraction for posterity lay in its assertion of

human rights and of man's participation in humanity and the cosmos, a notion which eclectic developments in Stoicism and Cicero's own predilections helped to foster. Cicero probably worked on the De legibus immediately after the De republica (cf. Leg. 1. 15), but did not publish it. (It does not appear in the list in Div. 2. 1 ff., and is not specifically mentioned in the letters.) In the three extant books (Macrobius quotes from a fifth book, and the reference to iudicia in 3. 47 has generally been taken to point to the subject of the fourth book) Cicero expounds the Stoic conception of divinely sanctioned Law, based on reason, and discusses legal enactments connected with religion and magistracies, drawing heavily on the 2nd-cent. BC Stoic Diogenes of Babylon.

Politically inactive under Caesar's dictatorship, the death of his daughter Tullia finally led Cicero to seek consolation in writing about philosophical subjects which had always interested him, from the early days of his studies under the Epicureans Phaedrus and Zeno (cf. EPICURUS), the Academics *Philon of Larissa, *Antiochus of Ascalon, at Athens and on Rhodes the Stoic *Posidonius, through the years of his association with Diodotus the Stoic (who lived and died in his own home), to the time immediately after the Civil War, when Gaius Matius urged him to write on philosophy in troubled times (Fam. 11. 27. 5). What had formerly been for Cicero a useful exercise (cf. Tusc. 2. 9, and his claim at Orat. 12 to be a product of the Academy rather than of the rhetoricians' workshops) and a source of oratorical material (cf. De or. 1. 5 and Orat. 113 ff.; the Paradoxa Stoicorum, published, it seems, as late as the beginning of 46, may be an exercise in the preparation of such material) became now a haven of refuge (Fam. 7. 30. 2), a doloris medicina (Acad. post. 1. 11). Cicero needed to reassure himself, and hoped as well to make a name for himself as a philosophical writer (at Off. 1. 2 ff. he admits his inferior philosophical knowledge, but contraposes his virtues as a stylist). But Cicero was well prepared for the task, having learnt Stoic dialectic from Diodotus, rhetoric and arguing both sides of a question from the Peripatetics, while the Academics had taught him to refute any argument. In addition Cicero had heard, and listened carefully, to the most charismatic philosophers of his time, the showmen of

the day. He had a profound admiration and respect for *Plato (deus ille noster—'our divine Plato': Att. 4. 16. 3) and *Aristotle. His claim to look to *Socrates (Acad. 1. 3) belies his sceptical method of inquiry and emphasis on ethics. He aimed above all at giving the Romans a philosophical literature and terminology, which would take the place of the Greek philosophers, on whom the Romans had been hitherto intellectually dependent. The surviving work of the Hellenistic philosophers suggests that Cicero would not be alone in following his Greek sources closely in order to engage them polemically. But some scholars have understood Cicero's words: 'ἀπόγραφα sunt, minore labore fiunt; verba tantum adfero quibus abundo' ('They are copies. They're no trouble. I just bring the words, and I've plenty of them': Att. 12. 52. 3) too seriously (i.e. without a hint of false modesty), and Shackleton Bailey has suggested that they do not even pertain to the philosophica. More trustworthy are Cicero's claims (Off. 1. 6) to follow the Stoics (in that work) not as a mere translator but drawing from Stoic sources as he thinks fit, and (Fin. 1. 6) to add his own criticism (iudicium) and arrangement (scribendi ordo) to the chosen authority.

Several lost works probably came first: a De gloria (a eulogy of *Cato the Elder); the Consolatio, an attempt to console himself for the loss of Tullia (and unique in being addressed to himself); and the Hortensius, a plea for the study of philosophy, which profoundly affected *Augustine (it turned him to God: Conf. 3. 4. 7). The list in Div. 2. 1 shows that Cicero swiftly proceeded with the construction of what is by his own description an encyclopaedia of Hellenistic philosophy: the protreptic Hortensius is followed by the Academica, on epistemology or theory of knowledge (especially concerned with the criterion of truth), originally in two books, entitled Catulus and Lucullus, of which only the second survives, but later recast in four books, of which we possess part of the first (Academica posteriora). It treats of the views of the New Academy after Arcesilaus, and in particular of *Carneades on the impossibility of attaining certain knowledge, but conceding some realia as more compelling or probable than others. The recommendation (Div. 2. 150) to give unprejudiced consideration to different theories before approving simillima *veri* appealed to Cicero, who sometimes portrayed himself as belonging to this philosophical school (*Tusc.* 2. 5, 4. 47). In fact Cicero remained generally true to Philon's early teaching, rejecting the possibility of certain knowledge, but retaining and asserting the right to adopt whatever position seemed most compelling on each occasion.

Thus in questions of ethics Cicero often inclined toward Stoic doctrine as he recoiled from the Epicurean, as is evident in the *De finibus bonorum et malorum*, where he compiles and answers in turn the theories on the *summum bonum* ('highest good') propounded by the Epicureans and Stoics, before giving the views of Antiochus' so-called 'Old Academy' in book 5. From this encyclopaedic survey of the various schools' positions on ethics, Cicero turned in the *Tusculan Disputations* to the problems of the psychology of the happy life: death, grief, pain, fear, passion, and other mental disorders, and of what is essential for happiness, including (according to the Stoics) virtue. Concerned largely to allay his own doubts, and impressed by Stoic teaching on these subjects, he writes here with a passionate intensity and lyrical beauty.

As in the case of the contemporary Epicurean *Philodemus, theological speculation stands for Cicero in the place of a full account of natural philosophy and physical causes (such as is found, for example, in *Lucretius, Epicurus, or Chrysippus, though *Tusc.* 1 also treats materialism in its concern for the material composition of the soul and a rational chain of causation). Thus Cicero next composes *De natura deorum* in three books, each devoted to the view of a different school (Epicurean, Stoic, Academic) on the nature of the gods and the existence of the divine, its role in human culture and the state. Having allowed Cotta to present the sceptical Academic view in book 3, after Velleius' presentation of the Epicurean in book 1, and Balbus' of the Stoic in book 2, Cicero rounds off the debate with a typically Academic expression of his own opinion: that the Stoic's argument is more likely to be right (*ad veritatis similitudinem ... propensior* 3. 95). In a later work, Stoic beliefs concerning Fate and the possibility of prediction are examined, with more use of anecdote and quotation perhaps indicative of a popular exposition, in the two books of the *De divinatione*, published just after Caesar's murder (*Div.* 2. 4).

In this case Cicero displays no sympathy with the views of the Stoics, whose commitment to the validity of divination was based on complex principles of logic and cosmic sympathy. Cicero's pious reaffirmation (2. 148) of his belief in the existence of a divine being, maintaining that it is prudent to keep traditional rites and ceremonies, belies his concerns in matters of theology and religion for the state above all else. Finally, the fragmentary *De fato* discusses the more specialized problem of volition and decides against Stoic determinism.

Equally specialized are the two genial and polished essays *Cato Maior de senectute* (written probably just before Caesar's murder and included in *Div.* list) and the *Laelius de amicitia*, which show once again Cicero's anxiety to reassure or occupy himself in times of stress and danger, and his last work on moral philosophy *De officiis* (finished November 44) aims at giving advice, based on Stoic precepts and in particular (for books 1 and 2) on the teachings of *Panaetius, on a variety of problems of conduct (ostensibly to Cicero's son).

These three works, along with the *Tusc.* and the *Somnium Scipionis*, were the most popular among readers in the Middle Ages, when the work of Cicero the politician and orator was almost forgotten, to be rediscovered in the Renaissance. Cicero's influence on European thought and literature ensured that what he found interesting and important in Greek philosophy became the philosophical curriculum of the Renaissance and Enlightenment. His achievement stands out as the creator of philosophical vocabulary in Latin, and as a philosophical stylist.   J.H.S.; D.O.

Cicero, Quintus (Quintus Tullius Cicero) (*c*.102–43 BC), younger brother of *Cicero and similarly educated (they were both in Athens in 79 BC), had none of his brother's genius. He was irascible and often tactlessly outspoken; yet he was a good soldier and an able administrator. Plebeian aedile in 65 and praetor in 62 (helped, no doubt, by the fact that his brother Marcus was praetor and consul respectively when he was elected), he governed Asia from 61 to 58, receiving two long letters of advice and criticism from his brother in Rome (*QFr.* 1. 1–2). He spent winter 57/6 in Sardinia as a legate (subordinate commander) of *Pompey, when Pompey received his corn commission, and was evidently a hostage for Marcus' good behaviour in politics after his recall from exile (*Fam.* 1. 9. 9). He was legate on *Julius Caesar's staff in Gaul from 54 to early 51, taking part in the invasion of Britain in 54 and winning deserved praise for his courage in holding out against the Nervii when the Gauls attacked the winter camps in 54 (*BGall.* 5. 40–52); though unwell, he drove himself so hard that his troops forced him to take some sleep at night (ibid. 40. 7). At Atuatuca a year later he took risks, probably with more excuse than Caesar allows, and was criticized (ibid. 6. 36–42). He was a valuable legate on Marcus' staff in Cilicia in 51/50, supplying (with C. Pomptinus) the military experience which Marcus lacked. He joined Pompey in the Civil War, was pardoned after Caesar's victory at Pharsalus and then, with his son, behaved badly in maligning his brother to Caesar (*Att.* 11. 9 f.). He returned to Rome in 47 by Caesar's permission. Victims of the proscriptions in 43, he and his son were betrayed by their slaves.

The twenty-seven surviving letters of Marcus to Quintus were written between 60 and 54, mostly when Quintus was serving abroad. Of the four short surviving letters of Quintus, one (*Fam.* 16. 16: 53 BC) congratulated Marcus on enfranchising Marcus Tullius Tiro and three (*Fam.* 16. 8: 49 BC; 16. 26 f.: 44 BC) were to Tiro. Quintus was a literary dilettante, writing four tragedies in sixteen days when in Gaul (*QFr.* 3. 5. 7). Though certainty is not possible (Balsdon, *CQ* 1963, 242 ff.), a strong case can be made for believing that neither Quintus nor, indeed, a contemporary wrote the *Commentariolum petitionis*, a long letter on Marcus' canvass for the consulship of 63. It none the less preserves some valuable information.

Like his brother, Quintus owned property near Arpinum. His marriage to Pomponia, who was older than he and the sister of Marcus' friend *Atticus, lasted from 69 to 44 and was never a happy one. It produced one son, a gifted boy whom his father indulged.

J.P.B.; M.T.G.

Cimon, wealthy and noble 5th-cent. BC Athenian, son of *Miltiades and Hegesipyle,

daughter of the Thracian king Olorus; Cimon and the historian *Thucydides, son of an Olorus, were thus related (*APF* 234 f.). His sister Elpinice married Callias; an unpublished ostracon (among other evidence) alleges incest between them ('let Cimon take his sister Elpinice and get out'). He married Isodice, a member of the famous Athenian family the Alcmaeonidae, and perhaps also an Arcadian woman. His sons by one of these were: Lacedaemonius, Eleos/Oulios, Thettalus, programmatic names (he had diplomatic ties with Sparta and Thessaly, and the Ionian name Oulios, see *SEG* 38. 1996 *bis*, recalls one justification of the Delian League by stressing Ionianism); three other sons by Isodice are historically dubious. On Miltiades' death in 489 he paid his 50-talent fine. He joined an embassy to Sparta in 479 and thereafter was often *stratēgos* (general) (see *AO*). In 478 he helped Aristides bring the maritime Greeks into the Delian League and commanded most of its operations 476–463. He drove the Spartan Pausanias out of Byzantium; captured Eion-on-the-Strymon from the Persian Boges (?476/5); and conquered Scyros, expelling the Dolopians (pirates), installing a cleruchy (settlement of Athenians), and bringing back the 'bones of Theseus' to Athens. Cimon's greatest achievement was the Eurymedon victory over Persia, c.466; this brought places as far east as Phaselis into the league. It is possible that he negotiated peace with Persia about now, that his peace was rejected by his domestic enemies at the end of the decade, and that the 450 Peace of Cimon's brother-in-law Callias (the so-called Peace of Callias) was a renewal of Cimon's peace. Next he subdued Thracian Chersonesus and reduced revolted Thasos in 465–463 (hence the hostility of Thasian Stesimbrotus, a source of *Plutarch), but was prosecuted on his *euthyna* (examination of accounts) by *Pericles for allegedly accepting bribes from Alexander I of Macedon; he was acquitted. He next persuaded Athens to send him (462) with a large hoplite force to help Sparta against the helots, now in revolt. But the Athenians were sent humiliatingly home on suspicion of 'revolutionary tendencies', and Cimon's ostracism followed (461). The exact connection between this and Ephialtes' political reforms is obscure, but Cimon was no hoplite conservative. True, he spent lavishly on entertainments and public works, as

part of rivalry with radical leaders like
*Themistocles, Ephialtes, and Pericles. Again,
some of Cimon's policies were reversed after
his ostracism: his pro-Spartan policy and his
peace with Persia (if he made it) were abandoned. But despite personal ties and sympathies with Sparta he was no enemy of the
democracy or the empire: Eurymedon was as
much the achievement of the naval *thētes* (the
lowest Athenian census class) as of hoplites;
hoplites and *thētes* admittedly competed for
military glory in the post-Persian War period
(ML 26, cf. *JHS* 1968, 51 ff.) but both were
excluded from top office until 458 so that
opposition is unreal; Sparta at least saw
Cimon and his hoplites as revolutionaries,
i.e. compromised by the reforms hatching
back home; and Cimon approved the Ionian
propaganda of the empire (cf. above on
Oulios), expanded it as much as Pericles, and
like him forcibly opposed secession from it.

In 458 Cimon tried to help fight for Athens
against Sparta at Tanagra but was rebuffed
and not yet recalled from ostracism (though
one tradition asserts this). When he did
return at the end of the 450s he arranged a
five-year truce with Sparta and fought Persia
on Cyprus where he died.

A.W.G.; T.J.C.; S.H.

Cinna (Lucius Cornelius Cinna) of patrician, but not recently distinguished, family,
fought successfully in the Social War and,
against the opposition of *Sulla, became
consul 87 BC. Trying to rescind Sulla's legislation as passed by force, he was driven out of
Rome by his colleague Gnaeus Octavius and
illegally deposed; Lucius Cornelius Merula
was elected to replace him. Collecting Italians
and legionaries, he was joined by Gnaeus
Papirius Carbo and *Sertorius, and by
*Marius whom he summoned back to Italy.
They marched on Rome and captured it late
in 87 after the death of Gnaeus Pompeius
Strabo and Quintus Caecilius Metellus Pius'
failure to relieve it. He punished those who
had acted illegally, but tried (not very
successfully) to stop indiscriminate violence
on Marius' orders. Consul 86 with Marius
and, after Marius' death, with Lucius Valerius
Flaccus, he sent Flaccus to fight against
*Mithradates VI, while he restored ordered
government in Italy. He gained the co-operation of the *equites* (knights) and the people

by financial reforms (carried by Flaccus and
Marcus Marius Gratidianus), and that of
eminent consulars by moderation and return
to *mos maiorum* ('ancestral custom'),
although he could not repair the economic
disruption of Italy due to the Social and Civil
Wars. Following Marius' precedent, he held
the consulship again in 85 and 84 with Carbo,
owing to the emergency caused by the
Mithradatic War and the threatening behaviour of Sulla, with whom he continued to
negotiate. Embarking on a campaign in Lib-
urnia early in 84, probably to train an army
for a possible conflict with Sulla's veterans,
he was killed in a mutiny. Sulla now rebelled
and the government disintegrated. Our uniformly hostile accounts of him derive from
Sullani or men who deserted him to join the
victorious Sulla.

E.B.

Claudian (Claudius Claudianus, b. *c.* AD
370), poet. A native of Alexandria, he came to
Italy *c*.394 and, turning from Greek to Latin,
scored an instant success by eulogizing his
young patrons, the consuls Probinus and
Olybrius (January 395). Thereafter he became
court poet under the emperor Honorius and
his minister Stilicho, for whom he produced
a series of panegyrics and other propagandist
poems. His efforts won him the title *vir clarissimus* (indicating senatorial rank), a bronze
statue in the forum Traiani (*CIL* 6. 1710), and
a rich bride selected by Stilicho's wife, Serena.
His death (*c*.404) may be inferred from his
silence in the face of Stilicho's subsequent
achievements.

Three of Claudian's panegyrics were
written on consulships held by Honorius in
396, 398, and 404; the consulships of Mallius
Theodorus in 399 and Stilicho in 400 were
similarly recognized. The marriage of
Honorius to Stilicho's daughter Maria in 398
was celebrated with four *Fescennini* (ribald
wedding verses) and an epithalamium (a
more formal wedding poem), doing propagandist work as well as fulfilling their traditional functions. Invectives against Rufinus
and Eutropius, Stilicho's rivals at the eastern
court of Arcadius, appeared in 396–7 and 399
respectively. The other main genre in which
Claudian worked, the epic, is represented by
De bello Gildonico (398), *De bello Getico* (402),
and the unfinished mythological poems of
uncertain date, *De raptu Proserpinae* and
Gigantomachia.

Claudian's poetry belongs firmly to the classical tradition, though it does not necessarily follow that *Augustine and Orosius (followed by many modern scholars) were right in supposing him a pagan. He is indebted particularly to the Greek rhetoricians of the later empire and to the Latin poets of the Silver Age; in diction and technique he is the equal of *Lucan and *Statius, in hyperbole he perhaps outdoes them. Set speeches and descriptions are the hallmark of his work. Though slanted in the propagandist manner, his writings are a valuable historical source for his period.   J.H.D.S.

Claudius (Tiberius Claudius Nero Germanicus), 10 BC–AD 54), the emperor Claudius I, was born at Lugdunum (Lyons) (1 August), the youngest child of Nero Claudius Drusus and of Antonia. Hampered by a limp, trembling, and a speech defect all perhaps due to cerebral palsy, and by continual illnesses, he received no public distinction from Augustus beyond the augurate, and was twice refused a magistracy by Tiberius. Enactments of AD 20, the *tabula Siarensis* (*ZPE* 55 (1984), 58 f., fr. 1, ll. 6 f.; 19–21) and the *senatus consultum de Cn. Pisone patre* (ed. W. Eck and others, 1996) 1. 148, like Tac. *Ann* 3. 18. 4, illustrate his low position in the imperial family. Claudius retained the status of a knight until on 1 July 37 he became suffect consul with his young nephew, the emperor *Gaius (1); for the rest of the reign he received little but insults. What role, if any, he played in planning the assassination of Gaius in 41 is disputed. After the murder he was discovered in the palace by a soldier, taken to the praetorian barracks, and saluted emperor while the senate was still discussing the possibility of restoring the republic. Senators did not easily forgive him for the way he came to power, but he had the support of the army: the revolt of Lucius Arruntius Camillus Scribonianus in Dalmatia (42) was short-lived. Claudius stressed his bond with guard and legions and, making up for previous inexperience, briefly took a personal part in the invasion of Britain (43). The capture of Camulodunum occasioned an impressive pageant, and Claudius made a leisurely progress back to Rome for his triumph (44). By the end of his principate he had received 27 salutations as *imperator*, more than any other emperor until *Constantine I. He was also consul four more times

(42, 43, 47, and 51), and revived the office of censor, which he held with his favourite Lucius Vitellius in 47–8.

Although he reverted from the pretentious absolutism of Gaius (whose acts, however, were not annulled wholesale), and stressed civility to the senate, the precariousness of his position made him liable to take sudden and violent action against threats real, imagined by himself, or thought up by advisers; offenders who were given a trial were often heard by few advisers in private. His early career and mistrust of the senate led him to rely on the advice of freedmen, especially Narcissus and Marcus Antonius Pallas, whose influence and wealth were hated; but his dependence on his third and fourth wives *Messallina and *Agrippina the Younger was due as much to their political importance as to uxoriousness. Messallina was the mother of his only surviving son Britannicus, born 41 (Claudius' earlier wives, Plautia Urgulanilla and Aelia Paetina, left him only with a daughter, Antonia. She was hard to dislodge for that reason, but fell in 48, in what looks like a struggle between freedmen on the one hand and senators and knights on the other. Agrippina, daughter of Claudius' popular brother *Germanicus, was a figure in her own right, and particularly desirable after the loss of face entailed by Messallina's fall. The son she brought with her was more than three years older than Britannicus, and in 50 he was adopted by Claudius as a partner for his own son to assure their joint accession to power; in 53 Nero married Claudius' daughter Claudia Octavia. But while Nero's career was accelerated, with a grant of proconsular power outside Rome coming in 51, Britannicus was pushed aside. Claudius' death on 13 October 54 conveniently made it impossible for him to give his natural son the toga of manhood, but the story that he was poisoned by Agrippina has been questioned.

In youth Claudius wrote works on Etruscan and Carthaginian history. From *Livy he acquired a knowledge of Roman history, and he was steeped in religion and tradition, but his celebration of the Secular Games (47), extension of the *pomerium* (the religious boundary of the city of Rome), and taking of the *augurium salutis* ('augury of security', 49) had the political purpose of reassuring the Roman people about the stability and success of his regime.

Claudius paid particular attention to the welfare of the populace. Building the harbour at Ostia and draining the Fucinus lacus (a large lake at the centre of Italy) were intended to secure or increase the grain supply, as was his offer of privileges to those who invested in the construction of grain ships.

Claudius' interest in government, from which he had been excluded, inclined him to intervene whenever he found anything amiss, and he berated senators who failed to take an active part in debate. He was particularly interested in jurisdiction, and was indefatigable, if emotional and inconsistent, in dispensing justice. Legislation had clear aims: to discourage sedition; to protect inheritance within the clan and the rights of individual property owners; more 'liberal' measures increased the rights of slaves, women, and minors. Arguments for his legislation invoked traditional *mores* and the upholding of status, but in his senatorial speech advocating the admission of Gauls to the senate, Claudius' preoccupation with the place of innovation in Roman life shows him coming to terms with changes in economy and society.

Claudius was noted for generosity with the citizenship, though his advisers also sold it without his knowledge. A few widespread grants of Latin rights, along with his favourable response to the request of long-enfranchised Gallic chieftains for permission to stand for senatorial office (resented by existing senators), made him seem more generous than he was: proved merit was his own criterion for grants. Administrative changes have also been given undue weight, as also the influence of the freedmen (i.e. ex-slaves), who were emerging in previous reigns and have wrongly been claimed to have become the equivalent of modern 'ministers' as part of a policy of 'centralization'. Claudius' grant of additional jurisdiction to provincial procurators, and the introduction of that title for equestrian governors of provinces, previously called 'prefects', simply relieved him of the job of hearing appeals and stressed the dependence of the governors upon their emperor.

Claudius added other provinces to the empire besides Britain, although that left few resources for an active policy against the Germans: the two Mauretanias (whose last king, Ptolemy, had been executed by Gaius),

Lycia (43), and Thrace (46); and he resumed overseas colonization. His dealings with Judaea and the Parthians, however, were inept. In Judaea the procurators who replaced the deceased King Agrippa I in 44 proved unsatisfactory, and by 54 Claudius' eastern governors had allowed the Parthians to gain control of Greater Armenia, a serious blow to Roman prestige.

Claudius was deified on death, enhancing his adoptive son's prestige, but in Nero's early years the failings of the regime (influence of women and freedmen, corruption, trials held in private, the bypassing of the senate, favour to provincials) were excoriated: the younger *Seneca's *Apocolocyntosis* reveals the tone. Under *Vespasian a more balanced view prevailed and Claudius' temple was completed, but *Tacitus, though he exploits Claudius' speeches, is merciless. Modern writers have overreacted, exaggerating his purposefulness in encouraging the development of the provinces; his accession and survival, preserving the imperial peace, and his recognition of social changes were his main domestic achievements.   J.P.B.; B.M.L.

Claudius Caecus, Appius, censor 312 BC before holding other high office; consul 307 and 296, praetor 295: in the latter two years he fought in Etruria, Campania, and Samnium. In 280, now old and blind, he successfully opposed peace with *Pyrrhus after the Roman defeat at Heraclea. It is not known whether the version of this speech known to Cicero was authentic. He is also credited with a work (probably in prose) containing a collection of moral essays.

Claudius has been rightly described as the first live personality in Roman history, and his censorship as sensational. As censor, he commissioned the building of the via Appia from Rome to Capua and the first aqueduct (aqua Appia). In drawing up the list of the senate he left out men regarded as superior to those included, even enrolling the sons of freedmen. He distributed the lower classes (*humiles*) through all the rural tribes, thus increasing their influence in the tribal assembly; the move was reversed by the censors of 304. He also transferred the cult of Hercules from private to public superintendence. Claudius probably supported the action of the aedile Gnaeus Flavius, also in 304, in publishing the details of legal procedure and a calendar of the days on which legal business could be conducted. He is said to have had a wide personal following (*clientela*).

All this may look democratic, but in 300 he opposed the admission of plebeians to the two main priestly colleges (*pontifices* and *augures*) and on two occasions attempted to secure the election of an all-patrician college. These moves can be explained either as part of his political conflict with Quintus *Fabius Maximus Rullianus or on the supposition that Claudius was trying to promote the interests of the people as a whole, not just those of the new plebeian nobility.   J.Br.

Cleisthenes, Athenian politician, of the Alcmaeonid family, son of Megacles and Agariste, daughter of Cleisthenes of Sicyon. He was archon under the tyrant Hippias (son of *Pisistratus) in 525/4 BC, but later in Hippias' reign the Alcmaeonids went into exile and put pressure on Sparta through the Delphic oracle to intervene in Athens and overthrow the tyranny. In the power vacuum which followed, Cleisthenes and Isagoras were rivals for supremacy; Isagoras obtained the archonship (a senior magistracy) for 508/7; but Cleisthenes appealed for popular support with a programme of reform. Isagoras appealed to King *Cleomenes I of Sparta, who came to Athens with a small force, invoked the hereditary curse of the Alcmaeonids, and forced Cleisthenes and others to withdraw; but he met with strong popular resistance and was forced to withdraw in turn, taking Isagoras with him. Cleisthenes returned, and his reforms were enacted and put into effect.

Cleisthenes' main achievement was a new organization of the citizen body. The four Ionian *phylai* or tribes (subdivisions of the citizen body) and other older units were left in existence but deprived of political significance. For the future each citizen was to be a member of one of 139 local units called demes (*demoi*), and the demes were grouped to form 30 new *trittyes* ('thirds') and 10 new *phylai*; citizenship and the political and military organization of Attica were to be based on these units (e.g. *Solon's council, *boulē,* of 400 became a council of 500, with 50 members from each tribe and individual demes acting as constituencies). The main purpose of the reform was probably to under-

mine the old channels of influence (and perhaps to give the Alcmaeonids an advantageous position in the new system); its main appeal to the ordinary citizens was perhaps the provision of political machinery at local level; and working this machinery educated the citizens towards democracy. The institution of ostracism (the mechanism in 5th-cent. Athens of banishing a citizen for ten years) is almost certainly to be attributed to Cleisthenes.

In the 5th cent. Cleisthenes came to be regarded as the founder of the democracy, but in the political disputes at the end of the century the democrats looked further back, to Solon or even to Theseus.   T.J.C.; P.J.R.

Clement of Alexandria (Titus Flavius Clemens) was born *c.* AD 150, probably at Athens and of pagan parents. He was converted to Christianity and after extensive travels to seek instruction from Christian teachers received lessons from Pantaenus, whose catechetical school in Alexandria was then an unofficial institution giving tuition to converts. Clement affects a wide acquaintance with Greek literature, since his writings abound in quotations from *Homer, *Hesiod, the dramatists, and the Platonic and Stoic philosophers. However, comparison with ps.-Justin's *De monarchia* and *Cohortatio ad Graecos* shows that he made much use of florilegia. His *Protrepticus* is a copious source of information about the Greek mysteries, though his wish to represent them as a perversion of Scriptural teachings must have led to misrepresentation. After ordination he succeeded Pantaenus as head of the school some time before 200, and held the office till 202, when, on the eve of the persecution under *Septimius Severus, he left Alexandria and took refuge, perhaps with his former pupil Alexander, then bishop of Cappadocia and later of Jerusalem. Clement died between 211 and 216.

Much of his writing is lost, but the following survive nearly complete: (1) The *Protrepticus* or 'Hortatory Address to the Greeks' (*c.*190), designed to prove the superiority of Christianity to pagan cults and way of life. (2) The *Paedagogus* or 'Tutor' (*c.*190–2), an exposition of the moral teaching of Christ, not only in general, but also with application to such details as eating, drinking, dress, and use of wealth. (3) The *Stromateis* or 'Miscellanies' (probably c.200–2) in eight books, the first seven attempting a construction of Christian philosophy with its centre in Christ the *logos* and the word of Scripture; book 5. 9, with its justification of allegory as a way of saying what cannot be spoken, points the way to negative theology; the eighth book is a fragment on logic. (4) The *Excerpta ex Theodoto*, which follow in one MS, is a collection of dicta by a Valentinian heretic, of whom Clement, who calls himself a Gnostic, seems not to disapprove. (5) *Eclogae propheticae* are also attached to this MS. (6) The *Quis dives salvetur?* is a homily urging detachment from (though not necessarily renunciation of) worldly goods. (7) The fragments of the *Hypotyposeis* ('Sketches') suggest an exegetical work consisting mainly of notes on passages from Scripture. Clement added little to dogma, but his philosophy points the way to *Origen, and, as in the case of the latter, prevented his being regarded as a saint.   M.J.E.

Cleomenes I, Agiad king of Sparta (reigned c.520–490 BC), son of Anaxandridas II by a second, bigamous union. His long, activist reign was one of the half-dozen most influential on record. He pursued an adventurous and at times unscrupulous foreign policy aimed at crushing Argos and extending Sparta's influence both inside and outside the Peloponnese. It was during his reign, but not entirely according to his design, that the Peloponnesian League came formally into existence. He embroiled Thebes with Athens and frustrated Thebes' plans for a united Boeotian federation by referring Plataea to Athens for alliance (probably in 519: Thuc. 3. 68). He intervened twice successfully in Athenian affairs, overthrowing the tyranny of Hippias (son of *Pisistratus) in 510 and expelling *Cleisthenes in favour of Isagoras in 508. But his attempt to restore Isagoras by a concerted expedition of Sparta's Peloponnesian and central Greek allies in c.506 was frustrated by the opposition of the Corinthians and of his Eurypontid fellow king Demaratus. A further Spartan proposal to restore Hippias in c.504 is not specifically attributed to Cleomenes but was anyway blocked by majority vote of Sparta's allies in the first certain act of the Peloponnesian League proper. In 494 Cleomenes defeated Argos at Sepeia near Tiryns and unscrupulously capitalized on his victory by burning several thousand Argive survivors to death in a sacred grove, for which impiety he was tried at Sparta and acquitted.

But he disliked overseas commitments, refusing to interfere in the affairs of Samos (c.515), or to support the Ionian Revolt against Persia (499); and he showed no certain awareness of the Persian danger before 491 when his attempt to punish Aegina for Medism (i.e. taking the Persian side) was thwarted by Demaratus. He thereupon bribed the Delphic oracle to declare Demaratus illegitimate and had him deposed, but the intrigue came to light and he fled Sparta, possibly to stir up revolt among the Arcadians. Recalled to Sparta, he met a violent end, perhaps at his own hands.   P.A.C.

Cleomenes III, Agiad king of Sparta (reigned c.235–222 BC). The son of Leonidas, he imbibed ideals of social revolution from his wife Agiatis, widow of his father's opponent Agis IV. Before implementing those ideals at home (and they were not for export), he was active abroad. He first moved in 229, when he annexed Tegea, Mantinea, Orchomenus, and Caphyae in Arcadia from the Aetolian Confederacy. Then, having provoked the Achaean Confederacy into war (228), he won victories at Mt. Lycaeum and Ladoceia (227). Now (winter 227/6) he seized quasi-despotic power at home and set up a 'Lycurgan' (i.e. traditional) regime. (Debts were cancelled, land was redivided, the citizen body was replenished from *perioikoi* (neighbouring peoples) and foreigners. A refashioned educational cycle and mess-regimen were reinstated (the so-called *agōgē*), the army re-equipped. The allegedly post-Lycurgan ephorate was abolished, the *gerousia* (council of elders) made subject to annual re-election, the diarchy transformed into a *de facto* monarchy. Cleomenes' military successes against Achaea in Arcadia were followed by the capture of Argos (225) and siege of Corinth (224). These provoked *Aratus (2) into opening negotiations with the Greeks' notional suzerain, *Antigonus Doson of Macedon, who reached the Isthmus, secured the revolt of Argos and placed Cleomenes on the defensive, though in winter 223 he took and destroyed Megalopolis. Despite a mass liberation of helots, Cleomenes' new model army proved no match for Antigonus at Sellasia north of Sparta in July 222, and he fled to the court of his patron *Ptolemy III Euergetes of Egypt. Imprisoned by Euergetes' successor, he broke out, tried in vain to stir up revolution in Alexandria, and committed suicide (winter 220/219).

Cleomenes' patriotism is not in doubt, and the ideals he proclaimed provoked eager support inside and outside Sparta, but it may be questioned how far he was a social and political reformer on principle.   P.A.C.

Cleon, Athenian politician, the son of a rich tanner. He was perhaps involved in the attacks on *Pericles through his intellectual friends in the 430s BC, and in the opposition to Pericles' strategy of refusing battle against the invaders in 431. In 427 he proposed the decree (overturned the next day) to execute all the men of Mytilene after the suppression of its revolt. In 426 he attacked the *Babylonians* of *Aristophanes (1) as a slander on the state. In 425, after the Athenians had got the better of the Spartans at Pylos, he frustrated the Spartan peace proposals, when *Nicias offered to resign the command to him he was obliged to take it, and in co-operation with Demosthenes, the general on the spot, he kept his promise and rapidly obtained the Spartans' surrender. In the same year he doubtless approved the measure greatly increasing the tribute paid by the allied states; and he was responsible for increasing the jurors' pay from two to three obols. In 423 he proposed the decree for the destruction of Scione (in Chalkidice, north Greece) and the execution of all its citizens. In 422, as general, he led an expedition to the Thraceward area, and recovered Torone and Galepsus, but he failed in an attack on Stagira and was defeated by the Spartan commander Brasidas and killed in a battle outside Amphipolis.

We have a vivid picture of Cleon in *Thucydides and Aristophanes, both of whom had personal reasons for disliking him. He was an effective, if vulgar, speaker, and seems to have been given to extravagant promises and extravagant accusations against opponents. He was one of the first of a new kind of politician, who were not from the old aristocracy, and whose predominance depended on persuasive speeches in the assembly and law-courts rather than on regular office-holding; when he did serve as general, the undisputed facts include both successes and failures.

                                        A.W.G.; T.J.C.; P.J.R.

Cleopatra (Cleopatra VII) (69–30 BC), the final and best known of the Ptolemies, was daughter of *Ptolemy XII (Auletes). On the latter's death in 51 she became queen, alone at first and subsequently with her younger brothers, first *Ptolemy XIII (who opposed Caesar) and then (47–45) with *Ptolemy XIV. A joint reign with *Ptolemy XV Caesar (Caesarion, reputedly Caesar's son) is recorded from 45 BC. Her later children by Mark *Antony were the twins Alexander and Cleopatra (born 40 BC after Antony's winter in Alexandria), and Ptolemy Philadelphus (born 36). In 37/6 she marked Antony's gift to her of Chalcis in Syria by instituting a double numeration of her regnal years (year 16 = 1). She died at her own hand (and the bite of a royal asp) soon after Octavian (see AUGUSTUS) took Alexandria on 3 August 30.

Best known for her successful relations first with *Julius Caesar who besieged and captured Alexandria in 48–47, and later with Mark Antony, following a colourful encounter at Tarsus (in Cilicia) in 41, she managed to increase her kingdom territorially in return for financial support. Caesar restored Cyprus to Egypt and in 34, in a magnificent ceremony at Alexandria, Cleopatra appeared as Isis to mark the division of the earlier kingdom of *Alexander the Great between the royal couple and their children. Cleopatra ruled Egypt and Caesarion Cyprus as Queen of Kings and King of Kings; Antony's children Alexander Helios (the Sun) and Ptolemy Philadelphus were named kings east and west of the Euphrates respectively, with Cleopatra Selene (the Moon) queen of Cyrene. The symbolism of the ceremony was more important than any reality.

Internally Cleopatra was strong, using her position as pharaoh to gain backing from all the people. To her title of Philopator ('father-loving') was added Philopatris ('loving her country') (*BGU* 14. 2377. 1) and her support for the traditional Egyptian bull-cults is recorded at both Memphis and Armant. In the final struggle against Octavian however she confiscated temple lands. In Greek she was known also as Thea Neotera, 'the younger goddess'. An expert linguist, she was reportedly the first Ptolemy to have known Egyptian, and *Plutarch reports it was her conversation rather than her looks which formed the secret of her success.

The legend of Cleopatra has proved even

more powerful than her historical record. Thanks to her successful liaisons with men of power she was named as the author of treatises on hairdressing and cosmetics. Her exploitation of Egyptian royal symbolism with its eastern tradition of luxury was used against her by her antagonists; for Roman poets she was 'monster' and 'wicked woman'. Her visit to Rome in 46–44 achieved little but embarrassment for Caesar. Following his murder, her attempts to aid the Caesarians in 42 were thwarted by *Cassius, and by contrary winds. The summons to Tarsus by Antony followed. Her liaison with Antony formed the focus of Octavian's propaganda, based on fear of Egyptian wealth. Yet the skilful manipulation of power by this queen preserved Egypt from the direct rule of Rome longer than might otherwise have been the case.   D.J.T.

Clodia, second of the three sisters of *Clodius, born c.95 BC, had married her first cousin Quintus Caecilius Metellus Celer by 62 (Cic. *Fam.* 5. 2. 6). Her bitter enemy *Cicero (but gossip said she had once offered him marriage, Plut. *Cic.* 29) paints a vivid picture of her in his *Letters* from 60 BC onwards, and above all in the *Pro Caelio* of April 56. Her affair with *Catullus—the identification with Lesbia is widely admitted—began before the death of Metellus in 59, which Clodia was said to have caused by poison: by the end of that year Marcus Caelius Rufus was her lover. After the Caelius case her political importance ceases, but she may have been still alive in 45 BC (Cic. *Att.* 12. 38, etc.).   G.E.F.C.; R.J.S.

Clodius (Publius Clodius Pulcher), youngest of six children of Ap. Claudius Pulcher. He was born c.92 BC (since quaestor in 61). In 68 he incited the troops of his brother-in-law Lucullus to mutiny in Armenia. When prosecuting *Catiline in 65 he was, according to Cicero, in co-operation with the defence. On his return to Rome he had been apparently friendly with *Cicero (Plut. *Cic.* 29), but in May 61 Cicero gave damaging evidence against him when he was on trial for trespassing on the Bona Dea festival disguised as a woman the previous December. However Clodius was narrowly acquitted by a jury said to have been heavily bribed. Next year, on returning from his quaestorian province of

Sicily, he sought transference into a plebeian *gens* (family): this was at first resisted, but in March 59 *Julius Caesar as *pontifex maximus* (the leading member of the most senior college of priests) presided over the *comitia curiata* (a special kind of assembly) at which the adoption was ratified. There were suggestions of subsequent disagreements with Caesar and *Pompey and of his departure from Rome, but in the event he was elected tribune for 58. His measures included free corn for the *plebs*, restoration of *collegia* (private clubs), repeal or modification of certain legislation (the *Leges Aelia et Fufia*), grant of new provinces to the consuls Aulus Gabinius and Lucius Calpurnius Piso Caesoninus, a bill exiling those who had condemned Roman citizens to death without popular sanction, a bill confirming the exile of Cicero (who departed in late March), the dispatch of *Cato the Younger to Cyprus, and grant of title of king and control of Pessinus to Brogitarus ruler of the Galatian Trocmi. Clodius then turned against Pompey, allowing the escape of the Armenian prince Tigranes, threatening Pompey's life, and (Cic. *Dom.* 40; *Har. resp.* 48) suggesting that Caesar's acts of 59 were invalid because of Marcus Calpurnius Bibulus' religious obstruction. These attacks on Pompey were continued in 57, especially over the question of Cicero's recall, and in the early part of Clodius' aedileship in 56; but after the conference of Luca (see *JULIUS CAESAR) his attitude changed and by agitation and violence he helped to bring about the joint consulship of Pompey and *Crassus in 55. He still continued to control large sections of the urban *plebs* (*plebs urbana*). He stood for the praetorship of 52 but owing to rioting the elections had not been held when he was murdered by *Milo on 18 January of that year. His clients among the *plebs* burned the senate-house as his pyre.

Clodius, who like two of his sisters used the 'popular' spelling of his name, probably saw the tribunate as a vital step in his political career: revenge on Cicero need not have been his main aim in seeking transfer to the *plebs*, nor (despite Cic. *Dom.* 41; *Sest.* 16) Caesar's aim in granting it. Moreover, the view that Caesar was at any time his patron seems misconceived. In 58–56 he may have been allied with Crassus; but he was surely both opportunist and independent, for before as well as after Luca he was friendly with various *optimates* (Cic. *Fam.* 1. 9. 10, 19), and in 53 he was supporting the candidates of Pompey for the consulship (Asconius, 26, 42). The one consistent motif is his courting of the urban *plebs* and the promotion of its interests. The daughter of his marriage to *Fulvia was briefly married to Octavian (later *Augustus) in 42.   G.E.F.C.; A.W.L.

Colotes, of Lampsacus (*c.*310–260 BC), pupil and devoted follower of *Epicurus. He countered *Arcesilaus (Plut. *Adversus Coloten* 1121e, 1124b; Diog. Laert. 9. 44) and the sceptical New Academy with Epicurean materialism and atomism, and sought to discredit all thinkers who, as he or his opponents thought, had cast doubt on the plain evidence of the senses, among whom he included Democritus, Cyrenaics, *Arcesilaus and his followers, *Parmenides, *Empedocles (against whom the Epicurean Hermarchus also wrote), *Socrates, Melissus, *Plato, and Stilpon. Several of his works are preserved among the fragments of the Epicurean library from Herculaneum: *Against Plato's Lysis*; *Against the Euthydemus* (both ed. W. Crönert in *Kolotes und Menedemos*, 1906); *Against the Gorgias*; *Against the Republic*, from which Proclus (*in Platonis Rempublicam commentarii* 2. 113. 12 f., 116. 19–21 Kroll) preserves Colotes' extensive attacks on Plato's use of myths: about Er in the *Republic*, Colotes wondered how a dead man can come back to life. Macrobius (*Commentarius Ex Cicerone in Somnium Scipioni* 1. 9–2. 4) reports that Cicero in consequence preferred to have his tale related by one roused from a dream. Plutarch in *Adversus Coloten* gives a detailed if unfavourable report of Colotes' treatise with the ungainly long title, 'On the Point that it is not Possible Even to Live According to the Doctrines of Other Philosophers', in which he extended a refutation of the scepticism and suspension of belief in certain knowledge (*epochē peri pantōn*) promulgated by the contemporary Arcesilaus in the New Academy, to a claim that no theory of knowledge other than the empiricism of Epicurus affords a secure basis for practical life. Colotes uses an argument from *apraxia*, 'inaction', a version of which Epicurus had already used against the ethical determinist in *On Nature* and which reappears in Lucretius (4. 507–10, cf. *Adversus Coloten* 1122c), according to which

to deny the truth of our impressions is to abolish knowledge, and without knowledge life itself becomes impossible. Thus he challenges the cognitive sceptic to show how suspension of belief is consistent with the requirements of life itself.   W.D.R.; D.O.

Columella (Lucius Iunius Moderatus Columella)(cf. *CIL* 9. 235) *fl.* AD 50, b. Gades (mod. Cádiz) in Spain (*Rust.* 8. 16. 9; 10. 185), author of the most systematic extant Roman agricultural manual (written *c.* AD 60–5) in twelve books. Book 1: introduction, layout of villa, organization of slave workforce; 2: arable cultivation; 3–5: viticulture (mainly) and other arboriculture; 6, 7: animal husbandry; 8, 9: *pastio villatica* (e.g. specialized breeding of poultry, fish and game, and bees); 10: horticulture (in hexameter verse); 11: duties of *vilicus* (slave estate-manager), calendar of farm work and horticulture; 12: duties of *vilica* (female companion of *vilicus*), wine and oil processing and food conservation. Another surviving book (the so-called *Liber de arboribus*) probably belonged to a shorter first version of the subject, while his works criticizing astrologers (11. 1. 31) and on religion in agriculture (if ever written, 2. 21. 5) are not extant. Columella defends the intensive slave-staffed villa—characterized by capital investment (1. 1. 18), close supervision by the owner (1. 1. 18–20), and the integration of arable and animal husbandry (6 *praef.* 1–2)—against influential contrary views on agricultural management (1 *praef.* 1). His calculation of the profits of viticulture (3. 3. 8–15) has aroused lively modern debate. But that Columella treats vines at greater length than cereals reflects the complexity of viticulture not the supposed demise of Italian arable cultivation. He owned several estates near Rome (2. 3. 3; 3. 9. 2) but had firsthand knowledge of agriculture elsewhere in Italy (cf. 7. 2. 3) and in the provinces, especially southern Spain (cf. 2. 15. 4), Cilicia, and Syria (2. 10. 18). Continually aware of the effects of various climatic conditions, soils, and land formations (e.g. 2. 9. 2–7), he does not describe just one ideal estate. The serious nature of his work is further illustrated by the ample bibliography of Greek, Punic, and Roman authors (1. 1. 7–14), while his practical experience ensured a critical use of all sources. Columella's stylish prose, citations of Virgil, and book of verse were designed to give his work greater credibility among contemporary literary landowners, e.g. *Seneca the Younger and his brother Gallio (3. 3. 3; 9. 16. 2); they do not undermine its practical worth.   M.S.Sp.

Commodus, Lucius Aurelius, sole emperor AD 180–92, one of twin sons born to *Marcus Aurelius and Annia Galeria Faustina in August 161, the first emperor 'born in the purple'. Given the title Caesar in 166, he was summoned to his father's side after the usurpation of Avidius Cassius in 175, received a grant of supreme power (*imperium*) and of tribunician power (*tribunicia potestas*) at the end of 176, and was consul in 177, now Augustus, and co-ruler. He was married in 178 to Bruttia Crispina, and left Rome with Marcus for the second Marcomannic War. On his father's death on 17 March 180 he became sole emperor, taking the names Marcus Aurelius Commodus Antoninus, rapidly made peace, and abandoned the newly annexed territories, holding a triumph in October 180.

Major wars were avoided during the reign, the exception being in Britain, where, following a breach of the northern frontier, victories were won by Ulpius Marcellus, for which Commodus assumed the title Britannicus in AD 184. There were minor disturbances on the Danube frontier and in Mauretania, and serious problems with banditry and deserters, as well as mutinies in the British army. Commodus at first retained his father's ministers, e.g. the guard prefect Taruttienus Paternus, but after an assassination attempt in 182, in which the emperor's sister Annia Aurelia Galeria Lucilla was implicated, Paternus was dismissed and soon killed along with many others. The guard prefect Tigidius Perennis effectively ran the government from 182 to 185, when he was lynched by mutinous troops. Marcus Aurelius Cleander, the freedman chamberlain, was the next favourite to hold power, even becoming guard prefect. After his fall in 190, following riots at Rome, power was shared by the emperor's favourite concubine Marcia, the chamberlain Eclectus, and (from 191) the guard prefect Quintus Aemilius Laetus. Commodus, by now obsessively devoted to performing as a gladiator, appeared to be dangerously deranged. Proclaiming a new golden age, he shook off his allegiance to his father's memory, calling himself Lucius Aelius Aurelius Commodus, as well as eight other names, including Hercules Romanus: each month was given one of these names; Rome itself became the *Colonia Commodiana*. Numerous senators had been executed; others feared the same fate, and Laetus, probably with the connivance of the future emperor Publius Helvius Pertinax and others, had Commodus strangled on the night of 31 December 192. His memory was at once condemned but was restored by *Septimius Severus in 195.   A.R.Bi.

Constantine I, 'the Great' (Flavius Valerius Constantinus) (*c.* AD 272/3–337), born at Naissus, was son of *Constantius I and Helena. When his father was appointed Caesar (293) Constantine remained as a tribune at the court of *Diocletian. He fought alongside *Galerius against Persia (298) and the Sarmatians (299), and was at Nicomedia in 303 and again in 305 when Diocletian abdicated. Constantius was now senior Augustus; his eastern partner Galerius reluctantly released Constantine for service with his father. Constantine, fearing interception by the western Caesar, Flavius Valerius Severus, hastened to Britain to aid his father against the Picts.

When Constantius died at York (Eburacum, 306), his troops proclaimed Constantine Augustus; Galerius gave this rank to Severus, but grudgingly conceded Constantine the title Caesar. Based mainly at Trier (Augusta Treverorum), Constantine ruled his father's territories of Spain, Gaul, and Britain. At Rome *Maxentius usurped power; Severus and then Galerius failed to dislodge him. For Constantine an alliance with Maxentius was welcome. The usurper's father, the former emperor *Maximian, returned to power, visited Constantine in Gaul (307), and gave him the title Augustus and his daughter Fausta in marriage. Constantine sheltered Maximian when driven from Rome after failing to depose his son (308). At the conference of Carnuntum Galerius gave the title Augustus to *Licinius; like *Maximin in the east, Constantine spurned the style *filius Augustorum* (son of the Augusti) and retained that of Augustus, which Galerius recognized (309/10). Meanwhile he defended the Rhine, warring against the Franks (306–7), raiding the territory of the Bructeri, and bridging the river at Cologne (Colonia Agrippinensis, 308). He was campaigning against the Franks (310) when Maximian tried to regain power. Constantine forced him to surrender and commit suicide. As the connection with the Herculian dynasty was now discredited, a hereditary claim to the throne was invented for Constantine: it was alleged that his father had been related to the emperor Claudius II. On the death of Galerius (311), Maximin and Licinius narrowly avoided war when partitioning his territories, and as Maximin looked for support to Maxentius, Constantine looked to Licinius. In 312 Constantine invaded Italy. Victorious over Maxentius's northern forces near Turin and Verona, he marched on Rome. Maxentius gave battle at Saxa Rubra, was defeated, and was drowned near the pons Mulvius. The senate welcomed Constantine as liberator and made him, not Maximin, senior Augustus. He took over the rule of Italy and Africa, and disbanded the praetorian guard which had supported Maxentius.

Two years earlier it had been given out that Constantine had seen a vision of his tutelary deity the sun-god Apollo accompanied by Victory and the figure XXX to symbolize the years of rule due to him. By the end of his life Constantine claimed to have seen a (single) cross above the sun, with words 'Be victorious in this'. At Saxa Rubra, Constantine as the result of a dream sent his soldiers into battle with crosses (and no doubt other symbols) on their shields; heavily outnumbered, he defeated Maxentius. No more, yet no less, superstitious than his contemporaries, he saw the hand of the Christian God in this, and the need to maintain such support for himself and the empire. From that moment he not merely restored Christian property but gave privileges to the clergy, showered benefactions on the Church, and undertook a massive programme of church building. At Rome a basilica was provided for the Pope where the barracks of the mounted branch of the praetorians had stood, and other churches, most notably St Peter's, followed. His religious outlook may have undergone later transformations, and was affected by his encounters with problems in the Church. In Africa he confronted the Donatist schism: the Donatists objected to the largess for their opponents and appealed to him. To the *vicarius* (supreme governor) of Africa, a

'fellow worshipper of the most high God', he wrote (314) of his fear that failure to achieve Christian unity would cause God to replace him with another emperor. Sincerity is not determinable by historical method; it is, in any case, not incompatible with a belief that consequential action may have political advantage. He had been present at Nicomedia when persecution began in 303; he knew that the problem with Christianity was that its exclusiveness stood in the way of imperial unity. If he threw in his lot with the Christians, there could be no advantage if they were themselves not united. Following a papal council in 313, his own council at Arles (Arelate) in 314, and his investigation into the dispute, he saw the refusal of the Donatists to conform as obtuse. From 317 he tried coercion; there were exiles and some executions. Totally failing to achieve his object, he left the Donatists to God's judgement (321). Weakness in the face of a movement widespread in Africa was seen when the Donatists seized the basilica Constantine built for the Catholics at Cirta; he left them in possession and built the Catholics another one.

At Milan (Mediolanum, 313) he met Licinius, and gave him his half-sister Constantia in marriage. Back at Nicomedia, Licinius published regulations agreed with Constantine on religious freedom and the restoration of Christian property (the so-called Edict of Milan). Licinius struck down Maximin, and the two emperors were left to rule in harmony. In 313 the Rhine frontier engaged Constantine's attention; in 314 after attending the council of Arles he campaigned against the Germans; in 315 he spent two months in Rome.

The concord with Licinius was unstable. A first war was decided in Constantine's favour by victories at Cibalae (316) and Campus Ardiensis. Licinius ceded all his European territories except for the diocese of Thrace. In 317 Crispus and Constantine, sons of Constantine, and Licinius II, son of Licinius, were made Caesars. Constantine spent 317–23 in the Balkans. Licinius became increasingly distrustful of him and suspicious of his own Christian subjects, whom he began to persecute. Constantine defeated a Gothic invasion (323) but was accused by Licinius of usurping his function; war followed. Constantine was victorious at Adrianople, in the Hellespont, and at Chrysopolis, and forced the abdication of Licinius at Nicomedia (324). Though his life was spared after his wife intervened with her brother, Licinius was later accused of plotting and executed, with his Caesar Martinianus (325); the Caesar Licinius II was executed in 326. Implication in the supposed plot may have been the excuse also for Constantine to remove one of the consuls of 325, Proculus. In a mysterious scandal, he even ordered the deaths of his son Crispus and his wife Fausta (326). Only one usurpation is recorded in the rest of his reign: Calocaerus in Cyprus (334), who was burnt alive by the emperor's half-brother Dalmatius.

On 8 November 324 Constantine made his third son Constantius II Caesar and founded Constantinople on the site of Byzantium. The need for an imperial headquarters near the eastern and Danubian frontiers had been seen by Diocletian, who preferred Nicomedia; Constantine will have recognized the strategic importance of Byzantium in his war with Licinius. The city's dedication with both pagan rites and Christian ceremonies took place on 11 May 330. From the beginning it was 'New Rome', though lower in rank. Pagan temples and cults were absent, but other features of Rome were in time reproduced (Constantius II upgraded the city council to equality with the Roman senate). To speak of the foundation of a capital is misleading; yet a permanent imperial residence in the east did in the end emphasize division between the empire's Greek and Latin parts.

In a reunited empire Constantine was able to complete Diocletian's reforms and introduce innovations. The separation of civil and military commands was completed. A substantial field army was created under new commanders, *magister equitum* (master of the horse) and *magister peditum* (in charge of the infantry), responsible directly to the emperor: its soldiers (*comitatenses*) had higher pay and privileges than the frontier troops (*limitanei*). The number of Germans seems to have increased, especially in the higher ranks. Praetorian prefects and *vicarii* (overall governors in charge of the dioceses or groups of provinces) now had purely civilian functions. In a reorganization of the government, the *magister officiorum* (master of the offices) controlled the imperial bureaux (*scrinia*), a new corps of guards (*scholae*) which replaced the praetorians, and a corps of couriers and agents (*agentes in rebus*); the

quaestor sacri palatii (quaestor of the sacred palace) was chief legal adviser; the *comes sacrarum largitionum* (count of the sacred largesses) and the *comes rei privatae* (in charge of the imperial domains) handled those revenues and expenditures not controlled by the praetorian prefects. The emperor's council (*consistorium*) had the above as permanent members, as well as *comites* (counts). These at first were men who served at court or as special commissioners, but the title 'count' was soon given freely as an honour. He also resuscitated the title of patrician. He tried vainly to stop corruption in the steadily growing bureaucracy. He gave senatorial rank freely, and reopened many civilian posts to senators who began to recover some of their lost political influence. From his reign survive the first laws to prevent tenant farmers and other productive workers, not to mention town councillors, from leaving their homes and work. His open-handedness harmed the economy: taxation (mostly in kind) rose inexorably despite the confiscation of the vast temple treasures. He established a gold coinage of 72 solidi to the pound, but the other coinage continued to depreciate.

Resident now in the more Christianized east, his promotion of the new religion became more emphatic. He openly rejected paganism, though without persecuting pagans, favoured Christians as officials, and welcomed bishops at court, but his actions in Church matters were his own. He now confronted another dispute which was rending Christianity, the theological questions about the nature of Christ raised by the Alexandrian priest Arius. To secure unity Constantine summoned the council which met at Nicaea in 325 (later ranked as the First Ecumenical Council), and proposed the formula which all must accept. Dissidents were bludgeoned into agreement; but Athanasius' view that his opponents had put an unorthodox interpretation on the formula was seen by Constantine as vexatious interference with attempts to secure unity. Even if his success in this aspect was superficial, he nevertheless brought Christianity from a persecuted minority sect to near-supremacy in the religious life of the empire.

He spent the generally peaceful last dozen years of his reign in the east or on the Danube, though he visited Italy and Rome (326), and campaigned on the Rhine (328/9). Victory over the Goths (332) was followed (334) by a campaign against the Sarmatians, many thousands of whom were then admitted within the empire as potential recruits. In 336 he fought north of the Danube, even recovering part of the lost province of Dacia. The empire's prestige seemed fully restored; a Persian war loomed but did not break out until after his death.

His youngest son Constans gained (333) the title Caesar already held by Constantine II and Constantius II. A believer in hereditary succession, Constantine groomed these to succeed along with his nephews Dalmatius (Caesar 335) and Hannibalianus, hoping they would rule amicably after his death. Baptized when death approached (such postponement was common at the time), he died near Nicomedia (22 May 337).   R.P.D.

Constantius I (Flavius Valerius; perhaps Flavius Iulius before 293; nicknamed, not before the 6th cent., Chlorus), born no later than AD 250, of Illyrian stock; stories of his relationship with the emperor Claudius II are fictions of *Constantine's propagandists. Constantius served as an army officer, as governor of Dalmatia, and possibly as praetorian prefect of Maximianus Augustus (*Maximian), whose daughter or stepdaughter Theodora he married, having put away Helena, the mother of Constantine I. On the establishment of the tetrarchy, *Diocletian appointed him Caesar, Maximian invested him at Milan (Mediolanum, 1 March 293), and he took charge of Gaul, basing himself mainly at Trier (Augusta Treverorum). His first task was to recover NE Gaul, held, with Britain, by the usurper Carausius. In summer 293 he stormed Boulogne; but Allectus, who murdered Carausius, retained Britain. Many of Carausius' defeated barbarian allies, Chamavi and Frisii, were settled within the empire. In 296, with Maximian guarding the Rhine, Constantius and his praetorian prefect, Asclepiodotus, took ship for Britain. Asclepiodotus, landing near Clausentum (Bitterne), routed and killed Allectus; Constantius, separated from his prefect, came up the Thames to London in time to destroy the survivors of the beaten army. Constantius showed mercy to Britain and restored its defences. His other campaigns included a spectacular victory over the Alamanni at Langres (302). He failed fully to implement in his territories Diocletian's edicts against Christians (304), merely demolishing some churches. On the abdication of Diocletian and Maximian (1 May 305) Constantius had Spain added to his territories but his rank as senior Augustus was curbed by the fact that both Caesars, Flavius Valerius Severus and Gaius Galerius Valerius Maximinus, were creatures of *Galerius Augustus, who also held Constantine as a virtual hostage. Constantius crossed to Britain and asked that his son be released. Constantine was able to reach him fast enough to assist in his last victory, over the Picts, and to be proclaimed emperor by the army at York (Eburacum) when Constantius died there (25 July 306). His premature death, and Constantine's proclamation, wrecked Diocletian's tetrarchic system. Constantinian propaganda bedevils assessment of Constantius, yet he appears to have been an able general and a generous ruler. By Theodora he had six children, half-siblings of Constantine; grandsons included Gallus Caesar, *Julian, and the usurper (350) Nepotian.   R.P.D.

Corbulo (Gnaeus Domitius Corbulo) through the six marriages of his mother Vistilia (Plin. *HN* 7. 162) was connected with many prominent families: one of his stepsisters married the emperor *Gaius (1). Probably suffect consul AD 39, in 47 he was legate of Lower Germany when he successfully fought against the Chauci led by Gannascus, but was not allowed by *Claudius to go further. A strict disciplinarian, he made his troops dig a canal between the Meuse and Rhine. Proconsul of Asia under Claudius, he was soon after *Nero's accession made *legatus Augusti pro praetore* (in effect, governor) of Cappadocia and Galatia with the command against Parthia in the war about the control of Armenia. This started in earnest only in 58, when Corbulo had reorganized the Roman army in the east. He captured Artaxata and Tigranocerta, installed Tigranes as king of Armenia, and received the governorship of Syria. But Tigranes was driven out of Armenia, the war was renewed in 62, and at Corbulo's request a separate general, Lucius Caesennius Paetus, was sent to Armenia. After Paetus' defeat, Corbulo obtained in 63 a *maius imperium* (authority greater than that of any other magistrate in the area) and was again put in charge of Cappadocia–Galatia, as well as Syria. He restored Roman prestige, and concluded a durable agreement with Parthia: Tiridates, the Parthian nominee to the throne of Armenia, admitted a Roman protectorate. Corbulo probably did not abuse his popularity, but his son-in-law Annius Vinicianus conspired. In October 66 Nero invited Corbulo to Greece and compelled him to commit suicide. His daughter Domitia Longina became wife of *Domitian in 70. It was the homage of the new dynasty to the name and influence of the greatest general of his time. The account of his achievements in Tacitus (*Ann.* bks. 12–15) and *Cassius Dio (bks. 60–3) derives ultimately to a great extent from Corbulo's own memoirs.   A.M.; G.E.F.C.; M.T.G.

Corinna, lyric poet, native of Tanagra in Boeotia, less probably Thebes (Paus. 9. 22; *Suda*). Tradition made her a pupil of Myrtis (*Suda*) and contemporary (perhaps older) and rival of *Pindar, whom she allegedly defeated (once, Paus. 9. 22; five times, Ael. *VH* 13. 25, *Suda*). Aelian's statement that Pindar retorted by calling her a 'Boeotian sow' is a biographical fancy derived from Pindar (*Ol.* 6. 90), likewise *Plutarch's anecdote (*De glor. Ath.* 4. 347f–348a) presenting her as adviser to the young Pindar (cf. Pind. fr. 29). Her traditional date has been contested. No Alexandrian scholar studied her work, and the earliest references to her belong to the 1st cent. BC (*Anth. Pal.* 9. 26; Prop. 2. 3. 21); the papyrus fragments consistently reflect the Boeotian orthography of the late 3rd cent. BC; her metre shows some affinities with Attic drama and her simple style is unlike that of Archaic choral poetry; the papyrus presents sporadic Atticisms (features characteristic of classical Athenian Greek). On present evidence the issue cannot be resolved. Her poetry was divided into five books. She was added by some as a tenth to the canon of nine lyric poets (e.g. *Anecd. Bekk.* 751; *peri diaphoras poiētōn* 18 ff.). Though the *Suda* speaks of epigrams, surviving fragments consist of lyric narratives dealing (almost exclusively) with local legends; titles attested are *Boeotus, Seven against Thebes, Euonymia, Iolaus, The Return Voyage, Orestes.* The dialect is predominantly epic, with some Boeotisms. Fr. 655 suggests that the narratives were sung by choirs of local girls. The largest papyrus preserves two narratives: the first tells of a singing contest between Cithaeron and Helicon, and the distress of the loser Helicon; the second contains a speech by the seer Acraephen to the river-god Asopus explaining the disappearance of the latter's nine daughters. The style is simple; fluent narrative, 'objective' in manner, with epithets sparse and unsurprising.   C.C.

Cornelia, second daughter of *Scipio Africanus, married Tiberius Sempronius Gracchus. Of her twelve children only three reached adulthood: Sempronia, who married *Scipio Aemilianus, and the two famous tribunes Tiberius *Gracchus and Gaius *Gracchus. After her husband's death she did not remarry (she is reported to have refused an offer by *Ptolemy VIII Euergetes II), devoting herself chiefly to the education of her children. Traditions about her attitude to the tribunes' political activities vary, but she made Gaius abandon his attack on Marcus Octavius (see Plut. *C. Gracch.* 4. 3). Some of her letters were admired by Cicero (*Brut.* 211), but Quintilian (1. 1. 6) no longer knew them. The authenticity of two fragments addressed to Gaius and preserved in *Nepos MSS must be regarded as uncertain. (See N. Horsfall, *Cornelius Nepos* (1989) 41 f.) After Tiberius' death she retired to a villa at Misenum (where she heard of Gaius' death) and devoted herself to cultural pursuits and correspondence and conversation with distinguished men (Plut. *C. Gracch.* 19). She was dead by 100 BC. The base of a statue of her seen by Pliny (*HN* 34. 31) survives (see *ILLRP* 336) and has been much discussed. (See M. Kajava, *Arctos* 1989, 119 ff.)   A.E.A.; E.B.

Cornelius Cinna, Lucius See CINNA.

Cornelius Dolabella, Publius See DOLABELLA.

Cornelius Fronto, Marcus See FRONTO.

Cornelius Gallus (Gaius Cornelius Gallus), said (not altogether reliably—see below) to have been born 70/69 BC at Forum Iulii, by which modern Fréjus is probably meant. In 43 he appears at Rome as a mutual acquaintance of Asinius Pollio and *Cicero (*Fam.* 10. 31. 6, 32. 5). In 41 he had some sort of supervision of the confiscations of land, which involved *Virgil's family farm, in Transpadane Gaul (Broughton, *MRR* 2. 377). In 30 as *praefectus fabrum* (prefect of engineers) he took an active military part in Octavian's (see AUGUSTUS) Egyptian campaign after the battle of Actium and laid out a Forum Iulium (this may have caused confusion about his birthplace) either in or near Alexandria; this he recorded in an inscription (*AE* 1964, 255), erased after his downfall, on an obelisk that is now in front of St Peter's at Rome. Octavian made him the first prefect (in effect, governor) of the new province of Egypt. He suppressed a rebellion in the Thebaid, marched south beyond the first cataract, negotiated the reception of the king of Ethiopia into Roman protection, and established a buffer-zone with a puppet king. He celebrated these achievements in a boastful trilingual inscription at Philae dated 15 April 29 (*CIL* 3. 14147 = *ILS* 8995) and in inscriptions on the Pyramids, and set up statues of himself all over Egypt. He was apparently recalled, and, because of the insolence to which his pride had encouraged him, was interdicted from the house and provinces of Augustus. He was then indicted (and condemned?) in the senate, and driven to commit suicide (27/6 BC).

He wrote four books of love-elegies, probably entitled *Amores*, addressed to Volumnia Cytheris, a freedwoman actress who had been the mistress of Mark *Antony 49–45 BC, under the pseudonym Lycoris. As well as one already-known pentameter, nine lines of these verses have been recovered from a papyrus, perhaps dating from the 20s BC, found in 1978 in a fortress in Egyptian Nubia and perhaps containing an anthology of quatrains from Gallus. These verses confirm the position of Gallus as creator (Ov. *Tr.* 4. 10. 53) of the new genre of love-elegy and his influence, long suspected, on *Propertius; the appearance of the word *domina* also confirms the long-held view that it was Gallus who, developing *Catullus, created the basic situation for Augustan elegists of the inamorata's dominance over the enslaved and helpless lover. There also seems to be a reference to the intended Parthian expedition of *Julius Caesar. Virgil in his tenth *Eclogue* (ll. 44 ff.— probably as far as 63), a consolation to Gallus on his desertion by Lycoris, according to the ancient Virgilian commentator Servius adapts lines (employing topics which appear

in later love-elegy) from Gallus' own elegiacs into hexameters; a misunderstanding of *Chalcidico versu* (l. 50), probably a reference to the alleged inventor of elegiac verse Theocles of Chalcis, as a reference to Euphorion is probably responsible for statements in ancient commentators that Gallus translated or imitated Euphorion, specifically a poem on the Grynean grove at Colophon (Serv. on *Ecl.* 6. 72). It is however likely that Gallus did occasionally imitate Euphorion and was introduced to him by his friend Parthenius, who wrote his *Erōtica pathēmata* for the use of Gallus in epic (i.e. hexameter) and elegiac verse (in fact Gallus apparently wrote no hexameter verse, whereas Euphorion, with insignificant exceptions, wrote nothing else); this seems to indicate a Propertian-style interest in mythological *exempla*. The style of the papyrus fragment is very plain, with none of the recherché obscurity of Euphorion; Quintilian (*Inst.* 10. 1. 93) regards Gallus as 'durior' ('harder') than Propertius and Tibullus.

The statement by Servius (on *Ecl.* 10. 1; *G.* 4. 1) that the Georgics originally ended with *laudes Galli* is probably due to another misunderstanding.   E.C.

Cornelius Nepos, the earliest extant biographer in Latin, lived *c*.110–24 BC. From Cisalpine Gaul, by 65 BC he was living in Rome and moving in literary circles: he corresponded with *Cicero and considered *Atticus a friend; Catullus dedicated verses to him. He kept out of politics.

WORKS (1) *De viris illustribus* ('On Famous Men'), at least sixteen books and with perhaps 400 lives, grouped according to categories (those of generals and historians are firmly attested), and including non-Romans. It was first published before the death of Atticus, probably in 34 BC; a second, expanded, edition appeared before 27 BC. Of this we have *De excellentibus ducibus exterarum gentium* ('On Eminent Foreign Leaders') and the lives of *Cato the Elder and Atticus from the Latin historians. (2) Lost works: *Chronica*, a universal history in three books (Catull. 1); *Exempla*, anecdotes in at least five books (Gell. *NA* 6 (7). 18. 11); fuller lives of Cato (Nep. *Cato* 3. 5) and Cicero (Gell. 15. 28. 2); a work on geography, cited by Pomponius Mela and *Pliny the Elder. His light verse (Plin. *Ep.* 5. 3. 6) was probably never published.

'An intellectual pygmy' (Horsfall), Nepos probably took the idea of a parallel treatment of foreigners from *Varro's *Imagines*. His defects are hasty and careless composition (perhaps less marked in his first edition) and lack of control of his material. He is mainly eulogistic, with an ethical aim, but also gives information about his hero's environment. As historian his value is slight; he names many sources, but rarely used them at first hand. His style is plain. His intended Roman readership is hard to locate—but middle-brow, with, at best, only a slight knowledge of Greece.   J.C.R.; G.B.T.; A.J.S.S.

Cornelius Scipio Aemilianus, Lucius See SCIPIO AEMILIANUS.

Cornelius Scipio Africanus, Lucius See SCIPIO AFRICANUS.

Cornelius Sulla See SULLA.

Crassus (Marcus Licinius Crassus), son of Publius Licinius Crassus (consul 97 BC, escaped from *Cinna to Spain, joined *Sulla after Cinna's death, played a prominent part in regaining Italy for him, and made a fortune in Sulla's proscriptions. After his praetorship he defeated *Spartacus (72–71 BC), but *Pompey, after crucifying many fugitives, claimed credit for the victory, deeply offending Crassus. Formally reconciled, they were made consuls 70 and presided over the abolition of Sulla's political settlement, though his administrative reforms were retained. During the next few years Crassus further increased his fortune and, relying on his connections, financial power, and astuteness, gained considerable influence. After 67, overshadowed by Pompey's commands (which he had opposed), he is associated by our sources with various schemes to expand his power and perhaps gain a military command. As censor 65, he tried to enrol the Transpadanes as citizens and to have Egypt annexed; he was foiled by his colleague Quintus *Lutatius Catulus (2) and their quarrel forced both to abdicate. Always ready to help eminent or promising men in need of aid, he shielded the suspects in the 'first conspiracy' of *Catiline and supported Catiline until the latter turned to revolution and a programme of cancelling debts. He may have supported the law of Publius Servilius

Rullus. A patron of *Julius Caesar (without, however, detaching him from Pompey), he enabled him to leave for his province in 62 by standing surety for part of his debts. On Caesar's return, he was persuaded by him to give up his opposition to Pompey, which during 62–60 had prevented both of them from gaining their political objectives, and to join Pompey in supporting Caesar's candidacy for the consulship. As consul (59), Caesar satisfied him by passing legislation to secure remission of one third of the sum owed by the *publicani* of Asia for their contract (Crassus presumably had an interest in their companies), and he now joined Pompey and Caesar in an open political alliance. After Caesar's departure for Gaul he supported *Clodius, who soon proved to be too ambitious to make a reliable ally and tried to embroil him with Pompey and Cicero. He welcomed Cicero on his return from exile, but in 56 alerted Caesar to the attempts by Cicero and others to recall him and attach Pompey to the *optimates* (lit. 'the best men', the office-holding upper class). Caesar and Crassus met at Ravenna and Pompey was persuaded to meet them at Luca and renew their alliance. The dynasts' plans were kept secret, but it soon became clear that Pompey and Crassus were to become consuls for a second time by whatever means proved necessary and to have special commands in Spain and Syria respectively assigned to them for five years, while they renewed Caesar's command for five years.

Late in 55, ignoring the solemn curses of the tribune Gaius Ateius Capito, Crassus left for Syria, determined on a war of conquest against Parthia. He won some early successes in 54 and completed financial preparations by extorting huge sums in his province. In 53 he crossed the Euphrates, relying on his long-neglected military skills and the recent ones of his son Publius Licinius Crassus. Although deserted by Artavasdes of Armenia and the king of Osroëne, he continued his advance into unfamiliar territory. After Publius died in a rash action, he himself was caught in Surenas (the Parthian king's hereditary commander) near Carrhae and, trying to extricate himself, died fighting.

After playing the game of politics according to the old rules, in which he was a master, he in the end found that unarmed power no longer counted for much in the changed conditions of the late republic, and he died while trying to apply the lesson. His death helped to bring Caesar and Pompey into the confrontation that led to the Civil War.   E.B.

Craterus (d. 321 BC), marshal of *Alexander the Great. First attested in charge of a Macedonian infantry *taxis*, he commanded the left of the phalanx at the battles of Issus (333) and Gaugamela (331). After the removal of Philotas and Parmenion, in which he played an unsavoury role, he assumed Parmenion's mantle and commanded numerous independent detachments during the campaigns in Sogdiana and India. At Opis (324) he was appointed viceroy in Europe in *Antipater's stead and commissioned to repatriate 10,000 Macedonian veterans. Alexander's death found him in Cilicia, and he could not participate in the Babylon settlement at which his role in Macedonia was (somewhat mysteriously) modified. In 322 he moved to Europe, where his forces were instrumental in winning the Lamian War. The following year he co-operated with Antipater, now his father-in-law, in the invasion of Asia Minor, where he died heroically in battle against *Eumenes of Cardia. A staunch defender of Macedonian tradition (and perhaps an uncomfortable figure at Alexander's court), he was intensely popular with the Macedonian rank and file, who cherished his memory.   A.B.B.

Crates of Mallus, son of Timocrates, was a contemporary of Demetrius of Scepsis (Strabo 14. 676) and *Aristarchus (2). He visited Rome as envoy of *Attalus II of Pergamum, probably in 159 BC, when his lectures, during his recovery after breaking his leg in the Cloaca Maxima, greatly stimulated Roman interest in scholarship (Suet. *Gram.* 2; see, however, Walbank, *HCP* 3. 415: the king may have been *Eumenes II and the date 168). He may have helped Eumenes II organize the library at Pergamum. He was mainly interested in *Homer, but we have no list of his writings. He also concerned himself with *Hesiod, *Euripides, *Aristophanes (1), and *Aratus (1), and laid claim to the title of *kritikos* ('critic'), which implied vastly wider interests than those of *grammatikos* ('grammarian'). Strabo 2. 5. 10 reports that he constructed a sphere to represent the world, on which the map of the land mass could be shown.

The Pergamenes and the Alexandrians were divided on the rival principles of 'analogy' and 'anomaly' in language. *Aristophanes (2) and *Aristarchus (2), of Alexandria, in editing Homer sought the correct form (or meaning) of a word by collecting and comparing its occurrences in the text, a procedure more novel in their age than in ours. Further, they tried to classify words by their types of form (cf. our declensions), in order by reference to the type to decide what was correct in any doubtful or disputed instance. Thus in Homer Aristarchus accented Κάρησος after Κάνωβος, πέφνων after τέμνων, οἰῶν after αἰγῶν; and similarly as to inflexions (see APOLLONIUS DYSCOLUS). Crates, on the contrary, borrowed his linguistic principles from the Stoics, and sought in literature a meaning which he already knew a priori. Not only words but literature likewise they thought a μίμησις θείων καὶ ἀνθρωπείων ('representation of things human and divine'; Diog. Laert. 7. 60), an accurate reflection of truth, and on this basis they carried to ludicrous extremes the allegorical method of interpretation, in order to secure the support of Homer for Stoic doctrines. In such features as inflexion they saw only confusion wrought upon nature's original products by man's irregular innovations and perversions. Cleanthes had named this unruly principle of language ἀνωμαλία ('anomaly'), illustrating it without much difficulty from the Greek declensions. This term and doctrine, and the allegorical method, were adopted by Crates and his school, to whom, consequently, the Alexandrian classification of forms (Crates seems to have written chiefly on noun anomalies) seemed futile in practice and wrong in principle.

The controversy gained importance with the growth of purism, and its extension from Greek to Latin; it is reflected in *Varro's *De lingua Latina*. Compromises attempted by both Greek and Roman scholars left the problem unsettled. 'Quare mihi non invenuste dici videtur, aliud esse Latine, aliud grammatice loqui' ('Therefore, it seems to me that the remark, that it is one thing to speak Latin and another to speak grammar, was far from unhappy') Quint. *Inst.* 1. 6. 27.
                                    P.B.R.F.; R.B.; N.G.W.

Cratinus was regarded, with *Aristophanes (1) and *Eupolis, as one of the greatest poets of Old Attic Comedy. He won the first prize six times at the City Dionysia (the main Athenian festival sacred to Dionysus) and three times at the Lenaea, another Dionysian festival (*IG* 2². 2325. 50, 121). We have 27 titles and over 500 citations. The precisely datable plays are: *Cheimazomenae* at the Lenaea in 426 BC (hyp. 1 Ar. *Ach.*), *Satyrs* at the Lenaea in 424 (hyp. 1 Ar. *Eq.*), and *Pytine* at the City Dionysia in 423 (hyp. 6 Ar. *Nub.*). Three more are approximately datable: *Archilochi* treats (fr. 1) the death of *Cimon as recent, and therefore comes not long after 450; *Dionysalexandros* (see below) attacked *Pericles for 'bringing the war upon Athens', and must belong to 430 or 429; and fr. 73 *Thraltae* suggests that Pericles has just escaped the danger of ostracism (ten-year exile). We do not know when Cratinus died; Ar. *Pax* 700 ff. speaks of him (in 421) as dead, but the context is humorous and its interpretation controversial. One category of titles is especially characteristic of Cratinus: *Archilochi, Dionysi, Cleobulinae, Odysses, Pluti,* and *Chirones*. In *Odysses* it appears from fr. 151 that the chorus represented Odysseus' crew; it is possible that the 'new toy' of fr. 152 was a model of his ship brought into the orchestra. The play is mentioned by Platonius (*Diff. com.* 7 and 12) as an example of 'Middle Comedy' ahead of its time, i.e. as containing no ridicule of contemporaries. There are papyrus fragments of *Pluti*, one of which indicates that the chorus explained its identity and role to the audience in the parodos. The hypothesis of *Dionysalexandros* is also largely preserved in a papyrus; in this play *Dionysus—as the title suggests—was represented as carrying Helen off to Troy; there was a chorus of satyrs. In *Pytine* Cratinus made good comic use of his own notorious drunkenness (cf. Ath. 39c), represented himself as married to Comedy, and adapted in self-praise the compliment paid to his torrential fluency and vigour by Ar. *Eq.* 526 ff.

Cratinus' language and style were inventive, concentrated, and allusive, and Aristophanes was obviously much influenced by him, but Platonius (*Diff. com.* 14) describes his work as comparatively graceless and inconsequential. It is clear from Ath. 495a, Hdn. 2. 945, and Galen, *Libr. Propr.* 17 that

Cratinus was the subject of commentaries in Hellenistic times.   K.J.D.

Critias (*c.*460–403 BC), one of the Thirty Tyrants (a short-lived extreme right-wing group which controlled Athens in 404–403 BC). Born of an old wealthy family to which *Plato also belonged (*APF* 8792) he, like his close friend *Alcibiades, was a long-time associate of *Socrates. He is often included with the sophists, and surviving fragments of his tragedies and other works evince an interest in current intellectual issues. Later scholars were uncertain whether some plays ascribed to him may have been the work of *Euripides (*Vit. Eurip.*); there is still disagreement about the authorship of *Sisyphus*, which included a speech giving a rationalistic account of the origin of human belief in the gods (*TGF* 1. 43 F 19).

Critias was implicated in the mutilation of the herms (415; see ANDOCIDES) but was released on the evidence of *Andocides. He played little or no part in the oligarchic coup in 411. In perhaps 408 he proposed the recall of Alcibiades. The latter's second exile in 406 was probably linked to Critias' own exile; he went to Thessaly where he may have assisted in a revolt by democratic forces. He was an admirer of Spartan ways, about which he wrote several works, and upon the Spartan defeat of Athens in 404 he returned from exile to become one of the Thirty Tyrants. In *Xenophon's narrative (*Hell.* 2. 3–4) he appears as the leader of the extremists, violent and unscrupulous, who proposes the execution of his colleague *Theramenes; but the account in *Ath. pol.* (34–40) does not mention him. He was killed fighting against Thrasybulus in spring 403. His reputation did not recover after his death; but Plato honoured his memory in several dialogues.   M.Ga.

Croesus, last king of Lydia (*c.*560–546 BC), son of Alyattes. He secured the throne after a struggle with a half-Greek half-brother, and completed the subjugation of the Greek cities on the Asia Minor coast. His subsequent relations with the Greeks were not unfriendly; he contributed to the rebuilding of the Artemisium at Ephesus and made offerings to Greek shrines, especially Delphi; anecdotes attest his friendliness to Greek visitors and his wealth. The rise of Persia turned Croesus to seek support in Greece and Egypt, but Cyrus the Great of Persia anticipated him: Sardis was captured and Croesus overthrown. His subsequent fate soon became the theme of legend: he is cast or casts himself on a pyre, but is miraculously saved by Apollo and translated to the land of the Hyperboreans or becomes the friend and counsellor of Cyrus.

P.N.U.; S.H.

Curtius Rufus, suffect consul AD 43, of obscure origin and alleged by some to be the son of a gladiator, entered the senate and won the praetorship, with the support of *Tiberius, who considered that he was 'his own parent' (Tac. *Ann.* 11. 21). Commander of the Upper Rhine army in 47, he employed his troops with digging for silver in the territory of the Mattiaci and was rewarded with the *ornamenta triumphalia* (insignia borne by a victorious general in his triumphal procession). Later, as an old man, he was proconsul of Africa, fulfilling a prediction made to him in his humble beginnings (Tac. *Ann.* 11. 21; Plin. *Ep.* 7. 27. 2), and died in office. In *Tacitus's obituary he is an unamiable *novus homo* (first man of his family to reach the consulship); the view that he was identical with Quintus Curtius Rufus, the historian of *Alexander the Great, now holds the field. (See next entry.)

R.S.; B.M.L.

Curtius Rufus, Quintus, rhetorician and historian, wrote during the 1st or early 2nd cent. AD (under *Claudius remains the preferred choice). His ten-book history of *Alexander the Great goes as far as the satrapy distributions at Babylon (323). The first two books (down to 333 BC) are lost (and there are substantial lacunae elsewhere), and in what remains there are no statements of biography and few on method. His work is extremely rhetorical, close in tone to the *Suasoriae* of *Seneca the Elder; it contains many speeches of varied length and quality, and the narrative is suffused with moralizing comments and arbitrary attributions of motive. There is little consistency (after strong criticism in the body of the work the final appreciation of Alexander is pure encomium), and the exigencies of rhetoric determine the selection of source material. Consequently he switches arbitrarily from source to source and sometimes blends them into a senseless farrago. He has

often been accused of deliberate fiction, but even in the speeches he used data from his regular sources and added an embroidery of rhetorical comment. He did not manufacture fact. He is by far the fullest derivative of the near-contemporary Alexander-historian Cleitarchus and preserves much that is of unique value (particularly on Macedonian custom); and he also records material common to *Arrian and probably made direct use of *Ptolemy I. But he very rarely names authorities and their identification in detail is hazardous. See also CURTIUS RUFUS (preceding entry).

A.B.B.

Cyprian (Thascius Caecilius Cyprianus), *c.* AD 200–58. Son of rich parents probably from the upper ranks of curial society (local elite) rather than of Roman senatorial rank, he became bishop of Carthage (248) soon after baptism and was quickly beset by Decius' persecution (248), for which his writings are a major source. His letters and tracts, from which much of the old Latin Bible can be reconstructed, deal mainly with difficulties within the Christian community resulting from the persecution, especially the terms and proper authority for restoration of apostates and the avoidance of a split between the rival advocates of laxity and rigour. In 256–7 his theology led to a split with Rome, whose bishop Stephen recognized the baptism of Novatianus' community (since 251 separated on rigorist grounds). In *Valerian's persecution (257) he was exiled to Curubis, but returned to Carthage and on 14 September 258 was executed there, the authorities treating him with the respect due to his class. More an administrator than a thinker, he writes with the effortless superiority of a high Roman official, liking correct procedure and expecting his clergy and *plebs* (and in practice his episcopal colleagues) to accept his authority. He speaks of bishops as magistrates, judges on behalf of Christ, and his language finds many analogies in Roman law. His application of juridical categories to the conception of the Church permanently influenced western Catholicism. His Life by his deacon Pontius, the earliest Christian biography, aims to show him as the equal of the glorious martyr Perpetua, pride of African Christianity.

J.F.Ma.

Cypselus, tyrant of Corinth, traditionally (and probably in fact) *c.*657–627 BC. He overthrew the aristocracy of the Bacchiadae, and established the earliest tyrant dynasty, and one of the longest lasting. *Herodotus' account, though its context is hostile, bears unmistakable signs of a favourable tradition in the folk-tale (which has eastern parallels) that his mother Labda, herself of Bacchiad descent, rescued him as an infant by hiding him in a *kypselē* (beehive) when the Bacchiadae tried to kill him. The story that he spent his youth in exile is probably invented: the Bacchiadae treated him as one of them, though his father Aetion was not; that enabled him to exploit discontent with their exclusive control. He drew active support only from wealthy Corinthians, but his popularity is reflected in Aristotle's view that he became tyrant 'through demagoguery': he had no bodyguard i.e. (perhaps) did not *need* one. His most important achievement was to remove the Bacchiadae: we hear little of his actions in power. He built a treasury at Delphi: Herodotus preserves an early favourable Delphic oracle. He founded colonies in north-west Greece with his bastard sons as founders and tyrants, and established a long-lasting Corinthian interest there: the most important was Ambracia; Anactorium and Leucas, where he had a canal dug through the spit which joins the mainland, were smaller foundations. He probably also devised the Corinthian tribal system, an early example of one based on domicile and not descent, upon which later institutions were based.   J.B.S.

Dd

Demades (*c.*380–319 BC) Athenian states-man, of major importance in the two decades following the Greek defeat at the battle of Chaeronea (338 BC). Of his early career nothing sure can be said, but by 338 he must have made his mark; taken prisoner in the battle, he was chosen by *Philip II of Macedo-nia as an envoy and used by the Athenians to negotiate the so-called Peace of Demades. From then on he was regularly called on by the city to get it out of troubles caused by those who did not share his view that Macedon was too strong militarily for the Greeks to revolt with a real chance of success. Having counselled against supporting Thebes' revolt of 335, he was able to dissuade *Alexander the Great from persisting in his demand for the surrender of *Demosthenes, *Hyperides, and other advocates of war. He opposed involvement in the revolt of Agis III (331), at which date he was treasurer of the military fund (*tamias tōn stratiōkotōn*) (*IG* 2². 1493). He seems to have sought the suspen-sion of the Exiles' Decree in 324 by proposing a flattering decree that Alexander be voted a god (which earned him a ten-talent fine), but his greatest service was successfully to negotiate with *Antipater the end of the Lamian War. In 319 he went on an embassy to Antipater to request the withdrawal of the garrison from Munichia, but *Cassander had him executed, a letter to *Perdiccas having come to light in which Demades urged him to move from Asia against Antipater and save the Greeks.

His policies of appeasement leagued him frequently with the prudent Phocion. Stories of his greed are dubitable, and the fact that, like Demosthenes, he was found guilty of appropriating some of the money deposited by Harpalus by no means proves that he had actually done so. All in all, he served Athens well and deserved the statue that had been erected in the Agora (Din. 1. 101).

He began life as a rower and received no formal training in rhetoric. He developed his great natural talent by speaking in the assem-bly. *Theophrastus opined that as an orator Demosthenes was worthy of the city, Demades too good for it. He published no speeches (cf. Cic. *Brut.* 36 and Quint. *Inst.* 12. 17. 49)—the fragment of a speech *Concerning the Twelve Years* (*Hyper tēs dōdekaetias*) is generally agreed not to be genuine—but many striking phrases were remembered.

G.L.C.

Demetrius the Besieger (Demetrius Poliorcetes), Demetrius I of Macedonia (336–283 BC), son of *Antigonus the One-eyed, was reared at his father's court in Phrygia and fled with him to Europe (322). He was married early (321/0) to Phila, daughter of *Antipater, widow of *Craterus and a potent political asset, and rapidly acquired military distinc-tion, commanding Antigonus' cavalry at Paraetacene and Gabiene (317/6). His inde-pendent commands began inauspiciously at Gaza (312), where he lost an army to *Ptolemy I, and subsequently (311) failed to displace *Seleucus I from Babylonia. However, in 307 he led the Antigonid offensive in Greece, lib-erating Athens from the regime of Demetrius of Phaleron, and in 306 his victory over a Ptolemaic fleet off Cyprus inspired his father to claim kingship for them both. These laurels were tarnished by setbacks in Egypt and, above all, Rhodes, where an epic year-long siege (305–4), which won Demetrius his reputation as 'the Besieger', was ended by negotiation. He was more effective as Anti-gonus' lieutenant in Greece (304–2), extending the alliance to Boeotia and Aetolia and reconstituting the League of Corinth (302) (see PHILIP II). Consequently he retained a base in the Isthmus when Anti-gonus' empire crumbled away after the defeat at the battle of Ipsus (301).

From this nadir his position strengthened when Seleucus married his daughter, Stratonice, and ceded Cilicia (299/8). Demetrius then reappeared in Greece (?295) to 'liberate' Athens from the tyranny of Lachares and defeated the Spartans. At this juncture he was invited to intervene in the dynastic turmoil in Macedon, where (thanks to Phila) he had himself proclaimed king after murdering the young Alexander V. He now held the throne for seven years (294–287) and devoted much of his energy to extending his control in central Greece (Thebes was twice besieged) and the west. But his primary ambition was the reconquest of Antigonus' empire, and by 288 a massive fleet of 500 ships was in preparation. At the news Seleucus, *Lysimachus and Ptolemy I allied against him, and his army refused to fight as Macedonia was invaded from east and west. Expelled from Macedon, he could not contain southern Greece, where the Athenians expelled his garrison from the city (but not Piraeus). Ptolemy arbitrated over a peace (287) and encouraged Demetrius to contest Asia Minor yet again. Plague and famine decimated his army, and he surrendered himself to Seleucus. The last two years of his life he spent in captivity, where drink and despondency accelerated his death. In his youth he was affable, accessible, the embodiment of Antigonus' propaganda of liberation. Later he fostered an aura of regal majesty (without his father's vindictive savagery), and his absolutist pretensions encouraged some of the most extreme manifestations of the ruler-cult. His chequered fortunes are a mirror of his age, when kingship meant conquest.   A.B.B.

Democritus, of Abdera in Thrace, b. 460–57 BC (Apollod. in Diog. Laert. 9. 41), 40 years after *Anaxagoras according to his own statement quoted by *Diogenes Laertius. He travelled widely, according to various later accounts, and lived to a great age. In later times he became known as 'the laughing philosopher', probably because he held that 'cheerfulness' (*euthymiē*) was a goal to be pursued in life. There is a story that he visited Athens—'but no one knew me' (Diog. Laert. 9. 36); this may be a reflection of the undoubted fact that *Plato, although he must have known his work, never mentioned him by name.

WORKS Diog. Laert. 9. 46–9 mentions 70 titles, arranged in tetralogies by Thrasyllus like the works of Plato, and classified as follows: Ethics, Physics, Unclassified, Mathematics, Music (which includes philological and literary criticism), Technical, and Notes. None of these works survives. Of his physical theories, on which his fame rests, only meagre quotations and summaries remain; the majority of texts that have come down to us under his name are brief and undistinguished moral maxims.

From the time of *Aristotle, Democritus and Leucippus are jointly credited with the creation of the atomic theory of the universe; it is now impossible to distinguish the contribution of each. Aristotle's account of the origin of the theory (*Gen. corr.* 1. 8) rightly relates it to the so-called Eleatic philosophers. *Parmenides argued that what is real is one and motionless, since empty space is not a real existent; motion is impossible without empty space, and plurality is impossible without something to separate the units. Division of what is real into units in contact, i.e. with no separating spaces, is ruled out because (*a*) infinite divisibility would mean there are no real units at all, and (*b*) finite divisibility is physically inexplicable. Against these arguments, says Aristotle, Leucippus proposed to rescue the sensible world of plurality and motion by asserting that empty space, 'the non-existent', may nevertheless serve to separate parts of what exists from each other. So the universe has two ingredients: Being, which satisfies the Eleatic criteria by being 'full', unchanging, and homogeneous, and Non-being or empty space. The pieces of real Being, since it is their characteristic to be absolutely indivisible units, are called 'atoms' (i.e. 'uncuttables'). They are said to be solid, invisibly small, and undifferentiated in material; they differ from each other in shape and size only (perhaps also in weight), and the only change they undergo is in their relative and absolute position, through movement in space.

By their changes of position the atoms produce the compounds of the changing sensible world. Compounds differ in quality according to the shape and arrangement of the component atoms, their congruence or otherwise (i.e. their tendency to latch together because of their shape), and the amount of space between them. It is a matter of controversy whether the atoms have a natural downward motion due to weight (as later in Epicurean theory: see EPICURUS,

Doctrines)) or move randomly in the void until their motion is somehow directed by collisions with other atoms. In the course of time, groups of atoms form 'whirls' or vortexes, which have the effect of sorting out the atoms by size and shape, like to like. Some of these are sorted in such a way as to produce distinct masses having the appearance of earth, water, air, and fire: thus worlds are formed—not one single world, as in most Greek cosmologies, but an indeterminate number scattered thoughout the infinite void, each liable to perish through random atomic motions, as they were originally formed. Leucippus and Democritus produced an account of the evolution within worlds of progressively more complex stages of organization, including human cultures (traces in Diod. Sic. 1. 7–8 and see Lucr. bk. 5).

The soul, which is the cause of life and sensation, is made of fine round atoms, and is a compound as perishable as the body. Perception takes place through the impact of *eidōla* (thin atomic films shed from the surfaces of sensible objects) upon the soul-atoms through the sense organs. Perceptible qualities are the product of the atoms of the sensible object and those of the perceiving soul. (A relatively full account is preserved in Theophr. *Sens.* 49–82.) They therefore have a different mode of existence from atoms and void—'by convention' as opposed to 'in reality'.

Little is known about Democritus' mathematics, although mathematical writings appear in the lists of his works; he must have been a diligent biologist, for Aristotle quotes him often.

Many surviving fragments deal with ethics, but they are mostly short maxims, hard to fit together into a consistent and comprehensive doctrine (see Havelock, *The Liberal Temper in Greek Politics* (1957), ch. 6 for a bold effort). His positions, as reported, are close to those of Epicurus, and it is hard to know whether this is historically genuine or a prejudice of the doxographers. His ethical ideal seems to include the idea that the soul-atoms should be protected from violent upheavals; wellbeing which leads to 'cheerfulness' (*euthymiē*) is a matter of moderation and wisdom (B 191). It is important not to let the fear of death spoil life, and to recognize the limits to which man is necessarily confined

(B 199, 203). Pleasure is in some sense the criterion of right action, but there must be moderation in choosing pleasures (B 189, 207, 224, 231). In social ethics, Democritus was apparently prepared to link his view of contemporàry society with his theory of the evolution of human communities; he saw that a system of law is by nature necessary for the preservation of society.

Democritus is a figure of great importance who has suffered intolerably from the triumph of his opponents, Plato, Aristotle, and the Stoics. He defended the infinite universe, plural and perishable worlds, efficient, non-teleological causes, and the atomic theory of matter, as opposed to the single, finite, and eternal cosmos of Aristotle, teleology, and the continuous theory of matter. The best brains preferred his opponents' arguments, and Epicurus and *Lucretius were his only influential followers until the post-Renaissance scientific revolution—by which time his books were lost.   D.J.F.

Demosthenes (384–322 BC), the greatest Athenian orator. When Demosthenes was 7 years old his father died, leaving the management of his estate to his brothers, Aphobus and Demophon, and a friend, Therippides. The trustees mismanaged the business, and Demosthenes at the age of 18 found himself almost without resources. He claimed his patrimony from his guardians, who spent three years in attempts to compromise. In the mean time, he was studying rhetoric and legal procedure under *Isaeus and at 21 he brought a successful action against his guardians, but two more years elapsed before he received the remnants of the property. By now he was engaged in the profession of *logographos* (speech-writer) and the reputation gained in private cases led to his being employed as an assistant to prosecutors in public trials.

From 355/4 onwards he came more and more to devote himself to public business. It is not clear how far Demosthenes' sympathies were engaged in his first public trials, the prosecutions of Androtion and Leptines in 355 and of Androtion's associate, Timocrates, in 353: *Against Androtion* and *Against Timocrates* he wrote for a Diodorus, and in any case the political tendency of the trials is unsure; *Against Leptines* Demosthenes did deliver himself, and, since Leptines' law was defended by Aristophon, it is possible that all three trials centred on his policy and that Demosthenes was one of his opponents. This would be consistent with the policy he supported in *On the Symmories* in 354/3: a rumour came that the king of Persia was preparing to attack Greece, as he had threatened to do in 356/5, and Demosthenes, arguing that the city was not properly prepared, opposed the advocates of war, certainly not the *Eubulus group, possibly that of Aristophon. In 353/2 he turned on Eubulus: *On the Syntaxis* seems directed partly against the allocation of surpluses to the *theōrika* (the fund from which grants were made to enable citizens to attend the theatre) —at § 30 he sneers about the public works of Eubulus— and partly against the policy of abstaining from all but essential military enterprises.

For the next few years Demosthenes was regularly on the losing side and of minor importance. Early in 352 in *For the Megalopolitans* he argued in favour of promising to support Arcadia, if Sparta carried out her plan of exploiting Thebes' preoccupation with the Third Sacred War: since Athens based her policy on concord with Phocis and Sparta, the decision to do no more than give a guarantee to Messenia was probably right. A few months later Demosthenes wrote *Against Aristocrates* for use in the attack on a proposal to honour Charidemus in gratitude for his offices in the cession of the Chersonesus by Cersobleptes: the speech is notable both as a source of information about the law of homicide and also for the manner in which it regards *Cersobleptes, not *Philip II of Macedonia, as the real enemy in the north. Demosthenes did not yet see what was plain to those he opposed. In late 352 Philip's attack on Cersobleptes carried him very near the Chersonesus, and Demosthenes' eyes were opened. In 351 he delivered the *First Philippic* which pleaded for more vigorous prosecution of the war for Amphipolis: his proposals were not accepted; deeper involvement in the long fruitless struggle may have seemed to endanger the power to defend the vital areas of Thermopylae and Chersonesus. Late in 351 in *On the Liberty of the Rhodians* he urged support of the Rhodian *dēmos* against the oligarchs supported by the Carian dynasty (see ARTEMISIA (2)) but the Persian attack on Egypt prompted caution, and Demosthenes' arguments were far from strong. In mid-349 Olynthus in north Greece, which had by then

lapsed from Philip's alliance, was attacked by Philip and appealed to Athens for help: in the three *Olynthiacs*, delivered in quick succession, Demosthenes demanded the fullest support and, in the last, an end to the law assigning surpluses to the *theōrika*; again he scathingly alluded to the works of Eubulus. There is, however, no reason to suppose that the three expeditions voted were not supported by Eubulus or indeed that they satisfied Demosthenes, and the implementation of his proposals might have brought even greater disaster than the loss of Olynthus. Early in 348 the party of Eubulus involved the city in a costly and inconclusive intervention in Euboea to prevent the island falling into the control of those hostile to Athens: Demosthenes later claimed to have been alone in opposing the expedition; either he was not truthful or he had taken a curious view of Athens' interests. One consequence of his opposition to Eubulus was that he became embroiled in an absurd wrangle with Midias, a prominent supporter of Eubulus, who had slapped his face at the Dionysia (an important festival of Dionysus) of 348: the case was settled out of court and the speech *Against Midias* was never delivered.

In mid-348, before the fall of Olynthus, Demosthenes successfully defended Philocrates when he was indicted under the *graphē paranomōn* (law against unconstitutional proposals) for his proposal to open negotiations with Philip, and in 347/6, when Demosthenes like *Aeschines was a member of the Council of 500, the partnership continued and Demosthenes played a leading part in securing acceptance of the Peace of Philocrates. On the two embassies to Macedon he cut a poor figure before Philip and got on badly with his fellow ambassadors, but the decisive moment came after the second embassy's return when in the assembly on 16 Scirophorion, it was known that Philip had occupied the Gates of Thermopylae and that Phocis could not be saved. Demosthenes was shouted down and Aeschines made the speech to which Demosthenes constantly recurred. What Demosthenes wanted that day is not clear: if he did want the city to denounce the new Peace, to march out to support Phocis attacked by the Macedonians and Thessalians from the north and the Thebans from the south, his judgement was seriously awry. From that day

Demosthenes determined to undo the Peace. Shortly after, however, in *On the Peace* he counselled caution, and for the moment contented himself with the attack on Aeschines from which he was forced to desist by the successful countercharge against his own associate, Timarchus.

The year 344 brought Demosthenes his opportunity to attack the Peace. Rumours reached Athens that Philip was preparing to intervene in the Peloponnese in support of Argos and Messene, and Demosthenes went on an embassy to those cities to warn them of the dangers of consorting with Philip: Philip protested, and shortly after Demosthenes' return the embassy of Python and all Philip's allies protested against his misrepresentations, and offered to turn the Peace into a Common Peace; first reactions were favourable, but in the assembly Hegesippus succeeded in having the status of Amphipolis referred to Philip—an oblique way of sabotaging the whole affair—while Demosthenes' contribution was the *Second Philippic* in which he denounced Philip as not worth an attempt at negotiation. (The alternative reconstruction would deny this conjunction and put Python's embassy in early 343.) In mid-343, after the success of *Hyperides' prosecution of Philocrates, Demosthenes judged the moment suitable to resume his attack on Aeschines; *On the False Embassy* sought to exploit the support of Eubulus' party for continuing the Peace and to suggest that Aeschines was really responsible for Philip's use of the peace negotiations to intervene in Phocis in 346. With the support of Eubulus and Phocion, Aeschines was acquitted by a narrow margin.

With the final collapse in early 342 of proposals to amend the Peace, Philip either began to intervene directly in Greece or was represented by Demosthenes as so doing, and amidst mounting hostility to Macedon Demosthenes went on an embassy to the Peloponnese to set about the organization of an Hellenic alliance for the war he was determined to have. For the moment his efforts came to little, but in 341 in *On the Chersonese* and shortly after, in the *Third Philippic*, he defended the aggressive actions of Diopeithes against Cardia by arguing that, since Philip's actions already amounted to war, it was absurd to heed the letter of the Peace. Not long after, he delivered the *Fourth*

Philippic (of which the authenticity was long doubted but is now widely accepted); in it Demosthenes appears so confident of his control that he dismissed the notion of harm being done by the theoric distributions in words inconceivable in 349, and he successfully demanded an appeal to Persia to join in attacking Philip. In 341/0 he also formed an alliance with Byzantium, and by autumn 340, when Philip finally declared war and seized the Athenian cornfleet, Demosthenes was in full charge of the war he had sought, though he was unable to restrain Aeschines from his unwise intrusion at Delphi into the rivalries of central Greece (see AESCHINES). In mid-339 he moved the suspension of the allocation of surpluses to the *theōrika*, and with Thebes unlikely to side with Philip after having expelled the Macedonian garrison from the Gates, Demosthenes could expect not to have to face Philip in Greece. The sudden seizure of Elatea in Phocis threw Athens into horrified perplexity, but Demosthenes proposed and effected alliance with Thebes, which he later pretended always to have wanted, and Athens and Thebes fought side by side at Chaeronea in autumn 338.

Demosthenes was present at the battle, and returned so quickly to organize the city's defences that Aeschines could accuse him of running away. He provided corn, repaired the walls, and was so much the man of the hour that he was chosen to deliver the solemn public Funeral Oration for 338. With Philip in Greece, the people looked to Demosthenes and he successfully met the frequent attacks on him in the courts. In 337/6 he was theoric commissioner, and Ctesiphon proposed that he be crowned at the Dionysia for his constant service to the city's best interests: perhaps encouraged by the opening of the Macedonian attack on Persia, Aeschines indicted Ctesiphon, but with the changing events of the next few months he preferred for the moment to let the case lapse. Demosthenes, hoping that the death of Philip was the end of Macedonian domination in Greece, sought to foment troubles for his successor, but *Alexander the Great quickly marched south and Demosthenes had to accept the new monarch. In 335 Demosthenes actively aided the Thebans in their revolt and narrowly escaped being surrendered to Alexander. From then on he seems to have looked to Persia to accomplish the liberation of

Greece: such at any rate seems to be the meaning of the many charges of receiving money from the Persians. Demosthenes gave no support to Agis III at any stage and, when Persia was crushed at the battle of Gaugamela (331) and the revolt of Agis collapsed, Athens was left in disastrous isolation. Aeschines seized the opportunity to renew his attack on Demosthenes through Ctesiphon. The case was heard in mid-330, and Demosthenes defended his acts in *On the Crown*, which is his masterpiece. He declined to fall into the trap of discussing recent events and with supreme art interspersed his discussion of events long past with lofty assertions of principle. Fewer than one-fifth of the jury voted for Aeschines, and he retired to Rhodes. Demosthenes was left in triumph, and the city settled down to acceptance of Macedonian rule, until in 324 word reached Greece that at the coming Olympian Games Nicanor was to make public a rescript ordering the restoration of exiles. Since this would affect the cleruchy (Athenian settlement) on Samos, an agitation began which was to end in the Lamian War. Demosthenes led a deputation as *architheōros* to protest. Subsequently he engaged in the discussion at Athens about divine honours for Alexander, having also taken the lead in dealing with the sudden appearance of Harpalus by proposing first that Harpalus be kept prisoner and his money stored on the Acropolis, and later that the venerable council of the Areopagus investigate the losses. It is difficult to assess Demosthenes' policy in this year: he may have foreseen the new uprising under Leosthenes and planned to involve Athens, but, since the especial ally of Leosthenes was Hyperides, who led the attack on Demosthenes in the prosecution of early 323, Demosthenes appears to have been at odds with the war-party. Equally unsure is his guilt in the Harpalus trial: the Areopagus declared him guilty of appropriating 20 talents, and he was found guilty and fined 50 talents, but, even if he did take the money, he may have intended to use it in service of the state; the whole affair is most obscure. He retired into exile, and lent his support to Hyperides in the creation of the alliance for the Lamian War. He was then recalled to Athens, but after the Macedonian victory at Crannon in 322 he left the city again, and was condemned to death by the decree of *Demades. Pursued by the agents of

*Antipater, he committed suicide in Calauria (322).

Modern opinions of Demosthenes' political importance have varied greatly, often in discernible relation to contemporary events. He has been lauded as a solitary champion of liberty and censured as the absurd opponent of progress. With the latter view English scholars have, happily, had little sympathy, but the high esteem in which the works of Demosthenes have been rightly held as works of art has tended to obscure the possibility that, while his devotion to liberty is one of the supreme monuments of liberty, his methods and his policies were not the best suited to attain their end, and that those of his opponents, which we must largely infer from his attacks, were no less directed to maintaining the city's power and independence, and perhaps more apt.

Demosthenes has much to say about Philip's success being due to bribery and was convinced that his own opponents had been corrupted, but in his obsession with this dubitable view he seems blind to the real problem of his day, which was how Greece could be united to counter effectively the military power of the new national state so far greater than the power of any single city-state. There was much to be said against Demosthenes' determination to involve the full military resources of Athens in a war in the north, in particular that in such a war Athens stood to gain most and the other Greeks would not unite for that result. For the defence of Greece itself against invasion there was a real hope of uniting the cities in a Common Peace, and this appears to have been the policy of Demosthenes' opponents. There was perhaps more enthusiasm than judgement in his military assessments, and since the defeat of Chaeronea appears to have produced a Greece that could never wholeheartedly unite in a war of liberation, it is possible that, if such a decisive battle was inevitable, his opponents might have united Greece for it more effectively. But the situation of Greece was tragic, and Demosthenes was certainly of heroic stature.

PRIVATE LAWCOURT SPEECHES (*dikai*). The series of private speeches begins with those against Aphobus and Onetor (363–362), in which Demosthenes claimed recovery of his property from his guardians, and continues throughout his life (*Against

Dionysodorus, 323–322). Several private speeches attributed (perhaps wrongly) to Demosthenes were delivered on behalf of the Apollodorus who was his opponent in the *For Phormion*. The speech *For Phormion* (350) and the first *Against Stephanus* (349; the second *Stephanus* is undoubtedly spurious) raise a question of professional morality. Pasion, the banker, appointed his chief clerk Phormion trustee for his sons; the elder son, Apollodorus, subsequently claimed a sum of money allegedly due to him, but Phormion proved that the claim had been settled some years previously. Apollodorus then prosecuted Stephanus, one of Phormion's witnesses, for perjury. If, as *Plutarch states, Demosthenes wrote *Stephanus A* as well as *For Phormion*, he was guilty of a serious breach of faith, for while the earlier speech extols Phormion's character, the later one contains insinuations against him. The evidence for the authenticity of *Stephanus A* is, however, inconclusive (cf. L. Pearson, *Antichthon* 1969, 18–26). Aeschines asserts that Demosthenes showed to Apollodorus a speech composed for Phormion, but this may be a misrepresentation of some attempt by Demosthenes to act as mediator.

The subjects of the private speeches include guardianship, inheritance, claims for payment, maritime loans, mining rights, forgery, trespass, assault, etc. In the *Callicles* (which has flashes of humour, seldom found in Demosthenes) the plaintiff alleges that the defendant has flooded his land by blocking a watercourse; in the *Conon*, a brilliant piece of writing, combining Lysianic grace (see LYSIAS) and Demosthenic force, some dissolute young rowdies and their father are summoned for assault.

Demosthenes had many rivals in his lifetime; but later critics considered him the greatest of the orators. His claim to greatness rests on his singleness of purpose, his sincerity, and his lucid and convincing exposition of his argument. In many instances he produces a great effect by the use of a few ordinary words. In his most solemn moments his style is at its plainest and his language most moderate. A master of metaphor, he uses it sparingly, and hardly at all in his most impressive passages. His style varies infinitely according to circumstances; sometimes as simple as Lysias, now polished like *Isocrates, again almost as involved as *Thucydides, he

follows no scholastic rule; long and short periods follow each other, or are mingled with passages in the running style not according to any regular system. Thus his carefully prepared utterances give an impression of spontaneity. Such was his control of language that he was generally able to avoid hiatus (where a word ending in a vowel precedes a word beginning with one) without any dislocation of the order of words. He had an instinctive aversion to a succession of short syllables, and even tribrachs are of comparatively rare occurrence.   G.L.C.

Dicaearchus, of Messina in Sicily, Greek polymath and prolific writer, pupil of *Aristotle and contemporary of *Theophrastus and *Aristoxenus: fl. *c.*320–300 BC. He spent some of his life in the Peloponnese. Fragments only survive of his works, but they show a remarkable range:

LITERARY AND CULTURAL HISTORY
(1) The *Life of Greece*, a pioneering history of culture in three books: it began with an idealized worldwide golden age and went on to trace the evolution of contemporary Greek culture, pointing the contribution of Chaldaeans and Egyptians as well as Greeks. (2) *On Lives*, in several books, treating *Plato, *Pythagoras, and other philosophers: he found 'juvenile' and 'vulgar' elements in the *Phaedrus*. The title suggests a discussion of different lifestyles rather than straightforward biographies, and he presented his subjects as men of action as well as of reflection. (3) *On Alcaeus*, perhaps including a commentary; this again treated wider aspects of cultural history. (4) Works on *Homer, form and titles unknown. (5) *Hypotheseis of the Plots of* *Sophocles and* *Euripides*, tracing the authors' reworkings of the myths. (6) *On Cultural Contests*, treating musical and poetic competitions. The last three works were important sources for later scholars of literature.

POLITICAL (1) *Tripoliticus*, apparently advocating a 'mixed' constitution with elements of monarchy, aristocracy, and democracy. (2) *Constitutions* of Pellene in Achaea, Corinth, Athens, and perhaps Sparta, though this last may have been part of (1), with Sparta exemplifying the mixed ideal. (3) *Olympicus* and *Panathenaicus*, more likely political dialogues named after their settings than public

orations. (4) *On the Sacrifice at Troy*, i.e.
*Alexander the Great's sacrifice before the
battle of the Granicus.

PHILOSOPHICAL (1) *On the Soul*, a dialogue on the corporeal nature and mortality
of the soul (this is one of the ways in which
he departed from Aristotelian teaching),
apparently consisting of two three-book parts
named after their settings *At Lesbos* and *At
Corinth*. (2) *On the Destruction of Humans*,
arguing that man is destroyed more by man
than by natural disasters. (3) *On Prophecy*,
accepting the possibility of the soul's prophetic power in dreams and in frenzy, but
doubting its moral value and advisability. (4)
Descent into the Trophonian Cave (an under-
ground sanctuary for oracular consultation
at Lebadea in Boeotia), including immoral-
ities of its priests. (5) A work on future things,
perhaps identical with (3) or (4). (6) *Letter*,
probably philosophical, to Aristoxenus.

GEOGRAPHICAL *Tour of the World*
(*periodos gēs*: the title may not be Dicaearchus' own), apparently including maps.
This established with some accuracy a main
parallel of latitude from the straits of Gibraltar to the Himalayas and the assumed eastern
Ocean. It included perhaps 'Measurements
of Mountains in Greece', whose heights he
overestimated.

Dicaearchus' learning was as remarkable
as his range and originality. He influenced
many subsequent writers, including
*Eratosthenes, *Panaetius, *Posidonius,
*Varro, *Josephus, and *Plutarch. *Cicero
admired him greatly, taking him as the model
advocate of the 'practical' life and
Theophrastus as that of the 'theoretical' (*Att.*
2. 16. 3).   C.B.R.P.

Didymus (1st cent. BC) belonged to the
school founded at Alexandria by *Aristarchus
(2) and himself taught there. A scholar of
immense learning and industry (cf. his nick-
names *Chalkenteros* ('Brazen-bowels') and
Bibliolathas ('Book-forgetting'), the latter
because of occasional self-contradictions due
to his having forgotten what he had said in
earlier books), he is said to have written 3,500
or 4,000 works. His importance for literary
history consists primarily in his compilation
of the critical and exegetical work of earlier
scholars. He was not an original researcher,
but rather a variorum editor and a transmitter of learning that might otherwise have

been lost. He was criticized by some later
scholars, e.g. Harpocration.

WORKS 1. He discussed Aristarchus'
recension of the Homeric text by comparing
copies and by examining Aristarchus' commentaries and special treatises. His results
were much used by the scholiasts. 2. Commentaries, with abundant mythological,
geographical, historical, and biographical
information, on *Homer, *Hesiod, *Pindar,
*Bacchylides, Choerilus, *Aeschylus,
*Sophocles, Ion of Chios, *Euripides,
Achaeus, Cratinus, *Aristophanes (1),
*Phrynichus, *Eupolis, *Menander, *Thu-
cydides, *Antiphon, *Isaeus, *Isocrates,
*Aeschines, *Demosthenes, *Hyperides,
*Dinarchus. Much of the oldest material in
the scholia to Pindar, Sophocles, Euripides,
and Aristophanes is ultimately derived from
Didymus. A papyrus fragment of his commentary on Demosthenes' *Philippics* illustrates his compilatory method; the quality of
the discussion leaves a great deal to be
desired. 3. Lexicography: *Lexeis tragikai* and
Lexeis kōmikai ('tragic expressions', 'comic
expressions'). These collections formed a
valuable source for scholiasts and lexicographers, e.g. Hesychius. *On Corrupt Expressions*, *On Expressions of Doubtful Meaning*,
Metaphorical Expressions, *On Proverbs*, a chief
source of the extant works of the *paroemiog-
raphers. 4. Grammar: *On Orthography*, *On
Analogy among the Romans*, *On Inflexions*.
5. Literature and antiquities: *On Lyric Poets*,
Xenē historia (on myths and legends), *Sympotic Miscellany* (*Symmikta symposiaka*), *On
the Axones of *Solon*, works on the death of
Aeneas, the birthplace of Homer, etc., and
a polemic against *Cicero, *Rep.*, which was
answered by *Suetonius; but this last may be
by his namesake Claudius Didymus.

J.F.L.; R.B.; N.G.W.

Dinarchus (*c.*360–*c.*290 BC), the last of the
canonical Ten Attic Orators. For the outline
of his life we largely depend on *Dionysius of
Halicarnasus *On Dinarchus*, chs. 2, 3, and 9.
He was born at Corinth but went to Athens
to study rhetoric under *Theophrastus and
from 336/5 on constantly and successfully
practised the profession of speech-writer
(*logographos*). As a metic (resident
foreigner), he was barred from a political
career nor was he able himself to speak in
court, but when after the Lamian War the

leading orators of the age, *Demosthenes and *Hyperides, had met their deaths, Dinarchus was left in unchallenged and lucrative supremacy and the period of rule by Demetrius of Phalerum, his friend and patron, was his heyday. When Demetrius had to retire from Athens at the coming of *Demetrius the Besieger in 307/6, Dinarchus, suspect for his wealth and perhaps even more his friendship with 'those who dissolved the democracy' (*FGrH* 328 F 66), deemed it expedient to remove to Chalcis and stayed there awaiting the opportunity to return. This was negotiated for him by Theophrastus in 292. With his eyesight failing, he stayed with his friend Proxenus, against whom he shortly filed a suit for the recovery of money lost in the house, the only time in Dinarchus' life that he appeared in court. That is the last we hear of him.

Dionysius knew of 87 speeches ascribed to Dinarchus of which he pronounced 60 genuine. We possess only three which scholars agree in assigning to him—*Against Demosthenes*, *Against Aristogiton*, and *Against Philocles*, all concerned with the investigations into the disappearance of the money deposited in Athens by Harpalus (324/3). Three of Dionysius' list are to be found in the Demosthenic Corpus (*Orationes* 45, 46, 58; cf. DEMOSTHENES), but scholars have been disinclined to ascribe them to Dinarchus.

Dinarchus marks the beginning of the decline in Attic oratory. He had little originality, except some skill in the use of new metaphors; he imitated his predecessors, especially Demosthenes (Hermogenes, *Id.* 2. 11 calls him *krithinos Dēmosthenēs*, 'a small-beer Demosthenes'), but developed no characteristic style of his own. He knew the technique of prose composition and had command of all the tricks of the orator's trade. He was competent up to a point, but his work is careless and lacking in taste. Thus, the arrangement of his speeches is incoherent; his sentences are long and formless, certain figures of speech, e.g. epanalepsis and asyndeton, are ridden to death, and his invective is so exaggerated as to become meaningless. Numerous minor plagiarisms are collected by Blass (*Att. Ber.*[2] 3. 2. 318–21); in particular, a passage about Thebes in *Demos.* 24 is based on Aeschin. 1. 133, and *Aristog.* 24 is suggested by Dem. 9. 41. G.L.C.

Dio Cassius See CASSIUS DIO.

Dio Chrysostom See DIO COCCEIANUS.

Dio Cocceianus, later called Chrysostom (*c.* AD 40/50–after 110), Greek orator and popular philosopher. Born of wealthy family in Prusa in Bithynia, Dio began a career as a rhetorician at Rome, but soon fell under the spell of the Stoic philosopher Gaius Musonius Rufus. Involved in a political intrigue early in the reign of *Domitian, he was banished both from Rome and from his native province, and spent many years travelling through Greece, the Balkans, and Asia Minor as a wandering preacher of Stoic-Cynic philosophy. Rehabilitated by *Nerva, he became a friend of *Trajan, but continued to travel widely as an epideictic orator. He later retired to his family estates in Bithynia and became a notable in the province (he figures in the *Letters* of *Pliny the Younger as the defendant in a prosecution arising out of a public building contract).

Of the 80 speeches attributed to him, two are actually the work of his pupil *Favorinus. Many are display-speeches, but others, e.g. those delivered before the assembly and council at Prusa, deal with real situations. His themes are varied: mythology, the Stoic-Cynic ideal monarch, literary criticism, popular morality, funeral orations, rhetorical descriptions, addresses to cities, etc. He sees himself as a teacher of his fellow men, and his stock ideas are the Stoic concepts of *physis* ('nature'), *aretē* ('virtue'), and *philanthrōpia* ('philanthropy'). His language and style are Atticist (i.e. they imitate classical Athenian Greek), though he avoids the extreme archaism of some representatives of the 2nd-cent. AD rhetorical revival known as the Second Sophistic, and often aims at an easy, almost conversational style, suggestive of improvisation. *Plato and *Xenophon are his main models. Dio idealizes the Hellenic past, and feels himself the heir to a long classical tradition, which he seeks to revive and preserve. His Stoic-Cynic philosophy has lost its erstwhile revolutionary *élan*, and become essentially conservative, though he still insists on the philosopher's right to free speech and criticism. His Greek patriotism is in no way anti-Roman. Like his contemporary *Plutarch, he reflects the attitudes and culture of the upper classes of the eastern half of the empire, who were beginning to reach out to a share in political power. He gives a vivid and detailed picture of the life of his times.

R.B.; N.G.W.

Diocles, physician from Carystus on Euboea; in several ancient medical canons (e.g. Vindicianus, *De med.* 2, fr. 2 Wellmann) he is placed second in fame only to *Hippocrates. His writings survive only in quotations, and there are serious problems of attribution in the case of certain fragments. Diocles was perhaps a contemporary of *Aristotle (*c.*384–322 BC) but his dates are highly controversial and the nature of his intellectual relationship to Aristotle and the Lyceum even more so. *Galen claims that he wrote the first anatomical handbook (2. 282 Kühn, fr. 23 W); he also wrote influential works on physiology, aetiology, medical semiotics and prognostics, dietetics, and botany. His practice was no less famous than his theory; a type of bandage for the head was named after him, as was a cunning spoon-like device for the removal of arrowheads. The relative sophistication of Diocles' method is evident in an unusual fragment preserved by Galen (6. 455 Kühn, fr. 112 W), where he seems to be arguing for more flexibility in the assignment of pathological effects to given causes on the ground that the mere presence of a certain smell, substance, or other quality does not necessitate uniform reactions in all parts of the body or in all patients. Galen praises him for his appreciation of the importance of practical experience, even in the light of his commitment to theory—a theory which advocated a cardiocentric view of intelligence, and attributed the management of the body to the interactions of the four qualities hot, cold, dry, and moist (fr. 8 W).   J.T.V.

Diocletian (Gaius Aurelius Valerius Diocletianus), originally named Diocles. Of obscure origins, born in Dalmatia perhaps in the early 240s AD, he rose to command the *domestici* (bodyguard) of the emperor Numerianus on the Persian campaign of 283–4. When Numerianus was killed by his praetorian prefect Aper, the army proclaimed Diocles Augustus at Nicomedia; he killed Aper. He campaigned (285) against Numerianus' brother Carinus, who was killed at Margus. A usurper Julianus was also removed, and Diocletian was sole emperor.

Visiting Italy, he proclaimed his comrade-in-arms *Maximian as Caesar and sent him to suppress the Bacaudae. Maximian was made Augustus (286) and spent the next years defending Gaul. Diocletian spent most of his reign on the Danube or in the east. In 287 he installed Tiridates III as king of Armenia and reorganized the Syrian frontier. He campaigned on the Raetian frontier (288); he fought the Sarmatians (285 or 289), and the Saracens (290).

But the problems of the empire remained serious. On 1 March 293 he established the 'tetrarchy' (system of four emperors). To the two Augusti, now known as Iovius and Herculius respectively to emphasize their quasi-divine authority, were added Caesars, *Constantius I and *Galerius; these were adopted into the Jovian or Herculian houses by the marriage of Galerius to Diocletian's daughter Valeria and of Constantius to Maximian's (?step-)daughter Theodora. The arrangement would provide an imperial presence in different areas; it might deter usurpers; and the Caesars might become acceptable to the armies and live to succeed as Augusti (but it is most unlikely that the Augusti had yet planned to abdicate). To raise the dignity of the imperial office Diocletian adopted an oriental court ceremonial (*adoratio*) and seclusion. Each tetrarch had his own staff (*comitatus*), and was often on the move in his territory, though Nicomedia, Trier (Augusta Treverorum), and Sirmium often provided an imperial residence; Rome was of lesser importance. In practice the empire was divided into two; Maximian and Constantius ruled the west, Diocletian and Galerius the east. Diocletian employed Galerius in Oriens until 299, thereafter on the Danube. Diocletian defeated the Sarmatians (294) and campaigned against the Carpi (296); many Bastarnae and Carpi were settled on Roman soil. In Egypt a revolt broke out (297) under Domitianus and Aurelius Achilleus; present in person, Diocletian suppressed this after a long siege of Alexandria, reorganized the administration of Egypt, and negotiated with the Nobatae on the extreme southern frontier (298). Meanwhile he had sent Galerius to deal with the situation on the Syrian frontier: the Persian king Narses had expelled Tiridates from Armenia. Though defeated in his first campaign, Galerius won a total victory (298) and added significant territories to the empire. Campaigning by Constantius continued on the Rhine, but from 298 there was a general lull in rebellions and wars; tetrarchic authority was secure.

Diocletian pursued systematically a long-established policy of dividing provinces into smaller units; by 314 there were about 100, twice the number of a century earlier. The purpose was to ensure closer supervision, particularly over law and finance, by governors and their numerous staffs; critics saw it as leading to never-ending condemnations and confiscations. All provinces were governed by equestrian *praesides* except Asia and Africa (by senatorial proconsuls) and the divisions of Italy (by *correctores*). To oversee the *praesides*, Diocletian grouped the provinces into twelve new 'dioceses', each under a new equestrian official, the *vicarius* or 'deputy' of the praetorian prefects. In the later part of his reign, Diocletian began an important reform, separating military from civil power in frontier provinces; groups of provincial armies were put under the command of *duces*, so that *praesides* were left with civilian duties only. Senators remained excluded from military commands. His conception of defence was conservative; he made little or no effort to increase the size of the élite field army (*comitatus*), which had been formed in the late 3rd cent. But a huge programme of building and reconstruction of defensive works was undertaken on all frontiers, and these were to be held by sheer force of numbers; the size of the Roman army was perhaps nearly doubled.

The army and the increase of administrative personnel were a heavy financial burden. Diocletian reformed the system of taxation to take inflation into account and to regularize exactions in kind. Taxation was now based on the *iugum*, a new concept, a unit of land calculated from its productivity as much as by its area, and on the *caput*, the unit of human resource. Most revenue and expenditure was now in kind; every year an assessment of all levies payable on each fiscal unit was declared (*indictio*) by the praetorian prefects. By the Currency Edict (301) Diocletian attempted to create a unified currency, doubling the value of at least some coins and decreeing that the retariffed currency be used both for paying debts to the *fiscus* and in private contracts. But he could not establish confidence in this revaluation. Late in 301 he tried to halt infla-

tion by the Price Edict. In great detail this fixed maximum prices and wages; despite savage penalties it became a dead letter, as goods disappeared from the market.

Many legal decisions show Diocletian's concern to maintain or resuscitate Roman law in the provinces. He was an enthusiast for what he understood of Roman tradition and discipline, to reinforce imperial unity: hence he decreed the suppression of the Manichees. This policy forms the backdrop to the persecution of Christians, undertaken possibly on the insistence of Galerius. Earlier attempts had been made to purge the court and the army, but the first persecuting edict, issued at Nicomedia (23 February 303), was designed to prevent the Church from functioning, by requiring the burning of Scriptures and the demolition of churches, and the banning of meetings for worship; recusants were deprived of any rank, and thus made liable to torture and summary execution and prevented from taking action in court; imperial freedmen were re-enslaved. In Gaul and Britain Constantius contented himself with demolishing churches, and the later edicts were not promulgated outside the areas controlled by Diocletian and Galerius. The second edict imprisoned all clergy; the third released them, but they were to sacrifice first. The fourth edict ordered a universal sacrifice, but implementation was patchy, most severe it seems in Palestine and Egypt.

Late in 303 Diocletian visited Rome for the only time, to celebrate with Maximian his *vicennalia* (the 20th anniversary of his accession). A collapse in health caused him to return to Nicomedia, where on 1 May 305 he abdicated (Maximian reluctantly did the same at Milan), leaving Constantius and Galerius as Augusti, with Flavius Valerius Severus and *Maximin as Caesars. He attended Galerius' conference at Carnuntum (308) but refused to reassume the purple and spent his last years at Salonae; remains of the palace he built survive. He died about 312. His wife Prisca and only child Valeria were exiled by Maximin and beheaded by *Licinius. Diocletian's genius was as an organizer; his measures did much to preserve the empire in the 4th cent., and many lasted much longer in the east. The tetrarchy as such broke down when Diocletian's personality was removed, but for most of the 4th cent. more than one emperor was the rule. His reforms were completed by *Constantine I, who introduced further innovations, most notably in the army and in religion.   R.P.D.

Diodorus Siculus, of Agyrium, Sicily (hence 'Siculus'), is the author of the *Bibliothēkē* ('Library'), a universal history from mythological times to 60 BC. Only 15 of the original 40 books survive fully (bks. 1–5; 11–20); the others are preserved in fragments. Despite his claim to cover all of known history, Diodorus concentrates on Greece and his homeland of Sicily, until the First Punic War (i.e. Roman war against Carthage), when his sources for Rome become fuller. But even in its fragmentary state, the *Bibliothēkē* is the most extensively preserved history by a Greek author from antiquity. For the period from the accession of *Philip II of Macedon to the battle of Ipsus (301) in Phrygia (where *Antigonus the One-Eyed was defeated by *Lysimachus and *Seleucus I), when the text becomes fragmentary, it is fundamental; and it is the essential source for classical Sicilian history and the Sicilian slave rebellions of the 2nd cent. BC. For many individual events throughout Graeco-Roman history, the *Bibliothēkē* also sheds important light.

Diodorus probably visited Egypt *c.*60–56 BC, where he began researching his history. By 56, he may have settled in Rome, completing the *Bibliothēkē* there around 30. He read Latin and had access to written materials in Rome, but, despite his admiration for *Julius Caesar, there is no evidence that he personally knew Romans of prominence. Diodorus originally intended to cover events to 46; perhaps the dangers of writing contemporary history of a turbulent period influenced his decision to conclude with the year 60.

Books 1–6 include the geography and ethnography of the *oikoumenē* ('inhabited world') and its mythology and paradoxology (account of marvels) prior to the Trojan War; bks. 1–3 cover the east, bks. 4–6 the west. Of special significance are the description of Egypt in bk. 1, drawn from Hecataeus of Abdera; the discussion of India in bk. 2, drawn from Megasthenes; passages from the works of Agatharchides of Cnidus in bk. 3; and the highly fragmentary Euhemeran material in bk. 6 (see EUHEMERUS).

The fully preserved historical books cover 480–302 and are organized annalistically, with Olympian, Athenian archon, and Roman consular years synchronized—often erroneously. The fragmentary final books, which draw on *Posidonius, are probably organized episodically. Occasionally including the same incidents from different authorities or failing to understand the organizational habits of an individual author, Diodorus created numerous, sometimes serious doublets.

The main source for most of the narrative of the Greek mainland is *Ephorus; *Hieronymus of Cardia is the prime authority for the outstanding narrative of the Diadochi (successors of *Alexander the Great). Sicily receives important independent attention, in which Diodorus employs *Timaeus extensively. For much of the later Roman period, Diodorus follows *Polybius closely, as the preserved Polybian text shows; he employs Posidonius for many events after 146. But the 19th-cent. belief that all of Diodorus' sources could be identified proved over-confident and attempts to make such identifications continue to provoke great controversy. Further, because few of his sources survive outside his own work, precisely what Diodorus has taken verbatim, what he has confused and entered in error, and what he has consciously interpolated are matters of great dispute. It appears at least that certain themes recur throughout the *Bibliothēkē* independently of Diodorus' current source. Character assessments, with a strong insistence on personal and collective morality, and an emphasis on the civilizing power of individual benefactors suggest late Hellenistic influence and therefore Diodorus' own philosophy.   K.S.S.

Diogenes (1), the Cynic (*c.*412/403–*c.*324/321 BC). The general distortions in the ancient traditions about Cynicism ('doggishness') multiply in the case of Diogenes, who provoked extremes of admiration, hostility, and imaginative invention. All accounts are controversial, but the ancient traditions show certain constants and *Diogenes Laertius 6. 70–3 preserves Diogenes' essential thought.

Accused with his father, moneyer at Sinope (south coast of he Black Sea), of 'defacing the currency' (a phrase which was to yield a potent metaphor), Diogenes was exiled some time after 362 and spent the rest of his life in Athens and Corinth. (His capture by pirates, consultation of Delphi, and discipleship of

*Socrates' follower *Antisthenes are fictitious.) He evolved a distinctive and original way of life from diverse, mainly Greek, elements: the belief (espoused by certain types of holy men and wise men) that wisdom was a matter of action rather than thought; the principle (advanced by various sophists, 5th-cent. primitivists, and Antisthenes) of living in accordance with nature rather than law/convention; the tradition, perhaps sharpened by contemporary disillusionment with the *polis* (city-state), of promulgating ideal societies or constitutions; a tradition of 'shamelessness' (reflected by the symbol of the dog in literature and by the supposed customs of certain foreign peoples); Socratic rejection of all elements of philosophy except practical ethics; Socrates' pursuit of philosophy in the agora rather than in a school; an anti-intellectual tradition; the tradition (variously represented by Odysseus, Heracles, the Spartans, and to some extent by Socrates) of physical toughness as a requirement of virtue; the image of the suffering hero and the wanderer (Odysseus, Heracles, various tragic figures); the tradition of mendicancy (represented both in literature and in life); the life of asceticism and poverty (as represented by various wise men and holy men and labourers); the tradition of the wise or holy man who promises converts happiness or salvation; and various humorous traditions (the jester's practical and verbal humour; Old Comedy's outspokenness and crudity; Socrates' serio-comic wit).

Diogenes pursued a life as close as possible to the 'natural' life of primitive man, of animals, and of the gods. This entailed the minimum of material possessions (coarse cloak, staff for physical support and protection, purse for food) and of sustenance (obtained by living off the land and by begging); performance in public of all natural functions; training in physical endurance, and a wandering existence in harmony with natural conditions. Freedom, self-sufficiency, happiness, and virtue supposedly followed. It also entailed not merely indifference to civilized life but complete rejection of it and of all forms of education and culture as being not simply irrelevant but inimical to the ideal life. Hence Diogenes' attacks on convention, marriage, family, politics, the city, all social, sexual, and racial distinctions, worldly reputation, wealth, power and authority, litera-

ture, music, and all forms of intellectual speculation. Such attacks are imposed by the Cynic's duty metaphorically to 'deface the currency'. Hence the modern implications of the word 'cynic' are misleading. Indeed, humane attitudes came easily to Diogenes (e.g. his advocacy of sexual freedom and equality stemmed naturally from rejection of the family).

Although proclaiming self-sufficiency, Diogenes tried to convert others by his own outrageous behaviour (which went beyond the requirements of the natural life), by direct exhortation employing all the resources of his formidable wit and rhetorical skills, and by various written works. Notwithstanding ancient and modern doubts, it is certain that Diogenes expounded his views in a *Politeia* ('Republic', reconstructable from Diog. Laert. 6. 72 and *Philodemus' *On the Stoics*) and several tragedies. Such writings, which compromise the ideal of the practical demonstration of philosophical truth and the formal rejection of literature, did not imply real debate with conventional philosophers. Diogenes sparred verbally with *Plato but dismissed his philosophy as absurd; his *Politeia*, while a serious statement of Cynic positions, parodied 'serious' philosophers' pretensions.

Diogenes' missionary activity entailed what his aggressiveness sometimes obscured: recognition of the common humanity of Cynics and non-Cynics. 'Philanthropy' (concern for one's fellow human beings) is integral to Cynicism and essential to Diogenes' celebrated concept of 'cosmopolitanism' (the belief that the universe is the ultimate unity, of which the natural and animal worlds, human beings, and the gods are all intrinsic parts, with the Cynic representing the human condition at its best, at once human, animal, and divine).

Ancient and modern reactions to Diogenes range from appreciation of his wit to admiration for his integrity, denial of his philosophical significance, revulsion at his shamelessness, dislike of the threat he posed to conventional social and political values, and misguided attempts to make him respectable. Yet, whatever the detailed distortions in the Stoic history of philosophy, it was right to locate Diogenes within the great tradition, as even Plato half-conceded when he dubbed him a 'mad Socrates' (Diog. Laert. 6. 54). J.L.Mo.

Diogenes (2), of Oenoanda in Lycia (near mod. Incealiler in Turkey), author of a massive Greek inscription presenting basic doctrines of Epicureanism (see EPICURUS). The inscription was carved in a stoa (colonnade), probably in the 2nd cent. AD. Between 1884 and 1895, 88 fragments were discovered, and were the basis of successive editions until the publication by M. F. Smith of 124 new fragments (1970–84).

The inscription occupied several courses of a wall *c.*80 m. (87 yds.) long. In the lowest inscribed course was a treatise on ethics dealing (*inter alia*) with pleasure, pain, fear, desire, dreams, necessity, and free will; beneath its columns was inscribed a selection of Epicurus' *Primary Tenets* and other maxims. Immediately above was a treatise on physics, the surviving sections of which include criticisms of rival schools and discussions of epistemology, the origins of civilization and language, astronomy, and theology. Above these main treatises were more maxims, letters of Epicurus (one, addressed to his mother, concerns her anxious dreams), at least three letters written by Diogenes to Epicurean friends, and Diogenes' defence of old age. Fragments survive also of Diogenes' instructions to his friends.

Diogenes records that he was ailing and aged when he set up the inscription, and that he was moved by a desire to benefit his fellows at home and abroad as well as future generations. Although most of the inscription remains buried, the recovered fragments illuminate Epicurean theory and the activity of the school under the Roman empire. See EPICURUS.   D.K.

Diogenes Laertius, also called Laërtius Diogenes, author of an extant compendium on the lives and doctrines of the ancient philosophers from *Thales to *Epicurus. Since he omits Neoplatonism and mentions no philosopher after Saturninus (a Pyrrhonian sceptic of the 2nd cent. AD), he probably lived in the first half of the 3rd cent. AD. Nothing whatever is known of his life, not even where and with whom he studied philosophy.

After an introduction on some non-Greek 'thinkers' such as the magi, and some of the early Greek sages, he divides the philosophers into two 'successions', an Ionian or eastern (bk. 1. 22 to bk. 7) and an Italian or western (bk. 8), and ends with the 'sporadics', import-

ant philosophers who did not found successions (bks. 9–10). This arrangement disperses the Presocratics in books 1, 2, 8, and 9. Book 10 is devoted entirely to Epicurus and preserves the texts of several of his works.

In 10. 138 Diogenes speaks of giving the finishing touch to his entire work; but the book is such a tissue of quotations industriously compiled, mostly from secondary sources, that it could have been expanded indefinitely. Diogenes usually drew his material on any one philosopher from more than one earlier compilation, depending by preference on such writers as Antigonus of Carystus, Hermippus, Sotion, *Apollodorus, Sosicrates of Rhodes, Demetrius of Magnesia, Diocles of Magnesia, Pamphila, and *Favorinus, all of whom were themselves industrious compilers. Thus Diogenes' material often comes to us at several removes from the original. Fortunately, he usually names his sources, mentioning over 200 authors and over 300 works by name. As a rule he changes sources continually. Hence his reliability and value also change from passage to passage. For example, his account of Stoic doctrine (8. 39–160) is reliable and his long quotations from *Epicurus are invaluable when separated from the inserted marginalia that sometimes interrupt the sense. But some Lives, as *Heraclitus', are mere caricatures, and some summaries of doctrine are vitiated by philosophic distortion: for instance, *Aristotle's doctrines are viewed through Stoic, perhaps also Epicurean, eyes.

Diogenes also wrote some wretched poetry, which he quotes more than 40 times and of which he published a separate edition, not extant (1. 39). It has been suggested that Diogenes was himself an Epicurean, or alternatively a Sceptic; but most probably he was an adherent of no school (cf. Barnes in *ANRW* 2. 36. 6. 4243–4).   H.S.L.; R.W.S.

Dion (*c.*408–353). Son of Hipparinus, *Dionysius I's father-in-law. A disciple of *Plato from 388/7, married Dionysius' daughter Arete and became his most trusted minister and diplomatist. His vast wealth and notorious Platonism, together with his austerity and ambition for his nephews, aroused the suspicion of *Dionysius II and of the 'old guard' monarchists. Hoping to convert Dionysius, he brought Plato to Syracuse (367/6), but the disclosure of an indiscreet letter to the Carthaginians led to his banishment. At Athens he associated with the Academy, and he was honoured at Sparta; but Plato failed to reconcile Dionysius with him, and he was dispossessed of his wife and property. Landing in western Sicily (357), and greatly augmenting his small force on the march, he seized Syracuse, less the citadel, in the absence of Dionysius, and was elected general plenipotentiary (with his brother). Dion soon quarrelled with the radical leader Heraclides and was forced to retire to Leontini. Recalled (355) to eject Dionysius' general Nypsius from Syracuse, he became master of the whole city; but his imperiousness, his exactions, his employment of Corinthian advisers, and his intention of establishing some form of Platonist aristo-monarchy, again alienated the *dēmos*. He had Heraclides murdered, but his supporters fell away and he was himself assassinated at the instigation of his Athenian friend Callippus, who (briefly) became the ruler of Syracuse. Austere, haughty, aloof, contemptuous of democracy, tainted by his long connection with tyranny; he was probably sincere in his own interpretation of Platonism; but he lacked the domestic support, the resources, and the devoted military force needed to establish a stable non-democratic regime; and his 'liberation' of Sicily brought only political and social chaos to the island, for nearly twenty years.   B.M.C.

Dionysius I of Syracuse, born c.430 BC, son of Hermocritus, a well-to-do Syracusan; wounded (408) in Hermocrates' attempted coup; secretary to the generals (406), he distinguished himself in the campaign against Carthage for possession of Akragas. By unscrupulous demagogy he secured the dismissal of the generals and his own election as general plenipotentiary (a title he may have used until 392), obtained a bodyguard, occupied and fortified the citadel (Ortygia), and assumed control of the state. With a large allied army, he failed to raise the siege of Gela (405), but crushed a revolt of the aristocracy (confiscating their properties), and concluded the Peace of Himilco, which stripped Syracuse of her possessions. Besieged in Ortygia by the rebellious Syracusans (404–3), he came to terms with them (less the exiled aristocracy), giving them, although dis-

armed, a measure of autonomy. After subjugating eastern Sicily (south of Messana (mod. Messina)) with a mercenary army (402–399), he prepared for war with Carthage, fortifying Epipolae, amassing war-material, building a huge fleet, rearming the Syracusans, hiring mercenaries, and forming matrimonial alliances with Syracuse (Andromache, sister of *Dion) and Locri Epizephyrii in south Italy (Doris). He invaded the Carthaginian province (397) and stormed Motya (Mozia), but (396) retired before Himilco to Syracuse; here, following the defeat of his navy off Catana (Catania), he was besieged until 395, when, with some Corinthian and Spartan aid, he overthrew Himilco's plague-stricken forces. He restored his east Sicilian empire (incorporating Messana), attacked Rhegium (Reggio) and countered a new Carthaginian threat (395–2); but when the Syracusan army mutinied, he concluded a peace with Carthage (392) that recognized his suzerainty of eastern Sicily. He again attacked Rhegium (390) and starved it into surrender (387), allied himself with the Lucanians, crushed the forces of the Italiot League on the Eleporus (Galliparo) (389), and incorporated Iapygia (southern Calabria) in his empire. The year 388 witnessed the fiasco of Dionysius' Delphic embassy. In 387 he helped Sparta to impose the King's Peace on Greece; and in 386 a palace conspiracy (probably) led to the banishment of some of his courtiers, including his brother Leptines (later recalled) and the historian *Philistus. To improve his supply of silver, timber, horses, and mercenaries, he extended his power into the Adriatic, founding colonies and establishing friendly relations with the Senones. He raided Pyrgi (384), the port of Etruscan Caere. The chronology and details of his greatest war (383– probably 375), against the Italiots and allied Carthage, are unclear, owing to a failure in the transmission of *Diodorus Siculus' text (15. 15–17, 24). Attacking Thurii, he lost his fleet in a storm, but he gained Croton. In Sicily he routed the Carthaginians at Cabala but was totally defeated at Cronium (Leptines was killed), and made a peace that established the Halycus (Platani) as the common frontier. He sent expeditions to Greece (369, 368), to assist Sparta against the Boeotians; and Athens, hitherto hostile, voted him a crown and (368) conferred her citizenship on him and his sons. He again invaded western Sicily

(368) and besieged Lilybaeum (Marsala), but his fleet was captured at Drepana (Trapani) and he concluded an armistice. At the Lenaea festival at Athens in 367 his play, *The Ransom of Hector*, won the prize, and a mutual defence treaty was negotiated, whose ratification was perhaps prevented by his death.

Dionysius, who probably styled himself *archōn* (ruler) of Sicily, was a born leader of men, in peace and war; orator and diplomat, planner and administrator, patron of religion, of his native city, of literature and the arts, a dramatist perhaps no worse than the generality in an age of decline—above all, the greatest soldier that, apart from the Macedonians, ancient Greece produced. He applied mind to warfare, introducing artillery, Phoenician siege-technique, and the quinquereme. He could handle large mercenary armies and small light-infantry detachments; he appreciated the importance of reconnaissance. If his subordinates had not constantly let him down, he might well have achieved his life's ambition, to drive the Carthaginians from Sicily. Dionysius represents the irruption onto the historical scene of the new individualism of his age. Portrayed by the anecdotal tradition, above all by the Academy (the philosophical school founded by *Plato) as the archetypal tyrant—paranoid, oppressive, obsessed with power—he looms through the historical tradition (Diodorus Siculus (and Polyaenus), going back through *Ephorus and *Timaeus to Philistus) rather as the first of the Romantic 'great men'; the precursor of *Alexander the Great, *Hannibal, and Napoleon: obsessed not with power but with glory.   B.M.C.

Dionysius II, tyrant of Syracuse (367–357 BC); born *c.*396, eldest son of *Dionysius I and Doris; married half-sister Sophrosyne. Unwarlike and short-sighted, he was estranged from his father, who is said (perhaps falsely) to have excluded him from public life and encouraged his debauchery. Inheriting an empire 'secured with bonds of adamant', he ruled successfully for ten years; making peace with Carthage (Halycus frontier), assisting Sparta (365), resisting the Lucanians, combating piracy in the Adriatic, and restoring Rhegium (mod. Reggio), renaming it Phoebia (honouring his supposititious father, Apollo). Encouraged by *Dion and *Plato himself, he conceived a passion

for philosophy, which split his court between the 'reformers' and the 'old guard', led by the historian *Philistus, and led to a rupture with Dion and eventually (360) with Plato. During his absence in Italy (357), Dion liberated Syracuse and dissolved his empire. Dionysius was confined to the citadel (Ortygia), which, after the death of Philistus (356), he entrusted to his son, and withdrew to Locri Epizephyrii in south Italy. In 346 he recovered Syracuse from his half-brother Hipparinus. The Locrians then revolted and massacred his family. Dionysius was again confined to Ortygia by Hicetas, and surrendered it to *Timoleon (344), retiring into private life in Corinth. Denigrated by the Academic tradition, Dionysius was neither an ineffectual ruler nor a despot (unless, perhaps, in Locri); but the abandonment of his father's crusade against Carthage deprived the regime of its purpose and its glamour, and it was weakened internally by division and by Dionysius' ill-advised attempt to reduce his soldiers' pay.   B.M.C.

Dionysius of Halicarnassus, Greek critic and historian, lived and taught rhetoric at Rome, arriving 'at the time *Augustus put an end to the civil war', and publishing the first part of his *Roman Antiquities* (*Rhōmaïkē archaiologia*) 22 years later (*Ant. Rom.* 1. 7). This great work was in twenty books, going down to the outbreak of the First Punic War (i.e. Roman war against Carthage); we have the first eleven (to 441 BC), with excerpts from the others. Dionysius used the legends of Rome's origins to demonstrate that it was really a Greek city, and his whole history is an erudite panegyric of Roman virtues. It is also very rhetorical, abounding in long speeches. He doubtless thought of it as exemplifying his literary teaching, which was directed towards restoring Classical prose after what he saw as the aberrations of the Hellenistic period. The treatises in which he developed this programme seem mostly to have been written before the *Antiquities*, though their chronology is much disputed. These are: (1) *On imitation* (*Peri mimēseōs*), in three books, of which only fragments survive; the judgements on individual authors coincide largely with those in Quintilian *Inst.* 10. 1; (2) a series of discussions of individual orators (*Lysias, *Isocrates, *Isaeus, *Demosthenes), prefaced by a programmatic statement of distaste for 'Asianic' (florid) rhetoric, hope for an 'Attic' revival, and the writer's consciousness that this happy change is due to the good taste of the Roman governing class; (3) a group of occasional works: *On Dinarchus*, *On *Thucydides* (important), two letters to Ammaeus (one on Demosthenes' alleged indebtedness to Aristotle, the other on *Thucydides), and a letter to Cn. Pompeius on *Plato, of whose 'dithyrambic' style Dionysius was very critical; (4) *On Arrangement of Words* (*De compositione verborum*, *Peri syntheseōs onomatōn*), the only surviving ancient treatise on this subject, full of interesting observations on euphony and onomatopoeic effects (note especially ch. 20, on *Odyssey* 11. 593–6); this was a fairly late work, but the second part of *Demosthenes* (35 ff.) presupposes it.

For all the traditional terminology and character of Dionysius' criticism—he frequently gives the impression of 'awarding marks' for good qualities narrowly and unimaginatively defined—he is an acute and sensitive stylistic critic, whose insights deserve attention; and he understood the importance of linking historical study (e.g. on questions of authenticity) with the purely rhetorical and aesthetic.   D.A.R.

Dionysius Thrax ('the Thracian') (*c*.170–*c*.90 BC), son of Teres, of Alexandria, was a pupil of *Aristarchus (2) and later a teacher of grammar and literature at Rhodes, where his pupils provided him with the silver for a model to illustrate his lectures on Nestor's cup (Ath. 489, 492, 501). His only surviving work is the *Technē grammatikē*, an epitome of pure grammar as developed by the Stoics and Alexandrians. The work is essentially Alexandrian, but there are traces of Stoic influence. It defines grammar as an *empeiria* (empiricist craft), but includes analogy (*analogia*; see CRATES) among its parts; classifies accents, stops, letters, and syllables; defines the parts of speech, with lists of their qualifications (cases, moods, etc.), and subdivisions, if any, giving examples; and concludes with some paradigms of inflexion. The ultimate aim of the grammarian is stated to be *krisis poiēmatōn*, which has generally been interpreted as meaning 'criticism of poetry'. There is no treatment of syntax in the work. It had, however, an immediate vogue which lasted until the Renaissance, and its authority was continued in the catechisms derived from

it which then took its place. Latin grammar early fell under its influence, and through Latin most of the modern grammars of Europe are indebted to it. Through Syriac and Armenian adaptations its influence spread far beyond Europe. An immense corpus of commentary grew up in Hellenistic, Roman, and Byzantine times around Dionysius' brief text. In recent years there has been controversy about its authenticity.

P.B.R.F.; R.B.; N.G.W.

Diophantus, of Alexandria (date uncertain, between 150 BC and AD 280), mathematician, wrote an algebraic work on indeterminate equations, *Arithmētika*, in thirteen books, of which six survive in Greek and four more in Arabic. The latter are numbered 4–7, and certainly represent Diophantus' original books 4–7. The Greek books are numbered 1–6 in the MSS, but of these only 1–3 represent Diophantus' original numbering, while '4–6' must be made up of extracts from the original 8–13. In the Greek (but not the Arabic) MSS the words for the unknown (*arithmos*) and its powers up to the sixth degree are represented by symbols, as is the operation for minus, so that the equations appear in a primitive algebraical notation, but it is likely that this was introduced in Byzantine times rather than by the author. Diophantus' method is to propose a problem, e.g. 'to find three numbers such that the product of any two of them plus their sum is a square' (2. 34), and then to go through every step of finding a single solution, in rational but not necessarily integer numbers. The method for finding more solutions is only implied by the example given. This procedure, using specific numbers, puts Diophantus in a tradition going back ultimately to Babylonian mathematics, and is in stark contrast to the abstract methods of classical Greek geometry. He does not recognize negative or irrational numbers as solutions. Books 1–3 contain linear or quadratic indeterminate equations, many of them simultaneous. Beginning with book 4 cubes and higher powers are found. The solutions often demonstrate great ingenuity. A small treatise by Diophantus on polygonal numbers is preserved, but a work on porisms to which he refers and which may be his own is lost.   G.J.T.

Dioscorides (Pedanius Dioscorides) (1st cent. AD), of Cilician Anazarbus, wrote an extensive, five-book work on the drugs employed in medicine. Dioscorides studied under Areius of Tarsus and travelled extensively collecting information about the medicinal uses of herbs, minerals, and animal products. His travels took him to the Greek mainland, Crete, Egypt, and Petra, but he mentions plants from much further afield. In the Preface he describes his travels as leading to a 'soldier-like life', a statement that led later writers to conclude, probably falsely, that he was once a physician in the Roman army.

Dioscorides' *Peri hylēs iatrikēs* (*Materia medica*, 'Materials of Medicine'), bks. 1–5, lists approximately 700 plants and slightly more than 1,000 drugs, and includes a letter to Areius that serves as an introduction. His method was to observe plants in their native habitats and to research previous authorities on these subjects. Finally he related the written and oral data to his clinical observations on the effects the drugs had on and in the body. He also provided data on preparations, adulterations, veterinary, and household usages. Dioscorides boasted that his method of organization was superior to that of previous works. His scheme was first to organize by categories, such as whole animals, animal parts and products, minerals, and plants—the last subdivided into roots, pot-herbs, fruits, trees, and shrubs. Within each category he arranged drugs according to their physiological reaction on the body. This arrangement by drug affinities was not explained and, as a consequence, many later copyists of his text rearranged his system according to the alphabet thereby obscuring the genius of his contributions. Dioscorides' information aims at medical precision, and his account is relatively free of supernatural elements, reflecting keen, critical observation of how drugs react. His medical judgements were well regarded until the 16th cent. Manuscripts of the *Materia medica* in Greek, Latin, and Arabic are often beautifully illuminated and indicate that Dioscorides' original text was accompanied by illustrations.   J.M.Ri.

Diphilus, of Sinope on the south coast of the Black Sea, brother of Diodorus of Sinope, New Comedy poet, born *c.*360–350 BC, lived most of his life at Athens, but died in Smyrna probably at the beginning of the 3rd cent. (the reference to him in Plaut. *Mostell.* 1149 is useless for establishing his death date: see M. Knorr, *Das griechische Vorbild der Mostellaria des Plautus* (1934), 7 f.). He wrote about 100 plays, winning three victories in the Lenaean festival at Athens (*IG* 2². 2325. 163 = 5 C 1 col. 4, 12 Mette). Some 60 titles are known, mostly typical of New Comedy; the nine or so with a mythical connection (e.g. *Danaides, Theseus*) need not all have been mythological burlesques: some could have taken their titles from a man aping a hero of myth (cf. Ath. 10. 421e on *Heracles*), others from a divine prologue (e.g. *Heros*). An unusual title is *Hairēsiteichēs* ('Wall-capturer'), which was altered to *Stratiōtēs* ('Soldier') when the play was rewritten, presumably for a second production (Ath. 11. 496f: the two titles appear as separate entries in the Piraeus book catalogue, *IG* 2². 2363 = test. 6 KA). Diphilus' reference to 'gilded *Euripides' (fr. 60 KA and Kock: cf. the parody in fr. 74 KA = 73 K) suggests gentle ridicule mingled with admiration. There are many interesting frs.: 17 KA and K, the nationality of the guests is important to a cook (cf. 42 KA = 43 K); 37 KA = 38 K, the unfilial conduct of Ctesippus, son of Chaereas; 70 and 71 KA = 69 and 70 K, *Archilochus and Hipponax anachronistically *Sappho's lovers; 91 KA and K, a lively description of an unattractive woman.

A play by Diphilus was the original of *Plautus' *Rudens*; his *Klēroumenoi* ('Men Casting Lots') of Plautus' *Casina*; *Synapothnēskontes* ('Men Dying Together') of Plautus' lost *Commorientes* (*Terence, in the *Adelphoe*, used a scene omitted by Plautus: cf. *Ad.* 6); and possibly *Schedia* ('Raft') of Plautus' *Vidularia*. Although Diphilus' originals may have been completely remodelled by Plautus, certain characteristics common to all the Roman adaptations can doubtless be attributed to the Greek poet: a delight in lively theatrical effects, with clearly contrasted scenes and characterization perhaps less sensitive than that of *Menander.

W.G.A.

Dolabella (Publius Corenelius Dolabella) allegedly born 69 BC (App. *BCiv.* 2. 129. 539), but certainly earlier. After a dissolute youth (*Cicero twice defended him), he divorced his wife in 50 and, against Cicero's wishes, married Cicero's daughter Tullia, embarrassing Cicero by (unsuccessfully) prosecuting Appius Claudius Pulcher. (Divorce followed in 46 and he never repaid the dowry.) After working for *Julius Caesar before 49, he was defeated commanding a fleet for him (49), then fought without distinction in Greece. Alleging illness, he returned, had himself adopted by a plebeian Lentulus (see D. R. Shackleton Bailey, *Two Studies in Roman Nomenclature* (1976) 29 ff.), and, as tribune 47, in Caesar's absence, provoked street fighting (which Mark *Antony failed to suppress) by proposing cancellation of debts—largely to escape his own creditors. Forgiven by Caesar, he accompanied him to Africa (but is not mentioned at Thapsus), then fought for him in Spain, was wounded, and utterly charmed him. He was rewarded with confiscated estates and picked to become consul when Caesar left for the east; but Antony blocked the election. On Caesar's death he seized the consulship and, securing recognition, courted the tyrannicides' supporters while negotiating with Antony. He thus obtained Syria for five years (and Cicero considered accepting a position on his staff (*legatio*): *Att.* 15. 11. 4). Crossing to Asia, he brutally assassinated the proconsul Gaius Trebonius and plundered the province. The senate now united to outlaw him (cf. Cic. *Phil.* 11). In May 43 he crossed into Syria, was soon besieged by *Cassius in (Syrian) Laodicea, and when, despite support from *Cleopatra, he could not hold it, committed suicide. He was the grandfather of the Publius Cornelius Dolabella who was prominent in the reign of *Tiberius.   E.B.

Domitian (Titus Flavius Domitianus), son of the emperor *Vespasian, was born on 24 October AD 51, and remained in Rome during his father's campaign against *Vitellius. Surrounded on the Capitol with his uncle, Flavius Sabinus, he managed to escape and on Vitellius' death was saluted as Caesar by the Flavian army, though the real power lay in the hands of Gaius Licinius Mucianus until Vespasian's arrival. In 71 he participated in the triumph of Vespasian and *Titus, and between 70 and 80 held seven consulships, being twice ordinary consul (73 and 80). Although Domitian exercised no formal power, he was clearly part of the dynastic plan, and there is no convincing evidence that he was kept in the background or consumed by jealousy of his brother, whom he succeeded smoothly in 81.

The literary sources, especially *Tacitus and *Pliny the Younger, represent a senatorial tradition hostile to Domitian. But this is a legitimate and important viewpoint, illustrating the tension between aristocratic officials and autocrat. *Suetonius' account, though basically hostile, is more balanced and suggests that a more favourable view did exist, apart from the flattery of poets like *Statius and *Martial.

Domitian was conscientious in the performance of his duties, adopting a stance of moral rectitude, maintaining public decency at shows, and showing respect for religious ritual; three Vestal virgins suffered capital punishment for breaking their vows of chastity; later, Cornelia, the chief Vestal, was buried alive. He promoted festivals and religious celebrations, showing particular devotion to Jupiter and Minerva, and performed the Secular Games; many public buildings were erected, completed, or restored, including the Capitol, the Colosseum, and a great palace on the Palatine. For the people there were frequent spectacles and banquets, though his cash grants were restrained. He raised military pay by a third, and bestowed by edict additional privileges on veterans and their families; he remained popular with the army and praetorians.

Domitian administered legal affairs diligently and tried to suppress corruption. Suetonius' contention that he achieved equitable provincial administration through careful supervision of officials and governors (*Dom.* 8. 2) has been challenged, but other evidence indicates that Domitian, although authoritarian in his attitude to the provinces (e.g. his abortive order to cut down at least half the provincial vineyards), tried to impress probity and fairness on his appointees; he sensibly granted rights of ownership to those who had appropriated tracts of unused land (*subseciva*); Pliny the Younger's letters to *Trajan show that Domitian's administrative decisions were generally endorsed. The role and influence of equestrians in the administration increased in his reign, but as part of a continuing trend rather than deliberate policy. The effectiveness of his management of imperial finances is disputed, but he probably left a surplus in the treasury; his confiscation of the property of his opponents was for political rather than financial reasons.

Domitian was the first reigning emperor since *Claudius in 43 to campaign in person, visiting the Rhine once, and the Danube three times. *Frontinus in his *Strategemata* reports favourably on Domitian's personal control of strategy and tactics. In 82/3 he fought a successful war against the Chatti on the middle Rhine, brought the Taunus area under Roman control, and accepted a triumph and the name 'Germanicus'. But the military balance was shifting towards the Danube, and in 85 the Dacians, under king Decebalus, invaded Moesia killing its governor, Oppius Sabinus. Domitian came in person in 85 and 86; and after the defeat and death of Cornelius Fuscus (praetorian prefect), Tettius Julianus, governor of Upper Moesia, won a victory at Tapae in 88. Since Domitian was facing trouble from the Marcomanni and Quadi in Pannonia, he made peace with Decebalus before launching a campaign against them (spring 89); at the end of 89 he celebrated another triumph. Then early in 92 a legion was destroyed in Pannonia by an incursion of the Sarmatian Iazyges and the Suebi, which was eventually contained under Domitian's personal direction. There was also considerable military activity in Britain, where *Agricola continued the invasion of northern Scotland; his recall in 84 after an unusually long governorship of seven years, probably reflects military needs elsewhere rather than imperial jealousy.

Domitian failed to find a working relationship with the senate. He was sometimes tactless and did not conceal the reality of his autocracy, holding ten consulships as emperor, wearing triumphal dress in the senate, having 24 lictors, and becoming censor for life in 85, symbolically in charge of the senate; his manner was arrogant, and he allegedly began an official letter: 'Our lord god orders that this be done'. There was a conspiracy in 87, and a rebellion in 89 by Lucius Antonius Saturninus, governor of Upper Germany. He apparently had little support among his troops and was easily crushed, but Domitian thereafter forbade two legions to be quartered in one camp. He became more ruthless against presumed opponents, and factions in the aristocracy produced many senators willing to act as accusers. The executions of at least twelve ex-consuls are recorded in the reign, mainly for dissent or alleged conspiracy, and not because they were Stoics, although Domitian did expel philosophers. The emperor himself observed: 'no one believes in a conspiracy against an emperor until it has succeeded'. The execution in 95 of Flavius Clemens, his cousin, whose sons he had adopted as heirs, was a mistake since it seemed that no one now was safe. A plot was formed by intimates of his entourage possibly including his wife, Domitia, and he was murdered on 18 September 96; his memory was condemned by the senate.   J.B.C.

Domitius Corbulo See CORBULO.

Domitius Ulpianus See ULPIAN.

Donatus, Aelius, the most influential grammarian of the 4th cent. AD, whose pupils included the future St *Jerome. His two *artes* ('treatises') attracted many commentators (e.g. Servius, Cledonius, Pompeius) and dominated grammatical learning in Europe until the re-emergence of *Priscian in the 12th cent. The *Ars minor*, intended for beginners, deals with the eight parts of speech in question-and-answer format; the *Ars maior* is more comprehensive and includes sections on the 'flaws' and 'virtues' of speech. Donatus also wrote commentaries on *Terence and *Virgil. The extant Terence commentary is only a much abridged version (lacking *Heautontimoroumenos*) compiled at an unknown date from (probably) two sets of marginal scholia in manuscripts of Terence; the original commentary cannot be reconstructed. From the Virgil commentary there survive only the dedicatory epistle, the 'Life' of Virgil (drawn from *Suetonius), and the introduction to the *Eclogues*. But the 'vulgate' commentary of *Servius contains much material from Donatus, and the augmented version of Servius ('Servius Danielis') contains still more. Some of the doctrine found in commentaries to Donatus' *artes*, and some of the more learned notes in glossaries (e.g. *Liber glossarum*), may also derive from the commentary on Virgil.   R.A.K.

Draco, according to Athenian tradition, was a lawgiver who introduced new laws in the year when Aristaechmus was archon (a senior magistrate), probably 621/0 BC. This was the first time that Athenian laws were put in writing. According to one account (*Ath. pol.* 4) he established a constitution based on the franchise of hoplites (heavy-armed infantry soldiers), but elsewhere he is only said to have made laws against particular crimes. The penalties were very severe: when asked why he specified death as the penalty for most offences, he replied that small offences deserved death and he knew of no severer penalty for great ones; and the 4th-cent. orator *Demades remarked that Draco wrote his laws in blood instead of ink (Plut. *Sol.* 17). *Solon repealed all his laws except those dealing with homicide.

Such was the tradition current in Athens in the 5th and 4th cents. BC. At that period no one doubted that the homicide laws then in force were due to Draco; this is shown by references in Athenian speeches, and also by an inscription of 409/8 which contains part of the current law and describes it as 'the law of Draco about homicide' (*IG* 1³. 104).

Modern scholars have treated the tradition with varying degrees of scepticism. Some have doubted whether Draco existed at all. The hoplite constitution is generally regarded as spurious (being perhaps an invention of 5th-cent. oligarchic propagandists). Most accept that Draco introduced laws about homicide and other offences, and some accept that the surviving inscription reproduces his homicide laws with little or no alteration; but details of his other laws cannot now be known. D.M.M.

Drusus (Claudius Drusus, Nero), second son of Tiberius Claudius Nero and *Livia, younger brother of *Tiberius, later emperor, was born in 38 BC about the time of Livia's marriage to Octavian (later *Augustus; see *PIR*² D 857 for the circumstances); his first name was originally Decimus. After Tiberius Nero's death in 33 he was brought up by Octavian. In 19 he was permitted to stand for magistracies five years before the legal ages, and in 18 was quaestor. In 15 BC with Tiberius he subdued the Raeti and Vindelici (Alpine tribes), and established the later via Claudia Augusta over the Alps into Italy. In 13, left in charge of the Three Gauls, he organized a census and on 1 August 12 (or 10, Wells, p. 267) founded an altar to Rome and Augustus at Lugdunum (Lyon). Augustus entrusted the conquest of Germany to him, while Tiberius subdued the Balkans (12–9). His chief bases were on the lower Rhine near Vechten, Vetera near Birten, then Mogontiacum (Mainz). In 12, after routing the Usipetes and Sugambri, who had raided Gaul, he sailed along a canal dug for the purpose (Fossa Drusiana, probably the Vecht), through the lakes into the sea, won over the Frisii, perhaps occupied Borkum at the mouth of the Ems, defeated the Bructeri in a naval encounter upstream, and invaded the country of the Chauci. His ships were stranded by the ebb tide but the Frisii helped him get away. He began the year 11 in Rome as urban praetor, then subdued the Usipetes, and after bridging the Lippe marched through the territory of the Sugambri and Cherusci to the Weser; he left behind forts at Aliso and among the Chatti. After celebrating an *ovatio* (a kind of minor triumph) and receiving the military honour of the *ornamenta triumphalia* (insignia carried by a general in his triumphal procession) he attacked the Chatti in 10 as proconsul, and returned to Rome with Augustus and Tiberius. In 9 as consul he fought the Chatti, Suebic Marcomanni, and Cherusci, and reached the Elbe; but died in camp after falling from his horse. Tiberius, hastening from Ticinum, reached him before his death.

Drusus' conquests were extensive and well-garrisoned. (Florus' claim (2. 30. 26) of 50 forts on the Rhine alone has not been substantiated.) The senate bestowed on him and his descendants the surname of Germanicus; but the achievements in Germany were largely swept away with *Quinctilius Varus in AD 9. He was popular, and his views considered 'republican'; Tiberius disclosed to Augustus a letter expressing them. He was buried in Augustus' mausoleum; a cenotaph was built at Mogontiacum. An unknown poet wrote his mother the *Consolation to Livia*. His wife Antonia bore him *Germanicus—who, emulating his father, in AD 15–16 tried to recover Roman territory in Germany—Livia Julia, and *Claudius.

A.M.; T.J.C.; B.M.L.

Ee

Elagabalus (Marcus Aurelius Antoninus), was the son of Sex. Varius Marcellus and Julia Soaemias Bassiana, niece of Julia Domna. Born probably in 203, as Varius Avitus Bassianus, he was holding the priesthood, hereditary in his mother's family, of the presiding deity of Emesa in Syria, in 218, when his mother and grandmother Julia Maesa used him as figurehead of a rebellion against Macrinus. He was proclaimed to be son of his mother's cousin *Caracalla (M. Aurelius Antoninus) and renamed after him. After the victory, he took the cult of the god by whose name he is known to Rome, which he reached in July 219. In late 220 his intention to make Elagabalus ('deus Sol invictus') supreme god of the empire aroused open hostility at Rome when he divorced his first wife Julia Paula and married the Vestal virgin Aquilia Severa, a 'sacred marriage' to match the union of the god with Juno Caelestis. He was forced to adopt his cousin Alexianus, renamed Alexander (26 June 221), and to divorce Aquilia in favour of a descendant of M. Aurelius, Annia Faustina; but by the end of 221 took Aquilia back and tried to get rid of Alexander. This provoked renewed outrage, which came to a head with his murder on 11 March 222 and replacement by Alexander. His flouting of conventions in the choice of officials, combined with disgust at the orgiastic ceremonial of the Syrian cult, had proved too much for senate, praetorians, and *plebs* alike.

A.R.Bi.

Empedocles (*c*.492–432 BC), a philosopher from Acragas (Agrigento) in Sicily. Most details of his life are uncertain. Book 8 of *Diogenes Laertius provides the largest selection of legends. Much of our biographical information (especially the manner of his death and claims that he was a doctor and prophet and considered himself a god) may have been extrapolated from his poetry. There is no reason to doubt his aristocratic background, that his family participated in the Olympian Games, that he was involved in political life, or that he was active in both the religious and the philosophical spheres. He apparently travelled to mainland Greece to recite at the Olympian Games and visited Thurii (south Italy) soon after its foundation in 443 BC. Pythagoreanism was clearly a philosophical inspiration. Equally important was *Parmenides, whose thought shaped the basic ideas underlying Empedocles' philosophy. There is no evidence that he was familiar with the work of *Zeno (1), Melissus, or the atomists; he probably knew the work of *Anaxagoras, certainly that of *Xenophanes.

According to Diogenes Laertius (8. 77), he was the author of two poems, *On Nature* and *Purifications.* (The *Suda* entry for Empedocles mentions only an *On Nature*, though it is often emended to agree with Diog. Laert.) Other authors refer to one poem or the other, not both. The relationship between these two poems is problematic, with no consensus about the distribution of the fragments. Hence the suspicions that *On Nature* and *Purifications* are alternate titles for a single work. Our sources also mention works of dubious authenticity: medical writings in prose and verse, tragedies, a hymn to Apollo, an *Expedition of Xerxes.* But the surviving fragments can be fairly well accommodated in the work(s) on natural philosophy and religion.

Empedocles is especially important for:

1. *His response to Parmenides*, who argued that no real thing could change or move and that the world was static. Empedocles accepted that *real* objects did not change; but against Parmenides he claimed that there could be several such things, his four 'roots' or elements, which moved under the influence of Love and Strife. All six of Empedocles' realities were often personified as gods. The events of the world's history result from the interaction of these entities.

2. *Introducing the notion of repeated world cycles.* The influence of Love and Strife alternated; hence the history of the cosmos was cyclical. The principal controversy about the details of the cosmic cycle centres on whether or not there is a recognizable 'world' during each half (under the increasing power of Love and under that of Strife). When Love is supreme, the world is a homogeneous whole; when Strife has conquered, the elements are completely separated.

3. *The claim that there are only four basic forms of perceptible matter:* earth, water, fire, and air. Unlike *Aristotle, who adopted his view, Empedocles thought that these forms of matter were unchangeable. Empedoclean matter is often treated as particulate; hence, despite his denial of void, there is reason to suspect that he influenced atomism (see DEMOCRITUS).

4. *The effluence theory.* A simple mechanism of pores and effluences was used to explain perception (effluences from sense-objects entering into the pores of sense organs), mixture, and many other natural processes. This notion had a major influence, especially on atomism.

5. *A theory of reincarnation and the transmigration of the soul.* Despite the claim that transmigration occurs, there is no clear indication of whether the *daimones* (spirits) which move from body to body survive for ever or only until the end of the current world cycle. His claim that even human thought is identifiable with the blood around the heart points to the physical nature of the transmigrating *daimōn*.   B.I.

Ennius, Quintus (239–169 BC), an immigrant of upper-class Messapian origin (south Italy) brought to Rome in 204 by Cato the Elder (consul 195) and given the citizenship in 184 by Quintus Fulvius Nobilior (consul 153). Cato found him serving in a Calabrian regiment of the Roman army in Sardinia. At Rome he made himself acceptable to the Cornelii, the Sulpicii, and the Caecilii as well as to the Fulvii. He lived in a modest house on the Aventine and taught Greek and Latin grammar to the young men of the great families. He composed plays for the public festivals down to the year of his death, although never, like *Livius Andronicus, acting roles in them. He also composed a large amount of non-dramatic verse and at least one work

in prose. Marcus Fulvius Nobilior took him on his staff to Aetolia in 189. Biographers noted a fondness for alcohol and declared him to have died of gout.

Three titles (*Caupunculus, Pancratiastes, Telestis* (?)) have the smell of the (Greek) New Comedy, New. To some of the twenty recorded tragic titles (*Achilles, Aiax, Alcmeo, Alexander, Andromacha, Andromeda, Athamas, Cresphontes, Erechtheus, Eumenides, Hectoris Lytra, Hecuba, Iphigenia, Medea, Melanippa, Nemea, Phoenix, Telamo, Telephus, Thyestes*) are attached fragments sufficiently extensive to indicate that Ennius had a particular liking for *Euripides and that he translated his tragedies in the free manner Latin poets had been using for half a century. Compared with Euripides, he seems to us to have written rather grandly. To Cicero's contemporaries, comparing him with *Pacuvius and *Accius, he seems to have made his personages use the everyday language (*Orat.* 36). He also wrote a play in the tragic style on an incident of early Roman history (*Sabinae*) and another on Nobilior's deeds in Aetolia (*Ambracia*). The character of the *Scipio* is disputed.

A narrative poem in fifteen units on the history of the Roman people from the loss of Troy to the seizure of Ambracia and the triumphal return of the elder Nobilior was intended by Ennius to do better what *Naevius had attempted in his *Carmen belli Poenici.* Its title, the (*libri*) *Annales,* appropriated that of the record which the pontifices (the senior college of priests) kept in notoriously simple prose of religiously significant events. Instead of the ancient *Camenae,* Ennius invoked the *Musae* (Muses), newly imported to Rome and given a home by Nobilior in a new temple on the Campus Martius. He represented himself as a reincarnation of Homer and replaced the Saturnian verse with a Latin version of the dactylic hexameter rather closer to the Homeric pattern than, say, the verses of the stage were to those of the Classical Athenian tragedians and comedians. The archaic vocabulary used by Livius and Naevius was pruned but some items survived, and many novelties appropriate to dactylic metrical patterns of an openly Greek origin were introduced. Books 1–3 took Ennius' story down to the expulsion of the last king and the foundation of the republic; 4–6 dealt with the reduction of Etruria and

Samnium and the seeing off of the Epirote king *Pyrrhus; 7–9 with the driving of the Carthaginians back to North Africa and the incorporation within the Roman state of the old Greek cities of southern Italy and Sicily; 10–12 with the campaigns of the first decade of the 2nd cent. on the Greek mainland and in Spain; 12–15 with the defeats inflicted on *Philip V, *Antiochus III the Great, and the Aetolian Confederacy. The poem emphasized the constant expansion of the Roman empire and the eclipse suffered by the Greek states which had sacked Troy and by their descendants. The gods of Olympus were made to support and assist the expansion. There was little on the other hand about the internal politics of the city of Rome. A number of Ennius' themes were foreign to the old Greek epic tradition. e.g. autobiography, literary polemic, grammatical erudition, and philosophical speculation.

Ennius added a further three books to the *Annales* in the last years of his life. These books featured the deeds of junior officers, rather than those of the generals, in the wars of the 180s and 170s against the Istrians, Ligurians, and other minor tribes.

Whereas it had been the custom to write epitaphs for leading men in Saturnian verses and even in senarii (verse in lines of six feet), Ennius composed pieces on *Scipio Africanus (d. 184) and on himself in a Latin version of the elegiac couplet. The notion that Scipio's soul may have been assumed into heaven went against conventional Roman doctrine on the after-life, as did the deification of Romulus narrated in the first or second book of the *Annales*.

The *Epicharmus* presented, in trochaic septenarii of the theatrical type, an account of the gods and the physical operations of the universe. The poet dreamed he had been transported after death to some place of heavenly enlightenment.

The *Euhemerus* presented a theological doctrine of a very different type in a kind of mock-simple prose modelled on the Greek of *Euhemerus of Messene and earlier theological writers. According to this doctrine the gods of Olympus were not supernatural powers still actively intervening in the affairs of men, but great generals, statesmen, and inventors of olden times commemorated after death in extraordinary ways. The relationship of such a view to what Ennius

expounded in the *Annales*, the epigrams, and the *Epicharmus* can only be guessed at.

The *Hedyphagetica* must have seemed to move from yet another philosophical position. It took much of its substance from the gastronomical epic of Archestratus of Gela, a work commonly associated with Epicureanism. A reference to Ambracia suggests Ennius' own mature experience. The eleven extant hexameters have prosodical features avoided in the more serious *Annales*.

The *Sota* employed a metrical form associated with Sotades and probably presented similar themes in a similar tone.

The remains of six books of *Saturae* show a considerable variety of metres. There are signs that Ennius sometimes varied the metre within a single composition. A frequent theme was the social life of Ennius himself and his upper-class Roman friends and their intellectual conversation. Some scholars have detected the influence of *Callimachus' *Iambi*. The character of the *Protrepticus/Praecepta* is obscure.

Ennius stands out among Latin writers for the variety of the works he produced. Some of his tragedies were still performed in the theatre during the late republic. The *Annales* was carefully studied by *Cicero, *Lucretius, *Catullus, *Virgil, *Ovid, and *Lucan, and its text was still available in the Flavian period. Recitations were given during the time of *Hadrian. Copies had become rare by the 5th cent., but a reader of Orosius' *Histories* obtained access to one. Commentators on Virgil's *Aeneid* liked to point out borrowings from the older poem. Nonius Marcellus is the only late writer who can be shown to have read any of the tragedies. *Apuleius was able to find in a library a copy of the *Hedyphagetica* and *Lactantius one of the *Euhemerus*.

H.D.J.

Epaminondas (d. 362 BC), Theban general, famous for his victories at the battles of Leuctra and Mantinea. Of his early career little is known. He is said to have been a pupil of Lysis of Tarentum, and to have saved the life of *Pelopidas at Mantinea, presumably during the Spartan siege in 385, but played a minor role in the liberation of Thebes in 379, and in the subsequent rebuilding of the Boeotian Confederacy. However, by 371 he was one of the boeotarchs (Boeotian federal officials), and, as such, represented Thebes at the peace conference in Sparta, walking out when *Agesilaus II refused to allow him to take the oath on behalf of the Boeotians as a whole.

Although all seven boeotarchs were at Leuctra, Epaminondas was clearly regarded as the architect of victory, and was re-elected for 370. Late in the year he went to the aid of the Arcadians, and was largely responsible for the crucial decision to press on with the invasion of the Spartan homeland—the first in historical times—and, above all, to free Messenia. In the summer of 369 he led a second invasion of the Peloponnese, which succeeded in further eroding Spartan influence, without quite matching previous triumphs. But his successes and, possibly, high-handed behaviour aroused jealousy, and he was not re-elected boeotarch for 368, though legend has it that while serving as an ordinary hoplite (heavy-armed infantryman) he was called upon to rescue the Boeotian army when it got into difficulties in Thessaly. Re-elected for 367, his third invasion of the Peloponnese finally put an end to Sparta's 300-year-old Peloponnesian League. The removal of the fear of Sparta, however, aroused old antagonisms, and by 362 Thebes found herself fighting many of her erstwhile allies in alliance with Sparta. At the battle of Mantinea, Epaminondas was killed in the moment of victory.

Though an innovative tactician, Epaminondas' strategic and political sense may be questioned. His attempt to challenge Athenian supremacy at sea in 364 had little lasting effect, and some of his dealings in the Peloponnese were questionable. But his traditional nobility of character presumably reflects how he appeared to contemporaries, and he possibly lacked the ruthlessness necessary to impose Thebes' will on her quarrelsome allies, once they ceased to fear Sparta. He may honestly have wanted to create an alliance of independent states in which Thebes would be no more than first among equals.   J.F.La.

Ephorus, of Cyme (c.405–330 BC), a historian whose now lost work is of great importance because *Diodorus Siculus followed it extensively. In antiquity, he was thought to have been a student of *Isocrates; there are in fact clear echoes of Isocratean sentiments in the Ephoran parts of Diodorus, and some of the character assessments found in Diodorus are in the Isocratean style. His pro-Athenian bias might also have come from Isocrates.

The 30-book *History* (*Historiai*) avoided the mythological period—although it included individual myths—beginning with the Return of the Heraclidae (descendants of Heracles) and reaching the siege of Perinthus, in 340. His son, Demophilus, completed the work with an account of the Third Sacred War. His work was grand in scope and far longer than 5th-cent. histories. According to *Polybius, he was the first universal historian, combining a focus on Greek history with events in the barbarian east. Ephorus may have been the first historian to divide his work by books, and he provided each with a separate proem. Individual books were apparently devoted exclusively to a particular area (southern and central Greece, Macedonia, Sicily, Persia), but within each book events were sometimes retold episodically, sometimes synchronistically.

Ephorus drew on a diversity of sources, historical and literary, at times using good judgement (he preferred the *Oxyrhynchus historian to *Xenophon), at other times making unfortunate choices (he coloured *Thucydides' account with material from 4th-cent. pamphleteers). Of special interest to Ephorus were migrations, the founding of cities, and family histories.

The *History* was widely quoted in antiquity and was generally complimented for its accuracy (except in military descriptions). It was known to Polybius and was extensively used by *Strabo, *Nicolaus of Damascus, Polyaenus, *Plutarch, and possibly Pompeius Trogus. But its greatest significance lies in the probability that Diodorus followed it closely for much of Archaic and practically all of Classical Greek history. In paraphrasing Ephorus, Diodorus supplies critical information, especially about 4th-cent. mainland history.

His other works include a history of Cyme (*Epichōrios logos*), a treatise on style (*Peri lexeōs*), and two books (*Peri heurēmatōn*) which aimed at satisfying the demand for popular information on diverse topics characteristic of the period.   K.S.S.

Epicharmus, a Sicilian writer of comedy, was active during the first quarter of the 5th cent. BC, as is clear from his reference to the

Anaxilas tyrant of Rhegium (fr. 98) and possibly to *Aeschylus (fr. 214). He was probably a native of *Syracuse (our earliest evidence for this is Theoc. *Epigr.* 18 and *Marm. Par.* 71), but other cities laid claim to him; Arist. *Poet.* 1448ᵃ32 is ambiguous, but may mean that the Sicilian Megarians (i.e. the people from Megara Hyblaea) regarded him as their own. Aristotle surprisingly says that he was 'much earlier than Chionides and Magnes', and if this is true he must have been an established poet during the last part of the 6th cent.

The titles, citations, and fragments of his plays (now significantly augmented by papyri) indicate that he was particularly fond of mythological burlesque; Heracles and Odysseus were the 'heroes' of some of these burlesques. *Logos and Logina* is shown by fr. 87 to have been mythological in character, a fact which could hardly have been guessed from its title. Some titles, like those of Attic comedies, are plurals, e.g. *Islands, Persians, Sirens.* No fragment enables us to decide beyond doubt how many actors these plays required or whether they required a chorus. The abundance of plural titles constitutes a prima facie case for a chorus. Certain fragments (6, 34) suggest that there *may* have been three actors on stage simultaneously, but this evidence is far from decisive. The scale of his plays is also uncertain. His language is Sicilian Doric, and is as colourful and sophisticated as that of Old Comedy; he uses a variety of metres *kata stichon* ('according to the line'), but there are no lyrics among the extant fragments.

A considerable number of philosophical and quasi-scientific works were attributed to Epicharmus in antiquity. The hard core of these may have been a collection of maxims made from his plays (cf. Theoc. *Epigr.* 18), but as early as the 4th cent. BC the *Pseudepicharmeia* were regarded as forged (Aristox. fr. 45 Wehrli), and continued to be so regarded by critical historians, though the less critical treated them without scruple as genuine works of Epicharmus. A certain Alcimus argued that *Plato derived much of his doctrine from Epicharmus (Diog. Laert. 3. 9 ff.), but it is hardly credible that the passages cited in support of this allegation were composed early in the 5th cent.; one of them (fr. 171) appears to parody the technique (*panu men oun,* 'yes, no doubt') of Platonic dialogue. The tradition that Epicharmus was a Pythag-

orean (see PYTHAGORAS) first appears in Plutarch (*Num.* 8).   K.J.D.

Epictetus (mid-1st to 2nd cent. AD), Stoic philosopher from Hierapolis in Phrygia; in early life a slave of Epaphroditus in Rome. Eventually freed by his master, he studied with Musonius Rufus. Epictetus taught in Rome until *Domitian banished the philosophers in AD 89. He set up a school at Nicopolis in Epirus, where his reputation attracted a following which included many upper-class Romans. *Arrian published the oral teachings (*Discourses, Diatribai*) of Epictetus. Four books of these survive, along with a summary of key teachings known as the *Manual* (*Encheiridion*). These writings and his personal reputation made an impact on the emperor *Marcus Aurelius; the *Manual* has been an important inspirational book in both ancient and modern times.

Epictetus' teaching took two forms. He taught basic works of Stoicism, especially those of Chrysippus, and shows considerable familiarity with technical matters. In the *Discourses*, however, great emphasis is placed on the need to put philosophical sophistication to work in reforming moral character; learning is of little value for its own sake.

Epictetus' philosophy was largely consistent with earlier Stoicism, although its idiom differs markedly. A major doctrinal innovation was his commitment to the innate character of moral beliefs; for earlier Stoics, such ideas were natural but not innate. Another novelty is in the organization of his teaching: Epictetus divided it into three 'themes' (*topoi*), concerning (1) the control of desires and passions, (2) actions, and (3) assent. Other leading ideas include: (*a*) a contrast between what is in the power of the agent and what is not; beliefs, desires, plans, reactions, and interpretations of experience are 'up to us', while events which happen to us are not. This leads him to emphasize the *use* we make of our presentations in contrast to their mere reception. (*b*) An intense focus on *proairesis*, the power of individual moral choice. (*c*) The Socratic claim that all men act according to what they believe to be good for them; hence, the proper response to moral error is an effort at education and not anger. (*d*) A powerful belief in divine providence. He interprets the rational, cosmic deity of Stoicism in a more personal sense with an emphasis on the need to harmonize one's will with that of the deity.

B.I.

Epicurus (b. Samos, 341 BC; d. Athens, 270 BC), moral and natural philosopher. His father Neocles and mother Chaerestrate, Athenians of the deme Gargettus, emigrated to the Athenian cleruchy (settlement) in Samos. As a boy he was taught by a Platonist, Pamphilus. He served as an ephebe (young man of 18–20 undergoing paramilitary training) in Athens, when Xenocrates was head of the Academy (the philosophical school founded by *Plato) and *Aristotle was in Chalcis (Euboea); the playwright *Menander was in the same class of the ephebate as Epicurus. He rejoined his family, who had then settled on the Asian mainland at Colophon. At this time or earlier he studied under Nausiphanes, from whom he learnt about the atomist philosophy of *Democritus. At 32 he moved to Mytilene in Lesbos, then to Lampsacus on the Hellespont; at both places he set up a school and began to acquire pupils and loyal friends.

About 306/7 he bought a house in Athens, with a garden that became the eponymous headquarters of his school of philosophy. Apart from occasional visits to Asia Minor, he remained in Athens until his death in 270, when he bequeathed his garden and school to Hermarchus of Mytilene (his will survives, in Diog. Laert. 10, the main source for his biography).

THE EPICUREAN SCHOOL (The Garden). He and his followers lived together, secluding themselves from the affairs of the city and maintaining a modest and even austere standard of living, in accordance with the Master's teaching. They included slaves and women. Contemporary Epicureans mentioned in the literature were his most devoted companion, Metrodorus of Lampsacus, who died before Epicurus; Leontius and his wife Themista, also of Lampsacus; Hermarchus, his successor; and a slave called Mys.

The school was much libelled in antiquity and later, perhaps because of its determined privacy, and because of Epicurus' professed hedonism. The qualifications that brought this hedonism close to asceticism were ignored, and members of rival schools accused the Epicureans of many kinds of profligacy. In Christian times, Epicureanism was anathema because it taught that man is mortal, that the cosmos is the result of accident, that there is no providential god, and that the criterion of the good life is pleasure. Hence such caricatures as Sir Epicure Mammon, in Ben Jonson's *Alchemist*, and the modern use of the word 'epicure'.

WRITINGS Diog. Laert. 10. 26 reports that Epicurus wrote more than any of the other philosophers—about 300 rolls. Most of these are now lost. Fragments of his 37 books *On Nature* survive in the volcanic ash at Herculaneum, and efforts to restore and interpret them, begun around 1800, are now in progress with renewed vigour. The following three letters and two collections of maxims have been preserved intact, the first four all in Diog. Laert. 10: (1) Letter to Herodotus (*Ep. Hdt.*): a summary of his philosophy of nature; (2) Letter to Pythocles (*Ep. Pyth.*): a summary of astronomy and meteorology; (3) Letter to Menoeceus (*Ep. Men.*): a less technical summary of Epicurean morality; (4) *Kyriai doxai* (*KD*), *Ratae sententiae* (*RS*), or *Principal Doctrines*: 40 moral maxims; (5) *Vatican Sayings* (*Sent. Vat.*): 81 similar short sayings identified in a Vatican manuscript by C. Wotke in 1888.

Present-day knowledge and appreciation of Epicurean philosophy depends very largely on the great Latin epic poem of his later follower, *Lucretius' *De rerum natura*.

DOCTRINES The purpose of philosophy is practical: to secure a happy life. Hence moral philosophy is the most important branch, and physics and epistemology are subsidiary. (For this tripartition, see Sext. Emp. *Math.* 11. 169, and for the comparative evaluation *KD* 11 and Diog. Laert. 10. 30).

1. EPISTEMOLOGY The main sources are *Ep. Hdt.*, Lucr. 4, and critical comments in Sext. Emp. *Math.* Epicurus held that sense perception is the origin of knowledge, and defended its reliability with a physical account of it. Physical objects, being made of atoms, give off from their surface thin films of atoms, called *eidōla*, which retain the shape and some other characteristics of their parent body and implant its appearance on the sense organs of the perceiver. This appearance is somehow transmitted to the soul-atoms which constitute the mind. The appearance itself is never false: falsehood occurs only in the opinion (*doxa*) the mind forms about it. If appearances conflict, a closer look or a sound argument or experience of the context may serve to 'counter-witness' all but one consistent set of opinions: in some cases (especially in astronomy, where no closer look is possible) we must accept that all beliefs not counter-witnessed are somehow true.

Epicurus was apparently not able to articulate an explanation of concept-formation and theorizing by minds made of atoms and void. The extant texts show frequent use of analogical reasoning, from phenomena to theoretical entities.

2. PHYSICS Epicurus adopted the atomist theories of Democritus, with some changes that can often be seen as attempts to answer Aristotle's criticisms.

The original atomist theory was a response to the Eleatic school of *Parmenides, *Zeno (1), and Melissus of Samos. Arguments about Being and Not-being show that there must be permanent elements—atoms of matter. Arguments about divisibility show that there must be indivisibles—construed by Epicurus as inseparable parts of atoms. The observed fact of motion proves that there must be empty space in which atoms can move.

Change is explained as the rearrangement of unchangeable atoms. The universe is infinite, both in the number of atoms and in the extent of space. Our cosmos, bounded by the region of the heavenly bodies, came into being through random collisions of suitable atoms, and it will some day dissolve again into its component atoms. It is one of an indefinite number of cosmoi, past, present, and future.

Atoms move naturally downwards at constant and equal speed because of their weight, unless they collide with others. But they would never collide unless some of them sometimes swerved from the straight downward path. (This postulate, which also accounts for the self-motions of animals (see below), is not mentioned in any surviving text of Epicurus, but is set out at some length by Lucretius, 2. 62–332, mentioned by other classical writers, and generally agreed to have been advanced by Epicurus himself.)

Gods exist, atomic compounds like everything else, but take no thought for this cosmos or any other, living an ideal life of eternal, undisturbed happiness—the Epicurean ideal. It is good for men to respect and admire them, without expecting favours or punishments from them.

Both creation, as in *Plato's *Timaeus*, and the eternity of the cosmic order, as in *Aristotle's world picture, are rejected: natural movements of atoms are enough to explain the origin and growth of everything in the world. A theory of the survival of the fittest explains the apparently purposeful structure of living things.

Epicurus was a thoroughgoing physicalist in his philosophy of mind. The soul is composed of atoms, all extremely small but distinguished by shape into four kinds: fire, air, and breath (but all somehow different from their ordinary namesakes), and a fourth, unnamed kind. At death the component atoms are dispersed.

The swerve of atoms somehow accounts for the possibility of actions performed by choice, by humans and some other animals: without the swerve, apparently, all actions would be as fully determined as the fall of a stone dropped from a height. How this works is a matter of continuing controversy.

3. MORAL PHILOSOPHY 'We say that pleasure is the beginning and end of living happily' (*Ep. Men.* 128). It is a datum of experience that pleasure is naturally and congenitally the object of human life. Since it is a fact, however, that some pleasures are temporary and partial, and involve pain as well, it is necessary to distinguish between pleasures, and to take only those which are not outweighed by pains. Pain is caused by unsatisfied desire; so one must recognize that those desires that are natural and necessary are easily satisfied; others are unnecessary. The limit of pleasure is the removal of pain; to seek always for more pleasure is simply to spoil one's present pleasure with the pain of unsatisfied desire. Pleasure is not so much the process of satisfying desires (*kinetic* pleasure) but rather the state of having desires satisfied (*katastematic* pleasure).

Pleasure of the soul, consisting mainly of contemplation or expectation of bodily pleasure, is more valuable than bodily pleasure. The ideal is *ataraxia*, freedom from disturbance. The study of philosophy is the best way to achieve the ideal. By teaching that the soul, made of atoms as the body is, dies with the body, it persuades us that after death there is no feeling: what happens after our death, like what happened before our birth, is 'nothing to us'. By teaching that the gods do not interfere and that the physical world is explained by natural causes, it frees us from the fear of the supernatural. By teaching that the competitive life is to be avoided, it removes the distress of jealousy and failure; by teaching one how to avoid intense emotional commitments, it frees us from the pain of emotional turmoil. (The main sources are Epicurus *Ep. Men.*, *KD*, and *Sent. Vat.*, and Lucretius 3 and 4.)

Epicurean moral philosophy thus finds room for most of the conventional Greek virtues of the soul; its main difficulty is to justify the virtues that are concerned with the well-being of other people—especially justice. Those who are wise will avoid injustice, Epicurus argues, because one can never be certain of remaining undetected. But Epicurean morality was less selfish than such statements made it appear. The Epicurean communities were famous even among their enemies for the friendship which bound members to each other and to the founder. See also DIOGENES (2) OF OENOANDA.

D.J.F.

Erasistratus, of Iulis on Ceos (about 315–240 BC?), is the only scientist other than *Herophilus to whom ancient sources attribute systematic scientific dissections of human cadavers. Celsus claims that Erasistratus, like Herophilus, also vivisected convicted criminals. The extant evidence leaves little doubt that he performed vivisectory experiments on animals. Often taking a functional approach to his anatomical discoveries, he combined detailed descriptions of parts with explanations of their physiological roles. Thus he not only gave the first reasonably accurate description of the heart valves but also demonstrated that their function is to ensure the irreversibility of the flow through the valves.

Three consistent features of Erasistratus' approach are his use of mechanistic principles to explain bodily processes, an Aristotelian teleological perspective, and the verification of an hypothesis by means of experiment. His major mechanistic principle is that matter naturally moves by means of 'following toward what is being emptied' (*pros to kenoumenon a kolouthia*), i.e. if matter is removed from any contained space, other matter will enter to take its place, since

a natural massed void (or 'vacuum') is impossible.

Using this principle, he united respiration, the vascular system, the nervous system, muscular activity, appetite, and digestion in a single, comprehensive physiological model, which he probably presented in his *General Principles* (*Hoi katholou logoi*). External air moves into the lungs through the windpipe and bronchial ducts as the thorax expands after exhalation. Some of the breath (pneuma) in the lungs then moves through the 'vein-like artery' (i.e. the pulmonary vein) into the left ventricle of the heart, when this ventricle expands after contraction. The pneuma in the left cardiac ventricle in turn is refined into 'vital' (*zōtikon*) pneuma before being pushed into the arteries when the heart contracts. Excess air in the lungs, having absorbed some of the superfluous body heat produced by the heart, is exhaled as the thorax contracts, but, in accordance with his principle that matter 'follows towards what is being emptied', fresh breath rushes into the thorax again as it expands. The pulmonary breathing cycle thus both cools the body and provides the arteries with life-sustaining pneuma.

The nerves, too, carry pneuma: some of the 'vital' pneuma is pumped through arteries from the left cardiac ventricle to the brain, where it becomes further refined into 'psychic' (*psychikon*) pneuma, which in turn is distributed to the body through the sensory and motor nerves. Appetite and digestion—both of which he also explains partly in terms of the principle that matter 'follows toward that which is being emptied'—provide the liver with liquid nutriment to process into blood, which then flows from the liver into the veins by the same mechanical principle. The arteries and the nerves, then, contain only pneuma, whereas the veins distribute only blood (as nutriment). The muscles, like other organic structures, consist of 'triple-braided' strands (*triplokiai*) of veins, arteries, and nerves. The pneuma carried to the muscles by arteries and nerves allows the muscles to contract or relax, thereby rendering voluntary motion possible.

In his pathology Erasistratus introduced several causes of diseases, all ultimately instances of different forms of matter (blood, pneuma, various liquids) that normally are rigorously separated, somehow not remaining separated. 'Plethora', a condition typically marked by excessive blood-nutriment in the veins, can cause inflammation, which can lead to fever, swollen limbs, diseases of the liver or stomach, epilepsy, and other ailments, in part because excessive blood in the veins can cause a dangerous spillover (*paremptōsis*) of blood into the arteries through inosculations (*synanastomōseis*) between veins and arteries, thus impeding the arterial flow of vital pneuma.

Like Herophilus, he argued that there are no diseases peculiar to women. In treating patients, his guiding principles (in part presented in *Hygieina* 1–2) were, first, to prevent plethoric conditions by means of regimen; secondly, to ensure, by relatively mild measures, the return to its proper place of matter that has gone astray. He emphasized the stochastic nature of symptomatology and therapeutics, opposed drastic measures, and rejected traditional uses of bloodletting, thereby provoking the notorious ire of *Galen. Other attested treatises include *On Fevers, On Expectoration of Blood, On Paralysis, On Dropsy, On Podagra, On the Abdominal Cavity*, and *On Divisions*.   H.V.S.

Eratosthenes, of Cyrene (*c.*285–194 BC), pupil of *Callimachus and Lysanias of Cyrene. After spending several years at Athens, where he came under the influence of *Arcesilaus and Ariston of Chios, he accepted the invitation of *Ptolemy III Euergetes to become royal tutor and to succeed *Apollonius Rhodius as head of the Alexandrian Library. He thus became a member of the Cyrenaean intelligentsia in Alexandria, of which the central figure was Callimachus. His versatility was renowned and criticized, and the eventual Alexandrian verdict was to describe him as *bēta*, 'B-class' (that is to say, not 'second rate' but 'next after the best specialist in each subject'), and *pentathlos*, an 'all-rounder'. Others, more kindly, called him 'a second Plato' (see PLATO). In more than one field, however, and particularly in chronology and mathematical and descriptive geography, of which, thanks to *Strabo, we know most, his work long retained much of its authority.

WORKS (almost entirely lost in direct quotation).

1. Literary criticism. Eratosthenes evidently attached considerable importance to his researches in this field, for we are told by *Suetonius that he was the first scholar to call himself by the proud title of *philologos*. His most important work seems to have been the treatise *On Ancient Comedy*, in at least twelve books; this dealt with literary, lexical, historical, and antiquarian matters, and problems of the authorship and production of plays.

2. Chronology. His *Chronographiai* represented the first scientific attempt to fix the dates of political and literary history. He also compiled a list of Olympian victors. In this field his most significant achievement (later abandoned) was to replace a partly mythical pre-historic chronology by one based on supposedly assured data (the fall of Troy).

3. Mathematics. He investigated a wide range of mathematical and geometrical problems and was accepted as an equal by *Archimedes, who addressed his *Methodus* to him, after the death of his earlier disciple Conon of Samos. In his *Platonicus* (perhaps a dialogue) he apparently discussed mathematical definitions and the principles of music. Among his geometrical works were the *On Geometrical Means* and *On the Duplication of the Cube*. The latter included his poem on that well-worn theme, addressed to Ptolemy III. In his *On the Measurement of the Earth* (probably a preliminary work to his *Geographica*) he treated mathematical geography, calculating with a higher degree of accuracy than his predecessors the circumference of the earth. He was the first systematic geographer, and the *Geographica* (three books) dealt with mathematical, physical, and ethnographical geography, being based on a division of continents on a geometrical basis into 'seals' (*sphragides*), a term perhaps borrowed from contemporary Ptolemaic terminology of land-measurement. The work opened with a sketch of the history of the subject, with especial reference to the Homeric poems, and this, along with the mathematically more exact work of *Hipparchus, formed the main source of Strabo's theoretical geography in books 1–2. For the Asiatic section his work was based to a considerable extent on the data provided by the bematists of *Alexander the Great and the early Seleucids.

4. Philosophy. His works in this field, the *Platonicus*, mentioned above, and the *Ariston* (named after the Chian philosopher Ariston, whom Eratosthenes had heard with some scepticism in Athens) were severely criticized by Strabo for their dilettanteism, but we know virtually nothing of their contents, and Strabo, as a good Stoic, was nettled by Eratosthenes' disenchantment with his Stoic teachers. Archimedes, in sending to Eratosthenes the text of his *Methodus*, called him 'a leader of philosophy' (*philosophias proestōs*), and there is no reason to regard this as polite condescension. It seems likely that these philosophical writings belong to the pre-Alexandrian phase of Eratosthenes' career.

5. Poetry. As a poet Eratosthenes for the most part eludes us, though his 'Alexandrian' characteristics are evident in theme and occasional quotation. His statement that the aim of poetry is to entertain, not to instruct, reflects a coherent *ars poetica*. His short epic *Hermes* described the birth of the god Hermes, his youthful exploits, and his ascent to the planets. The short epic *Anterinys* or *Hesiod* dealt with the death of *Hesiod and the punishment of his murderers. [Longinus] (*Subl.* 33. 5) praises the elegy *Erigone*, which told the myth of Icarius and his daughter, as 'a faultless little poem' (*dia pantōn amōmēton poiēmation*). These, however, have vanished, and the longest surviving fragments of his versatile muse are the delightful poem on the Duplication of the Cube (see above), and the short piece on the youth of Hermes.

Eratosthenes' intellectual calibre is seen both in chance utterances which reveal him as a man of insight and conviction (perhaps also of prejudice) and also in an occasional glimpse of a wide moral and political comprehension, notably in his comment in his *Geographica* (Strab. 66) that Greek and 'barbarian' (the Indians and the Arians, the Romans and the Carthaginians, 'with their wonderful political systems') should be judged by the unique criterion of morality and not of race. His candour and independence of judgement may go some way towards explaining that, although the names of some of his direct pupils are known, he seems to have established no lasting following associated with his name; we hear of no *Eratostheneioi*, as there were 'Callimacheioi', 'Aristarcheioi', and others.   P.M.F.

Eubulus (*c*.405–*c*.335 BC), probably the most important Athenian statesman of the period 355–342. In 355, after thirteen years' struggle to regain Amphipolis and the Thracian Chersonese and the brief but disastrous Social War, the imperialistic advocates of war were discredited and the state near bankruptcy. Rising under the aegis of Diophantus of the Athenian deme of Sphettus, Eubulus by means of his position as a theoric commissioner (treasurer of the fund from which grants were made to enable citizens to attend the theatre) gradually assumed control of the whole of Athens' finances, and raised public and private prosperity to a level probably not attained since the 5th cent. An extravagant version of the sort of methods he probably followed is to be found in *Xenophon's De vectigalibus*, but the most important guarantee of economic recovery was a law which made it difficult for the assembly to draw on the routine revenues of the state for inessential military operations. Thus he was able to employ the annual surpluses on a programme of public works: the distribution of money to the people (the theoric fund, Gk. *to theōrikon*) probably instituted in this period, engaged only a small part of the moneys controlled by the theoric commission. In the wider spheres of policy, to judge from the allusions of *Demosthenes, he sought to concentrate Athens' military resources on the defence of the essential interests of Athens and of Greece, and to exclude *Philip II from Greek affairs by uniting the Greeks in a Common Peace, his chief associates being Midias, *Aeschines, and Phocion. The expedition to Thermopylae in 352, the intervention in Euboea in 348, and the attempt to unite the Greeks against Philip II in 347/6 (or 348/7) are the chief fruits of this policy. Like almost all Athenian statesmen, he felt himself forced to accept the peace negotiated in 346 by Philocrates and Demosthenes. After Philip used the peace to intervene in Phocis, Demosthenes determined to renew the war, but Eubulus and his supporters sought to maintain and extend the peace. By mid-344 the opposition of Demosthenes and Hegesippus was beginning to weaken Eubulus' influence; in 343 the parties were fairly evenly balanced; but in 342 Demosthenes and the war-party were in full control. No more is heard of Eubulus after the battle of Chaeronea (338), and he may, like Aeschines, have retired from active politics. By 330 he was dead.   G.L.C.

Euclid, mathematician (date uncertain, between 325 and 250 BC). Nothing is known of Euclid's life: the biographical data linking him with Alexandria and *Ptolemy I are worthless inferences by late authors (*Pappus and *Proclus) who seem to have had no more information about him than we do. His fame rests on the *Stoicheia* or *Elements* which goes under his name. It is in thirteen books (bks. 1–6 on plane geometry, 7–9 on the theory of numbers, 10 on irrationals, 11–13 on solid geometry). The work as it stands is the classical textbook of elementary mathematics which remained the standard (in many languages and versions) for 2,000 years. It incorporates (and eliminated) many works on the 'elements' by writers predating Euclid, notably *Eudoxus, and it seems impossible to define precisely Euclid's own contribution, or to determine how much the extant version was changed after him (the recension by Theon of Alexandria was the basis of all printed editions before Peyrard's of 1814–18). Commentaries, of which fragments are preserved in the Arabic of an-Nayrīzī, were written by *Heron, Pappus, and Simplicius. The extant commentary of Proclus on book 1 is valuable chiefly for its citations from earlier lost writers. 'Book 14' of the *Elements* is by Hypsicles of Alexandria, 'book 15' a compilation from late antiquity.

Other geometrical works by Euclid are (1) *Data,* which defines 'given' for geometrical entities and proves what parts of a figure must be 'given' to determine the whole; it was an important part of the 'Domain of Analysis' outlined by Pappus (bk. 7); (2) *On Divisions* [*of Figures*], extant only in Arabic. Lost works are (1) *Pseudaria* ('Fallacies'); (2) *Topoi pros epiphaneia* ('Surface-loci'), of uncertain content; (3) a work on the four-line locus, important in the theory of conics; (4) *Porisms,* perhaps also auxiliary to conics. The 'four books on conics' attributed to him by Pappus (7. 30) is probably the latter's conjecture.

Other extant works by or attributed to Euclid are the following. (1) *Phaenomena,* on elementary spherical geometry as applied to astronomy. It has much in common with *On the Moving Sphere* by Autolycus of Pitane. (2) *Optics,* an elementary but influential treatise

on geometrical optics. (3) *Catoptrics,* a work on the optics of reflection which in its present form is a late compilation, but may contain 'Euclidean' material. (4) Two treatises on music, *Section of the Canon* and *Harmonic.* The Euclidean authorship of these is disputed.   G.J.T.

Eucratides I ('the Great'), Graeco-Bactrian king *c*.170–145 BC. His brilliant but warlike reign marked the climax of Greek rule in Bactria(-Sogdiana). Just. *Epit.* 61. 6. 1–5 compares him to Mithradates the Great of Parthia, while Apollodorus of Artemita (quoted at Strabo 15. 1. 3) calls him 'ruler of a thousand cities'. His parents Heliocles and Laodice, commemorated on a special series of his coins, are otherwise unknown; however, Laodice is portrayed wearing a diadem and was therefore from a royal family. Some believe her to be a sister of *Antiochus III the Great, but most scholars reject this view and associate her with either the family of Diodotus II or Euthydemus I. Eucratides apparently seized power in Bactria, and then waged wars in Sogdiana, Arachosia, Drangiana, Aria, and finally NW India. His principal adversary was probably King Demetrius I (son of Euthydemus I, though some argue for Demetrius II). After enduring a long siege, Eucratides overcame Demetrius and claimed the territories of Parapamisadae and Gandhara. It is likely that he also defeated the relatives of Demetrius I, including the ephemeral kings Euthydemus II, Agathocles, and Pantaleon. A campaign against Menander I is also possible.

The career of Eucratides may be traced in his voluminous coinage, which is among the finest and most innovative from antiquity. Besides commemorating his parents, he portrayed himself in heroic pose and added the epithet 'Great' to his royal title. His standard coin-type, the charging Dioscuri (Castor and Pollux), seems to celebrate the famous cavalry of Bactria. South of the Hindu Kush mountains, he issued rectangular and bilingual coins (Greek/Prakrit) on an Indian standard for local commerce. He also struck the largest known gold coin from the ancient world, a numismatic masterpiece weighing 20 staters (169 g.: almost 6 oz.).

Eucratides was brutally assassinated *c*.145 BC by one of his sons, probably Plato. Another son, Heliocles 'the Just', avenged the crime, but Bactria-Sogdiana soon fell victim to nomadic invaders from the north and Parthian encroachment from the west.　　F.L.H.

Eudoxus, of Cnidus (*c*.390–*c*.340 BC), was an outstanding mathematician and did important work in astronomy and geography; he was versatile in 'philosophy' in general. According to the not entirely trustworthy ancient biographical tradition (see especially Diog. Laert. 8. 86 ff.), he was a pupil of Archytas of Tarentum in geometry and of Philistion in medicine; he came to Athens to hear the Socratics when about 23, later spent time in Egypt studying astronomy with the priests, then lectured in Cyzicus and the Propontis, visited the court of *Mausolus, and finally returned to teach at Athens, where he was acquainted with Plato; he drew up laws for Cnidus, and died aged 52.

In geometry he invented the general theory of proportion, applicable to incommensurable as well as commensurable magnitudes, found in Euclid bk. 5 (scholion in Heiberg, *Euclidis Opera* 5. 280). This greatly helped to assure the primacy of geometry in Greek mathematics. He also developed the method of approach to the limit (misnamed 'method of exhaustion' in modern works) which became the standard way of avoiding infinitesimals in ancient mathematics, He was thus able to prove that cone and pyramid are one-third of the cylinder and prism respectively with the same base and height (Archim. *Method* pref.). Of his solution to the problem of doubling the cube nothing certain is known.

In astronomy he was the first Greek to construct a mathematical system to explain the apparent motions of the heavenly bodies: that of the 'homocentric spheres'. Simplicius' account of this (*in Cael.* 492. 31 ff.), which gives its title as *Peri tachōn* ('On Speeds'), reveals both the high level of mathematics and the low level of observational astronomy of the time: Eudoxus combined uniform motions of concentric spheres about different axes with great ingenuity to produce, for instance, a qualitatively correct representation of the retrogradations of some planets; but the underlying observational data are few and crude, and the discrepancies of the results with the actual phenomena often gross. Its adoption in a modified form by Aristotle was responsible for its resurrection

in later ages. More practical (and very influential) was Eudoxus' description of the constellations, with calendaric notices of risings and settings, which appeared in two versions, named *Enoptron* and *Phaenomena*. The latter is known through its adaptation by *Aratus (1) in his immensely popular poem of the same name; the commentary of *Hipparchus on both Eudoxus and Aratus is extant (see the edn. of Manitius (Teubner), 1894), p. 376 for refs. to Eudoxus). Another calendaric work was the *Oktaetēris* ('*Eight-year* [luni- solar] *Cycle*'). The papyrus treatise named *Eudoxou technē*, though composed much later, contains some elementary calendaric and astronomical information which may derive from Eudoxus. There is some evidence for Babylonian influence in Eudoxus' astronomical work.

The *Gēs periodos* ('Circuit of the Earth'), in several books, was a work of mathematical and descriptive geography.　　G.J.T.

Euhemerus, of Messene, perhaps wrote while in the service of *Cassander (311–298 BC), but was perhaps active as late as 280 BC. He wrote a novel of travel which was influential in the Hellenistic world. The substance of the novel is known from fragments, especially in *Diodorus Siculus, see below, and from an epitome by *Eusebius. Euhemerus described an imaginary voyage to a group of islands in the uncharted waters of the Indian Ocean and the way of life on its chief island, Panchaea. The central monument of the island, a golden column on which the deeds of Uranus, Cronus, and Zeus were recorded, gave the novel its title *Hiera anagraphē*, 'Sacred Scripture'. From this monument Euhemerus learnt that Uranus, Cronus, and Zeus had been great kings in their day and that they were worshipped as gods by the grateful people. Earlier authors had written of imaginary utopias but the utopia of Euhemerus was particularly relevant to the position of those Hellenistic rulers who claimed to serve their subjects and on that account to receive worship for their services. Euhemerism could be interpreted according to taste as supporting the traditional belief of Greek epic and lyric poetry which drew no clear line between gods and great men; as advancing a justification for contemporary ruler-cults; or as a work of rationalizing atheism. At the same time Euhemerus was influenced by the beliefs of the wider world which had been opened up by the conquests of *Alexander the Great, and his novel reflected the awareness of new ideas in an exciting situation.

The theory of god and man which was advanced by Euhemerus seems to have made little impression on the Greeks, but Diodorus, apparently taking the romance for fact, embodied it in his sixth book, which survives in fragments. In Latin it had more success after the publication of the *Euhemerus* of *Ennius, and euhemerizing accounts of such mythological figures as Faunus exist. The Christian writers, especially *Lactantius, liked to use it as evidence of the real nature of the Greek gods. Euhemerus' name survives in the modern term 'euhemeristic', applied to mythological interpretation which supposes certain gods (e.g. Asclepius) to be originally heroes.   H.J.R.; S.H.

Eumenes I (d. 241 BC), ruler of Pergamum, nephew and successor of Philetaerus, former treasurer of *Lysimachus (263). Eumenes extended Pergamene control in Mysia and Aeolis and defeated *Antiochus I near Sardis (262). Although he paid protection money to the Galatians he maintained a mercenary army, garrisoning *i. a.* the forts Philetaireia and Attaleia and controlling the port cities Elaia and Pitane. Pergamum enjoyed a constitution of democratic structure, though Eumenes, who as dynast stood outside the constitution, appointed the *stratēgoi* (chief magistrates) and so controlled the finances.
                                                         R.M.E.

Eumenes II (d. 158 BC), king of Pergamum (197–158), eldest son and successor of *Attalus I. Characteristic is the family solidarity of Eumenes, his mother Apollonis, and his three brothers, which gave unusual inner strength to the dynasty. Eumenes, immediately threatened by *Antiochus III the Great, was Rome's major ally in the war against him, culminating in the battle of Magnesia (189), and he made the greatest gains from the ensuing Peace of Apamea (188) which divided Seleucid territory north of the Taurus between Pergamum and Rhodes. Pergamum became immediately rich but also a guarantor of stability in the Roman interest. A new coinage, the cistophori ('basket-bearers'), introduced sometime after 188, marked Pergamum's new

economic role. Roman support did not mean peace: wars with Prusias I of Bithynia (187–183) and Pharnaces I of Pontus (183–179) were ended by Roman intervention. A major victory against Galatians (184) made the grateful Greeks call him Soter ('Saviour'); he celebrated it at home by extending the Pergamene temple of Athena Nikephoros ('Victory-Bringer') and making her festival pan-Hellenic. In the 170s Eumenes' building programme transformed Pergamum into a splendidly equipped capital city and produced the apogee of Pergamene plastic art (e.g. the Great Altar of Zeus); contacts with major Greek centres—Athens, Miletus, Delphi, Cos—were marked by massive gifts; diplomacy produced a successful coup, when he helped *Antiochus IV Epiphanes to succeed his murdered brother Seleucus IV in Syria (175).

Instrumental in influencing Rome to annihilate the Macedonian monarchy (The Third Macedonian War: 170–168), Rome's victory ironically rendered Eumenes' strength superfluous and suspicious, and the senate began to dismantle it. It courted his brother Attalus, refused to receive Eumenes, while encouraging Prusias, and declared the rebellious Galatians free, after Eumenes had just defeated them. In 160/59 *Attalus II became co-ruler, but the peak of Pergamene power was past.   R.M.E.

Eumenes of Cardia (*c.*361–316 BC), secretary to *Philip II and *Alexander the Great of Macedon. A royal favourite, bitterly resented by many native Macedonians, he received the prestigious command of a hipparchy of Companions (cavalry) during Alexander's last year, and after the king's death he attached himself to *Perdiccas, in whose interest he probably composed the Royal Diaries (*ephemerides*). Thanks to Perdiccas he was appointed satrap of Cappadocia and installed in office by the royal army (322). As head of the Perdiccan forces in Asia Minor he had successive victories over Neoptolemus and *Craterus (321) but was isolated after Perdiccas' death and condemned to death at Triparadeisus. Brought to bay in Cappadocia and besieged at Nora (319/18), he came to terms with *Antigonus the One-eyed, but immediately sided with *Polyperchon and accepted command of the 'Silver Shields', veterans of Alexander's hypaspists. These he controlled adroitly by representing himself simply as a medium for their deceased king and won the leadership of the coalition of satraps which resisted the expansionist ambitions of Peithon and Antigonus. In an epic campaign in the Iranian highlands the inconclusive battle of Paraetacene (317) was followed by Gabiene (early 316), where his Macedonians lost their baggage (and families) to Antigonus. Consequently Eumenes was surrendered to his death. Despite his political brilliance he had no lasting impact.   A.B.B.

Eunapius, Greek sophist and historian, was born at Sardis *c.* AD 345 and studied there under Chrysanthius, and later in Athens under Prohaeresius. When he returned to Sardis he entered the circle of local Neoplatonists, learned theurgy and medicine (he is sometimes described as an 'iatrosophist'), and mainly taught rhetoric. A fervent admirer of the emperor *Julian and a convinced opponent of Christianity, he wrote to defend his old faith. His History is now lost except for fragments, though much of its character can be recovered from later writers who used it (see below). It continued the work of Herennius Dexippus, and went in fourteen books from AD 270 to 404; it was finally concluded in about 414. A first edition had however appeared many years earlier, since the work is referred to in the *Lives of the Sophists* of *c.*396, and since traces of its influence can be detected in *Ammianus Marcellinus' account of Julian's Persian campaign; some scholars however ascribe the resemblances to Ammianus' direct use of one of Eunapius' sources, Julian's doctor *Oribasius. According to *Photius (*Bibl.* 77), who had seen both versions, the second edition of the History appeared in a toned-down form because of the very anti-Christian attitude of the first version, though it is not agreed whether the new edition was prepared by Eunapius himself, or what form the revisions took, since the surviving version of the History still seems very outspoken. Apart from his use of Oribasius' memoir on Julian's Persian campaign we know little about Eunapius' sources; he himself complained about the lack of reliable information on contemporary events in the western part of the empire (in which he contrasts sharply with his successor Olympiodorus). He was himself an important source, not only to the pagan Zosimus, but also to Christian historians, notably Philostorgius and Sozomen; the latter opens his History with an attack on the view of the conversion of Constantine I propounded by Eunapius (whom he does not name). Eunapius' *Lives of the Sophists* are extant in full. They follow *Philostratus' model and on the basis of first-hand information deal mainly with 4th-cent. Neoplatonists, of whom Eunapius gives an idealized picture in order to compete with the biographies of Christian saints. In particular, they trace a line of Neoplatonic descent from Iamblichus, to which the emperor Julian also adhered.   J.F.Ma.

Euphorion, of Chalcis in Euboia, Greek poet; b. 275 (*Suda*), pupil of the philosophers Prytanis and Lacydes and the poet Archebulus of Thera; he profited from the patronage of the wife of Alexander, ruler of Euboea, and was appointed librarian at Antioch by *Antiochus III the Great (who ruled 223–187). He was possibly given Athenian citizenship.

Euphorion was a scholar-poet in the tradition of *Callimachus: monographs on the Isthmian Games and other historical and mythological subjects are attested; he is also credited with a lexicon to *Hippocrates, and two of his epigrams appear in Meleager's anthology (*Garland, c.*100 BC). He was best known though for his hexameter poetry, of which only tantalizingly small fragments have been preserved; even the more extensive papyrus fragments discovered this century do not permit confident judgements on the nature or merits of his poems, which ancient readers found difficult (cf. Cic. *Div.* 2. 133, Clem. Al. *Strom.* 5. 8. 51). The *Suda* mentions only three works, *Hesiod, Mopsopia,* and *Chiliades,* but other sources yield over twenty titles, which however cast little light on the content of the poems. At least three (*Thrax, Curses* or *The Goblet-thief, Chiliades*) were curse-poems, recounting obscure mythological stories in abstruse terms (cf. Ovid's *Ibis*): *Chiliades* apparently predicted the certain punishment of Euphorion's adversaries by citing oracles which had been fulfilled after a lapse of a thousand years. His interest in recondite lore and aetiology is reminiscent of Callimachus, whose style he closely imitated; his diction is basically Homeric, with learned elaborations.   F.W.

Eupolis was regarded as one of the greatest poets of the Old Comedy (e.g. Hor. *Sat.* 1. 4. 1). His first play was produced in 429 BC (Anon. *De com.* 9 p. 7); he won three victories at the Lenaea and at least one at the City Dionysia (*IG* 2². 2325. 59, 126). The datable plays are: *Numeniae* at the Lenaea in 425 (hyp. 1 Ar. *Ach.*), *Maricas* at the Lenaea in 421 (schol. Ar. *Nub.* 551), *Flatterers* at the City Dionysia in 421 (hyp. 1 Ar. *Pax*), *Autolycus* in 420 (Ath. 216d), and *Baptae* after 424 (fr. 89 refers to Ar. *Eq.*) but before 415 (Aristid. *Or.* 3. 444 D relates a story which, though untrue, presupposes 415 as the last possible date for *Baptae*). *Cities* is probably to be dated *c.*420 BC; it has many personal references in common with Ar. *Nub.*, *Vesp.*, and *Pax*. *Demes* must be later than 418 (fr. 99. 30 ff. refers to the Mantinea campaign of that year) and earlier than 406 (fr. 110 shows that the younger Pericles is still alive); 412 is the most probable date. Eupolis died 'in the Hellespont, during the Peloponnesian War' (*Suda*), sometime after 415 (Eratosth. quoted in Cic. *Att.* 6. 1. 18). We have nineteen titles and nearly 500 citations, with substantial papyrus fragments of, and of commentaries on, *Maricas, Prospaltii*, and *Taxiarchi*.

Flatterers ridiculed Callias, son of Hipponicus, for cultivating the company of sophists—a comic poet's view of the kind of scene portrayed in Pl. *Prt.* 314 ff. *Maricas* was an attack on Hyperbolus, comparable with *Aristophanes (1)'s attack on *Cleon in *Knights*; like Aristophanes' *Lysistrata*, it had two opposed choruses. In *Demes* great Athenians of the past were brought up from the Underworld to give advice to the present. In *Taxiarchi* the soft-living Dionysus is subjected to hard military and naval training by the Athenian commander Phormion. Eupolis' style seemed 'abusive and coarse' to the author of Anon. *De com.* 33 p. 9, but 'highly imaginative and attractive' to Platonius, *Diff. com.* 1 p. 6.   K.J.D.

Euripides, Athenian tragic playwright.

CAREER Euripides was born probably in the 480s. He first took part in the dramatic competitions of the City Dionysia at Athens in 455 BC, the year after the death of *Aeschylus (Life 32: he came third; the plays included *Daughters of Pelias*, his first treatment of the story of Medea); he died in 407–6, leaving, like *Sophocles later in the same year, plays still unperformed (*Iphigeneia at Aulis, Alcmaeon in Corinth, Bacchae*: schol. Ar. *Frogs* 67), with which he won a last, posthumous victory (*Suda*, entry under the name). His first victory came only in 441 (*Marm. Par.* 60; plays unknown). He won again in 428 (hyp. *Hippolytus*), but in his lifetime won only four victories at the Dionysia (*Suda*): he was thus far less successful in the competition than Aeschylus (thirteen victories) or Sophocles (eighteen victories). In 438 he was defeated by Sophocles (hyp. *Alc.*; Euripides' plays were *Cretan Women, Alcmaeon in Psophis, Telephus, Alcestis*); in 431 he was third to Aeschylus' son, Euphorion, and Sophocles (hyp. *Med.*: his plays were *Medea, Philoctetes, Dictys, Theristae*); in 415 second to Xenocles (Ael. *VH* 2. 8; Euripides' plays were *Alexander, Palamedes, Trojan Women, Sisyphus*); in 409 second, perhaps to Sophocles (hyp. *Phoen.*; his plays included *Phoenissae* and perhaps *Oenomaus* and *Chrysippus*). In 408 he probably competed at the Dionysia for the last time with plays that included *Orestes* (schol. *Or.* 371). Soon afterwards he left Athens on a visit to Macedon, as guest of the Hellenizing king Archelaus, and wrote a play there about an eponymous ancestor of the king (much as Aeschylus had written a play about the foundation of the city of Aetna while in Syracuse as guest of the tyrant, Hieron). He never returned to Athens but died in Macedon. There is no good reason to accept the ancient tradition that he had left Athens an embittered man, finally despairing after a series of defeats by almost unknown playwrights (Satyr. *Vit. Eur.* fr. 39; Philodemus *de vitiis*, col. 13: Satyrus' Life is largely a work of fiction).

PLAYS Euripides wrote some ninety plays (*Suda*, entry under the name). By chance we have more than twice as many of them as we have plays by either Aeschylus or Sophocles. They fall into two categories: the first, a group of ten plays which have been transmitted to us in our medieval manuscripts complete with the accumulation of ancient notes and comments that we call *scholia*. They represent the same kind of volume of 'selected plays' as we have for the other two playwrights. They are: *Alcestis, Medea, Hippolytus, Andromache, Hecuba, Trojan Women, Phoenissae, Orestes, Bacchae*, and *Rhesus*. The last is probably not by Euripides; the plays are in their likely chronological order; *Bacchae* has lost its scholia and the end of the play is partly missing. The other nine plays are: *Helen, Electra, Heraclidae, Heracles, Suppliant Women, Iphigenia at Aulis, Iphigenia among the Taurians, Ion, Cyclops.* They have been transmitted in only a pair of closely related 14th-cent. manuscripts (known as L and P); they have no scholia and they are in a rough (Greek) alphabetical order. There is little doubt that they represent the chance survival of one volume (perhaps two) of the 'complete plays' of Euripides, which circulated in alphabetical order, as we know from ancient lists of plays and collections of '*hypotheseis*' (prefaces) to the plays (see Barrett, ed. *Hippolytos*, 45–61): they therefore represent a random sample of Euripides' work. Nine of the surviving plays are dated: *Alcestis* (438), *Medea* (431), *Hippolytus* (428), *Trojan Women* (415); *Helen* (412); *Phoenissae* (409); *Orestes* (probably 408); *Bacchae* and *Iphigenia at Aulis* (between 408 and 406). The remaining plays can be dated more roughly but with some confidence on the evidence of Euripides' writing of the verse of spoken dialogue in his plays. Statistical studies have shown that the tendency he clearly displays to write an ever freer, looser iambic verse line, by replacing 'long' syllables with pairs of 'short', is steadily progressive and not subject to sudden fluctuations (Dale, ed., *Helen*, with references to earlier work). The likely sequence (with approximate dates) is: *Heraclidae* (430), *Andromache* (426), *Hecuba* (424), *Suppliant Women* (422), *Electra* (416), *Heracles* (414), *Iphigenia among the Taurians* (413), *Ion* (410). The satyr-play *Cyclops* is late, probably around 408. We also have, mostly from papyrus texts, sizeable fragments of several other plays: *Telephus, Cretans, Cresphontes, Erechtheus, Phaethon, Alexander, Oedipus, Hypsipyle, Archelaus* (in their probable chronological order).

'REALISM', FRAGMENTATION, FORMALISM Ever since *Aristophanes (1)'s portrayal of Euripides, in his play *Frogs*, as an intellectual iconoclast who insisted on confronting the darker and more disturbing aspects of everyday reality (*Frogs* 959), and Aristotle's quotation of an opaque remark attributed to Sophocles, to the effect that he (Sophocles) presented men 'as they ought to be', while Euripides presented them 'as they are' (*Poet.* 1460[b]33 ff.), Euripides has tended to be read as a 'realist'. Plays such as *Trojan Women* (which sharply focuses on the savage brutality of war, in the middle of war); *Aeolus* (which takes incest as its theme: we know of it only from its 'hypothesis') and *Cretans* (whose action turns on sexual intercourse between a woman and a bull) have been cited in evidence. Moreover it has seemed obvious to many critics (already in antiquity: [Longinus], *Subl.* 15. 4–5) that a naturalistic treatment of human psychology, particularly female psychology, is another hallmark of Euripidean theatre: witness Medea, Phaedra, Hecuba, Electra, Creusa but also Ion, Orestes (in *Orestes*), and Pentheus. It is undoubtedly true that there are strands of 'realism' in Euripides' writing for the theatre: for example, Medea's presentation of herself as mistrusted 'foreigner' and oppressed and exploited 'woman' (*Med.* 214–58) and her subsequent slow, tortured progress to infanticide; Orestes sickened and eventually driven mad by the corrosive effects of guilt (*Or.* 34–45; 208–315, including the only 'mad scene' in extant Greek tragedy); or the voyeurism of Pentheus in *Bacchae*. But these are strands only in an extremely fragmented whole. For it is arguable that a vision of human experience as inherently fragmented and as defined by the co-existence of disparate, even contradictory, strands forms the very heart of Euripidean sensibility.

If we go back to *Medea* and read it attentively, we shall find that the Medea we have encountered in the passage already referred to exists, within the world of the play, alongside other Medeas: before the passage mentioned, she has been heard off-stage, giving incoherent voice only to pain and articulate only in universal cursing and damnation, of herself and her own children as well as of her enemies; immediately after it, she is transformed into a subtle adversary who patently and easily outwits her most powerful enemy. Subsequently she becomes successively brilliant orator, pathetic victim, devious manipulator, exultant (and uncanny) avenger, tormented mother until her final metamorphosis (involving a stunning *coup de théâtre*) into the demonic figure who, in an aerial chariot drawn by snakes, closes the play with prophecies and taunts sent down from beyond his reach upon the husband who deserted and humiliated her.

Hippolytus too introduces us to a similarly fragmented world: the play is framed by the appearance of two human-like divinities, cool, articulate, and frighteningly rational in their revenges; in between it is given over to humans, in three very disparate and distinct 'movements'. The first of these movements comprises the uncanny and disturbing passage across the stage of Hippolytus, who, it is clear, lives apart in a world of his own making and companioned by his own, personal, chorus; as he leaves, we are confronted, first, by a world of women, characterized by an intimacy which is warm and close but also painful, and by a Phaedra, who is successively delirious with hunger and unspoken sexual desire and then, immediately, rational, articulate, and analytical in presenting her decision to take her own life. That world is shattered by its own intimacies, which lead by slow degrees but with a sense of psychologically convincing inevitability first to deadly revelation and then to misguided intervention. The intervention goes terrifyingly astray. Phaedra dies and the world of women in which she has lived is replaced by a world of men, that of her husband and Hippolytus, the stepson with whom she had, by Aphrodite's will, fallen obsessively in love. This male world is characterized no longer by intimacy and warm relationship but by distance and cold rhetoric: in this world there is no communication, only speech-making and the cut-and-thrust of distichomythia (the formal exchange of pairs of lines). The scene ends in Theseus' invocation of a male divinity, his own father, to destroy his son and it is followed at once by the messenger's description of that destruction: the description demonstrates that divinity is not human, but bestial and capable of tearing men literally apart and of bringing about the annihilation of all that they have made.

Moreover, Euripidean 'realism' is conveyed to the reader/spectator through the medium of a marked, if equally fragmented, formalism. It has been a stumbling-block for many critics that Euripidean theatricality is expressed in stiffly formal, often detached, 'set pieces'. Euripides characteristically opens his plays with a markedly non-naturalistic 'prologue', in the form of a monologue, which acts as a kind of separate overture. Almost as characteristically he closes them with a detached tailpiece: the shape of the action is broken and brought to a halt by the intervention, sometimes (as in *Medea*) of a character

from that action, now transformed, but more often a divinity (as in *Hippolytus, Andromache, Suppliant Women, Electra, Iphigenia among the Taurians, Ion, Helen, Orestes, Bacchae*). The divinity often apparently makes a highly theatrical apparition off the ground in mid-air, the so-called '*deus ex machina*' (already a problem for Aristotle: *Poet.* 1454^{b}2 ff.). Confrontation between dramatic persons frequently takes the form of an exchange of symmetrical and brilliantly rhetorical speeches, transparently forensic in tone, a special kind of bravura set-piece which modern scholars have called an *agōn*.

INNOVATION AND RECURRENCE In *Frogs* Aristophanes presents Euripides (comically) as a compulsive innovator and subverter of tradition. In his handling of the traditional stories which he (like the other 5th-cent. playwrights) took as the material out of which to make his plays, he clearly innovates: Medea's infanticide; Heracles' killing of his wife and children after, not before, the labours; Electra's marriage to a peasant farmer; the trial of Orestes before the Argive assembly; Thebes, years after Oedipus' discovery of the truth, still inhabited by Iocasta, Oedipus, and Antigone (and by a transient chorus of Phoenician girls!)—all these seem to be Euripidean innovations. There is a kind of restlessness to Euripidean experimentation (*Phoenissae* provides a good example) that many critics have taken to be definitive of his theatrical imagination. But innovation is not in itself a peculiarly Euripidean trait: Aeschylus (especially in *Suppliant Women* and *Oresteia*) and Sophocles (especially in *Philoctetes*) both gave themselves the freedom to reshape traditional stories in order to create new fictional worlds for the tragic theatre.

At least as characteristic of Euripides is the tendency to create theatre, almost obsessively, out of recurring dramatic situations which echo and resonate with each other. Very often these situations have women at their centre, women as victims and/or deadly avengers: examples are *Medea, Hippolytus, Andromache, Hecuba, Electra, Trojan Women, Ion, Helen, Iphigenia at Aulis*. Sometimes structural echoing (as between *Medea* and *Hippolytus*), situational parallels (as between *Electra* and *Orestes* or between *Hecuba* and *Trojan Women*), or emotional resonances (as between *Medea* and *Ion*) almost give the impression that the later play is a reworking of the earlier. Similarly *Bacchae* recurs to the theme of divine revenge through the subjugation and perversion of human will that he had treated in *Hippolytus*. But these are not 'revivals' under another name. Each reworking offers a different vision of the human condition and these disparate visions are enacted in very different structural forms: the ending of *Hecuba*, for example, is quite other than, and carries a very different sense of 'closure' from, that of *Trojan Women*.

SPEECH AND SONG: THE LATE PLAYS The late plays of Euripides (roughly those of the last decade of his life, the plays that come after *Trojan Women* and *Heracles*) have thrown up major problems of interpretation and have led to strong critical disagreement. In so far as there has been a consensus, plays such as *Iphigenia among the Taurians*, *Ion*, and *Helen* have been characterized as 'escapist' or as 'tragicomedies', while others such as *Phoenissae*, *Orestes*, and *Iphigenia at Aulis* (*Bacchae*, it is agreed, is somehow 'different') have been called 'epic theatre' or 'melodrama'. The underlying assumption has been that Euripides has turned away from the painful realities of tragic experience to offer his audiences less demanding, more 'entertaining' forms of theatre: the very real sufferings caused by the Peloponnesian War between Athens and the Spartan alliance have often been invoked in explanation.

The late plays are also often seen as the moment in Athenian theatre history when the chorus goes into terminal decline: its songs become fewer, more 'irrelevant' to the action and more purely decorative in function. (The charge of 'irrelevance' has indeed been laid against Euripides' use of the chorus even in his earliest surviving plays, for example in the third *stasimon* of *Medea*, ll. 824–65.) The two issues (of the changing nature of late Euripidean theatre and the 'decline of the chorus') need to be taken together.

Sung and spoken text together form the 'script' of the Greek tragic theatre from the earliest surviving play, Aeschylus' *Persians* of 472 BC, to the last, Euripides' *Bacchae* and *Iphigenia at Aulis* and Sophocles' *Oedipus at Colonus*, and in almost all the plays that we have actors and chorus both sing and speak (it is generally assumed that the spoken lines marked 'Chorus' in our manuscripts were in fact spoken only by the chorus-leader). But song is the characteristic mode of choral utterance and speech that of actors. In the late plays of Euripides this distinction becomes very much less clear as actors are increasingly given arias and duets to sing and moments of great emotional intensity in these plays are marked by such songs. Thus, for example, Creusa's anguished and distracted aria of self-revelation at *Ion* 859–922; the recognition duet of Menelaus and Helen at *Helen* 625–97; the murder scene of *Orestes* 1246–1310; and the final encounter and last farewells of Antigone and Oedipus at *Phoenissae* 1539–81, 1710–57. Sung text is also used to convey young innocence at *Ion* 82–183 and *Phoenissae* 103–92. At the same time choral songs are becoming more infrequent, though the stanzas that form them are getting longer.

Moreover, Euripides increasingly uses 'astrophic' song, that is song not composed of the responding, metrically 'rhymed' stanzas that throughout the history of tragedy had characterized the song of both chorus and actors. We have external evidence that connects these changes to new developments in musical composition, developments that were seemingly designed to make possible freer, aurally less predictable vocal lines. The key figure in these developments appears to have been Euripides' younger contemporary, Timotheus of Miletus, who is plausibly associated with Euripides in a number of ancient anecdotes. Such music and the writing that goes with it, composed of long sentences, free in syntax, that seem to float without ultimate closure (they are brilliantly parodied by Aristophanes in *Frogs*), are clearly the medium for a different perception of human experience than that of the earlier plays. It is not that Euripides' perception is no longer 'tragic' (though a number of the late plays, such as *Ion*, *Iphigenia among the Taurians*, and *Helen*, do end with apparent 'happiness'); rather Euripides now seems to see human beings not just as articulately analytical in confronting suffering but simultaneously as living in a world of shifting, unstable, and often contradictory emotions. It is through song, and the associative juxtaposition of sensations, thoughts, and experiences that have always characterized Greek song, that such fleeting and unstable forms of consciousness are conveyed in the late plays.

Alongside this almost operatic use of song,

Euripides also employs in the late plays other new formal devices to create new versions of the tragic. They include vastly extended passages of stichomythia (exchanges of single lines, dialogue at its most tensely formal) and the use of metres taken from much older forms of tragedy, such as the trochaic tetrameter (*Or.* 729–806, which includes 25 successive lines divided between two speakers, shows both formal devices together). The result is a series of plays whose emotional atmosphere is much more difficult to seize and characterize. Their themes still include human isolation and inexplicable suffering, failures of communication, the victimization of women, and the drive to revenge, even the terrors of madness, themes that have marked earlier Euripidean theatre but in a bewildering variety of new dramatic modes.

The last two plays that we have, *Bacchae* and *Iphigenia at Aulis*, point up the paradoxical and disconcerting multiplicity of Euripides' theatrical imagination. *Bacchae* eschews almost all the formal innovations of the other late plays (though not the freer iambic verse nor the extended stichomythia scenes) and offers a vision of human experience that combines a stark and shocking view of the power of divinity with a luxuriant but ambiguous emotionalism which veers from joyful calm to exultant savagery: men and women are crushed and overwhelmed by collision with a divine power which they cannot comprehend. *Iphigenia at Aulis* takes us into another world. It makes much use of actor arias and duets (including an extended passage of sung text given to Agamemnon, as well as long arias for Iphigenia); it deploys greatly extended passages of stichomythia, much of it in trochaic tetrameters and involving free use of broken lines. The choral songs are more numerous than in other late plays and the first of them (the entry-song of the chorus) is very long. Above all it creates an emotionally charged but unstable world marked by botched deception and exciting disclosure, by an anti-hero, Agamemnon, who is tormented by indecision, and by a young Iphigenia, who combines a childlike innocence with heroic self-determination. The worlds of *Iphigenia* and of *Bacchae* barely touch and yet, in the theatre, they were juxtaposed, played one after the other before the same audience. They attest not merely the variety of Euripides' theatrical imagination

(to the very end of his life) but also a fact that we should always remember: that his audiences, like those of Aeschylus and Sophocles, were accustomed to the experience of tragedy not in the form of a single play but as a sequence of three disparate tragic fictions, rounded off by anti-tragic burlesque. The disparateness of Euripides' theatrical imagination plays to that expectation.

J.P.A.G.

Eusebius, of Caesarea (*c.* AD 260–339), prolific writer, biblical scholar and apologist, effective founder of the Christian genres of Church history and chronicle, and the most important contemporary source for the reign of *Constantine I. His intellectual formation at Caesarea in Palestine owed much to the influence of Pamphilus (martyred 310), by whom he was apparently adopted, and to their joint use of the library of *Origen. From his election as bishop of Caesarea *c.*313 until his death in 339, Eusebius played a significant role in ecclesiastical politics in the eastern empire. He attended and assented to the decisions of the council of Nicaea in 325, having been readmitted to communion after recanting his earlier views; but though he delivered a speech at the dedication of Constantine's church of the Holy Sepulchre in Jerusalem (335) and encomia for the emperor's *decennalia* (315–16) and *tricennalia* (335–36), he was probably not such a confidant of Constantine as has commonly been supposed. He was present at the council of Tyre in 335 as an opponent of Athanasius, and shortly afterwards at Jerusalem when Arius was readmitted to the church. His *Life of Constantine*, left unfinished at his death, sought to create the impression of a harmonious and consistent imperial religious policy from the accession of Constantine (306) to the reign of his three sons, beginning in September 337.

Eusebius wrote biblical commentaries, in which the profound influence exerted on him by Origen is tempered by his own historical perspective; his *Onomasticon*, 'a biblical gazetteer', is an important source for the historical geography of Palestine. The two editions (? before 303 and 325–6) of his lost *Chronicle*, represented by *Jerome's Latin version and by an Armenian translation, synthesized Old Testament, near-eastern, and Graeco-Roman history into a continuous chronological sequence accompanied by chronological tables. The object, as in his *Ecclesiastical History*, was to demonstrate that God's plan for salvation subsumed the whole of history. The same thinking lay behind his *Preparation for the Gospel* and *Proof of the Gospel* (after 313), apologetic works in which pagan philosophy is refuted and the Roman empire seen as the necessary background for the coming of Christ and the establishment of Christianity. The *Preparation* reveals Eusebius' immense debt to the library of Origen, with its many citations from Greek historians, *Philo Judaeus, and especially Middle Platonist philosophy. An early work, *Against Hierocles*, attacks the comparison of the pagan Apollonius of Tyana with Christ; in the *Preparation* the main target is *Porphyry, whose anti-Christian arguments Eusebius systematically set out to refute. The later *Theophany* (325–6 or later), extant in Syriac translation, and his last works repeat many of the same apologetic themes.

Eusebius' integrity as a historian has often been challenged, and indeed the later part of his ten-book *Ecclesiastical History* (which may have been begun in the 290s but only reached its final form in 324–5) was successively extended and clumsily revised as immediate circumstances changed. The *Life of Constantine*, in four books, has seemed so suspect on the grounds of bias and inconsistencies that Eusebian authorship has been denied. But the authenticity of the many documents cited or mentioned has been vindicated in one major case by the identification of the same text on papyrus, and modern scholarship is more willing than before to recognize the complexity of Eusebius's methods. The citation of documentary evidence marks both works off from secular historiography. However, Eusebius' aim was not so much objectivity as persuasion: close study of the reworking of parts of the *Ecclesiastical History* in the *Life of Constantine* shows that he deliberately developed and enhanced his own earlier argument in the light of later reflection. Both works reflect the powerful impact of Christian persecution on Eusebius' thought but unlike the *Ecclesiastical History*, which took its main shape before or during the persecution of 303–13, and went on to cover only the part of Constantine's reign up to the defeat of Licinius in 324, the much later *Life of Constantine* reflects Eusebius' mature,

if one-sided, understanding of the implications of a Christian imperial system.

A.M.C.

Eustathius (12th cent. AD), born and educated in Constantinople, was deacon at St Sophia and taught rhetoric (and probably grammar) in the patriarchal school until 1178, when he became metropolitan of Thessalonica, in which position he continued till his death (*c*.1194). His works of classical scholarship were written before 1178. Henceforward he devoted himself to the practical duties of his spiritual office and to combating the prevailing corruption of monastic life.

WORKS (1) Classical: *Commentary on Pindar*, of which only the introduction survives; this gives information on lyric poetry (especially *Pindar's) and Pindar's life, and shorter notes on the Olympian Games and the pentathlon. The *Commentary on Dionysius Periegetes* contains discursive scholia, valuable for citations from earlier geographers, historians, the unabridged *Stephanus of Byzantium, and the lost works of *Arrian. The *Commentaries on Homer's Iliad and Odyssey* (*Parekbolai eis tēn Homērou Iliada Odysseia*) are a vast compilation, in which the Iliad commentary is twice as long as that on the Odyssey. They are evidently based on Eustathius' lectures. Prefaces deal with the differences between the poems and with the cultural importance of Homer. The notes discuss chiefly questions of language, mythology (sometimes interpreted allegorically), history, and geography. Their value consists particularly in the assemblage of material drawn from the old scholia and the lost works of earlier scholars and lexicographers. His quotations from classical authors are taken mostly at second hand. He often illustrates a point by reference to the customs and observances of his own time and to contemporary vernacular Greek.

(2) His other works include an account of the conquest of Thessalonica by the Normans (1185), in which he was personally involved. It is a perceptive account of life in an occupied city, in which victors and vanquished alike are corrupted and demoralized. He also wrote polemics, e.g. the famous *Inquiry into Monastic Life*; letters to the emperor, church dignitaries, and others; speeches and addresses, homilies and tracts, some of which have historical value. Eustathius was the outstanding

scholar of his time, enthusiastic for traditional learning, for the preservation of
books, for sound principles of education, and
for the moral reawakening of monasticism.
He is regarded as a saint by the Orthodox
Church, and portrayed in a fresco in the
church of the Virgin in the Serbian royal
monastery of Gračanica (*c*.1321); see STE-
PHANUS OF BYZANTIUM; ARRIAN.

J.F.L.; R.B.

Evagoras, *c*.435–374/3 BC), an interesting
and important figure in Greek, Persian, and
Cypriot history. He was a member of the
Teucrid house (cf. Tod 194), the traditional
rulers of Cypriot Salamis. Exiled during his
youth, which fell in a period of Phoenician
domination, he gathered some 50 followers at
Soli in Cilicia, and with their help established
himself as ruler of Salamis in 411. His subsequent policy aimed at strengthening Hellenism in Cyprus by co-operation with Athens
(which honoured him *c*.407, perhaps for
shipping corn there); and his court became a
centre for Athenian *émigrés*, of whom Conon
was the most distinguished. A clash with

Persia was ultimately inevitable, but in his
early years he was not out of line with Persia,
and he postponed the confrontation by
assisting in the revival of Persian sea-power
culminating in the triumph of the battle of
Cnidus (394). Athens now honoured him for
his services as a 'Greek on behalf of Greece'.
War finally came *c*.391 and dragged on for
ten years. In alliance with Acoris of Egypt,
Evagoras at first more than held his own. He
not only extended his rule over the central
cities of Cilicia, but also captured Tyre and
dominated Phoenicia. In 382 Persia mobil-
ized an overwhelming force against him,
Evagoras lost control of the sea at Citium in
381, and was forced to sue for peace, obtaining
reasonably favourable terms, through dissensions among the Persian commanders. In 374
he was assassinated in a palace intrigue.

The most detailed source for his life, *Isocrates, Evagoras,* is not altogether reliable factually; but it, together with Isocrates' other
'Cyprian orations' the *To Nicocles* (Evagoras'
son) and the *Nicocles,* is an important document of early Greek kingship theory.

D.E.W.W.; S.H.

Ff

Fabius Cunctator See FABIUS MAXIMUS VERRUCOSUS.

Fabius Maximus Rullianus (Quintus Fabius Maximus Rullianus), consul 322, 310, 308, 297, 295 BC. Surviving accounts of his career are obscured by factual uncertainties; patriotic and family fictions; supposed clashes with Lucius Papirius Cursor, Appius *Claudius Caecus, and even Publius Decius Mus (his colleague in his last three consulships); and apparent duplicates of incidents from the career of Quintus *Fabius Maximus Verrucosus (Cunctator). Thus his supposed clash with Lucius Papirius Cursor in 325 (Fabius Pictor fr. 18 P) apparently owes much to Cunctator's quarrel with Marcus Minucius Rufus in 217 and his role as his son's legate in 292 is modelled on actions of both Cunctator and *Scipio Africanus. In 322 some sources attributed him major successes in Samnium and Apulia, and a triumph. As dictator in 315 he captured Saticula but was defeated by the Samnites at Lautulae. *Diodorus Siculus (19. 101. 3) alone attributes him a second dictatorship in 313 and the capture of Fregellae, Calatia, and Nola. In 310 he reputedly relieved Sutrium and forced Arretium (Artezzo), Cortona, and Perusia (Perugia) to a truce. The allocation of operations in Samnium and Etruria in 308 is uncertain and the prorogation of his command (and victory at Allifae) in 307 are difficult to accept. As censors in 304 he and Decius Mus reputedly reversed the tribal reforms of Appius Claudius Caecus and instituted the formal cavalry parade (*transvectio equitum*). In 297 and perhaps 296 he campaigned in Samnium, but in 295 he and Decius won a crucial victory over the alliance of Samnites, Etruscans, and Celts at Sentinum. He may be the Q. Fabios depicted in a military scene on an Esquiline tomb frieze.

A.D.

Fabius Maximus Verrucosus (Quintus Fabius Maximus Verrucosus, nicknamed 'Cunctator', see below), grandson or great-grandson of *Fabius Maximus Rullianus, as consul 233 BC celebrated a triumph over the Ligurians and unsuccessfully opposed the agrarian bill of Gaius *Flaminius. He was censor 230, consul for the second time 228, and dictator (probably) 221. In 218 he perhaps opposed an immediate declaration of war on Carthage. Dictator again in 217, after the Roman defeat at Lake Trasimene, he began his famous policy of attrition, believing that Hannibal could not be defeated in a pitched battle; this earned him the name 'Cunctator' (the Delayer). He allowed Hannibal to ravage the Campanian plain, but then blocked his exits; Hannibal, however, escaped by a stratagem. Opposition to Fabius' policy at Rome led to his *magister equitum* (master of the horse), Marcus Minucius Rufus, receiving *imperium* (a grant of military and civil authority) equal to his. When Minucius was enticed into a rash venture, Fabius rescued him. The traditional policy of fighting fixed battles was resumed in 216, but after the disaster at Cannae there was no alternative to Fabius' policy. With the help of his position as the senior member of the college of augurs—he is said to have been an augur since 265—he became suffect consul for the third time for 215, operating in Campania. He was re-elected for 214, helped to recapture Casilinum and had a number of successes in Samnium. In 213 he perhaps served as legate to his son. Direct control of affairs now passed to other men, but Fabius reached his final consulship in 209, when he recaptured Tarentum in south Italy and was made *princeps senatus* (first senator). In 205, together with Quintus Fulvius Flaccus, he strongly opposed *Scipio Africanus' plan to invade Africa. He was no doubt alarmed by Scipio's growing prestige, but genuinely believed that taking the war to Africa posed unnecessary dangers. It was Scipio who brought the war to an end, but Fabius' cautious strategy which made victory possible. Fabius died in 203. He had been *pontifex* (a member of the college of priests) since 216 as well as augur, a distinction unique until *Sulla and *Julius Caesar.   J.Br.

Favorinus (*c.* AD 85–155), sophist, philosopher, and man of letters. Born in Arelate (mod. Arles), he learned Greek in (?) Marseilles and worked exclusively in that language for the whole of his professional career; he may also have studied with Dio Chrysostom (see DIO COCCEIANUS) in Rome. His speaking tours took him to Athens, Corinth, and Ionia, where he contracted a bitter feud with his fellow sophist Polemon. He was a friend of *Plutarch, and the teacher and associate of Herodes Atticus, *Fronto, and Aulus *Gellius (who quotes and refers to him frequently in the *Noctes Atticae*). At Rome he moved in the circle of the emperor *Hadrian, was advanced to the rank of an *eques*, and held the office of a provincial high priest. About AD 130 he fell into disfavour, although it is disputed whether or not he was exiled. Under Antoninus Pius he recovered his status and influence. Though ancient sources speak of him as a eunuch, he is more likely to have been a sufferer from cryptorchism.

His extensive works (nearly 30 titles are attested) may be divided into three categories: (*a*) Miscellanies, principally the *Memoirs* and the *Miscellaneous History*, of which the first was devoted to stories about philosophers. These are the earliest known examples of the type of work later produced by Aelian and Athenaeus. (*b*) Declamations, comprising the *Corinthian* ('Dio', *Or.* 37), *Fortune* ('Dio', *Or.* 64), and *Exile* (*PVat. II*). (*c*) Philosophical works, ranging from *The Philosophy of Homer* and *Socrates and his Erotic Art* to *Plutarch, or the Academic Disposition, Cataleptic Phantasy*, and *The Pyrrhonian Modes*. The last three at least seem to have been substantial contributions to serious philosophical debate, in which Favorinus presented himself as an adherent of the 'old' scepticism of the Academy (the philosophical school founded by *Plato), as opposed to the 'new' scepticism of the Pyrrhonists (see PYRRHON OF ELIS).   M.B.T.

Flamininus, Titus Quinctius, brother of Lucius Flamininus (consul 192 BC). Born *c.*229 BC, military tribune 208 under Marcellus, then quaestor, probably at Tarentum, where he held praetorian *imperium* (supreme military and civil authority) for some years from 205. Decemvir for distributing land to *Scipio Africanus' veterans 201, he concurrently became triumvir (one of a board of three officials) to supplement the Roman colony at Venusia (200). In 198, against some opposition but with the support of the veterans he had settled, he was elected consul and sent to take over the war against *Philip V of Macedon with a new army and a new political approach. After driving Philip from a strong position in the Aous gorge separating Macedonia from Epirus, he moved towards central Greece against stiff resistance, but with his brother's help forced the Achaean Confederacy into alliance and now gained some further allies. Meeting Philip late in 198, he demanded the evacuation of all of Greece (unacceptable to Philip at this point), but apparently hinted to Philip that the senate might modify the terms. He instructed his friends in Rome to work for peace if he could not be continued in command and for war if he could complete it; he was prorogued, and the senate insisted on his terms. In spring 197, after gaining the alliance of most of Greece, he decisively defeated Philip by superior tactical skill at the battle of Cynoscephalae (Thessaly). He now granted Philip an armistice on the same terms, which the senate confirmed as peace terms. Advancing implausible excuses, he refused to allow his Aetolian allies to annex some cities promised to them. He thus secured a balance of power in the north, but gravely offended the Aetolians, making them eager to welcome *Antiochus III. In a spectacular ceremony (see Polyb. 18. 46) he announced the unrestricted freedom of the Greeks in Europe at the Isthmian games of 196 and persuaded a reluctant senate commission that this pledge had to be carried out if Greek confidence was to be retained against Antiochus, who was about to cross into Europe. He now initiated a diplomatic effort to keep Antiochus out of Europe and deprive him of the Greek cities in Asia Minor. The final settlement of Greece involved a difficult war against the Spartan ruler Nabis, nominally as head of an almost Panhellenic alliance. The settlement paralleled that with Philip: Nabis was left to rule Sparta, to secure a balance of power between him and Rome's Achaean allies. In 194 all Roman troops were withdrawn. Henceforth Flamininus was showered with honours (including divine honours) in Greece. He issued a commemorative gold coin with his portrait (*RRC* 548) and left for Rome to celebrate an unparalleled three-day triumph (Livy 34. 52). A bronze statue with a Greek inscription was erected to him in Rome by his Greek clients (Plut. *Titus* 1. 1).

In 193 he was entrusted with secret negotiations with Antiochus' envoys; when they refused his offer of undisturbed possession of Asia in return for withdrawal from Europe, he proclaimed to the Greek world that Rome would liberate the Greeks of Asia from Antiochus. Sent to Greece to secure the loyalty of the Greeks and of Philip, he was partly successful; but Demetrias in Thessaly, afraid of being surrendered to Philip, became an Aetolian bridgehead for Antiochus. He remained diplomatically active in 191–190, both in the war and in Peloponnesian affairs, handing Messene over to the Achaeans and annexing Zacynthus for Rome. In 189 he was censor. In 183, sent to Asia on an embassy, he unsuccessfully tried to intervene in Peloponnesian affairs on his way, then took it upon himself to demand the extradition of *Hannibal from king Prusias I of Bithynia. (Hannibal committed suicide.) With the senate working to substitute Demetrius, Philip's pro-Roman younger son, for Perseus, his elder son, as designated successor, he hatched a plot to substitute Demetrius for Philip as king (see Polyb. 23. 3, cf. 7; Livy 40. 23, denying the charge). The result was Demetrius' execution (181). After this failure he disappears from public affairs until his death (174).

A typical patrician noble, he saw his world in terms of personal ambition, Roman patriotism, family loyalty, and patron–client relationships. He was the first to develop a policy of turning the Greek world—cities, leagues, and kings—into clients of Rome and of himself, nominally free or allied, but subject to interference for Rome's advantage. The Greeks, whom he had liberated, he expected to follow his instructions even without a public mandate. Aware of Greek history and traditions, he attracted many Greeks by charm and tact, but aroused antagonism by

unscrupulous trickery. Midway between arrogant imperialists and the genuine philhellenes of a later period, he laid the foundations of the uneasy acceptance of Roman hegemony by the Greek world. E.B.

Flaminius (Gaius Flaminius) was the only politician before the Gracchi to mount a serious challenge to the senatorial establishment on behalf of the *populares* (popular politicians). The tradition, initially influenced by Quintus Fabius Pictor, presents a hostile picture of him, particularly so *Polybius, *Livy, and sources dependent on Livy, and it is hard to separate fact from fiction. A *novus homo* (first man of his family to reach the consulship), he was tribune of the *plebs* 232 BC, and, against opposition led by Q. *Fabius Maximus Verrucosus, carried a law distributing the *ager Gallicus*—land between Ravenna and Sena Gallica, confiscated from the Senones 50 years earlier—in individual lots to needy Roman citizens. Polybius describes the law as the beginning of the perversion of the people, and claims that it caused the Gallic invasion of 225. Praetor in 227, Flaminius was the first annual governor of Sicily. As consul in 223 he led the first Roman army to cross the river Po (Padus), and won a victory over the Insubres. Polybius is critical of his generalship. Later sources say that prodigies caused the senate to annul the results of the elections, and they sent a letter to the consuls ordering them to abdicate, but Flaminius refused to open it until after the battle. It is said that his triumph was voted by the people, and according to Plutarch the consuls were eventually forced to abdicate. He may have been appointed *magister equitum* (master of the horse) by the dictator Quintus Fabius Maximus Verrucosus, probably in 221, but they had to abdicate because of a portent during the procedure. As censor in 220 he built the via Flaminia and the Circus Flaminius. He is said to have been the only senator to support the law of Quintus Claudius in 218; this law forbade senators and their sons from owning ships capable of carrying more than 300 amphorae. Livy portrays him as being opposed by virtually the whole senate; in fact he may have had the support of the Scipios and their allies. He was elected consul for the second time for 217, is said to have neglected to take the auspices at Rome, to have entered office at Ariminum (Rimini), and to have ignored unfavourable omens. He took up position at Arretium (Arezzo), but *Hannibal marched past him towards the heart of Etruria. Flaminius followed, and because of morning fog was caught in ambush at Lake Trasimene. He was killed and 15,000 men with him. The defeat was ascribed to his neglect of religious observances.

J.Br.

Florus, name of three Latin authors, usually, but not unanimously, identified as the same man.

(1) Lucius Annaeus (Iulius in Cod. Bamberg) Florus, Roman historian, author of the *Epitome bellorum omnium annorum DCC* ('Abridgement of all the Wars over 1200 Years'); wrote no earlier than *Antoninus Pius to judge from pref. 8 and 1. 5. 5–8. His work is an outline of Roman history with special reference to the wars waged up to the reign of Augustus, with the suggestion that the latter had brought peace to the world. Some manuscripts describe it as an epitome of *Livy; but it is sometimes at variance with Livy. The author also made use of *Sallust, *Julius Caesar, and in one passage (pref. 4–8) probably *Seneca the Elder; and there are reminiscences of *Virgil and *Lucan. It is planned as a panegyric of the Roman people. 'The tone is pious and ecstatic, condensed Livy' (Syme, *Tacitus* 2. 503).

(2) Publius Annius Florus, poet and rhetorician, author of the imperfectly preserved dialogue *Vergilius orator an poeta* ('Was Virgil an Orator or Poet?'); born in Africa, he took part as a youth in the Capitoline Games under *Domitian, afterwards residing at Tarraco. Of the dialogue only a fragment of the introduction remains. It was probably written about AD 122; its diction closely resembles that of the *Epitome*.

(3) Annius Florus, poet-friend of *Hadrian, whose risky lines on the emperor beginning 'Ego nolo Caesar esse' ('I don't want to be a Caesar') had the honour of a retort from him (SHA *Hadr.* 16. 3). Other fragments are preserved (Riese, *Anth. Lat.* 1. 1, nos. 87–9 and 245–52). They are not sufficient to enable judgement to be passed on the author's poetry and hardly justify the theory that the famous *Pervigilium Veneris* is his work.   E.S.F.; G.B.T.; A.J.S.S.

Frontinus (Sextus Iulius Frontinus), perhaps from southern Gaul, served as urban praetor in AD 70 and then assisted in suppressing the revolt of Julius Civilis, receiving the surrender of 70,000 Lingones. Consul in 72 or 73, he served as governor of Britain (73/4–77) where he crushed the Silures in south Wales, establishing a fortress for Legio II Augusta at Caerleon, and then attacked the Ordovices. He may have accompanied *Domitian during his German campaign in 82/3, was proconsul of Asia in 86, and was subsequently appointed by *Nerva in 97 as *curator aquarum* (superintendent of aqueducts). He held his second, suffect, consulship in 98, and his third, ordinary, consulship in 100, both times with *Trajan. Pliny described him as one of the two most distinguished men of his day (*Ep.* 5. 1). He died in 103/4.

WORKS Frontinus wrote in an uncluttered, direct style about several technical subjects: the history, administration, and maintenance of the aqueducts of Rome (*De aquis urbis Romae*); he cites engineers' reports, official documents, plans, and senatorial decrees, with details of quantity, supply, and abuses of the system. The book is a source of the highest value for the study of the working of the Roman water-supply, and the history and administration of the city of Rome in general. It combines a rhetorical pride in the Roman achievement in this field with a willingness to list very technical statistics. In the *Strategemata* Frontinus discusses techniques of military command, using stratagems drawn mainly from past commanders, though including several recent examples, particularly from Domitian's campaigns in Germany; the work is divided into three books by categories: before battle, during and after battle, sieges; a fourth book contains maxims on the art of generalship. Doubts about its authenticity are probably unjustified. Frontinus claims to provide practical guidance for contemporary commanders, and the *Strategemata* may have served as a textbook in a society with no formal means of training men for public office. Another treatise on Greek and Roman military science is now lost. Frontinus was probably the author of several works on land-surveying, partly preserved in the *Corpus Agrimensorum* (collection of treatises about land-surveying), covering categories of land, land measurement and division, boundary marking, and types of dispute.   J.B.C., N.P.

Fronto (Marcus Cornelius Fronto) (*c.* AD 95–*c.*166), orator, suffect consul July–August 143; born at Cirta (Constantine) in Numidia (north Africa); completed his education in Rome; a leading advocate under *Hadrian, he was appointed tutor by *Antoninus Pius to *Marcus Aurelius (Caesar) and his adoptive brother Lucius Verus, remaining on intimate terms with them until his death, probably from the plague of 166/7.

Though famous for his oratory ('not the second but the other glory of Roman eloquence', *XII Panegyrici Latini* 8 (5). 14. 2, an allusion to *Cicero), Fronto is known today almost exclusively through his correspondence, chiefly with Marcus, but also with Pius, Lucius, and various friends. The letters expound and illustrate his stylistic theories: the orator must seek out the most expressive word in Early Latin texts, preferring the unusual to the commonplace provided it is not obscure or jarring (but new coinages are discountenanced); he must dispose his words in the best order and cultivate rhetorical figures, the *sententia* (a brief saying embodying a striking thought), and the image-like description (*eikōn*). Among Fronto's favourite authors are *Cato the Elder, *Plautus, *Ennius, and *Sallust; Cicero, though unsurpassed as a letter-writer, is criticized as an orator for taking insufficient pains to find 'unexpected and surprising words' (*insperata atque inopinata verba*, 57. 16–17). *Virgil is ignored, *Lucan and *Seneca the Younger damned.

The letters also illustrate Fronto's distaste for Stoicism, his distress at its hold on Marcus, his constant ill-health, his family joys and sorrows, and the difficulties of life at court. He complains (111. 17–20) that Romans have no capacity for affection (*philostorgia*), nor even a name for it; Marcus, silent on Fronto's rhetorical tuition, acknowledges that he has learnt from him the hypocrisy of courts and the coldness of Roman patricians (M. Aur. *Med.* 1. 11). Their own correspondence is marked by extreme displays of affection.

A few declamations and fragments of speeches have also survived, as has a draft for a panegyrical history of the Parthian War. Minucius Felix (*Oct.* 9. 6–7) quotes a speech alleging that Christian ritual included incest and murder; despite the entire absence of political advice from Fronto's letters, some have seen in this invective the origin of Marcus' persecution. At the opposite extreme, it has been dismissed as incidental forensic abuse; it might also have been a speech in loyal support of imperial policy.

Aulus *Gellius includes Fronto in five chapters of his *Attic Nights*; three are in book 19, perhaps making the connection seem closer than it was. His authority in questions of vocabulary is vividly conveyed, but the admiration expressed for Quadrigarius and Virgil is probably Gellius' own. Fronto reacts with dismay to a report that 'Gellius' (presumably Aulus) is trying to acquire and publish his works (182. 5–6).

Before his letters came to light in 1815, Fronto had been idealized as the wise counsellor of a philosophic emperor; afterwards an exaggerated reaction dismissed him as a futile twaddler. He was more remarkable for mastery of language and warmth of heart than for keenness of intellect or strength of purpose; but our few fragments of his speeches tend to justify his ancient fame.

L.A.H.-S.

Fulvia, offspring of two noble families, became the best-known of late republican ladies active in politics and a prototype of empresses. Born in the late 70s BC, she married P. *Clodius, supported his policies and called for vengeance after his assassination. Briefly married to Gaius Scribonius Curio, she married Mark *Antony after Curio's death, took an active part in his management of politics after Caesar's death and later in the proscriptions, greatly enriching herself. When Antonius took charge of the east, she supported his cause in Italy, ultimately combining with his brother Lucius Antonius (Pietas) in opposing Octavian (later *Augustus). Besieged with him at Praeneste, where her presence was exploited by hostile propaganda, she was allowed to join her husband after its fall, but was badly received by him and soon died. Her daughter by Clodius was briefly Octavian's first wife; Marcus Antonius Antyllus and Iullus Antonius were her sons by Antony. In later literature (especially Cass. Dio) she became the type of the wicked matron, contrasted with the virtuous Octavia.   E.B.

Gg

Gaius (1), the emperor, 'Caligula' (Gaius Iulius Caesar Germanicus), AD 12–41), son of *Germanicus and *Agrippina the Elder, born at Antium (31 August). In 14–16 he was on the Rhine with his parents and, dressed in miniature uniform, was nicknamed 'Caligula' ('Bootee') by the soldiers. He went with his parents to the east in 17 and, after Germanicus' death in 19, lived in Rome with his mother until her arrest in 29, then successively with *Livia and Antonia until he joined *Tiberius on Capreae. The downfall of Tiberius' favourite *Sejanus in 31 was to Gaius' advantage, and it was probably engineered by him and associates such as the prefect of the watch (*vigiles*) Macro, who also benefited. After the death of his brother Drusus Julius Caesar in 33 Gaius was the only surviving son of Germanicus and, with Tiberius Julius Caesar Nero 'Gemellus'—Claudius' claim not being considered—next in succession. He became *pontifex* (a member of the most important college of priests) in 31 and was quaestor two years later, but received no other training in public life. Tiberius made Gaius and Gemellus joint heirs to his property, but, supported by Macro, now prefect of the praetorian guard, Gaius was proclaimed emperor (16 March 37), Tiberius' will being declared invalid by the senate, although his acts as a whole were not invalidated; Gaius made an appropriately perfunctory effort to have him deified.

Gaius' accession was greeted with widespread joy and relief, and his civility promised well. One symbolic gesture was the restoration of electoral choice to the popular assemblies, taken from them in 14 (it failed and Gaius had to revert to Tiberian procedure). Gaius needed to enhance his authority and held the consulship four times, in 37 (suffect, so that the men in office in March were not disturbed), 39, 40 (sole consul), and 41; he became Pater Patriae (father of his country), a title refused by Tiberius, on 21 September 37. In the early months of his rule he honoured the memory of his mother, father, and brothers and spoke abusively of Tiberius. Antonia, a restraining influence, died on 1 May 37. In October Gaius was seriously ill; *Philo's view (*Leg.* 14, 22) that this unhinged him has been given too much attention. But the illness may have brought the succession question into prominence: some time before 24 May 38, Gaius executed both Macro and his rival Gemellus. In 39 Gaius quarrelled with the senate, revised his attitude towards Tiberius' memory, announcing the return of slandering the emperor as a treasonable offence. The same year he married his fourth wife, Milonia Caesonia, who had already borne him a daughter, proving her fertility. The autumn and winter of 39–40 Gaius spent in Gaul and on the Rhine; a conspiracy was revealed whose leader, Gnaeus Cornelius Lentulus Gaetulicus, commander of the Upper Rhine army, was executed. This conspiracy may be connected with the simultaneous disgrace of his brother-in-law (and possible successor) Marcus Aemilius Lepidus and of Gaius' surviving sisters *Agrippina the Younger and Julia Livilla. After his return to Rome (in ovation, on 31 August 40) Gaius was in constant danger of assassination, having no successor to avenge him, displayed increasing brutality, and was murdered in the palace on 22 or 24 January 41. His wife and daughter were also murdered.

The government of Gaius was autocratic and capricious, and he accepted extravagant honours which came close to deification. His reign has been interpreted as a departure from the Augustan Principate to a Hellenistic monarchy. Rather, Gaius seems to have been engaged in discovering the limits of his power ('for me anything is licit', Suet. *Calig.* 29). He was a person of the highest descent (he once banished *Agrippa from his ancestry by postulating incest between Augustus and his daughter *Julia), which helps to account for the unprecedented attention paid to his sisters, Julia Drusilla, whose death in 38 was followed by a public funeral and consecration, Livilla, and Agrippina; he possessed an exceptional intellect and a cruel and cynical wit; and he demanded exceptional homage and was savage if his superiority was not recognized. A gifted orator, who delivered Livia's funeral oration at the age of 17, he enjoyed writing rebuttals of successful speeches. By insisting on primacy in everything Gaius left even courtiers no role of their own. He had terrified the senators, humiliated officers of the praetorian guard (who carried out the assassination), and only the masses seem to have regretted his passing.

Gaius was a keen builder, interested in the state of Italy's roads and in Rome's water supply (he began the aqua Claudia and Anio Novus aqueducts). For the sake of the grain supply he began to improve the harbour at Rhegium (Reggio). He also completed the reconstruction of the theatre of Pompey and created a circus in the Vatican; other constructions were for his own pleasure, for instance the bridge of boats from Puteoli to Bauli (39), an ephemeral extravagance to outdo Xerxes or overawe a Parthian hostage.

Gaius' high expenditures were economically advantageous, ending the sluggishness of Tiberius' regime. His achievements abroad, with the exception of his deployment of client rulers, were negative. He probably raised two new legions (XV and XXII Primigeniae) for an invasion of Germany or Britain. However, his forays into Germany in the autumn of 39 may have been exercises intended to restore discipline after the fall of Gaetulicus and to commemorate the campaigns of Germanicus in 13–16 (the famous collection of sea shells, 'spoils of Ocean', probably alludes to the North Sea storms that Germanicus had encountered); here the Chauci and Chatti were still causing trouble in 41. The conquest of Britain was only mooted, and was considered achieved when Cunobelinus' (Cymbeline's) son Adminius came to render homage (Gaius could not afford to leave the centres of empire in 39–40). By deposing and executing Ptolemy of Mauretania he provoked a war that was brought to an end only in the next reign. For the Jews under Gaius see below.   J.P.B.; B.M.L.

GAIUS AND THE JEWS Soon after his accession, Gaius conferred a kingship in Palestine upon his friend, the Herodian *Julius Agrippa I. However, their understanding did not prevent discord between the inconsistent emperor and his Jewish subjects. A savage conflict between Jews and Greeks in Alexandria stood unresolved when Gaius died. The prefect, Aulus Avillius Flaccus, seemingly abandoning any pretence at even-handedness when Gaius succeeded, had backed the Greek side in the long-standing dispute with the Jews over citizen rights. Agrippa I, visiting en route for his kingdom, was mocked by the Greek crowd and a pogrom thereby unleashed. It was on the emperor's birthday that Jews who had survived the assaults on the Jewish quarter were rounded up in the theatre and made to eat pork. While Gaius did have Flaccus arrested and replaced in late 38, he disdainfully ignored the delegations sent to Rome by both groups, leaving his successor to investigate and settle the matter.

Among the Jews of Palestine, Gaius' policy was heading for disaster when he died. A statue of the emperor was to be placed in the Jerusalem Temple and worshipped: this was perhaps Gaius' reaction to the Alexandrian Jewish delegation (Josephus), perhaps a response to the destruction by Jews at Jamnia, of their pagan neighbours' altar to the emperor (Philo). Stalling by Publius Petronius, governor of Syria, apparently sympathetic to Jewish pleas, delayed developments; and the intervention of Agrippa, whose long and perhaps genuine letter to Gaius is quoted by *Philo, is alleged to have effected the abandonment of the plan. Philo claims that it was then reinstated by secret orders; but this he could scarcely have known. In general lines, however, the events are well documented: Philon was a participant, heading the Alexandrian Jews' delegation to Gaius, while *Josephus offers two distinct accounts of the events in Palestine.   T.R.

Gaius (2), the famous 2nd-cent. AD law teacher, was lecturing in 160/1 and still alive in 178. Though a Roman citizen, he was known, and apparently chose to be known, by the single undistinctive name 'Gaius'. Some phrases in his work read as if written in Rome; others point to an eastern province. The key to the puzzle may be that Gaius, who speaks of the school of Masurius Sabinus and Gaius Cassius Longinus as his teachers (*nostri* *praeceptores*), had his legal education in Rome but taught and wrote mainly in the east, Berytus (mod. Beirut), since Augustus a Roman colony with Italian status (*ius Italicum*), being a possible location. He is best known for his *Institutes* ('Teaching Course'), elementary lectures for students delivered in 160–1 but probably not published by himself. A 5th-cent. manuscript of these lectures, the most substantial legal work of the Principate to survive, was discovered in Verona in 1816 overwritten by later writing. Despite scribal errors most modern scholars regard the text as largely genuine. It is marked by clarity of style, attention to history, concern for classification, and a critical attitude to legal rules, for example the lifelong tutelage of women (*Inst.* 1. 190). It employs a 'Socratic' method of teaching (see SOCRATES) which often leaves unanswered the problem raised. A later work called *Res cottidianae* ('Everyday Matters'), at one time said to be of the 3rd cent. or later but now thought to be a genuine work of Gaius, refines and develops the sometimes loosely expressed text of the *Institutes*. Gaius was a prolific writer, the author of 30 books (*libri*) *Ad edictum provinciale* ('On the Provincial Edict'), a treatise *Ad legem XII tabularum* ('On the Law of the Twelve Tables'), and numerous other monographs. *Justinian's compilers excerpted 521 passages from his works.

Opinions differ as to his merits. He was no casuist; but his classifications are at least in part original. He invented or carried forward new types of legal literature, with an emphasis, natural if he was writing in the provinces, on imperial law. Gaius' *Institutes* were known in Egypt early in the 3rd cent. but, again perhaps because he was a provincial writer, none of his works are cited by later authors such as *Ulpian who would be likely to have known of them. In the 4th cent. his work spread to the west, and in 426 was officially recognized by the Law of Citations, which put him on a level with *Papinian, Paulus, Ulpian, and Modestinus as a writer whose work as a whole possessed authority. In Justinian's time he is affectionately called *Gaius noster* ('our Gaius') and Justinian's *Institutes* ('Teaching Course') are in effect a second edition of his work of that name. Through Justinian his has proved to be the most influential teaching manual for lawyers; and his classifications formed the basis of civil

law systems in Europe up to the time of the French and German codes.   T.Hon.

Galba (Servius Sulpicius Galba), the emperor (3 BC–AD 69), from an ancient patrician family, son of C. Sulpicius Galba and Mummia Achaica, through the empress *Livia's favour moved in the most elevated social circles of the Julio-Claudian era. He was governor of Aquitania, consul (33), governor of Upper Germany (40–2), and proconsul of Africa (44–5); his standing was recognized by the award of triumphal insignia and three priesthoods. Governor of Hispania Tarraconensis (north-east Spain) from 60, he was approached in 68 by Julius Vindex, who was instigating revolt against *Nero. Galba had his troops proclaim him as representative of the senate and people of Rome, and enrolled a new legion (eventually VII Gemina) in addition to the one in his province. Although Vindex was defeated, Nero's suicide and the support of Gaius Nymphidius Sabinus and the praetorians encouraged Galba to march on Rome, accompanied by *Otho, governor of Lusitania. Once in power, Galba tried to recover Nero's extravagant largess, but the execution of several opponents including Lucius Clodius Macer who had raised revolt in Africa, and the brutal killing of soldiers recruited by Nero from the fleet, cast a shadow. His avarice was notorious. He declined to pay the praetorians the donative promised by Nymphidius, saying that it was his practice to levy his troops not to buy them. He compounded this misjudgement by failing to control his own supporters, and by sending his newly recruited legion to Pannonia (south-west of the Danube). 'In everyone's opinion he was capable of being emperor had he never ruled' (Tac. *Hist.* 1. 49). When on 1 January the legions of Upper Germany, who felt that they had been cheated of their reward for defeating Vindex, renounced their allegiance, Galba decided to adopt a successor, choosing Lucius Calpurnius Piso Frugi Licinianus. Otho, coveting this role for himself, fomented revolt among the praetorians, who murdered Galba on 15 January 69.   J.B.C.

Galen, of Pergamum (AD 129–?199/216) in a spectacular career rose from gladiator physician in Asia Minor to court physician in the Rome of *Marcus Aurelius. The son of a wealthy architect, he enjoyed an excellent education in rhetoric and philosophy in his native town before turning to medicine. After studying medicine further in Smyrna and Alexandria, he began practising in Pergamum in 157, and went to Rome in 162. Driven out by hostile competitors, or fear of the plague, in 166, he returned in 169, and remained in imperial service until his death. A prodigious polymath, he wrote on subjects as varied as grammar and gout, ethics and eczema, and was highly regarded in his lifetime as a philosopher as well as a doctor.

Although *Plato and *Hippocrates were his gods, and *Aristotle ranked only slightly below them, he was anxious to form his own independent judgements, and his assertive personality pervades all his actions and writings. His knowledge was equally great in theory and practice, and based in part on his own considerable library. Much of our information on earlier medicine derives from his reports alone, and his scholarly delineation of the historical Hippocrates and the writings associated with him formed the basis for subsequent interpretation down to the 20th cent.

He made ambitious efforts to encompass the entirety of medicine, deriding those who were mere specialists or who rejected any engagement with theory. The best physician was, whether or not he knew it, also a philosopher, as well as a man good with his hands. Galen reports some spectacular surgical successes, like his removal of a suppurating breastbone, and he expected even moderate healers to be able to perform minor surgery. Although he rarely refrained from laying down the law on how to diagnose and treat patients, he equally stressed the inadequacy of general rules in an individual case. Although contemporaries credited him with almost miraculous skills in prognosis (which incorporated diagnosis), especially in what might be termed stress-related diseases, he replied that they were easily derived from Hippocratic first principles and that a sound diagnosis depended on close observation of every detail. His authoritative bedside manner would also have contributed to his success with patients.

Galen was particularly productive as anatomist and physiologist. Dissecting animals, especially monkeys, pigs, sheep, and goats, carefully and often, he collected and corrected the results of earlier generations by experiment, superior factual information, and logic. His physiological research was at times masterly, particularly in his series of experiments ligating or cutting the spinal cord. At others, his reliance largely on non-human anatomy, coupled with his belief that the basic structures of the human body had been described by Hippocrates, led him to 'see' things that were not there, e.g. the rete mirabile at the base of the human skull, cotyledons in the womb, and a connection between spleen and stomach.

His pathology, founded on the doctrines of the four humours and of three organic systems, heart, brain, and liver, explained disease mainly as an imbalance, detectable particularly through qualitative changes in the body. His pharmacology and dietetics were largely codifications of earlier learning, enlivened by personal observations and occasional novel ideas, as with his (unfulfilled and later influential) attempt to classify drugs according to twelve grades of activity.

His philosophy was equally eclectic. His major enterprise to create a logic of scientific demonstration, surviving only in fragments, went beyond Aristotle and the Stoics in both the range and precision of its arguments. Later authors credited him with innovations in syllogistic logic, and with powerful critiques of Peripatetic and Stoic ideas on motion. In his psychology, he favoured a Platonic tripartite soul over the Stoic unity, bringing the evidence of anatomy to support his case, in the same way as he used Aristotelian ideas on mixture to explain changes in the physical humours. His 'philosophical autobiography', On My Own Opinions, reveals the interactions between his medicine and his philosophy, as well as the limits he placed on certitude.

Galen's monotheistic views, his ardent belief in teleology, and his religious attitude—even anatomy was a veneration of God, and he was convinced of the personal protection of Asclepius—foreshadow the Middle Ages. His dominant influence on later generations, comparable only to that of Aristotle, is based on his achievements as scientist, logician, and universal scholar, and on his own self-proclaimed insistence on establishing a medicine that was beyond all sectarianism. The dissension of earlier science could be conquered by an eclectic rationality based ultimately on notions in which all shared, and be turned into a stable system of Galenic medical and practical philosophy.

L.E.; V.N.

Galerius (Gaius Galerius Valerius Maximianus; originally named Maximinus), of peasant stock, was born in the 250s AD on the Danube at a place he later renamed Romulianum after his mother Romula. A herdsman, tough and uneducated, he rose high in the army and (perhaps) became praetorian prefect of *Diocletian, to whom his loyalty was unswerving. On the establishment of the tetrarchy Diocletian proclaimed him Caesar (293); he divorced his wife and married Diocletian's daughter Valeria. He appears to have been in Egypt from 293–5. Defending the frontier with Persia against an attack by Narses, he was severely defeated between Carrhae and Callinicum (297), but raising reinforcements from the Balkans he attacked through Armenia, marched down the Tigris, advanced to Ctesiphon and returned up the Euphrates, gaining total victory (298). The peace treaty was entirely favourable to Rome: substantial territory was annexed. Thereafter he moved to the Danube provinces. Various campaigns against the Marcomanni, Carpi, and Sarmatians followed; he settled many Sarmatians within the empire. His religious views coincided with those of Diocletian. Prompted, it is said, by his mother, he urged Diocletian to begin the persecution of Christians at Nicomedia (303). On Diocletian's abdication, Galerius became Augustus (1 May 305); his subordination to *Constantius I meant little, as both Caesars, Flavius Valerius Severus and *Maximin, were his men (the latter son of his sister). Along with the Danubian provinces he now took on responsibility for Asia Minor. Senior Augustus from Constantius' death (306), he reluctantly accepted Constantine I as Caesar. The census conducted on Galerius' orders included city populations; at Rome this provoked the rebellion of *Maxentius, whom Galerius refused to recognize, sending the Augustus Severus against him. When Severus was defeated, Galerius invaded Italy but was forced to retreat (307). Summoning Diocletian, he attempted a new settlement of the empire at Carnuntum (11 November 308). Diocletian refused to resume the throne; Galerius appointed *Licinius Augustus, and

declared Maxentius a public enemy. Constantine (see CONSTANTINE I) and Maximin spurned the title *filii Augustorum* (sons of the Augusti), and Galerius recognized them as Augusti (309/10). Suffering from an agonizing illness, he issued an edict ending the Christian persecution (30 April 311) but died very shortly afterwards.

R.P.D.

Gallienus, Roman emperor (Publius Licinius Egnatius Gallienus), son of Valerian, appointed Augustus with him in AD 253. While his father lived, he commanded in the west and fought a series of successful campaigns on the Danube and Rhine. After the capture of Valerian by the Sasanid Persians (260), he faced serious invasions and internal revolts. He dealt with the most threatening of these (the rebellion of Ingenuus, the Alamannic invasion of Italy, and the advance on Rome of Macrianus senior) with dispatch, making excellent use of the generals he had promoted through the ranks. He then adopted a policy of studied inaction, in effect accepting a tripartite division of the empire. In the east, Septimius Odenaethus of Palmyra (see ZENOBIA) first disposed of Gallienus' remaining opponents (Ballista, Quietus) then, as *dux* and *corrector totius Orientis*, was allowed to supervise and defend the region in the emperor's name. In the west, Gallienus left the usurper Postumus in peace until the abortive campaign of 265, and did not trouble him thereafter. Gallienus thus gave himself the opportunity to consolidate his hold over his 'central' empire (Italy, North Africa, Egypt, the Danubian provinces, and Greece), and pursue significant military, political, cultural, and religious activities. In 268, however, he had to undertake a major campaign in the Balkans, where renewed Gothic invasions over the Black Sea and the Danube had, in 267, resulted in the sacking of Athens and other major Greek cities. He won an important victory on the Nestus, but was unable to exploit it because he had to return to northern Italy to deal with the mutiny of Aureolus. Though he quickly contained the insurrection, he was murdered by his staff officers as he besieged Aureolus in Milan.

The Latin literary tradition is uniformly hostile to Gallienus, probably because he excluded senators from military commands. Modern scholarship tended to rehabilitate his reputation, stressing his recognition of the need for change (e.g. in professionalizing the army, and making greater use of cavalry) and his prudent husbanding of scarce resources. Yet the disenchantment of his senior marshals—who owed their own careers to his patronage—indicates the need for caution; and recent studies have been more qualified in their assessment of him.

B.H.W.; J.F.Dr.

Gellius, Aulus, Roman miscellanist, born between AD 125 and 128, author of *Noctes Atticae* ('Attic Nights') in twenty books. Internal evidence suggests publication *c*.180; an apparent echo in *Apuleius' *Apology*, sometimes used to support an earlier date, can be otherwise explained. A probable reference in *Fronto apart, all knowledge of Gellius comes from his work: reconstruction of his life depends on the assumption, so far unfalsified, that his anecdotes, even if fictitious, are not anachronistic. There are slight but uncertain indications that he came from a *colonia* in Africa: however, most of his life was spent at Rome. He studied with Sulpicius Apollinaris, and knew Fronto; but the deepest impression was made on him by *Favorinus. He spent at least a year in Athens completing his education as a pupil of Calvenus Taurus; he visited Tiberius Claudius Atticus Herodes in his summer retreat at Cephisia, attended the Pythian Games of (probably) August 147, and enjoyed the life of a student and a tourist. After his return he was appointed a judge to try private cases (14. 2. 1); but his interest in the law is essentially antiquarian.

The *Noctes Atticae* (of which we lack the start of the preface, the end of bk. 20, and all bk. 8 except the chapter-headings) is a collection of mainly short chapters, based on notes or excerpts he had made in reading, on a great variety of topics in philosophy, history, law, but above all grammar in its ancient sense, including literary and textual criticism. According to his preface, Gellius conceived the notion of giving literary form to his notes during the long winter's nights in Attica (whence the title), but completed the project (some 30 years later) as an instructive entertainment for his children. Variety and charm are imparted by the constant changes of topic, purportedly reproducing the chance order of Gellius' notes (a cliché of such works), and by the use of dia-

logue and reminiscence as literary forms for conveying information; the dramatizations are generally fictitious, though in settings based on Gellius' own experience. The characters of Gellius' friends and teachers are finely drawn; the fictitious persons are less individual.

Gellius is well read in Latin, less so in Greek (though he shows some knowledge of Homeric scholarship); his judgement is sensible rather than incisive. His style blends the archaic, the self-consciously classical, and the new: he lifts words from early authors but also invents new ones, he construes *plenus* only with the genitive but occasionally admits *quod* clauses instead of accusative and infinitive. He shares the age's preference for Early Latin and *Sallust over Augustan and Silver writers, but admires *Virgil and will hear no ill of *Cicero (10. 3; 17. 5); most striking, however, is his liking for Claudius Quadrigarius, of whom he supplies almost half the extant fragments.

In later antiquity Gellius was diligently read by Nonius Marcellus, *Ammianus, and *Macrobius; in the Middle Ages he was excerpted in several florilegia. For the Renaissance he was a well-spring of learning and a model for humanistic writing; though displaced from his central position and disparaged along with his age, he has never lacked readers who relish not only the information he conveys, the quotations he preserves, and the reflections he arouses, but also the charm of his style and his infectious love of books.

L.A.H.-S.

Gelon, son of Deinomenes, greatest of Sicilian tyrants before *Dionysius I; he was the tyrant Hippocrates' master-of-horse, and on his death (*c*.491 BC), seized the tyranny of Gela. He formed an alliance with Theron of Acragas, married his daughter Damarete, and with him fought the Phoenicians of western Sicily. He restored the exiled aristocracy (*gamoroi*) of Syracuse (485), but seized the city, which became the seat of his power; his brother Hieron became ruler of Gela. He enlarged his empire by alliance (Leontini) and conquest (Camarina, a town called Euboea, and Megara Hyblaea were incorporated in the Syracusan state). He transferred half the population of Gela to Syracuse. In these ways he built up the strongest single military power in Hellas. The growth of his power, allied to Theron's, alarmed Anaxilas of Messana (Messina), Terillus of Himera, and the Phoenicians; and from 483, Carthage prepared for war. Gelon was prevented from helping the metropolitan Greeks against Xerxes by Hamilcar's arrival in NW Sicily; and he probably deposited a large sum at Delphi, to buy off Xerxes, if victorious. The victory of Himera (480) left Gelon, by alliances and the submission of his enemies, virtually the overlord of Sicily, and gave two generations of peace with Carthage. Gelon was now the accepted ruler of Syracuse (the story that he was acclaimed general plenipotentiary is much later, perhaps invented by *Philistus). He enfranchised 10,000 mercenaries, and built temples at Himera and Syracuse, where his public works, and peace, gave great prosperity, and his reign was looked back on as a golden age. He died in 478/7, and was succeeded by Hieron.   B.M.C.

Germanicus, Germanicus Iulius Caesar (before adoption Nero Claudius Drusus Germanicus), elder son of *Drusus and Antonia, was born 24 May 15 or 16 BC and adopted in AD 4 by his uncle *Tiberius. As Tiberius was immediately adopted by *Augustus, Germanicus became a member of the Julian *gens* (family) in the direct line of succession; and his career was accelerated by special dispensations. He served under Tiberius in Pannonia (7–9), and Germany (11). In 12 he was consul, and in 13, as commander-in-chief in Gaul and Germany, he won his first salutation as *imperator* (EJ 368: 'general', an honorific title) in a campaign against the Germans, clearing them out of Gaul and re-establishing order there. By now he was a popular figure, held like his father to entertain 'republican' sentiments, and his affability contrasted with Tiberius' dour reserve. But, though by no means incapable, he was over-emotional, and his judgement was unsteady. When, on the death of Augustus, the lower Rhine legions mutinied, his loyalty was proof against the (perhaps malicious) suggestion that he should supplant Tiberius, but his handling of the situation lacked firmness: he resorted to theatrical appeals and committed the emperor to accepting the mutineers' demands. On dynastic matters the two were at one, but their political style was different, and there was soon a marked difference of

view as to how Germany should be handled, Tiberius adhering to the precept of the dying Augustus that rejected immediate territorial advance.

In the autumn of 14 Germanicus led the repentant legions briefly against the Marsi. But he was eager to emulate his father and reconquer parts of Germany lost after the defeat of *Quinctilius Varus. He campaigned in the spring of 15 against the Chatti, Cherusci, and Marsi, and rescued the pro-Roman Cheruscan Segestes from Arminius. In the summer he attacked the Bructeri, reached the saltus Teutoburgiensis (district near mod. Kalkriese in Germany where Varus had been defeated), paid the last honours to Varus, and recovered legionary standards: after an indecisive battle with the Cherusci under Arminius, his forces suffered heavy losses on their way back. For the main campaign of 16 a great fleet was prepared and the troops were transported via his father's canal and the lakes of Holland to the Ems, whence they proceeded to the Weser and defeated Arminius in two battles at Idistaviso (near Minden) and somewhat to the north; the fleet suffered considerable damage from a storm on its homeward journey.

Although Germanicus claimed that one more campaign would bring the Germans to their knees, Tiberius judged that results did not justify the drain on Roman resources, and recalled him to a triumph (victory-procession, 26 May 17) and a command to reorder the 'overseas' provinces as proconsul with *maius imperium* (supreme military and civil authority, but subordinate to that of Tiberius). Germanicus entered on his second consulship (18) at Nicopolis in Epirus, crowned Zeno, son of Polemon, king of Armenia (so winning an *ovatio*—a lesser honour than a triumph), and reduced Cappadocia and Commagene to provincial status. In 19 he offended Tiberius by entering Egypt, which Augustus had barred to senators without permission, and by the informal dress he wore there; his reception was tumultuous (EJ 320(b), 379; Smallwood, *Docs. . . . Gaius* 370, lines 24–7). On his return to Syria the enmity between him and Gnaeus Calpurnius Piso, whom Tiberius had appointed governor as a check on Germanicus, led to his ordering Piso to leave the province. He fell mysteriously ill, and on 10 October died near Antioch, convinced that

Piso had poisoned him. His death—compared by some with that of *Alexander the Great—provoked widespread demonstrations of grief and in Rome suspicion and resentment; many honours were paid to his memory; his ashes were deposited in the mausoleum of Augustus at Rome. His reputation remained as an overwhelming political advantage to his brother and descendants.

Germanicus married *Agrippina the Elder, the daughter of *Agrippa and *Julia. She bore him nine children, among whom were Nero Julius Caesar (d. 31), Drusus Julius Caesar (d. 33), *Gaius (1) (later emperor), *Agrippina the Younger, Julia Drusilla, and Julia. Eloquent and studious, he wrote comedies in Greek (all lost) and Greek and Latin epigrams; he also translated into Latin the *Phaenomena* of *Aratus (1), bringing it up to date and adding further matter on the planets and the weather.   A.M.; T.J.C.; B.M.L.

Gracchus, Gaius Sempronius, younger brother of Tiberius *Gracchus, served under his cousin and brother-in-law *Scipio Aemilianus at Numantia. A member of his brother's land commission, he supported the plans of Marcus Fulvius Flaccus in 126 BC, then went to Sardinia as quaestor. Returning before his commander in 124, he was accused before the censors but acquitted, and elected tribune for 123 and again for 122, when he was joined by Flaccus, by then *consularis* (an ex-consul) and *triumphalis* (celebrator of a triumph, i.e. a victory procession at Rome). After laws meant to avenge his brother and secure himself against a similar fate, he embarked on a programme of reform, aided by friendly colleagues. The most important measures were: (1) a *lex frumentaria* (corn law) assuring citizens of wheat, normally at a subsidized price; (2) laws providing for the resumption of land distribution and the foundation of colonies, including one on the ritually cursed site of Carthage, which Gracchus himself, as commissioner, helped to establish; (3) laws regulating army service and providing for public works—all these to gain the support of the *plebs* and relieve poverty and exploitation; (4) a law to have the *decuma* ('tithe', a tax) of the new province of Asia sold by the censors in Rome; (5) laws (probably two) regulating *repetundae* (provincial corruption) trials, the second (passed by Manius Acilius Glabrio) introducing elements of criminal procedure

and taking juries from the *equites* (knights)—these to protect provincials from magistrates' rapacity, to secure the treasury's major revenue against peculation, and to set up members of the non-political class to control politicians; (6) a law to make the senate's designation of consular provinces immune to tribunician veto and to have it before the elections—this to remove the most important administrative decision of the year from personal prejudice. This law shows how far he was from being a 'democrat'.

Finally, in 122, he proposed to offer citizenship to Latins and Latin status to Italian allies, both to protect them from the excesses of Roman magistrates and to make them subject to his brother's agrarian law. The law was opposed by Gaius Fannius, whom he had supported for the consulship, and by *Livius Drusus (1), who outbid him with an unrealistic colonial programme. It was defeated, and Gracchus was not re-elected. In 121, with his legislation under attack, Gracchus, supported by Flaccus, resorted to armed insurrection. It was suppressed after the first use of the so-called *senatus consultum ultimum* ('ultimate decree' of the senate, in effect a declaration of a state of emergency); they and many of their supporters were killed, others executed after arrest.

Gaius Gracchus had more ambitious plans than his brother, whose memory he revered. He saw the need for major administrative reforms. A proud aristocrat, he wanted to leave the senate in charge of directing policy and the magistrates in charge of its execution, subject to constitutional checks and removed from financial temptation, with the people sharing in the profits of empire without excessive exploitation of the subjects. The ultimate result of his legislation was to set up the *publicani* (tax farmers) as a new exploiting class, not restrained by a tradition of service or by accountability at law. But this did not become clear for a generation, and he cannot be blamed for not foreseeing it.

                                                        E.B.

Gracchus, Tiberius Sempronius, son of Tiberius Sempronius Gracchus (consul 177 BC) and of *Cornelia, served at Carthage under his cousin *Scipio Aemilianus, who married his sister. As quaestor in Spain (137 BC), he used his father's connections to save the army of Gaius Hostilius Mancinus by a treaty later disowned by the senate on Scipio's motion. Thus attacked in his *fides* (good faith), he joined a group hostile to Scipio: his father-in-law Appius Claudius Pulcher, *princeps senatus* (First Senator) and augur (member of the college of official diviners); the consul for 133 Publius Mucius Scaevola and his brother Publius Licinius Crassus Dives Mucianus, both eminent lawyers and *pontifices* (members of one of the four major priestly colleges). As tribune 133, in Scipio's absence, he proposed, with their aid and advice, a law designed to solve Rome's interlocking problems: departure or expulsion of small landowners from their properties, leading to insuperable difficulties in recruiting armies; danger from increasing numbers of slaves; and lack of an assured food supply for the capital. The law reaffirmed the long-ignored limit of 500 *iugera* (*c.*135 *ha.*) of arable public land per person and instituted a commission (to which he, his brother Gaius (see above) and his father-in-law were ultimately elected) to find and confiscate surplus land and distribute it in small lots to poor citizens. A compromise offering 250 additional *iugera* for each child was withdrawn when it failed to secure its opponents' acceptance of the law. Following good precedent and with his eminent supporters' approval, he submitted the law to the *plebs* without previous discussion in the senate. It was vetoed by Marcus Octavius, taken to the senate for adjudication, and rejected. Gracchus none the less resubmitted it, and Octavius persisted in his veto, both contrary to *mos maiorum* (ancestral custom). To end the unprecedented impasse Gracchus had Octavius removed from office—again an unprecedented step, but without objection by the other tribunes, who did not veto it. When Pergamene envoys brought news of *Attalus III's death and will, leaving his estate to Rome, Gracchus (with whom they probably stayed owing to his father's *hospitium* (guest-friendship) with the dynasty) proposed to prejudge the issue of acceptance, ignoring the senate's traditional right to guide foreign affairs, and to distribute Attalus' property to Roman citizens, perhaps as equipment grants for his new allotment-holders.

He next sought re-election, to escape certain conviction on charges of *perduellio* (activity hostile to the state). This last unpre-

cedented step alienated earlier supporters and increased fear of tyranny among opponents. When the consul Scaevola refused to stop him by force, the *pontifex maximus* (senior *pontifex*) Publius Cornelius Scipio Nasica Serapio led a mob of senators and their clients 'to save the Republic'. Gracchus and many of his supporters were killed on the Capitol, others were later punished by a commission under Publius Popillius Laenas, consul 132. The land commission, however, continued unimpeded until 129 (see SCIPIO AEMILIANUS).

His tribunate marks the beginning of 'the Roman Revolution': the introduction of murder into politics and the breakdown of *concordia* (the tradition of not pushing legal powers to extremes) on which the republic was based. See also GRACCHUS, GAIUS.

E.B.

Grattius 'Faliscus' (less correct 'Gratius', Buecheler, *Rh. Mus.* 1880, 407: *CIL* 6. 19117 ff.: his connection with Falerii, based on 1. 40, and the epithet 'Faliscus' reported from a lost MS, are not universally accepted), Augustan poet contemporary with *Ovid before AD 8 (*Pont.* 4. 16. 34), has one extant work in about 540 hexameters, the *Cynegetica*. In it he treats of the chase and especially the management of dogs for hunting. It is difficult to decide whether he owes anything to *Xenophon (or pseudo-Xenophon) and the tradition of hunting literature; for his list of breeds of dogs he may have used an Alexandrian source. The Latin influence most operative upon him is that of *Virgil's *Georgics*; but he also borrowed from the *Aeneid* and Ovid, much less from *Lucretius. Authorities differ as to his influence on the similar poem by *Nemesianus.

The earlier part of his work, after a proem, deals with equipment for capturing game (nets, snares, spears, and arrows); the remaining part (150–541) deals with huntsmen, dogs, and horses. Here, the allotment of nearly 300 lines to dogs (their breeding, points, and ailments) justifies his title. Grattius diversifies his theme by the introduction of episodes, a eulogy on the chase, the accounts of two clever huntsmen (Dercylus (95 ff.) and Hagnon (213 ff.)), the homily on the deleterious effects of luxurious fare on human beings (somewhat amusingly juxtaposed with plain feeding for dogs), and two descriptive passages, a Sicilian grotto (430 ff.) and a sacrifice to the huntress Diana (483 ff.). The concluding portion on horses is mutilated. Grattius' diction—which includes numerous technical terms and *hapax legomena*—and versification are Augustan, but he does not always express himself lucidly. How far his inadequacies are to be ascribed to his exiguous MS tradition (Vindob. 277 (8th–9th cent.) is the sole independent witness) is uncertain.   A.Schi.

Gregory I, the Great, pope AD 590–604, of senatorial and papal family; probable prefect of Rome *c.*573; subsequently monk; deacon, 578; *apocrisiarius* (lit. 'delegate', a church official) at Constantinople, 579–585/6 (despite his poor Greek); then adviser to Pope Pelagius II. When pope, despite ill-health, he valiantly administered a Rome stricken by flood, plague, and famine, shrunken in population and isolated and threatened by Arian and pagan Lombards. He reorganized papal estates for Rome's supply, centralizing their administration through appointments, paid imperial troops, appointed officers, and negotiated with the Lombards. He devotedly served the Byzantine empire as the 'holy commonwealth', but sometimes acted independently of emperor and exarchs. Warfare and political fragmentation limited his powers, but expectation of the Day of Judgement sharpened his sense of spiritual responsibility for the world. As churchman, he upheld ecclesiastical discipline in Italy and Dalmatia, maintained authority in the vicariate of Illyricum, restructured the dioceses of his dwindling patriarchate, and laboured to convert Jews and pagan rustics. He urged Church reform on the Merovingians, reviving the vicariate of Arles at their request. He struggled (against imperial opposition) to end the Three Chapters schism in Venetia and Istria, and (with small success, and perhaps small need) to suppress African Donatism. He worked to convert the Lombards through queen Theodelinda, and organized a mission to the Anglo-Saxons (596). In the east, he maintained papal appellate jurisdiction, and was friendly with the patriarchs of Alexandria and Antioch. With Constantinople, he quarrelled over its patriarch's title Oecumenical, wrongly seen as challenging Rome's primacy. Generally, though, he was sensitive to local religious traditions.

A contemplative at heart, he saw episcopal duties as a necessary, but uncongenial extension of his monastic vocation into the secular world. His diaconal appointments favoured monks, alienating Rome's secular clergy. No original theologian, he was an eloquent moralizer and mystic, striving to make sense of his beleaguered world, and transmitting much patristic thought to the Middle Ages. His *Moralia in Iob* proved enormously popular; his *Cura pastoralis* remains a mirror for priest and bishop. His *Dialogues* (whose authenticity has been challenged) inspiringly portrayed the Italian Church as ascetic, preaching, thaumaturgic, but episcopally controlled. His *Homiliae in Ezechielem*, preached to the besieged city, movingly lament Rome's decay. He defended sacred art, reformed the Roman liturgy, and perhaps established a choir school. He conventionally condemned bishop Desiderius of Vienne for inappropriately teaching classical culture, and suspected its influence on potential monks, but conventionally acknowledged its utility in biblical studies; his straightforward, rhythmically skilful prose shows rhetorical training. (Many letters, though, are chancery-drafted.) A chief founder of the papal states, and of papal prestige in the post-Roman west, his leadership, and vigorous sense of Rome's political and Christian traditions, justified his epitaph as 'God's consul'.

S.J.B.B.

Hadrian (Publius Aelius Hadrianus), born AD 76, emperor 117–38. The Aelii of Italica (mod. Santiponce, near Seville) were among the earliest provincial senators; his mother Domitia Paulina was from Gades (mod. Cádiz). When his father died, Hadrian became the ward of *Trajan, his father's cousin, and of Publius Acilius Attianus (85). Early devotion to Greek studies earned the nickname, *Graeculus* ('little Greek'); a passion for hunting was apparent when he visited Italica (90). After the vigintivirate (a minor magistracy), he was tribune in Legio II Adiutrix (95) and V Macedonica (96). Sent to congratulate Trajan on his adoption in 97, he remained in Upper Germany as tribune of XXII Primigenia, under Lucius Julius Ursus Servianus, husband of his sister Paulina. In 100 he married Trajan's great-niece Sabina Augusta, a match arranged by Pompeia Plotina, a devoted supporter. As Trajan's quaestor (101) he had to polish his Latin (his 'rustic accent' was mocked). He joined Trajan for the First Dacian War (101–2); was tribune of the *plebs*; then legate of I Minervia in the Second Dacian War (105–6), perhaps being praetor *in absentia*. He governed Lower Pannonia and was suffect consul (108). When Trajan's closest ally Lucius Licinius Sura died, Hadrian took over as imperial speech-writer. In 112 he was archon at Athens, where he was honoured with a statue; its inscription (*ILS* 308 = Smallwood 109) confirms the career in the SHA. When the Parthian expedition began (October 113), he joined Trajan's staff, becoming governor of Syria at latest in 117; and was designated to a second consulship for 118. His position was thus very strong when Trajan died at Selinus in Cilicia on 8 August 117. The next day his adoption by Trajan was announced. A single aureus with the reverse HADRIANO TRAIANO CAESARI (*BM Coins, Rom. Emp.* 3. lxxxvi, 124) cannot dispel the rumours that Plotina had staged an adoption after Trajan died. Hadrian was disliked by his peers and had rivals, but the army recognized him; the senate had to follow suit. Plotina and the guard prefect Attianus took Trajan's body to Rome, while Hadrian faced the crisis in the east. He abandoned the new provinces (Armenia, Mesopotamia, and Assyria), dismissed Trajan's favourite Lusius Quietus from his command in Judaea, and probably wintered at Nicomedia, leaving Catilius Severus as governor of Syria. A rising in Mauretania, no doubt provoked by the dismissal of Quietus, a Moor, was suppressed by Hadrian's friend Quintus Marcius *Turbo. Britain was also disturbed; Quintus Pompeius Falco, governor of Lower Moesia, was probably sent to Britain to restore control when Hadrian reached the Danube in spring 118. He negotiated with the Roxolani and evidently evacuated the Transdanubian part of Lower Moesia annexed by Trajan. Gaius Julius Quadratus Bassus, governor of Dacia, had died campaigning; Hadrian summoned Turbo to govern part of Dacia, with Lower Pannonia. Dacia was divided into three provinces. Turbo, an equestrian, was given the same rank as a prefect of Egypt.

Meanwhile Attianus was active. Four ex-consuls, Gaius Avidius Nigrinus, Cornelius Palma Frontonianus, Publilius Celsus, and Lusius Quietus, were killed for plotting treason. When Hadrian reached Rome (9 July 118), the senate was hostile. He claimed not to have ordered the executions but took steps to win popularity. First came a posthumous triumph for Trajan's Parthian 'victory'. Crown-gold (*aurum coronarium*) was remitted for Italy and reduced for the provinces; a new, more generous, largess was disbursed to the *plebs*; overdue tax was cancelled on a vast scale; children supported by the *alimenta* (alimentary foundations for feeding children) received a bounty, bankrupt senators a subsidy; lavish gladiatorial games were held.

Hadrian, consul for the second time for

118, took as colleague Pedanius Fuscus, husband of his niece Julia: Fuscus was a likely heir. In 119 he was consul for the third and last time, and changed guard prefects. One new prefect was Septicius Clarus, to whom the younger Pliny had dedicated his Letters; *Suetonius Tranquillus, protégé of Pliny and Septicius' friend, became *ab epistulis* (in charge of imperial correspondence). The second prefect was Turbo: he was to take charge during Hadrian's absences, together with Marcus Annius Verus, a senator of Spanish origin, linked by kinship to Hadrian. Verus, consul for the second time in 121 and urban prefect, was rewarded by a third consulship in 126. On 21 April 121, the birthday of the city, Hadrian inaugurated a vast temple of Venus and Roma in the forum Romanum, designed by himself: one of many fields in which he dabbled and claimed expertise. A poet, he boasted of his cithara-playing and singing, was expert in mathematics—and in military science. A favourite occupation was debating with sophists or show-orators. *Favorinus yielded: 'who could contradict the Lord of Thirty Legions?' To the legions Hadrian now turned, leaving in 121 for the Rhineland. In Upper Germany and Raetia he erected a continuous palisade, Rome's first artificial *limes* (land boundary), symbolizing his policy of peace within fixed frontiers. Legions and *auxilia*—with a few exceptions—were to remain in the same bases, local recruiting became prevalent. Hadrian set out to improve discipline and training— *Arrian was to dedicate his *Tactica* to Hadrian, registering the emperor's innovations. In 122 he crossed to Britain, taking his friend Platorius Nepos, promoted from Lower Germany to Britain, and VI Victrix. The empress Sabina, the prefect Septicius, and Suetonius also went. An obscure imbroglio involving these three led to the men's dismissal. The main business was 'the wall to separate Romans and barbarians', as the SHA *vita* tersely puts it. Hadrian's Wall was far more elaborate than any other *limes*: the bridge at the eastern end of the wall bore his name, Pons Aelius (Newcastle upon Tyne)— perhaps he designed it. From Britain he made for Spain, via southern Gaul, where he commemorated his horse in verse and Plotina with a basilica (she died early in 123). He wintered at Tarragona, calling a meeting of delegates from the peninsula: military service

was on the agenda. Italica was not favoured with a visit, although—showing disdain— he granted it the status of *colonia* Roman colony). Conscious perhaps of the coming 150th anniversary of 27 BC, Hadrian now shortened his names to Hadrianus *Augustus: a claim to be a new founder of the empire.

A Moorish uprising was dealt with at this time, perhaps without his personal involvement. News from the east determined his next move. Perhaps visiting Cyrenaica *en route*—he resettled refugees from the Jewish uprising in a new city (Hadrianopolis)—his goal was the Euphrates, to confirm peace with Parthia. After an extensive tour of Asia Minor, he sailed (autumn 124) to Athens. There he was initiated in the Eleusinian mysteries, visiting many other cities before his return to Rome, via Sicily, in summer 125. He stayed in Italy for three years, touring the Po valley for six months in 127; during this period he created four 'provinces' in Italy, each with a consular governor. The senate was displeased—*Antoninus Pius abolished them. In 128 he accepted the title *pater patriae* ('father of the fatherland'); then began his last tour with a visit to Africa and Mauretania, creating another *limes*; he lectured the troops at Lambaesis, displaying his knowledge of manœuvres (Smallwood 328). Briefly at Rome in late summer, he crossed to Athens, where he wintered again, dedicated the temple of Olympian Zeus and assumed the name Olympius. After participating in the mysteries (spring 129), he went via Ephesus to Syria, wintering at Antioch, visiting Palmyra in spring 130, and going through Arabia and Judaea to Egypt. In Judaea he founded a Roman colony at Jerusalem (Aelia Capitolina), and banned circumcision: both measures to Hellenize the Jews—a fatal provocation. Hadrian was accompanied not only by Sabina but by a young Bithynian, Antinous: his passion for the youth, embarrassing to many Romans, was a manifestation of his Hellenism. After inspections of *Pompey's and *Alexander the Great's tombs, debates in the Museum, and hunting in the desert, a voyage on the Nile ended in tragedy: Antinous was drowned. Hadrian's extreme grief was only assuaged by declaring his beloved a god (duly worshipped all over the empire) and naming a new city on the Nile (perhaps already planned) Antinoöpolis.

Hadrian went from Egypt to Lycia; by the winter of 131–2 he was back at Athens, to inaugurate the Olympieum and founded the Panhellenion (an organization of Greek cities), the culmination of his philhellenism.

In 132 the Jews rebelled under Bar Kokhba, rapidly gaining control of considerable territory. Hadrian was briefly in Judaea, summoning his foremost general, Sextus Julius Severus, from Britain to crush the revolt. It lasted until 135; by then Hadrian had been back at Rome for a year, worn out and ill, staying mostly at his Tibur (Tivoli) villa. In 136 he turned his mind to the succession. The aged Servianus and his grandson Fuscus had aspirations; but Hadrian hated both and forced them to suicide. To universal surprise, he adopted one of the consuls of 136, as Lucius Aelius Caesar. It may have been remorse for the killing of Nigrinus, Aelius' stepfather, in 118. But Aelius died suddenly on 1 January 138. Hadrian now chose Aurelius *Antoninus (Pius) and ensured the succession far ahead by causing him to adopt in turn his nephew Marcus (= *Marcus Aurelius) and Aelius' young son Lucius (the future emperor Lucius Verus). Marcus, a favourite of Hadrian and grandson of Annius Verus, had been betrothed to Aelius' daughter. Hadrian died (10 July 138) with a quizzical verse address to his restless soul. He was buried in his new mausoleum (Castel Sant'Angelo) and deified by a reluctant senate. An intellectual and reformer (the Perpetual Edict, codified by Salvius Julianus, and the extension of Latin rights were major measures), by his provincial tours, amply commemorated on the coins, by his frontier policy, and promotion of Hellenism, he made a deep impact on the empire.   A.R.Bi.

Hamilcar Barca (probably = Semitic *Baraq*, lightning), father of *Hannibal, took over the command of the Carthaginian fleet in 247 BC and ravaged the coast of Bruttium. Landing in Sicily, he seized Heircte, near Palermo, where he held the Romans at bay by frequent skirmishes, and raided the Italian coast as far as Cumae. In 244 he seized Eryx in Sicily but was unable to raise the siege of Drepana. After the Carthaginian defeat at the battle of the Aegates isles in 241 he negotiated the peace terms and then resigned his command. When attempts to suppress the subsequent revolt of the mercenaries in the service of Carthage

failed, he was appointed to replace his enemy Hanno as commander (240). A bitter struggle, with appalling atrocities on both sides, ended in 238 or 237, when Hamilcar and Hanno were eventually persuaded to cooperate. After the end of the mercenary war he was sent to Spain, taking his 9-year-old son Hannibal with him. Starting from Gades (Cadiz), he conquered southern and southeastern Spain and founded a city at Acra Leuce (?Alicante). In 231 Rome sent an embassy to investigate the situation; Hamilcar replied that the aim of his conquests was to secure money with which to pay the indemnity for the First Punic War. He died in 229, drowned while retreating from the siege of Helice (?Elche). Although the story that he made Hannibal swear an oath never to be a friend of Rome is not incredible, it does not follow that Hamilcar was himself planning war with Rome. But after the loss of Sicily and Sardinia he wanted to add Spain's mineral wealth and manpower to Carthage's resources, thus enabling it to fight a new war effectively when war came.   H.H.S.; J.Br.

Hannibal, Carthaginian general. He was born in 247 BC, the eldest son of *Hamilcar Barca. After making Hannibal swear an oath never to be a friend of Rome, Hamilcar took him to Spain in 237, where he stayed during the commands of both his father and his brother-in-law Hasdrubal, marrying a Spaniard from Castulo. In 221 he assumed the supreme command in Spain on the death of Hasdrubal (confirmed by the popular assembly at Carthage) and reverted to his father's policy by attacking the Olcades, who lived on the upper Anas (Guadiana). In 220 he advanced beyond the Tagus (Tajo) as far as the Durius (Duero), defeating the Vaccaei and the Carpetani. Regarding Rome's alliance with Saguntum (Sagunto) as a threat to Carthage's position in Spain, he decided to defy her, and put pressure on Saguntum. He rejected a Roman protest, and after consulting Carthage began the siege of Saguntum in spring 219, knowing that war with Rome would result, and took the city eight months later.

Hannibal had decided, without waiting for a Roman declaration of war, to take the initiative by invading Italy; probably less with the object of destroying Rome than of detaching her allies (an expectation warranted by Carthage's experience in her wars with the Greeks) and so weakening her that she would give up Sicily, Sardinia, and Corsica, and undertake not to molest Carthage's North African and Spanish empire. He left his capital, Carthago Nova (mod. Cartagena) in May 218, with a professional army of 90,000 infantry and 12,000 cavalry (Iberians, Libyans, and Numidians) and elephants, leaving his brother Hasdrubal to hold Spain; and subdued, regardless of cost, the area between the Ebro and the Pyrenees. He remained there until September, presumably in the expectation of meeting and destroying the army of the consul Publius Cornelius Scipio before invading Italy. Then, with 50,000 infantry, 9,000 cavalry, and 37 elephants, he marched to the Rhône, avoided battle with Scipio (belatedly *en route* to Spain), and continued towards the Alps, which he crossed in about fifteen days, with great difficulty and enormous loss of life. The route he took remains a matter for conjecture: he seems to have marched up the valley of the Isère, past Grenoble, and then perhaps took the difficult Col du Clapier pass, having missed the easier Mt. Cenis pass. He arrived in the area of Turin about the end of October, defeated P. Cornelius Scipio (who had returned to Italy) in a cavalry skirmish at the Ticinus (Ticino) near Pavia, and then, having been joined by many Gauls, won the first major battle of the war at the Treb(b)ia, a little to the west of Placentia (Piacenza), against the combined forces of Scipio and Ti. Sempronius Longus (end of December). In May 217 Hannibal crossed the Apennines (losing an eye in the passage of the Arno), ravaged Etruria, and with the help of early-morning fog, trapped the consul Gaius *Flaminius in an ambush at Lake Trasimene. Flaminius and 15,000 men were killed and 10,000 captured. Hannibal proceeded to Apulia, and thence to Samnium and Campania, while the dictator Quintus *Fabius Maximus Verrucosus embarked on his strategy of following Hannibal but avoiding a pitched battle. Hannibal returned to Apulia (eluding Fabius) for the winter. In 216 he inflicted a devastating defeat on both consuls, who commanded over-strength armies, at Cannae; only 14,500 Romans and allies escaped death or captivity. After each battle he dismissed the Italian prisoners to their homes while holding the Romans (see e.g. Livy 22. 58).

Cannae led to the defection of southern Italy, including Capua (S. Maria Capua Vetere), the second city in Italy, and part of Samnium; but central Italy and all the Latin colonies remained loyal to Rome, and with Roman commanders avoiding another pitched battle, Hannibal achieved little in the following three years (215–213), although he concluded an alliance with *Philip V of Macedon (215), and helped to bring about the revolt of Syracuse (214). He received no assistance from Spain, where Hasdrubal was on the defensive, and little from Carthage. He failed to gain control of a port, despite attacks on Cumae, Neapolis (Naples), Puteoli (Pozzuoli) and Tarentum (Taranto), and his persistent assaults on Nola were repulsed; several towns were recaptured by Rome, notably Casilinum (Capua) and Arpi (near Foggia). In 212, however, he captured Tarentum by stealth, although the citadel remained in Roman control, and this was followed by the defection of three neighbouring Greek cities. In 211, in an attempt to relieve the siege of Capua (begun the previous year), Hannibal marched on Rome itself but failed to force the Romans to withdraw troops from Capua, and returned to the south; soon afterwards Capua fell, its fall being preceded by that of Syracuse. Hannibal was now being pressed ever further south—from 212–11 onwards, with one possible exception, he spent every winter in the extreme south of Italy—and suffered a further blow in 209 when Fabius recaptured Tarentum. In 208, however, he caught both consuls in an ambush in Lucania; one, Marcus Claudius Marcellus, was killed immediately, his colleague fatally wounded. In Spain, Publius Cornelius *Scipio Africanus had captured Carthago Nova (209) and defeated Hasdrubal at Baecula (Bailen) (208). Hasdrubal slipped out of Spain, but in 207 his defeat and death on the Metaurus (Metauro) dashed Hannibal's hopes of receiving reinforcements. Hannibal was now confined to Bruttium, where he stayed until 203—in 205 he could not prevent Scipio recapturing Locri Epizephyrii—when he was recalled to Africa to defend Carthage. After abortive peace negotiations with Scipio, he was decisively defeated at Zama (202), and successfully urged his countrymen to make peace on Rome's terms.

Hannibal now involved himself in domestic affairs; as sufete (chief magistrate) in 196 he introduced constitutional reforms to weaken the power of the oligarchs, and reorganized the state's finances so that the war indemnity could be paid to Rome without levying additional taxes. His enemies reacted by alleging to Rome that Hannibal was intriguing with *Antiochus III the Great of Syria. When a Roman commission of enquiry arrived, Hannibal fled, ultimately reaching Antiochus (195). He urged Antiochus to go to war with Rome; he asked for a fleet and an army with which to stir Carthage to revolt, or, failing that, to land in Italy. He accompanied Antiochus to Greece in 192, and advised him to bring Philip V into the war and invade Italy. In 190, bringing a fleet from Syria to the Aegean, he was defeated by the Rhodians off Side. The peace agreed between Rome and Antiochus provided for his surrender; he fled to Crete and then to Prusias I of Bithynia, whom he supported in his war with *Eumenes II of Pergamum. In 183 or 182 Titus Quinctius *Flamininus persuaded Prusias to surrender Hannibal, a fate which he pre-empted by taking poison.

Hannibal has been widely acknowledged, in both antiquity and modern times, as one of the greatest generals in history. He brought to perfection the art of combining infantry and cavalry, he understood the importance of military intelligence and reconnaissance and he commanded the unflagging loyalty of his troops. But he failed against Rome because all the assumptions upon which his policy and his strategy were based—that huge numbers of Gauls would follow him to Italy, that Carthage would recover the command of the sea and reinforce him from Africa and that Hasdrubal would bring him reinforcements from Spain, and, above all, that Rome's confederation would break up following Rome's defeat in the field—proved fallacious. Roman propaganda accused Hannibal of perfidy and cruelty; as far as the latter charge is concerned, although he could be chivalrous at times, his attitude to those who resisted him was uncompromising. But the record of Rome's treatment of defectors makes far grimmer reading.   B.M.C.

Hecataeus, son of Hegesander, of Miletus, the most important of the early Ionian prose-writers. For his date we depend on Herodotus' account (5. 36, 124–6) of his role in the planning of the Ionian Revolt (500–494 BC); his prudent opposition, based on geopolitical considerations, suggests a relatively senior figure.

Besides improving *Anaximander's map of the world, which he envisaged as a disc encircled by the river Oceanus, he wrote a pioneering work of systematic geography, the *Periēgēsis* or *Periodos gēs* ('Journey round the World'), divided into two books, *Europe* and *Asia* (which included Africa). (We do not know why *Callimachus regarded as spurious the text of the latter known to him.) This offered information about the places and peoples to be encountered on a clockwise coastal voyage round the Mediterranean and the Black Sea, starting at the Straits of Gibraltar and finishing on the Atlantic coast of Morocco, with diversions to the islands of the Mediterranean and inland to Scythia, Persia, India, Egypt, and Nubia. It is uncertain how far his information rested on his own observations, as is the extent of Herodotus' debt to his work. We have over 300 fragments, but many are merely citations in *Stephanus of Byzantium recording the occurrence of a place-name in the *Periēgēsis*.

His mythographic work (study of myth as history), the *Genealogies* (or *Histories* or *Heroologia*) occupied at least four books. We have fewer than 40 fragments; they reveal a rationalizing approach to the legends of families claiming a divine origin (including, apparently, his own (Hdt. 2. 143)). As is shown by his treatment of the stories of Geryon and Cerberus (frs. 26, 27), he evidently believed that behind the fabulous elaborations of tradition lay historical facts distorted by exaggeration or by literal interpretation of metaphors. His opening proclaims his intellectual independence (fr. 1): 'Hecataeus of Miletus speaks thus. I write what seems to me to be true; for the Greeks have many tales which, as it appears to me, are absurd.'

The fragments are too short to give a fair idea of his style; ancient critics regarded it as clear but much less varied and attractive than that of Herodotus.   S.R.W.

Hegesippus (c.390–c.325 BC), Athenian statesman, contemporary with *Demos-thenes, nicknamed *Krōbylos* ('Top-knot') from his old-fashioned hairstyle, an obscure but not unimportant figure. He was already a man of note in the 350s, and in 355 proposed the decree of alliance with Phocis. In the 340s he became prominent as a vigorous oppon-ent of *Philip II, and appears to have been one of the very few Athenian statesmen who opposed the making of the Peace of Philoc-rates (schol. to Dem. 19. 72). In 344/3 he played a decisive part in obstructing the offer of Philip, brought by Python of Byzantium, to turn the Peace into a Common Peace of all the Greeks. With Demosthenes' support, Hegesippus persuaded the Athenians to send him on an embassy to renew their claim on Amphipolis, which they had renounced in 346; as was to be expected, he was unceremo-niously received by Philip, and, when in early 342 Philip made the offer again, Hegesippus exerted himself to secure its final rejection. The speech *De Halonneso* ([Dem.] 7) is now generally agreed to be his contribution to the debate on that occasion (*Dionysius of Hali-carnassus, who accepted it as Demosthenic despite strong contrary indications of style, was not followed by *Libanius). The speech is misleadingly titled from the first topic with which it deals; it is really concerned to answer a letter from Philip *peri tēs epanorthōseōs Tēs eirēnēs* ('on the amendment of the peace') (§ 18 ff.) and manifests a complete refusal to assent to the decisions of 346. His policy was, in short, like that of Demosthenes, to seek a renewal of the war (cf. Plut. *Mor.* 187e and Aeschin. 2. 137). He was still active in politics after the battle of Chaeronea (338), but was not one of the demagogues whose surrender *Alexander the Great demanded in 335.

G.L.C.

Heliodorus, Greek novelist. His ten-book *Ethiopian Story of Theagenes and Charicleia* (*Aithiopika ta peri Theagenēn kai Charikleian*) closes with a signature naming his father as Theodosius 'of the race of the Sun' and their city as Phoenician Emesa. A 4th-cent. date can be argued, not from the Byzantine historian Socrates Scholasticus' (*Hist. eccl.* 5. 22) implausible identification of him with a bishop of Tricca, but from the possible use, in Heliodorus' account of the siege of Syene (9. 3 f.), of *Julian's description of the siege of Nisibis in *Orations* 1 and 3 (of AD 357). But more probably Julian used Heliodorus, allowing the date nearer 230 which is suggested by similarities to *Philo-stratus' *Apollonius* and *Achilles Tatius.

The central figure is Charicleia, born white and hence exposed by her mother the Ethiop-ian queen. Conveyed by a travelling Greek, Charicles, from Ethiopia to Delphi and there given a good Greek education, she became priestess of Artemis, at whose festival she and a Thessalian aristocrat, Theagenes, fall in love. Aided by a priest from Memphis, Cala-siris, searching for Charicleia at her mother's request, they elope, and after many novelistic adventures—pirates, brigands, lustful suitors, false deaths—they at last reach Ethi-opian Meroe, where they escape being sacri-ficed, and Charicleia, recognized by her parents, marries Theagenes.

Heliodorus masterfully launches his reader into mid-story, with a bizarre scene of blood, bodies, and booty on an Egyptian beach viewed through the eyes of mystified brigands. When the couple, seized by other brigands, seem about to reveal their story to readers and to Cnemon, an Athenian assigned to tend them, instead Cnemon tells his own tale, flowing from his stepmother's lust for him, a tale further entwined with theirs in the person of a slave Thisbe, whose murder is for some time thought to be Char-icleia's. We only learn how Charicleia and (much later) Calasiris reached Delphi, and left it, with Theagenes, for Egypt from Cala-siris' long narrative (2. 24. 5 to 5. 1) to the naïve listener Cnemon in Egyptian Chemmis, and further vital action—the discovery that Char-icleia is in Chemmis too (bought by their host Nausicles as Thisbe) delays its completion to 5. 17–32. Thereafter the linear narrative exploits surprise more than suspense, save that we always wonder if the couple will 'really' be reunited.

Recurrent metaphors from the tragic stage and assessments, by characters and author, of the gods' and Fate's role in the universe, invite us to read the work as elevated and deeply serious; Charicleia's outstanding beauty is idealistically conveyed, and just as Theagenes abhors the advances of others so Charicleia persistently defers sex with him until their goal of Ethiopia and marriage. Yet in some scenes Grand Guignol trespasses on the comic, recalling that Calasiris, in a sense a symbol for the author, and the work's only interesting character, combines true piety with mendacious trickery. The novel becomes a *tour de force* in which one literary trick succeeds another. Most are conventional—dreams, oracles, and examples of desriptions (the beach-scene, a carved jewel, siege-works, an oasis, a giraffe)—but Heliodorus' exploitation of them is unusually complex and subtle. His Atticism (imitation of Classical Athenian prose) is careful, and his long periods, with much especially participial subordination, are a better vehicle for extended narrative than the short sentences of Achilles and *Longus. Since Amyot's French translation (1547) there have been numerous others into modern languages, and Heliodorus has influenced both literature (e.g. Sidney's *New Arcadia*, Tasso's *Gerusalemme liberata*, Cervantes' *Persiles*) and painting (e.g. Dubois's Fontainebleau cycle).

E.L.B.

Hellanicus of Lesbos (*c.*480–395 BC) was a mythographer, ethnographer, and chronicler of major significance. Though his background was in the tradition of Ionian *historiē* begun by Hecataeus, he deserves to be ranked with *Herodotus and *Thucydides (Gell. *NA* 15. 23) in the effect he had on the development of Greek historiography. He wrote extensively, but only some 200 fragments have survived.

His five works of mythography (the study of myth as history)—*Phoronis*, *Deukalioneia*, *Atlantis*, *Asopis*, and *Troika*—brought together in a form that was definitive for later scholarship the efforts of earlier mythographers to collate and integrate the disparate corpora of *mythoi* into a coherent and chronologically consistent narrative. The effect of this creative activity upon the whole classical tradition is incalculable.

His ethnographic works (studies of peoples and places) were even more extensive, ranging from areas in Greece (Thessaly, Boeotia, Arcadia, and Lesbos) to foreign countries (Egypt, Cyprus, Scythia, and Persia). They were, however, less influential, partly because they were largely unoriginal, partly because they were overshadowed by the great work of Herodotus.

His other area of interest was the Universal Chronicle. Hellanicus pioneered the use of victor lists (Carnean Games at Sparta) and of magistrates (priestesses of Hera at Argos) to establish a common chronology for Greek history.

He combined all his talents late in life in Athens to create the first local history of Attica, based upon his ordering of the succession of mythical kings and the list of eponymous archons. His *Atthis* (called *Attikē Syngraphē* by Thucydides, 1. 97) covered in two books all Athenian history to the end of the Peloponnesian War. Its tone was influenced by Athenian national propaganda. Thucydides criticized Hellanicus but used his *Priestesses* (2. 2. 1, 4. 133. 2).   P.E.H.

Helvius Cinna, Gaius, a native apparently of Brescia and a friend of *Catullus, with whom he was probably in Bithynia in 57/6 BC (Catull. 10); he seems to have been there also in 66 BC at the end of the Mithradatic War and to have brought back the poet Parthenius to Rome. Cinna was a *doctus poeta*, 'learned poet', of the 'Alexandrian' school; Parthenius probably instilled in him the love of the exceedingly obscure *Euphorion, and he is the likely target of Cicero's barb at *cantores Euphorionis*, 'singers in the manner of Euphorion' (*Tusc.* 3. 45, July 45). His miniature epic *Zmyrna*, the work of nine years (Quint. *Inst.* 10. 4. 4; Catull. 95), was a masterpiece of the 'new' poetry and was much admired (Catull. 95; cf. Virg. *Ecl.* 9. 35). Its subject, the Cyprian legend of the incestuous love of Zmyrna (or Myrrha) for her father, gave opportunity for developing the Alexandrian interest in the psychology of passion, and its allusive learning was such that in Augustan times it already needed a commentary, which was provided by L. Crassicius (Suet. *Gram.* 19). Cinna sent off the young Asinius Pollio on a visit to Greece with a *propempticon* (travel poem); it too needed a commentary (supplied by the writer Julius Hyginus) in Augustan times. He also wrote light verse in a variety of metres. He was tribune in 44 BC and was lynched at Caesar's funeral because he was mistaken for the anti-Caesarian aristocrat Lucius Cornelius Cinna.

E.C.

Helvius Pertinax See PERTINAX.

Hephaestion (d. 324 BC), Macedonian noble. Arguably the most intimate friend of *Alexander the Great, he came to prominence after the death of the Macedonian general Philotas (330), when he shared command of the Companion cavalry with Cleitus the Black. Subsequently he had numerous independent commands, notably the commission to advance down the Kabul valley and bridge the Indus (327). One of the élite bodyguards, he was further distinguished by his elevation to the chiliarchy, the principal ceremonial role at court, and at the mass marriage of Susa (324) his bride (like Alexander's) was a daughter of Darius III, the Persian king. His sudden death at Ecbatana (autumn 324) plunged Alexander into a paroxysm of grief, and a colossally extravagant pyre was planned (but never executed) for his obsequies. His importance is measured by Alexander's affection. Nothing suggests that his abilities were outstanding.   A.B.B.

Heraclides Ponticus, 4th cent. BC philosopher of the Academy. Born of a wealthy and aristocratic family in Heraclea Pontica, he came to *Plato's Academy in Athens as a pupil of Speusippus. Like other Academics, he wrote a version of Plato's lectures *On the Good*; he also studied with *Aristotle, probably while Aristotle was still in the Academic school (he does not really belong to *Die Schule des Aristoteles*, the 'school of Aristotle'). He was placed in temporary charge of the Academy during Plato's third visit to Sicily (361/0) and after the death of Plato's successor *Speusippus (338) he was runner-up for the headship of the school. He returned to Heraclea. He was still alive at the time of Aristotle's death in 322.

The fragments of his writings, mostly dialogues, reveal the wide variety of his interests—ethical, political, physical, historical, and literary. Diog. Laert. 5. 86–8 gives a list of his writings; more are mentioned in other sources.

Heraclides' significance for posterity lies in four directions: in the distinctive form of his dialogues; in physics, particularly astronomy; in his eschatology; and in his contribution to the Pythagorean legend (see PYTHAGORAS). His dialogues were famous for their elaborate proems, their colourful use of historical personages, and the seductive quality of their anecdotes and myths. They influenced *Cicero, whose *De republica* may give some indication of their characteristics, and *Plutarch.

On astronomy, although the evidence is confused and even contradictory, it seems probable that Heraclides held (1) that the universe is infinite; (2) that the earth rotates on its axis once daily from west to east at the centre of the cosmos; (3) that the sun circles around the earth from east to west in the ecliptic once a year; and (4) that the planets Venus and Mercury move in circular orbits with the sun as centre. One repeated testimonium (113 Wehrli) says that he claimed along with certain Pythagoreans that each of the stars is a separate cosmos.

In physics he had a theory of 'seamless masses' (*anarmoi onkoi*), a term also found in testimonia about the physiology of the doctor Asclepiades of Prusias in Bithynia (1st cent. BC). Whatever significance they had for Asclepiades, it seems probable that for Heraclides they represented the elementary particles of Plato's *Timaeus*, which unlike atoms can somehow dissolve into fragments and regroup so as to form a different element.

In a way typical of 4th-cent. philosophy, Heraclides combined this interest in science with an interest in eschatology and in such shamanistic figures, real or invented, as Empedotimus, Abaris, Pythagoras, and *Empedocles. In the vision of Empedotimus (frs. 96 and 98 Wehrli) the soul is described as substantial light, having its origin in the Milky Way.

The list of his works in Diog. Laert. 5. 86 includes several ethical books: *On Justice, On Sōphrosynē, On Piety, On Virtue, On Happiness*, etc. There are also many books on music and poetry. Few fragments of these survive.

D.J.F.

Heraclitus (fl. *c.*500 BC), son of Bloson of Ephesus. Of aristocratic birth, he may have surrendered the (honorific) kingship voluntarily to his brother. He is said to have compiled a book and deposited it in the temple of Artemis. The surviving fragments are aphorisms, dense and cryptic. With implicit self-description, Heraclitus writes that the Delphic god Apollo 'neither says nor conceals, but gives a sign'. The fragments form a cross-referring network rather than a linear argument.

Heraclitus' central concept is that of *logos*, by which he apparently means at once his own discourse, connected discourse and thought in general, and the connected order in things that we apprehend. Most people, he holds, go through life like sleepers, experiencing the world with little understanding, each lost in a private vision. Waking up to the shared public order requires inquiry, sense-experience, and self-examination: 'I went in search of myself.'

The order we experience is a constant process of change; thus, stepping into the same river, we find different waters constantly flowing by us. Change, indeed, is necessary to the maintenance of cosmic order: 'the barley drink separates if it is not stirred.' Criticizing *Anaximander, who had contrasted the strife of the elements with their due order or *Dikē*, Heraclitus insists that *Dikē* is strife, and that nature is comparable to a taut bow, with tensions in opposite directions. Developing his dynamic conception of periodic orderly change, he selects fire as a basic element, in terms of which all things are measured, and whose measures are preserved over time. Stoic thinkers understood him to predict the periodic conflagration of the entire cosmos; they may have been right.

*Aristotle charged Heraclitus with denial of the Principle of Non-Contradiction because he asserts that certain opposites (the way up and the way down, day and night, etc.) are 'one'. Very likely, however, Heraclitus was charting the many ways in which opposites figure in our discourse. Sometimes one and the same thing will be seen to have opposite properties in relation to different observers; sometimes a thing will have opposite properties when viewed from different perspectives; sometimes one opposite cannot be understood or defined without reference to the other opposite. This excavation of the logical structure of language is part of inquiry into nature.

Heraclitus is the first Greek thinker to have a theory of *psychē* or 'soul' as it functions in the living person. He connects *psychē* with both *logos* and fire, and appears to think of it as a dynamic connectedness that can be overwhelmed by a 'watery' condition, which spells death. He connects this idea with praise of temperate living and of those who pursue 'ever-flowing fame' rather than bestial satiety. He attacks the cult of Dionysus and shows disdain for a central aspect of popular religion, saying 'corpses are more to be thrown away than dung'.

In politics he shows aristocratic sympa-thies, but insists on the importance of public law. All human laws, he insists, are nourished by one divine law—presumably speaking of the unitary divinity that he identifies with the changing order of nature.   M.C.N.

Hermesianax, of Colophon, Greek poet of the early 3rd cent. BC, pupil and friend of Philitas, author of *Leontion* and possibly also of *Persica* (fr. 12 Powell). *Leontion* (the title was apparently the name of his mistress) was in elegiacs, and in three books; it may have been modelled on the *Lyde* of *Antimachus. It exemplifies several of the typical features of Hellenistic poetry: a fondness for linguistic rarities, interest in love (esp. if unhappy), and stress on aetiology. Fr. 1 (from bk. 1) describes Polyphemus gazing out to sea, which suggests a reworking of the Polyphemus–Galatea story from Philoxenus (himself mentioned in fr. 7. 69–74); frs. 2 and 3 (Daphnis and Menalcas) may belong to the same book, possibly devoted to the love affairs of herdsmen. Book 2 included the tale of Arceophon's rejection by Arsinoë, and her subsequent metamorphosis into stone (fr. 4 = Ant. Lib. *Met.* 39) and possibly also the story of Leucippus' incest (fr. 5 = Parth. *Amat. narr.* 5). The longest fragment (7), 98 lines long, is preserved, in a corrupt form, by Athenaeus (13. 597b); it consists of a fanciful catalogue of love affairs of poets from Orpheus to Philitas, and of philosophers (*Pythagoras, *Socrates, Aristippus). Typically, the poets' subject-matter is presented as biographical evidence, and some of the pairings can hardly be meant to be taken seriously (e.g. *Homer and Penelope, *Hesiod and 'Ehoea'; *Alcaeus and *Anacreon are, anachronistically, rivals for the love of *Sappho; Socrates courts Aspasia). Fr. 8 mentions an elegy for the Centaur Eurytion, which strongly supports the ascription to Hermesianax of the newly recovered poem preserved in *PBrux.* 8934 and *PSorbonn.* 2254 (= *Suppl. Hell.* 970).   F.W.

Hermogenianus, Aurelius (?), a Roman lawyer of the late 3rd and early 4th cent. AD; of a systematic cast of mind, he came from the eastern empire and, to judge from evidence both of style and access to material, was *Diocletian's *magister libellorum* (master of petitions) from the beginning of AD 293 to the end of 294, after which he probably served *Maximian in the west in the same capacity.

He used the spare and uncompromising rescripts (replies to petitions) which he drafted in that capacity, along with some western material, as the basis for his compilation of imperial laws (*Codex Hermogenianus*), probably completed in Milan in 295. Two further editions were published in the author's lifetime, at least one more after his death. His *Codex* remained in use until superseded by *Justinian's *Codex* of 528, which incorporated many of its laws. Around 300 Hermogenianus wrote six books (*libri*) of *Iuris epitomae* ('Summaries of the Law'), a synopsis of classical legal writing, in which the sources are not identified. An inscription uncovered in Brescia in 1983 shows that an Aurelius Hermogenianus, probably the same man, became praetorian prefect under *Constantius Caesar not later than 305. He is important as the first lawyer who made an effort to reduce the law to a small number of basic principles, such as respect for the individual will, from which solutions to concrete problems could be deduced. This effort was further developed by the natural law and historical schools of jurisprudence from the 17th cent. onwards. T.Hon.

Herod the Great (*c.*73–4 BC), son of the Idumaean Antipater, was through him made governor of Galilee in 47 BC and then, with his brother, designated tetrarch by Mark *Antony. Herod escaped the Parthian invasion of 40, and, while the Parthian nominee, the Hasmonean prince Antigonus, occupied the throne, Herod was declared king of Judaea by Antony and the senate. In 37, having married Mariamme, granddaughter to both of the feuding Hasmoneans, Hyrcanus and Aristobulus, Herod took Jerusalem, with the assistance of Gaius Sosius. Octavian (the future *Augustus), whom Herod supported at the battle of Actium, confirmed his rule, adding a number of cities. In 23, Herod received territories north-east of the Sea of Galilee—Trachonitis, Batanea, and Auranitis. Herod's rule meant that the kingship and high priesthood were now again separate in Judaea, though the latter was in the king's gift: he promoted a new high-priestly class, centred on a handful of diaspora families, who thus acquired great wealth and standing. The palace élite, of mixed ethnic affiliation, also grew. Herod was an able administrator and a skilful financier. He taxed the country heavily, but also developed its resources, to which end his artificial harbour at Caesarea contributed. Spectacular building projects were a hallmark of his reign, including the rebuilding of Samaria as Sebaste, a characteristic string of fortress-palaces, most notably Masada, and Herodium, also his burial place. Jerusalem acquired an amphitheatre as well as a theatre, whose decorations aroused the suspicion of some Jews. But his greatest undertaking, the rebuilding of the Temple, was left entirely to priests, to preserve purity. There, offence was given by a golden eagle put over the gate at the very end of his reign, a time when tensions with the Pharisees, earlier his friends, were running high. Lavish donations outside Palestine established Herod as a benefactor on an empire-wide scale, as well as a flamboyant philhellene; the Olympian games and the city of Athens were among the beneficiaries. Through his personal good offices, his visits to Rome, and the mediation of *Nicolaus and of Marcus *Agrippa, Herod long retained Augustus' confidence. He may have been exempt from tribute. But, in 9 BC, an unauthorized war against the Nabataeans incurred imperial displeasure. Also increasingly unacceptable was his savagery towards the large family produced by his ten wives: intrigues led him to execute his favourite, Mariamme I, in 29, her two sons in 7, and his eldest son and expected heir a few days before his death. Serious disturbances then allowed Roman intervention, and the division of his kingdom between his remaining sons, Herod Antipas, Archelaus, and Philip, was formalized. T.R.

Herodas, or perhaps **Herondas,** composer of *mimiamboi* in choliambics (iambic trimeters in which the penultimate syllable is long). Seven poems survive more or less complete on a papyrus published in 1891, an eighth (*The Dream*) is partially legible, and there are scraps of others; they range in length from 79 to 129 verses and are transmitted with individual titles. Herodas was probably active in the middle of the 3rd cent. BC. Poem 2 and probably 4 are set on Cos; poem 1 is set outside Egypt but refers to the glories of Alexandria, and poem 8 very likely refers to the literary squabbles of the Alexandrian Museum; *Pliny the Younger names Herodas in the same context as Callimachus (*Ep.* 4. 3. 4). Herodas, like *Callimachus in his *Iamboi*, claims the poet Hipponax (6th cent BC) as his authorizing model for the use of choliambics (poem 8), and the *mimiamboi* are written in a creative, literary approximation to the Ionic of Hipponax. In style and theme, however, Herodas is more indebted to comedy and the mime tradition of Sophron of Syracuse (5th cent. BC); there is as yet no passage of Herodas that approaches the sexual and scatological explicitness of the Archaic iambus.

Each *mimiambus*, except poem 8, has more than one speaking 'part', even if minimally so (poem 2); each poem assumes the presence of mute extras. It has been hotly debated whether they were originally composed only to be read, to be performed by a single mime, or by a troupe. Their learned character suggests that Herodas envisaged the possibility of a reading audience—he may even have arranged them into a collection—but it is not possible to decide on internal grounds how they were originally performed; the onus of proof, however, falls on those who deny that some at least were acted by a small troupe of players.

(1) *The Procuress.* An old woman seeks to persuade a younger one to take a new lover while her current man (? husband) is away in Egypt. The theme is familiar from comedy and Roman elegy (Prop. 4. 5; Ov. *Am.* 1. 8). (2) *The Brothel-keeper.* A brothel-keeper prosecutes a client before a Coan court for stealing one of his girls and damaging his house. The speech is a masterpiece of shameless rhetoric and inversion of the topoi of legal oratory. (3) *The Schoolteacher.* A mother brings her truant son to school to be flogged for neglecting his studies in favour of gambling. (4) *Women Making a Dedication and Sacrifice to Asclepius.* Two women bring a thank-offering to the healing god and admire the artworks in his (probably Coan) temple, cf. Theoc. 15. (5) *The Jealous Woman.* A mistress threatens terrible punishment upon the slave who has been her lover because he has slept with another woman; he is begged off by the intercession of a young female slave. (6) *Women Visiting for a Chat.* A woman called Metro visits a friend (cf. Theoc. 15) to enquire where she got a wonderful leather dildo; after receiving the information she goes off in pursuit of the maker, Kerdon. (7) *The Shoemaker.* Metro brings some friends to

visit Kerdon in his shoe-shop; he shows them his wares. Our memory of poem 6 allows us to sense that more than shoes is involved here. (8) *The Dream.* A master (who turns out to be the poet) relates a dream in which his goat is killed by (?) 'goatherds' who then use its skin in the rustic game of *askoliasmos* (balancing on a wineskin), in which the dreamer himself wins the prize; the god Dionysus and Hipponax also seem to appear in the dream. He interprets the dream to mean that 'amidst the Muses [i.e. probably, 'in the Museum (of Alexandria)'] many men will tear at my songs, the products of my labour' (cf. Callim. fr. 1 Pf.), and he forecasts a position of honour for himself after Hipponax in the history of choliambic verse.

The very diverse background of the *mimiamboi* shows them to be typical of their age—both modern and archaizing, learned and 'low'. They are 'realistic' in the sense that the characters and what they say have 'real life' analogues, but they depend upon an audience which knows how stylized is the view of life presented—that it derives its particular flavour from the transference of comic themes to a mimic mode—and can appreciate the productive clash between versification and language on one side and subject-matter on the other. The *mimiamboi* were perhaps more widely read and appreciated in later antiquity than the very scanty external evidence suggests.   R.L.Hu.

Herodotus, of Halicarnassus (now Bodrum on the Aegean coast of Turkey), historian. 'Herodotus of Halicarnassus' are (in Greek) the first two words of a long historical narrative, the earliest we possess. It looks back to the fall of the Lydian kingdom in western Turkey in 545 BC and forwards to events in the early 420s, during the great war between Athens and Sparta, but it has as its focus and *raison d'être* (1. 1) the 'war between Greeks and non-Greeks', which we call the Persian Wars. We do not know exactly when it was written but it was already familiar in Athens in 425 BC, when *Aristophanes (1) parodied its opening chapters in one of his plays (*Ach.* 515 ff.). We know very little about the life of its author: he nowhere claims to have been an eyewitness or participant in any of the major events or battles that he describes (unlike *Aeschylus), but records conversations with those who were (8. 65, 9. 16) and with the grandsons of those involved in events of the late 6th cent. (3. 54; cf. 3. 160, 4. 43 where Herodotus' informant may well be the exiled grandson of the Persian Zopyrus, referred to in 3. 160). This fits with the dating of his birth traditional in antiquity ('a little before the Persian Wars', Dion. Hal. *Thuc.* 5; '484 BC', Gell. *NA* 15. 23). But the latter date is suspicious: it is 40 years before the foundation of the Athenian colony at Thurii in southern Italy in which Herodotus is said to have taken part and where he is said to have spent the rest of his life and died (Steph. Byz., entry under *Thourioi*: his grave was shown there; Aristotle, *Rh.* 3. 9, already refers to him as 'Herodotus of Thurii'); 40 years is an ancient biographer's formula for his subject's age at a turning-point in his life and the whole chronology may be imaginary. His birthplace, Halicarnassus in Caria, was a Greek city, founded some 500 years earlier, but by Herodotus' time it was subject to Persian control; it lay on the extreme western edge of the great empire that had its administrative centre three months' journey (5. 50) to the east, in Iran. Intermarriage with the neighbouring non-Greek population, who were Carians, was widespread (ML 32) and Herodotus was a cousin of the Halicarnassian epic poet Panyassis, who had a Carian name. He seems to have taken part in political struggles against the Persian-nominated tyrant Lygdamis, grandson of the *Artemisia (1) who figures prominently in his narrative (7. 99; 8. 68–9, 87–8, 93, 101–3); these struggles ended in Panyassis' death and Herodotus' exile. Most of what Herodotus tells us about himself concerns his travels and enquiries (see (3) below). He is likely to have died where his allusions to later events themselves end, in the 420s; he may well have been less than 60 when he died.

2. Herodotus' narrative is built from smaller narratives and from summaries of events that are peripheral to his main concern. These smaller narratives, often told in rich detail and equipped with verbatim reports of many conversations, are sometimes told in Herodotus' own person; sometimes in the special syntax which ancient Greek reserves for things reported on another's authority. They are generally linked by chronological succession (particularly, at the beginning, the succession of eastern kings), and as cause and effect; but some-

times they go temporarily backwards (effect is followed by its explanatory cause in another story) or move sideways, to take in events elsewhere which throw light on something in the main line of the story. Their starting-point is in answer to the question with which Herodotus ends his first sentence: 'What caused Greeks and non-Greeks to go to war?'. After surveying traditions (Persian and Phoenician, according to Herodotus) which traced the origin of the conflict to the reciprocal abduction of legendary princesses (Io, Europa, Medea, Helen: 1. 1–5), Herodotus declares his own view that the story cannot reliably be taken back beyond the reign of the Lydian king Croesus (1. 5), who began the process of absorbing the Greek communities of the Aegean coast into his kingdom and whose fall brought the power of Persia into contact with these communities, which were promptly forced into submission. The first book explains how these events occurred, deals with the Persian conquest of the Median kingdom which embroiled Lydia and led to its annexation by Persia, and continues the expansionist reign of the Persian king Cyrus the Great to his death in battle in 530 BC. Book 2 takes the form of a massive excursus on the geography, customs, and history of Egypt, which was the next target of Persian expansionism, under Cyrus' son and successor, Cambyses. Book 3 continues the reign of Cambyses down to his death in 522 BC, after a failed attempt to invade Ethiopia; it goes on to describe the turmoil that followed and the eventual emergence of Darius I as the new king of Persia, and deals with his administrative settlement of the empire (3. 88–97). Book 4 covers Darius' abortive attempt to subdue the nomadic Scythian tribes who lived to the north and east of the Danube and across southern Russia, and deals also with Persian expansion along the North African coast. Book 5 traces further Persian expansion, into northern Greece and the southern Balkans, and narrates the unsuccessful attempt of the Aegean Greek communities to free themselves from Persian control (the so-called Ionian Revolt: 5. 28–38, 98–6. 42): Herodotus signals, ominously, the fatal support that Athens gave to that revolt (5. 97). Book 6 begins the story that runs continuously to the end of Herodotus' narrative in book 9: the Persian determination to have revenge for Athenian interference in the affairs of its empire and the first seaborne attack on mainland Greece, which was defeated at Marathon in 490 BC. Books 7–9 embrace the huge expedition mounted in 480–479 by Darius' son and successor, Xerxes, and the Greek response to that threat; the opening engagements, at sea off Artemisium and on land at Thermopylae; the climactic battles of Salamis and Plataea, which forced the Persian army and navy to withdraw to the north; and the carrying of the war back across the Aegean, ending in the battle of Mycale, on the Turkish coast opposite Samos. At various points, episodes in the history of Greek communities not at first directly in contact with Persian power, such as Sparta, Athens, Corinth, and Samos, are interleaved, often at length, with the main narrative of Persian expansion as they explain how these communities became involved or failed for a time to be involved, until all are seamlessly joined together in books 7–9.

3. The stories from which Herodotus' narrative is built derive sometimes (as we have seen) from distinguished individuals, sometimes from 'collective' informants ('the Corinthians say . . .'; 'we Spartans have a story . . .'; 'I heard the story in Proconessus and Cyzicus . . .'). Occasionally his source may have been a document (for example, his description of the satrapy system set up by Darius to administer the Persian empire). But the overwhelming mass of his material must derive from oral tradition and that tradition will always have been local, even familial. Thus the overall conception of a narrative that would draw on these local traditions but would connect them so as to span more than 70 years and take in much of the known world was Herodotus' own, and it is his most brilliant and original achievement. Herodotus did not speak any language other than Greek but he writes of interpreters in Egypt (2. 154) and at the Persian court (3. 38, 140), where also there were Greek officials in high places. He writes repeatedly of what was told to him in an astonishing range of places: where he could, he preferred to trust what he could see for himself (2. 99; cf. 2. 147, 4. 81, 5. 59) and could enquire into (Herodotus' word for 'enquiry' is *historiē*, which brought the word 'history' into the languages of Europe). Where he could not, he listened. He writes of enquiries made in the northern Aegean, in southern Italy, round the shores of the Black Sea, in Egypt (where he travelled as far up the Nile as Elephantine, near Aswan: 2. 29), at Dodona in NW Greece, and at Cyrene in Libya; of things seen on the Dnieper in southern Russia; in Babylon on the Euphrates; at Tyre in Lebanon; of talking to Carthaginians and to the inhabitants of Delphi. He is familiar with the geography of Samos, of Attica, and of the Nile delta, which he compares to the mouth of the Acheloüs river in NW Greece, as well as to the coast of Turkey from Troy south to the Maeander. He takes for granted a detailed knowledge of the topography of Delos, of the Athenian Acropolis, and of Delphi. Everywhere he writes of what was said to him by 'the locals'. It is of the essence of Herodotus' method of *historiē* that he builds the process of enquiry into his narrative: he writes not only of his sources, their agreements and disagreements, but also of his own belief and disbelief at what he is told (he is, he writes, under an obligation to report what was said to him, but under no obligation to believe it: 7. 152. 3); sometimes too he records his inability to decide, or the impossibility of arriving at an answer to some question he is enquiring into (sometimes because it is beyond the reach of human memory; sometimes because it lies too far away, too far beyond the limits of his travels). Unlike *Thucydides, he does not present his account of the past as smoothly authoritative, the result of work not to be done again (Thuc. 1. 23) but as one man's struggle, not always successful, to discover and record what heroic men, non-Greek as well as Greek, have achieved, before those achievements are obliterated by time (1. 1).

4. It is not merely Herodotus' travels that cover an astonishing range but also his understanding of the variety of human experience. He does not disguise the fact that the Greek-speaking world was the cultural as well as the geographical centre of his perceptions. But he writes, almost always openmindedly, of the differences that distinguish Persians from Scythians, Babylonians, Indians, and Egyptians, as well as from Greeks. For Egypt, he has a model to help him understand the way their world works: it is simply the world of other men upside down; the Egyptians do the opposite of what is universal elsewhere, just as the Nile behaves in a way that inverts the behaviour of all other rivers by flooding in high summer (2. 35). He

is less sure of what makes Persian culture cohere but describes what seem to him its distinctive features (the features, that is, that make the Persians un-Greek: 1. 131–40). He is relatively unsuccessful too in grasping the 'ideologies' that made one religion different from another. That is hardly surprising: he records religious practice everywhere with precision, but he has nothing to teach him the 'meaning' of ritual, as he has for Greek religion in the epic poems of *Homer and *Hesiod (2. 53). He is sure that for all men, however much they know of other cultures, their own culture is superior (3. 38). But when he is faced with something totally alien to his experience and to Greek experience generally, such as the culture of the Scythian nomads, who have no aspect of permanence to their lives (no statues, altars, or temples, except to Ares, the god of war; no agriculture, no buildings, no walls or settlements even), though he can admire their ability to escape Persian domination by never staying to confront the enemy ('for the rest', he writes, 'I do not like them': 4. 46). They offer him no point of resemblance and they do not fit. None the less, he describes their culture also dispassionately. For Herodotus it is important that things should fit: he is at home with symmetries. He is persuaded of the truth of a story of young Nasamonian tribesmen wandering across the Sahara and finding a great river flowing west–east, because the river they found must have been the Nile. Its identity is guaranteed by the symmetry of its course with that of the Danube, which flows west–east from the Pyrenees and then turns south, as the Nile turns north, to flow out 'opposite the Nile' (2. 32–3)! But such a priori geography exists alongside acute empirical observation of the world around him, as in his defence of the proposition that the land of Lower Egypt is the product of the Nile's silting over ten or twenty thousand years (2. 11–12).

5. Herodotus' vast narrative coheres because it is strung on two lines of connection which pass through time. The first is kinship; the second reciprocity. Reciprocity is the demand that all men respond to what is done to them with like for like ('equals for equals', in Herodotus' own phrase: 1. 2): with good for good and with hurt for hurt. The demands of reciprocity are absolute, admit of no exceptions and, Herodotus believes, are common

to all men. They also outlive time, since they are inherited. The principle of reciprocity is essential to Herodotus' writing: to answer the question 'why did this happen?' it is necessary to ask the further question: 'to what previous act was this act a response?'. The chain of reciprocity may reach far back and encompass many people. Thus the search for a 'beginning' is common to all narrative and it is no surprise that, faced with the question 'why did non-Greeks and Greeks go to war (in the 5th cent. BC)?', Herodotus finds an answer in events far distant in space and more than three generations in the past, with Croesus of Lydia and his 'beginning of wrongful acts against Greeks' (1. 5). It is the logic of reciprocity that explains not only the two Persian invasions of Greece but also, for example, the bitter hostility between Athens and Aegina, which lasted from the mid-6th cent. until the Athenians expelled the Aeginetans from their island in 431 BC (5. 82–7: Herodotus describes it as 'owed from before') and the complex of obligations which tied Persia, Sparta, Corinth, and Corcyra (Corfu) together in their several relationships with Samos over more than a generation (3. 44–53, 139–40). For the most part, the question 'why?' is not a problem for Herodotus. Events that are too uncanny, shocking, or momentous for merely human explanation call into play the actions of divinity which are assumed also to be determined by the logic of reciprocity (1. 90–1, 6. 75, 82, 7. 133–7). He seems too to be at ease with the question of the 'meaning' of events. Both in his own person and also in the person of various 'warners' who appear in his narrative (men such as *Solon; the Egyptian pharaoh Amasis; Xerxes' uncle, the Persian Artabanus, and Croesus, after his downfall), the thread of events seems to be illuminated by general statements: 'human success stays nowhere in the same place', Herodotus (1. 5); 'divinity is jealous and disruptive', 'man is the creature of chance', and 'in everything one must look to the end', 'Solon' (1. 32); 'there is a cycle of human experience: as it revolves, it does not allow the same men always to succeed', 'Croesus' (1. 207). These look to add up to what D. Lateiner (*The Historical Method of Herodotus* (1989)) has called Herodotus' 'historical philosophy'. But they do not in reality fit together; rather they are what ancient Greeks called *gnōmai* (maxims) and their function is closer to that of the proverb than to any 'law' of historical process: they are not discountenanced by contradiction. Nor do references to 'what was going to be', or to motions of a man's 'portion', or 'what is assigned' make Herodotus a historical determinist. Rather they represent the story-teller's sense of the shape of his story. Closer perhaps to the heart of Herodotus' sense of things are 'wonder' (a very Herodotean word) at human achievement, the 'great and wonderful deeds of men' (1. 1) and the emotional undercurrent to events that so often gives his narrative a tragic colour: two compelling and haunting examples are the story of the deadly quarrel between *Periander, the tyrant of Corinth, and his own son (3. 49–53: characteristically, the story is introduced to explain another event, Corinthian and Corcyrean involvement in the affairs of Samos), and the astonishing moment at Abydos when Xerxes, in the act of mounting his great invasion of Greece and engaged in reviewing his vast invasion force, bursts into tears on reflecting that in a hundred years not one of these splendid warriors would be living (7. 45–7: his uncle, Darius' brother Artabanus, replies that more painful still is the fact that in so short a life there was not one who would not, again and again, wish himself dead to escape the distress of living).

6. The singularity of Herodotus' methods and achievement has always meant that he was problematic to his readers. He has been read with most enthusiasm and greatest understanding in periods of the rapid expansion of men's horizons, such as the Hellenistic period of *Alexander the Great's eastern conquests and in the Age of Discovery. But two adverse responses constantly recur: the first that he is a mere storyteller, charming perhaps but not a serious historian (that view, without the acknowledgment of charm, goes back to Thucydides (1. 21–2; cf. Aristotle, *Gen. an.* 3. 5)); the other view is that he is a liar. This view also has ancient supporters (especially *Plutarch in his bizarre essay, *On the Malice of Herodotus*: Plutarch's beloved city of Thebes does not emerge very well from Herodotus' account of events). But it was revived at the end of the last century by Sayce and is currently championed by Fehling and Armayor: Fehling's view would make the untravelled Herodotus the inventor of plausible-sounding encounters with 'those who

should know' about the fantastic events he wishes to pass off as veracious. There are problems, certainly, about believing everything that Herodotus says he saw or was told but they are not so great as the problem of recognizing Fehling's Herodotus in the text that we have. J.P.A.G.

Heron, of Alexandria, (fl. AD 62), mathematician and inventor, was known as *ho mechanikos* ('the inventor'). The following works are associated with his name. (1) *Metrica*, three books, on the measurement of surfaces and bodies, and their division in a given ratio. (2) *Definitions* (*Horoi*), defining geometrical terms and concepts. (3) *Geometrica*, (4) *Stereometrica*, and (5) *On Measures* (*Peri Metron*, all works of practical mensuration. (6) *Pneumatica*, on the construction of devices worked by compressed air, steam and water. (7) *On Automata-making* (*Peri automatopoiikes*), mostly on the construction of *thaumata* ('miracle-working' devices used especially in temples). (8) *Mechanica*, three books (extant only in Arabic, but extensively excerpted by *Pappus book 8), on how to move weights with the least effort, containing (book 1) the foundations of statics and dynamics, (book 2) the five simple machines, (book 3) the building of lifting-machines and presses. (9) *Dioptra*, on the construction and use of a sighting-instrument for measurement at a distance (with additions describing unrelated instruments, e.g. a hodometer). (10) *Catoptrica* (extant only in Latin translation), on the theory and construction of plane and curved mirrors. (11) *Belopoeica*, in the construction of war-catapults. Some of these, notably (3), (4) and (5), can hardly be by Heron in their present form, but all may well be based on treatises by him.

Other works by Heron no longer extant include a commentary on *Euclid's *Elements* (substantial remains in an-Nayrīzī's commentary on Euclid); *Baroulkos*, describing a machine for lifting huge weights by means of a combination of gear-wheels (parts are incorporated into *Mechanica* 1.1 and *Dioptra* 37); *On Water-clocks* (Proclus, *Hypotyp.* 120); and *Cheiroballistra*, another type of artillery weapon (fragmentarily preserved). The *Geodaesia* and *Liber geoponicus* are later compilations, largely extracts from the *Geometrica* and other mensurational works.

Heron, although very adept at both mathematics and applied mechanics, was probably not very original in either. But his mensurational works are of great importance as our main source for practical mathematics in Graeco-Roman antiquity. While classical 'Euclidean' mathematics aimed at constructing and proving theorems, 'Heronic' mathematics was directed towards solving practical problems, if necessary by approximation. Thus, Heron gives examples of approximations to irrational square- and cube- roots. He solves quadratic equations arithmetically, and gives the formula for the area of a triangle, $\triangle = \sqrt{\{(s(s-a)\ (s-b)\ (s-c)\}}$. The origins of this type of mathematics lie in Mesopotamia. In pneumatics, mechanics, and the other sciences too, though Heron often discusses theoretical matters, his purpose is utility and amusement; hence we get detailed descriptions, with figures, of devices such as siphons, a self-regulating lamp, a water-organ, pulley-systems, and a variety of mechanical toys. Although the discovery of the principles behind these, and perhaps many of the devices too, were due to Heron's predecessors, such as Ctesibius, here too he is of major importance as a source.   G.J.T.

Herophilus, of Chalcedon (*c.*330–260 BC), Alexandrian physician, pupil of *Praxagoras of Cos. He and *Erasistratus were the only ancient scientists to perform systematic scientific dissections of human cadavers. If the controversial but unequivocal evidence of several ancient authors is to be trusted, Herophilus also performed systematic vivisectory experiments on convicted criminals—experiments made possible, according to Celsus, only by royal intervention. Herophilus' numerous anatomical achievements included the discovery of the nerves. He distinguished between sensory and 'voluntary' (motor) nerves, described the paths of at least seven pairs of cranial nerves, and recognized the unique characteristics of the optic nerve. The first to observe and name the *calamus scriptorius* (a cavity in the floor of the fourth cerebral ventrical), he called it *kalamos* ('reed pen') because it resembles the carved out groove of a writing pen. His dissection of the eye yielded the distinction between cornea, retina, iris, and chorioid coat.

From his *Anatomica* 1 the first reasonably accurate description of the human liver is preserved. He also identified and named the duodenum (*dōdekadaktylon*). From *Anatomica* 3 fragments concerning the reproductive parts are extant. Using the analogy of the male parts, he discovered the ovaries, which he called the female 'twins' or testicles (*didymoi*, 'twins', being a traditional term for the male testicles). He likewise discovered the Fallopian tubes, but without determining their true course and function. In the male, he meticulously identified previously unknown parts of the spermatic duct system. *Anatomica* 4 seems to have dealt with the anatomy of the vascular system. Adopting Praxagoras' distinction between veins and arteries, he added basic observations on the heart valves, on the chambers of the heart, and on various vascular structures. The *torcular Herophili*, a confluence of several great venous cavities (sinuses) in the skull, was first identified and named (*lēnos*, 'wine vat') by Herophilus.

In his physiopathology, he appears to have accepted the traditional notion that an imbalance between humours or moistures in the body is a principal cause of disease, but he insisted that all causal explanation is provisional or hypothetical. The 'command centre' of the body is in the fourth cerebral ventricle (or in the cerebellum, which is indeed the region responsible for all muscular co-ordination and for the maintenance of equilibrium). From the brain, sensory and motor nerves proceed like offshoots. Neural transmissions, at least in the case of the optic nerve, are said to take place by means of *pneuma* (breath), which is ultimately derived from the air through respiration. Respiration is attributed to the natural tendency of the lungs to dilate and contract through a four-part cycle.

His *On Pulses* (*Peri sphygmōn*) became the foundation of most ancient pulse theories. A faculty (*dynamis*) flowing from the heart through the coats of the arteries causes the regular dilation (*diastolē*) and contraction (*systolē*) of the arteries, which thus 'pull', transport, and distribute a mixture of blood and *pneuma* from the heart throughout the body (the veins, by contrast, contain only blood). Using metrical analogies, he described the relations between diastole and systole as successively assuming pyrrhic, trochaic, spondaic, and iambic rhythms, viz. in infancy, childhood, adulthood, and old age. He had sufficient faith in the diagnostic value of the pulse to construct a portable clepsydra, adjustable for the patient's age, to measure the frequency of his patient's pulses.

Reproductive physiology and pathology are well represented in his extant fragments. His *Midwifery* (*Maieutikon*) apparently tried to demystify the uterus by claiming that it is constituted of the same material elements as the rest of the body and is governed by the same faculties. Although certain 'affections' (*pathē*) are experienced only by women (conception, parturition, lactation), there is no disease peculiar to women. He also discussed the normal duration of pregnancy, causes of difficult childbirth, and whether the foetus is a living being. *Tertullian charges him with possession of an instrument known as 'foetus-slayer' (*embryosphaktēs*) and implies that he performed abortions. Gynaecological issues are also addressed in his *Against Common Opinions* (*Pros tas koinas doxas*): menstruation is helpful to some women, harmful to others.

His semiotic system, known as a 'triple-timed inference from signs' (*trichonos seimeiōsis*), his descriptions of causes and symptoms of many physical and mental disorders, and his threefold classification of dreams are among many further achievements that provoked both acclaim and polemical responses throughout antiquity.
H.V.S.

Hesiod, one of the oldest known Greek poets, often coupled or contrasted with *Homer as the other main representative of early epic. Which was the older of the two was much disputed from the 5th cent. BC on (*Xenophanes in Gell. *NA* 3. 11. 2; Hdt. 2. 53; *Ephorus, *FGrH* 70 F 101, etc.): Homer's priority was carefully argued by *Aristarchus (2), and generally accepted in later antiquity. Hesiod's absolute date is now agreed to fall not far before or after 700 BC. Of his life he tells us something himself: that his father had given up a life of unprofitable sea-trading and moved from Aeolian Cyme to Ascra in Boeotia (*Op.* 633–40); that he, as he tended sheep on Mt. Helicon, had heard the Muses calling him to sing of the gods (*Theog.* 22–35, a celebrated passage); and that he once won a tripod for a song at a funeral contest at Chalcis in Euboea (*Op.* 650–60). For his dispute with Perses see below (2). He is said to have died in Hesperian Locris (Thuc. 3. 96,

etc.), but his tomb was shown at Boeotian Orchomenus (Arist. fr. 565 Rose, *Certamen* 14, Paus. 9. 38. 3). For the story of his meeting and contest with Homer see *Certamen Homeri et Hesiodi* (A. Rzach, Teubner ed. *Hesiod*⁵ (1913), 237 ff.). The poems anciently attributed to him are as follows (only the first three have survived complete, and only the first two have a good claim to be authentic):

1. The *Theogony* (*Theogonia*). The main part of the poem, which is prefaced by a hymn to the Muses (1–104; cf. the *Homeric Hymns*), deals with the origin and genealogies of the gods (including the divine world-masses Earth, Sea, Sky, etc.), and the events that led to the kingship of Zeus: the castration of Uranus by Cronus, and the overthrow of Cronus and the Titans, the 'former gods' (424), by the Olympians. This 'Succession Myth' has striking parallels in Akkadian and Hittite texts, and seems originally to have come from the near east. Hesiod's version shows some stylistic awkwardness and inconcinnity, but is not without power. Interlaced with it are the genealogies, which run smoother. The first powers born are Chaos, Earth, and (significantly) Eros (116–22). From Chaos and Earth, in two separate lines, some 300 gods descend; they include personified abstracts, whose family relationships are clearly meaningful. There is an interesting passage in praise of the un-Homeric goddess Hecate (411–52), further myths, notably the aetiological tale of Prometheus (521–616), and a detailed description of Tartarus (720–819). The poem ends with the marriages of Zeus and the other Olympians, and a list of goddesses who lay with mortal men. This last section, which refers to Latinus (1013), eponymous hero of the Latini, and led on to the *Catalogue* (below, 4), is agreed to be post-Hesiodic, though opinions vary as to where the authentic part ends.

2. The *Works and Days* (*Erga kai Hēmerai*), abbr. '*Op.*'. This poem, apparently composed after the *Theogony* (cf. 11–24 with *Theog.* 225), would be more aptly entitled 'the Wisdom of Hesiod'. It gives advice for living a life of honest work. Hesiod inveighs against dishonesty and idleness by turns, using myths (Prometheus again, with the famous story of Pandora, 42–105; the five World Ages, 106–201), parable (202–12), allegory (286–92), proverbial maxims, direct exhortation, and threats of divine anger. The sermon is osten-

sibly directed at a brother Perses, who has bribed the 'kings' and taken more than his share of his inheritance (37–9); but Perses' failings seem to change with the context (cf. 28 ff., 275, 396), and it is impossible to reconstruct a single basic situation. Besides moral advice, Hesiod gives much practical instruction, especially on agriculture (381–617, the year's 'Works'), seafaring (618–94), and social and religious conduct (336–80, 695–764). There is a fine descriptive passage on the rigours of winter (504–35). The final section, sometimes regarded as a later addition, is the 'Days' (765–828), an almanac of days in the month that are favourable or unfavourable for different operations. Some ancient copies continued with an *Ornithomanteia*, a section on bird omens. The poem as a whole is a unique source for social conditions in early Archaic Greece. It has closer parallels in near eastern literatures than in Greek, and seems to represent an old traditional type. (*Virgil's Georgics*, though much influenced by Hesiod, are shaped by the Hellenistic tradition of systematic treatment of a single theme.)

It has always been the most read of Hesiodic poems. There was even a 'tradition' that it was Hesiod's only genuine work (Paus. 9. 31. 4); but he names himself in *Theog.* 22, and links of style and thought between the two poems confirm identity of authorship. Both bear the marks of a distinct personality: a surly, conservative countryman, given to reflection, no lover of women or of life, who felt the gods' presence heavy about him.

3. The *Shield* (*Aspis*), abbr. '*Sc.*', is a short narrative poem on Heracles' fight with Cycnus, prefaced by an excerpt from the fourth book of the *Catalogue* giving the story of Heracles' birth (1–56). It takes its title from the disproportionately long description of Heracles' shield (139–320), which is based partly on the shield of Achilles (*Il.* 18. 478–609), partly on the art of the period *c*.580–570 (R. M. Cook, *CQ* 1937, 204 ff.; this proves that *Aristophanes (2) of Byzantium was right in denying the poem to Hesiod). Disproportion is characteristic of the work; the Homeric apparatus of arming, divine machination, brave speeches, and long similes is lavished on an encounter in which two blows are struck in all. Parts of the description of the shield betray a taste for the macabre.

4. The *Catalogue of Women* (*Gynaikōn Kat-*

alogos or *Ehoiai*) was a continuation of the *Theogony* in five books, containing comprehensive heroic genealogies with many narrative annotations. Numerous citations and extensive papyrus fragments survive. The poem was accepted as Hesiod's in antiquity, but various indications point to the period 580–520 BC.

5. Other lost poems. (*a*) Narrative: *Greater Ehoiai* (genealogical); *Melampodia* (at least three books; stories of famous seers); *Wedding of Ceyx*; *Idaean Dactyls*; *Aegimius* (at least two books; alternatively ascribed to Cercops of Miletus or Clinias of Carystus). (*b*) Didactic: *Precepts of Chiron* (addressed to Achilles); *Astronomy* (risings and settings—and myths?—of principal stars); *Greater Works*. A few fragments of most of these poems survive.   M.L.W.

Hesychius, of Alexandria, author of a lexicon of rare words found in poetry or in Greek dialects; probably to be dated to the 5th cent. AD, if the Eulogius whom he addresses in his introductory epistle is to be identified with Eulogius the *scholastikos*. The comprehensive scope of his design is indicated both in that epistle and in the title, *Alphabetical Collection of all Words*. The work, Hesychius says, was based on the specialist lexica of *Aristarchus (2), Heliodorus (1st cent. BC), Apion (1st cent AD), and Apollonius, son of Archibius (pupil of Apion), and on Diogenianus and Herodian; Hesychius seems to have added the interpretations of a number of proverbs which are included. The lexicon is known only from a 15th-cent. MS, badly preserved, and in many places interpolated (even obliterated) by expansions and other notes made by the first editor, Marcus Musurus (1514). Bentley showed that the biblical glosses in Hesychius are interpolations; less successful attacks have been made on the Latin and Atticist items. The original, as Hesychius says, included the sources of the rare words listed. The sources, however, have disappeared in the severe abridgement which has reduced the lexicon to a glossary, copious though that remains. Hesychius often preserves correct readings for which easier synonyms have been substituted in our extant MSS of Greek literature. His dialectal items are sometimes imperfect: he writes *F* either as *B* (less often *Y*) or as *Γ* (less often *T*), as e.g. Γοιδα· οὐκ οἶδα [sic cod.], Γισγόν [sic cod.]· ἴσον. Nevertheless, he is of the greatest value for the study of Greek dialects, the interpretation of inscriptions, and the criticism of poetic texts.   P.B.R.F.; R.B.

Hieron II, tyrant, later king, of Syracuse (c.271–216 BC); claimed, without grounds, descent from *Gelon. Between 275 and 271, Hieron was elected general, seized power as the result of a military coup, allied himself with the popular faction, and was perhaps elected general plenipotentiary. He attacked the Mamertines, and after a severe defeat and further preparation, routed them on the Longanus river (west of Messana) (265). He was then acclaimed king. Alarmed by the Mamertines' alliance with Rome, Hieron joined the Carthaginians in besieging Messana (264); but forced by the Romans to withdraw, and besieged in Syracuse, he came to terms (263), preserving much of his kingdom, but becoming in effect a subordinate of Rome. His loyalty to Rome in the First Punic War earned him the revision of his treaty (248): it became a *foedus aequum* (a treaty as between equals), he received additions to his kingdom and the indemnity still outstanding was remitted. Hieron maintained an efficient navy and policed the sea, enjoyed friendly relations with Carthage (after 241), Rhodes, and Egypt, improved (with the help of his friend *Archimedes) the defences of Syracuse, and enriched Syracuse and his kingdom by his building. He supplied Rome with grain, both before and during the Second Punic War, and co-operated with her at sea (218, 216) and sent troops and money (217, 216). He died shortly after *Hannibal's victory at Cannae (216); his son (and colleague) Gelon having predeceased him, he was succeeded by his grandson Hieronymus, and Syracuse abandoned her Roman allegiance. 'Naturally regal and statesmanlike' (*Polybius), Hieron was sufficiently realistic to jettison his early imperial aspirations in favour of loyalty to Rome and the prosperity and well-being of his people. His system of taxation, adopted by Rome after her annexation of Sicily (241)—the *lex Hieronica*—was regarded as both efficient and equitable.   B.M.C.

Hieronymus, of Cardia, historian and statesman, was in the entourage of his fellow Cardian (and relative?) Eumenes, one of the Successors, acting as his emissary at the siege of Nora (319/8 BC) and passing to the court of *Antigonus the One-eyed after Eumenes' death at Gabiene (316). He served with Antigonus in Syria (312/1) and at the battle of Ipsus (301), and under *Demetrius the Besieger governed Thebes after its revolt in 293. He ended his days with *Antigonus Gonatas. His great history spanned the period from *Alexander the Great's death (323) to at least the death of *Pyrrhus (272). It was *Diodorus Siculus' authority for Greek affairs in bks. 18–20, and was used extensively by *Plutarch, *Arrian, and Justin. The extant fragments only hint at its dimensions and content. The main evidence is Diodorus' digest of his work, which in bks. 18–20 abruptly rises to a quality not found elsewhere in the *Bibliothēkē*. Excellently informed (see, for instance, the description of the battle lines at Paraetacene and Gabiene, which Hieronymus witnessed), he supplied documentation such as the texts of Alexander's Exiles' Decree and Polyperchon's *diagramma* (edict) of 319/8, and carefully explained the motives of the various protagonists (particularly Eumenes and Antigonus the One-eyed). The lively and lucid narrative was varied by pertinent digressions like the descriptions of Alexander's funeral car and the Indian practice of suttee. He was not without bias, understandably favourable to Eumenes and Antigonus Gonatas, and markedly unsympathetic to Athenian democracy, but there is nothing to equal the sustained prejudice of *Polybius, his only Hellenistic rival in 'pragmatic history'. (For this term see POLYBIUS.)   A.B.B.

Hipparchus, astronomer (fl. second half of 2nd cent. BC). Born at Nicaea in Bithynia, he spent much of his life in Rhodes; his recorded observations range from 147 to 127. His only extant work, the *Commentary on the Phainomena of Eudoxus and Aratus*, in three books, contains criticisms of the descriptions and placings of the constellations and stars by those two (see ARATUS (1); EUDOXUS), and a list of simultaneous risings and settings. Valuable information on Hipparchus' own star coordinates has been extracted from it. Most of our knowledge of Hipparchus' other astronomical work comes from *Ptolemy (Claudius Ptolemaeus)'s *Almagest*.

Hipparchus transformed Greek astronomy from a theoretical to a practical science, by applying to the geometrical models (notably the eccentric/epicyclic hypothesis) that had been developed by his predecessors numerical parameters derived from observations, thus making possible the prediction of celestial positions for any given time. In order to do this he also founded trigonometry, by computing the first trigonometric function, a chord table. He constructed viable theories for the sun and moon, and, using several ingenious methods for determining the lunar distance (which he was the first to estimate accurately), developed a theory of parallax. He was thus able to compute both lunar and solar eclipses. For the planets, however, he refused to construct a theory, contenting himself with compiling a list of observations from which he showed the insufficiency of previous planetary models. He is famous for his discovery of the precession of the equinoxes, which is connected both with his investigations of the length of the year and his observations of star-positions.

Hipparchus was a systematic and careful observer, who invented several instruments, possibly including the plane astrolabe. He had a critical and original mind and a fertile mathematical invention. But he could not have achieved what he did without the aid of Babylonian astronomy, of which he displays a knowledge far deeper than any Greek before or after him, and the success of which in predicting phenomena he evidently wished to emulate. Not only did he have access to the wealth of Babylonian observational records (which he seems to have been instrumental in transmitting to the Greek world), but he also adopted many numerical parameters directly from Babylonian astronomy (e.g. the very accurate length of the mean synodic month, together with all the other mean motions in his lunar theory), and used a number of Babylonian arithmetical procedures, which were only later (by *Ptolemy (Claudius Ptolemaeus)) replaced with strictly geometrical methods. Hipparchus' skill in combining the Babylonian and Greek traditions in astronomy was crucial to the successful propagation of the science in that form for over a thousand years.

Hipparchus' geographical treatise, which we know mainly from Strabo, was a polemic against the *Geography* of *Eratosthenes, criticizing descriptive and especially mathematical details. Other works by him include an astronomical calendar of the traditional type, treatises on optics and combinatorial arithmetic, *On Objects Carried Down by their Weight*, and a catalogue of his own writings. He also wrote on astrology, and his establishment of methods for computation of celestial positions undoubtedly contributed to the enormous expansion of that 'science' in the Graeco-Roman world soon after his time.

G.J.T.

Hippocrates, of Cos, probably a contemporary of Socrates (469–399 BC), was the most famous physician of antiquity and one of the least known. The important early corpus of medical writings bears his name but many scholars insist that he cannot be confidently connected with any individual treatise, let alone with any specific doctrines. He remains for many a 'name without a work', in the words of Wilamowitz; and even in antiquity the nature of his personal contributions to medicine were the subject of speculation.

All kinds of anecdotes and medical doctrines have been connected at different times to the name of Hippocrates. One influential ancient biographical tradition, represented by a *Life of Hippocrates* (attributed to Soranus of Ephesus and probably a source for several much later commentators including the Byzantine scholar Johannes Tzetzes), maintains that he was taught medicine by his father and by the gymnastic trainer Herodicus of Selymbria, and that he sat at the feet of the sophist Gorgias of Leontini, the eponym of *Plato's dialogue. Hippocrates on this account worked throughout Greece, and is supposed to have died at Larissa in Thessaly. The evidence for his acquaintance with certain 5th-cent. sophists is supported by Cornelius Celsus (1st cent. AD), who claims that the historical Hippocrates was the first to separate medicine from philosophy, and much more strongly by *Plato, who mentions Hippocrates several times. Plato suggests that he taught medicine for a fee (*Prt.* 311b) and offers a cryptic glimpse into his medical thought, reporting that he claimed that one could not understand the nature of the body without understanding the nature of the whole (*Phdr.* 270c). This difficult passage in the *Phaedrus* attracted much comment in antiquity, and has continued to do so, since it represents the only early independent reference to Hippocrates' method.

The Anonymus Londinensis papyrus points to an ancient confusion about the historical Hippocrates' pathological doctrines. On one view, which is ascribed to *Aristotle (and which seems to be rejected as historically incorrect by the author of the papyrus), Hippocrates held that disease is caused by vapours given off by the residues of undigested food. The 'real' Hippocrates, claims the author of the papyrus, related disease to regimen, to one's way of life. And indeed, one influential modern scholar, W. D. Smith, has argued that the Hippocratic treatise *On Regimen* can be ascribed to Hippocrates himself, but his thesis has not found widespread support. Many scholars have sought to align parts of these characterizations of Hippocratic theory with particular Hippocratic treatises, but with limited success. Others, following other ancient witnesses, have seen the hands of Hippocrates' sons Thessalus, Dracon, and Polybus in other Hippocratic treatises.

To a large degree, modern ideas about Hippocrates' theory and practice have been shaped by those who wrote commentaries on him in antiquity. *Herophilus of Chalcedon is traditionally regarded as the first Hippocratic commentator, and the earliest surviving work of Hippocratic exegesis is the commentary on *Joints* by Apollonius of Citium. The best-known ancient commentator is *Galen, who presents us with an Hippocrates as the head of a medical school based in Cos and set against a rival school centred on Cnidus. Galen's Hippocrates is credited with profound philosophical as well as medical talents, in many cases anticipating Plato and Aristotle. He advocates a four-humour theory, based on an underlying four-element and four-quality theory similar to that associated with *Empedocles. Galen's reasons for presenting the kind of Hippocrates he did are very complex, and they are coloured by his own philosophical sympathies with Plato, Aristotle, and Stoicism.

There is also an ancient pseudepigraphic tradition which contains spurious anecdotal material about Hippocrates' life. The stories that he diagnosed lovesickness in King Perdiccas II of Macedon, halted the great Athenian plague of 432 BC by burning fires throughout the city before discovering an antidote, and that he was called by the insensitive people of Abdera to treat the supposed mad hilarity of the philosopher *Democritus, are very likely to be fictitious. In the Middle Ages, wildly anachronistic tales of his exploits in Rome were in circulation. There are many Hippocratic myths, then, and the Hippocratic 'question' remains unanswered because it is probably unanswerable.   J.T.V.

Histiaeus, tyrant of Miletus, loyal Persian functionary and ambitious empire-builder (c.515–493 BC), saved the Persian king Darius I's expedition beyond the Danube when fellow Greek autocrats pondered betraying their overlord (c.513). He protected Darius' interests in the undermanned western provinces of Anatolia, suitably rephrasing for Hellenic sensibilities oriental monarchy's commands, and gained Darius' gift of Edonian Myrcinus on the river Strymon, a hub for Ionian penetration and economic exploitation of the Thracian–Macedonian coastlands (Hdt. 5. 11, cf. 8. 85).

Suspected of potential rebellion or excessive power by rival Persian grandees, he was summoned to Susa, long detained, and honoured by Darius as his Aegean expert. Histiaeus overboldly promised (499) to regain the allegiance of Miletus and other Ionian cities that *Aristagoras, his appointed deputy and relative, had led into rebellion. Like *Hecataeus (Hdt. 5. 36), he appreciated Persian power and Hellenic inadequacies. Sent to pacify Ionia, after several Ionian repulses (6. 1–5) he dared not return to Susa and so departed for his Thracian project. Unlikely ever to have encouraged Aristagoras' premature mainland revolt, his absence from the defeat at Lade suggests realistic evaluation of the coalition's chances. He subsequently launched shipping-raids from Byzantium and descents on Chios, Thasos, and Lesbos that less resemble self-interested marauding than independent operations. He intended either to curry renewed favour with Darius or support faltering rebels. As he foraged near Atarneus, Persian units captured and impaled him (6. 26–30, 493).

Herodotus unsurprisingly found only hostile Greek and Persian sources. This first biography supplies sinister motives for Histiaeus' every mysterious move, but the biased narrative invites doubts about parochial malice. Herodotus acknowledges Histiaeus' steady services to Darius that led Harpagus and Artaphernes to execute him. Largely irrelevant to the Ionian Revolt, Histiaeus was none the less vilified both for starting it and for avoiding martyrdom in it.   D.G.L.

Homer The ancient world attributed the two epics, the *Iliad* and the *Odyssey*, the earliest and greatest works of Greek literature, to the poet Homer. Against this general consensus a few scholars at Alexandria argued for different authorship of the two poems; and modern critics, in the 150 years after Wolf (1795), went further and questioned the unity of authorship of each poem. However, the difficulties on which these 'analysts' based their discussions have been resolved through a greater understanding of oral poetry, and now most scholars see each as the work of one author. Whether he was the same for both remains uncertain. They have a great deal of common phraseology, but the *Odyssey* is less archaic in language and more repetitive in content, it views the gods rather differently, and for a few common things it uses different words. Such changes might occur in the lifetime of one person. As nothing reliable is known about Homer, perhaps the question is not important.

There is some agreement to date the poems in the second half of the 8th cent. BC, with the *Iliad* the earlier, about 750, the *Odyssey* about 725. This was the age of colonization in the Greek world, and it may be no accident that the *Iliad* shows an interest in the northeast, towards the Black Sea, while much of the *Odyssey* looks towards the west. In *Od.* 6. 7–10 many have seen an echo of the founding of a Greek colony. As to Homer himself, the *Iliad* at least suggests a home on the east side of the Aegean Sea, for storm winds in a simile blow over the sea from Thrace, from the north and west (9. 5), and the poet seems familiar with the area near Miletus (2. 461) as well as that round Troy (12. 10–33). Moreover, the predominantly Ionic flavour of the mixed dialect of the poems suits the cities of the Ionian Greek migration on the other side of the Aegean. Chios and Smyrna have the strongest claims to have been his birthplace.

2. The *Iliad* is the longer of the two by a third, consisting of over 15,600 lines, divided into 24 books. The book division seems to have been later than the original composition, although the books do in many cases represent distinct episodes in the plot (e.g. books 1, 9, 12, 16, 22, 24). There is now broad agreement that we have the poem virtually as it was composed, with the exception of book 10, where the evidence for later addition is strong. For the rest, an individual intelligence is shown by the theme of the anger of Achilles, begun in the quarrel with Agamemnon in 1, kept before us in the Embassy of 9, transferred from Agamemnon to Hector in 18, and resolved in the consolation of Priam, Hector's father, in 24; also by the tight time-scale of the epic, for, in place of a historical treatment of the Trojan War, the *Iliad*, from book 2 to 22, records merely four days of fighting from the tenth year, separated by two days of truce. Even the beginning and end add only a few weeks to the total.

Thus the action is concentrated, but the composition subtly expands to include the whole war, with echoes from the beginning in books 2 to 4, and the final books repeatedly looking forward to the death of Achilles and the fall of Troy. The centre is occupied by a single day of battle between 11 and 18, with the Trojans temporarily superior, Greek leaders wounded, their strongest and most mobile fighter (Achilles) disaffected, only Ajax and some warriors of the second rank holding the defence. The turning-point is in 16, when Patroclus, acting on a suggestion from Nestor in 11, persuades Achilles to let him go to the rescue of their comrades, and thus starts the sequence that leads to his own death (16), Achilles' return (18), Hector's death (22), and the conclusion of the epic (24).

3. High among the qualities of the *Iliad* is a vast humanity, which justifies comparison with Shakespeare. The poet understands human behaviour and reactions. There are numerous well-differentiated portraits of leading figures, introduced on the Greek side in the first four books, whose successes in action reinforce their heroic status, and whose personal feelings and relationships are expressed in the very frequent speeches. Figures of the second rank (e.g. Meriones, Antilochus) support the leaders; and a large number of minor characters, who appear only to be killed, add a sense of the pathos and waste of war, through background details, particularly reference to families at home. The Trojans have their leaders too, but

their efforts are essentially defensive, and the desperate situation of their city, and the threat to the women and children, contrast with the more straightforward heroics of the Greeks. Three women of Troy, Hecuba, Andromache, and Helen, appear at key moments in books 6 and 24, the first two also in 22.

There is also what Pope called 'invention', a constant brilliance of imagination infusing the reports of action, speeches of the characters, and descriptions of the natural world. The language has a kind of perfection, due to a combination of phrases worn smooth by traditional use and the taste and judgement of the poet; and features which had been technical aids to the oral bard seem to have assumed the form of art in the *Iliad*—the use of formulae and repeated story patterns, ring-composition in the construction of speeches, the pictorial effects of extended similes.

4. The *Odyssey*, about 12,000 lines long, was probably composed in its present form in imitation of the already existing *Iliad*. Its 24 books show exact construction. Four books set the scene in Ithaca ten years after the end of the war, and send Odysseus' son Telemachus to two of the most distinguished survivors, Nestor at Pylos and Menelaus at Sparta, in search of news of his father. The next four show Odysseus himself released from the island of Calypso and arriving at the land of the Phaeacians, a half-way house between the fairy-tale world of his adventures and the real world of Ithaca which awaits him. There, in 9 to 12, he recounts his adventures to the Phaeacians. That completes the first half; the second is devoted to Odysseus' return home, the dangers he faces, and his eventual slaughter of the suitors of his wife Penelope. In book 15, the two strands of the first half are brought together, when Telemachus returns from Sparta and joins his father.

For reasons difficult to guess, the quality of composition fades at the end, from 23. 296, which the Alexandrian scholars *Aristophanes (2) and *Aristarchus (2) confusingly describe as the 'end' of the *Odyssey*. However, at least two parts of the 'continuation' (i.e. what follows 23. 296) are indispensable for the completion of the story—the recognition of Odysseus by his old father Laertes, and the avoidance of a blood feud with the relatives of the dead suitors.

5. The *Odyssey* is a romance, enjoyable at a more superficial level than the heroic/tragic *Iliad*. We can take sides, for the good people are on one side, the bad on the other. Even the massacre of the suitors and the vengeance on the servants who had supported them are acceptable in a story of this kind. The epic depends very much more than the *Iliad* on a single character; and Odysseus has become a seminal figure in European literature, with eternal human qualities of resolution, intellectual curiosity, and love of home. Apart from books 9 to 12, the settings are domestic, Ithaca, Pylos, Sparta, and Scheria (the land of the Phaeacians). The effect of this is that the gentler qualities of politeness, sensitivity, and tact come into play, as in the delicate interchanges between Odysseus and Nausicaa (the princess on Scheria) and her parents. On the other hand, the boorish behaviour of the suitors shows a break-down of the social order.

For many readers the adventures are the high point. The Lotus-eaters, Cyclops, king of the winds, cannibal giants, witch Circe, Sirens, Scylla, and Charybdis are part of the folk-tale element in western consciousness. They are prefaced by a piratical attack on a people in Thrace, near Troy, and concluded on the island of the Sun, an episode which results in the elimination of Odysseus' surviving companions, leaving him alone to face the return home. In the middle, in book 11, comes the visit to the Underworld, where he sees figures from the past and receives a prophecy of the future.

The combination of precision of observation and descriptive imagination is on a par with the *Iliad*; examples are Odysseus in the Cyclops' cave, Odysseus in his own house among the suitors of his wife, the recognition by his old dog Argos. One gets the impression, however, more strongly with the *Odyssey* than the *Iliad*, that the tale has been told many times before, and some superficial inconsistencies may be the effect of variant versions (e.g. the abortive plans for the removal of the arms in 16. 281–98).

6. The dactylic hexameter has a complex structure, with from twelve to seventeen syllables in the lines, and some precise metrical requirements. Milman Parry demonstrated that features of composition, notably pervasive repetition in the phraseology, derive from the practice of illiterate oral bards, who would learn the traditional phrases

(formulae) in their years of apprenticeship. This explains many aspects that worried analytical critics since the days of the critics in ancient Alexandria; for repetition of a half-line, line, or sequence of lines had been taken by readers used to the practice of later poets as evidence for corruption in the text, and an adjective used inappropriately had seemed to be a fault, instead of the inevitable consequence of the use of formulae.

Of equal significance to the repetition of formulaic phrases in the composition of oral poetry is the repetitive, though flexible, use of what are called typical scenes, patterns in the story, sometimes described as 'themes'. These range from the four arming-scenes in the *Iliad* (in books 3, 11, 16, 19), scenes of arrival and departure, performance of sacrifices, descriptions of fighting, to the repeated abuse directed at Odysseus in the second half of the *Odyssey*. Such 'themes' performed a parallel function to the formulae, giving the experienced bard material for the construction of his songs in front of an audience.

Virtually all scholars now accept that oral poetry theory has added to our understanding. Difference remains about whether Homer himself was an illiterate bard, or whether his position at the end of a long tradition shows a bard using the possibilities of literacy while still retaining the oral techniques. The ultimate problem of the survival of the two epics is inextricably bound up with this question. Three possibilities divide the field. Either the poet composed with the help of writing, the Greek alphabet having become available at just the right time; or the poems were recorded by scribes, the poet himself being illiterate; or they were memorized by a guild of public reciters (rhapsodes) for anything up to 200 years (there being evidence for a written text in Athens in the 6th cent.).

7. The language in which the poems are composed contains a mixture of forms found in different areas of the Greek world. The overall flavour is Ionic, the dialect spoken on Euboea, other islands of the eastern Aegean such as Chios, and on the mainland of Asia Minor opposite them. Attic (Athenian) Greek was a subdivision of Ionic, but Atticisms (Athenian forms) in the epic dialect are rare and superficial. Second in importance to Ionic in the amalgam is Aeolic, the dialect of north Greece (Boeotia and Thessaly) and the northern islands such as Lesbos. Where Aeolic had a different form from Ionic, the Aeolic form mostly appears as an alternative to the Ionic in the epic language when it has a different metrical value. More deeply embedded are certain words and forms which belonged to the dialect of southern Greece in the Mycenaean age, sometimes described as Arcado-Cypriot, because it survived into historical times in those two widely separated areas of the Greek world.

The historical implications of all this are obscure. The geographical location during the Mycenaean age of the speakers of what later became Ionic and Aeolic was necessarily different from that in historical times; and the dialects themselves obviously developed differently in different areas. What is clear, however, is that the linguistic picture is consistent with that presented by oral theory. Some features are very ancient (often preserved in the formulaic phrases), some quite recent. An important conclusion is that late linguistic forms are not to be seen as post-Homeric interpolations, but more probably come from the language of the poet himself, while earlier ones had reached him through the tradition. It is noted that the similes in the *Iliad* contain a high proportion of 'late' forms.

8. The assumed date of the Trojan war falls in the 13th cent. BC, towards the end of the Mycenaean age; for the Mycenaean palaces on the mainland were destroyed from about 1200. There is thus a gap of some four and a half centuries between the date of composition of the *Iliad* (about 750) and the legendary past which is its setting. The 8th cent. is essentially more important for the epics than the 13th; but the history of the Mycenaean age and of the shadowy times that lay between is naturally of the greatest interest. Here archaeologist and historian combine. We have the extraordinary discoveries of Schliemann at Mycenae, and the excavations at Troy itself by Schliemann (1870–90), Blegen (1932–8), and Korfmann (1981–). Historical evidence from the 13th cent. has come to the surface. It is, however, unsafe to assume too close a connection with Homer. For the passage of time, and a retrospective view of a heroic age, have moved the picture nearer to fiction than reality. Only fossilized memories of the Mycenaean age survive in his work.

After the destruction of the palaces a long Dark Age intervened, lightened to some extent recently by the discovery at Lefkandi in Euboea of a city with important trade connections in the 10th and 9th cents. It must have been during the Dark Age that heroic poetry developed and spread, even if (as seems probable) it originated in the Mycenaean age. Historians see in the epics reflections of the society and political aspirations of this period, even of the 8th cent.

9. Hexameter poetry continued after Homer, with Hesiod and the *Homeric Hymns*, and the poems of the Epic Cycle, which described the two legendary wars of the heroic age, those against Thebes and Troy. The Theban epics are lost, but for the Trojan we have summaries of the contents of six poems (*Cypria, Aethiopis, Little Iliad, Sack of Troy (Iliu Persis), Returns (Nostoi), Telegony (Telegonia)*), which had been fitted round the *Iliad* and *Odyssey* to create a complete sequence from the marriage of Peleus and Thetis to the death of Odysseus. The summaries, attributed to 'Proclus' (perhaps a grammarian of the 2nd cent. AD), are found in some manuscripts of the *Iliad*. These cyclic epics were obviously later than the Homeric poems, and from a time when oral composition had ceased and public performance was by rhapsodes, not traditional bards. Their significance for us is that they represent the subject-matter of heroic poetry as it was before Homer; for the *Iliad* itself, being the individual creation of a poet of genius, was not typical. Thus, by a time reversal, the partially known later material can make some claim to priority over the earlier. A school of 'neoanalysts' argues that episodes in books 8 (rescue of Nestor), 17 (recovery of the body of Patroclus), 18 (mourning of Thetis), and 23 (funeral games) echo situations connected with Achilles in the repertoire of the oral bards, which later appeared in the cyclic *Aethiopis*. The importance of this is that it seems to give us an insight into the creativity of the *Iliad* poet.   M.M.W.

Horace (Quintus Horatius Flaccus) was born on 8 December 65 BC in Venusia in Apulia (mod. Venosa) and died on 27 November 8 BC (*Epist.* 1. 20. 26–7; Life). Thanks to the almost complete preservation of *Suetonius' Life and numerous biographical allusions in the poetry, we are relatively well informed about his life. His father was a freed slave (*Sat.* 1. 6. 6, 45–6), though this need not mean, as some have supposed, that he had come as a slave from the east. Even an Italian could have been enslaved as a result of the Social War (91–87 BC), in which Venusia was captured by Rome. Horace presents himself as brought up in the old Italian style (cf. *Sat.* 1. 4. 105–29 with Ter. *Ad.* 414–19) and his father may well have come from Italy itself. The father had a fairly small landholding in Venusia (*Sat.* 1. 6. 71) but in his role as *coactor* (public auctioneer) obtained what was clearly not an inconsiderable amount of money (*Sat.* 1. 6. 86, Life); otherwise he could not have afforded to send his son to Rome and then Athens for an education that was the equal of that of a typical upper-class Roman of the time (*Sat.* 1. 6. 76–80, *Epist.* 2. 1. 70 f.; Life). This ambitious education was clearly intended to help Horace to rise in society, and at first this plan met with success. While in Athens, Horace joined the army of *Brutus as a military tribune (*Sat.* 1. 6. 47 f.; Life), a post usually held by *equites* (knights). But all these high hopes were brought to nothing by the fall of Brutus and the loss of the family's property (*Epist.* 2. 2. 46–51). Horace counted himself lucky to be able to return to Italy, unlike many of his comrades-in-arms, and to obtain the reasonably respectable position of *scriba quaestorius* (*Sat.* 2. 6. 36 f.; Life: clerk to the quaestors). It was in this period that he wrote his first poems (*Epist.* 2. 2. 51 f.), which brought him into contact with *Virgil and the poet Varius Rufus. They recommended him to *Maecenas, then gathering around him a circle of writers; and when Maecenas accepted him into this circle in 38 BC (*Sat.* 1. 6. 52–62, 2. 6. 40–2), and later gave him the famous Sabine farm, his financial position was secure. His property put him in the higher reaches of the *equites* census (cf. *Sat.* 2. 7. 53) and he now possessed the leisure to devote himself to poetry. He was acquainted with many leading Romans, and on friendly terms with a considerable number of them, most notably his patron Maecenas. In his later years *Augustus also sought to be on close terms, as several letters written in a warm and candid tone attest (Life). But Horace knew well how to preserve his personal freedom. Augustus offered him an influential post on his personal staff (*officium epistularum*) but Horace turned this down (Life) and as *Epistle* 1. 7

demonstrates he showed a similar independence towards Maecenas.

WORKS *EPODES* The *Epodes* or *Iambi* (cf. *Epod.* 14. 7; *Epist.* 1. 19. 23) form a slender book of 17 poems. They include some of Horace's earliest poems, written before the encounter with Maecenas, but work on them continued throughout the 30s BC and poems 1 and 9 allude to the battle of Actium (31): the collection as a whole seems to have been published around 30 BC. Horace's formal model was *Archilochus, the founder of *iambus*, to whom he joins the 5th-cent. BC poet Hipponax (*Epod.* 6. 13 f.; *Epist.* 1. 19. 23–5). He thus introduced for the first time into Rome not only the metrical form of early Greek iambus, but also some of the matter (cf. *Epod.* 10, which is closely related to the disputed papyrus fragment Archilochus 79a Diels = Hipponax 115 West). Horace's adoption of this early form may be compared with the incorporation of classical and pre-classical motifs in the visual art of the day, but it did not represent a rejection of the Callimachean principle (see CALLIMACHUS) that every detail of a poem should be artistically controlled and contribute to the overall effect. Even the 'archaic' epodes are written in a style of painstaking elegance. The central theme of iambic poetry was traditionally invective, that is personal attack, mockery, and satire (*Epist.* 1. 19. 25, 30 f.; cf. Arist. *Poet.* 1448^{b}26 ff.), and Horace may have taken up the genre in his affliction after the battle of Philippi (42) as a way of preserving his self-respect in hard times. But only some of the *Epodes* are invectives (4, 5, 6, 8, 10, 12, 17), and even in these the targets are either anonymous or figures about whom we know next to nothing. Horace clearly avoids the sort of personal attacks on important contemporary figures that we find in *Catullus. A different aspect of early Greek poetry is taken up in *Epodes* 7 and 16. Just as the early Greek poets (including Archilochus: cf. fr. 109 West with *Epod.* 16. 17 ff.) on occasions addressed themselves to the general public, so in these poems Horace represents himself as warning and exhorting the Roman people. There are no iambic elements in the poems to Maecenas: *Epod.* 3 is a joke, *Epod.* 14 an excuse, and in *Epod.* 1 and 9 one friend talks to another in the context of the decisive struggles of 31 BC. Other epodes take up motifs from other contemporary genres (elegy in 11 and 15, pastoral

in 2) but with significant alterations of tone: Horace ironically breaks the high emotional level of the models with a detached and distant closure. *Epode* 13 anticipates a theme of the *Odes* (cf. *Carm.* 1. 7).

SATIRES Contemporaneously with the *Epodes*, Horace composed his two books of satires (*Satira*: 2. 1. 1, 2. 6. 17). He also calls them *Sermones*, 'conversations' (2. 3. 4, *Epist.* 1. 4. 1, 2. 1. 250, 2. 2. 60), which suits their loose colloquial tone that seems to slide from one subject to another almost at random. The first book contains ten satires, the second eight. The earliest datable reference is to the 'journey to Brundisium' undertaken with Maecenas and his circle in 38 or 37 BC and described at length in *Sat.* 1. 5, the latest is to the settlement of veterans after the civil war in 30 BC (*Sat.* 2. 6. 55 f.). Some of the poems may have been written before 38, but there is no evidence that any are later than 30. Horace's model is *Lucilius (1), but he represents himself as determined to write with greater care and attention to form (*Sat.* 1. 4, 1. 10, 2. 1), and thus, again, as a follower of Callimachus (cf. especially *Sat.* 1. 10. 9–15, 67–74). Another difference from Lucilius is that Horace's satires are less aggressive. While the pugnacious poet of the 2nd cent. took sides in the political struggles of his time, Horace chooses a purely private set of themes. In *Sat.* 1. 4 and 2. 1 he represents personal abuse as a typical element in satire, but declares that he himself does not attack any contemporary public figures. When he names people as possessed of particular vices, as in the *Epodes* they are either unknown or no longer alive, and it is clear that the names represent types rather than individual targets. The criticism of vice occurs less for its own sake than to show the way to a correct way of life through an apprehension of error. In these passages Horace comes close to the doctrines and argument-forms of popular philosophy (so-called diatribe), even if he rejects the sometimes fanciful tone of the Cynic-Stoic wandering preachers. His style is rather to tell the truth through laughter (*ridentem dicere verum*), and not only to show others the way but also to work at improving himself and making himself more acceptable to his fellow human beings (*Sat.* 1. 4. 133–8). The autobiographical aspect of many satires is another Lucilian element. Just like Lucilius, he makes his own life a subject for his poetry, and his personal situation is a central theme of poems like *Sat.* 1. 4, 1. 6, 1. 9, and 2. 6, and a partial concern in many others. Both books are arranged according to theme. In the first book, related poems are grouped together in three groups of three: 1–3 are diatribes, 4–6 are autobiographical, and 7–9 relate anecdotes, while in the last poem of the book Horace offers a retrospective look at the individuality of his satiric production. In contrast to the first book, the poems of the second book are mostly dialogues. They are arranged so that poems from the second half of the book parallel poems of the first in motif: in the dialogues of *Sat.* 1 and 5 an expert is asked for advice, the theme of 2 and 6 is the value of a simple life on the land, in 3 and 7 Horace faces some decidedly dubious representatives of popular philosophy who inflict long sermons on him, and the theme of 4 and 9 is the luxuriousness of contemporary Roman banqueting.

ODES (CARMINA) After the publication of the *Epodes* and *Satires* around 30 BC, Horace turned to lyric poetry. The earliest datable reference is in *Odes* 1. 37, which celebrates Augustus' defeat of *Cleopatra at Actium in 31 BC, though it is not impossible that some odes were written earlier than this: 1. 14, for instance, on the 'ship of state', whose situation fits best the time before Actium (though the poem is open to different interpretations, and it has even been doubted whether it is in fact a political allegory at all). At any rate, the first three books of the *Odes*, 88 poems in all, seem to have been published as a collection in 23 BC. The concluding poem, 3. 30, looks back on the work as a completed unit, and does not envisage a sequel. After the composition, at Augustus' bidding, of the *Carmen saeculare* in 17, however, a fourth book of 15 poems was added, which also seems to have been inspired by Augustus (Life).

Horace declares that his main literary model in the *Odes* was the early Greek lyric poetry from Lesbos, especially that of *Alcaeus (*Carm.* 1. 1. 33 f., 1. 32, 3. 30. 13 f.; *Epist.* 1. 19. 32 f.). He is indebted to this model for the metrical form of the *Odes* but he also begins a series of poems with an almost literal translation of lines by Alcaeus (the so-called 'mottoes'), which serve as a springboard for his own developments (e.g. 1. 9, 1. 18, 1. 37, 3. 12). He also takes over motifs from other early lyric poets, such as *Sappho (1. 13), *Anac-

reon (1. 23), and *Pindar (1. 12, 3. 4, and some of the higher-style poems in book 4). His view of this early poetry, however, is that of a poet trained in the modern contemporary Hellenistic style: the *Odes* are not written in the simple language of the archaic models but are full of the dense and sophisticated allusivity that was the inevitable result of the complex literary world of Augustan Rome. He also takes over a number of themes from Hellenistic poetry, especially from Greek epigram (cf. 1. 5, 1. 28, 1. 30, 3. 22, 3. 26).

Although the major themes of the *Odes* are the usual ones of ancient poetry, Horace's treatment of them is, as far as we can tell, markedly different. The hymns to the gods, for instance, are not meant for cult performance but encounter the world of Greek divinity more with aesthetic pleasure than in an act of pious worship. His love poetry takes a different line from that of his contemporaries. While Catullus and the elegists had tended to make a single beloved the focus of their life and poetry, Horace's poems are concerned with a variety of women (and boys). Although passionate obsession is not entirely alien to the *Odes*, typically Horace tries to free himself from extreme emotion and move himself and his beloved towards a calm and cheerful enjoyment of the moment. The sympotic poetry diverges distinctively from that of Alcaeus. Horace does not set out to drown his sorrows, but to give himself and his friends at the drinking-party a brief moment of freedom from care, in poems which, as earlier in the *Satires*, lead often to reflection on the right way to live one's life. Friendship is an important theme throughout the *Odes*: they are hardly ever soliloquies, but poems addressed to a friend offering help and advice. The political themes begun in the *Epodes* are taken further. Although Horace declines to celebrate Augustus or Agrippa in the traditional Roman form of panegyric epic (1. 6, 1. 12), from the time of the poem celebrating the defeat of Cleopatra (1. 37) on he offers explicit praise of the new ruler as one who had brought peace and through his policies maintained it. He also declares his support for the attempt by Augustus to restore 'ancient Roman' customs and morality (3. 1–6 and 3. 24). In the later *Ode* 3. 14, in the *Carmen saeculare*, and in the poems of book 4 the panegyric of the Augustan epoch comes even more to the fore, and it is celebrated as an epoch of peace, a second golden age.

Horace's *Odes* differ in one essential respect from the norms of modern, especially post-Romantic, lyric poetry. Modern lyric strives as far as possible for a unity of atmosphere within one poem, but this is found in Horace only in his shortest poems. More commonly, as F. Klingner (*Studien zur röischen und griechischen Literatur* (1964) 305–518) noted, within a single poem there are significant movements and changes in content, expression, and stylistic level. Poems written in high style with important content often conclude with a personal and apparently insignificant final turn. In other odes, the whole poem moves considerably from the content or atmosphere of the opening, most often from a distressed or agitated emotional level to a dissipation of tension. In other odes again, a concrete situation gives rise to thoughts which move far away from it, with the result that the meaning of the poem seems to rest on these general reflections rather than in the poem's situation. And a fourth possibility is a form of ring-composition: an opening section is followed by a second part very different in content and tone, and the final section then returns to the mood of the opening. A harmonious balance is also aimed at in the order of poems within the books. Poems of important content and accordingly a high stylistic register tend to be placed at the beginning and end of books, with lighter poems placed next to them for contrast (cf. 1. 4, 1. 5, 2. 4, 2. 5, 3. 7–3. 10 towards the beginning of books, 3. 26, 3. 28, 4. 12 towards the end). In contrast, the first book ends with the light, cheerful short sympotic poem 1. 38, preceded by the weighty victory poem 1. 37.

EPISTLES book 1 After the publication of the *Odes*, Horace returned to hexameter poetry and the conversational style of his earlier *Sermones*, but this time in the form of letters addressed to a variety of recipients. Although Lucilius had written satires in the form of letters, the notion of a complete book of verse epistles was comparatively novel. The poems are naturally not real letters actually sent to their addressees, but the choice of the letter-form was a literary device which gave Horace a concrete starting-point and a unified speech-situation. The dating of the collection is uncertain: the last line of *Epistles* 1. 20 refers to the consuls of 21 BC, and many

would place the publication in that year, but 1. 12. 26 seems to refer to the defeat of the Cantabri (NW Spain) in 19 BC (Cass. Dio 54. 11). In the programmatic *Epistle* 1. 1 Horace grounds his choice of the new form in his advancing old age: philosophical reflection and a concentration on questions of how to lead one's life now suit him better than the usual themes of lyric. The philosophical meditation that this declaration places at the centre of his work is an essential theme of the book, but not its only concern. Horace writes also more generally of the circumstances of his own life, and offers his friends various forms of counsel. Many elements recall the *Satires*, but the choice of the letter-form brings a more unified tone to the varied content. The last epistle (1. 20) is an address to the book itself, portrayed as a young slave eager to be free of its master.

EPISTLES book 2, ARS POETICA From *Satires* 1. 4 and 1. 10 on, poetry itself had been a constant concern of Horace's poetry, and this becomes the central theme of the two long poems of *Epistles* book 2 (2. 1 to Florus and 2. 2 to Augustus) and the *Ars poetica*. These poems are again hard to date: but *Epist.* 2. 2. 141 ff. contrasts a philosophical concern for the right way of life with the themes of lyric in similar terms to *Epist.* 1. 1 and the two poems are unlikely to be far apart chronologically. *Epist.* 2. 2 is thus probably written before Horace's resumption of lyric poetry in book 4 of the *Odes* (17 BC). On the other hand *Epist.* 2. 1. 132–7 probably alludes to the *Carmen saeculare*, and 2. 1. 252 seems to recall *Odes* 4. 14. 11 f. from the year 15. Thus the letter to Augustus (2. 1) seems to be later than the letter to Florus (2. 2). The dating of the *Ars poetica* is particularly controversial: in 301–9 Horace says that he is not currently writing (lyric) poetry, but this ironic remark can be situated either before or after *Odes* book 4. The interpretation of all three letters is difficult, because their logical articulation is deliberately obscured by the colloquial tone of a *sermo* or conversation and their various themes are interwoven without clearly marked transitions between them. The great commentary of C. O. Brink has however made many points clearer. In the letter to Augustus (2. 1), Horace complains that the taste of the contemporary public turns more to the cheap theatrical effects of earlier Latin writers than the authors of his own generation. He sees this as unfair, and accuses the older writers of being careless and deficient in taste. The letter to Florus (2. 2) is more personal. In it, Horace explains to his friend why he no longer writes poetry but has turned to philosophy, and offers a candid picture of the restrictions and difficulties of a poet's life at Rome. The *Ars poetica* begins with the proposition that every poem must be a unified whole (1–41), and after a few verses on the necessary ordering of material (42–4) turns to poetic language and the correspondingly appropriate style (45–118). Lines 119–52 then move via a sliding transition to the choice of material and its treatment, with examples taken both from epic and from drama. Lines 153–294 concentrate on the various genres of dramatic poetry, and in the final section (295–476), after another sliding transition, the reader is offered general rules for the poet's craft. This varied subject-matter is given unity by the recurring insistence on values such as appropriateness, clarity, and artistic composition. Horace's teaching lies in the tradition of *Aristotle's school, the Peripatetic, though the *Ars* does not draw directly on the extant *Poetics* and *Rhetoric* but on later versions of the school's doctrine, particularly (according to the ancient commentator Pomponius Porphyrio) the early Hellenistic philosopher Neoptolemus of Parium. There are striking parallels between the *Ars* and the meagre fragments we possess of Neoptolemus, but it is not impossible that other works also lie behind the *Ars*. At any rate, Horace's own contribution lies less in offering a new view of the existing tradition than in his poetic transformation of it through images and vignettes.

H.P.S.

Hyperides (389–322 BC), prominent Athenian statesman, rated by the ancients second only to *Demosthenes amongst the ancient canon of the Ten Orators. He studied rhetoric under *Isocrates and began his career by writing speeches for others. His political career opened with an attack on the politician Aristophon in 363/2. There were other, perhaps numerous, such prosecutions of leading figures, the most notable being his successful prosecution of Philocrates in 343 which heralded his future bitter opposition

to Macedon (see PHILIP II), and after the battle of Chaeronea (338) he assumed a leading role. Immediately after the action in which 1,000 Athenians had died and 2,000 were captured, he sought to provide replacements by making metics (foreign residents) citizens and freeing slaves; he was himself duly indicted for this unconstitutional measure but it showed his determination to resist, as did indeed his prosecution of Demades and other collaborationists and his vigorous plea to the Athenians not to accede to *Alexander the Great's demand in 335 for Demosthenes and others (amongst whom Hyperides was counted by *Arrian, but *Plutarch *Dem.* 23 makes it clear enough that he was not one). In 324/3 he led the attack on Demosthenes and others who were accused of appropriating the money deposited by the Macedonian Harpalus. Presumably he wanted it for the coming revolt against Macedon. Indeed Hyperides was the chief supporter of the Athenian general Leosthenes and of Athenian action in the Lamian War (323–322). Fittingly he was chosen to deliver the Funeral Oration of late 323, a speech of which much survives. With the collapse of the Greek resistance, Hyperides had to flee. He was captured and put to death, the Macedonian statesman *Antipater, in one version, first ordering the cutting out of the tongue which had so bitterly assailed him and Macedon, a not ignoble end for one of the heroes of Greek liberty.

WORKS Although in antiquity of the 77 speeches preserved under the name of Hyperides over 50 were regarded as genuine, except for a few fragments his work was unknown to moderns until 1847. Between that year and 1892 papyri were discovered containing several of his speeches, in whole or in part, most notably the all too fragmentary attack on Demosthenes of 324/3.

In general tone he is akin to *Lysias. He borrowed words and phrases from comedy, thus bringing his language into touch with the speech of everyday life. 'Longinus' *On the Sublime* draws attention to his wit, his suavity and persuasiveness, his tact and good taste. He can be sarcastic and severe without becoming offensive; his reproof often takes the form of humorous banter. He speaks with respect of his adversaries and avoids scurrilous abuse.

G.L.C.

Ii

Ion, of Chios, an unusually versatile poet and prose author, seems to have been born in the 480s BC and to have come to Athens about 466. He was dead by 421, when *Aristophanes (1) paid a graceful tribute to him at *Peace* 834–7.

WORKS included the following. (1) Tragedies and satyr-plays (*TrGF* 1². 95–114). The *Suda* says that Ion wrote 12 or 30 or 40 plays, the first in 451–448. He was defeated by *Euripides in 438, but on another occasion he is said to have won first prize in both tragedy and dithyramb and to have made a present of Chian wine to every Athenian citizen. He was admitted by later critics into a canon of five great tragedians. 'Longinus' found his plays faultless and elegant but sadly lacking in the inspired boldness of *Sophocles. We have eleven titles and some brief fragments, notably from the satyric *Omphale*. (2) Lyric poetry (Page, *PMG* 383–6). This included dithyrambs, encomia, paeans, and hymns. (3) Elegiac poetry (West, *IE*² 2. 79–82). This mainly consisted of drinking-songs, to judge from the surviving fragments. One song (fr. 27) was apparently written for a symposium (drinking party) given by *Archidamus II king of Sparta. (4) Perhaps comedies, but these rest only on one doubtful source. (5) The *Triagmos* (DK), a philosophical work, in prose, of *Pythagorean tendencies, in which Ion ascribed a threefold principle to all things. (6) A *Foundation of Chios* (*FGrH* no. 392), probably in prose. (7) *Epidemiai* or *Visits*, a book of reminiscences, in prose. This recounted Ion's meetings with, and impressions of, great men of his day, and was perhaps his most original work, and the most interesting to us. Surviving fragments describe meetings with *Cimon, *Aeschylus, and Sophocles, all of whom Ion admired (the conversation of Sophocles at a symposium on Chios is the subject of a long extract). Also mentioned, but not necessarily known to him in person, were *Themistocles, *Pericles (whom Ion disliked), the philosopher Archelaus, and *Socrates.   A.L.B.

Isaeus, Athenian speech-writer (*c.*420–340s BC).

LIFE The skimpy ancient biographical tradition ([Plut.] *Mor.* 839e–f, *Dionysius of Halicarnassus' critical essay *Isaeus*, and a Life preceding the speeches in the main MSS) preserves his father's name, Diagoras, but was uncertain whether he was Athenian or from Chalcis in Euboea. *Isocrates reportedly taught him, but he plainly also studied *Lysias' speeches and was himself a teacher of *Demosthenes and author of a *technē*, a speech-writer's manual. His working life extended from *c.*389 to the 350s, perhaps to 344/3 if a lengthy quotation by Dionysius traditionally printed as speech 12 was by him and is correctly dated. The ancient tradition had his activity extend down to the reign of *Philip II of Macedon.

WORKS As a professional speech-writer (*logographos*) in Athens, he specialized in inheritance cases. Some 64 speech-titles were known in antiquity, 50 of which were reckoned genuine. Eleven survive complete, of which four can be internally dated (speech 5 in 390 or 389, 6 in 364 or 363, 7 in 355 or 354, and 2 in the 350s), while stylometric criteria have been plausibly used by R. F. Wevers (*Isaeus: Chronology, Prosopography, and Social History* (1969)) to date the remainder. The subject-matter of his speeches is fundamental for Athenian social history, lying as it does where the study of Athenian legal practice converges with those of oratorical professionalism, property acquisition strategies, and private familial behaviour.

STYLE Dionysius chose him, with *Lysias and *Isocrates, to illustrate the older style of Attic oratory, and devoted a shrewd and sympathetic essay to him, comparing his style to that of Lysias. As he rightly said, though each speech is superficially lucid, he so 'uses insinuations and preliminary expositions and contrived divisions of material ... and embroiders his speeches by alternating argument with emotional appeal' that he gained 'a reputation for wizardry and deceit' (*Isaeus* 3 and 4). The accuracy of Dionysius' judgement can be confirmed by following the analyses in Wyse's classic edition, a masterpiece of sceptical deconstruction.   J.K.D.

Isocrates (436–338 BC), Athenian orator of central importance. Although he lacked the voice and the confidence ever to address a large audience and so played no direct part in the affairs of the state, his written speeches, which presumably were of some influence on public opinion, provide us with a most valuable commentary on the great political issues of the 4th cent. His system of education in rhetoric exercised a profound effect on both the written and the spoken word: his many pupils included the historians *Ephorus and *Theopompus, the atthidographer (historian of Athens) Androtion, and the orators *Hyperides and *Isaeus. Judgements of his importance have variously treated him as the prophet of the Hellenistic world, and as the specious adulator of personal rulers, but, admired or despised, he cannot be neglected in the study of his age.

LIFE As son of a rich man, he studied under Prodicus of Ceos, Gorgias of Leontini in Thessaly, Tisias, and the moderate oligarch, *Theramenes. He was also a follower of *Socrates. Thus, while the Peloponnesian War (between Athens and the Spartan alliance) was destroying both his father's fortune and his city's, he was receiving his education from teachers who included the critics of democracy and empire, and the effect was lasting.

In the 390s he turned his theoretical training to account and wrote speeches for others to use in the courts. Orations 16–21 belong to this early phase. Soon discontented with the profession of *logographos* (speech-writer), he began to train others in rhetoric. In *Against the Sophists* he advertised his principles, and of the early writings the *Helen* and *Busiris* displayed his skill on themes already treated by others. It was perhaps in this period before the King's Peace (386) that he opened a school on Chios. The *Panegyricus*, published in 380 after ten years of composition, was his version of a conventional subject celebrated by

Gorgias and Lysias; its demand that the Greeks unite under the shared hegemony of Athens and Sparta was familiar, and the long period of composition suggests that it was intended to be an enduring masterpiece of its kind, not, as some have supposed, a topical plea for the establishment of the Second Athenian Confederacy. One of Isocrates' most distinguished pupils was Timotheus, the Athenian general, whom at some stage Isocrates had accompanied on campaign and served by writing his dispatches to the Athenian people, and as a result of Timotheus' successes Athens was able in 375 to make the peace which embodied the principle of the shared hegemony. Despite the fact that Persia's position in the peace was unchanged, Isocrates lauded it, perhaps partly on personal grounds, and began to address pleas, very similar in form to the *Philippus* of 346, to eminent individuals begging them to assume the lead against Persia, first *Agesilaus II, then *Dionysius I, then Alexander of Pherae (cf. Speusippus' *Letter to Philip* 13) and later perhaps *Archidamus III (cf. *Epistle* 9, of doubtful authenticity). Their reaction is not recorded, nor that of other Greeks, but the ambitious proposals of the 4th-cent. tyrant Jason of Pherae suggest that Isocrates' pleas were to some not wholly impracticable.

In 373 when Thebes seized Plataea, he composed the *Plataïcus* purporting to be a speech to the Athenian assembly urging reprisals, and this may have been a sincere manifestation of antipathy to Thebes as a disruptive rival to Athens and Sparta. Likewise the *Archidamus* (366), the imagined speech of the future Spartan king about the Peace of 366/5, may reflect Isocrates' own inclinations. But other writings in this period can hardly be much more than rhetorical exercises, viz. the orations *To Nicocles* (*c*.372), *Nicocles* (*c*.368), and *Evagoras* (*c*.365); see EVAGORAS.

The failure of Athens in the Social War (357–355) and the perilous financial position of the state in 355 stirred Isocrates to denounce in the *De pace* the war policy of the imperialists as the way to bankruptcy, and to demand, in place of the limited peace being made with the allies, a Common Peace and the solution of economic difficulties by the foundation of colonies in Thrace: on the question of a Panhellenic crusade the speech is strikingly silent; the Persian ultimatum of 355 had ruled it out for the moment. The speech is a companion piece to the *Poroi* of *Xenophon; both writings illuminate the financial and foreign policy of *Eubulus. Shortly after, in the *Areopagiticus*, Isocrates advocated return to a sober constitution under which the Areopagus would exercise its ancient general supervision of all aspects of life: although some would ascribe the speech to the period before the Social War, it probably belongs to 354 when the supporters of the Athenian general Chares were beginning to raise their heads again, and in view of the impending prosecution of Timotheus Isocrates may have been in a gloomy mood about the future of Athens under its existing constitution. The treatise must have made a curious impression on his countrymen. Certainly by 353 Isocrates was very much on the defensive. By then he had amassed wealth unprecedented for his profession, and by the law of Periander (?357) he had become liable to frequent trierarchies (funding the costs of a warship for a year); challenged in 354/3 to an *antidosis* (a kind of legal challenge which might result in an exchange of properties), Isocrates had emerged from the court unsuccessful and, imagining himself as a second Socrates, felt moved to write his apologia in the *Antidosis* of 353, in which he criticized his rivals and gave some account of what he himself professed. This is the chief source of our knowledge of his system of education.

In 346 he published his most important treatise, the *Philippus*. Written between the voting of the Peace of Philocrates (346) and *Philip II of Macedon's intervention in Phocis in central Greece, it expounded afresh the programme of the *Panegyricus* and called on Philip 'to take the lead of both the concord of the Hellenes and the campaign against the barbarians' (§ 16) and to relieve the misery of Greece by planting colonies in the western satrapies of the Persian empire (§ 120). In the following year, when Philip instead of beginning the crusade had got himself wounded in war against northern barbarians, Isocrates sent a further letter (*Epistle* 2) urging Philip to begin the campaign against Persia and so acquit himself of slanderous accusations about his real intentions; there is no suggestion here that Isocrates thought of a League of Corinth as the necessary instrument for Philip's leadership of 'the concord of the Hellenes'. We do not know how Isocrates reacted to Philip's proposal to extend the

peace brought in 344 by his old pupil Python, but shortly after the collapse of this diplomatic initiative in early 342, he began the last of his great treatises, the *Panathenaicus*, the completion of which was delayed by illness until 339. It was in part personal apologia, in part a comprehensive comparison of Athens and Sparta greatly to the glory of the former. Nowhere did he manifest any further interest in the great theme of the *Panegyricus* and the *Philippus*. Events had disappointed him and the epistles *To Alexander* (?342) and *To Antipater* (?340) were purely personal. One last effort remained. After discussion with the Macedonian statesman Antipater, when after the battle of Chaeronea (338) he came to negotiate, Isocrates wrote an appeal to Philip (*Epistle* 3) to set about the programme of the *Philippus*. The Peace of Demades was the answer, and at the time of the annual burial of the dead in autumn 338 Isocrates starved himself to death.

SIGNIFICANCE In the realm of political ideas large claims have been made for Isocrates as the man who inspired Philip with the idea of attacking Persia, who envisaged not only the form of Hellenic league that established concord and defined the relation of Greece and the Macedonian kings but also the flowering of Greek culture in the Hellenistic world. These claims cannot be substantiated. The various writings addressed to Philip probably helped Philip to form a clearer idea of the nature and strength of the Panhellenist movement the support of which he needed, but that they did more is a conjecture against which Isocrates' own words in *Epistle* 3 (§ 3) contend. His ideas about the partnership of Philip and the Greeks appear from the treatises to have been very imprecise, and the fact that he was said to have sent substantially the same epistle to Philip as to *Agesilaus suggests that he sought little more than a good general for the campaign. As to the role of the new colonies, he appears not to have thought of a dispersion of Greeks beyond Asia Minor, and far from the leavening of barbary he spoke as if Greek cities would form separate free entities surrounded by barbarians, ruled as barbarians had to be ruled. For the colonies were to effect merely the removal from Greece of the impoverished, and he had no vision of the prosperity that could and did flow from the creation of new trading areas. On the other hand, Isocrates did provide answers to the two great problems of his age, viz. the discord (*stasis*) within cities due to poverty, and the discord between cities due to petty ambitions and rivalries, and one has only to compare the views of *Plato and *Aristotle to see that, naïve as Isocrates seems, he was by far the most practical; neither of the philosophers explained how cities were to be kept from destroying each other, and their plans for ensuring concord within the city by controlling the growth of population contrast unfavourably with Isocrates' proposals to settle in prosperity those whose poverty was the source of revolutionary violence.

Much has been made of the somewhat imprecise proposals for curing the ills of democracy in the *Areopagiticus*. It is to be noted that these proposals are part of a long tradition deriving from his early master, *Theramenes, and found fulfilment in the arrangements of the Athenian statesman Demetrius of Phalerum (late 4th cent): Isocrates was not alone. In his other writings the tone is very different, and this outburst may have been occasioned largely by the serious condition of Athens after the Social War.

In the history of education Isocrates has an important place. The details of his system remain somewhat obscure, but it would seem that his pupils received under his personal supervision a course of instruction which was neither purely speculative nor a mere training in rhetoric. He disdained the business of the lawcourts as well as 'astrology, geometry, and the like' which at best, he held, did no harm but were of no use 'either in personal matters or in public affairs', and he eschewed the logic-chopping of dialectic, 'the so-called eristic dialogues'. For him the true concern of higher education was 'discussion of general and practical matters', the training of men for discussion and action in the sphere of the practical. What exactly such 'great affairs' were he did not specify, but it would seem that the sort of matters discussed in his own speeches provided the themes for his pupils' speeches which were to be well, that is persuasively argued.

In all this he was in contrast to *Plato whose teaching was at once highly theoretical and essentially dogmatic. Plato aimed to teach men what to think, Isocrates how to argue. There was, not surprisingly, tension between the two and (though many have denied it) with delicate irony Plato in the *Phaedrus* (279a) sneered at Isocrates, who defended himself and his system in the *Antidosis*.

WRITINGS Of the 60 orations extant under his name in Roman times, 25 were considered genuine by *Dionysius of Halicarnassus, and 28 by the rhetor and historian Caecilius (1st cent. BC). Twenty-one survive today; six are court speeches. Of the nine letters extant the authenticity of 1, 3, 4, and 9 has been questioned but never disproved.

The works of Isocrates represent Attic prose in its most elaborate form. Dionysius (*Comp.* 23) compared it to 'closely woven material', or 'a picture in which the lights melt imperceptibly into shadows'. He seems, in fact, to have paid more attention to mere expression than any other Greek writer. He was so careful to avoid hiatus (where a word ending in a vowel precedes a word beginning with one) that Dionysius could find no single instance in the whole of the *Areopagiticus*; he was very sparing even in the elision of short vowels, and crasis, except of καί and ἄν, occurs rarely. Dissonance of consonants, due to the repetition of similar syllables in successive words, and the combination of letters which are hard to pronounce together, is similarly avoided. These objects are attained without any perceptible dislocation of the natural order of words. Another characteristic of the style is the author's attention to rhythm; though avoiding poetical metres, he considered that prose should have rhythms of its own, and approved of certain combinations of trochee and iambus. His periods are artistic and elaborate; the structure of some of the longer sentences is so complex that he overreaches himself; he sacrifices lucidity to form, and becomes monotonous. His vocabulary is almost as pure as that of *Lysias, but while the simplicity of Lysias appears natural, the smoothness of Isocrates is studied.   G.L.C.

Iulia, Iulius See JULIA, JULIUS.

Iunius See JUNIUS.

Jj

Jerome (Eusebius Hieronymus) (*c.* AD 347–420), biblical translator, scholar, and ascetic. Born into a Christian family at Stridon in Dalmatia, he was educated at Rome at the school of Aelius *Donatus, and later studied rhetoric. During a stay at Trier, where he had probably intended to enter imperial service, his Christianity took on greater meaning, and around 372, fired with ascetic zeal, he set out for the east. After two years or more at Antioch, he finally withdrew to the desert of Chalcis (Syria) to undertake the penitential life of an anchoritic monk. Here he began to learn Hebrew, with immense consequences for biblical scholarship. But after no more than a year or so he returned to Antioch, where he was ordained priest. Back in Rome in 382, he quickly won the confidence of Pope Damasus, at whose request he commenced work on what was to become the core of the Vulgate version of the Bible. There too he formed friendships with several aristocratic women who had dedicated themselves to Christianity and were living austere and simple existences. His association with the widow Paula in particular combined with other factors to put him in a bad light with the generality of Roman Christians, and following Damasus' death he was effectively hounded from the city (385). Paula followed him to Palestine, where, at Bethlehem, they founded a monastery and a convent. Here Jerome remained for the rest of his life, devoting himself to the ascetic way and to Christian learning.

Jerome was a prolific writer. In addition to his translations of Scripture, he produced numerous commentaries on books of the Bible, for which he drew heavily on previous commentators such as *Origen. Polemical works on a variety of religious issues reveal a bitter and vitriolic side to his nature. His surviving correspondence, which discloses a network of connections across the whole Mediterranean world and in high places, is of the greatest interest for the study of 4th- and 5th-cent. Christianity. Other works of importance include his translation and expansion of *Eusebius of Caesarea's *Chronicle* of world history, and the *De viris illustribus*, a catalogue of 135 mainly Christian writers.

The famous dream in which Jerome saw himself accused of being not a Christian but a 'Ciceronian' (see CICERO), and which seems to have resulted in his giving up reading pagan literature altogether for many years, is a reflection of the tension felt by many Christians of the time between their religious beliefs and their classical heritage. Over a long period Jerome himself succeeded in resolving this conflict, and perhaps more than any other of the Latin Fathers he can be seen as a man of the classical world who happened to be Christian. His classicism is evident not only in his frequent quotations from classical literature, but often in his style. While his scriptural translations and exegetical works tend to be simple and unadorned, other texts display the full fruits of rhetorical training and the verve of a great natural talent steeped in the best writings of an earlier age. If his enduring importance lay most of all in the Vulgate, in his teaching on celibacy, and in his contribution to western monasticism, he also ranks among the finest writers of Latin prose.   J.H.D.S.

Josephus (Flavius Iosephus) (b. AD 37/8) was a Greek historian but also a Jewish priest of aristocratic descent and largely Pharisaic education, and a political leader in pre-70 Jerusalem. Though a zealous defender of Jewish religion and culture, his writing is largely hostile to the various revolutionary groups, whom he regarded as responsible for the fall of the Temple: his theology centres on the idea that God was currently on the Romans' side. Participation in a delegation to Rome (*c.*64) impressed on him the impracticality of resistance. When the Jerusalem leaders put him in charge of Galilee, he played an ambiguous role. He was besieged at Jotapata, but when captured, evaded a suicide pact and, he claims, was freed when his prophecy of *Vespasian's accession came true. He remained close to *Titus until the fall of Jerusalem, making several attempts to persuade the besieged city to surrender. He was given Roman citizenship, and, after the war, an imperial house to live in in Rome, a pension, and land in Judaea.

He first wrote an account of the war, now lost, in Aramaic, for the Jews of Mesopotamia. Most, if not all, of the seven books of the Greek *Jewish War* appeared between 75 and 79. The first book and a half sketch Jewish history from the Maccabean revolt to AD 66. Much of the rest is based on Josephus' own experience, together with eyewitness reports from others and, probably, the diaries of Vespasian and Titus. The triumph at Rome over *Judaea capta* ('captive Judaea') is described in detail. The *Jewish Antiquities*, in twenty books, published in 93/4, is a history of the Jews from the Creation to just before the outbreak of revolt, ostensibly for Greek readers. The biblical history of the first ten books depends not only on the Hebrew and Greek Bibles, but also on current Jewish oral interpretation. For the post-biblical period, works of Jewish-Hellenistic literature such as the Letter of Aristeas, 2 Esdras, and 1 Maccabees are adapted. In the later part, there is a substantial dependence on the histories of *Nicolaus of Damascus. The famous *testimonium* to Jesus is partly or even wholly an interpolation. Appended to the *Antiquities* was the *Life*—not a full autobiography, but a defence of Josephus' conduct in Galilee, responding to his critics, especially Justus of Tiberias. The *Against Apion* was an apologia for Judaism in two books, demonstrating its antiquity in comparison with Greek culture, and attacking anti-Semitic writers, from the 3rd cent. BC to Apion. Josephus' writings were preserved by the early Church.

E.M.S.; T.R.

Juba II, king of Mauretania and son of Juba of Numidia, was led in *Julius Caesar's triumph in 46 BC when still an infant, and brought up in Italy; he received the Roman citizenship, apparently from Octavian (the future *Augustus), and accompanied him on campaigns. Perhaps first reinstated in Numidia, in 25 he received from Augustus the kingdom of Mauretania, at which parts of Gaetulia rebelled and were put down with the help of a Roman proconsul, Cossus Lentulus (consul 1 BC); and in 17 Juba seems to have taken part in the defeat of Tacfarinas. He married first (by 20 BC) Cleopatra Selene, the daughter of Mark *Antony and *Cleopatra VII, and secondly Glaphyra. He died *c.* AD 23 and was succeeded by Ptolemy, his son by Cleopatra.

Juba was also a person of deep learning, who sought to introduce Greek and Roman culture into his kingdom. His capital at Iol, refounded as Caesarea, and in the west Volubilis, where he may have had a second residence, became fine cities. His artistic collections were remarkable. He developed the production of the 'Gaetulian' purple, perhaps prepared by his invention from orchil. He wrote many books (now lost) in Greek: works on Libya, Arabia, and Assyria; a history of Rome; researches into language, drama, and painting; a treatise on the plant euphorbia, which he discovered and named after his doctor Euphorbus, brother of Antonius Musa, physician to Augustus; and *Homoiotetes*, a comparative study of antiquities, mainly Greek and Roman. *Pliny the Elder and *Plutarch were among the authors who used his writings. He organized an exploratory mission to the Canary Islands.

A.M.; T.J.C.; K.S.S.

Jugurtha, grandson of the Numidian King *Masinissa, outside the line of succession, served at Numantia under Scipio Aemilianus, hereditary patron of the Numidian dynasty, and on his recommendation was adopted by King Micipsa and given pre-eminent rank over his brothers. After Micipsa's death (118 BC) the 'legitimate' brothers Hiempsal and Adherbal objected to his primacy, but he had Hiempsal assassinated and attacked Adherbal, who fled to Rome to appeal for assistance. A commission under Lucius Opimius divided Numidia, giving the more primitive western part to Jugurtha and the more developed eastern part to Adherbal. In 112 Jugurtha attacked Adherbal, besieged him in Cirta, and despite two Roman embassies (one under the *princeps senatus* (First Senator) *Scaurus) captured Cirta and killed him. Some Italian businessmen who had helped in the defence were also killed, and this caused outrage in Rome and led to agitation for war by Gaius Memmius. In 112 the consul Opimius invaded Numidia, but soon gave Jugurtha a tolerable peace, perhaps through the efforts of his Roman friends, but certainly through hesitation over starting a long colonial war. Summoned to Rome under safe-conduct to reveal his protectors, Jugurtha was forbidden to speak by a tribune and, after having a pretender murdered, left hurriedly. In Numidia the war was incompetently waged by Spurius Postumius Albinus (consul 110), and his brother and legate Aulus was forced to capitulate in his absence. An outcry over aristocratic 'corruption' in Rome led to the institution of a commission of enquiry and the election of *Metellus Numidicus for 109. Metellus in two campaigns achieved considerable success, but got no nearer ending the war. His legate *Marius, profiting by this, intrigued to gain the consulship (107), promising quick victory, but he too was unable to deliver it, despite army reforms including the first enrolment of *proletarii* (the poorest citizens, previously exempt from military service) in the legions. The war was finally won when *Sulla persuaded Bocchus I to surrender Jugurtha to Marius. He was executed after Marius' triumph (104).

As Sallust saw, the Jugurthine War marks an important stage in the decline of the oligarchy and the organization of attacks on it. Above all, Marius' army reform unwittingly prepared the way for the use of armies loyal to their commander in politics and civil war.

E.B.

Julia (Iulia), only daughter of *Augustus (by Scribonia), was born in 39 BC and betrothed in 37 to Marcus Antonius Antyllus, son of Mark *Antony and *Fulvia. She was brought up strictly by her father and stepmother *Livia Drusilla. In 25 she married her cousin Marcus Claudius Marcellus and in 21 Marcus *Agrippa, to whom she bore Gaius Julius Caesar and Lucius Julius Caesar, Julia, Vipsania Agrippina, and Agrippa Julius Caesar (Agrippa Postumus). Her third marriage, to *Tiberius (in 11) is said to have been happy at first, but estrangement followed, and her behaviour may have contributed to Tiberius' decision to retire from Rome in 6. In 2 BC Augustus learned of her alleged adulteries

(e.g. with Iullus Antonius, second son of Mark Antony and Fulvia, and banished her to Pandateria; in AD 4 she was allowed to move to Rhegium. Scribonia voluntarily shared her exile. Augustus forbade her burial in his mausoleum, and Tiberius kept her closely confined and stopped her allowance, so that she died of malnutrition before the end of AD 14. *Macrobius (*Sat.* 2. 5) speaks of her gentle disposition and learning, and gives anecdotes attesting her wit.

T.J.C.; R.J.S.

Julia Agrippina See AGRIPPINA THE YOUNGER

Julia Avita Mamaea, younger daughter of Julia Maesa, wife of Gessius Marcianus, was mother of *Severus Alexander and became Augusta on his accession (AD 222). She enjoyed unusual prominence for an empress throughout her son's reign, sharing his popularity until military pressures turned the army against the dynasty; she was murdered with him in March 235.   A.R.Bi.

Julian 'the Apostate' (Flavius Claudius Iulianus), emperor AD 361–3, was born at Constantinople in 331, the son of a half-brother of *Constantine I, Julius Constantius. After his father's murder in dynastic intrigues of 337, Julian was placed by Constantius II in the care of an Arian bishop and from 342 was confined for six years on an imperial estate in Cappadocia. He impressed his Christian tutors there as a gifted and pious pupil, but his reading of the Greek classics was inclining him in private to other gods. In 351, as a student of philosophy, he encountered pagan Neoplatonists and was initiated as a theurgist Maximus of Ephesus. For the next ten years Julian's pagan 'conversion' remained a prudently kept secret. He continued his studies in Asia and later at Athens until summoned to Milan by Constantius to be married to the emperor's sister Helena and proclaimed Caesar with charge over Gaul and Britain (6 November 355). Successful Rhineland campaigns against the Alamanni and Franks between 356 and 359 proved Julian a talented general and won him great popularity with his army. When Constantius ordered the transfer of choice detachments to the east the army mutinied and in February 361, probably with tacit prompting, proclaimed Julian

Augustus. Constantius' death late that year averted civil war and Julian, now publicly declaring his paganism, entered Constantinople unopposed in December. A purge of the imperial court quickly followed, drastically reducing its officials and staff. In his brief reign Julian showed remarkable energy in pursuit of highly ambitious aims. An immediate declaration of general religious toleration foreshadowed a vigorous programme of pagan activism in the interest of Hellenism: the temples and finances of the ancestral cults were to be restored and a hierarchy of provincial and civic pagan priesthoods appointed, while the Christian churches and clergy lost the financial subsidies and privileges gained under Constantine and his successors. Though expressly opposed to violent persecution of Christians, Julian overtly discriminated in favour of pagan individuals and communities in his appointments and judgements: measures such as his ban on the teaching of classical literature and philosophy by Christian professors and his encouragement of charitable expenditure by pagan priests mark a determination to marginalize Christianity as a social force. His attempts to revive the role of the cities in local administration by restoring their revenues and councils and his remarkable plan to rebuild the Jewish Temple at Jerusalem are best appraised in the light of this fundamental aim.

Julian's military ambitions centred on an invasion of Persia intended to settle Rome's long-running war with King Sapor II. To prepare his expedition he moved in June 362 to Antioch, where his relations with the mainly Christian population deteriorated markedly during his stay. The expedition set out in March 363 but despite some early successes it was already in serious difficulties when Julian was fatally wounded in a mêlée in June 363. He left no heir (Helena died childless in 360, and Julian did not remarry), and after his death the reforms he had initiated quickly came to nothing.

Julian's personal piety and intellectual and cultural interests are reflected in his surviving writings, which show considerable learning and some literary talent. They include panegyrics, polemics, theological and satirical works, and a collection of letters, public and private. Of his anti-Christian critique, *Against the Galileans*, only fragments remain. His own philosophic ideology was rooted in Iamblichan Neoplatonism and theurgy. How forcefully it impinged on his public religious reforms is controversial: on one view, they were directed more to the founding of a Neoplatonist 'pagan Church' than to a restoration of traditional Graeco-Roman polytheism, and their potential appeal to the mass of contemporary pagans was correspondingly limited.   R.B.E.S.

Julianus (Lucius Octavius Cornelius Publius Salvius Iulianus Aemilianus), an important Roman lawyer of the 2nd cent. AD, came from Hadrumetum (Hammamet) in Africa (Tunisia) and was a pupil of the lawyer Javolenus Priscus. *Hadrian appreciated his legal expertise and made him quaestor at double the normal salary with responsibility for editing the praetor's edict, which was then enacted in permanent form by a decree of the senate in 131. He was a member of Hadrian's *consilium* (council) and one of the heads of the Sabinian school in succession to Javolenus. He was consul in 148, then governor of Lower Germany, followed by a period out of office which fits the likely date of composition of the *Digesta* ('Ordered Abstracts'), then governor of Nearer Spain about 161–4, and in 167/8 of Africa (Carthage). The future emperor Marcus Didius Severus Julianus was perhaps his nephew.

Beginning with excerpts from and comments on lesser writers (*Ex Minicio, Ad Urseium Ferocem*) his best-known work, the *Digesta* in 90 books (*libri*), follows the same order as Juventius Celsus' similar work, that of the edict followed by a section on separate laws and senatorial decrees. It is notable for its rich casuistry, based mainly on the discussion of cases taken from practice and teaching. Self-confident and original in his views, Julianus seldom cites other lawyers, even when he adopts their views, and his criticisms, more moderate than those of Celsus, are apt tactfully to omit the name of the victim. He was a typical Sabinian in his search for workable solutions and his acceptance of anomalies. No one is more often cited by his fellow lawyers and his work was annotated by, among others, Ulpius Marcellus, Cervidius Scaevola and *Paulus. For a time overshadowed by the late classics such as *Papinian, he is named only as a secondary authority in the Law of Citations of 426, but Justinian honoured him as the most eminent of Roman lawyers and the precursor of his own codification. T.Hon.

Julius Agricola See AGRICOLA.

Julius Agrippa I, Marcus (10 BC–AD 44), called 'Herod' in the Acts of the Apostles but 'Agrippa' on his coins. A grandson of *Herod the Great and eventually ruler of his former kingdom. He lived in Rome from childhood, under the patronage of Antonia the Younger, until the death of the elder (*Drusus in AD 23. Josephus narrates Agrippa's subsequent attempts to raise funds in Palestine and Italy. He was imprisoned by *Tiberius in 36 for a treasonable remark, but, when his friend *Gaius (1) acceded, appointed tetrarch (ruler) of those territories north-east of the Sea of Galilee which were previously ruled by his uncle Philip, and those of Lysanias. In 39 the substantially Jewish areas of Galilee and Peraea, until then under Herod Antipas, were added. Agrippa's appearance, when he passed through Alexandria, sparked off the anti-Jewish riots there. Shortly before Gaius' assassination, he dissuaded the emperor from desecrating the Temple. In 41 *Claudius, in whose accession Agrippa had been involved, added Judaea and Samaria, to complete his kingdom. But the emperor was later displeased by Agrippa's extension of the city wall in north Jerusalem and by his inviting client kings to Tiberias. Agrippa's dramatic death in the Caesarea amphitheatre is embroidered in tradition. His respect for Judaism was remembered longer than his benefactions to Caesarea, Sebaste, Berytus, and Heliopolis. Acts of the Apostles makes him responsible for the execution of James brother of John and Peter's imprisonment. T.R.

Julius Agrippa II, Marcus (b. AD 27/8), did not succeed his father *Julius Agrippa I in 44, but lived in Rome. There he supported the Jews before the emperor Claudius against the Samaritans and the procurator Cumanus. In 50 Agrippa was appointed king of Chalcis in the southern Beqa' valley, succeeding to the position of his uncle *Herod the Great. As controller of the Temple, he also received the right to appoint and depose high priests. In 53 his territory was exchanged for the area in the Lebanon and anti-Lebanon region once ruled by Philip (Herod's son) and then by his own father. *Nero added parts of Galilee and

of Peraea. Agrippa's coins carry the imperial portrait. He lavished attention on the Temple and had his Jerusalem palace close by. But in 66 he and his sister Berenice were expelled from the city by the Jewish leadership, having failed to persuade the Jews to tolerate Gessius Florus' conduct as procurator. Unable to prevent revolt, Agrippa supplied cavalry and archers to the Romans throughout the war, and accompanied Titus during its latter stages. He was rewarded by an enlargement of his territory. In 75, when Berenice went to live with Titus in Rome, Agrippa received praetorian status there. He supplied *Josephus with information for the *Jewish War* and commended the work on publication. Indications in Josephus that Agrippa was dead before the publication of the *Antiquities* and the Life (93/4) are compatible with the epigraphic evidence from his kingdom, and they discredit the Byzantine scholar Photius' statement (*Bibl.* 33) that Agrippa died in 100.

St *Paul appeared before him. T.R.

Julius Caesar (Gaius Iulius Caesar), born 100 BC (Suet. *Iul.* 88. 1), of a patrician family without social equals, as descendants of Venus and Aeneas, but with little recent political success. His father's sister Julia married *Marius, and her cousins Lucius Julius Caesar and Gaius Julius Caesar Strabo Vopiscus profited by his unforeseen success, but Caesar's father never became consul. *Cinna while in power, gave Caesar his daughter Cornelia in marriage and made him *flamen Dialis* (priest of Jupiter) as successor to Lucius Cornelius Merula—a post of supreme honour but normally precluding a consulship (no doubt thought unattainable). *Sulla, after his victory, annulled his enemies' measures, including this appointment, but as a fellow patrician spared Caesar's life, even though he refused to divorce Cornelia and voluntarily resign his priesthood.

Most of the next decade Caesar spent in Asia, studying and winning military distinction, including a victory over an advance force of *Mithradates VI and a *corona civica* (the Roman Victoria Cross); but two prosecutions of ex-Sullani (Gnaeus Cornelius Dolabella and Gaius Antonius), although unsuccessful, established his fame as an orator. In 73 he was co-opted a *pontifex* (member of one of the four chief colleges of the Roman priesthood), largely through family connections, and returned to Rome. Elected *tribunus militum* (military tribune), he supported amnesty for the associates of Marcus Aemilius Lepidus. As quaestor 69, before going to his province of Further Spain, he lost both his aunt Julia and his wife. He conducted their funerals in the grand aristocratic manner, stressing his aunt's (and thus partly his own) descent from kings and gods (Suet. *Iul.* 6. 1) and, for the first time since Sulla, displaying Marius' *imago* (wax funerary mask) and distinctions in public. (He no doubt similarly displayed Cinna's at Cornelia's funeral.) On his return from Spain he found the Latin colonies beyond the Po vigorously demanding Roman citizenship and supported their agitation, but did nothing to further their cause in Rome. He supported the laws of Aulus Gabinius and Gaius Manilius, conferring extraordinary commands on *Pompey (clearly a most useful patron), and he married Pompeia, a granddaughter of Sulla. With Pompey overseas, he courted another powerful ex-Sullan, *Crassus, Pompey's enemy, joining him in various political schemes in return for financial support, which enabled Caesar to spend large sums as curator of the Appian Way and as aedile (65). In 64, in charge of the murder court, he resumed his vendetta against Sulla by offering to receive prosecutions of men who had killed citizens in Sulla's proscription.

In 63 Quintus Caecilius Metellus Pius' death left the chief pontificate vacant, a post normally held by eminent ex-consuls. Although two (Publius Servilius Isauricus, to whom Caesar was bound in loyalty as to his old commander in Cilicia, and Quintus *Lutatius Catulus (2)) sought the office, Caesar announced his candidacy and through lavish bribery won the election. This and his election to a praetorship for 62 established him as a man of power and importance. He supported *Catiline, who advocated a welcome cancellation of debts, but covered his tracks when Catiline turned to conspiracy. The consul *Cicero, who to the end of his days was convinced of Caesar's involvement, had to proclaim his innocence. In his prosecution of Gaius Rabirius he left the legality of the so-called *senatus consultum ultimum* ('ultimate' i.e. emergency decree of the senate) in doubt, and when Cicero wanted the death penalty

under that decree for the conspirators betrayed by the Allobrogan envoys (the Allobroges were a Gallic tribe), Caesar persuaded most senators to vote against it, until a speech by *Cato the Younger changed their minds.

As praetor he joined the tribune Quintus Caecilius Metellus Nepos in agitating for the recall of Pompey against Catiline's forces. Suspended from office, he demonstratively submitted, and the senate, eager to avoid alienating him, reinstated and thanked him. In December, when Pompeia was *ex officio* in charge of the rites of the Bona Dea, from which men were strictly excluded, *Clodius gained access disguised as a woman—it was said, in order to approach Pompeia in her husband's absence—and was ejected. Caesar, while asserting the innocence of Clodius (a man congenial to him and worth cultivating) and of Pompeia, divorced her, proclaiming that his household must be free even from suspicion. With his consulship approaching, he could now seek a more advantageous marriage.

But first he had to go to his province of Further Spain. His creditors applied for an injunction to stop him from leaving, and he was saved from this unprecedented indignity by Crassus' standing surety for part of his debts: his provincial spoils would cover the rest. He now 'had to make a bigger profit in one year than *Verres had in three' and, largely neglecting his routine duties, he concentrated on attacking independent tribes. The booty enabled him to clear his debts and pay large sums into the treasury, all without incurring a risk of prosecution. About mid-60 he returned to Rome, was voted a triumph (victory-procession) by a co-operative senate, and prepared to claim his consulship. There was a technical obstacle: to announce his candidacy for the consulship he had to enter Rome long before the triumph could be arranged, but that would forfeit his *imperium* (grant of overriding military and civil authority) and right to triumph. The senate was ready to give him a dispensation, but his enemy Cato, although only an ex-tribune, arranged to be asked to speak and talked the proposal out. Caesar decided to put power before glory and entered the city.

He now could not afford to lose, so he needed allies and a massive infusion of money. A brilliant stroke secured both. In his absence Pompey and Crassus had failed—partly because each had opposed the other—

to obtain what they respectively wanted from the senate: ratification of Pompey's eastern settlement and land for his veterans, and a remission of part of the price offered for the tithe of Asia by the *publicani* (Roman tax-farmers). Caesar, on good terms with both, persuaded them to support his candidacy: he promised to give each what he wanted without harm to the other, provided they refrained from mutual opposition. Pompey now persuaded his wealthy friend Lucius Lucceius to join Caesar in his canvass: in return for paying the expenses for bribery (no doubt with Crassus' help), he could expect to succeed through Caesar's popularity. But Caesar's enemies, led by the upright Cato, collected a huge bribery fund for Cato's son-in-law Marcus Calpurnius Bibulus, who secured second place after Caesar.

As consul Caesar appealed to the senate for co-operation in formulating the laws to satisfy his allies. Frustrated by his enemies, he passed them in the assembly by open violence, aided by friendly tribunes. Bibulus withdrew to his house, announcing that he was stopping all future meetings of the assemblies by watching the sky for omens. This unprecedented step, of doubtful legality, was ignored by Caesar, who satisfied Pompey and Crassus and went on to pass further legislation, *i.a.* on *repetundae* (extortion) and on the publication of senate debates. Pompey and Crassus, satisfied (especially) with his assuming the onus for his methods, now joined him in an open alliance (sometimes erroneously called the 'First Triumvirate'). Pompey married Julia and Caesar married *Calpurnia (1), whose father, Lucius Calpurnius Piso Caesoninus, was made consul 58, with Pompey's aide Gabinius as colleague. For further insurance, Clodius was allowed to become a plebeian and tribune 58. Caesar's reward was a law of Vatinius, giving him Illyricum and Cisalpine Gaul for five years. The senate obligingly added Transalpine Gaul. Early in 58 attempts to prosecute Caesar were averted, and moderates in the senate attempted conciliation by offering to have his legislation re-enacted in proper form. But Caesar refused, since this would admit guilt and impair his *dignitas* (personal honour). The breach between him and the senate majority thus became irreparable.

A movement by the Helvetii (a Celtic people who in about 100 BC had migrated to an area in modern Switzerland) gave him an unforeseen chance of starting a major war, which after nearly a decade and many vicissitudes led to the conquest of the whole of Gaul. It was in Gaul that he acquired the taste and the resources for monarchy and trained the legions that could 'storm the heavens' (*BHisp.* 42. 7). Young Roman aristocrats flocked to him to make their fortunes, vast sums (sometimes made palatable as loans) flowed into the pockets of upper-class Romans and, as gifts, to cities and princes, to support Caesar's ambitions. The depleted treasury received none of the profits and was forced to pay for his legions. In his triumphs of 46 (see below) he displayed 63,000 talents of silver and spent about 20,000 of his own money (together enough to create the fortunes of 5,000 *equites* (members of the Roman order of knights), much of it booty from Gaul. Plutarch, on the basis of Caesar's figures, reports that a million Gauls were killed and another million enslaved. Requisitions of food and punitive devastations completed human, economic, and ecological disaster probably unequalled until the conquest of the Americas.

In Rome Caesar's position remained secure until 56, when his bitter enemy Lucius Domitius Ahenobarbus, confident of becoming consul 55, promised to recall and prosecute him, and Cicero, back from exile, hoped to detach Pompey from him. Crassus informed him of what was going on, and they summoned Pompey to Luca (mod. Lucca), where he was persuaded to renew the compact. Pompey and Crassus became consuls 55, receiving Spain and Syria respectively for five years, while Caesar's command was renewed for five years in Gaul; Pompey was to stay near Rome to look after their interests, governing Spain through legates. But the alliance soon disintegrated. Julia died (54) and Crassus, attacking Parthia, was killed at Carrhae (53). In 52 Pompey married a daughter of Caesar's enemy Quintus Caecilius Metellus Pius Scipio and made him his colleague as consul. Caesar now secured legal authorization to stand for a consulship in absence in 49; but the legality of this became doubtful, and his claim that it included the right to retain *imperium* (hence immunity from prosecution) was denied by his enemies. (The legal position is obscured by partisan distortion.) Pompey was gradually (perhaps reluctantly) forced to co-operate with them, to avoid a consulship by Caesar in 48, which would have left him irreversibly at Caesar's mercy. In 49 Caesar invaded Italy and started a civil war, nominally to defend the rights of tribunes who had been forced to flee to him for protection, but in fact, as he later admitted (Suet. *Iul.* 30. 4), to escape conviction and exile.

He rapidly overran Italy, where there were no reliable veteran legions to oppose him. As he moved down the peninsula, he kept making specious peace offers, retailed with considerable distortion in book 1 of his *Civil War.* Ahenobarbus was forced to surrender at Corfinium, and Pompey, knowing that Italy was untenable, to the chagrin of his aristocratic supporters crossed to Greece, hoping to strangle Italy by encirclement. Caesar broke it by defeating Pompey's legates in a brilliant campaign in Spain and then taking Massalia. In 48 he crossed to Greece, though Pompey controlled the seas, and besieged him at Dyrrhachium. A tactical defeat there turned into *de facto* strategic victory when Pompey withdrew to Thessaly, where both sides received reinforcements. Persuaded, against his better judgement, to offer battle at Pharsalus, Pompey was decisively defeated, escaped to Egypt and was killed. Caesar, arriving there in pursuit, intervened in a domestic conflict over the kingship and was cut off for months in Alexandria, until extricated by troops from Asia Minor and a Jewish force under Antipater (father of *Herod). He spent three more months in Egypt, chiefly with *Cleopatra VII, whom he established on the throne and who after his departure bore a son whom she named Ptolemy Caesar. Then, moving rapidly through Syria and Asia Minor, he reorganized the eastern provinces, easily defeated Pharnaces II (son of Mithradates) at Zela, and in September 47 returned to Italy. There he had to settle an army mutiny and serious social unrest, fanned during his absence by Marcus *Caelius Rufus and *Milo and after their death by *Dolabella.

Meanwhile the republican forces had had time to entrench themselves in Africa, where Metellus Scipio assumed command, aided by Juba I of Mauretania. Caesar landed in December. After an inauspicious beginning he gained the support of Bocchus II and Publius Sittius and, deliberately inviting blockade at Thapsus, won a decisive victory that led to the death of most of the republican leaders (including Scipio and Cato). On his return he was voted unprecedented honours and celebrated four splendid triumphs (20 September–1 October 46), nominally over foreign enemies, to mark the end of the wars and the beginning of reconstruction. But the younger Gnaeus Pompeius Magnus, soon joined by his brother Sextus *Pompey and Titus Labienus, consul for the second time, raised thirteen legions in Spain and secured much native support. In November Caesar hurriedly left Rome to meet them. The Pompeians were forced to offer battle at Munda (near Urso) and were annihilated with the loss of 30,000 men in Caesar's hardest-fought battle. After reorganizing Spain, with massive colonization, he returned to Rome and celebrated a triumph over 'Spain'.

Caesar had been dictator (briefly), nominally for holding elections, in 49, consul for the second time 48, and dictator for the second time after Pharsalus; he was consul for the third time and *curator morum* ('supervisor of public morals') in 46 and dictator for the third time (designated for ten years ahead, we are told: Cass. Dio 43. 14. 3) after Thapsus; he held his fourth, sole, consulship for nine months and his fourth dictatorship in 45, and was consul for the fifth time and (from about February) *dictator perpetuo* (dictator for life) in 44. The specification of his dictatorships after the first is lost in the *fasti* (official calendars and records of magistracies), but at least the third and fourth were probably, like Sulla's, *rei publicae constituendae* ('for settling the republic'). Apart from epigraphic evidence (see T. R. S. Broughton, *Magistrates of the Roman Republic* (1951–2) 3. 108), this is suggested by Cicero's references and by the fact that the work of reform began after Thapsus. The specification (if any) of the perpetual dictatorship is beyond conjecture. In addition to introducing the Julian calendar, his most lasting achievement, he considerably increased the numbers of senators, priests, and magistrates, for the first time since *c.*500 created new patrician families, founded numerous colonies, especially for veterans and the city *plebs*, and passed various administrative reforms. His great-nephew Octavian, adopted by Caesar in his testament in 45, was made a *pontifex* aged about 16 and, although he had no military experience, was designated *magister equitum* ('master of the horse', in effect the dictator's deputy) in 44, aged 18. Caesar, although he adopted the dress and ornaments of the old Roman kings, refused the invidious title of *rex* (king), but, thinking gods superior to kings (Suet. *Iul.* 6. 1), aimed at deification, which after gradual approaches he finally achieved shortly before his death (Cic. *Phil.* 2. 110: Mark *Antony was designated his *flamen* or priest). It was the culmination of increasingly unprecedented honours voted by the senate (Cass. Dio lists them at various points), perhaps in part to see how far he would go, and he accepted most of them.

He had no plans for basic social, economic, or constitutional reforms, except to graft his divine and hereditary rule onto the republic. The abyss this opened between him and his fellow *nobiles* made him uncomfortable, and he planned to escape from Rome to wage a major Parthian war. As all remembered the disruption caused by his temporary absences during the Civil Wars, the prospect of being ruled by an absent divine monarch for years ahead proved intolerable even to his friends. He was assassinated in the Curia (senate-house), in a widespread conspiracy hastily stitched together to anticipate his departure, on 15 March 44.

Caesar was a distinguished orator in the 'Attic' manner (i.e. claiming the orators of Classical Athens as models), believing in 'analogy' (grammatical regularity, on which he wrote a treatise) and in the use of ordinary words (Gell. *NA* 1. 10. 4). His speeches, at least some of which were published, and his pamphlet attacking Cato's memory, are lost. Seven books on the Gallic War (an eighth was added by Aulus Hirtius) and three on the Civil War survive, written to provide raw material for history and ensure that his point of view would prevail with posterity. Distortion at various points in the *Civil War* is demonstrated by evidence surviving in Cicero's correspondence. For praise of Caesar's style, see Cic. *Brut.* 262 (strongly tinged by flattery).

E.B.

Julius Caesar Germanicus See GERMAN-ICUS.

Julius Frontinus See FRONTINUS.

Julius Paulus See PAULUS.

Junius Brutus, Marcus See BRUTUS.

Justin Martyr (*c.* AD 100–65), a Christian apologist, flourished under *Antoninus Pius and died a martyr in Rome after his condemnation as a Christian by the city-prefect Quintus Junius Rusticus. At the beginning of his *First Apology* he tells us that he was born at Flavia Neapolis (the ancient Shechem in Samaria) of pagan parents. He seems never to have been attracted to Judaism, though he knows seven Jewish sects (*Trypho* 80. 4). His account of his early disappointments in philosophy (*Trypho* 3 ff.) is conventional, but he was certainly a Platonist (see PLATO) when converted to Christianity. The Stoics he knew and admired, but more for their lives and for their teachings, and his conversion owed much to the constancy of Christian confessors (*2 Apol.* 12).

After leaving Samaria, he set up a small school in Rome, and wrote two apologies, nominally directed to Antoninus Pius. One (*c.*155) defends Christianity in general against popular calumny and intellectual contempt; the second (*c.*162) is inspired by acts of persecution following denunciations of Christians to the authorities. It reveals that Christians served in the army and that Christian wives sometimes divorced their pagan spouses. Justin's pupil Tatian attributes his death to information given by Crescens, a Cynic rival (*Oratio* 19).

Justin's work is not so much a synthesis of Christianity, paganism, and Judaism as an attempt to discover an underlying homogeneity. This he effects by his doctrine of the Logos, which, as Christ, was present in many Old Testament epiphanies, and guarantees the unity of scriptural inspiration. (So he maintains in his *Dialogue with Trypho*, the first great work of Christian typology.) In the *Apologies* (esp. *2 Apol.* 13) he anticipates *Clement of Alexandria and the Alexandrian school by arguing that a 'spermatic *logos*', identical with or related to Christ, instructs every man in wisdom, so that even pagan philosophers foreshadowed Christian truth. Like the other apologists, he accepts the civil authorities, and at once explains and enhances the attraction of Christianity for

Greek-speaking intellectuals of the period. Because of his reputation, a number of feeble apologies were also attributed to him; of these the *De monarchia* and *Cohortatio ad Graecos*, unusually replete with Christian or Jewish forgeries, are occasionally a useful source of fragments from authentic pagan dramas.

W.H.C.F.; M.J.E.

Justinian (Flavius Petrus Sabbatius Iustinianus), eastern Roman emperor AD 527–65. He was born *c.*482 at Tauresium, near Bederiana in Thrace, a place subsequently graced with the city of Justiniana Prima (mod. Caricin Grad). His father Sabbatius married a sister of the future emperor Justin, who adopted his nephew. Under Anastasius he joined the *scholae* or guards, and became a *candidatus*, personal imperial bodyguard. During the succession dispute in 518 Justinian was offered the throne but supported his more senior uncle, whose position he helped secure by eliminating potential rivals, Amantius and Vitalian. From his residence in the palace of Hormisdas he was now the dominant influence on imperial decisions, as revealed by his correspondence with Pope Hormisdas that healed the Acacian schism. Promotion reflected his power, *comes* ('count') in 519, *magister militum praesentalis* ('general in attendance') in 520, consul in 521 when celebrations were exceptionally lavish, patrician and *nobilissimus* ('most noble') before 527. After 523 he married the former actress Theodora, but only after the empress Lupicina, who strongly opposed the match, had died and Justinian persuaded Justin to repeal the law prohibiting marriages between senators and actresses. Justinian, apparently a staunch Chalcedonian, married a Monophysite.

Justinian was crowned Augustus on 1 April 527, succeeded as sole emperor on Justin's death on 1 August, and soon began a campaign to enforce legislation against heretics, pagans, and male homosexuals, while in 530/1 permitting Monophysites exiled by Justin to return. Imperial success depended on God's favour, a recurrent concern throughout Justinian's reign, so that deviants must be corrected or eliminated, but Justinian's conception of orthodoxy was sufficiently flexible to encourage him repeatedly to attempt religious reunification. Negotiations with Monophysites were pursued in 531/2,

and in March 533 an imperial edict proclaimed the oneness of Christ, underlining this through the Theopaschite formula that the Christ who suffered in the flesh was one of the Trinity. This departure from rigid Chalcedonian doctrine seemed to presage toleration, but Monophysites failed to respond as intended. Further attempts at compromise began in the 540s, with Justinian's decision to secure condemnation of specific writings by three leading 5th-cent. opponents of Monophysites, Theodore of Mopsuestia, Theodoret of Cyrrhus, and Ibas of Edessa. This culminated in anathema for these so-called Three Chapters at the fifth ecumenical council in Constantinople in 553, when Pope Vigilius subscribed under extreme compulsion. This compromise, too, failed to reconcile Monophysites who now possessed a separate episcopal hierarchy, and created schism in Italy and Africa for about 50 years. Towards the end of his reign Justinian engaged in discussions with Nestorian bishops from Persia, and in his last year, concerned to achieve unity to the very end, he adopted the extreme Monophysite doctrine of Aphthartodocetism, that Christ's body was incorruptible: this prompted fresh expulsions of bishops, though now the victims were leading Chalcedonians.

After religion Justinian's second great passion was law and administration. In 528 he established a commission to codify all valid imperial constitutions from Hadrian to the present: the *Codex Iustinianus* was first promulgated in 529, with a revised edition in 534. A second commission, appointed to excerpt and codify the works of classical jurists, published the *Digest* in December 533 (see below). Thereafter Justinian continued to legislate energetically, with about 150 *Novels* (*Novellae*: 'new constitutions') promulgated on a wide variety of administrative, legal, ecclesiastical, and criminal matters in a confident assertion of the efficacy of imperial action. Justinian also imposed his image on Constantinople after the Nika riot (532) necessitated extensive reconstruction, with the architecturally innovative St Sophia as centre-piece.

Warfare occupied much of Justinian's attention: he inherited conflict with Sasanid Persia which, although briefly interrupted by the Endless Peace in 532, resumed in 540 and dragged on until 561/2. His greatest ambition was to reconquer the provinces of the western empire: Africa was quickly recovered from the Vandals in 533/4, but Ostrogothic Italy proved much harder in spite of apparent triumph in 540 and the peninsula was not secured until 561/2; part of Spain was fortuitously recovered in 551. While intending to concentrate aggressive warfare in the west Justinian devoted much money and energy to enhancing the defences of the Balkans and eastern frontier: Armenia, Mesopotamia, and Syria required protection from the Persians, Thrace, and Illyricum from raids by Bulgars, Gepids, and Slavs which on occasion even threatened the suburbs of Constantinople. Human and natural destruction had to be restored. *Procopius' *Buildings* provides a panegyrical survey of Justinian's efforts: fortifications were improved, but other components of an active defence may have been neglected. Beyond the frontiers diplomacy and money were exploited to maintain peace and dilute threats, with mixed success and adverse reaction from advocates of 'traditional' Roman aggression.

Justinian led an austere life, working hard for long hours and expecting the same of subordinates. He identified and exploited talent, John the Cappadocian and Peter Barsymas as administrators, *Tribonian the lawyer, the generals Belisarius and Narses, the architect Anthemius, and the writers *Procopius and Paulus the Silentiary. Their various efforts ensured that the long reign presented, in general, a successful façade, though in some areas the reality of the achievement is questionable. Justinian's most trusted assistant, Theodora, died in 548; thereafter the childless Justinian failed to attend to the most pressing concern for every prudent emperor from *Augustus onwards, namely the identification and grooming of a successor.

L.M.W.

Justinian's codification is a term loosely used to describe the three volumes (*Codex, Digesta* or *Pandectae, Institutiones*) in which Justinian (AD 527–65) tried to restate the whole of Roman law in a manageable and consistent form, though this restatement, which runs to over a million words, is too bulky and ill-arranged to count as a codification in the modern sense.

Ninety years after the Theodosian Code (see THEODOSIUS II) of 438 a new codex was needed to collect the laws enacted in the intervening period. Justinian, with a keen sense of his predecessors' neglect and his own superior dedication, seized the opportunity to carry out part of the programme envisaged by Theodosius II in 429. This involved including all imperial laws in one volume and ensuring that the laws in it were consistent with one another (C. *Haec* pref.). Within a few months of becoming emperor in 527, he ordered a commission of ten, mostly present or recent holders of public office, to prepare a comprehensive collection of imperial laws including those in the three existing codices (*Gregorianus, Hermogenianus,* and *Theodosianus*), so far as they were still in force, together with more recent laws (*novellae*). The laws were to be edited in a short and clear form, with no repetition or conflict, but attributed to the emperors and dates at which they had originally been issued. The commission contained some lawyers but its head was the politically powerful non-lawyer, John of Cappadocia. Within fourteen months the *Codex Iustinianus* in twelve books (*libri*) was finished and on 7 April 529 was promulgated as the exclusive source of imperial laws, the earlier codes being repealed (C. *Summa*). Its practical aim was to curtail lawsuits; and its compilation was widely regarded as a major achievement. It fitted a vision in which Justinian saw himself as rapidly restoring and extending the empire, in which process military and legal achievements would reinforce one another (C. *Summa* pref.). This 529 *Codex* does not survive, but the second edition of 534 does.

Besides the laws in the *Codex,* C. *Summa* allowed the writings of the old lawyers of authority to be cited in court. Their views not infrequently conflicted, the conflicts being settled by counting heads according to the Law of Citations of 426. In 429 Theodosius II had looked forward to a time when this voluminous material could be arranged under subject-headings and harmonized. Probably, though the matter is controversial, Justinian from the start intended to undertake the further project of collecting, condensing, and amending the rest of Roman law, provided someone could organize it: the incentive to outdo Theodosius still applied. At any rate, Justinian first arranged for the 50 most prominent conflicts between the old writers to be settled (*Quinquaginta decisiones*), then in December 530 (C. *Deo* *auctore*) ordered that these old works, which ran to over 1,500 books (*libri*), be condensed in 50 books and given the title *Digesta* ('Ordered Abstracts') or *Pandectae* ('Encyclopaedia'). For that purpose he set up a second commission consisting of élite lawyers under the quaestor *Tribonian, who had shown his mettle as a member of the earlier commission, along with another official, four law professors, and eleven advocates. They were to read the works of authority, none of them written later than about AD 300, and excerpt what was currently valid. As for the *Codex*, the commissioners were to edit the texts in a clear form with no repetition or contradiction. Thirty-nine writers were used for the compilation. The commission was not to count heads but to choose the best view, no matter who held it. In the upshot *Ulpian, who provided two-fifths of the *Digesta*, was their main source; *Paulus provided one-sixth.

The commission worked rapidly and the *Digesta* or *Pandectae* was promulgated on 16 December 533 (C. *Tanta/Dedōken*). The speed of the operation has led some scholars to suppose that the commissioners, instead of reading the original sources, worked from previous collections of material. But nothing on the required scale has been traced, and Tribonian would have dismissed reliance on secondary sources as disreputable, even supposing it escaped detection. Time was saved in another way. As F. Bluhme discovered in 1820, the works to be read were divided into three groups, extracts from which are generally kept together in the finished *Digesta*. The inference is that three subcommittees were appointed to read the three groups of works; and the operation was perhaps further subdivided within the committees. Justinian, in whose palace the commission was working, could be relied on to see that the timetable was kept to, as he did with the construction of Hagia Sophia.

The compilers had authority not merely to eliminate obsolete or superfluous texts but to alter those they kept. The extent to which they made use of this power is controversial. In any event, if the new version of a text differed from the old, the new prevailed, on the theory that Justinian was entitled to amend the previous law as he wished. But the amended texts were 'out of respect for antiquity' attributed to the original authors and books. This was a compromise, unsatisfactory from a scholarly point of view, which enabled Justinian to claim that everything in the *Digesta* was his, while in fact often reverting to the law as it was before 300.

The practical aims of the *Digesta* were to shorten lawsuits and provide a revised law syllabus to be used in the schools of Berytus (mod. Beirut) and Constantinople (C. *Omnem*). To complete the reform of law-teaching Justinian ordered Tribonian and two of the professors to prepare an up-to-date edition of *Gaius (2)'s lectures, the *Institutiones*, making use also of other elementary teaching books by writers of authority. The professors perhaps each drafted two books, while Tribonian brought the whole up to date by adding an account of recent legislation, especially Justinian's. The *Institutiones* like the *Digesta* was promulgated in December 533. It has survived and was for many centuries a successful students' first-year book. Then in 534 a second edition of the *Codex* of 529 was produced, which included the reforming laws of the intervening five years. This also has survived. The codification was now at an end. To avoid conflicting interpretations, commentaries on it were forbidden. Justinian however continued to legislate without pause, mainly in Greek, and private collections of his later laws (*novellae*) have been preserved.

His codification had a practical and a political aim. Its practical impact, though considerable, was limited by the fact that it was wholly in Latin. Hence in the Greek-speaking Byzantine empire few could make proper use of it until the coming of a Greek collection of laws, the *Basilica*, which in the 9th and 10th cents. at last fused the two main sources of law, *Codex* and *Digesta*. In the west Justinian's laws were in force for two centuries in parts of Italy and in North Africa until the expansion of Islam in the 7th cent.

The political aim of the codification was to renew, reform, and extend the Roman empire in its civil aspect. In this Justinian was in the long run successful, but not in the way he foresaw. He thought that the spread of Roman law depended on military conquest. In the west that proved short-lived; and when from the 11th cent. onwards his codification came to be taken as the basis of legal education and administration throughout Europe, it was not by force of arms but through its prestige and inherent rationality that his version of Roman law was adopted.

T.Hon.

Juvenal (Decimus Iunius Iuvenalis), Roman satirist. Known primarily for the angry tone of his early *Satires*, although in later poems he developed an ironical and detached superiority as his satiric strategy. The highly rhetorical nature of the *Satires* has long been recognized but only recently has the allied concept of the 'mask' (*persona*) been deployed (primarily by W. S. Anderson, *Essays on Roman Satire* (1982)) to facilitate assessment of the *Satires* as self-conscious poetic constructs, rather than the reflections of the realities of Roman social life for which they have often been read. This approach is reinforced by rejection of the biographical interpretation, in which Juvenal's 'life' was reconstructed from details in the *Satires*. In fact, virtually nothing is known of his life: he is the addressee of three epigrams of *Martial (themselves highly sophisticated literary constructions) which indicate his skill in oratory. The absence of dedication to a patron in Juvenal's *Satires* may suggest that he was a member of the élite. The few datable references confirm R. Syme's assessment that the five books were written during the second and third decades of the 2nd cent. AD (or later), at about the same time as *Tacitus was writing his *Annals*. There is no reason to doubt that the *Satires* were written and published in books. Book 1 comprises *Satires* 1–5, book 2 *Satire* 6 alone, book 3 *Satires* 7–9, book 4 *Satires* 10–12, and book 5 *Satires* 13–16 (the last poem is unfinished).

In book 1 Juvenal introduces his indignant speaker who condemns Rome (satire is an urban genre), especially the corruption of the patron–client relationship (in *Satires* 1, 3, 4, and 5) and the decadence of the élite (in 1, 2, and 4). *Satire* 1, following predecessors in the genre, provides a justification for satire and a programme of the angry tone and the victims of satirical attack. These include the 'outgroups' who transgress sexual and social boundaries, such as the passive homosexuals of *Satire* 2 and the social upstarts, criminals, and foreigners attacked by Umbricius in *Satire* 3 (Umbricius figures himself as the last true Roman, driven from an un-Roman Rome). The Roman élite are portrayed as paradigms of moral corruption: the selfish

rich are attacked in *Satires* 1 and 3 and the emperor *Domitian is portrayed as sexual hypocrite and autocrat in 2 and 4. Those dependent on these powerful men are not absolved from blame: the courtiers humiliated by Domitian by being asked to advise on what to do with an enormous fish in *Satire* 4, like the client humiliated by his wealthy patron at a dinner party in 5, are condemned for craven compliance.

The focus upon Roman men in book 1 is complemented by the focus upon Roman women in book 2, which consists of the massive *Satire* 6, comparable in length to a book of epic. The speaker fiercely (but unsuccessfully) attempts to dissuade his addressee from marriage by cataloguing the (alleged) faults of Roman wives. Here Juvenal develops his angry speaker in the ultimate rant which seems to exhaust the possibilities of angry satire; thereafter he adopts a new approach of irony and cynicism. Initially (in book 3) Juvenal's new, calmer persona takes up the same topics as treated in book 1, although his detachment invites a less stark perspective: clients and patrons (*Satires* 7 and 9) and the corruption and worthlessness of the élite (8). He then marks his change of direction explicitly at the start of book 4, where the speaker states his preference for detached laughter over tears as a reaction to the follies of the world; in the remainder of *Satire* 10 he accordingly demolishes first the objects of human prayer, then the act of prayer itself. His programmatic declaration is borne out by the 'Horatian' tone and topics (see HORACE) of *Satire* 11 (where an invitation to dinner conveys a condemnation of decadence and a recommendation of self-sufficiency) and 12 (where true friendship is contrasted with the false friendship of legacy-hunters). The speaker of book 5 becomes still more detached and cynical as he turns his attention to the themes of crime and punishment, money and greed. The opening poem, *Satire* 13, offers a programmatic condemnation of anger in the form of a mock consolation, which indicates clearly the development from book 1 where anger was apparently approved.

Juvenal claims that his satire replaces epic (*Sat.* 1) and tragedy (6. 634–61): his chief contribution to the genre is his appropriation of the 'grand style' from other more elevated forms of hexameter verse, notably epic. This contrasts markedly with the sometimes coarse language of *Lucilius (1) and the tone of refined 'conversation' adopted by Horace in his satirical writings. Juvenal's satiric 'grand style' mingles different lexical levels, ranging from epic and tragedy (e.g. the epic parody in *Satires* 4 and 12) to mundanities, Greek words, and occasional obscenities. His penchant for oxymora, pithy paradoxes, and trenchant questions makes Juvenal a favourite mine for quotations, e.g. *mens sana in corpore sano* (10. 356) and *quis custodiet ipsos custodes?* (6. 347–8): 'a healthy mind in a healthy body' and 'who guards the guards themselves?' The *Satires* also appropriate the themes and structures of other forms of discourse: they are rhetorical performances which develop for satiric ends material drawn from epic (*Homer, *Virgil, *Ovid) and pastoral poetry; situations and characters of comedy and mime; philosophical ideas and texts (including *Plato and the Hellenistic philosophical schools); and rhetorical set-pieces (consolation, persuasion, farewell speech).

Juvenal's *Satires* apparently present reassuring entertainment for the Roman male élite audience. However, inconsistencies written into the texts allow alternative views of Juvenal's speakers as riddled with bigotry (chauvinism, misogyny, homophobia) or as cynically superior. In literary history, Juvenal's significance is in bringing to fullest development the indignant speaker: his 'savage indignation' had a lasting influence on Renaissance and later satire (as Johnson's imitations of *Satires* 3 and 10, *London* and *The Vanity of Human Wishes*, indicate) and remains central to modern definitions of 'satire'.   S.M.B.

Ll

Labeo (Marcus Antistius Labeo), whose family came from Samnium in central Italy, was a leading Roman lawyer of the age of *Augustus and died between 10 and 22 AD. His father Pacuvius, also a lawyer, was killed fighting for the republican cause. As a member of a commission to reconstitute the senate in 18 BC he showed his independent spirit. Out of sympathy with the new order, his political career stopped at the praetorship: the consulship belatedly offered him by Augustus he refused. Sextus Pomponius (*Dig.* 1. 2. 2. 47) and Tacitus (*Ann.* 3. 75) contrast his attachment to republican principle with the obsequiousness of his contemporary Ateius Capito. Taught by his father, and by Gaius Trebatius Testa, and by others, he acquired expertise not only in law but in dialectics, language, literature, and grammar, which he brought to bear on legal problems. Author of many innovations, he divided his time equally between teaching in Rome and writing in the country, and composed in all some 400 books. He drew a line, as it were, under republican jurisprudence, which was henceforth cited largely through him. He was also, after Gaius Aquillius Gallus, the first important figure to devote himself to legal science to the exclusion of political concerns. Sextus Pomponius speaks of him as the founder of the Proculian school, presumably because of his intellectual breadth and attachment to principle. In time his works were superseded, so that, though much cited by *Ulpian, *Justinian's compilers had available for excerpting only his *Pithana* ('Persuasive Views') and *Posteriora* (posthumous works) selected and edited by Javolenus Priscus   T.Hon.

Lactantius (Lucius Caelius (Caecilius?) Firmianus also called **Lactantius),** *c.* AD 240–*c.*320, a native of North Africa, pupil of *Arnobius, one of the Christian apologists. Under *Diocletian he was officially summoned to teach rhetoric at Nicomedia; the date of his conversion is uncertain, but is earlier than the persecution of 303, when his Christianity caused him to lose his position at Nicomedia. He remained there until he moved to the west in 305; in extreme old age he was tutor (*c.*317) to Crispus, eldest son of *Constantine I.

Of Lactantius' numerous works on various subjects, only his Christian writings survive. He began these after the outbreak of the persecution. The *De opificio Dei* demonstrates providence from the construction of the human body. The *Divinae institutiones* (303–13), begun as a reply to attacks on Christianity by the philosopher and official Hierocles, was intended to refute all opponents past, present, and future. The order of composition of the books, like the date of the *Epitome*, is uncertain. The work shows knowledge of the major Latin poets, and above all of Cicero, but little of Greek apart from spurious Orphic and Sibylline poems. The *De ira Dei* (after 313) makes anger, as a disposition rather than a passion, an essential property of God. The *De mortibus persecutorum* (317/8) is designed to show that the fate of persecutors is always evil, and may therefore have exaggerated the role of the unfortunate emperor *Galerius in inspiring the persecution of his own times. One poem by Lactantius, the *Phoenix*, also survives.

At the Renaissance Lactantius, the most classical of all early Christian writers, came to be known as the Christian Cicero. Except in the *Epitome*, he shows little philosophic knowledge or ability, and has little of importance to say on Christian doctrine or institutions. The latter defect, at least, can be explained as the accustomed reserve of the Christian apologist when writing for hostile or unbelieving readers.   R.A.K.

Laodice, daughter of Mithradates II of Pontus, married *Antiochus III at Zeugma (221 BC) at a ceremonial royal wedding (Polyb. 5. 43. 1–4). The marriage was one of several examples (e.g. *Seleucus I) of the Seleucid dynasty's use of marriage alliances with non-Greek dynasties and kingdoms.

From the start of the Seleucid dynasty, the queen had won public honours and recognition from Greek cities in and outside the empire. A rare example of the powers of a Seleucid queen is given in Laodice's letter (*c.*195) to Iasus in Caria, after Antiochus' capture of the city, detailing her benefactions (*euergesia*), including the grant for ten years of corn, to be used by its sale (at fixed prices; i.e. no profiteering!) to found dowries 'for the daughters of needy citizens', plus the undertaking of further aid (carefully) in accordance with the king's wishes. This inscription (Austin 156, cf. *SEG* 26. 1226) gives an indication of the queen's power, who can in her own right communicate with cities by letter, like the governors of satrapies, and either from her own resources, or perhaps local crown resources, fund subsidies at a time of crisis.

There is now a growing corpus of inscriptional evidence for civic cults for Laodice (at Sardis, 213; Teos, 204–3; Iasus, *c.*195), which not only gives an official picture of a great queen, but may have prefigured and perhaps paved the way for Antiochus' inclusion, by 193, of Laodice in the first Seleucid state ruler-cult of the living king, his ancestors, and his queen.

Of Laodice's children, Seleucus IV and Antiochus IV reigned as kings, while her daughter, Cleopatra I, was married to *Ptolemy V.   s.s.-w.

Lepidus (Marcus Aemilius Lepidus), the triumvir, younger son of another Marcus Aemilius Lepidus (consul 78, who agitated against *Sulla's settlement and marched on Rome). As praetor 49 BC, he supported *Julius Caesar, then governed Hither Spain (48–7), intervening in the dissensions in Further Spain and returning to triumph. He was consul (46) and Caesar's 'master of the horse' (lieutenant and deputy of a dictator) (46–44). On Caesar's death he gave armed support to Mark *Antony, who in return contrived his appointment as *pontifex maximus* (the most prominent and influential member of the

four colleges of priests) in Caesar's place. He then left to govern the provinces assigned him by Caesar, Gallia Narbonensis and Hither Spain. When, after the war of Mutina, Antony retreated into Gaul, Lepidus assured Cicero of his loyalty to the republic but on 29 May 43 joined forces with Antony and was declared a public enemy by the senate. At Bononia (modern Bologna) in October he planned the Triumvirate with Antony and Octavian (see AUGUSTUS), accepting Further Spain with his existing provinces as his share of the empire; and demanding (or conceding) the proscription of his brother Lucius Aemilius Paullus. After triumphing again *ex Hispania* ('from Spain') he held a second consulship (42) and took charge of Rome and Italy during the campaign of Philippi. After their victory his colleagues deprived him of his provinces, on the rumour of a collusion between him and Sextus *Pompey, but nothing serious was proved; and after helping Octavian ineffectively in the war against Mark Antony's brother Lucius Antonius (Pietas), he was allowed by Octavian to govern Africa, where he had sixteen legions and won an imperatorial salutation. Kept out of the discussions at Tarentum over the renewal of the Triumvirate (37) and ignored in the arrangements, he asserted himself when summoned by Octavian to aid in the war against Sextus Pompeius. He tried to take over Sicily, but Octavian won over his army, ousted him from the Triumvirate and banished him to Circeii, though he later contemptuously allowed him to enter Rome. He kept his title of *pontifex maximus* until his death in 13 or 12, when Augustus took it over. Superior to his two partners in social rank and inherited connections, he lacked their ability to organize support and their total dedication to the pursuit of power.

G.W.R.; T.J.C.; E.B.

Libanius, born at Antioch in Syria (AD 314), died there (*c.*393), was a Greek rhetorician and man of letters who embodied in his work many of the ideals and aspirations of the pagan Greek urban upper classes of late antiquity. He belonged to a wealthy Antiochene family of town-councillors, and after a careful education at home was sent to study in Athens (336–40). Thereafter he taught rhetoric successively at Constantinople (340/1–346) and at Nicomedia. Recalled to

Constantinople by Constantius II, he was offered but declined a chair of rhetoric at Athens; in 354 he accepted an official chair of rhetoric in Antioch, where he passed the rest of his life. His pupils numbered many distinguished men, pagan and Christian alike. John Chrysostom and Theodore of Mopsuestia were almost certainly among them, *Basil and Gregory of Nazianzus probably, and *Ammianus Marcellinus possibly.

In his later years Libanius became a literary figure of renown throughout the Greek world, and was in correspondence with many of its leading figures, e.g. the emperor *Julian, for whom he had an unbounded admiration, and whose death was a bitter blow to him. In spite of his adherence to paganism, which for him was uncomplicated by Neoplatonist speculations, he enjoyed considerable influence under *Theodosius I, who granted him the honorary title of praetorian prefect. In general, however, he avoided involvement in the politics of the empire.

WORKS His 64 surviving speeches deal with public or municipal affairs, educational and cultural questions. Many are addressed to emperors or high government officials, with whom he intervenes on behalf of the citizens or the curials of Antioch (e.g. after the riot of 382). Some of these were never actually delivered, but were sent to their addressees and published. Other speeches include his funeral oration on Julian (*Or.* 17), his encomium of Antioch (*Or.* 11), and the autobiography which he composed in 374 (*Or.* 1). There also survive some 1,600 letters, 51 school declamations, numerous model rhetorical exercises and minor rhetorical works composed in the course of his teaching. The speeches and letters are a mine of information on social, political, and cultural life in the eastern half of the empire in the 4th cent. AD.

Deeply attached to old values, and seeing the rapidly changing world about him through the distorting lens of a pedantic and snobbish literary tradition, Libanius was vain, petty, and wrapped in finicking antiquarianism. Yet his sincerity, his freedom from vindictiveness, his never-failing readiness to use his eloquence to combat injustice, and a certain warmth of character which breaks through the restraints of classicizing purism make him attractive to the patient reader. He writes an Atticizing Greek

(imitating Classical Athenian prose) which is always the result of painstaking labour, and often tortuous and difficult. He was much esteemed as a model of style in Byzantine times.   R.B.

Licinius (Valerius Licinianus Licinius), Roman emperor, born of peasant stock in (new) Dacia perhaps in the 260s AD, became a close friend and comrade-in-arms of *Galerius, who at Carnuntum (308), when *Diocletian refused to leave retirement, created him a second Augustus in the tetrarchic system (rule by four emperors). Rather than attack *Maxentius in Italy, Alexander in Africa, or Constantine in Gaul, Licinius undertook the administration of the diocese (grouping of provinces) of Pannonia; it seems that he did not persecute Christians. On the death of Galerius (311) he and *Maximin raced to acquire Galerius' territories; Licinius obtained those in Europe, and faced Maximin across the Bosporus, but war was averted by negotiation. Against Maximin, he formed an alliance with *Constantine I. At Milan (February 313) he married Constantine's half-sister Constantia. His conference with Constantine was interrupted when Maximin invaded Europe. Licinius defeated him near Adrianople, taking over his Asiatic territories. Licinius and Constantine were now the only claimants to the empire. At Nicomedia on 15 June he informed his subjects that they had agreed on toleration for all religions, including Christianity, and that confiscated Christian property was to be restored. At the time Christian writers regarded Licinius as a Christian; though he prescribed a monotheistic prayer for use by the army, his later career shows that he was no convert. For obscure reasons he quarrelled with Constantine who defeated him (8 October 316) at Cibalae and then at Campus Adriensis, neither victory being decisive. After Cibalae, Licinius made the *dux limitis* (commander of a frontier army) Valens emperor, but Valens was executed before Licinius negotiated peace with Constantine early in 317. Licinius agreed to surrender all European territory except the diocese of Thracia. On 1 March 317 he made his infant son and namesake Caesar, and Constantine gave this title to his sons Crispus and Constantine II. Knowing that Constantine would never be happy until he was sole ruler, and suspecting that his own Christian subjects were disloyal, he embarked on a perfunctory persecution. The uneasy peace was broken when Constantine attacked in 324, won a decisive battle at Adrianople (3 July) and besieged Licinius in Byzantium. Licinius put up his *magister officiorum* ('master of the offices') Martinianus as emperor. Byzantium fell, and at Chrysopolis Licinius was defeated (18 September). He and Martinianus surrendered, and were sent to Thessalonica, where they were accused of plotting and executed in spring 325. Licinius' son was granted his life but executed in 326. A bastard son who had been legitimized and given high rank was enslaved.   R.P.D.

Licinius Crassus, Marcus See CRASSUS.

Licinius Lucullus, Lucius See LUCULLUS.

Licinius Valerianus, Publius (Roman emperor). See VALERIAN.

Livia (Livia Drusilla), wife of *Augustus, b. 58 BC. The granddaughter of Marcus *Livius Drusus (2), she first married in 43 or 42 Tiberius Claudius Nero, whom she accompanied on his flight after the Perusine War. She bore him *Tiberius, the future emperor, and *Drusus. In 39, in order to marry Octavian (the future Augustus), she was divorced though pregnant with her second son. Although she had no further children, she retained Augustus' respect and confidence throughout his life. As consort of the *princeps*, she became an effective model of old-fashioned propriety, her beauty, dignity, intelligence, and tact fitting her for her high position. She played a role in the Augustan system which was unusually formal and conspicuous for a woman, and on Augustus' death became a principal figure in his cult and (by his will) a member of his family, as Julia Augusta. She was believed to have interceded successfully on behalf of conspirators, but some took her influence on Augustus to be malign, and saw her as a ruthless intriguer (her grandson *Gaius (1) called her 'Ulixes stolatus', 'Odysseus in a matron's gown'), while the tradition grew up that she had manipulated the affairs of Augustus' household on behalf of her sons, especially Tiberius, to the extent of involvement in the deaths of Marcus Claudius Marcellus, Gaius

and Lucius Caesar, Agrippa Postumus and *Germanicus, and even of Augustus himself. But after AD 14 her continuing influence caused discord between her and Tiberius, who was even supposed to have retired from Rome in 26 chiefly to avoid her. She died in 29, but Tiberius' hostility ensured that her will was not executed until Gaius' reign, and that she was not deified until that of *Claudius.   N.P.

Livius Andronicus, Lucius, a freedman (ex-slave) of the Livii, commonly held to be the first to compose poems of the Greek type in Latin. He produced a comedy and a tragedy at the Ludi Romani of 240 BC and wrote the text of a hymn to Juno sung by 27 young women at a moment of crisis in 207. Ancient biographers presented him as a half-Greek from Tarentum who provided grammatical instruction in both Greek and Latin for the children of Marcus Livius Salinator (consul 207) and other aristocrats, and who played roles in the stage plays he composed. His prestige persuaded the Roman authorities to permit actors and stage-poets to assemble for religious purposes in the Aventine temple of Minerva.

Titles of three comedies (*Gladiolus, Ludius, †virgus†*) and ten tragedies (*Achilles, Aegisthus, Aiax, Andromeda, Antiopa, Danae, Equos Troianus, Hermiona, Ino, Tereus*) are transmitted. Varro knew of a tragedy in which Teucer figured. Livius composed for both genres iambic and trochaic verses of the kind that remained current in the Roman theatre until well into the 1st cent. BC. Ten words cited by Nonius from an *Equos Troianus* have been plausibly scanned in a mixture of trochaic and cretic short verses and attributed to an actor's monody. The alternating full and 'miuric' (with short penultimate syllable) hexameters cited by Terentianus Maurus from a hymn to Diana in an *Ino* have often been rejected as spurious.

Twenty-one fragments of a translation of *Homer's *Odyssey* in Saturnian verses are unambiguously transmitted. Others can be assigned with a fair degree of certainty. Livius ignored the 24-book division introduced at Alexandria. He seems to have kept fairly close to the general wording of the Homeric text but gave both the gods (*Mousa*= Camena) and the heroes (e.g. *Odysseus*= Ulixes) local names and took account of the differences between Roman and Greek notions of story-telling. A peculiarly Roman goddess of prophecy (Morta) replaced a general idea of destiny (*moira*). Conceptions shocking to Roman ears were toned down (e.g. Patroclus *theophin mēstōr atalantos*, 'counsellor equal to the gods' (3. 110), became *vir summus adprimus*, 'first-rate leading man'). Undignified reactions to external events were replaced (e.g. *Odysseos lyto gounata*, 'Odysseus' knees were loosened', became *Ulixi cor frixit*, 'Ulysses' heart froze'). Livius sought a much grander verbal style in his epic than in his tragic writings, introducing words (e.g. *insece, procitum, ommentans, dusmus*) and forms (e.g. the -*as* genitive singular) quite absent from the ordinary language.

*Cicero thought little of either the *Odyssey* translation or the plays (*Brut.* 71). An eminent schoolmaster of the middle of the 1st cent. BC nevertheless beat the former into the heads of his charges (Hor. *Epist.* 2. 1. 69–71). A revision set in dactylic hexameters of the Ennian type (see ENNIUS) and divided into 24 books was sometimes confused in the grammatical tradition with Livius' original work but seems to have had little general circulation. Those who tried to determine *Virgil's archaic models ignored Livius.

H.D.J.

Livius Drusus (1), **Marcus,** probably a descendant of Aemilius Paullus and Marcus Livius Salinator, as tribune (122 BC) combined with the consul Gaius Fannius in exploiting the people's reluctance to extend the citizenship as a weapon against Gaius *Gracchus. He proposed the establishment—never carried out—of twelve large citizen colonies and the exemption of Latins from corporal punishment, and brought about Gracchus' defeat in the tribunician elections. Consul (112) and proconsul, he fought in Macedonia, triumphing in 110. Elected censor (109) with *Scaurus, he died in office, whereupon Scaurus was forced to abdicate. His daughter married first Quintus Servilius Caepio, to whom she bore *Servilia, then Marcus Porcius Cato, to whom she bore *Cato the Younger.

E.B.

Livius Drusus (2), **Marcus,** son of the preceding, eldest of a circle of ambitious young nobles around Lucius Licinius Crassus, to whom he owed his oratorical training and some of his ideas. A brilliant, hard-working, and arrogant man, he became tribune 91 BC, having been quaestor and aedile, just after the conviction of his uncle Publius *Rutilius Rufus. With the encouragement of *Scaurus, who was himself in danger, and of Crassus he proposed a solution for all of Rome's major problems: 300 *equites* (knights) were to be raised to the senate (where their influence would be minimal) and criminal juries were to be chosen from the enlarged senate. Thus the *equites* would be eliminated as a political force, with the most ambitious creamed off and the rest deprived of power. He also proposed colonies and land distributions to provide for the poor, and the enfranchisement of all Italians. The ruling oligarchy was to reap the political benefit (he is called 'patron of the senate') and hold unchallenged leadership. But those who thought themselves adversely affected combined against him: extreme oligarchs, led by the consul Lucius *Marcius Philippus; *equites* rallied by Quintus Servilius Caepio (once Drusus' friend, but now an enemy); Italians unwilling to give up public land (*ager publicus*) as the price of citizenship; probably *Marius, the enemy of Rutilius. After Crassus' death in September Philippus gained the upper hand and had the laws already passed invalidated by the senate. Shortly after, Drusus was assassinated. The Social War and the commission of Quintus Varius were the immediate consequences. Drusus was the grandfather of *Livia Drusilla.

E.B.

Livy (Titus Livius), the Roman historian, lived 59 BC–AD 17 (although R. Syme has argued for 64 BC–AD 12). He was born and died at Patavium (mod. Padua), the most prosperous city of northern Italy, famed for its stern morality. Gaius Asinius Pollio criticized Livy's *Patavinitas* (Paduanism), but the import of this remark is unclear. An epitaph from Padua recording a T. Livius with two sons and a wife Cassia Prima may be his (*ILS* 2919). In a letter he urged his son to imitate *Demosthenes and *Cicero, and this or another son wrote a geographical work. A daughter married Lucius Magius, a rhetorician. We do not know when Livy came to Rome or how much time he spent there; but he was on good personal terms with *Augustus (see below) and encouraged the young *Claudius, future emperor, to write history. Apart from, perhaps before beginning, his major work he also wrote philosophical dialogues.

Livy entitled his work *Ab urbe condita libri* ('Books from the Foundation of the City'): it covered Roman history from the origins of Rome to 9 BC in 142 books. Of these only 1–10 and 21–45 survive (and 41 and 43–5 have lacunae caused by the loss of leaves in the 5th-cent. manuscript which alone preserves 41–5). We also have two fragments of manuscripts of late antiquity: one, some 80 lines of print, has been known since the 18th cent.; the other, much damaged and containing parts of a few sentences of book 11, was discovered in 1986. We also have passages cited or referred to by later writers, and two kinds of summary of the history. First, there is the so-called Oxyrhynchus Epitome, covering books 37–40 and 48–55, and preserved in a papyrus written in the first half of the 3rd cent. Second, there are the *Periochae* (summaries) of all books except 136 and 137. The *Periochae* were perhaps composed in the 4th cent. and are preserved in a normal manuscript tradition (the summary of the first book survives in two different versions). It is uncertain whether the authors were working directly from the text of Livy or from an earlier summary (or summaries). Conflicts between the summaries and the text of Livy himself can be attributed to errors by the epitomator or to the use of sources other than Livy. Comparison of the summaries with the extant books indicates that we cannot always assume that the summaries of the lost books provide a reliable indication of their contents. The summaries of the final books are very brief, reporting only some foreign wars and events concerning Augustus' family. Livy was also the major source for, among others, *Florus, Eutropius, and Obsequens (the so-called 'Livian tradition'). The whole work seems to have survived into the 6th cent.

From late antiquity, Livy's history was referred to by 'decades'. This is because ten books were the most that could be fitted into a parchment codex (thus the story of the transmission of the surviving parts varies from decade to decade). But it is disputed whether Livy himself conceived his work as consisting of significant units of five (pentads), ten, or even fifteen books. Book 5 ends with the recovery of Rome after the Gallic sack and book 6 begins with a 'second

preface'. The First Punic War began in book 16, while the Second War occupies the whole of the third decade, with the war against *PhilipV—the start of Rome's domination of the Hellenistic world—beginning in book 31; the war against *Antiochus III begins in book 36, and books 41–5 contain the whole of the reign of Perseus, the last Macedonian king. But there is no obvious break before books 11 and 26, and it is difficult to discern any pattern in the lost books. Livy was probably attracted by the possibility of beginning and/or concluding a pentad or decade with a significant historical event, but was not prepared to achieve that end by damaging the economy of his work—making books excessively long or short, skimping or padding his material.

Internal indications show that books 1–5 were completed between 27 and 25 BC. It may be, however, that some of the passages which date from that time were additions to an early draft. A note in the best manuscripts of the *Periochae* states that book 121 was said to have been published after the death of Augustus; if that is true (and it may come from Livy's preface) it is likely that this applies to the following books.

Apart from a few references to topography and monuments, indicating autopsy, Livy relied on literary sources; he did not regard it as his duty to consult documents. In books 31–145 it is clear that for events in the east Livy followed *Polybius closely, adapting his narrative for his Roman audience and making additions—sometimes tacitly—and noting variants from the 1st-cent. writers Quintus Claudius Quadrigarius and *Valerius Antias. The common view is that his procedure elsewhere was similar; he followed one main source—Antias, Gaius Licinius Macer, and (for books 6–10) Quadrigarius in the first decade, Lucius Coelius Antipater, Antias, or Quadrigarius in books 31–45—for longer or shorter sections, supplementing it from other sources. It is also thought that, apart from Antipater in the third decade, he did not use 2nd-cent. Roman writers directly: references to Quintus Fabius Pictor and Lucius Calpurnius Piso Frugi were derived from the 1st-cent. writers. Neither conclusion is certain: no Roman writer was so obviously superior on western events as was Polybius on eastern ones, and it could be that Livy sometimes produces an amalgam of the various works he had read (which in many cases had virtually the same story). A passage of the fourth decade (32. 6. 8) is hard to reconcile with the view that Livy read only Polybius, Antias, and Quadrigarius for events in Greece. There is a strong case for holding that he used *Cato the Elder directly for the latter's campaign in Spain in 195, and he could well have read other 2nd-cent. writers. Nor can it be excluded that he consulted Polybius directly throughout the third decade (most scholars agree that he did so for parts of books 24–30). If Livy did read 2nd-cent. historians, he did not necessarily conclude that discrepancies between them and later sources were to be resolved in favour of the former, though he was aware that Antias, and to a lesser extent Quadigarius, were fond of inflating enemy casualty figures.

Livy has been criticized for his failure to inspect the linen corselet which, according to Augustus, proved that Aulus Cornelius Cossus was not a military tribune when he dedicated the *spolia opima* (spoils offered by a general who slew an enemy leader in single combat) (4. 20). But Livy was writing tongue in cheek; it would have been out of the question to refute Augustus, who had political reasons for wanting Cossus not to have been a military tribune. Livy is also criticized for not inspecting the *libri lintei* ('linen books' cited as containing lists of magistrates) when his sources gave differing reports of their evidence (4. 23); it is quite possible that the books were no longer accessible. Nor are Livy's errors—anachronisms, geographical mistakes, misunderstandings of Polybius, and chronological confusions (sometimes caused by fitting Polybius' Olympiad years into a system based on Roman consular years)—all that numerous or striking in relation to the size of his work or in comparison with other writers.

It has often been said that it was Livy who fulfilled Cicero's desire that history should be written by an orator. Cicero wanted a style that 'flowed with a certain even gentleness', and *Quintilian was to write of Livy's *lactea ubertas* ('milky richness'). Livy, reacting against the contorted Thucydideanism of *Sallust (see THUCYDIDES), first introduced fully developed periodic structure into Latin historiography. He had the ability to use language to embellish his material (comparison of Livy with Polybius in individual passages

often shows the extent of Livy's originality) to convey an atmosphere and portray emotions. He gives special attention to major episodes, which are particularly numerous in the first decade—e.g. the rape of Lucretia, the attempted rape of Verginia, the stories of Coriolanus, Spurius Maelius, and Marcus Manlius Capitolinus. The mixture of direct and indirect speech is one of the features of his technique. Elsewhere the speed of action in a battle—his battle scenes are often stereotyped—can be conveyed by short vivid sentences, while the dry style normally adopted for lists of prodigies, elections, and assignments of provinces and armies is perhaps a deliberate imitation of early writers, criticized by Cicero for just this, or of the *annales maximi* (the chronicle kept by the *pontifex maximus*).

Part of Livy's style is achieved by the use of poetical or archaic words avoided by Cicero and *Julius Caesar. In this respect he is following in a tradition of historiography to which *Sallust also belonged. These usages are most common in books 1–10, least so in 31–45. This phenomenon, however, is not to be explained on the hypothesis that Livy began under the influence of Sallust, but later moved back to a more Ciceronian vocabulary. Rather, Livy makes particular use of vocabulary of this sort in those episodes which specially attracted him, and these became progressively less common as his work proceeded—the diplomatic and military details of the early 2nd cent. did not compare in excitement with the great (and largely fictional) stories of the first decade. But some such episodes do occur in the later books, and it is precisely there that we find the greatest concentration of non-Ciceronian usages, as for example in the story of the Bacchanalia in book 39 or the account of the death of Cicero preserved by *Seneca the Younger.

Livy was a patriotic writer, though in narrative he never refers to Roman troops as *nostri* or *exercitus noster* ('our men', 'our army'), and often, writing from their opponents' point of view, talks of the Romans as *hostes* ('enemy'). His aim was to chronicle the rise of Rome to mastery first of Italy, then of the rest of the Mediterranean world, and to highlight the virtues which produced this result and enabled Rome to defeat *Hannibal. Livy intended his work to be morally improving (pref. 10), but though there are many passages where he writes with this aim in mind, a moral purpose is not all-pervasive. He believed that a serious moral decline had taken place by his own time, and appears to have lacked confidence that Augustus could reverse it.

Livy doubtless shared Augustus' ideals, but he was by no means a spokesman for the regime. Tacitus (*Ann.* 4. 34) makes Cremutius Cordus, defending himself on a *maiestas* (treason) charge, claim that Livy felt free to praise *Brutus and *Cassius; Cordus also claims that Livy was so lavish in his praise of *Pompey that Augustus called him a Pompeian, and adds that this did not harm their friendship. There are signs that Livy regarded the rule of Augustus as necessary, but only as a short-term measure.   J.Br.

Longus, Greek writer of *The pastoral Story of Daphnis and Chloe* (*Poimenika ta kata Daphnin kai Chloēn*), which he presents as a guide's explanation of a painting he saw while hunting on Lesbos. His apparently detailed knowledge of Lesbian topography is imprecise and inconsistent, and although Longi appear on Lesbian inscriptions, ours may have been a visitor rather than resident. There are hitherto no papyri, but his mannered sophistic *apheleia* (simplicity), often using short rhyming and rhythmically balanced *cola*, suits the late 2nd or early 3rd cent. AD, as do similarities to passages in Aelian and Alciphron (though priority is disputed). Few accept Hermann's identification with the Hadrianic grammarian Velius Longus.

Longus' four books miniaturize and rusticate the standard novel. Daphnis and Chloe, foundlings brought up by shepherds on the estate of a Mytilenean aristocrat, gradually fall in love. Obstacles there are—rivals, abductions by pirates and by a task-force from Methymna. But everything happens on a few miles of coastline near Mytilene; the chief obstacle to union is their rustic naïvety; and the central theme is their gradual discovery of what love is, by precept, example, and experiment. This is represented as a grand plan of Love, and the Nymphs and Pan help the couple in trouble; Longus dedicates his work to all three. In book 3 Daphnis is sexually initiated by an older city woman, Lycaenion, but only after eluding further admirers and discovering their aristocratic urban

origins do Daphnis and Chloe return from their taste of Mytilene to a country wedding and a life in which their children too will be shepherds. Like the countryside and seasons to which they respond and the incidents which catalyse change, the couple's developing sexual awareness is described in lingering detail. That detail sometimes cloys, the careful motivation of actions sometimes seems contrived, and the teenagers' sexual naïvety may stretch credibility. The style too can be monotonous, albeit well suited to naïve monologues and pretty *ecphrases* (descriptions) of rustic scenes and seasons. But the Thucydidean narrative (see THUCYDIDES) of war between Mytilene and Methymna brings variety, and well-educated readers could enjoy recognizing the many allusions to earlier texts, especially to that Hellenistic pastoral poetry which Longus is crossing with the prose tradition of the novel. Despite the preface's claim, the text is written for entertainment rather than to instruct readers in love or allegorically (as argued by R. Merkelbach, *Dier Hirten des Dionysos* (1988)) in the Dionysiac mysteries.

Among the Greek novelists Longus vies with *Heliodorus for the palm. Readers can admire vivid and convincing detail while aware that they need not be convinced, and, as with *Achilles Tatius, Longus' description of physical attractions, bodies, and swelling emotions has attracted more than it has repelled (the latter included Wilamowitz, the former, Goethe, who in his *Gespräche mit Eckermann* recommended reading *Daphnis and Chloe* once a year). Since Amyot's French translation (1559) some 500 translations into modern languages and editions have appeared. In the 18th and early 19th cents. Longus influenced Bernadin de St Pierre (*Paul et Virginie*) and S. Gessner's pastoral idylls in rhythmical prose. Illustrators have been numerous and often distinguished, including Corot, Maillol, Chagall, though many know the story only from Ravel's ballet score (1912).   E.L.B.

Lucan (AD 39–65), the poet, was born at Corduba (mod. Córdoba), 3 November AD 39. His father, Marcus Annaeus Mela, was a Roman knight and brother of *Seneca the Younger. Mela came to Rome when his son was about eight months old. There Lucan received the typical élite education, ending with the school of rhetoric, where he was a great success; he probably also studied Stoic philosophy under Lucius Annaeus Cornutus, a connection of Seneca. He continued his studies at Athens, but was recalled by *Nero, who admitted him to his inner circle and honoured him with the offices of quaestor and augur. In AD 60, at the first celebration of the games called Neronia, he won a prize for a poem in praise of Nero. In AD 62 or 63 he published three books of his epic on the Civil War. Growing hostility between him and Nero, for which various reasons are given, finally led the emperor to ban him from public recitation of his poetry and from speaking in the lawcourts. Early in AD 65 Lucan joined the conspiracy of Gaius Calpurnius Piso, and on its discovery was forced to open his veins in April 65; as he died he recited some of his own lines on the similar death of a soldier.

WORKS Lucan was a prolific writer. Of the many titles fragments exist of the *Catacthonia* ('Journey to the Underworld'), *Iliaca*, *Orpheus*, and epigrams. The surviving epic *De bello civili* (the alternative title *Pharsalia* is probably based on a misunderstanding of 9. 985) contains ten books covering events in the years 49–48 BC beginning with *Julius Caesar's crossing of the Rubicon; the poem breaks off, almost certainly unfinished, with Caesar in Alexandria. The historical sources include *Livy's (lost) books on the period and Caesar's own *On the Civil War*, but Lucan freely manipulates historical truth where it suits his purpose, e.g. in introducing Cicero in *Pompey's camp on the eve of the battle of Pharsalus in book 7. The epic has no single hero; the three main characters are Caesar, an amoral embodiment of Achillean and elemental energy; Pompey, figure of the moribund republic and shadow of his own former greatness; and *Cato the Younger, an impossibly virtuous specimen of the Stoic saint.

The Civil War is narrated as a tale of unspeakable horror and criminality leading to the destruction of the Roman republic and the loss of liberty; this message sits uneasily with the fulsome panegyric of Nero in the proem, unless that is to be read satirically or as the product of an early stage of composition before Lucan fell out with the emperor. From the moment when Caesar is confronted at the Rubicon by a vision of the distraught

goddess Roma, in a scene that reworks Aeneas' vision of the ghost of Hector on the night of the sack of Troy, Lucan engages in continuous and detailed allusion to *Virgil's *Aeneid*, the epic of the birth and growth of Rome, in order to construct the *De bello civili* as an 'anti-*Aeneid*', a lament for the death of the Roman body politic as Roman military might is turned in against itself. Lucan's rhetorical virtuosity is exploited to the full to involve the audience (defined in the proem as Roman citizens, i.e. those most nearly concerned by the subject of civil war) in his grim tale. In an extension of tendencies present already in Virgil, an extreme of pathos is achieved through the use of lengthy speeches, apostrophe of characters in the narrative, and indignant epigrammatic utterances (*sententiae*) contravention of the objectivity associated with Homeric epic, Lucan as narrator repeatedly intrudes his own reactions, as in the shocked meditation on the death of Pompey in book 8. Related to the goal of *pathos* are the features of hyperbole and paradox. Hyperbole is expressive both of the vast forces involved in the conflict, presented as a 'world war', and of the greatness of the crimes perpetrated. Lucan's use of paradox is rooted in the conceptual and thematic antistructures of civil war, in which legality is conferred on crime, and the greatest exemplars of Roman military virtue, such as the centurion Scaeva in book 6, are at the same time the greatest criminals; but in this topsyturvy world paradox also extends to the physical, as in the sea-battle at the end of book 3 which turns into a 'land-battle' because the ships are so tightly packed. Realism is not a goal; Lucan's notorious abolition of the traditional epic divine machinery is not determined by the desire for a historiographical plausibility; rather, Lucan replaces the intelligibility of the anthropomorphic gods of Homer and Virgil with a darker sense of the supernatural, in a world governed by a negative version of Stoic Providence or Fate. Dreams, portents, and prophecies abound, as in the list of omens at Rome at the end of book 1, or in Appius Claudius Pulcher's consultation of the long-silent Delphic oracle in book 5; the Gothick atmosphere reaches a climax with the consultation in book 6 by Sextus *Pompey of the witch Erictho and her necromantic resurrection of a corpse. Death fascinates Lucan, in both its destructive and its heroic aspects; a recurrent image is suicide, viewed both as the symbol of Rome's self-destruction and as the Stoic's praiseworthy exit from an intolerable life (the paradoxes are explored in the Vulteius episode in book 4). The Roman spectacle of ritualized killing in the amphitheatre is reflected in the frequent gladiatorial imagery of the epic. In all of these features Lucan shows a close affinity with the writings, above all the tragedies, of his uncle *Seneca the Younger.

Lucan displays his learning in mythological episodes, such as the story of Hercules and Antaeus in book 4, in the geography and ethnography of the catalogues of books 1 and 3 and the description of Thessaly in book 6, and in the 'scientific' passages on the snakes of Libya in book 9 and on the sources of the Nile in book 10; but these 'digressions' usually have a further thematic and symbolic purpose. It is true that Lucan's style lacks the richness and colour of Virgil's, but his limited and repetitive range of vocabulary, often prosaic in tone, is deliberately geared to the bleak, remorseless, and unromantic nature of the subject-matter; a similar response may be made to the criticism of the monotony of Lucan's metre. Stylistic and metrical narrowness as a purposeful inversion of Virgilian norms finds an analogy in the device of 'negative enumeration', the listing of things that do not happen, but which might in normal circumstances be expected to happen, as in the description of the funereal remarriage of Cato and Marcia in book 2.

Lucan's epic was avidly read and imitated for centuries after his death; his admirers include *Statius (whose mythological epic on civil war, the *Thebaid*, is permeated with echoes of Lucan), Dante, Goethe, and Shelley. After a period of critical condemnation and neglect, the sombre baroque brilliance of the work is once more coming to be appreciated.

                                                   W.B.A.; P.R.H.

Lucian, of Samosata in Syria (b. *c.* AD 120), accomplished belletrist and wit in the context of the Second Sophistic (revival of Greek oratory in the 2nd–3rd cent. AD). The details of his life are extremely sketchy, and his own presentations of his biography are literary and therefore suspect. His native language was not Greek but probably Aramaic; but he practised in the courts, then as an itinerant lecturer on literary-philosophical themes as far afield as Gaul. He presents a 'conversion' to philosophy around the age of 40, and his natural milieu is Athens. He was known to *Galen for a successful literary fraud. We find him late in life in a minor administrative post in Roman Egypt; he survived the emperor *Marcus Aurelius.

WORKS Lucian's work is difficult both to categorize and to assign to any sort of literary 'development'. Throughout he is a master of sensibly flexible Atticism (the imitation of Classical Athenian Greek). His *œuvre* runs to some 80 pieces, most of which are genuine. While some can be classified under traditional rhetorical headings such as *meletai* ('exercises') and *prolaliai* ('preambles'), the most characteristic products of his repertoire are literary dialogues which fuse Old Comic and popular and/or 'literary' philosophy to produce an apparently novel blend of comic prose dialogue. But he is also an accomplished miniaturist, essayist, and raconteur: the *Enalioi dialogoi* ('Dialogues of the Sea-Gods') are particularly successful in exploiting the art of prose paraphrase of verse classics from *Homer to *Theocritus; the *Pōs dei historian syngraphein* ('How to Write History') gives a wittily commonsensical rather than commonplace treatment of a topical subject; while the *Philopseudeis* ('Lovers of Lies') successfully combines satire of superstition with racy novella. When he chooses he can be a lively and revealing commentator on his cultural and religious environment as when he attacks successful sophists, or figures such as Peregrinus or the oraclemonger *Alexander of Abonuteichos whom he sees as charlatans. In the *Alēthē diēgēmata* ('True Histories') he produced a masterpiece of Munchausenesque parody. His literary personality is engaging but elusive: he is cultivated but cynical, perhaps with a chip on his shoulder, but difficult to excel in his chosen field of versatile prose entertainment. His weakest moments to contemporary taste are perhaps as a repetitive and superficial moralist, his most successful when he plays with the full range of Classical Greek literature in a characteristically amusing way.   W.M.E.; R.B.; G.A.

Lucilius (1), **Gaius,** born probably in 180 BC at Suessa Aurunca on the northern edge of Campania, died in Naples 102/1 BC. His family was of senatorial status, a brother probably a senator, but Lucilius remained a knight (*eques*), a landowner with large estates who never sought political power himself. It is likely that Lucilius visited Greece. He saw service under *Scipio Aemilianus at the siege of Numantia in 134/3, continued to enjoy the close friendship of Scipio and his companion Gaius Laelius until the end of their lives, and attacked their enemies. He had other eminent friends in Rome such as Junius Congus and *Rutilius Rufus.

WORKS The extant fragments of Lucilius consist of some 1,400 lines, either isolated verses or small groups. They fall into two main collections, the first chronologically books 26–30 and the second books 1–21. In the first Lucilius used metres found in the *saturae* of *Ennius: the dramatic septenarius (bks. 26–7), a mixture of dramatic metres and hexameters (bks. 28–9). In book 30 he accepted the hexameter alone as the appropriate metre for satire and retained it for the whole of the later collection. References in the poems to historical events seem to confirm that the books in both collections are in chronological order. There are in addition fragments in elegiac couplets in books 22–5, probably epigrams and epitaphs. But in spite of the severe difficulties in the interpretation of poems in a problematical transmission, Lucilius appears as a powerful personality and a major writer.

As a personal poet following *Archilochus, Lucilius attacked enemies by name and described without inhibition his own amatory exploits. In an epistolary poem he reproached a friend for having failed to visit him when he was ill. By recounting such mundane personal experiences he resembles *Catullus, but sometimes, when appropriate, he used a persona. His account of a journey to Sicily (bk. 3) suggests a genuine travelogue. Lucilius vilified reprobate consulars such as Lucius Opimius and Gaius Papirius Carbo, also undisciplined tribes and dishonest political lobbying. In denouncing gluttony and extravagance he shows a censorial aptitude for popular moralizing. His definition of *virtus* ('excellence') proposes a Roman aristocratic ideal with Stoic undertones. He had philosopher friends in Athens but parodied Stoic terminology. Praised by *Pliny the Elder for his critical faculty, he wrote on principles of literary criticism and linguistic usage. Particularly noteworthy are Lucilius' own literary intentions, a polemic against tragedy, and his defence of personal attacks (parts of bks. 26 and 30), the 'Council of the Gods' (bk. 1) on the chequered career of Cornelius Lentulus Lupus, *princeps senatus* (First Senator) (d. *c.*125), and the parody of the trial of the Stoic Quintus Mucius Scaevola accused of provincial extortion by the Epicurean Titus Albucius (bk. 2), in which conflicting styles of rhetoric were ridiculed. Lucilius' style is conversational with some unbridled obscenity. He uses many Greek words including technical terms, and sometimes shows calculated elaboration and striking imagery.

At the end of the republic Lucilius was judged to be a writer of cultivated urbanity with characteristic Roman humour but formidable in his vituperation. *Horace discusses him in relation to his own writings: his predecessor's attack on named individuals and his improvisatory manner (*Sat.* 1. 4), his crude use of Greek words and unrefined style (*Sat.* 1. 10), and his autobiographical reflections and political invective (*Sat.* 2. 1). Towards the end of the 1st cent. AD there was a short-lived enthusiasm for Lucilius, in which many preferred him to Horace. Viewed by the satirists *Persius and *Juvenal as the archetypal master of the genre, Lucilius had put a stamp on verse satire which it has retained until the 20th cent.   M.Co.

Lucilius (2) **(Iunior), Gaius,** friend of *Seneca the Younger and the recipient of the *De providentia, Quaestiones naturales,* and *Epistulae morales*; was born in Campania, perhaps at Pompeii or Naples (Sen. *Ep.* 49. 1, 53. 1, 70. 1), without wealth or prospects (*QNat.* 4. pref. 14–15; *Ep.* 19. 5). He was some years younger than Seneca (*Ep.* 26. 7). Talent, literary style, and distinguished connections brought him into prominence (*Ep.* 19. 3). His own energy made him an *eques Romanus* (Roman knight, *Ep.* 44. 2). He was loyal to the memory and to friends or relatives of Gnaeus Cornelius Lentulus Gaetulicus after the latter's execution under *Gaius (1), and to victims of *Messalina or Narcissus under *Claudius (*QNat.* 4. pref. 15). Under Claudius and *Nero he held procuratorships in Alpes Graiae, Epirus, or Macedonia, Africa, and Sicily (*Ep.* 31. 9, 45. 2, 79. 1; *QNat.* 4. pref. 1). The date of his death is unknown.

Seneca uses Lucilius as a sounding-board for the philosophical progression of the *Epis-

tles. Many of them start from some question Lucilius has supposedly put—generally philosophical, but sometimes literary, linguistic, or social (*Ep.* 9, 29, 39, 43, 71, 72, 106, 108, 109, 111, 113, 114, 117). In spite of business (*Ep.* 17, 19, 22, 24), travel (*Ep.* 69, 84, 104), ill health (*Ep.* 78, 96), and a tendency to grumble (*Ep.* 21, 28, 44, 45, 60, 96, 103), he is depicted as a philosopher, perhaps an ex-Epicurean Stoic (see EPICURUS). On one occasion Seneca says to him 'meum opus es', 'you are my work' (*Ep.* 34. 2) which may also be read as testimony to Seneca's (re-)construction of his friend into the ideal philosophical neophtye and didactic addressee (cf. Griffin (see bibliog. below), 347–53). Seneca also warmly praises Lucilius' own philosophical work (*Ep.* 46).

Lucilius was also a poet (*QNat.* 4. pref. 14 and ch. 2. 2). Four Latin lines (two iambics and two hexameters) are preserved by Seneca (*Ep.* 8. 10, 24. 21; *QNat.* 3. 1. 1). It is unlikely that he is the same as the Lucil*l*ius of the Greek Anthology; but one Greek epigram of twelve lines (*IG* 14. 889 = *Epigr. Gr.* 810) inscribed on stone in Sinuessa with the genitive heading *Iounioros* may well be his. From the passage Sen. *Ep.* 79. 5–7 Wernsdorf and others have attributed the pseudo-Virgilian *Aetna* to Lucilius; but the wording suggests a poem including a description of Aetna rather than one devoted to Aetna *per se*.

A.M.D.; P.G.F., D.P.F.

Lucretius (Titus Lucretius Carus), Epicurean poet (see EPICURUS), author of the *De rerum natura (DRN)*, 'On the Nature of Things' (*c.*94–55 or 51 BC?). We know less about the life of Lucretius than about almost any other Latin poet. His full name is given only in the manuscripts of his work (pun on *Carus*, 1. 730 ?), and nothing is known of his place of birth or social status, though both have been the subject of much speculation. *Jerome's version of the *Chronicle* of *Eusebius puts his birth in 94 BC, and says that he was 44 when he died, but the *Donatus *Life of Virgil* puts his death in 55, on the same day that Virgil assumed the *toga virilis* (6, though there are textual problems), and a note in a 10th-cent. manuscript (H. Usener *Kl. Schr.* (1913), 156, 196–9) says that he was born 27 years before Virgil, i.e. 97 BC. The only secure date is a reference in a letter of *Cicero to his brother (*QFr.* 2. 10(9). 3) written in February

54, where he praises Lucretius' *poemata* as possessing both flashes of genius (*ingenium*) and great artistry (*ars*), that is, as combining the qualities of an inspired and a craftsmanlike poet. This is certainly a reference to *DRN* (an *Empedoclea* by one Sallustius is mentioned more critically in the same context), and although *poemata* could refer to just selections, the easiest hypothesis is that Lucretius' poem was published by this time. The poem has often been thought to be unfinished (there are problems especially in the prologue to book 4): if so, Lucretius may well have been dead by the time of the letter. But textual corruption rather than incompleteness may be responsible for the problems in the text.

Jerome (whose source was *Suetonius) also reports the story (made famous by Tennyson and others) of Lucretius writing *DRN* in brief intervals of sanity after having been driven mad by a love-potion given him by his wife, and eventually committing suicide. If this story is true, it is surprising that it was not used by *Ovid in his defence of the *Ars Amatoria* in *Tristia* 2 or by the Fathers of the Church attacking paganism and Epicureanism: it may be the result of a biographical reading of parts of books 3 and 4, or of confusion with Lucullus (cf. Plut. *Luc.* 43. 2). Nor is there any reason to believe Jerome's statement that Cicero edited *DRN* after its author's death. More biographical details are provided by the so-called 'Borgia Life' found in a British Museum printed book, but this is a Renaissance compilation (L. Canfora, *Vita di Lucrezio* (1993), 35–6).

The addressee of the *De rerum natura* (1. 25–43, 136–48; cf. 1. 411, 1052, 2. 143, 182, 5. 8, 93, 164, 867, 1282) is a Memmius, who must be Gaius Memmius, a prominent politician associated also with Catullus (28. 9). Memmius was praetor in 58, and a candidate for the consulship of 53: but after a complicated electoral pact that went wrong, he was found guilty of corruption in 52 and went into exile in Athens (E. S. Gruen in *Hommages à Marcel Renard* (1969), 2. 311–21; G. V. Sumner, *Harv. Stud.* 1982, 133–9). In the summer of 51, Cicero wrote to him on behalf of the Epicurean group in Athens, asking him not to demolish what was left of Epicurus' house (*Fam.* 13. 1. 3–4), and suggesting that Memmius was not on good terms with the Epicureans. It is not impossible that he had been annoyed by the dedication of *DRN*: despite its warm praise of him in the prologue, the poem is orthodox in its Epicurean condemnation of political life (3. 59–84, 995–1002, 5. 117–35). But in any case, *DRN* does not imply that Memmius was a convinced Epicurean (cf. 1. 102–3). There can be no clear distinction between Memmius as the didactic addressee and a more generalized second-person, but Memmius' public persona was relevant: *DRN* is not unpolitical (D. Minyard, *Lucretius and the Late Republic* (1985); D. P. Fowler, in M. Griffin and J. Barnes (eds.), *Philosophia Togata* (1989), 120–50).

The poem is in six books of hexameter verse (*c*.7,400 lines, about three-quarters the size of the *Aeneid*) and whether or not it failed to receive the final corrections of its author is substantially complete: it opens with an elaborate prologue, and the prologue to book 6 states explicitly that this is the final book (6. 92–5). The ending is abrupt, and textually corrupt: it is likely that 1247–51 are the actual concluding lines, and should be transposed after 1286, but if this is done, the ending contains a number of closural features, most notably a recall of the end of the funeral of Hector at the end of the *Iliad* (cf. P. G. Fowler, in F. Dunn, D. P. Fowler, and D. Roberts, *Classical Closure* (1997)). The ending on the plague at Athens and the many deaths it caused is in stark contrast to the opening description of the first day of spring and the appeal for help to Venus, but the polarity can be made to have point. The recurrent pattern of the cycle of coming-to-be and passing-away makes a final appearance, while the fixed temporal and spatial location in Athens, which represents the peak of civilization according to the opening of book 6, indicates the inevitable failure of the city-state to provide for the ultimate happiness of human beings.

As well as the great initial prologue to book 1, each of the other books also has a prologue, and the concluding section of each book in some way stands apart from the rest of the book (see especially the attack on love in book 4, and the final plague). Each book is a unity in terms both of structure and subject-matter. Book 1 deals with the basic metaphysical and physical premisses of Epicureanism, beginning with the proposition that nothing comes to be out of nothing, and concluding with a description of the collapse of our world

which is presented as a counterfactual consequence of the belief that all elements tend towards the centre of the earth but which anticipates the Epicurean accounts of the death of our world at the end of book 2 and in book 5. Book 2 deals with the motion and shape of the atoms, and how these are relevant to the relationship between primary and secondary qualities: it concludes with the important Epicurean doctrine of the infinite number of worlds in the universe, and the connected proposition that our world has both a birth and a death (recalling the end of book 1). Book 3 gives an account of the nature of the human soul, and argues both that it is mortal and that, because of this, death is not to be feared. Book 4 discusses a variety of psychological phenomena, especially perception, and argues against scepticism: as remarked above, it concludes with an attack on love, seen as a mental delusion. Book 5 argues for the mortality of our world, and then gives a rationalist and anti-providentialist account of its creation and early history, concluding with the section on the development of human civilization which is perhaps the most famous part of the poem. Book 6 then proceeds to account for those phenomena of our world which are most likely to lead to false belief in the gods—thunder and lightning, earthquakes, volcanoes, etc.—and ends with the aetiology of disease and the plague at Athens.

This clearly defined book-structure is more typical of prose philosophical treatises than of hexameter poetry, and it is replicated at levels both above and below that of the individual book. The books form three pairs, in which books 1 and 2 deal with atomic phenomena up to the level of the compound, books 3 and 4 deal with human beings, and books 5 and 6 deal with the world: there is thus a clear sense of expanding horizons, as we move from the atomic to the macroscopic level. The twin targets of the work as a whole are fear of the gods and of death (1. 62–135; cf. Epicurus, *RS* 1–2, *Ep. Men.* 133): the first and last pairs deal more with the former fear, by explaining phenomena that would otherwise be felt to require divine intervention in the world, while the central books, and especially book 3, tackle the fear of death head on. But the two motives are intermingled throughout the work. The six books may also be organized into two halves, with books 1–3

dealing with basic premises, books 4–6 with
what follows from those basic premises: the
problematic prologue to book 4 (repeated
almost verbatim from 1. 921–50), with its
stress on Lucretius' role as a poet and philosopher and its Callimachean imagery (see
CALLIMACHUS), thus functions as a 'proem in
the middle' for the second half (cf. G. B.
Conte *YClS* 1992, 147–59). The existence of
more than one possible structural analysis in
this way is typical of *DRN* as a whole (contrast
3. 31–40 with 5. 55–63).

Below the level of the book, the subject-
matter is carefully delineated and individual
propositions within sections signposted with
markers like *Principio*, 'First', *Deinde*, 'Next',
and *Postremo*, 'Finally': the verse, in contrast
to both the epic verse-paragraph and the neoteric focus on the single line, tends to group
itself into blocks of two or more verses, with
careful arrangement of words within the
block. This division of the text corresponds
to the Epicurean stress on the intelligibility
of phenomena: everything has a *ratio* or systematic explanation, the world can be analysed and understood. If we are to believe
Cicero, however, this is in marked contrast to
the formlessness of earlier Epicurean writing
in Latin (cf. Cic. *Acad. post.* 5 with Reid's
comm., and esp. *Fin.* 1. 22, 29, 2. 30, 3. 40).

Every major proposition in *DRN* can be
paralleled in other Epicurean sources, and
it is likely that the majority at least of the
arguments for these propositions also existed
in the Epicurean tradition. We do not know,
however, to what extent the poem had a single
main source, and if so, what that source was.
The title (cf. 1. 25) recalls that of Epicurus'
major treatise, the *Peri physeōs* or 'On Nature',
but the structure of that work as we know it
from papyrus fragments is not very similar
to that of *DRN*, and that presumably also
goes for any (lost) epitome. There is a much
closer correspondence, however, with the
extant *Letter to Herodotus* of Epicurus, passages of which are closely translated (e.g. 1.
159–60 = *Ep. Hdt.* 38), although *DRN* is
longer and the order of topics is sometimes
changed (e.g. in *Ep. Hdt.* 42–3 Epicurus treats
atomic shape before atomic motion, while
DRN reverses the order, 2. 62–729). One
plausible hypothesis is that the *Letter to Herodotus* provided the basic core of the poem,
but this was expanded from a variety of other
sources (cf. also D. Clay, *Lucretius and Epic-*

urus (1983)). Other prose philosophical and
scientific sources are also drawn on (e.g.
Plato's *Timaeus*, P. De Lacy in *Syzetesis: Studi
Gigante* (1983), 291–307, and the Hippocratic
corpus (see HIPPOCRATES), C. Segal, *CPhil.*
1970, 180–2) though we can never be certain
that some of this had not already been assimilated into the atomist tradition (cf. F.
Solmsen, *AJPhil.* 1953, 34–51). The final part
of book 3 in particular (cf. also the prologues
to 2 and 3 and the end of 4) contains material
from the so-called 'diatribe' tradition of practical philosophical rhetoric (cf. B. P. Wallach,
*Lucretius and the Diatribe against the Fear of
Death: De Rerum Natura III 830–1094* (1970);
T. Stork, *Nil igitur est ad nos* (1970); G. B.
Conte, *Genres and Readers* (1994)).

But *DRN* also draws on a wide range of
literary texts in both Greek (e.g. *Sappho fr.
31 LP in *DRN* 3. 152–8, *Aeschylus fr. 44 Nauck
in *DRN* 1. 250–61, *Euripides fr. 839 Nauck in
DRN 2. 991–1003, Callimachus fr. 260. 41 Pf.
in *DRN* 6. 753, Antipater of Sidon, *Anth. Pal.*
7. 713 in *DRN* 4. 181–2, and especially *Thucydides's account of the plague at Athens in 2.
47–53 at the end of *DRN* bk. 6) and Latin (e.g.
*Ennius, cf. 1. 117–26, O. Gigon, in *Lucrèce*,
Entretiens Hardt 24 (1978), 167–96, Pacuvius,
e.g. *Chryses* fr. 86–92 Ribbeck with 5. 318–
23). The main model is the lost philosophical
didactic poem of *Empedocles, the *Peri
physeōs* or 'On Nature' (cf. W. Kranz, *Philol.*
1943, 68–107; M. Gale, *Myth and Poetry in
Lucretius* (1994), 59–75): Empedocles' doctrine is criticized (1. 705–829), but he is
praised as a poet especially for his stance as a
'master of truth' offering an important secret
to his audience, in contrast to the stress on
form in Hellenistic didactic poetry (*Aratus
(1), *Nicander, etc.). Lucretius too writes to
save humanity (cf. 6. 24–34 on Epicurus):
although the work concentrates on physics
and natural philosophy, this ethical purpose
is clear throughout (cf. e.g. 2. 1–61, 3. 59–93,
5. 43–54). Epicurus was opposed to poetry as
a serious medium of enlightenment, and the
Epicurean stress on clarity and simplicity of
language and 'sober reasoning' in thought
creates problems for an Epicurean didactic
poem: by returning to the archaic models of
Empedocles and *Parmenides, Lucretius was
able to place himself in a tradition which
made the alliance of philosophy and poetry
more natural (though Empedocles' status as
a poet had itself been called into question

by *Aristotle, *Poet.* 1447^b 17 ff.). Many of the resources of poetry, particularly the recall to the phenomenal world implicit in the use of metaphor and simile, can easily be made consonant with the needs of Epicureanism: poet and philosopher alike must make the reader *see* (cf. 2. 112–41, A. Schiesaro, *Simulacrum et Imago* (1990)). The effect is a recontextualization of both the traditional devices of poetry and the basic elements of Epicurean epistemology, particularly the 'first image' (*Ep. Hdt.* 38) or prolepsis associated with each word, the basis for live metaphor (cf. D. Sedley, *Cron. Erc.* 1973, 5–83). The complexity and precision of Lucretius' imagery, always a central part of his claim to poetic excellence (D. West, *The Imagery and Poetry of Lucretius* (1969)), is thus also an aspect of his role as philosopher and scientist.

Nevertheless, the old conception of a conflict between Lucretius the poet and Lucretius the philosopher was not perhaps wholly wrong. The *De rerum natura* became an immensely important text in the Renaissance and modern periods because of its rationalism: when Abraham Cowley celebrated Bacon's victory over 'Authority' and superstition in his ode *To the Royal Society*, it was to Lucretius' image of Epicurus triumphing over *religio* to which he naturally turned (1. 62–79). Similarly, through Pufendorf, Hobbes, and Rousseau (cf. C. Kahn, in G. B. Kerferd (ed.), *The Sophists and their Legacy* (1981), 92–108), the account of the development of civilization in book 5 of *DRN*, and in particular the notion of the 'social contract', enabled historians and philosophers to free themselves from theist models of the foundations of human society. But that very stress on scientific rationalism as providing a single sure and certain (cf. *DRN* 6. 24–34, 4. 507–21) answer to the troubles of life has come under suspicion in the post-modern age. Lucretius the poet offers perhaps more ways of looking at the world than can be accommodated with comfort within the plain and simple truth of Epicureanism. Of necessity, his rationalism has its own sustaining myths, from the clear light of reason which pierces and disperses the clouds of ignorance (2. 55–61, 3. 14–17) to the secure citadel of the wise (2. 7–13), from the nurturing female powers of Venus, Mother Earth, and Nature (cf. 2. 589–660) to the hellish shadows of 'normal' life (3. 59–86). Nevertheless, those myths in themselves continue to offer a powerful vision of a world by no means providentially ordered for humanity, but in which all humans can find happiness.   P.G.F., D.P.F.

Lucullus (Lucius Licinius Lucullus), grandson of Lucius Licinius Lucullus (consul 151 BC), nephew of *Metellus Numidicus, for whose return from exile he pleaded. He served in the Social War under *Sulla and, as quaestor (88 BC), was the only officer who supported his march on Rome. As proquaestor in the east, he was Sulla's most reliable officer, charged with diplomatic missions, collecting ships and money, and letting *Mithradates VI escape from Gaius Flavius Fimbria in accordance with Sulla's policy. Aedile (79) with his brother Marcus Terentius Varro Lucullus, he gave splendid games. Praetor in 78, he became Sulla's literary executor and guardian of Faustus Cornelius Sulla, and then governed Africa. As consul in 74, he opposed tribunician agitation and, worried by the threats of *Pompey, sent him generous supplies to Spain; after complicated intrigues, he secured an *imperium* (grant of supreme military and civil authority) against the pirates for Marcus Antonius (Creticus) and the command against Mithradates for himself.

He relieved Marcus Aurelius Cotta, raised the siege of Cyzicus, then occupied much of Pontus, forcing Mithradates to flee to Armenia. In the province of Asia he tried to relieve the cities of financial ruin by drawing up a moderate and ultimately successful plan for payment of their debts and interest at moderate rates. After capturing Sinope, which he saved from plundering by his army, and Amaseia, he asked for a senate commission to organize the annexation of Pontus. When *Tigranes II allied himself with Mithradates, Lucullus marched through Cappadocia and invaded Armenia, and in a battle against Tigranes won 'the greatest victory the sun had ever seen' (Plut. *Luc.* 28. 8). He captured the new capital Tigranocerta, allowed his troops to plunder it and celebrated victory games there. Tigranes had to evacuate his earlier conquests, including Gordyene and Syria. But the enemy collected fresh forces and the king of Parthia threatened intervention. An invasion of the Armenian highlands had to be abandoned when the army mutinied, and the capture of Nisibis did not assuage them. His brother-in-law *Clodius incited rebellion, and in Rome public opinion was turned against him, chiefly by those who had incurred losses in his organization of Asia. His command was removed by stages (68–67); the army, hearing this, deserted him; and in the end he was superseded by Pompey under the law of Gaius Manilius.

Back in Rome, he had to divorce his wife (a sister of *Clodia) for adultery, and a second marriage, to a niece of Porcius *Cato the Younger, turned out no better. After long delays caused by his enemies, he finally triumphed in 63. But he took no leading part in politics, except for an attempt to oppose *Julius Caesar and stop the ratification of Pompey's eastern arrangements (59), which ended in humiliation. He now concentrated on living in refined luxury, but lapsed into insanity before his death (57/6).

He was an able soldier and administrator, an Epicurean, a lover of literature and the arts, and a generous patron. But he lacked the easy demagogy that was needed for success in both war and politics in his day.   E.B.

Lutatius Catulus (1), **Quintus,** of noble, but not recently distinguished, family, half-brother of two Julii Caesares (Lucius Julius Caesar and Julius Caesar Strabo Vopiscus), and married first to a Domitia, then to a Servilia, sister of Quintus Servilius Caepio; was three times defeated for the consulship before succeeding for 102 BC with the help of *Marius, married to a Julia and at the summit of his popularity. It was perhaps to improve his chances that he first extended the traditional funeral procession and eulogy of *nobiles* (see Polyb. 6. 53 f.) to a woman, his mother Popillia (Cic. *De or.* 2. 44). Defeated by the Cimbri on the upper Adige, he had to give up the Po valley; but in 101, joined by Marius (who treated him with courtesy) and helped by his legate *Sulla, he shared in the victory of the Vercellae (perhaps near Rovigo, on the lower Po). Marius and he triumphed jointly (101) and he built a portico on the Palatine out of the spoils. When Marius received most of the credit for the victory, Catulus became a bitter enemy of his, drawing his friends away from him. He probably fought under Lucius Caesar in the Social War, opposed Marius and *Cinna in 88–87, and after their return was prosecuted by

Marcus Marius Gratidianus and committed suicide.

A cultured man, interested in philosophy, art, and literature, and a patron of literary men (e.g. Aulus Licinius Archias and Antipater), though not the centre of a literary circle, he was a link between the friends of *Scipio Aemilianus, whom he knew in his youth, and the generation of *Cicero, who greatly admired him and introduced him as a character in the *De oratore.* He wrote light verse (two epigrams survive) and a (lost) monograph on his German campaign, and he was a competent orator.   E.B.

Lutatius Catulus (2), **Quintus,** son of (1) above, escaped from Rome at the return of *Cinna in 87 BC, but seems to have come back and become aedile. On *Sulla's return he joined him and brought about the cruel death of Marcus Marius Gratidianus in revenge for his father's. But he opposed lawless murders by the *Sullani.* Consul in 78, he opposed his colleague Marcus Aemilius Lepidus, carried a law against violence, and secured Sulla a solemn funeral, at which the power of his veterans was displayed. When Lepidus rebelled, Catulus, as proconsul (77), was chiefly responsible for his defeat. Henceforth he was an acknowledged leader of the *optimates* (lit. 'the best men', the office-holding upper class). He was entrusted with the rebuilding of the Capitoline temple and the Tabularium (public archive) and dedicated the buildings in 69 with lavish games. (Cf. *ILLRP* 367–8.) During the 70s he defended the Sullan settlement, but finally acknowledged the corruption of senatorial juries and accepted its modification (70). He opposed the laws of Aulus Gabinius (67) and Gaius Manilius (66)—Pompey had offended him in 77—and in 65, as censor, the attempts of his colleague *Crassus to enfranchise the Transpadanes and annex Egypt. In 63 he was ignominiously defeated by Caesar in an election for the chief pontificate. He tried to throw suspicion on Caesar as involved in the conspiracy of *Catiline but failed, and his *auctoritas* now declined: in 61 he was asked to speak in the senate after two men much junior to him. He died soon after. He was a mediocre orator (Cic. *Brut.* 222) and never equalled his father's cultural interests.

E.B.

Lycophron The name of Lycophron is associated with two writers of the Hellenistic age, the identity of whom is open to much debate. They are here distinguished as (a) Lycophron and (b) ps.-Lycophron.

(a) Lycophron, a native of Chalcis, of the early 3rd cent. BC, active in Alexandria, a member of the tragic Pleiad (canonical grouping of the city's eight or more tragic poets), author of a number of tragedies and satyr-plays, and also a grammarian and glossographer of the comic poets, of whom a few glosses survive. The titles of some of the plays are conventional, of others topical (including one on his friend Menedemus of Eretria and one called the *Cassandreis*, the theme of which is unknown). Only a few fragments survive.

(b) Ps.-Lycophron, author of the 'monodrama' *Alexandra*, written in the immediate aftermath of the victory of *Flamininus at Cynoscephalae over *Philip V of Macedon in 197/6 BC. The author, whose true name and place of origin are probably concealed beneath the impenetrably enigmatic biographical tradition concerning Lycophron, probably used the name, and some of the literary substance, of Lycophron (a), not in emulation, but as an ironic reminiscence of the earlier writer, who had combined the practice of tragedy and the elucidation of comedy. Only on this assumption of a deliberate pseudepigraphon can the full irony of his work be appreciated. His poem, cast in the form of a prophetic recitation by Cassandra in iambic trimeters, called in the title of the poem Alexandra, has acquired notoriety on account of its obscure and laboured style and vocabulary, in which individual episodes and persons are alike concealed in memorable metaphorical terms, which defy indisputable rationalization. The poem is nevertheless a powerful, indeed brilliant performance, in which tragic intensity, grim irony, and recondite learning combine to create a memorable *tour de force*.

The framework of the poem (ll. 1–30 and 1461–74) is provided by a report to Priam by a guard set to watch over Cassandra. The rest is Cassandra's prophecy, which falls into the following main divisions: ll. 31–364, the fall of Troy and consequent disasters; 365–1089, the sufferings of the Greeks who do not succeed in returning home; 1090–1225, the sufferings of the Greeks who do return home;

1226–80, the wanderings of Aeneas and the Trojans; 1283–1450, the struggles between Europe and Asia, culminating in the victory of Rome; 1451–60, Cassandra's lamentation on the uselessness of her prophecy.

Three major questions relate to (1) the sources, (2) the purpose, and (3) the occasion of the poem.

1. Sources: (a) stylistic, thematic, and linguistic sources. The use of the iambic trimeter is natural to its tragic theme, and the tragic type of 'monodrama' recitatif (whether iambic or lyric) was current in the Hellenistic age; these features therefore call for no comment here, though they could be illustrated in many ways. (b) For the role of Cassandra as prophetess of post-Homeric catastrophes the author could call on numerous Archaic and Classical sources, and it is inevitable that precise debts, probably incurred by direct loan and not through an intermediary compendium of post-Homeric legends, should be largely unassignable. We may also be certain that, the prophecy apart, many other sources also contributed to the substance of the poem, both in general, and in specific passages. For instance, *Herodotus' opening passage on the conflict of east and west probably provided the poet with that theme, essential to his version of Cassandra's prophecy, and *Timaeus may have been the channel through which many of the abstruse Western legends, based on *Nostoi* ('Returns' from Troy), which form so significant a part of the poem, reached him. The possibilities extend far beyond the range of our limited knowledge. (c) The poet's language, monstrously obscure and metaphorical, was no doubt his own: a deliberate and successful attempt to wrap the prophetic, Sibylline theme in language that readers might deem appropriate to the occasion, in which echoes of Homeric, lyric, and especially tragic language are evident. The ancients reckoned the poet as 'dark' (*skoteinos, ater*), and he would no doubt have agreed.

2. Intent. The poet's purpose in choosing the theme is not explicitly stated, but the emphasis on Italian legends, especially those connected with Odysseus, and other Greek heroes (irrespective of whether such legends came to him, for example, from a direct reading of an early poet or poets, from a careful study of Timaeus, in some ways a

kindred spirit, from an intermediate hand-book, or even perhaps by local traditions regarding the heroic past) and the prominence given to the decisive role played by Macedonia in subduing Persia, and of Rome in subduing Macedonia, seem to indicate that the ultimate purpose of the prophecy is to commemorate the recent and apparently decisive change in the world order which he associates with the victory of Roman arms.

3. Date. The date of composition has to be determined in the light of this presumed purpose. It has caused much debate and there is no reason, unless more evidence is forthcoming, why the controversy should cease. The problem is well known. Lycophron, as identified under (a), lived in the early 3rd cent. BC, yet the poet clearly refers to a widely recognized Roman supremacy. The two propositions are hardly reconcilable, and the 12th-cent. Byzantine commentator Tzetzes suggested that the relevant lines had been written by another Lycophron. Since the debate opened in modern times it has been continually discussed whether the lines referring to Rome are acceptable in the context of a date c.275 BC, whether the whole passage relating to Rome should be regarded as an interpolation added after Roman conquest of Greece had become a reality, or whether the whole poem should be dated to a period when that had happened. The suggestion made here as to authorship is based on the hard-won belief that the reference in the Rome passage to a 'unique Wrestler' refers to Titus Quinctius Flamininus, and was made in the immediate aftermath of his victory at Cynoscephalae in 197/6 BC, when his praises were being sung, statues being erected to him, and religious festivals in his honour, Titeia, being inaugurated all over Greece. The impact made by the politic and philhellene Titus, representative of a new ruling power linked by ties of mythological kinship to the Greek and Trojan past, provides the appropriate background for this speedily produced pro-Roman eulogy from the mouth of the Trojan Cassandra. Independent evidence derived from the use made of 3rd-cent. authors, seems to confirm this date.

P.M.F.

Lycurgus (c.390–c.325/4 BC), Athenian statesman, of great importance after the battle of Chaeronea (338). The principal evidence

about him is the 'Life' in [Plut.] *Lives of the Ten Orators* and the appended honorific decree of 307/6, the original of which is partially preserved (*IG* 2². 457). Clearly he played the major part in the control of the city's finances for a period of twelve years, raising the revenue to perhaps 1,200 talents a year, and financing projects by raising capital from individuals (*prodaneismoi*); scattered epigraphic evidence attests the wide range of his activities (note esp. *Syll.*³ 218, *IG* 2². 1627 and 1672, ll. 11 and 303). The powers by which he did it all are obscure. Some have inferred from *Hyperides fr. 118 (OCT Kenyon) and other passages that he was given a general but extraordinary commission to supervise the city's finances, but the manner of the allusions in *Ath. Pol.* to the financial officers tells against such a theory: the passage in Hyperides *In Dem.* (col. 28) frequently taken to describe Lycurgus' position should be referred to *Demosthenes' powers as theoric commissioner (in charge of *theōrika*, 'spectacle' grants). Probably he occupied different offices including the position of *tamias tōn stratiōtikōn* (steward of the military fund) and controlled the whole by personal influence (cf. Plut. *Mor.* 841c), which manifests itself to us in the varied decrees which he proposed. Whatever his powers, it is certain that he carried through a diverse building programme including the completion of the Skeuotheke (arsenal) begun by the politician Eubulus, the rebuilding of the theatre of Dionysus, the construction of docks, and the improvement of the harbours. The substantial increase in the navy in this period is ascribed to him. He concerned himself also with the arrangements for processions and festivals, and had statues of the three great tragic poets erected and an official copy made of their works (later borrowed by *Ptolemy II Philadelphus for the library of Alexandria and never returned). The common belief that Lycurgus instituted, or reformed, the corps of *ephēboi* (young men on military service) is ill grounded. In politics he was bitterly suspicious of Macedon and was one of those at first demanded by *Alexander the Great in 335. He prosecuted Lysicles who had been a general at Chaeronea and any who after the battle seemed to show signs of defeatism, and, when the revolt of the Spartan king Agis III in 331/0 put the city in turmoil, Lycurgus used the occasion to attack Leocrates, who had been absent from the city from 338 to 332 but probably not illegally, and very nearly had him condemned for treachery. The fragments of his speeches attest the wide range of his prosecution of corrupt practices. He died shortly before the Harpalus affair. According to a story contained in a letter ascribed to Demosthenes he was accused by his successor Menesaechmus of having left a deficit; his sons were condemned to repay the money, and were imprisoned when unable to do so. They were released on the appeal of Demosthenes. By 307/6 his great services were generally recognized.

works Of fifteen speeches regarded as genuine by the rhetor and historian Caecilius (1st cent. BC), the only one extant is *Against Leocrates*. The ancient opinion that Lycurgus was mercilessly severe in his prosecutions is supported by the study of this speech. His literary style was influenced by that of *Isocrates, but he is a much less careful writer, being often negligent in the matter of hiatus, and inartistic in the composition of his sentences. Evidently he cared more for matter than style. His disregard of proportion is shown by his inordinately long quotations from the poets.   G.L.C.

Lydus, i.e. **John the Lydian,** civil servant at Constantinople and Greek author (AD 490–c.560). John, son of Laurentius, native of Philadelphia in Lydia, was well educated in Latin and Greek before travelling to Constantinople in 511. He studied philosophy while awaiting admission to the *memoriales*, an administrative bureau, but when his compatriot Zoticus became praetorian prefect John enrolled as *excerptor* in the prefecture, receiving a privileged position with profitable opportunities (1,000 solidi from fees in 511/2); his patron also arranged a lucrative marriage. John's career progressed less spectacularly after Zoticus' retirement in 512, although his exceptional command of Latin was always an asset. For a time he served as a secretary in the imperial palace, before returning to the prefecture. Under *Justinian, John's literary skills received recognition with imperial requests to deliver a Latin panegyric before foreign dignitaries and describe a Roman victory at Dara (530); perhaps in 543 he was given a professorship at Constantinople, being permitted to combine this with work in the prefecture until retirement in 551/2.

The latter half of his bureaucratic career was soured by hatred for Justinian's powerful praetorian prefect, John the Cappadocian, who overhauled central and provincial administration in ways which John disliked, especially since literary learning was devalued. John's three extant works all have antiquarian leanings, though they are not therefore divorced from contemporary concerns. *De mensibus* discusses the Roman calendar, *De ostentis* deals with astrological matters, while *De magistratibus* charts the history of Roman administrative offices, with particular attention to the praetorian prefecture on which John provides valuable inside information.   L.M.W.

Lysander (d. 395 BC), Spartan general. His family, though of Heraclid origin, was poor and when young he was reputedly of *mothax* status, requiring sponsorship through the *agōgē* (Spartan public training). He subsequently became the *erastēs* ('lover') of *Agesilaus, younger son of King *Archidamus II. Appointed admiral in 408 or 407, he gained the friendship and support of Cyrus the Younger, commenced the creation of a personal following, and won a victory at Notion which led to the dismissal of *Alcibiades. Resuming command in 405, he transferred his fleet to the Hellespont and destroyed the Athenian fleet at Aegospotami. His personal success was celebrated through several monuments and dedications; at Samos he was worshipped as a god, perhaps the first living Greek ever to receive divine worship. Cf. also *Suppl. Hell.* nos. 51, 325, 565.

Lysander established 'decarchies' (ten-man juntas) of his oligarchical partisans in many cities. Obtaining Athens' surrender through blockade (spring 404), he secured the installation of the Thirty Tyrants, but his policy was overturned by King Pausanias' restoration of democracy in 403. At some (disputed) date before 396 the ephors withdrew support from the faltering decarchies. His continuing influence, however, led Sparta to support Cyrus' attempt at the Persian throne (401) and to make his protégé Agesilaus king. Hoping to restore the decarchies, he obtained for Agesilaus the command against Persia in 396. Resentful of Lysander's personal following, Agesilaus frustrated his plans, but gave him an important Hellespontine command where he persuaded the

Persian Spithridates to defect. Back in Sparta in 395, he was instrumental in starting war with Thebes. Invading Boeotia from Phocis, he was surprised and killed at Haliartus before the planned rendezvous with King Pausanias' forces.

An abortive scheme to increase his power by making the kingships elective was 'discovered' after his death by Agesilaus. The sources differ as to whether it was planned in 403 or 395; it may be an invention to discredit his posthumous reputation and supporters. Accurate interpretation of Lysander's career generally is impeded by the hostility of most sources to the imperial system he created.

                                                              S.J.Ho.

Lysias, Attic orator. The ancient biographical tradition, that he was born in 459/8 and died *c.*380 BC ([Plut.] *Vit. Lys.* 835c, 836a; Dion. Hal. *Lys.* 1, 12), is clear but problematic. The latter date is plausible; the former less so, and many scholars suggest that a man some fifteen years younger would have been more likely to engage in his range of activities after 403 (the speeches, and cf. also [Dem.] 59. 21–2). He appears as a character in *Plato's Phaedrus;* in the *Republic,* his father Cephalus is an elderly Syracusan, living as a metic (foreign resident) in Athens, and friend of assorted Athenian aristocrats: the search for dramatic dates, however, is probably vain.

Lysias and his brother Polemarchus left Athens after Cephalus' death to join the panhellenic colony of Thurii in southern Italy, where he is said to have studied rhetoric. They were expelled as Athenian sympathizers after the Sicilian expedition, and returned to Athens as metics in 412/1. In 403 the Thirty Tyrants arrested both brothers, alleging disaffection but really (according to Lys. 12. 6) in order to confiscate their substantial property. Polemarchus was executed; Lysias escaped, and gave financial and physical support to the democratic counter-revolutionaries. He was rewarded by *Thrasybulus' decree granting citizenship to all those who assisted in the restoration, but this grant was promptly annulled as unconstitutional.

WORKS Modern editions contain 34 numbered speeches, although the titles of about 130 others are known, and for several we possess sufficient fragments (either as citations or on papyrus) to determine the nature of the case. Lysias' activity as a speech-writer after 403 was largely confined to that of forensic logography, like his fellow metics *Isaeus and *Dinarchus, composing speeches for litigants to deliver in court; but his versatility was very great. Like *Demosthenes and *Hyperides, he wrote for both public and private cases. The two categories, however, are not formally distinguished in the corpus, where few private speeches remain: most striking is 1, in which a cuckolded husband pleads justifiable homicide after killing his wife's lover, and the attack in 32 on an allegedly dishonest guardian. Private cases are better represented among the fragments, including for instance the *Hippotherses,* which deals with Lysias' attempts to recover his confiscated property from those who had purchased it under the Thirty Tyrants. Underlying the public speeches are a variety of legal procedures, most notably the *dokimasia* or scrutiny of prospective officials, many of them compromised by their record under the oligarchies of the Four Hundred or the Thirty Tyrants (16, 25, 26, 31, and the fragmentary *Eryximachus*); other cases concern official malpractice (most notably 12, in which Lysias personally charged Eratosthenes, ex-member of the Thirty, with having killed Polemarchus). The shadow of the Thirty, indeed, hangs over much of Lysias' work, but attempts to discern a consistent political standpoint throughout the corpus have largely foundered.

Lysias' reputation attracted speeches. We are told ([Plut.] *Vit. Lys.* 836a) that no fewer than 425 were circulating in antiquity, but that only 233 of these were agreed to be genuine. Critics since *Dionysius of Halicarnassus (Dion. Hal. *Lys.* 11–12) have attempted to determine authorship on chronological, stylistic, or, more recently, stylometric grounds, but the search has proved largely inconclusive. K. J. Dover, *Lysias and the Corpus Lysiacum* (1968) has indeed argued that authorship itself may not be a simple concept, and that Lysias and his clients may have collaborated to varying degrees, but this view remains contentious. More important for most purposes (including for instance the use of the speeches as historical sources) is the authenticity not of authorship but of the texts themselves: with the exception of 11, perhaps of 15, and possibly of 6, all the forensic works seem to be genuine speeches, written to be delivered on the occasion they purport to be (though we should allow for the probability of unquantifiable revision).

CHARACTERISTICS Lysias was noted in antiquity as a master of the language of everyday life: this 'purity' of style led to his being regarded by later rhetoricians as the pre-eminent representative of 'Atticism' (the imitation of Classical Athenian Greek), as opposed to the florid 'Asiatic' school. Dionysius (*Lys.* 18) criticized him for lacking emotional power in his arguments, but this may be to miss the significance of his admitted mastery in narrative: by the time Lysias has finished telling a story, the audience has been beguiled by his apparent artlessness into accepting as true the most tendentious assertions. Dionysius noted his mastery of *ēthopoiia* (§ 8), by which he evidently meant the ability to portray character attractively, though there are signs in several speeches (notably 1 and 16) of an attempt also to capture the individuality of the speaker in the language given to him.   s.c.t.

Lysimachus (*c.*355–281 BC), Macedonian from Pella (late sources wrongly allege Thessalian origins), was prominent in the entourage of *Alexander the Great, achieving the rank of Bodyguard by 328. At Babylon (323) he received Thrace as his province, establishing himself with some difficulty against the Thracian dynast, Seuthes (322). He consolidated his power in the eastern coastal districts, suppressing a revolt among the Black Sea cities (313) and founding Lysimacheia in the Chersonese as a bulwark against the Odrysian monarchy (309). Though he assumed royal titulature (306/5), he made no mark in the wars of the Successors until in 302 he invaded Asia Minor and fought the delaying campaign against *Antigonus the One-eyed which enabled *Seleucus I to bring up his army for the decisive battle of Ipsus (301). His reward was the lands of Asia Minor north of the Taurus, the source of immense wealth, which he husbanded with legendary tight-fistedness and a degree of fiscal rapacity. These new reserves (Pergamum alone held 9,000 talents) supported his impressive coinage and allowed him to consolidate in Europe, where he extended his boundaries north until he was captured by the Getic king, Dromichaetes, and forced to surrender his Transdanubian acquisitions (292). In 287 he joined *Pyrrhus in expelling *Demetrius the

Besieger from Macedon and two years later occupied the entire kingdom. His writ now ran from the Epirote borders to the Taurus, but dynastic intrigue proved his nemesis, when he killed his heir, Agathocles, at the instigation of his second wife, *Arsinoë II, and alienated his nobility (283). Seleucus was invited to intervene and again invaded Asia Minor. The decisive battle at Corupedium (*c.* January 281) cost Lysimachus his life. Asia passed to the Seleucids while Macedonia dissolved into anarchy.   A.B.B.

Lysippus and **Lysistratus,** Sicyonian sculptors, active *c.*370–315 BC. The two, who were brothers, worked exclusively in bronze. Lysippus was by far the more prolific and famous, producing gods, heroes, agonistic victors, portraits, animals, and even metal vases; Lysistratus is known only for his portrait of Melanippe and for his innovative technique. He took plaster life-masks from his subjects, made adjustments on the wax castings thus obtained, and based his portraits on them (Plin. *HN* 35. 153). He also took casts from statues, presumably either for workshop consultation or for reproduction (and sale?).

Lysippus was also an innovator. Aggressively independent (Plin. *HN* 34. 61), he acknowledged the Doryphorus of Polyclitus as his master only ironically (Cic. *Brut.* 86, 296). This is consistent with *Pliny the Elder's report (*HN* 34. 65) that he abandoned Polyclitan four-square proportions for a slim physique and small head that made his figures look taller, and cultivated great precision of detail. This approach explains his success as a portraitist.

His works ranged in scale from an 18.3-m. (60-ft.) Zeus and a colossal Heracles for Tarentum to the 0.3-m. (1-ft.) Heracles Epitrapezius. Roman copies convey their appearance. Many copies of an Eros with a bow have been connected with his Eros at Thespiae, and his Kairos ('Opportunity') appears on reliefs and gems: winged, with a tuft of hair over the forehead but bald behind, and running with a balance supported on a razor, it illustrated the proverb 'Seize time by the forelock', but may also have embodied his artistic credo. His numerous athletes are represented by a contemporary marble version at Delphi of his Agias (erected 337–332) and by two copies of his Apoxyomenos;

the latter both thrusts his arms out into the observer's space and rocks from foot to foot. An original bronze athlete in Malibu (Getty Museum) is probably a school piece.

Among his portraits, a late classical *Socrates type ('B') may copy his statue for the Pompeion in Athens. He was *Alexander the Great's favourite sculptor, but few copies remain. If correctly attributed, the so-called Dresden type shows Alexander as crown prince (cf. Plin. *HN* 34. 63), the Schwarzenberg type as the heroic, leonine warrior (Plut. *Mor.* 335b), and the inscribed Azara type as a Zeus on earth (Plut. *Mor.* 335a). Bronze statuettes preserve several different body-types; all once held the spear that proclaimed his kingly authority and martial prowess

(Plut. *Mor.* 360d). An equestrian statuette in Naples has been connected with his group at Dium (in Macedonia) of the king and his 25 Companions who fell at the Granicus in 334, and a Hellenistic relief from Messene may reproduce his group at Delphi of *Craterus saving the king from a lion.

Attributions (all copies) include the Farnese Heracles, the Lateran Poseidon, a Dionysus in Venice, a seated Hermes from Herculaneum, the Berlin–Santa Barbara Dancer (cf. Plin. *HN* 34. 63), and several athletes. A revolutionary figure, Lysippus transformed the classical tradition in sculpture; his influence lasted into the Hellenistic period through his pupils.   A.F.S.

Mm

Macrobius, Ambrosius Theodosius, wrote (1) *De verborum Graeci et Latini differentiis vel societatibus,* (2) *Commentarii in Somnium Scipionis,* (3) *Saturnalia;* in the dedications of (1) and of Avianus' fables simply 'Theodosius'; in MSS of (2) and (3) styled *vir clarissimus et illustris* (the highest grade of senator); identical with Theodosius, praetorian prefect of Italy in AD 430 (Cameron), rather than with Macrobius, proconsul of Africa in 410 (Flamant); father of Flavius Macrobius Plotinus Eustathius, city prefect *c.*461, dedicatee of (2) and (3); grandfather of Macrobius Plotinus Eudoxius, who corrected a text of (2).

(1) *De differentiis.* This treatise, addressed to a Symmachus (? the orator *Symmachus' grandson, consul 446), comparing the Greek verb with the Latin, survives in extracts made at Bobbio and more extensively by Eriugena; it uses *Apollonius Dyscolus and may have been used by *Priscian. Another Bobbio fragment (*De verbo*), addressed to a scholar called Severus, comparing the Latin verb with the Greek, is not Macrobius' work, though possibly based on it.

(2) *Commentarii.* Having discussed how *Cicero's *Republic* differs from *Plato's, and what dreams are, Macrobius expounds the *Somnium* philosophically, discoursing on number-mysticism, oracles, moral virtue, astronomy, music, geography, and the soul (vindicating Plato against *Aristotle); he praises P. *Cornelius Scipio Aemilianus for uniting all the virtues, and the *Somnium* for uniting all the branches of philosophy. The main source is *Porphyry, in particular his commentary on *Timaeus;* but direct knowledge of *Plotinus has been established. Despite frequent inconsistencies and misapprehensions, the work was a principal transmitter of ancient science and Neoplatonic thought to the western Middle Ages.

(3) *Saturnalia.* This work is cast in the form of dialogues on the evening before the Saturnalia festival (16 December) of AD 383(?) and during the holiday proper. The guests include the greatest pagan luminaries of the time (Praetextatus, Symmachus, Nicomachus Flavianus), Avienus (variously identified with a son of Avienus the *Aratea* poet and with Avianus the fabulist, if in fact called Avienus), and the grammarian Servius, still a shy youth but praised in accordance with his later eminence; other names seem taken from Symmachus' letters (Dysarius the doctor, Horus the philosopher, Euangelus the boor). Macrobius himself plays no part. After a few legal and grammatical discussions the night before, the three days are devoted to serious topics in the morning, lighter ones, including food and drink, in the afternoon and evening. Having ranged over the Saturnalia, the calendar, and famous persons' jokes, the speakers devote the second and third mornings to *Virgil, represented as a master of philosophical and religious lore and praised almost without reserve in matters of rhetoric and grammar, including his use of earlier poets, Greek and Roman. The guests then turn to physiology, with special reference to eating and drinking. Sources include *Gellius (constantly used and never named), *Seneca the Younger's *Epistulae,* *Plutarch's *Quaestiones convivales,* Aelius *Donatus, and [*Alexander of Aphrodisias], *Physical Problems;* they are adapted to Macrobius' own purposes, as when matter from Gellius is used in a preface professing orderly exposition. The work expresses the nostalgia of the Christianized élite in a diminished Rome for the city's great and pagan past; the new religion is ignored. Macrobius' style is elegant, without the extravagance of a *Sidonius Apollinaris or a *Martianus Capella. Though much exploited by John of Salisbury, the *Saturnalia* was less read in the Middle Ages than the *Commentarii,* but returned to favour in the Renaissance.   L.A.H.-S.

Maecenas, Gaius Maecenas is his *nomen* or family name: 'Cilnius' (Tac. *Ann.* 6. 11) may be his mother's name, perhaps descended from an ancient Etruscan family, the Cilnii of Arretium (Livy 10. 3. 2). The poets call Maecenas scion of Etruscan kings (Hor. *Carm.* 1. 1. 1). Among Octavian's earliest supporters—he fought at the battle of Philippi (42 BC)—he was his intimate and trusted friend and agent. (See AUGUSTUS.) His great position rested entirely on this: he never held a magistracy or entered the senate, remaining an *eques* (Roman knight). He arranged Octavian's marriage with Scribonia, and represented him at the negotiations of the pact of Brundisium (40 BC) and that of Tarentum (37 BC), when he took along his poets (Hor. *Sat.* 1. 5). He went as envoy to Mark *Antony in 38, and in 36–33 and 31–29 he was in control of Rome and Italy in Octavian's absence, an unprecedented position: 'no title, only armed power' (Syme, *AA* 272). In 30, claiming to uncover a conspiracy, he executed the son of the triumvir *Lepidus . His enormous wealth must derive partly from the confiscations: by chance we hear that he acquired part of the possessions of the proscribed Marcus Favonius (schol. Juv. 5. 3). He bequeathed the emperor everything, including his magnificent house and grounds on the Esquiline hill at Rome, the famous *turris Maecenatiana*. Many inscriptions survive of his slaves and freedmen. Maecenas was famous, or notorious, for his luxury: wines, gourmet dishes (baby donkey, Plin. *HN* 8. 170), gems, fabrics, and love affairs (that with the actor Bathyllus became scandalous: Tac. *Ann.* 1. 54). Astute and vigorous at need, he cultivated an image of softness (Sen. *Ep.* 114). His name became proverbial as the greatest patron of poets (Martial 8. 55. 5). Absent from the *Eclogues*, he is the dedicatee of *Virgil's *Georgics*; unnamed in *Propertius 1, he is a rewarding and apparently exigent patron in 2. 1. Virgil introduced *Horace (Hor. *Sat.* 1. 6. 54), who dedicated to Maecenas *Satires* 1, *Epodes*, *Odes* 1–3, and *Epistles* 1. Maecenas gave Horace his Sabine estate. Horace gives the fullest picture of Maecenas and his circle, which included Lucius Varius Rufus, Plotius Tucca, Domitius Marsus, and his freedman Maecenas Melissus. Maecenas wrote poems which recall the metres and to some extent the manner of Catullus: extant fragments of two are addressed to Horace, intimate in

tone. He wrote in prose: *Prometheus* (? a Menippean satire); *Symposium*, Virgil and Horace being speakers; *De cultu suo*. His style was criticized for affectation: 'the preciosity and neuroticism of the author come through strongly in the fragments' (Courtney, *FLP*). They contain no trace of politics, but Maecenas must have been influential in inducing Virgil, Horace, and even Propertius to express support for the regime and the values it fostered. His influence is controversial in detail. He was an important intermediary between *princeps* and poets, who lost contact after his death. His wife Terentia, eventually divorced, was Aulus Terentius Varro Murena's sister; apparently Maecenas, departing from his usual discretion, warned her of the detection of her brother's conspiracy (23 BC). Thereafter his relations with Augustus, never openly impaired, seem to have been less close. He died in 8 BC. Two undistinguished *Elegies* on his death survive.   J.Gr.

Malalas (*c.* AD 480–*c.*570), author of an influential universal chronicle in Greek. John Malalas came from Antioch in Syria where legal expertise probably secured him administrative employment (Malalas is Syriac for 'rhetor', 'lawyer'). His eighteen-book *Chronographia* covers world history from the Creation to AD 563, where the single manuscript of a continuous text breaks off (12th-cent. Oxford MS Bodl. Baroccianus 182): the chronicle probably terminated in 565, less plausibly 574. Apart from lacunae, this MS is also an abridgement of the original, but Malalas was used by later Greek, Syriac, Coptic, Latin, and Slavonic writers and through these adaptations a fuller version of the original has been reconstructed.

The preface proclaims a dual purpose, to narrate the course of sacred history as presented in Christian chronography and present a summary of events from Adam to *Justinian. These motives coalesce in the chronological computations which present an unusual date for Christ's crucifixion, 6,000 years after Creation (normally *c.*5,500): this permitted Malalas to dismiss contemporary apocalyptic fears that the world would endure for only 6,000 years and hence end in the early 6th cent. Books 1–8 cover the period before Christ, with Greek mythology and history incorporated within a framework of Hebrew affairs. Books 9–10 treat the late

Roman republic and early empire, with special attention to the chronology of Christ's incarnation, while 11–17 narrate Roman imperial history from *Trajan to Justin I (uncle of Justinian); the account becomes increasingly detailed, and from Zeno's reign deserves credit as a major contemporary source, especially for events at Antioch to which Malalas naturally devoted much attention. Book 18 covers Justinian's reign, and at least in part represents a continuation, not necessarily by the same author: the focus of the narrative switches to Constantinople; after a very detailed, document-based account of Justinian's early years (527–32), it abruptly deteriorates into a series of brief notices until the mid-540s when fuller coverage resumes. Malalas' religious views seem orthodox, though theological matters were not a major concern. The *Chronographia* provides important evidence for the interests and attitudes of the educated administrative élite in the eastern empire.   L.M.W.

Manetho (fl. 280 BC), Egyptian high priest at Heliopolis in the early Ptolemaic period (see PTOLEMY), wrote a history of Egypt in three books (*Aigyptiaka*) from mythical times to 342. The human history was divided into 30 human dynasties (a 31st was added by a later hand) which still form the framework for ancient Egyptian chronology. The original, which contained serious errors and omissions, is lost and the fragments preserved in Christian and Jewish writers are frequently badly corrupted. Nevertheless, his importance in the preservation of Egyptian historical tradition is great, and his influence has been generally benign.

There also exist under the name of Manetho six books of didactic hexameters on astrology entitled *Apotelesmatika* ('Forecasts'). Probably they were composed between the 2nd and 3rd cents. AD. The sole extant MS transmits them in confused order: books 2, 3, and 6 are together a complete poem, and book 4 is another; books 1 and 5 are heterogeneous fragments. The author of the long poem gives his own horoscope (6. 738–50), from which it can be calculated that he was born in AD 80. By claiming knowledge of Egyptian sacred writings and addressing 'Ptolemy', the writer of book 5 seeks extra credibility by implying that he is the famous Manetho; and the whole collection came to

be attributed to the same source. The poems are bald catalogues of the likely duties, characteristics, and sexual proclivities of those born under the various combinations and conjunctions of planets and star-signs. The writer of book 4 is notable for his many new compound nouns and adjectives; but in general these poets have little to recommend them.   A.B.L.; N.H.

Manilius, Marcus, Stoic author of the *Astronomica*, a didactic astrological poem whose composition spans *Augustus' final years and *Tiberius' succession (1. 899 mentions P. *Quinctilius Varus' defeat in AD 9; ambivalent references at 1. 7 and 925–6 are disputed, but Augustus is probably alive at 2. 508–9, since Tiberius is not mentioned in 2; by 4. 763–6, 773–7 Tiberius is *princeps* or emperor). Manilius may mirror Virgil in choosing didactic at a period of political transition, and he uses his risky topic in support of a continuing Principate.

The technical content is as follows. Book 1: an introductory theodical account of creation and an astronomy influenced by *Aratus (1); book 2: the characteristics, conjunctions, and twelvefold divisions (*dodecatemoria*) of the zodiacal signs, the relationship of cardinals and temples to different areas of human life; book 3: a different circular system of twelve lots (*sortes*) of human experience, its adjustment, the calculation of the horoscope at birth, length of life, tropic signs; book 4: zodiacal influences at birth, the tripartite division of signs into decans, the 360 zodiacal degrees and their influence, the partition of the world and its nations among the signs, ecliptic signs; book 5: the influence on character of extra-zodiacal constellations at their rising (*paranatellonta*), a lacuna (709 ff.), stellar magnitudes. The proem to 5 demonstrates that Manilius settled for a five-book structure. Books 2–4 provide a zodiacal central section and the astronomical tour of 5 balances that of 1. Books 1–4 have extensive prologues, 1, 4, and 5 significant finales. Manilius may have abandoned an earlier plan for seven books to include a thorough treatment of planetary influences which can only have received about 200 lines in the lacuna at 5. 709 ff. But since book 5's extensive Andromeda myth and its closing depiction of stellar magnitudes as a hierarchical star-state analogous with human society echo the bee-state and Orpheus myth of *Virgil's last *Georgic*, book 5 should be the final book. Manilius' astrological sources are unclear. Egyptian, Hermetic, and Posidonian influences have been mooted, and some material only reappears in Arab astrological writings. If not himself the source of the astrological writer Firmicus Maternus (early 4th cent.), Manilius shares one with him. His repetitions, contradictions, inaccuracies, and omissions, notably of the promised planetary material, have been justifiably castigated. But his purpose and talents have been obscured by his complex subject and, for English-speakers, by Housman's sarcastic compliments about skilfully versified sums.

The *Astronomica* are no more a practical treatise than are Virgil's *Georgics*. Religious philosophy and political ideology are the driving forces. A blistering attack on *Lucretius' republican Epicurean poem underlies the poet's passionate Stoic hymns to the mystical order governing the multiplicity and diversity of creation. Astrology allows Manilius to link heavenly macrocosm with earthly and human microcosm and he claims the authority of a divinely inspired ascent to justify his vision. His hexameters are fine and his poetic range unusual. Exploiting didactic's formal elements—prologue, 'digression', and epilogue—he reworks Lucretius' and Virgil's greatest excursuses and *Cicero's *Somnium Scipionis*, but can also frame telling cameos of human foibles in comic and satiric vein, whilst his verbal point marks him as *Ovid's younger contemporary. Today Scaliger's view of Manilius, that he was as sweet as Ovid and more majestic, is returning to favour.   A.M.W.

Marcius Philippus, Lucius, grandson of Quintus Marcius Philippus and of Appius Claudius Pulcher, after a demagogic tribunate (*c.*105 BC) omitted the aedileship, hence (probably) failed to become consul 93. Elected for 91, he disliked *Livius Drusus (2)'s plans to enlarge the senate and enfranchise the Italians and led the opposition to him. After the death of Lucius Licinius *Crassus, he succeeded, as an augur, in having Drusus' laws invalidated. He is not heard of between 90 and 86: a provincial command may be conjectured. Collaborating with the government of *Cinna, he became censor with

Marcus Perperna in 86, registering the first of the newly enfranchised Italians. They struck his uncle Appius Claudius Pulcher, then in exile, off the senate list as a supporter of *Sulla. Together with Gnaeus Papirius Carbo and Quintus Hortensius Hortalus, he successfully defended *Pompey on a criminal charge. On Sulla's return he joined him, conquered Sardinia for him (82), and as the oldest living consular (except for the inactive Perperna) became a pillar of the Sullan establishment after Sulla's death, leading vigorous action against Marcus Aemilius *Lepidus and *Sertorius, against whom he persuaded the senate to send Pompey. He frequently, though unsuccessfully, urged the annexation of Egypt under the testament of *Ptolemy X Alexander I. Cicero greatly admired him, characterizes him as a good speaker (though eclipsed by Lucius Crassus and Marcus Antonius), and frequently quotes his witticisms.   E.B.

Marcius Turbo See TURBO, MARCIUS.

Marcus Aurelius emperor AD 161–80, was born in 121 and named Marcus Annius Verus. His homonymous grandfather, Marcus Annius Verus, from Ucubi (Espejo) in Baetica, consul for the third time in 126 and city prefect, a relative of *Hadrian and an influential figure, brought him up after his father's early death. His mother Domitia Lucilla inherited the fortune created by Cn. Domitius Afer. From early childhood Marcus was a favourite of Hadrian, who nicknamed him *Verissimus*. At the age of 15 he was betrothed at Hadrian's wish to Ceionia Fabia, daughter of the man Hadrian adopted as Lucius Aelius Caesar. In 138 Hadrian ordered his second heir *Antoninus Pius, whose wife was Marcus' aunt Annia Galeria Faustina, to adopt Marcus along with Aelius' son Lucius: he now became Marcus (Aelius) Aurelius Verus Caesar. When Hadrian died, Marcus was betrothed to Antoninus' daughter, his own cousin Annia Galeria Faustina, instead of Ceionia. Quaestor in 139, first elected consul in 140 and again in 145, he married in the latter year; his first child was born on 30 November 147; the next day he received *tribunicia potestas* (tribunician power) and *imperium* (a grant of supreme military and civil authority) and Faustina became Augusta (*fasti Ostienses*). Marcus was educated by a host of famous teachers, one being the orator *Fronto; many of their letters survive. His leaning to philosophy, already manifest when he was 12, became the central feature of his life. He was much influenced by Quintus Junius Rusticus (elected to a second consulship in 162), son or grandson of a Stoic 'martyr' of AD 93, and by the teaching of *Epictetus. Although Marcus is called a Stoic, his *Meditations* (see below) are eclectic, with elements of Platonism and Epicureanism as well. Further, he was much indebted to Antoninus, who receives a lengthier tribute than anyone else in the *Meditations* (1. 16; another version, 6. 30). His tranquil family life is vividly portrayed in his correspondence and recalled with affection in the *Meditations*. Faustina bore him further children; several died in infancy, but the couple had four daughters when Marcus succeeded Antoninus on 7 March 161; and Faustina was again pregnant.

Marcus at once requested the senate to confer the rank of co-emperor on his adoptive brother Lucius, as Hadrian had intended. Lucius took Marcus' name Verus, while Marcus assumed that of Antoninus. There were thus two Augusti for the first time, equal rulers, except that only Marcus was *Pontifex Maximus* (head of the college of priests) and he had greater *auctoritas* (prestige). The coinage proclaimed the *concordia Augustorum* (concord of the emperors), Lucius Verus was betrothed to Marcus' eldest daughter Annia Aurelia Galeria Lucilla, and the *felicitas temporum* (happiness of the times) was further enhanced when Faustina gave birth to twin sons on 31 August, their names honouring Antoninus (Titus Aurelius Fulvus Antoninus) and Lucius (Lucius Aurelius Commodus). But Antoninus' death had unleashed trouble on the frontiers: in Britain, dealt with by Sextus Calpurnius Agricola; Upper Germany, to which Marcus' close friend Aufidius Victorinus, Fronto's son-in-law, was sent; along the Danube; and, most seriously, in the east. The Parthians seized Armenia, defeated the governor of Cappadocia (who took his own life), and invaded Syria. It was decided that an expeditionary force was needed, to be led by Lucius Verus, with an experienced staff. Verus left Italy in 162 and was based at Antioch until 166 (with a visit to Ephesus in 164 to marry Lucilla), but was merely a figurehead. After the expul-

sion of the Parthians from Armenia by Statius Priscus (163), he took the title Armeniacus (accepted by Marcus in 164), crowning a new king, Sohaemus. Other generals, notably Avidius Cassius, defeated the Parthians in Mesopotamia: Ctesiphon was captured and Seleuceia on the Tigris sacked at the end of 165. Verus became Parthicus Maximus, Marcus following suit after a short delay. In 166 further success led to the title Medicus. But plague had broken out in the eastern army; the threat in the north was becoming acute—the despatch of three legions to the east had weakened the Rhine–Danube *limes* (frontier). Verus was obliged to make peace, celebrating a joint triumph with Marcus (12 October 166). Each became Pater Patriae (father of the fatherland) and Marcus' surviving sons, *Commodus (whose twin had died) and Annius Verus (b. 162), became Caesar.

Marcus planned a new campaign to relieve the Danube frontier. New legions, II and III Italicae, were raised in 165; V Macedonica, formerly in Lower Moesia, was moved to Dacia on its return from the east. But the plague, reaching Rome in 166, delayed the expedition until spring 168; meanwhile Pannonia and Dacia were both invaded. The emperors went to the Danube in 168 and reinforced the frontier, stationing the new legions in western Pannonia under Quintus Antistius Adventus (*ILS* 8977). They wintered at Aquileia, where the plague broke out; the praetorian prefect Furius Victorinus was a victim and *Galen, the imperial physician, refused to stay. At Verus' insistence, he and Marcus also left in January 169, but Verus had a stroke on the journey and died a few days later. Marcus deified him and obliged the widowed Lucilla to marry the Syrian *novus homo* (first man of his family to reach the senate) Tiberius Claudius Pompeianus, who had distinguished himself in Pannonia. In spite of further bereavement—his younger son Verus died—he pressed on with preparations, auctioning imperial treasures to raise funds, and returned north, to Sirmium, in autumn 169.

Apparently planning to annex territory beyond the Danube, he launched an offensive in spring 170, but incurred a severe defeat. The Marcomanni and Quadi of Bohemia and Slovakia invaded, outflanked Marcus and swept over the Julian Alps, sacking Opitergium (Oderzo) and besieging Aquileia. It was the worst such crisis since the German invasions at the end of the 2nd cent. BC. Desperate measures, led by Pompeianus and *Pertinax, cleared Italy, Noricum, and Pannonia. The Marcomanni were defeated as they tried to recross the Danube with their booty. But the Balkans and Greece were invaded by the Costoboci, requiring further emergency measures, and Spain was ravaged by the Moors, dealt with by Marcus' friend Victorinus. Marcus, based at Carnuntum, first used diplomacy to detach some tribes from the 'barbarian conspiracy'; some peoples were settled within the empire. The offensive, resumed in 172, is depicted at the start of the Aurelian column in Rome. In spite of the death of the praetorian prefect Vindex, the Marcomanni were defeated: victory was claimed, with the title Germanicus. In a battle against the Quadi Roman troops were saved by a 'rain miracle', shown on the column, later claimed to have been achieved by the prayers of Christian legionaries; Marcus gave the credit to the Egyptian Hermes 'Aerius'. In 173 he pacified the Quadi, moving to Sirmium in 174 to take on the Sarmatian Jazyges of the Hungarian plain. After some successes, he was obliged to make an armistice when Avidius Cassius, who had had special powers in the east, was proclaimed emperor. The revolt collapsed after three months, but Marcus, now Sarmaticus, toured the east, taking Faustina, who died in late 175 and was deified, and Commodus. He went through Asia and Syria to Egypt, returning via Athens to Rome. Here he held a triumph (23 December 176) and raised Commodus to Augustus. In summer 178, renewed warfare in the north took him northwards again. He remained, evidently planning to annex Marcomannia and Sarmatia, until his death (17 March 180).

Marcus has been universally admired, as a philosopher-ruler, to the present day, criticized only for leaving his unworthy son as successor. This no doubt seemed the best way to ensure stability, and he left Commodus experienced advisers, including his numerous sons-in-law. Despite Marcus' lack of military experience he took personal command against the first wave of the great *Volkerwanderung* that ultimately destroyed the empire, setting an example that inspired his contemporaries in the view of *Ammianus (31. 5. 14).

A.R.Bi.

MEDITATIONS Marcus is most famous for a work his subjects never saw, the intimate notebook in which he recorded (in Greek) his own reflections on human life and the ways of the gods, perhaps before retiring at night. The title *Meditations* is purely modern: Gk. *ta eis heauton* ('to himself'), found in our MSS, may not go back to the author, but is surely accurate. Internal evidence suggests that he was past his prime when he wrote (2. 2, and other references to his age or imminent death), and that at least parts were composed during his lengthy campaigns against the German tribes. It seems to have survived almost by accident; it was unknown to the writers of his time and for long afterwards, but seems to have surfaced in the 4th cent. (Them. *Or.* 6. 81c, not a certain allusion). In general the closest analogies for the thought are with *Epictetus, but Marcus is interested less in sustained exposition. The style, often eloquent and poetic, can also be compressed, obscure, and grammatically awkward. All of this is understandable if he was writing memoranda for his eyes alone.

Although divided by moderns into twelve 'books', the work seems not to have a clear structure. Brief epigrams are juxtaposed with quotations (usually of moral tags, occasionally of longer passages: esp. 7. 38–42, 11. 30–9) and with more developed arguments on divine providence, the brevity of human life, the necessity for moral effort, and tolerance of his fellow human beings. Frustratingly, these *pensées* are almost invariably generalized: we do not learn Marcus' secret thoughts about his family, members of the court, or military policy. We do, however, get some idea of his personality and preoccupations.

The first book of the *Meditations* is a different matter, being more coherent than the others; it may have been composed independently. Here Marcus goes through a list of his closer relatives and several teachers, recording what he owes to each—in some cases a specific lesson, but more often a general moral example. This list culminates in two long passages on what he owes to his predecessor *Antoninus Pius, and to the gods (1. 16 and 17). Though often allusive and obscure, these give us unique access to the mind of an ancient ruler, and the whole book is a precious personal document.

In the rest of the work, though technical discussion of Stoic doctrine is avoided, certain recurrent themes stand out: the need to avoid distractions and concentrate on making the correct moral choice; the obligation of individuals to work for the common good (e.g. 6. 54: 'What does not benefit the hive does not benefit the bee'); the unity of mankind in a world-city (4. 4; cf. G. R. Stanton, *Phronesis* 1968, 183 ff.); insistence on the providence of the gods, often combined with rejection of the Epicurean alternative that all is random movement of atoms (e.g. 6. 17, 8. 39). Duty and social responsibility are strongly emphasized; Marcus is keenly aware of the temptations of power (e.g. 5. 16, 6. 30 'do not be Caesarified'). Thoughts of providence lead him to contemplate the vastness of time and space, and the guiding pattern that according to the Stoics gives order to the universe (e.g. 10. 5). There is also a more melancholy note, of resignation and pessimism. Though determined to persevere in his moral efforts, the author is often resigned to their futility (8. 4; 9. 29 'who will change men's convictions?'). Hymns to the grandeur and order of the universe (4. 23, 5. 4) can give way to revulsion and disgust (8. 24). Above all, Marcus is fascinated by life's transience and the way in which all great men, even philosophers and emperors, pass on and are forgotten (4. 32, 33, 48, 50, etc.). His most lasting achievement is a work which has inspired readers as different as Sir Thomas Browne, Matthew Arnold, and Cecil Rhodes.

R.B.R.

Marius, Gaius, born *c.*157 BC near Arpinum, of a family probably of recent equestrian standing, but with good Roman connections, including *Scipio Aemilianus. He served with distinction under Scipio at Numantia and, with his commendation, won a military tribunate by election, perhaps serving under Manius Aquillius in Asia. Quaestor *c.*123, he was helped to a tribunate by the Metelli (119), but fiercely attacked the consul Lucius Caecilius Metellus Delmaticus when he opposed Marius' law ensuring secrecy of individual votes in the *comitia* (assembly). Because of this breach of *fides* (trust) he failed to gain an aedileship, but became (urban) praetor 115, barely securing acquittal on a charge of *ambitus* (bribery). Sent to Further Spain as proconsul, he showed aptitude at guerrilla warfare and added to his fortune. On his return he married a patrician Julia, a distinguished match. In 109 *Metellus Numidicus,

sent to fight a guerrilla war against *Jugurtha, chose Marius as his senior legate. But when Marius requested leave to seek a consulship, Metellus haughtily rebuffed him. Marius now intrigued against Metellus among his equestrian and Italian friends in Africa and Rome and won election for 107 by playing on suspicions of the aristocracy. He superseded Metellus in Numidia by special legislation. He ended the manpower shortage by the radical step of abolishing the property qualification for service and enrolled a volunteer army. After fighting for two years without decisive success, he captured Jugurtha through the diplomatic skill of his quaestor *Sulla, was elected consul for the second time for 104 by special dispensation, to deal with a threatened German invasion, and triumphed on 1 January.

He found an army reorganized and trained by Publius *Rutilius Rufus, his fellow legate under Metellus and his enemy, as consul 105; and, re-elected consul year after year, with friendly colleagues, he improved the army's equipment and organization and defeated the Teutones and Ambrones at Aquae Sextiae (mod. Aix-en-Provence) and, with Quintus *Lutatius Catulus (1), the Cimbri at the Vercellae (near Rovigo in northern Italy), in 102 and 101 respectively, consenting to celebrate a joint triumph with Catulus. His immense prestige attracted nobles like Catulus into his following and confirmed the loyalty of *equites* and *plebs*. He was elected to a sixth consulship (100), defeating Metellus' quixotic candidacy.

The tribune Lucius Appuleius *Saturninus had provided land for his African veterans in 103, and in 100 undertook to do so for the veterans of the German war. Marius gladly accepted his co-operation and was pleased when Metellus' intransigence in opposition led to his exile. But when Saturninus, with the help of Gaius Servilius Glaucia, threatened to establish independent power, Marius turned against them, rejected Glaucia's consular candidacy, and, when they tried to force through a law overruling him, 'saved the republic' by forcibly suppressing them. But his stubborn opposition to Metellus' return, delaying it while his friend Marcus Antonius was consul, alienated his optimate supporters. When the vote for Metellus' recall passed, he left for the east, 'to fulfil a vow', abandoning hope for a censorship. His firm words to *Mithradates VI earned him election to an augurate in absence and, with his *dignitas* restored, he returned. But he had frittered away his overwhelming stature. Some of his friends and clients were now attacked (Manius Aquillius, Gaius Norbanus; the prosecution of Titus Matrinius (Cic. *Balb.* 48 f.)), and although he successfully defended them, his noble friends deserted him. In 92, reaffirming his links with the *equites*, he assisted in the prosecution of P. Rutilius Rufus, and in 91 he seems to have opposed Marcus *Livius Drusus (2) with his equestrian friends, mobilizing his Italian followers against Drusus. When the senate openly expressed support for Sulla by allowing Bocchus I, king of Mauretania, to dedicate a group showing Jugurtha's surrender on the Capitol, Marius was prevented from violent opposition only by the outbreak of the Social War (91–87). In the war he was successful on the northern front, but when not offered supreme command, chose to retire.

With war against Mithradates imminent, Marius hoped to have the command and opposed the attempt of his relative by marriage Gaius Julius Caesar Strabo Vopiscus to win the consulship for 88. He found an ally in Drusus' friend Publius Sulpicius Rufus, tribune 88, in return for supporting his policies. When the *optimates* (lit. 'the best men', the office-holding upper class) chose Sulla for the consulship and command (he married Caecilia Metella, widow of the *princeps senatus* (First Senator) Marcus Aemilius *Scaurus), Sulpicius had the *plebs* transfer the command to Marius. Sulla responded by seizing Rome with his army. Marius, unprepared for this, had to flee (the flight was later embroidered with dramatic detail), finding safety at Cercina, a colony of his veterans off Africa. After the expulsion of *Cinna from Rome, Marius returned and joined him with an army collected among his veterans. He sacked Ostia and organized Cinna's capture of Rome. Both were proclaimed consuls for 86 and Marius was to supersede Sulla in the east. He now took terrible vengeance on his enemies, especially on faithless former friends; but his health gave out and he died before taking up his command.

A typical *novus homo* (first of his family to reach the senate and/or consulship), like *Cato the Elder before him and Cicero after him, Marius wanted to beat the nobles at their own game and win acceptance as a leader of their *res publica*. Unlike some aristocrats, from Gaius Sempronius *Gracchus to *Julius Caesar, he had no plans for reform. Although favouring rewards for soldiers without distinction between citizens and Italians, he opposed Drusus' attempt to enfranchise the Italians and left it to Saturninus to look after his veterans' interests. His reform of enlistment, due to momentary considerations, accidentally created the client army: it was Sulla who taught him the consequences. However, his early career first demonstrated the power inhering in an alliance of a successful commander with a demagogue and a noble following; and his opponents, in their attitude to him and to Sulla, revealed the lack of cohesion and of political principle besetting the *nobilitas* (the senatorial elite descended from consuls).   E.B.

Mark Antony See ANTONY, MARK.

Martial (Marcus Valerius Martialis), Latin poet, was born at Bilbilis in Spain on 1 March in a year between AD 38 and 41 (in 10. 24, written between 95 and 98, he celebrates his fifty-seventh birthday). He died in Spain, probably at Bilbilis, between 101 and 104 (book 12 is later than 101, but Plin. *Ep.* 3. 21 on Martial's death is not later than 104). Brought up in Spain, he came to Rome around AD 64 (10. 103 and 104, datable to AD 98, report that he had lived in Rome for 34 years). In Rome he was supported by *Seneca the Younger, then the most celebrated Spaniard in the city, and probably by other important patrons (4. 40, 12. 36): Gaius Calpurnius Piso, Memmius Regulus (consul in 63), and Vibius Crispus (consul in 61). Already in 65, however, the suppression of the Pisonian conspiracy brought ruin to the families of Seneca and Piso. Martial continued to be on friendly terms with the widow of *Lucan (Seneca's nephew and another victim) and with Quintus Ovidius, formerly connected with the circle of Seneca (7. 44, 45): it is possible that Martial's property at Nomentum and the neighbouring estate of Quintus Ovidius were both gifts from Seneca, who had considerable holdings in the area. These links do not, however, mean that Martial was connected with the intellectual opposition to *Domitian, whose favour he assiduously courted. The references to martyrs to republican freedom (*Pompey,

*Cicero, *Cato the Younger, *Brutus, *Porcia, Publius Clodius Thrasea Paetus) that occur from time to time in Martial are common in literature and by this date innocuous, or indeed had been taken over by Flavian propaganda against Nero. We do not know if Martial attempted a legal career: he expresses strong dislike of the idea, even when endorsed by another important Spaniard, *Quintilian (2. 90), but it was normally considered the most suitable career for an intellectual on the make. In the fifteen years and more that he spent in Rome before his first publications, he was probably already gaining renown and reward through occasional verse and panegyrics of the rich and powerful. He must already have been well known to have been able in 80 to celebrate with a book of epigrams an important public event, the opening games for the new Flavian amphitheatre. It was probably on this occasion that *Titus gave him the *ius trium liberorum* (legal privileges for parents of three children), an honour later confirmed by Domitian. After another two collections with particular purposes (*Xenia* and *Apophoreta*), in 86 he began publishing the series of twelve books of varied epigrams which are his principal claim to fame. They show already in existence a network of patronage and friendship involving a large cross-section of Roman upperclass society. He was also in contact with many of the most significant writers of the period: Quintilian, *Pliny the Younger, *Silius Italicus, *Frontinus, *Juvenal. There is no mention of *Statius, nor does Statius ever mention Martial, and this silence is usually taken to be a sign of personal enmity between two poets competing for the attentions of the same patrons. Martial's success, already apparently noteworthy before his poems were published in book form (2. 6), grew progressively, and he became extremely popular, being read even in the provinces by a wide public. His relationship with Domitian and the powerful freedmen of the court also grew, as his popular success gave him a central role in the literary scene and made it more and more natural that his epigrams should be used to celebrate official events connected with imperial propaganda. Martial complains that this success did not bring him financial reward: without any copyright in his works, he was dependent on patrons whose lack of generosity towards their clients

and refusal to respect the role and dignity of an intellectual and a poet he constantly laments. He represents himself, doubtless with considerable exaggeration, as just another *cliens* forced to roam the streets of Rome in search of tiny recompense for the humiliating attentions that had to be paid to his patrons. For a long time he rented a house like other persons of moderate means, but he had his property at Nomentum, and from 94 at least he also had a house in Rome: he had a number of slaves, and an honorary tribunate (3. 95. 9) conferred on him the social prestige of equestrian rank. After the death of Domitian he showed no hesitation in repudiating his earlier adulation and turning to Nerva (in book 11; an anthology of books 10 and 11 was also dedicated to Nerva, but this has not survived, though its opening epigrams were placed in book 12) and later Trajan (in a second edition of book 10 from which Domitian's name was expunged, the only version to survive, and in book 12). Both his personal position and his poetry were, however, too closely involved with the court of Domitian, and in the new regime Martial must have felt less at home. Tired of city life and, as ever, nostalgic for the idealized 'natural' life in Spain that he had always set against the falsity and conventionality of Rome, he decided to return there in 98. One of his patrons, Pliny the Younger, helped him with the expenses of the journey, and even in Spain he needed to depend on the generosity of friends, especially a widow, Marcella, who gave him a house and farm which finally enabled him to realize his dream of a free and natural existence. The contradictory and unnatural life of the capital was, however, the source of his poetry, and in book 12, composed in Spain, he expresses with a new bitterness his sense of delusion and emptiness at the loss of the cultural and social stimuli that had made him a poet in the first place.

WORKS *Epigrammaton liber* (modern title, *Liber de spectaculis*), published AD 80. This described the games for the opening of the Flavian amphitheatre (the Colosseum): we possess an incomplete selection of about 30 poems from the original volume.

Xenia and *Apophoreta* (now books 13 and 14), published in December of two different years (or less likely a single year) between 83 and 85. They claim to be collections of poetic tickets, each of a single couplet in elegiacs (except for two of the 127 *Xenia* and nine of the 223 *Apophoreta*), and designed to accompany gifts at the Saturnalia (festival of Saturnus). They present themselves as collections from which readers can select examples for their own use, and thus form part of the production of works designed to be of practical help to readers during the Saturnalian festivities (cf. Ov. *Tr.* 2. 471 ff.) but they merit literary appreciation for the ingenious brevity with which they characterize everyday objects (in the case of the *Xenia* usually foodstuffs, in the more varied and lively *Apophoreta* every type of gift).

Epigrammaton libri XII (around 1,175 poems in all), published probably as follows. Book 1 at the beginning of 96; 2 in 96–7; 3 in autumn 87, during a long stay at Imola; 4 in December 88; 5 in December 89; 6 in 90–1; 7 in December 92; 8 in January 94; 9 in autumn 94; 10 (lost first edition) in 95; 11 in December 96; 10 (second edition), April–October 98; 12, end of 101/102. Books 1, 2, 8, 9, 12 have prose prefaces.

Martial's production does sometimes include epigrams of the usual Greek type: epitaphs for friends and patrons, dedications celebrating both private and public events, and epideictic poems on contemporary or historical events, unusual happenings, or recoveries from illness. In these cases the traditional conventions are easily recognized, though the treatment may be original. In general, however, Martial's epigrams are very different from those of his Greek predecessors. His main model was *Catullus, not as a love-poet but as a writer who had brought full literary dignity to the minor poetry of autobiography and comic realism. He takes from Catullus many formal elements, above all his metres: as well as the elegiac couplets characteristic of Greek epigram and also predominant in Martial, he includes poems in hendecasyllables and scazons, both common metres in Catullus. Other metres are rare. Catullus had created a genre of minor poetry which joined the influence of the Greek epigram, iambic, and lyric traditions to the Roman tradition (itself influenced by Greek iambic poetry) of satirical verse full of personal and political polemic. Of the other models to whom Martial refers, we know little (Domitius Marsus) or scarcely anything (Albinovanus Pedo, Gnaeus Cornelius Len-

tulus Gaetulicus), but they presumably continued the Catullan tradition. Certainly this type of minor poetry on sentimental/ autobiographical, satirical, polemical, or complimentary themes was widely practised at Rome both by dilettante amateurs and by 'professional' poets as occasional verse for their patrons. Martial also had important models in late Hellenistic Greek epigram, which had already developed the tendency towards a clever final 'point' which marks much of his work: the Neronian poet Lucillius and his imitator Nicarchus had cultivated a new type of epigram mocking physical defects and typical characters from social and professional life. Their epigrams are perhaps a little cold and cerebral, but they conclude with striking final effects of surprise.

At first Martial's poems circulated privately, especially through oral delivery (2. 6), or were published in connection with particular events (*Liber de spectaculis*) or for particular 'practical' purposes (*Xenia, Apophoreta*). When he decided to publish them in collections of varied nature divorced from their (real or supposed) occasions, they ceased to be 'practical' verse and became 'literature', although the new form of presentation in its turn fulfilled roles as entertainment, polemic, or celebration on a higher and more lasting level. Martial's growing success with his readers encouraged the conviction that this type of minor poetry (which he always termed 'epigram', in contrast to the more varied terminology of other writers of the period) corresponded to a real need which the grander and more official genres could not satisfy. It was not a question of formal elegance or emotional intensity— the characteristics that had led *Callimachus and Catullus to affirm the greater dignity of the shorter forms—but of a need for realism, of a closer link between the pages of the text and everyday life (8. 3). The short epigram, able to treat incisively any and every aspect of life, could satisfy this need in a way that the more distant and conventional genres, which continued to produce variations on the same old mythological themes (4. 49, 9. 50, 10. 4), could not. The most typical form of the epigram in Martial, and the reason for his success, is the humorous realistic epigram on contemporary characters and behaviour which moves from witty entertainment to offer a lively and merciless picture of Roman society, revealing its multiple absurdities and contradictions through the mirror of the gestures and behaviour of the various social classes. Martial's attitude, unlike most social description in antiquity, is not moralizing, but he takes pleasure simply in recording with all his verbal art the complexities and contradictions of the spectacle of life. Both as a Spaniard born in a province which still retained a sense of the natural life of the country, and as an intellectual in a world where poets were valued less than he thought their due, Martial observes Rome from the outside. His ambitious view that his chosen poetic form, considered the lowest of all genres (12. 94. 9), might have greater validity than the great works promoted by official culture, and the merciless picture he offers of Roman society together give Martial's work a strongly anti-establishment tone, which, though frequently criticized by opponents, was well received by the general public, and eventually even by the higher classes and the court, albeit with a certain nervousness. A considerable part of his work in fact represents him as well integrated into the life of the upper classes, who were happy to see themselves described and celebrated in his verse even if at the same time it exposed many sordid aspects of the society of which these same classes were the highest representatives. The epigrams which Martial as a 'professional' poet offered to his patrons as a noble and cultured ornament of their lives give to us a particularly concrete and direct representation of Roman high society, with its houses, parks, possessions, and rituals. The many epigrams devoted to Titus and especially to Domitian are a fundamental document for the history of the imperial ruler-cult under the Flavians. The first-person of the comic or satirical poems is mostly simply a device to give vividness to the many social observations so that they appear to have been born from one man's experience, but there is also a more autobiographical 'I', not always easy to separate from the more general figure, the personality of a restless and unsatisfied poet who is proud of his merits but disappointed in society and convinced that he could have achieved much more in different circumstances. We are offered the picture of a simple and candid individual, qualities appropriate to a poet who constantly denounces the falsity and

paradoxes of a counterfeit life, a man of delicate affections and a strong sense of friendship, both often depicted in Horatian terms (see HORACE). Love (as opposed to sex) plays little part in the poems, but there are some epigrams of a subtle and sophisticated eroticism, mainly directed towards boys.

Martial's production is extremely varied, and offers both realism and fantasy, subtlety and extravagance. It is rarely that one has a sense of a poem having been written solely for piquant entertainment. His poetic language is influenced not only by Catullus but also by Horace, and above all by *Ovid; it has a cool mastery of expression which knows how to preserve the appearance of nature even when artifice is at its most obvious. His celebratory and adulatory poetry is clearly related to the precious mannerism of Flavian epideictic as we find it in some of Statius' *Silvae*, albeit with a greater lightness of touch. His realistic epigrams, while maintaining a high literary quality, open themselves to a lower and cruder language, including obscenity: in this area Martial is one of the boldest Latin poets, and, in general, many everyday objects and acts, and the words that describe them, enter Latin poetry for the first time with Martial. His most celebrated virtue is the technique with which he realizes his comic effects, either placing at the end of his epigrams a novel or surprising conclusion which throws an unexpected light on the situation being described, or else concentrating the entire sense of the poem at the end, in a pointed, antithetical, or paradoxical formulation of extraordinary density and richness of expression. This technique derives in part from later Greek epigram (see above), and also shows the same taste for point seen in contemporary rhetoric; Martial's brilliantly inventive use of it made him a model for the modern epigram, and indeed more widely for modern short poetry. The comic mechanisms that he employs, however, are not simply intellectual games, but also the means by which, on each occasion, the reality he is representing can be made the bearer of an intimate contradiction and incongruity, of a violent asymmetry with respect to reason and nature. They are thereby an original and efficacious means to give meaning to the myriad fragments of reality which had attracted his interest and which his large corpus offers in abundance. Within this vast canvas, the generic affinity with real life that epigram derives from its occasional nature is everywhere employed to the full, but realism is in productive tension with fantasy, play, and the grotesque, as the patterns of behaviour of everyday life are turned about in the brilliant paradoxes of Martial's wit.   M.Ci.

Martianus Minneus Felix Capella composed in Vandalic Carthage, probably in the last quarter of the 5th cent. AD, a prosimetrical Latin encyclopaedia of the seven Liberal Arts (grammar, dialectic, rhetoric—the medieval 'trivium'—and the 'quadrivium', geometry, arithmetic, astronomy, music. He subsequently composed a short metrical treatise. Both works were addressed to his son. The encyclopaedia, usually known as the *De nuptiis Philologiae et Mercurii*, but called the *Philologia* by its author, comprises a two-book introductory myth describing the ascent to heaven, apotheosis, and marriage of Philology to Mercury, as well as a seven-book introduction to the Liberal Arts, in which each subject is presented by an elaborately described female personification. The encyclopaedic books are pedestrian compilations, mostly from Latin sources, such as Aquila Romanus, Geminus, *Pliny the Elder, *Quintilian, and Julius Solinus; whether *Varro's lost *Disciplinarum libri* were also used is still debated. The myth is fantastic, imaginative, and curiously learned: while strongly influenced by Neoplatonic sources and doctrines on the ascent of the soul, it owes to the parodistic tradition of Menippean satire such features as councils of the gods, heavenly voyages, and wrangling philosophers. Martianus was pagan (he makes veiled allusions to Christianity as well as to Chaldaean theurgy, and elegizes over the silence of the oracles) and sufficiently well-read in Greek to translate Aristides Quintilianus' treatise on music. His baroque and intentionally abstruse periodic Latin proved extremely liable to corruption in the extensive and contaminated later manuscript tradition. The *Philologia* was very influential during the Carolingian period and the 12th-cent. Platonic revival, both as a textbook and as a literary source of mystic cosmology and images of the seven Liberal Arts. Two hundred and forty-one manuscripts of the *Philologia* have been examined and described by C. Leonardi (*Aevum* 1959, 443–89, and

1960, 1–99 and 411–524), and much work has been, and is being, done on the medieval commentaries.   D.R.S.

Masinissa, king of Numidia (238–148 BC). In about 213 he helped his father, in alliance with Carthage, to defeat Syphax, king of the western or Masaesylian Numidians, and then crossed to Spain, where he first appears in 211, commanding Numidian cavalry against Publius Cornelius Scipio (Livy 25. 34). He continued to serve the Carthaginians in Spain down to Ilipa in 206, but then defected to Rome, pledging his support to *Scipio Africanus himself should the Romans invade Africa (Livy 28. 34. 12 ff.).

Shortly afterwards, on the death of his father, he returned to Africa, and recovered control of his kingdom from his nephew, only to be driven out again by Syphax. There followed a series of adventures which, according to the more probable version, left him little more than a hunted fugitive. But in 204 he was able to join Scipio Africanus, when the latter landed in Africa (Livy 29. 29. 4), and thereafter his fortunes rapidly improved. His services to Rome culminated in the defeat and capture of Syphax after the battle of the 'Great Plains', and command of the Numidian cavalry on Scipio's right at the decisive battle of Zama.

His recognition as 'king' by Scipio was confirmed by the senate (Livy 30. 17. 12); and by the terms of the subsequent peace, everything which had belonged to him or his ancestors was to be restored to him. This virtually gave him *carte blanche* in his dealings with Carthage, and by loyally supporting Rome in her wars in Spain, Macedonia, and Greece, he usually, though not invariably, enjoyed her support. His continuous aggression eventually led to Carthage's resorting to war against him, contrary to her treaty with Rome, and though Masinissa was victorious—or perhaps because he was—war with Rome became inevitable, Masinissa living to see its outbreak, though not its end.

Tough, brave, and ruthless, Masinissa was obviously a skilled commander, particularly of cavalry, and a wily statesman. He was one of the very few Mediterranean potentates to grasp the overwhelming power of Rome, and, caught up in a titanic struggle between two great powers, managed to emerge with his own territory significantly enlarged. How far his ambitions extended is doubtful. Inscriptions show that he established diplomatic contacts with eastern Mediterranean kings, but his shrewdness would surely have precluded his thinking in terms of an empire stretching from Morocco to Egypt, as some have claimed. *Polybius (37. 10) and *Strabo (17. 3. 15) also praise his success in turning the Numidians into farmers, though he may have done no more than exploit areas already developed by Carthage. Although there are signs that even the Romans were becoming exasperated by, if not wary of, his ambitions, he managed to die in his bed, at the age of 90, and to bequeath his kingdom to his sons.

J.F.La.

Mausolus (Maussollos in inscriptions), son of Hecatomnus, satrap of Caria (SW Asia Minor). Ruler of Caria 377–353 BC, in conjunction with his sister and wife *Artemisia (2), and an important figure in the diffusion of Hellenism in 4th-cent. Asia Minor, who nevertheless promoted or retained the local Carian element. (He made dedications in Greek, but only at local, culturally mixed sanctuaries like Labraunda; he is not directly attested at the other important Carian sanctuaries Amyzon or Sinuri, though this may be chance because his brother Idrieus features at both places and his sister Ada and Hecatomnus at Sinuri.) Greek artists worked on his Mausoleum, though again this has some definitely non-Greek features.

He ruled under Persian auspices, and used the title satrap in inscriptions (Tod 138 = Syll.³ 167; Syll.³ 170). That he was a proper satrap has been denied on grounds such as that 'real' satraps did not rule jointly or were always Iranians, but these are not ancient definitions; it has further been urged that literary sources do not call him satrap, but the combination of FGrH 115 F 297 and A. Gell. 10. 18 imply that *Theopompus did. The same applies to other members of the Hecatomnid family. It is nevertheless true that Mausolus seems to act as a free agent in foreign and internal affairs, but that may merely indicate that the kings of Persia wisely left a lot to the men (and women) on the spot.

Mausolus moved his capital from Mylasa (mod. Milas) to Halicarnassus (mod. Bodrum), which he enlarged by the incorporation of other settlements (Callisthenes FGrH 124 F 25) in the 370s, perhaps announcing

thereby an interest in Aegean politics. He joined the Satraps' Revolt of the 360s, but seems to have smoothly returned to his Persian allegiance when things got rough. Thereafter his activities promoted or at least coincided with Persian interests, most notably when he fomented the Social War of 357–355 between Athens and its allies in the Second Athenian Confederacy. *Demosthenes in his Rhodian Speech (15) is our main source for this and he has every motive for exaggerating Mausolus' role, thus sparing Athens and the Rhodian democrats whom Mausolus had seduced away from their democratic solidarity with Athens and into the arms of Caria. But the fact of Mausolus' interference is certain (Diod. Sic. 16. 7, from *Ephorus, is independent corroboration). On Rhodes and elsewhere Mausolus' regime resulted in oligarchies, whether at his insistence or not. But Syll.³ 169 (from Mausolan Iasus) has a fairly democratic formula, cf. Michel 466 (assembly pay at the same city).

Mausolus' area of direct control was large and his sphere of influence larger, taking in, as we now know, Cnossus on Crete (ILabraunda no. 40, Greek text which starts 'it seemed good to Mausolus and Artemisia'). But he also had relations with communities in Pisidia (the Solymoi), Pamphylia (Phaselis), and Ionia (Erythrae, see Tod 155). Mausolus definitely annexed Rhodes, Chios, and Cos in the 350s (Dem. 15, cf. 5. 25). By the time of his brother Pixodarus (337), Lycia (SW Asia Minor) was included in satrapal Caria, but it is not certain that this was so under Mausolus, who was, however, on good terms with Caunus on the Lycia–Caria border (SEG 12. 471).

S.H.

Maxentius, Marcus Aurelius Valerius (b. c. AD 283), son of *Maximian, married *Galerius' daughter but was, like Constantius I's son *Constantine I, passed over when Diocletian and Maximian abdicated and Galerius and *Constantius I succeeded as Augusti (305). On Constantius' death Flavius Valerius Severus became Augustus, but Constantine's proclamation and the attempt by Severus to register the plebs at Rome provoked the praetorian guard to proclaim Maxentius as princeps or emperor (306). In 307 he took the title Augustus and reconferred this on his father, calling him from retirement to assist him. Severus failed to suppress Maxentius, who had him executed; Galerius invaded Italy but failed against Maxentius, who now controlled all Italy and Africa, but not Spain. Maximian secured an alliance with Constantine in Gaul by giving him the title Augustus and his daughter Fausta in marriage. In 308 Maximian quarrelled with his son, failed to depose him, and fled to Constantine; at Carnuntum Galerius declared Maxentius a public enemy. A revolt in Africa by the *vicarius* (provincial governor) Domitius Alexander (c.308–9) was defeated by Maxentius' praetorian prefect; famine at Rome was averted. Maximian's renewed attempt to become Augustus (310) caused Constantine to sever his alliance with the family and (312) invade Italy. He killed Maxentius' prefect near Verona, marched on Rome and defeated Maxentius' forces (said to have been four times as numerous) at Saxa Rubra; Maxentius was drowned near the Mulvian bridge. He may have been no soldier, and his need for cash caused resentment among senators, but Constantinian propaganda gives a wholly misleading impression of him. Twice in the interests of public order he intervened in squabbles in the Roman Church, but he tolerated Christianity and restored property to the Church.   R.P.D.

Maximian (Marcus Aurelius Valerius Maximianus). Born c. AD 250, the son of shopkeepers near Sirmium, he rose through the ranks of the army. An excellent general, he was called by his old comrade-in-arms *Diocletian to assist him as his Caesar (21 July 285), with responsibility for Italy, Africa, Spain, Gaul, and Britain. Sent against the insurgent Bacaudae in Gaul, he soon dispersed their irregular bands under Amandus and Aelianus; he repelled a German invasion of Gaul, and was promoted Augustus. Against the self-proclaimed emperor Carausius he was less successful: an expedition by sea failed, and the usurper was able to hold Britain and part of Gaul for some years, while Maximian was heavily engaged on the Rhine. He acted in close accord with Diocletian, with whom he conferred in 289 and 290/1 and to whom he remained utterly loyal.

In 293, under Diocletian's tetrarchic system, he received Constantius, probably his praetorian prefect since 288 and already married to his (?step-) daughter Theodora,

as his Caesar. In 296 he came to guard the Rhine while Constantius recovered Britain from Allectus, who had killed Carausius. After fighting in Spain in autumn 296, Maximian crossed to Africa to deal with a revolt by the Quinquegentanei and other Mauretanian tribes; c.299 he entered Rome in triumph, and there he began the building of the baths of Diocletian. Late in 303 Diocletian joined him in Rome to celebrate a joint triumph and the *vicennalia* (twentieth anniversary of his reign). Maximian enforced the persecution of Christians (303–5) in Italy and Spain, and with some severity in North Africa where they were numerous.

When Diocletian abdicated on 1 May 305, Maximian, at Milan, reluctantly did the same, but his son *Maxentius, proclaimed emperor at Rome (28 October 306), named his father Augustus for the second time and called him from retirement. In spring 307, assisting his son, Maximian forced Flavius Valerius Severus to abdicate at Ravenna; then, to secure for Maxentius an alliance with *Constantine against *Galerius, he went to Gaul (c. Sept.) and gave Constantine the title Augustus and his daughter, Fausta, in marriage. In April 308 Maximian failed to depose his son, with whom he had quarrelled, and fled to Constantine who sheltered him. Forced to abdicate again at the conference of Carnuntum (November 308), Maximian could not settle down to honourable inactivity. In revolt against Constantine he assumed the purple for the third time, but was quickly captured at Massilia and died by his own hand (c. July 310). Proclaimed *Divus* by Maxentius and the senate, his memory was damned by Constantine; after the Mulvian bridge his widow Eutropia swore that Maxentius had not been his son, and he was rehabilitated.   R.P.D.

Maximin (Gaius Galerius Valerius Maximinus), originally named Daia, born in Illyricum c. AD 270, son of a sister of *Galerius, was rapidly promoted in the army, and made Caesar when Galerius became Augustus (305). Charged with governing Syria and Egypt, he was resentful that Galerius made *Licinius Augustus (308). Spurning the title *filius Augustorum* ('son of the Augusti'), he had his troops proclaim him Augustus; Galerius recognized this (309/10). On Galerius' death (311), as senior Augustus he seized

Asia Minor while Licinius occupied Galerius' European territories; war with Licinius was averted, but to balance the latter's alliance with Constantine (see CONSTANTINE I) he drew closer to *Maxentius. Learning of the latter's defeat, and that the senate had made Constantine senior Augustus, he crossed the Hellespont. Defeated by Licinius near Adrianople (30 April 313), he fled and committed suicide at Tarsus. Like Galerius, he was an ardent pagan. In 306 and 308 he ordained that all in his dominions should sacrifice: city magistrates and census officials drew up lists and individuals were called on by name. From 307 he used the death penalty only rarely, but mutilated recusants and sent them to the mines; outside Egypt there were relatively few executions. When Galerius ended the persecution Maximin acquiesced but in autumn 311 recommenced. With little genuine support, he incited cities and provinces to petition against the Christians. 'Acts of Pilate' and confessions of ex-Christians to incest were published as propaganda. To revive paganism he organized the pagan priesthood hierarchically. The persecution was relaxed and then called off just before his defeat.   R.P.D.

Menander (?344/3–292/1 BC), the leading writer of New Comedy, although in his own time less successful (with only eight victories) than *Philemon. An Athenian of good family, he is said to have studied under the philosopher *Theophrastus and the playwright *Alexis, and to have been a friend of Demetrius of Phaleron, the pro-Macedonian regent of Athens from 317 to 307. Making his début probably in 324 or 323, he wrote over 100 plays, many of which must have been intended for performance outside Athens. Nearly 100 titles are known, but some may be alternatives attached to plays restaged (as happened frequently) after Menander's death.

Menander's plays were lost in the 7th and 8th cents. AD as a result of Arab incursions and Byzantine neglect, but in modern times many papyri have been discovered, attesting great popularity in Ptolemaic and Roman Egypt. These include one virtually complete play, Dyskolos ('Old Cantankerous': victorious at the Athenian Lenaea festival in 316), and large enough portions of six others to permit some literary judgement: Epitrepontes

('Arbitration', a mature work half-preserved intact and named after a brilliant scene), Perikeiromene ('Rape of the Locks', nearly half of its clear plot surviving), Samia ('Girl from Samos', four-fifths preserved), Aspis ('Shield', first half), Sikyonios ('Sicyonian', some 180 lines more or less complete, fragments of 250 or so others), and Misoumenos ('Man She Hated', tantalizing remains of a popular and exciting comedy, about 175 lines complete or comprehensible). There are smaller but important fragments of Dis Exapaton ('Double Deceiver'), Georgos ('Farmer'), Heros ('Hero'), Theophoroumene ('Girl Possessed'), Karchedonios ('Carthaginian'), Kitharistes ('Harpist'), Kolax ('Flatterer'), Koneiazomenai ('Drugged Women'), Perinthia ('Girl from Perinthus'), Phasma ('Phantom'), and of several still unidentified plays.

In addition ancient authors have preserved over 900 quotations, ranging from a single word to sixteen lines. Some are witty, some impressively moving, some sententious, but the lack of dramatic context normally prevents evaluation of serious or ironic intent. There also exist several collections of one-line maxims (monostichoi) attributed to Menander, but only a few of these actually originated with him.

It has always been difficult to assess how far his Latin adaptors *Plautus and *Terence modified Menander's works for the Roman stage, although the tattered fragments of Dis Exapaton now reveal that Plautus' adaptation at Bacchides 494–562 was freer than most scholars had previously imagined. Plautus' Cistellaria was based on Menander's Synaristosai ('Women Lunching Together'), Stichus on Adelphoi ('Brothers') 1, Terence's Adelphoe on Adelphoi 2, Andria on Andria ('Woman of Andros') and Perinthia, Eunuchus on Eunouchos ('Eunuch') and Kolax; Plautus' Aulularia has often been thought to derive from Menander.

Menander's plays are always set in contemporary Greece, often Athens or Attica, but although the characters are aware of events in the wider world, the plots focus on private domestic problems. These often include situations less common probably in real life than on the stage (foundling babies, raped or kidnapped daughters, for instance). There is always a love-interest, but the range of situations is wide—a young man in love with a country girl or an experienced courtesan, an older man believing his mistress has been unfaithful, a husband doubting the paternity of his wife's new baby. Yet love is often only one ingredient in the drama; thus in *Dyskolos*, Sostratos' infatuation shares the limelight with his developing friendship with Gorgias and Knemon's misanthropy.

Menander was a skilful constructor of plots, an imaginative deviser of situations, and a master of variety and suspense. He wrote for the theatre, highlighting the memorably emotive detail both in scenes of psychologically convincing dialogue and in long, vivid narrative speeches which sometimes recall the messengers of 5th-cent. tragedy. Tragedy may also have influenced the use of divine prologues, either beginning the play or following an appetite-whetting initial scene; these provided the audience with facts still unknown to the characters and enabled them to appreciate the irony of characters' ignorance.

Menander's plays were written in nonrealistic verse (mainly iambic trimeters), yet his lines give an illusion of colloquial speech, while variations of rhythm subtly modulate tone, emotion and presentation of character. In his earlier comedies at least he introduced variety by sometimes using, for both lively and serious scenes, the trochaic tetrameter; and the last scene of *Dyskolos* employs iambic tetrameters accompanied by pipes.

The characters are firmly rooted in a comic tradition of two-generation families, with important roles for slaves, courtesans, soldiers, parasites, and cooks. Although they retain hints of the traits that were developed in Middle Comedy, they are presented as credible individuals, and here two aspects of technique are significant. Menander often takes a type figure and either adds to it some unexpected touches (thus the courtesan Habrotonon in *Epitrepontes* is turned into a planning slave), or develops the expected traits in a new direction (thus the soldier Polemon in *Perikeiromene* characteristically boasts, but about his mistress's wardrobe, not military exploits). Secondly, although virtually every character speaks the same late Attic dialect, many of them are given individual turns of phrase that set them apart (e.g. in *Dyskolos* the cook Sikon's flamboyant metaphors and Knemon's simplistic exaggerations).

Menander attempts no profound psychological insights and leaves to his audiences the pleasure of deducing emotions and motives. Dialogue often moves so quickly that an alert brain is needed to grasp all the implications. A single sentence may simultaneously forward the action, describe another person, and illuminate the speaker. Characters are portrayed typically with mingled irony and sympathy, and although the dramatist is primarily an entertainer, he quietly inculcates a lesson that understanding, tolerance, and generosity are the keys to happiness in human relationships.   W.G.A.

Menippus, of Gadara (Syria), influential Cynic writer, probably of first half of 3rd cent. BC. An untrustworthy Life (Diog. Laert. 6. 99–101) makes him a pupil of Metrocles and associates him with Boeotian Thebes. Twice referred to as *spoudogeloios* or satirist (Strabo 16. 2. 29; Steph. Byz., entry under 'Gadara'), a term he might have applied to himself, he seems to have specialized in humorous moralizing; it is tempting, but perhaps dangerous, to assume that his works closely resembled those of Lucian in which he is a character. Very little is known of his work except titles, among which are: *Diathekai* or 'Wills' (parodying the wills of philosophers?); *Letters Artificially Composed as if by the Gods* (? cf. Lucian, *Saturnalia*); *Nekyia* or 'Necromancy' (presumably in the parodistic tradition of Crates and Timon, and possibly influential on *Horace, Sat. 2. 5, *Seneca the Younger, *Apocol.*, and various works of *Lucian; a trace of this work may survive at Diog. Laert. 6. 102); *Symposium* (cf. Ath. 14. 629 f); *Arcesilaus* (presumably Arcesilaus the head of the Academy); *Diogenous prasis* ('Sale of Diogenes') (Diog. Laert. 6. 29–30; cf. Lucian, *Sale of the Philosophers*). Menippus is said to have used *omnigenum carmen* in his works ('Probus' on Verg. *Ecl.* 6. 31, discussing *Varro's *Menippean Satires*), and there is no reason to doubt that, in keeping with the general Cynic tradition, both quotation and parody had a prominent role; the influence of Semitic and Arabic 'prosimetrum' has been suggested (cf. LUCIAN). It must be stressed that ancient theory did not use 'Menippean satire' to denote all prosimetric forms in the loose fashion still too common in modern scholarship.   R.L.HU.

Messal(l)a Corvinus, Marcus Valerius (64 BC–AD 8), Roman public figure. He first distinguished himself in the Philippi campaign (43–42 BC), following his hero *Cassius. Declining command of the republican army after this defeat, he transferred his allegiance first to *Antony, then at an uncertain date to Octavian (see AUGUSTUS). He fought against Sextus *Pompey (36) and in Illyricum (35–34), subdued the Alpine Salassi (?34–33), wrote pamphlets against Antony, and as consul with Octavian (31) took part in the battle of Actium. After a command in Syria (?30–29) he governed Gaul (?28–27), where he conquered the Aquitani, celebrating a triumph (victory procession) in September 27. In 26 or 25 he was made urban prefect but resigned after a few days, claiming that he was uncertain how to operate (Tac. *Ann.* 6. 11. 4) or, more bluntly, that the power was unsuitable for a citizen amongst citizens (Jerome, *Chron.* 164H). Thereafter he enjoyed less public prominence, but there was no public breach with Augustus. Already an augur and by 20 BC an arval brother, he became the first permanent *curator aquarum* (commissioner for the water-supply) in 11, and it was he who proposed the title of 'father of his country' for Augustus (2 BC): that record of independence perhaps contributed to his selection. He reconstructed part of the via Latina and several public buildings; he gained fame as an orator, though some found him lacking in concision and bite; he wrote his memoirs, dabbled in bucolic poetry, philosophy, and grammar, and was patron of an impressive literary circle—*Tibullus, Lygdamus, the young *Ovid, and his own niece Sulpicia. One of his protégés fêted him in the extant *Panegyricus Messallae*.   C.B.R.P.

Messal(l)ina, Valeria great-granddaughter of *Augustus' sister *Octavia on her father's and mother's sides, was born before AD 20. In AD 39 or 40 she married her second cousin *Claudius, then *c.*50 years old, and bore him two children, Claudia Octavia and Britannicus. Claudius alone was blind to her sexual profligacy (which *Juvenal travestied in Satires 6 and 10), even to her eventual participation in the formalities of a marriage service with the consul-designate Gaius Silius in AD 48. The freedman Narcissus turned against

her and, while Claudius was in a state of stunned incredulity, ensured that an executioner was sent. Encouraged by her mother Domitia Lepida, she committed suicide.

    J.P.B.; M.T.G.

Metellus Macedonicus (Quintus Caecilius Metellus Macedonicus), son of Quintus Caecilius Metellus, fought under *Paullus and was on an embassy sent to announce the victory of Pydna to the senate. He was probably tribune in the late 150s BC, setting up a special court (Val. Max. 6. 9. 10). As praetor 148, he was sent to Macedonia, probably with proconsular status, and remained until 146, defeating Andriscus and perhaps another pretender (Zonar. 9. 28. 8) and at least beginning the provincial organization of Macedonia. Called away to deal with the rebellion by the Achaean Confederacy, he won some successes, but had to hand over to Lucius Mummius and returned to Rome. Although he triumphed and was awarded the victor's additional name (*agnomen*), an honour unprecedented for a praetorian, he became consul only in 143, after two unsuccessful attempts. Sent to Hither Spain, he defeated a Celtiberian rebellion, but was said to have handed his army over in bad shape to his successor and enemy Quintus Pompeius. In 133 both of them were forced by the consul Lucius Furius Philus to go to Hither Spain as his *legati* (staff officers). In 133 he helped to suppress a slave rising and, although an enemy of *Scipio Aemilianus, fiercely opposed Tiberius *Gracchus. In 131 he and Pompeius were the first plebeian pair of censors. In that office (probably) he built a portico enclosing temples of Jupiter Stator and Juno Regina, the first temples in Rome faced with marble. A speech urging citizens to marry and raise children, assigned to Numidicus (below) by Gellius, is thought (probably correctly) to be one of his censorial speeches on account of a statement in a Livian *Periocha* (summary): *ORF*[4] p. 107. He was augur for at least 25 years and died in 115, leaving four sons, all of whom became consuls and two (Baliaricus and Caprarius) censors, as well as three daughters, all of whom married leading aristocrats. He thus, with Calvus (above), founded a dynasty that dominated Roman politics for over a generation.   E.B.

Metellus Numidicus (Quintus Caecilius Metellus Numidicus), son of Calvus and brother of Delmaticus. Elected consul 109 BC to finish the war against *Jugurtha, he won two battles and stormed several towns, with the help of his legates *Marius and Publius *Rutilius Rufus, but made little progress in guerrilla war. He insulted Marius, who asked for leave to stand for a consulship, and Marius now intrigued against him in Numidia and in Rome until he was elected consul 107 and, by a special law, appointed to supersede Metellus, who left before Marius' arrival. In Rome he was prosecuted, but acquitted, and allowed to triumph in 106 and take a triumphal *cognomen*. As censor 102, he tried to expel *Saturninus and Gaius Servilius Glaucia from the senate, but was prevented by his colleague (and cousin) Quintus Metellus Caprarius. In 100 he stubbornly refused to swear an oath to observe one of Saturninus' laws when the rest of the senate did and chose to go into exile. After Saturninus' death his return was long prevented by Marius and his friends, despite the pleas of his son Pius and other nobles. It was finally voted late in 99. He returned in glory, but henceforth kept out of politics.   E.B.

Milo (Titus Annius Milo), of a prominent family of Lanuvium in Latium (central Italy), as tribune 57 BC worked for *Cicero's recall from exile and, with Publius Sestius, organized armed gangs to oppose those led by *Clodius which had long prevented it. Fighting between Clodius and Milo in the city continued for several years, since—short of the *senatus consultum ultimum* ('ultimate decree' of the senate, in effect a declaration of emergency), impossible to pass—there was no legitimate way of using public force to suppress it. Both Milo and Clodius ascended through the official career, at times unsuccessfully prosecuting each other for *vis* (violence), until Milo's men met and defeated Clodius' near Bovillae (on the Appian Way, about 17 km. from Rome) in January 52. Clodius, wounded in the fighting, was killed on Milo's orders, chiefly to clear the way for Milo's candidacy for the consulship of 52, elections for which had been prevented by Clodius with *Pompey's support. After continued rioting Pompey was made sole consul and passed legislation including a strict law on *vis*, under which Milo was prosecuted.

Cicero, intimidated by Pompey's soldiers guarding the court, broke down and was unable to deliver an effective speech for the defence. (The speech we have was written later.) Milo was convicted and went into exile at Massalia (Marseille), where he ironically professed to enjoy the mullets. *Julius Caesar, in part out of loyalty to Clodius' memory, refused to recall him along with other political exiles, and in 48, while Caesar was away in the east, Milo joined Marcus Caelius Rufus in an attempt to raise rebellion among the poor in Italy and was killed.   E.B.

Miltiades, Athenian aristocrat and general, a member of the wealthy and powerful family of the Philaïdai. Archon (state official) in 524/3 BC, he was sent to recover control of Chersonesus by the Athenian tyrant Hippias in succession to his brother, Stesagoras, and his namesake and uncle, the elder Miltiades. There he married the daughter of the Thracian king, Olorus (see THUCYDIDES, *Life*). Subsequently he submitted to Persia, and served Darius I in the latter's Scythian campaign, allegedly supporting the Scythian suggestion that he and his fellow Greek tyrants should destroy the bridge over the Danube that Darius had left them to guard, though *Histiaeus of Miletus persuaded the majority not to agree. Shortly afterwards he was driven out of Chersonesus by a Scythian invasion, but returned when the nomads withdrew. He then appears to have joined in the so-called Ionian Revolt early in the 5th cent., and it was possibly then that he won control of Cycladic Lemnos. But he was forced to flee to Athens when the revolt was crushed, and was prosecuted for having held tyrannical power in Chersonesus. Acquitted, he was shortly afterwards elected one of the ten generals for the year 490/89, and, according to tradition, it was he who was responsible for the Athenian decision to confront the Persians at the battle of Marathon, for persuading the *polemarchos* (military leader) Callimachus to give his casting-vote for fighting, and for choosing the moment, possibly when the Persian cavalry was absent; modern scholars have also credited him with deploying the phalanx with strong wings and a weak centre with the deliberate intention of bringing about the 'double envelopment' which won the battle. However, some of the details of the story are possibly anachronistic—for example, the *polemarchos* was probably still the real commander-in-chief—and Miltiades' alleged military experience should not be exaggerated. He had never commanded a hoplite army of any size—and even *Herodotus does not make him responsible for the Athenian deployment, which, in any case, was probably defensive. Since Callimachus was killed, and Miltiades' son *Cimon subsequently became the most influential man in Athens in the 470s and 460s, one suspects that Miltiades' image as the victor of Marathon owes much to family tradition.

After the victory, he commanded an Athenian fleet in an attack upon Cycladic Paros, but having failed to take the town, and been severely wounded, he was brought to trial and condemned to pay a fine of 50 talents. He died of gangrene before he could pay, but his son dutifully discharged the debt.

J.F.La.

Mimnermus, Greek elegiac poet from Smyrna in W Asia Minor (fr. 9 West), later claimed by Colophon whose foundation he described (frs. 9. 3, 10). His name may commemorate the Smyrnaeans' famous resistance to the Lydian king Gyges at the river Hermus sometime before 660 BC, which would imply his birth at that time. He commented on a total solar eclipse (fr. 20), more likely that of 6 April 648 than that of 28 May 585. He was apparently still alive when *Solon (fr. 20 West) criticized a verse of his, but there is no sign that he survived the Lydian king Alyattes' destruction of Smyrna *c.*600. Ancient reckoning set his floruit in 632–629 (*Suda*). His poetry was divided into two books, probably corresponding to the titles *Smyrneis* and *Nanno* (cf. Callim. fr. 1. 11–12 pf.). The *Smyrneis* was a quasi-epic on the battle against Gyges, with elaborate proemium and ample narrative with speeches (frs. 13–13a). The shorter elegies stood under the collective title *Nanno,* said to be the name of a girl aulete whom Mimnermus loved; though she is not mentioned in fragments, and he also celebrated the charms of boys (cf. frs. 1. 9, 5, Hermesianax 7. 38 Powell, Alexander Aetolus 5. 4 f. Powell). He was especially famous for poems on the pleasures of love, youth, and sunlight. But fr. 14 seems to come from a call to arms, contrasting the citizens' present spirit with that of a hero of the Hermus battle. Mimnermus was also remembered as an aulete or oboist (Hipponax 153 West; Hermesianax 7. 37 f.; Strabo 14. 1. 28).

M.L.W.

Mithradates VI Eupator Dionysus (120–63 BC), elder son of Mithradates V Euergetes, king of Pontus in Asia Minor, was the greatest, most famous Pontic king, and Rome's most dangerous enemy in the 1st cent. BC. After murdering his mother and brother, his first major enterprise was the conquest of the Crimea and northern Black Sea. Ultimate control of most of the circuit of the Black Sea gave him almost inexhaustible supplies of men and materials for his military campaigns. In Cappadocia he continued to try to exert indirect control through agents: his creature Gordius, a Cappadocian noble; his sister Laodice; her son Ariarathes VII; and eventually his own son, whom he installed as king Ariarathes IX. For the more aggressive annexation of Paphlagonia he took as ally his most powerful neighbour, *Nicomedes (3) III of Bithynia, but subsequently fell out with him. A famous meeting with C. *Marius in 99/8, and the armed intervention of *Sulla in Cappadocia a little later, made it clear that war with Rome was inevitable, and he prepared carefully. While Italy was preoccupied by Social War (91–87), he annexed Bithynia and Cappadocia. Skilful diplomacy, masterful propaganda, and Roman overreaction enabled him to cast Rome in the role of aggressor and cause of the First Mithradatic War which followed (89–85). His armies swept all before them in Asia, where he ordered a massacre of resident Romans and Italians (the 'Asian Vespers'). He failed to capture Rhodes, but was welcomed in Athens and won over most of Greece. The Roman response came in 87, when Sulla arrived in Greece with five legions. He defeated the Pontic armies, besieged and captured Athens, and took the war to Asia. Mithradates surrendered at the Peace of Dardanus, and was allowed to retire to Pontus. The Second Mithradatic War (*c.*83–81) was no more than a series of skirmishes with Sulla's lieutenant Lucius Licinius Murena, but when *Nicomedes (4) IV of Bithynia died in 76 or 75 and bequeathed his kingdom to Rome, Mithradates again prepared for war. Having allied himself with Quintus *Sertorius, the Roman rebel in Spain, he invaded Bithynia in the spring of 73 (possibly 74), thus precipitating the Third Mithradatic War. The advance faltered immediately with a disastrous failure to capture Cyzicus, and the Roman forces, ably commanded by *Lucullus, pushed Eupator out of Pontus into Armenia, where he took refuge with King *Tigranes II, his son-in-law. He failed to win Parthian support, but was able to return to Pontus in 68. The great *Pompey, newly appointed to the Mithradatic command, easily defeated him, and forced him to retreat to his Crimean kingdom. He was said to be planning an ambitious invasion of Italy by land, when his son Pharnaces led a revolt against him. Inured to poison by years of practice, he had to ask an obliging Gallic bodyguard to run him through with a sword. Mithradates presented himself both as a civilized philhellene—he consciously copied the portraiture and actions of Alexander the Great—and as an oriental monarch, and although in many ways he achieved a remarkably successful fusion of east and west, he failed either to understand or to match the power of Rome.

                                                                B.C.McG.

Moschus, of Syracuse, elegant hexameter poet of the mid-2nd cent. BC; counted as second in the *Suda*'s canonical list of Three Bucolic Poets, between *Theocritus and Bion. Like most Hellenistic poets, he combined creative writing with scholarship; the *Suda* calls him a *grammatikos* (grammarian) and pupil of *Aristarchus (2), and he may be the Moschus whom Athenaeus (11. 485e) mentions as author of a work on Rhodian lexicography.

His masterpiece is the *Europa*, a 166-line pocket epic narrating the abduction of the Phoenician princess by Zeus in bull-form. It exhibits all the stigmata of the classic 'epyllion': neat exposition of the situation in time and space, brief but rhetorical speeches, dreams and prophecies of the future, a summary conclusion, and in particular the elaborate, 25-line *ekphrasis* (description) of the golden basket which Europa takes to the seaside meadow, inlaid by Hephaestus with scenes which (unbeknown to her) prefigure her own imminent fate. Echoes of *Homer dominate the poem, both at the linguistic level and in the way the heroine recalls Nausicaa; the influence of *Apollonius Rhodius and Theocritus can also be traced, besides that of earlier works like the *Homeric Hymn to Demeter* (flower-gathering) and Aeschylus (dream of the two continents; cf. Aesch. *Pers.* 176 ff.). The language is highly polished; indeed, polished can become precious, and (like *Catullus, in poem 64) Moschus is rather over-fond of certain stylistic mannerisms, e.g. iterative forms in -*eske*.

Five other shorter pieces have an eroticopastoral flavour; poem 1 ('Eros on the Run') is a cleverly-motivated description of the god's characteristics cast in the form of a 'Wanted' proclamation delivered by his mother Aphrodite. Also of considerable interest is the *Megara*, a 125-line hexameter dialogue between the wife of Heracles and his mother Alcmene, concerning their anxieties about the absent hero; but there is no justification for its traditional place in editions as 'Moschus IV'.   A.H.G.

Mucius Scaevola See SCAEVOLA, MUCIUS.

Munatius Plancus See PLANCUS, MUNATIUS.

Nn

Naevius, Gnaeus, stage poet of Campanian birth and obscure social attachments, possibly a client of the Claudii Marcelli. He saw military service in the last years of the First Punic War. His theatrical career began as early as 235 and was over by 204. Many stories were told of the insulting remarks he made about men of the nobility from the stage or in other contexts. Plautus, *Mil.* 210–12 was interpreted to refer to a spell by him in prison. He died in the Punic city of Utica.

Titles of 32 plays on themes of the Attic 'New' Comedy are transmitted (*Acontizomenos, Agitatoria, Agrypnuntes, †assitogiola†, Carbonaria, Chlamydaria, Colax, †cemetria†, Corollaria, Dementes, Demetrius, Dolus, Figulus, Glaucoma, Gymnasticus, Hariolus, Lampadio, Leo, Nagido, Neruolaria, †pellicus†, Personata, Proiectus, Quadrigemini, Stalagmus, Stigmatias, Tarentilla, Technicus, Testicularia, †tribacelus†, Triphallus, Tunicularia*). According to *Terence (*An.* 9–21), Naevius was one of those who set a precedent for treating an Attic model with some liberty. He put both dialogues and monologues into musically accompanied metres of the type used by his contemporary *Plautus. On occasion he made his Greek personages allude to features of Italian life. There is thus no need to deduce from an allusion to the tastes of the men of Praeneste and Lanuvium (Macrob. *Sat.* 3. 18. 6) that the *Hariolus* was a play of the kind composed by Titinius and Lucius Afranius, i.e. a *fabula togata* (a type of comedy set in Rome or Italy). The *Satyra* cited by Verrius Flaccus (Festus, p. 306. 29, Lindsay) is a mystery.

Six titles (*Danae, Equos Troianus, Hector proficiscens, Hesiona, Iphigenia, Lycurgus*) suggest tragedies of the Attic type. An account of Danae's disgrace (Non. p. 456. 25, Lindsay) seems to have been set in bacchiac verse rather than in spoken senarii. Naevius also composed original tragedies, one on the story of Romulus the first Roman king,

another (the *Clastidium*) on the defeat of a Gallic army in 222 by Marcus Claudius Marcellus. The latter may have been performed at funeral games for Marcellus in 208 or at the dedication in 205 of the temple of Virtus vowed by the consul before the battle of Clastidium.

Only one of the plays survived into the 1st-cent. BC stage repertoire. A narrative poem in Saturnian verses concerning the 264–241 war with Carthage, the *Carmen belli Poenici*, lasted longer. The grammarian Gaius Octavius Lampadio divided it into seven units towards the end of the 2nd cent. Naevius could hardly have been unaware of the pro-Carthaginian account of the war by Philinus of Acragas. Whether he knew of the Roman Fabius Pictor's has been the subject of much speculation. A digression filling a large part of the first of Lampadio's units, all the second, and a large part of the third related the early history of Rome and Carthage and provided a divine, perhaps even a cosmic, setting for the 3rd-cent. clash of arms. Naevius claimed inspiration by the Camenae (Roman goddesses identified with the Muses) and used a metrical and verbal style hard now to distinguish from that of *Livius Andronicus' translation of *Homer's *Odyssey*.

Despite strong criticism by *Ennius (Cic. *Brut.* 72) Naevius' poem continued to find readers in the 1st cent. BC. Two grammarians, a Cornelius and a Vergilius, composed commentaries on it (Varro, *Ling.* 7. 39). *Horace used its survival to make fun of the claims of Ennius' *Annals* (*Epist.* 2. 1. 53–4). The collectors of 'thefts' in *Virgil's *Aeneid* detected a number from Naevius. The matter was still of interest in the 5th cent. AD (cf. Macrob. *Sat.* 6. 2), but there is no evidence that the older poem itself could be found in any library of this time.   H.D.J.

Nemesianus, Marcus Aurelius Olympius, from Carthage, late in the 3rd cent. AD com-

posed four pastorals, long ascribed to *Calpurnius Siculus, and an incomplete didactic
poem on hunting (*Cynegetica*). He is
recorded as having distinguished himself in
poetic contests, and himself states an intention (apparently never fulfilled) to write an
epic on the deeds of the imperial brothers
Numerianus and Carinus (*Cyn.* 63–78). His
Cynegetica is datable to the period between
the death of the emperor Carus (283) and that
of Numerianus (284). If *Cyn.* 58–62 means—
as it surely does—that he has turned from
pastoral to didactic poetry, his *Eclogues* will
have been written first.

The *Eclogues*, four short poems, 319 lines
in all, are strongly influenced by *Virgil and
Calpurnius. In the first the shepherd Thymo-
etas' threnody on Meliboeus recalls the
praises of Daphnis in Verg. *Ecl.* 5. The second,
in which two young shepherds express their
longing for the girl Donace, shut up at home
by her parents, is indebted especially to Calp.
Ecl. 2 and 3. Verg. *Ecl.* 6 is the model for the
third, in which Pan sings in praise of Bacchus.
The fourth, like the second an amoebean
song, owes to Verg. *Ecl.* 8 the use of a refrain,
which was part of the Theocritean tradition
(see THEOCRITUS). Both Virgilian and Cal-
purnian elements appear in all four poems.

Of the *Cynegetica*, 325 lines survive. After
a long introduction, Nemesianus turns to the
necessities for hunting-dogs (he discusses
rearing, training, diseases, breeds), horses,
nets, and traps. The poem breaks off on the
verge of the chase. It is a vexed question
whether the poet used the work of Grattius
'Faliscus'; if so he is at least independent of
the order of the material in Grattius' poem.

Two fragments of a poem on bird-catching
(*De aucupio*, 28 hexameters) are also ascribed
to Nemesianus, though the attribution is
doubtful.

Nemesianus is essentially an imitator—
sometimes whole lines are borrowed from a
predecessor—but he is at least competent,
and his poems are not unattractive. With a
few exceptions, his diction and metre are clas-
sical.   J.H.D.S.

Nero (Nero Claudius Caesar), Roman
emperor AD 54–68, was born 15 December 37
of Gnaeus Domitius Ahenobarbus (consul
AD 32) and *Agrippina the Younger.

To strengthen his doubtful claim to the

throne, stories had been spread of his miracu-
lous childhood (Suet. *Ner.* 6; Tac. *Ann.* 11. 11)
and stress laid on his descent from the divine
*Augustus. In 49 his mother, as *Claudius'
new wife, was able to have *Seneca the
Younger recalled from exile in order to teach
her son rhetoric and to secure his betrothal
to Claudius' daughter Octavia; in 50 Lucius
Domitius Ahenobarbus was adopted by
Claudius, thus becoming Tiberius Claudius
Nero Caesar or, as he is sometimes called,
Nero Claudius Caesar Drusus Germanicus.
In the next year he assumed the *toga virilis*
(dress indicating manhood) at the early age
of 13 and was clearly marked out for the accession by being given the same privileges as
Augustus' grandsons Gaius and Lucius had
received. When Claudius died on 13 October
54, Nero was escorted into the praetorian
camp by the prefect Sextus Afranius Burrus.
The senate then conferred the necessary
powers on Nero and declared his adoptive
father a god and Agrippina his priestess.

The ancient tradition is unanimous in
regarding Nero's initial years of rule as excellent, a period hailed as a golden age by contemporary poets. Two 4th-cent. writers
ascribe to the later emperor *Trajan the view
that Nero surpassed all other *principes* for
a *quinquennium*, apparently referring to the
first five years. Of our three major ancient
authorities, *Suetonius and *Cassius Dio
suggest that the young emperor at first left
government to his mother and Dio adds that
Seneca and Burrus soon took over control,
leaving the emperor to his pleasures. *Tacitus,
however, regards the influence of Agrippina
(visible on coins of December 54 showing her
head facing Nero's on the obverse) as more
apparent than real and the role of his advisers
as one of guiding his activities, as in Seneca's
De clementia, and managing court intrigue
and public relations. Nero's first speech to
the senate, written by Seneca, is described
by Suetonius (*Ner.* 10) as a promise to rule
according to Augustan precedent; Tacitus
(*Ann.* 13. 4) adds a renunciation of the abuses
of the Claudian regime—excessive influence
of palace minions and monopolization of
jurisdiction by the emperor, in particular, the
trying of (political) cases behind closed
doors—and a pledge to share the responsibilities of government with the senate. The historian vouches for the fulfilment of these
promises, clearly interpreting the last, not in

the sense of a surrender of power by the *princeps* but of an attitude of respect towards that body. Symbolic of the new attitude was the legend '*ex s c*' ('in accordance with a senatorial decree') appearing regularly on the gold and silver coinage for the first ten years, though whether it is an authorization mark or relates to the types and legends is uncertain.

Nero at first heeded his advisers because they protected him from his domineering mother and indulged him within limits. She had always used the menace of rivals to threaten him, and the presence of a considerable number of dynastic claimants was inevitable under the Augustan Principate, which, not being an avowed monarchy, could have no law of succession to regulate the actual practice of hereditary succession. When Agrippina decided to show sympathy for Claudius' natural son Britannicus in 55, she sealed his doom, though the poisoning was not overt and could be dissembled, as by Seneca, who wrote praising Nero's clemency in the next year. In 59 Agrippina's resistance to his affair with Poppaea Sabina led Nero to enlist the prefect of the fleet of Misenum to drown her in a collapsible boat. When that failed, she was stabbed at her villa. This spectacular crime marked the end of the good part of Nero's reign, according to a contemporary view (Tac. *Ann.* 15. 67), echoed in the later tradition of the 'Quinquennium Neronis'. But for Tacitus, the political deterioration did not set in until 62 when a treason charge of the unrepublican sort, based on irreverence towards the emperor, was admitted for the first time in the reign, and Burrus died, thereby ending Seneca's influence as well. One of the new prefects, Ofonius Tigellinus, was seen by Tacitus as Nero's evil genius, rather like *Sejanus to *Tiberius. Nero now divorced his barren wife Octavia and married Poppaea who was pregnant: the child was a girl, Claudia Augusta, who was born in January of 41 and died four months later.

The death of his mother already made him feel freer to indulge his artistic passions. His enthusiasm for art, chariot-racing, and Greek athletics seems to have been genuine; he wanted to lead Rome from gladiatorial shows to nobler entertainments. At the Juvenalia, private games held in 59 to celebrate the first shaving of his beard, he sang and performed on the cithara (lyre) but also encouraged members of the upper classes to take lessons in singing and dancing. A year later he introduced for the first time at Rome public games in the Greek fashion to be celebrated every five years. In 61 he opened a gymnasium and distributed free oil to competitors. His interest in re-educating Rome was genuine: it was not until the second celebration of these games in 65 that the emperor himself performed, though he had already made his début in the Greek city of Naples a year earlier. His voice, described as 'slight and husky', may have been passable; his poetry was probably his own, for *Suetonius had seen his notebooks with their erasures (*Ner.* 52).

The emperor's popularity with the propertied classes had been further undermined by a fire which devastated the city and strained the economy. It broke out in the early hours of 19 June 64 in shops around the Circus Maximus, and spread north through the valley between the Palatine and the Esquiline hills. It lasted for nine days in all and reduced three of the fourteen regions of the city to rubble, leaving only four regions untouched. The emperor provided emergency shelter and helped with reconstruction, but he soon revealed that he would take the opportunity, not only to introduce a new code of safety for buildings, but to use land previously in private occupation for a grand palace and spacious parks (the Golden House or Domus Aurea) in the centre of Rome. The precious metal coinage shows the financial strain, to which the expense of the disastrous revolt of *Boudicca in Britain in 60 and the protracted wars with Parthia over Armenia contributed: both the gold and silver were reduced in weight and the silver content of the denarius lowered by more than 10 per cent. With rumours circulating that Nero had instigated the fire and recited his own poems over the burning city, Nero made the Christians scapegoats, burning them alive to make the punishment fit the alleged crime.

Nero never lost his popularity with the ordinary people of Rome, who loved his generosity and his games. The threat came from the upper classes and especially from senators governing provinces where the propertied élite had become discontent as a result of confiscations after the Rome fire: they are attested in Gaul, Spain, Africa, Britain,

Judaea, and Egypt. But meanwhile his paranoiac prosecutions in Rome led to a conspiracy in 65 to assassinate him and make Gaius Calpurnius Piso emperor. The scheme was betrayed. Piso and his accomplices, senators including *Lucan, knights, officers of the praetorian guard, and one of the prefects, Faenius Rufus, were executed. Nero now suspected all, and more deaths followed, including Seneca, *Petronius, and the Stoics Thrasea Paetus and Barea Soranus. In the year after Poppaea's death, Nero married Statilia Messallina, and, also in 66, Tiridates, a member of the ruling Parthian dynasty, came to Rome to receive the diadem of Armenia from Nero's hand. This represented an adjustment of Roman foreign policy in the east, where independent client kings had always been imposed on this buffer state with Parthia. In September of 66, despite another conspiracy at Beneventum, Nero himself left for Greece, to perform in all the Greek games. The highpoint of his tour was his liberation of Greece from Roman administration and taxation, announced at a special celebration of the Isthmian Games at Corinth on 28 November 67. The text of Nero's speech in Greek is preserved on an inscription (*ILS* 8794; *Syll.*³ 814; Sherk, *Hadrian* 71 for translation).

While in Greece *Vespasian was selected from the emperor's entourage to deal with a revolt in Judaea. But Nero deposed and executed three senatorial commanders, Gnaeus Domitius *Corbulo who had served him well in the east, and the Scribonii brothers who governed the two Germanies. Disaffection was rumbling in the west. At last Nero, in response to the warnings of his freedman Helius, returned to Italy. Soon after, in March of 68, Gaius Julius Vindex, governor of Gallia Lugdunensis, rose in arms. Although he was defeated two months later by the governor of Upper Germany, Nero's failure to respond decisively had encouraged others to defect. In Spain *Galba declared himself 'Legate of the Senate and Roman People', and in Africa Lucius Clodius Macer revolted. The praetorians were told that Nero had already fled abroad and were bribed by Gaius Nymphidius Sabinus, one of their prefects, to declare for Galba. The senate followed suit, decreeing Nero a public enemy. Nero took refuge in the villa of his freedman Phaon and there he committed suicide,

reputedly lamenting, 'What an artist dies with me!' (Suet. *Ner.* 48–9).

Nero's philhellenism earned him the devotion of many in the Greek-speaking provinces, and within the next twenty years, three false Neros appeared there, all playing the lyre and all attracting followers. But the Christians naturally hated him for their persecution of 64 and the Jews for the mistreatment that led to the revolt which ultimately lost them the Temple in Jerusalem.

M.P.C.; G.E.F.C.; M.T.G.

Nerva (Marcus Cocceius Nerva), Roman emperor AD 96–8, grandson of Marcus Cocceius Nerva, a close friend of *Tiberius, was born possibly in AD 35. His family, which came from the old Latin colony of Narnia and acquired distinction during the Civil Wars, had a remote connection with the Julio-Claudian dynasty. Nerva it seems did not serve as a provincial governor or hold any senior administrative post, but was influential as a confidant of *Nero, who admired his poetry and presented him with triumphal ornaments and other honours after the suppression of the conspiracy of Gaius Calpurnius Piso in 65. Despite this he was high in the Flavians' favour, being ordinary consul with *Vespasian in 71 and again in 90 with *Domitian.

Nerva was seemingly not party to the plot to murder Domitian and was approached by the conspirators only after several others had rebuffed them. But he had qualities of good birth, a pleasant disposition, and long experience in imperial politics, and immediately set out to be a contrast to Domitian, who had been detested by the upper classes and whose memory was damned by the senate. The slogans on Nerva's coinage ('Public Freedom', 'Salvation', 'Equity', 'Justice') reflect his wish to create a new atmosphere. He released those on trial for treason, banned future treason charges, restored exiles, returned property confiscated by Domitian, displayed moderation in the public honours he accepted, and took advice from leading men. He built granaries in Rome, dedicated the forum Transitorium begun by Domitian, distributed a largess to the people and the soldiers, removed the burden of the imperial post from communities in Italy, and initiated moves to buy up land for distribution to the poorest citizens; he may also have begun the alimentary scheme, which aimed to provide funds for the maintenance of poor children in rural Italy, although major responsibility for its execution probably lay with Trajan. According to Tacitus, Nerva combined two incompatible elements—liberty and imperial rule (*Agr.* 3).

However, Nerva was elderly and infirm and had no children. Naturally there was speculation about the succession, and further problems appeared. The desire for vengeance against supposed agents of Domitian came close to anarchy. The appointment of a senatorial committee in 97 to effect economies suggests that there were some financial difficulties, which arguably were the result of extravagance in Nerva's regime. The most serious signs of disquiet occurred among the soldiers, with whom Domitian had been popular. One army was close to mutiny on the news of his death, and subsequently there were rumours about the intentions of a governor of one of the eastern provinces in command of a substantial army (Philostr. *VS* 488; Plin. *Ep.* 9. 13). Coins celebrating 'Concord of the armies' probably express hope rather than confidence. There was also a plot against the emperor in Rome. Most ominously, rebellion broke out among the praetorians who had been stirred up by their prefect Casperius Aelianus into demanding the execution of the murderers of Domitian. Nerva had to accede, and was forced to give public thanks for the executions, thereby losing much of his authority and prestige. In October 97 amid gathering political crisis, he adopted *Trajan, whom he had previously appointed governor of Upper Germany, as his son, co-emperor, and successor. His own title *Germanicus*, granted for a minor victory over the Germans in Bohemia, was conferred on Trajan. It is impossible to discover the exact circumstances of Trajan's adoption. Pliny the Younger suggests that the empire was tottering above the head of an emperor who now regretted his elevation to imperial power (*Pan.* 6. 3, 7. 3), but this may have been exaggerated in order to please Trajan. However if Nerva's regime faced increasing discontent, his advisers would doubtless take into consideration Trajan's distinguished background and career, popularity with the troops, and proximity to Rome. Nerva's death on 28 January 98 marks an important point

in the development of the empire, since he was the last strictly Italian emperor.   J.B.C.

Nicander, of Colophon. Nicander says he was 'nurtured by the snow-white city of Claros' (*Theriaca* 958), and that he lives among 'the tripods of Apollo in Claros' (*Alexipharmaca* 11), indicating that he was probably a priest of Apollo at Claros (W. Asia Minor). Nicander of Colophon is not the Nicander, son of Anaxagoras, cited as an epic poet in a Delphian inscription (*Syll.*³ 452), dated 258 BC; internal evidence suggests a floruit for Nicander of Colophon of *c.*130 BC.

WORKS Surviving intact are two didactic poems in hexameters, the *Theriaca* and *Alexipharmaca*. Forming the subject-matter of the *Theriaca* are snakes, spiders, scorpions, presumably poisonous insects, and related creatures (centipedes, millipedes, solifuges), accompanied by remedies for their bites and stings; the *Alexipharmaca* retails botanical, animal, and mineral poisons and antidotes. Nicander is a gifted Homeric glossator, but he is neither zoologist nor toxicologist: the lost tracts *Poisonous Animals* and *Poisonous Drugs* by Apollodorus of Alexandria (early 3rd cent. BC) were plagiarized for specifics. Noteworthy are descriptions of several cobras, the black widow spider, a number of scorpions, the blister beetle (from which came the infamous aphrodisiac, *kantharis*), the velvet ant (a wingless wasp), the wind scorpion or solifuge, and others. Important are the accounts of opium, aconite, hemlock, and the thorn apple (*Datura stramonium* L.), showing careful study of widely known poisons. Extant as fragments or known only by title or subject are the metaphrastic epics *Oetaica*, *Thebaica*, *Sicelia*, *Cimmerians*, and *Europia*; *Ophiaca* was in elegiacs, retelling snake-legends; *Heteroeumena* ('Metamorphoses') was employed by Antoninus Liberalis and *Ovid; *Cicero (*De or.* 1. 69) admires Nicander's *Georgica*, used by *Virgil for his poem of the same name; and probably Nicander's *Melissurgica* ('Bee-keeping') underlies bk. 4 of Virgil's *Georgics*; Nicander's *Cynegetica* was a hunting-poem in elegiacs; the scholia on the *Theriaca* incorporate a *Hymn to Attalus* (fr. 104 Schneider), often cited as a Vita Nicandri; the scholiasts know a *Colophoniaca*, *Poets from Colophon*, *Glosses*, and *Temple Tools* (the last two in prose), and *Aetolica* has perished almost without a trace;

two epigrams in the Greek Anthology (7. 526; 11. 7) carry Nicander's name, the former about the Spartan Othryadas, the latter addressed to Charidemus about the boredom attending sex with one's own wife.

The *Suda* entry on Nicander (*v* 374) makes him a grammarian, poet, and physician, the last falsely adduced from his ersatz medical poems, or from Nicander's versifying of the pseudo-Hippocratic *Prognostics*. Nicander has little poetic talent; his efforts generally lack digressions, and in spite of some lofty subjects, there are woefully few similes and metaphors. His borrowing from Apollodorus indicates near-slavish dependence, and Nicander has little comprehension of the toxicology or zoology he carefully purloined. Yet as a grammarian and glossator, Nicander is among the most diligent of the Alexandrians in searching for puns, double meanings, and allusions in the Homeric epics, and like *Euphorion, Nicander frequently alters word-meanings, fitting fresh spellings into his lines, often violating the norms of Greek grammar. *Callimachus was Nicander's guide in handling metre.

Nicander's two poems became standard for later students of toxicology, and these obscure hexameters owe their survival to their ease on the memory: one recalled Nicander's scanned lines far more easily than (e.g.) the lengthy treatises of Apollodorus or the poisonous animals in Philumenus of Alexandria. Nicander's poems were authoritative until the Renaissance, even with the large scholiastic literature alongside, attempting to explain many of Nicander's patently murky terms. The scholia contain numerous quotations of lost authors, or unknown from other sources, and the delicious replication of superstitions about snakes, spiders, toads, frogs, salamanders, wasps, spiders, and so on are lodes for the folklorist and the historian of medicine, who note the meld of magic and therapeutics, also occasionally characteristic of *Dioscorides and *Galen.   J.Sca.

Nicias (*c.*470–413 BC), Athenian politician and general. During the period after the death of *Pericles he became the principal rival of *Cleon in the struggle for political leadership. He was a moderate and opposed the aggressive imperialism of the extreme democrats, his aim being the conclusion of peace with Sparta as soon as it could be attained on terms favourable to Athens. Elected frequently to serve as *stratēgos* (general), he led several expeditions in which, thanks to his cautious competence, he suffered no serious defeat and won no important victory. He was largely responsible for the armistice concluded in 423, and the Peace of 421 appropriately bears his name.

He now favoured a policy of retrenchment and objected to the ambitious schemes of *Alcibiades, who advocated Athenian intervention in the Peloponnese and later an expedition to Sicily. Despite his disapproval Nicias was appointed with Alcibiades and Lamachus to conduct this enterprise. Alcibiades was soon recalled, and little was accomplished in 415, but in 414 Syracuse was besieged and almost reduced to capitulation. The death of Lamachus, the arrival of the Spartan Gylippus, and the inactivity of Nicias, now seriously ill, transformed the situation, and in spite of the efforts of the Athenian general Demosthenes, who brought reinforcements in 413, the Athenians were themselves blockaded. Nicias, who refused to withdraw by sea until too late, led the vanguard in a desperate attempt to escape by land. His troops were overwhelmed at the river Assinarus, and he was subsequently executed. The narrative of *Thucydides, though giving due credit to Nicias for his selfless devotion, shows very clearly that the Athenian disaster was largely due to the inadequacy of his military leadership.

He was very wealthy (Xen. *Vect.* 4. 14 says he had 1,000 slaves working in the silver mines and spent lavishly; see esp. Plut. *Nic.* 3, mentioning the splendid festival procession he led to Delos, where Athens has recently re-established the festival of the Delia (Thuc. 3. 104). Thucydides may have this in mind when he speaks of Nicias' *aretē* (civic virtue, a notion which could include open-handed outlay on liturgies, the state offices funded by the incumbent himself). See Thuc. 7. 86. 5.
                                                                        H.D.W.; S.H.

Nicolaus of Damascus, versatile author; friend and historian of *Herod the Great; born *c.*64 BC of distinguished family, outstandingly well-educated. He became a Peripatetic and came into contact with leading figures of his day: he was tutor to the children of Mark *Antony and *Cleopatra VII (*FGrH* 90 T 2) and from 14 BC close adviser of Herod I, who employed him on diplomatic missions (F 136). Herod also studied philosophy, rhetoric, and history with Nicolaus and encouraged him to write (F 135). When Herod incurred *Augustus' displeasure on account of the campaign in Arabia in 8/7, Nicolaus succeeded in placating the emperor in Rome; in 4 he supported Herod Archelaus who had come to Rome to have his succession to the throne confirmed (F 136).

WORKS (1) *Historiai*, universal history in 144 books from the earliest times to the death of Herod the Great, the most comprehensive work of universal history since *Ephorus. Books 1–7, known through the Constantinian excerpts, dealt with the ancient east (Assyrians, Medes, Lydians, Persians) and early Greece (F 1–102). Sources: chiefly Ctesias of Cnidos and Xanthus of Lydia for the east, Ephorus and *Hellanicus for Greece. Only meagre fragments of books 8–144 are extant. Books 123–4, preserved in *Josephus *AJ* 14–17, contained the history of Herod the Great, for which Nicolaus, despite his tendentious and extenuating presentation (cf. T 12, F 96. 101 f.), was an excellent primary source: he drew on his own experiences and on the king's *hypomnēmata* or memoirs (*FGrH* 236). (2) *Ēthōn synagōgē* ('collection of (Strange Peoples') Customs'), dedicated to Herod and of Peripatetic character (F 103–24, all in Stobaeus). (3) *Bios* ('Life') *of Augustus*, apologetic and panegyric account based on Augustus' autobiography, which reached down to *c*.25 BC. The fragments (F 125–30, in the Constantinian excerpts) treat of the youth and education of Octavian (later *Augustus), *Julius Caesar's assassination, and the conflict between Octavian and Antonius until Octavian's levy of an army in Campania in 44; the terminal point and date of composition have been much discussed, but he probably wrote sometime between 25–20 BC (Jacoby) and AD 14 (Steidle). (4) *On My Own Life and Education*, autobiography (F 131–9). Education is seen from the viewpoint of Aristotelian ethics (see ARISTOTLE) and compared to 'a journey to one's own hearth' (F 132); an important source for the contemporary system of education. (5) (Lost) tragedies and comedies. (6) Philosophical writings, known through Greek fragments and, chiefly, texts in Arabic and Syriac: *On Aristotle's Phil-*

osophy, a handbook of paraphrases and commentaries, e.g. on natural philosophy, metaphysics, and the after-life. Nicolaus therefore plays an important part in the reception of Aristotle.   K.M.

Nicomedes, the name of several kings of Bithynia in Asia Minor:

(1) NICOMEDES I (*c*.279–*c*.255 BC), son of Zipoetes (before 315–*c*.279), who had taken the royal title in 298, inherited his father's struggle against *Antiochus I. He joined the Northern League, purchasing the aid of Heraclea Pontica by returning Cierus, invited the Gauls across the Bosporus, and assisted them to settle in Phrygia. He founded Nicomedia (mod. Izmit) *c*.265, and received honours at Cos and Olympia. At his death his son Ziaëlus (*c*.255–*c*.230) seized the throne in defiance of the guardians of his father's will in favour of his minor children, but continued his Hellenizing policy.

(2) NICOMEDES II EPIPHANES (149–*c*.127 BC), son of Prusias II of Bithynia, cultivated the favour of the Greek cities, and, a faithful ally, aided Rome in the war against Aristonicus in Macedonia (133–129), but his request for territory in Phrygia was refused in favour of Mithradates V of Pontus.

(3) NICOMEDES III EUERGETES (*c*.127–*c*.94 BC), son of Nicomedes II. His gifts to Greek cities won him the title Euergetes ('Benefactor'). Yet because of the condition of Bithynia, when *Marius requested aid from him against the Cimbri (104) he declared that most of his men had been seized and enslaved by Roman *publicani* (tax-collectors), and the senate decreed that no free man from an allied state should be held in slavery. His attempts to divide Paphlagonia with *Mithradates VI of Pontus and to win Cappadocia by marrying Queen Laodice were foiled by Roman intervention.

(4) NICOMEDES IV PHILOPATOR (*c*.94–75/4 BC), son of Nicomedes III. *Mithradates VI of Pontus promptly drove him out in favour of his brother Socrates (*c*.92), but a Roman commission under Manius Aquillius restored him (90–89). Under pressure from Aquillius and his Roman creditors he raided Pontic territory, and precipitated the First Mithradatic War (88). Restored by *Sulla in 85/4, he ruled thereafter in such peace as Roman officials and businessmen allowed him. *Julius Caesar was sent as envoy to him

to get ships for the siege of Mytilene (81/0). At his death (late 75 or early 74) he bequeathed his impoverished kingdom to Rome.   T.R.S.B.; S.M.

Nonnus, of Panopolis in Egypt (fl. AD 450–70), the main surviving exponent of an elaborate, metrically very strict style of Greek epic poetry that evolved in the Imperial period. His huge *Dionysiaca* is in 48 books, the sum of the books of the *Iliad* and *Odyssey*; Nonnus' stated intention is to rival *Homer, and to surpass him in the dignity of his divine, not human, subject (25. 253–63). The poem describes at length the antecedents of Dionysus' birth, the birth itself, and the new god's fight for recognition as a member of the pantheon in the face of hostility from Hera; the central section (books 13–40), which describes the war of Dionysus and his Bacchic forces against the Indians and their king Deriades, is Nonnus' equivalent of the *Iliad*.

Nonnus' highly rhetorical and extraordinarily luxuriant style is an attempt to create a new type of formulaic composition, recognizably similar to that of Homer but with greater variety and with far more lexical permutations. In his mythological learning and countless allusions to earlier poetry he is a true successor to Hellenistic writers of the Callimachean school (see CALLIMACHUS); the episodes that describe Dionysus' love affairs with youths and nymphs are influenced also by the novel.

Nonnus' other extant work is a hexameter version of St John's Gospel. Stylistic analysis suggests that it may be earlier than the *Dionysiaca*; but the *Dionysiaca* clearly lacks final revision. These two facts have led scholars to make ingenious conjectures about Nonnus' life, religion, and possible conversions. But there is evidence that amongst intellectuals in the 5th cent. it was not felt contradictory for a Christian to write heavily classicizing verse.   N.H.

Oo

Octavia, daughter of Gaius Octavius and Atia, and sister of Octavian (the future *Augustus), married (by 54 BC) Gaius Claudius Marcellus. In 40 Marcellus died and, to seal the Pact of Brundisium, she was immediately married to Mark *Antony. She spent the winters of 39/8 and 38/7 with him in Athens, and in 37 helped with the negotiations which led to the Pact of Tarentum. When he returned to the east, Antony left her behind. In 35 Octavian sent her to Antony with token reinforcements for his army; Antony forbade her to proceed beyond Athens. She rejected Octavian's advice to leave Antony's house, and though divorced by him in 32 brought up all his surviving children by Fulvia and *Cleopatra VII along with their two daughters and her three children by Marcellus. Her nobility, humanity, and loyalty won her wide esteem and sympathy. She died in 11 BC. The still-standing Porticus Octaviae in Rome (see Nash, *Pict. Dict. Rome*) was named after her.

G.W.R.; T.J.C.

Octavian See AUGUSTUS.

Old Oligarch is the modern name given to a short pamphlet about 5th-cent. BC Athens, preserved among the works of *Xenophon and sometimes referred to as ps.-Xenophon, *Constitution of the Athenians*. There are three chapters.

The work aims to show that the *demos* (people) or lower classes at Athens run affairs in their own interests, and it takes the curious form of a salute from an anti-democratic viewpoint. The author stresses the importance of the link between sea power and democracy: 'it is right that the poor and the *demos* have more power there than the noble and rich because it is the *demos* which mans the fleet' (1. 2).

The ostensible date is disputed (440s or—the more usual dating—mid-420s?). See however below.

It is hard to know what to make of the treatise: nothing else quite like it survives from the 5th cent. and it had little influence on later anti-democratic thought in antiquity (no contemporary author quotes it). It may belong in the category of symposium (drinking-party) literature, note the second person singular at 1.8—perhaps a sign that what we have is the dazzling second half of a kind of dialogue written to entertain. If so, we cannot be sure how seriously to take it or whether it constitutes good first-hand evidence for what it mentions. There are passages which would be valuable evidence for Classical Athens if they were straightforwardly usable (and they are often so used), e.g. 1. 10 on the licence allowed to slaves, 1. 16 on the use of the law-courts for the maintenance of the democracy, ch. 2 on sea power generally, 2. 18 on the refusal of the people to let dramatists mock the *demos* (something less than outright censorship may be meant), the figure of 400 trierarchs (3. 4), and occasional Athenian imperial toleration of non-democratic regimes (3. 11). But some of this could have been concocted out of *Thucydides, cf. e.g. 1. 8 with Thuc. 3. 45. 6 for the link between freedom and ruling others; and the end of 3. 11 (Messenians) could be elaborated from Thuc. 1. 102 ff. If the above doubts are justified, the 'date' question reduces to one of intended *dramatic* date and there may be no such single date, i.e. we cannot even press the argument from the assumed existence of the Athenian Empire. But the above is heretical and the usual view sees the pamphlet as good evidence for facts and attitudes about Athenian democracy.

S.H.

Olympias, daughter of Neoptolemus of Molossia in Epirus (NW Greece), married *Philip II of Macedon (*c.*357 BC) and bore him two children, *Alexander the Great and Cleopatra. Her husband's last marriage (to Cleopatra, niece of Attalus) led to a serious quarrel in which she retired to her native Epirus. Returning after Philip's assassination, she savagely murdered her erstwhile rival along with her infant daughter. After Alexander's departure (334) her relations with his viceroy, Antipater, were turbulent, and by late 331 she had resumed residence in Epirus, which she treated as her fief. There she remained until 317, when Polyperchon, Antipater's successor as regent, enlisted her aid against King Philip III's queen, Eurydice, who had disowned him and sided with Cassander, Antipater's son. She invoked the memory of her husband and son, and the royal couple fell into her hands without a blow. That goodwill disappeared after she forced Eurydice and her wretched consort to their deaths and conducted a bloody purge in Macedon. Her armies in turn melted away before Cassander and she was forced to surrender at Pydna (spring 316). She was condemned by the Macedonian assembly and killed by relatives of her victims. Implacably passionate in her political hatreds, she was passionately devoted to ecstatic Dionysiac cults, and her influence may have helped engender his son's belief in his divinity.   A.B.B.

Oribasius (c. AD 320–c.400), Greek medical writer. Born in Pergamum, he studied medicine at Alexandria under Zeno of Cyprus, and practised in Asia Minor. He became the personal physician of *Julian, who took him to Gaul (355). Closely involved in the proclamation of Julian as emperor (361), Oribasius accompanied him until his death in Mesopotamia (363). Banished for a time to foreign courts, Oribasius was soon recalled by the emperor Valens and continued to practise his profession until an advanced age. His principal works are a collection of excerpts from *Galen—now lost—and the *Collectiones medicae*, a vast compilation of excerpts from earlier medical writers, from Alcmaeon of Croton (c.500 BC) to Oribasius' contemporaries Philagrius and Adamantius. Both of these works were written at the behest of Julian. Of the 70 (or 72) books of the *Collectiones* only 25 survive entire; but the rest can be in part reconstructed from the *Synopsis ad Eustathium*, and the treatise *Ad Eunapium*, epitomes of the *Collectiones* in 9 books and 4 books respectively made by Oribasius himself, and from various excerpts and summaries, some of which are still unpublished. Oribasius was a convinced pagan, and his medical encyclopedia is a product of the vain effort of Julian and his circle to recall the classical past. For the medical historian its importance lies in the large number of excerpts from lost writers—particularly those of the Roman period—which it preserves, usually with a precise reference to the source; Oribasius adds nothing of his own. His work was constantly quoted and excerpted by early Byzantine medical writers, the *Synopsis* and the *Ad Eunapium* were twice translated into Latin in Ostrogothic Italy, and Syriac and Arabic translations of portions of Oribasius' work form one of the principal channels by which knowledge of Greek medicine reached the Islamic world.   R.B.; V.N.

Origen (Origenes Adamantius) (probably AD 184 or 185–254 or 255: Euseb. *Hist. Eccl.* 7. 1, Jerome, *De Vir. Ill.* 54) was born at Alexandria of Christian parents. Our chief source of information on his life is the sixth book of *Eusebius' *Ecclesiastical History*, together with the *Panegyric* by Gregory Thaumaturgus and the surviving book (translated by Rufinus) of the *Apology for Origen* which Eusebius wrote with Pamphilus (Migne, *PG* 17. 521–616). Educated by his father Leonides (who perished in the persecution of 202 under *Septimius Severus) and later in the Catechetical School of Alexandria under Pantaenus and *Clement of Alexandria, he became a teacher himself, with such success that he was recognized, first informally, then in 203 officially, as head of the school. He learned pagan philosophy from one Ammonius, perhaps not Ammonius Saccas but another Ammonius who was a Peripatetic (Porphyry, in Eus. *HE* 6. 19, *Vita Plotini* 20). The story of his self-castration in accordance with Matthew 19: 12 is supported by Eusebius (*HE* 6. 8), but doubted by Epiphanius (*Panarion* 64. 3). His career as a teacher was interrupted in 215 by *Caracalla's massacre of Alexandrian Christians. He withdrew to Palestine, but after a time was recalled by his bishop, Demetrius. Through his extensive literary work he now acquired such influence in the eastern Church as to become its unofficial arbiter, and, on a journey to Greece in this capacity, allowed himself to be ordained priest by the bishops of Caesarea and Jerusalem. Demetrius, who had not given his consent, took offence at this and perhaps also at parts of Origen's teaching. On obscure grounds, Origen was banished from Alexandria and deposed from the presbyterate, but the decision was ignored in Palestine, and Origen settled at Caesarea in 231. He continued his labours until, after repeated torture in the Decian persecution (250–1), his health gave way and he died at Tyre at the age of 69.

Origen's works were voluminous and of wide scope, but only a fraction has survived. He was a pioneer in textual criticism of the Bible, exegesis and systematic theology.

Critical. His chief work in this sphere was the *Hexapla*, begun before 233 and not completed till 244–5. In it were set out in six columns: (*a*) the Hebrew text of the OT, (*b*) the same transliterated into Greek characters, (*c*) and (*d*) the two Greek versions by Aquila and Symmachus, (*e*) the Septuagint, (*f*) the revision of this by Theodotion. Only fragments survive. A conservative redactor, Origen defended the Greek portions of Daniel against Sextus Julius Africanus.

Exegetical. He wrote commentaries on the greater part of Scripture. Some took the form of scholia on obscure passages, others of homilies on numerous books of the OT and NT, many of which are preserved in the original or in Latin translation by *Jerome or Rufinus. There were also elaborate commentaries on diverse books of the OT and on the Gospels of Matthew and John (parts survive). Origen sought, though not consistently, a moral sense pertaining to the soul and a typological sense to instruct the spirit, occasionally discarding the historical sense where data were in conflict.

Doctrinal. The *De Principiis* is an original exposition of Christianity written before Origen left Alexandria. Setting out from points of doctrine in the Church tradition, he proceeds by (often tentative) speculation to support these by rational inference by Scriptural quotation, and thus produce a system at once philosophical and pious. Large fragments of the Greek survive, but the only complete version is the Latin of Rufinus.

Apologetic. The *Contra Celsum*, written c.249, replies in detail to the learned attack of the Middle Platonist Celsus, which probably appeared in 176. This is the only extant work in which Origen avows his philosophic education. Part of the *Dialogue with Heraclides* was discovered on papyrus at Tura near Cairo in 1941.

Devotional. Two of Origen's works in this category, the *De oratione* and *Exhortatio ad martyrium*, have come down to us complete. The former was probably written c.231, the latter was addressed c.235 to his friends Ambrosius and Protoctetus, who suffered persecution under Maximin. His spiritualizing treatise *On the Pasch* was also discovered at Tura.

The *Philocalia* is a collection of excerpts from Origen's writings by Gregory of Nazianzus and *Basil of Caesarea. It preserves the original Greek of many passages otherwise known only in Latin, and shows what the Cappadocians found valuable in his teaching. But Origen had already come under attack by Methodius for his denial of a carnal resurrection, and at the end of the 4th cent. he was condemned by Epiphanius and (eventually) Jerome. The translations by his champion Rufinus are often freer and more periphrastic than those of Jerome, in the interests of orthodoxy and of clarity. Despite this advocacy, Origen was finally condemned under Justinian at the Council of Constantinople (553).   H.C.; M.J.E.

Otho (Marcus Salvius Otho, AD 32–69), whose father received patrician rank from *Claudius, was husband of *Poppaea Sabina and friend of *Nero. As Nero fell in love with his wife (afterwards divorced), he was sent to Lusitania as governor in 58 and remained there until Nero's death (68). He supported *Galba and hoped to be his heir. Disappointed, he organized a conspiracy among the Praetorians and was hailed emperor (15 Jan. 69). He tried to appear as the legitimate successor of Nero. Egypt, Africa, and the legions of the Danube and the Euphrates declared for him. But the legions of the Rhine had already chosen *Vitellius, and their military preparations were far advanced. By early March their advanced guard had crossed the Alps, and an Othonian expedition to southern Gaul achieved little. His generals Vestricius Spurinna and Annius Gallus held the line of the Po, but his armies from the Danube arrived only gradually. Though defeated in a minor engagement the Vitellians were soon heavily reinforced: yet Otho insisted on a decisive battle before he could oppose equal strength. His troops advanced from Bedriacum, *c*.35 km. (22 miles) east of Cremona, and were irretrievably defeated. He committed suicide on 16 Apr. 69.

Otho's profligacy seems not to have impaired his energy or his interest in government. But he was a slave to the Praetorians who had elevated him.

A.M.; G.E.F.C.; M.T.G.

Ovid (Publius Ovidius Naso, 43 BC–AD 17), poet, was born at Sulmo in the Abruzzi on 20 March. Our chief source for his life is one of his own poems, *Tr.* 4. 10. As the son of an old equestrian family, Ovid was sent to Rome for his education. His rhetorical studies under Arellius Fuscus and Porcius Latro, in which he evidently acquitted himself with distinction, are described by *Seneca the Elder (*Controv.* 2. 2. 8–12; cf. 9. 5. 17). His education was rounded off by the usual Grand Tour through Greek lands (*Tr.* 1. 2. 77–8, *Pont.* 2. 10. 21 ff.). After holding some minor judicial posts, he apparently abandoned public life for poetry—thus enacting one of the commonplaces of Roman elegiac autobiography. With early backing from *Messalla Corvinus (*Pont.* 1. 7. 27–8) Ovid quickly gained prominence as a writer, and by AD 8 he was the leading poet of Rome. In that year he was suddenly banished by *Augustus to Tomis on the Black Sea. Ovid refers to two causes of offence in his exile poetry: *carmen*, a poem, the *Ars Amatoria*; and *error*, an indiscretion. He has much to say concerning the first of these counts, especially in *Tr.* 2; concerning the second he repeatedly refuses to elaborate—though, since the *Ars* had already been out for some years in AD 8, the *error* must have been the more immediate cause. Amid the continuing speculation (cf. J. C. Thibault, *The Mystery of Ovid's Exile* (1964); R. Syme, *History in Ovid* (1978), 215–22), all that can be reconstructed from Ovid's own hints is a vague picture of involuntary complicity (cf. *Tr.* 2. 103–8) in some scandal affecting the imperial house. Tomis, a superficially Hellenized town with a wretched climate on the extreme edge of the empire, was a singularly cruel place in which to abandon Rome's most urbane poet. Public and private pleading failed to appease Augustus or (later)

*Tiberius: Ovid languished in Tomis until his death, probably (so *Jerome) in AD 17. Several of the elegies from exile are addressed to his third wife (connected somehow with the Fabian clan: *Pont.* 1. 2. 136), who remained behind him in Rome; Ovid also mentions a daughter and two grandchildren.

WORKS (ALL EXTANT POEMS WRITTEN IN ELEGIAC COUPLETS EXCEPT THE *Metamorphoses*). *Amores*, 'Loves'. Three books of elegies (15, 20, and 15 poems) presenting the ostensibly autobiographical misadventures of a poet in love. What we have in this three-book collection is a second edition, published not before 16 BC and perhaps somewhat later (1. 14. 45–9); work on the original five books mentioned in Ovid's playful editorial preface may have begun *c*.25 BC. (For the vexed chronology of all Ovid's amatory works see J. C. McKeown, *Amores* (1987) 1. 74–89.) The *Amores* continue the distinctive approach to elegy taken by Ovid's older contemporaries *Propertius and *Tibullus and by the shadowy *Cornelius Gallus before them (cf. *Tr.* 4. 10. 53–4); the frequent use of mythological illustration recalls especially Propertius. Corinna, the named mistress of Ovid's collection, owes much to Propertius' Cynthia and Tibullus' Delia; her name itself (along with the pet bird mourned in *Am.* 2. 6) acknowledges a debt to an important forerunner of the Augustan elegiac woman, *Catullus' Lesbia ('Lesbia' looks to *Sappho; 'Corinna' names another Greek female poet; see CORINNA). Erotic elegy before Ovid had featured a disjunction in the first-person voice between a very knowing poet and a very unknowing lover. Ovid closes this gap, and achieves a closer fit between literary and erotic conventions, by featuring a protagonist who loves as knowingly as he writes. Ovid's lover is familiar with the rules of the genre, understands the necessity for them, and manipulates them to his advantage. The result is not so much a parody of previous erotic elegy as a newly rigorous and zestful exploration of its possibilities.

Heroides, 'Heroines' (so called by Priscian, *Gramm. Lat.* 2. 544 Keil; but cf. *Ars Am.* 3. 345 *Epistula*. The correct form may have been *Epistulae Heroidum*, 'Heroines' Epistles'). Of the 'single *Heroides*' 1–14 are letters from mythological female figures to absent husbands or lovers; *Her.* 15, whose Ovidian authorship is in doubt, is from the historical but heavily mythologized Sappho. In their argumentative ingenuity these poems show us the Ovid who was a star declaimer in the schools; in that they speak of female subjectivity under pressure they also testify to an admiration for Euripidean tragedy (see EURIPIDES), and give us a glimpse of what we have lost in Ovid's own *Medea*. The heroines tend to be well known rather than obscure: some of the interest of the letters lies in locating the point at which they are to be 'inserted' into prior canonical works, usually epic or tragic, and in considering the operations of revision and recall. The epistolary format is sometimes archly appropriate ('what harm will a letter do?', Phaedra asks Hippolytus), sometimes blithely inappropriate (where on her deserted shore, one wonders, will Ariadne find a postman?); above all, perhaps, it effects a characteristically Alexandrian modernization by Ovid of the dramatic monologue by presenting the heroine as a writer, her impassioned speech as a written text, and the process of poetic composition as itself part of the action. Ovid claims the *Heroides* to be a new kind of literary work (*Ars Am.* 3. 346); they owe something to an experiment in Propertius (4. 3). The idea for the 'double *Heroides*' (16–21) may have come from the replies which Ovid's friend Sabinus is said to have composed for the 'single *Heroides*' (*Am.* 2. 18, a poem which probably places the 'single *Heroides*' between the two editions of the *Amores*). Formerly doubted, 16–21 are now generally accepted as Ovid's own, stylistic discrepancies with 1–14 being explained by a later compositional date (perhaps contemporary with the *Fasti*). Arguably it is in these paired letters that the potential of the epistolary format is most fully realized.

Medicamina Faciei Femineae, 'Cosmetics for the Female Face'. A didactic poem which predates the third book of the *Ars* (*Ars Am.* 3. 205–6). Only the first 100 lines survive, the latter 50 of which, a catalogue of recipes, show Ovid matching Nicander (in the *Theriaca* and *Alexipharmaca*) in virtuoso ability to make poetry out of abstruse drug-lore.

Ars Amatoria, 'Art of Love' (for the title cf. Sen. *Controv.* 3. 7. 2). A didactic poem in three books on the arts of courtship and erotic intrigue; the mechanics of sexual technique receive but limited attention (2. 703–32, 3. 769–808), perhaps reversing the proportions

of works such as the manual of Philaenis (*POxy.* 2891). Books 1–2, datable in their present form to about 1 BC (1. 171 ff.), advise men about women; book 3, presented as a sequel (3. 811 may or may not imply a substantial gap in real time), advises women about men—arguably with one eye still firmly upon the interests of the latter. The situations addressed owe much to previous elegy; at times the preceptor seems to explore the rules of love poetry as much as of love (*ars amatoria* functioning as *ars poetica*). Mythological illustration is more fully developed than in the *Amores*, anticipating the full-scale narratives of *Metamorphoses* and *Fasti*. The actors themselves are firmly located in contemporary Rome: the vivid specificity of the social milieux is sometimes more reminiscent of satire than of earlier elegy. As didactic, the *Ars* takes many traits from Virgil's *Georgics* and Lucretius. It has an irreverent and parodic feel, however, deriving not from the theme alone (other didactic poems, as Ovid was to point out (*Tr.* 2. 471 ff.), could be frivolous too) but from the combination of theme and metre. Conventionally, didactic was a subset of epic written in hexameters; Ovid's choice of elegiac couplets, as it signals a continuity with his own *Amores*, signals a felt discontinuity with mainstream didactic. As successor to the *Amores*, the *Ars* achieves much of its novelty through a reversal of the implied roles of poet and reader: in the *Amores* the reader oversees the poet's love affair; in the *Ars* the poet oversees the reader's love affair. It may be (for we cannot but read with hindsight derived from later events) that this newly direct implication of the Roman reader in the erotic text made the *Ars* the poem most likely to be picked on when the climate turned unfavourable to Ovid's work. The poet's attempts to forestall moral criticism in this area (1. 31–4; cf. *Tr.* 2. 245–52) seem disingenuous.

Remedia Amoris, 'Remedies for Love'. A kind of recantation of the *Ars Amatoria*; the poet now instructs his readers how to extricate themselves from a love affair. The *Remedia* (date between 1 BC and AD 2 indicated by 155–8) appropriately concludes Ovid's early career in erotic elegiac experimentation.

Metamorphoses, 'Transformations'. An unorthodox epic in fifteen books, Ovid's only surviving work in hexameters, composed in the years immediately preceding his exile in AD 8. The poem is a collection of tales from classical and Near Eastern myth and legend, each of which describes or somehow alludes to a supernatural change of shape. Metamorphic myths enjoyed an especial vogue in Hellenistic times and had previously been collected in poems (all now lost) by Nicander, by the obscure Boios or Boio (whose *Ornithogonia*, 'Generation of Birds', was apparently adapted by Macer, *Tr.* 4. 10. 43), and by Parthenius. In Ovid's hands metamorphosis involves more than just a taste for the bizarre. Throughout the poem (and with programmatic emphasis in the opening cosmogony) the theme calls attention to the boundaries between divine and human, animal and inanimate, raising fundamental questions about definition and hierarchy in the universe. Structurally the *Metamorphoses* is a paradox. The preface promises an unbroken narrative, epic in its scope, from the creation to the poet's own day; but throughout much of the poem chronological linearity takes second place to patterns of thematic association and contrast, book divisions promote asymmetry over symmetry, and the ingenious transitions (criticized by the classicizing Quintilian: *Inst.* 4. 1. 77) do as much to emphasize the autonomy of individual episodes as to weld them into a continuum. In some ways the poem's closest analogue (structurally; but also for its interest in the mythic explanation of origins) is *Callimachus' *Aetia*, whose avowed aesthetic, influential on all Augustan poetry, the *Metamorphoses* seems both to reject and to embrace (1. 4; E. J. Kenney, *PCPS* 1976, 46 ff.). There is a real flirtation with the Augustan model of epic teleology established in the *Aeneid*; but it can be argued that the metamorphic world of Ovid's poem is structurally and ideologically incompatible with such a vision. Wherever his sources are wholly or partly extant, Ovid's dialogues with the literary past repay the closest attention. He engages with an unprecedented range of Greek and Roman writing; every genre, not just epic, leaves its mark in the poem's idiom. But in the final analysis the *Metamorphoses* renders its sources superfluous: with its many internal narrators and internal audiences, with its repeated stress on the processes of report and retelling whereby stories enter the common currency, the primary intertextual

reading which the poem insists on is one internal to itself. As narrative it brilliantly captures the infinite variety and patterning of the mythological tradition on which it draws (and which, for many later communities of readers, it effectively supersedes). Ovid's poetic imagination, intensely verbal and intensely visual, finds here its finest expression. The *Metamorphoses* tells utterly memorable stories about the aspirations and sufferings which define and threaten the human condition; from the poem's characteristic aestheticization of those sufferings comes both its surface brightness and its profound power to disturb.

Fasti, 'Calendar'. A poetical calendar of the Roman year with one book devoted to each month. At the time of Ovid's exile it was incomplete, and only the first six books (January–June) survive. These show evidence of partial revision at Tomis (e.g. 1. 3, 4. 81–4); the silence which is abides 7–12 abides as a reminder of a life interrupted. The poem's astronomy (1. 2) is influenced by *Aratus (1)'s *Phaenomena*, its aetiological treatment of history and religion (1. 1) by Callimachus. These debts show Ovid at his most overtly Alexandrian; but, like Propertius in his fourth book (4. 2, 4, 9, 10), he is applying Callimachean aetiology to distinctively Roman material. The *Fasti* belongs equally in the tradition of *Varro's lost *Antiquitates*; and the figure without whom the poem is ultimately inconceivable is the emperor Augustus, whose recuperation and appropriation of Roman religious discourse constitutes the basis of Ovid's own poetic appropriation (1. 13–14). The restrictiveness of the day-to-day format as a determinant of both subject-matter and structure is repeatedly stressed by the poet (4. 417, 5. 147–8). However, comparison with other calendrical sources (cf. A. Degrassi, *Inscr. Ital.* 13, *Fasti et Elogia* (1963), esp. the *Fasti Praenestini* compiled by Verrius Flaccus) reveals the extent to which Ovid has been free to select and order his emphases; and the very fragmentation of the narrative material (e.g. the life of Romulus is split and chronologically shuffled between five or six different dates) offers an interesting contrast with the contemporaneous (and more fluid) *Metamorphoses*. The poet is a prominent character in his own poem: he appears in expository passages as an eager antiquarian weighing aetiological and etymological variants with himself or with interlocutors who range from the Muses (as in books 1–2 of Callimachus' *Aetia*) to random bystanders. Long mined for its detailed information about the perceived roots of Roman religion and ritual, the *Fasti* has begun to attract new attention both as a complex work of art and as an exploration of religious thinking at a time of ideological realignment.

Tristia, 'Sorrows'. A series of books dispatched from exile between AD 9 and 12, containing (so *Tr.* 1, 3, 4, 5) poems addressed by Ovid to his wife and to various unnamed persons in Rome. The 'sorrows' of the title are the past, present, and anticipated sufferings associated with the relegation to the Black Sea: the *Tristia*, like the later *Epistulae ex Ponto*, function as open letters in which the poet campaigns from afar for a reconsideration of his sentence. *Tr.* 2, addressed to Augustus, differs in format from the other four books. A single poem of over 500 lines, it uses an ostensibly submissive appeal for imperial clemency as the point of departure for a sustained defence of the poet's career and artistic integrity. The mood of the *Tristia* is deeply introspective, with all the rich opportunities for geography and ethnography subsumed within the narrative of an inner journey: the ships on which Ovid voyages into exile merge with his metaphorical 'ship of fortune' (1. 5. 17–18); the icy torpor and infertility of the Pontic landscape become indices of the poet's own (allegedly) frozen creativity. The books read at times as *post mortem* autobiography, with exile figured as death and the elegiac metre reclaiming its supposed origins in funereal lament. On one level the insistently self-depreciatory poetics (e.g. 1. 1. 3 ff.) offer an artful fiction of incompetence, extending a *topos* of mock modesty familiar from earlier literary programmes in the sub-epic genres. But only on one level. The pervasive imagery of sickness and barrenness, decay and death, though belied by the continued technical perfection of Ovid's writing, captures an erosion of the spirit which feels real enough, in and between the lines, in the later books from Tomis.

Epistulae ex Ponto, 'Epistles from Pontus'. Four books of poems from exile, differing from the *Tristia* only in that the addressees are named (1. 1. 17–18), and characterized with greater individuality. The letters in books 1–3 were gathered into a single collection ('without order': so claims 3. 9. 51–4) in AD 13; book 4 probably appeared posthumously (4. 9 written in AD 16).

Ibis. An elaborate curse-poem in elegiacs (perhaps AD 10 or 11) directed at an enemy whose identity is hidden under the name of a bird of unclean habits; both title and treatment derive from a lost work of Callimachus (55–62). As at the beginning of the *Tristia*, Ovid dramatizes a forced break with his former self: a previously benign poet now seeks to wound; his elegy has become a prelude to Archilochean iambic. In fact, the *Ibis* displays much continuity with Ovid's earlier work. The poem's ferociously dense catalogue of sufferings achieves a mythological comprehensiveness (despite its small compass) comparable to that of the *Metamorphoses* or *Fasti*; even its 'unOvidian' obscurity (57–60) comes across as a thoroughly Ovidian experiment (cf. G. Williams, *PCPS* 1992, 174 ff.).

Lost and spurious works. Our principal loss is Ovid's tragedy *Medea* (*Tr.* 2. 553). Two verses survive, one cited by Quintilian (*Inst.* 8. 5. 6), the other by *Seneca the Elder (*Suas.* 3. 7). The poet of the *Fasti* was among those who translated Aratus' *Phaenomena* into Latin hexameters; two brief fragments remain. It is most unlikely that either the *Halieutica* or the *Nux* is by Ovid (cf. J. A. Richmond in *ANRW* 2. 31. 4, 2744 ff., with bibliography).

Ovid is not only one of the finest writers of antiquity; he is also one of the finest readers. Not since Callimachus, perhaps, had a poet shown such understanding in depth and in detail of the literary traditions of which he was the inheritor; never was such understanding carried so lightly. In a national literature dominated by anxious gestures towards the past, Ovid's relationship with his predecessors is exuberantly unanxious. Moreover, the same revisionary energy which he brings to alien texts is applied no less to his own. Ovid constantly reworks himself, at the level of the poem (the *Ars* reframes the *Amores*, the *Remedia* the *Ars*), of the episode (cross-referential Persephones in *Metamorphoses* and *Fasti*), and even of the individual line and phrase (cf. A. Lueneburg, *De Ovidio sui imitatore* (1888)). This paradigm of self-imitation, together with the deceptively easy

smoothness and symmetry which he
bequeaths to the dactylic metres, make his
manner (once achieved) endlessly imitable to
later generations as a kind of Ovidian *koinē*.
What remains inimitable, however, is the
sheer wealth of the poet's invention. Ovid
devoted most of his career to a single genre,
elegy, so that by the time of the *Remedia* he
was already able to claim (*Rem. Am.* 395–6)
that 'elegy owes as much to me as epic does
to Virgil'. (The *Metamorphoses* still lay ahead,
an epic which—although it is much else
besides—can justly be said to be the epic of
an elegist.) But within elegy he achieved an
unparalleled variety of output by exploiting
and extending the range of the genre as no
poet had before—not by ignoring its traditional norms, but by carrying to new
extremes the Alexandrian and Augustan tendency to explore a genre's potentiality by
testing its boundaries.

No Roman poet can equal Ovid's impact
upon western art and culture; only the critics,
stuffy as *Quintilian (*Inst.* 10. 1. 88, 98), have
sometimes stood aloof. Especially remarkable in its appropriations has been the *Metamorphoses*—from   the   Christianizing
ingenuities codified in the 14-cent. *Ovide
moralisé* to the bold painterly narratives of
Titian's *poesie* in the Renaissance. In the
Anglophone world the terms of Ovid's reception in the modern era have largely been
defined by Dryden and Pope; behind these
influential Ovids can still be sensed the Naso
of Shakespeare's Holofernes, 'smelling out
the odoriferous flowers of fancy', and the
figure of 'Venus clerk, Ovyde' in Chaucer's
Hous of Fame. Though not immune to the
challenges which the 20th cent. has posed
to the continuity of the classical tradition,
Ovid's poetry, now entering upon its third
millennium, still reaches artists as well as
scholars: a 1979 preface to the *Metamorphoses*
by Italo Calvino is at once an academic essay
and an assimilation of Ovid's narrative aesthetic to Calvino's own 'postmodern' fiction
('Ovid and Universal Contiguity' translated
in *The Literature Machine* (1987), 146 ff.).

                                                                    S.E.H.

Oxyrhynchus, the historian from *Hellenica
of Oxyrhynchus*: two sets of papyrus fragments found at Oxyrhynchus in Egypt, both
2nd cent. BC: POxy 842 (London Papyrus,

found in 1906, edited by Grenfell and Hunt,
who named the unknown author P. =
Papyrus) and PSI 1304 (Florentine Papyrus,
found in 1942). Both belong to the same historical work dating from the first half of the
4th cent. BC and contain a total of about 20
pages of Greek history, with some gaps. The
London Papyrus deals with the political
atmosphere in Greece in 397/6, the naval war
between Athens under Conon and Sparta, the
conflict   between   Thebes   and   Phocis
(including a valuable excursus on the constitution of the Boeotian Confederacy, and
*Agesilaus' campaigns in Asia Minor. The
Florentine Papyrus deals with events of the
Ionian–Decelean War (final phase of the
Peloponnesian War), esp. the sea-battle at
Notium 407/6.

The Oxyrhynchus historian (henceforth
'P.') represents a valuable independent tradition parallel to *Xenophon, *Hell.* 1 and 2,
and is, via *Ephorus, the basis of *Diodorus'
books 13–14. P. wrote shortly after the events
related in his narrative; he is a primary author
whose work is based on autopsy and personal
research. The presentation is objective and
factual, the style moderate, no speeches, frequent excursuses; the chronological arrangement is by summers and winters, like
*Thucydides (quoted in ch. 2. of the Floren-
tine Papyrus). Hence it is a continuation of
Thucydides from 411 to 395. P. wrote after the
King's Peace in 387/6 (cf. 11. 2) and before the
end of the Third Sacred War in 346 (13. 3).

Numerous attempts have been made to
determine the author's identity. Among the
names put forward are Ephorus, *Theopompus, Androtion, Daimachus, Cratippus.
Ephorus and Theopompus are not primary
sources; Ephorus writes *kata genos*, that is he
arranged his material by topic; furthermore
P. is hardly a writer of universal history. Style,
ethos, and presentation exclude Theopompus. P. is no Atthidographer (historian
of Attica) either: Androtion arranged his
material by *archontes* (the senior Athenian
magistrate who gave his name to the year).
Daimachus, the local historian of Boeotia,
can be ruled out: P. does indeed show valuable knowledge of Boeotia and the Boeotian
Confederacy, but betrays no sympathy for
Theban policy (cf. 12. 4–5). Detailed knowledge of the situation at Athens, sympathy for
Conon, and the close continuation of Thucydides suggest an Athenian author (see above):

The most likely candidate is a Cratippus (*FGrH* 64) whom F. Jacoby called a 'später Schwindelautor', a late fraud—unjustly, since he seems to have been a historian of great importance. This identification is based on the correspondences between, on the one hand, what we know of Cratippus' work from T2 = Plut. *Mor.* 345c–e and (on the other) Ephorus in Diod. 13 and 14 (cf. Accame).

K.M.

Pacuvius, Marcus (*c.*130–220), stage poet and painter of South Italian birth, nephew and pupil of Quintus *Ennius. His family belonged to Brundisium, and he spent his last years in Tarentum. He seems to have had relations with Aemilius *Paullus (consul for the first time 182), or with Paullus' sons, and Gaius Laelius (consul 140).

Titles of 13 tragedies of the Attic Greek type (*Antiopa, Armorum iudicium, Atalanta, Chryses, Dulorestes, Hermiona, Iliona, Medus, Niptra, Pentheus, Periboea, Teucer, Thyestes* [?]) are transmitted. The themes of 8 relate to the Trojan War. *Cicero approved of the way in which, when translating *Sophocles' *Niptra*, Pacuvius made Ulysses' reaction to pain more appropriate to a great hero (*Tusc.* 2. 48). Several plots seem to have come from post-Euripidean pieces (see EURIPIDES). The *Paullus* must have dealt with some episode in the life of L. Aemilius Paullus or in that of his father. Fulgentius cites (*Serm. ant.* 12) a comedy *Pseudo*, while Pomponius Porphyrio (Hor. *Sat.* 1. 10. 46) and Diomedes (*GL* 1. 485. 32–4) refer to *saturae*. In the time of *Pliny the Elder the temple of Hercules in the forum Boarium boasted the possession of a painting by him (*HN* 35. 19).

Pacuvius' borrowings of Greek poetic vocabulary, neologisms (cf. e.g. the description of some dolphins as *Nerei repandirostrum incuruiceruicum pecus*, 'Nereus' snub-nosed, curved-necked flock') and unusual items of syntax brought him criticism from the grammatical purists of his own time. In the 1st cent. he was regarded as the greatest of the Latin tragic poets, surpassing *Accius in the artistry of his deployment of the high tragic style. Cicero cites a number of extended passages in his rhetorical and philosophical dialogues. The *Armorum iudicium, Chryses, Iliona*, and *Teucer* remained in the 1st-cent. BC repertoire. Nonius Marcellus (early 4th cent. AD?) had access to copies of the *Atalanta, Periboea, Dulorestes*, and *Her-*miona and possibly others. The several references to borrowings from Pacuvius in the late commentaries on *Virgil's *Aeneid* doubtless go back to the scholarship of the 1st cent. AD.

H.D.J.

Panaetius (*c.*185–109 BC), son of Nicagoras; a Stoic philosopher from Rhodes. At some point he was made a priest of Poseidon Hippios at Lindus. From a noble family, he studied with Crates of Mallus at Pergamum and with the leaders of the Stoic school at Athens, Diogenes of Babylon and his successor Antipater of Tarsus. He moved to Rome in the 140s and became, like *Polybius, part of the entourage of *Scipio Aemilianus. He accompanied Scipio on a major journey in the eastern Mediterranean (140/139). It is said that he lived alternately in Rome and Athens. In 129 he succeeded Antipater as head of the school. He died in Athens in 109.

Panaetius seems to have been more open to the views of *Plato and *Aristotle than were many Stoics, and to have questioned the earlier belief in a periodic world-conflagration. Unlike earlier Stoics, he doubted the efficacy of astrology and divination, though he retained a belief in divine providence. It is possible that he made some changes in moral psychology, in the direction of Platonic or Aristotelian dualism. But the evidence on this point is not as clear as for *Posidonius. In ethics, he is associated with a more practical emphasis on the moral situation of ordinary men and a reduced emphasis on the morally perfect sage. His account of the virtues also shows signs of revision, but not radical change. Books 1–2 of *Cicero's *De Officiis* were heavily influenced by Panaetius' *Peri kathēkontos* ('on duty'). His student Hecaton was influential in ethics.

B.I.

Papinian (Aemilius Papinianus), a leading lawyer of the Severan age and a close associate of the emperor *Septimius Severus, probably came, like him, from Africa and had some exposure to Hellenistic culture. He was assessor to a praetorian prefect, then from AD 194 to 202, to judge from their style, composed rescripts (replies to petitions), often of a highly technical character, for Septimius, latterly at least as *a libellis* (secretary for petitions). On the fall of Gaius Fulvius Plautianus in AD 205 he became praetorian prefect along with Quintus Aemilius Laetus, but on the death of Septimius in February 211 was dismissed by *Caracalla. After the murder of Caracalla's brother and joint emperor Septimius Geta in 212 he was prosecuted by the praetorians and, without protest from Caracalla, put to death, an event which entered into legend as the martyrdom of a just man.

Leaving aside some perhaps early writings on Greek road officials (*astynomikoi*) and adultery, Papinian is best known for 37 books of *Quaestiones* ('Problems'), which belong to the 190s and, between 206 and 212, nineteen of *Digesta responsa* ('Ordered Opinions'), not confined to his own practice but drawing on a wide range of sources. His efforts to explore the ethical basis of legal rules goes along with a more crabbed style than is usual with Roman lawyers, but when properly understood his reasoning is as impressive as his technical mastery. Papinian was long regarded as the greatest Roman lawyer, and Constantine I declared invalid the (at times critical) notes of Paulus and *Ulpian on his work. The Law of Citations of 426 gives him the leading position among the five writers of authority and a casting vote in case they are equally divided. Third-year law students, who had to study his work, were called Papinianists, but Justinian, while preserving this custom, rehabilitated Paulus' and Ulpian's notes on Papinian and esteemed *Julianus more highly.   T.Hon.

Pappus, of Alexandria (fl. AD 320), mathematical commentator. The most important of his surviving works is *Sunagōgē* (*Collection*), a compilation (probably made after his death) in eight books of eight originally separate treatises and commentaries on different parts of the mathematical sciences. Book 8, an introduction to mechanics, is referred to as a distinct work by Eutocius, and exists as such in Arabic translation (in a fuller version than the Greek). Book 1 is missing, but was perhaps Pappus' commentary on

*Euclid, *Elements* 10 (see below). Book 2, of which the first part is also missing, contains number games based on a lost work of *Apollonius of Perge with a notation for expressing large numbers. Book 3 is a miscellany of geometrical problems for the use of students, book 4 on higher geometry and special curves, book 5 on isoperimetric problems and the regular and semi-regular polyhedra, book 6 a commentary on the collection of astronomical treatises known as the 'Little [Domain] of Astronomy' (*Mikros Astronomoumenos*). Book 7, the longest and most interesting, entitled *Domain of Analysis* (*Analouomenos topos*), is a commentary on Hellenistic works of higher geometry, mostly lost. The *Collection* is invaluable (and of considerable influence in European mathematics) as a source for lost works from the great period of Greek mathematics. Pappus' own contributions, in the form of 'lemmas' and proofs, are mostly trivial, and it is probable that all significant theorems are taken from earlier works, even when unattributed.

Pappus wrote a commentary to *Ptolemy (Claudius Ptolemaeus)'s *Almagest*, of which the part on books 5 and 6 survives. This is superficial, but provides valuable information on lost works of *Hipparchus. His commentary to Euclid *Elements* 10, which survives in Arabic translation, is of interest because of its discussion of 'unordered irrationals', with references to a work of Apollonius on the same topic and to Theaetetus. Among other lost works are *Chōrographia oikoumenikē*, a universal geography used in an early Armenian text, and commentaries on the *Planispherium* of Ptolemy (Claudius Ptolemaeus) and the *Analemma* of Diodorus of Alexandria.   G.J.T.

Parmenides of Elea (S Italy) is said to have legislated for his native city and (*c*.450 BC) to have visited Athens in his sixty-fifth year (Pl. *Parm.* 127b). His philosophical poem, in hexameters, survives in large fragments. It opens with the narration of a journey taken by the initiate poet-speaker, apparently from the world of daily life and light to a mysterious place where night and day cross paths and opposites are undivided. Here he is greeted by a goddess whose instruction forms the remainder of the work. She urges him to cease relying on ordinary beliefs and to 'judge by reason the very contentious refutation' of those beliefs that she offers. Her address attends closely to logical rigour and connection. The proem is suffused with religious language, and one might conjecture that an initiation in reason is being substituted for the perception-suffused initiations of religious cult.

Every aspect of this difficult argument is disputed; one can only offer one plausible account. Central to the goddess's teaching is the idea that thought and speech must have an object that is there to be talked or thought about. This being the case, if something is sayable or thinkable, it must *be*: 'You cannot say or think that it is not.' On this basis, she concludes not only that nothingness or the non-existent cannot figure in our speech, but also that temporal change, internal qualitative variation, and even plurality are all unsayable and unthinkable—on the grounds that talk about all these will commit the speaker to making contrasts and entail the use of negative language. Thus, whatever can be talked or thought about must be 'without birth or death, whole, single-natured, unaltering, and complete'.

A subsidiary argument invokes an idea of sufficient reason to rule out cosmogony: if what is had a beginning in time, there must have been some reason for that beginning. But what reason could there be, if (by hypothesis) there was nothing there previously?

Having described the 'Way of Truth', the goddess then acquaints her pupil with the deceptive contents of mortal beliefs. The cosmogony that follows is not intended to have any degree of truth or reliability. It is presumably selected because it shows the fundamental error of mortals in its simplest form. The decision to 'name' two forms, light and night, commits mortals to contrastive negative characterizations.

Parmenides was a great philosophical pioneer, who turned away from the tradition of Ionian cosmogony to attempt something fundamentally different: a deduction of the character of what is from the requirements of thought and language. His views were developed further by his followers Melissus and the distinguished *Zeno. *Empedocles, *Anaxagoras, and *Democritus all felt the need to respond to his arguments in defending plurality and change, though they did so without addressing his fundamental concern about language and thought. The core of his argument thus remained untouched until *Plato's *Sophist*, in which the Eleatic Stranger proposes a new understanding of the relation between language and the world in order to break the strong grip of the argument of 'father Parmenides'.

M.C.N.

Paul, Saint St Paul was a convert from Pharisaic to Messianic Judaism as a result of a mystical experience (Gal. 1: 12 and 16) when he believed himself called to be the divine agent by whom the biblical promises about the eschatological ingathering of the pagans would be fulfilled. That transference of allegiance led him to renounce his previous religious affiliations (Phil. 3: 6 f.), even though the form of his religion remains in continuity with apocalyptic Judaism. We know him as the result of letters which he wrote over a period of about ten years to maintain communities of Jews and gentiles in Rome and several other urban centres in a pattern of religion which enjoined faithfulness to Jesus Christ as the determining factor in the understanding of the Mosaic Law. This subordination of the Law inevitably led to conflict with Jewish and Christian opponents who suspected him of antinomianism and apostasy. His doctrine of justification by faith was hammered out as a way of explaining his position in relation to the Jewish Law. He commended Christianity as a religion which was both the fulfilment of the Jewish tradition and also the negation of central precepts like food laws and circumcision, though he was emphatic in his rejection of idolatry. In his letters we have clear evidence of the emergence of identifiable Christian communities separate from Judaism with a loose adherence to the Jewish tradition as interpreted by Paul. At the end of his life he organized a financial offering for the poor in Jerusalem from the gentile churches he had founded. According to *Acts his journey to Jerusalem with this collection preceded his journey to Rome where later Christian tradition suggests that he died in the Neronian persecution. The letters in the New Testament which are widely assumed to be authentic are Romans, 1 and 2 Corinthians, Galatians, Philippians, 1 Thessalonians, and Philemon, and possibly Colossians and 2 Thessalonians. Ephesians, and 1 and 2 Timothy and Titus are probably pseud-onymous. This last group of documents indi-cates the direction of the Pauline tradition after the apostle's death when accredited teachers began to be ordained to ensure the preservation of the apostolic traditions and institutions in the face of emerging gnosti-cism and antinomianism.   C.C.R.

Paullus (Lucius Aemilius Paullus) became an augur in 192 BC and governed Further Spain as praetor in 191, with command pro-rogued for 190 and 189. A defeat in 190 was retrieved by a victory in the following year. Later in 189 he went to Asia as one of the ten commissioners who administered the settle-ment after the defeat of *Antiochus III the Great. On his return in 187 he, with a majority of the commission, unsuccessfully opposed the granting of a triumph to Gnaeus Manlius Vulso. Despite several attempts he did not reach the consulship until 182, when he oper-ated in Liguria; his command was prorogued for 181 when, despite having been besieged in his camp, he eventually forced the Ligurian Ingauni to surrender. In 171 he was one of the patrons chosen by the peoples of Spain to represent their complaints against Roman governors. He was elected to a second con-sulship for 168, and ended the Third Macedo-nian War by his victory at Pydna. His triumph was marred by the death of his two young sons; his two elder sons, by his first wife Papiria, had been adopted and became Quintus Fabius Maximus Aemilianus and Publius Cornelius Scipio Aemilianus. He was elected censor in 164 and died in 160, by no means a rich man; of the booty from the war against *Perseus he had kept for himself nothing but Perseus' library. Paullus had a great interest in Greek culture, giving his sons a Greek as well as a traditional Roman educa-tion, and undertaking an archaeological tour of Greece after the war with Perseus. That did not prevent him from willingly carrying out the senate's order to sack Epirus, and from sanctioning other acts of brutality by Roman troops. See also CATO THE ELDER   J.Br.

Paulus, Julius, a celebrated Roman lawyer whose origin is unknown. Taught by the lawyer Cervidius Scaevola (late 2nd cent. AD), he was active in Rome as advocate, teacher, and writer. Under *Septimius Severus he was assessor to *Papinian as praetorian prefect

and became a member of the emperor's council and perhaps head of the records office (*a memoria*). He was thus able to publish reports of cases decided by Severus (*Imperiales sententiae, Decreta*), in which he shows his sturdy independence. Though the matter is disputed, he was possibly made praetorian prefect by *Elegabalus in AD 219, when the emperor married Julia Cornelia Paula, whose name suggests that she was the lawyer's daughter. The marriage was dis-solved in 220. Paulus was banished but was recalled by *Severus Alexander (222–35), whom he served as counsellor while continu-ing to write.

His output in some five decades came to over 300 books (*libri*), including 16 on the civil law (*Ad Sabinum*) and 78 on the praetor's edict (*Ad edictum praetoris*), besides notes on earlier writers and dozens of monographs on particular topics. The big commentaries came early in his career, and the monographs often develop themes touched on in them. There are also 26 books of *Quaestiones* ('Problems') and 23 of *Responsa* ('Opinions') derived mainly from Paulus' extensive con-sultative practice. His fame attracted several spurious works, including the so-called *Pauli sententiae* ('Paul's Views'), compiled in the late 3rd cent. but endorsed by Constantine I as genuine. The Law of Citations of 426 named him as one of five lawyers whose corpus of work had authority, and *Justin-ian's compilers selected over 2,000 passages from him, some 17 per cent of the *Digesta*, often to supplement the account given by *Ulpian. His bent as a writer was academic, even doctrinaire, his tone sharp, his outlook basically cautious; but his remarkable range of interests ensured that his ideas were con-tinually evolving. Influenced by Aristotelian natural law and Stoic philosophy (see ARIS-TOTLE, he along with Ulpian helped to ensure the adaptation of Roman law to a cosmopol-itan society.   T.Hon.

Pausanias, Agiad king of Sparta 445–426 and 408–395 BC: his first reign was as minor during the temporary deposition of his father Pleistoanax. In 403 he undermined *Lysand-er's dominance in Athens by obtaining command of a Peloponnesian League exped-ition against the democratic resistance at Piraeus, promoting reconciliation between them and the Three Thousand in Athens, and securing a treaty which restored democracy and brought Athens into Sparta's alliance. Back in Sparta he was prosecuted but acquitted. In 395 his army arrived at Haliartus after Lysander's defeat and retired without battle, partly due to Athenian military opposition. Sentenced to death, he fled to Tegea. In exile he continued to oppose his enemies in Sparta. He interceded with his son Agesipolis I to save the democratic leaders at Mantinea in 385, and wrote a pamphlet which seemingly accused his enemies of violating traditional Lycurgan laws and advocated abolition of the ephorate. The pamphlet probably disseminated much basic documentation about Sparta, such as the 'Great Rhetra', but also contributed significantly to the distorted idealization of her society, the 'Spartan mirage'. S.J.Ho.

Pausanias the Periegete, periegetic or travel-writer from Magnesia by Mt. Sipylus in W Asia Minor (?) (fl. *c.* AD 150), wrote an extant *Description of Greece* (*Periēgēsis tēs Hellados*) claiming to describe 'all things Greek' (*panta ta Hellēnika*); in fact limited essentially to the province of Achaia with the omission of Aetolia and the islands. Contents: 1. Attica, Megara; 2. Argolis etc.; 3. Laconia; 4. Messenia; 5–6. Elis, Olympia; 7. Achaea; 8. Arcadia; 9. Boeotia; 10. Phocis, Delphi.

His chief concern in his selective account was with the monuments (especially sculpture and painting) of the Archaic and Classical periods, along with their historical contexts, and the sacred (cults, rituals, beliefs), of which he had a profound sense. His work is organized as a tour of the *poleis* (cities) and extra-urban sanctuaries of Achaia, with some interest in topography, but little in the intervening countryside. His concern for objects after 150 BC is slight, although contemporary monuments attracted his attention, especially the benefactions of *Hadrian. He wrote from autopsy, and his accuracy (in spite of demonstrable muddles) has been confirmed by excavation. Although his approach was personal, his admiration for old Greece (Athens, Sparta, Delphi, and Olympia figure prominently) and its great patriots (see 8. 52) belongs to the archaizing enthusiasm for the Greek motherland fanned by Greek high culture of the day and Hadrian's organization of Greek mother-

cities and their colonies, the Panhellenion, which attracted many overseas (especially Asian) Greeks to Antonine Achaia; presumably Pausanias wrote partly with these in mind. A.J.S.S.

Pelagius Now agreed to have been British by birth, educated in rhetoric and possibly in law, Pelagius settled in Rome after AD 380. Noted for his asceticism, though formally neither monk nor priest, he enjoyed (like *Jerome, Priscillian, and Rufinus) the patronage of Christian aristocrats, especially women, and responded similarly to their interest in scripture. His *Letter to Demetrias* is a vivid monument. His commentaries on Epistles of *Paul are straightforward and polished, following in a Roman tradition dating to Marius Victorinus and including Ambrosiaster, reminiscent of the 'Antiochene' school, but informed also by Latin translations of *Origen. He was inevitably engaged with protagonists of the controversy over Origen's theology. His asceticism was moderate, his attachment to freedom intense. He aroused the scorn of Jerome for the one and criticized *Augustine on account of the other. Anxious to maintain a balance between Manichaeism and a disparagement of virginity, he rejected current views of original sin, defending the justice of God and the individual's ability to rise by deliberate choice above moral weakness. Protected in Rome by his patrons, he left the city at the time of the Gothic sack in AD 410, taking brief refuge in Africa and seeing his supporter Cælestius condemned at the Council of Carthage in 411. Pelagius moved east and was supported at synods by John of Jerusalem in 415. Western enemies in both Africa and Rome were relentless, however, and were reinforced by imperial condemnation in 418 (*Coll. Quesnelliana* 14, 19, *PL* 56. 490–3, 499–500. See also *C.Th.* Sirm. 6 of AD 425). The remaining course of his life and the circumstances of his death are unknown. The soundness of his judgement has been hard to suppress, in spite of Augustine's reputation, and was proliferated in numerous pamphlets and defended by Julian of Eclanum. P.R.

Pelopidas, Theban general. First attested at the Spartan siege of Mantinea (386), he was exiled by the pro-Spartan junta (382). His contribution to the liberation of Thebes

(379/8) earned the first of thirteen boeotarch-ies (chief magistracies in the Boeotian Confederacy). Returning from an attack on Boeotian Orchomenus, he inflicted a psychologically important defeat on two Spartan *morai* at Tegyra (375). At the battle of Leuctra (about which he had a prophetic dream) he and the Sacred Band helped to execute *Epaminondas' battle-plan. After the historic Theban invasion of Laconia (370/69), he was (like Epaminondas) acquitted on a politically inspired charge of acting *ultra vires*. In 367 he visited King Artaxerxes II of Persia, extracting a rescript which suited Theban interests but proved hard to enforce. Latterly his special interest was Thessaly. In 369 he threatened the tyrant Alexander of Pherae and freed Larissa from King Alexander II of Macedon, receiving *Philip II as a hostage. In 368 he bargained with Ptolemaeus (Alexander's murderer), but was arrested by Alexander of Pherae (Boeotian military intervention eventually 'negotiated' his release). In 364 Thessalians under his command worsted Alexander of Pherae at Cynoscephalae, but he was killed. (The Thessalians erected his statue at Delphi, *SEG* 22. 460.) With Epaminondas (their friendship is much stressed in the tradition esp. Plut. *Pelop.*, for which see Westlake, *CQ* 1939, 11 ff.) he embodies the post-Leuctra 'Theban hegemony', though neither consistently exercised political control in Thebes.

C.J.T.

Perdiccas (d. 321 BC), son of Orontes, Macedonian noble of the princely house of Orestis, commanded his native battalion in the phalanx of *Alexander the Great. His military distinction, somewhat obscured by the hostile account of *Ptolemy I, won him elevation to the rank of Bodyguard by 330. Subsequently he ranked second only to *Craterus in his effectiveness as marshal and succeeded *Hephaestion in his cavalry command and his position as chiliarch (Grand Vizier). The settlement at Babylon (323) confirmed him in the chiliarchy with command of the central army and gave him custody both of the new king, Philip III Arrhidaeus, and the unborn child of Alexander. In 322 his position strengthened after his successful invasion of Cappadocia, but his dynastic intrigues alarmed the commanders in Europe, *Antipater and Craterus, who declared war in winter 322/1 (the chronology is disputed).

Perdiccas himself quarrelled with Ptolemy, whom he suspected of separatist ambitions, and invaded Egypt (summer 321). After protracted and costly operations around Pelusium and Memphis his troops were incited to mutiny, and he was killed.   A.B.B.

Periander, tyrant of Corinth *c.*627–587 BC, after his father Cypselus; he was for many the typical oppressive tyrant. Advice that he should eliminate rivals is said by *Herodotus to have been given to Periander by Thrasybulus of Miletus, who walked silently through a field of corn lopping off ears that were taller than the rest; *Aristotle made the advice pass in the opposite direction. Unlike his father, Periander recruited a bodyguard; he sent 300 Corcyraean boys to Lydia in W Asia Minor for castration as punishment when Corcyraeans killed his son; he himself killed his wife Melissa, made love to her corpse and took the fine clothes off Corinthian women to burn for her spirit. There was also, however, a more favourable tradition: he was in many lists of the seven sages, and 'he was neither unjust nor insolent, but hated wickedness' (Arist. fr. 611. 20 Rose). The burning of clothes probably reflects a more general attack on luxury, and restrictions on slave ownership may have been similar; his measures against idleness are a misinterpreted memory of the labour which his extensive building programme required: among other things, he constructed the diolkos (stone haulway for ships across the Isthmus) and an artificial harbour at Lechaeum, and levied dues upon the use of them. If Cypselus had not brought Corcyra under control after the aristocratic clan of the Bacchiadae fled there, Periander did, and installed his son as tyrant; this is the context of the joint Corinthian/Corcyraean foundations of Apollonia and Epidamnus. He founded Potidaea in N Greece, the only Corinthian colony in the Aegean. He had a warlike reputation; probably his activity in particular lay behind *Thucydides's account of early naval affairs, which attributes more or less the naval practices of his own day, including suppression of piracy, to Corinth. He attacked Epidaurus and captured its tyrant, his father-in-law Procles. He arbitrated between Athens and Mytilene in their dispute over Sigeum. He gave Thrasybulus of Miletus advice, and probably naval assistance, during his successful resistance to the

Lydian siege. On his death, the tyranny passed to his nephew Cypselus, also called Psammetichus, who was soon killed; opposition will have begun much earlier, under Periander himself.   J.B.S.

Pericles (*c.*495–429 BC), Athenian politician, was the son of Xanthippus and Agariste of the aristocratic Alcmaeonid family, niece of *Cleisthenes and granddaughter of Agariste of Sicyon and Megacles. He was *chorēgos* (paying for the production) for *Aeschylus' *Persae* in 472, but first came to prominence as one of the elected prosecutors of *Cimon in 463/2. In 462/1 he joined with Ephialtes in the attack on the council of the Areopagus.

According to *Plutarch he became popular leader and one of the most influential men in Athens after Ephialtes' death and the ostracism of Cimon. Little is recorded of him for some years, but it is reasonable to assume that he was in favour of the more ambitious foreign policy pursued by Athens in the 450s and of the further reforms of that decade. He is credited with a campaign in the Gulf of Corinth *c.*454 and with the sending out of cleruchies (colonies) to places in the Delian League, and with the introduction of pay for jurors and the law limiting citizenship to those with an Athenian mother as well as an Athenian father. His proposal for a congress of all the Greeks, which came to nothing because of opposition from Sparta (Plut. *Per.* 17: its authenticity has been challenged) perhaps belongs to the early 440s and was an attempt to convert the Delian League into a league of all the Greeks under Athens' leadership now that the Delian League's war against Persia had ended. In 446 he commanded the expedition to put down the revolt of Euboea; he returned to Athens when the Peloponnesians invaded, and was alleged to have bought off the Spartan king Pleistoanax; and he then went back to deal with Euboea.

Pericles was greatly involved in Athens' public building programme of the 440s and 430s. This was the issue on which opposition to him was focused by Thucydides son of Melesias, a relative of Cimon, but Thucydides was ostracized *c.*443 and the building continued. According to Plutarch, Pericles was elected general every year after that and was Athens' unchallenged leader; but it seems likely that attacks on Pericles and his friends, probably from the democratic end of the political spectrum, are to be dated to the early 430s. His mistress Aspasia and the sophist *Anaxagoras were perhaps prosecuted, the sculptor *Phidias was prosecuted and left Athens, and Pericles himself was charged with embezzlement but presumably acquitted.

In the 430s he led an expedition to the Black Sea. The policies pursued by Athens in the late 430s, which led to the outbreak of the Peloponnesian War between Athens and the Spartan alliance, are presumably his: *Aristophanes represents him as being particularly obstinate over the decree imposing sanctions on Megara, and Thucydides gives him a speech claiming that a policy of appeasement will not work. According to Thucydides his strategy for the Peloponnesian War was to stay inside the walls when the Peloponnesians invaded, and to rely on Athens' sea power and superior financial resources to outlast the Peloponnesians; but there are indications in the scale of Athens' expenditure and naval activity in the opening years of the war that Thucydides' picture may be distorted. In 430, when the hardship of the war was beginning to be felt, the Athenians deposed him from the generalship and attempted unsuccessfully to negotiate with Sparta; he was afterwards re-elected, but he was one of the many Athenians to suffer from the plague, and he died in 429.

Pericles was an aristocrat who became a democratic leader. He won the admiration of Cimon's relative, the historian *Thucydides, as a man who was incorruptible and far-sighted, and who led the people rather than currying favour with them (2. 65). Plutarch reconciled this with the less favourable picture given by *Plato by supposing that Pericles was a demagogue in the earlier part of his career and a great statesman in the later. He was an impressive orator. His manner was aloof, and he is said to have been uninterested in his family's concerns. His marriage (possibly to his cousin and *Alcibiades' mother, Deinomache) was unhappy, but he formed a liaison with the Milesian Aspasia, and when his two sons by his Athenian wife had died from the plague his son by Aspasia, Pericles, was made an Athenian citizen.

                                         A.W.G.; P.J.R.

Perseus, king of Macedonia (179–168 BC), elder son and legitimate successor of *Philip V, was born about 213/2. He took part in his father's campaigns against the Romans and then, as ally of Rome, against the Aetolians. Perseus stood against the pro-Roman policies and royal aspirations of his brother Demetrius (executed for treason by Philip in 180) and succeeded to the throne on Philip's death in 179. After renewing his father's treaty with Rome, he secured his popularity at home with a royal amnesty and set about extending his influence and connections in the Greek world at large. In the early 170s he married Laodice, daughter of Seleucus IV, gave his sister in marriage to Prusias (II) of Bithynia, won the goodwill of Rhodes, and restored Macedon's position in the Delphic Amphictiony. The mid-170s saw his popular involvement in social conflicts in Aetolia and Thessaly, his reduction of Dolopia, and a remarkable *tour de force* through central Greece. Perseus' success evoked at Rome hostile suspicion, evident from the early 170s and increasing thereafter as Perseus came to be for many an alternative focus to Rome in the states of Greece. Much of the expansion of Perseus' influence was at the expense of *Eumenes II of Pergamum, widely and correctly perceived theretofore as supporter of Rome. Eumenes denounced Perseus at length to the Romans (172) and provided them with a series of pretexts for war with Macedon, declared in 171. That Perseus had warlike designs against Rome must be doubted, as his susceptibility to the deceptive diplomacy of Quintus Marcius Philippus in the winter of 172/1 suggests. His aim was to restore the prestige of Macedon in Greece, and a situation wherein 'the Romans would be chary ... of giving harsh and unjust orders to the Macedonians' (Polyb. 27. 9. 3). Perseus' decision to accept war with Rome has, with reference to the military manpower available to Rome, been viewed as foolish; it has also, with different sort of reason, been compared to the decision of the Greeks in October 1940. His strategy of defence on the Macedonian frontiers was at first successful, and a cavalry victory in 171 revealed a groundswell of support in Greece. But his diplomacy won over only the Illyrian king Genthius, whose support proved of little moment. The Romans entered Macedonia, and the Macedonian phalanx fought its last battle on unfavourable ground at Pydna, on the morrow of the lunar eclipse in June 168. Perseus himself, after firing the royal records,

was taken on Samothrace later in the year. He graced the triumphal procession of Lucius Aemilius *Paullus in 167 and died in captivity a few years later at Alba Fucens.   P.S.D.

Persius Flaccus, Aulus (AD 34–62), Neronian satirist; see NERO. His ancient biography records that he was a rich equestrian of Etruscan stock who died young and who was connected with the Stoic opposition to Nero through his links with Publius Clodius Thrasea Paetus and the philosopher Lucius Annaeus Cornutus. However, Persius' satires are isolated and introverted works, more concerned with inner, philosophical freedom than with political liberty. The 'biting truth' he reveals (1. 107) is confined to moral crassness, literary bad taste, and his own failings.

Persius claims to take his lead from *Lucilius (1), but his language and ideas are similar to those of *Horace. He reduces Horace's 18 satires to 6 and a mere 650 hexameters, offering 'something more concentrated' (1. 120), with 'the taste of bitten nails' (1. 106). This format provoked violent reactions in antiquity: *Lucan admired the satires as 'real poetry'; *Martial considered them a precious elixir worth more than bulky epics; but *Jerome is said to have burned them because of their obscurity. Persius certainly stretches satire to un-Horatian extremes: his characters are either aged or immature, tutors or students; his ideal is uncompromising Stoicism, not easy Epicureanism (see EPICURUS); Horace's mocking conversations become diatribes filled with bitter spleen.

Persius opens with a prologue in limping iambics (scazons), the metre of cynical sneering, exposing satire as a hybrid, semi-poetic genre, and the patronage system as mutual back-scratching. (1) lifts the curtain on a disgusting orgy of modern poetry, in which specimens of literary decadence, possibly parodies of Nero's own works, corrupt Persius' avowedly straightforward style. His disgust with 'confused Rome' eventually explodes, and he mutters a cherished secret into a hole in the ground: all Romans have asses' ears. This echo of the Midas story prompted an ancient legend that Cornutus, who edited Persius after his death, had been forced to change a specific attack on Nero to this vaguer generalization. (2) strips bare the hypocrisy of Roman citizens who sacrifice to the gods in the hope of material gain, not

moral virtue. (3) is most often read as a dialogue between a lazy student in bed with a
hangover and a Stoic tutor who urges him to
pursue philosophy before it is too late
(though both may be voices inside Persius'
own head). (4) is a dialogue between a young
politician (*Alcibiades) and a philosopher
(*Socrates) where, again, self-knowledge is
encouraged. In (5) Persius pays homage to
his own tutor Cornutus, who has taught him
to use unadorned language. The two are
united by their devotion to Stoicism in a
topsy-turvy world where others are enslaved
to material desires. In (6), a Horatian-style
epistle to Caesius Bassus from the coastal
resort of Luna, Persius meditates on the contrast between his own tiny and worthless-
seeming legacy to his profligate heirs and the
infinite heaps of wealth coveted by others.

Persius is often regarded as a paragon of
Stoic virtue, but in fact he makes no secret of
his own imperfections; in the confusion of
different voices, he speaks as an erring
student as well as a stern tutor. It is a mistake
to try to extract clear messages from his disjointed outbursts. Although he claims to
aspire to bluntness, his language is a tortuous
mixture, full of jarring juxtapositions and
strained links (*iunctura . . . acri*, 5. 15); he uses
a dense tissue of images, often graphically
anatomical, to revitalize dead metaphors and
fuse disparate ideas. It was this black wit
which struck a chord with the church fathers,
and with later satirists, especially John
Donne.   E.J.G.

Pertinax, Publius Helvius, born in Liguria
AD 126, the son of a freedman; he abandoned
a career as a schoolteacher and sought a commission as a centurion; rejected, he gained
appointment as an equestrian officer in Syria
*c.*160. The wars of the 160s brought further
posts, in Britain and Moesia, followed by a
procuratorship and (*c.*169) command of the
classis Germanica (Rhine fleet). An inscription near Cologne (*AE* 1963. 52) records his
career to that point and a further procuratorship in Dacia. He was soon assisting Claudius
Pompeianus in clearing the Marcomannic
invaders out of Italy (170–1); he was made a
senator by *Marcus Aurelius and after further
success became consul (175); he then governed both Moesias, Dacia, and Syria. Dismissed in 182 by the praetorian prefect
Tigidius Perennis, he was in retirement until
185, when he governed Britain, suppressing
a major mutiny; he became prefect of the
alimenta (foundations for feeding children)
in Italy, proconsul of Africa, and, in 192,
prefect of Rome and consul for the second
time. Apprised in advance of the plot against
*Commodus, he was hailed emperor by an
enraptured senate in the night of 31 December 192. In spite of his humble origin, his
phenomenal career had won him unrivalled
respect. His attempts to redress the financial
crisis and restore discipline soon aroused
hostility from the guard. Two coups, on 3
January and in early March, failed, but on 28
March he was killed by mutinous soldiers.
*Septimius Severus assumed the name Perti-
nax shortly afterwards and deified him.

                                                    A.R.Bi.

Petronius, senator of consular rank and
courtier of *Nero. His praenomen is uncertain (at Tac. *Ann.* 16. 17 'Gaius' is supplied
from 16. 18, but it is more likely that a cognomen (family-name) has fallen out); Pliny, *HN*
37. 20, and Plut. *Mor.* 60 D seem to give the
praenomen (personal name) Titus to the
same man, and a Titus Petronius Niger is
attested as consul on Herculaneum tablets.
However, a document from Ephesus attests a
Publius Petronius Niger as suffect consul
with the same colleague in July of AD 62.
According to *Tacitus he had been outstanding for his indolence, though this did not
prevent him from being energetic as proconsul in Bithynia and as consul (*Ann.* 16. 18).
For a time he was influential enough to guide
Nero in his choice of pleasures, and even
when forced by the praetorian prefect
Ofonius Tigellinus' intrigues to commit
suicide in 66, he showed himself not merely
fearless but contemptuous of Stoic postur-
ings. Instead of a will full of flattery of Nero
or his current favourites, Petronius left a
document denouncing him in embarrassing
detail. Scholars have long ago discarded the
notion that this denunciation has anything
to do with the *Satyricon* (see PETRONIUS
ARBITER), which, however, reflects the phil-
hellenic atmosphere of the Neronian court,
having affinities with the *Odyssey* (see
HOMER) and the Hellenistic novel and being
set in places around the Bay of Naples.

                                                    M.S.S.; M.T.G.

Petronius Arbiter, author of the extant *Satyrica*, possibly identical with *Petronius, the politician and *arbiter elegantiae* at the court of Nero, forced to suicide in AD 66. Given that scholars now agree that the *Satyrica* belongs stylistically and in terms of factual detail to the Neronian period, and that *Tacitus' account of the courtier Petronius describes a hedonistic, witty, and amoral character which would well suit the author of the *Satyrica* (*Ann.* 16. 17–20), many find it economic to identify the two, but the matter is beyond conclusive proof; the occurrence of the name Titus Petronius Arbiter in the MSS of the *Satyrica* gives no aid, since this may simply be the supplement of a later copyist who had read Tacitus.

Of the *Satyrica* itself we seem to have fragments of books 14, 15, and 16, with book 15 practically complete, containing the *Cena Trimalchionis* ('Dinner of Trimalchio') (26. 6–78.8). The commonly used but misleading title *Satyricon* (sc. *libri*) conceals not the Greek *Saturikon* (neuter singular) but *Saturikōn* (neuter genitive plural) and alludes both to influence from Roman satire and (ironically) to Encolpius' far from satyric sexual capacity (see below for both). The whole work was evidently lengthy; one conjectural reconstruction has suggested twenty books and a length of 400,000 words. It is prosimetric in form, an inheritance from the similar satires of *Varro, though there is now extant a Greek low-life prosimetric fictional text in the Iolaus-papyrus, *POxy.* 42 (1974). The outline of the plot is naturally difficult to reconstruct; the main characters are the homosexual pair Encolpius (the narrator) and the younger Giton, who undergo various adventures in a southern Italian setting. They encounter a number of characters, some of whom, such as the unscrupulous adventurer Ascyltus and the lecherous poet Eumolpus, try to divide the lovers; Giton is not particularly faithful, and this, like the sexual orientation of the lovers and many other elements in the novel, constitutes an evident parody of the chaste fidelity of the boy–girl pairings of the ideal Greek novel. Encolpius seems to be afflicted with impotence as the result of the wrath of the phallic god Priapus, and there are several episodes describing his sexual failures; the wrath of Priapus is evidently a parody of the wrath of Poseidon in the *Odyssey*, and other parallels between Encol-

pius and Odysseus are present, particularly when he encounters a woman named Circe (126 ff.).

Many themes familiar from Roman satire appear, such as legacy-hunting (the episode set in Croton (Crotone), 116–41) and the comic meal (the *Cena Trimalchionis*); in the latter Encolpius, Giton, and Ascyltus attend a dinner given by the rich freedman (ex-slave) Trimalchio, probably in Puteoli, in the narrative of which both Trimalchio's vulgar and ignorant display of wealth and the snobbishness of the narrator emerge very forcibly, and which contains in a parody of *Plato's *Symposium* a collection of tales told by Trimalchio's freedman friends which gives some evidence for vulgar Latin, though Petronius has naturally not reproduced colloquial speech exactly. Several other inserted tales are told in the novel, especially those of the Pergamene Boy (85–7) and the Widow of Ephesus (111–12), suitably lubricious stories for their narrator Eumolpus, but also clearly drawing on the Hellenistic tradition of Milesian tales. The inserted poems in various metres sometimes appear to comment on the novel's action; the two longest, presented as the work of the bad poet Eumolpus, seem to relate to other Neronian writers, the 65-line *Troiae Halosis* (89) written in the iambic trimeters of Senecan tragedy, and the *Bellum Civile* in 295 hexameters (119–24), closely recalling *Lucan's homonymous epic on the same subject (and restoring the divine machinery which Lucan had excluded). Literary and cultural criticism is certainly a concern of the novel; there are prominent attacks on contemporary oratory, painting, and poetry (1–5, 88–9, 118).

Petronius' novel seems not to have been widely known in antiquity, though a more extensive text than ours was available; it was rediscovered between the 15th and 17th cents., with great impact. The fragmentary text which has come down to us is likely to have some degree of interpolation, though scholars disagree as to how much. A number of poems in various metres transmitted separately from the *Satyrica* are also attributed to Petronius.   S.J.Ha.

Phaedrus or **Phaeder, Gaius Julius** (*c.*15 BC–*c.* AD 50), a slave of Thracian birth (possibly from Macedonian Pydna: see 3, prol. 17 ff.), received a good schooling perhaps in Italy, became a freedman of Augustus, and composed five books of verse fables. Under *Tiberius, he offended *Sejanus through suspected allusions in his fables and suffered some unknown punishment. Scarcely noticed by Roman writers (he is not mentioned by either *Seneca the Younger or *Quintilian in their references to fable), he is first named (though identification is uncertain) by *Martial (3. 20. 5 *improbi iocos Phaedri*, 'the jokes of mischievous Ph.') and next by Avianus (*praefat.*). Prose paraphrases of his and of other fables were made in later centuries, in particular the collection entitled 'Romulus', and in the Middle Ages enjoyed a great vogue. The five books are clearly incomplete and thirty further fables (*Appendix Perottina*), included in N. Perotti's epitome of fables (*c.*1465) drawn from a MS now lost, have been shown to belong to them; additional fables deriving from Phaedrus are contained in the prose paraphrases.

Phaedrus' achievement, on which he greatly prides himself, lies in his elevation of the fable, hitherto utilized in literature only as an adjunct, e.g. in satire (cf. Hor. *Sat.* 2. 6. 79 ff., the town and country mouse; *Epist.* 1. 7. 29 ff., the fox and the corn-bin), into an independent genre. His fables, written in iambic senarii, consist of beast-tales based largely on '*Aesop', as well as jokes and instructive stories taken not only from Hellenistic collections but also from his own personal experience. His main source is likely to have been a collection of Aesopic fables compiled in prose by the Athenian Demetrius of Phaleron (late 4th cent. BC). Philosophic weight is sought by borrowings from the *chreiai* ('maxims') and diatribe; moral instruction is generally self-contained at the beginning (*promythia*) or ending (*epimythia*) of the tale. Besides his professed purpose of providing amusement and counsel, Phaedrus sometimes satirizes contemporary conditions both social and political. His work evidently evoked considerable criticism and retorts to his detractors are frequent. The presentation is animated and marked by a humorous and charming brevity of which Phaedrus is rightly proud (2 *prol.* 12, 3 *epil.* 8, 4 *epil.* 7), but which sometimes leads to obscurity. In language he stands in the tradition of *Terence; skilfully adapting the *sermo urbanus*, he shows a classical purity and clearness (apart from a frequent use of abstract nouns and occasional vulgarisms or other unorthodoxies). His iambic senarius goes back to the early metre of Latin comedy and is very regular.   A.Schi.

Phidias, Athenian sculptor, son of Charmides, active *c.*465–425 BC; reputed pupil of Hegias and Hageladas. His early works included the colossal bronze Athena Promachos on the Acropolis; her spear-point and helmet-crest were supposedly visible from Sunium, the southernmost promontory of Attica (Paus. 1. 28. 2). His Athena Lemnia, perhaps preserved in Roman copy, and his Marathon group at Delphi may also be early; some attribute the Riace bronzes to the latter.

Phidias' reputation rested chiefly on his chryselephantine Athena Parthenos and his Zeus at Olympia (Quint. 12. 10. 9). Both were of gold and ivory over a wooden core, with embellishments in jewels, silver, copper, enamel, glass, and paint; each incorporated numerous subsidiary themes to demonstrate the divinity's power. *Plutarch (*Per.* 13) puts Phidias in charge not merely of the Athena but of *Pericles' entire building programme. He certainly belonged to Pericles' inner circle, and at the least probably directed the Parthenon's exterior sculpture. The Athena recapitulated several of its themes. Almost 12 m. (40 ft.) high and draped in over a ton of gold, she was begun in 447 and installed in 438; descriptions by *Pliny the Elder (*HN* 36. 18) and *Pausanias (1. 24) have enabled the identification of many copies. Her right hand held a Nike (personified victory), and her left a spear and a shield embellished outside with the Amazonomachy and inside with the Gigantomachy. Lapiths and Centaurs adorned her sandals, and her base carried the Birth of Pandora in relief. A Gorgoneion occupied the centre of her aegis (all-round bib with scales, fringed with snakes' heads), and a sphinx and two Pegasi supported the three crests of her helmet; griffins decorated its cheek-pieces.

Plutarch (*Per.* 31 f.) reports that Pericles' enemies prosecuted Phidias for embezzling the Parthenos' ivory and for impiety, and that he died in prison; Philochorus dated his trial to 438, but says that he fled to Olympia, where the Eleans killed him after he made the Zeus (*FGrH* 328 F121). This seems more likely, for his workshop there belongs to the 430s and has yielded tools, terracotta moulds (for a colossal female statue), and even a cup bearing his name. As *Strabo (8. 353 f.) and Pausanias (5. 10. 2 ff.) describe it, the Zeus was even larger than the Parthenos. Enthroned, he held a Nike in his right hand and a sceptre in his left; coins and vase-paintings reproduce the composition. The throne was richly embellished with Graces, Seasons, Nikai, sphinxes and Theban children, the slaughter of the children of Niobe (of which marble copies survive), and an Amazonomachy; paintings by Panaenus (Phidias' brother) on the screens between its legs included Hellas (Greece) and Salamis, some of the Labours of Heracles, Hippodamia and Sterope, and Achilles and Penthesilea. Another Amazonomachy adorned Zeus' footstool, and the statue's base carried the Birth of Aphrodite.

Ancient critics regarded Phidias as the greatest and most versatile of Greek sculptors (Quint. 12. 10. 9, etc.). His pupils dominated Athenian sculpture for a generation, and Hellenistic and Roman neo-classicism looked chiefly to him. Attributions (all copies) include the Medici Athena, the 'Sappho-Ourania', the Kassel Apollo, and the Mattei-Sciarra Amazon (after Pliny's account of the contest at Ephesus, *HN* 34. 53).   A.F.S.

Philemon, 368/60–267/63 BC, New Comedy poet from Syracuse (*Suda* φ 327) or Soli in Cilicia (Strabo 14. 671), but granted Athenian citizenship before 307/6 (*IG* 2². 3073 = *Syll.*³ 1089 = 2 B 1a Mette). In a long life (97 or 99 or 101 years: sources differ) he wrote 97 comedies, of which over 60 titles are known; he won 3 times at the Athenian Lenaea festival, coming immediately after *Menander in the victors' list (*IG* 2². 2325. 161 = 5 C 1 col. 4. 10 Mette), while his first victory at the Dionysia festival is dated to 327 (*Marm. Par., FGrH* 239 B 7). Alciphron (4. 18) implies that Philemon received an invitation to the court of *Ptolemy I; it is not certain that this was taken up, although another anecdote (Plut. *Mor.* 449e, 458a) brings him before King Magas of Cyrene. Accounts of his death differ, but all agree that he was physically and mentally active to the end.

Most of the titles seem typical of New Comedy; only two (*Myrmidons, Palamedes*) sound like myth burlesques. Contemporary judgement awarded Philemon frequent victories over Menander, though this verdict was reversed by posterity (Quint. *Inst.* 10. 1. 72; Apul. *Flor.* 16.; Gell. *NA* 17. 4. 1). Just under 200 fragments survive, emphasizing the moralizing aspect of Philemon's thought: e.g. fr. 22 KA and K, a slave is a human being; 74 KA = 71 K, peace the only true good; 97 KA = 94 K, real justice. There are many gnomic lines and couplets, often lacking Menander's terse precision, and Jachmann's attack (*Plautinisches und Attisches* (1931), 226 f.) on Philemon's flat-footed, repetitive, and platitudinous verbosity is not unjustified. Of greater interest perhaps are the pompous cook who parodies *Euripides' *Medea* (82 KA = 79 K: see H. Dohm, *Mageiros* (1964), 122 ff.) and part of a long-winded prologue spoken by Air (95 KA = 91 K).

Of Philemon's capacities in complete plays Plautine adaptations (see PLAUTUS) furnish some evidence—*Mercator* (from Gk. *emporos*, Merchant), *Trinummus* (from *Thēsauros*, Treasure), and possibly *Mostellaria* (? from *Phasma*, Phantom). Here the fondness for surprises is probably the most interesting common factor; there is little, however, to make anyone quarrel with *Apuleius' judgement (*Flor.* 16) that Philemon's plays contained wit, plots neatly turned, recognitions (or solutions) lucidly arranged, realistic characters, maxims agreeing with life, and few seductions.

In Athens Philemon's comedies were revived after his death (B. H. Meritt, *Hesperia*, 1938, 116 ff. = 4a 25 Mette); in the 2nd cent. AD a statue was erected in his honour (*IG* 2². 4266). But it is an index of diminished popularity in comparison with Menander that there are far fewer quotations from Philemon in later writers, and no papyrus or other text identified with certainty as Philemon has been recovered, although several attributions have been suggested (cf. Austin, *CGFP* 244, 255, 296, 297); of these perhaps the second is the most plausible, in view of the long-windedness of part of that fragment.

W.G.A.

Philip II (382–336 BC), king of Macedon and architect of Macedonian greatness. In his youth he witnessed the near dissolution of the kingdom through civil war and foreign intervention, and spent some time (probably 369–367) as hostage in *Epaminondas' Thebes. The nadir came when his brother,

Perdiccas III, died in battle against Illyrian invaders (360/59), who occupied the north-western borderlands. On his accession (perhaps initially as regent for his nephew, Amyntas) his priority was to save Macedon from dismemberment by hostile powers, poised for the kill; and from the outset he displayed a genius for compromise and intrigue. The Athenians, who backed a pre-tender (Argaeus), were defeated in a skirmish near Aegae (mod. Vergina) but wooed by the return of their prisoners (and by hints that he would recognize their claims to Amphi-polis. Other belligerents (Paeonians and Thracians) were bought off, and Philip used the time he acquired to train a new citizen army in mass infantry tactics, introducing the twelve cubit pike (*sarisa*) as its basic weap-onry. His efforts bore fruit in 358, when he decisively defeated the Illyrians near Lake Lychnitis and used his victory to integrate the previously independent principalities of upper Macedonia into his kingdom. Their nobility joined the companions of his court and the commons were recruited into the army. Philip's increased power was immedi-ately deployed against Athens. While the city was enmeshed in the Social War (357–355) he annexed Amphipolis and Pydna in 357, captured Potidaea in 356, ceding it to the Olynthian federation in return for alliance, and acquired Methone (354)—at the cost of his right eye and permanent disfigurement. From the conquests came land which he dis-tributed in part to a new aristocracy, recruited from all parts of the Greek world Nearchus of Crete, Laomedon of Mytilene and Androsthenes of Thasos (all settled at Amphipolis). Most important was Crenides, the Thracian settlement by Mt. Pangaeus, which Philip occupied and reinforced in 356, naming it Philippi after himself. The exploit-ation of the neighbouring gold mines allegedly engrossed 1,000 talents *per annum*, which enabled him to maintain a large mer-cenary army and win the services of polit-icians in southern Greece.

Thessaly rapidly became an annexe of Macedon. An early marriage alliance with the Aleuadae family of Larissa brought an invita-tion to intervene in the murderous inter-necine war between the Thessalian League and the tyrants of Pherae. Initial defeats in 353 were redeemed in 352 by the great victory of the Crocus Field and the expulsion of Lycophron and Peitholaus from Pherae. In return Philip was appointed archon of Thes-saly with its revenues and superb cavalry at his disposal. In 349 he attacked another trad-itional enemy, Olynthus, and by September 348 had captured the city through internal treachery. The population was enslaved and Olynthus' land absorbed, but despite the shock of this exemplary treatment there was no response to the Athenian appeal for an international alliance against him, and in despondency the Athenians entered peace negotiations early in 346. Peace and alliance were concluded in April 346 (Peace of Philocrates) at the same time that Philip accepted an appeal to lead an Amphictionic campaign against the Phocians (allies of Athens). With masterly prevarication he delayed ratifying the peace until he was in the vicinity of Thermopylae, preventing the Athenians reinforcing their allies, and forced the Phocians to terms (July 346). The settle-ment which resulted left him master of Thermopylae with voting rights in the Amphictiony.

The years after 346 saw further expansion. Campaigns against the Illyrians (notably in 345) brought the Dardanians and Taulantians to subject status, and between 342 and 340 Philip crowned a long series of campaigns against the Thracians with a prolonged war in the Hebrus valley. The old Odrysian kingdom became a dependency under a Macedonian *stratēgos* ('general'); military colonies (notably Philippopolis/Plovdiv) were im-planted, and the Thracians supplied his largest pool of auxiliary troops. Meanwhile Philip's influence had expanded in southern Greece. He championed Megalopolis and Messenia against Sparta, supported a coup at Elis (343) and sent mercenaries to Euboea (343/2: date disputed). By 342 Athenian inter-pretations of his motives had more convic-tion. In 341 the Euboean regimes at Eretria and Oreos (Histiaea) were overthrown by an Athenian-led invasion and Athenian over-tures were sympathetically received in the Peloponnese. The situation became graver in 340, when Philip laid siege to Perinthus and Byzantium, and open war erupted in the late summer, when he commandeered the Athen-ian grain fleet. He left the sieges incomplete to launch a successful attack on the Scythian king Ateas, and returned to Macedon in mid-339.

The final act came when he assumed command of an Amphictionic expedition against the Locrians of Amphissa and used the campaign as a fulcrum to attack Thebes and Athens, now united in alliance against him. Its denouement was the battle of Chaeronea (August 338), fought with a fraction of the forces at his disposal, which destroyed Thebes as a military power and made him undisputed master of the Greek world. Garrisons at Corinth, Thebes, Ambracia, and (probably) Chalcis policed the settlement he imposed, and a conference at Corinth (summer 337) approved a common peace which guaranteed the stability of all governments party to it, prohibited constitutional change and entrenched Philip as executive head (*hegemon*) of the council (*synedrion*) which directed its enforcement. It was intended to perpetuate Macedonian domination and did so effectively. The meeting also witnessed Philip's proclamation of his war of revenge against Persia, a project doubtless long in gestation but only now publicized, and in 336 an expeditionary force crossed the Hellespont to begin operations in Asia Minor.

Philip's last year was overshadowed by domestic conflict. His love match with Cleopatra provoked a rift in the royal house which saw his wife *Olympias in angry retirement and the heir-apparent, Alexander (see ALEX-ANDER THE GREAT), in temporary exile in Illyria. There was a formal reconciliation; but tensions persisted, and Philip fell by an assassin's hand in autumn 336. The sources give personal motives, but there are also hints of a multiplicity of conspirators and the background to the murder is beyond speculation. He was interred at Aegae (many believe, in the splendid barrel-vaulted Tomb II in the Great Tumulus of Vergina), leaving his kingdom a military and economic giant but internally almost as distracted as it had been at his accession. A.B.B.

Philip V (238–179 BC), king of Macedon, son of Demetrius II and Phthia (Chryseis) and adopted by *Antigonus Doson, whom he succeeded in summer 221. He quickly showed that his youth did not betoken weakness in Macedon, initially against the Dardani and others in the north. The Social War (220–217), in which he led the Hellenic League against Aetolia, Sparta, and Elis, saw him establish his own authority in the face of intrigues amongst his ministers and brought him considerable renown at home and abroad. After the Peace of Naupactus (217), he sought to take advantage of Rome's discomfiture in Italy and to replace Roman with Macedonian influence along the eastern shore of the Adriatic: first by sea with limited success (after an aborted expedition in 216 he lost his fleet in 214) and later by land with considerably more (he captured Lissus on the Adriatic in 213). His treaty with *Hannibal (215) defined spheres of operation and interest but led to no useful action. Rome's alliance with the Aetolian League (211) did much to neutralize Philip's advantage on land, and the intervention of *Attalus I of Pergamum on the Roman–Aetolian side further distracted him. Remarkable energy and tactical skill were devoted to assisting and protecting his allies, the Achaeans against Sparta and those on the mainland against Roman–Aetolian rapacity. With the withdrawal of Attalus, a biennium of Roman inactivity (207–206), the development by *Philopoemen of a competent military force in Achaea, the balance shifted. After sacking Thermum (the religious and political centre of Aetolia), Philip forced terms on the Aetolians (206), and concluded the temporizing (on the Roman side at least) Peace of Phoenice in 205. Philip then turned eastward: he employed the piratical Dicaearchus to gain resources and from 203/2 sought to gain control of territory in the Aegean and Asia Minor subject to the infant *Ptolemy V; the nature and extent of his co-operation with *Antiochus III in this venture is disputed. This expansion, along with that achieved by his lieutenants on the mainland, alarmed many, especially Attalus and the Rhodians. Their naval engagements with Philip off Chios and Lade (near Miletus) in 201 were of mixed outcome, but their *démarche* at Rome late that year came at an opportune juncture: the Romans were victorious over Carthage and already inclined against Philip and towards the east. In 200 they declared war and lost no time in announcing that they had come as protectors of the Greeks; many believed them. After campaigns in Macedonia (199) and Thessaly (198), Philip was defeated at Cynoscephalae in Thessaly in 197. By the subsequent peace settlement the Romans confined him to Macedonia, exacted 1,000 talents indemnity, most of his fleet, and hostages, amongst them his younger son, Demetrius. After securing an alliance with the Romans, Philip co-operated with them, sending help against the Spartan king Nabis (195) and Antiochus and the Aetolians (192–189), and made acquisitions in Thessaly. For facilitating the advance of the Scipios (*Scipio Africanus and Lucius Cornelius Scipio Asiagenes through Macedon and Thrace (190) he had the rest of his indemnity remitted and his son restored. He then set about consolidating Macedon: finance was reorganized, populations were transplanted, mines reopened, central and local currencies issued. Accusations by his neighbours (especially *Eumenes II of Pergamum) led to constant interference by an already suspicious Rome. Adverse decisions by the senate in 185 convinced him that his destruction was intended and quickened his efforts to extend his influence in the Balkans by force and diplomacy. Meanwhile, the pro-Roman policy of Demetrius (fostered by *Flamininus and others who encouraged him to entertain hopes of succession) led to a quarrel with the crown prince Perseus and ultimately to Philip's reluctant decision to execute Demetrius for treason (180). From this Philip never recovered, and in 179, amidst an ambitious scheme for directing the Bastarnae against the Dardani, he died at Amphipolis. P.S.D.

Philistus, of Syracuse, *c.*430–356 BC, friend, adviser, officer, and historian of *Dionysius I and II. He successfully supported Dionysius I in his bid for power in 406/5 (T 3) and served for a long time as commander of the tyrants' stronghold in Ortygia (T 5c). He was exiled for personal reasons in *c.*386 and on his return put in charge of the organization of colonies along the Adriatic coast (T 5a). He served as Dionysius II's political adviser and *nauarchos* ('admiral', T 9b). A staunch opponent of *Plato's and *Dion's reforms (T 5c and 7), he died in 356 in the fight against the insurgent Syracusans, maybe through suicide (T 9c).

WORK *The History of Sicily (Sicelica)* contained two *syntaxeis* (parts), covering the time from the mythical beginnings until 363/2. The seven books of the first part brought the narrative down to the capture of Acragas (mod. Agrigento) by the Carthaginians in 406/5, the second part dealt in four books with the reign of the elder Dionysius from his accession to power in 406/5 until his death in 368/7 (T 11a). In addition there were two books on Dionysius the Younger reaching down to 363/2. The work was continued by Athanis or rather Athanas of Syracuse until *Timoleon's resignation in 337/6 (Dion. 15. 94. 4). Philistus showed very favourable tendencies towards the tyrants. Plutarch (Dion. 36. 3 = T 23a) calls him 'the greatest lover of the tyrants (*philotyrannotatos*) and more than any one else an admirer of luxury, power, wealth, and marriage alliances of tyrants'. Similar opinions are found in *Cornelius Nepos (Dion. 3. 1 = T 5d), *Diodorus (16. 16. 3 = T 9c), *Dionysius of Halicarnassus (T 16a) and *Pausanias the Periegete (1. 13. 8 = T 13a). The scant fragments that deal with Dionysius I (esp. F 57 and 58) also show Philistus' favourable attitude. He was nevertheless a very competent and important historian: the ancients regarded him unanimously as an imitator of *Thucydides, e.g. Dionysius of Halicarnassus (T 16), *Cicero (T17) and *Quintilian (T 15c). Many parts of Diodorus' narrative which are based on *Timaeus, e.g. the siege of Gela 13. 108–13, the building of the wall in Syracuse 14. 18, the preparations for the war against Carthage 14. 41–6, ultimately derive from the vivid and knowledgeable account of Philistus. Several details in Diodorus' account of the Sicilian expedition by Athens (12. 82–13. 10) which are not mentioned in Thucydides, but do appear in Diodorus' source *Ephorus, argue for Philistus as their source of origin. Only 76 direct fragments are extant, 42 of which in the geographical lexicon of *Stephanus of Byzantium: these contain scarcely more than place names. E. Meyer regarded this as 'one of the most serious losses for ancient historiography'. K.M.

Philitas (also spelt **Philetas**) of Cos, poet and scholar, born *c.*340 BC, became tutor of *Ptolemy II Philadelphus (b. Cos 308); reputedly also taught Zenodotus, *Theocritus, and Hermesianax. He presumably spent some time in Alexandria, but probably died in Cos, where a bronze statue or relief was erected in his honour.

WORKS (1) *Poetry.* Five titles are attested: *Hermes, Demeter, Telephus* (?), *Epigrammata,*

Paegnia; only small fragments are extant. *Hermes* (the reason for the title is unclear), in hexameters, narrated Odysseus's visit to Aeolus's island and his love-affair with his daughter Polymele (fr. 5 Pow. (= Parthenius, *Er. Path.* 2) is not necessarily a full or accurate summary). *Demeter*, a narrative elegy, recounted the goddess's mourning and search for Kore, including perhaps her visit to Cos. *Telephus* (if the title is right: Telephus was also the name of P.'s father) included a reference to the marriage of Jason and Medea. *Paegnia* and *Epigrammata* may have been alternative titles for the same collection of epigrams. It is not clear in which of his works Philitas may have written love-poetry to Bittis (cf. Hermesianax fr. 7. 77–8; Ovid, *Tr.* 1. 6. 2), or treated the subject of *bougonia* (fr. 22 Pow.), possibly alluded to by Theocritus (*Id.* 7. 78–89) and Virgil (*G.* 4. 281 ff.).

(2) *Prose.* Thirty-odd fragments survive of a work variously entitled *Ataktoi glōssai*, *Glōssai*, or *Atakta* (i.e. *Miscellaneous Glosses*: an alleged work *Hermēneia* may be identical) which explained Homeric glosses, dialect forms, and technical terms; this is already referred to as a standard work of reference in a 3rd-cent. comedy, the *Phoenicides* of Straton.

Although so little of his work has survived, it is clear that Philitas' influence on Hellenistic and Latin poetry was very great. He rather than *Antimachus came to represent the combination of literary scholarship and poetic creativity emulated by *Callimachus and other *poetae docti* or 'learned poets' (e.g. Propertius 3. 1. 1, 3. 3. 52). His poetry was admired for its learning, small scale, and high polish; *Demeter* in particular was highly esteemed (cf. Callimachus, fr. 1. 9–10) and is thought to be the object of many allusions by later poets. It has been conjectured that the character of Philetas in *Longus' novel *Daphnis and Chloe* may be the vehicle for reminiscences of P.'s poems, in which some scholars have detected pastoral elements.

F.W.

Philo (Philon), often known as Philo Judaeus, philosopher, writer and political leader, was the leading exponent of Alexandrian-Jewish culture, and, together with *Josephus, the most significant figure in Jewish-Greek literature. Philo's voluminous works were a formative influence on Neoplatonism and on Christian theology, from the

New Testament on. His family was prominent in the Jewish diaspora and in the service of Rome in the east. The two sons of his brother, Alexander the Alabarch, were Marcus Julius Alexander, husband of *Julius Agrippa I's daughter Berenice, and Tiberius Julius Alexander. The only fixed date in Philo's own life is AD 39/40, when, as an old man, he led the Jewish embassy to *Gaius (1); see section on *Gaius and the Jews*. Apart from those events, he himself seems to have confined his activities to the Alexandrian Jewish community. He made a pilgrimage to Jerusalem, but need not otherwise have had much contact with Palestine. Virtually all his surviving works were apparently preserved in the library of Caesarea built up by *Origen and then by *Eusebius, who catalogues most of them at *HE* 2. 18. Some three-quarters of the corpus consists of exposition of the Pentateuch, in three series, whose order of writing is obscure: *Quaestiones*, which are brief catechetical commentaries in the form of questions and answers, *Legum allegoria*, a more extended and systematic exegesis, and *Exposition*, which sets out the Mosaic laws. The *Life of Moses* was perhaps a separate enterprise, as also the *De vita contemplativa*, which describes the way of life of a group of Egyptian Jewish ascetics called the Therapeutai. Two tracts, *In Flaccum* and the *De legatione ad Gaium*, probably originally one composite work, give a graphic account of the persecutions of the Jews under Gaius and of their political consequences. The *In Flaccum* gives much space to the divine punishment inflicted on the persecutors of the Jews.

Philo operated within the Greek philosophical tradition and deployed an elaborate Greek literary language. At the same time, he was at home with the Greek Bible on which his commentaries were based. The sole authority of the Mosaic law was fundamental to him. The spuriousness of his Hebrew etymologies suggests, but does not prove, that he did not know Hebrew. His ontology was markedly Platonic: to provide a medium for the operation of a perfect God upon an imperfect world, he introduced a range of mediating powers, notably *dunameis* and the *logos*. Philo's ethics are close to Stoicism, but for him true morality is imitation of the Deity.

T.R.

Philochorus (*c.*340–260 BC), son of Cycnus, was a truly Hellenistic man. The mini-biography of him in the *Suda* reveals a man of religion (he was official prophet and diviner in 306), a patriot, who was arrested and put to death by *Antigonus Gonatas for supporting *Ptolemy II Philadelphus at the time of the Chremonidean War, and a scholar-historian, who wrote at least twenty-seven works, of which the most famous was his *Atthis*. His scholarly interests ranged from local history (of Attica, Delos, and Salamis) to chronography (Olympiads), cult (monographs on *Prophecy, Sacrifices, Festivals,* and the *Mysteries at Athens*) and literature (studies on *Euripides and *Alcman). He was the last atthidographer (writer on Attic history) and the most respected, to judge from the number of times his work was cited. Jacoby considered him 'the first scholar' to write an *Atthis*, though this may be unfair to his predecessors.

The *Atthis* was seventeen books long. We have over 170 fragments. From these we can form a good impression of the structure and character of his work. It was arranged in the standard chronological format of the genre, by kings and archons, and presented its information in succinct factual notices in unadorned prose, a good example of which can be found in Dion. Hal. *To Ammaeus* 1. 9. Despite his professional interest in religion, Philochorus only devoted two books to the early period down to *Solon, and two more to the end of the 5th cent. The fourth century, which had been treated in detail by Androtion, was also reduced to two books. The remaining eleven books covered the 60 years from 320–260. So, Philochorus' main interest was the period of his mature years. Unfortunately nothing of significance has survived from these books, because this period did not interest the later scholars who cited him.

In his research Philochorus used documents and his own experience for his own time. For the earlier period he used the *Atthis* of Androtion, as is shown by the frequency with which the two are cited together. By contrast he did not approve of the *Atthis* of his immediate predecessor, Demon, which he criticized in a monograph entitled *Atthis against Demon*. The fragments show that Philochorus was familiar with the works of *Herodotus, *Thucydides, *Ephorus, and *Theopompus. His *Atthis* was a source for the Hellenistic chronographers.   P.E.H.

Philodemus (*c.*110–*c.*40/35 BC), born at Gadara in Syria, died probably at Herculaneum; he came to Rome *c.*75 BC and eventually enjoyed the favour and powerful friendship of the Pisones. One of them, Lucius Calpurnius Piso Caesoninus (consul 58), was especially attached to him and was perhaps the owner of the magnificent villa at Herculaneum. *Cicero's somewhat ironical praise of Philodemus (*Pis.* 28. 68 ff.) shows that he was already well known to a Roman audience for his poetry in 55 BC. His connections with Piso brought Philodemus the opportunity of influencing the brilliant young students of Greek literature and philosophy who gathered around him and Siron at Herculaneum and Naples, as is shown by Philodemus' addresses to and the responses of Rufus Varius (who wrote a *De morte*), *Virgil (cf. his *Appendix* and *Georgics* 3), Plotius Tucca, and *Horace (who names Philodemus in his *Satires*). Although his prose work, discovered in about a thousand papyrus rolls in the philosophical library recovered at Herculaneum, is detailed in the strung-out, non-periodic style typical of Hellenistic Greek prose before the revival of the Attic (imitating Classical Athenian authors) style after Cicero, Philodemus like *Lucretius greatly surpassed the average literary standard to which most Epicureans aspired (see EPICURUS). In his elegant and often indecently frank erotic epigrams, some thirty-five of which are preserved in the *Anthologia Palatina*, together with a hundred or so incipits of these and additional epigrams in a papyrus from Oxyrhynchus, he displays taste and ingenuity worthy of his fellow-citizen Meleager. The success of these poems is proved by the allusions to, and imitations of, them in several passages of Horace, *Propertius, Virgil, and *Ovid. Although Cicero seems to imply that Philodemus' main activity was poetry, he makes clear that he also devoted himself, for Piso's benefit, to popularizing Greek philosophy, which he dealt with both systematically (Rhetoric, Poetics, Music, Ethics, Physics or, rather, Theology) and historically (in his comprehensive History of Philosophers, comprising an outline of the chronology of the Greek philosophical schools in ten books). His works covered a wide field, including in addition psychology, logic, aesthetics, and literary criticism. Particularly remarkable was his theory of art, which he conceived as an autonomous, non-philosophical activity, independent of moral and logical content, according to which artistic worth is determined not by its content or meaning, but by its form or aesthetic value. His particular originality is obscured by the fact that his works were not selected for preservation in the manner of other canonical authors. Philodemus succeeded in influencing the most learned and distinguished Romans of his age. No prose work of Philodemus was known until rolls of papyri, charred but largely legible, containing his writings, were discovered among the ruins of the villa at Herculaneum (now at Naples).   P.T.; D.O.

Philon, of Larissa in Thessaly (159/8–84/3 BC), the last undisputed head of the Academy (the philosophical school at Athens, founded by *Plato). Philon studied for eight or nine years in his native town under Callicles, a pupil of Carneades, before he went to Athens at the age of 24, to study under Clitomachus, whom he succeeded as head of the Academy in 110/9. In 88, during the Mithradatic wars (see MITHRADATES), he left for Rome, where he numbered among his pupils Catulus, father and son (see LUTATIUS CATULUS (1–2), Q.), and *Cicero, who became his most devoted pupil and follower. Philon probably remained in Rome until his death.

Although Philon may have published many books, none of them, not even their titles, have survived, and we know nothing about their form. Some of his teachings are represented in a long passage in *Stobaeus and in Cicero's *Academicus primus* and *Lucullus*.

Under the scholarchate of Philon, the sceptical Academy modified its attitude of strict suspension of judgement and adopted Carneades' account of the 'plausible impression' (Gk. *pithanon*, Lat. *probabile*) as an epistemological theory that would allow philosophers to accept the views they found most convincing, with the proviso that certain knowledge could not be achieved. This may have led to the revival of a more radical version of scepticism by Aenesidemus, who accused the Academics of his time of being 'Stoics fighting other Stoics' (Phot. *Bibl.* cod. 212). It was probably in the two books he wrote at Rome towards the end of his life that Philon went a step further and

claimed that knowledge (*katalēpsis*) was indeed possible, though not by the stringent standards of the Stoic definition. He proceeded to ascribe this view to the Academics from *Plato on, which provoked an angry reaction from his pupil Antiochus of Ascalon in the *Sosus*.

In accordance with the new fallibilism of his school, Philon also taught other philosophical subjects. Like the Stoics, he compared the philosopher to a doctor, and divided the teaching of ethics into five parts corresponding to the stages of a medical therapy (Ar. Did. in Stob. 2. 7. 2), from persuading the pupil of the benefits of philosophy through the elimination of erroneous beliefs and the implanting of healthy views about goods and evils to teaching about the goal of life (*telos*) and advice for everyday living. Cicero tells us that Philon also taught rhetoric alongside philosophy; a combination that Cicero obviously found congenial.

While Philon's mitigated scepticism may be discerned in later self-styled Academics like *Plutarch, his influence on the development of Middle Platonism remains doubtful.
G.S.

Philopoemen (*c.*253–182 BC), son of Craugis of Megalopolis, statesman and general of the Achaean Confederacy, called 'the last of the Greeks' by an anonymous Roman. Philopoemen's first known activity dates from the 220s, when he helped defend Megalopolis against the Spartan king *Cleomenes III (223) and impressed *Antigonus III Doson at the battle of Sellasia. He subsequently spent ten years in Crete as mercenary captain, perhaps serving Macedonian interests. During the First Macedonian War as hipparch (cavalry commander) of the Confederacy (209) and twice *strategos* (chief magistrate and general: 208/7 and 206/5) he defeated and killed the Spartan ruler Machanidas at Mantinea (207). Under Nabis Sparta continued to trouble the Peloponnese. Philopoemen campaigned against him both as volunteer (202/1) and as *strategos* (201/299) and, after six more years in Crete, again as *strategos* (193/2) when, after Nabis' murder by the Aetolians, he united Sparta with the Confederacy, against *Flamininus' wishes.

Sparta's entry to the Confederacy raised the problem of dealing with the masses of Spartans exiled by the social-revolutionary regimes of the last generation. Philopoemen wished to restore only Achaean supporters, but by adopting an uncompromising hostility to traditional Spartan concerns (in 188, after massacring a group of exiles at Compasion, he destroyed Sparta's city-walls and dismantled the characteristic education (*agōgē*) and legal systems, replacing them with Achaean institutions) he provoked opposition even among Achaean friends in Sparta. Spartan opponents appealed against Achaean policies to the Roman senate, which repeatedly suggested solutions, all of which Philopoemen and his supporters (especially Lycortas) rejected—indeed, they refused on principle to recognize any Roman competence in Achaean internal affairs, since Rome had formally recognized Achaean independence by granting a treaty. This rigorous and offensive attitude split Achaean politics also on this issue (Aristaenus, Callicrates), but Philopoemen died before a solution was reached. He was said to have been poisoned after being captured by renegade Messenians (182). At his public funeral Lycortas' son *Polybius carried the urn and later wrote a biography (not extant), and defended his memory in his *Histories*.   R.M.E.

Philoponus, John, *c.* AD 490 to 570s, a Christian Neoplatonist in Alexandria, influenced subsequent science down to Galileo by replacing many of *Aristotle's theories with an account centred on the Christian idea that the universe had an absolute beginning. But because his own Christian theology was unorthodox, he was anathematized in 680, and his scientific influence came to the West belatedly through the Arabs. Seven early commentaries on Aristotle survive, four described as taken from the seminars of his Alexandrian teacher Ammonius son of Hermeias, although he added his own ideas. The commentary on Aristotle's *Physics* (datable to 517) among others may have been revised after 529 to accommodate more anti-Aristotelian theories. In that year, the Christian emperor *Justinian closed the other great Neoplatonist school at Athens, and Philoponus published an attack on the Athenian Neoplatonist *Proclus, who had been Ammonius' own teacher. This attack (*Against Proclus On the Eternity of the World*) was followed by *Against Aristotle on the Eternity of the World*. The most influential of Philo-

ponus' anti-Aristotelian ideas concerned dynamics. Motion in a vacuum is theoretically possible. Again, projectiles are moved by an internal impetus impressed from outside, not by Aristotle's external forces. Later (*De opificio mundi*), Philoponus expanded impetus theory into a unifying system by having God impress different kinds of impetus into bodies at the time of the Creation. From 553, Philoponus concentrated on Christian theology in a series of heretical works which have survived mostly in Syriac. Some, including the *Arbiter* (= *Diaetētēs*) of that year, upheld the Monophysite view that Christ had only one nature, not two, one human and one divine. Later works, including *On the Trinity* (= *On Theology*) published in 567, are apparently committed to Tritheism, the view that the three members of the Trinity are three gods. Still later ones including *On the Resurrection*, written around 574, argued that we will have new resurrection bodies and, as immortal, will cease to be human. Philoponus never held the Alexandrian philosophy chair. He was known as Grammaticus, and two of his works on grammar survive, as do works on many other subjects.   R.R.K.S.

Philostrati Up to four members of this originally Lemnian family can be separated, but not securely. (1) Philostratus son of Verus, a writer of sophistic works of which probably none now survives. (2) His son Lucius Flavius Philostratus ('the Athenian'), who enjoyed both a distinguished local career and a place in the circle of Julia Domna, wife of *Septimius Severus. She commissioned his 'Life' of Apollonius of Tyana, a philosophic holy man of the 1st cent. AD; later he produced 'Lives of the Sophists', and he is probably the author of most of a number of minor pieces, including the *Heroikos*, a dialogue on the heroes of the Trojan War and their cults, a *Gymnastikos* (On Athletic Training) and 'Erotic Epistles'; he died under Philip the Arab (AD 244–9) (*Suda*). He mentions (3) Philostratus the Lemnian, probably great-nephew and son-in-law. Two sets of *Eikones*, descriptions of pictures, survive, attributed to two Philostrati who were grandfather and grandson, either (2) and the exceptionally well connected (3), or (3) and an otherwise unknown (4). Two *Dialexeis* and a brief dramatic dialogue 'Nero' also survive.

The *Life of Apollonius* offers pagan hagiography under a sophistic veneer, and remains suspect both in sources and details; the *Lives of the Sophists* offer the foundation for our knowledge of the Second Sophistic (Greek rhetorical revival of the 2nd–3rd cent.): they are sketches, sometimes affected and tendentious, of prestigious public speakers in action. The *Heroikos* offers an entertaining *aperçu* into how a sophistic writer might extend and 'correct' still vibrant Homeric materials. The first *Eikones* are often charming mythological sketches, purporting to instruct a child on the content of perhaps imaginary pictures; the later set are more perfunctory.

The *œuvre* of the Athenian Philostratus so far as we can judge it offers an illuminating glimpse into sophistic interests and the capacity to infiltrate them into a wide variety of literary fields. But fluency and charm are often at odds with idiosyncrasy and rhetorical bravura, as well as a constantly equivocal attitude to facts and 'the real world'. Philostratus ranks as something of an arbiter of sophistic tastes and values; he is also an index of sophistic shortcomings.

W.M.E.; R.B.; G.A.

Photius (*c*.810–*c*.893), the best of the Byzantine scholars and patriarch of Constantinople in AD 858–67 and 878–86. 'At the pressing entreaty of the Caesar (Bardas), the celebrated Photius renounced the freedom of a secular and studious life, ascended the patriarchal throne, and was alternately excommunicated and absolved by the synods of the East and West. By the confession even of priestly hatred, no art or science, except poetry, was foreign to this universal scholar, who was deep in thought, indefatigable in reading, and eloquent in diction' (Gibbon, ch. 53). His most important work is the *Bibliotheca*, 'Library' (not his title; the alternative *Myriobiblion*, 'Ten Thousand Books', has even less justification), 'a living monument of erudition and criticism' (Gibbon, as above). It is a hastily compiled, ill-arranged critical account in 280 chapters of books read by Photius in the absence of his brother, Tarasius, for whose information, and at whose request, the work was composed. There is conflicting evidence about the date of composition. Theology and history predominate; oratory, romance, philosophy, science, medicine, and lexicography also come within its

scope. Besides its intrinsic value (the criticisms are often felicitous and acute, both from the literary and the bibliographical point of view), it has a considerable adventitious importance as the best or sole source of our information about many notable lost works; it mentions some sixty non-theological works not now surviving. Poetry is almost entirely neglected; but there is other evidence that Photius had read at least the usual school authors, *pace* the implication of Gibbon's remark cited above. The *Lexicon*, which is an earlier work, is a glossary based ostensibly and in fact indirectly upon Aelius Dionysius, Pausanias, and Diogenianus, but immediately drawn from such later compilations as Timaeus' Platonic lexicon, and chiefly from the *Sunagōgē*. The *Lexicon* was long known only from the *Codex Galeanus* at Cambridge, defective at the beginning. Part of the missing portion was then supplied by MSS in Athens and Berlin, and finally in 1959 a MS containing the complete *Lexicon* was found at Zavorda in Macedonia. Some aspects of Photius' scholarship can be illustrated from his *Letters* and *Amphilochia*.

P.B.R.F.; R.B.; N.G.W.

Phrynichus, an early Athenian tragic poet. The *Suda* says that he won his first victory between 511 and 508 BC, was the first to introduce female characters in tragedy, and invented the trochaic tetrameter (the last claim, at least, being certainly false). *Themistocles was his *choregos* (financial backer) for a victorious production in 476 (Plut. *Them.* 5), probably near the end of his career.

At least two of his tragedies were on historical subjects. Soon after 494, when the city of Miletus, which had been aided by Athens, was sacked by the Persians, Phrynichus produced a *Capture of Miletus*, which, according to *Herodotus 6. 21, so distressed the Athenians that they fined him a thousand drachmas 'for reminding them of their own troubles'. The hypothesis to the *Persians* of *Aeschylus quotes Glaucus of Rhegium as saying that Aeschylus modelled the play on the *Phoenician Women* of Phrynichus, but that Phrynichus began his play with a eunuch who related the defeat of Xerxes I of Persia while setting out chairs for the royal councillors (but there may be a confusion here between Phrynichus' *Phoenician Women* and his *Persians*).

Plays on mythical subjects included *Egyptians* and *Danaids* (titles which recall Aeschylus' Danaid tetralogy); *Alcestis*, which influenced *Euripides' *Alcestis* (at least at lines 74–6); *Women of Pleuron*, concerning Meleager; *Actaeon, Antaeus*, and *Tantalus*.

He was remembered for the beauty of his lyrics (Ar. *Wasps* 220, 269, *Birds* 748–51) and for inventive choreography (Ar. *Wasps* 1490, Plut. *Quaest. Conv.* 8. 9. 3). In general he seemed to *Aristophanes (1) to exemplify the 'good old days' of tragedy (also *Thesm.* 164–6, *Frogs* 910, 1299 f.).   A.L.B.

Phylarchus, from Athens or Naucratis in Egypt, Greek historian who lived in the 3rd cent. BC. The fragments are collected in *FGrH* 81. He wrote *Historiai* covering the period from *Pyrrhus' death, 272, to the death of the Spartan king Cleomenes III in 220/19, thereby continuing *Hieronymus of Cardia and Duris of Samos; he adopted Duris' tragic and sensational mode of presentation: cf. Polyb. 2. 56–63 = F 53–6. Phylarchus' partisanship of Cleomenes and his anti-Achaean bias were harshly criticized by *Polybius (see above), himself not an admirer of the king, who denounces Phylarchus' arbitrary and erroneous reporting. His work included numerous digressions of all kinds: miraculous events (F 10, 17, 35), strange animal tales (F 4. 26–28. 38. 61), multifarious anecdotes (F 12, 31, 40, 41, 75), love affairs (F 21, 24, 30, 32, 70, 71, 81). Phylarchus' reliability cannot be rated very highly: despite Strasburger, Polybius' reproach of *terateia* ('sensationalism') is justified. *Plutarch used Phylarchus as his chief authority for the *Agis and Cleomenes* and as one of his sources for the *Pyrrhus* and *Aratus*. Pompeius Trogus also drew on him. The Atticists' low opinion of his style may account for the loss of his work. Only 60 fragments are extant.

Shorter works: *The History of Antiochus and Eumenes of Pergamum* (probably a supplement to the *Historiai* dealing with *Antiochus III the Great, 223–187, and *Eumenes II, 198–160/59); *Mythical Epitomes*, apparently a brief mythical story; *Agrapha* ('Unwritten'), maybe a compilation of mythical traditions which had received no previous literary treatment, cf. fr. 47; *On Inventions*.   K.M.

Pindar, lyric poet, native of Cynoscephalae in Boeotia. He was born probably in 518 BC (*Suda*, fr. 193, if the latter refers to Pindar). The tradition (one of several competing accounts) that he lived to the age of 80 is at least roughly correct, since his last datable composition (*Pyth.* 8) belongs to or shortly after 446. On the basis of *Pyth.* 5. 72 it is widely believed that he belonged to the aristocratic family of the Aegeidae. He achieved panhellenic recognition early; at the age of 20 he was commissioned by the ruling family of Thessaly to celebrate the athletic victory of a favourite youth, Hippocleas (*Pyth.* 10). His commissions covered most of the Greek world, from Macedonia and Abdera in Thrace in the north (fr. 120–1, *Pae.* 2) to Cyrene in Africa in the south (*Pyth.* 4, 5, 9), from Italy and Sicily in the west (*Ol.* 1–5, 10, 11, *Pyth.* 1, 2, 3, 6, *Nem.* 9, *Isthm.* 2) to the seaboard of Asia Minor in the east (*Ol.* 7, *Nem.* 11, fr. 123). He probably travelled a great deal, but we have little information on his movements. He is already a classic for *Herodotus (3. 38), and was regarded by many in antiquity as the greatest of the nine poets of the lyric canon (Quint. 10. 1. 61, Dion. Hal. *On imitation* 2).

The Alexandrian editors divided Pindar's works into 17 books: hymns, paeans, dithyrambs (2 books), *prosodia* (processional songs, 2 books), *partheneia* (maiden-songs, 3 books), *hyporchemata* (dance songs, 2 books), encomia, *threnoi* (dirges) and *epinicia* (victory songs, 4 books). Of these, the only books to survive intact are the choral victory songs composed for the formal celebration of victories in the four panhellenic athletic festivals. His patrons were the great aristocratic houses of the day, and the ruling families of Cyrene, Syracuse, and Acragas. The scale of this section of the corpus indicates the value which Pindar, in common with other Greeks, placed on athletics as a testing ground for the highest human qualities. The victory ode was normally performed either at the athletic festival shortly after the victory or after the victor's return to his native city. Since time for composition and choir training was limited, the former type tends to be brief. Odes composed for performance after the victor's return are usually, though not invariably, lengthier and more elaborate. The longer odes usually have three sections, with the opening and closing sections devoted to the victor and his success and the central section usually containing a mythic narrative. The opening is always striking, often elaborate, consisting either of an abrupt announcement of victory or a focusing process which sets the victory against a general background, usually through a hymnal invocation or a preparatory list of objects, experiences, or achievements (*priamel*). In the sections devoted to the victor conventional elements recur. The god of the games is honoured. Place of victory and event are announced, with details frequently surrendered slowly in order to maintain a forward tension (description of victory is rare, however). Earlier victories by the patron or other members of his family are listed; such lists are carefully crafted to avoid monotony. The city is praised, and in the case of boy victors the father and usually the trainer. Self-praise by the poet is also common. More sombre notes, surprising to the modern reader, are struck. The poet often reminds the victor of his mortality or offers prayers to avert misfortune; these elements reflect the archaic fear of divine envy and awareness of the psychological dangers of success; they function both to warn and to emphasize the extent of the achievement. *Gnomai* (succinct generalizations) are frequent. Recurrent themes are the impossibility of achievement without toil, the need for divine aid for success, the duty to praise victory, the vulnerability of achievement without praise in song, the importance of inborn excellence and the inadequacy of mere learning. The effect of this moralizing is to give the ode a pronounced didactic as well as celebratory quality.

Pindar usually chooses myths dealing with the heroes of the victor's city. As with most Greek lyric, the myth is not narrated in full. Usually a single incident is selected for narration, with other details dealt with briskly. Even the lengthy quasi-epic myth of *Pyth.* 4 proceeds by a series of scenes, not an even narrative. Audience familiarity with the myth is assumed. Unlike his contemporary *Bacchylides, Pindar regularly adopts an explicit moral stance with reference to the events narrated. The role of myth in the odes varies. Sometimes the myth has only a broad relevance to the victor, in that the deeds of the city's heroes highlight the tradition which has produced the victor's qualities. On occasion

myth presents a negative contrast to the victor (such as the Tantalus myth in *Ol.* 1, the Orestes myth of *Pyth.* 11). Often it appears to reflect an aspect of the victory or the victor's situation as developed in the direct praise.

The fragmentary nature of the rest of the corpus makes it difficult to generalize about other genres. The same moralizing quality is present. The structure where ascertainable corresponds to the tripartite structure of the victory odes. The myth is in most cases uncontroversial, since it arises from the location and occasion of the performance.

His poems are written in regular stanzas, either strophic or triadic. With the exception of *Isthm.* 3 and 4, no two poems are identical metrically. Most are composed in the dactylo-epitrite or aeolic metres. His manner of writing is both dense and elaborate. Words are used sparingly. Compound adjectives abound. The style is rich in metaphor, and rapid shifts of metaphor are common. Transition between themes is rapid, and is often effected by formalized claims to be constrained by time or rules of composition or to have lost the way. As his earliest and last datable compositions (*Pyth.* 10 and 8) show, he adhered throughout his life to a conservative set of standards. His thought impresses not for its originality but the consistency and conviction with which he presents the world view of the aristocrat of the late Archaic period. His religion is the traditional Olympian religion, combined in *Ol.* 2 with the dirges with elements of mystery cult and Orphico-Pythagorean belief.   C.C.

Pisistratus, tyrant of Athens, claimed descent from the Neleids of Pylos and Pisistratus, archon at Athens 669/8 BC. He first came to prominence through his success in the war against Megara (*c.*565). In a period of aristocratic faction between Lycurgus and the *Pedieis* (party 'of the Plain') and Megacles and *Paralioi* (coast party), he created a third faction, the *Hyperakrioi* or *Diakrioi* (referring to 'hill country', probably NE Attica: the factions probably reflect regional bases of support, Hdt. 1. 59). He first seized power with the bodyguard granted him by the Athenians (*c.*560). Ousted by the other two factions, he returned again with Megacles' allegiance and, if we can extract anything from the ruse in *Herodotus (1. 60), a claim to the protection of Athena. However the alliance with the Alcmaeonid family disintegrated and he went into a 10-year exile, settling Rhaecelus in Macedonia, mustering support from Eretria, other cities (e.g. Thebes) and from the mines of Mt. Pangaeus (*Ath. Pol.* 15; Hdt. 1. 64). Armed with money and Argive mercenaries, he landed near Marathon, *c.*546, defeated opposition at the battle of Pallene, and established the tyranny for 36 years. He died in 527.

Sources agree that Pisistratus' rule, financed by a 5 per cent tax and perhaps family resources from the Strymon area, was benevolent and law-abiding (esp. Thuc. 6. 54; a 'golden age', *Ath. Pol.* 16. 7). Despite the mention of exiles (Hdt. 1. 64), he seems to have achieved a *modus vivendi* with other aristocratic families (who are later found holding archonships). Strained relations with the Philaids may have been eased by *Miltiades' colonization of the Chersonesus (Hdt. 6. 34–41), whose strategic importance suggests it had Pisistratus' blessing. Athenian interests were strengthened by Pisistratus' control of Naxos (Hdt. 1. 64), and recapture of Sigeum, foreshadowing Athens' later maritime expansion. He lent money to poor farmers and instituted travelling judges (*Ath. Pol.* 16).

From the 560s, Athens begins to acquire a monumental appearance and become a panhellenic artistic centre (J. Herington, *Poetry into Drama* (1985), ch. 4). The archaeological record indicates rapidly increasing prosperity, as Attic black figure becomes (from the 560s) the dominant exported pottery. How much can be linked to Pisistratus' personal efforts, rather than to the indirect effects of internal peace and external expansion, is uncertain and controversial, and purely archaeological evidence is inconclusive. The Panathenaea festival, reorganized in 566/5, and City Dionysia festival prospered, but Pisistratus cannot securely be credited with establishing the former, nor erecting the (so-called 'old') temple of Athena on the Acropolis built about the same time. The beginning of Athenian coinage, attested archaeologically by 550, might imply the ruler's support. It is likely, however, that, like other archaic aristocrats, he used religious cult to consolidate his position (Davies *APF* pp. 454–5; D. Lewis, *Hist.* 1963, 22 ff.) or enhance *polis* (city-state) cohesion; and that he was a great builder, like his sons. He purified the Ionian religious centre of Delos and instituted a festival there (Thuc. 3. 104). Other cults to Apollo were probably fostered by him in Athens, that of Pythian Apollo and (perhaps) Apollo Patroos (first temple built, in the Agora, *c.*550); and perhaps other cults (see H. Shapiro, *Art and Cult under the Tyrants in Athens* (1989)). It has been suggested, purely on pottery evidence, that he claimed special association with Heracles (J. Boardman, *Rev. Arch.* 1972, 57 ff.) as well as Athena's protection. Of secular buildings, as well as the Enneakrounos fountain-house (Paus. 1. 14. 1), he can probably be associated with other building in the Agora in the third quarter of the 6th cent., including the Stoa Basileios and the mysterious 'Building F': in short with the further clearing of the Agora and its development as civic centre.   R.Th.

Plancus, Lucius Munatius, of senatorial family, served under *Julius Caesar in the Gallic and Civil Wars, was probably praetor late 47 BC, and in 45 was one of Caesar's six prefects of the city (see *RRC* 475). Proconsul of Gallia Comata ('Long-haired Gaul') after Caesar's death, he invaded Raetia, winning a minor victory, and founded the colonies of Lugdunum and Raurica (later Augusta Raurica). In letters to Cicero (*Fam.* 10) he asserted his loyalty to the republic, while advising peace with Mark *Antony. He left D. Junius Brutus Albinus, probably after Octavian's march on Rome, joining Antony and *Lepidus. In the triumviral proscriptions he was said to have put his brother's name on the list. In December 43 he triumphed (over Gaul or Raetia), became consul 42 with Lepidus, and then or later restored the temple of Saturn out of his triumphal spoils (*ILLRP* 43; cf. Suet. *Aug.* 29. 5). In the Perusine War he failed to assist Lucius Antonius (Pietas), then escaped with Fulvia to Antony in Greece. After governing Asia (40) and, during Antonius' Parthian campaign, Syria as Antonius' deputy (35: he is said to have ordered the execution of Sextus *Pompey), he joined Antonius in Alexandria and outdid himself in flattery of *Cleopatra VII. Before the battle of Actium he joined Octavian with his nephew Marcus Titius, later claiming that he had refused to fight for Cleopatra. In 27 he moved that Octavian be called Augustus. In 22 he was censor, with Paullus Aemilius Lepidus. He was buried at Caieta (mod.

Gaeta), where his tomb inscription was found (*ILS* 886). His son Lucius was consul AD 13, his daughter Munatia Plancina married Gnaeus Calpurnius Piso (see GERMANICUS).   G.W.R.; T.J.C.; E.B.

Plato of Athens, *c.*429–347 BC, descended from wealthy and influential Athenian families on both sides. His own family, like many, was divided by the disastrous political consequences of the Peloponnesian War between Athens and the Spartan alliance. His stepfather Pyrilampes was a democrat and friend of *Pericles, but two of his uncles, *Critias and Charmides, became members of the Thirty Tyrants. At some point Plato renounced ambition for a public career, devoting his life to philosophy. The major philosophical influence on his life was Socrates, but in three important respects Plato turned away from the example of *Socrates. He rejected marriage and the family duty of producing citizen sons; he founded a philosophical school, the Academy; and he produced large quantities of written philosophical works (as well as the shadowy 'unwritten doctrines' produced at some point in the Academy, for which we have only secondary evidence).

Plato's works are all in the form of dialogues in which he does not himself appear. The philosophical point of this is to detach him from the arguments which are presented. Plato is unique among philosophers in this constant refusal to present ideas as his own, forcing the reader to make up his or her own mind about adopting them—a strategy which works best in the shorter dialogues where arguments are presented in a more lively way. For Plato this detachment and use of dialogue is not a point of style, but an issue of epistemology: despite various changes of position on the issue of knowledge, he remains convinced throughout that anything taken on trust, second-hand, either from others or from books, can never amount to a worthwhile cognitive state; knowledge must be achieved by effort from the person concerned. Plato tries to stimulate thought rather than to hand over doctrines.

This detachment also makes Plato himself elusive, in two ways. First, we know very little about him personally. Later biographies are patently constructed to 'explain' aspects of the dialogues. The seventh of a series of

'letters by Plato' has been accepted as genuine by some scholars, and has been used to create a historical background to the dialogues. But such 'letters' are a recognized fictional genre; it is very unwise to use such material to create a basis for the arguments in the dialogues, which are deliberately presented in a detached way. To try to explain the dialogues by appeal to a 'life and letters', though tempting since antiquity, is to miss the point of Plato's procedure, which is to force us to respond to the ideas in the dialogues themselves, not to judge them by our view of the author.

Second, the dialogues themselves are extremely varied and interpretatively often quite open. Since antiquity there has been a debate as to whether Plato's philosophical legacy should be taken to be one of a set of doctrines, or of continuing debate and argument. The middle, sceptical Academy read Plato for the arguments, and Plato's heritage was taken to be a continuation of the practice of argument against contemporary targets. The dialogue most favourable to this kind of interpretation is the *Theaetetus*, in which Socrates presents himself as a barren midwife, drawing ideas out of others but putting forward none himself. However, even in antiquity we find the competing dogmatic reading of Plato, in which the dialogues are read as presenting pieces of doctrine which the reader is encouraged to put together to produce 'Platonism', a distinctive system of beliefs. The dogmatic reading has to cope with the diverse nature of the dialogues and the unsystematic treatment of many topics, with apparent conflicts between dialogues and with the changing and finally disappearing role of Socrates as the chief figure. These problems are often solved by appeal to some development of Plato's thought, although there have been 'unitarians' about Plato's ideas since Arius Didymus declared, 'Plato has many voices, not, as some think, many doctrines' (Stobaeus, *Eclogae* 2. 55. 5–6).

Since the 19th cent. much energy has been expended on the chronology of the dialogues, but, in spite of computer-based work, no stylistic tests establish a precise order. In any case a chronology of the dialogues is only interesting if it tracks some independently established development of Plato's thought, and attempts to establish this easily fall into circularity where they do not rest on the dubious 'life and letters'. Stylistically, however, the dialogues fall into three comparatively uncontroversial groups: (1) the 'Socratic' dialogues, in which Socrates is the main figure, questioning others about their own positions but arguing for none himself, though characteristic views of his own emerge. This group includes *Ion, Laches, Lysis, Apology, Euthyphro, Charmides, Menexenus, Hippias Major, Hippias Minor, Protagoras, Crito, Cleitophon, Alcibiades, Lovers, Hipparchus* (the last two are often doubted as Plato's work, and since the 19th cent. this has been true of the *Alcibiades*, never doubted in antiquity). Two dialogues generally regarded as transitional between the Socratic and middle dialogues are *Gorgias* and *Meno*. Two dialogues which use the Socratic format but have much in common with the later works are *Euthydemus* and *Theaetetus*. (2) the 'middle' dialogues, in which Socrates remains the chief figure, but, no longer undermining others' views, sets out, at length, many positive ideas: this group includes *Phaedo, Republic, Symposium,* and *Phaedrus*. (3) the 'later' dialogues, in which Socrates retreats as the main interlocutor, and Plato deals at length, sometimes critically, with his own ideas and those of other philosophers, in a newly detailed and increasingly technical and 'professional' way: this group includes *Cratylus, Parmenides, Sophist, Statesman, Philebus,* and *Laws*. *Timaeus* and *Critias* are most often put in this group, but there are arguments for placing them with the middle dialogues.

There is no uncontroversial way of presenting Plato's thought. Many aspects of his work invite the reader to open-ended pursuit of the philosophical issues; others present her with more developed positions, substantial enough to be characterized as 'Platonic' even for those who reject the more rigid forms of the dogmatic reading. While no brief survey of Plato's varied and fertile thought can be adequate, some major themes recur and can be traced through several works.

ETHICAL AND POLITICAL THOUGHT
Plato is throughout insistent on the objectivity of values, and on the importance of morality in the individual's life. The 'protreptic' passage in the *Euthydemus* anticipates the Stoics in its claim that what are called 'goods' (health, wealth, and so on) are not really so; the only good thing is the virtuous person's

knowledge of how to make use of these things in a way consonant with morality. The assumption is explicitly brought out that everyone pursues happiness, though we have, prior to philosophical reflection, little idea of what it is, and most confuse it with worldly success; the choice of virtue is embodied in the worldly failure Socrates. Many of the Socratic dialogues show Socrates trying to get people to rethink their priorities, and to live more morally; he is sure that there is such a thing as virtue, though he never claims to have it. He further identifies virtue with the wisdom or understanding that is at its basis, the unified grasp of principles which enables the virtuous to act rightly in a variety of situations, and to explain and justify their decisions and actions.

In the *Protagoras*, we find the claim that this wisdom will be instrumental in achieving pleasure; this view is examined respectfully, and although we find attacks on the idea that pleasure could be our end in the *Phaedo* and *Gorgias*, Plato reverts to some very hedonistic-seeming thoughts in the *Philebus* and *Laws*. Arius Didymus compares Plato with *Democritus as a kind of hedonist, and clearly he is tempted at times by the idea that some form of pleasure is inescapably our aim, although after the *Protagoras* he never thinks that our reason might be merely instrumental to achieving it. Apart from cryptic and difficult hints in the *Philebus*, he never achieves a substantive characterization of the virtuous person's understanding.

In some of the early and middle dialogues Plato conflates the wisdom of the virtuous individual with that of the virtuous *ruler*; the skill of running one's own life is run together with that of achieving the happiness of others. The culmination of this is the *Republic*, where individual and state are similar in structure, and the virtuous individual is produced only in the virtuous state. Later Plato divides these concerns again, so that the *Philebus* is concerned with individual, and the *Laws* with social morality.

Plato's treatment of social and political matters is marked by a shift of emphasis between two strands in his thought. One is his conviction that the best solution to political problems is the exercise of expert judgement: in an individual life what is needed is overall grasp based on correct understanding of priorities, and similarly in a state what is needed is expert overall understanding of the common good. This conviction is triumphant in the *Republic*, where the rulers, the Guardians, have power to run the lives of all citizens in the state in a very broadly defined way: laws serve the purpose of applying the Guardians' expert knowledge, but do not stand in its way. Expert knowledge gives its possessor the right to enforce on others what the expert sees to be in their true interests, just as the patient must defer to the doctor and the crew to the ship's captain.

Plato is also, however, aware of the importance of law in ensuring stability and other advantages. In the *Crito* the Laws of Athens claim obedience from Socrates (though on a variety of unharmonized grounds). In the *Statesman* Plato admits that, although laws are in the real world a clog on expertise, they embody the past results of expertise and are therefore to be respected, indeed obeyed absolutely in the absence of an expert. In the *Laws*, where Plato has given up the hope that an actual expert could exist and rule uncorrupted by power, he insists that problems of political division and strife are to be met by complete obedience to laws, which are regarded as the product of rational reflection and expertise, rather than the haphazard product of party strife.

Plato's best-known contribution to political thought is his idea, developed in the *Republic*, that individual (more strictly the individual's soul) and state are analogous in structure. Justice in the state is the condition in which its three functionally defined parts—the rulers, the rulers' auxiliaries, and the rest of the citizens (the producers)—work in harmony, guided by the expert understanding of the rulers, who, unlike the others, grasp what is in the common interest. Analogously, justice in the individual is the condition where the three parts of the individual's soul work in harmony. What this condition will be will differ for members of the three classes. All the citizens have souls whose parts are: reason, which discerns the interest of the whole or at least can be guided by grasp of someone else's reason which does; 'spirit', the emotional side of the person; and desire, the collection of desires aimed at their own satisfaction regardless of the interests of the whole. For all, justice consists in the rule of reason, and the subordination of spirit and the desires; but what this demands is different

for the rulers, who understand and can articulate the requirements of reason, and for the producers, who do not. It is notable that Plato identifies this condition of soul, which he calls psychic harmony, with justice, quite contrary to Greek intuitions about political justice. In the *Republic*, the citizen's justice consists in identifying his or her overall interest, to the extent that that is possible, with the common interest, and this idea is taken to notorious lengths in the central books, where the rulers are to live a life in which individuality is given the least possible scope. Opinions have always differed as to whether the *Republic* is a contribution to political theory, or a rejection of the very basis of political theory, one which refuses to solve political conflicts, but unrealistically eliminates their sources. The *Republic* has always been most inspiring as a 'pattern laid up in heaven' for individuals to use in the pursuit of individual justice.

KNOWLEDGE AND ITS OBJECTS In the early dialogues, Socrates is constantly in search for knowledge; this is provoked, not by sceptical worries about knowledge of matters of fact, but by the desire to acquire, on a larger and deeper scale, the kind of expert knowledge displayed by craftspeople. Socrates does not doubt that such globally expert knowledge, which he calls wisdom, exists, nor that it would be most useful in the understanding and running of one's life, but he never claims to have it, and in the Socratic dialogues differences show up between it and everyday kinds of expert knowledge. Sophists, particularly Hippias, are ridiculed as people who uncontroversially have everyday skills, but are shown up as totally lacking in the kind of global understanding which Socrates is seeking.

Socrates' conception of wisdom is an ambitious one; the person with this expert knowledge has a unified overall grasp of the principles which define his field and (as is stressed in the *Gorgias*) he can give a *logos* or account of what it is that he knows, enabling him to explain and justify the judgements that he makes. In several dialogues this demand for giving a *logos* becomes more stringent, and prior conditions are set on an adequate answer. The person who putatively has knowledge of X is required to give an answer as to what X is which is in some way explanatory of the way particular things and kinds of thing are X. The answer is said to provide a 'form' which is itself in some way X, indeed X in a way which (unlike the Xness of other things) precludes ever being the opposite of X in any way. A number of complex issues arise over these 'forms', hotly disputed by scholars and with respect to which the text gives suggestive but incomplete suggestions.

In the Socratic dialogues there is a noteworthy mismatch between the goal of wisdom and the method that Socrates employs; for the latter is the procedure of *elenchus*, the testing of the opponent's views by Socrates' tenacious arguments. But the *elenchus* is a method that shows only inconsistency between beliefs; it has no resources for proving truth. Its result is negative; we have demonstrations as to what friendship, courage, piety, and the like are not, but none as to what they are. In the *Meno* a different approach emerges; the theory of 'recollection' stresses that a person can get knowledge by thinking in a way not dependent on experience, and therefore entirely through his own intellectual resources. Although the *Meno* is not careful to restrict knowledge entirely to such *a priori* knowledge, Plato goes on to develop an account of knowledge in which the model of skill is replaced by that of non-empirical, particularly mathematical reasoning. In the *Phaedo* and *Republic* Plato stresses both the non-empirical nature of the objects of knowledge, the forms, and the structured and hierarchical nature of knowledge. Understanding now requires grasp of an entire connected system of thought, and insight into the difference between the basic and the derived elements, and the ways in which the latter are dependent on the former. As the conditions for having knowledge become higher, knowledge becomes an ever more ideal state; in the *Republic* it is only to be achieved by an intellectually gifted élite, who have spent many years in unremittingly abstract intellectual activities, and have lived a life strenuously devoted to the common good. In the *Republic* Plato's account of knowledge, theoretically demanding yet practically applicable, is his most extensive and ambitious.

In later dialogues this synthesis, though never repudiated, lapses. In the *Statesman* we find that theoretical and practical knowledge are now carefully separated; in the *Laws* a continued stress on the importance of math-ematics does little work, and contrasts with the work's extensive and explicit reliance on experience. The *Theaetetus* examines knowledge with a fresh and lively concern, attacking various forms of relativism and subjectivism, but without reference to the *Republic* account.

Plato continues to talk about forms, but in elusive and often puzzling ways. The one sustained passage which appears to discuss forms as they appear in the *Phaedo* and *Republic* is wholly negative—the first part of the *Parmenides*, where various powerful arguments are brought against this conception of forms, and no answers are supplied. Whatever Plato's own opinion of these arguments (some of them resembling arguments in early *Aristotle), forms in later dialogues revert to a role more like their earlier one. They are the objective natures of things, the objects of knowledge, and are to be grasped only by the exercise of thought and enquiry, not by reliance on experience. *Statesman* 262b–263d discusses the way that language can be misleading: there is no form of foreigner, since 'foreigner' simply means 'not Greek', and things are not put into a unified kind by not being Greek. There is no single method, other than the continued use of enquiry, to determine which of our words do in fact pick out kinds that are natural, rather than merely contrived. However, Plato, though never renouncing forms as a demand of objectivity in intellectual enquiry, ceases to attach to them the mystical and exalted attitudes of the middle dialogues.

SOUL AND THE COSMOS Throughout the dialogues Plato expresses many versions of the idea that a person's soul is an entity distinct from the living embodied person, attached to it by a relation which is inevitable but unfortunate. In the *Phaedo* several arguments for the soul's immortality show that Plato is dealing indiscriminately with a number of different positions as to what the soul is: the principle of life, the intellect, the personality. The latter two are the ideas most developed. Soul as the intellect is the basis of Plato's tendency to treat knowledge as what transcends our embodied state; in the *Meno* learning a geometrical proof is identified with the person's soul recollecting what it knew before birth. Soul as the personality is the basis of Plato's use of myths of transmigration of souls and afterlife rewards and punishments. In the middle dialogues these two ideas are united: the *Phaedrus* gives a vivid picture of souls caught on a wheel of ongoing rebirth, a cycle from which only philosophical understanding promises release.

Plato's use of the idea that souls are immortal and are endlessly reborn into different bodies is a metaphorical expression of a deep body–soul dualism which also takes other forms. He tends to draw sharp oppositions between active thinking and passive reliance on sense-experience, and to think of the senses as giving us merely unreflected and unreliable reports; the middle dialogues contain highly coloured disparagements of the world as revealed to us through the senses. However, there is also a strain in Plato which sets against this a more unified view of the person. In the *Symposium* he develops the idea that erotic love can be sublimated and refined in a way that draws the person to aspire to philosophical truth; in the *Phaedrus* he holds that this need not lead to repudiation of the starting-point. In the *Republic* the soul has three parts, two of which are closely connected with the body; but in the final book only the thinking part achieves immortality.

The *Timaeus*, an account of the natural world cast in the form of a description of how it was made by a creator god, treats the world itself as a living thing, with body and soul, and a fanciful cosmic account is developed. Other later dialogues, particularly the *Philebus*, also introduce the idea that our souls are fragments of a cosmic soul in the world as a whole. Many aspects of the *Timaeus*' cosmology depend on the assumption that the world itself is a living thing.

LATER PROBLEMS AND METHODS The later dialogues do not display the same literary concerns as the Socratic and middle ones, nor do they contain the same themes. Rather, Plato moves to engaging with the ideas of other philosophers, and his own earlier ones, in a way strikingly unlike his earlier way of doing philosophy by his earlier use of dialogue. In the later works the dialogue form is often strained by the need for exposition, and they are sometimes heavy and pedagogical. However, dialogue is often used brilliantly for long stretches of argument, as in the *Parmenides* and *Sophist*.

The *Sophist* presents, in a passage of challenging argument, Plato's solution to *Parmenides' challenge about the coherence of talking about not-being. The *Timaeus* takes up the challenge of cosmology, replying to earlier thinkers with different cosmological assumptions. More fanciful treatment of cosmology is found in the *Statesman*. The *Cratylus* discusses questions of language and etymology in a semi-playful but systematic way. The unfinished *Critias* and the *Statesman* take up questions of political theory, discussing them by means previously rejected, like fiction and accounts which take folk memory and myth seriously. The *Philebus*, discussing the place of pleasure in the good life, does so in a context of Pythagorean metaphysics. The *Laws* sketches an ideal state with considerable help from the lessons of history and of actual politics. These works show a larger variety of interests than hitherto, and an increased flexibility of methodology. Plato in these works shows both a greater respect for the view of others and an enlarged willingness to learn from experience, tradition and history. *Laws* 3 is a precursor of Aristotle's detailed research into political history. It is not surprising that we find many ideas which remind us of his pupil Aristotle, and the latter's methods and concerns, from the 'receptacle' of the *Timaeus*, suggestive of matter, to the treatment of the 'mean' in the *Statesman*.

Plato is original, radical, and daring, but also elusive. His ideas are locally clear and uncompromising, and globally fragmented, perennially challenging the reader to join in the dialogue and take up the challenge, following the argument where it leads.   J.A.

Plautus (Titus Maccius Plautus), comic playwright, author of *fabulae palliatae* (comedies) between *c.*205 and 184 BC; plays by Plautus are the earliest Latin works to have survived complete. The precise form of his name is uncertain, and in any case each element of it may have been a nickname (see A. S. Gratwick, *CQ* 1973, 78 ff.). He is said to have come from Sarsina in Umbria, inland from Ariminum (Jerome, Festus; an inference from the joke at *Mostellaria* 769 f.?), made money in some kind of theatrical employment, lost it in a business venture, and been reduced to working in a mill (Gell. *NA* 3. 3. 14 f., probably all fictitious). Gell. *NA* 3. 3 records that 130 plays were attributed to him but that the authenticity of most was disputed; Varro had drawn up a list of 21 plays which were generally agreed to be by Plautus, and there can be little doubt that these are the 21 transmitted in our manuscripts and listed at the end below (though Varro himself believed some others to be genuine as well). Nearly 200 further lines survive in later quotations (many of one line or less), attributed to over 30 named plays.

The *didascaliae* (production notices) give dates of 200 BC for *Stichus* (at the Plebeian Games) and 191 for *Pseudolus* (Megalesian Games), on the dedication of the temple of Cybele. There is general agreement that *Cistellaria* and *Miles Gloriosus* are relatively early plays, *Bacchides, Casina, Persa, Trinummus,* and *Truculentus* late, but the dating of most plays is quite uncertain; the criteria usually invoked are (alleged) contemporary references and relative frequency of *cantica* (parts with musical accompaniment), but neither yields indisputable results.

The plays are nearly all either known or assumed to be adaptations of (Greek) New Comedy, with plots portraying love affairs, confusion of identity and misunderstandings; the strongest candidates for (Greek) Middle Comedy are *Amphitruo* (Plautus' only mythological comedy) and *Persa* (because of the reference to a Persian expedition into Arabia at line 506). For eight plays the prologue names the author or title, or both, of the Greek original: *Diphilus is named as the author for *Casina* and *Rudens*, *Philemon for *Mercator* and *Trinummus*, the otherwise unknown Demophilus for *Asinaria*; titles alone are given for *Miles Gloriosus* and *Poenulus*; the prologue of *Vidularia* is very fragmentary but seems to have given at least the title of the original. In addition, *Bacchides, Cistellaria,* and *Stichus* are known to be based on plays by *Menander, and *Aulularia* is widely believed to be. We cannot always be sure what titles Plautus himself gave his plays, but in about half these cases he seems to have changed it from the Greek original, and the titles of nearly all his plays have at least been Latinized. Scholars influenced by *Terence's invocation of Plautine precedent at *Andria* prologue 18 used to think they could show that Plautus had in some cases incorporated material from another Greek play into his adaptation; it is now commoner to believe in free invention of some material

by Plautus. Attempts have even been made to show that he sometimes took no specific Greek original as his model, so far without success. But he adapted his models with considerable freedom and wrote plays that are in several respects quite different from anything we know of New Comedy. There is a large increase in the musical element. The roles of stock characters such as the parasite appear to have been considerably expanded. Consistency of characterization and plot development are cheerfully sacrificed for the sake of an immediate effect. The humour resides less in the irony of the situation than in jokes and puns. There are 'metatheatrical' references to the audience and to the progress of the play (e.g. *Pseudolus* 388, 562 ff., 720–1), or explicit reminders (as at *Stichus* 446–8) that the play is set in Greece. Above all, there is a constant display of verbal fireworks, with alliteration, wordplays, unexpected personifications (e.g. *Rudens* 626, 'Twist the neck of wrongdoing'), and riddling expressions (e.g. *Mercator* 361, 'My father's a fly: you can't keep anything secret from him, he's always buzzing around'). Both the style of humour and the presentation of stock characters may well have been influenced by the *Atellana* (low-life masked comedies), but the verbal brilliance is Plautus' own.

The Greek originals have not survived, but a tattered papyrus published by Handley in 1968 contains the lines on which *Bacchides* 494–561 are based (from Menander's *Dis Exapaton*, 'The Double Deceiver'), for the first time enabling us to study Plautus' techniques of adaptation at first hand, and confirming the freedom of his approach. Plautus has preserved the basic plot and sequence of scenes, but he has cut two scenes altogether and has contrived to avoid a pause in the action where there was an act-break in the original. The tormented monologue of a young man in love has had some jokes added to it. Passages spoken without musical accompaniment in the original Greek are turned into accompanied passages in longer lines. The play is still set in Athens, and the characters have Greek-sounding names; but Plautus has changed most of them, in particular that of the scheming slave who dominates the action, called Syrus (The Syrian) in Menander's play; Plautus calls him Chrysalus (Goldfinger) and adds some colour elsewhere in the play by punning on this name. Chrysalus even boasts of his superiority to slaves called Syrus (649)!

The plots show considerable variety, ranging from the character study of *Aulularia* (the source of Molière's *L'Avare*) to the transvestite romp of *Casina*, from the comedy of mistaken identity in *Amphitruo* and *Menaechmi* (both used by Shakespeare in *The Comedy of Errors*) to the more movingly ironic recognition comedy of *Captivi* (unusual in having no love interest). *Trinummus* is full of high-minded moralizing; *Truculentus* shows the triumph of an utterly amoral and manipulative prostitute. In several plays it is the authority-figure, the male head of the household, who comes off worst: *Casina* and *Mercator* show father and son competing for the love of the same girl, while at the end of *Asinaria* the father is caught by his wife as he tries to share his son's beloved; other plays (above all *Bacchides*, *Epidicus*, *Mostellaria*, and *Pseudolus*) glorify the roguish slave, generally for outwitting the father. These plays have been seen as providing a holiday release from the tensions of daily life, and their Greek setting must have helped: a world in which young men compete with mercenary soldiers for a long-term relationship with a prostitute was probably quite alien to Plautus' first audiences, a fantasy world in which such aberrations as the domination of citizens by slaves could safely be contemplated as part of the entertainment.

Plautus is at his most exuberant in the *cantica*, operatic arias and duets written in a variety of metres, with considerable technical virtuosity, and displaying many features of high-flown style. They often do little or nothing to advance the action, and we know of nothing like them in Greek New Comedy. *Cantica* come in many contexts, e.g. in the mouths of young men in love (as at *Cistellaria* 203–28, *Mostellaria* 84–156, *Trinummus* 223–75), or of 'running slaves', who rush on to the stage in great excitement to deliver an important piece of news but take the time to deliver a lengthy monologue about its importance (as at *Mercator* 111–30, *Stichus* 274–307, *Trinummus* 1008–58). Chrysalus has two strikingly boastful *cantica* at *Bacchides* 640–66 and 925–77. Some of his boasting is embroidered with triumph-imagery and other peculiarly Roman references; it is part of the fantasy of Plautus' Greek world that it can include Italian elements. Thus at *Pseudolus* 143 and 172 the pimp Ballio in addressing the members of his establishment speaks as a Roman magistrate issuing an official edict, and at *Menaechmi* 571 ff. the complaints about the duties of a patron are concerned entirely with social problems at Rome in Plautus' day. But such explicit comment on Roman matters is rare.

Plautus' plays continued to be performed with success at Rome at least until the time of Horace, and they were read by later generations. The earliest surviving manuscript is the 6th-cent. 'Ambrosian palimpsest'. Plautus was well known in Renaissance Italy, particularly after the rediscovery of twelve plays in a manuscript found in Germany in 1429, and his plays were performed and imitated all over Europe until the seventeenth century, and more sporadically thereafter. Terence was more widely read in schools, but both contributed to the development of the European comic tradition.   P.G.M.B.

Pliny the Elder (AD 23/4–79), Gaius Plinius Secundus, prominent Roman equestrian, from Novum Comum (mod. Como) in Gallia Cisalpina, commander of the fleet at Misenum (Roman naval base in the bay of Naples), and uncle of *Pliny the Younger, best known as the author of the 37-book *Naturalis Historia*, an encyclopaedia of all contemporary knowledge—animal, vegetable, and mineral—but with much that is human included too: *natura, hoc est vita, narratur* ('Nature, which is to say Life, is my subject', *pref.* 13).

Characteristic of his age and background in his range of interests and diverse career, Pliny obtained an equestrian command through the patronage of Quintus Pomponius Secundus (consul 41), and served in Germany, alongside the future emperor *Titus. Active in legal practice in the reign of *Nero, he was then promoted by the favour of the Flavians (and probably the patronage of Licinius Mucianus, whose works he also often quotes) through a series of high procuratorships (including that of Hispania Tarraconensis), in which he won a reputation for integrity. He became a member of the council of *Vespasian and Titus, and was given the command of the Misenum fleet. When Vesuvius erupted on 24 August 79, duty and curiosity combined, fatally; he led a detachment to the disaster-area, landed at

Stabiae, and died from inhaling fumes. For his career and death two letters of his nephew (Pliny, *Ep.* 3. 5 and 6. 16) are the primary source (also Suet. *Rel.* fr. 80 Reifferscheid).

Throughout this career Pliny was phenomenally productive of literary work. His cavalry command produced a monograph on the use of the throwing-spear by cavalrymen, piety towards his patron demanded a biography in two books. The *Bella Germaniae* in 20 books recounted Roman campaigns against the Germans, and was used by *Tacitus in the *Annales* and *Germania*. *Studiosi* in 3 long books (two rolls each) was a collection of *sententiae* from *controversiae* for use by orators, and *Dubius sermo*, reconciling the claims of analogy and anomaly in Latin diction, reflect his period of legal employment—and the dangers of composing anything less anodyne in the latter years of Nero. The years of his procuratorships produced a 31-book history continuing the historian Aufidius Bassus and covering the later Julio-Claudian period; and, dedicated to Titus, the *Naturalis Historia*.

Pliny was clearly impressed by scale, number, comprehensiveness, and detail. It is characteristic that he claims that there are 20,000 important facts derived from 2,000 books in his work (*pref.* 17), but this is a severe underestimate. The value of what he preserves of the information available to him (the more so since he usually attributes his material to its source) far outweighs the fact that when he can be checked against the original (as with *Theophrastus, for instance), he not infrequently garbles his information through haste or insufficient thought. To give only four examples: our study of ancient agriculture, medicine, the techniques of metallurgy, and the canon of great artists in antiquity, would all be impoverished if the work had perished. So dependent are we on him for many technical fields, that it becomes essential to remember that, mania for inclusiveness notwithstanding, his was a selection of what was available to him (and is indeed—creditably—slanted where possible towards his own experience). The argument from literary silence about many matters of economic and social importance is thus often essentially an argument from the silence of Pliny, and therefore methodologically very limited. It still has to be said that he can scarcely be blamed for not applying the

standards of empirical enquiry to ancient medical lore, or for sharing widespread misconceptions about the world. Indeed, one of the interesting aspects of the work is the eloquent witness that he provides for precisely these pre-scientific ways of thinking.

Pliny was no philosopher. It may indeed be thought refreshing to have a view of the ancient world from an author who did not have some claim to the philosophical viewpoint; certainly the sections where Pliny's thought is least accessible are often those where subject matter such as the Cosmos or the Divine take him away from the relatively concrete. Even here, though, there is an engaging personality at work, and there are enough asides and reflections on the world to give an impression of the author which, though it resembles, to an extent, the persona adopted by other Latin technical writers such as *Vitruvius or *Frontinus (and is deeply conscious of what literary work it is proper to expect from an important equestrian, but not a senator) is still highly individual: as is the style and the imagery, which was often misunderstood in later antiquity, and can still baffle today. The standard ethical diatribe against luxury and aristocratic excess of the man from the municipality is given vivid historical and geographical colour, and if the Roman past is idealized it is partly through the evocation of an image of the *populus Romanus* which is among the least hostile treatments of the many in any ancient author. The themes of the sufficient excellence of the natural endowment of Italy, and the terrible moral threat posed by the differential value of the exotic, form a laconic and memorable conclusion to book 37 (described in book 1, end as *Comparatio naturae per terras; comparatio rerum per pretia*, 'nature compared in different lands; products compared as to value').

Vita vigilia est (*pref.* 18): Life is being awake. The *Naturalis Historia* is a monument to keeping alert, and to the useful employment of time. Pliny's energy and diligence astonished his nephew, were intended to impress his contemporaries, and still amaze today; they were, moreover, not just a contingent habit of mind, but intended as an ethical statement. For all his defects of accuracy, selection, and arrangement, Pliny achieved a real summation of universal knowledge, deeply imbued with the mood of the time, and the greatness of his work was speedily recognized. It was a model for later writers such as Julius Solinus and Isidorus, and attained a position of enormous cultural and intellectual influence in the medieval west.

N.P.

Pliny the Younger (*c.* AD 61–*c.*112), Gaius Plinius Caecilius Secundus, is known from his writings and from inscriptions (e.g. *ILS* 2927). Son of a landowner of Comum (mod. Como), he was brought up by his uncle, *Pliny the Elder, of equestrian rank, who adopted him, perhaps in his will. He studied rhetoric at the feet of *Quintilian and Nicetes at Rome. After the usual year's service on the staff of a Syrian legion (*c.*81), he entered the senate in the later 80s through the patronage of such distinguished family friends as Verginius Rufus and *Frontinus. He practised with distinction in the civil courts all his life, specializing in cases relating to inheritance, and conducted several prosecutions in the senate of provincial governors charged with extortion. He rose up the senatorial ladder, becoming praetor in 93 (or less probably 95) and consul in 100, and he also held a series of imperial administrative appointments, as *praefectus aerari militaris,* in charge of the army pension fund (*c.*94–6), *praefectus aerari Saturni,* in charge of the state treasury (*c.*98–100), and *curator alvei Tiberis,* i.e. in charge of the banks of the river Tiber (*c.*104–6). He was thrice a member of the judicial council of Trajan (*c.*104–7), who sent him as *legatus Augusti* to govern Bithynia-Pontus (*c.*110), where he apparently died in office (*c.*112). His career, very similar to that of his friend *Tacitus, is the best-documented example from the Principate of municipal origins and continuing ties, of the role of patronage, of the nature of senatorial employment under emperors tyrannical and liberal, and of the landed wealth that underpinned the system.

Pliny published nine books of literary letters between 99 (or 104) and 109 at irregular intervals, singly or in groups of three. Some letters comment elegantly on social, domestic, judicial, and political events, others offer friends advice, others again are references for jobs or requests for support for his own candidates in senatorial elections, while the tone is varied by the inclusion of short courtesy notes and set-piece topographical descriptions. Each letter is carefully composed (*Ep.* 1. 1), with great attention to formal style; Pliny uses the devices of contemporary rhetoric, with intricate arrangement and balance of words and clauses in sentences and paragraphs. Letters are limited either to a single subject treated at appropriate length, or to a single theme illustrated by three examples (cf. *Epp.* 2. 20; 3. 16; 6. 31; 7. 27). Great care was also taken with the sequence of letters within each book. Pliny and his friends regularly exchanged such letters (*Ep.* 9. 28), which Pliny distinguished from boring business letters (*Ep.* 1. 10), from mere trivialities (*Ep.* 3. 20), and from the philosophical abstractions of *Seneca the Younger's letters (*Ep.* 9. 2). The letters do have their origins in day-to-day events, but Pliny aimed to create a new type of literature. He set out to write not an annalistic history, but a picture of his times with a strong moral element. He censures the cruelty of slave masters, the dodges of legacy hunters, and the meanness of the wealthy, but the targets of his criticisms are normally anonymous. He dwells for preference on positive aspects of the present, the benign role of Trajan, the merits of friends and acquaintances, the importance of education, and the literary life of Rome. Other letters describe the public life of senatorial debates, elections and trials, without concealing the weaknesses of senators, and recount, in a manner anticipating Tacitus, heroic episodes of the political opposition to *Domitian, with which Pliny liked to claim some connection.

Pliny was also active in other fields of literature. He wrote verses enthusiastically, publishing two volumes in the manner of his protégé *Martial, of which he quotes a few indifferent specimens. His surviving speech, the *Panegyricus,* the only extant Latin speech between *Cicero and the late imperial panegyrics, is an expanded version of the original he delivered in the senate in thanks for his election to the consulship. Rhetorically a success (its popularity in the late-Roman rhetorical schools is responsible for its survival), it contrasts Trajan with the tyrannical Domitian. It is a major statement of the Roman political ideal of the good emperor condescending to play the role of an ordinary senator.

The tenth book of letters contains all of Pliny's correspondence with Trajan: the first fourteen letters date between 98 and *c.*110, the remainder to Pliny's governorship of Bithynia-Pontus. The letters are much simpler in style than those in books 1–9 and were not worked up for publication, which probably occurred after Pliny's death. The provincial letters are the only such dossier surviving entire, and are a major source for understanding Roman provincial government. Each letter concerns a particular problem, such as the status of foundlings or the condition of civic finances, on which Pliny sought a ruling from Trajan. In *Ep.* 10. 96 Pliny gives the earliest external account of Christian worship, and the fullest statement of the reasons for the execution of Christians.

A.N.S.-W.; S.R.F.P.

Plotinus (AD 205–269/70), Neoplatonist philosopher. The main facts of his life are known from *Porphyry's memoir (prefixed to editions of the *Enneads*). His birthplace, on which Porphyry is silent, is said by *Eunapius and the *Suda* to have been Lyco or Lycopolis in Egypt, but his name is Roman, while his native language was almost certainly Greek. He turned to philosophy in his 28th year and worked for the next eleven years under Ammonius Saccas at Alexandria. In 242–3 he joined Gordian III's unsuccessful expedition against Persia, hoping for an opportunity to learn something of eastern thought. The attempt was abortive, and at the age of 40 he settled in Rome as a teacher of philosophy, and remained there until his last illness, when he retired to Campania to die. At Rome he became the centre of an influential circle of intellectuals, which included men of the world and men of letters, besides professional philosophers like Amelius and Porphyry. He interested himself also in social problems, and tried to enlist the support of the emperor Gallienus for a scheme to found a Platonic community on the site of a ruined Pythagorean settlement in Campania (see PYTHAGORAS).

WRITINGS Plotinus wrote nothing until he was 50. He then began to produce a series of philosophical essays arising directly out of discussions in his seminars, and intended primarily for circulation among his pupils. These were collected by Porphyry, who classified them roughly according to subject, arranged them rather artificially in six *Enneads* or groups of nine, and eventually published them *c.*300–5. From this edition

our manuscripts are descended. An edition by another pupil, the physician Eustochius, is known to have existed (schol. *Enn.* 4. 4. 30); and it has been argued by some scholars that the extracts from Plotinus in *Eusebius, *Praep. Evang.* are derived from this Eustochian recension. Save for the omission of politics, Plotinus' essays range over the whole field of ancient philosophy: ethics and aesthetics are dealt with mainly in *Enn.* 1, physics and cosmology in *Enns.* 2 and 3; psychology in *Enn.* 4; metaphysics, logic, and epistemology in *Enns.* 5 and 6. Though not systematic in intention, the *Enneads* form in fact a more complete body of philosophical teaching than any other which has come down to us from antiquity outside the Aristotelian corpus. Plotinus' favourite method is to raise and solve a series of 'difficulties': many of the essays give the impression of a man thinking aloud or discussing difficulties with a pupil. Owing to bad eyesight, Plotinus never revised what he wrote (Porph. *Vita Plot.* 8), and his highly individual style often reflects the irregular structure of oral statement. Its allusiveness, rapid transitions, and extreme condensation render him one of the most difficult of Greek authors; but when deeply moved he can write magnificently.

PHILOSOPHICAL DOCTRINE In the 19th cent. Plotinus' philosophy was often dismissed as an arbitrary and illogical syncretism of Greek and oriental ideas. Recent writers, on the other hand, see in him the most powerful philosophical mind between *Aristotle and Aquinas or Descartes; and in his work a logical development from earlier Greek thought, whose elements he organized in a new synthesis designed to meet the needs of a new age. These needs influenced the direction rather than the methods of his thinking: its direction is determined by the same forces which resulted in the triumph of the eastern religions of salvation, but its methods are those of traditional Greek rationalism. Plotinus attached small value to ritual, and the religious ideas of the Near East seem to have had little direct influence on the *Enneads*, though E. Bréhier (*La Philosophie de Plotin*, 1928; Eng. trans. 1958) would explain certain parallels with Indian thought by postulating contact with Indian travellers in Alexandria. To Christianity Plotinus makes no explicit reference; but *Enn.* 2. 9 is an eloquent defence of Hellenism against Gnostic superstition.

Plotinus holds that all modes of being, whether material or mental, temporal or eternal, are constituted by the expansion or 'overflow' of a single immaterial and impersonal force, which he identifies with the 'One' of the *Parmenides* and the 'Good' of the *Republic* (see PLATO), though it is strictly insusceptible of any predicate or description. As 'the One', it is the ground of all existence; as 'the Good', it is the source of all values. There is exact correspondence between degrees of reality and degrees of value, both being determined by the degree of unity, or approximation to the One, which any existence achieves. Reality, though at its higher levels it is non-spatial and non-temporal, may thus be pictured figuratively as a series of concentric circles resulting from the expansion of the One. Each of these circles stands in a relation of timeless dependence to that immediately within it, which is in this sense its 'cause'; the term describes a logical relationship, not an historical event. Bare Matter is represented by the circumference of the outermost circle: it is the limiting case of reality, the last consequence of the expansion of the One, and so possesses only the ideal existence of a boundary.

Between the One and Matter lie three descending grades of reality—the World-mind, the World-soul, and Nature. The descent is marked by increasing individuation and diminishing unity. The World-mind resembles Aristotle's Unmoved Mover: it is thought-thinking-itself, an eternal lucidity in which the knower and the known are distinguishable only logically; within it lie the Platonic Forms, which are conceived not as inert types or models but as a system of interrelated forces, differentiations of the one Mind which holds them together in a single timeless apprehension. The dualism of subject and object, implicit in the self-intuition of Mind, is carried a stage further in the discursive thinking characteristic of Soul: because of its weaker unity, Soul must apprehend its objects successively and severally. In doing so it creates time and space; but the World-soul is itself eternal and transcends the spatio-temporal world which arises from its activity. The lowest creative principle is Nature, which corresponds to the immanent World-soul of the Stoics: its consciousness is faint and dreamlike, and the physical world is its projected dream.

Man is a microcosm, containing all these principles actually or potentially within himself. His consciousness is normally occupied with the discursive thinking proper to Soul: but he has at all times a subconscious activity on the dreamlike level of Nature and a superconscious activity on the intuitive level of Mind; and his conscious life may lapse by habituation to the former level or be lifted by an intellectual discipline to the latter. Beyond the life of Mind lies the possibility of unification, an experience in which the Self by achieving complete inward unity is momentarily identified with the supreme unity of the One. This is the Plotinian doctrine of ecstasy. The essays in which he expounds it, on the basis of personal experience, show extraordinary introspective power and are among the classics of mysticism. It should be observed that for Plotinus unification is independent of divine grace; is attainable very rarely, as the result of a prolonged effort of the will and understanding; and is not properly a mode of cognition, so that no inference can be based on it.

Plotinus also made important contributions to psychology, particularly in his discussion of problems of perception, consciousness, and memory; and to aesthetic, where for Plato's doctrine that Art 'imitates' natural objects he substitutes the view that Art and Nature alike impose a structure on Matter in accordance with an inward vision of archetypal Forms. His most original work in ethics is concerned with the question of the nature and origin of evil, which in some passages he attempts to solve by treating evil as the limiting case of good, and correlating it with Matter, the limiting case of reality.

E.R.D.; J.M.D.

Plutarch (Lucius (?) Mestrius Plutarchus) of Chaeronea; b. before AD 50, d. after AD 120; philosopher and biographer. The family had long been established in Chaeronea, and most of Plutarch's life was spent in that historic town, to which he was devoted. He knew Athens well, and visited both Egypt and Italy, lecturing and teaching at Rome. His father, Autobulus, his grandfather, Lamprias, and other members of his family figure often in his dialogues; his wide circle of influential friends include the consulars Lucius Mestrius Florus (whose gentile name he bore),

Quintus Sosius Senecio (to whom the *Parallel Lives* and other works are dedicated), and Gaius Minicius Fundanus, as well as magnates like the exiled Commagenian prince Julius Antiochus Philopappus. For the last thirty years of his life, Plutarch was a priest at Delphi. A devout believer in the ancient pieties and a profound student of its antiquities, he played a notable part in the revival of the shrine in the time of Trajan and Hadrian; and the people of Delphi joined with Chaeronea in dedicating a portrait bust of him 'in obedience to the decision of the Amphictions' or councillors of the Amphictiony, the regional organization in charge of the sanctuary (*Syll.*³ 843 A). Late authorities (*Suda*, Eusebius) report that he received *ornamenta consularia* (decorations of consular rank) from Trajan, and was imperial procurator in Achaia under Hadrian; whatever lies behind this, he was a man of some influence in governing circles, as he was in his writing an active exponent of the concept of a partnership between Greece, the educator, and Rome, the great power, and of the compatibility of the two loyalties.

The 'Catalogue of Lamprias', a list of his works probably dating from the 4th cent., contains 227 items. Extant are 78 miscellaneous works (some not listed in the Catalogue) and 50 Lives. We have lost the Lives of the Caesars (except *Galba* and *Otho*) and some others (notably *Epaminondas*, *Pindar*, *Daiphantus*), and probably two-thirds of the miscellaneous works. Nevertheless, what remains is a formidable mass; Plutarch was a very prolific writer, especially (it seems) in the last twenty years of his life. The relative chronology of his works however is very difficult to establish (C. P. Jones, *JRS* 1966, 61–74). For a complete list of titles, see e.g. any volume of the Loeb *Moralia*, or D. A. Russell, *Select Essays and Dialogues* (World's Classics, 1993), pp. xxiii–xxix. In what follows, we can only mention a few. (The numbers attached to the titles refer to the order of treatises in all editions.)

1. The group of *rhetorical* works—epideictic performances—includes 'The Glory of Athens' (22), 'The Fortune of Rome' (20), 'Against Borrowing Money' (54). Plutarch's richly allusive and metaphorical style does not seem very well adapted to rhetorical performance, and these—with the exception of 'Against Borrowing' which is a powerful,

satirical piece—are not very successful; it is often thought, though without clear evidence, that Plutarch's epideictic rhetoric was something that he gave up in later life.

2. The numerous treatises on themes of popular moral philosophy are derivative in content, but homogeneous and characteristic in style. Among the best are 'Friends and Flatterers' (4), 'Progress in Virtue' (5), 'Superstition' (14), 'The Control of Anger' (29), 'Talkativeness' (35), 'Curiosity' (36), and 'Bashfulness' (38). In 'Rules for Politicians' (52), Plutarch draws both on his historical reading and on his own experience, to give advice to a young man entering politics. The warm and sympathetic personality never far beneath the surface appears particularly in 'Consolation to my Wife' (45) and 'Advice on Marriage' (12). Plutarch's teaching is less individualistic than that of many ancient moralists: family affections and friendly loyalties play a large part in it.

3. Many of Plutarch's works are *dialogues*, written not so much in the Platonic tradition as in that of *Aristotle (and indeed *Cicero), with long speeches, a good deal of characterization, and the frequent appearance of the author himself as a participant. The nine books of 'Table Talk' (46) are full of erudite urbanity and curious speculation. 'Socrates' Daimonion' (43) combines exciting narrative (liberation of Thebes from Spartan occupation in 379/8; see PELOPIDAS) with philosophical conversation about prophecy (a favourite theme) and an elaborate Platonic myth (see PLATO) of the fate of the soul after death (Plutarch attempted such myths elsewhere also, especially in 'God's Slowness to Punish' (41)). 'Eroticus' (47) also combines narrative with argument, this time in a near contemporary setting: the 'kidnapping' of a young man by a widow who wishes to marry him forms the background to a discussion of heterosexual and homosexual love in general. Delphi is the scene of four dialogues, all concerned with prophecy, *daimones*, and divine providence; and it is in these (together with *Isis and Osiris* (23)) that the greater part of Plutarch's philosophical and religious speculation is to be sought.

4. He was a Platonist, and a teacher of philosophy; and the more technical side of this activity is to be seen in his interpretation of the *Timaeus* (68) and a series of polemical

treatises against the Stoics (70–2) and Epicureans (73–5).

5. We possess also important antiquarian works—'Roman Questions' and 'Greek Questions' (18), mainly concerned with religious antiquities—and some on literary themes ('On Reading the Poets' (2) is the most significant).

Plutarch's fame led to the inclusion in the corpus of a number of *spuria*, some of which have been very important: 'The Education of Children' (1) was influential in the Renaissance; 'Doctrines of the Philosophers' (58) is a version of a doxographic compilation to which we owe a lot of our knowledge of Greek philosophy, while 'Lives of the Ten Orators' (55) and 'Music' (76) are also important sources of information.

The 'Parallel Lives' remain his greatest achievement. We have 23 pairs, 19 of them with 'comparisons' attached. Plutarch's aims are set out e.g. in *Alexander* 1: his object was not to write continuous political history, but to exemplify individual virtue (or vice) in the careers of great men. Hence he gives attention especially to his heroes' education, to significant anecdotes, and to what he sees as the development or revelation of character. Much depends of course on the sources available to him (*Alcibiades* is full of attested personal detail, *Publicola* is thin and padded out, *Antony* full of glorious narrative, especially about *Cleopatra VII, Phocion* and *Cato Maior* full of sententious anecdotes), but the general pattern is maintained wherever possible: family, education, début in public life, climaxes, changes of fortune or attitude, latter years and death. The *Lives*, despite the pitfalls for the historian which have sometimes led to despair about their value as source material, have been the main source of understanding of the ancient world for many readers from the Renaissance to the present day.

Indeed, Plutarch has almost always been popular. He was a 'classic' by the 4th cent., and a popular educational text in Byzantine times. The preservation of so much of his work is due mainly to Byzantine scholars (especially Maximus Planudes). His wider influence dates from Renaissance translations, especially Amyot's French version (*Lives* 1559, *Moralia* 1572) and Sir T. North's English *Lives* (1579; largely based on Amyot) and Philemon Holland's *Moralia* (1603).

Montaigne, Shakespeare, Dryden, Rousseau, and Emerson are among Plutarch's principal debtors. In the 19th cent., however, his influence, at least among scholars, diminished: he was seen as a derivative source both in history and in philosophy, and his lack of historical perspective and his rather simple moral attitudes earned him much disrespect. Recent scholarship has done much to reverse this negative view; as understanding of his learning and the aims and methods of his writing has deepened, so he has come again to be seen, not as a marginal figure, but as a thinker whose view of the classical world deserves respect and study.   D.A.R.

Pollux, Julius, of Naucratis in Egypt (2nd cent. AD), scholar and rhetorician. His *Onomasticon* was composed in the lifetime of *Commodus, to whom are addressed epistles prefixed to each of its ten books: that introducing book 8 indicates that the author's appointment to a chair of rhetoric at Athens (not before AD 178) preceded the completion of the work. In books 8–10 he replies to Phrynichus the Arab's criticism of points in 1–7. As an example of Atticism (study and imitation of Classical Athenian Greek) and other profitable vices of the age he comes under Lucian's lash in Rhetorum Praeceptor, a Teacher of Rhetoric: cf. ch. 24—'I am no longer called Potheinos—the Desired One— but have become the namesake of the children of Zeus and Leda'; i.e. the Dioscuri, Castor and Pollux. Like his other works, the *Onomasticon* in its original form has perished: the extant manuscripts are derived from four incomplete, and interpolated copies, all descending from an early epitome (abridgement) possessed (and interpolated) by Arethas, archbishop of Caesarea, c. AD 900. The arrangement is by topic, not alphabetical. The work partly resembles a rhetorical handbook, e.g. in its collections of synonyms and of subject-vocabularies, in collections of compounds (*homo-* and some others), in the fifty-two terms for use in praising a king, or the thirty-three terms of abuse to apply to a tax-collector. The story of Heracles' discovery of purple is added expressly as a light relief for the student. Wider philological and encyclopaedic interests appear in the citations from literature and in the treatment of music and the theatre. Besides these, his subjects include religion, private and public law, human anatomy and ethics, war, the sciences, arts, crafts and trades, houses, ships, husbandry, cookery, children's games, and a host of other matters. The sections on stage antiquities (book 4) and on the Athenian constitution (book 8) are of especial interest to scholars. But the work is predominantly a thesaurus of terms, not of information. It is also mainly derivative, but useful to us because the sources no longer survive.

P.B.R.F.; R.B.; N.G.W.

Polybius (*c.*200–*c.*118 BC), Greek historian of Rome's rise to Mediterranean dominion and of the world in which that happened. His father, Lycortas of Megalopolis, was a leading figure of the Achaean Confederacy in the 180s and, along with *Philopoemen, one of the architects of the doomed Achaean attempt to treat with Rome on a basis of equality during those years. Polybius bore Philopoemen's ashes to burial in 182, was appointed in 180 as envoy to Alexandria, and in 170/69 served as Hipparch of the Confederation. After Rome's victory over *Perseus of Macedon at Pydna, he was denounced as insufficiently friendly to the Romans by the Achaean politician Callicrates, and became one of the thousand prominent Achaeans deported to Rome and subsequently detained without trial in various towns of Italy. Polybius became friend and mentor to *Scipio Aemilianus, was allowed to remain in Rome during his captivity, and formed part of the 'Scipionic Circle'. He probably accompanied Scipio to Spain (151) and to Africa (where he met *Masinissa), returning to Italy over the Alps in *Hannibal's footsteps. After the release of the surviving detainees in 150 Polybius witnessed the destruction of Carthage (146) in Scipio's company and undertook an exploratory voyage in the Atlantic. He helped to usher in the Roman settlement of Greece after the sack of Corinth (146), visited Alexandria and Sardis, and may have been at Numantia (mod. Garray in Spain) in 133. He is reported to have died at the age of 82 after falling from a horse.

His minor works—an early encomiastic biography of Philopoemen, a work on tactics, a history of the Numantine war, and a treatise on the habitability of the equatorial region—are all lost. Of his *Histories* a substantial amount survives; he is the only Hellenistic historian of whom a significant amount does

remain. Only books 1–5 of the original forty survive intact. After that we are dependent upon excerpts and occasional quotations by other writers. The 'Excerpta Antiqua' are a continuous abridgement of books 1–18 and provide the majority of what remains of books 6–18. For the remainder the main source is the slightly later collection of excerpts, by a number of hands under various headings and from many Greek historians along with Polybius, made for the emperor Constantine VII Porphyrogenitus (AD 912–50). From five books there are no excerpts at all (17, 19, 26, 37, 40); they were presumably lost already. A few quotations from 19, 26, and 37 are found in other authors. Book 34 (devoted to geographical matters) was much referred to, especially by *Strabo; it survives only in quotations. Books 17 and 40 have perished without trace. For the arrangement of what does survive of books 7–39, a matter beset with difficulty, see F. W. Walbank, *A Historical Commentary on Polybius* 3. (1979) 1–62.

Polybius' original purpose was to tell the story of (that is, to describe and explain) Rome's rise to world dominion, to answer the question 'how and by a state with what sort of constitution almost the whole of the known world was conquered and fell under the single rule of the Romans in a space of not quite 53 years' (1. 1. 5; from the beginning of the 140th Olympiad in 220 to the end of the Macedonian monarchy in 167: books 3–30). He was profoundly impressed by this process, both by the simple fact of the end of the monarchy that had dominated the affairs of Greece for almost two centuries and by the way in which the course of events seemed almost calculated to produce the final result. A metaphor of supernatural guidance is often invoked in the form of *tychē* (fortune), which, though sometimes very close to seeming an active, even a vengeful, agent, is never invoked as an explanation of anything. He later extended his purpose to show how the Romans exercised their dominion, how the world under them reacted to it, and how both were affected (books 30–39; book 40 contained a recapitulation and chronological survey). For his task Polybius developed both a structure and a kind of history. Given his theme and his belief that the process at issue was fundamentally unitary, the structure must allow at once for universality and focus.

This was made possible by combining chronological and geographical organization in an original way. Vertically, the arrangement is by Olympiads, each Olympiad containing four numbered years; these years were not rigidly fixed but were adapted to the flow of events. Horizontally, the framework is geographical. Within each year there is a fixed progression from west to east: first, events in Italy (with Sicily, Spain, and Africa), then Greece and Macedonia, then Asia, then Egypt. Books 1 and 2 are something apart. They focused primarily on Rome from the first Punic war to 220, providing a background for those little acquainted with the Romans and an explanation of how the Romans could with reason come to develop the aim for universal dominion (*hē tōn holōn epibolē*, 1. 3. 6, etc.) that informed their actions after the Hannibalic war.

For the kind of history he wrote Polybius invented the term *pragmatikē historia*, 'pragmatic history'. This kind of inquiry involves study of documents and written memoirs, geographical study (especially autopsy), first-hand knowledge of some events, and the most careful examination of eye-witnesses about the rest. The focus is upon political actions (*hai praxeis hai politikai*, 12. 25e), but the scope of 'political' was for Polybius very wide indeed, as may be inferred from the breadth of his account of the Roman *politeia* in book 6: this embraced military, economic, religious, social, and political institutions and practice. (It also included the formulation of the theory of a tripartite constitution, incorporating elements of monarchy, aristocracy, and democracy, that influenced political thinking for the next two thousand years.) Apprehension of all these was needed in order to describe things properly and, above all, to explain them. For Polybius the historian's primary task was explanation. 'The mere statement of a fact may interest us, but it is when the reason is added that the study of history becomes fruitful: it is the mental transference of similar circumstances to our own that gives us the means of forming presentiments about what is going to happen . . .' (12. 25b). This resembles *Thucydides (1. 22), as does Polybius' insistence upon true and accurate narration of historical action (both deed and speech), but Polybius goes beyond his predecessor in his insistence upon the element of explanation and beyond every-

body in his explicit formulation (3. 6–7) about beginnings (*archai*) and reasons (*aitiai*). (*Prophasis* is reserved for 'pretext'.) Beginnings are actions; actions are preceded by decisions to act; decisions to act are processes involving various elements: a proper explanation, for Polybius, must delineate these processes and identify these various elements. In dealing with the wars that led to Rome's dominion Polybius adheres rigorously to his principles: he aims to explain in a properly multifaceted way rather than to assign responsibility.

Having brought the writing of history to a methodological acme (and having access to Rome and Romans in a way that his Greek predecessors and contemporaries did not), Polybius was regularly critical of past and contemporary historians, often polemically and sometimes excessively, whether for their method or their bias (book 12 is the most concentrated statement about method and what survives of it contains much hostile criticism of *Timaeus). From bias he was himself manifestly not free, whether positive (as for Philopoemen, Scipio Aemilianus, or the Achaean Confederacy as a whole) or negative (as for Titus Quinctius Flamininus, the Aetolian Confederacy, many of Rome's opponents and supporters alike, and the lower classes generally). But he was, though of course not neutral, honest, and he was, above all, concerned about the effect of undisputed dominion upon the society that wielded it and upon those who inhabited the world in which it was wielded.   P.S.D.

Polyclitus, Argive sculptor, active *c.*460–410 BC. Supposedly a pupil of Hageladas, Polyclitus worked exclusively in metal; all his works were in bronze except the Hera of Argos (after 423), which was in chryselephantine. He made gods, heroes, and athletes, and his statues of mortals were unsurpassed (Quint. 12. 10. 9). His reputation rested largely on a single work, the *Doryphorus* or Spearbearer; he also wrote a book called the Canon, or Rule, that explained the principles of his art, apparently basing it on this statue. In it, he stated that 'perfection comes about little by little through many numbers' (Philon Mechanicus 4. 1, 49. 20), and described a system of proportion whereby, starting with the fingers and toes, every part of the body was related mathematically to every other and to the whole (Galen, *De plac. Hipp. et Plat.* 5, p. 3. 16 Kühn).

The Doryphorus (perhaps an Achilles) is nowhere described in detail; we only know that it was a nude, 'virile boy', 'suitable for both war and athletics', and 'aimed at the mean' (Plin. *HN* 34. 55; Quint. 5. 12. 21; Galen, *De temperamentis*, p. 566. 14 Kühn). Since 1863, however, it has been unanimously identified with a youth known in over 50 copies, the best in Naples (from Pompeii), Berlin, and Minneapolis. A bronze herm by Apollonius is the best copy of the head. He stands on his right leg with his left relaxed; his right arm hangs limp and his left is flexed to hold the spear; his head turns and inclines somewhat to his right. This compositional scheme, which unifies the body by setting up cross-relationships between weight-bearing and relaxed limbs, is called chiastic after the Greek letter *chi* (χ), and thereafter becomes standard practice in Greek and Roman sculpture. His proportional scheme was equally influential (though no single reconstruction of it has yet gained universal acceptance), as was his system of modelling, which divided the musculature into grand (static) and minor (mobile) forms, alternating in ordered sequence throughout the body. Though sculptors such as Euphranor and *Lysippus introduced their own variations upon this ideal, the Polyclitan ideal remained widely influential, and was particularly popular in Roman imperial sculpture. This and the longevity of Polyclitus' own school accounts for *Pliny the Elder's observation that later artists followed his work 'like a law' (*HN* 34. 55).

*Varro criticized Polyclitus' work as being 'virtually stereotyped' (Plin. *HN* 34. 56—an inevitable consequence of a rigorously applied ideal), and a series of copies that apparently reproduce his other statues bear this out. These include his Diadoumenos (a victor binding a fillet around his head), Discophoros, Heracles, and Hermes; the 'Westmacott Boy' in the British Museum may copy his statue of the boy-boxer Cyniscus at Olympia. His Amazon, placed first in the contest at Ephesus, is plausibly identified in the Sosicles (Capitoline) type, who rests on a spear held in her right hand. The Hera is described by Pausanias (2. 17), but no secure copies of her survive, presumably because antiquity rated her inferior to the great chryselephantine statues of *Phidias (cf. Strabo 8. 372).   A.F.S.

Polycrates, tyrant of Samos, son of Aeaces, seized power *c.*535 BC, with his brothers Pantagnotus and Syloson, but soon made himself tyrant. Almost unrivalled in magnificence (Hdt. 3. 125, 122), he made Samos a great naval power, subjected neighbouring islands (Hdt. 3. 39, 122; Thuc. 1. 13), including Rheneia near Delos which he dedicated to Apollo (Thuc. 1. 13; 3. 104). He formed a defensive alliance with Amasis, king of Egypt, but seems to have broken it off deliberately (contrast the moralizing tale of Polycrates' ring in Hdt. 3. 39 ff.) when the Persian king Cambyses tried to acquire Egypt, and supplied Samian ships. The Samians mutinied and went over to Sparta; Sparta and Corinth, apparently to prevent Polycrates medizing, tried to overthrow him, unsuccessfully (525 BC). He was lured to the mainland, *c.*522, by the satrap (Persina provincial governor) Oroetes, who pretended to be plotting against King Darius I, and was crucified. He pursued a piratical and opportunist thalassocracy (see Hdt. 3. 39 for piracy), upset by the gradual extension of Persian power, which he tried to court. He attracted artists, craftsmen, and poets (*Anacreon, Ibycus, Theodorus). The three famous building achievements praised by *Herodotus (3. 60), the great temple of Hera, the harbour mole, and the tunnelled aqueduct bringing water to the city, may all in fact be attributable to Polycrates (as Arist. *Pol.* 1313[b]), though the chronology on which this hinges is disputed.   R.Th.

Polyperchon, son of Simmias, Macedonian from Tymphaea (close to Epirus, and on the east side of N. Pindus), campaigned with *Alexander the Great. After the battle of Issus (333 BC) he was given command of the Tymphaean battalion of the phalanx, which he retained until 324. Already of advanced years, he returned with the veterans demobilized at Opis (324). As Craterus' second-in-command he acted as governor in Macedonia during the first coalition war (321–19), and was rewarded for his loyalty and military success with the regency, to which the dying *Antipater appointed him over the head of *Cassander. In the war which ensued he encouraged democratic revolution at Athens (318), but was frustrated at Megalopolis and withdrew to Macedon. There he invoked the aid of *Olympias against the challenge from queen Eurydice, wife of Philip III, but shared her unpopularity and lost his army—and Macedon—to Cassander (spring 316). Returning to the Peloponnese, he surrendered the regency to *Antigonus the One-eyed (315); and in 309 he invaded Macedon, hoping to replace Cassander with Heracles (an illegitimate son of Alexander), but murdered his charge in return for recognition by Cassander and ended his life (at an uncertain date) in comparative obscurity in the Peloponnese.   A.B.B.

Pompey the Great, Gnaeus Pompeius Magnus, b. 106 BC (the official *cognomen* (surname) meaning 'the Great', in imitation of *Alexander, was assumed after 81 BC). He served with his father Gnaeus Pompeius Strabo at Asculum (89) and brought a private army of three legions from his father's veterans and clients in Picenum to win victories for *Sulla in 83. He was then sent *pro praetore* (as a magistrate substituting for a praetor) to Sicily, where he defeated and killed Gnaeus Papirius Carbo, and from there to Africa, where he destroyed Gnaeus Domitius Ahenobarbus and King Iarbas. Though Pompey was still an *eques* (Roman knight), Sulla grudgingly allowed him to triumph (12 March 81); and in 80, after the death of his wife Aemilia, Sulla's stepdaughter, he married Mucia Tertia, a close connection of the Metelli. He supported Marcus Aemilius *Lepidus for the consulship of 78, for which Sulla cut him out of his will, but assisted *Lutatius Catulus (2) to overcome Lepidus next year. Later in 77 he was sent *pro consule* (i.e. as a magistrate substituting for a consul) to reinforce Quintus Caecilius Metellus Pius against *Sertorius in Spain. Thence he returned in 71 and attempted to steal from *Crassus the credit for finishing off the Slave War. He was rewarded with a second triumph and as his first magistracy, despite his youth, the consulship of 70, with Crassus as his colleague. They restored the legislative powers which Sulla had removed from the tribunes; and Lucius Aurelius Cotta reversed another of Sulla's arrangements by ending the senate's monopoly of representation on the courts: judges were now to be drawn equally from senators, *equites*, and *tribuni aerarii* (a group similar to the *equites*).

Pompey took no consular province. But in 67 the Gabinian law empowered him to deal with piracy. The command, for three years, covered the whole Mediterranean, and gave him unprecedented powers; but Pompey's campaign required only three months. In 66 a law of the tribune Gaius Manilius gave him the Asiatic provinces of Cilicia, Bithynia, and Pontus, earlier held by *Lucullus, and the conduct of the war against *Mithradates VI. Pompey's eastern campaigns were his greatest achievement. Mithradates was defeated immediately, and though attempts to pursue him over the Caucasus failed, he committed suicide in the Crimea in 63. Pompey founded colonies, annexed Syria, settled Judaea, and laid the foundation of subsequent Roman organization of the East (though he reached no agreement with Parthia).

In 62 he returned, disbanded his army, and triumphed, no longer a *popularis* (popular politician) as hitherto (for the new role, Cic. *Att.* 2. 1. 6). He made two requests: land for his veterans, and ratification of his eastern arrangements. But he had divorced Mucia for adultery, allegedly with *Julius Caesar; and the Metelli, aided by Lucullus and *Cato the Younger, frustrated him until in 60 Caesar succeeded in reconciling him with Crassus. In 59 the three men formed a coalition and Pompey married Caesar's daughter Julia. His demands were satisfied by Caesar as consul; but his popularity waned, and in 58/7 *Clodius flouted and attacked him. In 57, after securing *Cicero's return from exile, he received control of the corn-supply for five years with proconsular *imperium* and fifteen legates. But no army was attached, nor could he secure the commission to restore *Ptolemy XII Auletes in Egypt. In April 56 the coalition with Caesar and Crassus was renewed at Luca. Pompey became consul with Crassus for 55, and received both Spanish provinces for five years; he governed them through legates, staying in the suburbs of Rome. After Julia's death in 54 he declined a further marriage alliance with Caesar, and the death of Crassus in 53 increased the tension between Caesar and Pompey. In 52 after Clodius' murder Pompey was appointed sole consul, with backing even from Cato. Pompey's immediate actions—the trial of *Milo and his legislation on violence, on bribery, and on the tenure of magistracies—were not necessarily intended specifically to injure Caesar, but the prolongation of his *imperium* (grant of supreme military and civil power) for five years from this date destroyed the balance of power, and he took as his colleague Quintus Caecilius Metellus Pius Scipio, whose daughter Cornelia he married about the time that he became consul. At first he resisted attempts to recall Caesar, but his desire to pose as the arbiter of Caesar's fate was challenged in 50 by Gaius Scribonius Curio, who insisted that both or neither should lay down their commands. Unable to accept the implications of parity, Pompey conditionally accepted from the consul Gaius Claudius Marcellus the command of the republic's forces in Italy. In 49 he transported his army from Brundisium to Greece and spent the year mobilizing in Macedonia. He met Caesar on the latter's arrival in 48 with a force powerful in every arm, and inflicted a serious reverse when Caesar attempted to blockade him in Dyrrachium. But later (9 August), perhaps under pressure from his senatorial friends, he joined in a pitched battle at Pharsalus (Thessaly), and was heavily defeated. He fled to Egypt, but was stabbed to death as he landed (28 September 48).

The violence and unconstitutional character of Pompey's early career invite comparison with *Augustus whose constitutional position his powers often prefigured: in 67 he had 15 (or even 24) legates; from 55 he governed Spain through legates, and while doing so was made consul in 52. But still more significant was his wealth and his unofficial power: by 62 in Spain, Gaul, Africa and the east, and parts of Italy, there were colonists and clients bound to him by the relationship of *fides* (loyalty) and surrounding him with a magnificence unsurpassed by a Roman senator hitherto; the climax was reached with the dedication of his theatre in the Campus Martius in 55. His military talents are hard to evaluate. Other commanders—Metellus, Crassus, Lucullus—often paved the way to his successes, and at Pharsalus he clearly panicked. Logistics seem to have been his strong point, as in the campaign against the pirates. But in politics he showed a mastery which it was easy for clever men to underrate (e.g., for all its brilliance, the epigram of Marcus Caelius Rufus in Cic. *Fam.* 8. 1. 3: 'he is apt to say one thing and think another, but is not clever enough to keep his real aims from showing'). 'Moderate in everything but in seeking domination' (Sallust, *Histories* 2. 14),

by superb skill and timing he rose from his lawless beginnings to a constitutional pre-eminence in which he could discard the use of naked force. His aim was predominance, but not at the expense of at least the appearance of popularity. He did not wish to overthrow the republican constitution, but was content if its rules were bent almost but not quite to breaking-point to accommodate his extraordinary eminence. His private life was virtually blameless, and two women, Julia and Cornelia, married to him for dynastic ends, became deeply attached to him, and his love for Julia was noted by contemporaries. Cicero, though he never understood Pompey's subtleties, remained a devoted admirer; and despite the disappointments of the war years Pompey's death brought from him a muted but moving tribute: 'I knew him to be a man of good character, clean life, and serious principle' (*Att.* 11. 6. 5).

G.E.F.C.; R.J.S.

Pompey, Sextus (Sextus Pompeius Magnus Pius), younger son of *Pompey and Mucia Tertia, was born probably *c.*67 BC. Left in Lesbos with his stepmother Cornelia during the campaign of Pharsalus (48), he accompanied his father to Egypt and after his murder went to Africa; after Thapsus (46) he joined his brother Gnaeus Pompeius Magnus in Spain, and during the campaign of Munda (45) commanded the garrison of Corduba. Subsequently he contrived to raise an army, partly of fugitive Pompeians, and won successes against *Julius Caesar's governors in Further Spain, Gaius Carrinas, who was suffect consul in 43, and after him C. Asinius Pollio. In summer 44 *Lepidus arranged a settlement between him and the senate, under the terms of which he left Spain; but instead of returning to Rome, he waited on events in Massalia with his army and fleet. In April 43 the senate made him its naval commander, with the title *praefectus classis et orae maritimae* ('prefect of the fleet and the sea coast') (see *RRC* 511); but in August he was outlawed under the Pedian law and then used his fleet to rescue fugitives from the proscriptions and to occupy Sicily, at first sharing authority with the governor Pompeius Bithynicus, but later putting him to death; and using the island as a base for raiding and blockading Italy. He repelled an attack by Octavian's general Quintus Salvidienus Rufus in 42, supported Antony against Octavian in 40 (when his lieutenant Menodorus occupied Sardinia) and in 30 concluded the Pact of Misenum with the triumvirs *Antony, Octavian (later *Augustus), and Lepidus, who conceded to him the governorship of Sicily, Sardinia and Corsica, an augurate (member of the college of official Roman diviners) and a future consulship (see *ILLRP* 426) in return for the suspension of his blockade. In 38 Octavian accused him of breaking the pact and again attacked him, but was defeated in sea fights off Cumae and Messana. In 36 the attack was renewed, and after *Agrippa's victory off Mylae, Octavian's defeat off Tauromenium, and Lepidus' occupation of southern and western Sicily, the war was decided by the battle of Naulochus (3 September). Sextus escaped with a few ships to Asia, where he attempted to establish himself, but was forced to surrender to Marcus Titius, who put him to death.

Sextus was, like his father, an able and energetic commander. His brief career was spent entirely in the continuation—symbolized by his adoption of the surname Pius (he gives his name as Magnus Pompeius Magni f. Pius, 'Magnus Pompeius Pius son of Magnus')—of an inherited struggle. Despite his long absence from and blockade of Italy, he seems to have been popular in Rome. His wife was Scribonia, daughter of Lucius Scribonius Libo.   T.J.C.; R.J.S.

Pomponius, Sextus, a Roman lawyer of the 2nd cent. AD who wrote under *Hadrian, *Antoninus Pius, and *Marcus Aurelius. A teacher and prolific writer, the author of over 300 books (*libri*), he seems not to have given *responsa* (consultative opinions) nor to have held public office. His relation to the Sabinian and Proculian schools is problematic; but there is (disputed) evidence that he was at one time an associate of *Gaius (2) (*Dig.* 45. 3. 39). His *Enchiridium* (Introduction to Law), from which Justinian's compilers excerpted a long passage (*Dig.* 1. 2. 2), is of great interest for its account of the history of the Roman constitution and the legal profession. It was the first and for long the only work on legal history. But the text, perhaps taken from a student's notes of lectures shortly before 131 AD, is garbled and contains many errors. Pomponius' large-scale commentaries included thirty-nine books of readings on

Quintus Mucius (see SCAEVOLA), thirty-five on Masurius Sabinus' *ius civile* (Civil Law), and perhaps 150 on the praetor's edict: we know of a citation from book 83 which deals with a topic that comes little more than halfway through the edict. *Ulpian, an admirer, made great use of this work, which was not available to Justinian's compilers. There were also extensive casuistic works, *Epistulae* (Letters) and *Variae lectiones* (Varied Readings). In all Justinian's compilers included over five hundred passages from Pomponius in their *Digesta*. Dealing meticulously with unlikely as well as likely hypotheses, Pomponius' work not only founded the study of legal history but made a solid contribution to the analysis and structure of Roman private law.   T.Hon.

Pomponius Atticus See ATTICUS.

Poplicola Potitus, Lucius Valerius, and Marcus Horatius Barbatus were consuls in 449 BC, immediately after the Second Decemvirate. Livy (3. 55. 3 ff.) ascribes to them three laws: (1) measures passed by the *plebs* in a tribal assembly were to be binding on the entire people (cf. Dion. Hal. *Ant. Rom.* 11. 45. 1 ff.); (2) no magistrate was to be elected who was not subject to appeal (cf. Cic. *Rep.* 2. 54); (3) severe penalties were to be inflicted on those harming the tribunes or other plebeian officers. *Diodorus Siculus (12. 26. 1) says nothing of these measures and their historicity is controversial. The first is also ascribed to *Publilius Philo (339) and Quintus Hortensius (287/6), though some suppose that the *lex Valeria Horatia* established either the legislative powers of the *comitia tributa* (assembly of the *plebs*) or the validity of plebiscites that received patrician or senatorial sanction. The measure on *provocatio* (also ascribed to a tribune (C. Duillius)) depends on the fictions of the tyrannous Second Decemvirate (supposedly not subject to *provocatio*) and the creation of the right of *provocatio* in 509. The third law may reflect a tradition which ascribed the creation of the tribunate to the Second Secession. Cumulatively, all three laws replicate for the aftermath of the Decemvirate the same creation or reinforcement of key popular rights that supposedly followed the overthrow of the monarchy in 509 (when a Valerius and Horatius were also reputedly consuls). The role of

Valerius and Horatius in negotiating the end
of the Second Secession and Second Decemvirate will certainly be annalistic fiction, as
also the story that the people, not the senate,
granted them triumphs for victories over the
Aequi and Volsci (Valerius) and Sabines
(Horatius).   A.D.

Poppaea Sabina, daughter of Titus Ollius
(d. AD 31), and named after her maternal
grandfather Gaius Poppaeus Sabinus (consul
AD 9, governor of Moesia 12–35), was married
first to Rufrius Crispinus, prefect of the praetorians under Claudius, by whom she had a
son later killed by *Nero. By 58, during her
second marriage, to the future emperor
Otho, she became mistress of Nero (so Tac.
Ann. 13. 45 f.; another version in *Hist.* 1. 13).
It was allegedly at her instigation that Nero
murdered *Agrippina the Younger in 59 and
in 62 divorced, banished, and executed
Claudia Octavia. Nero now married Poppaea,
who bore a daughter Claudia in 63; both
mother and child received the surname
Augusta but the child died at four months.
Through Poppaea's influence, her native
Pompeii became a colony. *Josephus, who
secured a favour from her in Rome, apparently attests to her Jewish sympathies
(though the word *theosebes* is problematic),
but she actually did the Jews a disservice in
securing her friend's husband, Gessius
Florus, the procuratorship of Judaea in 64
(*Vita* 16; *Ant. Jud.* 2. 195). In 65, pregnant
again, she is supposed to have died from a
kick which Nero gave her in a fit of temper,
and was accorded a public funeral and divine
honours.   T.J.C.; M.T.G.

Porcia was daughter of *Cato the Younger
and wife first of Marcus Calpurnius Bibulus
and from 45 BC of *Brutus. She shared the
political ideals of her father and her husbands, insisted on being let into the secret of
the plot to murder *Julius Caesar, and took
part with her mother-in-law *Servilia in the
conference of republicans at Antium on 8
June 44. When Brutus sailed for the east she
returned to Rome, where she became ill and
in the early summer of 43 took her life,
perhaps by inhaling fumes from a brazier
(Plut. *Brut.* 53, Cic. *Ad Brut.* 1. 9. 2, 17. 7). The
less good tradition makes her do this on the
news of Brutus' death in 42.   T.J.C.

Porcius Cato See CATO.

Porphyry (AD 234–*c.*305), scholar, philosopher, and student of religions. He was born
probably at Tyre; originally bore the Syrian
name Malchus; studied under Cassius Longinus at Athens; became a devoted disciple of
*Plotinus with whom he studied in Rome
(AD 263–268). His varied writings (sixty-nine
titles can be listed with reasonable certainty)
may be put into the following categories.

  1. Commentaries and introductions to
*Aristotle: only the influential *Isagoge* and
the shorter commentary on the *Categories*
survive. There are fragments of a larger commentary on the *Categories* and of commentaries on *De interpretatione, Ethics, Physics,*
and *Metaphysics.*

  2. Commentaries on *Plato: extensive fragments of a *Timaeus* commentary, evidence
for commentaries (or at least treatment of
select topics) on *Cratylus, Parmenides,
Phaedo, Philebus, Republic,* and *Sophist.*

  3. Our edition of Plotinus' *Enneads*
arranged into sets of nine treatises; also a lost
commentary on the *Enneads.*

  4. Historical work includes scholarly
research on chronology which may have
formed a separate work (*Chronica*) or part of
his *Against the Christians* and a history of
philosophy down to Plato, from which the
extant *Life of Pythagoras* (see PYTHAGORAS)
is an excerpt.

  5. His metaphysical works are almost
entirely lost but included treatises on the
principles, matter, the incorporeal, the soul
and the surviving *Sententiae,* a succinct, but
probably incomplete, introduction to Plotinian metaphysics which displays some divergences from Plotinus. An anonymous
commentary on the *Parmenides,* even if not
by Porphyry himself, suggests strongly that
Porphyry is the ultimate source for some
important developments in the concepts of
being, existence, and transcendence with particular reference to the One and Nous. It can
no longer be held that Porphyry made no
original contribution to philosophy.

  6. Although his publications on religion
have been commonly interpreted as pointing
to an intellectual development from credulous superstition to critical rejection, a fairer
assessment of the evidence demonstrates a
consistent interest and respect for most traditions allied to a searching but constructive

critique of the workings and significance of many pagan rituals. *On Abstinence* (a treatise on vegetarianism) and the *Letter to Marcella* show a traditional piety, *On Statues* a conventional interest in ritual symbolism, *Philosophy from Oracles* acceptance of ritual with some questioning, the *Letter to Anebo* a searching critique of ritual religion, and *De regressu animae* a limitation of the scope of theurgy. Porphyry raised but did not solve the problem of the relationship of philosophy to religion. In *Against the Christians* he used historical criticism e.g. to establish the lateness of the Book of Daniel. Elsewhere he similarly proved the 'Book of Zoroaster' to be a forgery.

7. Philological works include *Homeric Enquiries*, a landmark in the history of Homeric scholarship (see HOMER); an allegorizing interpretation of the Cave of the Nymphs in the Odyssey; writings on grammar, rhetoric, and the history of scholarship.

8. Extant works on technical subjects are a commentary (incomplete) on *Ptolemy (Claudius Ptolemaeus)'s *Harmonica*; an introduction to Ptolemy's *Tetrabiblos* and a treatise on the entry of the soul into the embryo (formerly attributed to *Galen but probably by Porphyry).   A.SM.

PORPHYRY'S MUSIC THEORY Like *Augustine and other Christian fathers, Porphyry was suspicious of real music but held musical theory in high esteem. In arguing that Ptolemy (Claudius Ptolemaeus)'s *Harmonics* relies heavily on unacknowledged sources, his incomplete *Commentary* preserves much important earlier material (selections translated in A. Barker, *Greek Musical Writings*, 2 (1989)). It became well known in the Renaissance for championing a non-Ptolemaic, partly qualitative theory of pitch.   A.D.B.

Porsen(n)a, Lars, king of Clusium, who besieged Rome at the beginning of the republic in a vain attempt to reinstate the exiled *Tarquinius Superbus. The standard version of the story is that Porsenna was so impressed by the heroism of Romans such as Horatius Cocles and Gaius Mucius Scaevola that he gave up the siege and made peace with the Romans. He withdrew from Rome, and instead sent his forces, under the command of his son Ar(r)uns, against the Latin town

of Aricia. This expedition ended in failure, however, when Arruns was defeated and killed by the Latins and their allies from Cumae. The survivors of his army made their way back to Rome, where they were hospitably received. There are many contradictory elements in this romantic tale, which is further complicated by an alternative tradition which maintained that the Romans had surrendered to Porsenna (Tac. *Hist.* 3. 72), and that he imposed a humiliating treaty on them (Plin. *HN* 34. 139). This unflattering version, which is unlikely to have been invented by the Romans, has given rise to a modern theory that Porsenna used Rome as a base from which to launch his attack against the Latins, and that it was his defeat at Aricia that finally caused him to withdraw. The battle of Aricia is probably an authentic event, since it appears to have been independently recorded in Greek sources, but it is unlikely that Porsenna's original aim was to restore the Tarquins. Since Tarquinius Superbus was closely associated with Porsenna's enemies, the Latins and Aristodemus, it is more probable that, so far from attempting to restore the Roman monarchy, Porsenna actually abolished it, and that the republic emerged after his withdrawal.

T.J.Co.

Posidonius (*c.*135–*c.*51 BC), Stoic philosopher, scientist, and historian. A Syrian Greek from Apamea on the Orontes (Syria), he was educated at Athens under *Panaetius, but settled in Rhodes, a prosperous free city with already a reputation for philosophy and science. Granted citizenship, he took a significant part in public life as *prytanis* ('president', a magistrate's title), and as a member of at least one embassy to Rome in 87/6. Probably in the 90s he embarked on long tours of research to the west, visiting certainly Spain, southern Gaul, and of course Rome and Italy. Thereafter his School in Rhodes became the leading centre of Stoicism, and a general mecca not only for intellectuals, but for the great and powerful of the Roman world such as *Pompey and *Cicero.

The range of his writing is astonishing. In addition to the conventional departments of philosophy (Natural philosophy, ethics, logic), he wrote penetratingly on astronomy, meteorology, mathematics, geography, hydrology, seismology, zoology, botany, anthropology, and history. Some thirty titles survive over this field, but no complete work. This has led to a crux of methodology in Posidonian scholarship. Earlier this century research inspired by K. Reinhardt concentrated on a wide range of supposed echoes of Posidonian influence conjectured from horizontally parallel passages in later authors as the main tool for reconstructing his philosophy; but the uncertainty and dangerously subjective nature of this process, although at times illuminating, produced contradictory results. A fresh start has been made by the collection and study of the attested fragments which form a more secure base for what can be accepted as evidence, and offer a new picture.

Posidonius has been dubbed unorthodox in his Stoicism, but this is a misconception. He was not so regarded by his contemporaries, and he did not diverge from the fundamental tenets. He believed rather in the development of philosophy by continued interpretation in the light of subsequent criticism of the basic ideas of the founders and 'the old authorities'. At that level there had always been divergence of interpretation in the Stoa, as between Ariston and Chrysippus. So Posidonius had strikingly original things to say within the context of Stoic natural philosophy in defence of the ultimate principles as material without quality or form; on problems of destruction, generation, continuity and change related to the individual; on the problem of 'now' in time viewed as a continuum; on a finite cosmos surrounded by infinite void; and in logic, on the criterion of truth, dialectic, and on the relational syllogism.

On the other hand he was convinced that in ethics Chrysippus had seriously distorted Stoicism with his monolithic rational psychology which defined emotion as mistaken judgement, and so failed to explain the cause and operation of emotions and hence the major questions in moral behaviour. Posidonius argued for a return to irrational faculties of mind with affinities towards pleasure and power. These were natural, but not good. Only our rational affinity for moral virtue he recognized as good and absolute. Hence the uncompromising Stoic end of virtue alone is preserved, despite some ancient and modern misunderstandings. Posidonius claimed that he could now explain the mechanics of moral

choice, moral responsibility (since the root of evil lies within us), and moral education which required behavioural therapeutics as well as rational argument. His attack on Chrysippus in his book *On Emotions* as culled from *Galen's De Placitis* rests on three grounds: respect for the facts, consistency derived from deductive proof, and understanding sprung from explanation of the causes of phenomena. Posidonius was himself famed for all three in antiquity. They are the key for the coherence of his own work.

In the first place, he promoted logic from being the organon or tool of philosophy to that organic part of it which as bones and sinews supplied the articulation and dynamic of its structure. From the model of Euclidean mathematics, in whose foundations he was much interested, he regarded axiomatic deductive proof as the top-down causal explanation of the cosmic nexus. The tools of philosophy, and this is explicitly stated, now become the special sciences, a completely original concept peculiarly apposite for the material continuum of the Stoic universe. The sciences were thus necessary for natural philosophy, and the two complementary, but not equal. For while science supplied the descriptive factual pattern of phenomena as the cosmic map on which their rational organization may be traced, and so included the plotting of their immediate relationship of antecedent causation, and even offered possible alternative explanatory hypotheses at that level, only philosophy could provide final and complete explanation of causes or aetiology by its incontrovertible method of deductive proof from assured axiomatic premisses established by the natural philosophers. These procedures demanded precise distinction between different kinds of cause, but the details of the synthesis and interaction of natural philosophy and science are largely missing because of the lack of interest of reporters like *Strabo. Some of Posidonius' own research in the sciences is remarkable, such as a lunar theory of the periodicity of tides which held sway until Newton; or his ingenious method of measuring the circumference of the earth leading to the establishment of latitudinal bands. *On Ocean* was an extraordinary work ranging from the astronomical establishment of geographical zones and so physical and climatic conditions, to human geography and anthropology. It is one of the lost books of antiquity one would most like to recover.

The same relationship holds for history and ethics, for history with its descriptive framework of actual social behaviour was his necessary tool for moral philosophy. The *History* was a major work in its own right of 52 books covering the period from 146 BC probably to the mid-80s and possibly unfinished. Its scope was all-embracing of the Mediterranean-centred world, from the histories of Asia Minor to Spain, Egypt and Africa to Gaul and the northern peoples, Rome and Greece. It was packed with formidable detail of facts and events, both major and minor, global and local, and of social and environmental phenomena. But the unifying factor of the huge canvas, factually drawn and sharply critical of credulous legend was, as *Athenaeus implied and the tone and presentation of the brief Athenian tyranny of Athenion in 88 BC demonstrates, a moralist's view of historical explanation, where events are caused by mind and character in the relationship between ruler and ruled, and by tribal or racial character in social movement and motives. Hence his detailed interest in ethnology (Italian, Roman, Gallic, Germanic), i.e. ethology operating as cause. Again, such studies offer immediate historical explanation; final aetiology and principal causes come from the philosophical study of psychology and ethics.

His style, vivid, forceful and highly coloured, still gleams fitfully through the fragments. It so impressed such an authority as Cicero that he importuned Posidonius to write up his cherished consulate. The manner of declining showed a diplomat of enviable tact.

Posidonius' position in intellectual history is remarkable not for the scattered riches of a polymath and savant, but for an audacious aetiological attempt to survey and explain the complete field of the human intellect and the universe in which it finds itself as an organic part, through analysis of detail and the synthesis of the whole, in the conviction that all knowledge is interrelated.

A dominant figure in his lifetime, his subsequent reputation and influence have been overstressed to pandemic proportions and require re-examination; but the impact was considerable and continued at least to the 6th cent. AD. In mainstream Stoicism he did not supplant Chrysippus of Soli, and it was often outside the School, and not least in the sciences and history that he was consulted. The riches of the details tended to obliterate the grand design.   I.G.K.

Praxagoras of Cos, a physician of the second half of the 4th cent. BC. He is known only through the testimony of others, but it seems likely that he was a teacher of the great anatomist *Herophilus of Chalcedon, and what little is known of him suggests that he was himself an anatomist of importance. *Galen rather grudgingly acknowledges this, at the same time attacking his view that the nerves originate in the heart. He made important observations about the connection of the brain and spinal cord, and drew a distinction (perhaps being the first to do so) between veins and arteries, and their functions. He argued that the venous vascular system carried blood around the body, the arterial, *pneuma*. Details are lacking, but blood was apparently a product of healthy digestion, and *pneuma* was derived from inspired air, supplemented possibly by certain gaseous byproducts of digestion. *Pneuma* assumed a special status in Praxagoras' physiology, and was associated with the generation and communication of movement both in the arteries and the heart, and throughout the body. Praxagoras' complex physiological and pathological system ascribed the origins of most diseases to alterations in the state of humours, brought about by imperfect digestion. The four humours were themselves divided into as many as eleven sub-categories on grounds of taste, colour, and other properties. Little is known of his therapeutic practice, but it seems to have reflected closely his theoretical concerns with redressing highly complex humoral imbalances by means of dietary regulation and purging.   J.T.V.

Praxiteles, Athenian sculptor, probably son of the sculptor Cephisodotus, active *c*.375–330 BC. *Pliny the Elder dates him to 364–361, perhaps after his Aphrodite of Cnidus ('Cnidia'). He worked in both bronze and marble, though was more successful at the latter (Plin. *HN* 35. 133); he paid great attention to surface finish, by preference employing the painter Nicias for the final touches (*HN* 35. 133). A prolific artist, he specialized in statues of the younger gods, particularly Aphrodite, Dionysus, and their respective circles, and in portraits, though some architectural sculpture is also attributed to him.

His masterpiece was the Cnidia (Pliny, *HN* 36. 30 f.; ps.-Lucian, *Amores* 13; etc), supposedly modelled on his mistress Phryne; reproductions on local coins have led to the identification of numerous copies. Chief among them is the so-called Venus Colonna in the Vatican, though recent research suggests that it and others like it may copy a Hellenistic version rather than the Cnidia herself. Displayed amid gardens in a colonnaded, circular shrine, remains of which have been discovered on the site, the goddess was completely nude. Sculptors of the previous generation had occasionally represented her in transparent drapery or baring a breast, and Praxiteles himself may have already shown her topless if the Arles Aphrodite is correctly attributed to him and is earlier than the Cnidia. In the Cnidia, he simply took the final, logical step: the essence of the love-goddess was her body, so it must be revealed. His pretext was apparently her cult-title 'Euploia', referring to her 'fair voyage' from Cyprus; accordingly, he showed her at the bath, with a hydria beside her, holding her cloak in her left hand.

No certain originals by Praxiteles exist: the base of his Apollo group from Mantinea and the bronze Marathon boy are probably workshop pieces, and the Aberdeen and Leconfield heads could be by his sons. The Hermes at Dionysus at Olympia, long attributed to him on the basis of *Pausanias 5. 17. 3, is almost certainly post-Praxitelean; among other anomalies, Hermes' shoes are unparalleled in the 4th cent. but have clear descendants in the second. A bust from Eleusis, however, may be his 'Eubuleus', cut down from a free-standing statue after the Costobocian sack of AD 170. His Apollo Sauroctonos survives in copy, and other plausible attributions (all copies) include two satyrs, the Arles Aphrodite, the Dresden and Gabii Artemis types, and the Palatine Eros; the Apollo Lycius, recognized from *Lucian, *Anach. 7, is often added to them on stylistic grounds even though no text specifies its author.

Praxiteles' vision of a dreamy Elysium inhabited by divine beings remote from the cares of mortals anticipates the philosophy of

*Epicurus, and was widely influential. His fastidious manner was often imitated, particularly in Alexandria, where it tended to degenerate into a facile slurring of surfaces enlivened by a luminous polish. His canon for the female nude (wide hips, small breasts, oval face, centrally-parted hair etc.) remained authoritative for the rest of antiquity.

A.F.S.

Priscian (Priscianus Caesariensis, 5th–6th cent. AD) was the most prolific and important member of the late Latin grammarians. His grammatical works have been edited by Heinrich Keil (*Grammatici Latini* 2, 3), and they amount to over 1,000 printed pages in all.

Born in Mauretania, Priscian spent most of his life as a teacher of Latin in Constantinople (Byzantium), then the capital of the eastern Roman empire. His surviving works include the *Institutio de nomine et pronomine et verbo*, the *Praeexercitamina*, a set of grammatical exercises based on each first line of the twelve books of the *Aeneid*, and the *Institutiones grammaticae*. The *Institutio* was an important authority for the teaching of Latin in the early Middle Ages before the much longer and more comprehensive *Institutiones* (974 printed pages) became widely known in and after the Carolingian age.

This work comprises eighteen books, the first sixteen setting out, after a brief introduction to orthography, the eight Latin word classes (parts of speech) in great detail. Books 17 and 18 provide an account of the syntax of Latin, the first systematic treatment of Latin syntax of which we have knowledge.

The *Institutiones* represents a summation in Latin of the whole of grammatical theory and practice as it had developed in the Graeco-Latin world hitherto. The two books on syntax were, as Priscian acknowledges, very largely based on the work of the Alexandrian Greek grammarian *Apollonius Dyscolus. The original purpose of the *Institutiones* was the teaching of Latin to Greek speakers, as is shown by repeated references to classical Greek texts. Latin was still the official language of the eastern empire, but by the 8th cent. it had become largely unused and unremembered except by some scholars.

In western Europe it became, along with the shorter grammars of Donatus, the authority for the teaching of grammar and of Latin, the *lingua franca* of educated medieval Europe. Several hundred individual manuscripts are known to have existed, and the work was subjected to many epitomes and commentaries. In the later Middle Ages it became the linguistic basis of the scholastic speculative grammars, particularly in the University of Paris. This arose gradually through the attempted philosophical explanation by commentators on Priscian's descriptive account of Latin, after the study of the Aristotelian texts became more widespread and profound.

The established and intended purpose of Priscian's teaching and writing had become void after a few centuries in the east, but his principal work remains of the greatest importance in the western Middle Ages for the teaching of Latin and for philosophical grammar, some of whose concerns, e.g. universal grammar, are still with us today.

R.H.R.

Probus (Marcus Aurelius Probus), Roman emperor, b. Sirmium AD 232, commanded the eastern army in 276. He challenged Florianus after the death of the emperor Tacitus and, as the better general, emerged as sole emperor (autumn).

He was an active warrior-emperor. In Gaul from 277 to 278, he expelled Alamannic and Frankish invaders and restored the Rhine frontier. Between 278 and 280 he defeated the Burgundians and Vandals in Raetia and campaigned on the middle Danube. In 280 he moved to Syrian Antioch, whence he directed the suppression of Isaurian banditry in SE Asia Minor and nomadic incursions into Upper Egypt. His main intention was probably to deal with the Persian question, but he soon had to leave Syria to subdue mutinies on the Rhine and in Britain. Another rebellion, by Saturninus, in his rear, also failed. In 281 he celebrated a triumph in Rome. In 282 he was at Sirmium when Carus claimed the purple in Raetia. Probus was killed by his own troops (autumn).

His problems with the army suggest growing military discontent. This is traditionally ascribed to Probus' disciplinarian tendencies and his use of soldiers as labourers on agricultural and civil-engineering schemes. However, possibly he also seemed to his troops and officers to be increasingly careless of the empire's real needs. Indeed, though in his military, civil, and religious policies he projected himself as the authentic successor of *Aurelian, his end is reminiscent of that of *Gallienus. His main historical significance is his acceleration of the settlement of barbarians on Roman territory.

J.F.DR.

Proclus, Neoplatonist philosopher (AD 410 or 412–485). Born in Lycia (SW Asia Minor) of wealthy parents, he was destined for the law, but after some study in Alexandria, came to Athens in search of philosophical enlightenment, where he spent the rest of his life. He studied with Plutarch of Athens and Syrianus, whom he succeeded as head of the Platonic school (*diadochos*) in 437. His importance as a creative thinker has sometimes been exaggerated: most of the new features which distinguish his Neoplatonism from that of *Plotinus, such as the postulation of triadic 'moments' within each hypostasis, or of 'henads' within the realm of the One, are traceable, at least in germ, to Iamblichus or Syrianus. But he is the last great systematizer of the Greek philosophical inheritance, and as such exerted a powerful influence on medieval and Renaissance thought, and even, through Hegel, on German idealism. His learning was encyclopaedic and his output vast. Extant works include the following:

1. Philosophical treatises: *Elements of Theology*, a concise summary of Neoplatonic metaphysics; *Platonic Theology*, a more elaborate account of the same; *Elements of Physics*, based on *Aristotle's theory of motion; *Opuscula: On Providence, On Fate*, and *On Evil*, long known only in William of Moerbeke's Latin trans., but now rediscovered in Greek, plagiarized by Isaac Sebastocrator.

2. Commentaries on *Plato: *On the Timaeus; On the Republic*, really a series of independent essays; *On the Parmenides; On the Alcibiades; On the Cratylus* (excerpts).

3. Scientific works: *Outline of Astronomical Theories; Commentary on the First Book of *Euclid's Elements*. There are also a commentary on *Ptolemy (Claudius Ptolemaeus)'s *Tetrabiblos* and a work on eclipses, which have received no modern edition.

4. Literary works: *Hymns; Chrestomathia*, a handbook of literature extant in epitome only, authorship disputed.

J.M.D.

Procopius, Greek historian, born in Caesarea in Palestine *c.* AD 500. After a thorough rhetorical and legal education—where he studied we do not know—he obtained by 527 a post on the staff of *Justinian's great general Belisarius, and soon became his *assessor* and counsellor, and carried many difficult and sometimes dangerous missions for his commander. After accompanying Belisarius on his Persian (527–31), African (533–6), and Italian (536–40) campaigns, he returned to Constantinople by 542, where he may have continued to pursue an official career. His fortunes no doubt fluctuated with those of his great patron, who incurred the enmity of Justinian's empress, Theodora. He is not to be identified with the Procopius who was prefect of the city in 562. The date of his death is unknown.

His principal work is his *History of the Wars of Justinian* in eight books. Books 1–2 deal with the first Persian war, 3–4 with the war against the Vandals in Africa, 5–7 with that against the Goths in Italy; these were probably published in 551. Book 8 contains supplementary material and a short history of the years 551–3. The *History* deals primarily with Justinian's campaigns, but there are many digressions on the political scene in Constantinople and on events elsewhere in the empire. Procopius, as Belisarius' confidant, had direct and comprehensive acquaintance with military affairs and was favourably placed to interrogate eyewitnesses of what he had not himself seen. These are the main sources upon which his *History* relies. But he also made use of documents and other written sources in Greek and Latin, and probably also in Syriac. His strength lies in clear narrative rather than in analysis. Procopius was a careful and intelligent man, generally of balanced judgement, though he had a slight prejudice in favour of his hero Belisarius. His attitude is somewhat old-fashioned and backward-looking. His claim to a sincere desire to establish the truth is somewhat vitiated by the very different picture which he paints of Justinian's regime in his *Secret History*, written at the same time as books 1–7 of his *History of the Wars*. It is a virulent, uncritical, and often scurrilous attack on the whole policy of Justinian and on the characters of the emperor and his consort, which can only have been circulated clandestinely so long as Justinian was alive. It provides a kind of sub-text to the *History of the Wars*, and reveals Procopius as a diehard, if occasionally almost paranoiac, adherent of the aristocratic opposition, which had briefly shown its hand at the time of the Nika riot of 532. Whether this was his attitude since his youth or had been occasioned by his later experience we do not know. The general reliability of his account of military events is unlikely to have been seriously affected by his reservations concerning Justinian's regime. His work *On Justinian's Buildings*, was composed (*c.*553–5) at the emperor's behest, and is panegyrical in tone. Whether this betokens a change in the author's views or merely proves his ability to ride two different horses at once, we cannot tell. The work is a first-class source for the geography, topography, and art of the period, and Procopius displays an unexpected talent for lucid architectural description.

All the works are written in a classicizing but generally clear Greek, with many echoes and reminiscences of earlier historians, particularly *Thucydides. Procopius, however, is no imitative epigone, but a historian of the first rank, helped rather than hindered by the literary tradition within which he wrote.

R.B.

Propertius, Sextus, born between 54 and 47 BC, at Asisium, where his family were local notables (4. 1. 121 ff.). His father died early, and the family property was diminished by Octavian (see AUGUSTUS)'s confiscations of 41–40 BC (4. 1. 127 ff.)—not so diminished however that Propertius needed to earn a living. In the two last poems of book 1 the poet notably identifies with the side vanquished by Octavian at Perusia in 41 BC. It is the first sign of a political independence that continues throughout his life, despite involvement in *Maecenas' circle. As the Augustan regime toughened, Propertius' modes of irreverence become more oblique, but irreverence towards the government is maintained none the less: see e.g. 2. 7, 2. 15. 41 ff., 3. 11, 4. 9.

Propertius' first book was probably published before Oct. 28 BC; the latest events mentioned in books 2, 3, and 4 belong to the years 26, 23, and 16 respectively. Propertius was certainly dead by 2 BC (Ov. *Rem. Am.* 764).

It is as a love poet that Propertius is best

known. He celebrated his devotion to a mistress whom he called Cynthia (a name with
Apolline and Callimachean associations; see
CALLIMACHUS). Apuleius says her real name
was Hostia (*Apol.* 10). Many of the incidents
suggested in the poems seem conventional,
but there is no reason to doubt Cynthia's basic
reality. Her social status is uncertain.

Characteristic of Propertian love poetry is
the claim to be the slave of his mistress (1.
1 etc.), and the claim that love is his life's
occupation; it replaces the normal career
move of a young equestrian (service in the
cohort of a provincial governor, *militia*).
Propertius distils this last point by referring
to love as his *militia* (esp. 1. 6. 29 f.). Typical
too of his love poetry is his use of mythology:
he cites figures and events from myth as
'romantic standards', as examples of how
things in a romantic world might be.

Book 1, consisting almost entirely of love
poems, is addressed to a variety of friends,
most prominently a Tullus (1. 1, 1. 6, 1. 14, 1.
22; 9. 3. 22) who seems to have been nephew
to Lucius Volcacius Tullus, consul in 33 BC
with Octavian. Book 2 (which some think
an amalgamation (by a later hand) of two
books), still largely devoted to love poems,
evidences his entry to the circle of Maecenas
(2. 1), but there is no suggestion that he was
ever economically dependent on the great
patron in the way that *Virgil and *Horace
were. Book 3 also contains a prominent poem
to Maecenas (3. 9), but book 4 omits all
mention of his name. Maecenas fades from
Propertius' poetry as he fades from Horace's:
this is probably due to the great patron's loss
of favour with Augustus in the wake of the
conspiracy of 23 BC.

Book 3 shows a greater diversity of subject-
matter than the first two books, and it is here
that Propertius first makes an ostentatious
claim to be a Roman Callimachus (3. 1 and 3.
3). Some scholars think the claim is not very
justified: Horace had claimed to be the
Roman *Alcaeus (*Ode* 3. 30); with some
humour Propertius responds by making his
claim to be the first Roman to adopt the
mantle of another Greek poet. The many
non-Cynthia poems in book 3 one
might note 3. 18 on the death of Augustus'
nephew Marcus Claudius Marcellus. It is
hard to imagine Propertius writing this a few
years earlier. The toughening of the Augustan
regime and the fading influence of the medi-

ating Maecenas was having its effect. But
Propertius can still be irreverent (see above).
The concluding poems of the book recall
book 1 in various ways, and mark the end
both of the affair with Cynthia and of his
career as a love-poet (or so it seems).

Book 4 is more successful than book 3, and
in it Propertius has a more valid claim to
be called a Roman Callimachus. It consists
partly of poems descended from Callimachus' *Aetia*; but these are Roman *Aetia* (1, 2,
4, 6, 9, and 10), one (6) indeed explaining the
aition of the Temple of Apollo as a thank-
offering for the victory at Actium. 4. 6 is an
example of Propertius' later subtle irreverence. It is largely devoted to an account of the
battle of Actium, but tells it all in the manner
of Callimachus, a style wholly unsuited to the
subject-matter. The total result is amusing to
those with literary taste. To these aetiological
poems are added poems on various subjects.
The two in which he returns to the theme of
Cynthia (7 and 8) are among Propertius' most
original, and the speech from beyond the
grave by Cornelia (11) is moving, though
marred by textual corruption.

Some Romans, though not *Quintilian,
thought Propertius the most 'refined and
elegant' of the Roman elegists (Quint. 10. 1.
93; cf. also Plin. *Ep.* 9. 22). Such epithets apply
to many of his poems, but others seem to the
modern reader obscure and jagged. Part of
this is the reader's fault. The poet's wit is a
demanding one. Other and real obscurities
are due to a very corrupt manuscript tradition. The fact remains that Propertius is
difficult in a way that *Tibullus is not, and—
perhaps owing to his Callimachean aspirations—often seems to cultivate complexity
and convolution.

His vivid re-creation of his affair with
Cynthia, his literary range, and his political
independence make Propertius one of the
most captivating of the Latin poets.

R.O.A.M.L.

Prosper Tiro (*c.* AD 390–*c.*455), of Aquitaine,
became a monk and may have taken deacon's
orders. At Marseille he supported *Augustine's doctrine of Grace against more moderate interpretations put forward in John
*Cassian's *Collationes* (426). In 431 he jour-
neyed to Rome to seek Pope Celestine's
support for Augustinianism, and on the
accession of Leo I (440) he returned to Rome

where he acted as the Pope's secretary. According to Gennadius he drafted Leo's letters against Eutyches.

He was important, first as a champion of Augustine in the 'Semi-Pelagian' controversy (427–32), and second as the compiler of the Chronicle. Though he did not know Augustine he wrote (427/8) telling him that Pelagianism (see PELAGIUS) was rife in Marseille, and after Augustine's death (430) Prosper wrote three books in his defence. He attacked the anti-predestinarian views of John Cassian in a sarcastic work, *Contra Collatorem*, a reference to Cassian's *Collationes*. After the latter's death in 435 his *Expositio super Psalmos* contained more friendly estimates of his views, but also expressed Prosper's distaste for the current misbeliefs of Nestorius, the Donatists, and Pelagians. While at Rome he popularized Augustine's memory in two works of extracts from Augustine's writings, *Liber Sententiarum ex operibus Sancti Augustini delibatarum* and *Epigrammata ex sententiis Sancti Augustini*, the latter in verse.

At Rome he compiled his Chronicle; down to 378 it was based on *Jerome's translation of *Eusebius' Chronicle, and thereafter to 417 borrowed from Sulpicius Severus and Orosius. He continued it first to 443 and finally to 455. From 417 to 455, Prosper's jejune entries are valuable for contemporary events, e.g. the intrigues which led to the invasion of Africa by the Vandal leader Gaiseric (429) and also for the early years of Leo's pontificate. The tendency of the work is heavily anti-heretical. This coupled with vindication of St Augustine rather than historical accuracy was his main interest.

His lasting memorial lay in the canons of the Council of Orange (529), which were based partly on the *Epigrammata*. His style, often modelled on Cicero, was good and the author's liveliness of spirit survives the rather rigid framework of his subjects.   W.H.C.F.

Protagoras of Abdera (*c*.490–420 BC), the most celebrated of the sophists. He travelled widely throughout the Greek world, including several visits to Athens, where he was associated with *Pericles, who invited him to write the constitution for the Athenian colony of Thurii. The ancient tradition of his condemnation for impiety and flight from Athens is refuted by *Plato's evidence (*Meno*

91e) that he enjoyed a universally high reputation till his death and afterwards. He was famous in antiquity for agnosticism concerning the existence and nature of the gods, and for the doctrine that 'Man is the measure of all things', i.e. the thesis that all sensory appearances and all beliefs are true for the person whose appearance or belief they are; on the most plausible construal that doctrine attempts to eliminate objectivity and truth altogether. It was attacked by *Democritus and Plato (in the *Theaetetus*) on the ground that it is self-refuting; if all beliefs are true, then the belief that it is not the case that all beliefs are true is itself true. In the *Protagoras* Plato represents him as maintaining a fairly conservative form of social morality, based on a version of social contract theory; humans need to develop social institutions to survive in a hostile world, and the basic social virtues, justice and self-control, must be generally observed if those institutions are to flourish.   C.C.W.T.

Psellus, Michael (baptismal name Constantine) (AD 1018–after 1081), Byzantine man of letters. Born and educated in Constantinople, he became an imperial secretary and probably also gave private tuition in philosophy and other subjects. Psellus belonged to a group of young intellectuals, pupils of John Mauropous, which included the future patriarchs John Xiphilinus and Constantine Leichoudes. They played a prominent role—though probably less prominent than Psellus would have us believe—in the revival of higher learning in the 11th cent., and entertained hopes of exercising real power during the enlightened reign of Constantine IX Monomachus (1042–55). Their hopes were not fulfilled, and Psellus found it politic to retire to a monastery in Bithynia in 1054–5. Constantine IX granted him the title of *hypatos tōn philosophōn* ('highest of philosophers'), which seems to have been largely honorific, though it may have implied some kind of supervision of higher education and some teaching duties.

Psellus was an erudite, wide-ranging, and immensely productive writer. Many works attributed to him are still of doubtful authenticity. His authentic works include:

1. Historiography. A brief and jejune chronicle of traditional form, probably an early work. His *Chronographia*, a lively and

colourful account of the years 976–1077, in which the causes of events are sought in the interplay of character, ambitions, emotions, and intrigues. The latter part of the *Chronographia* owes much to the author's personal observation, and he somewhat exaggerates his own part in the events which he recounts. Though not always entirely reliable, the work represents a new departure in medieval Greek historiography.

2. Rhetoric. Numerous panegyrics, funeral orations, and other occasional pieces, together with some 500 letters, which provide a lively picture of Byzantine life as well as of the author himself.

3. Philosophy. Commentaries on works of *Plato and *Aristotle, a philosophical miscellany, *De omnifaria doctrina* (*didaskalia pantodapē*); the remarkable and original *De operatione daemonum* (*Peri energeias daimonōn*), and numerous minor treatises.

4. Scientific and literary. Treatises on mathematics, music, astronomy, alchemy, medicine, jurisprudence, as well as studies on Athenian judicial terminology and on the topography of Athens.

5. Miscellaneous. Homeric paraphrases, rhetorical exercises, occasional verse, didactic, satirical and epigrammatic. Psellus was a man of encyclopaedic learning and great literary gifts. At a time when scholarship was at a low ebb after the advances in the 10th cent., he had a keen though self-conscious love of classical and patristic literature, and was passionately devoted to Plato and the Neoplatonists. His own style owed much to imitation of Plato, Aelius *Aristides, and Gregory of Nazianzus. More than any other man he laid the foundations of the Byzantine literary and philosophical renascence of the 12th cent. R.B.

Ptolemy (Claudius Ptolemaeus), wrote at Alexandria, between AD 146 and *c.*170, definitive works in many of the mathematical sciences, including astronomy and geography. Ptolemy's earliest work, the *Canobic Inscription*, is a (manuscript) list of astronomical constants dedicated by him in 146/7. Most of these are identical with those of the *Almagest*, but a few were corrected in the latter, which must have been published *c.*150. This, entitled *Mathematikē suntaxis* ('mathematical systematic treatise': the name 'Almagest' derives from the Arabic form of *hē megistē* sc.

suntaxis), is a complete textbook of astronomy in thirteen books. Starting from first principles and using carefully selected observations, Ptolemy develops the theories and tables necessary for describing and computing the positions of sun, moon, the five planets and the fixed stars. The mathematical basis is the traditional epicyclic/eccentric model. In logical order, Ptolemy treats: the features of the geocentric universe and trigonometric theory and practice (book 1); spherical astronomy as related to the observer's location on earth (2); solar theory (3); lunar theory, including parallax (4 and 5); eclipses (6); the fixed stars, including a catalogue of all important stars visible from Alexandria (7 and 8); the theory of the planets in longitude (9–11); planetary stations and retrogradations (12) and planetary latitudes (13). Commentaries by *Pappus and Theon of Alexandria are partly preserved. The *Almagest* is a masterpiece of clear and orderly exposition, which became canonical, dominating astronomical theory for 1,300 years, in Byzantium, the Islamic world, and later medieval Europe. Its dominance caused the disappearance of all earlier works on similar topics, notably those of *Hipparchus (to which Ptolemy often refers). Hence Ptolemy has been erroneously considered a mere compiler of the work of his predecessors. He should rather be regarded as a reformer, who established Greek astronomy on a valid (i.e. geometrically rigorous) basis, replacing in one sweep the confusion of models and methods which characterized practical astronomy after Hipparchus. He was an innovator in other ways, notably in introducing the 'equant' for the planets to produce remarkable agreement of theory with observation.

2. Other astronomical works are (*a*) *Planetary Hypotheses* (*hupotheseis tōn planōmenōn*), in two books (only the first part of book 1 extant in Greek, the whole in Arabic), a résumé of the results of the *Almagest* and a description of the 'physical' models for use in constructing a planetarium. At the end of book 1 he proposes the system of 'nested spheres', in which each body's 'sphere' is contiguous to the next: he is thus able to compute the absolute distances of all heavenly bodies out to the fixed stars (in the *Almagest* this is done only for sun and moon). This feature was generally accepted through-

out the Middle Ages, and determined the usual view of the (small) size of the universe to Dante and beyond. (*b*) *Planispherium* (extant in Arabic and medieval Latin translations), describing the stereographic projection of the celestial sphere on to the plane of the equator (the theoretical basis of the astrolabe). (*c*) *Analemma* (extant only in Latin translation from the Greek, except for some palimpsest fragments), an application of nomographic techniques to problems of spherical geometry encountered in the theory of sundials. (*d*) *procheiroi kanones* (*Handy Tables*), a revised and enlarged version of the *Almagest* tables, extant in the edition by Theon of Alexandria; Ptolemy's own rules for their use survive. (*e*) *phaseis aplanōn asterōn*, on the heliacal risings and settings of bright stars, and weather predictions therefrom. This was part of traditional Greek astronomy, but Ptolemy introduced rigorous trigonometrical methods. Only the second of two books survives.

3. The *Geography* (*geōgraphikē huphēgēsis*), in eight books, is an attempt to map the known world. The bulk (books 2–7) consists of lists of places with longitude and latitude, with brief descriptions of important topographical features. Although, as Ptolemy tells us, it was based in part on the work of Marinus of Tyre (otherwise unknown), it seems probable that Ptolemy was the first to employ systematically latitude and longitude as terrestrial co-ordinates. Book 1 includes instructions for drawing a world map, with two different projections (Ptolemy's chief contribution to scientific map-making). Book 8 describes the breakdown of the world map into 26 individual maps of smaller areas. The maps accompanying the existing manuscripts are descended from a Byzantine archetype; whether Ptolemy himself 'published' maps to accompany the text is disputed. The work is certainly intended to enable the reader to draw his own maps. Given the nature of its sources (mainly travellers' itineraries), the factual content of the *Geography* is inevitably inaccurate. The main systematic error, the excessive elongation of the Mediterranean in the east–west direction, was due to one of the few astronomical data utilized, the lunar eclipse of 20 September 331 BC observed simultaneously at Carthage and Arbela (Mesopotamia): the faulty report from Arbela led Ptolemy to assume a time

difference of three (instead of two) hours between the two places, leading to a 50 per cent error in longitude. Although the general outlines of areas within the Roman empire and immediately adjacent are moderately accurate, there are numerous individual distortions, and beyond those areas the map becomes almost unrecognizable. A notorious error is a southern land-mass connecting Africa with China (making the Indian Ocean into a lake). Nevertheless, the *Geography* was a remarkable achievement for its time, and became the standard work on the subject (revised innumerable times) until the 16th cent.

4. Other surviving works. (*a*) *apotelesmatika* (*Astrological Influences*) or *tetrabiblos* (from its four books) was the astrological complement to the *Almagest*, and although not as dominant, was influential as an attempt to provide a 'scientific' basis for astrological practice. *Karpos* (*Fruit*, Latin *Centiloquium*), a collection of 100 astrological aphorisms, is spurious. (*b*) *Optics*, in five books, is extant only in Latin translation from the Arabic, from which book 1 and the end of book 5 are missing. Book 1 dealt with the theory of vision (using the doctrine of 'visual rays'); book 2 deals with the role of light and colour in vision, books 3 and 4 with the theory of reflection in plane and spherical mirrors, book 5 with refraction. This contains some remarkable experiments, including some to determine the angles of refraction between various media. In comparison with the earlier optical work of *Euclid, Ptolemy's treatise is greatly advanced in mathematical refinement and the representation of physical and physiological reality, but it is difficult to estimate its originality, because of the loss of such works as the *Catoptrics* of *Archimedes. It had considerable indirect influence on medieval and later optics through the work of ibn al-Haytham (Alhazen), which incorporated and greatly improved on it. A slight philosophical work, *peri kritēriou kai hēgemonikou* (*On the Faculties of Judgement and Control*) is attributed to Ptolemy. (*d*) *Harmonics* (see below).

5. Lost works. Excerpts from a work on Euclid's 'parallel postulate' are given by *Proclus, *Comm. in Eucl.* Simplicius (*in Ar. de caelo* 9) mentions a work *peri diastaseōs* (*On Dimension*), in which Ptolemy 'proved' that there are only three dimensions. *Suda*

(see below the title) says that he wrote *mēch-anika* in three books; this is probably the same as the *peri ropōn* mentioned by Simplicius (*in Ar. de caelo* 710). Simplicius also mentions a work *peri tōn stoicheiōn* (*On the Elements*) (*in Ar. de caelo* 20).   G.J.T.

PTOLEMY'S harmonics Ptolemy's *Harmonics* is outstanding in its field, and significant in the history of scientific thought for its sophisticated blend of rationalist and empiricist methodology. While rejecting Aristoxenian empiricism (see ARISTOXENUS) outright, insisting with the Pythagoreans that musical structures must be analysed through the mathematics of ratio and shown to conform to 'rational' principles, Ptolemy criticizes the Pythagoreans for neglecting perceptual evidence: the credentials of rationally excogitated systems must ultimately be assessed by ear. He pursues this approach with meticulous attention to mathematical detail, to the minutiae of experimental procedures, and to the design and use of the special instruments they demand.

Book 1 establishes the ratios of concords and melodic intervals, and divisions of tetrachords in each genus. Here and in book 2 Ptolemy's criticisms of earlier theorists preserve important information, especially about Archytas and Didymus. Book 2 analyses complete two-octave systems. Perhaps mistakenly, it dismisses as musically insignificant the contemporary conception of *tonoi* as 'keys', thirteen (or fifteen) transpositions of identical structures: on Ptolemy's view their role is to bring different species of the octave into the same central range, and there can be only seven. Three invaluable chapters (1. 16, 2. 1, 2. 16) analyse attunements actually used by contemporary performers. Experimental instruments are discussed as they become relevant throughout books 1–2, and in 3. 1–2. The rest of book 3 extends harmonic analysis to the structures of all perfect beings, especially the soul and the heavens. Ideas from book 1, modified and abbreviated, survived into the Middle Ages through *Boethius' paraphrase: in the Renaissance the work became a major focus of musicological controversy.   A.D.B.

Ptolemy (Ptolemaeus) The name of all the Macedonian kings of Egypt.

PTOLEMY I SOTER ('Saviour') (367/6–282 BC), son of Lagus and Arsinoë, served

*Alexander the Great of Macedon as an experienced general and childhood friend. At Susa in 324 he married Artacama (also called Apame), daughter of the Persian Artabazus, whom he later divorced. He later married the Macedonian Eurydice (6 children) and subsequently Berenice I, mother of the dynastic line. On Alexander's death (323) he hijacked the conqueror's corpse and, taking it to Memphis in Egypt, established himself as satrap in place of Cleomenes. In the following year he took Cyrene and in 321 repulsed the invasion of *Perdiccas. In the complex struggles of Alexander's successors he was not at first particularly successful. In 295 however he recovered Cyprus, lost in 306 to *Demetrius the Besieger, and from 291 he increasingly controlled the Aegean League of Islanders. Ptolemy took the title of King (*basileus*) in 305; this served as the first year of his reign. Responsible for initiating a Greek-speaking administration in Egypt, he consulted Egyptians (*Manetho and others), exploiting their local expertise. The cult of Sarapis, in origin the Egyptian Osiris-Apis, was probably developed under Soter as a unifying force. There are few papyri from his reign, but hieroglyphic inscriptions from the Delta (especially the 'Satrap Stele') present him as a traditional pharaoh. In Upper Egypt he founded Ptolemais Hermiou (modern El-Mansha) as a second Greek administrative centre. Moving the capital from Memphis to Alexandria, he brought Egypt into the mainstream of the Hellenistic world.   D.J.T.

PTOLEMY I AS HISTORIAN Ptolemy I wrote a history of the reign of *Alexander the Great. Much about it is obscure, notably its title, dimensions and even its date of composition. Apart from a single citation in *Strabo our knowledge of it is wholly due to *Arrian who selected it, along with Aristobulus of Cassandreia, as his principal source. The work was evidently comprehensive, covering the period from at least 335 BC to the death of Alexander, and it provided a wealth of 'factual' detail, including most of our information about the terminology and organization of the Macedonian army. The popular theory that Ptolemy based his work upon a court journal rests ultimately on his use of the Ephemerides (Day-books) for Alexander's last illness. Rather the narrative, as it is reconstructed from Arrian, suggests that Ptolemy had propagandist aims (not surprisingly, given his skill at publicity). He emphasized his personal contribution to the campaign and tended to suppress or denigrate the achievements of his rivals, both important in an age when service under Alexander was a considerable political asset. There is also a tendency to eulogize Alexander (whose body he kept interred in state) and gloss over darker episodes like the 'conspiracy' of the Macedonian general Philotas. The king accordingly appears as a paradigm of generalship, his conquests achieved at minimum cost and maximum profit, and Ptolemy continuously figures in the action. His account is contemporary and valuable; but it is not holy writ and needs to be controlled by other evidence.　　　　　A.B.B.

PTOLEMY II PHILADELPHUS ('Sisterloving') (308–246 BC), son of Ptolemy I and Berenice I, born on Cos, first married *Lysimachus' daughter Arsinoë I, mother to Ptolemy III, Lysimachus, and Berenice, and then his sister Arsinoë II, who brought him her Aegean possessions. He became joint ruler with his father in 285, succeeding to the throne in 282. Externally, he expanded the Ptolemaic overseas empire in Asia Minor and Syria, fighting two Syrian Wars, against the Seleucid king *Antiochus I (274–271) and, with less success, against Antiochus II in 260–253; in 252 his daughter Berenice II was married to Antiochus II. The Chremonidean War (267–261) against Macedon in Greece and the western Aegean involved some Ptolemaic losses. Cyrene was re-established under Ptolemaic rule (250); Red Sea trading-posts were founded. Internally, an increasing number of Greek and demotic Egyptian papyri illuminate a developing bureaucracy and control of the population through a tax-system based on a census and land-survey. Land, especially in the Fayūm, was reclaimed and settled with military cleruchs and in gift-estates. It was a period of experiment and expansion. Royal patronage benefited Alexandria; the Pharos, Museum, Library, and other buildings graced the city, which developed as a centre of artistic and cultural life. Honouring his parents with a festival, the Ptolemaieia (279/8), Philadelphos further instituted a Greek royal cult for himself and Arsinoë II.

PTOLEMY III EUERGETES ('Benefactor') (b. 284 BC), son of Ptolemy II and Arsinoë I, ruled from early 246 until his death in February 221. His wife was Berenice II of Cyrene. They had at least six children, including Ptolemy IV and the young Berenice whose death resulted in the priestly Canopus Decree (238) which details her honours as an Egyptian goddess and prescribes a calendar (not adopted) of 365 days with an extra day every four years. In the Third Syrian War against *Seleucus II (246–241) Euergetes acquired important towns in Syria and Asia Minor, but this represented the limit of Ptolemaic expansion. The Alexandrian Serapeum was founded in his reign.

PTOLEMY IV PHILOPATOR ('Fatherloving') (c.244–205 BC), son of Ptolemy III and Berenice II, succeeded in 221 and married his sister Arsinoë III in 217. His success in the Fourth Syrian War (219–217), started when *Antiochus III invaded Palestine, brought internal problems. In the battle of Raphia (217), which restored Coele Syria to Egypt, the substantial use of native Egyptian troops was seen to mark a turning point in the internal cohesion of Egypt. From 206 Thebes was lost to central control for twenty years. In Alexandria Philopator's construction of the Sema, a tomb centre for Alexander and the Ptolemies, further strengthened the dynastic cult. Philopator was murdered in a palace coup by Sosibius and Agothocles and news of his death was kept secret for several months.

PTOLEMY V EPIPHANES ('Made manifest') (210–180 BC), son of Ptolemy IV and Arsinoe III, succeeded as a child following his father's murder. He married a Seleucid princess, Cleopatra I, in 193. His official succession was followed by revolts within Egypt and by the Seleucid and Macedonian kings' joint enterprise to seize Egypt's external possessions. Most Ptolemaic possessions in the Aegean and Asia Minor were lost and, following the battle of Panium in 200, also Palestine. Following the Macedonian ceremony of coming-of-age (anakleteria) in Alexandria, in 197 Epiphanes was crowned at Memphis in a traditional Egyptian ceremony. The priestly Rosetta Decree which followed (196; see OGI 90), marked the start of a more explicit policy in which Ptolemy and priests cooperated in both their interests. Thebes was recovered in 186.

PTOLEMY VI PHILOMETOR ('Motherloving'), son of Ptolemy V and Cleopatra I, started his reign still a child in joint rule with his mother (180 BC); on her death in 176 he married his sister Cleopatra II. His reign was marked by struggles both at home (with his brother, Ptolemy VIII Euergetes II) and abroad. Antiochus IV invaded Egypt twice (169–168, initially with the support of Philometor), and in July 168, formally crowned as king, he only left when Rome intervened. The temporary reconciliation of the brothers, with a joint reign of Ptolemies VI and VIII and Cleopatra II from 169–164, could not discount this new influence on Egyptian affairs. Ejected in 164, Philometor visited Rome to plead for his throne. In 163 the brothers finally agreed to disagree, with Philometor restored to Alexandria and his brother ruling Cyrene. Philometor kept his throne but died fighting Alexander Balas in Syria in 145. Whatever his personal qualities, he had been unable to prevent an unsettled reign full of turmoil; besides dynastic troubles there were rebellion and revolts in Alexandria and throughout the country.

PTOLEMY VII NEOS PHILOPATOR ('Young father-loving'), son of Ptolemy VI and Cleopatra II, ruled briefly together with his father in 145 and following Philometor's death; he was speedily liquidated by his uncle Ptolemy VIII.

PTOLEMY VIII EUERGETES II ('Benefactor') (c.182/1–116 BC), also called Physcon ('Potbelly'), was younger brother of Ptolemy VI. He ruled jointly with Ptolemy VI and Cleopatra II in 170–164, alone in 164–163, and in Cyrene from 163 until 145 when he succeeded his brother in Egypt. He married his brother's widow (his sister) Cleopatra II and then took her daughter (his niece) Cleopatra III as a second wife. The ensuing civil war (132–130) brought devastation to the countryside as well as Alexandria. A joint reign of Euergetes and the two Cleopatras followed from 124 until his death. Continually hostile to the Alexandrians (who had favoured Philometor in 163), he was responsible for severe destruction, persecutions and expulsions (including many of the intelligentsia). The long amnesty decree of 118 (*PTeb.* 5) represents a traditional response to trouble.

PTOLEMY IX SOTER II ('Saviour') (142–80 BC), also known as Lathyrus ('Chickpea'), was the elder son of Ptolemy VIII and Cleopatra III. He married two of his sisters, first Cleopatra IV, probably the mother of Berenice IV (Cleopatra Berenice), and then Cleopatra V Selene, who bore him two sons. (The mother of Ptolemy XII was probably a concubine.) On the death of his father (116), although not her favourite, his dominant mother installed him joint-ruler with her and, briefly, with Cleopatra II, who died soon after. In 107, ejected by his mother in favour of his brother, he fled to Cyprus and became embroiled in Palestinian affairs. Victorious against his mother and the Jews, he re-established himself in Egypt in 88 BC. With Thebes in revolt, Soter elicited aid from Memphis, and in 86 he celebrated an Egyptian 30-year jubilee (a Sed Festival) in that city. He remained on the throne until his death.

PTOLEMY X ALEXANDER I (c.140–88 BC), younger brother of Ptolemy IX, from 116 served as governor of Cyprus, until recalled by his mother to Egypt in 107. A short joint reign ended in October 101 with the death of his mother (murdered by Alexander according to the more sensational accounts). Ptolemy X then married his niece, Cleopatra Berenice, daughter of his exiled brother Ptolemy IX. Their joint rule was ended when he in turn was expelled in 88. Attempts to retake Egypt from Syria and Asia Minor were unsuccessful; he died soon after at sea. Continual dynastic conflict is reflected in the bull-cults of Egypt; strongly supported by Soter II, during the rule of Alexander these suffered from neglect.

PTOLEMY XI ALEXANDER II (c.100/99–80 BC), the younger son of Ptolemy X by an unnamed wife, left the kingdom of Egypt (including Cyprus) to Rome. Briefly succeeding his uncle Ptolemy IX in 80, he was established by *Sulla as joint ruler with and husband of his stepmother Cleopatra Berenice. He murdered her within three weeks and was in turn murdered by the Alexandrians.

PTOLEMY XII NEOS DIONYSUS (AULETES, 'Fluteplayer'), son, by a mistress, of Ptolemy IX, succeeded Alexander II in 80 and married his sister Cleopatra Tryphaena ('the opulent one'). His cultivation of friendly relations with Rome led to his expulsion by the Alexandrians in 58. After visiting Rome, where his restoration became a mainstream political issue, and through heavy expenditure, in 55 he was restored by Aulus Gabinius, Roman governor of Syria. Auletes was the first Ptolemy to adopt Theos ('god') in his Greek titulature. His use of Egypt's wealth in pursuit of his throne brought hardship on the country.

PTOLEMY XIII (63–47 BC), younger brother of *Cleopatra VII, who married and briefly ruled with him from 51. He sided with the nationalists against Cleopatra VII and *Julius Caesar in the Alexandrian war and, on defeat, was drowned in the Nile.

PTOLEMY XIV (*c*.59–44 BC), the younger of Cleopatra VII's two young brothers, was appointed governor of Cyprus in 48. In 47 Caesar made him his sister's husband and consort. He was murdered on her orders.

D.J.T.

PTOLEMY XV CAESAR, nicknamed 'Caesarion' (Little Caesar), eldest son of *Cleopatra VII, who claimed *Julius Caesar as his father and gave him the royal names of God Philopator and Philometor ('loving his father and his mother'). Born 47 BC, he later appears as co-ruler; from 36 his years may be separately numbered. In the 'Donations of Alexandria' (34: see ANTONY) he was named 'king of kings', with Cleopatra 'queen of kings'. Antony asserted Caesar's paternity to the senate, claiming Caesar had acknowledged it, and setting up Caesar's natural son as a rival to his adopted son Octavian for the loyalty of Caesarians. It was denied by Gaius Oppius and by later official tradition. The facts are beyond recovery. In 30 he officially came of age and was told to escape to India via Ethiopia. But he was overtaken or betrayed by his tutor to Octavian (see AUGUSTUS), who had him executed.

T.J.C.; E.B.

Publilius Philo, Quintus, was consul in 339, 327, 320, and 315 BC, and the first plebeian praetor in 336. He reputedly served on a commission to organize debt relief in 352 and as dictator in 339 passed three laws: (1) one censor must always be plebeian; (2) the sanction accorded by patrician senators (*patrum auctoritas*) must now be given before the presentation of legislation to the centuriate assembly (thus limiting patrician obstruction); (3) decisions of the plebeian assembly (*plebiscita*) were to be binding on the whole people. The last of these duplicates the measure of Quintus Hortensius in 287/6 BC and is probably fictitious. Publilius' dictatorship is also suspect but if he passed the first two measures (perhaps as consul), this marks a significant development in plebeian

use of a curule magistracy for political reform.

In 339 Philo also triumphed (i.e. was awarded a victory procession) for a victory over the Latins and in his censorship (332) enrolled new Latin citizens and created two new tribes (the Maecia and Scaptia). In 327–6 he besieged Naples and Palaeopolis and through his contacts with philo-Roman elements secured their surrender: the Greek interests attested by his *cognomen* Philo may have assisted here and he triumphed in 326 as the first historical proconsul. The victories in Campania and Apulia credited to him and Lucius Papirius Cursor by some sources in 320 constitute a suspect revenge for the Caudine Forks but his re-election with Cursor for 315 testifies to his standing and reputation.

A.D.

Publilius Syrus (not Publius, Wölfflin *Philol.* 1865, 439) was brought to Rome (perhaps from Antioch, *Pliny the Elder *HN* 35. 199) as a slave in the 1st cent. BC. According to *Macrobius (*Saturn.* 2. 7. 6–10) he was freed for his wit and educated by his master and composed and performed his own mimes throughout Italy. Invited by *Julius Caesar to perform at the games of 46 BC he challenged other mime-writers to improvise on a given scenario and was declared victor by Caesar over his chief rival Laberius. Only two of his titles are recorded, *Putatores* (Nonius 2. 133) and *Mumurco* ('The mutterer'?, *Priscian, *Inst.* K. 2. 532. 25), and no fragments that indicate the action or themes of his mimes. It became a commonplace (Cassius Severus in *Seneca the Elder, *Contr.* 7. 3. 8, *Seneca the Younger, *Ep. Mor.* 8. 9–10) that his aphorisms expressed moral teaching better than serious dramatists, and a set of fourteen maxims is quoted by *Gellius (*NA* 17. 14: cf. Macrobius 2. 7. 11). (Trimalchio's 'quotation' from Publilius at Petronius *Sat.* 55 is spurious.)

In the 1st cent. AD apophthegms uttered by various dramatic roles in the mimes were selected and alphabetically arranged as proverbial wisdom for schoolboys to copy or memorize. These formed a fixed syllabus with e.g. the distichs of *Cato the Elder, so that in the 4th cent. *Jerome learned in class a line which he quotes twice *aegre reprehendas quod sinas consuescere* (Hieron. *Ep.* 107. 8; 128. 4). It is difficult to distinguish original

Publilian *sententiae* from accretions due to paraphrase of genuine verses, or insertions of Senecan and pseudo-Senecan ideas (see SENECA THE YOUNGER), or distortions of the original iambic senarii and trochaic septenarii that led copyists to mistake them for prose.

One would not expect a common ethical standard among maxims spoken by different characters in a mime. Some contradict others, as proverbs often do. Although many advocate selfish pragmatism, their prevailing terseness of expression gives them an undeniable attraction. J.W.D.; E.F.

Pyrrhon of Elis (*c.*365–275 BC), the founder of Greek Scepticism. He was a painter early in his life, but then studied with a certain Bryson (it is not clear which) and with the Democritean Anaxarchus, with whom he travelled to India in the train of *Alexander the Great. There he is said to have encountered the 'gymnosophists' and 'magi' who were thought to have influenced his later philosophical views. He returned to his native town and lived a quiet and modest life, honoured and respected by his fellow citizens.

Pyrrhon wrote nothing, and what we know of him goes back to the writings of his main pupil, Timon of Phlius. Later accounts of Pyrrhon's philosophy tend to be heavily influenced by the philosophers of the Pyrrhonist revival after Aenesidemus. From a passage attributed to Timon we learn that Pyrrhon claimed that nothing can be found out about the nature of things because neither our senses nor our opinions are true or false. Hence we should be without opinions or inclinations, saying about all things that they no more are than they are not. This attitude will result first in non-assertion, then in tranquillity. The claim that things cannot be known is stated without reservations, and the emphasis lies on the alleged result of suspending judgement—tranquillity. This accords well with the rest of our evidence from Timon, who satirized all other philosophers by contrasting their empty talk and fruitless worries with the supreme calm and serenity of Pyrrhon. Later Pyrrhonists took care to soften the dogmatic tone of Pyrrhon's statements about the impossibility of finding the truth, and to reject the anecdotes that had grown around Pyrrhon's lifestyle, arguing that he would live in accordance with appearances and hence have no grounds for

departing from ordinary customs. We do not have an account of Pyrrhon's arguments for the claim that things are unknowable, but it is likely that he used some of the examples of conflicting appearances and opinions familiar to philosophers since the time of the sophists and Democritus. Those materials were later systematized in the ten Modes of inducing suspension of judgement by Aenesidemus. G.S.

Pyrrhus of Epirus (319–272 BC), son of Aeacides and Phthia, most famous of the kings of the Molossi (an Epirote tribe), chief architect of a large, powerful, and Hellenized Epirote state, and builder of the great theatre at the oracle of Dodona. After reigning as a minor from 307/6 to 303/2, he was driven out and followed for a time the fortunes of *Demetrius the Besieger. With the support of *Ptolemy I, whose stepdaughter Antigone he married, and of *Agathocles of Syracuse, he became joint king with Neoptolemus, whom he soon removed. Early in his reign he annexed and retained southern Illyria, probably as far as Epidamnus. He tried to emancipate Epirus from Macedonia. By intervening in a dynastic quarrel in Macedonia Pyrrhus obtained the frontier provinces of Parauaea and Tymphaea, together with Ambracia, Amphilochia, and Acarnania. On the death of Antigone he acquired Corcyra and Leucas as the dowry of his new wife, Lanassa daughter of Agathocles, and made alliances with the Dardanian chief Bardylis and the Paeonian king Audoleon, whose daughters he also married. Conflict with Demetrius (from 291), now king of Macedon, saw substantial gains in Thessaly and Macedonia, but these were largely lost later to *Lysimachus (284).

Appealed to by the Tarentines (as his uncle Alexander of Epirus and the Spartans *Archidamus III and Cleonymus before him), Pyrrhus went to assist them in their Hellenic struggle against Rome. With a force of 25,000 infantry, 3,000 horse, and 20 elephants he defeated the Romans at Heraclea (280), though not without loss, and won the support of the Samnites, Lucanians, Bruttians, and Greek cities of the south. He marched towards Rome, but prolonged negotiations failed to secure peace. In 279 he defeated the Romans again, at Ausculum, but again with heavy losses. Late in the same year he received an appeal from Syracuse and in

278 sailed to Sicily, where he fought the Carthaginians, then allies of Rome, and Mamertines. In 276 he abandoned the campaign (perhaps by then a lost cause) and returned to Italy, whither he was urgently summoned by his allies in the south. After more losses (including eight elephants and his camp) in battle with the Romans at Malventum (renamed thereafter Beneventum) in 275, he returned to Epirus with less than a third of his original force. A garrison was left behind at Tarentum, signifying perhaps future intent, but the Italian manpower at Rome's disposal had triumphed decisively. Pyrrhus himself embarked upon a new attempt at Macedonia. Initial success and a brief time as king there in 274 gave way to unpopularity after he plundered the royal tombs at Aegae (mod. Vergina), and in 273 he marched into the Peloponnesus. Following a failed attack on Sparta he went to Argos, where in 272 he died, struck on the head by a tile thrown from the roof of a house; in the same year Tarentum fell to the Romans.   P.S.D.

Pythagoras, son of Mnesarchus, one of the most mysterious and influential figures in Greek intellectual history, was born in Samos in the mid-6th cent. BC and migrated to Croton (mod. Crotone) in c.530 BC. There he founded the sect or society that bore his name, and that seems to have played an important role in the political life of Magna Graecia (Greek S. Italy) for several generations. Pythagoras himself is said to have died as a refugee in Metapontum. Pythagorean political influence is attested well into the 4th cent., with Archytas of Tarentum.

The name of Pythagoras is connected with two parallel traditions, one religious and one scientific. Pythagoras is said to have introduced the doctrine of transmigration of souls into Greece, and his religious influence is reflected in the cult organization of the Pythagorean society, with periods of initiation, secret doctrines and passwords (*akousmata* and *symbola*), special dietary restrictions, and burial rites. Pythagoras seems to have become a legendary figure in his own lifetime and was identified by some with the Hyperborean (far-northern) Apollo. His supernatural status was confirmed by a golden thigh, the gift of bilocation, and the capacity to recall his previous incarnations. Classical authors imagine him studying in

Egypt; in the later tradition he gains universal wisdom by travels in the east. Pythagoras becomes the pattern of the 'divine man': at once a sage, a seer, a teacher, and a benefactor of the human race.

The scientific tradition ascribes to Pythagoras a number of important discoveries, including the famous geometric theorem that still bears his name. Even more significant for Pythagorean thought is the discovery of the musical consonances: the ratios 2 : 1, 3 : 2, and 4 : 3 representing the length of strings corresponding to the octave and the basic harmonies (the fifth and the fourth). These ratios are displayed in the *tetractys*, an equilateral triangle composed of 10 dots; the Pythagoreans swear an oath by Pythagoras as author of the *tetractys*. The same ratios are presumably reflected in the music of the spheres, which Pythagoras alone was said to hear.

In the absence of written records before Philolaus of Croton in the late 5th cent., it is impossible to tell how much of the Pythagorean tradition in mathematics, music, and astronomy can be traced back to the founder and his early followers. Since the fundamental work of Walter Burkert, it has been generally recognized that the conception of Pythagorean philosophy preserved in later antiquity was the creation of *Plato and his school, and that the only reliable pre-Platonic account of Pythagorean thought is the system of Philolaus. *Aristotle reports that for the Pythagoreans all things are numbers or imitate numbers. In Philolaus we read that it is by number and proportion that the world becomes organized and knowable. The basic principles are the Unlimited (*apeira*) and the Limiting (*perainonta*). The generation of the numbers, beginning with One in the centre, seems to coincide with the structuring of the cosmos. There must be enough cosmic bodies to correspond to the perfect number 10; the earth is a kind of heavenly body, revolving around an invisible central fire. This fact permitted Copernicus to name 'Philolaus the Pythagorean' as one of his predecessors.

Plato was deeply influenced by the Pythagorean tradition in his judgement myths, in his conception of the soul as transcending the body, and in the mathematical interpretation of nature. The *Phaedo* and the *Timaeus*, respectively, became the classical formulations for the religious and cosmological aspects of the Pythagorean world view. In the *Philebus* (16c) begins the transformation of Pythagoras into the archetype of philosophy. This view is developed by *Speusippus, who replaces Plato's Forms by Pythagorean numbers. Hence *Theophrastus can assign to Pythagoras the late Platonic 'unwritten doctrines' of the One and the Infinite Dyad, and these two principles appear in all later versions of Pythagorean philosophy.

In the 1st cent. BC, Publius Nigidius Figulus revived the Pythagorean tradition in Rome, while in Alexandria the Platonist Eudorus attributed to the Pythagoreans a supreme One, above the two older principles of One and Dyad. This monistic Platonism was developed by the Neopythagoreans: Moderatus of Gades in the 1st cent. AD, Nicomachus of Gerasa and Numenius of Apamea in the 2nd cent. Their innovations were absorbed into the great Neoplatonic synthesis of *Plotinus, and thereafter no distinction can be drawn between Pythagoreans and Neoplatonists. Porphyry and Iamblichus both composed lives of Pythagoras in which he is represented as the source of Platonic philosophy.

There is an important pseudonymous literature of texts ascribed to Pythagoras, Archytas, and other members of the school. This begins in the 3rd cent. BC and continues down to Byzantine times. A number of these texts have survived, thanks to the prestige of their supposed authors.   C.H.K.

PYTHAGOREANISM   (RELIGIOUS ASPECTS) Pythagoreanism is the name given to the philosophical and religious movement(s) allegedly derived from the teachings of Pythagoras. Reliable tradition on the early form of Pythagoreanism, coming chiefly from *Aristotle and his school, presents Pythagoras and his followers as a religious and political association in S. Italy (chiefly Croton) where they gained considerable political influence, until their power was broken in a catastrophe in about 450 BC. From then on, Pythagoreanism survived in two distinct forms, a scientific, philosophical form (the so-called *mathēmatikoi*) which in the 4th cent. manifested itself in the thinking of Philolaus and Archytas of Tarentum and the Pythagoreans whom Plato knew and followed, and a religious, sectarian form

(*akousmatikoi*, those following certain oral teachings (*akousmata* or *symbola*), which manifested itself in the migrant Pythagoristai of Middle Comedy. After the analysis of W. Burkert, it is universally recognized that scientific Pythagoreanism is a reform of its earlier, religious way ascribed to Hippasus of Metapontum around 450 BC.

Despite the fact that many pseudepigraphical Pythagorean writings are dated to Hellenistic times, the continuity of any form of Pythagoreanism after the Classical age is disputed. Neopythagoreanism existed at any rate in the late Hellenistic (the Roman Publius Nigidius Figulus, founder of Neoplatonism according to Cic. *Tim.* 1) and early imperial epochs (Apollonius of Tyana); through the alleged derivation of Pompilius Numa's teaching from that of Pythagoras, it gained popularity in Rome; prominent Neoplatonists such as *Porphyry and his pupil Iamblichus wrote on Pythagoreanism (*De vita Pythagorica*). The hexametrical collection of life rules, under the title Golden Words (*Chrusē Epē*) ascribed to Pythagoras himself, appears at the same date.

While among the philosophical disciplines of the mathematici, arithmetic, theory of number and music are prominent and influential, the doctrines of the acusmatici laid down rules for a distinctive life style, the 'Pythagorean life'. The originally oral *akousmata* (collected by later authors; a list in Iambl. *V. Pyth.* 82–6) contained unrelated and often strange answers to the questions 'What exists?', 'What is the best thing?', 'What should one do?' Prominent among the rules of life is a complicated (and in our sources not consistent) vegetarianism, based on the doctrine of metempsychosis and already ascribed to Pythagoras himself during his life-time (Xenophanes, DK 21 B 7); total vegetarianism excludes participation in sacrifice and marginalizes those who profess it, at the same time all the more efficiently binding them together in their own sectarian group. Metempsychosis and, more generally, an interest in the afterlife connects Pythagoreanism with Orphism; Plato associates vegetarianism with the Orphic life-style (*bios Orphikos*, Plat. *Laws* 6. 783 C), and authors from about 400 BC onwards name Pythagoreans as authors of certain Orphic texts.

F.G.

Qq

Quinctilius Varus, Publius (consul 13 BC),
of a patrician family that had been of no
importance for centuries. He owed his career
to the favour of *Augustus. He was consul 13
BC with the future emperor *Tiberius; like
him, Varus was at the time the husband of a
daughter of *Agrippa. Later he married
Claudia Pulchra, the grand-niece of
Augustus, and was able to acquire some political influence (his two sisters made good marriages, cf. Syme, *AA*, Table XXVI). Varus
became proconsul of Africa (?7–6 BC), and
then legate (governor) of Syria. When Judaea
revolted after the death of *Herod the Great
he marched rapidly southwards and dealt
firmly with the insurgents (Joseph. *BJ* 2. 39 ff.,
etc.). Varus is next heard of as legate of the
Rhine army in AD 9. When marching back
with three legions from the summer-camp
near the Weser, he was treacherously attacked
in difficult country by the Germanic chief
Arminius, whom he had trusted. The Roman
army was destroyed in the *Teutoburgiensis
Saltus* (an area near mod. Kalkriese), and
Varus took his own life (Dio 56. 18–22; Vell.
Pat. 2. 117–20; Florus 2. 30). The defeat had
a profound effect on Augustus (the regime
noticeably deteriorates in the last few years).
Varus was made the scapegoat for the signal
failure of Augustus' whole German policy. He
is alleged to have been grossly extortionate in
Syria, torpid and incompetent in his German
command (Vell. Pat. 2. 117. 2).   R.S.; E.B.

Quinctius Flamininus, Titus See FLAMIN-
INUS.

Quintilian (Marcus Fabius Quintilianus),
Roman advocate and famous authority on
rhetoric. He was born around AD 35 at Calag-
urris (Calahorra) in Spain. His father seems
to have been an orator also (*Inst.* 9. 3. 73), but
his relationship to the Quintilianus named
by *Seneca the Elder (*Controv.* 10 pr. 2) is not
to be known. The young Quintilian may have

been taught in Rome by the grammarian
Remmius Palaemon (schol. on Juv. 6. 452); he
certainly attached himself there to the orator
Domitius Afer (e.g. *Inst.* 5. 7. 7), who died in
59. At some point he returned to Spain, if
*Jerome is correct in saying that he was
brought to the capital by *Galba in 68. Jerome
also states that he was the first rhetorician
to receive a salary from the *fiscus* (imperial
funds), a practice instituted by *Vespasian
(Suet. *Vesp.* 18). His school brought him
unusual wealth for one of his profession (Juv.
7. 188–9). He taught for twenty years (*Inst.* 1
pr. 1), numbering *Pliny the Younger among
his pupils, and retired with unimpaired
powers (2. 12. 12), perhaps in 88, to write his
masterpiece. *Domitian made him tutor to
his two great-nephews and heirs (4 pr. 2), the
sons of Flavius Clemens, through whom he
gained the *ornamenta consularia* (honorary
decorations of a consul) (Auson. *Grat. Act.*
31). His wife died while not yet 19, leaving two
little sons; the younger child died aged five,
the elder aged nine, and his overwhelming
grief at these losses is touchingly expressed in
the preface to *Inst.* 6. The date of his own
death is not known, but is generally assumed
to have been in the 90s.

WORKS 1. *De causis corruptae eloquentiae*,
'On the causes of the corruption of eloquence', not extant (it is not, as was once
thought, the *Dialogus*, now firmly attributed
to *Tacitus; some idea of its contents can be
gained from allusions to it in the *Institutio*.

2. A (lost) speech *pro Naevio Arpiniano*
(*Inst.* 7. 2. 24), whose publication Quintilian
acknowledges as authentic, as opposed to
other speeches circulating under his name. He
also defended the Jewish queen Berenice
(4. 1. 19) and a woman accused of forgery (9.
2. 73).

3. Two books on rhetoric, taken down
without his permission from his lectures by
over-zealous students (1 pr. 7), now lost.

4. The extant *Institutio Oratoria*, 'Training

in Oratory', written and probably published before Domitian's death in 96 (note the flattery of the emperor in 10. 1. 91) and dedicated to Victorius Marcellus (suffect consul 105); its composition took rather more than two years, after which it was put aside for some time (see the letter to the bookseller Trypho which prefaces the work). It covers the training of an orator from babyhood to the peak of his career. Book 1 discusses the education of the child, a practical, humane, and fascinating section, and goes on to the technicalities of grammar, which Quintilian clearly found of great interest. In Book 2 the boy enters the school of rhetoric; there is a memorable chapter on the Good Schoolmaster (2. 2), and Quintilian gives a balanced account of the virtues and vices of declamation, before going on to a discussion of *rhetorikē*, drawing on the prolegomena to Greek rhetorical handbooks. Book 3 names his authorities and goes into much detail on the *status*-lore, besides giving most of what Quintilian has to say on deliberative and epideictic oratory. Books 4–6 take us through the parts of a speech, with appendices on various topics, including the arousal of emotions and of laughter. Invention thus dealt with, Quintilian proceeds to arrangement in Book 7, with much on the different kinds of *status*, and to style in books 8 and 9, full of examples from prose and poetry. Book 10, the most accessible of all, shows how the student is to acquire a 'firm facility' by reading, writing, and imitating good exemplars. The first chapter ends with a famous critique of Greek and Latin writers; Quintilian's concern is to direct his readers towards predecessors who will be useful in the acquisition of oratorical techniques; hence what might otherwise seem strange judgements, brevities ('some prefer Propertius'), and omissions: despite this limitation, many of his dicta have become classics of ancient criticism. The Greek section is derivative; the Latin, in which Quintilian is often at pains to show how Roman writers can stand up to Greek counterparts, is more original. In Book 11 the traditional five parts of rhetoric are rounded off with discussion of memory and delivery; fascinating details of dress and gesture are here preserved. There is also an important chapter on propriety. The final book shows the Complete Orator, *vir bonus dicendi peritus* (12. 1. 1: 'the good man skilled in speaking') in

action, a man of the highest character and ideals, the consummation of all that is best in morals, training, and stylistic discernment; Quintilian's insistence on eloquence as a moral force is here at its most impressive.

Quintilian's style, never less than workmanlike, is not without its variety and power. But it was content that most concerned him. Deeply imbued in Ciceronian ideas, and reacting sharply against the trends of his own century, his great book is a storehouse of sanity, humane scholarship and good sense. Its influence in the Middle Ages was limited by gaps in the manuscripts most widely available at that period: but after Poggio's discovery of a complete text at St Gall in 1416 it grew in fame, and it was important until the end of the 18th cent. R.G.A.; M.W.

Quirinius, Publius Sulpicius, consul 12 BC, a *novus homo* (roughly, first member of his family to become a senator and/or consul) from Lanuvium (on his career cf. Tac. *Ann.* 3. 48). Quirinius defeated the Marmaridae (Florus 2. 31), perhaps as proconsul of Crete and Cyrene (*c.*15 BC). Between 12 BC and AD 2 he subjugated the Homanadenses, 'Cilician' brigands on Lake Trogitis (Strabo 569). The precise date of this war and the command held by Quirinius are disputed. It has been argued that he must have been legate of Syria at the time; but the war could have been conducted only from the side of Galatia, which province, though normally governed by imperial legates of praetorian rank, might easily have been placed under a consular. Quirinius prudently paid court to *Tiberius on Rhodes, succeeded Marcus Lollius as guide and supervisor of Gaius Caesar (see AUGUSTUS) in the east (AD 2), and shortly after married Aemilia Lepida, a descendant of *Sulla and *Pompey. Legate of Syria in AD 6, he supervised the assessment of Judaea when that territory was annexed after the deposition of Archelaus (Joseph. *AJ* 17. 1 ff., cf. *ILS* 2683 = EJ 231 (tr. D. Braund, *From Augustus to Nero*, no. 446); also Acts 5: 37, which mentions the insurrection of Judas the Galilaean 'in the days of the taxing'). In order to reconcile and explain Luke 2: 1 and establish a date for the Nativity before the death of *Herod the Great (i.e. before 4 BC), various attempts have been made to discover an earlier governorship of Syria by Quirinius, and, by implication, an earlier census in

Judaea. The acephalous (= top missing) elogium from Tibur (*ILS* 918 = EJ 199; tr. D. Braund, no. 362) sometimes attributed to Quirinius more probably honours Piso (above), and in any case could not prove two governorships of Syria. Quirinius lived to a wealthy and unpopular old age. In 21 he died and was granted a public funeral on the motion of Tiberius, who recounted his meritorious services (Tac., above).   R.S.; B.M.L.

Rr

Rhianus of Crete, poet and scholar; born *c.*275 BC at Bene (?= Lebena) or Ceraea; began life as a slave, working as attendant at a wrestling-school, but was later educated and became a schoolteacher. One of his epigrams (70 Powell) mentions Troezen, and it has been conjectured that he moved to mainland Greece.

WORKS Rhianus produced an influential edition of *Homer, more conservative than Zenodotus of Ephesus'. He also wrote epigrams (66–76 Powell), mostly on erotic themes, but was best known as a prolific writer of epic poetry. Only small fragments (mostly geographical names) survive of his *Heracleia* (probably in 14 books), possibly modelled on that of Panyassis of Halicarnassus, and of the ethnographical epics *Thessalica* (at least 16 books), *Achaïca* (at least 4 books), and *Eliaca* (at least 3 books). We are better informed about the *Messeniaca* (at least 6 books): two papyrus fragments (*Suppl. Hell.* 923, 946) have been plausibly attributed to it, and the travel-writer Pausanias used it as a source for his narrative (4. 14–24) of the 'Second Messenian War'. It recounted the uprising of the Messenians, led by Aristomenes, against Spartan rule, the siege and fall of their stronghold on Mt. Hira, the adventures of the defeated insurgents, and Aristomenes' death in Rhodes. (Historians generally place these events in the early 5th cent.; but H. T. Wade-Gery (in E. Badian (ed.), *Ancient Society and its Institutions* (1966), 289–302) argues for a dating *c.*600.) We cannot determine which elements in Pausanias can be ascribed to Rhianus, but such episodes as Aristomenes' affair with the priestess (4. 17. 1), his escape from prison (4. 18. 5–6), and the adulterous intrigue of the herdsman double-agent (4. 20. 5–10) have a poetic flavour. It is not known to which, if any, of the epics the longest fragment (1 Powell) belongs: some regard it as a complete poem; its 21 lines, on human folly, written in straightforward Homerizing style with an admixture of Hesiodic diction, are sometimes interpreted as an attack on the pretensions of Hellenistic monarchs.

Rhianus represents a type of poetry very different from that of *Callimachus, but the scantiness of his surviving fragments makes aesthetic judgements hazardous.   F.W.

Rufus, Quintus Curtius See CURTIUS RUFUS.

Rutilius Claudius Namatianus, the author of an elaborate poetical itinerary in elegiacs conventionally referred to as the *De reditu suo* (the original title is lost), was a member of an aristocratic Gallo-Roman family, possibly from Toulouse (Tolosa). He held the offices of *magister officiorum* (master of the offices) (*c.* AD 412) and *praefectus urbi* (city-prefect) (414). His poem has come down to us in an incomplete state. The beginning of the first book is lost, and 644 lines survive; of the second book two portions are extant, the first 68 lines and a further fragment of 39 half-lines first published in 1973. The poem recounts the voyage undertaken by the author in 417 (though the date has been disputed) from Rome to Gaul, where his estates had suffered from barbarian inroads; his party has reached Luna on the bay of La Spezia when the main part of the text breaks off. The account of the journey and the descriptions of the places visited or passed are interwoven with personal and historical reflections of the poet. The poem is most notable, however, for its intensely pro-Roman, classical outlook. In its existing form it opens with a long eulogy of Rome, most of it presented as an address to the city by the poet on the point of departure. This attitude, combined with other features of the work, such as the invective against the Jews, the monks of Capraria, and Stilicho (*de facto* ruler of the western empire 395–408), who had burned the Sibylline books, strongly suggests that Namatianus was an adherent of the old paganism; but he need not have been an extreme opponent of Christianity. At all events, his poetic stance is located solidly in the classical tradition, as is his style. He is an elegant poet, schooled in the best verse of the classical period, but possessing originality and flair, and capable of rising to impressive heights. The rhetorical tone of parts of his work is typical of his time.   J.H.D.S.

Rutilius Rufus, Publius, born 160 BC or soon after, studied philosophy under *Panaetius (becoming a firm Stoic), law under Publius Mucius Scaevola (becoming an expert juris-consult), and oratory under Servius Sulpicius Galba (without becoming an effective speaker), then served as military tribune under *Scipio Aemilianus at Numantia. His wife was a Livia, probably a sister of *Livius Drusus (1), and his sister married a Cotta, to whom she bore Gaius, Lucius, and Marcus Aurelius Cotta. Despite his connections, he was defeated for the consulship of 115 by *Scaurus, prosecuted him, and was in turn prosecuted by him (both unsuccessfully) for *ambitus* (bribery). In 109–108 he and *Marius served with distinction as legates (subordinate commanders) under *Metellus Numidicus in Numidia, where they became bitter enemies. As consul 105 he restored Roman morale after the disaster of Arausio and introduced military reforms (among them arms drill), on which Marius later built his own army reforms and his German victories. As legate of Quintus *Scaevola he was left in charge of Asia when Scaevola returned to Rome, and he offended the *publicani* (tax-farmers) by strictly controlling their activities. (The date should be in and after Scaevola's consulship, since no ex-consul is ever recorded as serving under a praetor.) In 92 he was prosecuted for provincial extortion *repetundae* (the prosecution was encouraged by Marius), took *Socrates as his model in his defence, and was convicted by the court manned by *equites* (Roman knights). He went into exile at Smyrna and there wrote a largely autobiographical and highly personal history of his time, much used by later historians of the period. His conviction marked the bankruptcy of the equestrian courts first instituted by Gaius *Gracchus and led to the attempted reform by his nephew *Livius Drusus (2).   E.B.

Ss

Sallust (Gaius Sallustius Crispus), Roman historian, probably 86–35 BC. A Sabine from Amiternum, he probably derived from the municipal aristocracy. The earliest certain information of his career concerns his tribunate in 52, when he acted against *Cicero and *Milo (Asc. *Mil.* 37, 45, 49, 51 C). He was expelled from the senate in 50; *Inv. in Sall.* 16 alleges immorality, but the real grounds were probably his actions in 52. He now joined *Julius Caesar, commanding a legion in 49. As praetor in 46 he took part in the African campaign, and was appointed the first governor of Africa Nova. On his return to Rome he was charged with malpractice, allegedly escaping only on Caesar's intervention (Cass. Dio 43. 9. 2, *Inv. in Sall.* 19). With no immediate prospect of advancement, Sallust withdrew from public life—the proems of both *Cat.* and *Iug.* defend that decision—and turned to historiography.

In his first two works he avoided the usual annalistic presentation, preferring the monograph form introduced to Rome by Coelius Antipater. The first, the *Bellum Catilinae* (*c.*42/1 BC), treats the conspiracy of *Catiline, 'especially memorable for the unprecedented quality of the crime and the danger' (*Cat.* 4. 4). This is set against, and illustrates, the political and moral decline of Rome, begun after the fall of Carthage, quickening after *Sulla's dictatorship, and spreading from the dissolute nobility to infect all Roman politics (*Cat.* 6–14, 36–9). There are no doubts about the guilt of the 'conspirators', and Sallust so far accepts the assessment of Cicero, who must have been one of his principal sources (supplemented by oral testimony, *Cat.* 48. 9). But Cicero himself is less prominent than might be expected; the heroes are Caesar and *Cato the Younger, the two examples of *virtus* ('excellence') which stand out from the moral gloom of their day (53–4), and their speeches in the final debate are presented at a length which risks unbalancing the whole (51–2).

Sallust's even-handedness between the two men would have struck contemporaries familiar with the fiercely polarized propaganda since Cato's death.

The second monograph, the more ambitious and assured *Bellum Iugurthinum* (*c.*41–40 BC), again emphasizes moral decline. The Jugurthan War (see JUGURTHA) is chosen 'both because it was great, bloody, and of shifting fortunes, and because it represented the first challenge to the arrogance of the nobility' (*Iug.* 5. 1): a strange judgement, but one which reflects the work's interest in the interrelation of domestic strife and external warfare. The military narrative is patchy and selective. Politics are presented simply but vigorously, with decline again spreading from the venal nobility. This decline is presented more dynamically than in *Cat.*, as several individuals fail to live up to promising beginnings: Jugurtha himself, *Marius, Sulla, and even *Metellus Numidicus, who comes closest to being a hero. Speeches and especially digressions divide the work into distinct panels, and implied comparisons—Gaius Memmius and Marius, Metellus and Marius, Marius and Sulla—further plot the changes in political and military style. For sources Sallust perhaps used a general history and the autobiographies of *Scaurus, *Rutilius Rufus, and Sulla; some geographical notions, but not much more, may derive from *Posidonius. Little seems owed to the 'Punic books' mentioned at 17. 7.

Sallust's last work, the *Histories*, was annalistic (arranged by years). It covered events from 78, perhaps continuing Cornelius Sisenna, though it included a retrospect of earlier events. The last datable fragment, from book 5, concerns the year 67, hardly his chosen terminus. Speeches and letters survive entire, though the other fragments are scrappy. He again emphasized the decline of the state after Sulla, and was not generous to Pompey.

The 'Invective against Cicero' ascribed to Sallust in the manuscripts and cited as genuine by *Quintilian (4. 1. 68, 9. 3. 89) is not appropriate to Sallust in 54 (its ostensible date); its author was probably an Augustan rhetorician. The authenticity question is more difficult with the two 'Letters to the elderly Caesar', purportedly of 46 (or 48) and c.50 BC, but they too are most likely later works, probably declamations of the early empire.

As a historian Sallust has weaknesses. His leading theme is decline, but this is presented schematically and unsubtly; his characters have vigour, but seldom convince. The interpretation of Roman politics is often crude; but if the *nobiles* (elite of senators descended from consuls) come in for most criticism, this is because they set the pattern; their more popular opponents were no better. Still, the choice of the monograph form was enterprising, and he avoids the danger of drifting into biography; the use of particular episodes to illuminate a general theme is deft; he shows an increasing grasp of structure; the rhetoric, especially in speeches and letters, has concentration and verve; and the man has style. The influence of *Thucydides is pervasive, though he cannot match his model's intellectual depth. Many stylistic features are also owed to the Roman tradition, particularly *Cato the Elder. The characteristics are noted by ancient writers (*testimonia* in A Kurfess Teubner edn., pp. xxvi ff.): archaisms, 'truncated epigrams, words coming before expected, obscure brevity' (Sen. *Ep.* 114. 17), recherché vocabulary, rapidity. He won many admirers in later antiquity and was the greatest single influence on *Tacitus.   C.B.R.P.

Salvius Julianus See JULIANUS, SALVIUS.

Sapor (*Shabuhr*), name of kings of the Iranian Sasanid dynasty, of which the most famous was Sapor I (reigned AD 240–72), son of Artaxerxes I (*Ardashir*) and co-regent with him 240/1 (?). He continued, with spectacular success, his father's policy of aggression against Rome, taking full advantage of the internal crisis in the Roman empire. After Hatra and the Roman outposts in Mesopotamia fell to the Sasanians in the late 230s and early 240s, the emperor Gordian III started a counter-offensive, but was beaten and died in the battle of Misiche (244). The subsequent peace treaty between Sapor and the emperor Philip forced the Romans to pay a great amount of ransom. A further attack by Sapor led to the occupation of Armenia, the devastation of Syria, and the first conquest of Antioch (252/3). The third campaign of the Sasanid 'King of Kings, King of Iran and Non-Iran' saw the capture of *Valerian (260) and Persian raids into Syria, Cilicia, and Cappadocia. It was left to Septimius Odaenathus, dynast of Palmyra, to play the major role in forcing Sapor to withdraw from Roman territory (262–6). In addition to his military achievements (listed in his great inscription at Naqš-i Rustam, the *Res Gestae Divi Saporis*, and depicted in his famous rock-reliefs), Sapor was famed for his grandiose building operations (he used the labour of Roman captives) and for his relations with the religious leader Mani, who began his preaching in the Persian empire at the time of Sapor's investiture.   J.Wi.

Sappho, lyric poet. Born on the E Greek island of Lesbos in the second half of the 7th cent. BC, she was hailed in antiquity as 'the tenth Muse' (*Anth. Pal.* 9. 506), and her poetry was collected into nine books (arranged according to metre) in the canonical Alexandrian edition. Only one complete poem and some substantial fragments survive, culled from quotations in other writers or from papyrus finds.

Most of her poems were for solo performance, and many refer to love between women or girls. Other subjects include hymns to deities and apparently personal concerns such as her brother's safety (fr. 5). Wedding songs, and snatches from a lament for Adonis (fr. 140), are clearly for several singers. Fr. 44, describing the marriage of Hector and Andromache, is unusual in its narrative length and proximity to epic poetry.

Little about her life is certain: biographies (*POxy.* 1800, *Suda*, 'Sappho') are late and sometimes contradictory. She may have had some involvement in the aristocratic power struggles of Lesbos (fr. 71), leading to a period of exile in Sicily (*Marm. Par.* 36). She was probably married, though only a brother and (probably) a daughter, Cleis, figure in the poems. The story of her suicide for love of Phaon, a mythical ferryman, is almost certainly fictional.

Her sexual inclinations have occasioned

much speculation from antiquity to the present. From Attic comedy onwards she was credited with an implausible selection of male lovers. She is described as a lover of women only in post-Classical times, and in later European tradition was often regarded as heterosexual.

Her own poetry remains the major source for the controversial question of how she related to the companions (fr. 160) who formed her audience. An important parallel is *Alcman's *partheneia* (maiden-songs) written for girls' choruses, in which the singers praise each other in erotic terms. Sappho's term for her companions is *parthenos* (girl). This, and the frequent references to partings and absence in her poems, suggest that most of her circle shared their lives for only a limited period before marriage. Homoeroticism was probably institutionalized at this stage of life, as it was elsewhere for young men. The group's preoccupations—love, beauty, poetry—are indicated by the divinities most often invoked in Sappho: Aphrodite, the Graces, and the Muses.

But despite the likely educational and religious function of her group, Sappho herself emerges from the poems as far from the chaste headmistress figure constructed by 19th- and early 20th- cent. German philology. In fr. 1, the poet names herself in a prayer enlisting Aphrodite's help in winning the love of an unresponsive girl. In fr. 16 the singer links her own love for the absent Anactoria with that of Helen for Paris, and fr. 31 famously charts the singer's despair as she watches a beloved girl sitting next to a man. Sappho's love poetry differs from that of male writers in the almost complete absence of a sharp distinction between lover and beloved.

Poems such as these reveal an accomplished poet who can achieve effects of great subtlety beneath an apparently simple surface; other, less complex poems (frs. 102, 114) seem influenced by folk-song. Like her contemporary *Alcaeus she writes in a literary Aeolic dialect. Her work was admired in antiquity for its euphony (Dion. Hal. *Comp.* 23) and she was credited with musical invention; the Sapphic stanza was used by later poets such as *Horace. Notable imitations include *Catullus (1) 51, 61, and 62, while *Ovid's imaginary epistle from Sappho to Phaon (*Her.* 15) was the progenitor of many subsequent fictions about her.   M.Wil.

Saturninus (Lucius Appuleius Saturninus), of praetorian family and a good popular orator, as quaestor at Ostia (probably 105 BC) was superseded in his *cura annonae* (office of supervising the food supply) by *Scaurus and turned against the ruling oligarchy. As tribune 103 he sought the favour of *Marius by passing a law assigning land to his African veterans. Probably in that year, but possibly in 100, he passed a grain law against violent opposition by optimate tribunes and a law setting up a permanent *quaestio* (tribunal) on *maiestas* (treason), directed (if in 103) against unpopular nobles. He and Gaius Servilius Glaucia continued turbulent action in 102 and 101. *Metellus Numidicus tried, as censor, to expel them from the senate, but was prevented by his colleague. Tribune again in 100, he again co-operated with Marius by proposing to settle the veterans of his German war in Transalpine Gaul and to give Marius a limited (and probably traditional) right to enfranchise non-Roman colonists. An oath of obedience, to be taken by all magistrates and senators, was attached to the law. Marius found an evasive formula allowing senators to swear it without disgrace, but Metellus refused and went into exile. Marius and Saturninus were later suspected of conspiring to bring this about. With the help of Glaucia, now praetor and supported by the *equites* (knights) because of his *lex Servilia de repetundis* (extortion law), Saturninus also proposed colonies and land assignments for Roman and Italian veterans of other armies that had fought in Thrace and Sicily and of *proletarii* (poor citizens normally exempt from military service). Re-elected tribune for 99, he hoped to have Glaucia as consul, but Marius, now suspicious of their ambitions, rejected Glaucia's candidacy as illegal. After having Memmius, a hostile candidate, murdered in the electoral assembly, Saturninus, by massive use of force in the *concilium plebis* (plebeian assembly), tried to pass a law allowing Glaucia's candidacy. In the resulting riot, the senate, on the motion of the *princeps senatus* (first senator) Scaurus, passed the *senatus consultum ultimum* (the 'ultimate decree' of the senate, in effect a declaration of emergency)—its first use against a tribune in office—and Marius organized an attack on the agitators. On receiving an official promise (*fides publica*) of safety, they surrendered to him and were imprisoned in the senate-house, but were murdered by a mob without receiving any protection from Marius (probably autumn 100). This embittered their surviving adherents against Marius. Saturninus' colonies were not founded, but his land assignments seem to have been recognized.

In foreign policy he has been (implausibly) suspected of having tried to start a major war in the east in which Marius could command. More credibly, the law found at Cnidus in Asia Minor and at Delphi has been ascribed to his circle. He or a relative adopted a son of Publius Decius Subulo, and a relative of his married Marcus Aemilius Lepidus, father of *Lepidus, the triumvir.   E.B.

Scaevola, Quintus Mucius, called **'Pontifex',** son of Publius Mucius Scaevola, whom he surpassed both as an orator and a lawyer. In his most famous case, the *causa Curiana* (Cic. *De or.* 1. 180 f.), he defended the strict wording of a will, against the defence of *aequitas* (equity) and intention by Lucius Licinius *Crassus. As consuls (95 BC), he and Crassus passed the *lex Licinia Mucia* instituting a *quaestio* (tribunal of inquiry) against aliens who had been illegally enrolled as citizens. Perhaps on the motion of Aemilius *Scaurus, he was sent as proconsul to govern Asia, either after his praetorship, or more probably after his consulship. He reorganized the troubled province with the aid of his legate Rutilius and, departing after nine months, left Rutilius in charge. When Rutilius was prosecuted in 92, he escaped prosecution, probably through his remote connection with *Marius and because of his high prestige, and in 89 he became *pontifex maximus* (head of the most important of the priestly colleges at Rome), the last civil lawyer known to have held this office. After Marius' death he was threatened by Gaius Flavius Fimbria, but escaped harm and remained in Rome under the government of *Cinna and Gnaeus Papirius Carbo, loyal to the government and advising compromise with *Sulla. He was killed by Lucius Junius Brutus Damasippus in 82, probably when on the point of joining Sulla.

Scaevola, known in legal circles as 'Quintus Mucius', was perhaps the leading lawyer of the later Roman republic. His eighteen books (*libri*) on the civil law (*De iure civili*) was the most famous legal treatise of the period and was still the subject of commentary by the lawyer Sextus Pomponius and others in the 2nd cent. AD. He also compiled a book of definitions (*Horoi*: the title comes from the Stoic philosopher Chrysippus). He was the first lawyer to give serious attention to classification; thus, he distinguished five types of guardianship. But, despite his grounding in Greek, especially middle Stoic, culture he did not succeed in reducing the civil law to a system, though he helped to make it morally more acceptable. Thus he fixed on the conscientious head of a family (*diligens paterfamilias*) as the pattern of correct behaviour in avoiding harm to others. His large legal practice was attended by many pupils including Gaius Aquil(l)ius Gallus and, after his father P. Mucius Scaevola's death, *Cicero.
                                                 E.B.; T.Hon.

Scaurus (Marcus Aemilius Scaurus) of patrician, but recently impoverished and undistinguished family, according to Cicero had to work his way up like a *novus homo* (first man from his family to reach the consulship). He amassed wealth (not always reputably), gained the support of the Caecilii Metelli, and became consul (with a Metellus) 115 BC, defeating Publius Rutilius Rufus. As consul he humiliated the praetor Publius Decius Subulo, triumphed over Ligurian tribesmen and was made *princeps senatus* (First Senator) by the censors (one a Metellus) although probably not the senior patrician alive. He also began building a road (via Aemilia Scauri) linking the via Aurelia and the via Postumia. Increasingly powerful in the senate, he married Caecilia Metella and became the leader of the Metellan family group, then at the height of its glory. Though himself suspect because of his negotiations with *Jugurtha, he became chairman of one of the tribunals set up by Gaius Mamilius Limetanus. Censor 109, he refused, until forced, to resign on the death of his colleague *Livius Drusus (1). About 105, he received a *cura annonae* (office of supervising the food-supply), superseding the quaestor Saturninus. In 100 he moved the *senatus consultum ultimum* ('ultimate decree' of the senate, in effect a declaration of emergency) against Saturninus and his supporters. In the 90s he went on an embassy to Asia and on his return may have brought about the mission of Quintus Mucius Scaevola. After Rutilius' conviction (92) he avoided prosecution by Quintus Servilius Caepio and became one of the chief advisers of *Livius Drusus (2). Attacked by Quintus Varius, he crushed him with a haughty reply. He was dead by late 89, when Metella married *Sulla. Throughout his life he was involved in numerous trials, not always successful in prosecution, but never convicted. He was the last great *princeps senatus*: 'his nod almost ruled the world' (Cic. *Font.* 24).

He wrote an autobiography, perhaps the first, but it was soon forgotten. Cicero's admiration for him has coloured much of our tradition, but a very different view is found in (e.g.) Sallust, *Iug.*   E.B.

Scipio Aemilianus (Publius Scipio Aemilianus Africanus (Numantinus)), born 185/4 BC as second son of *Paullus, adopted as a child by Publius Cornelius Scipio, son of *Scipio Africanus, as his elder brother was by a Quintus Fabius Maximus. In 168 he fought under Paullus at Pydna. Back in Rome, he met *Polybius, who became his friend and his mentor in preparing him for a public career. (See esp. Polyb. 31. 23 ff.) In 151, though asked by the Macedonians, as Paullus' son, to settle their problems that soon led to the war with Andriscus, he instead volunteered for arduous service as a military tribune under Lucius Licinius Lucullus in Spain, thus persuading others to volunteer. In the fighting he won a major decoration, the *corona muralis* (for the first man to scale an enemy wall in battle). When sent to request elephants from *Masinissa, he renewed Africanus' patronal relations with him and vainly tried to mediate peace between him and Carthage after a battle he had witnessed. In 149 and 148 he served as a military tribune under Manius Manilius in Africa and again distinguished himself both in the fighting, where he won a rare distinction, the *corona graminea*, a grass crown for a soldier who raised a siege (Plin. *HN* 22. 6 ff., 13), and in diplomacy, persuading a Carthaginian commander to defect. After Masinissa's death he divided the kingdom among his three legitimate sons according to the king's request. Coming to Rome to stand for an aedileship for 147, he was elected consul, contrary to the rules for the *cursus honorum* (Roman career path), by a well-organized popular demand that forced the senate to suspend the rules. He was

assigned Africa by special legislation and, after restoring discipline and closing off the enemy's harbour, he overcame long and desperate resistance and early in 146 captured Carthage after days of street-fighting. After letting his soldiers collect the booty, he destroyed the city and sold the inhabitants into slavery. Anyone who should resettle the site was solemnly cursed. With the help of the usual senate commission he organized the province of Africa and after giving magnificent games returned to celebrate a splendid triumph, earning the name 'Africanus' to which his adoptive descent entitled him. He distributed some captured works of art among cities in Sicily and Italy (Cic. *Verr.* passim; *Syll.*[3] 677; *ILLRP* 326).

Probably in 144–3 he headed an embassy to the kings and cities of the east, perhaps even as far as the territory contested between Parthians and Seleucids (Lucil. 464 Marx), with *Panaetius as his personal companion. After his return he presumably guided senate policy in those areas, especially towards Pergamum, the Seleucids, and the Jews. (We have no evidence on its formulation and little on its execution.) In 142 he was censor with Lucius Mummius, who mitigated some of his severity. They restored the Aemilian Bridge and adorned the Capitol (temple of Jupiter).

In 136 he secured the rejection of the peace in Spain negotiated for Gaius Hostilius Mancinus by his cousin and brother-in-law Tiberius *Gracchus. This deeply offended Gracchus, even though Scipio saved him from personal disgrace. In 135, again by special dispensation and without campaigning for the office, he was elected consul 134 and sent to Numantia, with an army consisting chiefly of his own clients because of the shortage of military manpower. He starved Numantia into surrender in just over a year, destroyed it, and sold the survivors into slavery, returning in 132 to celebrate a second triumph and acquire the (unofficial) name 'Numantinus'. By approving of Gracchus' murder he incurred great unpopularity. It was increased when, in 129, defending the interests of Italian clients holding public land, he was responsible for a senate decree that paralysed the agrarian commission by transferring its judiciary powers to the consuls, usually hostile or absent. When, soon after, he was found dead, various prominent persons, including his wife (Gracchus' sister) and *Cornelia (Gracchus' mother), were suspected of responsibility, though the funeral laudation written by his friend Laelius specified natural death. (See E. Badian, *JRS* 1956, 220.)

His personal morality and civil and military courage made him an unlikely friend of *Cato the Elder. But he was a patron of poets and philosophers, with a genuine interest in literature (he was himself an able orator) and in Greek philosophy, as transmitted by Polybius, which he combined with a traditional aristocratic Roman outlook. He believed in the 'balanced constitution', with the people entitled to choose their leaders (Polyb. 6. 14. 4 and 8: hence his willingness to accept extraordinary appointments) and to take charge of criminal trials (Polyb. 6. 14. 5 ff.: hence his support for the ballot law of Lucius Cassius Longinus Ravilla). But he could foresee the ultimate fall of Rome (Astin 251 f.; cf. Polyb. 6. 9. 12 ff.), which could be delayed by stopping signs of decay, especially the decline in aristocratic morality (see *ORF* [1] 21, esp. nos. 13, 17, 30, and cf. Polyb. 6. 8. 4 f.) and the danger of the democratic element, under the tribunes (cf. Polyb. 6. 16. 5 ff.), leading the state into anarchy and tyranny (cf. Polyb. 6. 9. 2 ff.— and an aristocratic Roman fear of a leader's excessive popularity producing *regnum*, 'monarchy'). Utterly ruthless towards Rome's enemies, he believed in loyal patronage (both for Rome and for himself) over client-friends, whether monarchs like *Attalus II and Masinissa or Italian allies. Cicero, in *De republica*, depicts him as the ideal Roman statesman (cf. also *De senectute* and *De amicitia*) and sets him in a group of aristocrats and their cultured clients (esp. *Amic.* 69) that modern scholars turned into the 'Scipionic Circle'.   E.B.

Scipio Africanus (Publius Scipio Africanus), son of Publius Cornelius Scipio and nephew of Gnaeus Cornelius Scipio Calvus, husband of the daughter of Lucius Aemilius Paullus, father of Publius Cornelius Scipio, Lucius Cornelius Scipio, and of two daughters, married to Publius Cornelius Scipio Nasica Corculum and Tiberius Sempronius Gracchus (father of the *Gracchi), respectively. He was born in 236 BC and is said to have saved his father's life at the battle of the Ticinus in 218 and, as military tribune, to have rallied the survivors of the battle of Cannae at

Canusium. He was curule aedile 213, and in 210 was appointed by the people to the command in Spain, the first person to have received consular *imperium* (a grant of supreme military and civil authority) without having previously been consul or praetor. In Spain he resumed the aggressive policy of his father and uncle; in 209 he captured Carthago Nova (mod. Cartagena), the main Carthaginian supply base in Spain, by sending a wading party across the lagoon, which, he had discovered, normally ebbed in the evening. In 208, employing tactics which marked a major break with traditional Roman practice, he defeated Hasdrubal Barca at Baecula (Bailen), north of the Baetis (Guadalquivir). When Hasdrubal escaped towards the Pyrenees and the route to Italy, he decided not to pursue him. In 206 he defeated Mago and Hasdrubal the son of Gisgo at Ilipa, just north of Seville. Thereafter only mopping-up operations remained in Spain; a mutiny in his army was quelled, and the ringleaders executed. Scipio crossed to Africa to solicit the support of Syphax, and met *Masinissa in western Spain.

Elected consul for 205, Scipio wanted to carry the war to Africa. Opposition in the senate was led by Quintus *Fabius Maximus Verrucosus and Quintus Fulvius Flaccus, but he was assigned Sicily with permission to invade Africa if he saw fit. Denied the right to levy new troops, he crossed to Sicily accompanied only by volunteers, returning to southern Italy to recapture Locri (Epizephyrii); the subsequent behaviour of Pleminius briefly threatened Scipio's own position. In 204 he landed in Africa, began the siege of Utica, and wintered on a nearby headland. Hasdrubal and Syphax encamped a few miles to the south; in the course of feigned peace negotiations Scipio discovered the details of their camps, which were made of wood or reeds, and in the spring of 203 a night attack led to their destruction by fire and the death of large numbers of Carthaginian troops. Later Scipio defeated Hasdrubal and Syphax at the battle of the Great Plains, *c*.120 km. (75 mi.) west of Carthage. He now occupied Tunis, but was forced to use his transport ships to block a Carthaginian attack on his fleet at Utica, losing 60 transports. During an armistice, peace terms were agreed, and accepted at Rome, but in the spring of 202 an attack by Carthage on

Roman ships, and subsequently on envoys sent by Scipio to protest, led to the resumption of hostilities. Hannibal had now returned to Carthage, and after further abortive peace negotiations Scipio defeated him at the battle of Zama; peace was concluded on Rome's terms. Scipio received the *cognomen* (surname) Africanus and returned to Rome to celebrate a triumph.

Scipio now had great prestige at Rome. The so-called 'Scipionic legend' (in its later form Scipio is the son of Jupiter) had already come into existence. The capture of Carthago Nova, when Scipio is said to have told his troops that Neptune had appeared to him in a dream and promised him help, led to the belief that he was divinely inspired. The Iberians had saluted him as a king, but there is no evidence that he ever envisaged playing other than a traditional role in Roman politics. His success, however, meant that he had many enemies among the nobility, some alarmed by the stories circulating about him, others merely jealous of his success. He was elected censor in 199 but his tenure of the office was unremarkable: he became *princeps senatus* (first senator), a position confirmed by the following two pairs of censors. Consul for the second time in 194, he wanted to succeed *Flamininus in Greece, believing that a continued military presence was necessary as security against *Antiochus III the Great, but the senate voted that the army should be withdrawn. Scipio campaigned in northern Italy during his consulship, but achieved little. As an ambassador to Africa in 193 he failed, perhaps deliberately, to settle a dispute between Carthage and Masinissa; the story that he also went to Asia in that year and met Hannibal should be rejected. In 190 he volunteered to go to Asia as a legate under his brother Lucius Cornelius Scipio Asiagenes. He rejected a bribe, which Antiochus offered him in order to secure a favourable peace; shortly before the battle of Magnesia Antiochus returned his captive son Lucius Cornelius Scipio. He took no part in the battle itself because of illness, but was chosen to present the Roman peace terms after Antiochus' defeat. At Rome there now began a series of conflicts between the Scipio brothers (and their allies) and their opponents, among whom Cato the Elder was prominent, culminating in the much debated 'trials of the Scipios'. The accusations involved the embezzlement of public funds and, perhaps, the taking of bribes from Antiochus. It is probable that Publius was attacked in the senate in 187, and Lucius put on trial (in what way and with what result is uncertain), and that Publius was accused in 184, but avoided trial by retiring into voluntary exile at Liternum (in Campania), where he died the following year.   J.Br.

Sejanus (Lucius Aelius Seianus), d. AD 31, of Volsinii (mod. Bolsena). Sejanus' father was an *eques* (knight), Lucius Seius Strabo, his mother the sister of Quintus Iunius Blaesus, suffect consul AD 10, and connected with Aelii Tuberones and Cassii Longini. Sejanus, who had attended Augustus' grandson Gaius in the east, was made Strabo's colleague as prefect of the guard by *Tiberius in AD 14, and soon, on his father's appointment as prefect of Egypt, became sole commander; by 23 he had concentrated the guard in barracks near the porta Viminalis. After the death of Tiberius' son Drusus in 23 (murder was later imputed) his influence was paramount; a succession of prosecutions eliminated opponents (chiefly adherents of the elder *Agrippina). Tiberius allegedly refused to allow a marriage with Drusus' widow Livia Julia (25), but retired from Rome in 26, further increasing Sejanus' influence (he allegedly encouraged the move); honours and oaths were offered to him as to Tiberius. In 29 Agrippina and her eldest son Nero Julius Caesar were deported; her second, Drusus Julius Caesar, was imprisoned in 30. That year Sejanus was elected consul for 31 with Tiberius amid engineered demonstrations; a grant of proconsular power followed, and he hoped for tribunician power. In October, however, Tiberius, allegedly warned by his sister-in-law Antonia, sent a letter to the senate which ended by denouncing him (certainly of plotting against *Germanicus' youngest son, *Gaius (1) 'Caligula' (the future emperor)). Sejanus was arrested, the guard having been transferred to Macro, 'tried' in the senate, and executed; the punishment of Livilla and of adherents, real or alleged, followed; even his youngest children were killed. Tiberius acted quickly and in fear of the outcome. Sejanus has been suspected of planning a coup against him; more probably he intended a gradual accession to partnership, involving Livia Julia's son Tiberius Julius Caesar Nero 'Gemellus'.   J.P.B.; B.M.L.

Seleucus I (**Nicator:** Conqueror) (*c*.358–281 BC), son of Antiochus (unknown), fought with *Alexander the Great in the latter's campaigns from Asia Minor to Persia, Bactria, Sogdiana, and 'India', as a general. Subsequently he was to replay this 'conquest' as he, and his son, *Antiochus I, brought the eastern 'Upper Satrapies' of the former Persian empire gradually under Seleucid control and colonization, wisely negotiating after invasion (*c*.306) of the Indus region a settlement with the Maurya Indian ruler Sandracottus (Chandragupta), founder of the empire of the Mauryas. The detailed interpretation of the terms of this peace is uncertain, but Seleucus ceded the Indus valley, desert Gedrosia, Gandhara, the Swat valley tribes of the Parapamisadae, and east (i.e. desert) Arachosia.

After Alexander's death, Seleucus gained the satrapy of Babylonia (321), which was to form the core of his later kingdom. There he initially supported *Antigonus the One-eyed, but was ousted by him (316) and fled to Egypt. He regained Babylonia (312) with a small task force in a spectacular exploit and thence took Media, Susiana, and perhaps Persis too; as a Babylonian chronicle shows, fighting against Antigonus continued until a battle (308) left Seleucus in control of Babylonia. Seleucus then embarked on further campaigns to the 'Upper (i.e. eastern) Satrapies', to Bactria-Sogdiana, and the Indus region (above). He founded Seleuceia on Tigris (*c*.305) as a royal capital, returning westwards to join the coalition of 'separatist' generals against Antigonus.

The victory of Ipsus (301) gave Seleucus north Syria and access to the Mediterranean through Syria and Cilicia. He built Antioch in Syria (300) as another of his royal capitals to serve the then limits of his kingdom. Campaigns and colonization by Seleucus, Antiochus, and their officers, continued in the Upper Satrapies (e.g. Media, Sogdiana-Bactria, the Arab-Persian Gulf). Seleucus finally won Asia Minor with the victory of Corupedium over *Lysimachus (281). A new Babylonian chronicle fragment reveals Seleucus' military objectives after Corupedium as 'Macedon, his land,' apparently aiming at the reconstitution of Alexander's unified empire of Macedon and Asia. He launched a campaign, but was assassinated by Ptolemy Ceraunus, who wanted Macedonia for himself.

Seleucus was married to the Bactrian princess Apame, mother of his successor and eldest son, the half-Iranian Antiochus I, a prototype of the dynastic-marriage alliances with non-Greek dynasties that the Seleucids pursued as a continuing policy in their relations with non-Greek peoples in and beyond their realms. Seleucus had prepared Antiochus for the throne since he acted as crown prince (*mār šarri*) in Babylonia before he was appointed co-regent (292/1–281/0), a mechanism that facilitated the Seleucid succession and continued to be utilized. Seleucus' second marriage to Stratonice, daughter of *Demetrius the Besieger (290s), seems mainly to have been directed by politics, i.e. a (temporary) pact with Demetrius. It is uncertain if Apame was still alive. However, Stratonice was passed to Antiochus as queen and wife, and Antiochus was dispatched to the eastern satrapies as king with full royal authority (and armies). This is probably to be understood as a recognition of the need to consolidate in the Upper Satrapies and for royal authority to do it, leaving Seleucus free to deal with problems in Syria and Anatolia.

Seleucus was certainly one of the ablest of the Successors ('the greatest king of those who succeeded Alexander': Arr. *Anab.* 7. 22. 5). Apart from his military victories, he took great care to 'respect' and utilize local traditions (e.g. the Babylonian kingship and Babylonian traditions) and to proffer patronage to non-Greek communities and their sanctuaries as well as Greek ones.

    G.T.G.; S.S.-W.

Seleucus II (Callinicus: Gloriously Victorious) (*c*.265–225 BC) was the eldest son of Antiochus II and Laodice. In his reign (beginning in 246), a separate kingdom of Bactria, led by a Greek usurper, Diodotus, claimed independence from the Seleucids, at least by the early 230s. Seleucus also faced trouble in Parthia, where the nomadic Parthians had infiltrated and were slowly carving out an emerging realm from the Seleucid satrapy. Seleucus campaigned against them, claiming victories the reality and extent of which are difficult to assess. A recently published Babylonian astronomical diary also reveals that between 238 and 235 some kind of serious military revolt was taking place, one of the centres being Babylon. Seleucus was further hampered throughout his reign by dynastic troubles; first the ambitions of his step-brother which produced the invasion of *Ptolemy III with its spectacular (though ephemeral) successes ('Third Syrian War,' 246–241) and, later, those of his younger brother Antiochus Hierax in Asia Minor. Seleucus spent his reign on campaign, but it remained for his son *Antiochus III ('The Great') to restore the kingdom. However, the Seleucid policy of patronizing Greek and non-Greek places continued—notably e.g. Babylon, whence comes a Babylonian chronicle fragment referring to a letter from the king to the chief administrator of the great sanctuary of Esagil, attesting the king's support for Babylonian religious rites and his close relations with the Babylonian administrator. Seleucus II, like other contemporary monarchs, also provided massive material relief and aid (plus 10 warships) to *Rhodes after a devastating earthquake (Polyb. 5. 83. 8–9).   G.T.G.; S.S.-W.

Sempronius Gracchus, Gaius and **Tiberius** See GRACCHUS.

Seneca the Elder (Lucius Annaeus Seneca), writer on declamation, was born of equestrian family at Corduba (mod. Córdoba) in Spain about 50 BC. Of his life we know little; he was certainly in Rome both as a young man and after his marriage, and his knowledge of the contemporary schools of rhetoric implies that he spent much time in the capital. His family wealth was increased by his marriage to Helvia, a fellow countrywoman, by whom he had three sons, Lucius Annaeus Novatus (Gallio), Lucius Annaeus Seneca (*Seneca the Younger), the philosopher, and Marcus Annaeus Mela, the father of the poet *Lucan. He died around AD 40, after the death of Tiberius and before the exile of his second son.

His history of Rome 'from the start of the civil wars almost up to the day of his death', is lost. The partly preserved *Oratorum et rhetorum sententiae divisiones colores* (Sayings, Arguments, Colours of the Orators and Rhetors), written for his sons in his old age, originally comprised ten books devoted to *controversiae* (debates), each with a preface,

and at least two devoted to *suasoriae* (speeches of advice). Only five books (1, 2, 7, 9, and 10) of the *Controversiae* (together with seven of the prefaces) and one of the *Suasoriae* have survived more or less in full: an abridgement made later for school use (perhaps 4th cent.) gives us some knowledge of the missing books of *controversiae*. As the cumbersome title suggests, the material is grouped under three rubrics. For each theme, striking and epigrammatic extracts from various speakers are followed by the author's analysis of the heads of their arguments and by remarks on their 'colours' or lines of approach to the case. Extracts from Greek declaimers are often placed at the end, and the whole is spiced with comments and anecdotes of Seneca's own.

Seneca's sons were primarily interested in epigram, and his book is biased towards smart sayings. Only in *Controv.* 2. 7 does he seem to have set himself to reproduce a complete speech, and that is cut short by our manuscripts. The accumulated *sententiae*, vividly illustrative of an important aspect of Silver Latin, tend to cloy. Relief is provided by the excellent prefaces, which sketch with graphic detail the characters of the major declaimers on whom Seneca, relying (it seems) only on a phenomenal memory, primarily drew. Elsewhere Seneca's own stories and digressions give priceless information on declamatory practice and on the literary scene of the early empire. His literary criticism is conservative and somewhat mechanical, and he is out of sympathy with a good deal of what he preserves for us. High points include the assessment of the orator Cassius Severus and his comparative failure as a declaimer (*Controv.* 3 pref.); the sections on *Ovid in the school of Arellius Fuscus (ibid. 2. 2. 8–12); and a series of accounts of the death of *Cicero, including a fine extract from the poet Cornelius Severus (*Suas.* 6. 16–26).   C.J.F.; M.W.

Seneca the Younger (Lucius Annaeus Seneca) was born at Corduba (mod. Córdoba) in southern Spain between 4 BC and AD 1. He was born into a wealthy equestrian family of Italian stock, being the second son of *Seneca the Elder and Helvia; his brothers were Lucius Annaeus Novatus, later known as Iunius Gallio after his adoption by the orator of that name, and Lucius Annaeus

Mela, the father of the poet *Lucan. He was happily married to a woman younger than himself, Pompeia Paulina; the evidence for an earlier marriage is tenuous. He had one son, who died in 41.

He was brought to Rome by his mother's stepsister, the wife of Gaius Galerius, prefect of Egypt from 16 to 31. Little is known about his life before AD 41. In Rome by AD 5, he studied grammar and rhetoric and was attracted at an early age to philosophy. His philosophical training was varied. He attended lectures by Attalus the Stoic and by Sotion and Papirius Fabianus, both followers of Sextius who had founded the only native Roman sect a generation before: Seneca was to describe it as a type of Stoicism. It is not known when he met Demetrius the Cynic, whom he was to write about in his Neronian works. At some time he joined his aunt in Egypt, who nursed him through a period of ill health. About 31 he returned with her, survivors of a shipwreck in which his uncle died. Some time later, through her influence, he was elected quaestor, considerably after the minimum age of 25. By the reign of *Gaius (1), he had achieved a considerable reputation as an orator, perhaps also as a writer (if some of the lost works can be dated so early), and in 39, according to a story in *Cassius Dio, his brilliance so offended the emperor's megalomania that it nearly cost him his life (political motives have been conjectured). In 41 under *Claudius he was banished to Corsica for alleged adultery with Julia Livilla, a sister of Gaius, and remained in exile until 49, when he was recalled through the influence of *Agrippina the Younger and made praetor. He was appointed tutor to her son *Nero, then 12 years old and ready to embark on the study of rhetoric. In 51 Burrus, who was to become Seneca's congenial ally and colleague during his years of political influence, was made prefect of the praetorian guard; and with Nero's accession in 54, Seneca exchanged the role of tutor for that of political adviser and minister.

During the next eight years, Seneca and Burrus managed to guide and cajole Nero sufficiently to ensure a period of good government, in which the influence of his mother was reduced and the worst abuses of the Claudian regime, the irregularities in jurisdiction and the excessive influence and venality of the court, were corrected. Though

he ensured that Nero treated the senate with deference, and was himself a senior senator, having held office as suffect consul for the unusual term of six months in 55 or 56, he did not regularly attend senatorial meetings. Nor is Dio's conception of his role as initiating legislation and reform plausible. Rather, as *amicus principis* (friend of the emperor), writing the emperor's speeches, exercising patronage, and managing intrigue, Seneca's power was ill-defined but real. His relatives received important posts, as did the *equites* (knights) to whom he addressed most of his works. De clementia probably gives some idea of the way in which Nero was encouraged to behave himself, but Seneca's reputation was tarnished by Nero's suspected murder of Britannicus in 55 and certain murder of his mother in 59. As Nero fell under the influence of people more willing to flatter him and to encourage his inclination to seek popularity through exhibitionism and security through crime, Seneca's authority declined and his position became intolerable. In 62 the death of Burrus snapped his power, and Seneca asked to retire and offered to relinquish his vast wealth to Nero. The retirement was formally refused and the wealth not accepted until later; in practice he withdrew from public life and spent much time away from Rome. In 64, after Nero's sacrilegious thefts following the Great Fire in July, Seneca virtually retired to his chamber and handed over a great part of his wealth. He devoted these years to philosophy, writing, and the company of a circle of congenial friends. In 65 he was forced to commit suicide for alleged participation in the unsuccessful Pisonian conspiracy (named after Gaius Calpurnius Piso); his death, explicitly modelled on that of *Socrates, is vividly described by Tacitus (*Ann.* 15. 62–4) who, though sympathetic, clearly found it rather histrionic and preferred the ironic behaviour of *Petronius a year later.

Seneca's extant works comprise, first, the ten ethical treatises which are found in the Ambrosian MS (C. 90 inf.) under the name *dialogi*. They are, with the exception of the *De ira* ('on anger'), comparatively short, and their general content is readily inferred from their traditional titles; the dating is in many cases controversial. They comprise (in the manuscript order): *De providentia* ('on providence'), undatable and dedicated to

Gaius Lucilius (Iunior), maintaining that no evil can befall the good man; *De constantia sapientis* ('on the constancy of the wise man'), addressed to Annaeus Serenus, written sometime after 47 and probably before 62; *De ira* in three books, dedicated to Seneca's brother Novatus, probably in the early years of Claudius' reign (before 52); *Ad Marciam de consolatione* ('to Marcia, on consolation'), a belated and politically inspired attempt to console the daughter of Cremutius Cordus for the death of her son, probably his earliest extant work written in 39 or 40; *De vita beata*, incomplete, addressed to Novatus (now called Gallio) and probably in part an apologia, dating to after the attack on Seneca by Publius Suillius Rufus in 58 (Tac. *Ann.* 13. 42); *De otio*, of which only eight chapters survive, dating before 62, if addressed to Serenus (whose name has been erased in the MS), like *De tranquillitate animi* ('on tranquillity of mind'), which begins with Serenus describing his moral conflicts; *De brevitate vitae* ('on the brevity of life'), addressed to Paulinus, *praefectus annonae* (officer in charge of the grain supply) under Claudius and Nero and (now or later) Seneca's father-in-law, dated by some to 49, more plausibly to 55; *Ad Polybium de consolatione*, written about 43 to Claudius' freedman (see POLYBIUS), in hopes of flattering him into supporting Seneca's recall from exile; *Ad Helviam de consolatione*, addressed to his mother who is consoled on his exile.

Beside the Ambrosian *dialogi*, we have four other prose works. *De clementia* recommends the practice of the virtue to Nero in December 55/56 (after many suspected he had murdered Britannicus): of the original three books, only the first (which has affinities with Hellenistic essays *On kingship*) and the beginning of the second (a technical philosophical analysis of the virtue) survive. The codex Nazarianus (Vat. Pal. 1547), the fundamental source for the text of this treatise, also contains the *De beneficiis*, an elaborate work in seven books, often dry but informative about the Roman social code. It is addressed to Aebutius Liberalis and was written sometime after the death of Claudius, with 56 as a *terminus post quem* for book 2, and before *Ep.* 81. 3 (summer of 64). The *Natural questions*, dedicated to Lucilius and written during the period of Seneca's retirement, deals mainly with natural phenomena, though ethics often

impinge on physics, and is of great scientific and some literary interest. The text is corrupt and broken, and the original books, apparently eight in number, have a disturbed sequence. To the same period belongs the longest of the prose works, the *Epistulae morales*, consisting of 124 letters divided into 20 books; more were extant in antiquity. Their advertised recipient is again Lucilius, but the fiction of a genuine correspondence is only sporadically maintained. Though the form was inspired by *Cicero's letters to *Atticus (cited by Seneca), their antecedents are to be found rather in the philosophical letters of *Epicurus and *Horace and in the tradition of popular philosophical discourse (sometimes misleadingly called diatribe). Despite the artificiality of the letter-form, the variety and informality of these essays have made them the most popular of Seneca's prose works at all times.

In a category of its own is the obscurely entitled *Apocolocyntosis*, a Menippean satire written in a medley of prose and verse. It is an original and amusing skit on the deification of Claudius, containing serious political criticism and clever literary parody (even of Seneca himself).

Other prose works have been lost, for the titles or fragments of over a dozen survive. These included letters and speeches, a *Vita patris*, some ethical works, geographical treatises on India and Egypt, and books on physics and natural history.

The bulk of Seneca's prose work is philosophical in content and an important source for the history of Stoicism. He put his literary skills, human experience, and common sense at the service of his protreptic and paedagogic purpose: though orthodox in doctrine and sometimes learned and technical, his works aim primarily at moral exhortation. The moralizing is given all the force which an accomplished rhetorician can provide and is enlivened by anecdote, hyperbole, and vigorous denunciation. The style is brilliant, exploiting to the full the literary fashions of the day while remaining essentially individual, and has an important place in the history of European prose. Non-periodic and highly rhythmical, antithetical, and abrupt, it relies for its effect on rhetorical device, vivid metaphor, striking vocabulary, paradox and point; the point, a product of the philosophical as much as the rhetorical tradition, is at times refined to excess by the unflagging ingenuity of the writer. Aimed at immediate impact, the structure is often deliberately loose and need not imply an inability to develop a sustained theme. Seneca's contribution to forging a philosophical vocabulary in Latin (see LUCRETIUS) was considerable. The ultimate beneficiaries were the Latin Church Fathers.

His most important poetical works are his tragedies: the corpus contains *Hercules [furens]*, based generally on the *Hercules furens* of *Euripides; *Troades*, combining the sacrificial plot elements from Euripides' *Troades* and *Hecuba*; *Phoenissae*, an unfinished text without choral odes whose two long acts recall both *Sophocles' *OC* and Euripides' *Phoenissae*; *Medea*, close in action and characterization to Euripides' *Medea*; *Phaedra*, the Euripidean myth, but with a Phaedra both more shameless and more repentant than in the *Hippolytus Stephanephorus*; *Oedipus*, close in action to Sophocles' play; *Agamemnon*, unlike *Aeschylus' play in the role played by Aegisthus, the scenes between Cassandra and the Trojan chorus, and the final act; *Thyestes*, with no known model; and *Hercules Oetaeus*, a pagan passion-play whose derivative language and overextended action suggest rather an imitator than Seneca himself. A tenth drama the only surviving *praetexta* (serious drama based on a Roman historical subject), *Octavia*, based on the events of AD 62, can hardly be by Seneca, who is a character of the drama. Absent from the oldest MS (Etruscus), it implies knowledge of events that occurred after Seneca's death, and lacks Seneca's richness of verbal invention and dramatic development.

Recent scholarship has argued against judging the tragedies in relation to their famous Greek predecessors, realizing that Seneca did not adapt individual Greek tragedies, but drew inspiration from the whole tragic corpus, especially from *Euripides. More significant is his debt to Roman poetry: he did not admire and probably did not use the now lost republican tragedians; it is more likely that he learned from the metrical and dramatic techniques of Varius Rufus' *Thyestes* or *Ovid's *Medea*. There is unmistakable influence from Ovid's *Heroides* (*Medea*, *Phaedra*) and from episodes of violence and passion in the *Aeneid* and *Metamorphoses*:

thus *Troades* makes full use of *Aeneid* 2, and *Thyestes*, while it may reflect Ennius' or Varius' lost versions of the myth, undoubtedly adapts the language and psychology of Ovid's Tereus in *Met.* 6.

The tragedies cannot be dated absolutely, though the parody of the lament from *Hercules furens* in *Apocolocyntosis* implies dating of that early play before 54: Fitch's relative dating based on metrical practice (*AJPhil.* 1981, 289–307) suggests that at least *Thyestes* and *Phoenissae* may be Neronian.

Seneca largely observes a post-classical pattern of five acts, opening with an expository monologue or prologue scene. Acts are divided by choral odes in anapaests, sapphics, or asclepiads: lyric is also used for special scenes, such as the glyconics of the wedding procession and Medea's own polymetric incantations in *Medea*, and the anapaestic monodies of Hippolytus' hymn to Artemis and Andromache's supplication. While the plays show many features of post-classical stagecraft (cf. Tarrant, *Harv. Stud.* 1978, 213–63), and could be staged, discontinuity of action, with unanswered speeches and unexplained exits, suggests rather that they were primarily intended to be recited (wholly or in excerpts) or read. This is also consistent with Seneca's variable practice in indicating when the chorus is a witness to or absent from dialogue scenes and specifying its group identity: *Agamemnon* and *Hercules Oetaeus* have two different choruses.

The plays have been called 'rhetorical': certainly their most conspicuous feature is the passionate rhetoric of the leading characters, displayed both in terse stichomythia and extended harangues. They have been claimed as Stoic, since the dominant theme is the triumph of evil released by uncontrolled passion and the spread of destruction from man to the world of nature around him. Certainly Seneca both praises the beneficial persuasive effect of poetry (*Ep.* 108. 9, citing the Stoic Cleanthes on the power of verse to concentrate the impact and brilliance of a thought) and exonerates drama from the charge of fostering harmful emotions (*De ira* 2. 2. 5, distinguishing the audience's emotional response as preliminary or conditional). However, although the plays reflect Stoic psychology, ethics, and physical theories, their predominantly negative tone and representation of life makes it unlikely that they were composed as Stoic lessons (*contra* Marti *TAPA* 1945, 216–45).

The tragedies exercised a powerful influence over the Renaissance theatres of Italy, France, and Elizabethan England, where the 'Tenne Tragedies' adapted from Seneca by various translators coloured the diction and psychology of Marlowe, Shakespeare, and Ben Jonson. Compared with both life and entertainment in the late 20th cent. the violence and extravagance of Senecan as of Elizabethan tragedy no longer seem as shocking, grotesque, or incredible as they did to readers in earlier generations.

Besides the tragedies we have 77 epigrams, a few handed down under Seneca's name, and others attributed to him. Apart from the three epigrams specified as Seneca's in the Codex Salmasianus, their authenticity is highly dubious.

Seneca was a talented orator, statesman, diplomat, financier, and viticulturist, a prolific and versatile writer, a learned yet eloquent philosopher. Yet his style can weary us, as it did the generation of *Quintilian and *Tacitus, and as a man, he has continued to be criticized as a hypocrite as he was in antiquity: he preached the unimportance of wealth but did not surrender his until the end; he compromised the principles he preached by flattering those in power and by condoning many of Nero's crimes. Yet, as he says himself, effective exhortation can include preaching higher standards than can be realistically expected, and most moral teachers have urged attention to their words rather than to their example. Moreover, his teaching is more subtle and complex than is sometimes appreciated: he does not require the sacrifice of wealth, only the achievement of spiritual detachment from worldly goods; he advocates giving honest advice to rulers, while avoiding offence and provocation. Moreover, he confesses to having abandoned his youthful asceticism, to giving in on occasion to grief and anger, to being only on the first rung of moral progress. Above all, he conveys, as few moralists have, a sympathy with human weakness and an awareness of how hard it is to be good. For his disciples, then and later, Seneca's power as a healer of souls has more than made up for his shortcomings as a model of virtue.

L.D.R.; M.T.G.; E.F.

Septimius Severus, Lucius, emperor AD 193–211. The Septimii were of Punic origin, his mother's family (Fulvii) of Italian descent. His equestrian grandfather, probably identical with the poet *Statius' friend Septimius Severus, was the leading figure at Lepcis Magna under *Trajan; his father held no office, but two Septimii were already senators when Severus was born (145). One of them secured senatorial rank for him from M. Aurelius; he and his brother Publius Septimius Geta had normal careers under Marcus and Commodus. Consul in 190, by now with a second wife, Julia Domna, and two young sons, he became governor of Pannonia Superior in 191 through the praetorian prefect Quintus Aemilius Laetus, a fellow-African. Twelve days after *Pertinax's murder (28 March 193) he was proclaimed emperor at Carnuntum (9 April) as avenger of Pertinax, whose name he assumed. Backed by all sixteen Rhine and Danube legions he marched on Rome, securing the support of Clodius Septimius Albinus, governor of Britain, by granting him the title *Caesar*. By 1 June, 60 miles north of Rome, Severus was recognized by the senate; Pertinax's successor Didius Severus Julianus was murdered, and Severus entered Rome without opposition on 9 June 193. The praetorian guards were dismissed and a new guard, twice as large, was formed from the Danubian legions; three new legions (I–III Parthicae) were raised, one of which (II Parthica) was to be based at Alba, near Rome. This, together with increases in the *vigiles* (fire fighters), urban cohorts, and other units, radically enlarged the capital's garrison. Army pay was raised (for the first time since AD 84) and the men gained new privileges, e.g. the right to marry. Then Severus moved against Pescennius Niger, proclaimed emperor in Syria in April 193. Advance forces under Lucius Fabius Cilo halted Niger at Perinthus; his base at Byzantium was besieged by Marius Maximus with troops from Moesia. By the end of 193 Severan generals defeated Niger at Cyzicus and Nicaea; Egypt had recognized Severus by February 194. The final encounter (spring 194), near Issus, was followed by Niger's death. Syria was divided into two provinces, Coele and Phoenice, Antioch and other cities that had supported Niger being punished. Severus now launched a campaign against the Parthian vassals who had backed Niger. Most of

Osroëne was annexed, perhaps other parts of N. Mesopotamia too. Severus became *Parthicus Arabicus* and *Parthicus Adiabenicus* in 195. In the same year he proclaimed himself son of the deified Marcus and brother of the deified Commodus, renamed his elder son *Caracalla Marcus Aurelius Antoninus and made him Caesar, and gave his wife the title 'mother of the camp'. This clearly dynastic move led his ally Albinus Caesar to rebel and cross to Gaul with the British army. Severus hurried back west for this final civil war, won at the battle of Lugdunum (1) (19 February 197).

In a purge of Albinus' supporters 29 senators, and numerous others in Gaul, Spain, and Africa were executed. Severus left for the east in summer 197 for his Second Parthian War, invading in winter and capturing Ctesiphon, on 28 January 198. On this day, the centenary of Trajan's accession, he became *Parthicus Maximus*, raised Caracalla to the rank of Augustus, and made Publius Septimius Geta Caesar. The new province of Mesopotamia was garrisoned by two of the new legions (I and III Parthicae), with an equestrian prefect as governor. Two attempts to capture Hatra failed. After a lengthy stay in Syria, the imperial party entered Egypt before the end of 199, remaining for about twelve months: the province was reorganized, notably by the grant of a city council to Alexandria. At the end of 200 Severus returned to Syria for another year; he was consul for the 3rd time at Antioch, with Caracalla as colleague, on 1 January 202.

Back at Rome in early summer 202 he celebrated *decennalia* with lavish victory games (declining a triumph, although the arch in the Forum had already been voted by the senate), followed by Caracalla's marriage to Fulvia Plautilla, daughter of the seemingly all-powerful praetorian prefect Gaius Fulvius Plautianus. In the autumn the imperial family sailed for Africa: their native Lepcis, Carthage and Utica received *ius Italicum* (legal equality with, and privileges of, towns in Italy), while Severus crushed the desert tribes beyond Tripolitania. From 203 to 208 he remained in Italy, holding Secular Games in 204. Early in 205 Plautianus was killed and replaced by *Papinian, who, with his fellow-jurists *Ulpian and *Paulus, made the Severan era a golden age of Roman jurisprudence. In 208 minor hostilities in Britain gave

an excuse for another war, which Severus supposedly thought would benefit his quarrelling sons. The entire family, with Papinian, elements of the guard and other troops, crossed to Britain that year and took up residence at Eburacum (York). Severus and Caracalla led two campaigns in northern Scotland, with the professed intention of conquering the whole of Britain; a new advance base was built at Carpow on the Tay, and victory was claimed in 210 with the title *Britannicus* for Severus and his sons, the younger becoming Augustus at last to ensure a joint succession. Long a victim of gout, Severus died at York on 4 February 211, leaving his sons the advice 'not to disagree, give money to the soldiers, and ignore the rest'.   A.R.Bi.

Sergius Catilina See CATILINE.

Sertorius, Quintus (*c.*126–73 BC), an *eques* (Roman knight) from Sabine Nursia (Norcia), distinguished himself in the Cimbrian Wars under Quintus Servilius Caepio and *Marius, and under Titus Didius in Spain. Quaestor in 91, then a senior officer in the Social War between Rome and her Italian allies, he was thwarted by *Sulla in his candidacy for a tribunate (89 or 88) and joined *Cinna. He shared responsibility for the capture of Rome (87) and subsequent executions, but ended the indiscriminate terror of Marius' slave-bands. He became praetor (probably) in 85; kept in Italy by Sulla's impending return, he criticized, unsuccessfully, the Cinno-Marian leaders for their conduct of the civil war and finally took command of Spain (winter 83/2). Proscribed and driven out (81), he went to Mauretania as a *condottiere*. Invited by the Lusitanians and anti-Sullan Roman exiles, he returned to Spain (80) and soon gained widespread support among the natives, owing to his bravery, justice, and skill in exploiting their religious beliefs. (His white doe was regarded as a sign of divine inspiration.) Through crafty employment of guerrilla methods (and, for naval support, 'Cilician' pirates) he was successful against many Roman commanders, notably Quintus Caecilius Metellus Pius in Farther Spain, and by 77 he held most of Roman Spain. He tried to Romanize Hispanian leaders and acted throughout as a Roman proconsul, relying heavily on Roman and Italian exiles in the province; creating a 'counter-senate' from among them, he made Spain the focal point of resistance against the post-Sullan regime in Rome. When approached by *Mithradates VI he concluded an alliance, yet refused to surrender Asia to him (76/5). The arrival of Marcus Perperna Veiento with substantial remnants of the army of Marcus Aemilius Lepidus enabled him to take the offensive against *Pompey—now commanding in Hither Spain—whom he defeated at Lauro (77). But costly failures, of his own and his lieutenants, in several pitched battles (76) soon forced him to revert to guerrilla warfare, with waning success after 75. Losing the confidence of his Roman and Hispanian followers alike and embittered by failure, he became increasingly despotic and was assassinated by Perperna.   C.F.K.

Servilia, daughter of Quintus Servilius Caepio and Livia, daughter of *Livius Drusus (1), who was the mother of *Cato the Younger. Born c.100 BC, she married first Marcus Junius Brutus, to whom she bore *Brutus, then Decimus Junius Silanus; her daughters by Silanus married, respectively, Publius Servilius Isauricus, *Lepidus, and *Cassius Longinus, the tyrannicide. *Julius Caesar was her lover for many years and remained on good terms with her after: it was rumoured (implausibly) that Brutus, for whom he showed particular favour, was his son, and she profited in his sale of the Pompeians' confiscated estates (Cic. Att. 14. 21. 3). She may have been discreetly involved in high politics before the Civil War, and after Caesar's death Cicero's letters show her playing a leading part in the tyrannicides' deliberations, always protecting her son's interests. (She prided herself on descent from Gaius Servilius Ahala, a celebrated tyrannicide of early Roman history). After her son's death at Philippi she fell from power (cf. Nep. Att. 11. 4) and we hear no more about her. But for a short time, at least, she was the most powerful woman of her generation.

                                T.J.C.; E.B.

Severus (emperor). See SEPTIMIUS SEVERUS, L.

Severus, Sulpicius, Latin historian who was born in Aquitania c. AD 360. A member of a prominent family, he studied law in Bor-

deaux and became a convert to Christianity c.389 together with his friend Paulinus of Nola. After the death of his aristocratic wife, he organized under the influence of Bishop Martin of Tours a sort of monastic life on his own estates for himself and his friends. In old age he seems to have passed through a period of Pelagianism (a Christian heresy). He died c. AD 420. Gennadius wrote a brief biography of him (Vir. ill. 19), and we have also thirteen letters to him by Paulinus. His extant works are: (1) a life of (Saint) Martin of Tours which is an apology for asceticism and is supplemented by three letters on Martin's miracles and death and by a dialogue which compares Martin's feats with those of the Egyptian hermits; (2) a universal chronicle to AD 400 which is an important source for the history of 4th-cent. events, esp. the heresy of the Priscillianists (Severus disapproved of the execution of Priscillianus). The whole book is an interesting attempt to present a 'breviarium' of history from the Christian point of view: it uses Christian chronographers, especially St *Jerome, but also pagan writers. J. Bernays suggested (Ges. Abhandl. 2. 1885, 81 ff.) that for the destruction of Jerusalem in AD 70 Sulpicius followed the lost account of *Tacitus. *Sallust and Tacitus are his models in the matter of style.   A.M.; A.J.S.S.

Severus Alexander (Marcus Aurelius Severus Alexander), Roman emperor AD 222–35. Son of *Julia Avita Mamaea by her second husband, the procurator Gessius Marcianus of Arca Caesarea in Syria, b. c. AD 209, his names were Gessius Alexianus Bassianus until his adoption in 221 by his cousin *Elagabalus, when he became Marcus Aurelius Alexander Caesar. Made emperor on Elagabalus' murder in March 222, he took the further name Severus and was called 'son of the deified Antoninus' (Caracalla). His mother, under whose influence he remained throughout his reign, set out to recreate a 'senatorial regime', with a council of sixteen. Elderly senators such as Marius Maximus and *Cassius Dio were prominent. The jurist *Ulpian became praetorian prefect but, at latest in early 224, was killed by the guard; Dio was obliged to hold his second consulship (229) outside Rome to avoid the same fate and expressed concern at growing military indiscipline at the end of his History (bk. 80). Alexander was married in late 225 to

Gnaia Seia Herennia Sallustia Orba Barbia Orbiana Augusta, whose father may even have been made Caesar; but she was banished two years later when her father attempted a coup. A major new threat resulted from the collapse of Parthia and the revival of Persia under the Sasanids, *c*.224–5. In 231 Alexander launched a Persian expedition. The war, in which he took only a nominal part, ended in 233; although not a great success, it maintained Roman control over the province of Mesopotamia. Meanwhile the Alamanni were threatening Upper Germany and Raetia. A further expedition was necessary. Alexander wintered in Germany in 234–5, but before the campaign could begin was murdered outside Mainz, with his mother, in an uprising led by the equestrian commander Gaius Julius Verus Maximinus (February or March 235). His memory was condemned, but he was deified in 238 after Maximinus' death.   A.R.Bi.

Sextus Empiricus, Pyrrhonist Sceptic (see PYRRHON) and medical doctor. Nothing is known about his life, but the name 'Empiricus' shows that he was a member of the Empiricist school of medicine. *Diogenes Laertius (9. 116) tells us that his teacher was Herodotus, also a doctor. Most scholars now agree that Sextus' works were written towards the end of the 2nd cent. AD.

Sextus' extant works are traditionally cited under two titles:

1. *Outlines of Pyrrhonism,* abbrev. *PH,* in three books; the first offers a general outline of Pyrrhonist scepticism, including the Modes of Aenesidemus and Agrippa, and a discussion of the differences between Pyrrhonism and other schools or philosophers alleged to have held similar views; the second and third books contain refutations of dogmatic philosophies, divided by subject-matter: epistemology and logic, philosophy of nature, ethics.

2. *Adversus Mathematicos (Against the professors,* abbrev. *M),* in eleven books, originally no doubt two different works. *M* 7–11 (also entitled *Against the dogmatists*), is a critique of dogmatic philosophies parallel to but more detailed than *PH* 2–3; *M* 1–6 (*Against the professors*) criticizes other disciplines, as follows: grammar (1), rhetoric (2), geometry (3), arithmetic (4), astrology (5), music (6). Sextus' books on medicine and on the soul are lost.

Sextus is the only Pyrrhonist philosopher whose work has survived. The first book of *PH* offers a detailed and subtle defence of scepticism, its aims, and methods. Though Sextus obviously draws upon his predecessors and doxographical works, he is an intelligent compiler who writes clearly and concentrates on argument rather than on anecdotes. His discussions of the doctrines of other schools have preserved a wealth of information, in particular about Stoic logic and Hellenistic epistemology. Much work still needs to be done to explore the various strands of Pyrrhonism between Aenesidemus and Sextus that seem to lie behind his exposition, as well as the connections between Pyrrhonism and the ancient schools of medicine.   G.S.

Sextus Pompeius See POMPEY, SEXTUS.

Sidonius Apollinaris (Gaius Sollius Modestus Apollinaris Sidonius) was a leading political and literary figure in 5th-cent. Gaul, whose career and writings are central to the period. Born at Lyons *c*.430, he was educated with fellow-nobles at Lyons and Arles. Through his marriage with Papianilla (*c*.450), he entered the family of Eparchius Avitus (Augustus 455–6), in whose honour he composed his first published panegyric (*Carm.* 7), delivered at Rome on 1 January, 456. He held offices at the courts of Avitus and Majorian, but returned to Gaul after Majorian's fall in 461. His participation in a Gallic embassy to Anthemius in 467 led to a renewal of contacts with eminent Roman senators, his panegyric in honour of Anthemius, and his prefecture of Rome in 468. However, his support for the traitor Arvandus, whose illicit contacts with the Goths at Toulouse were uncomfortably close to Sidonius' own dealings, led to Sidonius' final withdrawal to Gaul, where he was consecrated bishop of Clermont in 470. Baptism by Faustus of Riez and participation in the Christian philosophical seminars at Vienne of Claudianus Mamertus in the 460s had prepared the Christian aristocrat for his new role, which he performed with diligence and compassion, concentrating on preaching and patronage, but avoiding theological controversy. His first five years were dominated by the Gothic siege of Clermont, resistance to which was led by Sidonius and his brother-in-law, Ecdicius. After the surrender of the city by the emperor's negotiators in 475, described by Sidonius as 'enslavement', the bishop was confined at Liviana, near Carcassonne, but was later released and allowed to return as bishop to Clermont, under Gothic supervision.

WORKS (1) *Carmina*, issued as a collection in 469, consisting of (*a*) panegyrics of Anthemius, Majorian, and Avitus, with prefaces, in reverse chronological order, and (*b*) occasional poems on both serious and trivial themes; (2) *Epistulae* in nine books, the first seven collected *c.*477, the last two issued separately and concluding after 481; (3) *Missae*, now lost but known to Gregory of Tours.

His excessive fondness for literary conceits may irritate, but Sidonius' originality was greater than his detractors allow, given the constraints of the literary conventions within which he operated. While the panegyrics were modelled on *Claudian, and his more literary letters on *Pliny the Younger, Sidonius' later writings increasingly incorporated Christian themes, often allusively, into the classical tradition and his collected correspondence was to form a bridge between the classical productions of Pliny, *Fronto, and *Symmachus and the episcopal collections of the 6th cent. Moreover, with their strong focus on aristocratic social behaviour and ambitions and the expanding role of the Germanic courts, Sidonius' writings mirror the conflict of traditional values with new realities and the effects on Gallic society of the Germanic presence and the declining power of Rome.   J.D.H.

Silius Italicus, Tiberius Catius Asconius (*c.* AD 26–102), Roman politician and poet, author of the *Punica*, an epic poem of 17 books on the Second Punic War, at over 12,000 lines the longest poem in Latin. Before turning to the composition of poetry in retirement Silius had an outstanding public career (the evidence for his life comes from *Martial's epigrams and a distinctly tepid death-notice in *Pliny the Younger, *Ep.* 3. 7). Zealous in prosecution under *Nero, he was the last consul appointed by the emperor in AD 68, at an early age for a *novus homo* (roughly, first member of his family to become a senator and/or consul). In the turmoil of the next year he was engaged in tense high-level negotiations between *Vitellius and *Vespasian's brother (Tac. *Hist.* 3. 65); his support for Vitellius did not harm him, for he reached the peak of a senator's career under Vespasian, as proconsul of Asia (*c.*77). One of his sons followed him to the consulate, and there were hopes for the second son, disappointed by death (Mart. 8. 66, 9. 86). He retired to Campania, where he owned many villas, and spent his last years as an artistic connoisseur, attracting adverse comment for conspicuous consumption. He owned one of *Cicero's villas and the tomb of *Virgil, whose memory he revered (Mart. 11. 48). Many assume that he began his poem in the late 80s on the rather shaky grounds that only then does Martial start referring to his poetic activity (4. 14); the praise of the Flavian dynasty at 3. 593–629 suggests that the poem was either published before Domitian's death (September 96) or, more probably, still not fully revised at the poet's death some years later. Afflicted by an incurable ailment, Silius starved himself to death at the age of 76, perhaps as late as 103. The Stoicism often attributed to him is based on no external evidence other than a hostile story told by *Epictetus about one Italicus, whom there is no need to identify with the poet (Arr. *Epict. Diss.* 3. 8. 7).

With *Livy's third decade as the principal historical source, and Virgil's *Aeneid* as the principal poetic model, the *Punica* traverses the entire Second Punic War, casting itself as the fulfilment of the curse with which Dido conjures eternal enmity between her people and Aeneas' (*Aen.* 4. 622–9). A mythological dimension is immediately present, therefore: Hannibal is not just a formidable human antagonist but the hellish tool of Juno's unassuaged hate, and the gods participate throughout. Silius' decision not to follow *Lucan's removal of the gods as characters has attracted the censure of modern critics, but it is symptomatic of his forswearing of Lucan's nihilism in favour of a more traditional view of divine sanction for imperial destiny (debts to Lucan are ubiquitous, however, especially in the Caesarian portrayal of Hannibal). The poem celebrates Roman fortitude by displaying such mighty heroes as Marcus Atilius Regulus, *Fabius Maximus Verrucosus, Marcellus, and *Scipio Africanus, and by organizing the mass of 15 years' history to centre on the catastrophic defeat at

Cannae in 216 BC (bks. 8–10, with seven books before and after): nostalgia for a simpler and nobler past is shot through with the apprehension that Rome's victory over Carthage held the seeds of contemporary decline.

Discovered only in 1417, the *Punica* had some esteem as a paradigm of courtly virtue until the end of the 16th cent., but for centuries its reputation has been in steep decline, and it is now scarcely read. Recent attempts at rehabilitation have concentrated on Silius' thematic concerns, structural skill, and professional engagement with his tradition. Further systematic and detailed study, especially of his language, is needed before Silius' achievement and stature can be convincingly reassessed.   D.C.F.

Simonides, Greek poet, from Iulis on Ceos (mod. Kea); son of Leoprepes, grandson or descendant of Hylichus (Callim. frr. 64. 8; 222), uncle of *Bacchylides (Strab. 10. 5. 6). If he worked at the court of Hipparchus (see PISISTRATUS) ([Pl.], *Hipparch.* 228c; Arist., *Ath. Pol.* 18. 1), his career began before 514 BC; his praises of Eualcidas of Eretria (fr. 518) date before 498, his *Battle of Plataea* (frr. 10–17 W²) in or after 479; he finished at the court of *Hieron II, and his tomb was shown at Acragas (Callim. fr. 64. 4). Tradition made him live to be 90; most sources set his birth c.556 (others c.532).

No poem of Simonides survives intact, except the epigrams attributed to him; even the *Suda's* list of works (which should preserve the outlines of the Alexandrian edition) is garbled. But the fragments make it clear that Simonides commanded a wide variety of genres. In choral lyric, he composed epinicians, of which he and perhaps Ibycus are the first known practitioners; dithyrambs, with which according to a (Hellenistic) epigram (xxvii Page) he won at least 57 competitions; *thrēnoi* (laments); paeans; encomia; Partheneia and the like (cf. Ar. *Av.* 919). His elegies, which occupied at least one book, included some pieces for the symposium (drinking party), and some historical (on the battles of Artemisium. Many epigrams, especially epigrams relating to the Persian Wars, were collected under Simonides' name; the epitaph for the seer Megistias (vi Page) may be genuine (cf. Hdt. 7. 228. 4). Simonides' clients included cities, individual athletes like

Eualcidas and Astylus of Croton (fr. 506), tyrants like Anaxilas of Rhegium (fr. 515), and various Thessalian dynasts, e.g. the Aleuadae and the Scopadae (Theoc. 16. 42–7). Xenocrates of Acragas (fr. 513) and the Corinthian Oligaethidae (fr. 519A, 21+22) commissioned poems from him, and also from *Pindar (*Isthm.* 2, *Pyth.* 6; *Ol.* 13). Tradition connected him with *Themistocles and *Pausanias; poetic enemies included Timocreon (fr. 10 W; Arist. fr. 75).

For the next generation, Simonides belonged to the classic (old-fashioned) poets (Ar. *Nub.* 1355; Eup. fr. 148 KA). He had the reputation of a money-grubber (Xenoph. fr. 21 W; Ar. *Pax* 698 f.), and at some stage Pindar's attack on the 'Muse for hire' was applied to him (*Isthm.* 2. 6, Callim. fr. 222). He acquired also the reputation of a sage, like Bias and Pittacus (Pl. *Resp.* 335e); various apophthegms were ascribed to him, mostly cynical; the saying 'painting is silent poetry and poetry painting that speaks' (Plut., *Mor.* 346f) forms the starting point of Lessing's *Laokoon.* He was credited further with discovering the third note of the lyre; the long and double letters; and the art of memory (Callim. fr. 64; *Suda*).

What little remains of Simonides shows a professional poet of great scope and range, much in demand over his long life, spanning the tyrants and the new democracy. Ancient critics admired him for simple pathos (Quint. *Inst.* 10. 1. 64), and that appears in noble verses for the dead of Thermopylae (fr. 531). But the tragic threnody of Danaë (fr. 543), and the devious gnomic textures of *To Scopas* (fr. 542), show other talents; in the elegies, lush eroticism (frr. 21–2 W²) contrasts with the pocket epic *Plataea,* whose form (a hymn to Achilles introducing a narrative of the campaign) enforces the parallel between the Trojan and Persian Wars, and between *Homer and Simonides.   P.J.P.

Socrates (469–399 BC), Athenian public figure and central participant in the intellectual debates so common in the city in the middle and late 5th cent. His influence has been enormous, although he himself wrote nothing.

Socrates' philosophy and personality reached a broad ancient audience mainly through the dialogues a number of his associates wrote with him as protagonist. These were numerous and popular enough for *Aristotle to classify them in the *Poetics* as a species of fiction in their own right. But apart from the works of *Plato, only a few fragments survive of the dialogues of *Antisthenes, Aeschines of Sphettus, and Phaedon of Elis, and nothing of the dialogues of Aristippus, Cebes of Thebes, and many others. In addition to Plato, most of our own information about Socrates comes from *Aristophanes (1) and *Xenophon, both of whom also knew him personally, and from Aristotle, who did not.

Socrates was the son of Sophroniscus and Phaenarete, of the deme (rural district) of Alopece. Though Plato and Xenophon depict him as a poor man, he must at some time have owned sufficient property to qualify for service as a hoplite (i.e. able to supply his own weapons and armour as an infantryman) in the battles of Potidaea, Amphipolis, and Delium, through which he acquired a reputation for courage. He was married to Xanthippe and was the father of two sons.

As a citizen, Socrates seems to have avoided active participation in politics. He was, however, one of the Presidents of the assembly when the generals at the sea-battle at Arginusae were put to trial for abandoning the bodies of the Athenian dead there. Socrates (who was foreman or *epistatēs* of the *prytaneis* on the crucial day, Xen. *Hell.* 1. 7. 15 and *Mem.* 1. 1. 18, 4. 4. 2; Pl. *Ap.* 32b) alone voted against the illegal motion to try the generals as a single group, and the generals were executed. After the defeat of Athens by the Spartan alliance in the Peloponnesian War, he openly ignored an order by the Thirty Tyrants to arrest an innocent citizen (Pl. *Ap.* 32c–d).

Socrates' circle included a number of figures who turned against democracy in Athens, including *Critias, Charmides, and *Alcibiades. This may well have been the underlying reason why he himself was tried and put to death by drinking hemlock in 399 BC. He was charged with impiety, specifically with introducing new gods and corrupting young men. This charge may have masked the political motives of his accusers, since the amnesty of 403 BC prohibited prosecution for political offences committed before that date.

Socrates' execution prompted Plato and Xenophon to create portraits intended to refute the formal charge under which he was tried and to counter his popular image, which may have been inspired by Aristophanes' *Clouds*. Aristophanes had depicted Socrates engaged in natural philosophy and willing to teach his students how 'to make the weaker argument stronger'—a commonplace charge against the sophists. Both Plato and Xenophon were intent on distinguishing Socrates as radically as possible from other members of the sophistic movement, with whom he may actually have had some affinities. But their strategies differ. In both authors, Socrates devotes himself, like the sophists, to dialectical argument and the drawing of distinctions. In both, he refuses, unlike the sophists, to receive payment. In Xenophon, however, he uses argument to support, in contrast to the sophists, a traditional and conventional understanding of the virtues. In Plato, on the other hand, it is a serious question whether he holds any views of his own, and his main difference from the sophists is that, unlike them, he never presents himself as a teacher of any subject.

Plato's and Xenophon's portraits, inconsistent as they are with Aristophanes', are also inconsistent with each other. This is the root of 'the Socratic problem', the question whether we can ever capture the personality and philosophy of the historical Socrates or whether we must limit ourselves to the interpretation of one or another of his literary representations. For various reasons, in the mid-19th cent. Plato replaced Xenophon as the most reliable witness for the historical Socrates, even though it is accepted that our knowledge of the latter can be at best a matter of speculation. And, though recent attempts to rehabilitate Xenophon are not lacking, most contemporary scholars turn to Plato for information on Socrates' ideas and character.

That character is cool, distant, reticent, and ironic, in contrast to Xenophon's more conventional, straightforward, almost avuncular figure. Plato's Socrates refrains from expounding complicated positive views of his own, preferring instead to question those who claim to have such views themselves. In Plato's early or 'Socratic' dialogues his questions mainly concern the nature and teachability of *aretē* ('virtue', 'excellence', or perhaps 'success') and what produces it, both in one's person and in one's activities, and its species—courage, wisdom, piety, self-control, and the like. By means of the procedure of question and answer which came to be known as the *elenchus*, Socrates refutes all those who claim to know what *aretē* is by showing their views to be internally inconsistent.

The Platonic Socrates is utterly serious about *aretē* and the nature of the good and happy life. His commitment to do what is, by his best lights, the right thing to do in all cases is unwavering. This commitment ultimately cost him his life: according to Plato's *Apology*, he antagonized his jury by insisting that his life had been as good as any human being's and that far from having committed any wrongs he had brought the greatest benefits to Athens.

Socrates seems to have been convinced that wisdom and virtue were ultimately the same—that if one knows what the good is, one will always do it. His argument was that the good, or *aretē*, either leads to or is itself part of the happy life. Since everyone wants to be happy above everything else, no one who knows what the good is will not choose to do it. This 'intellectualist' approach to ethics implies that there is no such thing as 'weakness of the will'. It is impossible to know the better and choose the worse: the only reason people choose a worse course of action is that they are ignorant of what is better. This is one of the 'Socratic paradoxes', which contradict everyday experience but have proved surprisingly intransigent to analysis and refutation.

Plato's Socrates consistently denied that he had the knowledge of *aretē* that he considered necessary for the good and happy life. He sometimes referred to this knowledge as 'divine', in opposition to the 'human' knowledge he himself possessed and which consisted in his awareness of his own ignorance. This, he claimed, made him wiser than others, who were both ignorant of *aretē* and ignorant of their very ignorance. In the *Apology* he claimed that this was the meaning of the Delphic oracle saying that no one in Athens was wiser than he was.

Socrates often, in both Plato and Xenophon, referred to a 'divine sign', a *daimonion*, which prevented him from taking certain courses of action—he attributes his reluctance to participate in active politics to this sign's intervention. His religious views, even though they sometimes overlapped with those of tradition (he acknowledged the authority of Apollo, for example, when he received the Delphic oracle), must have been quite novel, since he appears to have thought that the gods could never cause evil or misery to each other or to human beings. He also seems, as we see in Plato's *Euthyphro*, to claim that the gods' approval or disapproval does not render actions right or wrong. On the contrary, rightness and wrongness are established independently, and the gods, knowing what these are, both engage in the former and shun the latter and approve of human beings for acting likewise.

Socrates' moral seriousness is counterbalanced by a worldly personality who enjoys good food and company—goods which he is also willing to forgo without complaint if they are not available or if they conflict with the much more important pursuit of *aretē*. He had an uncanny ability, as we see in both Plato and Xenophon, not to do anything wrong, and his relation to positive philosophical views was fundamentally ambiguous. These features, along with the vividness with which Plato portrays his complex personality, are doubtless responsible for the fact that so many ancient philosophical schools, from the Academic Sceptics and the Cyrenaics to the Stoics and the Cynics, considered him as the person most closely approximating their respective ideal.

With the renewed study of Greek texts in the Renaissance, Socrates became an influence on modern philosophy as well. He provides the first model of a philosopher primarily devoted to the pursuit of ethical issues. His pursuit is systematic, and his emphasis on the necessity of knowing the definitions of the virtues if we are to decide securely what does and what does not fall under them provided an impetus for the development of logic. In addition, he still constitutes the paradigmatic figure in whom philosophy, even in its most abstract manifestations, is never severed from the concerns of life. He lived and—most importantly— he died in accordance with his philosophical principles. Plato's lively portrait makes it believable that such a life is possible. But since his principles are not always clear and we cannot be certain whether he himself knew exactly what they were, Socrates continues to constitute a mystery with which anyone interested in philosophy or in the writings of the Greeks must contend.   A.N.

Solon, Athenian politician and poet, was of noble descent but, whether or not the tradition that he was of moderate means is correct, came to sympathize with the poor. He was prominent in the war against Megara for the possession of Salamis, urging the Athenians to renewed effort when they despaired of success (*c*.600 BC). In 594/3 he was archon, and the link between his archonship and his reforms is probably to be accepted, though some have wanted to put the reforms 20 years later. He is said to have spent the 10 years after his reforms in overseas travel, during which his measures were not to be altered: if he continued to travel after that, he may have met Amasis of Egypt and Philocyprus of Cyprus, but if he died *c*.560/59 he is unlikely to have met Croesus of Lydia (though that tradition is as old as Hdt. 1. 29–33). It may be true that he was in Athens at the time of the troubles in which *Pisistratus first seized power, and tried to warn the Athenians against Pisistratus.

For *Herodotus Solon was a sage, a lawgiver, and a poet; *Thucydides does not mention him. It was at the end of the 5th cent. that the democrats began to think of him as their founding hero: if 4th-cent. writers had access not only to his poems but also to the *axones* (revolving pillars) on which the laws were inscribed, they will have had a firm basis for their accounts of him, even though they were capable of anachronistic misinterpretation, and though the orators tended to ascribe to him all the laws current in the 4th cent.

Solon's *seisachtheia* ('shaking-off of burdens') is represented as a cancellation of all debts, but should probably be seen as the liberation of the *hektēmoroi* ('sixth-parters'), men in a state of servitude who had to give a sixth of their produce to an overlord: their obligation was abolished and they became the absolute owners of their land; men who had been enslaved for debt (many of them, perhaps, *hektēmoroi* who had defaulted on their obligation) were freed, and for the future enslavement for debt was banned. Grants of citizenship to immigrant craftsmen, and a ban on the export of agricultural products other than olive oil, encouraging the growth of olives, will have helped to move Athens from a largely self-contained towards a trading economy. Behind an alleged series of changes in Athens' measures, weights, and

coinage we should perhaps see legislation for the use of standard measures and weights (not necessarily different from those already in use in Attica); but even the earliest coins are almost certainly later than the time of Solon.

Solon organized the Athenian citizens in four property classes (*pentakosiomedimnoi*, *hippeis*, *zeugitai*, and *thētes*), and made these the basis of all political rights, to break the monopoly of the noble families: the major offices were reserved for the two highest classes; the *zeugitai* were eligible for the minor offices; the *thētes* could not hold office but could attend the assembly and *ēliaia* (meetings of Athenian citizens to try legal cases). He may have included an element of allotment in the appointment of the archons, to improve the chances of candidates who were rich but not noble. He probably created a new council of 400 to prepare business for the assembly, and provided for regular meetings of the assembly.

He compiled a new code of laws, superseding the more severe laws of *Draco except in the area of homicide, and probably extending written laws into areas not touched by Draco. He created a category of public lawsuits, in which any citizen might prosecute, in contrast to the private lawsuits in which only the injured party or his family could prosecute; and he provided for appeals against the verdicts of magistrates to the *ēliaia* (possibly a judicial meeting of the assembly).

Solon shows in his poems that he was trying to achieve a compromise between the demands of the rich and privileged and of the poor and unprivileged, and that he satisfied neither: the *hektēmoroi* were not given the total redistribution of land which some had wanted, but their liberation angered the deprived overlords; the nobles were reluctant to share political power with the non-nobles, and there was trouble over appointments to the archonship in the years that followed; tension continued until the three seizures of power by Pisistratus, between *c*.561/0 and *c*.546/5. Nevertheless, in the creation of a free peasantry, the weakening of the aristocracy and the strengthening of the assembly and the judicial system, Solon laid the foundations for the successful and stable society of Classical Athens.　　A.W.G.; T.J.C.; P.J.R.

Sophocles, Athenian tragic playwright.

CAREER Sophocles' career in the theatre was a remarkably long one. He first competed against *Aeschylus in 468 BC (*FGrH* 239 *Marm. Par.* A 56; Plut. *Cim.* 8. 7: also his first victory in the competition) more than a decade before Aeschylus' death; he lived to compete for the last time at the Dionysia festival of 406 BC, dressing his chorus and actors in mourning, we are told, to mark the death of *Euripides, news of which had just reached Athens (*Life of Eur.* 3. 11 ff., ed. E. Schwartz, *Scholia in Euripidem*, 1 (1887)). He died a few months later (Ar. *Frogs* 82; hyp. 2 (second hypothesis ('preface')) to the *Oedipus at Colonos*); he was born in the 490s BC (probably 496 or 495: *Marm. Par.* A 56).

He wrote more than 120 plays (*Suda*) and won at least 20 victories, 18 at the City Dionysia (*IG* 2². 2325): he was thus markedly the most successful of the three great 5th-cent. playwrights. He was second often and never third (i.e. last). He is said to have given up acting in his own plays early in his career (because he did not have a sufficiently powerful voice) and to have written frequently for a particular actor, Tlepolemus, so as to draw on his strengths as a performer (Schol. Ar. *Clouds* 1267). He also figures in the public life of Athens when already in his fifties: he was one of the Treasurers of Athena in 443–442 BC and a general, with *Pericles, probably in 441/0 (*FGrH* 324 Androtion F 38), during the revolt of Samos. In the political crisis that followed the defeat of the Athenian armada at Syracuse in 413 he is said to have been one of the ten 'advisers' (*probouloi*) appointed to deal with the state of emergency (Arist. *Rhet.* 1419ᵃ25). There are a number of stories of his friendships with other leading figures of the day, e.g. with the younger tragic playwright, *Ion of Chios, who wrote a memoir of his conversations with him (Athen. 13. 603 ff.: cf. the scene in *Plato in which Cephalus, the father of the orator *Lysias, reports having been present at a conversation which included the aged Sophocles (Pl. *Resp.* 1. 329a–c). He was apparently a priest of the hero Halon (Life) and welcomed the new cult of the healing god Asclepius and the snake which symbolized him into his own house while a sanctuary was built (Plut. *Num.* 3: probably in 420–19). After his death he was given the honours of a hero cult himself, with the new name Dexion (*Etym. Magn.*). We

must be wary of ancient 'biographical' data (many of which are cautionary fictions: M. Lefkowitz, *Lives of the Greek Poets*, 1981) but with Sophocles there seems to be just enough reliable material to construct a public persona.

PLAYS Paradoxically facts are scarcer when it comes to Sophocles' theatrical output. We have dates for only two of the seven surviving plays (the last two): a victory with *Philoctetes* in 409 (hyp.) and another with *Oedipus at Colonos* in 401 (a posthumous victory, the play being produced by his grandson, Sophocles: hyp. 2). We know of victories in 447 (*IG* 2². 2318: plays unknown) and 438 (over Euripides: hyp. Eur. *Alc.*: plays again unknown); and with *Antigone* at a date unknown; also of defeats in 459 (*POxy.* 2256, fr. 3; by Aeschylus with the *Supplices* trilogy; Sophocles' plays of this year are uncertain); in 431 (hyp. Eur. *Med.*; by *Euphorion, Aeschylus' son: Euripides was third) and in the year of *Oedipus Tyrannus* (by Philocles, Aeschylus' nephew; date unknown). We have no evidence at all for the dates of *Ajax, Oedipus Tyrannus, Electra,* and *Trachiniae* and only unreliable and unconvincing anecdotal evidence for *Antigone*.

THEATRICALITY Readings of Sophocles in the earlier part of this century tended to be determined by the influence of *Aristophanes (1)'s passing remark about him, only months after his death, as 'easy-going' or 'relaxed' (*Frogs* 82) and by the judgement of later ancient critics of style which identified Sophocles' with the 'middle, well-blended' style, neither grand and austere (like Aeschylus and *Thucydides) nor smooth and pedestrian (like *Isocrates and Euripides: Dion. Hal., *Comp.* 21–4; cf. Dio Chrys. *Or.* 52. 15, for a reading of *Philoctetes* which sets Sophocles 'midway between' Aeschylus and Euripides). Sophocles thus emerged as 'middling'— stable, harmonious, and at ease with experience. Such readings ignored the frequently discomforting nature of much Sophoclean theatre (esp. in *Antigone, Oedipus Tyrannus,* and *Trachiniae,* for example) and largely denied his insistent theatricality. Sophocles is the master of the enacted metaphor—metaphors of blindness in the two Oedipus plays and *Antigone,* of bestiality in *Trachiniae*— which is momentarily 'realized' in the text as it is performed. The theatricality of such pervasive dramatic metaphors emerges in moments such as the messenger speech of *Oedipus Tyrannus* and the immediately following scene with the entry of the now blinded but 'seeing' Oedipus (*OT* 1223–1415), and in the first stasimon of the chorus in *Trachiniae* (497–530), where Deianira herself is imagined as an 'abandoned calf' helplessly watching two beast-men fighting in a 'game' (like a wrestling match at Olympia) for the right to take her. Such moments are moments of stunning theatrical power, and 'middling' is not a word to apply to them. Sophocles can produce equally powerful effects of the eerie and uncanny: e.g. in the opening scene of *Ajax*, where the unseen Athena manipulates a puppet-like Ajax and is resisted by the matching subtlety of Odysseus (1–133): the scene becomes even eerier in retrospect when Tecmessa reports it as if Ajax had been speaking to a vacancy, 301–6).

Much of Sophoclean theatricality resides in his dramatic use of significant objects and significant actions, especially exits and entrances. *Electra*, for example, is a play of thwarted recognition and its centrepiece enacts a sinister game of illusion, of disguises and deceptions. The game involves not only a brilliantly theatrical messenger speech evoking and narrating, in the bravura style of such speeches, distant events which culminate in the violent death of Orestes and which we know have not occurred (680–763), but also the bringing of Orestes' 'ashes', carried in an urn by the unrecognized Orestes himself. The urn is taken by Electra whose grief for her dead brother and lament for the irreparable loss of her own hoped-for future are directed to it, focused on the 'little weight' which is his tomb and which she now holds in her hands (1126–69). She begs to be allowed to join him in it, 'nothing with nothing', and even when Orestes struggles to disclose himself and to be recognized, she will not let go of it. The urn is 'what is closest' to her (1205–8). The fusing of game-playing, irony, and intensity of tragic emotion is mediated through the simple 'prop'. Other such powerfully meaningful props are the sword in *Ajax* and the bow in *Philoctetes*. Sophocles' dramatic imagination is before all else physical and concrete. It reveals much about him that in *Philoctetes* the isolation and the loss of identity of the hero is figured in physical terms by the deserted, uninhabited island with its cave and sea, its springs, rocks, and

wild animals, whereas in the Philoctetes plays of Aeschylus and Euripides Lemnos remains the inhabited island of ordinary experience.

Entrances and exits were always, given the layout of the theatre space, of more importance in Greek tragedy than in later forms of built theatre. Sophocles' use of them is, however, markedly his own. The entrance of the self-blinded Oedipus in *Oedipus Tyrannus*, immediately after one of Sophocles' most powerful messenger speeches, has already been mentioned (*OT* 1287 ff.). The final entrance of Creon, carrying the body of his son, in *Antigone* (1257 ff.) is another *coup de théâtre*: it follows almost without pause on the exit of his wife, turning away in silence from the messenger's narrative of her son's death. As Creon enters, he is instantly met by the same messenger emerging from the palace to announce his wife's death and by the 'rolling out' of the theatrical device called the *ekkyklēma*, carrying a tableau of his wife's body and the sword with which she has this moment killed herself. Entering and carrying one body, he confronts another.

Sophocles' last two plays offer a unique sense of space and 'place where', in relation to which alone the action has meaning. The deserted island of Lemnos in *Philoctetes* and the grove of the Semnai at Colonos in *Oedipus at Colonos* are heavily loaded with meaning as places to be left or reached. In both plays entrances and exits are thus equally full of significance. In *Oedipus at Colonus* the act of entering unknowingly upon sacred ground and above all that of leaving it are given dramatic weight by the slow measured extension of the blind Oedipus' movements (153–202). Later in the play the entry of Ismene is similarly extended, this time from the moment the figures on stage first catch sight of her (in the approach to the acting area) until she is within range of speech and touch (310–29). These are adagio movements; in *Philoctetes*, it is the suddenness, for example, of Odysseus' entries at 974 (in mid-line) and 1293 that gives them their theatrical quality. But in *Philoctetes* it is above all the thwarted exit that defines the theatricality of the play. The play's action requires that Philoctetes leave Lemnos for Troy. That exit is four times launched, delayed, and then thwarted (645–750; 877–926; 982–1056; 1362–1410: the final exit, at Heracles' urging, at 1449–71). Each thwarted exit is different in its implications from each of the others and the last, completed exit is itself ambiguous in its meaning.

LANGUAGE, FORM AND STRUCTURE The language that Sophocles deploys in his plays has, arguably, a greater range than that of either Aeschylus or Euripides, from the baroque sonorities of Ajax' great 'deception speech' (*Ajax* 646–92) or the messenger's opening proclamation of his news in *Oedipus Tyrannus* (1223–31) to the rambling, self-defensive preambles of the guard in *Antigone* (223–47; 388–405). It is a language which is often difficult, even inscrutable (especially in its syntax and particularly in the songs of the chorus); it is never less than formal and it does not yield its sense easily. But it has a flexibility that is very much Sophocles'. It is a mark of Sophoclean writing that it operates within highly formalized structures but uses those structures with masterly tact and subtlety. Sophocles uses the iambic trimeter of tragic dialogue for the most part in its severe form (without, that is, the fluid resolutions that Euripides increasingly used to free the verse) but he treats such formal boundaries as line-end, for example, with a relaxed ease; clauses, even prepositional phrases, may run over into the next line; occasionally a final vowel at the end of one line may be elided (i.e. run into) the opening vowel of the next. The pulse of the verse is kept steady but the rhythmical structure of the whole speech is given a new fluidity by Sophocles' informal treatment of metrical pause. So too with dialogue: like the other tragedians, Sophocles only divides a line between speakers as a sign of greatly heightened emotional tension but the length of the speeches that are exchanged is left much more fluid than those of Euripides, for example.

The fusion of formal symmetries with a more 'naturalistic' use of speech is well illustrated by the pivotal scene of *Oedipus Tyrannus* which embraces the quarrel between Oedipus and Creon, the entry and intervention of Jocasta, and the following dialogue between Oedipus and Jocasta (512–833). With the entry first of Creon and then of Oedipus the quarrel develops from Oedipus' opening speech of denunciation into a rapid, heated exchange of short speeches which keeps drifting into and out of the formal severities of *stichomythia* (the tightly controlled exchange of single lines); it culminates in Creon's long

speech of reasoned self-defence and Oedipus' curt proclamation of death, not exile, as Creon's punishment. This in turn leads at once into a vicious exchange of tense, broken lines, a choral intervention in spoken iambics and Jocasta's entry. The three characters now present (most of our sources attribute to Sophocles the innovation of using three actors: Arist. *Poetics* 1449ᵃ15) engage in dialogue with a marked tendency towards symmetry. The formal severity of the scene is suddenly tightened still more when the chorus break in again, this time in song, and confront, first Oedipus, then Jocasta in a mixture of sung and spoken dialogue; the two confrontations, which respond with precise symmetry, are separated by the final, spoken exchanges between Oedipus and Creon, ending in another broken verse and Creon's exit. The chorus in song briefly assure Oedipus of their absolute loyalty, and Jocasta then begins a new scene of spoken, loosely structured dialogue in which it gradually emerges, with a high degree of psychologically persuasive 'naturalness', that it may be Oedipus himself who killed his own predecessor as king, Jocasta's first husband, Laius.

The idea of flexibility in the deployment of a tightly controlled formal structure applies also to resonances and responsions between plays. Sophocles turned three times to the cycle of traditional stories associated with Thebes, not to produce a continuous 'trilogy' in the manner of Aeschylus but to explore certain recurring themes (the plays are sometimes called the 'Theban plays' or even the 'Theban trilogy'; both titles mislead, the second grossly: if the traditional chronology has any basis in fact the plays were written in the order: *Antigone*, *Oedipus Tyrannus*, *Oedipus at Colonos* and may well have been separated by decades). *Antigone* is often taken to be a broken-backed and structureless play (who is its 'hero'—Antigone, who disappears barely two-thirds of the way through the play, at l. 943 and never reappears, or Creon, who is alienated from us almost from the first by the brutal autocracy of his language? Similar questions have been raised over *Trachiniae*); *Oedipus Tyrannus*, ever since Aristotle (*Poetics* 1452ᵃ17–32), has been read as the paradigm of a well-structured play. But in important ways Sophocles uses these two differently structured theatrical experiences to explore closely related themes. *Oedipus Tyrannus* has a smoothly pivotal structure in which, with no appearance of discontinuity, we turn from one issue (the salvation of Thebes from plague brought on by pollution) to another (is Oedipus guilty both of parricide and incest?). Antigone seems very different: it is more like a revolving stage on which, from Antigone's exit under sentence of death at 582, one character is replaced by another (Antigone–Haemon–Antigone–Tiresias–Messenger–Eurydice–Creon) until in the closing scene of the play all but Tiresias and the dead Antigone are assembled together in final confrontation with death and, for Creon, tragic recognition. But the two plays are tightly bound together by common themes (pollution through violent death; human blindness to truth; the impenetrability of the divine and the opaqueness of the riddling language of divinity); in both plays humans are left for carrion to devour, and boundaries between the two worlds of gods and men are thereby crossed with deadly results; in both the bonds of kinship have been distorted into horrific travesties of family. Antigone ends in inescapable bleakness; Oedipus Tyrannus, more positively, with Oedipus re-confronting the world in his blindness.

TRAGEDY AND 'RECOGNITION' *Aristotle in the Poetics makes much use of the idea of 'recognition' (anagnōrisis) in his analysis of the tragic effect. The idea is not of much help in reading Aeschylus and of intermittent usefulness in Euripides. But in Sophocles (as arguably in *Homer's Iliad) it is an illuminating critical tool. In play after play, one or more characters is brought to a realization that he or she has misperceived the nature of reality and the realization is almost always associated with pain, suffering, and death. The idea of recognition is more often than not also associated with relationships between man and divinity. Between the two worlds of gods and men there is communication, in the imagined world of Sophoclean theatre: it comes in the form of dreams, oracles, and the reading of signs by seers such as Tiresias. Men and women try to guide their decisions by their understanding of such communications. But such understanding is almost always false: the language and the signs used by divinity are everywhere ambiguous, however simple in appearance, and are systematically and readily mis-

understandable, even if they are to hand. In Ajax, at a crucial moment, men learn too late of the seer's reading of Athena's intentions and Ajax dies; in Trachiniae both Deianira and Heracles only perceive the true meaning of a series of oracles and non-human communications when it is too late and the recognition cannot save them from the consequences of catastrophically mistaken action. In Antigone, both Antigone and Creon believe that they are acting as the gods require of them: Antigone dies with that belief shaken and perhaps foundering (919–27) and Creon confronts his misreading of the requirements of divinity only when not just Antigone but his son and wife also are already dead (1257–76). In Philoctetes the oracle is never brought sharply into focus but none the less haunts the play; in Oedipus Tyrannus the simplicities of the oracle's language become utterly opaque when read through the lens of Oedipus' 'knowledge' of the truth about himself. The recurring pattern of Sophoclean tragedy is that all falls into place and coheres only in retrospect: recognition comes after the event.

RECEPTION Successful in his lifetime, Sophocles continued to be a powerful presence in the Greek tragic theatre in the following century. His plays seem to have been frequently revived, and the leading parts in them were taken by great actors of the period, such as Polus and Theodorus (Dem. De fals. leg. 246–7; Epictetus Diss. fr. 11 Schenkl; Gell. NA 6. 5). For Aristotle, the Oedipus Tyrannus is a paradigm of how to maximize the tragic effect, even in reading (Poetics 1453^{b}2). Indeed Sophocles seems to have been read and performed through much of European history. Oedipus Tyrannus was the first drama to be performed in Palladio's Teatro Olimpico at Vicenza in the 17th cent. Antigone has haunted the European imagination for centuries (George Steiner, Antigones (1984)) and in the last century and subsequently Freud's reading of Oedipus Tyrannus as the enactment of a universal male fantasy has been widely influential (though not among classical scholars: for a rebuttal of Freudian readings of the play, see J.-P. Vernant, 'Oedipus without the complex', in Myth and Tragedy in Ancient Greece (1988), 85 ff.). In this century, Electra caught the imagination of Hugo von Hofmannsthal and of Richard Strauss, Trachiniae that of Ezra Pound. The readings that such continuous interest in Sophocles has led to have been extremely various: they attest the richness, as well as the inscrutability, of his text.   J.P.A.G.

Spartacus, a Thracian gladiator and former Roman auxiliary soldier, who led a revolt which began in the gladiatorial schools at Capua in 73 BC. He was first supported by fighters of Thracian and Celtic extraction, but later acquired adherents from slaves and even the free proletariat in the countryside of southern Italy (many of these would have been working the large estates or *latifundia* devoted to stockraising in that area). Ultimately his army was estimated at figures ranging from 70,000 to 120,000. In 73 he defeated two Roman commanders and ranged over southern Italy. In 72, although his Celtic lieutenant Crixus was defeated, he himself overcame both consuls and reached Cisalpine Gaul, whence, it is said, he hoped his followers would disperse to their homes. They, however, preferred to continue to ravage Italy. Spartacus, accordingly, returned south and after at least one major victory, devastated Lucania and would have invaded Sicily, if he had succeeded in obtaining transport from the pirates. In 71 *Crassus, after trying to cut off Spartacus in Bruttium, caught and destroyed his army in Lucania subsequently crucifying any survivors he captured. Spartacus himself was killed, though his body was never found. Pompey on his return from Spain annihilated others who had escaped. This rebellion was outstanding for its scale and temporary success. It was quite unlike the other small outbreaks by gladiators of which we have evidence and resembled more the major slave-revolts in Sicily of 137–3 and 104–1 BC, inasmuch as it drew in a depressed rural population. Spartacus quickly became a legend: he was competent, brave, physically powerful, and humane with those he led.   E.T.S.; A.W.L.

Speusippus (*c.*407–339 BC), Athenian philosopher, son of Eurymedon and of *Plato's sister Potone. He accompanied Plato on his last visit to Sicily (361) and succeeded him as head of the Academy from 347 to 339. Of his voluminous writings (Diog. Laert. 4. 4) only fragments and later reports remain, but Aristotle treats him with respect and it is clear that he continued and helped to shape some major philosophical interests which the Academy had acquired under Plato.

(*a*) DEFINITION Speusippus argued that, since a definition is designed to identify its subject and differentiate it from everything else, it can only be established by knowing everything there is. This can hardly have been intended, as some ancient critics thought, to refute all attempts at defining. More probably it was this view of definition which prompted Speusippus in his ten books of *Homoia* ('Similar Things') to set about collecting the observable resemblances between different sorts of plant and animal, for he may have thought (as *Aristotle sometimes did, *An. Post.* B 13) that a species can be defined by discovering a set of characteristics which it shares with various other species, taken collectively, but not with any one other species.

The Academy's interest in definition had led to the recognition that some expressions have more than one meaning. Speusippus marked this by drawing distinctions comparable to, but fuller than, those familiar from Aristotle's logic. Where a single word is in question, it may have one sense or more than one (*synōnyma, homōnyma*); where more than one word is in question, they may stand for one thing or for quite different things, or one may derive its sense from the other (*polyōnyma, heterōnyma, parōnyma*). This in itself would give Speusippus his place at the birth of logic in the Academy.

(*b*) PHILOSOPHY AND EXACT SCIENCE Speusippus wrote on Pythagorean mathematics (see PYTHAGORAS), endorsing the search for the elements of numbers which Plato had taken over from the Pythagoreans (see the newly discovered fragment of Speusippus, *Plato Latinus* 3. 40 1–5). But he refused to equate numbers with Platonic Ideas, which like others in the Academy he rejected; and he further denied the claim, which Aristotle ascribes to the Pythagoreans and Plato, that the elements of number are the elements of everything else. Other sorts and levels of reality, he argued, need other sorts of element. Hence Aristotle accuses him of making the universe 'episodic', disconnected; but it is Speusippus' theory that underlies Aristotle's attempt in *Metaph. A* to show that it is not strictly true, but only true 'by analogy', that all things have the same elements.

(*c*) ETHICS In the Academic debate which can be heard behind Plato's *Philebus* and the ethical writings of Aristotle Speusippus makes two appearances. He holds, first, that pleasure is neither good nor evil in itself, and second, that goodness is to be found only in the final stages of development and not in the origins.

Under all these heads it is likely that the best of his work has been digested in that of Aristotle and his successors, and in particular that his biological observations in the *Homoia* were largely absorbed in the treatises of the Lyceum.   G.E.L.O.; S.H.

Statius, Publius Papinius, Roman poet. Born between AD 45 and the early 50s in the distinctively Greek city of Naples, Statius was the son of a man who had a glittering career first as a professional poet on the Greek festival circuit, and then as a teacher in Naples and in Rome, where the family moved when Statius was in his teens (*Silv.* 5. 3). Although Statius did not follow either of these careers, his debt to his father's inheritance is manifest particularly in the *Silvae*, where the often impromptu praise-displays of the Greek festivals blend with the Roman tradition of friendship poetry to produce something new in Latin literature. Popular from a young age as a poet in Rome, he may have composed a pantomime libretto for Paris, *Domitian's favourite (executed AD 83: Juv. 7. 82–7). He was victorious in the poetry competition at Domitian's annual Alban games (prob. March 90), but suffered a mortifying failure in the much more prestigious Capitoline games, almost certainly later in the same year (*Silv.* 3. 5. 31–3). By now he had married Claudia, widow of another poet, who brought him a step-daughter (he had no children of his own). The poem to Claudia (*Silv.* 3. 5), persuading her to leave Rome and follow him to Naples, speaks of her devoted support, and her nursing of Statius in illness. His epic, the *Thebaid*, was published in 91/2, after many partial recitations and many years of work (one for each of the twelve books he says, with suspicious symmetry, *Theb.* 12. 811–12). There followed the occasional poems of the *Silvae*. Books 1–3 were published together in 93 or 94; Book 4 was published in 95, by which time he had left Rome for Naples; and Book 5 (together with his unfinished second epic, the *Achilleid*) was published after his death, which is conventionally dated before the assassination of Domitian (Sept. 96).

WORKS   *LOST WORKS* The pantomime libretto *Agave* has not survived (if it was ever written); nor have his poems for the Neapolitan, Alban, or Capitoline games, although we may have a fragment of the Alban piece in four hexameter lines from a Statian poem on Domitian's German wars quoted by Valla on Juvenal 4. 94 (cf. *Silv.* 4. 2. 65–7).

THEBAID The only surviving Roman epic which can securely be said to have been published as a completed work by its author, the *Thebaid* recounts the war between the sons of Oedipus over the kingship of Thebes. Statius may well have begun the poem before he turned 30; it is an acutely self-conscious masterpiece, which has only recently begun to emerge from the neglect that overtook it after its prolonged popularity in the Middle Ages and Renaissance. The poem extravagantly explores human violence and madness. Its cosmic framework draws upon *Ovid's *Metamorphoses* to chart the problematic boundaries of human possibilities, and its political framework draws upon *Virgil and *Lucan (Statius' near-contemporary) to probe the imperial themes of absolutism and civil war. Seneca's tragedies (see SENECA THE YOUNGER) are the principal source for the atmosphere of doomed familial insanity. The diverse problems of succession and authority which face the brothers, the audience, and the poet reflect upon one other throughout, and this self-awareness renders nugatory the traditional criticism of Statius as derivative. In the divine action above all Statius shows himself to be a bold critic and innovator, undermining his inherited epic apparatus and experimenting with allegorical modes in ways which were to be profoundly influential in the Middle Ages. The verse is superbly accomplished, the style too aestheticized for many. In both respects Statius is rather nearer to Ovid, and further from Virgil, than his contemporaries *Valerius Flaccus and *Silius Italicus.

SILVAE Thirty-two poems, of which twenty-six are in hexameters, the standard metre for post-classical Greek encomiastic poetry. The only popular poem in the collection has been the exceptional poem to Sleep (5. 4). The poems evince a not very intimate acquaintance with a not very large or eminent group, marking noteworthy moments such as marriage, official advancement, or bereavement, and celebrating the taste shown in artistic acquisition or architectural construction. In the service of these quasi-professional relationships Statius marshals the panoply of Greek praise-poetry inherited from his father, boasting self-deprecatingly of the impromptu production of the requisite verses (*Silv.* 1 *Pr.*). Generally knowing and light in touch, rather than ponderous, the poems none the less usually avoid banter and ease. Domitian, an intimidating and distant personality, receives six poems which modern taste has found repellent for sycophancy, though a more charitable reading might focus on the anxiety behind them: 4. 2, thanking the emperor for an invitation to dinner in 94, betrays relief after four long years since the last sign of favour at Alba.

ACHILLEID The plan was to tell the whole life of Achilles, but the poet died before even getting his hero to Troy, and the epic breaks off some 160 lines into the second book. The charming, almost novelistic fragment represents a striking departure from the more elevated and passionate *Thebaid*.   D.C.F.

Stephanus of Byzantium was a Greek grammarian, probably a contemporary of *Justinian, and a publicly appointed teacher in Constantinople. Nothing is known in detail of his life except that he was a Christian. He is the author of *Ethnica*, in sixty books, an alphabetical list of place-names together with the adjectives derived from them. The original work, which contained information on foundation-legends, etymologies, changes of name, oracles, historical anecdotes, proverbs, etc., is lost. The surviving epitome, consisting mainly of jejune entries, was compiled some time between the 6th and 10th cents. AD. It may be the work of one Hermolaus, mentioned in the *Suda*, but some scholars believe that it is actually a conflation of at least two epitomes (abridgements), made on slightly different principles. There are fragments of the original extensive text embedded in the *De Administrando Imperio* and *De Thematibus* of Constantine Porphyrogenitus.

Stephanus was neither a geographer—he makes no direct use of *Ptolemy (Claudius Ptolemaeus)—nor a historian—he puts down side by side information dating from different epochs—but a grammarian. His prime interest is the correct formation of ethnic adjectives, for which he has two criteria, morphological regularity and regional usage. His direct sources, which he sometimes mentions, include Herodian, Oros of Miletus, Philo of Byblos *On Cities*, Dionysius Periegetes, *Strabo, historians from *Hecataeus to *Polybius, and lost grammarians and antiquarians. He is not entirely uncritical in his handling of his sources, but his main value is as a compilation of material from writers whose works are lost. The surviving epitome was used by the *Etymologicum Magnum*, *Eustathius, and probably the *Suda*. The last writer to use the original version was Constantine Porphyrogenitus. The *Ethnica* are preserved in a large number of manuscripts, mainly dating from the Renaissance. There is no satisfactory critical edition.   R.B.

Stesichorus, Greek lyric poet, active *c.*600–550 BC. Greek tradition made him later than *Alcman, and contemporary with *Sappho and *Alcaeus (*Suda*); Simonides (fr. 564) referred back to him and to *Homer. He was connected with Mataurus in Bruttium (Steph. Byz., *Suda*), and with Himera in Sicily (already Pl., *Phdr.* 244a); Arist. *Rh.* 1393[b] tells an anecdote of him and Phalaris. His tomb was shown at Himera (Poll. 9. 100) or Catana (Antip. Thess., *Anth. Pal.* 7. 75, etc.). Some said that his real name was Teisias (*Suda*).

Stesichorus' works were collected in 26 books (*Suda*); nothing now survives but quotations and some fragmentary papyri. The poems are cited by title, not by book-number. That suggests substantial pieces, and what detail we know confirms it. *Geryoneis* apparently reached at least 1300 lines; *Oresteia*, and perhaps *Helen*, occupied two books. The titles cover a whole range of major myths: *Helen, Wooden Horse, Sack of Troy, Homecomings, Oresteia* belong to the Trojan cycle, *Geryoneis, Cycnus,* and *Cerberus* to the adventures of Heracles, *Eriphyle, Europia,* and the untitled fragment about Eteocles and Polynices to the Theban story; *Boar-hunters* was concerned with Meleager, *Funeral Games for Pelias* with the Argonauts.

These poems represent a kind of lyric epic. Their metre, 'Doric' dialect, and triadic form seem to attach them to the 'choral lyric' tradition represented by Alcman and *Pindar. But their large scale and narrative sweep recall the traditional epic; their language is often

Homeric, their metres dactylic (fr. 222A even has some quasi-hexameters); it has been argued that such long pieces must have been performed, like epic, by a solo poet or reciter, not by a chorus. The prehistory of this form is obscure, and Stesichorus seems to have no successors: perhaps this was a unique attempt to transfuse epic material into a new medium. Not only is his diction 'Homeric' in general; he seems to know at least individual passages of the *Iliad* and *Odyssey* as we have them. Thus fr. 209 reworks the departure of Telemachus from Sparta (*Od.* 15. 164 ff.); Geryones borrows rhetoric from Sarpedon (S11; *Il.* 12. 322 ff.) and dies like Gorgythion (S14; *Il.* 8. 306–8), his mother speaks as Hecuba (S13; *Il.* 22. 83). Ancient critics duly called Stesichorus 'Homeric'; *Quintilian (*Inst.* 10. 1. 62) praises his dignity but criticizes his diffuseness. Certainly the few continuous pieces suggest a narrative well spaced with direct speech. In the '*Thebaid*' (fr. 222A) Oedipus' widow proposes a compromise between her warring sons, the sons agree, Tiresias predicts disaster if the bargain is broken, Polynices leaves, and travels towards Argos: this takes 100 lines, of which the speeches occupy 70. In *Geryoneis* Heracles crosses Ocean in the cup of the Sun, kills the triple Geryones, and drives away his cattle: there is time for a heroic speech by Geryones, and a lament by his mother, before Heracles destroys his heads one by one. Stesichorus came from the fringes of the Greek world: that may explain the idiosyncratic form, and the idiosyncratic versions of myth which the tragedians later borrowed (see frs. 193, 217). His influence has been suspected in the metopes of the temple of Hera at Foce del Sele and in Attic vase-painting of the later 6th cent.; one of the Tabulae Iliacae (a Roman monument of the 1st cent. AD found near Bovillae, for which see N. Horsfall, *JHS* 1979, 26 ff.) claims to represent his *Sack of Troy*.

P.J.P.

Strabo of Amaseia in Pontus, author of a *Geographia* in 17 books, by far the most important source for ancient geography, a priceless document of the Augustan age, and a compendium of important material derived from lost authors.

The family was prominent in the politics of Pontus since before the time of *Mithradates VI. Born about 64 BC, he studied grammar under Aristodemus of Nysa, and later at Rome under Tyrannio of Amisus, and philosophy under Xenarchus of Seleuceia (his teachers were Peripatetic; his views align him with the Stoics). He knew *Posidonius, whose work he used, and from whom he may have drawn his idea of a conjoint interest in history (with its ethical implications) and geography (historical notes (*hypomnēmata*) in 47 books, 43 after the conclusion of *Polybius, were his first work). The empires of Romans and Parthians allowed him to do for the Augustan empire what *Eratosthenes had been able to do in the aftermath of *Alexander the Great (1. 2. 1 [14]).

In the debate over how to do geography, however, he is very critical of Eratosthenes (and many other experts), though, compared with them, he is inclined to be amateurish about mathematics and cosmology, in general preferring the practical to the theoretical and the particular to the general, which locates him in the *periēgēsis* tradition (see HECATAEUS), and leads him to call his work 'chorography'. He therefore lays little stress on geographical wonders, and in searching for detailed information retails long passages of by then out-of-date description, which can make the interpretation of his evidence very hazardous. He travelled extensively, but does not bother to make very frequent boasts about autopsy (but see 2. 5. 11 [117]); a long stay in Egypt in the 20s when his patron Aelius Gallus was prefect, and several visits to Rome, are noteworthy; he has been thought to have returned to Amaseia and remained there until his death (after AD 21). Parts at least of the *Geographia* were composed under Tiberius.

This experience of the patronage of Roman leaders and education among the foremost intellectuals (many Greeks of Asia like himself) made Strabo (almost certainly a Roman citizen, with a Latin *cognomen* (surname)) an eloquent witness of the ways in which the Augustan settlement related to, depended on, and forever changed the plurifarious Mediterranean world of the late republic. Accommodation to Rome was part of the training of all his contemporaries, and he inherited the tradition of Panaetius, Polybius, and Posidonius. Beside *Nicolaus of Damascus and *Dionysius of Halicarnassus and in the same circles of patronage as the latter (Aelius Gallus, Quintus Aelius Tubero, the circle of *Sejanus and *Tiberius) he made his job the interpretation of Greek and Roman to each other in a way that looks forward to *Plutarch and *Cassius Dio, and at the same time uses the geographical necessities of Roman power to justify and explain the patriarchal hegemony of Augustus. It is no coincidence that this turning-point in Roman imperial power produced the *chef d'œuvre* of ancient geography.

Strabo emphasizes the usefulness of geography for statesmen and generals, those 'who bring together cities and peoples into a single empire and political management' (1. 1. 16 [9]). He speaks from knowledge of the central concerns of Roman government and is a precious witness to them (as on the lack of profit to be had from lands on the fringes of the inhabited world such as Britain, 2. 5. 8 [115–16]). It is now clear (against the once influential view of Ettore Pais, which relegated him to an Anatolian milieu) that he is speaking from and about the centre of imperial power. The work is an extraordinary achievement—he likens it himself, apologetically (1. 1. 23 [13–14], *kolossourgia*), to a colossal statue whose detailing is less significant than the overall effect—and justifies his more ambitious claim to have fused the disciplines to produce out of a historical and chorographical framework a philosophy of geography.   N.P.

Straton of Lampsacus, philosopher, head of the Peripatetic school after *Theophrastus until his death (c.287–269 BC). The preserved list of his books (Diog. Laert. 5. 59–60) includes ethics, cosmology, zoology, psychology, physics, and logic; his work on physics and cosmology earned him the name 'The Natural Philosopher.' Fragments (but only fragments) of several of his books survive; a substantial portion of his doctrine about the void may be preserved in the introduction to *Heron's *Pneumatica* (see H. B. Gottschalk, *Strato of Lampsacus: Some texts* (1965)).

He rejected *Aristotle's theory of place and contradicted him in asserting the existence of void in the cosmos. This has been taken as a concession to the atomists, but it seems unlikely; Straton argued only for 'disseminate void'—i.e. void interstices of small dimensions separating particles of matter. His reasoning was drawn chiefly from the penetration of apparently solid objects by 'physical powers' such as heat and light. The

origin of the theory is Theophrastus' theory of 'pores', rather than anything in the atomists.

Straton argued that the processes of nature were to be explained by natural causes, not by the action of any god. This is mainly an attack on the Stoics, but it also dispenses, apparently, with the very limited part played by Aristotle's divine unmoved movers of the heavens. Straton rejected the universal teleology of the Stoics; the evidence is not sufficient to decide to what extent he denied that kind of teleology which is the characteristic feature of Aristotelian biology.

He was an orthodox Aristotelian in his view of the cosmos as unique, uncreated, and geocentric. Like the Stoics, he modified the Aristotelian theory of the natural motions of the primary bodies to give to fire and air not absolute lightness but simply less weight than the other two elements; and he dispensed with the fifth body (aether) with its natural circular motion.

He was the last head of the Peripatetic school to do important original work. His theory about the void, his most famous contribution, was important in the history of physiology through its adoption by *Erasistratus, and in technology through its adoption by Heron.   D.J.F.

Suetonius (Gaius Suetonius Tranquillus) (b. *c.* AD 70), Latin biographer. Suetonius was the son of the equestrian Suetonius Laetus, tribune of Legio XIII at Bedriacum in AD 69, and originated perhaps from Pisaurum in Umbria or, more likely, Hippo Regius (mod. Bône) in Numidia. From the correspondence of *Pliny the Younger, he appears already to have attracted attention in Rome as an author and scholar by *c.* AD 97, and also to have gained experience in advocacy. Perhaps intending to pursue the equestrian *cursus* (career path), he secured through Pliny's patronage a military tribunate in Britain *c.*102, which in the event he declined to hold; *c.* AD 110, however, he probably travelled with Pliny to Bithynia as a member of the provincial governor's retinue, gaining soon after, again through Pliny's intercession, the *ius trium liberorum* (fictional grant of the privileges conferred on parents of three children). In the late years of *Trajan's reign and under *Hadrian, Suetonius held three important

posts in the imperial administration, the sec-
retaryships *a studiis*, *a bibliothecis*, and *ab
epistulis* (in charge of literary matters, the
imperial libraries, and correspondence), as
a fragmentary inscription found in 1952 at
Hippo Regius records (*AE* 1953. 73). As *ab
epistulis* he is likely to have accompanied
Hadrian to Gaul, Germany and Britain in
AD 121–2, but then for unknown reasons was
dismissed from office when Hadrian simultaneously deposed as praetorian prefect
Gaius Septicius Clarus, the dedicant of Suetonius' collection of imperial biographies, the
Caesares. He presumably continued to write
until his death, perhaps c. AD 130, but if a
public career continued nothing is known of
it.

WORKS 1. *De viris illustribus*, a now
incomplete set of biographies of Roman men
of letters arranged in categories—grammarians and rhetoricians, poets, orators, historians, philosophers—probably written before
the *Caesares* (below). The segment *De grammaticis et rhetoribus* is preserved independently, and a few other lives, variously
abbreviated or corrupted, are known from
manuscripts of other authors' works: thus
Terence, Horace, Lucan, and the Donatus
Virgil are generally regarded as deriving from
the section on poets. *Jerome drew on the
work in his *Chronicle*, naming from it 32
poets, from *Ennius to *Lucan, fifteen
orators, from *Cicero to Gnaeus Domitius
Afer, and six historians, from *Sallust to
*Pliny the Elder. The full collection, however,
may have contained as many as a hundred
lives. A particular interest in the age of Cicero
and *Augustus and, to a lesser extent, in the
Julio-Claudian era has been discerned in the
work, while the relationship between authors
and the public world in which they lived may
have been its principal theme.

2. *De vita Caesarum* (the *Caesares*), a set
of twelve imperial biographies from *Julius
Caesar to *Domitian, composed in the early
2nd cent. and complete except for the first
few chapters of Caesar (lost between the 6th
and 9th cents.).

3. Lost works, in Greek as well as Latin,
some known from a list in the *Suda* (under
'Trankullos'), others from random citations
in later authors. They included other apparently biographical works, on kings and
famous courtesans; works on such institutions as Greek games, the Roman year,

Roman customs, spectacles, and public
offices; and works perhaps of a lexicographical sort, on the names and types of clothes,
on physical defects, on weather-signs, on the
names of seas and rivers, and on the names
of winds. There was too a work on Cicero's
Republic. Several of these may have comprised the *Pratum* or *Prata* (*Meadows*), a miscellany probably also known as *De variis rebus*
(*On Various Subjects*).

Suetonius was a scholar of wide-ranging
antiquarian interests. But it is as an imperial
biographer that he must be principally
judged. Little that is safe can be said of the
literary tradition, or traditions, in which he
worked, since apart from *Cornelius Nepos
he is the first Latin biographer whose work
has survived. Consequently the *Caesares* have
to be evaluated largely in their own historical
context, with Suetonius' exposure to the
heart of imperial government during his
years of administrative service very much in
the forefront of consideration.

A striking feature of the biographies is
their thematic, rather than strictly chronological, arrangement: after an introductory
section on ancestry and a second on the subject's early life and pre-accession career, a
sequence of recurring rubrics follows, in
which Suetonius details the emperor's
accomplishments and his personal characteristics, often providing anecdotes to illustrate
general statements. The lives conclude with
an account of the subject's death, sometimes
accompanied by a description of his physical
appearance and personal idiosyncracies.
Though the framework of presentation varies
from life to life, the principle of organization
is consistent throughout.

The repetition from life to life of common
topics, especially those such as the building
operations or the public entertainments for
which a particular emperor was responsible,
suggests that the topics themselves had
special significance for Suetonius and his
contemporaries; and through comparison
with other sources such as the *Res Gestae* of
Augustus and the *Panegyric* of Pliny the
Younger, where an ideal standard of imperial
comportment is clearly perceptible, it
emerges that Suetonius used the topics to
judge his subjects against a set of popular
expectations of imperial behaviour that had
taken shape by the time the *Caesares* were
composed. *Tiberius, for example, is repeat-

edly criticized for having failed to live up to expectation, whereas even *Nero and Domitian, rulers on whom Suetonius' final judgement is damning, can nevertheless be commended for having successfully met some of their imperial responsibilities. Suetonius' concern with such aspects of private behaviour as the subject's sexual and religious tastes has been taken also to reflect the increasing Hellenization of upper-class Roman society.

In modern times, simplicity has been seen as the main characteristic of Suetonius' writing, in the absence of any obvious literary artistry. He is notable for citing earlier writers verbatim and quotes liberally from various documents—the letters of Augustus for instance—in Greek as well as Latin. (Suetonius may have exploited his period of administrative service under Trajan and Hadrian to seek out archival material for his biographies.) The Flavian lives are much shorter than those of the Julio-Claudians, and they in turn are less substantial than those of Caesar and Augustus. This again suggests that Suetonius' main historical preoccupation was the period from which the Principate ultimately appeared as a new form of government.

Suetonius, however, was not in the first instance a historian, and he should not therefore be compared with Sallust, Livy, or Tacitus. His principal concern was to collect and present material pertinent to the biographical goal of realistically illustrating imperial performance and personality, and in this he stands apart from the historians; for while fully capable of detailed analysis and sustained narrative composition if he wished, he had no interest in the moralistic or didactic as they did. As one author later expressed it, while the historians wrote *diserte* ('eloquently'), Suetonius wrote *vere* ('truthfully') (SHA *Prob.* 2. 7). Suetonius was followed as an imperial biographer by Marius Maximus, who wrote a sequence of imperial biographies, no longer extant, from Trajan to Commodus, and by the author, or authors, of the 4th-cent. *Historia Augusta*. He served also as the model for Einhard's *Life of Charlemagne* in the 9th cent., and lost his position in Europe as the classic biographer only when Plutarch's lives were translated into the vernacular languages.   K.R.B.

Sulla (Lucius Cornelius Sulla Felix), born *c.*138 BC of an old, but not recently prominent, patrician family, after a dissolute youth inherited a fortune from his stepmother, which enabled him to enter the aristocratic career. Chosen by C. *Marius as his quaestor (107) he distinguished himself in the Numidian War, finally securing the surrender of *Jugurtha by Bocchus I through diplomacy and thus ending the war. He again served under Marius against the Germans in 104 and 103, then joined the army of Quintus Lutatius Catulus, probably dispatched by Marius to advise Catulus, and enabled him to join in the final victory. Omitting the aedileship, he failed to become praetor for 98, but succeeded through lavish bribery in becoming urban praetor urbanus 97. He was assigned Cilicia *pro consule* (in place of a consul), then instructed to instal Ariobarzanes in Cappadocia. He accomplished this largely with local levies and displayed Roman power to the eastern kingdoms, including (for the first time) Parthia. A Chaldaean's prophecy that he would attain greatness and die at the height of good fortune influenced him for the rest of his life. He stayed in Cilicia for several years, perhaps until 92. On his return he was prosecuted, but the prosecution was abandoned. In 91 the senate, promoting him against Marius, granted Bocchus permission to dedicate a group showing the surrender of Jugurtha on the Capitol. Marius' reaction almost led to fighting, but the Social War supervened (Plut. *Sull.* 6).

In the war Sulla distinguished himself on the southern front and in 89, promoted especially by the Metelli, gained the consulship of 88 with Quintus Pompeius Rufus, whose son married Sulla's daughter. Sulla himself married Caecilia Metella, widow of *Scaurus, and was now one of the leading men in the state.

Given the command against *Mithradates Eupator by the senate, he was deprived of it by the tribune Publius Sulpicius Rufus, who transferred it to Marius in order to gain Marius' aid for his political plans. Sulla pretended to acquiesce, but finding support among his troops, who hoped for rich booty in Asia, he marched on Rome and took the unprepared city by force. His officers, except for his quaestor (his relative Lucullus), deserted him, and his methods shocked even his supporters. He had Sulpicius killed in office and his allies hunted down (Marius escaped to Africa), then passed several laws by armed force. General opposition compelled him to send his army away and allow the election of his enemy *Cinna as consul 87, over his own candidate Publius Servilius Vatia; and he failed to gain control of the army of Gnaeus Pompeius Strabo. Leaving Rome and ignoring a summons to stand trial, he embarked for Greece, where Quintus Braetius Sura, a legate of the commander in Macedonia, had already driven the enemy back to the sea. Sulla's hope of safety lay in winning the eastern war: he ordered Sura to return to Macedonia and took charge of the fighting.

Outlawed, but not molested, under Cinna, he agreed (it seems) to refrain from attacking Lucius Valerius Flaccus on his march against Mithradates. He himself twice defeated Mithradates' general Archelaus and sacked the Piraeus and (in part) Athens. After Lucullus had saved Mithradates from Gaius Flavius Fimbria, who had taken over Flaccus' army, he made peace with the king at Dardanus (85), granting him his territory, recognition as an ally, and impunity for his adherents in return for surrender of his conquests and support for Sulla with money and supplies. He then dealt with Fimbria, reconciled his own army (disgruntled at the peace with the enemy of Rome) by quartering it on the cities of Asia, which he bled of their wealth, and on hearing of Cinna's death abandoned negotiations with the government and openly rebelled (84). Invading Italy, he was soon joined by most aristocrats—especially Quintus Caecilius Metellus Pius, *Crassus, and *Pompey—and within a year defeated all the loyalist forces. Finding the Italians hostile, he swore not to diminish their rights of citizenship, but massacred those who continued resistance (especially the Samnites) and imposed severe penalties and confiscations on whole communities. After securing Rome through his victory at the Colline gate, he was appointed dictator under a law of the *interrex* Lucius Valerius Flaccus, whom he made his *magister equitum* (master of the horse), and was voted immunity for all his actions, past and future. He continued and legalized his massacres by publishing proscription lists (sometimes fraudulently added to by subordinates, whereby citizens were outlawed and their wealth confiscated).

During 81 he enacted a legislative programme designed to put power firmly in the hands of the senate, whose numbers (traditionally 300, but now much reduced) he raised to 600 by adlecting *equites* (knights) supporting him. In addition to minor reforms, he (1) curbed the tribunate by requiring the senate's approval for tribunician bills, limiting the veto (*intercessio*) and debarring ex-tribunes from other magistracies, thus making the office unattractive to ambitious men; (2) restored the *quaestiones* (standing courts), the number of which he raised to at least seven, to the enlarged senate; (3) increased the number of praetors to eight and that of quaestors to twenty, chiefly to ensure that tenure of provinces was not (in general) prolonged beyond one year; (4) laid down a stricter *cursus honorum* (career path for senators), making the quaestorship as well as the praetorship compulsory before the consulship could be reached at a minimum age of 42; (5) made quaestors automatically members of the senate, thus abolishing the censors' right of selection, and did away with the powerful post of *princeps senatus* (acknowledged first senator); (6) subjected holders of *imperium* (military and civil authority) outside Italy to stricter control by the senate. His veterans were settled on confiscated land (especially in Campania and Etruria) as guarantors of his order. Then, believing in the old prophecy that he now had not long to live, he gradually divested himself of power and restored constitutional government, becoming consul (with Metellus Pius) in 80 and returning to private status in 79. He retired to Campania, where he died of a long-standing disease in 79. His funeral was impressively staged to display the power of his veterans, especially in view of the agitation of the consul Marcus Aemilius Lepidus. In fact, his constitutional settlement, weakened by concessions during the 70s, was overthrown in 70 by his old adherents Pompey and Crassus; but his administrative reforms survived to the end of the republic and beyond.

Despite his mystical belief in his luck (hence his *agnomen* or additional name Felix and the *praenomina* (forenames) of his twin children, from *faustus*, 'fortunate'), despite his arrogance and ruthlessness, Sulla never aimed at permanent tyranny: he did not even put his portrait on his coins. He wished his settlement to succeed, and he thought it out carefully, no doubt with the help of his associates (some of the group that had supported Livius Drusus (2)), to eliminate the 'two-headedness' (thus Varro) that Gaius*-Gracchus had introduced into the republic and to restore a strengthened senate to unchallenged power. His arrangements were consistent, practical, and neither visionary nor reactionary. Yet he had no appreciation of deep-seated problems: he made no attempt to remove the threat of client armies, such as had supported his own rebellion, by putting the senate in charge of providing for veterans, and he seems actually to have abolished the provision of corn to the poor at a controlled price. His own example not only set a precedent for the use of client armies against the republic, but helped to destroy the morale of those on whom resistance to an imitator would depend. After sparing the only powerful enemy of Rome for his personal advantage, he had prepared the ground for that enemy's resurgence by ruining the cities of Asia; he had weeded out those most loyal to the republic in Rome and Italy and rewarded and promoted those who, for whatever reason, had joined in his rebellion. A sense of duty and public service could not be expected of those now making up the senate who had welcomed the opportunities for power and enrichment provided by a rebel; and a generation later it became clear that Italy, having suffered for its loyalty to the republic, was unwilling to defend Sulla's beneficiaries and their corrupt successors against Caesar when he followed Sulla's example.

That example did instil a horror of civil war that lasted for a generation: his beneficiaries praised his rebellion that had brought them to power, but shuddered at his cruelty after victory. Yet that memory was bound to fade. His career and the effects of his victory ultimately made another civil war almost inevitable, and a politic *clementia* now made a successful rebel unobjectionable to the majority.   E.B.

Sulpicius Galba (emperor). See GALBA.

Sulpicius Quirinius See QUIRINIUS.

Sulpicius Severus See SEVERUS, SULPICIUS.

Symmachus, Quintus Aurelius (c. AD 340–402), Roman senator, orator, and epistolographer, and leading proponent of the pagan religious cause against the Christian emperors, was educated by a Gallic teacher and enjoyed a highly successful political career. After visiting the court of Valentinian I in 369–70, where he delivered the three panegyrics of which fragments survive and made the lasting acquaintance of *Ausonius, he was proconsul of Africa (373) and prefect of Rome (383–4). Despite his support in a lost panegyric for the usurper Magnus Maximus, he was made consul in 391. In the last decade of his life, through his extensive correspondence and personal contacts he tirelessly promoted the interests of his family and friends; the letters in which he arranged the praetorian games of his son are of special interest. He died in 402, shortly after leading an embassy to the imperial court at Ravenna during the first occupation of north Italy by Alaric. The letters of Symmachus were edited by his son Quintus Fabius Memmius Symmachus, who arranged them after the manner of *Pliny the Younger, in nine books of private letters, the tenth being composed of letters addressed to the emperor. These include the 49 *relationes* addressed to Valentinian II during Symmachus' tenure of the urban prefecture, the most famous being *Relatio* 3, in which he argued for the restoration of the Altar of Victory to the senate-house. Symmachus failed to win over Valentinian against the influence of *Ambrose of Milan, whose own two letters on the subject are also extant. Symmachus' religious attitudes seem to focus upon the maintenance of the public cults of Rome and their priesthoods. In this he would contrast—though this may be a misleading impression—with the more varied religious tastes of the leading pagan senator Vettius Agorius Praetextatus, and he did not follow his intimate friend Nicomachus Flavianus into armed opposition to *Theodosius I in 393/4. Nevertheless, Symmachus' public career is marked by a high level of integrity and courage, in which he was not afraid to speak directly in criticism to emperors. His correspondence, for long dismissed as artificial and highly formal without much substantial content, is a fine monument to the character of senatorial influence and the literary culture of senators, though it reveals much less than one would wish of Symmachus' private tastes. Among his 130 known correspondents (others are anonymous), Symmachus included many of the most important political figures of his day, from cultivated court officials to barbarian generals. Symmachus' son, the editor of the letters, married a grand-daughter of Nicomachus Flavianus, and his daughter married Flavianus *iunior*. The names of the two families are preserved on the two leaves of an ivory diptych, respectively in the Victoria and Albert, and Cluny, Museums.   J.F.Ma.

Tt

Tacitus, Latin historian.

1. Publius(?) Cornelius Tacitus was born *c.* AD 56, probably in Narbonese or Cisalpine Gaul. He was in Rome at latest by 75, where an uninterrupted career under *Vespasian, *Titus, and *Domitian (*Hist.* 1. 1. 3) brought him to the praetorship in 88, by which time he was also a member of the prestigious priesthood, the college of the *Quindecimviri sacris faciundis* (guardians of the Sibylline books). During 89–93 he was absent from Rome (*Agr.* 45. 5), presumably holding government posts. In 97 he was suffect consul and pronounced the funeral oration upon Lucius Verginius Rufus. We know of no other office held by Tacitus, till seniority brought him the proconsulship of Asia for 112–13 (*IMylasa* 365, with W. Eck, *ZPE* 45 (1982), 139–53). The date of his death is unknown, but can scarcely have been before 118 (see below).

2. Early in 98 Tacitus published his first work, the *Agricola* (*De vita Iulii Agricolae*), a biography of his father-in-law Gnaeus Julius *Agricola, governor of Britain for seven years from 77 (or 78). That governorship, culminating in the decisive victory of mons Graupius, forms the work's central core (chs. 18–38). But the work is more than a panegyric of a dead man. The opening chapters, without naming Domitian, declare that recent times were hostile both to the performance and to the chronicling of great deeds. The final chapters develop that theme: a fierce invective against Domitian is followed by a moving *consolatio* for the dead Agricola; and the final words, again linking subject and biographer, affirm that Agricola will live on through Tacitus' biography.

Later in the same year came the *Germania* (*De origine et situ Germanorum*). In its first half (to 27. 1), after arguing briefly that the Germans are indigenous and racially pure, Tacitus describes their public and private life. Comparisons, implicit and explicit, between Germans and contemporary Roman society abound, not always to the advantage of the latter. However, the *Germania* is not to be seen as a mirror of morals (or, as some have argued, a historical excursus): its second half, devoted entirely to describing individual tribes, confirms that it is an ethnographical monograph, in which (naturally enough) a foreign people is viewed through Roman eyes.

The third of Tacitus' *opera minora*, the *Dialogus* (*Dialogus de oratoribus*), was perhaps written *c.*101/2; the belief that its neo-Ciceronian style (see CICERO) indicates an early, pre-Domitianic, date has now been discarded. It is an urbane and good-natured discussion about the causes of the contemporary decline in oratory; following the fiction of Cicero's *De oratore*, Tacitus affects to recall a discussion he heard as a young man in 75. Of its three speakers Marcus Aper champions modern oratory, while Vipstanus Messalla affirms that the decline can be remedied by a return to old-fashioned morals and education. Curiatius Maternus, in whose house the discussion takes place, ascribes the decline to political changes: in the late republic oratory had flourished amid virtual anarchy; now, under a benevolent and all-wise ruler, great oratory was no longer needed. While that may come closest to Tacitus' own view, it is simplistic to equate Maternus with Tacitus. Ambivalences attach to the opinions of all three speakers, and Tacitus characteristically leaves readers to elicit their own answers.

3. By about 105–6 Tacitus was collecting material for a historical work, almost certainly the *Histories* (Plin. *Ep.* 6. 16 and 20); the date of its completion is unknown, but may be *c.*109–10. When complete it comprised twelve or fourteen books, covering the years 69–96; only the first four and a quarter books survive, bringing the narrative to 70.

The subject-matter of bks. 1–3, dealing with the civil wars between *Galba, Otho,

*Vitellius, and Vespasian, is predominantly military, and it is for his handling of this material that Mommsen called Tacitus 'most unmilitary of writers'. It is true that the reader is repeatedly puzzled or irritated by the absence of information on chronology, topography, strategy, and logistics. But Tacitus did not write according to the canons of modern historiography. His aim is to provide a narrative that will hold the reader's attention. By that standard chs. 12–49 of bk. 1 (perhaps matched by the graphic description of the night battle of Cremona and the storming and sacking of the city in 3. 19–34) present a sustained narrative of unsurpassed pace and brilliance. From the moment when a handful of soldiers proclaim Otho emperor (27. 2) till Tacitus delivers his obituary over the murdered Galba (49. 4 'omnium consensu capax imperii, nisi imperasset': 'by universal consent fitted to rule—had he not ruled') the ebb and flow of fortune and emotion are portrayed with masterly skill.

The loss of the later books is particularly frustrating, since they deal with a time when Tacitus was himself close to the centre of political activity. From what survives we can surmise that he was no less hostile to Domitian than he had been in the *Agricola*, and that the senate, despite loud professions of independence, was quick to back down when faced by imperial opposition (4. 44. 1). And though Vespasian alone of emperors is said to have changed for the better (1. 50. 4), it is unlikely that Tacitus thought his reign without blemish.

4. At the beginning of the *Histories* (1. 1. 4) Tacitus had spoken of going on to write of *Nerva and *Trajan. In the event he chose to go back to the Julio-Claudian dynasty from the accession of *Tiberius. The *Annals* (more exactly *Ab excessu divi Augusti*; the titles *Historiae* and *Annales* date only from the 16th cent.) originally consisted of eighteen (or sixteen) books—six for Tiberius, six for Gaius and Claudius, six (or four) for Nero. Of these there are lost most of 5, all of 7–10, the first half of 11, and everything after the middle of 16. Whether Tacitus completed the *Annals* is not known; nor do we know the date of composition, though two passages (2. 56. 1 and 4. 5. 2) seem datable to 114 and 115 respectively. That would suggest that the last books can scarcely have been written before

the early years of *Hadrian's reign, perhaps *c.*120.

The six books of Tiberius' reign are structured as two triads. The dichotomy, marked by the striking opening of bk. 4, emphasizes that the reign took a decisive turn for the worse in AD 23 with the rise to power of the ambitious *Sejanus. But even the excellence of the earlier years is attributed to Tiberius' concealment (*dissimulatio*) of his true character. Whether that explanation, which does not originate with Tacitus, is consistent with Tacitus' claim to write impartially (*Ann.* 1. 1. 3 'sine ira et studio') is open to question; but it is skilfully used to probe the ambiguities of Tiberius' behaviour, as the emperor sought to combine a *de facto* autocracy with a show of constitutional republicanism.

For *Claudius, Tacitus accepted the traditional picture of an emperor dominated by his wives and freedmen and gave great (perhaps excessive) prominence to the sexual scandals of *Messal(l)ina and the dynastic scheming of *Agrippina the Younger. But in much of his dealings with the senate Claudius emerges as a pedantically thoughtful personality, e.g. 11. 13 and 24 (in the latter case uniquely we can compare Tacitus' version with the speech that Claudius actually delivered (*ILS* 212)).

*Nero's portrait also is simple: an initial quinquennium of mostly good government ends with the murder of Agrippina in 59, which frees Nero to follow his own desires (14. 13. 2). His extravagance, sexual depravity, and un-Roman innovations are depicted with verve and disapproval. Tacitus also pillories the servility of a senate that congratulates Nero when his mother is murdered (14. 12; cf. 59. 4 and 16. 16), while Publius Clodius Thrasea Paetus' attempts to uphold senatorial independence (13. 49; 14. 12, 48–9; 15. 20 and 23) lead only to his condemnation.

If political debate is less sharp in the Neronian books, foreign affairs and Nero's flamboyant behaviour fully extend Tacitus' descriptive powers. Their impact is strengthened by the organization of incidents into larger continuous units, a structural feature first observable in the Claudian books (so Messalina's final excesses in 11. 26–38 and the account of British affairs, covering several years, in 12. 31–40); similarly, in the Neronian books: British affairs in 14. 29–39 and the annual accounts of Gnaeus Domitius

*Corbulo's eastern campaigns, and (at home) Agrippina's murder (14. 1–13), the Great Fire of Rome and its aftermath (15. 38–45), and the Pisonian conspiracy (15. 48–74).

5. Though none of the sources used by Tacitus has survived, many scholars from Mommsen onwards have held that for continuous sections of his narrative Tacitus followed an unnamed single source; Cluvius Rufus, *Pliny the Elder, Aufidius Bassus, and Fabius Rusticus are among the names that have been suggested. Close and sustained similarities between Tacitus and *Plutarch for the reigns of Galba and Otho make the theory plausible for the period of the civil war, but it is unlikely that Tacitus restricted himself to a single source thereafter, since already at *Hist.* 2. 101 he expresses scepticism of pro-Flavian accounts. For the *Annals*, especially from bk. 6, similarities between Tacitus, *Suetonius, and *Cassius Dio suggest frequent, though not continuous, use of a common source (see also Tacitus' own statement at 13. 20. 2). However, it is probable that Tacitus proceeded differently with different types of material. For senatorial business the *acta senatus* (official record of proceedings) would provide a starting-point, but no more; their bureaucratic language and official version of events would be repugnant to Tacitus. For the private life of the emperor and his family the more lurid and sensational items could be published only after his death, when different versions would multiply (see *Ann.* 14. 2. 1–2 for Agrippina, and *Hist.* 1. 13 and *Ann.* 13. 45 for *Poppaea Sabina). For military matters formal reports in the *acta senatus* could be supplemented from elsewhere (e.g. *Pliny the Elder's twenty volumes on wars in Germany or Corbulo's memoirs of his eastern campaigns). But convention also allowed the ancient historian licence to elaborate or invent incidents to make his narrative more colourful and exciting (cf. *Ann.* 4. 46–51 with Caesar, *BGall.* 7. 69 ff. and Sallust, *Hist.* 2. 87). Yet, whatever the source, the resulting narrative is, by selection, arrangement, and interpretation, wholly Tacitean.

6. Though regret for the lost freedoms of the republic is evident throughout Tacitus, he accepted the necessity of the rule of one man (*Hist.* 1. 1. 1; *Ann.* 4. 33. 2) and praised those few who served the state honourably but without servility (*Ann.* 4. 20. 3; cf. *Agr.* 42. 4). Yet pessimism and hints of a darker

underlying reality are ever-present: motives are rarely simple; innuendo often suggests that the less creditable explanation is the more probable; and an awareness of the gulf in political life between what was professed and what was practised informs all his writing and finds fitting expression in a unique prose style.

7. Tacitus' style is marked by a fastidious and continuous avoidance of the trite and hackneyed. Elevation is lent to his language by archaic and poetic words and an admixture of neologisms, while his extensive use of metaphor more closely resembles poetic than prose usage. In much of this he follows *Sallust, at times even echoing whole passages: so at *Ann.* 4. 1. 3 his portrait of Sejanus recalls (but modifies) Sallust's picture of *Catiline at *Cat.* 5. But to Sallust's renowned brevity Tacitus adds a greater compression of thought. The sinewy strength of his language is reinforced by a deliberate rejection of balance (*concinnitas*) in favour of syntactical disruption (*variatio*), a device he uses with special effectiveness to underline alternative motives. The same aim is served by a peculiarly Tacitean type of sentence construction in which the main syntactical statement stands at or near the beginning, and then has appended to it (by various syntactical means, of which the ablative absolute is one of the most common) comments that suggest motives or record men's reactions (for extended examples cf. *Ann.* 3. 3. 1 and 14. 49. 3). This type of sentence allows Tacitus to concentrate, often with sardonic comment, on the underlying psychology of men's actions and is tellingly employed in his portrait of Tiberius.

8. The surviving texts of Tacitus' works reached the age of printing by three tenuous threads. A Carolingian manuscript of the minor works came from Hersfeld in Germany to Rome c.1455, but disappeared after numerous 15th-cent. copies had been made; whether the 9th-cent. quire of the *Agricola* that survived till the 1940s was part of that manuscript is uncertain. *Annals* 1–6 depend on a single manuscript, the first Medicean, written in Germany (possibly Fulda) c.850, and now in the Laurentian Library in Florence. *Annals* 11–16 and *Histories* 1–5 (numbered consecutively as bks. 11–21) also depend on a single manuscript, the second Medicean, written in a Beneventan

script in the 11th cent.; modern attempts to show that any 15th-cent. manuscript is independent of the second Medicean seem unfounded.   R.H.M.

Tarquinius Priscus, Lucius, the fifth king of Rome (traditionally 616–579 BC), was believed to be the son of Demaratus of Corinth, who fled to Tarquinii (mod. Tarquinià) to escape the tyranny of *Cypselus. Tarquin himself migrated to Rome with his entourage, including his wife Tanaquil, and became the right-hand man of King Ancus Marcius. When Marcius died, Tarquin was chosen, by the regular procedure, as his successor. The story provides interesting examples of the horizontal mobility that characterized élite society in the Archaic period, when high-ranking individuals and groups could move freely from one community to another without loss of social position. This phenomenon, which is documented in the Etruscan cities by contemporary inscriptions, is consistent with the Demaratus story, which is in any case made plausible by archaeological evidence of cultural and trade relations between Etruria and Greece (especially Corinth). It also makes the traditional account of Tarquin's accession at Rome far more likely than the alternative modern theory of an Etruscan conquest of Rome, for which there is no supporting evidence. On the other hand, the connection between Demaratus and Tarquin may be artificial; it cannot be historical if the two Tarquins who ruled at Rome were father and son, as the oldest tradition maintained (Quintus Fabius Pictor fr. 11 Peter). As king, Tarquin is said to have increased the size of the senate and raised the number of cavalry centuries from three to six; and he conducted successful wars against the Latins, Sabines, and Etruscans. *Dionysius of Halicarnassus makes him conquer the Etruscans, but this version, which is not found in *Livy, is doubtless exaggerated. He is also said to have started the construction of the temple of Jupiter Capitolinus, a task completed by his son; but this is probably a compromise designed to overcome the fact that the same building was attributed by different versions of the tradition to both Tarquins. This process of duplication is evident elsewhere, for instance in the case of the drainage works they are both said to have carried out (Cassius

Hemina fr. 15 Peter; Plin. *HN* 36. 107). Tarquin was assassinated by the sons of Ancus Marcius, but their bid for the throne was thwarted by Tanaquil, who secured it for her favourite Servius Tullius. This bizarre story is made all the more odd by the fact that Tarquin himself is credited with two sons, Lucius (*Tarquinius Superbus) and Arruns. Of his two daughters, one married Servius Tullius, the other Marcus Brutus and thus became the mother of Lucius Junius Brutus, the founder of the republic.   T.J.Co.

Tarquinius Superbus, Lucius, traditionally the last king of Rome (534–510 BC). According to the oldest sources (Quintus Fabius Pictor fr. 11 Peter) he was the son of *Tarquinius Priscus, although on the traditional chronology that is impossible (Dion. Hal. 4. 6–7). It follows either that Superbus was in fact the grandson of Priscus (thus Piso fr. 15 P. = Dion. Hal. 4. 6–7), or, more probably, that the traditional chronology of the regal period is unsound. Tarquin is said to have pursued an aggressive foreign policy; he captured several Latin towns and reorganized the Latin League into a regular military alliance under Roman leadership (Livy 1. 52), a state of affairs that is reflected in the first treaty between Rome and Carthage (Polyb. 3. 22: 509 BC). The text of the treaty he made with the Latin town of Gabii is supposed to have survived until the time of *Augustus. He is also famous for having completed the temple of Capitoline Jupiter, and notorious for his tyrannical rule which eventually led to his downfall. Terracottas from the temple site at Sant'Omobono may belong to the reign of Superbus; in any event they confirm that the later Roman kings were flamboyant rulers who modelled themselves on contemporary Greek tyrants. This proves that Superbus' reputation as a tyrant is not (or not entirely) the result of secondary elaboration in the annalistic tradition in an artificial attempt to assimilate Rome and Greece.

After his expulsion from Rome Tarquin fled to Caere, and persuaded Veii and Tarquinii to attack Rome. After their defeat at Silva Arsia, he appealed to Lars *Porsenna, whose assault on Rome is said to have been aimed at restoring Tarquin to power; but this cannot have been so if Porsenna succeeded in taking the city, and it is hard to reconcile with the story that Tarquin then turned to his son-in-law Octavius Mamilius, dictator of the Latins, since the Latins had vanquished Porsenna. After the defeat of Mamilius at Lake Regillus, Tarquin took refuge with Aristodemus of Cumae, where he died in 495 BC.   T.J.Co.

Terence (Publius Terentius Afer), the Roman playwright, author of *fabulae palliatae* ('dramas in a Greek cloak') in the 160s BC. The *Life* by *Suetonius records that he was born at Carthage, came to Rome as a slave in the household of a senator called Terentius Lucanus, was soon freed, but died still young on a visit to Greece in 159. As usual, we have no way to check this information; his Carthaginian birth may have been an incorrect deduction from his *cognomen* or surname (*Afer*, 'the African'). He was patronized by prominent Romans, and his last play, *Adelphoe*, was commissioned by *Scipio Aemilianus and his brother for performance at the funeral games for their father Aemilius *Paullus in 160. The previous year, his *Eunuchus* had been an outstanding success, marked by a repeat performance and an unprecedentedly large financial reward. His one known failure was *Hecyra*, which twice had to be abandoned in the face of competition from rival attractions (first a tightrope walker and boxers, then a gladiatorial show); Terence's account of these misfortunes in his prologue for the third production is exceptional evidence for conditions of performance at the time.

All his six plays survive. Their dates are given by the *didascaliae* (production notices), which are generally accepted as reliable in spite of some difficulties: *Andria* ('The Girl from Andros', Megalesian Games 166); *Hecyra* ('The Mother-in-Law', Megalesian Games 165, revived in 160 at Aemilius Paullus' funeral games and again later that year); *Heautontimorumenos* ('The Self-Tormentor', Megalesian Games 163); *Eunuchus* ('The Eunuch', Megalesian Games 161); *Phormio* (Roman Games 161); and *Adelphoe* ('The Brothers', Aemilius Paullus' funeral games in 160). *Hecyra* and *Phormio* were based on originals by Apollodorus of Carystus, the other four on plays by *Menander; Terence preserved the Greek titles of all but *Phormio* (named after the main character; Apollodorus' title was *Epidikazomenos*, 'The Claimant at Law'). All the plays were produced by

Ambivius Turpio, with music by one Flaccus, slave of Claudius.

In adapting *Andria*, Terence added material from Menander's *Perinthia* ('The Girl from Perinthos'); for his *Eunuchus* he added the characters of the parasite and the soldier from Menander's *Kolax* ('The Toady'); and in *Adelphoe* he added a scene from *Diphilus' *Synapothnēskontes* ('Comrades in Death'). We learn this from the prologues to these plays, where he defends himself against charges of 'spoiling' the Greek plays and of 'theft' from earlier Latin plays. But he made more radical changes than these. The commentary by *Donatus provides some further information, e.g. that the first 20 lines of *Andria* are an entirely original creation, and that Terence has converted monologue to dialogue in the central scene of *Eunuchus* (539–614). The extent and implications of these and other changes are much disputed; it is a mark of Terence's skill that we cannot be sure of the boundaries of inserted material even when he tells us that it has been added. It is widely believed that he made significant changes to the endings of several plays (particularly *Eun.* and *Ad.*), but the meagre fragments that survive of his Greek originals force us to rely heavily on intuition about what Menander and Apollodorus are likely to have done.

One clear innovation was Terence's use of a prologue to conduct feuds with his critics; he never used one to tell the spectators about the background to the plot. It has been suggested that he preferred to exploit effects of surprise rather than irony and to involve his audience more directly in the emotions of characters (most notably in *Hecyra*, where it is laid bare how women are misunderstood, maligned, and mistreated by men). But the scope for ironic effect varies from play to play; in some cases he includes essential background information in the mouths of the characters at an early stage. It seems more likely that he dispensed with expository prologues because he regarded them as an unrealistic device. Consistent with this is his avoidance of direct audience address in his plays, though he does include some 'metatheatrical' remarks at *An.* 474–94 and *Hec.* 865–8.

There is a world of difference between Terence and *Plautus. In general, Terence seems to have preserved the ethos of his originals more faithfully, with well-constructed plots, consistent characterization, and very few overtly Roman intrusions into the Greek setting. Like Plautus, he increased the proportion of lines with musical accompaniment; but he hardly ever used lyric metres, and he was more sparing in his use of setpiece cantica (operatic interludes). His plays repay thoughtful study and give a sympathetic portrayal of human relationships (*Haut.* and *Ad.* both deal with questions of openness and tolerance between fathers and adolescent sons). On the other hand, he added stock characters and boisterous scenes to *Eun.* and *Ad.*, and he appealed to the precedent of Plautus and others when accused of *contaminatio*; he was not faithful enough to the Greek originals for some of his contemporaries. He deserves his reputation for *humanitas*, a humane sympathy for the predicaments of human beings, but his plays are also lively and entertaining situation comedies.

Terence's greatest contribution to the development of literary Latin was the creation of a naturalistic style far closer to the language of everyday conversation than that of Plautus or the other authors of *palliatae*, with much exclamation, aposiopesis, and ellipsis; many of its features are paralleled in *Cicero's letters and *Catullus's shorter poems. But he did also sometimes use a more ornate and repetitive style, both in the plays themselves and above all in the prologues, which are highly elaborate rhetorical pieces with much antithesis, alliteration, etc. He does not reproduce the fantastic verbal exuberance of Plautus.

Terence was widely read for many centuries after his death, above all for his style and moral sentiments. Over 650 manuscripts of his plays survive, including a number with famous miniature illustrations. In the 10th cent. the nun Hrothswitha of Gandersheim wrote six Christian comedies in imitation of Terence, and he was both imitated and revived in the Renaissance. He held a central place in the European school curriculum until the 19th cent.   P.G.M.B.

Tertullian (Quintus Septimius Florens Tertullianus) (AD *c.*160–*c.*240), born in or near Carthage, the son of a centurion. The tradition that he was a lawyer rests chiefly on the questionable authority of *Jerome. None

the less, he uses brilliant gifts of advocacy, rhetoric, and irony in favour of the rigorist party among the Carthaginian Christians. From the first he was steeped in the spirit of the martyrs. His *Ad martyres, Ad nationes,* and *Apologeticus* (all written *c.*197) defended Christianity against pagan charges of atheism, black magic, and sedition, while maintaining that only in martyrdom could the Christian be assured of his salvation. Next (198–205) he devoted himself largely to Christian ethical problems. His *De oratione, Ad uxorem, De paenitentia,* and *De baptismo* all make high demands on the Christian life.

Tertullian's sole authority, apart from his verbal and intellectual acumen, was the Bible. Where, as in the *De anima,* he cites Stoics with approval, it is as the confirmation, not the source, of his beliefs. His *De testimonio animae* is a classic exposition of the view that all men have innate knowledge of God; yet heresy is found, in his *De praescriptione haereticorum,* to result from the illegitimate substitution of philosophy for the 'rule of faith' (*regula fidei*). This was followed by works against the followers of the Platonizing Christian Valentinus, and (between 207 and 211) five books against the arch-heretic Marcion. Against Marcion's belittlement of the Old Testament and violent emendation of the New, he argues for the integrity of scripture and a unity of purpose between the 'just' Father and the 'good' Son.

At some time he joined the Montanists, disciples of a new era of the Spirit, from whom they claimed to be receiving immediate direction. His action may have been precipitated by disgust with Catholic laxity, and perhaps by a dispute with the clergy at Rome. Yet, to judge by his subsequent reputation, there was never a formal schism. The transition seems to have taken place by 207. Believing that it was time for man to regain his unfallen image, he wrote his *Ad Scapulam* (212) to a local pagan governor in defence of religious freedom; his *De fuga in persecutione* and *De corona militis* against Christians who complied with the authorities; and his *De ieiunio* and *De monogamia* to enjoin a rigour in discipline that went beyond scriptural teaching.

His important doctrinal writings of this period are the *De carne Christi, De resurrectione carnis, De anima,* and *Adversus Praxean,* all notable for their hostility to dualistic thought. Body and soul are one, God himself is a body (though its matter is Spirit), and the body of Christ that died on the cross is identical with the risen one. His last surviving work, *De pudicitia*, was probably directed against measures by Callistus, bishop of Rome (217–22), to relax the Christian penitential system. The work is fundamental for its theology of a gathered Church and the study of the western doctrine of the Holy Spirit.

Tertullian seems to have lived to a ripe old age, and finally to have broken with the Montanists to found his own sect of Tertullianists, more rigorous than they. With the possible exception of Minucius Felix, he is the first Latin churchman, and, as a favourite of both *Cyprian and *Augustine, exercised a great and abiding influence upon Christian theology in the west. He shares with his contemporary Hippolytus a hatred of Callistus, an aversion to all philosophy, a rebellious spirit harnessed to a strong ecclesiology, and a belief in the importance of distinguishing the persons of the Godhead (see *Adv. Praxean*). The affinity illustrates the close relations between north Africa and the capital in this period; he is, however, unparalleled in both the originality and the difficulty of his Latin style.   w.h.c.f.; m.j.e.

Thales of Miletus, the most scientific member of the Seven Sages, was credited in antiquity with the prediction of a solar eclipse (Hdt. 1. 74. 2) that modern scholars have dated in 585 BC. He was reported to have advised the Ionian Greeks to form a political union (Hdt. 1.170. 3). Thales acquired legendary status as engineer, geometer, and astronomer; in *Aristotle's view he was the first natural philosopher and cosmologist. Since Thales left no written work (with the dubious exception of a navigational handbook, a *Nautical Astronomy* in hexameter verse), it is impossible to know how much historical basis there is for the achievements attributed to him in the ancient tradition. These include various geometrical discoveries and feats of mensuration (e.g. calculating the height of the pyramids by the length of their shadow), the study of solstices and measurement of the astronomical seasons, and several physical theses: that the earth floats on water, that a magnetic stone has a *psychē* (soul) since it makes things move, that all things are full of

gods, and that water is the *archē*, the beginning or first principle of all things (Arist. *Metaph. A* 3, 983^{b}20 ff.). The primeval importance of water can be paralleled in Egyptian and Babylonian myths, as in the first verses of Genesis. The figure of Thales remained in popular memory as a marker of the moment when oriental science and myth were being transformed into the beginnings of Greek geometry, astronomy, and cosmology.   c.h.k.

Themistius, Greek philosopher and rhetorician, was born in Paphlagonia *c.* AD 317 of a cultured family of pagan landowners, and studied in the eastern provinces and in Constantinople, where he opened a school (*c.*345). Attracting the attention of the imperial government, he was soon appointed to an official chair and became a member of the Constantinopolitan senate. His eloquent and often constructive exposition of the ideology of monarchy in a succession of panegyrics and other speeches won and retained for him the favour of every emperor from Constantius II to *Theodosius I, who appointed him prefect of the city (383–4) and entrusted him with the education of his son, the future emperor Arcadius. He travelled widely in the empire, in attendance on the imperial court and on official missions, such as that to the Roman senate in 357. He died in Constantinople about 388.

In spite of his professed admiration for *Plato, Themistius found the pragmatic and realistic approach of *Aristotle more congenial, and he was little influenced by contemporary Neoplatonism, with its other-worldly overtones. In his early years as a teacher he wrote explanatory paraphrases of many of Aristotle's works, setting a pattern of exegesis which continued to be followed throughout the Middle Ages. A convinced but unfanatical pagan, he yet refrained from overt attacks on Christianity except in an address to *Julian, now lost, which evoked from the emperor the celebrated letter (253–67 Spanheim) setting out the principles of his proposed restoration of paganism.

Of his numerous works there survive: 34 speeches, mainly official addresses to emperors, but including an interesting funeral oration on his father (*Or.* 20); and paraphrases of Aristotle's *Posterior Analytics*, *Physics*, *De anima* (in the Greek original),

De caelo and *Metaphysics XII* (in a medieval Hebrew translation made from an Arabic version). Themistius was neither a great philosopher nor a great statesman, yet his speeches are valuable as sources for the history of his time and as specimens of pagan political ideology in the Christian empire, and his Aristotelian paraphrases embody material from lost commentaries. R.B.

Themistocles (*c.*524–459 BC), Athenian politician, was a member of the ancient Lycomid family but by a non-Athenian mother. *Herodotus' informants accused him of corruption and said that in 480 he had 'recently come to the fore', though he was archon in 493/2; but *Thucydides admired him for his far-sightedness and considered him one of the greatest men of his generation.

As archon, Themistocles began the development of the Piraeus as Athens' harbour; it may be that *Phrynichus' *Capture of Miletus* and subsequent trial, and *Miltiades' return to Athens from the Chersonesus and his subsequent trial, belong to 493/2 and that Themistocles was involved in these episodes. In the ostracisms of the 480s he regularly attracted votes but was not himself ostracized (altogether, 2,264 ostraca against him are known, including a set of 190 prepared by fourteen hands): the expulsion of Xanthippus (father of *Pericles) in 484 and Aristides in 482 may represent a three-cornered battle in which Themistocles was the winner. Attempts to connect him with a change from direct election to partial sortition in the appointment of the archons, in 487/6, have no foundation in the sources; but he was behind the decision in 483/2 to spend a surplus from the silver mines on enlarging Athens' navy from 70 to 200 ships—allegedly for use against Aegina, but these ships played a crucial part in the defeat of the Persian navy in 480.

In 480 he was the general who commanded Athens' contingents in the Greek forces against the invading Persians: on land in Thessaly, and then on sea at Artemisium and at Salamis; he interpreted an oracle to predict victory at Salamis, argued for staying at Salamis rather than retiring beyond the isthmus of Corinth, and tricked the Persians into throwing away their advantage by entering the straits. The Decree of Themistocles inscribed at Troezen in the 3rd cent.

probably contains authentic material but has at least undergone substantial editing. In the winter of 480/79 he received unprecedented honours at Sparta, but in 479 we hear nothing of him and Athens' forces were commanded by Aristides and Xanthippus.

After the Persian War there are various stories of his coming into conflict with Sparta (in the best attested he took delaying action at Sparta while the Athenians rebuilt their city walls), while the Delian League was built up by the pro-Spartan *Cimon. In the main tradition the cunning, democratic Themistocles is opposed to the upright, aristocratic Aristides, but there are indications that Aristides was now a supporter rather than an opponent of Themistocles. About the end of the 470s Themistocles was ostracized, went to live at Argos, and 'visited other places in the Peloponnese' (Thuc. 1. 135. 3), where an anti-Spartan alliance was growing. When Sparta became alarmed, and claimed to have evidence that he was involved with Pausanias in intrigues with Persia, he fled, first westwards to Corcyra and Epirus but then via Macedonia and the Aegean Sea to Asia Minor. The Athenians condemned him to death in his absence; after 465 the new king, Artaxerxes I, made him governor of Magnesia on the Maeander, where coins bearing his name and portrait were issued. He probably died a natural death, though there was a legend that he committed suicide; after his death, his family returned to Athens. Democracy did not become an issue while he was in Athens, but there are links between him and the democratic, anti-Spartan politicians who came to power at the end of the 460s.

A.R.B.; P.J.R.

Theocritus, poet from Syracuse, early 3rd cent. BC (working at the Alexandrian court in the 270s); creator of the bucolic genre, but a writer who drew inspiration from many earlier literary forms, cleverly blending them into a new amalgam which nevertheless displays constant invention and seeks variety rather than homogeneity. Thirty poems and a few fragments, together with twenty-four epigrams, are ascribed to him, several (e.g. 19, 20, 21, 23) clearly spurious and others (e.g. 25, 26) of doubtful authenticity. A scholar called Artemidorus boasts in an epigram transmitted along with the ancient scholia (which are very full and learned) that he has rounded up 'the Pastoral Muses' so that 'scattered once, all are now a single fold and flock'; his edition no doubt included a good deal of anonymous material in the most distinctive of the various Theocritean styles (rural sketches written in the Doric dialect alongside the master's work, and authorship is sometimes hard to determine.

A near-contemporary of the great innovator *Callimachus, Theocritus too was a remaker of the Greek poetic tradition, though his own method of propagating the gospel of tightly organized, perfectly finished writing on a miniature scale was to demonstrate by implicit example rather than engage in neurotic combat against real or imaginary enemies. The closest he comes to a manifesto, and a text that is central for understanding his art, is poem 7 in the collection, which bears the title *Thalysia*, 'The Harvest Home'. Cast in elusively autobiographical form, it describes a journey undertaken by a conveniently assumed persona, 'Simichidas', during his younger days on the island of Cos. On the road he meets a Cretan called Lycidas, 'a goatherd—nor could anyone have mistaken him for anything else, since he looked so very like a goatherd'. The two engage in a song contest, preceded by a discussion of the current state of poetry; Philitas and 'Sicelidas of Samos' (a near-anagram for Asclepiades) are mentioned, and Lycidas praises his young companion for his refusal to write Homeric pastiche (see HOMER). The result of the 'competition' is a foregone conclusion, for Simichidas is promised his prize in advance; just as well, since his clumsy party-piece is no match for the smiling Lycidas' sophisticated song. And no wonder: for as F. Williams showed, focusing earlier partial insights into a conclusive picture, Lycidas is Apollo, the god of poetry himself, and his epiphany in the poem marks it out as an account of the 'poet's consecration' (*Dichterweihe*) of the kind *Hesiod and *Archilochus had received from the Muses (*CQ* 1971, 137–45).

Other poems in the bucolic main sequence (1–7) also contain passages with programmatic implications—in particular the meticulous description of the wonderfully carved cup in poem 1, whose scenes (especially the culminating picture of the boy concentrating on weaving a tiny cage for a singing cricket, oblivious to all else) seem intended as a visual correlative of Theocritus'

poetic agenda. There are also pieces which refer more directly to the problems of the writer in the Hellenistic world. Poem 16 imaginatively reworks themes from *Simonides in appealing for patronage to *Hieron II of Syracuse, and 17 is a similar request to *Ptolemy II Philadelphus, less inspired overall but with a splendidly impish portrayal of the afterlife which the king's father is fancied to be enjoying on Mt. Olympus with *Alexander the Great and Heracles as his heavenly drinking-companions (16–33). Life in contemporary Alexandria, and praise of its enlightened ruler, is again the theme of 14, an exploratory transposition of a scene of New Comedy into hexameter form; while 15, one of the two 'urban mimes' in the collection which develop the form invented by Sophron in the 5th cent., gives us a glimpse of the annual Adonis festival in Ptolemy's palace. We watch the celebration, and hear the hymn (T. is fond of encapsulated song) through the eyes and ears of a pair of suburban housewives, Gorgo and Praxinoa, who have spent the first part of the poem (he is no less fond of diptychal composition) stunning the reader by the banality of their conversation.

The other mime (2) is also a diptych, this time cast as a monologue. A young Alexandrian woman, Simaetha, instructs her servant Thestylis in the performance of a magic ritual designed to charm back a wandering lover—or else destroy him; then, after the slave's departure with the drug, she recalls the occasion of her first sight of the youth, and her seduction. Both the incantations and the first part of the solo scene are punctuated with refrains appropriate to the situation, a hypnotic feature that recurs in the song on the death of Daphnis in 1. The poem is an excellent example of Theocritus' originality in expanding the catchment area of material to be considered 'fit for poetry'; the effect was permanent, and echoes of the double perspective here (the ironic yet fundamentally humane vision of the author laid over the distressed naïveté of the girl; cf. 11) can still be traced in Tiresias' description of the similarly squalid seduction in Eliot's *The Waste Land*. Though (like all of Theocritus' work) the piece is primarily designed for an audience of sophisticated readers, there is an emotional power here that makes it performable.

But Theocritus was also interested in staking a claim on more 'mainstream' territory, as his choice of the hexameter as his regular vehicle suggests (the only exceptions to this rule are three rather contrived experiments in Aeolic lyric, 28–30). Epic remained the ultimate challenge. Two poems (13, on Hylas; and 22, the second part of which narrates the fight between Polydeuces and Amycus) take up Argonautic subjects, and must relate somehow to the contemporary long poem by *Apollonius Rhodius—perhaps Theocritus is showing his less radical rival how to do it properly. *Pindar (*Nem.* 1) is recast into epic and updated in the treatment of Heracles' cradle-confrontation with the snakes in 24; only as babies or lovers (cf. Menelaus in the Spartan epithalamium, 18) can the traditional heroes retain their tenuous grasp on the Hellenistic imagination. The rhetorical sequence at 16. 47–57 makes all clear: two lines for Homer's *Iliad* (and even here the emphasis is given to the losers, and to the *handsomest* Greek fighter at Troy, Cycnus, never even mentioned in Homer's poem) are followed by six for the *Odyssey*, with the peasants given pride of place over the eponymous hero.

New, yet in some ways older, characters are brought forward to supplant the epic warrior: Daphnis (1), Hylas (13), and Adonis (15), each of whom swoons in erotic death, and Polyphemus (6, 11), who joins Simaetha and the goatherd in 3 as a failed lover and displaces Odysseus from centre-stage. Instead of the bloody duels of epic, the new model of competition is the agonistic singing of the goatherds. Old false ideals and fantasies are pared away, and the new ones that Theocritus puts in their place are justified, paradoxically, by their very self-conscious artificiality. In an age of uncertainty and unbelief, Theocritus offers three beacons by which life may be orientated: love (which must ultimately fail, through rejection or death), personal determination, and art. Each of these is symbolically figured in turn on the cup, the *aipolikon thaēma* ('marvel for goatherds'), at 1. 27–55.

At some point in the ancient tradition Theocritus' poems acquired the generic title *eidyllia*, 'vignettes'; in so far as the transliteration 'idylls' may conjure up a misleading image of rustic languor and passivity it is perhaps best avoided as a label for the poems of this energetic, engaged, and acutely intelligent writer.   A.H.G.

Theodosius I, 'the Great', the son of count Theodosius, was born *c.* AD 346. He was promoted early, serving as *dux* ('duke' or military commander) of Moesia Superior in 374. On his father's sudden disgrace and execution in 376 he retired to the family properties at Cauca but in 378, after the defeat and death of the emperor Valens at Adrianople, the emperor Gratian appointed him *magister militum* (master of infantry) to fight the Goths, and shortly afterwards (19 January 379) proclaimed him Augustus of the eastern parts, including the dioceses of Dacia and Macedonia. For the next few years Theodosius conducted campaigns against the Goths, basing himself at first at Thessalonica (379–80), then at Constantinople. Failing to eject the Goths from the empire, on 3 October 382 he signed a treaty with them, recognizing them as federates and assigning them lands in Thrace and Lower Moesia. In 386 he signed a treaty with Persia, whereby the long-disputed kingdom of Armenia was partitioned between the two empires. Both these treaties are shown on the base of the obelisk of Theodosius, erected in the hippodrome at Constantinople in 390, as triumphs of Roman arms. When the usurper Magnus Maximus killed Gratian in 383 and occupied the Gauls, Theodosius for a time recognized him, but when in 387 Maximus expelled Valentinian II from Italy, he marched west, defeated Maximus at Siscia and Poetovio, and put him to death at Aquileia. Theodosius stayed in the west for three years, and made a state visit to Rome in 389, the occasion of the delivery to him of the panegyric of the Gallic rhetorician Pacatus, and of cordial relations between the emperor and even pagan members of the senatorial aristocracy; *Symmachus, who had praised Maximus in a panegyric, was made consul for 391. At this time Valentinian II was established in Gaul, while Theodosius' elder son Arcadius, whom he had proclaimed Augustus in 383, had been left in nominal control of the east. Theodosius returned to Constantinople in 391, but again had to march west in 394 to subdue the usurper Eugenius, who had displaced Valentinian. He again left Arcadius in the east and took with him to the west his younger son Honorius, proclaimed Augustus in 393. He defeated Eugenius at the river Frigidus on 6 September 394 but died at Milan on 17 January 395, to be succeeded by his sons Arcadius and Honorius in east and west respectively.

Theodosius was a pious Christian and, unlike his predecessor Valens, an adherent of the Nicene creed, an allegiance which he owed to his origin and upbringing in the west. He was also surrounded by westerners, relatives and others, to whom he gave advancement, many of them individuals of intense personal piety. He was baptized very early in his reign, during a serious illness at Thessalonica. On 27 February 380 (before he had come to Constantinople) he issued a constitution declaring that the faith professed by Pope Damasus and by Peter, bishop of Alexandria, was the true Catholic faith. He deposed Demophilus, the Arian bishop of Constantinople, and recognized as bishop the Nicene protagonist, Gregory of Nazianzus. On 10 January 381 he ordered that all churches be surrendered to the Catholic bishops as defined by himself. He then called a council of about 150 bishops at Constantinople, which ratified Theodosius' action but refused to accept Gregory of Nazianzus. Theodosius asked them to produce a short list and chose Nectarius, a former senator of Constantinople, as bishop.

Theodosius was very severe against heretics, issuing eighteen constitutions against them; he even ordained the death penalty for some extremist sects. Towards the pagans his policy was at first ambivalent. He did not forbid sacrifice, but was so severe against divination as to prevent it. He did not close the temples, but allowed fanatical Christians, including his own praetorian prefect Cynegius, to destroy them, or granted them to petitioners. In a law issued at Milan in 391 he abruptly closed all temples and banned all forms of pagan cult. This step was probably taken under the influence of *Ambrose, bishop of Milan, who had obtained great ascendancy over him since his arrival in the west. Late in 388 Ambrose forced him to leave unpunished the bishop of Callinicum, who had burned down a synagogue, and in 390, when Theodosius ordered retributive killings at Thessalonica to avenge the death in a riot of the general Butheric, he refused him communion until he had done penance.

Theodosius' death was followed by what is often seen as the formal division of the Roman empire into eastern and western parts. His settlement with the Goths had long-term effects, as under their leaders the Goths installed themselves ever more intimately into the political structure and society of the Roman empire. His religious policies mark a significant step in the developing alliance between Church and State, and were greeted with delight by Christian writers like *Orosius and *Augustine, and with dismay by Eunapius. But he was brought to the throne at a time of major crisis, overcame it to the benefit of the empire, and imposed his personality on Roman history.   J.F.Ma.

Theodosius II, son of Arcadius, born in AD 401, was proclaimed Augustus in 402. He succeeded his father in 408 and reigned rather than ruled the empire until his death in 450. He was very piously educated by his elder sister, Pulcheria, who exercised a strong influence over him until the early 440s. For a time he was also much influenced by his wife Eudocia, whom he married in 421. During the earlier part of his reign the empire was in fact governed by Anthemius, praetorian prefect of the east from 405 to 414, and then probably by Helion, master of the offices from 414 to 427. From the early 440s the emperor was controlled by Chrysaphius, an imperial eunuch, and Nomus, master of the offices.

The chief military events of the reign were two successful Persian wars (421–2 and 441), the defeat of the usurper John in the west, and the installation of Valentinian III at Rome (425), an unsuccessful naval expedition against the Vandals (441), and a series of wars and negotiations with Rua and Attila, kings of the Huns. The Roman armies proved helpless against the Huns, and peace was obtained only by paying ever increasing subsidies (350 lb. gold per annum from 422, 700 lb. from 434, 2,100 lb. from 443).

The chief ecclesiastical events were the condemnation of Nestorius, bishop of Constantinople, by the council of Ephesus in 431, and of Flavian, bishop of Constantinople, by the second council of Ephesus in 449; Cyril and Dioscurus, bishops of Alexandria, were moving spirits in these two councils.

In 429 a commission was appointed under Antiochus, praetorian prefect and former quaestor, to codify all laws issued since 312. This attempt to reform the law failed, but in 435 a second commission under the same Antiochus Chuzon carried out the task and in 438 the Theodosian Code (see below) was promulgated in both parts of the empire.

A.H.M.J.; W.L.

THE THEODOSIAN CODE (Codex Theodosianus) was a collection of some 2,500 imperial laws collected and published between AD 429 and 438 on the authority of Theodosius II. By about 400 it had become clear that a new collection was needed to supplement the *Codex Gregorianus* and *Hermogenianus* of a century earlier. The law in the western and eastern parts of the empire had to be harmonized, its bulk reduced, forgeries eliminated, and a decision reached on which imperial laws were general, and so entitled to prevail over corrupt or improvident concessions to petitioners (*rescripta, adnotationes*). Given the disorder of the western empire, the eastern government took the initiative. In March 429 Theodosius II in Constantinople set up a commission, consisting of eight officials or ex-officials and a practising advocate, to collect all the general laws they could find from Constantine onwards, arrange them in chronological order under subject-headings, and shorten them so that only the operative part remained (*Cod. Theod.* 1. 1. 5). They were not to harmonize conflicting laws, but it was envisaged that ultimately the new *Codex*, together with the *Gregorianus*, the *Hermogenianus* and the writings of lawyers of authority would be fused in a harmonious whole.

By December 435 the available laws had been collected from various sources, eastern and western. *Cod. Theod.* 1. 1. 6 of that date shows that Theodosius then reconstituted his commission as a body of sixteen charged with proceeding to the next stage, that of editing the projected codex; but some scholars have supposed that Theodosius abandoned the original project as a failure and began again. The laws were to be edited so as to make them clear and elegant. By the end of 437 the commission had completed the *Codex* in sixteen books (*libri*) divided into subject-headings. In February 438 Theodosius promulgated it in a law addressed to the senate of Constantinople (*Nov. Theod.* 1), in which he thanked the eight commissioners who had seen the project through to the end, chief among them its guiding spirit Antiochus Chuzon, a lawyer from Antioch. The *Codex* was then presented to the senate of Rome, which acclaimed it for the increased certainty and security it brought.

The Theodosian Code could not by itself arrest the decline of the western empire, but in its own terms it was a success. It set out the text of all general laws in force since Constantine, thus resolving doubts about what was general, and hampering falsification. The texts were dated so that conflicts between them could be settled on the basis that the later prevails over the earlier. The Code provided for mutual recognition of future laws by west and east, though the system for ensuring this broke down. Theodosius did not go on to the ambitious project, adumbrated in 429, of a harmonious restatement of the whole law; but even a hundred years later *Justinian was able to achieve this only in part. Justinian included much of the Theodosian Code in his own *Codex*, but repealed the rest. Outside his sphere of authority Alaric II embodied about a quarter of it in his *Lex Romana Visigothorum* (Roman Law according to the Visigoths) of 506 and it helped to mould the law in the other kingdoms that replaced the western Roman empire.

T.Hon.

Theognis, elegiac poet, of Megara. Chronographers dated him *c.*550–540 BC, making him synchronous with Phocylides (with whom he was often coupled as a moralist); historical allusions have been held to point to a much higher dating (*c.*640–600). A corpus of some 1,400 verses survives in manuscript tradition, labelled as Theognis' work. A few scholars have tried to defend the unity of the collection, but everything points to its being a composite from two or three ancient (Hellenistic) anthologies of elegiac excerpts, Theognis being only one of many poets represented. Crucial points are: (1) Theognis habitually addresses a friend Cyrnus, also called Polypaides (see 19–26). In some parts of the collection (19–254, 319–72, 539–54, 805–22, 1171–84b) nearly every item contains this address, whereas elsewhere it is absent for long stretches. (2) Several pieces are identifiable from other sources as the work of *Tyrtaeus, Mimnermus, *Solon, and perhaps Euenus. (3) Some pieces clearly date from as late as the Persian Wars (757–64, 773–82; 903–30 is also surely 5th-cent.). (4) Many items are duplicated, with or without the textual divergences typical of anthologies. The corpus divides into five clear sections. 1–18: addresses to gods, gathered at the beginning. 19–254: nearly all Cyrnus-poems, serious in tone, with the first and last excerpts chosen to serve as prologue and epilogue. 255–1022: a much more heterogeneous and disorderly collection, with a few Cyrnus-blocks here and there. 1023–1220: similar in character, but with a high proportion of couplets duplicated elsewhere. (1221–30: added by editors from other sources.) 1231–1389: amatory poems, mostly addressed to boys. This section survives only in the 10th-cent. MS A (where it is designated 'book 2') and was unknown until Bekker's edition of 1815.

The addresses to Cyrnus, plus a few pre-Hellenistic citations naming the author, allow us to identify some 308 verses as Theognis'. Some of the rest may be his, but it is prudent to treat the greater part as anonymous and to call the corpus 'the Theognidea', not 'Theognis'. Theognis addresses Cyrnus in three roles: adviser, lover, and confederate. He makes many allusions to political turbulence. He appears as a 'squirearch', a man of standing in Megara, but subject to criticism and hostility, eventually betrayed by those he trusted, dispossessed of his estates in a civic upheaval, and forced into exile, where he dreams of revenge. He expects his verses to circulate at banquets everywhere, far into the future (237 ff.). Many of the anonymous Theognidea too were clearly composed for convivial gatherings. Drinking and merry-making are frequent themes. Other pieces are reflective or philosophic. The love poems of 'book 2' are often banal, but sometimes touching. The collection as a whole contains many delightful things. It may be taken as a representative cross-section of the elegiac poetry circulating in social settings between the late 7th and early 5th cent., and it is our best source for the ordinary man's ideas about life, friendship, fate, death, and other matters.

M.L.W.

Theophrastus (372/1 or 371/70–288/7 or 287/6 BC) of Eresus in Lesbos, associate and successor of *Aristotle. In spite of a tradition that he had been a pupil of *Plato, it is probable that he first joined Aristotle when the latter was at Assos. He became head of the Lyceum (see ARISTOTLE, § 5) when Aristotle withdrew from Athens on the death of *Alexander the Great. His most famous pupil was

the Athenian politician Demetrius of Phalerum, through whose influence he, though a metic (resident foreigner), was allowed to own property. He was also on friendly terms with *Cassander and *Ptolemy I. He was succeeded as head of the school by *Straton.

Theophrastus shared in, continued, and extended Aristotle's activity in every subject. His surviving works cover only a small part of the range of interests indicated by the lists of book-titles preserved in the biography by *Diogenes Laertius (5. 36–57) and by numerous reports in later authors. The extent to which he consciously diverged from Aristotle on major issues is a subject of debate; it is likely that he saw himself as continuing and developing Aristotle's work of discussion and observation. Much of his writing seems, like the extant *Metaphysics*, to have raised questions rather than categorically asserting a position.

Together with Eudemus of Rhodes, Theophrastus made important modifications to Aristotle's modal logic. His research in propositional logic anticipated and probably influenced the Stoic Chrysippus of Soli; but it was Chrysippus rather than Theophrastus who made this the foundation of a new logical system. Theophrastus certainly rejected Aristotle's Unmoved Mover, and argued—though not necessarily against Aristotle—that teleological explanation could not be applied to every aspect of the natural world. He retained a belief in the divinity of the heavens and the eternity of the universe; the evidence for his rejecting the fifth, heavenly element (the *aithēr*) and regarding fire as fundamentally different in kind from the other sublunary elements is uncertain. He raised objections to Aristotle's definition of place; Simplicius (6th-cent. AD commentator) was able to interpret him as anticipating Damascius' explanation of place in terms of position in the universe as an organic whole, but again it is unclear how far Theophrastus saw himself as introducing a new theory of place to supplant Aristotle's. He differed from Aristotle in involving material effluences in his explanation of the sense of smell. His collection of information about earlier philosophers (of which the extant treatise *On the Senses* formed part), undertaken in the context of his own philosophical concerns, was fundamental for later doxographers. His work on meteorology was exploited by *Epicurus and thence by *Lucretius.

In botany, the only area in which most of Theophrastus' work survives intact, he so far surpassed his predecessors that the history of the subject in the west can be said effectively to begin with him. In zoology he was apparently more concerned with the behaviour and habitat of living creatures, and with physiological processes, than with anatomical description. His interest in human behaviour is shown by his best-known surviving work, the *Characters*—a series of sketches of thirty more or less undesirable types of personality; its connections with systematic ethics, with rhetorical portrayal, or with the writing of comedy are still debated. (The preface and some of the contents are Byzantine interpolations.) His work on friendship was used by *Cicero, who elsewhere portrays him as laying more emphasis on the importance of fortune and external goods for happiness than did Aristotle; rhetorical exaggeration may, however, be suspected here. He was best known in the Middle Ages for an attack on marriage preserved by *Jerome (included in the compilation which angered Chaucer's Wife of Bath); this may have been one side of a debate rather than a statement of Theophrastus' own views. The same may also apply to arguments for vegetarianism based on the affinity between men and animals, asserting that justice is relevant to relations between men and animals where Aristotle had denied this. These arguments have led some to see Theophrastus as the source of the Stoic ethical theory of 'appropriation' (*oikeiōsis*), but the connection is doubtful. Theophrastus developed Aristotle's theory of the virtues of rhetorical style, wrote on rhetorical delivery, which Aristotle had neglected, and supplemented his political studies by the collection of laws and customs and the analysis of action in times of crisis.   R.W.S.

Theopompus of Chios, important Greek historian of the 4th cent. BC, the main exponent of rhetorical historiography alongside *Ephorus. According to a short *vita* (life) by *Photius (*Bibl.* 176 = T 2) he was born in 378/7, and was still young when he and his father Damasistratus were exiled from Chios for *lakōnismos* (sympathizing with Sparta). At the instigation of *Alexander the Great he

was allowed to return in 333/2 when he was 45 years old. After Alexander's death he was exiled a second time; 'driven out from everywhere' he eventually reached the court of *Ptolemy I, who wished to have the 'troublemaker' done away with. Theopompus was saved by the intervention of some friends and died probably shortly after 320. According to ancient tradition (cf. T 1, 5 a) he was a pupil of *Isocrates and worked for a long time as an orator (fr. 25). Extant titles of epideictic speeches are (T 48): *To Euagoras, Panathenaicus, Laconicus, Olympicus*; in addition he wrote political pamphlets (T 48): *Letters from Chios, Panegyric on *Philip II, Advice for Alexander*; and also an *Invective against *Plato and his School* (T 7. 48; fr. 259).

HISTORICAL WORKS (1) *Epitome of *Herodotus* in two books (T 1, fr. 1–4), the first demonstrable epitome of an earlier work in antiquity; (2) *Hellenica* in twelve books: a continuation of *Thucydides from 411 to 394, namely the sea battle of Cnidus, which marked the end of Sparta's short-lived hegemony (T 13 and 14). With this work Th. entered into competition with *Xenophon, *Hellenica* (1–4. 2), but he wrote in far greater detail than Xenophon. Only nineteen partly trivial fragments are extant (frs. 5–23), hence it is impossible to draw any definite conclusions as to contents, arrangement, bias, style, and quality. The *Hellenica* of the Oxyrhynchus Historian (see OXYRHYNCHUS, THE HISTORIAN FROM), frequently ascribed to Theopompus by modern scholars, is certainly not identical with this work; (3) *Philippica* or rather *Philippikai historiai* ('The History of Philip') in 58 books, Theopompus' main work, published late, after 324 (fr. 330); numerous fragments (frs. 24–396) and c.500 lines of verbal quotations are extant. It was not merely a history of *Philip II of Macedon, but a universal history including 'the deeds of Greeks and barbarians' (fr. 25) centring on Philip II: when *Philip V later had only the accounts of Philip II's exploits excerpted, the number of books was reduced to fifteen (T 31).

CHARACTERISTICS (1) Theopompus had a universal conception of history; he focused not only on political and military events but showed an interest in ethnography, geography, cultural history, history of religion, day-to-day life, memorabilia, *thaumasia* (marvels), even myth (fr. 381). (2) He was fond of extensive digressions of all kinds: especially noteworthy are the digressions on *thaumasia* (bk. 8 and part of 9; fr. 64–84); 'On the Athenian demagogues' (bk. 10; frs. 85–100); and the three books on Sicilian history, covering the tyranny of *Dionysius I and II 406/5–344/3 (cf. frs. 184, 183–205). (3) The rhetorical character of Theopompus' historical writing was very marked. He goes in for meticulous and skilful stylization, including numerous Gorgianic figures of speech reminiscent of the sophist Gorgias of Leontini (cf. e.g. 34, frs. 225, 263). (4) There is much moralizing in Theopompus. He incessantly denounced the moral depravity of leading politicians. (5) Political tendencies: Theopompus' attitude was that of a conservative aristocrat with Spartan sympathies. Philip II's patriarchal monarchy came closest to a realization of his ideal political and social system. Theopompus venerated him: 'Europe had never before produced such a man as Philip son of Amyntas' (fr. 27).

SOURCES The accounts of contemporary history are frequently based on autopsy, personal research and experiences (test. 20a): Theopompus spent some considerable time at Philip's court (T 7) and travelled throughout Greece (fr. 25); for the earlier periods he used historical and literary material such as speeches, comedies, and pamphlets. He was one of the most widely read and influential Greek historians in Graeco-Roman times. *Dionysius of Halicarnassus (*Pomp.* 6 = T 20) praises him for veracity, erudition, meticulous research, versatility, and his personal enthusiasm as well as for the purity, magnificence, and grandeur of his style. He does, however, find fault with Theopompus' invectives and excessive digressions. Pompeius Trogus, in Augustan times, called his own history *Historiae Philippicae* in imitation of Theopompus.   K.M.

Theramenes (d. 404/3 BC), Athenian politician, son of Hagnon. He played an active part in establishing the Four Hundred (a revolutionary oligarchic council set up to rule Athens) in 411, but four months later he was active in overthrowing them and establishing the Five Thousand, a more moderate but still not fully democratic regime which succeeded the Four Hundred briefly. When full democracy was restored in 410 he was in the Hellespont, assisting in the recovery of Athens'

naval supremacy. At Arginusae (406) he commanded only a single ship, but was one of those instructed to rescue survivors and corpses after the battle. Failure to achieve that was probably due only to bad weather, but later the blame was disputed between Theramenes and the generals, and after a largely illegal trial six generals were put to death. Xenophon blames Theramenes for orchestrating this miscarriage of justice; but in *Diodorus Siculus' account his role is less sinister, and *Aristophanes in the *Frogs* next spring treated him lightly, as an adroit politician. In 404 he was sent to negotiate with *Lysander, and afterwards brought back the final terms of peace from Sparta. He was involved in setting up the oligarchy of the Thirty Tyrants, and was himself one of the Thirty, but he soon quarrelled with the extremists, especially Critias, who had him executed.

His frequent changes of side were criticized both by democrats like *Lysias and by oligarchs like *Critias, but in the 4th cent. he could be defended as a moderate seeking a genuine political mean. The 'Theramenes papyrus' is probably part of a defence of him, written early in the 4th cent. by a man who knew Lys. 12 and 13 (but other interpretations have been proposed). If he was sincere, he was at least guilty of misjudgement, and must bear a share of the blame for the internal troubles which weakened Athens in the last years of the Peloponnesian War between Athens and the Spartan alliance.

                 A.A.; P.J.R.

Thrasybulus (d. 388 BC), son of Lycus, Athenian general and statesman. (Xenophon, *Hell.* 4. 8. 25 calls him Thrasybulus of (the deme of) Steiria to distinguish him from Thrasybulus of Collytus, *Hell.* 5. 1. 26, and modern books often do the same.) In 411 he was a leader of the democratic state formed by the navy at Samos in opposition to the oligarchy of the Four Hundred. He was responsible for the recall of *Alcibiades and contributed largely to the naval success of the following years.

He was banished by the Thirty Tyrants and fled to Thebes, where he organized a band of 70 exiles and occupied the Athenian borderfort of Phyle (late autumn, 404). When his followers had increased to a thousand, he seized the Piraeus and defeated the troops of the Thirty. Thanks to an amnesty proclaimed at the instance of Sparta, he led his men to Athens, and the democracy was restored. During the Corinthian War he played a prominent part in reviving Athenian imperialism, and in 389/8 he commanded a fleet which gained many allies but suffered from lack of financial support. At Aspendus his troops plundered the natives, who murdered him in his tent.

Thrasybulus showed ability and gallantry as a military leader. He was a staunch champion of democracy but was wise enough to make concessions in order to restore Athenian unity. In his last years he failed to appreciate that the imperialistic policy to which he gave his support was far beyond the material resources of Athens at that time.

H.D.W.; S.H.

Thucydides, author of the (incomplete) History of the War (Peloponnesian War) between Athens and Sparta, 431–404 BC, in eight books.

LIFE He was born probably between 460 and 455 BC: he was general in 424 (4. 104) and must then have been at least 30 years old; while his claim in 5. 26. 5 that he was of years of discretion from beginning to end of the war perhaps suggests that he was not much more than grown up in 431. He probably died about 400. He shows no knowledge of 4th-cent. events. The revival of Athenian sea power under Conon and Thrasybulus, from 394 on, made the decision of Aegospotami (405) less decisive than it seemed to Thucydides (compare e.g. 5. 26. 1 with Xen. *Hell.* 5. 1. 35). Of the three writers who undertook to complete his History, only *Xenophon took his view that the story ended in 404 (or 401). *Theopompus took it down to 394, and so probably did Cratippus (Plut. *Mor.* 345d). If, as seems likely, the very respectable author Oxyrhynchus Historian is Cratippus (see OXYRHYNCHUS, THE HISTORIAN FROM), then both his work and Theopompus' are on a very much larger scale than Xenophon's, a scale like Thucydides' own. This fact, as well as considerations of language and outlook, makes it likely that Xenophon wrote his continuation (*Hell.* books 1–2) earlier than the others, and indeed, before the battle of Coronea in 394. But if this be so, then Thucydides cannot have lived more than a year or so into the 4th cent. Marcellinus, in his Life,

ch. 34, says that Thucydides was 'over 50' when he died. If he was born about 455 and died about 400, this will be true. The figure may be from Cratippus, who evidently gave some biographical data: Marcellinus quotes him just before (33) for the view that Thucydides died in Thrace.

Thucydides, then, was part of that ardent youth whose abundance on both sides seemed to him to distinguish the war he wrote of. Something of his ardour may be felt in 2. 31: his pride in the soldier's profession and his devotion to the great commander, *Pericles.

He caught the plague, some time between 430 and 427, but recovered, and in 424 failed in the task of saving Amphipolis from Brasidas. Not to have been a match for Brasidas does not prove him a bad soldier: from his history one receives the impression of a first-rate regimental officer, ashore or afloat, who saw war as a matter of style; perhaps his defence of the generals before Megara in 4. 73. 4 (cf. 108. 5) says worse of his judgement of problems of high command than his failure against Brasidas. He was exiled for this (424 winter) and returned twenty years later, after the war was over, and died within a few years.

He had property and influence in the mining district of Thrace (4. 105. 1). His father's name was Olorus (4. 104. 4), the name of *Cimon's Thracian grandfather; his tomb was in Cimon's family vault. It is almost certain he was related by blood to Cimon, and probably to Thucydides the statesman (*JHS* 1932, 210); born in the anti-Pericles opposition, he followed Pericles with a convert's zeal.

PARTS OF THE HISTORY The incomplete history falls into five parts: A, an introduction (book 1); B, the ten years war (2. 1–5. 24); C, the precarious peace (5. 25–end); D, the Sicilian War (6 and 7); E, fragment of the Decelean War (8). It is convenient to take first B and D, the two complete wars.

B is enclosed between two statements that 'the continuous war has herein been described'. It was therefore provisionally finished (if these are Thucydides' words). It contains one allusion to the fall of Athens (2. 65. 12) and several allusions to events late in the twenty-seven years: these are no doubt additions made to an already existing narrative, since one passage certainly (2. 23. 3) was not written as late as the last decade of the century. The narrative gets rather more summary after Thucydides' exile (424): e.g. after the futile embassy to Artaxerxes I of Persia (4. 50) nothing is said of the important negotiations with Darius II.

D is the most finished portion. As it stands it is adapted to a history of the whole war (6. 7. 4, 6. 93. 4, 7. 18. 4, cf. 7. 9 etc., also 7. 44. 1, 7. 87. 5), and twice at least refers to events of 404 or later (7. 57. 2, 6. 15. 3–4). But these may be revisions and it has been suggested that Thucydides published it separately; and this opinion, though little held now, is not disproved. B and D are connected by C, sequel to B and introduction to D, and provided accordingly with a second preface. For symptoms of incompleteness, see below. C covers five and a half years, very unequally. Its two outstanding features are the description of the Mantinea campaign, and the Melian Dialogue. The former should perhaps be regarded, with B and D, as a third completed episode. The latter foreshadows the dramatic style of D; but if we read 5. 111 with 8. 27 we shall draw no facile moral (see 8. 27. 5).

E has the same symptoms of incompleteness as C and, moreover, stops abruptly in the middle of a narrative. It is very full, covering barely two years in its 109 chapters.

A consists of (1) 1. 1–23, a long preface, illustrating the importance of Thucydides' subject by comparison with earlier history (the so-called 'archaeology') and stating his historical principles; (2) the causes of the war—that is, for the most part, an account of the political manœuvres of 433–432; he adds important digressions, especially 1. 89–117, a history of the years 479/8–440/39 (the so-called *pentekontaetia*, partly to illustrate his view that the war was an inevitable result of Athens' power, partly to make his history follow without interval on that of *Herodotus (1. 97. 2). The second motive perhaps explains the length of another digression (1. 128–38) on the fate of Pausanias and *Themistocles.

INCOMPLETENESS E stops in mid-narrative, in winter 411: Thucydides intended to go down to 404 (5. 26. 1). It shares with (roughly) C two peculiarities, absence of speeches and presence of documents, which are thought to show incompleteness; for these see below. The plan to make of BCDE a continuous history of the twenty-seven years is only superficially achieved, even to 411: e.g.

there is nothing of Atheno–Persian relations between 424 and 412, vital though these were (2. 65. 12). We shall see below that Thucydides kept his work by him and revised continually; so he left double treatments of the same theme, one of which he meant no doubt to suppress—e.g. the tyrannicides, the killers of Pisistratus' son Hipparchus (1. 20, 6. 54–59); possibly 1. 23. 1–3 is a short early variant of 1. 1–19; 3. 84 of part of 82–3 (E. Schwartz, *Das Geschichtswerk des Thukydides* (1919) 286 f.). It may be even suspected that 8. 82. 2 is a less accurately informed version of 86. 4–5 and the two have been merely harmonized by 85. 4. If this last suspicion were just, it would be good evidence that Thucydides' remains were put into shape by an editor, whose hand may be further suspected in the misplacement of 3. 17, in 1. 56–7 (whose author—as it stands—surely misconceived the course of events), perhaps even in 1. 118. 2 (where the last sentence seems to leap from the 450s to 432); an editorial hand has, indeed, been suspected wholesale. Though no single case is quite decisive, it is unlikely Thucydides left his unfinished work in need of no editing. If we look for an editor, one thinks naturally of Xenophon, who wrote the continuation (it seems) immediately after Thucydides' death; the suggestion was made in antiquity (Diog. Laert. 2. 57). His soldierly (if not his intellectual) qualities might commend him to Thucydides, but if it was indeed he, he worked with extreme piety, and his hand is very little apparent. Xenophon's limits and virtues alike disqualify him for the authorship of 1. 56–7.

SPEECHES AND DOCUMENTS Ancient craftsmen, and Thucydides notably, aimed at exactness; but in his speeches, Thucydides admits (1. 22. 1) that exactness was beyond his powers of memory. Here, then, as in reconstructing the far past (1. 20–1), he had to trust to his historical imagination, whose use generally he planned to avoid 'what I think they would have said': this meant applying to the speeches the sort of rationalizing schematism that, e.g., *Hecataeus of Miletus applied to geography; and even here, he promises he will control its use as rigorously as he can by the tenor of the actual words. It is much debated whether he made this profession early or late; and it has been much explained away. But it is unreasonable to doubt that from the start Thucydides took notes himself, or sought for hearers' notes, of the speeches he considered important. But since he used speeches dramatically, to reveal the workings of men's minds and the impact of circumstance, it is clear that verbatim reports would not have served even if he could have managed to get them, and he was bound to compromise (unconsciously) between dramatic and literal truth. It is likely that, as his technique developed, dramatic truth would tend to prevail; it is tempting to put his profession of method early, a young man's intention. Even so, while we cannot suppose that, at a moment when morale was vital, Pericles used the words in 2. 64. 3; while it is unlikely that the Athenian debater at Melos developed exactly the same vein of thought as Phrynichus before Miletus (5. 111– 8. 27); while Pericles' first speech (1. 140 ff.) is perhaps composite, and hard to assign to a single occasion; it is yet dangerous to treat the speeches as free fiction: their dramatic truth was combined with the greatest degree of literal truth of which Thucydides was capable. He tried to re-create real occasions.

There are no speeches in E, and (except the Melian Dialogue) none in C: Cratippus (a younger contemporary) says Thucydides had decided to drop their use. Modern critics treat their absence as a symptom of incompleteness; they would have been added had he lived. But it is possible that these parts without speeches are experiments in new techniques. Thucydides may have felt, as many readers do, that the narrative of the ten years is a compromise between the methods of tragedy and of a laboratory notebook, so that between the profoundest issues and the particular detail, the middle ranges (e.g. an intelligible account of strategy) are neglected. In the later narrative the methods are more separated. The Sicilian War was capable of almost purely dramatic treatment; C and E evidently not. And in consequence in E at least a new technique is developed, less like either drama or chronicle, more of an organized narrative, with more of the writer's own judgements of values and interpretations of events. It is questionable if E would be improved by speeches, that is, could be profitably (or at all?) transformed into the style of B or D: was Cratippus perhaps right about Thucydides' intention?

This would not prevent some of the speeches in books 1–4 being composed (or revised) very late. The new experiment would not entail eliminating the dramatic from those books; Thucydides experimented to the end and never solved his problem. It is commonly thought that the Funeral Speech (2. 35 ff.) was written or rewritten after Athens' fall; and 2. 64. 3 surely was. The Corcyra debate (1. 31–44), on the contrary, has good chances of being an actual report, written up soon after delivery. Though some speeches aim at dramatic characterization (in the manner of Gorgias of Leontini, 4. 61. 7: Laconic i.e. Spartan, 1. 86), all are in Thucydides' idiom. But the personalness of this idiom is often overestimated (J. H. Finley, *Thucydides*[2], 1947).

It is noteworthy that those portions which lack speeches have (instead?) transcriptions of documents: that is, E and (roughly speaking) C.[1] If, then, we take C and E as experiments in a new method, the experiment begins in the latter part of B. These documents are usually thought (like the absence of speeches) a sign of incompleteness, since they offend against a 'law of style' which forbids the verbatim use of foreign matter in serious prose. We need not debate the general validity of this law: with so inventive a writer as Thucydides, his laws of style are to be deduced from his practice, and 5. 24. 2 (cf. 2. 1) suggests that the end of B is provisionally finished. Are they part of the experiment? One may be surprised (though grateful) that Thucydides thought the full text of the Armistice (4. 118–19) worth its room. One of the documents (5. 47) is extant in fragments (*IG* i[3]. 83) and confirms the substantial accuracy of the copies. One conflicts gravely with the narrative (5. 23, 5. 39. 3): it would seem the narrative was written in ignorance of the exact terms, and has not been revised.

'EARLY' AND 'LATE' Thucydides says (1. 1. 1) he began to write his history as soon as war started; and it is at least arguable that much of the existing narrative, in all five parts of the work, was written, substantially as we have it, very soon after the events. But he worked slowly, and, as he says at 1. 22. 3, laboriously; correcting in the light of better

---

[1] Not exactly C: C ends with the Melian Dialogue (which in colour belongs to D?) and B has documents instead of speeches in its latter part, i.e. after the occasion of Thucydides' exile.

information (we only detect this process where it is incomplete; e.g. 5. 39. 3 was due for correction in the light of 5. 23) or of later events (1. 97. 2; 4. 48. 5, where the qualification ὅσα γε may have been put merely *ex abundanti cautela*, from excess of caution, but more likely when the troubles started again in 410). If his point of view, or his method, changed materially during this process, it becomes of importance to know from which point of view this or that portion is written. More than a century ago, Ullrich called attention to this, believing that an important change of approach came with his discovery (announced in the second preface, 5. 26) that the war had not ended in 421.

Two criteria have been used to determine earliness or lateness: (*a*) reference to, or ignorance of, datable events or conditions; (*b*) the stage in Thucydides' own development which a passage reveals.

(*a*) References to late events cannot be written early, but they may be inserted in early contexts: e.g. those who think D early regard 6. 15. 3–4 and 7. 57. 2 as additions. Ignorance of late events is very much harder to establish: those same who think D early may suspect in 6. 41. 3 ignorance of *Dionysius I's tyranny, or even (a very slippery question) in 6. 54. 1 ignorance of Herodotus' history—but cannot prove their suspicions; yet where such ignorance is certain (see below), we may be sure that the narrative (or line of thought) which warrants them was conceived early. The results of this method are modest: e.g. (1) 1. 10. 2 was not written after the catastrophe of 404: therefore the war against which earlier wars are being measured is not the completed twenty-seven years, and the 'end of war' mentioned in 1. 13. 3–4, 1. 18. 1, is presumably 421; (2) 2. 23. 3 was not written after the loss of Oropus in 411: therefore some of the narrative of B was written much as we have it before 411; (3) 2. 65. 12 refers to the fall of Athens: therefore B received additions down to 404 at least.

(*b*) More has been hoped from the second method. Thucydides worked from his twenties to his fifties, his material growing under his eyes: there must surely be some intellectual or spiritual growth, some change of outlook. The best exponent of this method is Schwartz, who gives (*Das Geschichtswerk des T.*, 217–42) an eloquent account of Thucydides' growth. The danger of this method is

evident: in the ablest hands it yields quite different results (E. Meyer, *Forschungen* 2 (1899, no. v); Schwartz, *Das Geschichtswerk des T.*), and its first postulate may be doubted, namely, that Thucydides' opinion on the 'true cause' of the war (1. 23. 6) was not formed till after the fall of Athens. No doubt that was his view after 404; no doubt 1. 23. 6 and 1. 88 were written (inserted?) pretty late. But much the same view is expressed by the Corcyran envoy in 1. 33. 3 (cf. 42. 2); and whether the envoy said it or not it was surely Pericles' view. Pericles believed that if Athens used her opportunity in 433 she was bound to provoke in Sparta an enmity that must be faced; all his career, against Cimon and his successors, he had fought for his conviction that Athens and Sparta were natural enemies and Greece not large enough for both. His admirers held that this clear principle (1. 140. 1) was obscured in debate by the irrelevant particulars (1. 140. 4–141. 1). We have not to consider whether Pericles was right: rather, the effect on Thucydides. The devout disciple saw the story unfold in the terms his master had foreseen (2. 65). How far such a 'Pericles-fixation' may have warped Thucydides' judgement, see below.

If this first postulate go, the second will follow it, namely that only after 404 was Pericles given the importance he now has in books 1–2, since after 404 Thucydides started to rewrite his History as a 'defence of Pericles' (Schwartz 239). It hardly needs to be said that many hold to these postulates and the present writer's disbelief is as subjective as their belief. If these are untrue, truer postulates may be found: the attempt to re-create Thucydides' experience should (and will) never be dropped.

TRUTHFULNESS Perhaps no good historian is impartial; Thucydides certainly is not, though singularly candid. His tastes are clear: he liked Pericles and disliked *Cleon. He had for Pericles a regard comparable to Plato's for *Socrates and an equal regard for Pericles' Athens. These things were personal: but in principle, concentrations of energy (like Athens or *Alcibiades) were to his taste. Their impact on a less dynamic world was likely to be disastrous—but whose fault was that? The world's, he says, consistently (1. 99; 1. 23. 6 etc.; 6. 15; 6. 28; cf. 2. 64. 3–5): and though this consistency may surprise us, we need not quarrel with it. Such judgements are rare, since Thucydides conceives his task as like medical research (see below, and cf. 3. 82. 2) where blame is irrelevant; the disconcerting simplicity of 2. 64. 3 (power and energy are absolute goods) is the more striking.

We need not here investigate Thucydides' possible mistakes. The present writer believes that Pericles (having planned an offensive war) lost his striking power, first because Potidaea revolted, next because of the plague. Forced to the defensive, he left that as his testament. Thucydides was reluctant to face the fact of this failure, and accepted the testament, siding with the defeatist officer class against the revived offensive of Cleon (4. 27. 5, 28. 5, 65. 4, 73. 4; cf. 5. 7. 2). This is why Pericles' huge effort against Epidaurus (6. 31. 2; motive, cf. 5. 53) is recorded as a minor futility (2. 56. 4); why Phormion's first campaign in Acarnania (2. 68. 7–9; of 432?) is left timeless; why we hear nothing of the purpose of the Megara decree; why, when that nearly bore fruit at last, Thucydides suggests that the capture of Megara was of no great moment (4. 73. 4; but cf. 72. 1).

Such criticisms hardly detract much from his singular truthfulness. Readers of all opinions will probably agree that he saw more truly, inquired more responsibly, and reported more faithfully than any other ancient historian. That is a symptom of his greatness, but not its core. Another symptom is his style: it is innocent of those clichés of which *Isocrates hoped to make the norm of Attic style; in its 'old-fashioned wilful beauty' (*Dionysius of Halicarnassus) every word tells. Like English prose before Dryden and Addison, it uses a language largely moulded by poets: its precision is a poet's precision, a union of passion and candour. After Thucydides history mostly practised the corrupting art of persuasion (cf. Isoc. 4. 8): his scientific tradition survived in the antiquarians, of whom he is the pioneer (1. 8. 1, 2. 15. 2, 3. 104. 4–6, 6. 55. 1), but the instinctive exactness of early Greek observation was lost. To combine his predecessors' candour of vision with his successors' apparatus of scholarship was a necessity laid on him by his sense of the greatness of his subject: he could no more distort or compromise with what he wished to convey than Shakespeare or Michelangelo could.

Thucydides would no doubt prefer to substitute, for these great names, the practice of any honest doctor. He was not modest, but in his statement of his principles he is singularly unaware of his unique equipment, and claims rather that he has spared no pains. The proper context for this statement (1. 20–2) is, first, his very similar statement about his own account of the plague (2. 48. 3), and then the physician *Hippocrates' maxim, 'ars longa vita brevis'. The 'art' which outlasts individual lives is the scientific study of man: the physician studied his clinical, Thucydides his political, behaviour. To know either so well that you can control it (and civilization is largely made up of such controls) is a task for many generations: a piece of that task well done is something gained for ever (1. 22. 4).

H.T.W.-G.

STYLE In a famous sentence (*Thuc.* 24) *Dionysius of Halicarnassus gives as the four 'tools' in Thucydides' workshop τὸ ποιητικὸν τῶν ὀνομάτων, τὸ πολυειδὲς τῶν σχημάτων, τὸ τραχὺ τῆς ἁρμονίας, τὸ τάχος τῶν σημασιῶν, 'poetical vocabulary, great variety of figures, harshness of word-order, swiftness in saying what he has to say'. The first, third, and fourth of these criticisms are undoubtedly true. Thucydides' style has a poetical and archaistic flavour (it is often difficult to distinguish clearly between the two), as a reader sees at once when he turns from Thucydides to *Andocides and *Lysias. His consistent use of αἰεί for ἀεί, ξύν for σύν, and σσ for ττ is one of the signs of this tendency. 'Roughness' is to be seen in his bold changes of construction and his violent hyperbata, in which he wrests an emphatic word from its natural place in the sentence to give it more prominence (1. 19 κατ᾽ ὀλιγαρχίαν, 1. 93. 4 τῆς θαλάσσης). 'Speed' is perhaps the most striking of all his characteristics. He achieves an extreme concision, hardly to be paralleled in Greek prose except in the gnomic utterances of *Democritus. A sentence like δοκεῖ... καταστροφή (2. 42. 2) is gone in a flash, and no orator, composing for the ear, could have risked such brevity. At 2. 37. 1 (μέτεστι ... προτιμᾶται) two antitheses are telescoped into one. τὸ πολυειδὲς τῶν σχημάτων is much more open to question, especially as Dionysius has just before credited Thucydides with the use of the θεατρικὰ σχήματα, 'showy figures of speech' (parisosis (balance of clauses), paronomasia (play on words), and antithesis), affected by Gorgias and other writers of the sophistic school. Thucydides' thought is, it is true, markedly antithetical in cast (e.g. 1. 70. 6), and antithesis is sometimes strained (e.g. 2. 43. 3). But, unlike the Gorgianists, he has no affection for merely external antithesis, and he often deliberately avoids formal balance (e.g. 4. 59. 2). He eschews almost entirely certain other common adornments of style. He is too austere to use metaphor at all freely, or asyndeton (more suited to the spoken word). He does employ certain devices of assonance, neither, like Gorgias, as ἡδύσματα, nor, like Demosthenes, for emphasis pure and simple, but for the emphasizing of a contrast (3. 82. 8 εὐσεβεία ... εὐπρεπεία, 6. 76. 2 κατοικίσαι ... ἐξοικίσαι, 76. 4 ἀξυνετωτέρου ... κακοξυνετωτέρου). He has a strong leaning, as Dionysius observed (*Amm.* 2. 5), towards abstract expression (e.g. 3. 82–3), sometimes carried to the length of personification (πόλεμος 1. 122. 1, ἐλπίς 5. 103. 1). He probably coined abstracts (especially in -σις) freely, as *Euripides did, according to the fashion of the late 5th cent., and sometimes used them out of season (7. 70. 6 ἀποστέρησιν, and the odd-looking negatived abstracts, 1. 137. 4 οὐ διάλυσιν, etc.). Like *Antiphon, he experimented freely with the use of neuter adjective, or even participle (1. 142. 8 ἐν τῷ μὴ μελετῶντι), to convey an abstract idea. His periods are usually loosely constructed (e.g. 3. 38. 4–7), of clauses longer in actual words, and far richer in content, than those of other Greek prose-writers (e.g. 2. 43. 2–6).   J.D.D.

[The above entry in the *OCD* by Wade-Gery and Denniston, which goes back essentially to 1949, is an established classic and it seems an impertinence to attempt to replace it. But merely to reprint it would be unhelpful when Thucydides has been so intensively worked on. What follows is therefore a sketch of work on Thucydides in the quarter-century since the 2nd edition of the *OCD*. We do not attempt a survey of work up to 1970, confining ourselves to a mention of the great historical commentary on Thucydides (*HCT*), begun by A. W. Gomme (bk. 1, 1945; bks. 2–5.24, 1956) and then completed by A. Andrewes and K. J. Dover (bks. 5.25–7 (1970); bk. 8 (1981)). Note also the important new edition of the text of Thucydides by G. Alberti (so far bks. 1–2, 1972; bks. 3–5, 1992). But the standard edn. of the whole of Thucydides remains the Oxford Classical Text by H.

Stuart-Jones, repr. 1942 with critical apparatus revised by J. E. Powell.]

The most noticeable feature of Thucydidean scholarship since 1970 is the move away from preoccupation with the 'composition question' (the identification of layers of the History, with attempts to date them) to study of Thucydides' text as a complete literary whole. There is a parallel here with the move in Homeric scholarship (see HOMER) over the same period away from 'analytical' approaches and towards a 'unitarian' interest in the architecture of the two great poems. Of the 1970 Thucydides bibliography (not reprinted here), it is striking how many items addressed themselves to questions of composition, a topic to which Wade-Gery's *OCD* article was itself an influential contribution. One discussion which appeared just too late for the 2nd edn. was the relevant section of O. Luschnat's 1970 survey, *RE* Suppl. 12, 1147 ff. The related question, whether Thucydides' work was finished, has continued to attract study, notably in Andrewes's contribution to the final (1981) volume of Gomme, Andrewes, and Dover, *HCT*, with the reply by H. Erbse, *Thukydidesinterpretationen* (1989). (See also ch. 5 of Dover, *Greece and Rome New Survey* no. 7 (1973), an admirable general survey of Thucydides.) And H. H. Rawlings III, *The Structure of Thucydides' History* (1981) has speculated about the possible content of the unwritten books 9 and 10. But even this was part of a wider attempt to detect patterning within the larger existing structure.

F. M. Cornford, *Thucydides Mythistoricus* (1907) was an early attempt to treat Thucydides as a literary text to which methods used on tragedy and epic could be applied. More recent works include H.-P. Stahl, *Thukydides: Die Stellung des Menschen im geschichtlichen Prozess* (1966), a book which allotted as much space to narrative as to speeches. And H. Strasburger's studies of the 1950s (collected now in Strasburger, *Studien zur alten Geschichte* (1982)), and H. Kitto, *Poiesis* (1966). V. Hunter in 1973 set the tone for two decades by the title of her book *Thucydides the Artful Reporter*; Herodotus had for centuries found himself periodically in the pillory for alleged distortion and invention, but Thucydides' authoritative and apparently scientific manner had usually been respected. Now it was suggested that Thucydides might simply have made things up, particularly his imputations of motive. This approach was also pursued by C. Schneider, *Information und Absicht bei Thukydides* (1974). (Cf. below on the narratological problem of 'restricted access'.) Historical as well as historiographic issues are affected: thus whereas de G. E. M. de Ste. Croix, *The Origins of the Peloponnesian War* (1972) had sought to justify Thucydides (and threw in an excellent introductory section on Thucydidean methodology), E. Badian, *From Plataea to Potidaea* (1993), a collection of essays going back to the 1980s, is in complete contrast, an acute demonstration by a historian of the consequences of distrusting Thucydides.

Now the lid was off. One way of going further was to challenge the premiss that ancient historiography had pretensions to being an exact or any sort of science: perhaps (A. J. Woodman, *Rhetoric in Classical Historiography* (1988)) it was merely a branch of rhetoric with a different aim from factual description; perhaps, indeed, the 'facts' are nothing of the sort. (This is not just an 'ancient' problem; but enough documentary evidence exists to control Thucydides and reassure us that there was indeed a Peloponnesian War.)

Another more acceptable approach has been to disregard the signs of incompleteness in Thucydides and insist in post-modern fashion (W. R. Connor, *CJ* 1977) on the autonomy of the text: whatever the authorial intention, we have a long speech-punctuated narrative of Greek prose containing patterns, significant repetitions, ring-composition, etc. See Connor, *Thucydides* (1984), but cf. also S. Hornblower, *Thucydides* (1987) for an attempt to combine literary criteria with recognition of the composition problem and its implications.

The detailed work of Colin Macleod (*Collected Essays* (1983)) deserves a special word; there has been no finer treatment of the rhetoric of the Thucydidean speeches. On rhetorical issues note also W. K. Pritchett's excellent *Dionysius of Halicarnassus on Thucydides* (1975).

More recently still narratology has been tried on Thucydides. Narratology is nothing more frightening than the study of a branch of rhetoric, specifically of the principles underlying narrative texts. First used on modern, then on ancient, novels, it was applied in 1987 to *Homer* by I. de Jong

(*Narrators and Focalizers: The Presentation of the Story in the Iliad* (1987)), who demonstrated how narratology can help us see how Homer achieves his famously objective manner. The technique has been most fully applied to Thucydides by T. Rood, *Thucydides: Narrative and Explanation* (1998), but see already the short essay by Connor in M. Jameson (ed.), *The Greek Historians* (1985) (using, however, the term 'narrative discourse' not narratology), and Hornblower in S. Hornblower (ed.), *Greek Historiography*. Some narratological terms and insights are familiar to Thucydideans under other names; e.g. 'restricted access' means the difficulty encountered by a non-omniscient narrator interested in an agent's motives. The usual response, e.g. in messenger speeches in tragedy (and in Thucydides?) is for the narrator silently to assume an omniscient pose. But the greatest narratological weapon has been focalization, i.e. the point of view or perspective from which an event is described. Choice of Homeric (and Thucydidean?) vocabulary can sometimes be explained by the wish to present events or express emotions from a certain standpoint, which may or may not be that of the author rather than that of the imagined or historical agent. (Dover, *The Greeks and their Legacy* (1988), 74 ff. has ingeniously pointed to one purely linguistic way of determining whether a motive reflects Thucydides' own view or that of an agent's.) Again, all this is not quite new: in the 18th cent. Adam Smith in lectures on rhetoric distinguished between 'direct' and 'indirect' narration. And H. D. Westlake, *Studies in Thucydides and Greek History* (1989), ch. 14, shows that problems of 'personal motives in Thucydides' can be usefully studied in very plain language. There is much work still to be done, but provided it is recognized that there was a relation between what Thucydides says and a real world which existed in the 5th cent. BC, only good can come of the recognition that his text is susceptible to literary 'close reading'. (A valuable survey of the impact of new literary approaches is J. L. Moles JACT *Bulletin*, autumn 1993.)

The broad trends indicated above do not at all exhaust recent Thucydidean work. There have been full-length commentaries on bks. 1–3 (1991) and 4–5.24 (1996) by S. Hornblower (translates all Greek commented on). See also the commentaries on book 2 by J. S. Rusten (1988: markedly linguistic) and P. J. Rhodes (1988: markedly historical; see also his commentary on book 3, 1994); these two illuminate by exact methods traditionally applied, as does the outstanding monograph of K. Maurer, *Interpolation in Thucydides* (1995). On the important topic of the 4th-cent. and Hellenistic reception of Thucydides, Luschnat 1970 (see above) is less good than the older but shorter work of H. Strebel, *Wertung und Wirkung des Thukydideischen Geschichtswerkes* (1935): see Hornblower, *JHS* 1995. Other monographs include: L. Edmunds, *Chance and Intelligence in Thucydides* (1975), M. Ostwald, *ANAΓKH in Thucydides* (1988); Hornblower, *Harv. Stud.* 1992 (on religion esp. Delphi); L. Kallet-Marx, *Money, Expense and Naval Power in Thucydides' History* 1–5.26 (1993); J. Ziolkowski, *Thucydides and the Tradition of the Funeral Oration at Athens* (1981); N. Loraux, *The Invention of Athens* (1986). On Thucydides' indebtedness to Herodotus see C. Pelling in M. Flower and M. Toher (eds.), *Georgica* (1991) and Hornblower, *Commentary on Thucydides*, vol. 2 (1996), Introduction, section 2 and annexes A and B. This survey may end with the suggestion that two areas needing more work are Thucydides' detailed intertextual relation to Homer and to Herodotus.

                                                                                          s.h.

Tiberius, the emperor (Tiberius Julius Caesar Augustus), was the son of Tiberius Claudius Nero and *Livia Drusilla, born 16 November 42 BC. Livia was divorced and married Octavian (the future *Augustus) in 38 shortly before the birth of Tiberius' brother *Drusus. After public service in Spain with *Augustus (Suet. *Tib.* 8), Tiberius was quaestor in 23 BC, five years earlier than normal. From 20 BC, when he crowned the Roman nominee Tigranes in Armenia, until AD 12, when he returned to Rome after retrieving the situation on the Rhine after the Varian disaster (AD 9; see QUINCTILIUS VARUS), Tiberius' military career was uniformly successful. In 15 and 14 BC he completed with Drusus the conquest of the Alps; from *Agrippa's death in 12 until 9 BC he was reducing Pannonia; from Drusus' death to 7 BC and again from AD 4 to 6 he campaigned in Germany. Between AD 6 and 9 he was engaged in suppressing the revolts of Pannonia and Illyricum.

After Agrippa's death Tiberius divorced Vipsania Agrippina to marry Augustus' daughter *Julia; their son died in infancy. After his second consulship (7 BC), Tiberius was granted tribunician power and *imperium* (supreme military and civil authority) in the east for five years for a diplomatic mission, the restoration of Roman authority in Armenia, but the attempt to advance Augustus' grandson and adopted son Gaius Caesar to a premature consulship, made with or without the emperor's approval, helped provoke Tiberius' withdrawal to Rhodes. He returned to Rome, still out of favour, in AD 2. By spring AD 4 both Augustus' adopted sons were dead and he adopted Tiberius, together with Agrippa Postumus, while Tiberius adopted his nephew *Germanicus. Tiberius received tribunician power for ten years, renewed in AD 13 for a further ten; concurrently he held proconsular *imperium*, in 13 made equal to that of Augustus.

When Augustus died in AD 14 Tiberius was thus in full power. The nature of the embarrassing 'accession debate' (Tac. *Ann.* 4. 37 f.) of 17 September remains unclear: a fresh conferment of power, or a political discussion of the (less autocratic) form to be taken by the new Principate. Certainly, he abolished Augustus' advisory council, which in his last months had made authoritative decisions; matters came directly to the senate. Abroad, Tiberius' dislike of extravagant honours (Tac. *Ann.* 4. 37 f.) was tempered by precedent and a need to conciliate his subjects which could prevent him making his wishes clear, as to Gytheum in Laconia in AD 15 (EJ 102 (trans. D. Braund, *Augustus to Nero, 31 B.C.–A.D. 68* (1985), 127)).

Tiberius respected Augustus and exploited his memory when taking unpopular steps (Tac. *Ann.* 1. 14. 6–15. 1). In dealing with the Germans he followed the policy of containing the empire that Augustus laid down in his political testament (Tiberius may have helped to draft it). This conflicted with the views of Germanicus, who was recalled in AD 16. Augustus' methods of coping with Britain and Armenia were also followed: on his mission to the east (AD 17–19) Germanicus established another Roman nominee in Armenia, who survived successfully until 35; further negotiations, backed up by the threat of force, were conducted by Lucius Vitellius. Tiberius did not shrink from annexing dependent monarchies: Germanicus took over Commagene and Cappadocia, which made it possible to halve the Roman sales tax.

Two innovations in provincial administration are credited to Tiberius: prorogations of governors, and governorships in absence. Both were due to a shortage of satisfactory candidates, deplored by Tiberius (Tac. *Ann.* 6. 27). The second was clearly deleterious and the first kept some poor governors in office (e.g. Pontius Pilate in Judaea).

The most notorious feature of Tiberius' principate was the incidence of trials before the senate (introduced by Augustus), some *extra ordinem* (Marcus Scribonius Libo Drusus in 16; *Sejanus in 31), most for diminishing the majesty (*maiestas*) of the Roman people, the emperor, his family, or other notables, by whatever means, however trivial; at first some were discouraged by the emperor (e.g. Tac. *Ann.* 1. 73 f.). That of Gnaeus Calpurnius Piso, also accused in AD 20 of extortion and of poisoning Germanicus, is documented not only in Tac. *Ann.* 3. 8–19, but in the decree embodying the senate's decisions and approved by the emperor (W. Eck and others, *SC de Cn. Pisone patre* (1996)), which affords an unappetizing insight into the atmosphere of the reign.

Tiberius' reign opened with army mutinies, soon suppressed; the revolt in Gaul (AD 21) was minor. Two factors undermined his principate. Tiberius inherited a poor military and economic situation: the German war was unprofitable; politicians were short of cash and were resorting to prosecutions to obtain it (cf. Tac. *Ann.* 2. 34), there was unrest at Rome due to grain shortages, and provincials were chafing under tax burdens (cf. the revolt of 21). Tiberius' answers (gifts to individuals, treasury disbursements when senators became unable to pay their debts in 33 (Tac. *Ann.* 6, 16 f.), and public economy), were inadequate, and his marked frugality (though personally generous, he built little, and gave donations and games sparingly) increased his unpopularity.

Second, there had been family jealousy since 7 BC, and the people and many senators favoured his stepsons. Rivalry after AD 4 led to the downfall of Agrippa Postumus and his adherents. Feared by former opponents, Tiberius could not make politicians trust his

moderatio and *clementia* (moderation and clemency). They looked forward to the succession of Germanicus (Tiberius was 55 in AD 14). On his death in AD 19 and that of Tiberius' son Drusus Julius Caesar in 23 the succession question opened up again, with the sons of Germanicus pitted against Sejanus, who seems to have supported Drusus' surviving son Tiberius Julius Caesar Nero Gemellus. Instead of confronting the problem, Tiberius, encouraged by Sejanus, retired to Campania and then to Capreae (mod. Capri, AD 27), never to enter Rome again. While he was at the mercy of Sejanus and his freedmen, the struggle went on at Rome, until Nero Julius Caesar and Drusus Julius Caesar and their mother *Agrippina the Elder were disgraced (AD 29–30) and Tiberius was given evidence that Sejanus was attempting the downfall of Germanicus' youngest son Gaius (31; Suet. *Tib.* 61), who then became the only likely successor. A purge of Sejanus' followers (and of supporters of Gemellus and rivals of Gaius' chief aide Macro) continued until Tiberius' death on 16 March 37, which was greeted with rejoicing.

Tacitus delivers a favourable verdict on Tiberius' principate down to Sejanus' ascendancy; the five 'ages' ending with a death are another device for moving from promising beginning to disastrous end, like the hypocrisy (*dissimulatio*) also imputed to him.

Tiberius was a forceful orator, a poet (neoteric), a connoisseur, and perhaps a Sceptic (he was careless of religious ritual); he kept his intellect and relish for irony (Philon, *Leg.* 142; Tac. *Ann.* 6. 6). Stories of vice on Capreae (and Rhodes) may be discounted; real defects, a cultivated sense of superiority, relentlessness and lack of affability, meditated ambiguity of language, remained.

J.P.B.; B.M.L.

Tibullus, Albius, born between 55 and 48 BC. An anonymous and corrupt Life, possibly derived from *Suetonius, tells us that he was good-looking (confirmed by Hor. *Epist.* 1. 4. 6) and something of a dandy; also that he was of equestrian rank and won *dona militaria* (military awards). The Life is preceded by an epigram of Domitius Marsus, which fixes the date of Tibullus' death in 19 BC (cf. also the lament in Ov. *Am.* 3. 9).

Tibullus implies that his patrimony was

diminished, presumably by Octavian's confiscations of 41–40 BC (1. 1. 41 f.); cf. *Propertius. But his claims to poverty, *paupertas*, should not be taken too seriously. He no more than Propertius seems to have been reduced to economic dependence. *Horace indeed suggests that he was well-off, and possessed a villa at Pedum between Tibur and Praeneste (*Epist.* 1. 4; he is also probably the addressee of *Odes* 1. 33). Tibullus refused, or did not attract, the patronage of *Maecenas, and instead addresses himself to *Messalla Corvinus. He set out to the east in Messalla's entourage, but fell ill at Corcyra and returned to Italy (1. 3); it is uncertain whether he served under him in Gaul (1. 7. 9 and Life).

Tibullus' MSS contain three books, of which the third was divided into two by Italian scholars of the 15th cent.; these are commonly called the *Corpus Tibullianum* and only the first two belong to Tibullus himself. The dates of publication are uncertain: book 1 refers to Messalla's triumph (25 September 27 BC), book 2 to the installation of his son as one of the *quindecimviri sacris faciundis* or guardians of the Sibylline books (perhaps not long before Tibullus' death). It seems likely that Tibullus' first book appeared after Propertius' first, but before the completion of Propertius' second. Propertius 2. 5. 25 ff. seems a retort to Tibullus 1. 10. 61 ff. (on the question of the acceptability of violence in love-affairs).

Tibullus' first book deals with his love for a mistress, Delia (1, 2, 3, 5, 6); surprisingly and provocatively it professes comparable devotion to a boy, Marathus, too (4, 8, 9). Apuleius tells us that Delia existed and that her name was Plania (*Apol.* 10). We need not doubt this, though her attributes (and those of Marathus, for that matter) seem pretty conventional. Book 2 celebrates a different mistress, whom the poet calls Nemesis (3, 4, 6). Nothing certain can be said about the social status of any of these lovers (but for Delia cf. 1. 6. 68, which suggests that she is not a *matrona*).

Tibullus, like Propertius, expresses the belief that love must be his life's occupation (e.g. 1. 1. 45 ff.), and, like Propertius, he claims love to be his *militia* (1. 1. 75 f.), in spite of his actual forays into the world of action; like Propertius too he presents himself as the slave of his lovers (1. 5. 5 f., 1. 9. 21 f.). In his use both of military and servile figures Tibullus

is more specific than Propertius. For example his servile declarations express willingness to undergo servile punishments, and some scholars detect an intended, almost Ovidian humour (cf. OVID) in his use of both figures.

Unlike Propertius, Tibullus makes virtually no use of mythology. Propertius' romantic, impossible dream had been that Cynthia would be like heroines of myth. Tibullus' impossible dream is that Delia will join him in his country estate to enjoy a rural idyll (esp. 1. 5. 21 ff.). Tibullus' aspirations to live the country life, expressed in more than one poem, separate him from the urban *Catullus and Propertius.

Apart from the love poems, books 1 and 2 contain poems in honour of Messalla (1. 7, 2. 5), an elegy on the blessings of peace (1. 10), and a charming representation of a rustic festival and the poet's song at it (2. 1). Book 2 is only just over 400 lines long, and may be either defective or posthumous.

The third book is a collection of poems from the circle of Messalla. It begins with six elegies by Lygdamus, and also contains the *Panegyricus Messallae* (panegyric for Messalla), five poems on the love of Sulpicia (Messalla's niece and ward) for Cerinthus (known as the Garland of Sulpicia), and six short poems by Sulpicia herself. The poems on Sulpicia are conceivably by Tibullus. The book concludes with an elegy of quality purportedly by Tibullus, and an anonymous epigram.

In *Quintilian's view, Tibullus was the most 'refined and elegant' of the Roman elegists (10. 1. 93). The judgement is justified by the smooth finish of his poems; no other Roman poet writes with such refined plainness. Yet his simplicity is sometimes deceptive: the transitions by which he glides from one scene or subject to another often baffle analysis.

The almost total loss of *Cornelius Gallus makes it difficult to estimate Tibullus' originality, but it was probably considerable. Certainly his plainness, his eschewal of myth, and his rural emphasis contrast strongly with Catullus and Propertius.   R.O.A.M.L.

Tigranes II 'the Great', son of Tigranes I (App. *Syr.* 48) (or of Artavasdes I). Shortly after 100 BC he was set on the throne of Armenia by the Parthians (with whom he had been a hostage for some years) in return for the cession of 'seventy valleys' (Strabo 532). He rapidly consolidated his power, forming an alliance with *Mithradates VI of Pontus, whose daughter, Cleopatra, he married. The interference of the two kings in Cappadocia led to Roman intervention and a *démarche* by *Sulla. Tigranes turned his attention to expansion at the expense of Parthia, temporarily weakened by invasions on its eastern frontier. He ravaged Media as far as Ecbatana and Assyria as far as Media Atropatene, and Osroëne. In 83 he occupied Syria, Phoenicia, and Cilicia, ejecting warring Seleucid rivals. Greek cities that sided with him were given autonomy and coinage rights, but others, e.g. Soli in Cilicia and Cappadocian Mazaca, were destroyed and their inhabitants transferred to his new southern metropolis Tigranocerta. The empire of Tigranes, 'King of Kings', proved to be ephemeral. In 69 his alliance with Mithradates involved him in war with Rome. *Lucullus captured Tigranocerta, but the issue remained undecided until *Pompey in 66 succeeded in separating the Armenian and Pontic kings. Tigranes' son rebelled and fled to Pompey; together they marched on Artaxata and Tigranes finally surrendered (66). He lost all his territories except Armenia proper, though he later recovered Sophene and Pompey recognized his claim to Gordyene and the seventy valleys. Henceforward, though engaging in frontier disputes with Parthia, he remained a peaceful vassal of Rome until his death in *c.*56.

E.W.G.; B.M.L.

Timaeus of Tauromenium (mod. Taormina) in Sicily, *c.*350–260 BC, the most important western Greek historian; son of Andromachus, the dynast who refounded Tauromenium in 358. Andromachus gave Timoleon a warm welcome in 345 and lent him his support (T 3). Timaeus was exiled in *c.*315 probably on account of his hostility towards *Agathocles after the tyrant had captured Tauromenium (fr. 124d) and spent at least fifty years of his exile at Athens (fr. 34), where he studied under Philiscus of Miletus, a pupil of *Isocrates (T 1), and wrote his great work of history. It is conceivable that he returned to Sicily in *c.*265 but not certain. Timaeus died, allegedly at the age of 96 (T 5), shortly after 264 (see below).

WORKS 1. *Olympionikai*: a synchronic list of Olympian victors, Spartan kings and ephors, the Athenian archons, and the priestesses of Hera in Argos (Polyb. 12. 11. 1 = T 11, frs. 125–8). Thereafter it became standard practice to date historical events by the years of the Olympian Games. 2. (*Sikelikai*) *Historiai* = *Sicilian History* in 38 books from mythical times to the death of Agathocles 289/8 (T 6–8). He also wrote a 'separate account' on the '(Roman) Wars against *Pyrrhus' and the events until the epochal year 264 (T 9), where *Polybius's history starts, 'a fine Timaei' (from where Timaeus left off) (cf. Polyb. 1. 5. 1; 39. 8. 4 = T 6).

The arrangement is known only in outline: the five books of the introduction (*prokataskeuē*) dealt with the geography and ethnography of the west and accounts of 'colonies, the foundation of cities, and their relations' (T 7). Books 6–15 contained the earlier history of Sicily until *Dionysius I's accession to power in 406/5; books 16–33 treated the tyranny of Dionysius I and II (406/5–344/3) and events down to Agathocles. The last five books 34–8 were devoted to the history of Agathocles (T 8). The work is known through 164 fragments, the extensive use made of it by *Diodorus Siculus (4–21 for the Sicilian passages), and Polybius's criticism in book 12.

CHARACTERISTICS 1. *Subject-matter*: Timaeus did not restrict his treatment to Sicily but dealt with the whole west including Carthage. Most importantly he was the first Greek historian to give a comprehensive if summary account of Roman history until 264 (T 9b). Hence Aulus *Gellius (*NA* 2. 1. 1 = T 9c) even talks of 'historical works which Timaeus wrote in Greek on the history of the Roman people'. 2. *Conception of history*: Timaeus took an extremely broad view of history, including myth, geography, ethnography, political and military events, culture, religion, marvels, and the unbelievable *paradoxa*. 3. *Sicilian patriotism*: Timaeus frequently distorted events in favour of the Siceliots (fr. 94) and conversely wrote less favourably about the Athenians and Carthaginians (on the Sicilian expedition, cf. Meister, *Gymnasium* 1970, 508 ff.); he always emphasized the contribution of the western Greeks to Greek intellectual life (e.g. *Pythagoras, frs. 12 ff., 131 f.; *Empedocles, frs. 14, 134; Gorgias of Leontini, fr. 137). 4. *Hatred of tyrants*: Timaeus, a conservative aristocrat, distorted not only the historical picture of Agathocles, who had exiled him (fr. 124), but also of other tyrants, e.g. Hieron I and Dionysius I (frs. 29, 105). 5. *Historical classification of his work*: Timaeus' work displays rhetorical, tragic, and 'pragmatic' (frs. 7, 151) features (cf. Polyb. 12. 25; frs. 22, 31) in equal proportion, hence it is an excellent example of the early blend of different kinds of historiography. 6. *Historical criticism*: Timaeus was the first Greek historian critically to appraise almost all of his predecessors, historians and other writers alike. He frequently went too far, which earned him the nickname *Epitimaeus* ('slanderer'); he was first so called by Ister (later 3rd cent. BC, T 1, 11, 16). He was especially vehement in the attacks on his immediate predecessor Philistus (fr. 38, T 18, fr. 154).

Timaeus in turn was criticized by Polybius (book 12) for factual errors, his harsh criticism, and his historical methods (mere book-learning, want of autopsy, lack of political and military experience).

Timaeus was 'the most important historian between *Ephorus and Polybius' and became 'the standard authority on the history of the Greek West for nearly five centuries' (L. Pearson, *The Greek Historians of the West* (1987)). Of Greek authors he was used by e.g. *Callimachus, *Lycophron, *Eratosthenes, Agatharchides, Polybius, *Posidonius, Diodorus Siculus, *Strabo, and *Plutarch; of Roman writers by Quintus Fabius Pictor, *Cato the Elder, *Cicero, *Cornelius Nepos, *Ovid, and Gellius. The writings of Ister (T 10), Polemon of Ilium (T 26) in reaction to his work as well as Polybius, book 12, bear witness to Timaeus' great impact on historiography.   K.M.

Timoleon, Corinthian who expelled *Dionysius II from Syracuse, put down other tyrants in Sicily, and defeated Carthage: the truth about him is not easy to discern behind our adulatory sources. In the mid-360s BC he assassinated his brother Timophanes, who exercised a brief tyranny of uncertain character at Corinth. Nothing more is known of him until two decades later, when Syracusan exiles asked Corinth for help against Dionysius II. Corinth chose Timoleon, and gave him seven ships—without crews; they were joined by two from Corcyra and one from Leucas. Some of the 700 mercenaries he recruited were remnants from the Third Sacred War. He landed at Tauromenium in 344, defeated Hicetas, tyrant of Leontini, at Adranum, and made for Syracuse. Corinth and states of north-west Greece sent large reinforcements; Syracuse was taken, and Dionysius sent into exile at Corinth. A large Carthaginian army invaded Sicily, and Timoleon led a smaller force to victory over it at the river Crimisus. Some of the booty was sent to Corinth: part of the inscription recording its dedication is preserved (*SEG* 11. 126 A). Carthage gave assistance to tyrants of other Sicilian cities against him, but he agreed terms with the Carthaginians which limited them to the west of the island, probably to the same area as under Dionysius I, and most of the remaining tyrants were killed or expelled. He established a new Syracusan constitution. It is described as democratic, but that is unlikely: he himself had wide powers, probably as *stratēgos autokratōr* (supreme commander), and he secured help from two Corinthians in devising it: Corinthians had no experience of democracy. He invited settlers from mainland Greece to assist in the repopulation not only of Syracuse, but of other Sicilian cities: a figure of 60,000 is credibly reported; after the serious decline of the first half of the century Greek Sicily enjoyed a resurgence which can be traced in the archaeological record well after Timoleon himself. A further consequence was numismatic: coins of Corinthian type (*pegasi*), minted both at Corinth and in north-west Greece, seem first to have reached Sicily in quantity with Timoleon's forces; they became the standard coins of the island, and continued to arrive and circulate in huge numbers until the reign of *Agathocles. Timoleon resigned his office, allegedly because of blindness, died in the mid- to late 330s, and was buried in the Syracusan agora.   J.B.S.

Titus (Titus Flavius Vespasianus), Roman emperor, AD 79–81. Born on 30 December 39, he was the elder son of *Vespasian and was brought up at court along with Britannicus, *Claudius' son. He had considerable physical and intellectual gifts, especially in music and singing so that at one stage some viewed him as potentially a second *Nero. He married Arrecina Tertulla, daughter of the praetorian prefect of *Gaius (1); and she bore him a daughter, Julia. After her death he married Marcia Furnilla, whom he later divorced. He spent his early career as a military tribune in Germany and Britain, and it was probably in Lower Germany that he established his friendship with *Pliny the Elder, who subsequently dedicated the *Natural History* to him. Although only of quaestorian rank, he joined his father in 67 in his mission to suppress the Jewish revolt, taking command of legio XV Apollinaris and displaying great personal bravery. He was dispatched to convey Vespasian's congratulations to Galba, but turned back on hearing of the turmoil in Rome, pausing to consult the oracle of Venus at Paphos, whose allegedly encouraging response he brought to his father. He was closely involved in preparations for the Flavian bid for power which culminated on 1 July 69 when Vespasian was first acclaimed emperor by the troops in Egypt. Titus, however, remained in Judaea to take charge of the military operations and after the Flavian victory was created consul in his absence and given proconsular *imperium* (supreme military and civil authority). In 70 he captured Jerusalem and was hailed as *imperator* (general, an honorific title) by his troops. His exploits on campaign were recorded by the Jewish historian *Josephus, who had been befriended by the Flavians.

Hostile observers thought that Titus might use the affection of his troops to seize power for himself, since the soldiers in the east were demanding that he take them all back with him, but there is no sign of any disloyalty to his father. Once back in Rome he celebrated a triumph (victory procession at Rome) with Vespasian and was elevated to share his position, receiving the tribunician power (dated from 1 July 71), holding seven consulships with him, and sharing the office of censor; he also became leader of the young men along with his brother, *Domitian. He was appointed praetorian prefect, a post normally held by equestrians, and incurred hostility because of his ruthless suppression of the alleged conspiracy of Aulus Caecina Alienus and Eprius Marcellus. He was also disliked for his liaison with Berenice, whom he had met in Judaea and who came to Rome in 75, where she probably remained until 79.

Titus succeeded smoothly after Vespasian's death on 23 June 79, and belied the fears of some by the quality of his administration. He ended, however unwillingly, his affair with Berenice, banished informers, and refused to accept treason charges. He declined to put any senator to death or confiscate property, and had a courteous relationship with the senate. Titus once memorably remarked, on observing that he had benefited no one all day, 'Friends, I have lost a day' (Suet. *Tit.* 8). He dedicated the Colosseum begun by Vespasian, built baths, and provided lavish public spectacles. He reacted energetically to alleviate the natural disasters which occurred during his reign, the eruption of Vesuvius in 79 and a serious fire and plague in Rome in 80. There were rumours that Titus' relationship with his brother Domitian was sometimes strained and even that he was poisoned, but his death on 13 September 81 is likely to have been from natural causes. He was remembered with affection as the 'delight and darling of the human race' (Suet. *Tit.* 1), though *Cassius Dio shrewdly commented that had he lived longer his regime might not have been judged so successful.   J.B.C.

Trajan (Marcus Ulpius Traianus), Roman emperor AD 98–117, was born probably in 53 at Italica (mod. Santiponce, nr. Seville) in Spain, the son of Marcus Ulpius Traianus, a distinguished consular under the Flavians. His unusually long period of service as a military tribune (though hardly ten years as *Pliny the Younger alleges) included a time in Syria during the governorship of his father *c.*75. While legionary legate in Spain he marched against Lucius Antonius Saturninus, governor of Upper Germany, who revolted against Domitian in 89. He was consul in 91, and then having been appointed by *Nerva in 97 as governor of Upper Germany, was adopted by that emperor, who faced growing discontent among the praetorians, as his son and co-ruler, and became *consul ordinarius* (one of the two senior consuls) for the second time in 98. After Nerva's death Trajan first inspected the armies in Pannonia and Moesia, and on his arrival in Rome re-established strict discipline by disposing of the praetorian mutineers against Nerva.

As emperor his personal conduct was restrained and unassuming, qualities also exhibited by his wife Plotina, who from about 105 had the title *Augusta*. He was courteous and friendly with individual senators, and treated the senate with respect, avoiding confiscations of property and executions. Pliny's speech (*Panegyric*) delivered in 100, the year of Trajan's third consulship, gives a senatorial appreciation of his excellent qualities. Trajan intervened to help children who had been maltreated by their fathers, and free-born children exposed at birth, and made further exemptions from the inheritance tax. He required that candidates for public office in Rome should have at least one third of their capital invested in Italian land, and he perpetuated the alimentary scheme, probably instituted by Nerva, through which sustenance was provided for poor children in Italian communities. Trajan undertook many utilitarian and celebratory building projects, including baths, a canal to prevent the river Tiber from flooding, a new harbour at Ostia, the via Traiana which extended the via Appia from Beneventum to Brundisium, a forum and basilica in Rome dedicated in 112, and a column depicting the Dacian Wars. He was generous to the Roman people, extending the corn doles, paying out enormous largesse partly financed by the booty of the Dacian Wars and the treasure of Decebalus, and providing lavish spectacles; to celebrate the Dacian victory he gave games on one hundred and twenty-three days in which ten thousand gladiators fought.

The correspondence between Trajan and Pliny, who had been specially appointed to resolve administrative and financial problems in the communities in Bithynia, shows the kind of attitude towards provincial administration that the emperor had inspired in his officials, even if the emperor's replies were not directly composed by Trajan himself. They exhibit justice, fairness, and personal probity: 'You know very well that it is my established rule not to obtain respect for my name either from people's fears and anxieties or from charges of treason' (Plin. *Ep.* 10. 82). The letters about the treatment of Christians (10. 96–7) illustrate the fair-minded attitude of the emperor and his governor.

Experienced in military command, Trajan took a personal interest in the troops, whom he described as 'my excellent and most loyal fellow-soldiers', in instructions issued to governors about the soldiers' testatory privileges (*Digest* 29. 1). Two new legions were formed, both named after himself—II Traianic Brave and XXX Ulpian Victorious, and on campaign the emperor took personal charge, marching on foot at the head of his men. Trajan's reign was marked by two great wars of conquest, in Dacia and Parthia. His inva-

sion in 101 of Decebalus' Dacian kingdom beyond the Danube could be justified on the grounds that the accommodation with the Dacians reached by Domitian was unsatisfactory to long-term Roman interests, and that Decebalus' power was increasing. However his principal motive may have been to win military glory. Trajan crossed the Danube at Lederata and marched north-east to Tibiscum and Tapae; there is insufficient evidence to demonstrate the presence of a second invasion column. The Dacians resisted with great determination and courage and inflicted heavy losses on the Romans in a pitched battle. In 102 Trajan resumed campaigning and by threatening Decebalus' capital at Sarmizegethusa forced the king to accept a peace by which he surrendered some territory and became a vassal of the Romans (Cass. Dio, 68. 9). Leaving garrisons behind, Trajan returned to Rome where he celebrated a triumph, accepted the title *Dacicus*, and issued coins depicting the defeat of Dacia. In 105 the emperor renewed the war, ostensibly because Decebalus was contravening the treaty, and crossed the Danube on a bridge built by Apollodorus at Drobeta (mod. Turnu-Severin). After Sarmizegethusa had fallen to the Romans, Decebalus committed suicide and his treasure was captured. Coins now proclaimed 'the capture of Dacia', and the area was turned into a Roman province with a consular governor and two legions (IV Flavia Felix and XIII Gemina). On the site of a legionary fortress about 30 km. (18 mi.) to the west of the Dacian fortress of Sarmizegethusa a new colony was established, which served as the capital of the province. At Adamklissi a community called *Municipium Tropaeum Traiani* was set up, and a trophy containing a dedication to Mars the Avenger made by Trajan in 107/8. In Rome, Trajan's column celebrated the emperor's prowess and the glorious achievement of the Roman army; his ashes were to be deposited in its base.

Expansion continued with the annexation of Arabia in 106 by Aulus Cornelius Palma Frontonianus, the governor of Syria. Elsewhere in the east, contacts between Rome and Parthia, the only sophisticated empire on the periphery of Roman territory, had been characterized by diplomatic rapport and avoidance of serious warfare during the previous 150 years. The kingdom of Armenia,

between the two empires on the upper
Euphrates, though sometimes prey to Parthian influence and intervention, was generally ruled by a Roman nominee. Trajan took
exception to the attempts of King Osroes of
Parthia to establish control of Armenia, and
refusing all diplomatic advances arrived in
Antioch early in 114. Without major opposition he incorporated Armenia into the
empire and then launched an attack on
Parthia through Mesopotamia while the Parthian king was beset with civil strife. In the
campaigns of 115–16, the Romans crossed the
Tigris into Adiabene and then advanced
down the Euphrates, capturing the Parthian
capital, Ctesiphon. Trajan was acclaimed
imperator ('general', an honorific title), and
accepted the title *Parthicus*. At least one new
province (Mesopotamia) was created, and
possibly another (Assyria); coins celebrated
the 'capture of Parthia', and 'Armenia and
Mesopotamia brought into the power of the
Roman People'. The emperor advanced to the
Persian Gulf, but his success proved transi-
tory as serious uprisings occurred in the captured territory to the army's rear, and a major
insurrection of the Jews in the eastern provinces spread to Mesopotamia in 116. Trajan
tried to contain the military situation, and
Lusius Quietus had some success in northern
Mesopotamia while a vassal king, Parthamas-
pates, was imposed on the Parthians.
However, as the situation remained precarious, Trajan decided to retreat. Parthamas-
pates proved short-lived, despite
grandiloquent Roman coins proclaiming a
'king granted to the Parthians', and with his
health declining Trajan decided to return to
Italy; but in early August he died suddenly
at Selinus. *Cassius Dio explained Trajan's
aggrandizement in the east as a desire to win
glory and this remains the most likely explanation for a man who had already achieved
great military success. The policy was a disastrous failure but criticism was muted because
he was generally popular with senators. By
114 the appellation 'Best' (*Optimus*), which
had appeared early in the reign, had become
one of his official titles, and is recalled in the
ritual acclamation of the senate—'May you
be even luckier than Augustus and even better
than Trajan'. J.B.C.

Tribonian, the main architect of *Justinian's
codification of Roman law in the 6th cent.

AD, was a lawyer from Side in Pamphylia who
practised as an advocate and rose to be *magister officiorum* (master of offices) and in September 529 quaestor (minister of justice). He
was a member of the commission to prepare
Justinian's *Codex* of imperial laws (AD 528–
9), and in 530 Justinian put him in charge of
the preparation of the *Digesta* of legal writings (530–3), which he supervised throughout. He seems also to have played a full part
(though this is disputed) in the detailed work
of excerpting and editing the texts of earlier
lawyers, of which he had a large personal
collection and a deep knowledge. In 533 he
headed a commission of three to prepare an
up-to-date version of *Gaius's *Institutes*, and
in 534 produced a second edition of the
Codex. Accused of corruption and innovation, he was removed from office in January
532 as a sop to the public at the time of the
Nika riots, but continued to work on the
codification and by 535 had resumed the
office of quaestor, which he held until his
death in 541 or 542, continuing to draft new
slaws (*Novellae*). An erudite and self-confident man and a writer in the grand style in
both Latin and Greek, Tribonianus, who is
said to have been anti-Christian, was steeped
in Neoplatonic philosophy of an Aristotelian
type (see ARISTOTLE). In the Renaissance he
was accused of ruining Roman law by introducing changes into the classical legal texts,
originally written 250 to 500 years earlier,
when they were incorporated in Justinian's
Digesta. On a balanced view, however, the
changes he made, apart from shortening and
eliminating what was obsolete, were limited;
they consisted largely in developing ideas
found in the earlier writers, with whom Tribonianus considered himself to be on a par.
T.Hon.

Tullius Cicero See CICERO.

Turbo, Quintus Marcius, from the Caesarian colony Epidaurum in Dalmatia, is first
recorded as centurion in Legio II Adiutrix
and rose through the primipilate, becoming
praefectus vehiculorum (supervisor of the
postal service), tribune in the *vigiles* (fire
brigade) and urban cohorts at Rome, and
commander of the imperial horse guard, then
procurator of the *ludus magnus* (a training
school for gladiators) and prefect of the *classis
Misenensis* (fleet based at Misenum) under

*Trajan, the latter post taking him to the east for the Parthian War, at which time he was already one of *Hadrian's friends (SHA *Hadr.* 4. 2). In AD 116 he was given the first of several special missions, to suppress the Jewish revolts in Egypt and Cyrenaica; shortly after Hadrian's accession the next year he was sent to deal with an uprising in Mauretania. Next he had a special command in Pannonia (Lower) and Dacia, with a rank equivalent to prefect of Egypt (SHA *Hadr.* 6. 7, 7. 3). In 119 he became praetorian prefect and held this post for many years, although ultimately incurring Hadrian's dislike. Turbo, who had the additional names Fronto Publicius Severus, evidently had two adopted sons, one of whom became a senator, the other a procurator; the latter's career-inscription (*AE* 1946, 113) was long mistakenly attributed to Turbo himself until its incompatibility with one of Turbo's own numerous inscriptions (*AE* 1955, 225) was recognized. He is mentioned by *Fronto, *Cassius Dio, *Eusebius (*Hist. eccl.* 4. 2) and the *Historia Augusta*.

A.R.Bi.

Tyrtaeus, Spartan elegiac poet of the mid-7th cent. BC. His works are said to have filled five books; some 250 lines or parts of lines survive in quotations and papyri. They are of great historical interest in relation to two crises affecting Sparta at the time. One was civic unrest that threatened the authority of the kings and elders. In a poem that later came to be entitled *Eunomia* ('Law and Order') (frs. 1–4 W), Tyrtaeus reminded the citizens of the divine right by which the kings ruled, and of the oracle which had laid down the constitutional roles of kings, council, and demos; fr. 4. 3–9 quotes the four-line hexameter oracle, padded out with pentameters, and corresponding to part of the Rhetra in Plut. *Lyc.* 6. The other crisis was the Second Messenian War. Here too Tyrtaeus functioned as a sort of state poet, exhorting the Spartans to fight to the death for their city (frs. 10–14, 18–24). Callinus was making similar use of elegy at the same period on the other side of the Aegean. Tyrtaeus addresses the fighting men as if they were already on the battlefield, and it is not impossible that this was the case. Certainly in the 4th cent. BC, when Tyrtaeus was an established classic, Spartan armies on campaign were made to listen to recitations of his poetry (Lycurg. *Leoc.* 107, cf. Philochorus *FGrH* 328 F 216).

Besides elegies, the *Suda* credits Tyrtaeus with 'martial songs'. This probably refers to the anapaestic and iambic chants which accompanied armed dances and processions at certain Spartan festivals (in the Hellenistic age, at any rate; fragments in Page, *PMG* nos. 856–7, 870). These were apparently sometimes attributed to Tyrtaeus (Dio Chrys. *Or.* 2. 29 and schol. 2. 59; Ath. 630f; Poll. 4. 107); but their language does not look archaic.

M.L.W.

Uu

Ulpian (Domitius Ulpianus) came from Tyre in S. Phoenicia where an inscription honouring him has recently been found. He followed an equestrian career in Rome, drafting rescripts (replies to petitions) for *Septimius Severus, to judge from their style, from AD 202 to 209, and at least from 205 onwards did so as secretary for petitions (*a libellis*). In contrast with *Papinian, on Severus' death at York in 211 he sided with *Caracalla, who in 212 by the *constitutio Antoniniana* extended Roman citizenship to all free inhabitants of the empire. Presumably in response to this extension, which suited his outlook, Ulpian was galvanized into activity in the following years (213–17), systematically composing more than two hundred books (*libri*) in which he expounded Roman law for the benefit, among others, of the new citizenry, emphasized its rational and universal character and appealed to its basis in natural law. Probably under *Elagabalus he became *praefectus annonae* (responsible for the corn supply), in which capacity he is attested in March 222, early in the reign of *Severus Alexander, who in the same year made him praetorian prefect and set him over the two existing prefects. The resulting clashes allowed the praetorian troops, with whom he lacked authority, to mutiny and murder him in 223.

His commentaries on the praetor's edict (*Ad edictum praetoris*) and the civil law (*Ad Sabinum*), in 81 and 51 books respectively, were on an even greater scale than Paulus'. He also wrote important works *De officio proconsulis* ('On the Duties of the Provincial Governor') and on other officials, besides monographs and manuals for students both elementary and advanced. He had an exalted idea of a lawyer's calling: lawyers were 'priests of justice' devoted to 'the true philosophy'. His fame was immediate and lasting, his works more widely used than those of any other lawyer. A number of spurious works, such as the six books of *Opiniones* ('Opinions'), some of which may have been composed by authors of the same name, were credited to him. One of five jurists whose works were endorsed by the Law of Citations in 426, he was a principal source for Justinian's *Digesta*, of which he provided more than two-fifths (see JUSTINIAN). His clarity and forthright self-confidence make him an attractive writer, inspired by cosmopolitan tendencies, a search for consensus, and a regard for private rights. His work, both comprehensive and closely documented, foreshadows Justinian's *Digesta* which incorporated so much of it. For these reasons he has proved the most influential of Roman lawyers, having done more than anyone to present the law in a form in which it could be adapted to the very different needs of medieval and Renaissance Europe.　　　T.Hon.

Vv

Valeria Messal(l)ina See MESSAL(L)INA.

Valerian (Publius Licinius Valerianus), Roman emperor, ruled AD 253–60. An elderly (in his 60s) noble senator of great experience, he was sent to Raetia to gather troops to help Trebonianus Gallus against Aemilius Aemilianus. On the death of Gallus, he was hailed as emperor by his men, and marched on Italy. Following the murder of Aemilianus, Valerian and his adult son, *Gallienus, were universally recognized as Augusti (autumn 253). Both strove to serve the empire in circumstances that, as growing external pressures exacerbated internal economic, political and moral weaknesses, were becoming ever more difficult. However, their joint reign saw the nadir of the 3rd-cent. 'crisis'.

In 254 Valerian moved east to repair the damage done by the Persians under Gallus and Aemilianus, and to repel new Gothic raids (in 253/4, 254/5, 256) down the eastern and western coasts of the Black Sea into Asia Minor. The strain he was under is reflected in his persecution of Christianity (rescripts of 257, 258), and his increased reliance on Odaenathus of Palmyra (see ZENOBIA). It was perhaps the need for peace which tempted him to negotiate personally with the Sasanid Persian king Sapor I when the latter again invaded the empire in strength, and which led to his capture, with most of his general staff (summer 260). Valerian was subjected to various humiliations, and died a prisoner.

In outlook remarkably similar to the emperor Decius, Valerian may be seen as the last of the senatorial warrior-emperors, who had pursued a combined civilian and military career in the best republican tradition. As Gallienus recognized, new problems demanded new solutions. However, Valerian's courage in captivity in part redeems his incompetence, and may indeed have brought a breathing-space for his empire.   J.F.DR.

Valerius Antias, Roman historian of the 1st cent. BC. His work, known only through quotations and allusions in later authors, covered the history of Rome from the origins down to 91 BC at least. The reign of Pompilius Numa was treated in book 2, and the Hostilius Mancinus affair (136 BC) in book 22. Since the whole occupied at least 75 books, the scale of the narrative must have increased as it reached the author's own times. For earlier periods Antias' treatment was far less expansive than that of *Livy or *Dionysius of Halicarnassus. Livy mentions him frequently, but usually to disagree with him on points of detail and to criticize his tendency to exaggerate numbers (e.g. of battle casualties). He may nevertheless have been one of Livy's main sources, although the evidence for this is not conclusive. In general the character of his work is hard to judge, and he remains a little-known figure. His first name is not recorded, and scholars disagree on the date at which he was writing. Most experts place him in the age of *Sulla (following Velleius 2. 9. 6), but others date him to the 40s BC on the grounds that he is nowhere mentioned by *Cicero—not necessarily a strong argument. Most modern attempts to characterize Antias and his work are founded on a priori conjectures and inferences from passages of Livy that are assumed to be based on him. The resulting theories, about his social standing, his rhetorical aims, his glorification of the Valerian clan, his chauvinism, and his conservative political bias, are all based on circular reasoning and have no secure foundation in the evidence.   T.J.CO.

Valerius Flaccus (Gaius Valerius Flaccus Setinus Balbus), Roman poet, author of the *Argonautica*, an epic poem on the voyage of Jason and the Argonauts to Colchis in search of the Golden Fleece. There is no external evidence for his biography apart from *Quintilian's remark (c. AD 95) that 'we have recently suffered a great loss in Valerius Flaccus' (10. 1. 90); since Quintilian can use 'recent' of Caesius Bassus' death in AD 79 (10. 1. 96), the conventional dating of Valerius' death to the early 90s is without foundation. The evidence of the poem itself is controversial. The conventional claim that Valerius was a *quindecimvir sacris faciundis* (guardian of the Sybilline books) is based on lines in the proem which by no means dictate such a conclusion (1. 5–7). The one certainty is the reference in a simile to the eruption of Vesuvius, which occurred on 24 August 79 (4. 507–9; cf. 3. 208–9). The date of the composition of the proem, which alludes to *Vespasian, *Titus, and *Domitian, is keenly contested, with advocates for a date under each of the three. The most that can be securely stated is that the *Argonautica* is a Flavian epic (a fact of more than chronological importance).

Indebted to the *Argonautica* of *Apollonius Rhodius (and perhaps of Publius Terentius Varro Atacinus, but moulded above all by Virgil, Valerius' poem follows the Argonauts' expedition through many famous adventures to the point where Jason absconds from Colchis with Medea. The poem breaks off at 8. 467 as Medea is persuading Jason not to hand her back to her brother Absyrtus. The conventional view is that the poet died before finishing his work, although the latest editor believes that the poem was completed in eight books, with the second half of the last book lost in transmission.

The poem owes much to Apollonius' *Argonautica* as a quest with a strong interest in the problems of epic heroism. Valerius, though, departs radically from Apollonius when he concentrates on Argo as the first ship, harbinger of human civilization (1. 1–4), placing his poem in a long and energetic Roman tradition of appropriation of the golden age and iron age myths. A cosmic frame is provided by Jupiter's concern for the expedition, which will reproduce on earth the patterns of order and dominance guaranteed universally by his own recent victory in the Gigantomachy. The cycles set in train by Argo's voyage will carry on down to the contemporary world of the Roman empire (1. 537–60), where the Flavian house likewise rules after the chaos of civil war. Hyperbolically inflating Apollonius' interest in aetiology, Valerius recounts the origin of warfare and imperial institutions, so that the poem is studded with overt references to contemporary Roman practices (in marked contrast with *Statius' *Thebaid*). Valerius exploits Virgil's *Georgics* and *Seneca the Younger's *Medea* to stress the ambivalence of iron age achievement, for navigation is a violation of natural boundaries, and hence either magnificent or impious in its audacity. In cunning and ironic counterpoint to these grand themes is the love story which overtakes the narrative in book 5. Valerius rises to the daunting challenge of going where Apollonius, Virgil, and Ovid had gone before, exploiting his great goddesses to present a sombre and frightening image of Medea's passion.

Valerius has unjustly suffered from being viewed as a doggedly earnest imitator of mightier models; his self-awareness and wry humour have gone largely unnoticed, although he has been commended for the poise of his versification and the acuity of his observation.   D.C.F.

Valerius Maximus, in *Tiberius' reign composed a handbook of illustrative examples of 'memorable deeds and sayings', *Factorum ac dictorum memorabilium libri IX.* He was a friend of a Sextus Pompeius whom, if he is correctly identified with the Sextus Pompeius who was consul in AD 14, he accompanied to his governorship in Asia (Val. Max. 2. 6. 8: AD 24/5?), composing his book after his return. It is dedicated to Tiberius, to whom constant flattery is addressed; and the violent denunciation of a conspirator usually identified with *Sejanus (9. 10. *Externa* 4) suggests, if this identification is correct, that it was published soon after his downfall in 31. The subject-matter has no clearly defined plan, but is divided under headings mostly moral or philosophical in character (e.g. Omens, Moderation, Gratitude, Chastity, Cruelty), usually illustrated by Roman (*domestica*) and foreign (*externa*) examples. The latter, chiefly Greek, are admittedly less important, and in keeping with the strongly national spirit of the compilation are outnumbered by the *domestica* by two to one. Valerius' chief sources seem to have been *Livy and *Cicero, but there are indications of many others, such as *Varro, Coelius Antipater, Pompeius Trogus, and several Greek writers. His use of this material is almost entirely non-critical, and varies greatly in extent and accuracy. The work has been condemned as shallow, sententious, and bombastic, full of the boldest metaphor and rhetorical artifices of the silver age, especially forced antitheses and far-fetched epigrams, only occasionally relieved by touches of poetic fancy or neat passages of narrative or dialogue; but its sources and alignment have begun to attract attention. The variety and convenience of the compilation ensured some measure of success in antiquity, and considerably more in the Middle Ages. It is referred to by *Pliny the Elder, *Plutarch, and others. Most significant, however, is the existence of two later epitomes. The first is by Julius Paris (4th cent.?) and has attached to it a summary on Roman names, *De praenominibus*, ascribed to a certain C. Titius Probus and elsewhere erroneously included in MSS as book 10 of Valerius' own work. The second, by Ianuarius Nepotianus (5th cent.?), breaks off early in book 3.   G.C.W.; B.M.L.

Valerius Messal(l)a See MESSAL(L)A.

Valerius Poplicola See POPLICOLA.

Varro, Marcus Terentius (116–27 BC), was born at Reate, in the Sabine territory northeast of Rome. After studying at Rome with L. Aelius, the first true scholar of Latin literature and antiquities, and at Athens with the Academic philosopher *Antiochus of Ascalon, Varro began a public career that brought him to the praetorship and, ultimately, to service on the Pompeian side (see POMPEY) in the Civil War. Having received *Julius Caesar's clemency after Pharsalus, he was asked to plan and organize the first public library at Rome. But this project went unrealized, and after Caesar's assassination he was proscribed by Mark *Antony: his library at Casinum was plundered, but he escaped to live the rest of his life in scholarly retirement. He had completed 490 books by the start of his 78th year (Gell. 3. 10. 17): 55 titles are known in all, and his *œuvre* has been estimated to include nearly 75 different works totalling *c.*620 books (Ritschl, *Opuscula* 3. 485 ff.).

WORKS Varro's combination of methodical analysis, vast range, and original learning made him Rome's greatest scholar. His writings covered nearly every branch of inquiry: history (*De vita populi Romani*, on Roman 'social history'; *De gente populi Romani*, placing Rome's remote past in a Greek

context), geography, rhetoric, law (*De iure civili lib. XV*), philosophy, music, medicine, architecture, literary history (*De poetis*, *De comoediis Plautinis*), religion, agriculture, and language (at least 10 works on this last alone). The achievements of the Augustans and of later authors, in both poetry and prose, are scarcely conceivable without the groundwork that he laid.

Only two of his works survive substantially:

1. *De lingua Latina*, in 25 books, of which books 5–10 are partly extant (5 and 6 entirely). Book 1 provided an introduction; 2–7 dealt with etymology, and the connection between words and the entities they represent; 8–13, with inflectional morphology and the conflict (which Varro probably exaggerated) between 'anomalists' and 'analogists'; 14–25, with syntax and the proper formation of 'propositions' (*proloquia*, a topic derived from Stoic dialectic). Varro dedicated books 2–4 to his quaestor, the subsequent books to Cicero; the work was published before *Cicero's death, probably in 43.

2. *De re rustica* (3 books: 37 BC), a treatise on farming in dialogue form, intended as an agreeable entertainment for men of Varro's own class. It deals with agriculture in general (book 1), cattle- and sheep-breeding (book 2), and smaller farm-animals (birds, bees, etc.: book 3). The work, which survives entirely and shows some amusing strokes of characterization, reveals very strikingly Varro's fondness for analysing his subjects into their parts, and those parts into their sub-parts: though this analysis is sometimes carried to unhelpful lengths, it also represents a new stage in the logical organization of prose at Rome.

Among Varro's lost works the following are especially noteworthy:

1. *Saturae Menippeae* (150 books: prob. 81–67 BC), humorous essays on topics of contemporary vice and folly, mingling verse with prose; Varro professed to imitate the 3rd-cent. Cynic philosopher Menippus of Gadara. Ninety titles and 600 fragments survive

2. *Antiquitates rerum humanarum et divinarum* (41 books: 47 BC). Of the first 25 books, on human (i.e. Roman) antiquities, little is known: the introductory book was followed

by four segments of (probably) six books each, on persons (*de hominibus*: the inhabitants of Italy), places (*de locis*), times (*de temporibus*), and things (*de rebus*). The remaining sixteen books, dedicated to *Julius Caesar as *pontifex maximus* (head of one of the four most important priestly colleges at Rome), took up the human construction of the divine: another book of general introduction, then five triads, on priesthoods (27–9), holy places (30–2), holy times (33–5), rites (36–8), and kinds of gods (39–41). Among the lost works of republican prose, the *Antiquitates* is perhaps the one we most sorely miss.

3. *Logistorici* (76 books: 44 BC?), a series of dialogues on various subjects, each taking its name from a noted person: e.g. *Marius de fortuna, Tubero de origine humana, Curio de cultu.*

4. *Hebdomades vel de imaginibus* (15 books: 39 BC), a collection of 700 portraits of celebrated Greeks and Romans, in which each portrait was accompanied by an epigram; the number 7 played an important (if now obscure) role in the work's organization (cf. Gell. 3. 10. 1).

5. *Disciplinae* (9 books), a late work surveying the essential terms and principles of the learned 'disciplines' that a free man should command: these *artes liberales* included 'grammar', rhetoric, dialectic, arithmetic, geometry, astronomy, music, medicine, and architecture. R.A.K.

Varus See QUINCTILIUS VARUS.

Vegetius (Flavius Vegetius Renatus), wrote an *Epitoma rei militaris* in four books, which is the only account of Roman military practice to have survived intact. The work was written after AD 383 but before 450, when Eutropius undertook a critical revision at Constantinople, and the single emperor who is its addressee may be *Theodosius I (383–95), the occasion perhaps being his visit to Italy from August 388 to June 391.

Book 1 discusses the recruit, book 2 army organization, book 3 tactics and strategy, book 4 fortifications and naval warfare. Vegetius examines important themes—the maintenance of discipline and morale, vigilant preparations in enemy territory, establishing a camp, campaign planning, tactical adaptability in battle, conducting a retreat, and the use of stratagems. He also quotes some

general maxims which 'tested by different ages and proved by constant experience, have been passed down by distinguished writers' (3. 26). Vegetius is convinced of the relevance of this approach. The emperor had instructed him to abridge ancient authors, and sought instruction from past exploits despite his own achievements.

Vegetius was not himself a soldier or historian, but served in the imperial administration, perhaps as *comes sacrarum largitionum* (a finance official). He took an antiquarian interest in the army, ignoring the detailed changes accomplished by *Diocletian and *Constantine I, and for his manual collected material from many sources and chronological periods without adequate differentiation and classification. This impairs his value as a source for the organization and practices of the Roman army. He mentions some of his sources: *Cato the Elder, *Frontinus, Taruttienus Paternus (praetorian prefect of *Marcus Aurelius), and the ordinances of *Augustus, *Trajan, and *Hadrian. But there is no reason to assume that he always consulted these at first hand or that they were his only sources. The 'old legion' (*antiqua legio*) to which Vegetius refers (2. 4–14), and which is clearly not from his own day, should probably be dated to the late 3rd cent.

An interesting feature of Vegetius' treatise is the significant influence which it had upon the military thinking of the Middle Ages and the Renaissance. J.B.C.

Velleius Paterculus, Roman historical writer, provides details of himself in his work. Among his maternal ancestors were Minatus Magius of Aeclanum and Decius Magius of Capua (2. 16. 2–3); his paternal grandfather was Gaius Velleius, *praefectus fabrum* (chief of engineers) to *Pompey, *Brutus, and Tiberius Claudius Nero, father of the emperor *Tiberius (2. 76. 1); the senator Capito, who helped to prosecute the Caesaricide *Cassius in 43 BC, was a paternal uncle (2. 69. 5). Velleius himself was born in (probably) 20 or 19 BC. Having begun his career as military tribune around the turn of the millennium (2. 101. 3), he joined the staff of Gaius Caesar in the east (2. 101–102. 1); later he became *praefectus equitum* (commander of auxiliary cavalry), as his father had been, and spent AD 4–12 serving under the future emperor Tiberius in Germany (twice), Pannonia, and Dalmatia (2. 104. 3, 111. 3, 114. 2, 115. 5). In AD 6, having completed his service as an equestrian officer, he returned briefly to Rome and was elected quaestor for AD 7 (2. 111. 4); in AD 12 he and his brother Magius Celer Velleianus, who had also served in Dalmatia (2. 115. 1), took part in Tiberius' Illyrian triumph (2. 121. 3); and, when *Augustus died in AD 14, both brothers were already designated 'candidates of Caesar' (*candidati Caesaris*) for the praetorship of AD 15 (2. 124. 4). Nothing further is certainly known of him, apart from the fact that he dedicated his work to Marcus Vinicius, the consul of AD 30, the presumed year of its publication. There is no evidence for the suggestion that he was executed in the aftermath of *Sejanus' fall in AD 31; the suffect consuls of AD 60 and 61 are thought to be two sons.

Velleius' work begins with Greek mythology and ends in AD 29, a span of time which he encompassed in only two volumes. 'I hardly know any historical work of which the scale is so small, and the subject so extensive', said Macaulay. Like *Cornelius Nepos and *Florus he is thus a writer of summary history, something to which he draws frequent attention (1. 16. 1, 2. 29. 2, 38. 1, 41. 1, 52. 3, 55. 1, 66. 3, 86. 1, 89. 1, 96. 3, 99. 4, 108. 2, 124. 1). Almost all of book 1 is now lost: not only do we lack the preface and very beginning of the narrative but a vast lacuna has deprived us of his history of Rome between the time of Romulus (1. 8. 4–6) and the battle of Pydna in 168 BC (1. 9), although a stray fragment on *Cimon (1. 8. 6) shows that he continued to refer to Greek history at least as late as the 5th cent. BC. Book 1 is separated from book 2 by two excursuses, which would be notable even in a full-length history (1. 14–15 on Roman colonization; 1. 16–18 on Greek and Latin literature); and book 2 begins, as the narrative part of book 1 had ended (12–13), with the destruction of *Carthage in 146 BC, which Velleius, like *Sallust, saw as a turning-point in Roman history. Although the following years to 59 BC are dispatched in a mere 40 chapters, which notably include three further excursuses of varying length (2. 9 and 36. 2–3 on Roman authors, 2. 38–9 on Roman provincialization), Velleius devotes increasing amounts of space to *Julius Caesar (2. 41–59), Augustus (2. 59–93), and especially

Tiberius (2. 94–131), whose career forms the climax of his work. Whether he intended seriously to write his own full-length history, as he often promises (2. 48. 5, 89. 1, 96. 3, 99. 3, 103. 4, 114. 4, 119. 1), is uncertain.

Though Velleius constantly imitates the phraseology of both Sallust and *Cicero, it is the fullness and balance (*concinnitas*) of the latter's style that he aimed generally to reproduce. His sentences, replete with antithesis and point, are often long and involved; and he has a gift for pithy characterization. Yet readers have been dismayed by the successive rhetorical questions (e.g. 2. 122) and exclamations (e.g. 2. 129–30) in his account of Tiberius, which in general, like his treatment of Sejanus (2. 127–8), has been regarded as mere panegyric. On such grounds Sir Ronald Syme and most other 20th-cent. scholars have dismissed with contempt his work as a whole.

Yet in imperial times the traditional patriotism of Roman historians was inevitably focused on the emperor of the day, who in Velleius' case was also his former commander; and his account of Tiberius is valuable in presenting the establishment view of events for which Tacitus, from the safer perspective of the 2nd cent. AD, supplies an opposition view. Even so the prayer, which forms the unconventional conclusion to his work (2. 131), is arguably a recognition of the political crisis of AD 29, while the treatment of Sejanus, which is not a panegyric of the man but a defence of his elevation by Tiberius, betrays some of the very unease which it seems designed to dispel.

Velleius, like *Polybius, travelled widely (cf. 2. 101. 3); he was a senator, like Sallust and *Tacitus, and held magisterial office; like *Thucydides he witnessed and took part in a significant number of the events he describes (cf. 2. 104. 3, 106. 1, 113. 3, 118. 1). He thus enjoyed many of the advantages conventionally associated with the ideal historian. He regularly provides information on topics about which we would otherwise be ignorant; and he is the only Latin historian of Roman affairs to have survived from the period between *Livy and Tacitus. These seem reasons enough to justify his more favourable assessment in recent years.

Velleius' text depends upon a single codex, designated M, discovered by Beatus Rhenanus at Murbach in 1515 but now lost. From a lost copy of the codex derive both Amerbach's apograph (1516) and Rhenanus' first edition (dated 1520, Basel), the latter containing Burer's collation of the edition with M. The relative merits of apograph and first edition are disputed.   A.J.W.

Verres, Gaius, perhaps the son of one of *Sulla's new senators who, as an ex-*divisor* (distributor of bribes), had considerable influence. He may be the moneyer VER (*RRC* 350, dated 86 BC), an issue usually (but implausibly) assigned to an ex-tribune. Quaestor in 84, he deserted Gnaeus Papirius Carbo for Sulla, appropriating his *fiscus* (public funds). As legate (eventually *pro quaestore*) of Gnaeus Cornelius Dolabella in Cilicia, he helped him plunder his province and Asia, but on their return helped to secure his conviction. As urban praetor (74), he is charged by *Cicero with having flagrantly sold justice. Assigned Sicily as proconsul (73–71), he exploited and oppressed the province (except for Messana, in league with him) and even Roman citizens living or trading there by all means at his disposal. Unwisely offending some senators and ill-treating clients of *Pompey, he yet evaded the effect of a senate decree censuring him, passed on the motion of the consuls of 72, and was again prorogued. On his return, he used his great wealth (much of it acquired in Sicily) and his connections, and exploited the hostility of leading nobles (especially most of the Metelli) to Pompey, to gain strong and eminent support. Quintus Hortensius Hortalus, consul designate for 69 with a friendly Metellus (Quintus Caecilius Metellus Creticus), defended him against a prosecution launched in the *quaestio repetundarum* (extortion court) by Cicero (70) and tried to drag the case on into his year of office. Outwitted by Cicero's speed and forensic tactics, and despite the efforts of a Metellus as Verres' successor in Sicily, he found the case caught up in the popular agitation for jury reform and succumbed to Pompey's influence exerted against Verres. On his advice, Verres fled into exile at Massalia. Cicero nevertheless published the second *actio* (oration) he had prepared, to drive home Verres' guilt and demonstrate his own skill and efforts. The evidence in fact seems overwhelming. But after his victory Cicero conciliated Verres' many noble supporters by

agreeing to a low assessment of damages (Plut. *Cic.* 8. 1).

His *Verrines* give us our best insight into provincial administration and its abuses in the late republic. After Verres' proconsulship Sicily ceased to be Rome's main granary. Verres died at Massalia, allegedly proscribed for his stolen art treasures by Mark *Antony.   E.B.

Vespasian (Titus Flavius Vespasianus), emperor AD 69–79, was born on 9 November, AD 9, at Sabine Reate. His father, Flavius Sabinus (names also borne by Vespasian's elder brother), was a tax-gatherer; his mother also was of equestrian family, but her brother entered the senate, reaching the praetorship. Vespasian was military tribune in 27, serving in Thrace, quaestor in Crete in the mid-30s, aedile (at the second attempt) in 38, and praetor in 40. Claudius' freedman Narcissus now advanced his undistinguished career, and he became legate of legio II Augusta at Argentorate, commanding it in the invasion of Britain in 43 and subduing the south-west as far as Exeter (43–7); for this he won triumphal ornaments and two priesthoods. He was suffect consul in November–December 51 and is next heard of as an unpopular proconsul of Africa (*c*.62; any unemployment may be due to the deaths of Narcissus and *Vitellius and the eclipse of other supporters during the ascendancy of *Agrippina the Younger. In 66 he accompanied Nero to Greece and allegedly offended him by falling asleep at one of his recitals, but at the end of the year he was entrusted with suppressing the rebellion in Judaea. By mid-68 he had largely subdued Judaea apart from Jerusalem itself but conducted no further large-scale campaigns.

Vespasian now settled his differences with the governor of Syria, Gaius Licinius Mucianus. They successively recognized *Galba, *Otho, and Vitellius, but the idea of using the eastern legions to attain power became a plan in the spring of 69. On 1 July the two Egyptian legions under Tiberius Julius Alexander proclaimed Vespasian; those in Judaea did so on 3 July, and the Syrian legions a little later. Mucianus set out with a task-force against Italy while Vespasian was to hold up the grain ships at Alexandria and probably Carthage. However, the Danubian legions declared for Vespasian, and the legionary legate Marcus Antonius Primus invaded Italy. After his crushing victory at Cremona the city was brutally sacked. Primus fell from favour in 70 and took the blame. It was alleged that Primus' invasion was against orders (certainly Mucianus would have opposed his action), but victory could never have been bloodless. Primus pressed on, entering Rome on 21 December, the day after Vitellius' death. The senate immediately conferred all the usual powers on Vespasian, though he dated his tribunician years from 1 July, negating the acts of senate and people and treating his legions as an electoral college.

A fragment of an enabling law has survived (ILS 244 = EJ 364, trans. D. Braund, *Augustus to Nero* no. 293) conferring powers, privileges, and exemptions, most with Julio-Claudian precedents. It is disputed whether this was part of the original tralatician grant of powers, surviving only in Vespasian's case, or of a supplementary grant, due to difficulties with the senate, conferring by law the right to perform acts never questioned in a Julio-Claudian but which from Vespasian might be challenged. It sanctioned all he had done up to the passing of the law and empowered him to act in whatever way he deemed advantageous to the Roman people. Vespasian's standing was lower than that of any of his predecessors and the law took the place of the *auctoritas* (prestige, influence) he lacked. Vespasian was careful to publicize a number of divine omens which portended his accession; he frequently took the consulship, however briefly, and accumulated imperatorial salutations. Vespasian insisted that the succession would devolve on his son (Suet. *Div. Vesp.* 25; sons, Dio Cass. 65. 12). Controversy over the dynastic principle, part of a wider controversy over the role of the senate in government, may have caused his quarrel with doctrinaire senators like Helvidius Priscus, who was exiled and later executed.

Vespasian returned to Italy in the late summer of 70. While at Alexandria he had been concerned with raising money, and his sales of imperial estates and new taxes caused discontent there. He claimed that forty thousand million sesterces (so Suet. *Div. Vesp.* 16. 3) were needed to support the state. He increased, sometimes doubled, provincial taxation and revoked imperial immunities. Such measures were essential after the costs

incurred by Nero and the devastation of the civil wars; contemporaries inevitably charged Vespasian with 'avarice'. He was able to restore the Capitol, burnt in December 69, to build his forum and temple of Peace, and to begin the Colosseum. An attempt by senators in 70 to diminish expenditure by the state treasury, so promoting senatorial independence, was promptly vetoed.

It may have been in part for financial reasons that in 73–4 he held the censorship with *Titus. But both as censor and previously, he recruited many new members, Italian and provincial, to the senate, and conferred rights on communities abroad, notably a grant of Latin rights to all native communities in Spain.

Vespasian restored discipline to the armies after the events of 68–9. Before his return Mucianus had reduced the praetorian guard, enlarged by Vitellius, to approximately its old size, and they were entrusted to Titus on his return. The legions were regrouped so that Vitellian troops would not occupy dangerous positions. In the east Vespasian by the end of his reign had substituted three armies (six legions) in Syria, Cappadocia, and Judaea for the single army (until Nero's time only four legions) in Syria. After the Jewish and Rhineland rebellions (see TITUS) had been suppressed, Vespasian continued imperial expansion with the annexation of northern England, the pacification of Wales, and an advance into Scotland (see AGRICOLA), as well as in south-west Germany between Rhine and Danube.

On his death on 23 June 79 he was accorded deification, though Titus did not act at once (he had been Vespasian's colleague since 71 and the ceremony, last held on Claudius' death in 54, may have seemed discredited). Unassuming behaviour had partially conciliated the aristocracy, although some of his friends were informers or otherwise disreputable; Tacitus, *Hist.* 1. 50, claims that he was the first man to improve after becoming emperor, and the reign seems to have been tranquil after conflicts with the senate had been won. The years after 75 were marred (as far as is known) only by Titus' execution of Aulus Caecina Alienus and his forcing Marcellus to suicide.

Vespasian was industrious, and his simple life a model for contemporaries. Matching his rugged features he cultivated a bluff manner, parading humble origins and ridiculing a man who corrected his accent. His initial appointments show astuteness in building a powerful party of which the core was his own family. To have ended the wars was an achievement, and Pax ('Peace') was a principal motif on his coinage. His proclaimed purposes were the restoration and enhancement of the state, and he made no great break with tradition. In style of government, however, and in the composition of the governing class, the reign paved the way for the 2nd cent.

Nothing is known of Vespasian's education (he was no orator, but could quote *Homer), but his sons were cultivated, and he attended to the needs of Rome and the empire by founding chairs of rhetoric and philosophy and by granting fiscal privileges to teachers and doctors.

Vespasian's wife Flavia Domitilla was alleged to be only of Latin status until her father Liberalis proved her Roman citizenship. Besides his two sons she bore a daughter also named Flavia Domitilla; wife and daughter died before Vespasian's accession. He then lived with an earlier mistress, Caenis, a freedwoman of Antonia.   G.E.F.C.; B.M.L.

Vipsania Agrippina See AGRIPPINA THE ELDER.

Vipsanius Agrippa See AGRIPPA.

Virgil (Publius Vergilius Maro) (70–19 BC), Latin poet. The contemporary spelling of Virgil's name was with an *e*: the first occurrence with an *i* is on an honorific inscription to *Claudian in Greek (*CIL* 6. 1710 = *ILS* 1. 2949). Virgil is traditional in English, but the slightly historicizing Vergil is preferred by some modern critics. Virgil and his friends in any case punned on *virgo*, a virgin (*G*. 4. 564, perhaps 1. 430, *Donatus' 'Life' of Virgil, *Vit. Verg.* 11). Varius Rufus is said to have written on Virgil (Quint. 10. 3. 8) and there were other accounts by friends and acquaintances (cf. Gell. *NA* 17. 10. 2): the extant lives go back in part to *Suetonius, *De poetis*. Much (but not all) of the information in them derives from interpretation of the poems (including the spurious ones in the *Appendix Vergiliana*), and few details, however circumstantial, can be regarded as certain.

Nevertheless, Virgil is said to have been born on 15 October 70 BC in Andes, a village near Mantua. *Macrobius (*Sat.* 5. 2. 1) says that he was 'born in the Veneto of country parents and brought up amongst the woods and shrubs', and his father is variously described as a potter and a courier who married the boss's daughter (*Vit. Verg.* 1), but the real status of the family is uncertain. His mother was a Magia: both the *gentes* (lineages) covered a spectrum of social levels. Virgil is said to have been educated in Cremona and Milan before coming to Rome (*Vit. Verg.* 7) and the family would clearly have had to be sufficiently well-off for such an education to be feasible. At some stage Virgil was associated with the Epicurean (see EPICURUS) community in Naples (see M. Gigante, *Stud. Ital.* 1989, 3–6: his name appears in a papyrus from Herculaneum with Plotius Tucca, Varius Rufus, and *Quinctilius Varus); *Catalepton* 5 and 8, if either genuine or based on a sound biographical tradition, have him fleeing from the normal rhetorical education of a Roman to Epicurean retirement (cf. *G*. 4. 563–4, where he is again (?) enjoying *otium*, leisure, in Naples).

After the defeat of the tyrannicides (the murderers of *Julius Caesar in 42 BC, Octavian (see AUGUSTUS) attempted to settle members of his army on confiscated land, a controversial move which led to the Perusine War: full-scale war between Mark *Antony and Octavian was only narrowly (and temporarily) avoided by the treaty of Brundisium in 40 BC. Virgil's first collection of poems, the *Eclogues*, probably appeared around 39–38 BC (controversial: see R. J. Tarrant and G. W. Bowersock in *Harv. Stud.* 1978, 197–202) in the midst of the turmoil: the confiscations are a central topic in *Eclogues* 1 and 9. In the first poem, a slave Tityrus says that he has to thank a young man for freedom and security (1. 42): in the context of the times, this can only be Octavian. Other poems mention a Varus (6. 7, 9. 27), presumably the jurist Publius Alfenus Varus, suffect consul 39 BC, Gaius Asinius Pollio (4. 12, and probably the addressee of 8—for the controversy, see Tarrant and Bowersock), consul 40 BC, one of Antony's most important supporters and an architect of the Peace of Brundisium, and the important *eques* and poet *Cornelius Gallus (6. 64–73, 10 *passim*). These three men are said to have been involved in the distribution of land, though the arrangements are uncertain and the Virgilian commentators our only source (cf. *MRR* 2. 377–8). The biographical tradition says that Virgil's father's land was amongst the land confiscated, and some personal experience of loss is suggested by *Ecl.* 9. 27–9 'Mantua, all too near to unhappy Cremona' and *G.* 2. 198 'the land unfortunate Mantua lost', but it is impossible to know how many of the details derive from allegorical reading of the poems.

At some time after the publication of the *Eclogues*, Virgil entered the circle of *Maecenas, and thus of the future Augustus. He is mentioned several times in the first book of *Horace's *Satires*, published at the end of the decade; in 1. 6. 55 he is said to have introduced Horace to Maecenas, and in 1. 5 (40, 48) he is described as joining the 'journey to Brundisium'. The dramatic date of the latter poem is 38 or 37, depending on which of the two possible diplomatic missions it is associated with (cf. I. M. L. M. DuQuesnay, in T. Woodman and D. West, *Poetry and Public in the Age of Augustus* (1984), 39–43). In the concluding satire of the book (1. 10. 45, cf. 81) Virgil is one of the poets whose achievements Horace contrasts with his own: 'to Virgil the Muses who delight in the countryside have granted tenderness and charm' (*molle atque facetum*, trans. P. M. Brown). The sixteenth of Horace's *Epodes* (*Iambi*), also published at the end of the 30s, parodies *Ecl.* 4 in a context which highlights the violent alternation of hope and despair which characterized the decade.

The publication of Virgil's second major work, the *Georgics*, is usually dated to 29 BC; the battle of Actium (31 BC) is referred to in *Georgics* 3. 28–9 and according to the Donatus life, Virgil read the poem to Octavian 'after his return from the victory at Actium' (*Vit. Verg.* 27): Octavian reached Italy in the summer of 29 BC, and celebrated a great 'triple triumph' in August of that year, though the description of his achievements as depicted on the metaphorical temple at the opening of *Georgic* 3 (26–39) can plausibly be dated before or after this triumph. There was a story that the work had originally ended with praise of Cornelius Gallus, which was removed after his fall and suicide in 26 BC (Servius on *Ecl.* 10. 1; *G.* 4. 1) but this is

unlikely to be true (J. Griffin, *Latin Poets and Roman Life* (1985), 180–2).

Like the *Eclogues*, the *Georgics* are a constant presence in the poetry of the 20s BC, but by the time that the final poem of *Propertius' second (?) book of elegies is published some time after Gallus' death (2. 34. 91–2), 'something greater than the *Iliad* is being brought to birth' (2. 34. 66), that is, the *Aeneid*. Macrobius quotes a letter from Virgil to Augustus declining to send any samples as more work is needed; this may be a reply to the letter of Augustus quoted at *Vit. Verg.* 31 asking for a sketch or fragment, and to be dated to 27–25 BC since Augustus is described as away from Rome in Spain. It is possible, however, that more scepticism as to the genuineness of these letters is in order. Horace, *Odes* 1. 3 addresses a ship carrying a Vergilius to Greece; if this is taken to be Virgil, the bold enterprise of the ship's journey may also be read metapoetically of the vast undertaking of the *Aeneid*. The tradition claims that books 2 (or 3), 4, and 6 were recited to Augustus, the reference to the young Marcus Claudius Marcellus in 6 causing Octavia to faint (*Vit. Verg.* 32; Servius on *Aen.* 4. 323, 6. 861); this episode, whether true or not, must be set after the death of Marcellus in 23 BC. Virgil himself, however, died in 19 BC, with the poem apparently felt to be unfinished: 'in the 42nd year of his life, intending to finish the *Aeneid*, he decided to go off to Greece and Asia Minor, and to spend three straight years simply in correcting the poem, to leave the rest of his life free for philosophy. But when he had set out on his trip, he met Augustus in Athens returning to Rome from the east, and decided not to go off, and even to return with Augustus. He visited a small town near Megara in very hot sun and caught a fever; this was made worse by his continued journey, to the extent that he was somewhat sicker when he put into Brundisium, where he died on 20 September' (*Vit. Verg.* 35). He was buried at Naples 'within the second milestone on the road to Puteoli' (*Vit. Verg.* 36: this does not fit the tomb known to tradition), and is said to have composed his own epitaph on his death-bed:

Mantua me genuit, Calabri rapuere, tenet nunc

Parthenope; cecini pascua rura duces.

Mantua bore me, Calabria snatched me away, now

Naples holds me; I sang of pastures, fields, and kings.

Varius Rufus and Plotius Tucca were said to have 'emended' the *Aeneid* after Virgil's death, but without making any additions. The tradition also preserves the famous story that Virgil wished to burn the *Aeneid* on his death-bed: like everything else in the tradition, this may or may not be true.

Propertius' prophecy came to pass on the publication of the *Aeneid*: Virgil became the Roman *Homer, the *Aeneid* in particular serving as the great Roman classic against which later epic poets and in a sense all Latin poets had to situate themselves (cf. P. Hardie, *The Epic Successors of Vergil* (1993), cf. e.g. Pliny, *Ep.* 3. 7. 8 on Silius' veneration). Schoolboys studied it, even in Roman Egypt (R. Cavenaile, *Corpus Papyrorum Latinorum* (1958), 7–70), and its opening words became a common graffito on the walls of Pompeii (R. P. Hoogma, *Der Einfluss Vergils auf die Carmina Latina Epigraphica* (1952)). Already in his lifetime Virgil is said to have been famous (Tac. *Dial.* 13. 3) and his friendship with the great brought him considerable wealth: according to Valerius Probus' life (15–16) he was given ten million sesterces by Augustus (cf. Hor. *Epist.* 2. 1. 245–7 with Helenius Acro's comm.). As with Homer, all human learning came to be seen as condensed in the *Aeneid*, a view which finds full expression in Macrobius' *Saturnalia*: the ancient biographical tradition already shows a tendency to see Virgil as a *theios anēr*, a divine genius, and this became pronounced in the Middle Ages, with the legends of Virgil the Magician (D. Comparetti, *Virgilio nel Medievo²*, ed. G. Pasquali (1937–41; 1st edn. trans. E. F. Benecke 1895); cf. also C. G. Leland, *The Unpublished Legends of Virgil* (1879); J. W. Spargo, *Virgil the Necromancer* (1934); V. Zabughin, *Virgilio nel rinascimento italiano* (1921–3)). The text of the *Aeneid* was consulted as an oracle in the *sortes Vergilianae* (cf. SHA *Hadr.* 2. 8).

A number of portraits of Virgil are known (*Enc. Virg.* V** 103–4; see below, bibliography after *Enc. Virg.*): there is no reason to believe that any are based on a genuine likeness, but the tradition describes him as a valetudinarian who never married and preferred sex with boys (variously identified amongst the characters of the poems). All of this, naturally, tells us more about Roman constructions of gender and culture than about 'the man Virgil'.

THE LITERARY WORKS *THE ECLOGUES*
If any of the poems in the *Appendix Vergiliana* are genuine (which is unlikely), they may have been juvenilia, but essentially Virgil enters world literature with his first collection, the *Eclogues*, published probably around 39–38 BC (see above): ten short hexameter poems (the longest is 111 lines long) in the pastoral genre. The original title was *Bucolica*, 'cowherd songs' (*Eclogae*, N. Horsfall, *BICS* 1981, 108); *eclogae* means 'selections (from a larger corpus)' and it is unfortunate that a version of this later title has become usual in English. *Bucolica* as a title signals a clear allusion to pastoral (in Greek *ta bukolika*) and to *Theocritus in particular (cf. the refrain 'begin the bucolic song' in *Idyll* 1; in Moschus 3. 11 the pastoral poet Bion is called a cowherd, *boukolos*), and the collection makes constant reference to Theocritus' *Idylls*: commentators note four separate echoes in the first line. But the intertextuality with earlier Roman poetry is as dense: the opening lines are also significantly Lucretian (cf. G. Castelli, *RSC* 1966, 313–42; 1967, 14–39; see LUCRETIUS) and the 'Song of Silenus' in the sixth poem seems to interact with a broad selection of contemporary poetry, hints of only some of which are we able to pick up (cf. D. O. Ross, *Backgrounds to Augustan Poetry* (1975), 25; P. E. Knox, *Ovid's Metamorphoses and the Tradition of Augustan Poetry* (1986), 11–26).

This combination of the Greek and the Roman, the ancient and the contemporary, and the rustic and the sophisticated is typical of the collection as a whole. Although we do not know exactly in what form the poems of Theocritus and the other bucolic poets circulated in Rome (cf. A. F. S. Gow, *Theocritus* (1952), 1. lix–lxii, lxvi–lxxii), it is likely that any edition included both the strictly pastoral poems like the first idyll, urban mimes like 15, and the encomiastic poems 16 and 17. In one sense, Virgil carries this mixture further: just as Theocritus addresses his friend Nicias in the frame of *Idyll* 11, Virgil addresses Varus in 6 (though there Virgil is called 'Tityrus' himself by Apollo) and Pollio (?) in 8, but his contemporaries also make an appearance *within* the bucolic setting (3. 84–91, 6. 64–73, 9. 47, 10 *passim*). *Idyll* 7, the nearest equivalent in Theocritus, is much less explicit. In another sense, however, Virgil is more consistently pastoral: the encomiastic birth poem 4, explicitly *paulo maiora*, 'a little greater (in theme)', is still more consistently pastoral than Theocritus 16 or 17 (cf. *Ecl.* 4. 3, 21–2, 42–5, 55–9).

The ten poems are intricately arranged around the central poem 5; the first and ninth poems deal with the subject of the land confiscations, 2 and 8 contain long laments by star-crossed lovers, 3 and 7 are both 'amoebean' (i.e. with exchanges of song), and 4 and 6 are the most obviously 'elevated' of the collection. Poem 5, another amoebean exchange, describes the apotheosis of Daphnis; 10 concludes the collection with Cornelius Gallus taking on the role of dying lover played by Daphnis in Theocritus, *Idyll* 1. Some supplement this patterning with numerological correspondences, of varying suggestiveness (cf. J. Van Sickle, *The Design of Virgil's Bucolics* (1978)); certainly *Eclogue* 4, which is 63 (9 × 7) lines long, is structured around the magical number seven, but this has special point in relation to its oracular tone and subject-matter. The collection equally responds, however, to a serial reading. There is a clear movement from the first poem, where Tityrus describes how his land was saved, to the ninth, where Moeris says that he was not so fortunate: 'our poems, Lycidas, have as much power amongst the weapons of Mars as they say the Chaonian doves have when the eagle comes' (9. 11–13), with a pun on the 'eagle' of the legionary standard). Poem 6 opens with a 'proem in the middle' (cf. G. B. Conte, *YClS* 1992, 147–59) which echoes the opening of *Callim-achus' Aetia* and establishes the pastoral *deductum carmen*, 'fine-spun song', as the equivalent to Callimachus' 'slender muse' (*Ecl.* 6. 5, cf. 6. 8). At the end of the collection, Gallus gives in to love (10. 69), the poet rises from his pastoral ease in the shade (75–6), and the goats are told to go home, now fed to satiety (77).

As this suggests, the *Eclogues* are highly 'artificial' and metaliterary, and the relation of the world of song to the world outside is a central concern. Virgil toys with a variety of partial identifications in the poems: in 5. 86–7 Menalcas claims to have written *Eclogues* 2

and 3 and in 9. 10 Lycidas says that the same character 'saved all with his poems' but Apollo calls the narrator Tityrus in 6. 4 and it is not hard to see him in the idle singer of an empty day in the first poem (cf. *G.* 565–6); in a broader sense he is also the helpless Corydon of 2 and the magical Silenus of 6. Interwoven with and inseparable from the literary texture are the celebrated descriptive passages that so appealed to Romantic enthusiasts like Samuel Palmer, the buzzing bees and cool springs of the pastoral world (cf. e.g. 1. 51–8). The union of the two was an inheritance from Theocritus which Virgil passed on to the west, particularly through Renaissance imitators like Mantuan and especially Sannazaro; although 'Arcadia' is mentioned only rarely in the poems (7. 4, 26, 10. 31, 33, cf. 4. 58–9, 10. 26) and its significance is disputed (B. Snell, *The Discovery of the Mind*, trans. T. G. Rosenmeyer, ch. 13; D. Kennedy, *Hermathena* 1984, 47–59; R. Jenkyns, *JRS* 1989, 26–39), the *Eclogues* came to signify Arcady as a place where poetry and love meet with or avoid the worlds of politics, cities, and empires.

One of the *Eclogues* came to have particular significance for later readers: *Eclogue* 4, with its description of the birth of a child whose lifetime will see a return of the world to the golden age. There were several possible candidates for the identification of the child even for contemporary readers (cf. E. Coleiro, *An Introduction to Vergil's Bucolics with an Edition of the Text* (1979), 222–32: the modern favourite is an anticipated son of Mark Antony and Octavia, a hope already dashed by the time of the *Eclogues*' publication), but the poem can equally be read as a broader allegory of renewal; Christian readers naturally saw reference to the birth of Jesus (cf. Coleiro, 232–3; Constantine, *Oratio ad sanctum coetum* 19–21, *PL* 8. 454–66). The influence of Jewish messianic writing on the poem is nowhere a required hypothesis, but is not in itself unlikely (cf. R. G. M. Nisbet, *BICS* 1978, 59–78).

THE GEORGICS Virgil's call to himself to 'rise' at the end of the *Eclogues* (10. 75 *surgamus*) was answered by a rise in generic level with his next work, the *Georgics*, a didactic poem in four books on farming (book 1: crops, book 2: trees and shrubs, book 3: livestock, book 4: bees). Again there are Hellenistic Greek models: little can be said of the

lost *Georgica* of *Nicander (fragments in A.
F. S. Gow and A. F. Scholfield, *Nicander*
(1953), 145–61), but it is clear even from the
fragments that we have of Callimachus' *Aetia*
that that was an important model (four-
book structure, and especially the links
between the proem to the third and conclusion to the fourth book of each work: R. F.
Thomas, *CQ* 1983, 92–113) and *Aratus (1)'s
Phaenomena was both a central Hellenistic
text (translated by *Cicero and Publius Terentius Varro Atacinus) and of particular relevance to the discussion of weather in book 1
(cf. also the translation of a passage from
*Eratosthenes at *G.* 1. 233–51). But there was
also now an important archaic model in
*Hesiod's *Works and Days* (cf. 2. 176 *Ascraeum
... carmen*, 'Hesiodic song'), and the relationship to Lucretius' *De rerum natura* is so
central that the *Georgics* may be seen as an
anti-Lucretius (cf. P. R. Hardie, *Virgil's
Aeneid: Cosmos and Imperium* (1986), 157–67,
and in general J. Farrell, *Vergil's Georgics and
the Traditions of Ancient Epic* (1991)).
Lucretius' confident exposition of the power
of reason is 'remythologized' into a more
sceptical and yet more accepting attitude
towards the natural world and its traditional
divinities (2. 490–4).

Just as Aratus' *Phaenomena* had been based
on a prose treatise of *Eudoxus and the *De
rerum natura* on Epicurean texts, especially
the *Letter to Herodotus*, so the *Georgics* also
have important prose models, though none
is as central as in those texts. Virgil's sources
for the agricultural lore were various (L. A.
Jermyn, *G&R* 1949, 50) but the most significant was *Varro's *Res rusticae*, published in 37
BC and influential especially in books 3 and 4
(but note also *Rust.* 1. 1. 4–7 with the opening
invocation of the gods in *G.* 1. 8–23, and *Rust.*
1. 69. 2–3 with the end of the first book). The
didactic narrator is portrayed as a saviour-
sage, taking pity on 'the farmers ... ignorant
of the path' (1. 41, with Lucretian overtones:
cf. Hardie, 158) but the practical advice avoids
technical precision (in contrast to the fragments of Nicander) and the addressee is the
extremely unrustic Maecenas (1. 2, 2. 41, 3. 41,
5. 2; cf. also L. P. Wilkinson, *The Georgics of
Virgil* (1969), 52–5; S. Spurr, *G&R* 1986, 171–
5). As with the *De rerum natura*, the central
concern is rather the place in the world of
human beings and their possibilities of happiness.

In the established manner of didactic
poetry, passages of direct instruction are
interspersed with 'digressions', descriptive or
reflective passages with a more figured relationship to the main theme, such as Jupiter's
paternal disruption of the golden age (1. 121–
59) or the 'praises of Italy' (2. 136–77). In
particular, on the Lucretian model, the concluding section of each book stands out: the
troubles of Italy in 1 (464–514), the virtues
of the country life in 2 (475–540), the Noric
plague in 3 (478–566), imitating the end of the
De rerum natura: for book 3 as a microcosm
of that work, cf. M. Gale, *CQ* 1991, 414–26),
and especially the 'epyllion' (mini-epic) of
Aristaeus and Orpheus that ends book 4 (315–
58). This last section dramatizes (but also in
part deconstructs) the opposition between
the successful conquest of nature through
hard work (Aristaeus) and the pathos of loss
and failure (Orpheus) which can be traced
throughout the *Georgics* and which has led to
a debate over the 'optimism' or 'pessimism'
of the work which parallels similar disputes
over the *Aeneid* (cf. D. O. Ross, *Virgil's Elements* (1987); C. Perkell, *The Poet's Truth* (1989);
T. Habinek, in M. Griffith and D. J. Mastron-
arde (eds.), *Cabinet of the Muses* (1990), 209–
23; and R. F. Thomas, *CPhil.* 1991, 211–18). The
contemporary relevance of this is reinforced
by a constant comparison between the bee
society of book 4 and Rome (cf. J. Griffin,
Latin Poets (1985), 163–82).

The poem concludes with an epilogue
(modelled in part on the conclusion to Callimachus' *Aetia*) in which Virgil contrasts
Augustus' 'thundering' on the Euphrates (cf.
R. F. Thomas and R. Scodel, *AJPhil.* 1984, 339;
J. Clauss, *AJPhil.* 1988, 309–20) with his own
easeful retirement in Naples (4. 559–64) and
looks back to the *Eclogues*, depicted as the
playful work of his youth (565–6). At the
opening of *Georgics* 3 he had promised to
write a political epic (3. 46–8), a familiar
enough turn in the *recusatio* (refusal to
handle a topic), but just as Callimachus at the
end of the *Aetia* prophesies a move 'down' to
the *Iambi* (fr. 112), so at the end of the *Georgics*
we are left feeling that for Virgil the next
move would be 'up' in the hierarchy of genres
(cf. Farrell, *Vergil's Georgics*).

AENEID Virgil's final work was the *Aeneid*
(in Latin *Aeneis*), an account in twelve books
of hexameter verse of the flight of Aeneas
from Troy and his battles in Italy against

Turnus to found a new home, the origin of Rome. As an epic, the *Aeneid* occupies the summit of ancient generic classification. Epic was the sustained narration of great events ('kings and heroes' according to Callimachus fr. 1) by an inspired, omniscient, but distanced narrator; it was also the genre in which the anxiety of influence was greatest, since any epic was inevitably read against Homer's *Iliad* and *Odyssey*, by common consent the greatest poems of antiquity. Intertextuality with both poems is intense: the standard study takes 60 pages just to list the most obvious parallels (G. N. Knauer, *Die Aeneis und Homer* (1964), 371–431). The basic armature is that of the *Odyssey* (note also the focus on the hero in the title, though that has other implications: cf. *Aristotle, Poetics* 1451[a] 20): the first half of each epic describes the wanderings of the hero, the second his fight for victory in his home (cf. also the 'overlap' in the book-structure in the middle of each: *Od.* 13. 1–91 with *Aen.* 7. 1–36, and contrast *Apollonius Rhodius, 3. 1), and Aeneas is harried by Juno as Odysseus is by Poseidon, but the anger of Juno (cf. 1. 4, 11) also corresponds to the anger of Achilles (and Apollo) in the *Iliad*, and the end of the poem is more like the battle between Achilles and Hector in *Iliad* 22 than the killing of the suitors in *Odyssey* 22 (*contra* F. Cairns, *Virgil's Augustan Epic* (1989), 177–214). One may also contrast the first six books as 'Odyssean' with the second half as 'Iliadic' (cf. K. W. Gransden, *Virgil's Second Iliad* (1984): for a different version of this opposition, cf. D. Quint, *Epic and Empire* (1993)). But the correspondences with both epics go much further and much deeper (cf. Knauer, *Aeneis*; ANRW 2. 31. 2 (1981), 870–918; A. Barchiesi, *La traccia del modello* (1985); R. R. Schlunk, *The Homeric Scholia and the Aeneid* (1974)). The relationship is signalled in the famous opening words of the poem, *arma virumque cano*, 'arms and the man I sing', where 'arms' points to the *Iliad*, 'man' to the *Odyssey* (and 'I sing' perhaps to 'Cyclic' epic, cf. *Ilias parva* fr. 1).

Two other epics are also of importance: the *Argonautica* of Apollonius Rhodius (cf. D. Nelis, *The Aeneid and the Argonautica of Apollonius Rhodius* (1996)) and *Ennius' *Annales* (E. Norden (ed.), *Aen.* 6 (1926), 365–75; M. Wigodsky, *Vergil and Early Latin Poetry* (1972), 40–79). The relationship with Ennius is of great ideological significance (cf. G. B.

Conte, *The Rhetoric of Imitation* (1986), 141–84). But the range of material whose traces may be interpreted in the *Aeneid* is vast: other earlier epics like Greek 'cyclic' epic (E. Christian Kopff, ANRW 2. 31. 2 (1981), 919–47) and *Naevius' *Punica* (M. Barchiesi, *Nevio Epico* (1962), 50–1 and *passim*), Greek and Roman tragedy (Wigodsky, 80–97; A. König, *Die Aeneis und die griechische Tragödie* (1970); P. Hardie, *PVS* 1991, 29–45), Hellenistic poetry (W. Clausen, *Virgil's Aeneid and the Tradition of Hellenistic Poetry* (1987)), lyric and elegy (F. Cairns, 129–76), and many other genres (cf. N. Horsfall, *G&R* 1991, 203–11). The *Aeneid* thus both preserves the narrower generic norms of epic and expands the genre towards the variety that critics like M. Bakhtin have reserved for the modern novel, a process taken further by *Ovid (J. Solodow, *The World of Ovid's Metamorphoses* (1988), 25). The included genres maintain, however, their separate ideological implications.

Although the particular version of the Aeneas legend presented in the *Aeneid* has become canonical, the versions of the myth in the preceding tradition were many and varied (N. M. Horsfall, in J. N. Bremmer and N. M. Horsfall, *Roman Myth and Mythography*, BICS Suppl. 52 (1987), 12–24), and the reconstruction of the matrix of possibilities against which the *Aeneid* situates itself has always been a standard critical procedure (cf. esp. R. Heinze, *Virgil's Epic Technique*, trans. H. and D. Harvey and F. Robertson (1993); N. Horsfall, *Virgilio: l'epopea in alambicco* (1991)). It is clear that many of the details offered by Virgil were by no means the standard ones in his day, that his 'sources' were multiple, and that there was no compunction against free invention. The *Aeneid* is not therefore a 'safe' text to use for the investigation of early Latin history and cult. The story as told by Virgil takes the reader, as in the *Odyssey, in medias res*. Aeneas on his way to Italy is blown off course to North Africa by a storm instigated by Juno (book 1). There he meets Dido, and tells her the story of the fall of Troy (book 2) and his subsequent wanderings (book 3). He and Dido become lovers, and he forgets his mission; Mercury is sent to remind him, and his departure leads to Dido's tragic suicide (book 4). In book 5, the threat of another storm forces Aeneas to put into Sicily, where funeral games are celebrated for his dead father Anchises; after Juno instigates the Trojan women to burn the ships, part of the group are left behind in Sicily and Anchises appears in a dream to urge Aeneas to visit the Sibyl of Cumae (near Naples). The first half of the epic concludes with the consultation of the Sibyl and their visit to the underworld, where Aeneas meets his father and receives a vision of the future of Rome (book 6).

The events of the second half are described by Virgil as a 'greater work' (7. 44, *maius opus*). Landing in Latium, Aeneas sends a successful embassy of peace to the Latin king Latinus; but Juno uses the Fury Allecto to stir up the young Rutulian king Turnus and Latinus' wife Amata to encourage war. Aeneas' son Iulus kills a pet stag while hunting, and from that small spark a full-blown war develops. Before battle commences we are given a catalogue of Italian forces (book 7). In book 8 Aeneas, advised by the god of the river Tiber in a dream, visits the Arcadian king Evander, who is living on the future site of Rome; Evander's young son Pallas joins the Trojan forces, and Aeneas receives a gift of armour from his mother Venus, including a shield which again depicts future events in the history of Rome, most notably the battle of Actium (book 8). In the succeeding books of fighting, emphasis falls on the terrible cost of the war, as the young lovers Nisus and Euryalus die in a night expedition (book 9), Turnus kills Pallas, and Aeneas kills both the equally tragic youth Lausus and his father the evil Mezentius (book 10), and Turnus' ally the female warrior Camilla is killed by an arrow to her breast (book 11). Finally in book 12 Aeneas and Turnus meet in single combat, despite Juno's attempts to delay the duel; Aeneas is victorious, and hesitates over sparing Turnus until he sees the sword-belt that Turnus had taken from the dead Pallas. In a paroxysm of love and anger, he slaughters Turnus.

Throughout the *Aeneid*, as this summary suggests, there is a strong narrative teleology, reaching beyond the events of the story to the future Rome. 'Fate' is a central concept; it coincides with the will of Jupiter, though the exact relationship is kept vague (C. Bailey, *Religion in Vergil* (1935), 204–40). Juno, pained and angry at past events (1. 25–8), attempts always to retard the progress of the story, as a sort of 'counter-fate' (7. 294, 313–16). She is always doomed to failure; at the

end of the epic she is reconciled to the fate of Aeneas (12. 808–28) but we know that this is only temporary (10. 11–15: D. Feeney, in *Oxford Readings in Virgil's Aeneid* (1992), 339–62). Onto the opposition between the king and queen (1. 9) of heaven may be projected many other oppositions in the poem: heaven and hell, order and disorder, work (J. Griffin, *Latin Poets* (1985), 163–82), the pain and loss suffered by individuals are at least equally as prominent in the poem. The question of the relationship between individual and community is raised in a different form by the question of the poem's relationship to the new autocratic rule of Augustus. The purpose of the *Aeneid* was commonly seen in antiquity as to praise Augustus (Servius, *Aen.* pref.), who receives explicit eulogy from Jupiter (1. 286–96, though *Caesar* in 286 is ambiguous), Anchises (6. 791–805), and the primary narrator in the description of Aeneas' divine shield (8. 671–728). Much of the imagery of the *Aeneid* can be related to Augustan symbolic discourse (P. Hardie, *Virgil's Aeneid: Cosmos and Imperium*; P. Zanker, *The Power of Images in the Age of Augustus* (1988)) and there are many typological links between Augustus and Aeneas and other figures such as Hercules (cf. G. Binder, *Aeneas und Augustus* (1971); K. W. Gransden, *PVS* 1973–4, 14–27; J. Griffin, *Latin Poets* (1985), 183–97). On the other hand, many have again seen the poem's tragic elements as incompatible with a celebration of power. It is impossible to separate the question of the *Aeneid*'s political tendency—in its crudest form, whether we make it pro- or anti-Augustan—from the wider ideological issues mentioned above, and again the debate cannot be resolved by an appeal to text or history (cf. D. Kennedy, in A. Powell (ed.), *Roman Poetry and Propaganda in the Age of Augustus* (1992), 26–58).

Finally, these same issues have also surfaced in relation to the philosophical aspects of the *Aeneid*. Just as the *Georgics* may be read as a reply to the *De rerum natura*, so the *Aeneid* may be seen as again 'remythologizing' Lucretian rationalism (P. Hardie, *Virgil's Aeneid: Cosmos and Imperium, passim*); as Aeneas rejects retirement in Carthage or Sicily for his fate in Italy, so the *Aeneid* turns from 'ignoble ease' to harsh commitment (cf. 6. 851 with *De rerum natura* 5. 1130, though there is more than one way of reading the intertextuality). Several passages of the

Aeneid are explicitly philosophical in their language, most notably Anchises' account of the soul in 6. 724–51; this contains both Stoic and Platonic elements, and such eclecticism is typical and unsurprising in a period where the two schools pulled closer with figures such as *Antiochus of Ascalon and *Posidonius. But the debates over the philosophy of the *Aeneid* have concentrated on ethics and the theory of the passions, especially anger. Is the *Aeneid* essentially a Stoic text, which deprecates emotion? Or is it rather Peripatetic, and thereby endorsing a right measure of anger (A. Thornton, *The Living Universe* (1976), esp. 159–63)? Others have looked to Cynicism (F. Cairns, *Virgil's Augustan Epic* (1989), 33–8) or the Epicurean theory of anger as presented in *Philodemus' *De ira* (cf. G. K. Galinsky *AJPhil.* 1988, 321–48; M. Erler, *GB* (1991)). Any decision on these matters involves a consideration of the poem's imagery, as well as explicit statement by characters and the narrator; and once again the evaluation of these images is not a simple one. A similar ambivalence attends the depiction of the gods: although they may at times function as metaphors for psychological activity on the human plane (G. W. Williams, *Technique and Ideas in the Aeneid* (1983)), they cannot simply be reduced to allegory (D. Feeney, *The Gods in Epic* (1991), 129–87).

The classic status of the *Aeneid* is at once apparent from the parody of its opening line (and 7. 41) as the epitome of epic openings in the first of Ovid's *Amores* (date uncertain, but perhaps before 7 BC: cf. Mckeown on *Am.* 1. 1. 1–2). Intertextuality with the *Aeneid* is the central way in which Ovid's *Metamorphoses*, Lucan's *De bello civili* (see LUCAN), and especially the works of the Flavian epicists generate meaning: the *Aeneid* is figured as the official voice of the empire, to be subverted or recuperated (cf. P. Hardie, *The Epic Successors of Virgil*). But just as all Greek literature everywhere of necessity situates itself against Homer, so traces of the *Aeneid* can be seen in every genre of verse and prose, Christian as well as pagan (cf. W. Suerbaum, *ANRW* 2. 31. 1 (1986), 308–37; W. F. Jackson Knight, *Roman Virgil* (1966), 362–98). Inevitably, this role as a machine for generating meaning in others, a stable backdrop for new dramas, may lead to a simplification of the possibilities of the original text, but equally the links between parts of the *Aeneid* established by imitations often offer the possibility of new critical insights into the *Aeneid* itself (cf. P. Hardie, in A. J. Boyle (ed.), *The Imperial Muse: Flavian Epicist to Claudian* (1990), 3–20).

FORTUNA Virgil's works, but especially the *Aeneid*, retained their classic status throughout the Middle Ages and Renaissance as prime examples of pastoral (cf. A. M. Patterson, *Pastoral and Ideology* (1988); S. Chaudhuri, *Renaissance Pastoral and its English Developments* (1989)), didactic (cf. J. Calker, *The English Georgic* (1969)), and most obviously epic, from Dante to Milton (cf. T. M. Green, *The Light in Troy* (1982); D. Quint, *Epic and Empire* (1993)). Many aspects of this reception in the various vernaculars were studied in the publications connected with the bimillenary celebrations of 1981–2 (lists in A. Wlosok, *Gnomon* 1985, 127–34 and *Enc. Virg.* V**(1991), 114–18: cf. C. Martindale, *Virgil and his Influence* (1984) and *Redeeming the Text* (1993)). Although in English literature the Augustan period is most obviously an *aetas Vergiliana*, he has played a surprisingly important role in the modern period, from Eliot to Hermann Broch (T. Ziolkowski, *Virgil and the Moderns* (1991)); if no major work stands in relation to the *Aeneid* as Joyce's *Ulysses* does to the *Odyssey*, the tactics that novel adopts towards its model are entirely Virgilian. For Eliot as for Milton and Dryden Virgil was *the* classic; if this centrality has given way first before vernacular heroes (Shakespeare, Dante) and then before a more general scepticism towards the canon, Virgil continues to possess the alternative canonic virtue of continual reinterpretation and cultural reuse (cf. W. Suerbaum, *Vergils Aeneis, Beiträge zu ihrer Rezeption in Gegenwart und Geschichte* (1981)).   D.P.F., P.G.F.

Vitellius, Aulus (AD 15–69), Roman emperor in 69, son of Lucius Vitellius, an influential figure under the Julio-Claudians, was friendly with *Gaius (1), *Claudius, and *Nero. Consul in 48, he became proconsul of Africa, then served as legate to his brother in the same post. *Galba appointed him governor of Lower Germany in November 68, perhaps thinking that his reputed indolence made him less of a political threat. Vitellius won over the disaffected soldiers in the province by an ostentatious display of generosity. On 2 January 69 Vitellius was proclaimed emperor by his troops, and quickly won the support of the legions of Upper Germany, which had refused allegiance to Galba on 1 January. His main supporters were the legionary legates Fabius Valens and Aulus Caecina Alienus, and soon most of the western provinces and Africa were on his side. Galba had been replaced by *Otho, who committed suicide on 16 April after his army had been defeated at Bedriacum by the Vitellian forces. After an indisciplined march Vitellius entered Rome in July; he made offerings to Nero, and had himself created consul in perpetuity. Hostile sources emphasize Vitellius' gluttony, indolence, and incompetence, though he displayed restraint in dealing with Otho's supporters. He replaced the existing praetorian guard with sixteen cohorts recruited from his German legions. But he did nothing to placate troops who had been defeated or betrayed at Bedriacum, and detachments of the three Moesian legions summoned by Otho returned to their bases having agitated against Vitellius at Aquileia.

At the beginning of July *Vespasian was saluted emperor and soon all the troops in the east supported him. The legions in Pannonia, Dalmatia, and Moesia rapidly deserted Vitellius, and under the leadership of Marcus Antonius Primus, invaded Italy. Vitellius failed to block the Alpine passes, leaving the defence of Italy to Valens, who was ill, and Caecina, who occupied Cremona and Hostilia with an army including four legions and legionary detachments; he aimed to defend the line of the river Po, but collaborated with the Flavians. Although the Ravenna fleet defected, Caecina's army refused to follow his lead and arrested him. Junior officers led the army back to Cremona, near which in a hard-fought battle (October 69) the Vitellian forces were defeated. Valens was captured while trying to escape to Gaul. As the Flavians advanced on Rome there were steady desertions from Vitellius' cause, though his praetorians remained loyal. Vespasian's brother, Flavius Sabinus, prefect of the city, persuaded Vitellius to abdicate, but the agreement was frustrated by the mob in Rome, and some of the emperor's soldiers who forced Sabinus and his supporters to take refuge on the Capitol, where the temple of Jupiter was burnt down. The Flavian army now attacked the city and overcame Vitellian resistance in fierce street fighting. On 20 December

Vitellius was dragged through the streets, humiliated, tortured, and killed.   J.B.C.

Vitruvius (Pol(l)io), a Roman architect and military engineer, in which capacity he served *Julius Caesar. He built a basilica at Fanum Fortunae; but his fame rests chiefly on a treatise, *De architectura*, on architecture and engineering, compiled partly from his own experience, partly from work by the early-Hellenistic architect Hermogenes (to whom he is heavily indebted) and other Greek authors to which his own experiences have been added, sometimes in a disjointed fashion. It is hardly a handbook for architects: rather a book for people who need to understand architecture. Perhaps its main function was place-seeking from Octavian (see AUGUSTUS), to whom it is addressed. His outlook is essentially Hellenistic, and there is a marked absence of reference to important buildings of Augustus' reign, though he knows of Roman technical developments, such as concrete construction (which he mistrusts). *De architectura*, the only work of its kind which has survived, is divided into ten books. Book 1 treats of town-planning, architecture in general, and of the qualifications proper in an architect; 2 of building-materials; 3 and 4 of temples and of the 'orders'; 5 of other civic buildings; 6 of domestic buildings; 7 of pavements and decorative plaster-work; 8 of water-supplies; 9 of geometry, mensuration, astronomy, etc.; 10 of machines, civil and military. The information on materials and methods of construction in 2 and 7, and on rules of proportion in 3 and 4, is of great value.

Vitruvius' importance as an architect is very nearly matched by his significance as a historian of many different departments of ancient science and philosophy, ranging from mathematics to astronomy, to meteorology and medicine. Just as the Hippocratic doctors appreciated the importance of environment to good health, Vitruvius appreciated that in its general and most humane form, architecture included everything which touches on the physical and intellectual life of man and his surroundings.

Often, his encyclopaedic concern with covering a subject thoroughly seems odd to us. In book 2. 1–2 of the *On Architecture* he suggests that the architect who uses bricks needs to be familiar with pre-Socratic theories of matter if he is to understand how his materials can be expected to behave. The doxographies are combed for suitable information. In book 9, the highly abstract geometry of Plato is put to the use of the surveyor—something of which Plato himself might hardly have approved. Similar practical use is made of the mathematics of Archytas, *Eratosthenes, *Democritus, and *Archimedes, and Vitruvius remains an important source for our knowledge of a great many early Greek scientists. (It was Vitruvius who preserved the famous story of Archimedes' discovery in his bathtub of a way of detecting the adulteration of *Hieron II of Syracuse's golden crown (9, Pref. 9–12).) And

so Vitruvius goes on, often employing the theories of the most anti-banausic Greek thinkers to elucidate his very practical subject. Astronomy is necessary for an understanding of the use of sundials, and surveying instruments; astrology for the insights it offers into the organization of human life; machines and their principles (book 10) because of their utility in the manipulation of materials. As he notes at 10. 1. 4, all machines are created by nature, and the revolutions of the universe ultimately set them in motion. For a man with interests practical and theoretical in equal measure, understanding the nature of nature was central to all.   R.A.T.; J.T.V.

Xx

Xanthus, a Hellenized Lydian from Sardis, older contemporary of *Herodotus. Author of *Lydiaca* in 4 books on the origin and history of the Lydian people, maybe down to the capture of Sardis by Cyrus the Great in 547/6. According to *Ephorus (*FGrH* 70 F 180 = Xanthus T 5) he was used by Herodotus, but the fragments do not admit of definite conclusions. Xanthus lived to the time of *Thucydides (Dion. Hal. *De Thuc.* 5 = T 4). The fragments show a desire to support partly mythical native traditions with geological, linguistic (F 16), rationalistic and scientific (F12, 13) arguments: this is Xanthus' chief contribution to historical methodology. It is certain that he was used by *Nicolaus of Damascus, but in what way and to what extent has been much discussed, resulting in various reconstructions of the *Lydiaca*: cf. Herter on one side, von Fritz on the other. There are conspicuous correspondences with regard to some details of the early history of Lydia and the royal genealogy—cf. e.g. Nicolaus *FGrH* 90 F 15, 16, 22 and Xanthus F 16–18. But in other parts one finds unmistakable differences—cf. e.g. Nicolaus F 71 and Xanthus F 15. The 'melodramatic and fantastic tales' (von Fritz) about the Lydian kings Ardys, Gyges, and Croesus in Nicolaus F 44, 47, 68, which historians usually trace back to Xanthus, display such significant differences in style and mode from the genuine and partially very early attested fragments of Xanthus that an immediate influence can be ruled out. One may assume the existence of a Hellenistic adaptation as the source for Nicolaus. *On Empedocles* (Diog. Laert. 8. 63) and *Magica* (Clem. Alex. *Strom.* 3. 11. 1) are not very well attested and consequently their historicity is in doubt.   K.M.

Xenophanes of Colophon, poet, theologian, and natural philosopher, left Ionia at the age of 25, probably after the Persian Conquest in 545 BC, and led a wandering life for 67 years, as he tells us himself in a preserved passage from an elegiac poem (DK 21 B 8). He lived in several cities in Sicily, and is reported to have composed an epic on the colonization of Elea, but the tradition that he was the teacher of *Parmenides is doubtful. He is credited with being the first author of satirical verses (*Silloi*). The extant fragments, in various metres and genres, include two long elegiac passages on how to conduct a civilized symposium and on the civic importance of his own work and wisdom (*sophiē*).

A skilful poet in the tradition of *Tyrtaeus and *Solon, Xenophanes carried the Ionian intellectual enlightenment to Magna Graecia (the Greek settlements of Italy). His natural philosophy is a somewhat simplified version of the new Milesian cosmology, supplemented by interesting inferences from observed fossils. The origin of things is from earth and water; meteorological and celestial phenomena (including sun, moon, and stars) are explained by clouds formed from the sea. In theology and epistemology he was an original and influential thinker. He attacks *Homer and *Hesiod for portraying the gods as behaving in ways that are blameworthy for mortals. He mocks anthropomorphic conceptions of deity, and undermines the supernatural interpretation of natural phenomena. In place of the Homeric pantheon he offers the vision of a supreme god, 'greatest among gods and men, like unto mortals neither in body nor in mind' (fr. 23), who without effort sways the universe with his thought. Moderns have imagined him a monotheist, but he seems rather to have preached a harmonious polytheism, without conflict among the gods. In our ignorance of Milesian speculation about the gods, Xenophanes appears as the first thinker systematically to formulate the conception of a cosmic god, and thus to found the tradition of natural theology followed by *Plato, *Aristotle, and the Stoics. Pursuing a theme of archaic poetry, Xenophanes is the first to reflect systematically on the distinction between human opinion or guesswork (*dokos*) and certain knowledge.   C.H.K.

Xenophon LIFE Xenophon, son of Gryllus, from the Athenian deme (rural district) of Erchia, was born into a wealthy but politically inactive family around 430 BC. He presumably served in the cavalry and certainly (like other affluent young men) associated with *Socrates. This background did not encourage enthusiasm for democracy. He apparently stayed in Athens under the Thirty Tyrants and fought the democratic insurgents in the civil war (404–403). The political amnesty of 403/2 theoretically protected him, and material in *Hellenica* and *Memorabilia* shows that (like *Plato) he was critical of the Thirty, but insecurity was surely one reason why he accepted the suggestion of a Boeotian friend, Proxenus, to enrol as a mercenary with Cyrus the Younger. He was thus among the 10,000 Greeks involved in Cyrus' rebellion and defeat at Cunaxa (401). When Tissaphernes liquidated the Greek generals, Xenophon emerged as a replacement and led the survivors through Mesopotamia, Armenia, and northern Anatolia to Byzantium and then into service with the Thracian Seuthes. He alleges a wish to go home at this stage but for various reasons neither did so nor availed himself of Seuthes' offers of land and marriage-alliance. Consequently, when the Spartans under Thibron arrived in Anatolia for a war of 'liberation' (399) and took over the Cyreans (i.e. Cyrus' veterans), he became a Spartan mercenary. Nothing is known of his role in ensuing campaigns except that he self-defensively endorsed criticisms which led to Thibron's dismissal. Subsequent Spartan commanders, Dercylidas and *Agesilaus, were more to his taste and he forged close associations with them. In 394 Agesilaus returned home to confront rebellion amongst Sparta's allies and Xenophon fought for the Spartan cause at Coronea against, among others, his fellow-Athenians. Exiled as a result of this (if not, as some think, earlier, as part of an Athenian attempt to win Persian goodwill) he was settled by the Spartans at Scillus, near Olympia. (His estate and the sanctuary funded by booty from his Asiatic adventures are described idyllically in *Anab.* 5. 3. 5 ff.) As a Spartan protégé (he was

their *proxenos* (diplomatic representative) at Olympia and his children were allegedly educated in Sparta) he became vulnerable during the disturbances which followed the battle of Leuctra (371), was expelled, and spent the rest of his life in Corinth. There was, however, a reconciliation with Athens. Works such as *Cavalry Commander* and *Ways and Means* disclose a sympathetic interest in the city; and in 362 his son Gryllus was killed fighting in the Athenian cavalry at Mantinea. The posthumous eulogies this earned were in part a tribute to his father.

WORKS Most famous in antiquity as a 'philosopher' or mercenary-leader (ostensibly regarded as a perfect model for the young by *Dio Cocceianus, and systematically 'imitated' by *Arrian), Xenophon produced a large output, all known parts of which survive. The chronology is only vaguely established. Most works fall into three categories: long (quasi-)historical narratives, Socratic texts (surely Athenocentric works, not mere by-products of contact with supposed Socratic 'cells' in Elis or Phlius), and technical treatises. There are also monographs (encomium; non-Socratic political dialogue; politico-economic pamphlet; institutional analysis), though their secondary relation to the major categories is obvious. Many are the earliest (or earliest surviving) examples of particular genres. The clearest common features are (1) intimate relationship with Xenophon's personal experiences and (2) taste for didactic discourse. Xenophon's moral system is conventional, underpinned by belief in the gods and the importance of omen and ritual: divine power (often anonymous and not infrequently singular) is everywhere in Xenophon's writings, though not absolutely stultifyingly— when consulting the oracle at Delphi about going to Asia he famously framed the question so as to get the 'right' answer; and at the climactic moment in *Anabasis* where the Greeks reach the sea they are too excited to think of sacrificing to the gods. But it is not these things in their own right so much as issues of leadership (by states as well as individuals) or military skill which engage his didactic muse. That even purely practical pursuits have a moral component because they have social implications is a characteristic Xenophontic perception; and the would-be leader must, whatever else, earn his right to lead by superior wisdom and a capacity to match or outdo his subordinates in all the tasks which he demands of them.

In antiquity his style was judged to be simple, sweet, persuasive, graceful, poetic, and a model of Attic (Athenian) purity. This is understandable, though there are deviations from standard Attic and some would call the style jejune; both rhetoric (e.g. *Hell.* 7. 5. 1–27) and narrative can sometimes be awkward. The range of stylistic figures employed is modest (simile is quite common, with a penchant for animal comparisons). The overall effect (style *and* content) can seem naïve. A (perhaps *the*) central question, which divides modern readers into two camps, is how far style and content are really *faux-naif* and informed by humour and irony. One should perhaps reflect that (*a*) Xenophon's emergence as a leader in N. Mesopotamia in late summer 401 must disclose special qualities and (*b*) 4th-cent. Greece was full of men of 'upper-class' origin and of (ex-)mercenaries, and possibly not short of men who were both, but only one of them produced five (modern) volumes of varied, sometimes innovatory, writing. We should give Xenophon the benefit of the doubt, and conclude that there was more, not less, to him than there appears.

Hellenica. A seven-book history of Greek affairs, in two linguistically distinguishable parts, perhaps created at widely differing times, the first possibly as early as the 380s, the second in the mid-350s. (*a*) 1. 1. 1–2. 3. 10 covers the Peloponnesian War (between Athens and the Spartan alliance) from 411 to the destruction of Athens' walls, the overthrow of democracy and the surrender of Samos (404). The opening narrative links imperfectly with Thuc. 8. 109, but the intention can only be to 'complete' the Thucydidean account (see THUCYDIDES), though this is achieved with little reproduction of Thucydides' historiographical characteristics. (*b*) 2. 3. 11–7. 5. 27 continues the story, covering the Thirty Tyrants (404–403), Sparta's Asiatic campaigns (399–394), the Corinthian War and King's Peace (395–387/6), Spartan imperialism in Greece (386–379), the rise of Thebes (379–371) and the Peloponnesian consequences of Leuctra (371–362). The text ends at Mantinea (362), with Greece in an unabated state of uncertainty and confusion. The account is centred on Sparta and charac-

terized by surprising omissions (e.g. the name of *Epaminondas the architect of Leuctra is not given at all in book 6 where the battle is described; the liberation of Messenia; Athens' Aegean policies in 378–362), a tendency to expose the shortcomings of all states, including Sparta, and recurrent hostility to imperial aspirations. A curious amalgam of straight history and political pamphlet, it was relatively little read in antiquity, and its modern status has declined in recent years. But it remains an indispensable source, and the tendency to regard the presumed qualities of *Hellenica Oxyrhynchia* (see OXYRHYNCHUS, THE HISTORIAN FROM) as a reason for simply preferring alternative historical traditions should be questioned.

Anabasis. An account (date uncertain)—perhaps initially circulated under the name Themistogenes (cf. *Hell.* 3. 1. 2)—of Cyrus' rebellion and the fate of his Greek mercenaries, dominated in 3–7 by Xenophon's personal role in rescuing the army. The work's motive is not overtly stated. Apologia and self-advertisement are evident (there were other, and different, accounts in circulation); there is implicit endorsement of the panhellenist thesis that Persia was vulnerable to concerted attack and of a more general view about Greek superiority over barbarians (the army is an emblematic *polis* on the move); and a didactic interest in leadership and military stratagem is obvious (though the account of Cunaxa is strangely flawed). Equally striking is the care taken to construct a varied and genuinely arresting narrative. The work's modern reputation has suffered from traditional use in language learning (cf. *Julius Caesar's Gallic War*).

Cyropaedia. A pseudo-historical account of the life of the Persian king Cyrus the Great, often invoked in accounts of the background of the Greek novel. (There is even a significant, though sketchily narrated, 'love interest' in the story of Panthea and Abradatas.) The institutional framework preserves useful information about the Persian empire (though the oriental decor is not as pronounced as it might be; need for compromise with Greek suspicion of the orient makes difficulties here), but the story-line as it stands flagrantly contradicts other source material (e.g. Cyrus acquires Media by inheritance not conquest, and he dies in bed not battle); suggestions that it may sometimes represent alternative historical tradition (not mere invention) are optimistic. The chief concern (cf. 1. 1. 1) is with techniques of military and political leadership, which are exposed both paradigmatically and through passages of explicit instruction (often involving dialogue). There is also some suggestion that even Cyrus can be corrupted by the acquisition of empire, and a final chapter (post-362) excoriates contemporary Persian vices. Very popular in antiquity (and sometimes thought important enough to have prompted a response from Plato in parts of *Laws*), *Cyropaedia* has been found dull in modern times. But a revival of interest is under way, and it is arguably a litmus-test for true appreciation of Xenophon in general.

Apology. A brief (perhaps very early) work with a purported extract from the courtroom defence of Socrates against charges of religious deviance and corruption of the young sandwiched between a preliminary dialogue with Hermogenes and various carefree observations made after the trial was over. The stated purpose is to explain the *megalēgoria* ('big-talking') which previous writers agreed was a feature of Socrates' reaction to prosecution and show why he did not fear death. (Opportunity is also found to note the prosecutor Anytus' son's history of alcohol abuse.)

Symposium. 'In writing of great men it is proper to record not only their serious activities but their diversions' (1. 1), and entertainment at Callias's party is a mixture of cabaret (music, song, and dance, a sexually titillating tableau of Dionysus and Ariadne and more-or-less serious conversation about the guests' account of their most prized assets, e.g. beauty, wealth, poverty, making people better, recitation, joke-telling, skill at procuring). There is much explicit or implicit reference to personal relationships (doubtless a feature of real sympotic conversation), so Socrates' eventual discourse on common and celestial love is an unsurprising development, though the Platonic model is probably relevant.

Socratic Memoirs. A collection of conversations, probably not planned as a coherent whole. 1. 1–2 explicitly address charges advanced at Socrates' trial, but the whole work presents him as respecting the gods and helping (not corrupting) his fellow-men. Broad thematic patterns are visible—1 dwells

on religion and moderate life-style, 2 on friendship and family, and 3 on Socrates' help to 'those ambitious of good things', while 4 is more disparate (education; the existence of god; temperance; justice) and pretentious—but the pleasure of the work is in its individual vignettes and convincing (not necessarily authentic) picture of a down-to-earth Socrates equally happy debating with sophists, courtesans, and victims of the collapse of Athenian imperialism, and concerned with practicalities as well as philosophy. (As with Plato, drawing the line between genuine Socratic conversational subjects and Xenophontic ones is not easy.)

Oeconomicus. A conversation with Critobulus (1–6) establishes the importance of agriculture. Socrates then reports a conversation with Ischomachus—itself containing a conversation between Ischomachus and his wife (7–10)—covering household organization, the daily pursuits of a rich Athenian, the role of bailiffs, and technical details of cereal and fruit cultivation. Much of it is effectively about leadership—a harder skill than agriculture, as Ischomachus remarks. The work is an important (though, given Socratic—and Xenophontic—unconventionality, slippery) source for social history. Particularly notable is Ischomachus' wife, married young so she will be a *tabula rasa* on which her husband can write what he will, but accorded a significant—if sex-stereotyped—role in the running of the household.

Cavalry Commander deals with the management and improvement of the Athenian cavalry force (which ought—9. 3—to include foreign mercenaries). After comments on recruitment (1. 2, 9–13), securing good horses (1. 3–4, 14–16), general horsemanship (1. 5–6, 17–21), armament (1. 7, 22–3), discipline (1. 7, 24), the need for good phylarchs (brigade-commanders) and political allies (1. 8, 25–6) and tactical formations (2. 1–9) Xenophon formally turns to the cavalry-commander's duties (3. 1 ff.). There follow sections on festival performances (3), conduct of marches and intelligence-gathering (4), deception (5), inducing respect of subordinates by knowledge and example (6), the defence of Attica and more general tactical/strategic points (7, 8. 17–25), horsemanship (8. 1–8), questions of numerical advantage (8. 9–16). Treatment of topics is inexhaustive, unsystematic and inclined to repetition (e.g. numerical issues appear in 5. 1 f., 7. 5 f., 8. 9 f.). Characteristically Xenophon begins and ends with the gods, asserts that no art should be practised more than warfare (8. 7)—gymnastics are frivolous—and stresses the importance of leadership qualities.

On Horsemanship. 'Instruction and exercises' for the private and apparently rather ignorant individual (the specific addressees are 'younger friends': 1. 1). It is the earliest surviving such work (one by Simon is an acknowledged predecessor) and covers purchase, housing and grooming (1–6), mounting, riding, galloping and jumping (7–8), correction of vivacity and sluggishness (9), dressage and manipulation of appearance (10–11), and equestrian armour and weaponry (12). Its precepts are well regarded by modern experts.

On Hunting. A technical treatise dealing with nets (2), dogs and their training (3, 4. 11, 7), and the timing and conduct of the hunt (5–6, 8). The hunter is on foot, the normal prey a hare (an animal of notably good organic design: 5. 29), though Xenophon also mentions deer, boar and the wild cats of Macedonia, Mysia and Syria (9–11). He disapproves of the hunting of foxes (6. 3). The activity is non-utilitarian (quick capture shows perseverance, but is not real hunting: 6. 8), intensely pleasurable—the sight of a hare running is so charming that to see one tracked, found, pursued, and caught is enough to make a man forget all other passions (5. 33)—and a divine invention which promotes military, intellectual, and moral excellence (1, 12). A contrast is drawn with the corrupt verbal wisdom of 'sophists' (a group not treated elsewhere in Xenophon as a coherent evil), and the hunter beats the politician in point of ethical standing and social value (13). Suspicions about the work's authenticity are unfounded.

Agesilaus. Posthumous encomium of 'a perfectly good man' (1. 1). An uneven chronological account (long stretches in close verbal parallel to passages of *Hellenica*) is followed by a survey (with some anecdotal examples) of principal virtues (piety, justice, continence, courage, wisdom, patriotism, charm, dignity, austerity). Little solid information is offered which is not in *Hellenica*, but a new gloss (sometimes Panhellenic, occasionally critical) is put on already familiar facts. The work (like *Isocrates' Evagoras*) is normally regarded as an important contribution to the development of biography. See AGESILAUS.

Hiero. A dialogue version of the 'wise man meets autocrat' scenario (cf. *Herodotus on *Solon and the Lydian king Croesus, see Hdt. 1. 29 ff.) in which, contrary to expectation, Hiero refutes Simonides' claim that it is pleasant to be a tyrant, while Simonides supplies suggestions for improving the situation, not least by manipulation of public opinion. The original readers will inevitably have thought of 4th-cent. Syracusan tyranny (*Dionysius I and II), but this may not be a specifically intended subtext.

Ways and Means. Politicians claim that poverty compels Athens to treat other cities unjustly. So Xenophon advises alleviation of that poverty through innocent means, particularly (*a*) attracting revenue-creating foreign residents and (*b*) using state-owned slaves in the Laurium silvermines to increase income and generate a dole (*trophē*) for citizens. The economic plan (a curious mixture of the apparently familiar and completely alien) has been much criticized; but the primary imperative is political—to devise a new imperialism based on peace and consensual hegemony.

Constitution of the Spartans. An account of the Spartan system (attributed to a single lawgiver, Lycurgus) which demonstrates the rationality of its consistent contradiction of normal Greek practices. The tone is laudatory except in a final chapter (misplaced in the manuscripts) which notes the decline from Lycurgan values associated with 4th-cent. imperialism.

(The non-Xenophontic *Constitution of the Athenians*, conceding that democracy, though repellent, was rational in Athenian circumstances, was allowed into the corpus by a later editor as a companion piece. The treatise is often called the 'Old Oligarch' (see separate entry OLD OLIGARCH).)   C.J.T.

Xenophon Ephesius ('the Ephesian'), Greek novelist, author of *The Ephesian story of Anthia and Habrocomes* (*Ta kata Anthian kai Habrakomēn Ephesiaka*). Mention (2. 13. 3) of an eirenarch (police magistrate), an office not attested before *Trajan, together with the early place in the genre's development suggested by Xenophon's unambitious treatment of his story, indicates a date between AD 100 and 150: so far no papyri have been published. The *Suda* calls him a historian and alleges other works, specifying only one, *On the city of Ephesus*, and gives Ephesus as his origin, though the novel's knowledge of Ephesus has been argued to be second-hand. Xenophon tells, as omniscient narrator, how the young lovers from Ephesus were sent abroad by their parents soon after marriage in response to an oracle, became separated whilst on a voyage, and were conveyed round much of the Mediterranean world (even Italy), surviving all sorts of trials (shipwrecks, attacks by pirates and brigands, enslavement, advances by powerful suitors) and remaining faithful to each other.

Reunited at last in Rhodes they returned to Ephesus, to live happily ever after.

Occasional incoherence in a generically typical plot has been explained by the hypothesis that our text is an abridgement (the *Suda* reports ten books) or by Xenophon's clumsiness. His characterization is indeed unimpressive, and abridgement hardly explains some weaknesses in plot (e.g. the parents' decision to dispatch the couple on a journey that an oracle predicts as disastrous). His language, although often drawing on the vocabulary of the Athenian *Xenophon, has too many later features to be seen as Atticizing (deliberately imitating Classical Athenian Greek).   E.L.B.

Zz

Zeno (1) of Elea (S Italy) is portrayed by *Plato (*Prm.* 127b) as the pupil and friend of *Parmenides, and junior to him by 25 years. Their fictional meeting with a 'very young' *Socrates (ibid.) gives little basis for firm chronology. We may conclude only that Zeno was active in the early part of the 5th cent. BC. Whether the work from which Plato makes him read was his only book is uncertain.

The most famous of Zeno's arguments are the four paradoxes about motion paraphrased by *Aristotle (*Ph.* 6. 9), which have intrigued thinkers down to Bertrand Russell in our era. The Achilles paradox proposes that a quicker can never overtake a slower runner who starts ahead of him, since he must always first reach the place the slower has already occupied. His task is in truth an infinite sequence of tasks, and can therefore never be completed. The Arrow paradox argues that in the present a body in motion occupies a place just its own size, and is therefore at rest. But since it is in the present throughout its movement, it is always at rest. The Dichotomy raises the same issues about infinite divisibility as the Achilles; the Arrow and the Stadium (an obscure puzzle about the relative motion of bodies) are perhaps directed against the implicit assumption of indivisible minima.

According to Plato Zeno's method was to attack an assumption by deriving contradictory consequences from it (*Prm.* 127d–e). Simplicius quotes fragments in which Zeno adopts precisely this strategy against the hypothesis of plurality (*In Phys.* 139–41). Thus fr. 3 proves that if there are many things their number is both limited and unlimited. Frs. 1 and 2 evidently formed parts of a more elaborate argument from the same hypothesis. Each member of a plurality must be self-identical and one and therefore (grounds for this inference are not preserved) so small as to be without magnitude. Anything with magnitude, by contrast, has an infinite number of parts, each possessing magnitude, and must accordingly itself be so large as to be infinite. No other examples survive, although it is conceivable that the paradoxes of motion originally took the form of antinomies (cf. Ding. Laert. 9. 72) about plurality.

Plato's assessment of the purpose of Zeno's book is now usually accepted. He reads the antinomies as assaults on common sense; more specifically as an indirect defence of Parmenidean monism against outraged common sense (*Prm.* 128a–e). But perhaps Zeno intended not so much to shake belief in the existence of plurality and motion as to question the coherence of our understanding of these phenomena. On either interpretation Aristotle was right to see in Zeno the founder of dialectic (Diog. Laert. 8. 57).

M.Sch.

Zeno (2) of Citium (Cyprus), (335–263 BC), founder of Stoicism. He came to Athens in 313 and is said to have studied with or been influenced by various philosophers, notably Crates the Cynic, *Antisthenes the Socratic, and the Academics Xenocrates and particularly Polemon, who seems to have stressed the notion of nature. Zeno taught in the *Stoa Poikilē* ('Painted Colonnade') which gave its name to Stoicism. He was well respected at Athens, and in old age was invited by *Antigonus Gonatas to go to his court, but sent two students instead.

Zeno's writings established Stoicism as a set of ideas articulated into three parts: logic (and theory of knowledge), physics (and metaphysics), and ethics. Later Stoics developed some of his ideas in differing ways until an orthodoxy on fundamentals was established by the writings of Chrysippus. Stoicism is holistic in method: logic, say, or ethics can be developed in relative independence, but are ultimately to be seen to fit into the set of Stoic ideas as a whole, while no part serves as foundation for the others. Stoicism is materialist, regarding everything as part of a universal natural system subject to deterministic laws; however, it is also teleological and compatibilist. In method and epistemology it is uncompromisingly empiricist, but again shows no reductive tendencies, laying great stress on reason and its capacities; Stoic logic is one of its most distinctive and original contributions. Stoic ethics lays great stress on the difference of kind in value between virtue and other kinds of advantage such as health and wealth, although these are natural for us to pursue. This difference is such that virtue even without these is sufficient for happiness; thus stress on the importance of virtue leads to radical redefinition of happiness, our final end. The Stoics stressed the role of rules and principles in moral reasoning; early writings of Zeno stressed that even basic moral rules could have justified exceptions, but later Stoics downplayed this, and distanced themselves from Zeno's *Republic*, in which an ideal community, radically rejecting convention, was developed.   J.A.

Zenobia (Septimia), or in Aramaic *Bath Zabbai,* one of the great women of classical antiquity (*PLRE* 1. 990 f.). The second wife of Septimius Odaenathus of Palmyra, on his death in AD 267, in suspicious circumstances, she secured power for herself in the name of her young son, Septimius Vaballathus. As long as Zenobia kept the east secure, *Gallienus and Claudius Gothicus were prepared to accept her regime, including its bestowal upon Vaballathus of his father's Roman titles, and hence of the claim to be more than just king of Palmyra. However, in 270 Zenobia exploited the political instability that followed the death of Claudius to expand beyond Syria by taking over Egypt and much of Asia Minor, and further to enhance Vaballathus' Roman titles, while continuing to recognize *Aurelian as emperor. When Aurelian finally moved against her in 272, her forces failed to stop him at Antioch and Emesa, and—now calling her son *Augustus* and herself *Augusta*—she was besieged in Palmyra. She was captured while attempting to escape, shortly before the fall of the city. She was spared. Many tales were told of her subsequent life; little is certain, though it is likely that she was paraded in Aurelian's triumph.   J.F.D.

Zonaras, Johannes, Byzantine historian and canonist of the 12th cent. A commander of the body-guard and imperial secretary, he was probably forced to retire into monastic life after the failure of the conspiracy to make Anna Comnena empress in AD 1118. Living in exile on an island far from the capital he devoted himself to writing. He composed an authoritative commentary to Byzantine canon law, commentaries on the poems of Gregory of Nazianzus and on the terminology of religious poetry. Various other exegetic books and lives of saints go under his name; he is also the author of at least one religious poem. As a historian he wrote a universal history from the creation to AD 1118. Zonaras never claimed to be more than a compiler. For Greek history he mainly used *Herodotus, *Xenophon, *Plutarch, and *Arrian. For Roman history to the destruction of Carthage he excerpted Plutarch and the first twenty-one books of *Cassius Dio, for which he is our only important source. He was compelled to omit the history of the late Roman republic because he did not have the relevant books of Dio (he only gives some excerpts from Plutarch's *Pompey* and *Caesar*), but was able to use Dio's books 44–68 and is, together with Xiphilinus, our main source for the reconstruction of Dio's books 61–8. For the period after *Domitian he followed Xiphilinus instead of the original Dio. He added information from other sources (e.g. *Eusebius). Petrus Patricius was his chief source for the period between *Severus Alexander and *Constantine I. The rest derives from various chronicles, not all of which have been identified. Zonaras is especially important as a source for the period AD 450–550. His excerpts are faithful in content, but stylistically independent. See CASSIUS DIO.

Zonaras is not the author of the lexicon that usually goes under his name, a compilation probably made between 1204 and 1253, and much used by the Byzantines.   A.M.

Zosimus, Greek historian. Little is known of his life except that he had been *advocatus fisci* (lawyer acting for the central imperial treasury) and obtained the dignity of *comes* ('count'). His identification with either the sophist Zosimus of Ascalon or the sophist Zosimus of Gaza is very unlikely. He wrote a history (*Historia nova*) of the Roman empire from *Augustus reaching as far as AD 410, where his extant text terminates just before the sack of Rome by Alaric. He completed his work after 498, if indeed he refers to the abolition of the *auri lustralis collatio* (2. 38), and *c.*518, since the work is quoted in the chronicle of Eustathius of Epiphania, written apparently in the early years of Justin II. Book 1 summarizes the history of the first three centuries of the empire (the section of *Diocletian is lost); in books 2–4 he gives a more precise account of the 4th cent. and in books 5–6 a narrative of the years 395–410 for which he is our most important historical source. His excursus on the secular games (2. 1–6) derives from Phlegon of Tralles, and for the fourth and early fifth centuries he used extensively and uncritically the histories of *Eunapius and Olympiodorus, enabling the reconstruction of the texts and attitudes of these writers. His view of events is determined, even at the late date at which he wrote, by his paganism. He sees the decadence of the empire as a consequence of the rejection of paganism. He is naturally hostile to *Constantine I and *Theodosius I and favourable to *Julian, reproducing in these attitudes those of Eunapius. As he reached 407 he changed his source from Eunapius to Olympiodorus, and his view of Stilicho changed correspondingly from one of hostility to one of favour. The same moment is marked by a change in emphasis from eastern to western events, and by the appearance, from then to the end of his surviving text, of Latin transcriptions and quoted phrases.   J.F.Ma.

Chronology

<table>
<tr><td colspan="2">

GREECE AND THE EAST
BC

*c.*1575–1200 Mycenaean civilization in Greece
*c.*1575–1100 New Kingdom in Egypt
*c.*1450 Mycenaeans take over palace settlements of Minoan Crete

*c.*1270 Troy VI, perhaps the Troy of legend, destroyed
*c.*1100–776 'Dark Age' of Greece
*c.*1050–950 Migration of Ionian Greeks to the eastern Aegean

*c.*825–730 Colonization of the West begins
776 First Olympian Games

*c.*750–700 Homer and Hesiod active
*c.*744–612 Assyrian empire at its height
*c.*740 Greek alphabet created from a Phoenician (Semitic) source
*c.*700 Greeks begin to colonize Black Sea area

*c.*700–600 Society remodelled at Sparta (Lycurgus)
*c.*680–625 The first tyrannies: Pheidon at Argos and Cypselus at Corinth
621/20 Draco's laws at Athens
*c.*610–575 Alcaeus and Sappho active on Lesbos
594/3 Solon's reforms at Athens
587 Capture of Jerusalem by Nebuchadnezzar; beginning of Jewish Diaspora
585 Thales of Miletus predicts eclipse of the sun
*c.*560–510 Tyranny of Pisistratus and his sons at Athens
*c.*557–530 Cyrus founds Persian empire
*c.*546/5 Persians conquer Ionian Greeks

</td></tr>
</table>

ROME AND THE WEST
BC

*c.*1500–1200 Bronze-age 'Apennine' culture in western central Italy

*c.*1300 Earliest Celtic culture emerges on Upper Danube

*c.*1000 Hill-top settlements are established on the hills of Rome, including the Palatine
*c.*900–600 Iron-age 'Villanovan' culture in western central Italy
*c.*800–700 Celtic culture spreads to Spain and Britain
753 Traditional date for founding of Rome

*c.*700 Palatine settlement expands; the Forum is laid out as a public meeting place
700–500 Etruscan civilization in Italy; their alphabet stimulates the spread of writing in Italy

*c.*600 Latin city states begin to emerge in central Italy; organization of Roman calendar and major priesthoods

GREECE AND THE EAST
BC
....

*c.*534 First tragedy performed at City
    Dionysia in Athens

*c.*530 Pythagoras emigrates to South Italy

508 Reforms of Cleisthenes at Athens

499 Ionian Revolt against Persian rule

*c.*499–458 Aeschylus active (d. 456/5)

498–446 Pindar active

490 First Persian invasion of Greece; Battle
    of Marathon

*c.*487 State provision of comedies at City
    Dionysia in Athens begins

480–479 Second Persian invasion of
    Greece; battles of Thermopylae, Salamis,
    Plataea, and Mycale

478/7 Athens founds Delian League against
    Persia

*c.*468–406 Sophocles active (d. 406)

467 Cimon defeats Persians at Eurymedon

*c.*465–425 Phidias active

462/1 Ephialtes and Pericles initiate political
    reform at Athens

*c.*461–446 First Peloponnesian War

*c.*460–430 Herodotus writes his history

*c.*460–410 Polyclitus active

*c.*455–408 Euripides active (d. 406)

454 Treasury of the Delian League moved
    to Athens; growth of Athenian empire

447 Building of the Parthenon begins

431 Second Peloponnesian War begins

*c.*431–400 Thucydides writes his history

*c.*430 Democritus, Hippocrates, Socrates,
    and Protagoras active

430–426 Plague at Athens; death of Pericles
    (429)

*c.*427–388 Aristophanes active

415–413 Athenian expedition to Sicily

405 Battle of Aegospotami

405–367 Dionysius I is tyrant of Syracuse

404 Athens surrenders to Sparta; the Thirty
    Tyrants

*c.*404–355 Xenophon active

403 Democracy restored at Athens

399 Trial and execution of Socrates

395–386 Corinthian War

387 Plato (*c.*429–347) founds the Academy

386 King's Peace allows Persia to rule in
    Asia Minor

378 Foundation of Second Athenian
    Confederacy

377–353 Mausolus rules Caria

ROME AND THE WEST
BC
....

509 Expulsion of last king and founding of
    the Republic

494 First secession of the plebeians

493 Treaty between Rome and Latins
    establishes peace and military alliance

*c.*450 Codification of the Twelve Tables;
    Rome on the offensive against
    neighbouring tribes

*c.*400 Earliest genuine archival records in
    Rome

396 Romans destroy Veii, inaugurating
    conquest of Etruria

390/386 Sack of Rome by Celts brings only
    temporary setback to Roman expansion

GREECE AND THE EAST
BC

c.375–330 Praxiteles active
371 Sparta defeated by Thebes at Battle of
     Leuctra
c.370–315 Lysippus active
c.360–324 Diogenes the Cynic active
359–336 Philip II is king of Macedon
338 Philip defeats Athens and Thebes at
     Chaeronea
336 Alexander ('the Great') becomes king
     of Macedon (d. 323)
335 Aristotle (384–322) founds the Lyceum
334 Alexander crosses into Asia
331 Foundation of Alexandria
326 Alexander crosses the Indus
c.324–292 Menander active
c.323–281 Alexander's 'Successors' divide
     his empire
323–31 Egypt ruled by the Ptolemies
322 Death of Demosthenes (b. 384)
321 Seleucus gains satrapy of Babylon;
     beginning of Seleucid empire
c.310 Zeno (335–263) founds Stoicism
c.307 Epicurus (341–270) founds his school
     at Athens
301 Antigonus I killed at Battle of Ipsus
c.300 Euclid active

c.287 Theophrastus dies (b. c. 371)
281 Battle of Corupedium: Seleucus finally
     wins Asia Minor
281/80 Achaean Confederacy revived
c.277/6–239 Antigonus Gonatas is king of
     Macedon
274–217 Four Syrian Wars fought between
     Ptolemies and Seleucids
c.270–245 Apollonius of Rhodes writes
     Argonautica

c.247–AD 224 Arsacids rule Parthia
241–197 Attalus I rules Pergamum
229 Illyrian piracy attracts Roman
     intervention in the East
227/6 Cleomenes III reforms Spartan state

ROME AND THE WEST
BC

341–338 Latin War; Latin League is
     dissolved

326–304 Second Samnite War

300 All Latium under Roman control
298–290 Third Samnite War
295 Battle of Sentinum, decisive for
     supremacy in Italy

275 Pyrrhus driven back to Epirus by the
     Romans
272 Capture of Tarentum, the final act in
     the Roman conquest of Italy

264–241 First Punic War; first gladiatorial
     games (264) in Rome
260 Rome builds large navy

241 Sicily becomes first Roman province

218–201 Second Punic War; Hannibal
     invades Italy
216 Crushing victory over Romans at
     Cannae
206 Carthaginians defeated in Spain
c.205–184 Career of Plautus

GREECE AND THE EAST
BC
....

200 Palestine comes under Seleucid rule

194 Eratosthenes, natural philosopher, dies
      (b. c.285)

after 184 Great Altar of Pergamum
171–167 Third Macedonian War
168/7 Judaean Revolt against Antiochus IV
      Epiphanes, led by the Maccabees
166–188 Delos flourishes as free port

146 Macedonia a Roman province; Achaean
      War; destruction of Corinth
142 Jews expel Seleucids; ruled by
      Hasmonean high priests (to 63)

120–63 Mithradates VI King of Pontus

89–85 First Mithradatic War
88 Sack of Delos
86 Sack of Athens

64 Syria a Roman province

47 Library of Alexandria burnt

ROME AND THE WEST
BC
....

204 Scipio invades Africa
c.204–169 Career of Ennius
202 Scipio defeats Hannibal at Zama
200–197 Second Macedonian War between
      Rome and Philip V

192–188 Syrian War between Rome and
      Antiochus III
191 Rome completes conquest of Cisalpine
      Gaul

167 Kingdom of Macedon destroyed at
      Battle of Pydna
166–160 Plays of Terence
155–133 Celtiberian War leaves most of
      Iberia in Roman hands
149–146 Third Punic War; Carthage
      destroyed

133 The tribune Tiberius Gracchus
      proposes land reform; annexation of Asia
121 Murder of Gaius Gracchus
c.118 Death of Polybius (b. c.200)
112–106 War against Jugurtha of Numidia
107–100 Marius consul six times
91–89 Social War
88–82 Civil war between Sulla and Marius
      (d. 86)

81 Sulla dictator; proscriptions
73–71 Revolt of Spartacus
70 Crassus and Pompey consuls
70 Cicero's Verrine Orations delivered
63 Consulate of Cicero; conspiracy of
      Catiline; Pompey's settlement of the East
60 First Triumvirate (Pompey, Caesar and
      Crassus)
58–51 Caesar campaigns in Gaul; writes his
      commentarii
55–54 Caesar's invasions of Britain
55 (or 51) Death of Lucretius
54 Catullus dies (b. c.84)
49 Caesar crosses the Rubicon; Civil War
48 Caesar defeats Pompey at Pharsalus
44 Caesar made perpetual dictator;
      murdered (15 March); Cicero attacks
      Antony in his Philippics
43 Octavian seizes the consulship; Second
      Triumvirate (Octavian, Antony, and
      Lepidus); murder of Cicero (b. 106)
42 Republicans defeated at Philippi

GREECE AND THE EAST

BC

40 Parthians capture Jerusalem; Rome intervenes backing Herod the Great as King of Judaea

30 Egypt a Roman province

AD

6 Judaea a Roman province

c.30 Philon ('Philo'), Jewish writer, active; traditional date for crucifixion of Jesus of Nazareth

37/8 Josephus, Jewish Greek historian, born

c.48 Birth of Plutarch

66 First Jewish revolt begins against Roman rule

66–8 Nero's tour of Greece

70 Destruction of the Temple at Jerusalem

73/4 Fall of Masada ends first Jewish Revolt

106 Arabia a Roman province

135 Revolt of Bar Kokhba in Palestine suppressed

146–c.170 Ptolemy's writings on astronomy and geography

ROME AND THE WEST

BC

31 Octavian defeats Antony and Cleopatra at Actium

28–23 Vitruvius writes de Architectura

27 Octavian's first constitutional settlement; he is given the name Augustus

23 Augustus' second constitutional settlement

20 Diplomatic triumph in Parthia

19 Death of Virgil (b. 70)

13–9 Roman control established up to the Danube

8 Death of Horace (b. 65)

2 Forum of Augustus dedicated

AD

9 Loss of three legions in Germany; Rhine–Danube becomes empire's northern frontier

14–37 Tiberius emperor

17 Death of Livy (b. 59 BC); death of Ovid (b. 43 BC)

37–41 Gaius ('Caligula') emperor

41–54 Claudius emperor

54–68 Nero emperor

64 Fire in Rome

65 Suicides of Seneca (b. 4 BC/AD 1) and Lucan (b. 39)

c.65 Death of St Paul in Rome

69 Civil war

69–79 Vespasian emperor

79 Pompeii and Herculaneum destroyed by the eruption of Vesuvius; death of Pliny the Elder (b. 23/4)

81–96 Domitian emperor

98–117 Trajan emperor

c.110–120 Tacitus writes Histories and Annals

c.112 Death of Pliny the Younger (b. c.61)

113 Trajan's Column dedicated

117–138 Hadrian emperor; Suetonius and Juvenal active; the Pantheon built; Hadrian's Wall built (Britain); Soranus (physician) active

138–161 Antoninus Pius emperor

GREECE AND THE EAST
AD

150 Pausanias the travel writer flourishes

c.200 Mishnah, the first great Rabbinic compilation, is written

224/5 Origen (b. c.184/5) dies, Sasanid dynasty seizes power in Persia (224)
267 Athens sacked by Herulian Goths

c.300 Eusebius of Caesarea, Christian apologist, active; Christianity takes hold in Asia Minor
324 Constantinople founded

393 Olympian games abolished

420 Jerome, biblical translator (b. 347), dies in Palestine

Rome and the West
AD

161–180 Marcus Aurelius emperor; Galen is court physician
180–192 Commodus emperor
193–211 Septimius Severus emperor
198–217 Aurelius Antoninus ('Caracalla') emperor
c.202 Cassius Dio begins his Roman History
222–235 Aurelius Severus Alexander emperor
235–284 Period of anarchy
284–305 Diocletian emperor
293 Tetrarchy established
306–337 Constantine I emperor
313 Edict of Milan: Christianity tolerated

354 Augustine of Hippo born (d. 430)
395 Division of the empire between East and West
410 Sack of Rome by Alaric the Goth

476 Last Roman emperor in the West deposed
527–565 Justinian eastern emperor; codification of Roman law

MAPS

Map 1 GREECE AND THE AEGEAN WORLD

SAMOTHRACE

IMBROS

PSARA

CHIOS

Chios

ICARIA

MYCONOS

NAXOS

AMORGOS

THERA

D   E   F

Byzantium
Chalcedon

Perinthus

PROPONTIS

R. SANGARIUS

Lampsacus

Sestus   HELLESPONT

Abydus

Cyzicus

Elaeus

Sigeum   **Troy**

M Y S I A

P H R Y G A

Assus   Gargara

LESBOS

Mytilene   **Pergamum**

R. CAICUS

Eresus

Pitane

L Y D I A

Cyme

Phocaea

R. HERMUS

Smyrna   **Sardis**

Clazomenae

Erythrae   Teos   Colophon
Lebedus   Claros

R. CAYSTER

SAMOS

Ephesus

Samos

R. MAEANDER

Magnesia

Miletus

C A R I A

Didyma

Myndus   Halicarnassus

COS

L Y   D

Cnidus   I

Xanthus   C I A

Ialysus   **Rhodes**

Camirus

RHODES

Lindus

a

b

c

d

Map 2 THE HELLENISTIC WORLD

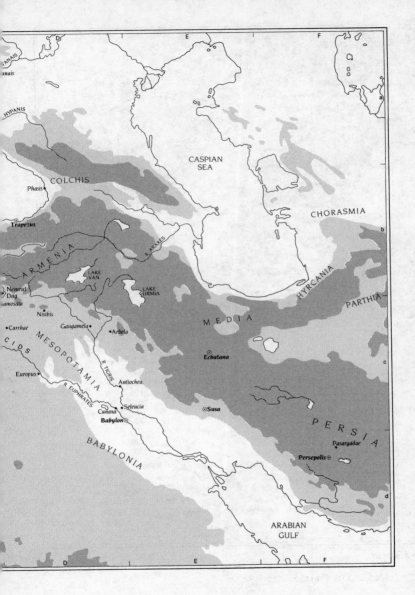

Map 3 ITALY

Map 4 THE ROMAN EMPIRE (Western Provinces)

Map 5 THE ROMAN EMPIRE (Central and Eastern Provinces)

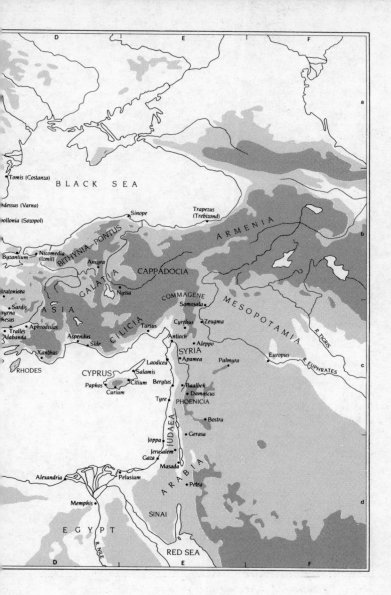

BLACK SEA

Tomis (Costanza)

dessus (Varna)

ollonia (Sozopol)

Sinope

Trapezus
(Trebizond)

ARMENIA

Byzantium

Nicomedia
(Izmit)

BITHYNIA–PONTUS

Ancyra

GALATIA

CAPPADOCIA

tratonicea

Nyssa

COMMAGENE

Sardis

Samosata

MESOPOTAMIA

myrna

ASIA

Aphrodisias

Cyrrhus

Zeugma

esus

CILICIA

Tarsus

Tralles

Antioch

Alabanda

Aspendus

Aleppo

R. TIGRIS

Xanthus

Side

SYRIA

RHODES

Laodicea

Apamea

Palmyra

Europus

R. EUPHRATES

CYPRUS

Salamis

Berytus

Baalbek

Paphos

Citium

Damascus

Curium

Tyre

PHOENICIA

Bostra

Joppa

Gerasa

JUDAEA

Jerusalem

Gaza

Masada

ARABIA

Alexandria

Pelusium

Petra

Memphis

SINAI

EGYPT

R. NILE

RED SEA